COMPARATIVE EQUALITY AND ANTI–DISCRIMINATION LAW:

CASES, CODES, CONSTITUTIONS, AND COMMENTARY

by

DAVID B. OPPENHEIMER
Clinical Professor of Law
University of California, Berkeley

SHEILA R. FOSTER
Vice Dean
Albert A. Walsh Professor of Law
Fordham University

SORA Y. HAN
Assistant Professor of Criminology, Law & Society
University of California, Irvine

Contributing Authors:

Winfried Brugger
Professor of Public Law, Philosophy of Law and Theory of State
Universität Heidelberg
Institut für Staatsrecht, Verfassungslehre und Rechtsphilosophie

Marie Mercat–Bruns
Associate Professor of Law
Conservatoire National des Arts et Métiers, Chaire de Droit Social–Paris
Sciences–Po Ecole de Droit

Sophie Robin–Olivier
Professeur à l'Ecole de Droit de la Sorbonne (Paris 1)

Marie–Christine Pauwels
Associate Professor of American Cultural Studies
Université Paris Ouest Nanterre la Défense

FOUNDATION PRESS
2012

THOMSON REUTERS™

© 2012 By THOMSON REUTERS/FOUNDATION PRESS

      1 New York Plaza, 34th Floor

      New York, NY 10004

      Phone Toll Free 1–877–888–1330

      Fax 646–424–5201

      foundation–press.com

Printed in the United States of America

ISBN 978–1–60930–061–6

Mat #41181611

For
Marcy, Alex, Joel, Jordan and Miriam
D.B.O.

Rosalind and Tyler
S.R.F.

Monty, Azure and Kieran
S.Y.H.

PREFACE

Why Study Comparative Equality Law?

This casebook is the first of its kind to examine the development of laws around the world grappling with social inequality based on human differences. By taking a comparative approach, we hope to contribute to a richer and more nuanced understanding of the meaning of equality, both as a legal principle and a practical discourse. This casebook, then, is not designed to compare in any explicit way different kinds of inequalities. While this might be necessary at certain points, comparing, for example, gender inequality with religious inequality, is precisely not the object of this book's comparative approach. Rather, our approach adopts the more traditional object of comparative law's study of foreign or multiple legal systems. That is, by bringing together the study of equality with the study of multiple legal systems, we are interested in understanding how equality is embedded in different legal systems around the world. We are interested in understanding what kinds of cultural, social and historical forces shape and have shaped inequality, in particular national contexts; what kinds of relationships the law has had to these inequalities; how different legal systems conceptualize equality, and how these conceptualizations have changed over time; and finally, how current laws on equality are being challenged, reformed, and reimagined.

Will legal reforms based on the principle of equality both nationally and internationally continue to march forward, only to eclipse the grounded insights of all the peoples and organizations struggling for real equality? Or can these reforms be made to truly reflect the needs, desires, and political imaginations of those historically and presently waved aside by the law? Will the proliferation of new technologies, new legal discourses, new forms of social contact, new modes of exclusion (along side their enduring precedents) render obsolete the ideal of equality, or provide us with increased opportunities to give it new meanings? Will we sacrifice the growing international sensibility in the US to legal formalism, or allow it to teach us how social differences of sexuality, race, gender, age, class, nation, religion, ability (the list can go on) challenge, and thus enrich, democratic life?

We also adopt the spirit of comparative law's methodological origins. Comparative law's pursuit of the knowledge of various legal systems necessitated an interdisciplinary approach, in contrast to more doctrinally-based legal study. In his article, "Nothing New in 2000? Comparative Law in 1900 and Today",[1] David Clark finds that the basic concepts and aims of comparative law that give the field such methodological richness today have not changed much in the past century. Comparative law has always relied on legal history and the social sciences to understand legal developments in context, even as it aspired to become a pure science. It has also always been

---

1. 75 Tulane Law Review 871, 893–895 (2000).

concerned with analyzing public law, even as issues of governance and community have been generally overshadowed by concerns with private law. And finally, it has always preferred selective rather than total legal rapprochement, even as it gravitates towards a unitary vision of the world. At its heart, although definitely not always in practice, comparative law has tried to understand law in social, cultural and historical context, has pursued questions of public good, and has been sensitive to the dangers of universalism. Indeed, *The Oxford Handbook of Comparative Law*[2] identifies over a dozen different kinds of approaches that have informed comparative law; sketches out subject areas spanning succession law to antitrust law, labor law to constitutional law; and outlines how comparative law is diversely engaged by scholars and practitioners in the Americas, Europe, and East Asia.

Pierre Legrand, in his article "How to Compare Now" argues for what he calls " 'deep' comparative inquiries", and makes the important observation that "the practice of comparative legal studies should reveal a proclivity on the part of the comparatist towards an acknowledgement of 'difference'."[3] He suggests that centering the problem of difference is perhaps the only way to do a truly comparative legal project. Or perhaps it is only by an attempt to address the social reality of difference, and all the tragic and unjust effects it has had in ordering the various national cultures of the world, that the comparative legal project can hope to have value. Thus, always returning the comparative analysis to questions of marginalization and exclusion that social differences have historically produced, we depart from comparative law's conflicted investments in a harmonizing worldwide legal system. We do not propose or even ask the question of a universal principle of or global system of rules on equality. Rather, we put forth the more humble exploratory task of understanding the age-old relationship between law and equality, what it is and what it could be in our time of globalization, by highlighting the existing legal pluralism underwriting equality across various national borders.

There are several compelling reasons why the study of comparative equality law emerges with unprecedented urgency today.

The first is historical. It is undisputable that populations constituted according to varying types of difference—racial, ethnic, gender, sexual, and religious, to name a few—have gained nominal legal recognition. Post-war international norms now codified in well-known conventions like the Convention on the Elimination of All Forms of Discrimination Against Women provide the world's nations with specific ideals of equality that many have incorporated into their domestic laws. In mature democracies such as the United States and France, anti-discrimination law and popular discourse have decades-long elaborations of how to enforce and effectively provide for equal rights and national status for its various minorities. More recent constitutional democracies like India, Brazil and South Africa display similar efforts, but with the benefit of the many lessons learned from failed

---

2. Mathias Reimann and Reinhard Zimmermann, eds., Oxford University Press, 2006.

3. *Legal Studies*, vol. 16, no. 2 (1996)

legal strategies of their older peers. And still other more nascent nations articulate constitutional provisions for equality so that they might be included in the international community. Legal equality for minorities has become a standard measure of a nation's political legitimacy and a testament to the genuineness of a nation's democratic spirit. Thus, examining these various visions and legislations of equality across national borders for the kind of legal landscape of equality that emerges there is to try to put our finger on the present state of laws effecting minority populations as well as to grasp at an historical sense of why equality remains as important today as it did during times when official exclusion, discrimination and domination of minorities went largely unchallenged.

The second is ethical. Mature, recent, and nascent democracies alike struggle to provide for real equality, albeit in different ways and for different reasons. Perhaps it is because we live in a world in which democratic capitalism for the most part goes unchallenged that it is easier to find comfort in the sameness of official declarations of equality than it is to find inspiration in the differences in struggles against inequality. An import-export model of comparative analysis risks becoming too comfortable with similarities that can lead only to the crudest expectations of legal reform, and loses sight of the reality that in order for equality to have traction on the ground we must insist on different legal cultures, strategies and visions. And so we caution throughout against the tendency of comparative law's attention to national similarities and differences to fold over into importing and exporting law, especially with respect to exporting legal approaches to equality from the global North to the global South. Instead, with each glimpse of a nation's laws in the materials that follow, we hope that their differences from each other open up both new and old questions about what real equality might be, in a particular time, in a particular place.

But even more than this, we hope that they provoke a more worldly curiosity about the cultural specificities and historical legacies that each of these completely local articulations of equality issue forth, for those specificities and legacies are also reflected in the roots and routes of the many minorities struggling for equality here. This casebook attempts to bring home the ethical implications of thinking globally about equality. In order to improve the capacity for American law to shift social, cultural and political institutions that continue to either actively or passively perpetuate inequalities, we should look to other nations' laws and histories for lessons we might learn. For example, India's incorporation of Sharia law in adjudicating issues of gender difference might at least provide American law with interesting questions about how we negotiate religious pluralism through a First Amendment secularism, as well as gender discrimination through formalized equal protection doctrine. There are a host of other examples: from the South African prohibition of "unfair discrimination" to the British balance between freedom of religious worship and a State religion; from the Canadian justification for affirmative action to the German view of hate speech; and from the Turkish position on religious expression in public places to the Mexican Supreme Court's reliance on equality to permit abortion. Which is to say, even if it does not seem feasible to simply transplant another nation's doctrine or analysis into ours, gaining a knowledge about these other legal approaches opens up questions for us that might not have occurred to us otherwise.

Lastly, the third reason is practical. Courts are increasingly looking towards jurisprudence outside their national systems for guidance on how to negotiate the issues arising from our increasingly multicultural societies. Although this remains a minority position in the US, the role of "foreign" law in our Supreme Court's decision making is a lively controversy. And other countries, such as Brazil, India and South Korea have more long-standing traditions of a transnational jurisprudence. These legal developments are, no doubt, a result of committed people and vibrant political organizations who continue to fight the world over for what the promise of equality might deliver in the everyday lives of marginalized men, women and children. When one scratches the surface of the cases, laws and scholarship contained in this book, we see the labor of this tireless commitment. And it is in order to contribute to these efforts that we invite a comparative study of equality law that might make more accessible new strategies, discourses, partnerships, and knowledge.

As the reader works through the casebook, we suggest some general questions that might help to guide a comparative analysis.

1. How exactly does a particular nation define, analyze and justify its particular notion of equality?

2. How does one nation's notion of equality resonate with another's? And how does it depart?

3. What are the shortcomings of each, and how does identifying these shortcomings perhaps yield points of reconsideration and reform?

4. Is this comparison helpful for thinking about new definitions, strategies, analyses and justifications? If yes, why? If no, why not?

5. Who are the individuals or people of these cases? What is their biography or history? What are the cultural and social contexts in which they are making their claims of equality?

6. What is the political history of a particular nation's legal system? And how does equality fit into this history? How does the substantive equality issue (religious, gender, or employment for example) emerge from and shape the legal notion of equality? And the cultural or social understanding of equality?

7. And finally, what other information would we need to have a fuller understanding of a particular nation's equality jurisprudence? To make a comparison more productive, or explain why a comparison perhaps might not be appropriate?

The opening chapter of the casebook introduces a discussion about the meaning of equality. What have commentators on the human condition said about equality, hoped for equality? What of these various articulations of equality, spanning centuries and continents, makes sense to us today? From this introductory chapter, we move into a more focused examination of how the ideals of equality have been legally determined. In contrast to social and cultural notions of equality, the law must articulate clear definitions, procedures and standards for how equality will be guaranteed and remedied. What are the procedural requirements, standards of proof, and evidentiary rules in a particular legal system that enables an experience of inequality to be turned into a legal claim, into a justiciable issue? These, we will see, differ from nation to nation, and provide a prerequisite knowledge of a particular legal system before moving on to more substantive issues.

The chapters then shift to the development of equality in various parts of social life. Chapters III and IV engage two issues among the most heavily litigated in the wake of mid-twentieth century civil rights and decolonization movements: employment discrimination and affirmative action. In educational and employment settings around the globe, we see the legal development of equality through notions like proportionality, historical redress, and merit. We see the interface between race and class, gender and identity, and difference and assimilation–all further complicating but adding to the possibility of discovering deeper legal commitments to equal distribution of socio-economic opportunities.

In Chapters V and VI, we encounter the reach of law in the name of equality into issues traditionally regarded as those of the private sphere: marriage and reproduction. Legal approaches to discrimination and equal treatment within these contexts are cast in terms of nature, happiness, health and national values. Less about equal socio-economic opportunity, and more about equal recognition of various kinds of human intimacies, these chapters reveal how various nations struggle to negotiate in their laws fundamental definitions of what life, family and political community are and should be.

Then, in Chapters VII, VIII and IX, we move on to the difficulties of guaranteeing equality in societies built on various liberties of self-expression, whether religious, personal, or political. Secularism, extremist ideologies, and public displays of personal bigotry all push on the limits of the liberal ideal that individuals are free to be and express who they are to the extent that it does not encroach on another's freedom or a state's obligation to its governed. These materials compellingly raise core questions about a nation's political structure and how we understand the relationship between the state and civil society, between the public domain of cultural expression and government regulation of it, between human singularity and the kinds of constraints a society places on individuals equally, perhaps at the expense of a meaningful diversity that allows an individual to flourish as a unique person. Finally, we close with Chapter X, which outlines more explicitly how issues of political organization between local agencies, intermediary governments, and national or supranational institutions effect legal articulations and enforcements of equality.

The source materials presented here are, obviously, only fragments of the legal knowledge on equality. They are clearly delimited by our own institutional and national locations, as well as our scholarly areas of interest. They are even more delimited by our linguistic abilities. But even if our language was not limited to a mono-, bi-or tri-lingualism, the field of equality law is unevenly translated and published, with translations of laws written outside of the Romance languages sorely missing. (This is not even to raise the question of translations of customary law). And even within the dominant languages, there will always be the problem of whether 'equality' in English means the same thing as the French term, 'égalité', or the Japanese term, 'byodoo', or the German term, 'gleichheit', or the Arabic term, 'mousawaa'. These difficulties, we think, are an invitation to scholars and students interested in issues of equality to support and develop multi-lingualism and study-abroad programs in liberal arts and legal education. Our knowledge and legal practice depends on it.

We hope that these fragments cohere into a constellation of legal forms of equality that directs interested readers towards any number of research projects and legal cases that wait to be undertaken. These are the cases and materials that tarry at the margins of the constitutional law classroom, and at the margins point us towards more nuanced and engaged understandings of diversity, social justice and democratic equality to come.

ACKNOWLEDGMENTS

This casebook has its origins in a reader initially prepared in 2005 for a course in Comparative Equality Law. The course was first taught by David Oppenheimer (then at Golden Gate University School of Law, now at Berkeley Law) and Sophie Robin–Olivier of the University of Paris (then at Nanterre/Paris X, now at the Sorbonne/Paris I) as part of a summer program in comparative law sponsored by Paris X and Golden Gate. In 2007 Sheila Foster of Fordham Law School joined the faculty of the comparative law program and joined the comparative equality project as a co-author. Sora Han of the University of California, Irvine, joined us in the program and project in 2008.

The reader would never have become a book without the help of many many collaborators. Professor Robin–Olivier collected material on French and European law, European federalism, and sources of European law. Professor Winfried Brugger of the University of Heidelberg (who, sadly, passed away in 2010 before the book was completed) contributed material on hate speech, and an essay on comparative secularism. Professor Marie–Christine Pauwels of Paris X drafted material on French secularism. Professor Marie Mercat–Bruns of Sciences–Po law school in Paris drafted material on French and European age discrimination in employment. Professor Eric Christiansen of Golden Gate University contributed to the materials on same-sex marriage. Alvaro Oliveira of the European Commission, Fulbright Scholar Costanza Hermanin, and Professors Isabelle Rorive and Emmanuelle Bribosia of the Free University of Brussels read many of our discussions of European law and corrected numerous errors. (Those that remain are solely our responsibility.) Dennis Dalton, Bernard Freamon, Gary Kates, Ian Haney Lopez, Ethan Schulman, and Stephanie Wildman helped us locate passages on the meaning of equality. Susie Squier helped identify relevant cases and commentary from British law, drawing on her experience with the UK Equalities Office. Victoria Plaut helped guide us through the science of bias. Joy Milligan helped us organize our discussion of secularism and equality. Noga Firstenberg helped us conceptualize how federalism shapes equality discourse. Participants in the Berkeley comparative law anti-discrimination law study group and in the Harvard/EUI workshop on the evolution of anti-discrimination law in Europe and the United States helped add depth to many of the chapters.

As we used the materials in the classroom, we often invited colleagues to team teach a class with us, and to help us refine the materials. We received helpful feedback, new ideas on approach, and often inspiration from the many friends and colleagues who joined us. We are grateful to them all, and in particular to Richad Antonius, Susanne Baer, Jean–Claude Beaujour, Florence Bellivier, Sandra Johnson Blake, Sabine Broeck, Winfried Brugger, Marie Mercat Bruns, Jesse Choper, Eric Christiansen, Willy Fletcher, James Goldston, Joe Grodin, Barbara Havelkova, Sophie Latraverse, Catharine McKinnon, Rachel Moran, Charles Ogletree, Alvaro Oliveira, Eva Paterson, Timothy Simon, Nadine Strossen, Kendall Thomas, and Frederic White.

Maryanne Gerber, Michael Daw, and Melissa Beuoy of the Golden Gate Law Library spent countless hours finding material, which was often then scanned, processed or otherwise digitized by Golden Gate staff members Mateo Jenkins and Sandra Derian, and by Berkeley Law staff member Joelle Brown, and our amazing editor Ayn Lowry.

We were assisted by law students Pauline Abadie, Yaser Ali, Ashu Arora, Swapna Balepur, Gael Bizel, Stephanie Brauer, Daniela Carrasco, Nicholas Cerutti, Michelle Chang, Candace Chen, Margaret Chen, Lynn Damiano, Lindsay Dazel, Elisabeth Decarvalho, Jeffrey Douglas, Lacey Ellis, Arusha Gordon, Simona Grossi, Esther Hagege, Britt Harwood, Sean Heneghan, Natalie Kwan, Trent Latta, Benedicte Magdelaine, Natalie Minez, Nadege Morvant, Deepti Nigan, Ariella Perry, Rory Quintana, Felipa Quiroz, Arvind Sabu, Khadeeja Shaikh, Julie Ann Talbo, Margaux Roussel, Fanxi Wang, and Yofi Weinberg, and by Criminology, Law and Society doctoral student, Kathryn Henne.

Although we do not cite or rely on Wikipedia as authority, since its articles are anonymous, we found it to be very helpful in identifying primary and secondary sources, and wish to thank its community of volunteer writers and editors.

This casebook is a work in progress, and reflects the substantial contribution of the students who have taken the course with us. We are grateful to them. Each of us is grateful to our co-authors, for committing to make this a truly collaborative project. We learned so much from each other, and in the process enriched each other's lives, as well as our work.

David B. Oppenheimer
Berkeley, California, January 2012

Sheila R. Foster
New York, N.Y., January 2012

Sora Y. Han
Oakland, California, January 2012

Copyright permission acknowledgments

Jack M. Balkin and Reva B. Siegel, "The American Civil Rights Tradition: Anticlassification or Antisubordination?" 58 *University of Miami Law Review* 9, 9–14 (2003). By permission of University of Miami Law Review.

Gu Baochang et al., "China's Local and National Fertility Policies at the End of the Twentieth Century," 33 Population & Development Review 129, 130, 132–133 (2007). By permission of publisher. Copyright © 2007, John Wiley and Sons.

Mostapha Benhenda, "For Muslim Minorities, it is Possible to Endorse Political Liberalism, But This is Not Enough," 11:2 Journal of Islamic Law and Culture 71–87 (2009). Electronic copy available at: http://ssrn.com/abstract=1574982, ISSN 1753–4534 online. By permission of author.

Karima Bennoune, "Secularism and Human Rights: A Contextual Analysis of Headscarves, Religious Expression, and Women's Equality Under International Law," 45 *Columbia Journal of Transnational Law* 367, 389–392 (2007). By permission of author and Columbia Journal of Transnational Law.

Jagdish Bhagwati, "Secularism in India: Why is it Imperiled?" in The Future of Secularism (Oxford University Press, 2009). By permission of publisher.

Winfried Brugger, "On The Relationship Between Structural Norms And Constitutional Rights In Church–State–Relations," in *Religion in the Public Sphere: A Comparative Analysis of German, Israeli, American and International Law* (eds. Winfried Brugger & Michael Karayanni, 2007, pp. 31–48, citations omitted). By permission of Springer–Verlag GmbH.

Eric C. Christiansen, "Ending the Apartheid of the Closet: Sexual Orientation in the South African Constitutional Process," 32 NYU J Int'l L & Pol 997, 997–1000, 1042–1043, 1046, 1051–1052, 1056, 1058 (2000). By permission of author and New York University Journal of International Law and Politics.

Linda Clarke, "Sexual Harassment Law in the United States, the United Kingdom and the European Union: Discriminatory Wrongs and Dignitary Harms," 36 *Common Law World Review* 79, 80–84; 86–88, 89–94, 97–98 (2007). By permission of Vathek Publishing.

Conseil Representatif des Associations Noires, "Should the French Government Collect Racial Population Data?" Found at http://www.lecran.org/newsdesk_info.php?newsdesk_did=79. By permission of Le Cran.

Hendrik Cremer, "A Constitution Without Race: Proposal for an Amendment of Article 3," German Institute of Human Rights Policy Paper No.16 (April 2010). Found at http://www.institut-fuer-menschenrechte.de/fileadmin/user_upload/Publikationen/Policy_Paper/policy_paper_16_ein_grundgesetz_ohne_rasse.pdf. By permission of Hendrik Cremer, Deutsches Institut für Menschenrechte.

Gareth Davies, "(Not Yet) Taking Rights Seriously: The House of Lords in Begum v. Headteacher and Governors of Denbigh High School, on

Religious Clothing in Schools" Human rights & human welfare: a forum for works in progress. Working paper no. 37, pp. 20–27, http://ssrn.com/abstract=945319. By permission of author.

Owen M. Fiss, "Groups and the Equal Protection Clause," 5 *J. Phil. & Pub. Affairs*, 107 (1976). By permission of author.

Bernard K. Freamon, "Conceptions of Equality and Slavery in Islamic Law: Tribalism, Piety, and Pluralism," (2007). By permission of author.

Julius Grey, "The Paradoxes of Reasonable Accomodation," *Options Politiques* (Septembre 2007), pp. 34–35. Found at http://www.irpp.org/po/archive/sep07/grey.pdf. By permission of the Institut de recherché en politiques publiques.

Angela P. Harris, "Loving Before and After the Law," 76 *Fordham Law Review* 2821, 2821–2822 (2008). By permission of author and Fordham Law Review.

Kristin Henrard, "Equal Rights Versus Special Rights? Minority Protection and the Prohibition of Discrimination," (Report Prepared for European Commission, Directorate–General Employment, Social Affairs and Equal Opportunities, June 2007, pp. 22–29; 55–59, footnotes omitted). Copyright © European Communities, 2007.

Benjamin Hensler, "Nao Vale a Pena? (Not Worth the Trouble?) Afro–Brazilian Workers and Brazilian Anti-discrimination Law," 30 HASTINGS INT'L & COMP. L. REV. 267, 287–289 (2007). By permission of author and Hastings International and Comparative Law Review.

Tanya Katerí Hernández, "Multiracial Matrix: The Role Of Race Ideology In The Enforcement Of Antidiscrimination Laws, A United States–Latin America Comparison," 87 *Cornell L. Rev.* 1093, 1129 (2002). By permission of author.

Therese Hesketh, Li Lu, and Zhu Wei Xing, "The Effect of China's One Child Policy After 25 Years," 353 NEW ENG. J. MED. 1171, 1171–1172 (2005). By permission of Massachusetts Medical Society.

John T. Jost, Laurie A. Rudmanb, Irene V. Blairc, Dana R. Carneyd, Nilanjana Dasguptae, Jack Glaserf & Curtis D. Harding, "The Existence of implicit bias is beyond reasonable doubt: A refutation of ideological and methodological objections and executive summary of ten studies that no manager should ignore," 29 *Research in Organizational Behavior* 39–69 (2009). www.sciencedirect.com. By permission of Elsevier: Copyright © 2009, Elsevier.

Pamela S. Karlan & George Rutherglen, "Disabilities, Discrimination, And Reasonable Accomodation," 46 *Duke Law Journal* 1, 2–5 (1996). By permission of authors.

Laura Kessler, "The Attachment Gap: Employment Discrimination Law, Women's Cultural Caregiving, and The Limits of Economic and Liberal Legal Theory", 34 *U. Mich. J.L. Ref.* 371, 386–389 (2001). By permission of author.

William C. Kidder, The Struggle for Access from Sweatt to Grutter: a History of African American, Latino, And American Indian Law School Admissions, 19 *Harvard BlackLetter Law Journal* 1 (2003). By permission of Harvard University/Law School.

Linda Hamilton Krieger, "The Content of Our Categories: A Cognitive Bias Approach to Discrimination and Equal Employment Opportunity," 47 *Stan. L. Rev.* 1161, 1187–1188 (1995). By permission of author and Stanford Law Review.

Andrzej Kulczycki, "The Abortion Debate in Mexico," 26 *Bulletin of Latin American Research*, 50, 57–59 (2007). By permission of Society for Latin American Studies.

Charles R. Lawrence III, "The Id, The Ego And Equal Protection: Reckoning With Unconscious Racism," 39 *Stan. L. Rev.* 317, 322, 323, 355–362 (1987). By permission of author and Stanford Law Review.

Robert Leckey, "Thick Instrumentalism and Comparative Constitutionalism: The Case of Gay Rights," 40 *Colum. Hum. Rts. L. Rev.* 425, 452–455 (2009). By permission of author.

R.A. Lenhardt, "Beyond Analogy: Perez v. Sharp, Antimiscegenation Law, and the Fight for Same–Sex Marriage," 96 CALIFORNIA LAW REVIEW 839, 840–45, 854–62 (2008). By permission of author and California Law Review.

Pierre Marois (President, Commision des droits de la personne et des droits de la jeunesse), "Religion, Private Schools and the Duty of Reasonable Accomodation: Looking Beyond the Trees to the Forest," *Le Devoir* (June 15, 2005). Found at www.cdpdj.qc.ca/en/publications/docs/article_religion_accommodation.pdf. By permission of Commision des droits de la personne et des droits de la jeunesse.

Jonathan L. Marshfield, "Authorizing Subnational Constitutions in Transitional Federal States: South Africa, Democracy, and the Kwazulu–Natal Constitution," 41 VAND. J. TRANSNAT'L L. 585 (2008), pp. 591–599. By permission of Vanderbilt Journal of Transnational Law.

Mari Matsuda, "Looking Beyond the Bottom: Critical Legal Studies and Reparations," 22 *Harvard Civil Rights—Civil Liberties Law Review* 323, 393–397 (1987). By permission of Harvard University/Law School.

Sharmila L. Murthy, "Iraq's Constitutional Mandate to Justly Distribute Water: The Implications of Federalism, Islam, International Law and Human Rights," 42 GEO. WASH. INT'L L. REV. 749 (2011), pp. 759–769. By permission of author and George Washington International Law Review.

Smita Narula, "Equal by Law, Unequal by Caste: The "Untouchable" Condition in Critical Race Perspective," 26, *Wis. Int'l L.J.* 255, 273, 274, 280–81, 295. By permission of author and Wisconsin International Law Journal.

Vasuki Nesiah, "Federalism and Diversity in India," in AUTONOMY AND ETHNICITY: NEGOTIATING COMPETING CLAIMS IN MULTI-ETHNIC STATES, Ghai, Yash, ed. (2000 Cambridge University Press), pp. 54–59. By permission of Cambridge University Press.

90 BVerfGE 241 (1994), German Federal Constitutional Court (German Holocaust Denial Case). By permission of Sir Basil Markesinis, QC, FBA (as translator).

Martha C. Nussbaum, "The Prohibition Era (Review of Covering: The Hidden Assault on Our Civil Rights, by Kenji Yoshino)," *The New Republic*, March 20, 2006. By permission of author and The New Republic. The author's book, *Philosophical Interventions* (Oxford University Press, January 2012), includes this article.

Colin O'Cinneide, "Age discrimination and the European Court of Justice: EU Equality Law Comes of Age," LAW AND EUROPEAN AFFAIRS, 2009–2010/2, p. 253–254, p.269. By permission of author and Law and European Affairs.

Charles J. Ogletree, Jr., "Repairing the Past: New Efforts in the Reparations Debate in America," 38 *Harvard Civil Rights–Civil Liberties Law Review* 279, 282–3 (2003). By permission of author and Harvard University/Law School.

Robert Post, "Prejudicial Appearances: The Logic of American Antidiscrimination Law," 88 *California Law Review* 1, 2–3, 8–13 (2000). By permission of author and California Law Review.

Robert C. Post & Reva B. Siegel, "Equal Protection by Law: Federal Antidiscrimination Legislation After Morrison and Kimel," 110 YALE L.J. 441 (2000), pp. 442–455. By permission of authors and Yale Law Journal.

Darren Rosenblum, *"Parity/Disparity: Electoral Gender Inequality On The Tightrope Of Liberal Constitutional Traditions"*, 39 *University of California Davis L. Rev.* 1119, 1159–1160. By permission of author.

Daniel Sabbagh, "Affirmative Action and the Group–Disadvantaging Principle," *Issues In Legal Scholarship, The Origins and Fate of Antisubordination Theory* (2003). Found at www.bepress.com/ils/iss2/art14. By permission of author and The Berkeley Electronic Press (bepress).

Daniel Sabbagh, "Affirmative Action at Sciences Po (Institut D'études Politiques De Paris), "FRENCH POLITICS, CULTURE AND SOCIETY, Fall 2002 v20 i3 p52–58. By permission of author and Berghan Books.

Michael Selmi, "Proving Intentional Discrimination: The Reality of Supreme Court Rhetoric," 86 *Georgetown Law Journal* 279, 283–285 (1997). By permission of author and the Georgetown Law Journal.

South Asian Human Rights Documentation Centre, "Prevention of Atrocities Act: Unused Ammunition," http://www.hrdc.net/sahrdc/hrfeatures/HRF83.htm (August 2003). By permission of South Asian Human Rights Documentation Centre, conditioned on acknowledgment of the source.

Sandra F. Sperino, "Rethinking Discrimination Law," http://ssrn.com/abstract=1759458. By permission of author.

D.K. Srivastava, "Progress of Sexual Harassment Law in India, China and Hong Kong: Prognosis for Further Reform," 51 *Harvard International Law Journal Online* 172, 175–76 (August 11, 2010). By permission of Harvard University/Law School.

Excerpt from "Count Stanislas—Marie—Adelaide de Clermont–Tonnerre's Speech on Religious Minorities (December 23, 1789)," from The French Revolution and Human Rights: A Brief Documentary History, Lynn Hunt, editor and translator. Copyright © 1996 by Bedford/St. Martin's. Reprinted with permission of the publisher.

Julie C. Suk, "Procedural Path Dependence: Discrimination and the Civil–Criminal Divide," 85 *Washington University Law Review* 1315, 1335–1339 (2008). By permission of author and Washington University Law Review.

The Unconstitutionality of the Total Criminalization of Abortion, Colombia Constitutional Supreme Court decision 2006, C–355/2006, Women's Link Worldwide, pp. 14–16, 20–21, 25, 27–28, 31–32, 34–36, 38, 41, 43, 48–51, 53–57, 61, 66–67. Translation by Women's Link Worldwide, with thanks to their counsel Monica Roa.

Tanya M. Washington, "All Things Being Equal: The Promise of Affirmative Efforts to Eradicate Color–Coded Inequality in the United States and Brazil," 21 NATIONAL BLACK LAW JOURNAL 1, 8–10, 34–35 (2009). By permission of author.

Wendy W. Williams, "The Equality Crisis: Some Reflections on Culture, Courts and Feminism," 14 *Women's Rights Law Reporter* 151, 168–170 (1992). By permission of author.

Kenji Yoshino, "Covering: The Hidden Assault on Our Civil Rights," 111 *Yale Law Journal* 769, 771–775 (2002). By permission of author and Yale Law Journal Company Inc.

Karthigasen Govender, "Achieving Substantive Equality in a Society Founded Upon Inequality: The South African Constitutional Experience", (1997). http://law.wustl.edu/Library/Guides/Equality/papers.html. By permission of author.

SUMMARY OF CONTENTS

TABLE OF CONTENTS

TABLE OF CASES

Principal cases are in bold type. Non-principal cases are in roman type. References are to Pages.

xxxiii

TABLE OF STATUTES

TABLE OF AUTHORITIES

COMPARATIVE EQUALITY AND ANTI–DISCRIMINATION LAW:

CASES, CODES, CONSTITUTIONS, AND COMMENTARY

CHAPTER I

WHAT IS EQUALITY IN THE LAW?

What are we talking about when we talk about equality in the law? The word and/or ideal of equality appears in most, if not all, constitutions of countries and states across the world. The guarantee of equality thus cuts across regional, cultural, and ideological differences. However, paradoxically, what exactly equality entails can also be highly dependent upon the particular regional, cultural, and ideological setting in which it is invoked and applied. At times it can even seem an "empty" ideal given its uneven and varied interpretations and applications.

Consider the most often-cited phrase in the founding document of the United States—the 1776 Declaration of Independence—which states, "We hold these truths to be self-evident, that all men are created equal." Its French equivalent, the 1789 Declaration of the Rights of Man, states in its first article that "Men are born and remain free and equal in rights." Yet Thomas Jefferson, the principal author of the American declaration, and an important contributor to the French declaration, was himself a slave owner, and took as his mistress one of his slaves when she was a teenager. This alone should alert us that the principle of equality may be divorced from the application. At the least, equality potentially contains varied and shifting meanings and even contradictions and tensions across time, geography, and context.

Ideas and applications of equality span a conceptual range that is impossible to capture completely here. In the materials and problems presented in chapters II–X, we will see a variety of concepts or models of equality discussed and applied. We will see equality described in terms of equal opportunity, equal outcomes, individual equality, group equality, measuring differences, refusing to measure differences, subordination, diversity, unity, respect, dignity, tolerance, social structures, institutions, individual decisions, individual rights, group rights, human rights, civil rights, color-blindness, racism-blindness, color-consciousness, reparations, obligations, damages, accommodation, discrimination, reverse discrimination, positive discrimination, affirmative action, prejudice, ignorance, bigotry, and cognitive bias. No doubt this list is incomplete.

Yet even within (and certainly between) these different ideas of legal equality there exists a tension between formal and substantive notions of equality. This tension is highlighted in this chapter before we begin confronting the problems and applications of equality in the following chapters. By formal equality, we mean the application of equality rules and norms that are agnostic about, or indifferent towards, the status of groups differently situated in society or the social structure. By substantive equality we mean the creation and application of equality rules and norms explicitly designed to identify and address the social status of groups

1

differently situated in a society. We view formal and substantive equality not as polar extremes but rather as a spectrum, along which articulations and applications of equality fall. The difference between the two is a useful heuristic device, or framework, for our discussion throughout the book.

This chapter asks us to consider a number of different concepts of equality and the ways in which the tension between formal and substantive equality plays out between and within them. The excerpts that follow— most quite brief, though a few somewhat longer—are statements by a variety of jurists, artists, politicians, professors and activists that describe different conceptions of equality. Their divergent views are offered to introduce you to a few of the many ways in which equality is framed and debated, both within the law and within our broader societies. This is not a comprehensive list but rather an illustrative one designed to get us thinking about equality and some of the themes that will run throughout the rest of the book.

As you read these materials, you may find it helpful to consider a variety of problems in which we are required to apply these concepts of equality. Consider the following:

- An African–American job applicant is denied a job for which he has applied and for which he is well qualified. The employer offers as a defense that there were better applicants, but cannot produce applications or other objective evidence on which it relied. Who should bear the burden of proving the employer's reason for its decision?

- In a State where same-sex marriage is authorized by law, a county clerk refuses to issue a marriage license to a same-sex couple because it violates his religious views. Should the clerk be required to issue the license (or disciplined for his refusal)? Whose equality rights are affected by the decision?

- A school district routinely assigns students from a minority group to "special education" classes, in which there is less academic instruction. The assignments are made based on intelligence tests administered to all incoming students. Is the district engaged in segregation? Is the assignment policy a violation of the minority children's rights? Does the decision affect the majority group children? Do they have rights that must be respected?

- An employer provides no medical leaves of any kind to its employees, reasoning that the inconvenience to customers and other employees makes the cost of such leaves prohibitive. The policy has its greatest impact on women employees in their twenties and thirties, who cannot take leave, and are thus terminated, if they choose to have children. Does the employer's policy violate the principle of equality?

- A medical school reserves a percentage of its seats for students from a disadvantaged minority group. Does the policy violate the rights (or reasonable expectations) of the majority group applicants? Does it violate the principle of equality?

- A national legislature passes a law making it a crime for a woman to go abroad to have an abortion. Does the law violate the principle of equality? What if the nation has legally adopted a state religion and that religion prohibits abortion?

- A national legislature passes a law authorizing clergy from certain religions to perform marriage ceremonies that will be legally recognized by the state. Members of other religions must marry in a civil ceremony for their marriage to be recognized. Does the law violate the principle of equality?

- A national constitution guarantees freedom of religion in private places, while prohibiting any public display of religious conviction, including the growing of beards for religious reasons. Does the law violate the principle of equality? May the state refuse citizenship to a man who is otherwise eligible but has grown a beard for religious reasons?

- A national legislature passes a law providing that hateful speech based on political views is protected by the liberty interest in free speech, but that hateful speech based on gender, race, ethnicity or religion is not. Does the law violate the principle of equality?

- A judge orders an employer to pay for a full-time interpreter to support the work of a deaf or hearing-impaired employee, who is well qualified to perform her work if an interpreter is provided. Competing businesses do not incur this expense. Is there a violation of the principle of equality?

Each of these problems is drawn from the chapters that follow, and in each case the application of the principle of equality has been applied (or probably would be applied) differently in the U.S. system as compared with other national legal systems. If we keep these examples in mind as we consider this chapter's readings on equality, it may help us better understand the comparisons that follow.

A. EQUALITY AS EQUAL CITIZENSHIP

On a very basic level, the concept of equality under the law simply requires that the government treat every individual with equal concern and respect, including giving each individual the rights necessary to fully participate in society. Doing so not only upholds the dignity of the individual in a democratic society but also helps to remove the social, economic, and political barriers that some individuals face on account of socially disadvantaging differences. Historically, however, courts and commentators have disagreed over whether equality requires not just the extension of basic political and civil rights but also being attentive to the social status of individuals whom the law and society have regarded as inferior. Consider the excerpts below in light of this conflict.

The Red Lily

(1894)

■ ANATOLE FRANCE (JACQUES ANATOLE FRANÇOIS THIBAULT)

The law, in its majestic equality, forbids the rich as well as the poor to sleep under bridges, to beg in the streets, and to steal bread.

Plessy v. Ferguson

163 U.S. 537 (1896)

■ JUSTICE BROWN delivered the opinion of the Court.

The object of the [Fourteenth] amendment was undoubtedly to enforce the absolute equality of the two races before the law, but, in the nature of things, it could not have been intended to abolish distinctions based upon color, or to enforce social, as distinguished from political, equality, or a commingling of the two races upon terms unsatisfactory to either. Laws permitting, and even requiring, their separation, in places where they are liable to be brought into contact, do not necessarily imply the inferiority of either race to the other. * * * We consider the underlying fallacy of the plaintiff's argument to consist in the assumption that the enforced separation of the two races stamps the colored race with a badge of inferiority. If this be so, it is not by reason of anything found in the act, but solely because the colored race chooses to put that construction upon it.

————

The Social Contract

(1762)

■ JEAN-JACQUES ROUSSEAU

[E]ach man, in giving himself to all, gives himself to nobody; and as there is no associate over whom he does not acquire the same right as he yields others over himself, he gains an equivalent for everything he loses, and an increase of force for the preservation of what he has. If we then discard from the social compact what is not of its essence, we shall find that it reduces itself to the following terms: "Each of us puts his person and all his power in common under the supreme direction of the general will, and, in our corporate capacity, we receive each member as an indivisible part of the whole." At once, in place of the individual personality of each contracting party, this act of association creates a moral and collective body, composed of as many members as the assembly contains votes, and receiving from this act its unity, its common identity, its life and its will."

————

Speech Announcing Submission of the Voting Rights Act

(March 15, 1965)

■ LYNDON B. JOHNSON

There is no Negro problem. There is no Southern problem. There is no Northern problem. There is only an American problem.

And we are met here tonight as Americans—not as Democrats or Republicans; we're met here as Americans to solve that problem. This was the first nation in the history of the world to be founded with a purpose.

The great phrases of that purpose still sound in every American heart, North and South: "All men are created equal." "Government by consent of the governed." "Give me liberty or give me death." And those are not just clever words, and those are not just empty theories. In their name Americans have fought and died for two centuries and tonight around the world they stand there as guardians of our liberty risking their lives. Those words are promised to every citizen that he shall share in the dignity of man. This dignity cannot be found in a man's possessions. It cannot be found in his power or in his position. It really rests on his right to be treated as a man equal in opportunity to all others. It says that he shall share in freedom. He shall choose his leaders, educate his children, provide for his family according to his ability and his merits as a human being.

To apply any other test, to deny a man his hopes because of his color or race or his religion or the place of his birth is not only to do injustice, it is to deny Americans and to dishonor the dead who gave their lives for American freedom. Our fathers believed that if this noble view of the rights of man was to flourish it must be rooted in democracy. This most basic right of all was the right to choose your own leaders. The history of this country in large measure is the history of expansion of the right to all of our people.

Many of the issues of civil rights are very complex and most difficult. But about this there can and should be no argument: every American citizen must have an equal right to vote. There is no reason which can excuse the denial of that right. There is no duty which weighs more heavily on us than the duty we have to insure that right. Yet the harsh fact is that in many places in this country men and women are kept from voting simply because they are Negroes. * * *

What happened in Selma is part of a far larger movement which reaches into every section and state of America. It is the effort of American Negroes to secure for themselves the full blessings of American life. Their cause must be our cause too. Because it's not just Negroes, but really it's all of us, who must overcome the crippling legacy of bigotry and injustice.

And we shall overcome.

———

Speech on Religious Minorities

(December 23, 1789)

■ Count Stanislas-Marie-Adélaide de Clermont-Tonnerre

Sirs, in the declaration that you believed you should put at the head of the French constitution you have established, consecrated, the rights of man and citizen. In the constitutional work that you have decreed relative to the organization of the municipalities, a work accepted by the King, you have fixed the conditions of eligibility that can be required of citizens. It would seem, Sirs, that there is nothing else left to do and that prejudices should be silent in the face of the language of the law; but an honorable member has explained to us that the non-Catholics of some provinces still experience harassment based on former laws, and seeing them excluded from the elections and public posts, another honorable member has protested against the effect of prejudice that persecutes some professions. This prejudice, these laws, force you to make your position clear. I have the honor to present you with the draft of a decree, and it is this draft that I defend here. I establish in it the principle that professions and religious creed can never become reasons for ineligibility. . . .

There is no middle way possible: either you admit a national religion, subject all your laws to it, arm it with temporal power, exclude from your society the men who profess another creed and then, erase the article in your declaration of rights [freedom of religion]; or you permit everyone to have his own religious opinion, and do not exclude from public office those who make use of this permission. . . .

But, they say to me, the Jews have their own judges and laws. I respond that is your fault and you should not allow it. We must refuse everything to the Jews as a nation and accord everything to Jews as individuals. We must withdraw recognition from their judges; they should only have our judges. We must refuse legal protection to the maintenance of the so-called laws of their Judaic organization; they should not be allowed to form in the state either a political body or an order. They must be citizens individually. But, some will say to me, they do not want to be citizens. Well then! If they do not want to be citizens, they should say so, and then, we should banish them. It is repugnant to have in the state an association of non-citizens, and a nation within the nation. . . . In short, Sirs, the presumed status of every man resident in a country is to be a citizen. (Edited and translated by Lynn Hunt.)

————

Conceptions of Equality and Slavery in Islamic Law: Tribalism, Piety, and Pluralism

(2007)

■ BERNARD K. FREAMON

Muslims assert that the idea of universal human equality is a core precept in the Islamic belief system and a central tenet of the *Shari'a*. Islamic egalitarianism, in place since the time of the Prophet Muhammad, greatly facilitated Islam's spectacular growth in the first century after the death of the Prophet and it has continued to be a powerful catalyst for the expansion of the religion over the past fourteen hundred years. The ritual of the *Hajj*—the pilgrimage to Mecca—is perhaps the best demonstration of the importance of the egalitarian ethos in Islamic religious belief and practice. Every year several million Muslims—men and women, youngsters and octogenarians, princes and paupers, scholars and illiterates, black, white, brown, and yellow—travel to Mecca as *hajjis* or religious pilgrims in a once-in-a-lifetime sacrifice of time, money, and the routine comfort of daily life. Upon arrival at Mecca's precinct gates, each *hajji* discards his or her worldly possessions and concerns, humbly donning the pilgrim's simple garb and entering into the Islamic status of *Ihram*. Every *hajji* then performs the sacred ritual in as near a state of perfect physical equality with every other pilgrim as conditions will allow. The *Qur'an*, at verse 22:25, explicitly mandates this equality, providing that "... we have made [the Sacred Mosque] (open) to (all) men—equal is the dweller there and the visitor from the country...."

Participation in this ritual gives each Muslim pilgrim a profound understanding of the basic sameness of all human kind. The *Hajj* celebrates this basic equality in a way that is not replicated in any other human event on earth. Some have described it as a "dress rehearsal" for Judgment Day, when all human beings will stand as equals before God and all will be fairly and justly called to account for their deeds. The *Hajj* thus cogently demonstrates that Islam's uncompromising conception of the oneness of God fosters a similarly uncompromising conception of the oneness of humanity.

Theological assertions of universal human equality are certainly not unique to the Islamic religion. Judaism and Christianity also make the same claim. Yet, Islam is exceptional in that, early in its existence, the Prophet Muhammad and several of his successors effectively translated the religion's theological egalitarianism into tangible assertions of political, social, and legal equality that were quite progressive for their time. These assertions made the religion very attractive to outsiders, particularly those who had been victims of harsh and depredatory treatment in their own communities.

―――――

NOTES

1. Anatole France uses irony to express very simply the idea of equality under the law. The law should not tolerate inequality between two classes of people, or two individuals regardless of their social class. But (in)equality of what exactly? The idea of equal citizenship might suggest that, at the least, every individual in a society be guaranteed the same rights and social goods as any other. But, even then, we must decide what social goods are important, and whether goods need be tangible or whether equality also guarantees certain intangible goods, like "dignity." Thus, one might see the formal-substantive tension expressed in these excerpts as citizenship as legal equality versus citizenship as "belonging." The latter evokes more clearly Professor Kenneth Karst's idea of equality in social "status," measured in part by the reduction of inequalities that impose stigma or caste, as discussed further in note 6.

2. Rousseau's argument is described by Enlightenment historian Gary Kates as follows: "Rousseau defines the relationship of liberty and equality in such a way that liberty is possible only when individuals relate to each other on the basis of strict equality." Consider how Rousseau's view

conflicts with the arguments over student speech codes, taken up in the discussion of hate speech in Chapter IX, which articulate that equality and liberty are necessarily in conflict.

3.   Count Tonnerre's speech to the French National assembly on religious equality and citizenship previews a theme we will consider more fully in chapter VIII—how should the state provide equality rights to religious minorities? Tonnerre's answer was that their religious practices must be largely abandoned in exchange for citizenship. This remains the prevailing answer in France today. Is this an equal bargain for religious minorities?

4.   The *Plessy* court's interpretation of the guarantee of equal protection in the United States Constitution is highly formalistic in its distinction between "political" and "social" equality. As Reva Siegel has argued, this type of formalism was employed as a way to give newly freed slaves legal equality without disturbing the social segregation that was the norm in the country.

> "Distinctions among civil, political, and social rights functioned more as a framework for debate than a conceptual scheme of any legal precision. But it was generally understood that civil rights were those rights exercised by economic man, such as the capacity to hold property and enter into contracts, and to bring suit to defend those rights in the legal system. Voting was the core political right. Social rights were those forms of association that, white Americans feared, would obliterate status distinctions and result in the "amalgamation" of the races.
>
> White Americans reasoning about the fate of the emancipated slaves drew such distinctions precisely because their commitment to abolish slavery was not a commitment to recognize African–Americans as equals in all spheres of social life; in the years before and after the Civil War, white Americans of widely varying political views reiterated their conviction that emancipating African–Americans entailed granting the freedmen some form of legal equality, but assuredly did not require granting them 'social equality.' "

Reva Siegel, *Why Equal Protection No Longer Protects: The Evolving Forms Of Status-Enforcing State Action*, 49 STANFORD L. REVIEW 1111, 1119–1121 (1997).

5.   You might see President Johnson's speech in support of giving African Americans the right to vote as an example of the formalism embedded in the civil/political/social rights distinction. Consider, however, that the right to vote was guaranteed to the newly freed slaves by the 15th Amendment to the United States Constitution, which was ratified in 1870. Passage of the Voting Rights Act of 1965 was deemed necessary to address the intransigence of southern states in resisting allowing African Americans to vote freely. The Voting Rights Act specifically sought to address, and outlaw, the various mechanisms—poll taxes, literacy requirements, violence, etc.—that Southern states employed as a way of intimidating African Americans from exercising their right to vote.

6.   Regarding stigma and equality, Professor Kenneth Karst argues that "[c]itizenship, in its narrowest sense, is a legal status. In relation to

the rights of citizenship, all citizens are equal ... The essence of equal citizenship is the dignity of full membership in the society." * * *

"The principle of equal citizenship presumptively insists that the organized society treat each individual as a person, one who is worthy of respect, one who "belongs." Stated negatively, the principle presumptively forbids the organized society to treat an individual either as a member of an inferior or dependent caste or as a nonparticipant. Accordingly, the principle guards against degradation or the imposition of stigma." * * *

"In its most typical application, the principle of equal citizenship will operate to prohibit the society from inflicting a status harm on members of a group because of their group membership. But even in these applications, the main energies released by the equal citizenship principle are individualistic. When one is freed from stigma, her sense of individual identity is strengthened precisely because she is no longer defined by others in terms of the stigma...." Kenneth Karst, *Equal Citizenship under the Fourteenth Amendment*, 91 Harvard Law Review 1, 5–8 (1977).

7. The United States Supreme Court in *Brown v. Board of Education*, 347 U.S. 483 (1954), took an important step toward guaranteeing a more substantive vision of equality in citizenship when it said, in invalidating racial segregation in grade and high schools: "To separate [Black children] from others of similar age and qualifications solely because of their race generates a feeling of inferiority as to their status in the community that may affect their hearts and minds in a way unlikely ever to be undone." The precedential value of this language in *Brown* has arguably declined over time as the U.S. Supreme Court settled on a rule that all racial classifications are inherently suspect, even if they are designed to address the differential social status of African Americans or other stigmatized racial groups in society.

B. Equality as Neutrality

Even if we agree that equal citizenship guarantees some degree of "belonging," there may be different means of guaranteeing that belonging. One ongoing question addressed by equality law is whether the demand of equality mandates that the law should, in effect, be blind to group differences such as race and ethnicity. An emerging norm would require that the law treat whites and blacks, for example, on the same terms as a way of guaranteeing them equality before the law and undoing stereotypical assumptions about racial differences. Such "colorblindness" would forbid (or presumptively restrain) the government from classifying individuals by race, except for compelling purposes.

On the other hand, others question whether equality can be achieved without legal recognition, or being explicitly conscious, of race where differences in the social status of groups exist or persist due to historical discrimination. Does equality require that the law tolerate differential treatment of social groups to provide for, or equalize, opportunity among groups where their group membership has been a cause of disadvantage? Or does taking account of group differences serve only to entrench those differences (and their social stigma) in the law and in society? The excerpts below provide some contours of the debate around whether the law should be neutral (or "colorblind") in light of differential social status and advantages between racial and ethnic groups.

————

Plessy v. Ferguson
163 U.S. 537 (1896)

■ JUSTICE HARLAN, dissenting

The white race deems itself to be the dominant race in this country. And so it is, in prestige, in achievements, in education, in wealth, and in power. So, I doubt not, it will continue to be for all time, if it remains true to its great heritage, and holds fast to the principles of constitutional liberty. But in the view of the constitution, in the eye of the law, there is in this country no superior, dominant, ruling class of citizens. There is no caste here. Our constitution is color-blind, and neither knows nor tolerates classes among citizens. In respect of civil rights, all citizens are equal before the law. The humblest is the peer of the most powerful.

————

McDonald v. Santa Fe Trail Transportation
427 U.S. 273 (1976)

■ JUSTICE MARSHALL delivered the opinion of the Court.

Title VII of the Civil Rights Act of 1964 prohibits the discharge of "any individual" because of "such individual's race," ... Its terms are not limited to discrimination against members of any particular race. Thus although we were not there confronted with racial discrimination against whites, we described the Act in *Griggs v. Duke Power Co.*, 401 U.S. 424, 431 (1971), as prohibiting "(d)iscriminatory preference for Any (racial) group, Minority or Majority." Similarly the EEOC [the Equal Employment Opportunity Commission], whose interpretations are entitled to great deference, has consistently interpreted Title VII to proscribe racial discrimination in private employment against whites on the same terms as racial discrimination against nonwhites, holding that to proceed otherwise would constitute a derogation of the Commission's Congressional mandate to eliminate all practices which operate to disadvantage the employment opportunities of any group."

————

Regents of the University of California v. Bakke
438 U.S. 265 (1978)

■ JUSTICE BRENNAN, dissenting

Our Nation was founded on the principle that "all Men are created equal." Yet candor requires acknowledgment that the Framers of our

Constitution, to forge the 13 Colonies into one Nation, openly compromised this principle of equality with its antithesis: slavery. The consequences of this compromise are well known and have aptly been called our "American Dilemma." Still, it is well to recount how recent the time has been, if it has yet come, when the promise of our principles has flowered into the actuality of equal opportunity for all regardless of race or color.

The Fourteenth Amendment, the embodiment in the Constitution of our abiding belief in human equality, has been the law of our land for only slightly more than half its 200 years. And for half of that half, the Equal Protection Clause of the Amendment was largely moribund so that, as late as 1927, Mr. Justice Holmes could sum up the importance of that Clause by remarking that it was the "last resort of constitutional arguments." Worse than desuetude, the Clause was early turned against those whom it was intended to set free, condemning them to a "separate but equal" status before the law, a status always separate but seldom equal. Not until 1954—only 24 years ago—was this odious doctrine interred by our decision in *Brown v. Board of Education* and its progeny, which proclaimed that separate schools and public facilities of all sorts were inherently unequal and forbidden under our Constitution. Even then inequality was not eliminated with "all deliberate speed." In 1968 and again in 1971, for example, we were forced to remind school boards of their obligation to eliminate racial discrimination root and branch. And a glance at our docket and at dockets of lower courts will show that even today officially sanctioned discrimination is not a thing of the past.

Against this background, claims that law must be "color-blind" or that the datum of race is no longer relevant to public policy must be seen as aspiration rather than as description of reality. This is not to denigrate aspiration; for reality rebukes us that race has too often been used by those who would stigmatize and oppress minorities. Yet we cannot ... let color blindness become myopia which masks the reality that many "created equal" have been treated within our lifetimes as inferior both by the law and by their fellow citizens.

————

Regents of the University of California v. Bakke

438 U.S. 265 (1978)

■ Justice Blackmun, dissenting

I suspect that it would be impossible to arrange an affirmative-action program in a racially neutral way and have it be successful. To ask that this be so is to demand the impossible. In order to get beyond racism, we must first take account of race. There is no other way. And in order to treat some persons equally, we must treat them differently. We cannot—we dare not—let the Equal Protection Clause perpetuate racial supremacy.

————

City of Richmond v. J.A. Croson

488 U.S. 469, 520–521, 527–529 (1989)

■ JUSTICE SCALIA, concurring

The difficulty of overcoming the effects of past discrimination is nothing compared with the difficulty of eradicating from our society the source of those effects, which is the tendency—fatal to a Nation such as ours—to classify and judge men and women on the basis of their country of origin or the color of their skin. A solution to the first problem that aggravates the second is no solution at all. I share the view expressed by Alexander Bickel that "[t]he lesson of the great decisions of the Supreme Court and the lesson of contemporary history have been the same for at least a generation: discrimination on the basis of race is illegal, immoral, unconstitutional, inherently wrong, and destructive of democratic society." A. Bickel, THE MORALITY OF CONSENT 13 (1975). At least where state or local action is at issue, only a social emergency rising to the level of imminent danger to life and limb—for example, a prison race riot, requiring temporary segregation of inmates, can justify an exception to the principle embodied in the Fourteenth Amendment that "[o]ur Constitution is color-blind, and neither knows nor tolerates classes among citizens," (citing *Plessy v. Ferguson*, HARLAN, J., dissenting). * * *

It is plainly true that in our society blacks have suffered discrimination immeasurably greater than any directed at other racial groups. But those who believe that racial preferences can help to "even the score" display, and reinforce, a manner of thinking by race that was the source of the injustice and that will, if it endures within our society, be the source of more injustice still. The relevant proposition is not that it was blacks, or Jews, or Irish who were discriminated against, but that it was individual men and women, created equal, who were discriminated against. And the relevant resolve is that that should never happen again. Racial preferences appear to even the score (in some small degree) only if one embraces the proposition that our society is appropriately viewed as divided into races, making it right that an injustice rendered in the past to a black man should be compensated for by discriminating against a white. Nothing is worth that embrace. Since blacks have been disproportionately disadvantaged by racial discrimination, any race-neutral remedial program aimed at the disadvantaged as such will have a disproportionately beneficial impact on blacks. Only such a program, and not one that operates on the basis of race, is in accord with the letter and the spirit of our Constitution.

———

Commencement Speech at Howard University

(1965)

■ LYNDON B. JOHNSON

But freedom is not enough. You do not wipe away the scars of centuries by saying: Now you are free to go where you want, and do as you desire, and choose the leaders you please. You do not take a person who, for years, has been hobbled by chains and liberate him, bring him up to the starting line of a race and then say, "You are free to compete with all the others," and still justly believe that you have been completely fair. Thus it is not enough just to open the gates of opportunity. All our citizens must have the ability to walk through those gates. This is the next and the more profound stage of the battle for civil rights. We seek not just freedom but opportunity. We seek not just legal equity but human ability, not just equality as a right and a theory but equality as a fact and equality as a result. For the task is to give 20 million Negroes the same chance as every other American to learn and grow, to work and share in society, to develop their abilities—physical, mental and spiritual, and to pursue their individual happiness. To this end equal opportunity is essential, but not enough, not enough.

————

Should the French State Collect Racial Population Data?

http://www.lecran.org/newsdesk_info.php?newsdesk_id=79

■ CONSEIL REPRESENTATIF DES ASSOCIATIONS NOIRES

[EDITORS' NOTE: In France, the census is prohibited from collecting information on race or ethnicity, because the idea of racial identity is regarded as offensive to the French Republican commitment to equality, which recognizes the only legitimate French identity as French citizenship. (A second reason sometimes offered is the trauma of the Holocaust, when French collaboration in the expulsion and murder of French Jews was facilitated by the existence of government records disclosing religion.) The following questions and answers, advocating the collection of racial data by the French state, are from the English language section of the web site of the Conseil Representatif des Associations Noires (CRAN, the Representative Council of Black Associations), an NGO founded at the time of the 2005 Paris riots to represent the interests of over 100 black organizations in France.]

Q. When one says that "in France Black people are invisible," what does it mean?

In principle to have dark skin in metropolitan France is not the best way to go unnoticed. The paradox is that as individuals, Black people in France are visible and yet as a social group remain invisible. As a social group it seems as if they were not supposed to exist: the French Republic doesn't officially recognize minorities, and doesn't record them as such. One could be satisfied with invisible populations, or at least see no problem with it, as long as social and specific difficulties concerning them be recorded, identified, recognized. However it is not the case. And instead of remaining a quiet and normal status, invisibility is wrong.

Q. Isn't to talk about "Black people" a misuse of language?

To the question "Who is Black?" we respond neither with nature arguments (which could refer to a "biologizing" race concept), nor with culture arguments (which could refer to an infinite variety of cultural differences among human individuals). Our response uses socio-political arguments. In societies where Blacks are part of the minority, a Black person is said to be as such, while a Black population made of men and women sharing a common social experience is that of discriminations because of the skin colour. Black people have in common to live in societies that consider them to be as such. Most of the time, they have no choice but to be the way they are perceived by others. To paraphrase Sartre, a Black person is an individual that others consider as Black.

Q. Is there a "black issue" in France?

No, there isn't, but France has an issue with its black populations. This issue has complex historical roots, linked to slavery and colonisation. Our goal is to alert volunteers in order to improve the tough situation of these populations, and fight against race discrimination.

Q. What is "race discrimination"?

Discrimination refers to an unfavourable treatment applied to a person because of his or her real or supposedly social belonging. Race discrimination is an unfavourable treatment based on race (for example the colour of the skin or any other type of phenotype distinction). Thus race discrimination can affect black persons, no matter their origin or nationality. Let's take the example of a black woman who is declined a job because of the fact that "customers wouldn't appreciate her skin colour." Here, this woman is the victim of race discrimination, not because of her origin, but because of her skin colour. Unlike racism which is an ideology, discrimination is a concrete act.

Q. How to fight against race discriminations?

First of all to fight against race discriminations requires studying these acts targeting individuals who don't look "right." This fight aims at being effective in order to put an end to moral damages. It is more concrete and pragmatic than fighting against racism. Its difficulty stands first of all in the recognition of race discriminations in order to find an efficient answer to them. And there is the rub in France, in that we lack statistical tools allowing us to measure discriminations and assess the efficiency of anti-discriminatory policies. To base one's assessment on testimonies is not enough, no matter how numerous and how much they match. These testimonies do not allow us to measure and compare discriminations from one year to the other.

Two major types of anti-discriminatory policies are possible and desirable. First, a sanction policy against discriminatory behaviour. The penal code acknowledges and curbs race discriminations, but one must admit that the justice of our country remains little active in the application of anti-discriminatory laws. Not enough lawsuits succeed. Judges are not well trained and often seem too little motivated with investigations and decisions concerning discrimination cases. Secondly, a policy which intends to actively promote diversity. This policy is called "affirmative action" in the USA and "positive discrimination" in France. No matter what terminology, it is about coming up with devices that help putting an end to the lack of diversity within too many political, economical and social authorities. The nature of these devices must become the core subject of a great national debate.

Q. Isn't an ethno-racial statistics dangerous?

Ethno-racial statistics is used in many countries. Its goal isn't to put people in biological and irreducible categories but to measure discriminations in order to better act against them. Demographers don't give their opinion concerning the nature of "race" or "ethnicity" and don't give any ontological verdict concerning their substance either. They only stand as a referent that helps characterizing and intervening on specific wrongdoings. These statistics are anonymous: they help measuring discriminations, but not identifying individuals.

Q. Who will decide on whether one is black or not?

Ethno-racial statistics is based on self-declaration: in the USA or in Great Britain, only concerned parties respond to those questions. Nobody decides for their group and responses are only optional.

——————

NOTES

1. Justice Scalia's dictate in a recent opinion on the constitutionality of race-conscious affirmative action programs—that "In the eyes of government, we are just one race here. It is American"—mirrors the French universalism (or formalism?) embedded in its refusal to classify citizens by race or to collect racial statistics. *Adarand Constructors, Inc. v. Pena*, 515 U.S. 200 (1995) (Scalia, concurring). Yet the question remains, as other commentators note, what position the law should take vis-à-vis the glaring social inequalities that track race and ethnicity in most modern societies. As Justice Blackmun argues, can societies and governments get beyond racism only by taking race into explicit account in addressing racial and ethnic inequalities? Or does focusing on race, particularly racial remedies (like affirmative action) do more harm than good to their targeted beneficiaries? *See, for example,* Ward Connerly, *One Nation Indivisible* (2001) http://www.hoover.org/publications/digest/4510836.html.

2. France is not the only country which refuses to collect racial data for the Census or for purposes of measuring racial and ethnic discrimination. As Tanya Hernandez notes, many Latin American nations refuse to collect census data according to racial identity, or otherwise collect systematic information on the status of its racial and ethnic populations. She explains that part of the reason is that any focus on race is believed to be adverse to maintaining a racially harmonious environment. However, she argues that without census data aggregated by race it is difficult to illustrate how significant the problem of racism by skin color is in these countries. In addition, the absence of census racial data effectively precludes the use of statistical evidence to prove a discrimination claim in court. *Tanya Kateri Hernández, Multiracial Matrix: The Role Of Race Ideology In The Enforcement Of Antidiscrimination Laws, A United States–Latin America Comparison*, 87 Cornell L. Rev. 1093, 1130–1131 (2002).

3. The refusal to collect racial data, either for the Census or to identify the existence of racial and ethnic discrimination, arguably has both positive and negative effects on a diverse society. Consider David Oppenheimer's observations as an American who has spent time in France observing and discussing this issue with French residents:

> From my limited time spent in France my own impression is that there is more racial and ethnic integration than in the United States. In particular, inter-racial friendships and intimate relationships appear to be more common in France than in the United States, and appear to be less controversial. Nonetheless, even a visitor sees enormous differences in the social status of non-whites in France. Nor do the French disagree; in my interviews, most of the French Muslims and French citizens of African descent (including North African and sub-Saharan African) with whom I spoke regard discrimination as a serious problem, as did many "non-minority" French citizens. Polling data confirms that these responses are representative. For example, according to a 2007 poll conducted by TNS–Sofres, over half of black French respondents stated that they had experienced racial discrimination. According to a 2006 poll, conducted by the European Union (the "Euro-barometer"), 80 percent of French respondents believe that ethnic origin discrimination is widespread in France, and over half believe that it had become worse in the prior five years. According to a 2003 poll by TNS–Sofres, 71 percent of French respondents believe that a person from North Africa or Africa faces increased discrimination.
>
> Whether we describe them as "minorities" or "visible minorities" or "immigrants" (a term sometimes extended to non-immigrant French citizens who are descended from non-European ancestors), or "blacks and Arabs" or "Africans" or "North and sub-Saharan Africans" or some other term of outsider identity, there are a substantial number of French citizens who are distinguished from French citizens of European descent by their skin color and ancestral origins. These French citizens are widely believed, and by some data revealed, to be less likely to have high-paying and/or high-status jobs, less likely to attend top schools and universities, and less likely to live in high-quality housing, as compared with lighter-skinned French citizens. Although the dark-skinned population of France is believed to be substantial, there are only a handful of dark-skinned French citizens elected to the National Assembly from the constituencies within continental Europe. (There are a few more elected from the overseas Departments in the Caribbean, the Indian Ocean, the South Pacific, and South America.) In the first poll ever taken of self-identified French blacks, they overwhelmingly responded that they were discriminated against because of their color.
>
> Housing segregation is sufficiently entrenched that an affirmative action admissions program that provides preferences to students who live in economically disadvantaged neighborhoods ("banlieues") can substitute for a race-based program in recruiting students perceived as not being "native French" to an elite (and largely white) school. The

riots that began in the suburbs of Paris in the fall of 2005 and spread to many minority neighborhoods were widely understood around the globe and within France to be race riots, and a wake-up call for France.

In the wake of the riots and the growing evidence of intolerable inequality, why not begin collecting racial identity data, and thus measuring discrimination and inequality?

David Oppenheimer, *Why France Needs To Collect Data On Racial Identity . . . In A French Way*, 31 HASTINGS INT'L & COMP. L. REV. 735, 743–746 (2008).

4.   In order to permit affirmative action policies (known as "positive action" in Europe), the European Union has adopted three provisions excepting affirmative action from the prohibition of discrimination, one in their constitutive treaty, two by legislation. The Treaty on the Functioning of the European Union provides at Article 157:4 "With a view to ensuring full equality in practice between men and women in working life, the principle of equal treatment shall not prevent any Member State from maintaining or adopting measures providing for specific advantages in order to make it easier for the underrepresented sex to pursue a vocational activity or to prevent or compensate for disadvantages in professional careers." Note that the treaty provision applies to gender, but not race, ethnicity or color. Similar language is found in Article 5 of European Union directive 2000/43/EC, which prohibits race and ethnic origin discrimination in employment and other sectors, and in Article 7 of Directive 2000/78/EC, which prohibits discrimination in employment (but not other sectors) based on religion or belief, age, disability and sexual orientation.

————

A Constitution Without Race: Proposal for an Amendment of Article 3

GERMAN INSTITUTE OF HUMAN RIGHTS POLICY PAPER No.16 (April 2010), *available at* http://www. institut-fuer-menschenrechte.de/fileadmin/user_upload/Publikationen/Policy_Paper/policy_ paper_16_ein_grundgesetz_ohne_rasse.pdf

■ HENDRIK CREMER

1.   Changing the formulation of the ban on discrimination in the Constitution

The German Institute of Human Rights recommends an amendment of the ban on discrimination in Article 3, Section 3, Clause 1 of the Constitution: the term "race" should be removed, without altering the protective scope of the clause. Art. 3, Sec. 3, Cl. 3 currently provides: "No one shall be favored or discriminated against on account of . . . his race."

This provision aims to combat racism and eliminate discrimination. At the same time, the wording of the provision conjures up a vision of humankind that is based on the notion of different "races." Yet only racist theories are based on the assumption that there are different human "races."

The formulation of Art. 3 Sec. 3 thus leads to an irresolvable contradiction. Parties who suffer racial discrimination must claim that they were discriminated against on account of their race; they have to assign themselves to a particular race and are therefore forced to use racist terminology.

The point of the discussion about the term "race" is not an intellectual mind game, but a change of perspective: racism cannot be credibly fought when the term "race" is retained. This is more so because use of the term makes the concept of human races appear acceptable, and can help feed racist thinking.

Some EU states have already decided to refrain from using the term in their legislation. In Germany, too, there is wide awareness of the problems of the term. An amendment of the Constitution, which is the foundation of the legal system of Germany, would be a signal to finally break the habit of using the term, and end the apparent acceptance of race concepts.

The German Institute of Human Rights recommends the striking of the term "race" from Art. 3 Sec. 3 Cl.1, and that the provision should be formulated in the following way:

> **"No one shall be favored or discriminated against *in a racist manner*, or on account of his sex, descent, language, home country and origin, beliefs, and religious or political views."**

* * *

3. Conclusion

The use of the term "race" in the ban on discrimination in the Constitution can promote racist thinking, because it suggests that there are different human "races." As long as the term is used in relation to people, it will trigger irritation and lack of understanding, culminating in personal injury. Moreover, its use is by no means necessary. The European Parliament has already recommended that the term should no longer be used in EU documents and human rights texts. Countries like Finland, Sweden and Austria have already distanced themselves from the term in their national legislation.

In the end, the term "race" cannot be interpreted in a sensible way. Every theory that is based on the existence of different human races is in itself racist. It is therefore time for a departure from the concept through amending Art. 3, Sec. 3, Cl. 1, so that the Constitution can instead prohibit *racist* discrimination or favoring. This would help the protection against racist discrimination and the fight against racism to have greater effect. (Translation by Fanxi Wang)

————

NOTES

1.   For more detail on the German debate on the nature of the term "race," see Hendrik Cremer, *". . . and To Which Race Do You Belong?" The Problem of the Term "Race" in Legislation*, German Institute of Human Rights Policy Paper No. 10 (2d ed. 2009).

2.   The European Union Directive implementing the principle of equal treatment between persons irrespective of racial or ethnic origin provides, "The European Union rejects theories which attempt to determine the

existence of separate human races. The use of the term "racial origin" in this Directive does not imply an acceptance of such theories." (*EC Directive 2000/43/EC* of 29 June 2000, Preamble, Part (6).) Does the language of the preamble satisfactorily answer the Cremer critique?

C.   Equality as Antisubordination

In 1976, Professor Owen Fiss of the Yale Law School published an essay that gave rise to a new theory of equality law, which he called the "group-disadvantaging principle" and is now known as antisubordination theory. Fiss asserted that courts were improperly interpreting the Equal Protection Clause of the Constitution as a requirement that the government not discriminate against an individual based on his/her classification (such as a racial classification). This is described as the non-discrimination principle. Today others would describe it as the "anticlassification" principle (embedded in the equality as neutrality notion discussed above). Fiss argued that the purpose of the Fourteenth Amendment's Equal Protection Clause was to protect subordinated groups (principally African Americans) from governmental acts that contributed to their subordination. The difference in the theories of what "equality" means can be described on two axes. One—does the constitution protect groups, or individuals? Two—does the Equal Protection Clause require strict scrutiny of government action when the government acts against a suspect class, or, alternatively, when it makes a suspect classification? What follows is a small portion of Fiss's own words on the subject and contemporary perspectives on the role of antisubordination analysis in equality jurisprudence.

————

Groups and the Equal Protection Clause

5 J. Phil. & Pub. Affairs. 107 (1976)

■ Owen M. Fiss

This is an essay about the structure and limitations of the antidiscrimination principle, the principle that controls the interpretation of the Equal Protection Clause . . .

The words—no state shall "deny to any person within its jurisdiction the equal protection of the laws"—do not state an intelligible rule of decision. In that sense the text has no meaning. The Clause contains the word "equal" and thereby gives constitutional status to the ideal of equality, but that ideal is capable of a wide range of meanings. This ambiguity has created the need for a mediating principle, and the one chosen by courts and commentators is the antidiscrimination principle. When asked what the Equal Protection Clause means, an informed lawyer—even one committed to Justice Black's textual approach to the First Amendment—does not repeat the words of the Clause—a denial of equal protection. Instead, he is likely to respond that the Clause prohibits discrimination.

One purpose of this essay is simply to underscore the fact that the antidiscrimination principle is not the Equal Protection Clause, that it is nothing more than a mediating principle. I want to bring to an end the identification of the Clause with the antidiscrimination principle. But I also have larger ambitions. I want to suggest that the antidiscrimination principle embodies a very limited conception of equality, one that is highly individualistic and confined to assessing the rationality of means. I also want to outline another mediating principle—the group-disadvantaging principle—one that has as good, if not better, claim to represent the ideal of equality, one that takes a fuller account of social reality, and one that more clearly focuses the issues that must be decided in Equal Protection cases.
* * *

The antidiscrimination principle has structural limitations that prevent it from adequately resolving or even addressing certain central claims of equality now being advanced. For these claims the antidiscrimination principle either provides no framework of analysis or, even worse, provides the wrong one.

The Permissibility of Preferential Treatment

One shortcoming of the antidiscrimination principle relates to the problem of preferential treatment for blacks. This is a difficult issue, but the antidiscrimination principle makes it more difficult than it is: the permissibility of preferential treatment is tied to the permissibility of hostile treatment against blacks. The antidiscrimination principle does not formally acknowledge social groups, such as blacks; nor does it offer any special dispensation for conduct that benefits a disadvantaged group. It only knows criteria or classifications; and the color black is as much a racial criterion as the color white. The regime it introduces is a symmetrical one of "color blindness," making the criterion of color, any color, presumptively impermissible. Reverse discrimination, so the argument is made, is a form of discrimination and is equally arbitrary since it is based on race. * * *

In my judgment ... preferential and exclusionary policies should be viewed quite differently under the Equal Protection Clause. Indeed, it would be one of the strangest and cruelest ironies to interpret that Clause in such a way that linked in some tight, inextricable fashion the judgments about the preferential and exclusionary policies. This dilemma can only be avoided if the applicable mediating principle of the Clause is clearly and explicitly asymmetrical, one that talks about substantive ends, and not fit, and one that recognizes the existence and importance of groups, not just individuals. Only then will it be possible to believe that when we reject the claim against preferential treatment for blacks we are not at the same time undermining the constitutional basis for protecting them. Of course, even if the antidiscrimination principle were not the predominant interpretation of the Clause, it might still be possible to formulate a claim against preferential treatment. The element of individual unfairness to the rejected applicants inherent in preferential treatment could be considered a cost in evaluating the state action in the same way as a loss of liberty or dignitary harm might be. The failure of the state to include other disadvantaged groups, such as the Chicanos, might also become significant. But the impenetrable barrier posed by the seemingly symmetrical antidiscrimination principle would be gone. The stakes would not be so high. * * *

In attempting to formulate another theory of equal protection, I have viewed the Clause primarily, but not exclusively, as a protection for blacks. In part, this perspective stems from the original intent—the fact that the Clause was viewed as a means of safeguarding blacks from hostile state action. The Equal Protection Clause (following the circumlocution of the slave-clauses in the antebellum Constitution) uses the word "person," rather than "blacks." The generality of the word chosen to describe those protected enables other groups to invoke its protection; and I am willing to admit that was also probably intended. But this generality of coverage does not preclude a theory of primary reference—that blacks were the intended primary beneficiaries, that it was a concern for their welfare that prompted the Clause.

It is not only original intent that explains my starting point. It is also the way the courts have used the Clause. The most intense degree of protection has in fact been given to blacks; they have received a degree of protection that no other group has received. They are the wards of the Equal Protection Clause, and any new theory formulated should reflect this practice. I am also willing to speculate that, as a matter of psychological fact, race provides the paradigm for judicial decision. I suspect that in those cases in which a claim of strict scrutiny has been or reasonably could have been made, it is commonplace for a judge to reason about an equal protection case by thinking about the meaning of the Clause in the racial context and by comparing the case before him to a comparable one in the racial area. Moreover, the limitations or inadequacies of the antidiscrimination principle surface most sharply when it is used to evaluate state practices affecting blacks.

Starting from this perspective, a distinctively racial one, it strikes me as odd to build a general interpretation of the Equal Protection Clause ... on the rejection of the idea that there are natural classes, that is, groups that have an identity and existence wholly apart from the challenged state statute or practice. There are natural classes, or social groups, in American society and blacks are such a group. Blacks are viewed as a group; they view themselves as a group; their identity is in large part determined by membership in the group; their social status is linked to the status of the group; and much of our action, institutional and personal, is based on these perspectives.

I use the term "group" to refer to a social group, and for me, a social group is more than a collection of individuals, all of whom, to use a popular example, happen to arrive at the same street corner at the same moment. A social group, as I use the term, has two other characteristics. (1) It is an entity (though not one that has a physical body). This means that the group has a distinct existence apart from its members, and also that it has an identity. It makes sense to talk about the group (at various points of time) and know that you are talking about the same group. You can talk about the group without reference to the particular individuals who happen to be its members at any one moment. (2) There is also a condition of interdependence. The identity and well-being of the members of the group and the identity and well-being of the group are linked. Members of the group identify themselves—explain who they are—by reference to their membership in the group; and their well-being or status is in part determined by the well-being or status of the group. * * *

I would therefore argue that blacks should be viewed as having three characteristics that are relevant in the formulation of equal protection theory: (a) they are a social group; (b) the group has been in a position of perpetual subordination; and (c) the political power of the group is severely circumscribed. Blacks are what might be called a specially disadvantaged group, and I would view the Equal Protection Clause as a protection for such groups. Blacks are the prototype of the protected group, but they are not the only group entitled to protection. There are other social groups, even as I have used the term, and if these groups have the same characteristics as blacks—perpetual subordination and circumscribed political power—they should be considered specially disadvantaged and receive the same degree of protection. What the Equal Protection Clause protects is specially disadvantaged groups, not just blacks. A concern for equal treatment and the word "person" appearing in the Clause permit and probably require this generality of coverage.

Some of these specially disadvantaged groups can be defined in terms of characteristics that do not have biological roots and that are not immutable; the Clause might protect certain language groups and aliens. Moreover, in passing upon a claim to be considered a specially disadvantaged group, the court may treat one of the characteristics entitling blacks to that status as a sufficient but not a necessary condition; indeed the court may even develop variable standards of protection—it may tolerate disadvantaging practices that would not be tolerated if the group was a "pure" specially disadvantaged group. Jews or women might be entitled to less protection than American Indians, though nonetheless entitled to some protection. Finally, these judicial judgments may be time-bound. Through the process of assimilation the group may cease to exist, or even if the group continues to retain its identity, its socioeconomic and political positions may so improve so as to bring to an end its status as specially disadvantaged.

———

The American Civil Rights Tradition: Anticlassification or Antisubordination?

58 University of Miami Law Review 9, 10–14 (2003)

■ JACK M. BALKIN and REVA B. SIEGEL

A fairly standard story about the development of antidiscrimination jurisprudence since the 1970s argues that the views of Fiss and other antisubordination theorists were rejected by the U.S. Supreme Court, which adopted a contrary and inconsistent theory of equality. This approach is sometimes called the anticlassification or antidifferentiation principle. Roughly speaking, this principle holds that the government may not classify people either overtly or surreptitiously on the basis of a forbidden category: for example, their race. We add the word "surreptitiously" because a law that does not explicitly classify by race may nevertheless be motivated by an invidious purpose to differentiate on the basis of race, and most people think that this also counts as a violation of the anticlassification or antidifferentiation principle.

When Fiss talks about the anticlassification approach in his 1976 article, he calls it the "antidiscrimination" principle. In hindsight, this choice of words was quite unfortunate, because there is no particular reason to think that antidiscrimination law or the principle of antidiscrimination is primarily concerned with classification or differentiation as opposed to subordination and the denial of equal citizenship. Both antisubordination and anticlassification might be understood as possible ways of fleshing out the meaning of the antidiscrimination principle, and thus as candidates for the "true" principle underlying antidiscrimination law.

[W]e challenge the common assumption that, during the Second Reconstruction, the anticlassification principle triumphed over the antisubordination principle. We argue instead that the scope of the two principles overlap, that their application shifts over time in response to social contestation and social struggle, and that antisubordination values have shaped the historical development of anticlassification understandings. Analyzed from this historical vantage point, American civil rights jurisprudence vindicates both anticlassification and antisubordination commitments, even as the antisubordination principle sits in perpetual judgment of American civil rights law, condemning its formalism, compromises, and worldly limitations, and summoning it to more socially transformative ends. * * *

The idea of distinguishing between anticlassification and antisubordination principles arose at a critical juncture in American race history. Fiss authored his path-breaking article proposing the "group disadvantaging principle" in 1976, two decades after *Brown*, when American law had discredited prominent and overtly discriminatory practices enforcing racial segregation. At this juncture in the struggle over disestablishing Jim Crow, the Court faced important questions about the constitutionality of two kinds of practices: practices that employed racial criteria to integrate formerly segregated institutions and practices that preserved the racial segregation of institutions through formally neutral rules that made no overt reference to race. The stakes were high. Depending on how the Court dealt with the legality of affirmative action and the legitimacy of facially neutral practices with a disparate impact on racial minorities, the Constitution would either rationalize or destabilize the practices that sustained the racial stratification of American society now that the most overt forms of segregation were abolished.

The questions facing the Court put at issue the very meaning of *Brown* and the civil rights movement. If the Court read *Brown* as invalidating segregation on the ground that it violated an anticlassification principle, then facially neutral practices with disparate impact on racial minorities would be presumptively constitutional, while affirmative action would not. On the other hand, if the Court read *Brown* as invalidating segregation on the ground that it violated an antisubordination principle, then affirmative action would be presumptively constitutional, while facially neutral practices with a disparate impact on minorities would not.

In point of fact, segregation under Jim Crow violated both the anticlassification and antisubordination principles. Cases like *Brown* and *Loving* contained language condemning the practice of classifying citizens by race as well as language condemning practices that enforced subordination or inflicted status harm. For example, *Brown* argued that "[t]o separate [Negro children] from others of similar age and qualifications solely because of their race generates a feeling of inferiority as to their status in the community that may affect their hearts and minds in a way unlikely ever to be undone." *Loving* argued that "[t]he fact that Virginia prohibits only interracial marriages involving white persons demonstrates that the racial classifications must stand on their own justification, as measures designed to maintain White Supremacy." Depending on whether one emphasized the anticlassification or antisubordination discourse in *Brown* and *Loving*, the cases seemed to resolve the disputes facing the Court quite differently.

Fiss advanced the group-disadvantaging principle as a framework for understanding *Brown*, so that *Brown* could be doctrinally elaborated in ways that would continue the work of disestablishing racial segregation. By developing the antisubordination values of cases like *Brown* and *Loving* into an independently justified "group-disadvantaging principle" and differentiating that principle from an anticlassification principle, Fiss sought to guide the Court in resolving the central questions of racial equality it faced in the mid–1970s. Fiss and the audience of *Groups and the Equal Protection Clause* understood the anticlassification and antisubordination principles to have divergent practical implications for the key issues of the moment: The anticlassification principle impugned affirmative action, while legitimating facially neutral practices with a racially disparate impact, while the antisubordination principle impugned facially neutral practices with a racially disparate impact, while legitimating affirmative action. Given the way Fiss and his audience understood the practical entailments of the two principles, it seems plausible to say that, during the 1970s and 1980s, the Court decided to vindicate anticlassification rather than antisubordination commitments. . . . If one defines the anticlassification and antisubordination principles solely with reference to these doctrinal debates, one might well conclude that the Court has never embraced the antisubordination principle in its Fourteenth Amendment case law. Yet if we step back from this particular group of cases, we will discover that this view fundamentally mischaracterizes the development of American antidiscrimination law. In fact . . . antisubordination values have played and continue to play a key role in shaping what the anticlassification principle means in practice.

Sometimes . . . courts have implemented the anticlassification principle in a fashion that preserves status relations. But often, and particularly as the civil rights agenda expands, the judiciary has applied the anticlassification principle in ways that dismantle status relations. . . . As social protest delegitimates certain practices, courts are often moved, consciously or unconsciously, by perceptions of status harm to find violations of the anticlassification principle where they saw none before. Considered from this historical vantage point, American civil rights jurisprudence vindicates both anticlassification and antisubordination commitments.

————

Groups, Politics, and the Equal Protection Clause

Issues In Legal Scholarship (2003), Abstract
http://www.bepress.com/ils/iss2/art19

■ SAMUEL ISSACHAROFF and PAMELA S. KARLAN

In some ways, what's remarkable is how much of the current debate follows the tracks Owen [Fiss] laid down over a quarter-century ago. *Groups* and the Equal Protection Clause identified two mediating principles that might "stand between the courts and the Constitution to give meaning and content to an ideal embodied in the text." One, which Owen called the "antidiscrimination principle," saw the clause as primarily a limitation on the government's power to classify individuals (that is, to make discriminations among them). The other, the "group-disadvantaging principle" that Owen championed, saw the clause as essentially a prohibition on the creation or perpetuation of subordinate classes. Much of the contemporary debate over affirmative action, for example, plays out along precisely these lines. Opponents of affirmative action emphasize its use of a "suspect classification" (race) to deprive individuals of the right to be judged on their own merits. Supporters stress the continuing disadvantaged condition of blacks and Hispanics and argue that race-conscious action is necessary to bring members of traditionally excluded groups into the educational and economic mainstream.

————

Affirmative Action and the Group–Disadvantaging Principle

Issues In Legal Scholarship (2003)
http://www.bepress.com/ils/iss2/art14

■ DANIEL SABBAGH

[A]ffirmative action inevitably relies on a historical, sociological and political judgment as to which reference groups ought not to be overrepresented at the bottom of the economic and occupational hierarchy in order to avoid the self-perpetuation of morally unacceptable, structural inequalities. For all "groups" are not of a similar kind. Some of them are only statistical aggregates in which case the distinctive feature of their "members" is defined on a quasi-random basis, and will be considered arbitrary by insiders and outsiders alike (think of the group of people with blond hair and brown eyes). Others are associations set up to promote the interests or ideas shared by their members, who typically affiliate themselves with some organizational structure specifically designed to that end (political parties, unions, etc.). Only a few of them are ascriptive, status groups whose existence, far from being the product of a foundation of any kind, remains largely independent from the will of their individual members and whose impact on their social experience and subjective identity is still particularly powerful. In Fiss' characteristically eloquent prose,

"There are natural classes, or social groups, in American society and blacks are such a group. Blacks are viewed as a group; they view themselves as a group; their identity is in large part determined by membership in the group; their social status is linked to the status of the group; and much of our action, institutional and personal, is based on these perspectives."

Naturally, one may well disagree over exactly which groups would qualify for a description of this kind. Yet, the margin of disagreement is not infinite. . . .

"black men and women (. . .) are not free to choose for themselves in what roles—or as members of which social groups—others will characterize them. They are black, and no other feature of personality or allegiance or ambition will so thoroughly influence how they will be perceived and treated by others, and the range and character of the lives that will be open to them."

Thus, Fiss' restrictive conception of social groups does provide an answer to the slippery-slope argument: the only groups that should benefit from affirmative action policies under the anti-caste principle enclosed in the Fourteenth Amendment are those whose membership of which stands as a crucial feature of the individual's identity insofar as it shapes others' expectations toward her.

NOTES

1.   The difference between "anticlassification" (or antidiscrimination), on the one hand, and "antisubordination," on the other hand, is a classic illustration of the formal/substantive equality divide. It is tempting to draw a stark line in the sand when reading a court's interpretation of the meaning of equality as either an illustration of formal equality or of substantive equality. However, Balkin and Siegel urge us to look deeper to see how formalism—e.g. application of the anticlassification rule—might, in some cases, contain strands of a concern for a more substantive equality. One example of this is the *Loving v. Virginia* case, 388 U.S. 1 (1967), discussed by Balkin and Siegel, excerpted in chapter V, and in which the United States Supreme Court invalidated laws prohibiting interracial marriages not just as a violation of the rule against racial classifications but also as wrongfully perpetuating an ideology that was at the heart of the subordination of Blacks in American society. In doing so, the Court rejected the State of Virginia's formal equality argument used to defend the antimiscegenation statute. The State argued that the statute treated blacks and whites equally by applying the same penalty to them for violating the ban on interracial marriage. The Court's rejection of that argument is accomplished by application of the anticlassification rule, which triggered a searching inquiry ("strict scrutiny") into the true purpose and effect of the statute, white supremacy. *Brown v. Board of Education* is another example,

as Balkin and Siegel point out, of how the Court imported antisubordination analysis into anticlassification analysis to invalidate "separate but equal" in part because of its impact on the "hearts and minds" of Black children in society.

2. Another area where the relationship between anticlassification/antidiscrimination and antisubordination has historically played out is affirmative action admissions policies, and in an earlier era, race-conscious student assignment policies to counteract segregated schools. A close look at the Court's jurisprudence similarly reveals a shifting terrain of the tension between formalist and more substantive visions of whether the anticlassification rule prohibits using race-conscious policies to ameliorate racial segregation and subordination:

"[D]uring the very period when the Supreme Court was adopting the strict scrutiny framework set forth in *McLaughlin* and *Loving*, federal courts were routinely upholding the right of state and local governments to implement race-conscious policies intended to lessen de facto public school segregation. Courts, in other words, understood equal protection as a race-asymmetric constraint on governmental action; they understood that the purpose of equal protection doctrine was to prevent the state from inflicting certain forms of status harm on minorities.

But this understanding of the presumption against racial classification began to shift by the end of the 1960s, in response to escalating national conflicts over race and the rise of a new generation of desegregation initiatives aimed at post-secondary and professional education. Constitutional challenges to voluntary desegregation initiatives, which appeared as soon as those initiatives began, suddenly had legal traction. Until the 1970s, race-conscious assignment policies were either understood as licit forms of racial classification, or not counted as "invidious classifications" at all. Amidst a national conversation about what harms and whose harms the Equal Protection Clause would redress, judges began to analyze university admissions practices as racial classifications subject to the presumption of unconstitutionality."

Reva B. Siegel, *Equality Talk: Antisubordination and Anticlassification Values in Constitutional Struggles Over Brown*, 117 HARVARD LAW REVIEW 1470, 1514–1515 (2004).

3. The concept that Fourteenth Amendment scrutiny should be elevated in cases involving "statutes directed at particular religious ... national ... or racial minorities" [demonstrating] "prejudice against discrete and insular minorities" was first articulated by the Supreme Court in footnote four of Justice Harlan Stone's majority opinion in *United States v. Carolene Products Co.*, 304 U.S. 144 (1938). Justice Stone reasoned that discrete and insular minority groups lacked the political power to protect themselves through the democratic process. This same concept is behind Dr. King's explanation of why civil rights advocates were obligated to obey just laws, but not unjust laws. As he explained in the *Letter From Birmingham Jail*, "An unjust law is a code that a numerical or power majority group compels a minority group to obey but does not make

binding on itself. This is difference made legal. By the same token, a just law is a code that a majority compels a minority to follow and that it is willing to follow itself. This is sameness made legal." http://www.stanford.edu/group/King/frequentdocs/birmingham.pdf.

4.   Does the decision to define certain categories as protected by anti-discrimination law reveal whether the intent is to protect against classification or subordination? Consider the Charter of Fundamental Rights of the European Union, which provides in Article 21:1.

> "Any discrimination based on any ground such as sex, race, colour, ethnic or social origin, genetic features, language, religion or belief, political or any other opinion, membership of a national minority, property, birth, disability, age or sexual orientation shall be prohibited."

D.   EQUALITY AS EQUAL TREATMENT

The question of gender equality raises slightly different arguments and tensions that revolve around the question of how to treat biological, physiological, and social differences between men and women. Should the law be "blind" to those differences and treat men and women the same? Or does equality law require that members of certain groups be treated differently in order to be treated the same? Treating men and women the same, despite differences, might in fact undermine stereotypes traditionally associated with some differences between men and women and which have hindered their opportunities in society. On the other hand, failing to recognize and explicitly account for those differences and the ways in which they have curtailed equal opportunities for men and/or women may perpetuate existing inequalities. Consider the questions raised by equality as sameness through the excerpts below.

Equality and Difference: The Case of Pregnancy

1 Berkeley Women's Law Journal 1, 26 (1985)

■ HERMA HILL KAY

Philosophers recognize that, just as the concept of equality requires that equals be treated equally, so it requires that unequals be treated differently. To treat persons who are different alike is to treat them unequally. The concept of formal equality, however, contains no independent justification for making unequals equal. A different concept, that of equality of opportunity, offers a theoretical basis for making unequals equal in the limited sense of removing barriers which prevent individuals from performing according to their abilities. The notion is that the perceived inequality does not stem from an innate difference in ability, but rather from a condition or circumstance that prevents certain uses or developments of that ability. As applied to reproductive behavior, the suggestion would be that women in general are not different from men in innate ability. During the temporary episode of a woman's pregnancy, however, she may become unable to utilize her abilities in the same way she had done prior to her reproductive conduct. Since a man's abilities are not similarly impaired as a result of his reproductive behavior, equality of opportunity implies that the woman should not be disadvantaged as a result of that sex-specific variation.

———

Bradwell v. Illinois

83 U.S. 130, 140–142 (1872)

■ MR. JUSTICE BRADLEY, concurring in the result

[EDITORS' NOTE: Myra Bradwell's application for membership in the Illinois bar was rejected because of her sex. In this opinion, Justice Bradley concurs with the Supreme Court's 8–1 decision rejecting her challenge to the bar's decision.] [T]he civil law, as well as nature herself, has always recognized a wide difference in the respective spheres and destinies of man and woman. Man is, or should be, woman's protector and defender. The natural and proper timidity and delicacy which belongs to the female sex evidently unfits it for many of the occupations of civil life. The constitution of the family organization, which is founded in the divine ordinance, as well as in the nature of things, indicates the domestic sphere as that which properly belongs to the domain and functions of womanhood. The harmony, not to say identity, of interest and views which belong, or should belong, to the family institution is repugnant to the idea of a woman adopting a distinct and independent career from that of her husband. So firmly fixed was this sentiment in the founders of the common law that it became a maxim of that system of jurisprudence that a woman had no legal existence separate from her husband, who was regarded as her head and representative in the social state; and, notwithstanding some recent modifications of this civil status, many of the special rules of law flowing from and dependent upon this cardinal principle still exist in full force in most States.

In the nature of things it is not every citizen of every age, sex, and condition that is qualified for every calling and position. It is the prerogative of the legislator to prescribe regulations founded on nature, reason, and experience for the due admission of qualified persons to professions and callings demanding special skill and confidence. This fairly belongs to the police power of the State; and, in my opinion, in view of the peculiar characteristics, destiny, and mission of woman, it is within the province of the legislature to ordain what offices, positions, and callings shall be filled and discharged by men, and shall receive the benefit of those energies and responsibilities, and that decision and firmness which are presumed to predominate in the sterner sex.

———

Muller v. State of Oregon

208 U.S. 412 (1908)

■ MR. JUSTICE BREWER, delivered the opinion of the Court

[EDITORS' NOTE: Muller was convicted of employing women employees at his laundry for over ten hours in one day, in violation of a state "protective" law. Relying on a lengthy brief filed by future Justice Louis Brandeis, collecting social science data on working conditions for women, the Court upheld the Oregon law, and Muller's conviction.]

That woman's physical structure and the performance of maternal functions place her at a disadvantage in the struggle for subsistence is obvious. This is especially true when the burdens of motherhood are upon her. Even when they are not, by abundant testimony of the medical fraternity continuance for a long time on her feet at work, repeating this from day to day, tends to injurious effects upon the body, and, as healthy mothers are essential to vigorous offspring, the physical well-being of woman becomes an object of public interest and care in order to preserve the strength and vigor of the race.

Still again, history discloses the fact that woman has always been dependent upon man. He established his control at the outset by superior physical strength, and this control in various forms, with diminishing intensity, has continued to the present. As minors, though not to the same extent, she has been looked upon in the courts as needing special care that her rights may be preserved. Education was long denied her, and while now the doors of the schoolroom are opened and her opportunities for acquiring knowledge are great, yet even with that and the consequent increase of capacity for business affairs it is still true that in the struggle for subsistence she is not an equal competitor with her brother. Though limitations upon personal and contractual rights may be removed by legislation, there is that in her disposition and habits of life which will operate against a full assertion of those rights. She will still be where some legislation to protect her seems necessary to secure a real equality of right. Doubtless there are individual exceptions, and there are many respects in which she has an advantage over him; but looking at it from the viewpoint of the effort to maintain an independent position in life, she is not upon an equality. Differentiated by these matters from the other sex, she is properly placed in a class by herself, and legislation designed for her protection may be sustained, even when like legislation is not necessary for men, and could not be sustained. It is impossible to close one's eyes to the fact that she still looks to her brother and depends upon him. Even though all restrictions on political, personal, and contractual rights were taken away, and she stood, so far as statutes are concerned, upon an absolutely equal plane with him, it would still be true that she is so constituted that she will rest upon and look to him for protection; that her physical structure and a proper discharge of her maternal functions—having in view not merely her own health, but the well-being of the race—justify legislation to protect her from the greed as well as the passion of man. The limitations which this statute places upon her contractual powers, upon her right to agree with her employer as to the time she shall labor, are not imposed solely for her benefit, but also largely for the benefit of all. Many words cannot make this plainer. The two sexes differ in structure of body, in the functions to be performed by each, in the amount of physical strength, in the capacity for long continued labor, particularly when done standing, the influence of vigorous health upon the future well-being of the race, the self-reliance which enables one to assert full rights, and in the capacity to maintain the struggle for subsistence. This difference justifies a difference in legislation, and upholds that which is designed to compensate for some of the burdens which rest upon her.

————

Sail'er Inn, Inc. v. Kirby

5 Cal.3d 1 (1971) California Supreme Court

■ PETERS, J., expressing the unanimous view of the Court.

Laws which disable women from full participation in the political, business and economic arenas are often characterized as "protective" and beneficial. Those same laws applied to racial or ethnic minorities would readily be recognized as invidious and impermissible. The pedestal upon which women have been placed has all too often, upon closer inspection, been revealed as a cage.

————

United States v. Virginia

518 U.S. 515, 533–534 (1996)

■ JUSTICE GINSBURG delivered the opinion of the Court.

"Inherent differences" between men and women, we have come to appreciate, remain cause for celebration, but not for denigration of the members of either sex or for artificial constraints on an individual's opportunity. Sex classifications may be used to compensate women for particular economic "disabilities [they have] suffered," to "promot[e] equal employment opportunity," to advance full development of the talent and capacities of our Nation's people. But such classifications may not be used, as they once were, to create or perpetuate the legal, social, and economic inferiority of women.

————

Nguyen v. Immigration and Naturalization Service

533 U.S. 53, 72 (2001)

■ JUSTICE KENNEDY delivered the opinion of the Court.

To fail to acknowledge even our most basic biological differences—such as the fact that a mother must be present at birth but the father need not be—risks making the guarantee of equal protection superficial, and so disserving it. Mechanistic classification of all our differences as stereotypes would operate to obscure those misconceptions and prejudices that are real. The distinction embodied in the statutory scheme here at issue is not marked by misconception and prejudice, nor does it show disrespect for either class. The difference between men and women in relation to the birth process is a real one, and the principle of equal protection does not forbid Congress to address the problem at hand in a manner specific to each gender.

———

Nguyen v. Immigration and Naturalization Service

533 U.S. 53, 72 (2001)

■ Justice O'Connor, dissenting

It is, of course, true that the failure to recognize relevant differences is out of line with the command of equal protection. But so too do we undermine the promise of equal protection when we try to make our differences carry weight they simply cannot bear.

———

NOTES

1. The U.S. Supreme Court is not engaging in the formalism of neutrality or "anticlassification" in its gender jurisprudence as it is in its race jurisprudence. In recognizing that there are real, or relevant, differences that the state may legitimately take into account, the Court recognizes both the biology of sexual difference and also that certain social differences on the basis of gender matter. While we might be wise to continue to reject biological determinism for race, is it safe to say that there are "real" racial differences (disparities) in American society? Why might we be able to acknowledge gender differences but not racial ones?

2. One might argue that the line between a sex-based distinction that "celebrates" gender differences and one that "denigrates" or restrains the opportunity of one sex is not always clear. One way to understand the tightrope that the United States Supreme Court is walking in its attempt to parse out the difference between an invidious and a more benign form of differential treatment is to think in terms of whether the sex difference relied upon embodies a "perfect proxy"—that is, whether the assumption underlying the difference is true of all women or no women; all men or no men. As Mary Ann Case persuasively argues, the Court has used the term "stereotype" to look for imperfect proxies, or overbroad generalizations. She has found that "[e]ven a generalization demonstrably true of an overwhelming majority of one sex or the other does not suffice to overcome the presumption of unconstitutionality the Court has attached to sex-respecting rules: virtually every sex-respecting rule struck down by the Court in the last quarter century embodied a proxy that was overwhelmingly, though not perfectly, accurate.... [A]s well as being descriptively less than perfectly accurate, these generalizations also embody outdated normative stereotypes (i.e., 'fixed notions concerning the roles and abilities of

males and females' or 'the accidental byproduct of a traditional way of thinking about females')." Mary Ann Case, *"The Very Stereotype the Law Condemns": Constitutional Sex Discrimination Law as a Quest for Perfect Proxies*, 85 CORNELL L. REV. 1447, 1449–1451 (2000).

3.   Professor Julie Suk observes, "American antidiscrimination doctrine is skeptical of paternalistic policies that restrict the choices of individuals belonging to protected groups in the name of their protection. Mandatory maternity leave betrays the sex stereotype of women as caregivers, and such stereotypes seem to offend the identitarian conception of sex equality that aspires to undo women's traditional identities as caregivers. At the same time, the absence of mandatory maternity leave has adverse distributive consequences for women; it makes it difficult for women to choose to take adequate maternity leaves, due to well-founded fears of being penalized in the labor market for such choices. The lack of adequate maternity leave in the United States notoriously disadvantages women workers and thereby undermines the redistributive conception of equality." Julie C. Suk, *Antidiscrimination to Equality: Stereotypes and the Life Cycle in the United States and Europe*, 60 AM. J. OF COMP. LAW ___ (2012).

4.   The Convention on the Elimination of All Forms of Discrimination against Women (CEDAW), adopted in 1979 by the UN General Assembly, attempts to guarantee gender equality between women and men through ensuring women's equal access to, and equal opportunities in, political and public life—including the right to vote and to stand for election—as well as education, health and employment. Over 185 countries have joined the Convention, although notably the United States is not a signatory. Quotas of some form exist in over one hundred of CEDAW's State signatories, including in France which amended its constitution in 2000 to require that half of all political candidates be women. For a list of countries that have adopted quotas, see *http://www.quotaproject.org/*. Think about the adoption of quotas by a country like France in light of its "universalist" equality mandate—i.e., its belief that all citizens are equal before the law and its anathema to identity classifications on the basis of race or ethnicity. Why doesn't a law that attempts to enforce gender parity not violate this universalism? Or does it? An early attempt to institute a 25% quota for women in France was rejected by its Constitutional Council as violating the principle of equality under French law which does not require that "different people be treated differently." For a nice summary of the reasoning of the Council *See* Darren Rosenblum, *Parity/Disparity: Electoral Gender Inequality On The Tightrope Of Liberal Constitutional Traditions*, 39 UNIVERSITY OF CALIFORNIA DAVIS L. REV. 1119, 1159–1160 (2006). However, as Professor Rosenblum explains, "the flourishing of feminist theory in France fed reconsideration of the relationship between gender and universalism." He explains that:

> The practical establishment of Parity as an element of French universalism arose as feminists shifted from a quota requirement of one-fifth or one-quarter of candidates to the fifty percent Parity proposal. In so doing, their efforts reflected respect of the universalism underlying French constitutional theory. Parity, unlike quotas, was not to establish some minority representation, but rather to give represen-

tation to women. . . . In feminist theory terms, Parity . . . re-conceptualiz[ed] representation in terms of society's composition of men and women, instead of centering on the uniquely feminine identity in each woman. Although Parity seems to convey an essentialist structure of gender, culture and law, its advocates' vision of a dual universal may move toward de-essentializing essentialism in the context of political representation as well.

Critics of this redefined universalism alleged that it was nothing more than communitarianism, American style. French constitutional theory centers on the civic creed of universalism in contrast to the communitarianism prevalent in the United States, where society finds itself broken up into groups based on ethnicity, race, or sexual orientation. . . . Feminists countered that women are not a group, but rather women cut across all interest groups and would not be a unified element in the legislature. In the end, advocates succeeded with this argument—that women are half of the universal, and do not constitute a group that would conflict with French universalist traditions. Rosenblum, *supra*, at 1163–1165.

E.   EQUALITY AS ACCOMMODATION

Equality might be framed as a demand to affirmatively accommodate certain differences so that these differences become essentially cost-free in society and in the market of equal opportunity. To reduce the opportunity costs of certain differences, accommodation would require taking explicit account of a particular difference as a way of reducing barriers in certain settings arising from that difference. A stronger version of accommodation would force fundamental restructuring of a workplace or other setting to allow those with certain differences to participate on an equal footing with others. Accommodation has its costs, however, as some of the commentators below point out. These excerpts illustrate some of the contours of the debate over whether and how the law might accommodate differences of religion, race, ethnicity, disability and gender where those differences restrict an individual's opportunities in society.

———

Religion, Private Schools and the Duty of Reasonable Accommodation: Looking Beyond the Trees to the Forest

Published in LE DEVOIR (June 15, 2005)
Found at www.cdpdj.qc.ca/en/publications/docs/article_religion_accommodation.pdf

■ PIERRE MAROIS

(President, Commision des droits de la personne et des droits de la jeunesse)

It is appropriate to emphasize that reasonable accommodation is a legal duty that arises from the right to equality. It is one of the tools used in Quebec to manage, in a civilized way, the conflicts that inevitably occur given the growing diversity within society.

Reasonable accommodation is based on a simple observation: although all human beings are equal, they are not identical. This observation has repercussions in daily life. For example, the courts have ruled that pregnant female employees must be accommodated to allow them to continue working without being penalized; if they have to miss a few hours of work for a medical examination, the employer must accommodate them if this can be done without unduly affecting the operation of the enterprise. The same applies to people with disabilities, who may have to be accommodated by changes to their job tasks or to the workplace. . . .

Religious particularities are also taken into account to encourage everyone to play an active role in society, just as the needs linked to pregnancy or disability are now recognized. A refusal to take religious particularities into account could have the opposite effect, namely that of placing some people on the margins of society, and this must be avoided. In its 1995 opinion, the Commission took into account the risks that, if students were forbidden to wear an Islamic veil at school, they could be excluded from the right to public education. . . .

Obviously, we must still look at the question of how far accommodation can extend. The duty of accommodation does not mean that all particularities must be accepted unconditionally. As the Commission pointed out in 1995, "In the case of religion, rights and freedoms can soon be transformed into sacred absolutes placing constraints on society as a whole." The duty of reasonable accommodation has a limit, defined by the notion of undue hardship.

The Paradoxes of Reasonable Accommodation

Options Politiques (Septembre 2007), pp. 34–35
Located at: http://www.irpp.org/po/archive/sep07/grey.pdf

■ Julius Grey

Many calls for accommodation come from the proponents of muddled political correctness—the friends of multiculturalism, diversity and communitarianism. For them, the existence of permanent ethnic and religious groups and of collective rights attached to them is a public good. Reasonable accommodation is one of the ways of maintaining differences and the negotiation of the degree of accommodation is, in the nature of things, the domain of the lobbies. This model of Canada is what Joe Clark meant when he said that Canada is a "community of communities." The opponents of accommodation, especially in Quebec, are often inspired by French republicanism, by notions of secularism, of equality and of integration of newcomers as equals into our society. They abhor the idea that civil society should become a permanent negotiating session between powerful lobbies. . . .

It is the thesis of this essay that reasonable accommodation is desirable for two reasons—individual freedom and effective integration of immigrants.

In a democratic society, individual freedom is surely one of the fundamental values. Telling a person what to wear, how to decorate their homes, what to eat and when to celebrate holidays is an unnecessary interference with personal liberty * * *

The second reason for accommodation is equally important—the integration of immigrants. Accommodating kirpas, kirpans, kerchiefs, turbans, religious holidays and so on allows the individuals in question easy access to public institutions and public employment. This, in turn, integrates them in the mainstream and, in the next generation, most of their children do not require accommodation.

This process is assisted by the fact that accommodation prevents the development of a sense of alienation or, in extreme cases, perception of persecution, which is sometimes evident in isolated minorities, and that the availability of many types of employment promotes economic equality, which is the most important condition for successful integration.

All of this, of course, points to certain limits as to the type of accommodation that merits the adjective "reasonable." Most will agree that demands for accommodation should not be too onerous. For instance, individuals should be able to claim a few days for religious observance; society could not cope with a request for 50 days a year. Similarly, one could not permit truly dangerous objects in the name of religion (e.g., a sharpened sword instead of a kirpan).

What has less often been pointed out is that accommodation that ghettoizes groups—for instance by the creation of separate schools, hospitals, courts—is undesirable. Indeed, a burka or a veil that covers the face, as opposed to a kerchief, is very problematic, because it constitutes a barrier to social integration. It is very surprising that, in their opposition to accommodation, Quebec republicans fixated on the rather innocuous kirpan, and not on the expensive and morally questionable subsidies to private schools. * * *

It is becoming increasingly clear that multiculturalism is not only a chimera, but also a dangerous one. No society has ever been successful in the long run unless it integrated its citizens and eliminated barriers to marriage between them.

The word "assimilation," which is odious when force is used, should be rehabilitated as a description of what happens to citizens of varied origins in an open society. When the Anglo Saxons, the Scandinavians, the Celts and the Normans fused to form the English nation, and when the Romans, Celts and Germanic Franks became the French, both attained a cultural and social cohesion that no multicultural society can imitate. Of course, assimilation is not a one-way street. The immigrants adopt the language and culture of the majority, but the majority is also modified, and indeed permeated, by the contribution of the immigrants. It is obvious that the waves of immigration of the 20th century have left an indelible mark on Canada and on the descendants of the two majority groups of the early 1900s. That is perhaps another reason, a pedagogical one, to permit manifestations of new cultures in our schools and other institutions, since much of what they bring will become part of us.

————

Trans World Airline v. Hardison

432 U.S. 63 (1977)

■ Justice Marshall, dissenting

The accommodation issue by definition arises only when a neutral rule of general applicability conflicts with the religious practices of a particular employee. In some of the reported cases, the rule in question has governed work attire; in other cases it has required attendance at some religious function; in still other instances, it has compelled membership in a union; and in the largest class of cases, it has concerned work schedules. What all these cases have in common is an employee who could comply with the rule only by violating what the employee views as a religious commandment. In each instance, the question is whether the employee is to be exempt from the rule's demands. To do so will always result in a privilege being allocated according to religious beliefs, unless the employer gratuitously decides to repeal the rule in toto. What the statute says, in plain words, is that such allocations are required unless undue hardship would result.

————

The Equality Crisis: Some Reflections on Culture, Courts and Feminism

14 Women's Rights Law Reporter 151, 168–170 (1992)

■ Wendy W. Williams

Feminists split over the validity of the Montana statute [requiring employers to provide pregnant employees with leaves of absence]. Some of us felt that the statute was, indeed, incompatible with the philosophy of the PDA ["Pregnancy Discrimination Act"]. Others of us argued that the PDA was passed to help pregnant women, which was also the objective of the Montana statute. Underneath are very different views of what women's equality means; the dispute is therefore one of great significance for feminists.

The Montana statute was meant to help pregnant women. It was passed with the best of intentions. The philosophy underlying it is that pregnancy is central to a woman's family role and that the law should take special account of pregnancy to protect that role for the working wife. And those who supported the statute can assert with great plausibility that pregnancy is a problem that men don't have, an extra source of workplace disability, and that women workers cannot adequately be protected if pregnancy is not taken into account in special ways. They might also add that procreation plays a special role in human life, is viewed as a fundamental right by our society, and therefore is appropriately singled out on social policy grounds. The instinct to treat pregnancy as a special case is deeply imbedded in our culture, indeed in every culture. It seems natural, and right, to treat it that way.

Yet, at a deeper level, the Supreme Court in cases like *Gilbert*, and the feminists who seek special recognition for pregnancy, are starting from the same basic assumption, namely, that women have a special place in the scheme of human existence when it comes to maternity. Of course, one's view of how that basic assumption cuts is shaped by one's perspective. What businessmen, Supreme Court Justices, and feminists make of it is predictably quite different. But the same doctrinal approach that permits pregnancy to be treated worse than other disabilities is the same one that will allow the state constitutional freedom to create special benefits for pregnant women. The equality approach to pregnancy (such as that embodied in the PDA) necessarily creates not only the desired floor under the pregnant woman's rights but also the ceiling which the [Montana . . .] case threw into relief. If we can't have it both ways, we need to think carefully about which way we want to have it.

Nevada Department of Human Resources v. Hibbs
538 U.S. 721, 737 (2003)

■ Chief Justice Rehnquist delivered the opinion of the Court.

By creating an across-the-board, routine employment benefit for all eligible employees, Congress sought to ensure that family-care leave would no longer be stigmatized as an inordinate drain on the workplace caused by female employees, and that employers could not evade leave obligations simply by hiring men. By setting a minimum standard of family leave for all eligible employees, irrespective of gender, the FMLA attacks the formerly state-sanctioned stereotype that only women are responsible for family caregiving, thereby reducing employers' incentives to engage in discrimination by basing hiring and promotion decisions on stereotypes.

Tennessee v. Lane
541 U.S. 509 (2004)

■ Justice Ginsburg, concurring.

Including individuals with disabilities among people who count composing "We the People," Congress understood in shaping the ADA, would sometimes require not blindfolded equality, but responsiveness to difference; not indifference, but accommodation.

Disabilities, Discrimination, and Reasonable Accommodation
46 Duke Law Journal 1, 2–5 (1996)

■ Pamela S. Karlan & George Rutherglen

[H]ow the law defines discrimination makes a big difference in the kinds of remedies it provides. The Americans With Disabilities Act (ADA), the newest comprehensive federal antidiscrimination statute, offers a fundamentally different approach to—and a fundamentally different remedy for—invidious discrimination than prior legal regimes. The older statutes generally prohibit discrimination in employment on other grounds: Title VII of the Civil Rights Act of 1964 (Title VII) on the basis of race, national origin, sex and religion; the Age Discrimination in Employment Act of 1967 (ADEA) on the basis of age. In language that tracks the earlier language of Title VII and the ADEA, the ADA forbids employers from taking an individual's disability into account by "limiting, segregating, or classifying a job applicant or employee in a way that adversely affects the opportunities or status of such applicant or employee because of the disability of such applicant or employee." But unlike Title VII, the ADA also requires employers to take some disabilities into account by providing "reasonable accommodations" to disabled workers who request them; it defines discrimination to include "not making reasonable accommodations to the known physical or mental limitations of an otherwise qualified individual. . . ." And the potential sweep of reasonable accommodations is quite broad: beyond "making existing facilities . . . readily accessible to and usable by individuals with disabilities" accommodations may include "job restructuring, part-time or modified work schedules, . . . [or] the provision of qualified readers or interpreters. . . ." Put somewhat differently, under the civil rights statutes that protect women, blacks, or older workers, plaintiffs can complain of discrimination against them, but they cannot insist upon discrimination in their favor; disabled individuals often can.

Two examples clarify this point. Suppose that one "essential function" of the job of sack handler is to carry fifty-pound sacks from the company loading dock to a store room. If a male worker is physically disabled by a back ailment, and thus unable to carry the sacks the full distance, the company can be required to make the reasonable accommodation of providing the worker with a dolly on which to transport the sacks. By contrast, if a female worker cannot lift the same heavy cartons hoisted by her male counterparts, no accommodation is required and firing her because she cannot do the job as it then stands does not constitute impermissible sex discrimination. As long as the heavy lifting requirement is job-related, an employer may impose such a qualification even if it excludes a disproportionate percentage of female applicants. But even if the requirement is job-related, the employer may be compelled to modify it in order not to exclude a disabled applicant who could perform the job as modified.

Consider also a job that requires its occupant to read various documents and prepare reports. The employer may be required to accommodate a blind or dyslexic worker by providing her with an assistant to read documents to her. But suppose a black employee—as a direct result of having attended inferior, poorly funded public schools beset by the lingering effects of de jure segregation—lacks adequate reading comprehension and writing skills. Even if he could certainly understand the documents if they were read to him and could communicate his reports orally, because he is the victim of "environmental, economic, and cultural disadvantages" and "is unable to read [at the appropriate level] because he . . . was never taught to read," he is not disabled and therefore is not entitled to any accommodation of his impairments.

We point out these contrasts between the safeguards of "traditional" civil rights laws and the protections accorded by the ADA not to show that disabled individuals are somehow receiving unwarranted benefit or even an unfair advantage over other groups that have experienced exclusion from full economic participation, but rather to suggest that the emerging law of reasonable accommodation may shed light on antidiscrimination law generally. The ADA's focus on a "flexible, interactive process" of employer-employee negotiation and liberal modification of physical, logistic, and attitudinal barriers that preclude full equality of opportunity may provide a model for thinking about traditional affirmative action as well.

————

NOTES

1.   The feminist debate in the United States over the accommodation of pregnancy in the workplace has shifted toward a more substantive debate about how to accommodate women's "caregiving" role in society. Contemporary feminist legal scholars now critique the push to accommodate pregnancy as limited because it failed to address the barriers to women's full participation in the workplace beyond the immediate, physical events of pregnancy and childbirth. As one feminist scholar points out:

> The persistent attachment gap resulting from women's disproportionate caregiving responsibilities at home has had tangible negative economic and social consequences for women. The part-time, temporary, or otherwise contingent jobs to which women are often limited generally provide lower hourly wages than full-time positions, tend to be less stable, and are less likely to offer health insurance, childcare benefits, pension benefits, or opportunities for advancement. Even for women who work full-time, career interruptions for nurturing responsibilities often translate into lower seniority, wages, and salaries vis-à-vis male coworkers. Such interruptions occur not just during a woman's childbearing years, but later in life as well. Older women who reduce their work hours or exit the workforce at the height of their earning capacity to care for elderly parents experience not only short-term losses of wages, but also potentially long-term reductions in pension income.
>
> Furthermore, women's disproportionate responsibility for caregiving at home has consequences well beyond their reduced economic well-being. The "feminization of poverty" weakens women's bargaining power within marriage, leaves women vulnerable to sexual abuse and domestic violence, and can decrease the likelihood of women gaining or keeping the custody of their children upon divorce. Moreover, because women are the primary caretakers of children in our society, the marginalization of women's wage work has resulted in the widespread poverty of children in America. Finally, the failure of our law to recognize women's work/family conflicts has, in large part, shifted the burden of caregiving from one class of women to another—

that is, from economically privileged women able to conform to the rigid expectations of the American workplace to low-paid domestic and childcare workers who disproportionately are poor women and women of color. . . . [T]he law's response to the labor force attachment gap and the resulting marginalized economic status of women and children has been minimal.''

Laura Kessler, *The Attachment Gap: Employment Discrimination Law, Women's Cultural Caregiving, And The Limits Of Economic And Liberal Legal Theory*, 34 U. Mich. J.L. Ref. 371, 386–389 (2001).

2. In 1993, Congress passed the gender-neutral Family Medical and Leave Act which requires employers to provide up to twelve weeks of unpaid leave in a twelve-month period for the care of family members with serious health conditions, for an employee's own serious health condition, or for the birth or adoption of a child. 29 U.S.C. § 2601–2654 (1994). While the Act specifically recognizes that "the primary responsibility for family caregiving often falls on women, and such responsibility affects the working lives of women more than it affects the working lives of men," contemporary feminists question whether the gender neutrality of the Act nevertheless perpetuates the myth that women and men share caregiving equally and thus fails to address the discriminatory structure of the workplace which continues to favor non-caregivers (who are mostly men) *See* Kessler, *supra*, at 420–421.

3. A stronger version of accommodation, as embodied in the American With Disabilities Act and developed in Quebec for its cultural and religious minorities, does require (in some circumstances) a fundamental restructuring of institutions and societal norms to accommodate "difference." But when does accommodation for certain differences undermine equality for others? In the context of a recent public debate on reasonable accommodation, the Quebec Council on the Status of Women, a provincial body that advises the government on issues relating to women, proposed that the Quebec charter be changed to ban public employees from wearing visible religious symbols within workspaces. Such symbols would include large Christian crosses, Sikh turbans, Jewish yarmulkes, and the common headscarf which conceals the hair and neck of Muslim women. The Council argued that abolition of these symbols was an important step toward ensuring equality between men and women in Quebec. According to the Quebec Council on the Status of Women, Islamic symbols such as the headscarf send "a message of the submission of a woman, which should not be conveyed to young children as part of a secular education, which is required to promote equality between men and women." Conseil du statut de la Femme, *Right to Equality Between Women and Men and Freedom of Religion,* www.csf.gouv.qc.ca/fr/english/. This proposal and its debate sparked an outcry from the Muslim community who felt targeted and increasingly isolated from the broader society. A group of feminists has published a statement opposing the Council's proposal because, among other reasons, "regulating women's public religious expression is gender discrimination insofar as it takes away women's freedom and inhibits their civic participation." *See* The Simone de Beauvoir Institute, Concordia University, *"Reasonable Accommodation: A Feminist Response"* (November

2007).   http://artsandscience1.concordia.ca/wsdb/documents/Reasonable Accommodations.pdf This issue is discussed further in chapter VIII.

4. As Professor Karlan and Rutherglen explain, the right to accommodation is central to the prohibition of discrimination against persons with disabilities. In *Eldridge v. British Columbia*, (1997, Docket 24896), the Supreme Court of Canada held that under the Charter of Rights and Freedoms in Canada, the government was obligated to provide sign interpreters to deaf patients at medical facilities. The Charter provides:

15.   (1) Every individual is equal before and under the law and has the right to the equal protection and equal benefit of the law without discrimination and, in particular, without discrimination based on race, national or ethnic origin, colour, religion, sex, age or mental or physical disability.

The Court relied on two theories, reasonable accommodation and adverse impact, which will be discussed in Chapter II. For a discussion of *Eldridge*, see Arlene B. Mayerson and Silvia Yee, *The ADA and Models of Equality*, 62 OHIO STATE L.J. 535 (2001).

5.   Under the United Nations Convention on the Rights of Persons with Disabilities, discrimination is defined as follows: "Discrimination on the basis of disability" means any distinction, exclusion or restriction on the basis of disability which has the purpose or effect of impairing or nullifying the recognition, enjoyment or exercise, on an equal basis with others, of all human rights and fundamental freedoms in the political, economic, social, cultural, civil or any other field. It includes all forms of discrimination, including denial of reasonable accommodation.

6.   The failure to provide reasonable accommodation to persons with disabilities is also required under the Equality Act of the United Kingdom (2010) at section 21(2), as are accommodations for religious requirements relating to sex, marriage and sexual orientation (schedule 9, para. 2). Are these two forms of accommodation comparable? In a case where a Registrar refused to perform same-sex marriages because it offended her religious beliefs, her claim that she was entitled to religious accommodation was rejected. *See Ladele v. London Borough of Islington*, UKEAT/0453/08/RN (EAT), [2009] EWCA Civ 1357 (CA) (discussed in Emmanuelle Bribosia and Isabelle Rorive, *In Search of a Balance Between the Right to Equality and Other Fundamental Rights*, European Network of Legal Experts in the Non–Discrimination Field (2010)).

7.   What other groups might reasonably seek accommodation as a means of achieving equality? When should it be provided?

F.   EQUALITY AS DIVERSITY

In the United States we have seen increasing acceptance of the idea that promoting racial and ethnic diversity is a positive social goal. But recognition of diversity requires recognition of the legitimacy of a particular identity. In France and other countries, as we have seen, there is resistance to viewing individuals as members of an identity group. Several of these excerpts address the idea that equality should entail some degree of recognition (and even celebration) of different identities as members of specific racial, ethnic, religious, and sexual groups. However there are strong and weak versions of this diversity principle that map onto the formal/substantive tension we have seen reflected in other conceptions of equality, and as the excerpts below reveal.

Lesbian and Gay Equality Project v. Minister of Home Affairs

Constitutional Court of South Africa Case CCT 60/04 (Dec. 1, 2005)

■ JUDGMENT, JUSTICE SACHS

Respect for human rights requires the affirmation of self, not the denial of self. Equality therefore does not imply a levelling or homogenisation of behaviour or extolling one form as supreme, and another as inferior, but an acknowledgement and acceptance of difference. At the very least, it affirms that difference should not be the basis for exclusion, marginalisation and stigma. At best, it celebrates the vitality that difference brings to any society. The issue goes well beyond assumptions of heterosexual exclusivity, a source of contention in the present case. The acknowledgement and acceptance of difference is particularly important in our country where for centuries group membership based on supposed biological characteristics such as skin colour has been the express basis of advantage and disadvantage. South Africans come in all shapes and sizes. The development of an active rather than a purely formal sense of enjoying a common citizenship depends on recognising and accepting people with all their differences, as they are. The Constitution thus acknowledges the variability of human beings (genetic and socio-cultural), affirms the right to be different, and celebrates the diversity of the nation.

Wygant v. Jackson Board of Education

476 U.S. 267 (1986)

■ JUSTICE STEVENS, dissenting

[I]n our present society, race is not always irrelevant to sound governmental decisionmaking ... In the context of public education, it is quite obvious that a school board may reasonably conclude that an integrated faculty will be able to provide benefits to the student body that could not be provided by an all-white, or nearly all-white, faculty. For one of the most important lessons that the American public schools teach is that the diverse ethnic, cultural, and national backgrounds that have been brought together in our famous melting pot do not identify essential differences among the human beings that inhabit our land. It is one thing for a white child to be taught by a white teacher that color, like beauty, is only "skin deep"; it is far more convincing to experience that truth on a day-to-day basis during the routine, ongoing learning process.

In this case, the collective-bargaining agreement between the Union and the Board of Education succinctly stated a valid public purpose— "recognition of the desirability of multi-ethnic representation on the teaching faculty," and thus "a policy of actively seeking minority group personnel." * * *

It is argued, nonetheless, that the purpose should be deemed invalid because, even if the Board of Education's judgment in this case furthered a laudable goal, some other boards might claim that their experience demonstrates that segregated classes, or segregated faculties, lead to better academic achievement. There is, however, a critical difference between a decision to exclude a member of a minority race because of his or her skin color and a decision to include more members of the minority in a school faculty for that reason.

The exclusionary decision rests on the false premise that differences in race, or in the color of a person's skin, reflect real differences that are relevant to a person's right to share in the blessings of a free society. As noted, that premise is "utterly irrational" and repugnant to the principles of a free and democratic society. Nevertheless, the fact that persons of different races do, indeed, have differently colored skin, may give rise to a belief that there is some significant difference between such persons. The inclusion of minority teachers in the educational process inevitably tends to dispel that illusion whereas their exclusion could only tend to foster it. The inclusionary decision is consistent with the principle that all men are created equal; the exclusionary decision is at war with that principle. One decision accords with the Equal Protection Clause of the Fourteenth Amendment; the other does not. Thus, consideration of whether the consciousness of race is exclusionary or inclusionary plainly distinguishes the Board's valid purpose in this case from a race-conscious decision that would reinforce assumptions of inequality.

Regents of the University of California v. Bakke

438 U.S. 265 (1978)

■ Appendix to Opinion of POWELL, J.

Harvard College Admissions Program

* * * The belief that diversity adds an essential ingredient to the educational process has long been a tenet of Harvard College admissions. Fifteen or twenty years ago, however, diversity meant students from California, New York, and Massachusetts; city dwellers and farm boys; violinists, painters and football players; biologists, historians and classicists; potential stockbrokers, academics and politicians. The result was that very few ethnic or racial minorities attended Harvard College. In recent years Harvard College has expanded the concept of diversity to include students from disadvantaged economic, racial and ethnic groups. Harvard College now recruits not only Californians or Louisianans but also blacks

and Chicanos and other minority students. Contemporary conditions in the United States mean that if Harvard College is to continue to offer a first-rate education to its students, minority representation in the undergraduate body cannot be ignored by the Committee on Admissions.

In practice, this new definition of diversity has meant that race has been a factor in some admission decisions. When the Committee on Admissions reviews the large middle group of applicants who are "admissible" and deemed capable of doing good work in their courses, the race of an applicant may tip the balance in his favor just as geographic origin or a life spent on a farm may tip the balance in other candidates' cases. A farm boy from Idaho can bring something to Harvard College that a Bostonian cannot offer. Similarly, a black student can usually bring something that a white person cannot offer. The quality of the educational experience of all the students in Harvard College depends in part on these differences in the background and outlook that students bring with them.

In Harvard College admissions the Committee has not set target-quotas for the number of blacks, or of musicians, football players, physicists or Californians to be admitted in a given year. At the same time the Committee is aware that if Harvard College is to provide a truly heterogeneous environment that reflects the rich diversity of the United States, it cannot be provided without some attention to numbers. It would not make sense, for example, to have 10 or 20 students out of 1,100 whose homes are west of the Mississippi. Comparably, 10 or 20 black students could not begin to bring to their classmates and to each other the variety of points of view, backgrounds and experiences of blacks in the United States. Their small numbers might also create a sense of isolation among the black students themselves and thus make it more difficult for them to develop and achieve their potential. Consequently, when making its decisions, the Committee on Admissions is aware that there is some relationship between numbers and achieving the benefits to be derived from a diverse student body, and between numbers and providing a reasonable environment for those students admitted. But that awareness does not mean that the Committee sets a minimum number of blacks or of people from west of the Mississippi who are to be admitted. It means only that in choosing among thousands of applicants who are not only "admissible" academically but have other strong qualities, the Committee, with a number of criteria in mind, pays some attention to distribution among many types and categories of students.

————

Grutter v. Bollinger

539 U.S. 306 (2003)

■ Justice O'Connor delivered the opinion of the Court

* * * The Law School's assessment that diversity will, in fact, yield educational benefits is substantiated by respondents and their amici. Our scrutiny of the interest asserted by the Law School is no less strict for taking into account complex educational judgments in an area that lies

primarily within the expertise of the university. Our holding today is in keeping with our tradition of giving a degree of deference to a university's academic decisions, within constitutionally prescribed limits. * * *

The Law School's claim of a compelling interest is further bolstered by its amici, who point to the educational benefits that flow from student body diversity. In addition to the expert studies and reports entered into evidence at trial, numerous studies show that student body diversity promotes learning outcomes, and "better prepares students for an increasingly diverse workforce and society, and better prepares them as professionals." *Brief for American Educational Research Association et al. as Amici Curiae 3*; see, e.g., W. Bowen & D. Bok, *The Shape of the River* (1998); *Diversity Challenged: Evidence on the Impact of Affirmative Action* (G. Orfield & M. Kurlaender eds. 2001); *Compelling Interest: Examining the Evidence on Racial Dynamics in Colleges and Universities* (M. Chang, D. Witt, J. Jones, & K. Hakuta eds.2003).

These benefits are not theoretical but real, as major American businesses have made clear that the skills needed in today's increasingly global marketplace can only be developed through exposure to widely diverse people, cultures, ideas, and viewpoints. *Brief for 3M et al. as Amici Curiae 5*; *Brief for General Motors Corp. as Amicus Curiae 3–4*. What is more, high-ranking retired officers and civilian leaders of the United States military assert that, "[b]ased on [their] decades of experience," a "highly qualified, racially diverse officer corps ... is essential to the military's ability to fulfill its principle mission to provide national security." *Brief for Julius W. Becton, Jr., et al. as Amici Curiae 5*. The primary sources for the Nation's officer corps are the service academies and the Reserve Officers Training Corps (ROTC), the latter comprising students already admitted to participating colleges and universities. At present, "the military cannot achieve an officer corps that is both highly qualified and racially diverse unless the service academies and the ROTC used limited race-conscious recruiting and admissions policies." * * *

Covering

111 Yale Law Journal 769, 771–775 (2002)

■ Kenji Yoshino

Assimilation is the magic in the American Dream. Just as in our actual dreams, magic permits us to transform into better, more beautiful creatures, so too in the American Dream, assimilation permits us to become not only Americans, but the kind of Americans we seek to be. Justice Scalia recently expressed this pro-assimilation sentiment when he joined a Supreme Court majority to strike down an affirmative action program. Calling for the end of race-consciousness by public actors, Scalia said: In the eyes of government, we are just one race here. It is American. (Packed into this statement is the idea that we should set aside the racial identifications that divide us—black, white, Asian, Latino—and embrace the Americanness that unites us all.)

This vision of assimilation is profoundly seductive and is, at some level, not just American but human. Surrendering our individuality is what permits us to enter communities larger than the narrow stations of our individual lives. Especially when the traits that divide us are, like race, morally arbitrary, this surrender seems like something to be prized. Indeed, assimilation is not only often beneficial, but sometimes necessary. To speak a language, to wear clothes, to have manners—all are acts of assimilation.

This assimilationist dream has its grip on the law. The American legal antidiscrimination paradigm has been dominated by the cases of race, and, to a lesser extent, sex. The solicitude directed toward racial minorities and women has been justified in part by the fact that they are marked by "immutable" and "visible" characteristics—that is, that such groups cannot assimilate into mainstream society because they are marked as different. The law must step in because these groups are physiologically incapable of blending into the mainstream. In contrast, major strands of American antidiscrimination law direct much less concern toward groups that can assimilate. Such groups, after all, can engage in self-help by assimilating into mainstream society. In law, as in broader culture, assimilation is celebrated as the cure to many social ills. One would have to be antisocial to argue against it.

I believe gays may have theorized some dimensions of the relationship between assimilation and discrimination differently from either racial minorities or women. This is because gays are generally able to assimilate in more ways than either racial minorities or women. In fact or in the imagination of others, gays can assimilate in three ways: conversion, passing, and covering. Conversion means the underlying identity is altered. Conversion occurs when a lesbian changes her orientation to become straight. Passing means the underlying identity is not altered, but hidden. Passing occurs when a lesbian presents herself to the world as straight. Covering means the underlying identity is neither altered nor hidden, but is downplayed. Covering occurs when a lesbian both is, and says she is, a lesbian, but otherwise makes it easy for others to disattend her orientation.

Of these three forms of assimilation, covering will probably be least familiar. The term and concept come from sociologist Erving Goffman's groundbreaking work on stigma. Goffman observed that even persons who are ready to admit possession of a stigma . . . may nonetheless make a great effort to keep the stigma from looming large. Thus a lesbian might be comfortable being gay and saying she is gay, but might nonetheless modulate her identity to permit others to ignore her orientation. She might, for example, (1) not engage in public displays of same-sex affection; (2) not engage in gender-atypical activity that could code as gay; or (3) not engage in gay activism.

As Goffman realized, these modes of assimilation are not always easily distinguishable from one another. For example, Goffman recognized that the same action could be either passing or covering depending on the knowledge of the audience before whom it was performed. A woman who refrains from holding hands with her same-sex partner may thus pass with respect to those who do not know her orientation but cover with respect to those who do. This does not mean that the modalities of assimilation are indistinguishable. Rather, it means that one must know not only the performance of the actor, but also the literacy of the audience, to make that distinction . . .

The classical model of identity is also a model of discrimination. If individuals have multiple ways of modulating their identities, discrimination against them will take multiple forms, including the demands to convert, to pass, and to cover. The form of assimilation required of an identity will often be correlated to the strength of the animus against it. When discriminatory animus against an identity is particularly strong, it may require conversion. When that animus is weaker, it may permit individuals to retain the targeted trait, but require them to pass. When the animus is weaker still, it may permit individuals to retain and disclose their trait, but require them to cover it.

―――――

The Prohibition Era (Review of Covering: The Hidden Assault on Our Civil Rights, by Kenji Yoshino)

The New Republic, March 20, 2006

■ Martha C. Nussbaum

In 1998, a Missouri court granted custody to a lesbian mother, after finding that "the children were unaware of Mother's sexual preference, and Mother never engaged in any sexual or affectionate behavior in the presence of the children." Many courts have gone the other way, after determining that same-sex parents engaged not in overt sexual conduct that would be inappropriate for any parent to display before any child, but in displays of affection, such as hugging or holding hands, which clearly revealed the parent's sexual orientation. Courts in these cases are not demanding that same-sex parents stop being gay, or even that they pretend not to be gay. Instead, they are making a demand that Kenji Yoshino (following Erving Goffman) calls a demand for "covering": a demand not to express their identity in public and visible ways.

The repression of a minority, Yoshino argues, does not end when it is permitted to exist in society, and is no longer forced to "convert" to some other way of being and acting. Nor does it end when members of the group are not expected to "pass," concealing their minority identity from all but chosen intimates. Even when minorities who reveal their group membership openly are tolerated, they are often required to assimilate in ways that "cover" that identity. Thus, it was all right for the lesbian mother to be known as a lesbian, but not all right for her to hold hands with her partner. It is often all right for African Americans to be prominent in the workplace, but they have to dress for success and play nice, conforming their behavior to a stereotype invented by the dominant culture.

An interesting example that came too late for inclusion in Yoshino's account of "covering" has been the media's treatment of the Olympic medal-winning speed skater Shani Davis. White society was all set to pat itself on the back when an African American finally medaled in the lily-white sport, and Davis would have been warmly welcomed into its bosom had he been cheerful, docile, and grateful. Stories of how Davis overcame his "gang-infested" neighborhood (he comes from my own neighborhood, Chicago's Hyde Park, a multiracial university community that can be criticized as boring but not as gang-infested) were trotted out to prepare the way for a warm reception. Instead of gratitude and proper "white" behavior, however, Davis was spiky, brusque, and clearly annoyed at the press's quite ridiculous treatment of his origins. He talked to Chicago newspapers, which treated him with respect and got his story right, but he turned a cold shoulder to the others. ("Are you angry, Shani?" a network reporter asked, as if that would be the unforgivable sin, when the white community was being so very nice). A similar treatment often befalls African Americans who wear cornrows, or "talk black," or in other ways refuse to make the majority comfortable.

Similar stories can be told about other minorities. There was once a time when Jews were forced to convert to Christianity if they wanted to escape persecution. Overlapping with this time were times when many Jews persisted in their religion but kept it secret, "passing" as Christian, while revealing their Jewish identity to intimates. By far the most significant form of discrimination suffered by Jews in Europe and North America in the modern era, however, is the form that Yoshino calls "covering": they may be full and equal (sort of) members of Protestant society if they talk and dress like WASPs, and do not flaunt their religion before others; in short, if they are not "too Jewish." In the mid-twentieth century, upwardly mobile Jewish parents gave their children WASP names, urged them to avoid their too-Jewish peers, and made sure they went to WASP schools where they would get the "right" social connections. I know older Jews who flinch, even today, before "out" Jews of their own generation, because the expressions and mannerisms of those Jews are exactly what their parents drilled them not to display.

Women, too, encounter a demand for "covering," but in a more complicated, mixed-up form. At times, women are urged to adopt stereotypical male behavior. A female law student is urged to be aggressive and talkative, to wear a black suit, to mask her emotions, not to have children or to say nothing about them if she does. But at other times (and in other careers), women are penalized if their dress and manner are not "feminine" enough. How on earth any sane person could ever decode these social rules is beyond me. Our confusion is clearly revealed by Yoshino's lists of women's "masculine" and "feminine" characteristics, since many professional women possess most of the items on both lists: they avoid pastels and floral designs, and they are aggressive, ambitious, assertive, athletic, competitive, individualistic, and self-reliant; but they also wear earrings and makeup, are sympathetic and yielding, and perform "nurture" functions at work, "like counseling and mentoring." So who would be surprised that women get criticized and downgraded from both directions: sometimes for being "too masculine," sometimes for being not "masculine" enough?

The story of any minority's progress, argues Yoshino, can be charted by examining these three stages: first, the demand for conversion; second, the demand for "passing"; third, and last, the demand for "covering." Not all three categories apply to all groups. Women were never asked to "convert," for obvious reasons, or even to "pass," and African Americans had no realistic option of "conversion." Most minorities in America today, according to Yoshino, no longer face demands for conversion or passing—but all, to some extent, face the demand for covering, for assimilation to majority norms. And this demand, while less oppressive than the other two, is profoundly unfair, burdening minorities in ways that majorities are not burdened.

Moreover, the demand is fraught with psychological danger. How can a person really have equality when she has to push some of her most deeply rooted commitments under the rug, treating them as something shameful and socially inappropriate? Surely the lives of gays in America have improved markedly now that they are typically not subjected to enforced conversion procedures, and may even be "out" with impunity; but being "out," as Yoshino rightly shows, is a spectrum, and the law professor whose colleagues tolerate his known gayness but who urge him not to engage in gay politics, or not to teach sexual-orientation law, or not to "flaunt" his orientation through public displays of affection, encounters a demand that is constricting. So, Yoshino concludes, we should not pat ourselves on the back because we tolerate people who are different, when we are imposing demands that deform and humiliate. Instead we must think about how we can produce a society where people are free to be themselves.

———

NOTES

1. Is "diversity" an empty concept? Diversity simply means difference, variety, or heterogeneity. This means that, in theory, diversity embraces all differences. For instance, in university admissions policies, race has been placed "on the same footing for consideration" as other "qualities" such as exceptional personal talents, unique work or service experience, leadership potential, maturity, demonstrated compassion, rural school attendance, non-mainstream political views, ability to communicate with the poor, and other qualities deemed "different." The concept thus leaves it up to the institution to determine which differences matter most. In theory, a school might attain diversity by accepting more racial minorities or by accepting more tuba players or athletes. Some have argued that diversity needs a "mediating principle" to give it substance in addressing the historical disadvantages of groups like African Americans. *See generally* Sheila Foster, *Difference and Equality: A Critical Assessment of the Concept of Diversity* 1993 Wisconsin Law Review 105. In practice, however, the diversity rationale has been used as a justification for upholding race-conscious affirmative action plans.

2. If an employer or educational institution succeeds in "diversifying" itself by hiring/admitting people of varying types of "difference"—racial, ethnic, sexual, etc.—under what circumstances might some individuals still feel the need to "cover" their identities? Does diversity address the problem of "covering?"

3. Who are the intended beneficiaries of diversity? Is the purpose to give minority group members an opportunity to join a majority-dominated college or workplace, or to improve the experience of the majority? One critique of the Harvard admissions plan adopted by Justice Powell's decision in *Bakke* is that its purpose was to improve the educational experience of Harvard's overwhelmingly white student body by admitting some Black and Chicano students, which would help give the white students a broader view of the world. Is this unfairly cynical? This issue is discussed further in chapter IV.

4. In his dissent to the *Grutter* decision, Justice Thomas describes the University of Michigan Law School's diversity admissions policy as an "aesthetics" policy, designed to produce a classroom racial mix that is pleasing to observe. See *Grutter v. Bollinger*, 539 U.S. 306, 354–355, n. 3 (dissenting opinion of THOMAS, J.). He argues that if the Law School really cared about promoting diversity, it could achieve it through random admissions, giving up its elite status by becoming less selective, or it could stop using the LSAT, which has a discriminatory impact on Blacks and Latinos. Do you agree? Why doesn't Michigan (and other highly selective law schools) give up using a test that produces such discriminatory results? This issue is discussed further in chapter IV.

5. In 2006, in response to the *Grutter* decision, which permitted the University of Michigan to use racial and ethnic diversity in admitting students, the voters of Michigan passed the "Michigan Civil Rights Initiative," which banned affirmative action by the State University system. Exit polls show that the initiative had strong support from white voters, and strong opposition from Black voters. It was narrowly opposed by women, and strongly supported by men. See http://www.insidehighered.com/news/2006/11/08/michigan.

6. California and Washington have also passed voter initiatives banning affirmative action in State Universities, including diversity-based affirmative action. Can a court find that the voters have violated the Equal Protection Clause by voting to end a policy that helped minorities? The Supreme Court said yes, in some circumstances (*see Hunter v. Erickson*, 393 U.S. 385 (1969); *Washington. v. Seattle Sch. Dist. No.1*, 458 U.S. 457 (1982)), but in the case of the California initiative the Ninth Circuit and the California Supreme Court both ruled that the initiative did not violate the principle of equality, even where it was supported by white voters and opposed by non-white voters. *See Coalition for Econ. Equity v. Wilson*, 122 F.3d 692, 702 (1997); *Coral Constr., Inc. v. City and County of San Francisco*, 113 Cal.Rptr.3d 279 (2010). New litigation on the issue is pending, as of February 2012, in the Sixth and Ninth Circuits.

G. REPARATIVE EQUALITY

One approach to achieving equality is to attempt to repair the harm caused by inequality through reparations, as part of a restorative justice process. When societies have undergone fundamental change, the demand for reparations has at times been an important, and controversial, part of the change process. Examples include reparations paid by the United States to Japanese Americans incarcerated during World War II, victims of the Nazi Holocaust, and the South African Truth and Reconciliation Commission. Continuing claims for reparations include claims in the United States for slavery, for race riots, for the genocide against the American Indians, and for the military conquest of Hawaii. Dr. King's "I Have a Dream" speech, often used as a defense of "color-blindness," can also be described as a call for reparations.

Repairing the Past: New Efforts in the Reparations Debate in America

38 Harvard Civil Rights–Civil Liberties Law Review 279, 282–3 (2003)

■ Charles J. Ogletree, Jr.

Reparations for African Americans are controversial and highly divisive, not just among whites but also among African Americans. For example, since its introduction in 1989, H.R. 40, Representative John Conyers's reparations bill, has failed to generate broad support or approval each year that he has filed it in Congress. At the state and local level, the reparations movement has been dramatically different. The movement has gained public moment in recent years, as evidenced by the growing number of legislative initiatives and remains a compelling argument for social justice.

At its most basic level, reparations seek something more than token acknowledgement of the centuries of suffering of African Americans at the hands of the state and federal governments, corporations, and individuals during the three centuries of chattel slavery and Jim Crow. As Randall Robinson notes in his book *The Debt: What America Owes to Blacks,* many of our greatest public monuments, including the White House, the Capitol, and the Jefferson Memorial, were built by slaves. Sadly and remarkably, the nation's Capital offers no tribute to these who constructed our nation's most venerable monuments. The sacrifices of the African American community for the American nation during slavery, Reconstruction, and Jim Crow are too often forgotten.

This is not a casual oversight. Randall Robinson argues persuasively that it is more insidious. The national consciousness of the terrible history of slavery and Jim Crow has been deliberately repressed into a national subconscious as an ugly part of our national history that we choose to ignore.

The failure to acknowledge this history greatly influences the national debate about race. If we refuse to consciously confront the nation's complicity in enslaving millions of its subjects and brutalizing millions of its citizens during Jim Crow, then we cannot engage in a conscientious discussion or race. To invoke our nation's responsibility for discrimination is not to play the "victim" card but to demand the same treatment that other races and ethnicities receive. Accordingly, the first goal of reparations is to remember and celebrate these forgotten African Americans and insist that our nation fully acknowledge their many contributions to our country's economic and political well-being.

But reparations can—and must—go further than educating the public and erecting monuments to the nation's slave forefathers and foremothers. Reverend Martin Luther King Jr. lamented our failure to recognize these historic contributions when he pleaded that for genuine social reconciliation to occur, American must engage in a process of acknowledging its past and repairing the enduring injustices it has created at home.

———

I Have a Dream

Speech delivered on August 28, 1963

■ Rev. Dr. Martin Luther King, Jr.

In a sense we have come to our nation's capital to cash a check. When the architects of our republic wrote the magnificent words of the Constitution and the Declaration of Independence, they were signing a promissory note to which every American was to fall heir. This note was a promise that all men would be guaranteed the inalienable rights of life, liberty, and the pursuit of happiness.

It is obvious today that America has defaulted on this promissory note insofar as her citizens of color are concerned. Instead of honoring this sacred obligation, America has given the Negro people a bad check which has come back marked "insufficient funds." But we refuse to believe that the bank of justice is bankrupt. We refuse to believe that there are insufficient funds in the great vaults of opportunity of this nation. So we have come to cash this check—a check that will give us upon demand the riches of freedom and the security of justice. We have also come to this hallowed spot to remind America of the fierce urgency of now.

———

[EDITORS' NOTE: Justice Scalia's indirect reply to Dr. King and Professor Ogletree is that there is no creditor or debtor race in American law. Consider the following excerpts in light of the continuing debate over reparations for slavery.]

Adarand Constructors, Inc. v. Pena

515 U.S. 200 (1995)

■ Justice Scalia, concurring in part and concurring in judgment

In my view, government can never have a "compelling interest" in discriminating on the basis of race in order to "make up" for past racial discrimination in the opposite direction. Individuals who have been wronged by unlawful racial discrimination should be made whole; but under our Constitution there can be no such thing as either a creditor or a debtor race. That concept is alien to the Constitution's focus upon the individual.

———

Looking Beyond the Bottom: Critical Legal Studies and Reparations

22 Harvard Civil Rights—Civil Liberties Law Review 323, 393–397 (1987)

■ MARI MATSUDA

Reparations is a "critical legalism," a legal concept that has transformative power and that avoids the traps of individualism, neutrality and indeterminancy that plague many mainstream concepts of rights or legal principles. Reparations avoid standard liberal pitfalls because, first, it is a concept directed at remedying wrongs committed against the powerless. Unlike "free speech" or "due process," payment for past injustice is a one-way value. Those on the bottom—minority group members, political outsiders, the exploited—will receive reparations.

Second, reparations doctrine supports group rights rather than individual rights and thus escapes some of the ideological traps of traditional rights thinking.

Finally, reparations is at its heart transformative. It recognizes the crimes of the powerful against the powerless. It condemns exploitation and adopts a vision of a more just world. The reparations concept has the aspirational, affirming, idealistic attraction of rights rhetoric, without the weak backbone. While rights rhetoric turns to dust time and again, reparations theory, should we accept and internalize it, may prove more dependable.

This progressive tilt of reparations, however, can mask lurking dangers. Some detect a certain commodifying vulgarity in throwing money at injured people.... Reparations, one could argue, promotes the idea that everyone has a price, that every wound is salved by cash, that success merely means more money.

The practical shortage of resources in the injured communities weighs against the commodification risk. Monetary grants will not compensate for the terrible losses sustained. No sum can make up for loss of freedom or sovereignty. The award serves a largely symbolic function, much as the passing of a pig in a Pacific-island apology ceremony. The judgment states, "Something terrible has happened for which we are responsible. While no amount can compensate for your loss, we offer here a symbol of our deep regret and our continuing obligation."

Resistance to commodification is important. If reparations are viewed as an equivalent exchange for past wrongs, continuing claims are terminated. Any obligation to victim-groups would end since their injury is transformed into a commodity and the price paid. A reparations claim would become a dangerous gamble for victims, and a welcome res judicata opportunity for perpetrators. One generation could sell away their claim at bargain-basement prices, to the detriment of future generations, in an effort to cash in at the earliest opportunity. Commodification must be resisted if reparations are to be more than a coercive quit-claim mechanism.

A related and indeed troubling objection to reparations comes from looking to the bottom. Some thoughtful victim group members are inclined to reject reparations because of the political reality that any reparations award will come only when those in power decide it is appropriate. Hayden Burgess, a native Hawaiian nationalist lawyer, suggests that any award of cash reparations is inadequate, for it ignores the Hawaiian's primary need: restoration of the Hawaiian government and removal of the United States presence in Hawaii. Rather than a top-down model of reparations granted by the United States, Burgess prefers negotiations between the Hawaiians and the United States as equals, perhaps mediated by a neutral third party in an international forum, to determine an appropriate remedy for the overthrow of the Hawaiian government. Burgess suggests that self-determination for the Hawaiian people is guaranteed by international law, and that self-determination includes the right to negotiate with the United States for the return of the Hawaiian Islands. Reparations would merely enforce the role of the United States as lawgiver and patron.

Reparations awards, in this view, portray the government as benign and contrite. Reparations buys off protest, assuages white guilt, and throws responsibility for continued racism upon the victims. "We paid you, why are you still having problems? It must be in your genes."

To avoid this corruption, victims must define the remedies, and the obligation of reparations must continue until all vestiges of past injustice are dead and buried. Reparations is not, then, equivalent to a standard legal judgment. It is the formal acknowledgment of historical wrong, the recognition of continuing injury, and the commitment to redress, looking always to victims for guidance.

Finally, there is the difficult problem of the effect of reparations to one group upon other victim groups that remain uncompensated. Just as affirmative action in employment and college admission—a form of reparations—may impact negatively on the white underclass, monetary reparations to one victim group may result in a new group slipping to the bottom.

Reparations will result in a new form of disadvantage only if they are made outside of a broader consciousness that always looks to the needs of the bottom. A critical theory of reparations recognizes economic as well as racial injustice. It looks to human experience to guide compensation to those in need. Such an approach would view each reparations award to a successful claimant group as a step forward in the long journey toward substantive equality. Thus, progressive Hawaiians view awards already made to Native Americans on the mainland United States not as a chunk taken out of a limited fund, leaving less for Hawaiians, but as a symbol of the possibility of reparations for Hawaiians as well. The arguments that victims will have to make and perpetrators will have to accept before any reparations are awarded will raise consciousnesses about the obligation and need to correct past wrongs. Each separate commitment to the concept of reparations thus internalizes new norms and moves us closer to the end of all forms of victimization.

A theory of reparations formulated in consideration of both a victim's consciousness and the insights of critical legal theorists provides a critical legalism, moving us away from repression and toward community.

————

Postamble to the Constitution of the Republic of South Africa Act No. 200 of 1993

(Interim Constitution)

This Constitution provides a historic bridge between the past of a deeply divided society characterised by strife, conflict, untold suffering and injustice and a future founded on the recognition of human rights, democracy and peaceful co-existence and development opportunities for all South Africans irrespective of colour, race, class, belief or sex.

The pursuit of national unity, the well-being of all South African citizens and peace require reconciliation between the people of South Africa and the reconstruction of society. The adoption of this Constitution lays the secure foundation for the people of South Africa to transcend the divisions and strife of the past, which generated gross violations of human rights, the transgression of humanitarian principles in violent conflicts and a legacy of hatred, fear, guilt and revenge.

These can now be addressed on the basis that there is a need for understanding but not for vengeance, a need for reparation but not for retaliation, a need for ubuntu [translated by Desmond Tutu as "open and available" and "the essence of being human"] but not for victimisation. In order to advance such reconciliation and reconstruction, amnesty shall be granted in respect of acts, omissions and offences associated with political objectives and committed in the course of the conflicts of the past. To this end, Parliament under this Constitution shall adopt a law determining a firm cut-off date, which shall be a date after 8 October 1990 and before 6 December 1993, and providing for the mechanisms, criteria and procedures, including tribunals, if any, through which such amnesty shall be dealt with at any time after the law has been passed.

With this Constitution and these commitments we, the people of South Africa, open a new chapter in the history of our country.

[EDITORS' NOTE: These provisions were preserved in Schedule 6, section 22 of the Constitution of the Republic of South Africa Act No. 108 of 1996 (the Constitution), which provided that: *Notwithstanding the other provisions of the new Constitution and despite the repeal of the previous Constitution, all the provisions relating to amnesty contained in the previous Constitution under the heading "National Unity and Reconciliation" are deemed to be part of the new Constitution for the purposes of the Promotion of National Unity and Reconciliation Act, 1995 (Act 34 of 1995), as amended, including for the purposes of its validity.*]

————

NOTES

1.   Are there different theories, or versions, of reparations reflected in these passages? If so, can you articulate them? Can you place them along the scale of formal and substantive notions of equality?

2.   In 1942, pursuant to an order by President Franklin Roosevelt (Executive Order 9066), the United States imprisoned (or detained or interred) over 100,000 American citizens of Japanese ancestry and Japanese residents living on the Pacific coast, sending them to prison camps (or detention or interment or war relocation camps). The Supreme Court upheld the constitutionality of the order, in *Korematsu v. United States*, 323 U.S. 214 (1944). In 1988 Congress passed the Civil Liberties Act of 1988, which provided reparations payments of $20,000 to each surviving detainee. Approximately 60,000 victims lived to receive reparations payments. Why were the reparations payments limited to survivors? Is there a principle of equality that explains this limitation?

3.   The *Korematsu* case was a prosecution by the United States of Fred Korematsu, an American citizen of Japanese ancestry who was prosecuted for failing to appear for "resettlement" in the camps. His conviction was affirmed by the United States Supreme Court, based on evidence submitted by the United States that U.S. citizens of Japanese descent could not be trusted to be loyal to the United States in the war with Japan. In the 1980's UCSD Professor Peter Irons uncovered evidence that the government "deliberately omitted relevant information and provided misleading information" to the Court. In 1983 the U.S. District Court for the Northern District of California overturned the original conviction. The holding of the Supreme Court decision, however, is undisturbed. For legitimate military purposes, the government may single out an ethnic, national or racial group for group imprisonment without trial.

4.   In 1921 the Greenwood section of Tulsa Oklahoma, then known as the "Black Wall Street," was pillaged and burned by white police, troops, and rioters. Uncounted numbers of Black residents were killed, and hundreds if not thousands were injured. The survivors were imprisoned in internment camps. In 1997 a "Tulsa Race Riot Commission" was formed. It recommended reparations payments to the surviving victims and the descendants of victims, and a scholarship fund for descendants and others affected by the riots. In response, the Oklahoma Legislature passed the "1921 Tulsa Race Riot Reconciliation Act," which provided for 300 scholarships, but no direct reparations payments. A lawsuit was filed in the United States District Court seeking reparations as recommended by the Commission; it was dismissed as untimely. For more on the Greenwood reparations claims, see http://www.okhistory.org/trrc/freport.htm; Alfred L. Brophy and Randall Kennedy, *Reconstructing the Dreamland: The Tulsa Race Riot of 1921*, RACE REPARATIONS, AND RECONCILIATION (2002).

5.   The largest reparations payments for racist acts by a state were the payments made by Germany to the survivors and descendants of the victims of the Holocaust. Since an initial settlement in 1952, Germany has paid an estimated $60 billion to the victims of Nazi persecution. See website of the Conference on Jewish Material Claims Against Germany at

http://www.claimscon.org/index.asp?url=about_us. Long after the original agreement, additional payments were demanded and paid, with some paid by the German state, others by German companies to their Holocaust era slave laborers, Swiss banks and Italian insurance companies to the descendants of their murdered depositors or policy holders, and museums all over Europe to the original owners (or their descendants) of artworks confiscated (stolen) by the German state. New claims continue to be negotiated over fifty years after the original agreement, as historical records surface that bring new evidence to light. Does the continuing viability of these claims help answer some of the concerns raised by Professor Matsuda that initial payments will be inadequate and will serve as *res judicata* as to further claims?

6.   Among the still unresolved Holocaust reparations claims is a claim against the French National Railroad, which transported over 70,000 Jews from France to German death camps in 1942 through 1944. The victims were transported in cattle cars, but were charged the price of passenger tickets. A class action brought in the United States is pending. An earlier case was brought against the railroad in France, where a lower court decision in favor of the victims was reversed by the highest administrative court (Conseil d'Etat). http://cacambo.over-blog.net/article–7318368.html. In January 2011 the railroad publicly apologized to French Holocaust victims for its role. The apology is expected to improve its bid to build bullet trains in the United States. See http://www.nytimes.com/2011/01/26/world/europe/26france.html.

————

I Will Give You A Talisman

Mahatma Gandhi, Last Phase, Vol. II (1958), P. 65

■ MAHATMA GANDHI

I will give you a talisman. Whenever you are in doubt, or when the self becomes too much with you, apply the following test. Recall the face of the poorest and the weakest man whom you may have seen, and ask yourself, if the step you contemplate is going to be of any use to him. Will he gain anything by it? Will it restore him to a control over his own life and destiny? In other words, will it lead to swaraj [freedom] for the hungry and spiritually starving millions? Then you will find your doubts and your self melt away.

————

Faces at the Bottom of the Well

(1992), p. 12

■ DERRICK BELL

We must see this country's history of slavery, not as an insuperable racial barrier to blacks, but as a legacy of enlightenment from our enslaved forebears reminding us that if they survived the ultimate form of racism, we and those whites who stand with us can at least view racial oppression in its many contemporary forms without underestimating its critical importance and likely permanent status in this country.

To initiate the reconsideration, I want to set forth this proposition, which will be easier to reject than refute: *Black people will never gain full equality in this country. Even those herculean efforts we hail as successful will produce no more than temporary "peaks of progress," short-lived victories that slide into irrelevance as racial patterns adapt in ways that maintain white dominance. This is a hard-to-accept fact that all history verifies. We must acknowledge it, not as a sign of submission, but as an act of ultimate defiance.*

————

NOTES

1. This chapter begins and ends with statements about equality based on wealth or poverty. Anatole France's ironic statement about equality law prohibiting the rich from stealing bread is bookended with Gandhi's talisman that we ask how our actions will affect the poor. What is the relationship between income equality and the various forms of identity equality discussed in the preceding pages?

2. Both Gandhi and Bell suggest a political ethic that, in coming to terms with the immensity of the problem of oppression, racism and inequality, provides us with a source for resistance, public service, and social change. How might the imperative to find inspiration from the "faces at the bottom of the well" or to "recall the face of the poorest and the weakest man" shift our understanding of legal equality? Or social equality? How does it reframe our understanding of legal advocacy for equality?

CHAPTER II

WHAT IS INEQUALITY?—PROVING DISCRIMINATION

INTRODUCTION

Our legal theories on the meaning of equality and inequality are translated into pragmatic questions of responsibility when equality laws are enforced in the courts. Most often, enforcement takes the form of litigating equality rights under constitutional provisions and anti-discrimination statutes. These are usually challenges to private or public acts of discrimination in employment, housing, education, voting, access to public accommodations, and the provision or withholding of public services or benefits. The common question in determining whether the plaintiff has established a violation of a constitutional provision or statute is whether s/he has proven discrimination. But what does proof of discrimination require? Should we require evidence of the intent to discriminate? If so, should we require a malicious intent, or merely the intent to differentiate? Does this equate with proof of a discriminatory motive? If so, must it be a conscious motive? Or is unintended discrimination, such as applied stereotyping, sufficient? That is, can discrimination be negligent? Alternatively, is it enough to show that there was a difference in treatment, whether intended or not? And if a difference is demonstrated, who should hold the burden of explaining or justifying it? How we answer these questions may depend on whether we see equality rights as individual or group rights. Consider these problems as you read the material that follows.

PROBLEMS

- A school district requires all incoming first grade students to take a standardized intelligence test. Ninety percent of the students from the local majority group test between the 30th and 95th percentile, while ninety percent of the children from the local minority group generally test between the 20th and 40th percentile. The school requires students testing below the 30th percentile to attend a special school, which provides fewer academic courses, and fewer opportunities for academic or vocational advancement. The result is that the main school is mostly made up of majority group students, most of whom advance to the university, while the special school is mostly made up of minority group members, most of whom drop out of school at age 16. Can the minority group members prove discrimination? Does it matter whether the test was adopted for the purpose of segregating the minority students, or whether it was adopted merely with knowledge of the likely results, or whether it was adopted by officials who had no idea what the results would be? If the officials testified that they had no idea what the results would be, would you believe them? If not, how would you prove what they knew?

- An employer has office workers, most of whom are from the majority group, and laborers, most of whom are from a minority group. The employer provides two cafeterias, one for office workers and one for laborers. Can the minority group members prove discrimination? What if the food quality is better in the office workers' cafeteria? What if the employer needs to provide better food to the office workers to keep them from quitting? What if the employer provides different bathrooms for the two groups?

- Again, an employer has office workers and laborers. In this case, the office workers are all majority group women, and the laborers are all minority men. Can either group prove discrimination? Could both?

- A minority group member applies for a job and is not selected. Should the employer be required to explain its reasons? What (if anything) should the employee be required to show before the employer is required to provide an explanation? What if the employer offers an explanation which the applicant demonstrates is false? Should we assume that the actual reason for the hiring decision is the applicant's minority status?

- A minority group member applies for a job and is not selected. A statistician studies the employer's most recent 500 hiring decisions and testifies that there is a 95% likelihood that the decision was based on the applicant's minority status. Should this be sufficient to prove discrimination? What if there was a 51% likelihood?

- An employer's decision-making process encourages supervisors to use their subjective evaluation of who is ready for management in making promotion decisions. Most of the supervisors are men, most of the supervisors choose men as ready for promotion, and very few women are promoted. Can a class of women prove discrimination? Can any individual woman prove discrimination?

- A night club sets up a velvet rope to screen potential patrons. Patrons must meet a certain dress code. Has there been a violation of the equality principle? Patrons must look ''hot.'' Has there been a violation of the equality principle? African Americans are less likely to be admitted than whites. Can any of the rejected patrons prove discrimination?

- A graduate school requires applicants to take its own admission test, which it administers only on Saturday mornings. A potential applicant objects that as an observant Jew she is precluded from taking the test. Can she prove discrimination? What if a musician objects that he plays late into the night on Fridays, and cannot take the test on Saturdays until afternoon? Can he prove discrimination?

- A woman of African descent applies for a job for which she is well qualified, attaching her resume, which includes a photo clearly indicating her skin color. She is rejected. She re-submits it, using a photo of a white friend. She is contacted for an interview. When she appears at the interview, the employer rejects her because she committed an act of dishonesty in submitting a substitute photo. Can she prove discrimination?

A. INTENTIONAL & UNINTENTIONAL (OR DIRECT AND INDIRECT) DISCRIMINATION

Most forms of discrimination are characterized through two dominant legal frameworks. The first is often described in the United States as "intentional" discrimination. It is comparable (but not identical) to what Europeans describe as "direct" discrimination. The second is commonly described in the U.S. as "unintentional," "adverse impact" or "effects" discrimination. It is comparable (but again not identical) to what is often called "indirect" discrimination outside the U.S. As you read the following materials think about what types of conduct, and states of mind, these theories are trying to capture.

————

Griggs v. Duke Power Co.

401 U.S. 424 (1971)

■ BURGER, C.J., delivered the opinion of the Court.

The objective of Congress in the enactment of Title VII [of the 1964 Civil Rights Act] is plain from the language of the statute. It was to achieve equality of employment opportunities and remove barriers that have operated in the past to favor an identifiable group of white employees over other employees. Under the Act, practices, procedures, or tests neutral on their face, and even neutral in terms of intent, cannot be maintained if they operate to 'freeze' the status quo of prior discriminatory employment practices. * * * The Act proscribes not only overt discrimination but also practices that are fair in form, but discriminatory in operation. The touchstone is business necessity. If an employment practice which operates to exclude Negroes cannot be shown to be related to job performance, the practice is prohibited. * * * [G]ood intent or absence of discriminatory intent does not redeem employment procedures or testing mechanisms that operate as 'built-in headwinds' for minority groups and are unrelated to measuring job capability.... Congress directed the thrust of the Act to the consequences of employment practices, not simply the motivation. More than that, Congress has placed on the employer the burden of showing that any given requirement must have a manifest relationship to the employment in question.

————

Washington v. Davis

426 U.S. 229 (1976)

■ JUSTICE WHITE delivered the opinion of the Court.

As the Court of Appeals understood Title VII, employees or applicants proceeding under it need not concern themselves with the employer's possibly discriminatory purpose but instead may focus solely on the racially differential impact of the challenged hiring or promotion practices. This is not the constitutional rule. We have never held that the constitutional standard for adjudicating claims of invidious racial discrimination is identical to the standards applicable under Title VII, and we decline to do so today. * * * The central purpose of the Equal Protection Clause of the Fourteenth Amendment is the prevention of official conduct discriminating on the basis of race. . . . But our cases have not embraced the proposition that a law or other official act, without regard to whether it reflects a racially discriminatory purpose, is unconstitutional solely because it has a racially disproportionate impact. * * * Disproportionate impact is not irrelevant, but it is not the sole touchstone of an invidious racial discrimination forbidden by the Constitution. Standing alone, it does not trigger the rule, that racial classifications are to be subjected to the strictest scrutiny and are justifiable only by the weightiest of considerations.

Massachusetts v. Feeney

442 U.S. 256 (1979)

■ JUSTICE STEWART delivered the opinion of the Court.

* * * The sole question for decision on this appeal is whether Massachusetts, in granting an absolute lifetime preference to veterans, has discriminated against women in violation of the Equal Protection Clause of the Fourteenth Amendment. * * *

The appellee's ultimate argument rests upon the presumption, common to the criminal and civil law, that a person intends the natural and foreseeable consequences of his voluntary actions. Her position was well stated in the concurring opinion in the District Court:

"Conceding . . . that the goal here was to benefit the veteran, there is no reason to absolve the legislature from awareness that the means chosen to achieve this goal would freeze women out of all those state jobs actively sought by men. To be sure, the legislature did not wish to harm women. But the cutting-off of women's opportunities was an inevitable concomitant of the chosen scheme-as inevitable as the proposition that if tails is up, heads must be down. Where a law's consequences are that inevitable, can they meaningfully be described as unintended?" 451 F.Supp., at 151.

This rhetorical question implies that a negative answer is obvious, but it is not. The decision to grant a preference to veterans was of course "intentional." So, necessarily, did an adverse impact upon nonveterans follow from that decision. And it cannot seriously be argued that the Legislature of Massachusetts could have been unaware that most veterans are men. It would thus be disingenuous to say that the adverse consequences of this legislation for women were unintended, in the sense that they were not volitional or in the sense that they were not foreseeable.

"Discriminatory purpose," however, implies more than intent as volition or intent as awareness of consequences. *See United Jewish Organizations v. Carey*, 430 U.S. 144 (concurring opinion). It implies that the decisionmaker, in this case a state legislature, selected or reaffirmed a particular course of action at least in part "because of," not merely "in spite of," its adverse effects upon an identifiable group. Yet, nothing in the record demonstrates that this preference for veterans was originally devised or subsequently re-enacted because it would accomplish the collateral goal of keeping women in a stereotypic and predefined place in the Massachusetts Civil Service.

NOTES

1. Does the *Griggs* case require employers to engage in affirmative action to avoid liability for unintentional discrimination? Stephan and Abigail Thernstrom have made this claim: "In 1964 Congress had been concerned about 'the *consequences* of employment practices, not simply the motivation,' Justice Burger claimed. It was an audacious rewriting of the statutory history.... The Civil Rights Act had maintained the traditional distinction between practices that were intentionally racist and those that were normal to the world of business and thus legitimate. Yet *Griggs* branded all aptitude tests and other sorting mechanisms—whatever the intent behind them and however fairly they were administered—as discriminatory devices if they were not indisputably job-related and if proportionately more blacks than whites failed them. * * * And thus while Title VII did not refer to affirmative action except as an available remedy for proven wrongs, with *Griggs* the Court took a significant step toward encouraging employers to rely on race in deciding whom to hire." Stephan & Abigail Thernstrom, AMERICA IN BLACK AND WHITE: ONE NATION, INDIVISIBLE at 432 (1997).

2. The relevant language of the U.S. employment discrimination law, Title VII of the 1964 Civil Rights Act, provides: "It shall be an unlawful employment practice for an employer (1) to fail or refuse to hire or to discharge any individual, or otherwise to discriminate against any individual with respect to his compensation, terms, conditions, or privileges of employment, because of such individual's race, color, religion, sex, or national origin; or, (2) to limit, segregate, or classify his employees or applicants for employment in any way which would deprive or tend to deprive any individual of employment opportunities or otherwise adversely affect his status as an employee, because of such individual's race, color, religion, sex, or national origin." The term "discriminate" is not defined by the Act. Title VII is discussed further in chapter III.

3. The basic international treaty prohibiting racial discrimination is the International Convention on the Elimination of All Forms of Racial Discrimination, which was adopted in 1965, and entered into force in 1969. It does provide a definition of discrimination. "Article 1, Section 1. ... the term 'racial discrimination' shall mean any distinction, exclusion, restriction or preference based on race, color, descent, or national or ethnic origin which has the purpose or effect of nullifying or impairing the recognition,

enjoyment or exercise, on an equal footing, of human rights and fundamental freedoms in the political, economic, social, cultural or any other field of public life." Should the U.S. Congress adopt this definition for Title VII? Should the U.S. courts?

4. The distinction between direct and indirect discrimination in Europe is explained in a June 2000 Directive of the Council of the European Union, which appears below. The European Union is a political and economic union. It is governed by the European Parliament, the Council of the European Union (heads of subject area ministries), and the European Commission (the executive body, consisting of 27 commissioners overseeing a staff of approximately 25,000 civil servants). The Council meets as the "European Council" up to four times a year, when it brings together heads of state or government. The Council and Commission sit in Brussels. The Parliament sits in Brussels, Strasbourg and Luxembourg (the latter for administrative offices). The European Union was previously named the European Community (EC) or European Economic Community (EEC). The Council of the European Union, on the basis of a proposal by the European Commission, is empowered to pass anti-discrimination Directives by unanimity and with the agreement of the European Parliament. The member states must then transpose the terms of the Directives into national law. The European Court of Justice may determine that a member state has failed to comply with a Directive, either by failing to transpose it correctly or completely, or by failing, through its national courts, to properly enforce it. *See* the Treaty on the Functioning of the European Union, Article 19 (originally added by the Treaty of Amsterdam).

5. European Union law is subject to the jurisdiction of the European Court of Justice (ECJ), which sits in Luxembourg. The Court consists of 27 judges, one from each member state. The judges are assisted by eight Advocates–General, who prepare independent opinions to help guide the Court in its decision-making. Their opinions, like the opinion of Advocate General Miguel Poiares Maduro which appears below, are not binding on the Court, but are highly influential.

6. The European Court of Human Rights ("ECtHR") is the high court of the Council of Europe. The Council consists of 47 European States that have signed the European Convention of Human Rights, and are thus bound by the human rights decisions of the Court. The Court sits in Strasbourg, France. It has 47 judges, with one selected by each member State. For more on the Council, *see* www.coe.int. It should not be confused with the European Court of Justice ("ECJ"), which is the high court of the 27 member European Union.

7. The United States has a long history of anti-discrimination legislation. Why then, should we look toward Europe in examining approaches to anti-discrimination law? Consider these observations by Professor Grainne de Burca: "The past decade and a half has witnessed a dramatic development and expansion of European antidiscrimination law. At the regional level, both the European Union and the Council of Europe have adopted important new instruments. Notably, the European Union has enacted a Charter of Fundamental Rights and an ambitious series of legislative measures, and the Council of Europe has adopted Protocol no. 12 to the European Convention on Human Rights that complements and expands the

existing antidiscrimination provision of Article 14 ECHR. These high-profile legal and political moves have both generated and been accompanied by significant domestic and transnational mobilization around European antidiscrimination norms. Funded in some cases by the EU Commission, and in other instances by major foundations and organizations like the Open Society Institute, strategic litigation in the fields of race, sexual orientation and disability discrimination has been brought by NGOs and legal activists before national and regional tribunals, including the European Court of Human Rights in Strasbourg and the European Social Charter's European Committee on Social Rights. These initiatives have sought to build in particular on the strategies and perceived successes of the movement for gender equality across Europe in previous decades. With a raft of new legislation and treaty provisions, new institutions such as the EU Fundamental Rights Agency, renewed civil society activism and a string of notable judicial victories for equality advocates, the condition of European antidiscrimination law and policy today—despite Europe's economic and financial woes—seems energetic and the outlook optimistic." Grainne de Burca, *The Trajectories of European and American Antidiscrimination Law*. Electronic copy available at: http://ssrn.com/abstract=1950697.

————

Council Directive 2000/43/EC of 29 June 2000

(Implementing the principle of equal treatment between persons irrespective of racial or ethnic origin)

Article 2—Concept of discrimination

1. For the purposes of this Directive, the principle of equal treatment shall mean that there shall be no direct or indirect discrimination based on racial or ethnic origin.

2. For the purposes of paragraph 1:

    (a) direct discrimination shall be taken to occur where one person is treated less favourably than another is, has been or would be treated in a comparable situation on grounds of racial or ethnic origin;

    (b) indirect discrimination shall be taken to occur where an apparently neutral provision, criterion or practice would put persons of a racial or ethnic origin at a particular disadvantage compared with other persons, unless that provision, criterion or practice is objectively justified by a legitimate aim and the means of achieving that aim are appropriate and necessary.

————

Council Directive 2006/54/EC of 5 July 2006

(Replacing Council Directive 97/80/EC of 15 December 1997)

Article 1: Purpose

The purpose of this Directive is to ensure the implementation of the principle of equal opportunities and equal treatment of men and women in matters of employment and occupation.

2(b).... "indirect discrimination": where an apparently neutral provision, criterion or practice would put persons of one sex at a particular disadvantage compared with persons of the other sex, unless that provision, criterion or practice is objectively justified by a legitimate aim, and the means of achieving that aim are appropriate and necessary.

Coleman v. Attridge Law

Case C–303/06

■ Opinion of ECJ Advocate General, Poiares Maduro, Delivered on 31 January 2008

- * * * 19. The Directive prohibits direct discrimination, harassment and indirect discrimination. The distinguishing feature of direct discrimination and harassment is that they bear a necessary relationship to a particular suspect classification. The discriminator relies on a suspect classification in order to act in a certain way. The classification is not a mere contingency but serves as an essential premise of his reasoning. An employer's reliance on those suspect grounds is seen by the Community legal order as an evil which must be eradicated. Therefore, the Directive prohibits the use of those classifications as grounds upon which an employer's reasoning may be based. By contrast, in indirect discrimination cases the intentions of the employer and the reasons he has to act or not to act are irrelevant. In fact, this is the whole point of the prohibition of indirect discrimination: even neutral, innocent or good faith measures and policies adopted with no discriminatory intent whatsoever will be caught if their impact on persons who have a particular characteristic is greater than their impact on other persons. It is this 'disparate impact' of such measures on certain people that is the target of indirect discrimination legislation. The prohibition of such discrimination ties in with the obligation of employers to accommodate those groups by adopting measures and designing their policies in a way that does not impose a burden on them which is excessive compared with that imposed on other people. In this way, while the prohibition of direct discrimination and harassment operates as an exclusionary mechanism (by excluding from an employer's reasoning reliance on certain grounds) the prohibition of indirect discrimination operates as an inclusionary mechanism (by obliging employers to take into account and accommodate the needs of individuals with certain characteristics).

D.H. and Others v. The Czech Republic

(13 November 2007)

■ Grand Chamber, European Court of Human Rights

* * *

3.   The applicants alleged, inter alia, that they had been discriminated against in the enjoyment of their right to education on account of their race or ethnic origin.

12.   According to documents available on the Internet site of the Roma and Travellers Division of the Council of Europe, the Roma originated from the regions situated between northwest India and the Iranian plateau. The first written traces of their arrival in Europe date back to the fourteenth century. Today there are between eight and ten million Roma living in Europe. They are to be found in almost all Council of Europe member States and indeed, in some Central and East European countries, they represent over 5% of the population. The majority of them speak Romani, an Indo–European language that is understood by a very large number of Roma in Europe, despite its many variants. In general, Roma also speak the dominant language of the region in which they live, or even several languages.

13.   Although they have been in Europe since the fourteenth century, often they are not recognised by the majority society as a fully-fledged European people and they have suffered throughout their history from rejection and persecution. This culminated in their attempted extermination by the Nazis, who considered them an inferior race. As a result of centuries of rejection many Roma communities today live in very difficult conditions, often on the fringe of society in the countries where they have settled, and their participation in public life is extremely limited.

14.   In the Czech Republic the Roma have national-minority status and, accordingly, enjoy the special rights associated therewith. The National Minorities Commission of the Government of the Czech Republic, a governmental consultative body without executive power, has responsibility for defending the interests of the national minorities, including the Roma.
* * *

133.   In the instant case, the applicants did not claim that the competent authorities had at the relevant time harboured invidiously racist attitudes towards Roma, or that they had intended to discriminate against Roma, or even that they had failed to take positive measures. All the applicants needed to prove—and, in their submission, had proved—was that the authorities had subjected the applicants to differential adverse treatment in comparison with similarly situated non-Roma, without objective and reasonable justification.

[EDITORS' NOTE: We will read additional parts of the D.H. case later in this chapter, and return to it in other chapters. The case is an important example of the meaning of "discrimination" under the European Convention on Human Rights, in the case law of the ECtHR. Focus on the court's conclusion here, that D.H. did not have to prove invidious racist attitudes, and that it was sufficient to prove differential adverse treatment without objective and reasonable justification.]

———

Bilka—Kaufhaus GmbH v. Weber von Hartz

ECJ Case 170/84 (May 13, 1986)

■ European Court Of Justice

* * *

3. It appears from the documents before the court that for several years Bilka, which belongs to a group of department stores in the Federal Republic of Germany employing several thousand persons, has had a supplementary (occupational) pension scheme for its employees. . . .

4. According to the version in force since 26 October 1973, part-time employees may obtain pensions under the scheme only if they have worked full time for at least 15 years over a total period of 20 years.

5. Mrs. Weber was employed by Bilka as a sales assistant from 1961 to 1976. After initially working full time, she chose to work part time from 1 October 1972 until her employment came to an end. Since she had not worked full time for the minimum period of 15 years, Bilka refused to pay her an occupational pension under its scheme.

6. Mrs. Weber brought proceedings before the German labour courts challenging the legality of Bilka's refusal to pay her a pension. She argued *inter alia* that the occupational pension scheme was contrary to the principle of equal pay for men and women laid down in Article 119 of the EEC Treaty. She asserted that the requirement of a minimum period of full-time employment for the payment of an occupational pension placed women workers at a disadvantage, since they were more likely than their male colleagues to take part-time work so as to be able to care for their family and children.

7. Bilka, on the other hand, argued that it was not guilty of any breach of the principle of equal pay since there were objectively justified economic grounds for its Decision to exclude part-time employees from the occupational pension scheme. It emphasized in that regard that in comparison with the employment of part-time workers the employment of full-time workers entails lower ancillary costs and permits the use of staff throughout opening hours. Relying on statistics concerning the group to which it belongs, Bilka stated that up to 1980 81.3% of all occupational pensions were paid to women, although only 72% of employees were women. Those figures, it said, showed that the scheme in question does not entail discrimination on the basis of sex.

8. On appeal the proceedings between Mrs. Weber and Bilka came before the Bundesarbeitsgericht; that court decided to stay the proceedings and refer the following questions to the court:

> May there be an infringement of Article 119 of the EEC Treaty in the form of 'indirect discrimination' where a department store which employs predominantly women excludes part-time employees from benefits under its occupational pension scheme although such exclusion affects disproportionately more women than men? * * *

[The court concludes that the denial of pension benefits to part-time workers results in full-time workers being paid more per hour than part-time workers.]

29.   If, therefore, it should be found that a much lower proportion of women than of men work full time, the exclusion of part-time workers from the occupational pension scheme would be contrary to Article 119 of the Treaty where, taking into account the difficulties encountered by women workers in working full-time, that measure could not be explained by factors which exclude any discrimination on grounds of sex.

30.   However, if the undertaking is able to show that its pay practice may be explained by objectively justified factors unrelated to any discrimination on grounds of sex there is no breach of Article 119.

31.   The answer to the first question referred by the national court must therefore be that Article 119 of the EEC Treaty is infringed by a department store company which excludes part-time employees from its occupational pension scheme, where that exclusion affects a far greater number of women than men, unless the undertaking shows that the exclusion is based on objectively justified factors unrelated to any discrimination on grounds of sex. * * *

35.   According to the Commission, in order to establish that there has been no breach of Article 119 it is not sufficient to show that in adopting a pay practice which in fact discriminates against women workers the employer sought to achieve objectives other than discrimination against women. The Commission considers that in order to justify such a pay practice from the point of view of Article 119 the employer must ... put forward objective economic grounds relating to the management of the undertaking. It is also necessary to ascertain whether the pay practice in question is necessary and in proportion to the objectives pursued by the employer.

Eldridge v. British Columbia

Supreme Court of Canada (1997)

■ The Judgment of the Court was delivered by La Forest J.

[T]his Court has also concluded that a discriminatory purpose or intention is not a necessary condition of a s. 15(1) violation; see *Andrews*, *supra*, at pp. 173–74, and *Rodriguez v. British Columbia (Attorney General)*, [1993] 3 S.C.R. 519 (S.C.C.), at pp. 544–49 (*per* Lamer C.J.); see also *O'Malley v. Simpsons–Sears Ltd.*, [1985] 2 S.C.R. 536 (S.C.C.), at p. 547. A legal distinction need not be motivated by a desire to disadvantage an individual or group in order to violate s. 15(1). It is sufficient if the *effect* of the legislation is to deny someone the equal protection or benefit of the law. As McIntyre J. stated in *Andrews*, *supra*, at p. 165, "[t]o approach the ideal of full equality before and under the law ... the main consideration must be the impact of the law on the individual or the group concerned." In this the Court has staked out a different path than the United States Supreme Court, which requires a discriminatory intent in order to ground an equal protection claim under the Fourteenth Amendment of the Constitution; *see*

Washington v. Davis, 426 U.S. 229 (U.S. Sup. Ct. 1976), *Arlington Heights v. Metro Housing Department*, 429 U.S. 252 (U.S. Sup. Ct. 1977), and *Personnel Administrator of Massachusetts v. Feeney*, 442 U.S. 256 (U.S. Sup. Ct. 1979).

————

NOTES

1. What types of conduct are the two main forms of discrimination—direct vs. indirect, or disparate treatment vs. disparate impact—designed to prevent? Are there different types of intentional conduct, or states of mind, at issue in these cases?

2. In the advisory opinion authored by Advocate General Poiares Maduro, he adopts a concept from U.S. Constitutional law: when a decision is made based on a "suspect classification" our concern is with the exclusion of minorities, but when a decision is made that constitutes indirect (or unintentional) discrimination, the concern is with a failure to be inclusive of minorities. He thus compares the duty to avoid indirect discrimination with a duty of accommodation. Do you agree?

3. How would the *Bilka* case be decided in the United States? The answer might depend on whether she sued under Title VII, using *Griggs*, or under the Constitution. For Title VII law on unintentional sex discrimination, *see Los Angeles Dept. of Water and Power v. Manhart*, 435 U.S. 702 (1978). Why should it matter which source of law she used?

4. Consider the effect of the *Washington v. Davis* rule in a case in which Title VII does not apply. For example, people convicted of felonies in the United States are disproportionately Black and Hispanic, and many studies demonstrate that the criminal justice system discriminates against non-whites, but in the absence of proof of intentional discrimination, there is no violation of the Constitution. And, consider the secondary effects of that systemic discrimination. For example, many States ban anyone convicted of a felony from voting. In the State of Washington, the felony voting ban disenfranchised 24% of the State's Black men. But in the absence of proof that the ban was adopted for the purpose of disenfranchising Black voters, the ban was upheld. *See Farrakhan v. Gregoire*, 623 F.3d 990 (9th Cir. 2010 en banc).

5. Former Solicitor General (and current Yale Law Professor) Drew Days writes: "The current requirement that discriminatory intent be shown means that the courts must accord extraordinary deference to government programs and policies that produce particularly severe consequences for some of the least fortunate and most defenseless groups in society with respect to things that really matter: food, housing, health care and education. Were America a country without a shameful history of overt, systematic discrimination against some of these same groups, we might be justified in resisting any call for government to explain itself. Since that is not the case, asking government to defend its policies, including its decision to reject more evenhanded and equally effective measures, accords more with the spirit of the equal protection clause than

does the current rule. Such an approach would not mean that the courts would necessarily reject the government's policy decisions, just that reasons would have to be given." Drew S. Days III, Dimensions of Equality: Doctrines of Limitation (1992).

6. Professor Days suggests that we should at least ask government for an explanation when a government program or policy has a discriminatory impact. Another approach is to ask government to examine the likely consequences of its programs or policies before adopting them; in essence, requiring an equality impact statement. *See, e.g., Marc Mauer, Racial Impact Statements as a Means of Reducing Unwarranted Sentencing Disparities*, 5 Ohio State Journal of Criminal Law 19 (2007).

7. The UK "public sector equality duty," found at section 149 of the UK Equality Act of 2010, which took effect in April 2011, requires public bodies in England, Scotland and Wales to "have due regard to the need to (a) eliminate discrimination, harassment, victimisation and any other conduct that is prohibited by or under this Act; (b) advance equality of opportunity between persons who share a relevant protected characteristic and persons who do not share it; (c) foster good relations between persons who share a relevant protected characteristic and persons who do not share it." The duty applies to age, disability, gender, gender reassignment, pregnancy and maternity, race, religion or belief and sexual orientation. *See* http://www.equalities.gov.uk Will the adoption of a policy that has a discriminatory impact be judged as a violation of the obligation to act with due regard to the need to eliminate discrimination and advance equality? The parameters of the duty of due regard, and how it will be applied, remain uncertain.

8. Most of the readings in this section are concerned with proving unintentional or indirect discrimination. But in many discrimination cases the critical question is whether the claimant was subjected to adverse treatment because of his/her race, and the primary source of evidence is comparative treatment. Is differential treatment evidence of discrimination? We will discuss this question further in section B. Is differential treatment itself direct discrimination? Compare the decisions in *Spivey v. Beverly Enterprises, Inc.*, 196 F.3d 1309 (11th Cir. 1999) with *Webb v. EMO Air Cargo (UK) Ltd*, Case C–32/93 (ECJ 1994). In *Spivey*, the plaintiff brought a pregnancy discrimination claim. Her employer had terminated her from her job as a nurse's assistant because she had been restricted from lifting over 25 pounds by her physician, because she was pregnant. If she had been injured on the job, her employer would have assigned her to light duty. The Court of Appeals affirmed an order of summary judgment for the employer, reasoning that there was no proof of disparate treatment because she was treated the same as any other employee would have been who could not lift over 25 pounds. The court further found there was no proof of disparate impact because she "failed to present statistical evidence to demonstrate that this policy in practice has a disproportionate impact on pregnant employees." In *Webb*, an employee was hired to temporarily replace a pregnant employee. The new employee discovered and disclosed a few weeks later that she too was pregnant, and was immediately terminated. The European Court of Justice held that "dismissal of a female worker

on account of her pregnancy constitutes direct discrimination on grounds of sex and the situation of a woman who finds herself incapable, by reason of pregnancy discovered very shortly after the conclusion of her employment contract, of performing the task for which she was recruited cannot be compared with that of a man similarly incapable for medical or other reasons, since pregnancy is not in any way comparable with a pathological condition, and even less so with unavailability for work on non-medical grounds."

B.   The Role of Inference

Very rarely does a claimant have direct proof of discriminatory animus. In the absence of such evidence, a claimant's ability to prove discrimination will often depend on the procedural and evidentiary burdens allocated to each party. As we will see, these questions, in turn, are influenced by whether we regard discrimination as common or rare. If we regard discrimination as common, we may easily conclude from circumstantial evidence of differential treatment that the cause of the differentiation was improper discrimination. But if we are skeptical of claims of discrimination, we may more readily accept alternative explanations, or even no explanation at all, when members of minority groups or women are treated differently than others. Consider what assumptions the courts made on these questions in deciding the following cases.

McDonnell Douglas Corporation v. Green

411 U.S. 792 (1973)

■ Justice Powell delivered the opinion for a unanimous Court.

[While employed by McDonnell Douglas, Green participated in a "stall-in" and a "lock-in"—demonstrations protesting the company's hiring practices. He was subsequently laid off. When the company advertised a position in the newspaper, Green applied.]

In this case respondent, the complainant below, charges that he was denied employment "because of his involvement in civil rights activities" and "because of his race and color." Petitioner denied discrimination of any kind, asserting that its failure to re-employ respondent was based upon and justified by his participation in the unlawful conduct against it. Thus, the issue at the trial on remand is framed by those opposing factual contentions. The two opinions of the Court of Appeals and the several opinions of the three judges of that court attempted, with a notable lack of harmony, to state the applicable rules as to burden of proof and how this shifts upon the making of a prima facie case. We now address this problem.

The complainant in a Title VII trial must carry the initial burden under the statute of establishing a prima facie case of racial discrimination. This may be done by showing (i) that he belongs to a racial minority; (ii) that he applied and was qualified for a job for which the employer was seeking applicants; (iii) that, despite his qualifications, he was rejected; and (iv) that, after his rejection, the position remained open and the employer continued to seek applicants from persons of complainant's qualifications. . . .

The burden then must shift to the employer to articulate some legitimate, nondiscriminatory reason for the employee's rejection. * * *

On remand, respondent must, as the Court of Appeals recognized, be afforded a fair opportunity to show that petitioner's stated reason for respondent's rejection was in fact pretext. Especially relevant to such a showing would be evidence that white employees involved in acts against petitioner of comparable seriousness to the 'stall-in' were nevertheless retained or rehired. Petitioner may justifiably refuse to rehire one who was engaged in unlawful, disruptive acts against it, but only if this criterion is applied alike to members of all races.

Other evidence that may be relevant to any showing of pretext includes facts as to the petitioner's treatment of respondent during his prior term of employment; petitioner's reaction, if any, to respondent's legitimate civil rights activities; and petitioner's general policy and practice with respect to minority employment. On the latter point, statistics as to petitioner's employment policy and practice may be helpful to a determination of whether petitioner's refusal to rehire respondent in this case conformed to a general pattern of discrimination against blacks. In short, on the retrial respondent must be given a full and fair opportunity to demonstrate by competent evidence that the presumptively valid reasons for his rejection were in fact a cover up for a racially discriminatory decision.

————

Furnco Construction Corporation v. Waters

438 U.S. 567 (1978)

■ JUSTICE REHNQUIST delivered the opinion of the Court.

A *prima facie* case under McDonnell Douglas raises an inference of discrimination only because we presume these acts, if otherwise unexplained, are more likely than not based on the consideration of impermissible factors. And we are willing to presume this largely because we know from our experience that more often than not people do not act in a totally arbitrary manner, without any underlying reasons, especially in a business setting. Thus, when all legitimate reasons for rejecting an applicant have been eliminated as possible reasons for the employer's actions, it is more likely than not the employer, who we generally assume acts only with some reason, based his decision on an impermissible consideration such as race.

————

St. Mary's Honor Center v. Hicks

509 U.S. 502 (1993)

■ JUSTICE SCALIA delivered the opinion of the Court.

We granted certiorari to determine whether, in a suit against an employer alleging intentional racial discrimination in violation of

§ 703(a)(1) of Title VII of the Civil Rights Act of 1964, the trier of fact's rejection of the employer's asserted reasons for its actions mandates a finding for the plaintiff. * * *

[Hicks, a black man, worked at a halfway house operated by St. Mary's. He was discharged, and brought a Title VII race discrimination action. The trial court found that he had established a *prima facie* case of discrimination, which required that an inference of discrimination be drawn, and that the employer had articulated a non-discriminatory reason for his discharge—that Hicks had violated work rules. The trial court further found that the reason offered by St. Mary's was not the true reason for the discharge; it was a pretext. But the trial court concluded that the actual reason for the discharge was a personality conflict, not racial discrimination.]

... [A]lthough the *McDonnell Douglas* presumption shifts the burden of production to the defendant, "[t]he ultimate burden of persuading the trier of fact that the defendant intentionally discriminated against the plaintiff remains at all times with the plaintiff." * * *

The factfinder's disbelief of the reasons put forward by the defendant (particularly if disbelief is accompanied by a suspicion of mendacity) may, together with the elements of the prima facie case, suffice to show intentional discrimination. Thus, rejection of the defendant's proffered reasons will permit the trier of fact to infer the ultimate fact of intentional discrimination, and the Court of Appeals was correct when it noted that, upon such rejection, "[n]o additional proof of discrimination is required," But ... a presumption does not shift the burden of proof, and ignores our repeated admonition that the Title VII plaintiff at all times bears the "ultimate burden of persuasion." * * *

Respondent contends that "[t]he litigation decision of the employer to place in controversy only ... particular explanations eliminates from further consideration the alternative explanations that the employer chose not to advance." The employer should bear, he contends, "the responsibility for its choices and the risk that plaintiff will disprove any pretextual reasons and therefore prevail." It is the "therefore" that is problematic. Title VII does not award damages against employers who cannot prove a nondiscriminatory reason for adverse employment action, but only against employers who are proven to have taken adverse employment action by reason of (in the context of the present case) race. That the employer's proffered reason is unpersuasive, or even obviously contrived, does not necessarily establish that the plaintiff's proffered reason of race is correct. * * *

■ Justice Souter, with whom Justice White, Justice Blackmun, and Justice Stevens join, dissenting.

Twenty years ago, in *McDonnell Douglas Corp. v. Green*, 411 U.S. 792 (1973), this Court unanimously prescribed a "sensible, orderly way to evaluate the evidence" in a Title VII disparate-treatment case, giving both plaintiff and defendant fair opportunities to litigate "in light of common experience as it bears on the critical question of discrimination." *Furnco Constr. Corp. v. Waters*, 438 U.S. 567, 577 (1978). We have repeatedly reaffirmed and refined the *McDonnell Douglas* framework, most notably in *Texas Dept. of Community Affairs v. Burdine*, 450 U.S. 248 (1981), another unanimous opinion. *See also Postal Service Bd. of Governors v. Aikens*, 460 U.S. 711 (1983); *Furnco, supra*. But today, after two decades of stable law in this Court and only relatively recent disruption in some of the Circuits, the Court abandons this practical framework together with its central purpose, which is "to sharpen the inquiry into the elusive factual question of intentional discrimination," *Burdine, supra*, at 255, n. 8. Ignoring language to the contrary in both *McDonnell Douglas* and *Burdine*, the Court holds that, once a Title VII plaintiff succeeds in showing at trial that the defendant has come forward with pretextual reasons for its actions in response to a prima facie showing of discrimination, the factfinder still may proceed to roam the record, searching for some nondiscriminatory explanation that the defendant has not raised and that the plaintiff has had no fair opportunity to disprove. Because the majority departs from settled precedent in substituting a scheme of proof for disparate-treatment actions that promises to be unfair and unworkable, I respectfully dissent.

Proving Intentional Discrimination: The Reality of Supreme Court Rhetoric

86 Georgetown Law Journal 279, 283–285 (1997)

■ MICHAEL SELMI

[T]he Court's jurisprudence relating to proving discrimination developed primarily in the early 1970s based on loose assumptions that discrimination provided an explanation for otherwise unexplained deviations from what would be expected in a race-neutral world. Based on this assumption, the Court not only developed a formal and now familiar model of proof to adjudicate employment discrimination cases, but also created similar models to identify discrimination violative of the Equal Protection Clause in jury selection, voting, and housing. These models all relied on basic evidentiary principles that could be adapted to address discrimination that is subtle or overt, conscious or unconscious, intentional or unintentional, and brought as both constitutional and statutory claims.

... In essence, these models suggested that deviations from race-neutral expectations, when the deviations were in the form of significant statistical disparities or procedural irregularities, could be seen as the product of discrimination because our history suggested that discrimination was the most likely explanation when the deviations were otherwise unexplained. Consequently, these models functioned properly only when the courts applying them were willing to see discrimination as a viable explanation for social and political conditions—a fact that was revealed most clearly in the Court's recent employment discrimination case, *St. Mary's Honor Center v. Hicks*. *Hicks* altered the standards for proving employment discrimination under Title VII in a way that will likely make it more difficult to prove claims of discrimination. Combined with recent Supreme Court decisions in the affirmative action and voting rights contexts, the *Hicks* case signals a judicial presumption that discrimination no longer offers an explanation for otherwise unexplained racial disparities.

Although the recent cases strongly indicate that the Court no longer considers discrimination to be a vital part of contemporary American social and political life, it would be a mistake to see these cases as representing a dramatic shift from the Court's past practice or attitude. Rather, these cases are best seen as the culmination of the way in which the Court has defined discrimination over the last twenty years. . . .

As a practical matter, the result is that the Court now sees unlawful discrimination in the affirmative use of race, as occurs in the affirmative action cases or through racial redistricting, but is much less likely to identify discrimination in cases in which African–Americans are the victims of subtle discrimination. Indeed, despite a broad consensus that discrimination today is generally perpetrated through subtle rather than overt acts, the Court continually refuses to adapt its vision to account for the changing nature of discrimination; as a result, it appears unable to see discrimination that is subtle rather than overt. In this way, the Court has never moved beyond its view of the world prior to the passage of civil rights legislation in the 1960s when explicit barriers prevented African–Americans and women from fully participating in social and economic life. As long as such blatant barriers do not exist, the Court has difficulty seeing discrimination. This limited vision explains why the Supreme Court can now see discrimination when a college denies admission to women, or when a state restricts access to its political process for gay men and lesbians, but not when the lone African–American supervisor in an organization is fired and the employer's reasons for firing him are disproved, or when Latinos are disqualified from serving on juries because of their ability to speak Spanish. The cases in which the Court identified violations all involved explicit barriers that constituted familiar examples of discrimination, while the latter cases required the Court to draw inferences of discrimination based on circumstantial evidence—an inference the Court has repeatedly demonstrated it is unwilling to make.

———

Council Directive 2000/43/EC of 29 June 2000

(Implementing the principle of equal treatment between persons irrespective of racial or ethnic origin)

Article 1—Purpose

The purpose of this Directive is to lay down a framework for combating discrimination on the grounds of racial or ethnic origin, with a view to putting into effect in the Member States the principle of equal treatment.

Article 8—Burden of proof

1. Member States shall take such measures as are necessary, in accordance with their national judicial systems, to ensure that, when persons

who consider themselves wronged because the principle of equal treatment has not been applied to them establish, before a court or other competent authority, facts from which it may be presumed that there has been direct or indirect discrimination, it shall be for the respondent to prove that there has been no breach of the principle of equal treatment.

2. Paragraph 1 shall not prevent Member States from introducing rules of evidence which are more favourable to plaintiffs.

3. Paragraph 1 shall not apply to criminal proceedings.

————

Handels-og Kontorfunktionrernes Forbund i Danmark v. Dansk Arbejdsgiverforening for Danfoss

ECJ Case 109/88 (October 17, 1989)

■ EUROPEAN COURT OF JUSTICE, Judgment of the Court

The Faglige Voldgiftsret [Industrial Arbitration Board] referred several questions to the Court for a preliminary ruling on the interpretation of Council Directive 75/117 (Equal pay for men and women) [replaced in 2009 by Directive 2006/54/EC with similar provisions].

* * * The [employer] paid the same basic salary to employees in the same salary class. In exercise of the option provided for by the collective agreement between the employers' association and the employees' union it paid individual salary supplements to its employees based on their mobility, training and length of service. The result was that the average wage of men was 6.85% higher than that of women. * * *

The burden of proof (questions 1 (a) and 3 (a))

It appeared from the documents that the case between the parties to the main action had its origin in the fact that the machinery for individual supplements applied to basic salaries was implemented in such a way that a woman was unable to identify the reasons for a difference between her salary and that of a man doing the same work.

In those circumstances the questions put by the national court were to be understood as asking whether Directive No. 75/117 was to be interpreted as meaning that where an undertaking applied a system of remuneration a feature of which was a complete lack of transparency, the employer had to show that its salary practice was not discriminatory if a woman showed that in relation to a relatively large number of employees the average wage of women was less than that of men.

In a situation such as that with which the appeal was concerned women would be deprived of any effective means of enforcing the principle of equal pay before the national court if the fact of showing that there was a difference between the average wages did not mean that the employer had to show that its salary practice was in fact not discriminatory.

The concern for effectiveness underlying Directive No. 75/117 meant that it had to be interpreted as meaning that there had to be adjustments to the national rules on the burden of proof in special situations where such adjustments were necessary for the effective implementation of the principle of equality.

To show that its salary practice did not systematically put women at a disadvantage the employer had to show how it had applied the criteria for additional payments and would thus be led to make its salary system transparent.

The Court held:

"Council Directive 75/117 of 10 February 1975 on the approximation of the laws of the Member States relating to the application of the principle of equal pay for men and women must be interpreted as meaning that:

1. where an undertaking applies a system of pay which is totally lacking in transparency, it is for the employer to prove that his practice in the matter of wages is not discriminatory, if a female worker establishes, in relation to a relatively large number of employees, that the average pay for women is less than what for men.

Wong v. Igen Ltd.

2005 WL 353346 (CA (Civ Div)), [2005] 3 All E.R. 812, [2005] (18 February 2005)

■ Court of Appeal (United Kingdom)

Held, giving judgment accordingly, that

(1) the new provisions in the Discrimination Acts as amended, which implemented European Directives, provided that if an applicant showed that he had been treated less favourably than others in circumstances which were consistent with that treatment being based on grounds of race or sex, the tribunal should draw an inference that such treatment was discriminatory unless the respondent could satisfy the tribunal that there was an innocent explanation.

(2) The provisions required the tribunal to go through a two stage process. The first stage required the complainant to prove facts from which the tribunal could, apart from the section, conclude in the absence of an adequate explanation that the respondent had committed, or was to be treated as having committed, the unlawful act of discrimination. If the complainant proved those facts, the second stage required the respondent to prove that he did not commit or was not to be treated as having committed that act.

Republic of France

Labor Code Section L122–45

... In the event of litigation relating to [discrimination in employment], the employee ... must present facts permitting an inference of direct or indirect discrimination. The burden then falls on the defendant to prove that its decision is justified by objective elements without any discrimination.

————

NOTES

1. Under U.S. law, all employment is assumed to be "at will" absent a contractual or statutory exception. In Europe, most employees are protected against discharge except for good cause. Does this help explain the different approaches to the burden of proof? The *Green* case was a hiring case, as are most European employment discrimination claims; European claims of discriminatory discharge are rare because discharge is rare in Europe, and requires good cause even in the absence of anti-discrimination laws. But *Hicks* involved a termination. Does the Green test make more sense when the employer knows little about the employee, while the *Hicks* test makes sense when the decision was likely to have been the result of multiple factors?

2. Michael Selmi argues that "statistical disparities or procedural irregularities could be seen as the product of discrimination because our history suggested that discrimination was the most likely explanation when the deviations were otherwise unexplained." Has that view changed? If it has, why? Has the society changed, or the point of view of the judges deciding the cases (or both)?

3. Note the relationship between the EC Council Directives, the French Code section, the British Court of Appeals decision, and the decision of the European Court of Justice. Recall that the Council, on the basis of a proposal by the European Commission, by unanimity and with the agreement of the European Parliament, is empowered to pass anti-discrimination Directives. The member states must then transpose the terms of the Directives into national law. The European Court of Justice may determine that a member state has failed to comply with the Directive, either by failing to transpose it, or by failing, through its national courts, to properly enforce it. *See* Treaty on the Functioning of the European Union, Article 19 (originally added by the Treaty of Amsterdam). The requirement of unanimity in the European Council means that any of the 27 member states may block a proposed Directive from moving forward.

4. In India, Section 12 of the Protection of Civil Rights Act provides that if any offense prohibited by the Act is committed against a member of an untouchable caste, the court presumes that it was committed on the ground of untouchability unless the contrary is proved. What social reality would justify such a strong presumption?

5. Why do French and European Union law shift the burden of proof to the employer, while U.S. law shifts only the burden of production? The following excerpt by Professor Suk suggests that the advantage of a shifting burden may be counteracted by procedural rules that favor plaintiffs in U.S. civil litigation.

————

Procedural Path Dependence: Discrimination and the Civil–Criminal Divide

85 Washington University Law Review 1315, 1335–1339 (2008)

■ JULIE C. SUK

The main problem that arises for plaintiffs claiming discriminatory hiring in the civil context [in France] is that parties cannot compel discovery of evidence in the adversary's hands to acquire evidence that would prove the elements of one's own case. In other words, bearing the burden of proof means bearing the burden of presenting evidence of the elements of one's case. And, in stark contrast to litigants in the United States, a civil litigant does not have access to relevant evidence that is in the hands of the adversary through the discovery devices that American lawyers rely on to get evidence that eventually supports one's allegations at trial.

Several rules in the French Code of Civil Procedure, understood through the principles that underlie these rules, make it highly unusual for one party to obtain evidence from the adversary that will help establish its own case. Article 2 of the French Code of Civil Procedure provides that

"The parties conduct the suit under the burdens they carry. It is up to them to accomplish the procedural acts in the forms and time frames required." This article is understood to establish the party-driven nature of the proceedings, which is elaborated by Article 9, providing, "The burden is on each party to prove, consistent with the law, the facts necessary to the success of its claim." An equitable proceeding requires each party to prove, without the aid of the court or the other party, the facts upon which the claim depends. Some Americans assume that the civil law judge plays a central role in civil proceedings, largely because civil procedure rules do, in letter, authorize the judge to investigate facts. However, a strong norm of judicial neutrality emerges from the *Code de procédure civile*'s imposition of burdens on the parties, which in reality limits the judge's liberty of investigation.

Even though the 2001 statute provides for burden shifting, the plaintiff must still "present" elements of fact that leave the factfinder to infer that discrimination occurred, and it is now clear that this requires the presentation of some evidence, not mere allegations. It is only after the plaintiff has submitted some evidence of such facts that the burden shifts to the employer to prove that there was an objective nondiscriminatory reason for the adverse action.

Practically speaking, the plaintiff has to present evidence of disparity in treatment. Without establishing that there was any disparity in the treatment of candidates belonging to one protected category and candidates belonging to another group, there would be no inference of discrimination. The evidence may be rebuttable, but nonetheless, it is the plaintiff's duty to prove disparity in treatment.

Very often, reliable evidence of differential treatment correlated with one of the protected categories is difficult to find, especially for a job candidate who is an outsider to the enterprise in question. How does an outsider obtain evidence that the employer has granted interviews to candidates of a particular racial group? How does he obtain evidence that the employer is lying when he tells the candidate of color that the position is no longer vacant? French civil procedure has traditionally favored written proof of fact. But the documents that would tend to prove these allegations are often in the hands of the employer—for instance, personnel files or internal memoranda indicating which candidates were interviewed and which candidates were not.

French civil procedure makes it very difficult to obtain documentary evidence that is in the hands of the adversary. Article 132 requires each party to disclose documents which support their own factual allegations. A party can compel the disclosure of a document if the adversary is relying on it to prove a fact that the adversary alleges. Finally, the investigating judge is authorized to issue investigatory orders with regard to facts on which the resolution of the dispute depends if one party requests such an order. This power seems to encompass the judge's power to require the production of documents by an employer that would tend to support the plaintiff's factual allegation of disparate treatment, such as personnel or payroll records. But the judge's power to order the production of documents is limited by Article 146, which provides "[i]n no case can an investigatory order be issued for the purpose of supplying the deficiency of a party in administering proof." As a result, ordering a defendant to produce documents to support plaintiffs' alleged facts, where plaintiff has no other evidence in his own possession to support these allegations, is seen as the judge's attempt to supply plaintiff with helpful evidence for which plaintiff alone is responsible. Many decisions of the *Cour de cassation* have held such investigatory orders to be improper.

Raouf Lachhab, [a claimant described earlier in the article] as a result of his double-CV experiment, may have some evidence of the employer's disparate treatment of Alsaciens and Arabs: namely, his own testimony, oral or written, that he sent the two CVs, and was rejected first but invited for an interview under a new name. But under French rules of civil procedure, a party cannot be a witness in his own case. The judge does have the power, however, to issue an investigatory order requiring a party to appear for questioning before the judge. Still, such orders are subject to the limitation that the judge cannot use the investigatory orders to supply a party with missing evidence that the party bears the burden of presenting.

The 2001 statute, in addition to easing the burden of proof in employment discrimination cases, explicitly provides that "the judge shall form his conviction after having ordered, in case of need, all investigatory orders that he deems useful." Although the statute encourages judges to issue investigatory orders when necessary in light of the burden-shifting framework introduced by the same statute, a recent empirical study of anti-discrimination litigation since the adoption of the 2001 statute reveals that investigatory orders in employment discrimination cases are almost nonexistent. Civil judges are accustomed to the norm of refraining from issuing investigatory orders when the orders appear to help one party fill in the deficiencies of proof for which that party bears the burden pursuant to Article 146. As a result, even though the 2001 statute reaffirms the judge's discretion to issue orders he "deems useful," civil judges are likely to exercise this discretion in very limited circumstances, in light of the Code of Civil Procedure's traditional understanding of the civil judge's role.

Another problem facing employment discrimination plaintiffs in civil proceedings is that certain forms of evidence have been deemed inadmissible by the *Cour de cassation*. For example, recordings that are made without the adverse party's knowledge have been rendered illicit....

Article 9 of the Code of Civil Procedure requires each party to prove the facts necessary to the success of its claims *"conformément à la loi,"* consistent with the law. Thus, if a plaintiff obtains a document through illegitimate means, for example by theft (which encompasses copying the employer's documents without the employer's consent), the evidence is inadmissible. Although courts have permitted employees to present copies of employer documents with which he is familiar through the exercise of his functions as employee, this exception is of no use to the job candidate complaining of discriminatory hiring.

C.   Second Class Citizenship

When does the government provision of separate, but arguably materially equal, social goods to different social groups constitute proof of discrimination or inequality? One way to argue and prove inequality in the law is to demonstrate that such separate but equal treatment is based solely on a status distinction that is (or should be) impermissible, because such distinctions tend to rest upon a presumption of inferiority of one group. These types of claims are difficult to make as they depend upon the Court reasoning in some ways like a social scientist would. Below are two examples, in different eras and contexts, of successful claims that a "separate but equal" regime of public goods is inherently unequal under constitutional guarantees of equality, in part because it would render one group "second class citizens."

———

Brown v. Board of Education of Topeka

347 U.S. 483 (1954)

■ Chief Justice Warren delivered the unanimous opinion of the Court.

In each of the cases, minors of the Negro race, through their legal representatives, seek the aid of the courts in obtaining admission to the public schools of their community on a nonsegregated basis. In each instance, they have been denied admission to schools attended by white children under laws requiring or permitting segregation according to race. This segregation was alleged to deprive the plaintiffs of the equal protection of the laws under the Fourteenth Amendment. In each of the cases other than the Delaware case, a three-judge federal district court denied relief to the plaintiffs on the so-called 'separate but equal' doctrine announced by this Court in *Plessy v. Ferguson*, 163 U.S. 537. Under that doctrine, equality of treatment is accorded when the races are provided substantially equal facilities, even though these facilities be separate. In the Delaware case, the Supreme Court of Delaware adhered to that doctrine, but ordered that the plaintiffs be admitted to the white schools because of their superiority to the Negro schools.

The plaintiffs contend that segregated public schools are not 'equal' and cannot be made 'equal,' and that hence they are deprived of the equal protection of the laws. * * *

In approaching this problem, we cannot turn the clock back to 1868 when the Amendment was adopted, or even to 1896 when *Plessy v. Ferguson* was written. We must consider public education in the light of its full development and its present place in American life throughout the Nation. Only in this way can it be determined if segregation in public schools deprives these plaintiffs of the equal protection of the laws. * * *

To separate [Black children] . . . from others of similar age and qualifications solely because of their race generates a feeling of inferiority as to their status in the community that may affect their hearts and minds in a way unlikely ever to be undone. The effect of this separation on their educational opportunities was well stated by a finding in the Kansas case by a court which nevertheless felt compelled to rule against the Negro plaintiffs:

'Segregation of white and colored children in public schools has a detrimental effect upon the colored children. The impact is greater when it has the sanction of the law; for the policy of separating the races is usually interpreted as denoting the inferiority of the Negro group. A sense of inferiority affects the motivation of a child to learn. Segregation with the sanction of law, therefore, has a tendency to (retard) the educational and mental development of Negro children and to deprive them of some of the benefits they would receive in a racial(ly) integrated school system.'

Whatever may have been the extent of psychological knowledge at the time of *Plessy v. Ferguson*, this finding is amply supported by modern authority.[11] Any language in *Plessy v. Ferguson* contrary to this finding is rejected.

We conclude that in the field of public education the doctrine of 'separate but equal' has no place. Separate educational facilities are inherently unequal. Therefore, we hold that the plaintiffs and others similarly situated for whom the actions have been brought are, by reason of the segregation complained of, deprived of the equal protection of the laws guaranteed by the Fourteenth Amendment.

---

11. K. B. Clark, *Effect of Prejudice and Discrimination on Personality Development* (Midcentury White House Conference on Children and Youth, 1950); Witmer and Kotinsky, *Personality in the Making* (1952), c. VI; Deutscher and Chein, *The Psychological Effects of Enforced Segregation: A Survey of Social Science Opinion*, 26 J.PSYCHOL. 259 (1948); Chein, *What are the Psychological Effects of Segregation Under Conditions of Equal Facilities?*, 3 INT. J. OPINION AND ATTITUDE RES. 229 (1949); Brameld, EDUCATIONAL COSTS, IN DISCRIMINATION AND NATIONAL WELFARE (MacIver, ed., 1949), 44–48; Frazier, THE NEGRO IN THE UNITED STATES (1949), 674–681. *And see generally* Myrdal, AN AMERICAN DILEMMA (1944).

In Re Marriage Cases

43 Cal.4th 757 (2008) California Supreme Court

[W]e note at the outset that the constitutional issue before us differs in a significant respect from the constitutional issue that has been addressed by a number of other state supreme courts and intermediate appellate courts that recently have had occasion, in interpreting the applicable provisions of their respective state constitutions, to determine the validity of statutory provisions or common law rules limiting marriage to a union of a man and a woman. [citations omitted] These courts, often by a one-vote margin, have ruled upon the validity of statutory schemes that contrast with that of California, which in recent years has enacted comprehensive domestic partnership legislation under which a same-sex couple may enter into a legal relationship that affords the couple virtually all of the same substantive legal benefits and privileges, and imposes upon the couple virtually all of the same legal obligations and duties, that California law affords to and imposes upon a married couple.... [T]he legal issue we must resolve is not whether it would be constitutionally permissible under the California Constitution for the state to limit marriage only to opposite-sex couples while denying same-sex couples any opportunity to enter into an official relationship with all or virtually all of the same substantive attributes, but rather whether our state Constitution prohibits the state from establishing a statutory scheme in which both opposite-sex and same-sex couples are granted the right to enter into an officially recognized family relationship that affords all of the significant legal rights and obligations traditionally associated under state law with the institution of marriage, but under which the union of an opposite-sex couple is officially designated a "marriage" whereas the union of a same-sex couple is official-ly designated a "domestic partnership." The question we must address is whether, under these circumstances, the failure to designate the official relationship of same-sex couples as marriage violates the California Consti-tution.

... As past cases establish, the substantive right of two adults who share a loving relationship to join together to establish an officially recog-nized family of their own—and, if the couple chooses, to raise children within that family—constitutes a vitally important attribute of the funda-mental interest in liberty and personal autonomy that the California Constitution secures to all persons for the benefit of both the individual and society.

Furthermore, in contrast to earlier times, our state now recognizes that an individual's capacity to establish a loving and long-term committed relationship with another person and responsibly to care for and raise children does not depend upon the individual's sexual orientation, and, more generally, that an individual's sexual orientation—like a person's race or gender—does not constitute a legitimate basis upon which to deny or withhold legal rights. We therefore conclude that in view of the substance and significance of the fundamental constitutional right to form a family relationship, the California Constitution properly must be interpreted to guarantee this basic civil right to all Californians, whether gay or hetero-sexual, and to same-sex couples as well as to opposite-sex couples.

... Furthermore, the circumstance that the current California statutes assign a different name for the official family relationship of same-sex couples as contrasted with the name for the official family relationship of opposite-sex couples raises constitutional concerns not only under the state constitutional right to marry, but also under the state constitutional equal protection clause.

... As we shall explain, although we do not agree with the claim advanced by the parties challenging the validity of the current statutory scheme that the applicable statutes properly should be viewed as an instance of discrimination on the basis of the suspect characteristic of sex or gender and should be subjected to strict scrutiny on that ground, we conclude that strict scrutiny nonetheless is applicable here because (1) the statutes in question properly must be understood as classifying or discriminating on the basis of sexual orientation, a characteristic that we conclude represents—like gender, race, and religion—a constitutionally suspect basis upon which to impose differential treatment, and (2) the differential treatment at issue impinges upon a same-sex couple's fundamental interest in having their family relationship accorded the same respect and dignity enjoyed by an opposite-sex couple.

Under the strict scrutiny standard, unlike the rational basis standard, in order to demonstrate the constitutional validity of a challenged statutory classification the state must establish (1) that the state interest intended to be served by the differential treatment not only is a constitutionally legitimate interest, but is a compelling state interest, and (2) that the differential treatment not only is reasonably related to but is necessary to serve that compelling state interest.... Applying this standard to the statutory classification here at issue, we ... conclude that the purpose underlying differential treatment of opposite-sex and same-sex couples embodied in California's current marriage statutes—the interest in retaining the traditional and well-established definition of marriage—cannot properly be viewed as a compelling state interest for purposes of the equal protection clause, or as necessary to serve such an interest.

A number of factors lead us to this conclusion. First, the exclusion of same-sex couples from the designation of marriage clearly is not necessary in order to afford full protection to all of the rights and benefits that currently are enjoyed by married opposite-sex couples; permitting same-sex couples access to the designation of marriage will not deprive opposite-sex couples of any rights and will not alter the legal framework of the institution of marriage, because same-sex couples who choose to marry will be subject to the same obligations and duties that currently are imposed on married opposite-sex couples.

Second, retaining the traditional definition of marriage and affording same-sex couples only a separate and differently named family relationship will, as a realistic matter, impose appreciable harm on same-sex couples and their children, because denying such couples access to the familiar and highly favored designation of marriage is likely to cast doubt on whether the official family relationship of same-sex couples enjoys dignity equal to that of opposite-sex couples.

Third, because of the widespread disparagement that gay individuals historically have faced, it is all the more probable that excluding same-sex couples from the legal institution of marriage is likely to be viewed as reflecting an official view that their committed relationships are of lesser stature than the comparable relationships of opposite-sex couples.

Finally, retaining the designation of marriage exclusively for opposite sex couples and providing only a separate and distinct designation for same-sex couples may well have the effect of perpetuating a more general premise—now emphatically rejected by this state—that gay individuals and same-sex couples are in some respects "second-class citizens" who may, under the law, be treated differently from, and less favorably than, heterosexual individuals or opposite-sex couples.

Under these circumstances, we cannot find that retention of the traditional definition of marriage constitutes a compelling state interest. Accordingly, we conclude that to the extent the current California statutory provisions limit marriage to opposite-sex couples, these statutes are unconstitutional.

———

NOTES

1. The California Supreme Court decision on same-sex marriage excerpted above was issued in June 2008. It was not the last word on same-sex marriage in California. In November 2008 the California electorate narrowly passed a California Constitutional amendment declaring that "marriage" was reserved for couples consisting of a man and a woman. In June 2009 the California Supreme Court upheld the amendment, ending the State's practice of same-sex marriage. The Court held that the state constitution could deprive same-sex couples of the term "marriage" but could not deprive them of any of the benefits of marriage. *See Strauss v. Horton*, 46 Cal.4th 364 (2009). Consider the Court's 2008 language on "second class citizenship." Does it still apply? Does the Court's decision permit the state constitution to create two levels of citizenship for California couples who wish to marry?

2. The question of whether restricting marriage to male/female couples is an equality violation is the subject of Chapter V.

3. Following the 2009 decision of the California Supreme Court upholding the State Constitutional amendment, a case was filed in federal court claiming a violation of the Fourteenth Amendment of the United States Constitution. The court ruled that the California amendment was unconstitutional. *See Perry v. Schwarzenegger*, 704 F. Supp. 2d. 921 (N.D. Ca. 2010). The *Perry* decision was affirmed by the United States Court of Appeals for the Ninth Circuit. The case is discussed further in chapter V.

4. Footnote 11 in *Brown* cites psychological evidence gathered by Drs. Kenneth and Mamie Clark on the effects of school segregation. The Court relied on this evidence in concluding that segregation made Black children second class citizens. Consider what other kinds of evidence would help prove second class citizenship. For more on the work of the Clarks, *see* the

Library of Congress website on the *Brown* case, at http://www.loc.gov/exhibits/brown/brown-brown.html.

5. How much have psychological racial attitudes changed since the 1950's? For a review of how young children exhibit racial bias, *see* Po Bronson & Ashley Merryman, *See Baby Discriminate*, NEWSWEEK Sept. 5, 2009. For a broader discussion of the psychology of bias, *see* section D, *infra*.

6. What exactly is the link between equal citizenship and access to marriage? Does the Court in *In re Marriage Cases* adequately explain this link? Consider the following articulation of why the right to marry the partner of one's choice is a central aspect of equal citizenship:

> "Since the founding of the nation, marriage has played both a central role in the American political imagination and the political economy of the United States—so much so that it makes sense to view marriage as a practice of national citizenship. 'Citizenship,' as Linda Bosniak and others have noted, can usefully be understood as comprising a number of different dimensions. First, there is legal citizenship: formal or nominal membership in an organized political community. Second, there is citizenship as the possession and enjoyment of certain political, civil, and social rights. A third meaning of citizenship is active engagement in the life of the political community. Finally, citizenship has been used to describe "the affective ties of identification and solidarity that we maintain with groups of other people in the world."
>
> Marriage is intertwined with all four dimensions of citizenship. Most of the legal scholarship has focused on the relationship between marriage and the first dimension of citizenship: the effect of legal marriage on national citizenship and vice versa. However, I will focus on the second, third, and fourth dimensions. The right to marry—as the current debate over same-sex marriage and earlier debates over interracial marriage, polygamy, and slave marriage illustrate—is a right central to citizenship; or, more precisely, legal exclusion from the right to marry the partner(s) of one's choice is understood both by those excluded and the excluders as a denial of full citizenship. Marriage also has been central, I will suggest, to the third dimension of citizenship: active engagement in the public life of the community. If the fundamental unit of political citizenship is the individual voter, the fundamental unit of the U.S. economy is the household, and the ideal type of this household has long been the married couple, with or without children. From the late nineteenth century until the present day, the nuclear family has been treated as the basic unit of labor power; as feminist economists have pointed out, wives' unpaid labor in the home subsidizes and makes possible husbands' full-time wage labor. As business corporations brought the "consumer society" into being, advertisers sought to connect family roles and "family values" to shopping and buying, making the nuclear family central to mass consumption and vice versa. In both realms—the realm of citizenship as rights and the realm of citizenship as participation in public life—marriage is important symbolically and materially.

Moreover ... these second and third dimensions of citizenship have important consequences for Bosniak's fourth dimension of citizenship, which concerns the politics of group identity. Bosniak refers primarily to the voluntary aspects of identity: how people affiliate themselves with others and come to an understanding of themselves as members of groups. As Iris Marion Young has shown, however, group identity formation is only partly voluntary. Identities are also imposed on individuals, through ideas and images that circulate through national culture and local and regional subcultures. Social and legal practices of inclusion and exclusion, in turn, play an important part in shaping these ideas and images. Bosniak's fourth dimension of citizenship can thus be understood as a kind of "cultural imaginary" in which some group identities come to be identified with national citizenship and other identities are identified as outside the bounds of citizenship. Angela P. Harris, *Loving* Before and After the Law, 76 Fordham Law Review 2821, 2821–2822 (2008).

7. Recall the note earlier in this chapter on *Farrakhan v. Gregoire*, 623 F.3d 990 (9th Cir. 2010 en banc) (disenfranchisement of Black voters through a ban on voting by ex-felons is not a violation of the Constitution unless adopted for a discriminatory purpose). Is this another form of second class citizenship?

8. The term "second class citizenship" implies that the protected party is a "citizen," but equality may be denied based on a lack of citizenship, particularly for persons present in a nation state without legal residence. The Fourteenth Amendment provides that "no State ... [may] deny to any person within its jurisdiction the equal protection of the laws." Does this mean that the equal protection clause applies to non-citizens? Yes, *see Plyer v. Doe*, 457 U.S. 202 (1982) (Non-citizen children of illegal immigrants may not be denied access to free public education). However, although the 1964 Civil Rights Act prohibited discrimination in employment on the basis of national origin, it does not prohibit discrimination based on citizenship. *See, Espinoza v. Farah Mfg. Co.*, 414 U.S. 86, 92 (1973) (Employer may restrict hiring to U.S. citizens, refusing to hire non-citizen legal residents).

9. The Fourteenth Amendment also provides that "all persons born or naturalized in the United States and subject to the jurisdiction thereof, are citizens of the United States and the State wherein they reside." A number of state legislatures are considering bills that would deprive birth certificates to children born to non-citizens who lack permission to reside in the United States ("illegal aliens"), and a bill is pending in Congress that would declare such children as "not subject to the jurisdiction of the United States," and thus not citizens. While most countries in North and South America grant citizenship based on birth ("jus soli"), in most of the rest of the world a child's citizenship is derived from the parent's citizenship.

10. In *Wards Cove Packing v. Atonio*, 490 U.S. 642 (1989) the Court reinstated a judgment for the defendant, an Alaska fishing cannery, in which the office workers were all white, the cannery workers were all non-white, and the living conditions for office workers and cannery workers were dramatically different.

In dissent, Justice Stevens wrote:

"Respondents constitute a class of present and former employees of petitioners, two Alaskan salmon canning companies. The class members, described by the parties as 'nonwhite,' include persons of Samoan, Chinese, Filipino, Japanese, and Alaska Native descent, all but one of whom are United States citizens. Fifteen years ago, they commenced this suit, alleging that petitioners engage in hiring, job assignment, housing, and messing practices that segregate nonwhites from whites in violation of Title VII. Evidence included this response in 1971 by a foreman to a college student's inquiry about cannery employment:

'We are not in a position to take many young fellows to our Bristol Bay canneries, as they do not have the background for our type of employees. Our cannery labor is either Eskimo or Filipino, and we do not have the facilities to mix others with these groups.'

Some characteristics of the Alaska salmon industry described in this litigation—in particular, the segregation of housing and dining facilities and the stratification of jobs along racial and ethnic lines—bear an unsettling resemblance to aspects of a plantation economy. Indeed the maintenance of inferior, segregated facilities for housing and feeding nonwhite employees strikes me as a form of discrimination that, although it does not necessarily fit neatly into a disparate impact or disparate treatment mold, nonetheless violates Title VII. Respondents, however, do not press this theory before us." *Wards Cove Packing v. Antonio, id.* at 663 fn.4.

Was Justice Stevens suggesting an analytical approach to employment discrimination law based on second-class citizenship?

11.   We have already encountered the International Convention on the Elimination of All Forms of Racial Discrimination. You may recall that Article 1, Section 1 defined discrimination to mean "any distinction, exclusion, restriction or preference based on race, colour, descent, or national or ethnic origin which has the purpose or effect of nullifying or impairing the recognition, enjoyment or exercise, on an equal footing, of human rights and fundamental freedoms in the political, economic, social, cultural or any other field of public life." Article 1, Section 2 provides: "This Convention shall not apply to distinctions, exclusions, restrictions or preferences made by a State Party to this Convention between citizens and non-citizens."

————

D.H. and Others v. The Czech Republic

(13 November 2007)

■ Grand Chamber, EUROPEAN COURT OF HUMAN RIGHTS

* * * 25. * * * In their grounds of appeal, the applicants explained that they had been placed in special schools under a practice that had been established in order to implement the relevant statutory rules. In their submission, that practice had resulted in *de facto* racial segregation and

discrimination that were reflected in the existence of two separately organised educational systems for members of different racial groups, namely special schools for the Roma and "ordinary" primary schools for the majority of the population. That difference in treatment was not based on any objective and reasonable justification, amounted to degrading treatment and had deprived them of the right to education (as the curriculum followed in special schools was inferior and pupils in special schools were unable to return to primary school or to obtain a secondary education other than in a vocational training centre). Arguing that they had received an inadequate education and an affront to their dignity, the applicants asked the Constitutional Court (Ústavní soud) to find a violation of their rights, to quash the decisions to place them in special schools, to order the respondents (the special schools concerned, the Ostrava Education Authority and the Ministry of Education) to refrain from any further violation of their rights and to restore the status quo ante by offering them compensatory lessons.

NOTES

1. The *D.H.* case, like the *Brown* case, stems from a system of exclusion and subordination of broad application. The Roma in Europe are often treated as second-class citizens, or as non-citizens. They are involved in a civil rights movement across Europe, which includes a strategic litigation effort that includes over 500 anti-discrimination lawsuits, filed in 15 countries. For more on these efforts, see the website of the European Roma Rights Center (ERRC) at www.errc.org.

2. Across the globe, women are usually under-represented in national legislative bodies, and among national leaders. Does that under-representation lead to (or constitute) a form of second-class citizenship? In Europe, this question is the subject of great debate. Several European States, including Norway, France, Germany, and Greece, have passed laws requiring various forms of parity among candidates for elective office. (For further discussion of these laws, see Chapter IV.)

The European Commission, (the executive arm of the European Union) created a special research project in 2007 to examine whether women were being denied equality of citizenship in Europe. The project, named "femcit" has as its principal aims:

"To produce an interdisciplinary understanding of gendered citizenship in a multicultural and changing Europe, in terms of six dimensions of citizenship: political, social, economic, ethnic/religious, bodily/sexual, and intimate citizenship. To develop an integrative analysis of the interrelationships between these six dimensions. To investigate how different and changing notions and practices of citizenship have been articulated by contemporary women's movements. To evaluate the impact of European feminist women's movements on citizenship discourses and practices since the 1960s. To undertake cross-national and comparative studies, as well as national case studies of gendered citizenship. To assess the current state of women's citizenship in Europe, with particular attention to differences of race/ethnicity, class, sexuality, religion, region and nationality. And to develop policy recommendations to promote women's full citizenship and gender-fair citizenship." Femcit has issued a series of research studies making the case that European women lack citizenship equality. *See* www.femcit.org.

3.   Another example of second-class citizenship is the Indian caste system, described here by the U.S. Library of Congress country study of India.

> "Although many other nations are characterized by social inequality, perhaps nowhere else in the world has inequality been so elaborately constructed as in the Indian institution of caste. Caste has long existed in India, but in the modern period it has been severely criticized by both Indian and foreign observers. Although some educated Indians tell non-Indians that caste has been abolished or that 'no one pays attention to caste anymore,' such statements do not reflect reality.

> Caste has undergone significant change since independence, but it still involves hundreds of millions of people. In its preamble, India's constitution forbids negative public discrimination on the basis of caste. However, caste ranking and caste-based interaction have occurred for centuries and will continue to do so well into the foreseeable future, more in the countryside than in urban settings and more in the realms of kinship and marriage than in less personal interactions.

> Castes are ranked, named, endogamous (in-marrying) groups, membership in which is achieved by birth. There are thousands of castes and subcastes in India, and these large kinship-based groups are fundamental to South Asian social structure. Each caste is part of a locally based system of inter-dependence with other groups, involving occupational specialization, and is linked in complex ways with networks that stretch across regions and throughout the nation.

> ... Many castes are traditionally associated with an occupation, such as high-ranking Brahmans; middle-ranking farmer and artisan groups, such as potters, barbers, and carpenters; and very low-ranking 'Untouchable' leatherworkers, butchers, launderers, and latrine cleaners. There is some correlation between ritual rank on the caste hierarchy and economic prosperity. Members of higher-ranking castes tend, on the whole, to be more prosperous than members of lower-ranking castes. Many lower-caste people live in conditions of great poverty and social disadvantage."

India, James Heitzman and Robert L. Worden, editors. INDIA: A COUNTRY STUDY, Washington: GPO for the Library of Congress, 1995, http://countrystudies.us/india/89.htm.

4.   To counter discrimination against the "untouchable" castes, the Indian Parliament passed the Protection of Civil Rights Act of 1955. It grants to all persons:

- Access to any place of public worship open to people of the same religion

- Ability to worship in the same manner as people of the same religion
- Access to shops, public restaurants, hotels, etc.
- Use of utensils in eateries
- Practice of any profession
- Use of tanks, wells, taps, etc.
- Use of or access to any places of public charity
- Use of or access to any facility partly or wholly maintained by State funds or dedicated to the use of the general public
- Use of any public conveyance
- Ability to live or build a home in any locality
- Access to any religious school open to the general public
- Ability to practice any social or religious custom
- Admittance to any hospital
- Ability to buy any good or hire any service

The Act also punishes:

- Preventing or obstructing another person from exercising a right that accrues to him now that untouchability has been abolished
- Insulting a person belonging to a Scheduled Caste on grounds of 'untouchability'
- Boycotting or excommunicating another person to enforce untouchability
- Preaching 'untouchability' directly or indirectly
- Justifying 'untouchability' on historical, philosophical, or religious grounds

In 1989, the Indian Parliament passed the Prevention of Atrocities Act, prohibiting atrocities such as

- Forcing an individual to drink or eat any inedible or obnoxious substance
- Dumping excreta or any other obnoxious substance in premises or a neighborhood
- Parading individuals naked
- Wrongfully occupying land and dispossessing
- Compelling begging or the performance of bonded labour
- Forcing or intimidating to vote in a particular way
- Instituting false or vexatious legal proceedings
- Intentionally insulting or intimidating with intent to humiliate

See, Sanjoy Ghose, *Untouchability and the Law*, 13 Interights Bulletin: A Review of the International Centre for the Legal Protection of Human Rights 98, 99 (2001).

5. Recall the debate in the French National Assembly in 1789 on the relationship between citizenship and religion, which was discussed in

Chapter I. Count Tonnerre argued that all persons could practice their religion privately, and that French Jews could be citizens, but only if they agreed to give up "their own judges and laws.... We must refuse everything to the Jews as a nation and accord everything to Jews as individuals. We must withdraw recognition from their judges; they should only have our judges.... [and] if they do not want to be citizens, they should say so, and then we should banish them." This is regarded as an early expression of what is now known as French Republicanism, the political ideal of equal citizenship, and of citizenship as the only legitimate form of public identity. For French Jews, was this equality?

6. Count Tonnerre is still debating. Consider this excerpt from an article by Mostapha Benhenda:

> "Conceptions of liberal citizenship are attractive in pluralistic societies. According to them, members of the society do not need to share the same cultural, ethnic or religious background in order to find acceptable terms of political cooperation. Instead, conceptions of liberal citizenship build civic ties on abstract and universal values. The essential feature of good liberal citizens is their allegiance to the principles underlying the political institutions of liberal democracy. What only matters is their loyalty to the fundamental law of their democratic country, their loyalty to their constitution.

> On the other hand, in Western democracies, there are a significant number of Muslim citizens. Their parents are mainly immigrants from Africa and Asia. They have cultural and ethnic differences with their fellow non-Muslim citizens, which sometimes hinder their integration in Western societies. Since conceptions of liberal citizenship are neutral with respect to these differences, they seem promising for integrating Muslim minorities. Indeed, the focus of these conceptions is elsewhere: they ask for a morally grounded allegiance to the principles embodied by democratic institutions. Therefore, in order to examine whether this promise of integration is fulfilled, we have to ask whether Muslim minorities have moral grounds to endorse or reject constitutional principles. In particular, an interesting question seems to be whether Muslims endorse these constitutional principles qua Muslims; that is to say, how they view the relationship (or absence of relationship) between the conditions of liberal citizenship and their religious position.

> * * * The norms of religious doctrine cannot legitimately be determined by empirical circumstances, but rather must be drawn from the sources of Muslim doctrine. Otherwise, we may well get integration and stability, but on the wrong basis. This confusion between sources and context is well illustrated by the expression "Islam of France" (Islam de France) that is sometimes proposed as a model opposed to "Islam in France" (Islam en France). It suggests that there is a distinctive religion, called "Islam of France," which takes France as its reference. In other words, "Islam of France" leaves the determination of its values to the country in which it is settled. In this way, it is difficult to see how these values could be taken as authoritative."

Mostapha Benhenda, *For Muslim minorities, it is possible to endorse political liberalism, but this is not enough*, 11:2 Journal of Islamic Law and Culture 71–87 (2009) Electronic copy available at: http://ssrn.com/abstract=1574982, ISSN 1753–4534 online.

D.   The Role of Prejudice, Bias and Stereotyping

Most of us understand discrimination and inequality to be premised on bias or prejudice against members of a social group. Yet, this is simply a starting point for analysis under the law. We might ask whether we want courts to require that bias or prejudice manifests itself as conscious or unconscious, and whether bias or prejudice against some groups is more egregious than against others. If we consider most bias and prejudice to be largely unconscious, or part of our everyday cognitive thought processes, how can courts determine whether such attitudes result in discriminatory acts or conduct?

————

Prejudicial Appearances: The Logic of American Antidiscrimination Law

88 California Law Review 1, 2–3, 8–13 (2000)

■ Robert Post

[Consider] a story that begins in Santa Cruz [California] in January of 1992, when the City Council proposed an ordinance that would prohibit discrimination against persons on the basis of "personal appearance." First advanced by a Santa Cruz group called the Body Image Task Force, the proposed law quickly became known in the media as "the 'purple hair ordinance' or the 'ugly ordinance.'" It provoked an intense and raucous controversy about the merits of what was called "anti-lookism."

Anti-lookism cuts deeply into the social fabric. Social relationships characteristically transpire through the medium of appearances; an ability to interpret the many meanings conveyed by appearances is required for fluency in the language of social life.... The presentation of appearances in everyday life is not merely a matter of the external surfaces of the self, for appearances are also connected to identity...

The draft Santa Cruz ordinance proposed to render appearances invisible. It would do so not merely in the context of the state's treatment of its citizens, but also in the context of ordinary employment and housing transactions among private persons. It is no wonder, then, that the ordinance prompted cries of outrage. "If someone has 14 earrings in their ears and their nose—and who knows where else—and spiky green hair and smells like a skunk," commented Kathy Manoff, owner of a small restaurant, "I don't know why I have to hire them." Newspaper editorials scorned the ordinance as extending "the power of the state over private judgments that are perfectly normal discriminatory responses to human eccentricities." Columnist Joseph Farah wondered, "Let's say you're a newspaper editor looking for someone to cover the police beat. An experienced professional journalist wants the job, but he shows up for the interview wearing a dress. Does he get a chance to be our ace crime reporter?"

Supporters of the proposed ordinance, however, insisted that it merely forbade superficial judgments based upon "stereotypes." They argued that because the real worth of persons did not inhere in their external appearance, important decisions regarding employment and housing ought not to depend upon such an irrelevant characteristic, particularly when decisions based upon appearance so often merely express "simple bigotry." The efforts of employers to "control the look of their workforce" were said to "smack of the kind of mentality that kept blacks and other minorities out of the public eye for years until civil rights protections were enacted."

* * * Anti-discrimination law in America characteristically presents itself according to a very definite logic. It is a logic that springs from a firm sense of the social reality of prejudice. Anti-discrimination law seeks to neutralize widespread forms of prejudice that pervasively disadvantage persons based upon inaccurate judgments about their worth or capacities.

The unfairness of prejudice is particularly manifest when it is directed against immutable traits, like race or sex. But prejudice can be unfair even if it is directed against traits that are within the control of a person. American anti-discrimination laws, for example, typically prohibit discrimination based upon religion and marital status, even though neither trait is "immutable." In this regard, obesity is an interesting borderline case. It is plain that there is widespread prejudice against the obese, so that obesity is a deeply stigmatizing characteristic. Anti-discrimination laws sometimes forbid discrimination based upon obesity when (and only when) the characteristic is conceptualized as a disability that is beyond the control of a person; sometimes they prohibit such discrimination if obesity is categorized as a disability, even if the disability is partially within the control of a person; and sometimes, as in the case of the Santa Cruz ordinance, antidiscrimination laws flatly forbid discrimination based upon "weight." Such statutes regard prejudice against the obese as unfair even if obesity is completely within the voluntary control of a person. Although this is not the occasion to elaborate the point, I suspect that legal judgments of unfairness depend upon whether a stigmatizing attribute is viewed as somehow essential or integral to a person, as is their religion.

Prejudice against a stigmatizing characteristic, such as race or sex, can manifest itself through invidious judgments of the "differential worth" of persons who display the characteristic, or it can manifest itself through "faulty" judgments about the capacities of such persons. American anti-discrimination law understands itself as negating such prejudice by eliminating or carefully scrutinizing the use of stigmatizing characteristics as a ground for judgment. The classic constitutional formulation of this perspective is Justice White's opinion for the Court in *Cleburne v. Cleburne Living Center, Inc.*, in which he writes that statutory classifications of "race, alienage, or national origin"

> are so seldom relevant to the achievement of any legitimate state interest that laws grounded in such considerations are deemed to

reflect prejudice and antipathy—a view that those in the burdened class are not as worthy or deserving as others. For these reasons and because such discrimination is unlikely to be soon rectified by legislative means, these laws are subject to strict scrutiny and will be sustained only if they are suitably tailored to serve a compelling state interest. . . .

Legislative classifications based on gender also call for a heightened standard of review. That factor generally provides no sensible ground for differential treatment. "What differentiates sex from such non-suspect statuses as intelligence or physical disability . . . is that the sex characteristic frequently bears no relation to ability to perform or contribute to society" . . . Rather than resting on meaningful considerations, statutes distributing benefits and burdens between the sexes in different ways very likely reflect outmoded notions of the relative capabilities of men and women. A gender classification fails unless it is substantially related to a sufficiently important governmental interest.

Judicial interpretation of Title VII, which is the portion of the Federal Civil Rights Act of 1964 that prohibits employment discrimination on the basis of "race, color, religion, sex, or national origin," displays a similar orientation. "In passing Title VII," the Court has said, "Congress made the simple but momentous announcement that sex, race, religion, and national origin are not relevant to the selection, evaluation, or compensation of employees." The point of rendering such factors irrelevant is to "target" and eliminate "stubborn but irrational prejudice." In the words of one federal district court:

"In our society we too often form opinions of people on the basis of skin color, religion, national origin . . . and other superficial features. That tendency to stereotype people is at the root of some of the social ills that afflict the country, and in adopting the Civil Rights Act of 1964, Congress intended to attack these stereotyped characterizations so that people would be judged by their intrinsic worth." * * *

Taken as a whole, American anti-discrimination law thus follows a simple but powerful logic. * * *

In essence, the logic of American anti-discrimination law requires employers to regard their employees as though they did not display socially powerful and salient attributes, because these attributes may induce irrational and prejudiced judgments. * * *

In fact what anti-discrimination law seeks to uncover is an apprehension of "individual merit." That is why the author of the Santa Cruz ordinance understood it as forcing employers to judge employees "on the basis of real criteria," which "is their ability to perform the job." American anti-discrimination law pushes employers toward functional justifications for their actions. * * *

Price Waterhouse v. Hopkins

490 U.S. 228 (1989)

■ JUSTICE BRENNAN announced the judgment of the Court and delivered an opinion, in which JUSTICE MARSHALL, JUSTICE BLACKMUN, and JUSTICE STEVENS join.

* * * Ann Hopkins had worked at Price Waterhouse's Office of Government Services in Washington, D.C., for five years when the partners in that office proposed her as a candidate for partnership. [By a vote of the partners, she was denied partnership, and subsequently informed that she would not be re-proposed for partnership.] * * *

[S]ome of the partners reacted negatively to Hopkins' personality because she was a woman. One partner described her as "macho"; another suggested that she "overcompensated for being a woman"; a third advised her to take "a course at charm school." Several partners criticized her use of profanity; in response, one partner suggested that those partners objected to her swearing only "because it's a lady using foul language." Another supporter explained that Hopkins "ha[d] matured from a tough-talking somewhat masculine hard-nosed mgr to an authoritative, formidable, but much more appealing lady ptr candidate." But it was the man who, as Judge Gesell found, bore responsibility for explaining to Hopkins the reasons for the Policy Board's decision to place her candidacy on hold who delivered the *coup de grace*: in order to improve her chances for partnership, Thomas Beyer advised, Hopkins should "walk more femininely, talk more femininely, dress more femininely, wear make-up, have her hair styled, and wear jewelry."

Dr. Susan Fiske, a social psychologist and Associate Professor of Psychology at Carnegie–Mellon University, testified at trial that the partnership selection process at Price Waterhouse was likely influenced by sex stereotyping. * * *

In the specific context of sex stereotyping, an employer who acts on the basis of a belief that a woman cannot be aggressive, or that she must not be, has acted on the basis of gender.

As to the existence of sex stereotyping in this case, we are not inclined to quarrel with the District Court's conclusion that a number of the partners' comments showed sex stereotyping at work. As for the legal relevance of sex stereotyping, we are beyond the day when an employer could evaluate employees by assuming or insisting that they matched the stereotype associated with their group, for " '[i]n forbidding employers to discriminate against individuals because of their sex, Congress intended to strike at the entire spectrum of disparate treatment of men and women resulting from sex stereotypes.' " *Los Angeles Dept. of Water and Power v. Manhart*, 435 U.S. 702, 707, n. 13 (1978), quoting *Sprogis v. United Air Lines, Inc.*, 444 F.2d 1194, 1198 (CA7 1971). An employer who objects to aggressiveness in women but whose positions require this trait places women in an intolerable and impermissible catch 22: out of a job if they behave aggressively and out of a job if they do not. Title VII lifts women out of this bind.

————

The Id, The Ego and Equal Protection: Reckoning With Unconscious Racism

39 Stan. L. Rev. 317, 322, 323, 355–362 (1987)

■ Charles R. Lawrence III

Americans share a common historical and cultural heritage in which racism has played and still plays a dominant role. Because of this shared experience, we also inevitably share many ideas, attitudes, and beliefs that attach significance to an individual's race and induce negative feelings and opinions about non-whites. To the extent that this cultural belief system has influenced all of us, we are all racists. At the same time, most of us are unaware of our racism. We do not recognize the ways in which our cultural experience has influenced our beliefs about race or the occasions on which those beliefs affect our actions. In other words, a large part of the behavior that produces racial discrimination is influenced by unconscious racial motivation.

There are two explanations for the unconscious nature of our racially discriminatory beliefs and ideas. First, Freudian theory states that the human mind defends itself against the discomfort of guilt by denying or refusing to recognize those ideas, wishes, and beliefs that conflict with what the individual has learned is good or right. While our historical experience has made racism an integral part of our culture, our society has more recently embraced an ideal that rejects racism as immoral. When an individual experiences conflict between racist ideas and the societal ethic that condemns those ideas, the mind excludes his racism from consciousness.

Second, the theory of cognitive psychology states that the culture— including, for example, the media and an individual's parents, peers, and authority figures—transmits certain beliefs and preferences. Because these beliefs are so much a part of the culture, they are not experienced as explicit lessons. Instead, they seem part of the individual's rational ordering of her perceptions of the world. The individual is unaware, for example, that the ubiquitous presence of a cultural stereotype has influenced her perception that blacks are lazy or unintelligent. Because racism is so deeply ingrained in our culture, it is likely to be transmitted by tacit understandings: Even if a child is not told that blacks are inferior, he learns that lesson by observing the behavior of others. These tacit understandings, because they have never been articulated, are less likely to be experienced at a conscious level. * * *

[The challenge is] how a court would identify those cases where unconscious racism operated in order to determine whether to subject an allegedly discriminatory act to strict scrutiny.

I propose a test that would look to the 'cultural meaning' of an allegedly racially discriminatory act as the best available analogue for and evidence of the collective unconscious that we cannot observe directly. This test would evaluate governmental conduct to see if it conveys a symbolic message to which the culture attaches racial significance. The court would analyze governmental behavior much like a cultural anthropologist might: by considering evidence regarding the historical and social context in which the decision was made and effectuated. If the court determined by a preponderance of the evidence that a significant portion of the population thinks of the governmental action in racial terms, then it would presume that socially shared, unconscious racial attitudes made evident by the action's meaning had influenced the decisionmakers. As a result, it would apply heightened scrutiny.

The unconscious racial attitudes of individuals manifest themselves in the cultural meaning that society gives their actions in the following way: In a society that no longer condones overt racist attitudes and behavior, many of these attitudes will be repressed and prevented from reaching awareness in an undisguised form. But as psychologists have found, repressed wishes, fears, anger, and aggression continue to seek expression, most often by attaching themselves to certain symbols in the external world. Repressed feelings and attitudes that are commonly experienced are likely to find common symbols particularly fruitful or productive as a vehicle for their expression. Thus, certain actions, words, or signs may take on meaning within a particular culture as a result of the collective use of those actions, words, or signs to represent or express shared but repressed attitudes. The process is cyclical: the expression of shared attitudes through certain symbols gives those symbols cultural meaning, and once a symbol becomes an enduring part of the culture, it in turn becomes the most natural vehicle for the expression of those attitudes and feelings that caused it to become an identifiable part of the culture.

Cognitive theory provides an alternative explanation of why the racial meaning the culture gives an action will be evidence of the actor's unconscious racial motivation. According to cognitive theory, those meanings or values that are most deeply ingrained in the culture are commonly acquired early in life through tacit lessons. They are, therefore, less recognizable and less available to the individual's consciousness than other forms of knowledge. Looked at another way, if the action has cultural meaning, this meaning must have been transmitted to an individual who is a member of that culture. If he professes to be unaware of the cultural meaning or attitude, it will almost surely be operating at an unconscious level.

Thus, an action such as the construction of a wall between white and black communities in Memphis [citing *City of Memphis v. Greene*, 451 U.S. 100 (1981)] would have a cultural meaning growing out of a long history of whites' need to separate themselves from blacks as a symbol of their superiority. Individual members of the city council might well have been unaware that their continuing need to maintain their superiority over blacks, or their failure to empathize with how construction of the wall would make blacks feel, influenced their decision. But if one were to ask even the most self-deluded among them what the residents of Memphis would take the existence of the wall to mean, the obvious answer would be difficult to avoid. If one told the story leading to the wall's construction while omitting one vital fact—the race of those whose vehicular traffic the barrier excluded—and then asked Memphis citizens to describe the residents of the community claiming injury, few, if any, would not guess that they were black.

The current racial meanings of governmental actions are strong evidence that the process defects of group vilification and misapprehension of costs and benefits have occurred whether or not the decisionmakers were conscious that race played a part in their decisionmaking. Moreover, actions that have racial meaning within the culture are also those actions that carry a stigma for which we should have special concern. This is not the stigma that occurs only because of a coincidental congruence between race and poverty. The association of a symbol with race is a residuum of overtly racist practices in the past: the wall conjures up racial inferiority, not the inferiority of the poor or the undesirability of vehicular traffic. And stigma that has racial meaning burdens all blacks and adds to the pervasive, cumulative, and mutually reinforcing system of racial discrimination.

Some may question the competence of courts to apply a test that asks them to interpret the meaning of human behavior. Although some legal scholars have warmly embraced economics, most remain skeptical about the utility of social sciences and the ability of courts to understand and interpret complex social science data. But the interpretation of cultural meaning is not so foreign a task for courts as it first appears. Indeed, construction of text is the most basic of judicial tasks. And while most judicial interpretation involves determining the meaning of written text, legal theorists have recognized that meaningful human behavior can be treated as a 'text-analogue.' The context in which both written and social text is read can give it meaning beyond its authors' original intention: the social text of human action, like the written text, is judged not just by those who are present when it takes place but by all who come to know of it.

In fact, courts frequently interpret the meaning of social phenomena. In establishment clause cases, the Court determines whether a governmental practice advances or inhibits religion by inquiring into the meaning the culture gives that practice: When a municipality includes a creche in its annual Christmas display, will most observers understand the creche as 'a symbol of Christian beliefs and a symbol of the city's support for those beliefs,' or will they interpret the display as merely depicting 'the historical origins of a traditional event long recognized as a National Holiday?' In determining the scope of the 'zones of privacy' that the Fourteenth Amendment's due process clause protects, the Court has interpreted the concept of the family by referring to the meaning that the history and traditions of our culture have given it. The Court has also defined the scope of the Fourth Amendment's protection against warrantless search and seizure by asking whether an individual has a 'reasonable expectation of privacy' in the searched premises.

In considering the constitutionality of statutes and regulations challenged on sex discrimination grounds, the Court has held that the legislature may not make overbroad generalizations that 'demean the ability or social status of the affected class.' It determines whether legislation transgresses this prohibition by asking whether the law 'tends to perpetuate the stereotyped view' of women. This question is not answered by determining whether the legislature intended to stereotype women but by interpreting the contemporary community consensus regarding the message the legislation conveys—that is, its cultural meaning. The legislation can only perpetuate a stereotype if it triggers existing preconceptions in the culture: men as breadwinners and women as dependents, men as property managers and women as homemakers, young men as sexually aggressive and women as weak and in need of protection, women as nurses and men as not.

Given that courts engage in cultural anthropological inquiry so often, why is there such resistance to a similar inquiry in racial discrimination cases? One possible explanation lies in the fact that social scientists can rarely prove the causal relationships that support their hypotheses. For example, courts have looked to social science to prove whether or not integrated schools will improve the educational achievement of black children and whether or not differential school expenditures will make a difference in students' educational opportunities. Our misgivings about allowing judicial decisions to turn on social science evidence are prompted, in large part, by social science's inability to prove or disprove such propositions.

If the proposed cultural meaning test required the courts to rely upon social scientists to conclusively demonstrate causal relationships between challenged governmental actions and harm to blacks, it would be subject to similar criticism concerning the inadequacy of social science methodology. But there is another kind of judgment or analysis that historians, economists, sociologists, anthropologists, and other social scientists make. This is interpretive judgment. As Ronald Dworkin has explained, causal judgments assert a causal connection between two independently specifiable social phenomena. An interpretive judgment, on the other hand, locates a particular phenomenon within a category of phenomena by specifying its meaning in the society within which it occurs.

Two of the more successful defenders of the *Brown* decision, Charles Black and Edgar Cahn, have argued that the question of the Court's reliance on social science evidence was beside the point: the constitutional rights at stake rested not upon that evidence but upon the insulting and degrading quality of segregation itself. But Dworkin points out that to argue that segregation is unconstitutional because it is an insult is not to argue that *Brown* was based on a value judgment distinct from a social science judgment. He notes that what Black and Cahn meant was that the decision rested on interpretive, not causal, judgments. To say that we don't need evidence for the proposition that segregation is an insult to the black community is not to say that we don't need to know it or that there is nothing to know. 'There is a fact of the matter, namely that segregation is an insult, but we need no evidence for that fact—we just know it. It's an interpretive fact.'

It is this type of interpretive judgment that the cultural meaning test requires. The search for cultural meaning is necessarily an interpretive task. The distinction between causal and interpretive analysis is crucial, because the objections to the use of social science evidence to prove causal relationships do not apply to interpretive judgments such as the judgment that a particular practice will have a racially insulting meaning. Moreover, much of what judges do entails this kind of interpretation: It requires the same skills they employ when they decide a case by characterizing or interpreting a line of precedent in the way that seems most true to them.

————

Negligent Discrimination

141 Penn. L. Rev. 899 (1993)

■ DAVID B. OPPENHEIMER

If whites are frequently unaware of their own racism, a theory of employment discrimination that focuses on an intent to discriminate provides no remedy for most discrimination. Yet the victims of unconscious discrimination have suffered the same economic damages, and often the same emotional damages, as the victims of knowing bigotry. The nature of the wrong committed by the employer who decides not to hire African Americans, or women, or members of ethnic or religious minority groups, because of a self-acknowledged prejudice, may be greater than that of the employer who is merely unaware of his own propensities, but the harm caused by the unconscious discrimination is largely the same. Intentional, bigoted decisions may be appropriately the subject not only of compensatory but of punitive damages as well, and thus properly distinguished. But the primary problem of employment discrimination should be focused on determining liability, and assessing proper damages, where most discrimination occurs, at the level of unconscious discrimination. * * *

[T]he analogy of Title VII to other employment torts is obvious. The central purpose of Title VII is to right the wrong created by discrimination, and to make its victims whole by permitting a civil action for damages. Although the source of this cause of action is an act of Congress, rather than the common law, the action is, like any other tort action, an action to redress a civil wrong, not based on contract, for which damages are sought. Examination of the theories under which Title VII actions may be brought reveals that the Court has clearly recognized Title VII as providing tort-like actions under theories of intentional tort and strict liability, while implicitly recognizing a wide range of inchoate negligence theories. * * *

The law of negligence requires persons who choose to become employers to enter into the employment relationship with care, in order to protect those persons seeking employment, those who become employed, and the general public. When a failure to exercise due care in the manner of choosing employees, or maintaining or terminating their employment, causes harm, the employer is responsible for the costs of that harm. * * *

It is a fundamental tenet of our legal system that fault is not equated with an intent to cause harm. We recognize that people often cause substantial harm without any wrongful intent. When the harm is caused as a result of failing to meet a minimum standard of care, which we require to provide ourselves with a reasonably safe and good society, we term that conduct negligence. When employers fail to meet their obligation of due care to protect their employees, and the public, from an undue risk of harm, they are negligent. Duties to use due care to protect employees' health and safety are frequently imposed by statute. One such duty is the requirement imposed by Title VII to treat employees and applicants equally, without regard to race, color, religion, sex, or national origin. Employers who, without intending harm, breach this duty by treating women or minorities less favorably than white men, have, in the absence of an available privilege, engaged in negligent discrimination. * * *

Whenever an employer fails to act to prevent discrimination which it knows, or should know, is occurring, which it expects to occur, or which it should expect to occur, it should be held negligent. Liability should also be recognized when an employer breaches the statutorily established standard of care by making employment decisions which have a discriminatory effect, without first scrutinizing its processes, searching for less discriminatory alternatives, and examining its own motives for evidence of stereotyping.

When a woman or minority job applicant is rejected, the rejection should act as a triggering device, requiring the decision maker to instantly stop and examine his or her own motives. If the decision cannot be justified with a reasonable, nondiscriminatory reason, such as bona fide qualifications, the decision may have been negligently reached. If a prohibited basis for decision making played a role in the decision, consciously or unconsciously, Title VII liability should be imposed.

Where an employer has created job screening procedures which fail to correct for unconscious discrimination, and such discrimination influences the process, the employer ought to be subject to negligence liability. The same standard should apply to employee evaluations, where stereotypes can easily influence subjective evaluations critical to job or career advancement. Similarly, when a female or minority employee is disciplined, the employer ought to take particular care in determining that the decision to impose discipline, and the level of discipline imposed, has not been improperly influenced by discrimination. Where unconscious motivations abound, self-conscious and cautious procedures are necessary.

The Content Of Our Categories: A Cognitive Bias Approach to Discrimination and Equal Employment Opportunity

47 Stan. L. Rev. 1161, 1187–1188 (1995)

■ LINDA HAMILTON KRIEGER

The emergence of social cognition theory represented a profound shift in psychologists' thinking about intergroup bias.... [U]ntil well into the 1970s, intergroup prejudice was generally understood as stemming from motivational processes. Stereotypes of members of "outgroups" were seen as developing out of prejudice, and as serving to rationalize it. While psychologists such as Gordon Allport recognized that stereotyping was functionally similar to categorization, stereotypes were seen as something "special," discontinuous with "normal" cognitive process. Before the 1970s, few psychologists seriously entertained the notion that normal cognitive processes related to categorization might in and of themselves produce and perpetuate intergroup bias.

This is a central premise of social cognition theory—that cognitive structures and processes involved in categorization and information processing can in and of themselves result in stereotyping and other forms of biased intergroup judgment previously attributed to motivational processes. The social cognition approach to discrimination comprises three claims relevant to our present inquiry. The first is that stereotyping, as Vinacke suggested in 1957, is nothing special. It is simply a form of categorization, similar in structure and function to the categorization of natural objects. According to this view, stereotypes, like other categorical structures, are cognitive mechanisms that all people, not just "prejudiced" ones, use to simplify the task of perceiving, processing, and retaining information about people in memory. They are central, and indeed essential to normal cognitive functioning.

The second claim posited in social cognition theory is that, once in place, stereotypes bias intergroup judgment and decisionmaking. According to this view, stereotypes operate as "person prototypes" or "social schemas." As such, they function as implicit theories, biasing in predictable ways the perception, interpretation, encoding, retention, and recall of information about other people. These biases are cognitive rather than motivational. They operate absent intent to favor or disfavor members of a particular social group. And, perhaps most significant for present purposes, they bias a decisionmaker's judgment long before the "moment of decision," as a decisionmaker attends to relevant data and interprets, encodes, stores, and retrieves it from memory. These biases "sneak up on" the decisionmaker, distorting bit by bit the data upon which his decision is eventually based.

The third claim follows from the second. Stereotypes, when they function as implicit prototypes or schemas, operate beyond the reach of decisionmaker self-awareness. Empirical evidence indicates that people's access to their own cognitive processes is in fact poor. Accordingly, cognitive bias may well be both unintentional and unconscious.

————

Nagarajan v. London Regional Transport

[1999] IRLR 572, HL

■ UNITED KINGDOM HOUSE OF LORDS

[Mr. Nagarajan applied for the position of Travel Information Assistant and was interviewed but not selected. He brought an action before the Industrial Tribunal under the Race Relations Act of 1976. The Tribunal found that the interviewers were influenced, "consciously or unconsciously" by the fact that he had brought prior actions against the L.R.T. The Employment Appeal Tribunal and Court of Appeal found that the claimant was required to prove conscious discrimination. The House of Lords [or Law Lords, subsequently renamed the United Kingdom Supreme Court] reversed the Court of Appeal and reinstated the decision of the Industrial Tribunal.]

Lord Nicholls of Birkenhead

The first point raised is whether conscious motivation is a prerequisite for victimisation under section 2 of the Act.

[I]n every case it is necessary to enquire why the complainant received less favourable treatment. This is the crucial question. Was it on grounds of race? Or was it for some other reason, for instance, because the complainant was not so well qualified for the job? Save in obvious cases, answering the crucial question will call for some consideration of the mental processes of the alleged discriminator. Treatment, favourable or unfavourable, is a consequence which follows from a decision. Direct evidence of a decision to discriminate on racial grounds will seldom be forthcoming. Usually the grounds of the decision will have to be deduced, or inferred, from the surrounding circumstances.

The crucial question just mentioned is to be distinguished sharply from a second and different question: if the discriminator treated the complainant less favourably on racial grounds, why did he do so? The latter question is strictly beside the point when deciding whether an act of racial discrimination occurred. For the purposes of direct discrimination under section 1(1)(a), as distinct from indirect discrimination under section 1(1)(b), the reason why the alleged discriminator acted on racial grounds is irrelevant. Racial discrimination is not negatived by the discriminator's motive or intention or reason or purpose (the words are interchangeable in this context) in treating another person less favourably on racial grounds. In particular, if the reason why the alleged discriminator rejected the complainant's job application was racial, it matters not that his intention may have been benign. For instance, he may have believed that the applicant would not fit in, or that other employees might make the applicant's life a misery. If racial grounds were the reason for the less favourable treatment, direct discrimination under section 1(1)(a) is established. * * *

I turn to the question of subconscious motivation. All human beings have preconceptions, beliefs, attitudes and prejudices on many subjects. It is part of our make-up. Moreover, we do not always recognise our own prejudices. Many people are unable, or unwilling, to admit even to themselves that actions of theirs may be racially motivated. An employer may genuinely believe that the reason why he rejected an applicant had nothing to do with the applicant's race. After careful and thorough investigation of a claim members of an employment tribunal may decide that the proper inference to be drawn from the evidence is that, whether the employer realised it at the time or not, race was the reason why he acted as he did. It goes without saying that in order to justify such an inference the tribunal must first make findings of primary fact from which the inference may properly be drawn. Conduct of this nature by an employer, when the inference is legitimately drawn, falls squarely within the language of section 1(1)(a). The employer treated the complainant less favourably on racial grounds. Such conduct also falls within the purpose of the legislation.

Members of racial groups need protection from conduct driven by unrecognised prejudice as much as from conscious and deliberate discrimination. Balcombe L.J. adverted to an instance of this in *West Midlands Passenger Transport Executive v. Singh* [1988] I.R.L.R. 186, 188. He said that a high rate of failure to achieve promotion by members of a particular racial group may indicate that 'the real reason for refusal is a conscious or unconscious racial attitude which involves stereotyped assumptions' about members of the group.

NOTES

1. Recall that in *Brown*, the Court relied on then-current scientific evidence of the impact of segregation on Black children to conclude that segregation is harmful. The primary evidence was work by psychologists Kenneth and Mamie Clark in which Black children who had attended segregated schools were less likely to respond positively to Black dolls than Black children who had attended integrated schools ("the doll tests.") The most important scientific evidence on racism today is the work derived from the implicit association test ("IAT"), which measures a person's psychological response to race. *See* Anthony G. Greenwald & Linda Hamilton Krieger, *Implicit Bias: Scientific Foundations*, 94 CALIFORNIA LAW REVIEW 945 (2006). To take the test yourself, see https://implicit.harvard.edu/implicit/.

2. For more on the effect of implicit bias on workplace equality, *see* Linda Hamilton Krieger & Susan T. Fiske, *Behavioral Realism in Employment Discrimination Law: Implicit Bias and Disparate Treatment*, 94 CAL. L. REV. 997 (2006), Christine Jolls & Cass Sunstein, *The Law of Implicit Bias*, 94 CAL. L. REV. 969 (2006).

3. For a skeptical view, *see* Samuel R. Bagenstos, *Implicit Bias, "Science," and Antidiscrimination Law*, 1 HARV. L. & POL'Y. REV. 477 (2007). In response to critics of implicit bias theory, a group of several well-known social scientists published an article: Jost, Rudman, Blair et al., *The Existence of Implicit Bias is Beyond Reasonable Doubt: A Refutation of Ideological and Methodological Objections and Executive Summary of Ten Studies That No Manager Should Ignore*, 29 RESEARCH IN ORGANIZATIONAL BEHAVIOR 39–69 (2009), www.sciencedirect.com. They argued, in part:

* * *

2.1. Managerial decisions concerning callback interviews

A pair of behavioral economists garnered widespread media attention when they reported the results of an audit study in which they submitted 5,000 bogus resumes in response to over 1,300 employment advertisements published in Boston and Chicago area newspapers in the following job categories: sales, administrative support, clerical, and customer services (Bertrand & Mullainathan, 2004). The resumes submitted were either relatively high or low in prior work experience and resume quality, and they bore names that were pre-tested to be stereotypical either of European Americans (*e.g.*, Brendan, Todd, Meredith) or African Americans (*e.g.*, Darnell, Rasheed, Tamika). Results of this experiment revealed that job candidates with white names were

50% more likely than equally qualified candidates with black names to receive invitations for job interviews. The magnitude of discrimination was relatively constant across occupation, industry, employer size, and city.

It seems unlikely that the huge racial gap in callbacks demonstrated by Bertrand and Mullainathan (2004) could be explained by the low levels of explicit, self-reported prejudice captured by public opinion surveys cited by Tetlock and Mitchell (2009). However, one cannot be perfectly certain that the discriminatory behavior exhibited by the 1,300 employers in Boston and Chicago was a function of implicit rather than explicit racial biases. Fortunately, two subsequent studies provide more direct evidence that the kinds of race-based hiring biases identified by Betrand and Mullainathan are linked to implicit prejudice. First, in a follow-up study, Bertrand, Chugh, and Mullainathan (2005) found that scores on an implicit stereotyping task involving race and intelligence were correlated with students' likelihood of selecting resumes with African American names, especially among participants who felt rushed while completing a resume selection task.

Second, Rooth (2007) conducted an illuminating field study using human resource personnel as participants. He examined whether job applicants were contacted for interviews and also administered the IAT to employment recruiters in a Swedish replication and extension of the Bertrand and Mullainathan (2004) study. Using either common Arab or Swedish male names, Rooth (2007) submitted a series of otherwise comparable applications for several different job openings in Stockholm and Gothenburg. The occupations were selected to be highly skilled or unskilled, and they varied in the extent to which they were commonly held by Arabs (*e.g.*, teachers, accountants, restaurant workers, and motor vehicle drivers). From a total of 1,552 submitted applications, in 522 cases at least one applicant was contacted by the employer and invited for an interview. When only one applicant was contacted, 217 times this candidate was Swedish (42%) and only 66 times was he or she an Arab (13%); thus, Swedish applicants were three times more likely than Arab applicants to be offered interviews.

Several months later, Rooth (2007) located a subset (26%) of the specific managers responsible for making recruitment decisions for these jobs and paid them to participate in a study "about the recruitment process" in which both implicit and explicit stereotyping measures were administered. Results indicated that managers' scores on an Arab–Swedish IAT—in which the same names used in the job applications were paired with words that were stereotypic of Arabs (*e.g.*, lazy, slow) vs. white Swedes (hardworking, efficient)—significantly predicted their likelihood of providing interview opportunities to Arab applicants [formula removed]. A single standard deviation increase in IAT scores was associated with a 12% reduction in the probability of inviting an Arab applicant for an interview. By contrast, explicit measures of stereotyping and prejudice were not predictive of interview decisions.

2.2. Hiring preferences, budget cuts, verbal slurs, social exclusion, and physical harm

* * *

If it is true that managers at least sometimes behave like other decision-makers, then a set of studies by Rudman and her colleagues warrant serious attention on the part of organizational researchers and practitioners. Rudman and Glick (2001) found that although research participants regarded female managerial applicants who presented themselves as confident, competitive, and ambitious (i.e., agentic) as highly qualified for a leadership role, the participants still discriminated against them (relative to men who were identically described) with respect to hiring decisions because the agentic women were perceived as dislikable and therefore thought to be deficient with respect to social skills. Furthermore, the likelihood of discrimination was increased to the extent that participants possessed implicit gender stereotypes concerning agentic (vs. "communal") characteristics (*see also* Jost & Kay, 2005). These findings suggest that the prescription for female "niceness," which is often internalized at an implicit, unexamined level of awareness, penalizes agentic women in the workplace (*see also* Eagly & Karau, 2002; Fiske, Bersoff, Borgida, Deaux, & Heilman, 1991; Heilman, Wallen, Fuchs, & Tamkins, 2004; *Price–Waterhouse v. Hopkins*, 1989).

. . . Rudman and Ashmore gauged implicit negative stereotypes using the IAT and found that these were related to the likelihood of performing behaviors that are unambiguously harmful toward minority groups. In the first study, implicit bias scores significantly predicted self-reported racial discrimination, including verbal slurs such as expressing racially or ethnically offensive comments and jokes ($r = .34$, $p < .01$, $n = 64$), excluding others from social gatherings and organizations because of their ethnicity ($r = .30$, $p < .05$, $n = 64$), and engaging in threat, intimidation, nonverbal hostility (e.g., giving 'the finger'), and even physically harming members of minority groups and/or their property ($r = .25$, $p < .05$, $n = 64$). In the second study, participants were asked for their recommendations about how to spread university budget cuts across several student organizations, including the marching band, drama club, political action groups, and, as the focal dependent variables, Jewish, Asian, and black student organizations. Rudman and Ashmore found that implicit bias scores predicted the likelihood that participants would engage in economic discrimination by disproportionately slashing budgets for the Jewish ($r = .38$, $n = 89$, $p < .05$), Japanese ($r = .30$, $n = 89$, $p < .05$), and black ($r = .18$, $n = 126$, $p < .05$) student associations. In both studies, the IAT again possessed strong incremental validity, predicting harmful and discriminatory behavior even after adjusting for explicit racial and ethnic attitudes.

4.   For more on how courts can use implicit bias research as evidence, *see* Jerry Kang, IMPLICIT BIAS: A PRIMER FOR COURTS, NATIONAL CENTER FOR STATE COURTS (2009) http://www.scribd.com/doc/45313723/Implicit–Bias–A–Primer-for-Courts–Kang#.

5.   Among the notable cases in which U.S. lawyers have used implicit bias evidence to attempt to prove discrimination is Dukes v. Wal–Mart Stores, Inc., 222 F.R.D. 137 (N.D.Cal. 2004), aff'd, Wal–Mart Stores v. Dukes, 509 F.3d 1186 (9th Cir. 2007), aff'd en banc, 603 F.3d 571 (9th Cir.

2010), rev'd, 131 U.S. 2541 (2011). In their motion for class certification, the plaintiffs relied on reports by several expert witnesses, including Professor William T. Bielby, a professor of sociology at the University of California, Santa Barbara. Here is a portion of Dr. Bielby's report on sources of workplace gender bias.

One way gender bias affects career outcomes is when stereotypes are allowed to affect personnel decisions. Gender stereotypes are beliefs about traits and behaviors that differ between men and women. For example, men are believed to be competitive, aggressive, assertive, strong, and independent, while women are thought to be nurturing, cooperative, supportive, and understanding. Men are assumed to place a high priority on their careers, while women are assumed to be more strongly oriented towards family, even though research demonstrates that the commitments of men and women with similar job opportunities and family situations are virtually identical.

These kinds of stereotypes are relevant to how men and women advance in careers with Wal–Mart. For example, if women are believed to be committed to and constrained by family circumstances, and men are not, women will not be given the same consideration as men for management positions that are believed to interfere with family obligations, especially if there is no reliable and systematic way to assess employees' interests in management positions.

When women perform successfully in male-dominated contexts, their accomplishments are more likely to be attributed to luck, help from others, or special circumstances rather than to their ability, whereas comparable performance by men is more likely to be attributed to their superior skills. Moreover, stereotypical behaviors that are believed to be typical of men are often viewed as inappropriate for women. For example, it is less acceptable for a married woman with young children to place a high priority on her career than it is for a married man. Similarly, a woman who behaves in a competitive, assertive, and independent manner often elicits disapproval from those around her.

Because of gender stereotypes, individuals tend to ascribe "masculine" traits to men and "feminine" traits to women, and individuals tend to assume that the prevalence of "masculine" traits among women and "feminine" traits among men is rare. A large body of research demonstrates that the tendency to invoke gender stereotypes in making judgments about people is spontaneous and automatic. As a result, people are often unaware of how stereotypes affect their perceptions and behavior, and individuals whose personal beliefs are relatively free of prejudice or bias are susceptible to stereotypes in the same ways as people who hold a personal animosity towards a social group.

In the employment context, career barriers resulting from gender stereotypes and gender bias are likely to be consequential for women working in traditionally male domains, such as the middle to upper managerial and professional ranks of large corporations, engineering divisions of firms, in the military, and in historically male-dominated industries such as skilled crafts and construction trades. At Wal–Mart, women comprise a majority of employees overall and about two-thirds of those in hourly positions, but they comprise only about a third of those in salaried management positions, and most higher level management positions have a low representation of women.

A large body of social science research demonstrates that stereotypes are especially likely to influence personnel decisions when they are based on informal, arbitrary, and subjective factors. In such settings, stereotypes can bias assessments of a woman's qualifications, contributions, and advancement potential, because perceptions are shaped by stereotypical beliefs about women generally, not by the actual skills and accomplishments of the person as an individual. In decision-making contexts characterized by arbitrary and subjective criteria and substantial decision-maker discretion, individuals tend to seek out and retain stereotyping-confirming information and ignore or minimize information that defies stereotypes.

Social research establishes clearly that the historical representation of women in a job has a substantial impact on compensation and other job rewards, mobility prospects, and workplace culture. In retailing, management has historically been viewed as "men's work" while women were viewed as appropriate for cashier and clerk positions. Wal–Mart's founder, Sam Walton, described the traditional view of men's and women's roles in the industry as follows:

> "In the old days, retailers felt the same way about women that they did about college boys, only more so. In addition to thinking women weren't free to move, they didn't think women could handle anything but the clerk jobs because the managers usually did so much of the physical labor—unloading trucks and hauling merchandise out of the stockroom on a two-wheeler, mopping the floors and cleaning the windows if necessary."

Experimental studies on stereotyping show that male and female job applicants with identical personal traits are matched according to their gender to jobs that are considered predominantly-male and predominantly-female. And studies done in both experimental and natural settings demonstrate the impact of "sex role spillover," whereby gender-linked traits associated with male-dominated occupations can profoundly affect the working climate for women.

A large body of research in industrial sociology, dating back to the 1950s, shows that individuals who find their opportunities for advancement blocked respond by lowering their goals and aspirations, and by lowering their commitment to their work compared to others with more promising career prospects. *See* http://walmartclass.com/staticdata/reports/r3.html.

E. THE ROLE OF STATISTICS

State of Alabama v. United States

304 F.2d 583 (5th Cir. 1962), aff'd per curiam, 371 U.S. 37

■ BROWN, CIRCUIT JUDGE

In the problem of racial discrimination, statistics often tell much, and Courts listen.

International Brotherhood of Teamsters v. United States

431 U.S. 324 (1977)

■ JUSTICE STEWART delivered the opinion of the Court.

* * * As of March 31, 1971, shortly after the Government filed its complaint alleging systemwide discrimination, the company had 6,472 employees. Of these, 314 (5%) were Negroes and 257 (4%) were Spanish-surnamed Americans. Of the 1,828 line drivers, however, there were only 8 (0.4%) Negroes and 5 (0.3%) Spanish-surnamed persons, and all of the Negroes had been hired after the litigation had commenced. With one exception a man who worked as a line driver at the Chicago terminal from 1950 to 1959 the company and its predecessors *did not employ a Negro on a regular basis as a line driver until 1969*. And, as the Government showed, even in 1971 there were terminals in areas of substantial Negro population where all of the company's line drivers were white. A great majority of the Negroes (83%) and Spanish-surnamed Americans (78%) who did work for the company held the lower paying city operations and serviceman jobs, whereas only 39% of the nonminority employees held jobs in those categories.

The Government bolstered its statistical evidence with the testimony of individuals who recounted over 40 specific instances of discrimination. Upon the basis of this testimony the District Court found that "(n)umerous qualified black and Spanish-surnamed American applicants who sought line driving jobs at the company over the years, either had their requests ignored, were given false or misleading information about requirements, opportunities, and application procedures, or were not considered and hired on the same basis that whites were considered and hired." Minority employees who wanted to transfer to line-driver jobs met with similar difficulties.

The company's principal response to this evidence is that statistics can never in and of themselves prove the existence of a pattern or practice of discrimination, or even establish a prima facie case shifting to the employer the burden of rebutting the inference raised by the figures. But, as even our brief summary of the evidence shows, this was not a case in which the Government relied on "statistics alone." The individuals who testified about their personal experiences with the company brought the cold numbers convincingly to life.

In any event, our cases make it unmistakably clear that "(s)tatistical analyses have served and will continue to serve an important role" in cases in which the existence of discrimination is a disputed issue. *Mayor of Philadelphia v. Educational Equality League*, 415 U.S. 605. *See also McDonnell Douglas Corp. v. Green*, 411 U.S., at 805. *Cf. Washington v. Davis*, 426 U.S. 229, 241–242. We have repeatedly approved the use of statistical proof, where it reached proportions comparable to those in this case, to establish a prima facie case of racial discrimination in jury selection cases, *see, e. g., Turner v. Fouche,* 396 U.S. 346; *Hernandez v. Texas,* 347 U.S. 475; *Norris v. Alabama,* 294 U.S. 587. Statistics are equally competent in proving employment discrimination.

————

McCleskey v. Kemp

481 U.S. 279 (1987)

■ JUSTICE POWELL delivered the opinion of the Court.

This case presents the question whether a complex statistical study that indicates a risk that racial considerations enter into capital sentencing determinations proves that petitioner McCleskey's capital sentence is unconstitutional under the Eighth or Fourteenth Amendment.

I

McCleskey, a black man, was convicted of two counts of armed robbery and one count of murder in the Superior Court of Fulton County, Georgia, on October 12, 1978. * * *

* * * McCleskey proffered a statistical study performed by Professors David C. Baldus, Charles Pulaski, and George Woodworth (the Baldus study) that purports to show a disparity in the imposition of the death sentence in Georgia based on the race of the murder victim and, to a lesser extent, the race of the defendant. The Baldus study is actually two sophisticated statistical studies that examine over 2,000 murder cases that occurred in Georgia during the 1970's. The raw numbers collected by Professor Baldus indicate that defendants charged with killing white persons received the death penalty in 11% of the cases, but defendants charged with killing blacks received the death penalty in only 1% of the cases. The raw numbers also indicate a reverse racial disparity according to the race of the defendant: 4% of the black defendants received the death penalty, as opposed to 7% of the white defendants.

Baldus also divided the cases according to the combination of the race of the defendant and the race of the victim. He found that the death penalty was assessed in 22% of the cases involving black defendants and white victims; 8% of the cases involving white defendants and white victims; 1% of the cases involving black defendants and black victims; and 3% of the cases involving white defendants and black victims.

Similarly, Baldus found that prosecutors sought the death penalty in 70% of the cases involving black defendants and white victims; 32% of the cases involving white defendants and white victims; 15% of the cases involving black defendants and black victims; and 19% of the cases involving white defendants and black victims.

Baldus subjected his data to an extensive analysis, taking account of 230 variables that could have explained the disparities on nonracial grounds. One of his models concludes that, even after taking account of 39 nonracial variables, defendants charged with killing white victims were 4.3 times as likely to receive a death sentence as defendants charged with killing blacks. According to this model, black defendants were 1.1 times as likely to receive a death sentence as other defendants. Thus, the Baldus study indicates that black defendants, such as McCleskey, who kill white victims have the greatest likelihood of receiving the death penalty.

II

McCleskey's first claim is that the Georgia capital punishment statute violates the Equal Protection Clause of the Fourteenth Amendment. He argues that race has infected the administration of Georgia's statute in two ways: persons who murder whites are more likely to be sentenced to death than persons who murder blacks, and black murderers are more likely to be sentenced to death than white murderers.

As a black defendant who killed a white victim, McCleskey claims that the Baldus study demonstrates that he was discriminated against because of his race and because of the race of his victim. In its broadest form, McCleskey's claim of discrimination extends to every actor in the Georgia capital sentencing process, from the prosecutor who sought the death penalty and the jury that imposed the sentence to the State itself that enacted the capital punishment statute and allows it to remain in effect despite its allegedly discriminatory application. We agree with the Court of Appeals, and every other court that has considered such a challenge, that this claim must fail.

A.

Our analysis begins with the basic principle that a defendant who alleges an equal protection violation has the burden of proving "the existence of purposeful discrimination." *Whitus v. Georgia*, 385 U. S. 545 (1967). A corollary to this principle is that a criminal defendant must prove that the purposeful discrimination "had a discriminatory effect" on him. *Wayte v. United States*, 470 U. S. 598 (1985). Thus, to prevail under the Equal Protection Clause, McCleskey must prove that the decisionmakers in his case acted with discriminatory purpose. He offers no evidence specific to his own case that would support an inference that racial considerations played a part in his sentence. Instead, he relies solely on the Baldus study.
* * *

V.

Two additional concerns inform our decision in this case. First, McCleskey's claim, taken to its logical conclusion, throws into serious question the principles that underlie our entire criminal justice system. The Eighth Amendment is not limited in application to capital punishment, but applies to all penalties. *Solem v. Helm*, 463 U. S. 277, 289–290 (1983); *see Rummel v. Estelle*, 445 U. S. 263, 293 (1980) (Powell, J., dissenting). Thus, if we accepted McCleskey's claim that racial bias has impermissibly tainted the capital sentencing decision, we could soon be faced with similar claims as to other types of penalty. Moreover, the claim that his sentence rests on the irrelevant factor of race easily could be extended to apply to claims based on unexplained discrepancies that correlate to membership in other minority groups, and even to gender. Similarly, since McCleskey's claim relates to the race of his victim, other claims could apply with equally logical force to statistical disparities that correlate with the race or sex of other actors in the criminal justice system, such as defense attorneys or judges. Also, there is no logical reason that such a claim need be limited to racial or sexual bias. If arbitrary and capricious punishment is the touchstone under the Eighth Amendment, such a claim could—at least in theory—be based upon any arbitrary variable, such as the defendant's facial characteristics, or the physical attractiveness of the defendant or the victim, that some statistical study indicates may be influential in jury decisionmaking. As these examples illustrate, there is no limiting principle to the type of challenge brought by McCleskey.

■ Justice Brennan, with whom Justice Marshall joins, and with whom Justice Blackmun and Justice Stevens join in all but Part I, dissenting.

    * * *

II

At some point in this case, Warren McCleskey doubtless asked his lawyer whether a jury was likely to sentence him to die. A candid reply to this question would have been disturbing. First, counsel would have to tell McCleskey that few of the details of the crime or of McCleskey's past criminal conduct were more important than the fact that his victim was white. Furthermore, counsel would feel bound to tell McCleskey that defendants charged with killing white victims in Georgia are 4.3 times as likely to be sentenced to death as defendants charged with killing blacks. In addition, frankness would compel the disclosure that it was more likely than not that the race of McCleskey's victim would determine whether he received a death sentence: 6 of every 11 defendants convicted of killing a white person would not have received the death penalty if their victims had been black, while, among defendants with aggravating and mitigating factors comparable to McCleskey's, 20 of every 34 would not have been sentenced to die if their victims had been black. Finally, the assessment would not be complete without the information that cases involving black defendants and white victims are more likely to result in a death sentence than cases featuring any other racial combination of defendant and victim. The story could be told in a variety of ways, but McCleskey could not fail to grasp its essential narrative line: there was a significant chance that race would play a prominent role in determining if he lived or died.

The Court today holds that Warren McCleskey's sentence was constitutionally imposed. It finds no fault in a system in which lawyers must tell their clients that race casts a large shadow on the capital sentencing process. The Court arrives at this conclusion by stating that the Baldus study cannot "prove that race enters into any capital sentencing decisions or that race was a factor in McCleskey's particular case." Ante at 481 U. S. 308. Since, according to Professor Baldus, we cannot say "to a moral certainty" that race influenced a decision, we can identify only "a likelihood that a particular factor entered into some decisions," and "a discrepancy that appears to correlate with race." This "likelihood" and "discrep-

ancy," holds the Court, is insufficient to establish a constitutional violation.
* * *

V

... [I]t has been scarcely a generation since this Court's first decision striking down racial segregation, and barely two decades since the legislative prohibition of racial discrimination in major domains of national life. These have been honorable steps, but we cannot pretend that in three decades we have completely escaped the grip of a historical legacy spanning centuries. Warren McCleskey's evidence confronts us with the subtle and persistent influence of the past. His message is a disturbing one to a society that has formally repudiated racism, and a frustrating one to a Nation accustomed to regarding its destiny as the product of its own will. Nonetheless, we ignore him at our peril, for we remain imprisoned by the past as long as we deny its influence in the present.

It is tempting to pretend that minorities on death row share a fate in no way connected to our own, that our treatment of them sounds no echoes beyond the chambers in which they die. Such an illusion is ultimately corrosive, for the reverberations of injustice are not so easily confined. "The destinies of the two races in this country are indissolubly linked together," [*Plessy v. Ferguson*], at 560 (Harlan, J., dissenting), and the way in which we choose those who will die reveals the depth of moral commitment among the living.

The Court's decision today will not change what attorneys in Georgia tell other Warren McCleskeys about their chances of execution. Nothing will soften the harsh message they must convey, nor alter the prospect that race undoubtedly will continue to be a topic of discussion. McCleskey's evidence will not have obtained judicial acceptance, but that will not affect what is said on death row. However many criticisms of today's decision may be rendered, these painful conversations will serve as the most eloquent dissents of all.

———

Brown v. City of Oneonta, New York

221 F.3d 329 (2d Cir. 2000)

[AMENDED OPINION]

■ WALKER, CIRCUIT JUDGE:

* * * Oneonta, a small town in upstate New York about sixty miles west of Albany, has about 10,000 full-time residents. In addition, some 7,500 students attend and reside at the State University of New York College at Oneonta ("SUCO"). The people in Oneonta are for the most part white. Fewer than three hundred blacks live in the town, and just two percent of the students at SUCO are black.

On September 4, 1992, shortly before 2:00 a.m., someone broke into a house just outside Oneonta and attacked a seventy-seven-year-old woman. The woman told the police who responded to the scene that she could not identify her assailant's face, but that he was wielding a knife; that he was a black man, based on her view of his hand and forearm; and that he was young, because of the speed with which he crossed her room. She also told the police that, as they struggled, the suspect had cut himself on the hand with the knife. A police canine unit tracked the assailant's scent from the scene of the crime toward the SUCO campus, but lost the trail after several hundred yards.

The police immediately contacted SUCO and requested a list of its black male students. An official at SUCO supplied the list, and the police attempted to locate and question every black male student at SUCO. This endeavor produced no suspects. Then, over the next several days, the police conducted a "sweep" of Oneonta, stopping and questioning non-white persons on the streets and inspecting their hands for cuts. More than two hundred persons were questioned during that period, but no suspect was apprehended. Those persons whose names appeared on the SUCO list and those who were approached and questioned by the police, believing that they had been unlawfully singled out because of their race, decided to seek redress. * * *

Plaintiffs ... contend that defendants utilized an express racial classification by stopping and questioning plaintiffs solely on the basis of their race. Plaintiffs assert that the district court erred in requiring them to plead the existence of a similarly situated group of non-minority individuals that were treated differently in the investigation of a crime.

* * * Plaintiffs do not allege that upon hearing that a violent crime had been committed, the police used an established profile of violent criminals to determine that the suspect must have been black. Nor do they allege that the defendant law enforcement agencies have a regular policy based upon racial stereotypes that all black Oneonta residents be questioned whenever a violent crime is reported. In short, plaintiffs' factual premise is not supported by the pleadings: they were not questioned solely on the basis of their race. They were questioned on the altogether legitimate basis of a physical description given by the victim of a crime. Defendants' policy was race-neutral on its face; their policy was to investigate crimes by interviewing the victim, getting a description of the assailant, and seeking out persons who matched that description. This description contained not only race, but also gender and age, as well as the possibility of a cut on the hand. In acting on the description provided by the victim of the assault—a description that included race as one of several elements—defendants did not engage in a suspect racial classification that would draw strict scrutiny. The description, which originated not with the state but with the victim, was a legitimate classification within which potential suspects might be found.

* * * The Equal Protection Clause, however, has long been interpreted to extend to governmental action that has a disparate impact on a minority group only when that action was undertaken with discriminatory intent. See *Washington v. Davis*, 426 U.S. 229, 239–41 (1976). Without additional evidence of discriminatory animus, the disparate impact of an investigation

such as the one in this case is insufficient to sustain an equal protection claim.

———

D.H. and Others v. The Czech Republic

(13 November 2007)

■ Grand Chamber, European Court of Human Rights

* * *

18. ... [T]he total number of pupils placed in special schools in Ostrava came to 1,360, of whom 762 (56%) were Roma. Conversely, Roma represented only 2.26% of the total of 33,372 primary-school pupils in Ostrava. Further, although only 1.8% of non-Roma pupils were placed in special schools, in Ostrava the proportion of Roma pupils assigned to such schools was 50.3%. Accordingly, a Roma child in Ostrava was 27 times more likely to be placed in a special school than a non-Roma child.

According to data from the European Monitoring Centre for Racism and Xenophobia (now the European Union Agency for Fundamental Rights), more than half of Roma children in the Czech Republic attend special schools.

The Advisory Committee on the Framework Convention for the Protection of National Minorities observed in its report of 26 October 2005 that, according to unofficial estimates, the Roma represent up to 70% of pupils enrolled in special schools.

Lastly, according to a comparison of data on fifteen countries, including countries from Europe, Asia and North America, gathered by the OECD in 1999 and cited in the observations of the International Step by Step Association, the Roma Education Fund and the European Early Childhood Research Association, the Czech Republic ranked second highest in terms of placing children with physiological impairments in special schools and in third place in the table of countries placing children with learning difficulties in such schools. Further, of the eight countries who had provided data on the schooling of children whose difficulties arose from social factors, the Czech Republic was the only one to use special schools. The other countries concerned almost exclusively used ordinary schools for the education of such children.

175. The Court has established in its case law that discrimination means treating differently, without an objective and reasonable justification, persons in relevantly similar situations (*Willis v. the United Kingdom*, no. 36042/97, § 48, ECtHR 2002–IV; and *Okpisz v. Germany*, no. 59140/00, § 33, 25 October 2005). However, Article 14 does not prohibit a member State from treating groups differently in order to correct "factual inequalities" between them; indeed in certain circumstances a failure to attempt to correct inequality through different treatment may in itself give rise to a breach of the Article ("*Case relating to certain aspects of the laws on the use of languages in education in Belgium*"), judgment of 23 July 1968, Series A no. 6, § 10; *Thlimmenos v. Greece* [GC], no. 34369/97, § 44, ECtHR 2000–

IV; and *Stec and Others v. the United Kingdom* [GC], no. 65731/01, § 51, ECtHR 2006–...). The Court has also accepted that a general policy or measure that has disproportionately prejudicial effects on a particular group may be considered discriminatory notwithstanding that it is not specifically aimed at that group (*Hugh Jordan v. the United Kingdom*, no. 24746/94, § 154, 4 May 2001; and *Hoogendijk v. the Netherlands* (Dec.), no. 58461/00, 6 January 2005), and that discrimination potentially contrary to the Convention may result from a de facto situation (*Zarb Adami v. Malta*, no. 17209/02, § 76, ECtHR 2006–...).

176. Discrimination on account of, inter alia, a person's ethnic origin is a form of racial discrimination. Racial discrimination is a particularly invidious kind of discrimination and, in view of its perilous consequences, requires from the authorities special vigilance and a vigorous reaction. It is for this reason that the authorities must use all available means to combat racism, thereby reinforcing democracy's vision of a society in which diversity is not perceived as a threat but as a source of enrichment (*Nachova and Others v. Bulgaria* [GC], nos. 43577/98 and 43579/98, § 145, ECtHR 2005–...; and *Timishev v. Russia*, nos. 55762/00 and 55974/00, § 56, ECtHR 2005–...). The Court has also held that no difference in treatment which is based exclusively or to a decisive extent on a person's ethnic origin is capable of being objectively justified in a contemporary democratic society built on the principles of pluralism and respect for different cultures (*Timishev*, cited above, § 58).

177. As to the burden of proof in this sphere, the Court has established that once the applicant has shown a difference in treatment, it is for the Government to show that it was justified (see, among other authorities, *Chassagnou and Others v. France* [GC], nos. 25088/94, 28331/95 and 28443/95, §§ 91–92, ECtHR 1999–III; and *Timishev*, cited above, § 57).

179. The Court has also recognised that Convention proceedings do not in all cases lend themselves to a rigorous application of the principle *affirmanti incumbit probatio* (he who alleges something must prove that allegation— *Aktaş v. Turkey* (extracts), no. 24351/94, § 272, ECtHR 2003–V). In certain circumstances, where the events in issue lie wholly, or in large part, within the exclusive knowledge of the authorities, the burden of proof may be regarded as resting on the authorities to provide a satisfactory and convincing explanation (*Salman v. Turkey* [GC], no. 21986/93, § 100, ECtHR 2000–VII; and *Anguelova v. Bulgaria*, no. 38361/97, § 111, ECtHR 2002–IV). In the case of *Nachova and Others*, cited above, § 157), the Court did not rule out requiring a respondent Government to disprove an arguable allegation of discrimination in certain cases, even though it considered that it would be difficult to do so in that particular case in which the allegation was that an act of violence had been motivated by racial prejudice. It noted in that connection that in the legal systems of many countries proof of the discriminatory effect of a policy, decision or practice would dispense with the need to prove intent in respect of alleged discrimination in employment or in the provision of services.

180. As to whether statistics can constitute evidence, the Court has in the past stated that statistics could not in themselves disclose a practice which could be classified as discriminatory (*Hugh Jordan*, cited above, § 154).

However, in more recent cases on the question of discrimination, in which the applicants alleged a difference in the effect of a general measure or *de facto* situation (*Hoogendijk*, cited above; and *Zarb Adami*, cited above, §§ 77–78), the Court relied extensively on statistics produced by the parties to establish a difference in treatment between two groups (men and women) in similar situations.

Thus, in the *Hoogendijk* decision the Court stated: "[W]here an applicant is able to show, on the basis of undisputed official statistics, the existence of a prima facie indication that a specific rule—although formulated in a neutral manner—in fact affects a clearly higher percentage of women than men, it is for the respondent Government to show that this is the result of objective factors unrelated to any discrimination on grounds of sex. If the onus of demonstrating that a difference in impact for men and women is not in practice discriminatory does not shift to the respondent Government, it will be in practice extremely difficult for applicants to prove indirect discrimination."

181.   Lastly, as noted in previous cases, the vulnerable position of Roma/Gypsies means that special consideration should be given to their needs and their different lifestyle both in the relevant regulatory framework and in reaching decisions in particular cases (*Chapman v. the United Kingdom* [GC], no. 27238/95, § 96, ECtHR 2001-I; and *Connors v. the United Kingdom*, no. 66746/01, § 84, 27 May 2004).

In *Chapman* (cited above, §§ 93–94), the Court also observed that there could be said to be an emerging international consensus amongst the Contracting States of the Council of Europe recognising the special needs of minorities and an obligation to protect their security, identity and lifestyle, not only for the purpose of safeguarding the interests of the minorities themselves but to preserve a cultural diversity of value to the whole community.

188.   In these circumstances, the Court considers that when it comes to assessing the impact of a measure or practice on an individual or group, statistics which appear on critical examination to be reliable and significant will be sufficient to constitute the prima facie evidence the applicant is required to produce. This does not, however, mean that indirect discrimination cannot be proved without statistical evidence.

189.   Where an applicant alleging indirect discrimination thus establishes a rebuttable presumption that the effect of a measure or practice is discriminatory, the burden then shifts to the respondent State, which must show that the difference in treatment is not discriminatory (see, mutatis mutandis, *Nachova and Others*, cited above, § 157). Regard being had in particular to the specificity of the facts and the nature of the allegations made in this type of case (*ibid.*, § 147), it would be extremely difficult in practice for applicants to prove indirect discrimination without such a shift in the burden of proof.

194.   Where it has been shown that legislation produces such a discriminatory effect, the Grand Chamber considers that, as with cases concerning employment or the provision of services, it is not necessary in cases in the educational sphere (*see, mutatis mutandis, Nachova and Others*, cited

above, § 157) to prove any discriminatory intent on the part of the relevant authorities (*see* paragraph 184 above).

195.   In these circumstances, the evidence submitted by the applicants can be regarded as sufficiently reliable and significant to give rise to a strong presumption of indirect discrimination. The burden of proof must therefore shift to the Government, which must show that the difference in the impact of the legislation was the result of objective factors unrelated to ethnic origin.

Why France Needs to Collect Data on Racial Identity.... In A French Way

31 Hastings International and Comparative Law Review 735, 736–37 (2008)

■ DAVID B. OPPENHEIMER

"[1] Statistics by ethnic categories are dangerous because they stigmatize people and are likely to support xenophobic or racist behavior. [2] Statistics by ethnic categories are necessary to fight against discrimination."—Laurent Thévenot

* * * It is central to the French ideal of equality and citizenship that the state refrain from making distinctions based on race or ethnicity. The principle has its roots in the revolution of 1789 and the resulting Declaration of the Rights of Man and Citizen. The most recent French Constitution, adopted in 1958 carries forward this principle, banning all distinctions based on racial identity. The French state is therefore generally barred from collecting data that we regard as commonplace in the United States. This bar was recently affirmed by the Conseil Constitutionnel, which rejected part of a bill passed by the French parliament permitting the collection of statistics reporting racial and ethnic identity for the purpose of measuring discrimination.

But to bar state recognition of race is not to eliminate racism. While racial/ethnic/religious discrimination and inequality may be difficult to measure in France, most observers agree that it is a serious problem. And, to comply with European law, France has now adopted legislation prohibiting "indirect" employment discrimination, and thus adopting the "adverse impact" theory of anti-discrimination law. Such discrimination is commonly proven by examining racial or ethnic identification data; for example, by comparing workforce data collected through a national census with employer utilization data to prove employment discrimination. Yet such data are not currently available in France.

Rihal v. London Borough of Ealing

[2004] EWCA Civ 623, Case No: A1/2003/2111 EATRF

In The UK Supreme Court Of Judicature

Court Of Appeal (Civil Division)

■ APPEAL FROM THE EMPLOYMENT APPEAL TRIBUNAL

[The employment tribunal found racial discrimination under Great Britain's Race Relations Act based partially on a disparity between the local population, which was 40% nonwhite, the senior management in other local departments, which was 25% nonwhite, and the senior management of the defendant's local housing department, which was virtually all white. The Court of Appeal affirmed the tribunal's decision.]

Lord Justice SIDLEY, concurring:

"The sharp ethnic imbalance revealed by Ealing's own figures was enough to entitle—indeed arguably to require—the tribunal to look for a convincing non-racial reason. In a well-run organisation there will be procedures, training and monitoring data capable of reassuring a tribunal that everyone has been treated on an equal footing and that any imbalances are caused by fortuitous or extraneous factors. When the tribunal failed to find an acceptable non-racial reason for the imbalance of which Mr. Rihal's history formed part, they were entitled to infer that there was none" (at Par. 53).

————

NOTES

1. Has Lord Justice Sidley stated a rule equally applicable in the United States? Would it be applicable in France?

2. How does the majority opinion's reasoning for rejecting McClesky's Eighth Amendment claim based on statistical evidence relate to assumptions about direct versus indirect (or intentional versus unintentional) discrimination? To the law's prohibition against exclusion versus the duty to accommodate?

3. In an important 1990 article, Professor Vicki Schultz asked how we should make sense of statistical evidence of the existence of sex segregation in the workplace—of "men's work" and "women's work"—with women's work occupying the lower rungs of the job market, by wage and status. Why does it exist, she asks, "Who is responsible for it? Is it an injustice, or an inevitability?"

Professor Schultz begins to construct an answer to her question by discussing the case of *EEOC v. Sears, Roebuck & Co.*, 628 F.Supp. 1264 (N.D. Ill. 1986), *aff'd*, 839 F.2d 302 (7th Cir. 1988), in which the EEOC relied on statistical evidence in an attempt to prove that Sears engaged in sex discrimination by hiring mostly men into commissioned sales jobs, and mostly women into non-commissioned jobs. Sears countered by offering a "lack of interest defense," which was accepted by the district court, which concluded that women didn't want commissioned jobs. Schultz locates the defense in a history of rejecting statistical proof of sex discrimination dating to the commencement of Title VII litigation. Employers successfully argued that, as Schultz puts it, women, "grow up wanting to do women's work, and we can't force them to do work they don't want to do."

> "Judges' failure to recognize the influence of historical discrimination on women's work aspirations has led them to adopt an anti-institutional, individualistic approach to evaluating evidence and con-

ceptualizing discrimination in sex segregation cases. The definition of discrimination is limited to taking specific actions to bar women from exercising what are imagined to be preexisting preferences for nontraditional work.... To a large extent, however, the structures of the work world that disempower most working women from ever aspiring to nontraditional work are left unexamined.

This approach was not inevitable. Before the first sex discrimination case raising the lack of interest argument was decided, the courts had already decided a landmark series of race discrimination cases addressing the same argument. In these early race discrimination cases, the courts applied evidentiary standards that presumed that continuing patterns of racial segregation were attributable to historical labor market discrimination, rather than to minorities' independent preferences for lower-paying, less-challenging jobs. This approach recognized that human choices are never formed in a vacuum and that people's work aspirations are inevitably shaped by the job opportunities that have historically been available to them, as well as by their experiences in the work structures and relations of which they have been a part." Vicki Schultz, *Telling Stories About Women and Work: Judicial Interpretations of Sex Segregation in the Workplace in Title VII Cases Raising the Lack of Interest Argument*, 103 Harv. L. Rev. 1749, 1751–56, 1758–59, 1769–70, 1840–43 (1990).

4. Do the approaches to proving discrimination set forth in this chapter work well? Consider this critique from Professor Sandra Sperino:

"The current discrimination frameworks remain largely unconnected to this changing practical and theoretical landscape. The division of discrimination claims into intentional claims and disparate impact claims ignores that discrimination may result from a combination of unconscious bias and traditionally conceived intentional bias or perhaps through unconscious bias alone. Neither disparate impact nor disparate treatment recognizes the possibility of negligent discrimination. Structural discrimination is not fully captured within any of the frameworks.

In the individual disparate treatment context, the courts largely seem to assume discrimination as a fairly constant bad motive that resides in an individual. The proof structures appear tied to a concept of discrimination that seeks to ferret out a single decisionmaker (or small group of decisionmakers) who acted with a certain kind of animus toward an individual plaintiff. This narrow concept of intent ignores the possibility of disparate influences and structural discrimination. None of the proof structures appropriately capture intersectional discrimination.

Further, courts have failed to fully explore whether the substantive equality model underlying disparate impact applies in other contexts or whether the current disparate impact tests fairly captures all conduct that might limit or tend to limit a plaintiff's opportunities. Plaintiffs unable to offer proof of specific practices that create gross statistical disparities under the disparate impact framework are largely left with models based on formal equality." Sandra F. Sperino, *Rethinking Discrimination Law*, http://ssrn.com/abstract=1759458.

5.   The Constitution of India, adopted following India's independence, abolished the practice "untouchability." From 1931–2010, the Indian Census thus asked no questions about caste. But in 2010 the cabinet decided that the 2011 census would ask people to voluntarily self-identify their caste, in order to help the government enforce anti-discrimination laws, and effectuate affirmative action programs. *See* http://www.bbc.co.uk/news/world-south-asia–11241916.

F.   DISCRIMINATION AS CRIME

Procedural Path Dependence: Discrimination and the Civil–Criminal Divide

85 Washington University Law Review Vol. 1315, 1340 (2008)

■ JULIE C. SUK

E.   *Advantages of Criminal Procedure*

[M]any features of French criminal procedure make it easier for victims of discrimination to unearth the evidence from which disparate treatment may be inferred. Most importantly, the *Code de procedure pénale* construes a far more active role for the *juge d'instruction*, the judge investigating the crime, than the limited investigatory role of the civil judge under the *Code de procédure civile*. Furthermore, recordings made without the adversary's knowledge are admissible in criminal proceedings, unlike in civil proceedings. In addition, the principle of the *"liberté des preuves,"* freedom of means of proof, makes it more common in criminal proceedings for witness testimony to be utilized. Finally, the possibility for victims and associations to participate in criminal proceedings as civil parties, with damages awarded upon a conviction, makes it efficient for plaintiffs to pursue remedies through criminal law.

A victim of discrimination can file a complaint with the prosecutor, who then enlists a *juge d'instruction*, an investigating judge, to investigate the complaint. The *juge d'instruction* is strictly separate from the judge who hears the case at trial. The victim of discrimination can also go directly to the *juge d'instruction*. The rules of criminal procedure make investigation by the *juge d'instruction* mandatory for all *crimes* but discretionary for *délits*. Because discrimination is a *délit*, not all claims of discrimination require investigation. But if a victim goes directly to the *juge d'instruction* and files a complaint as a civil party, the judge will ordinarily initiate an investigation.

Article 81 of the Code of Criminal Procedure provides that the *juge d'instruction* is to proceed, consistent with the law, in all acts of investigation that he judges useful for the manifestation of truth. This duty is in stark contrast with the principles underlying the Code of Civil Procedure, which charges the parties with the primary duty of establishing the facts in dispute between them. The Code of Criminal Procedure also puts the search for truth at the center of the judge's role, whereas the Code of Civil Procedure construes the judge's role as facilitating the resolution of a dispute between equal private parties. Accordingly, the *juge d'instruction* has very broad powers to investigate, which she is obliged to utilize as she sees fit to discover the truth. She questions the accused, as well as witnesses, whom she can require to appear for questioning. She also has broad search and seizure power. Article 94 allows her to order searches of any place where objects may be discovered that will lead to the revelation of the truth. Although some documents cannot be discovered due to various forms of professional privilege, the judge can order the police to seize all nonprivileged documents that appear useful for the revelation of the truth.

Thus, in an employment discrimination case, investigation by the *juge d'instruction* is very useful for uncovering evidence of both disparate treatment and discriminatory intent that is in the hands of the employer. In the cases that have resulted in findings of employer liability for discrimination, there is usually evidence, either documentary or testimonial, that could not have emerged in a civil proceeding. For instance, in 2002, the owner of "Hotel La Villa" was convicted of racial discrimination in hiring after an investigation uncovered the CVs of various applicants for a porter job that were marked "Black," or "Black, non, non!" In another case resulting in conviction of an Ikea recruiter, the investigation uncovered an e-mail memorandum concerning the recruitment of employees responsible for the distribution of a catalogue. The e-mail stated, "For this type of work, do not recruit persons of color since it's unfortunate to say that people open their doors to them less easily and it is important that we work quickly." In June 2006, a salon owner was convicted of racial discrimination after an investigation authorized by the *juge d'instruction*. The investigation consisted of oral interviews with the alleged victim, the defendant, and third-party witnesses. The alleged victim, a black woman, testified that she had appeared at the salon with her CV in response to a job advertisement she received from an employment agency, and that the salon owner said she was no longer looking for an employee. A friend of the victim, a white woman, testified she applied for the same job the next day, describing her qualifications as identical to those of the victim. The salon owner offered her an interview for the job. The defendant salon owner admitted: "Yes, I refused her application because I was looking for a white employee because that corresponds better to the clientele." When asked why she thought a black hairdresser would harm the salon or its clients, the defendant answered, "I don't know. I feel better with people of my color." She was then asked, "Are you racist?" She replied, "No, not necessarily."

Recently, the Paris Court of Appeals convicted the cosmetics giant L'Oréal, two of its subsidiaries, and temporary employment agencies, for racial discrimination in hiring, reversing a trial court's acquittal. In that case, a criminal investigation revealed a document and testimony by witnesses that the company was searching for a woman of the "type BBR." This expression, standing for "bleu, blanc, rouge," the colors of the French flag, is commonly associated with the Front National, an openly anti-immigrant political party in France. The document came to light because an employee of L'Oréal who had worked in recruitment had brought the matter to SOS–Racisme's attention, which led to the filing of a criminal charge. The recruiter testified the company had specifically instructed her not to hire persons of color. Initially, the trial court acquitted all the defendants on the grounds that the proceeding had only presented "suppositions and approximations." However, the Court of Appeals held that the facts constituted discrimination in hiring.

Furthermore, recordings made during testing operations are valid forms of evidence in criminal proceedings, in contrast to the civil context. The *Cour de cassation* has determined that recordings made without the knowledge of the employer do not constitute a crime of violating the private life of the employer. In that case, the recording consisted only of a telephone conversation discussing the possible firing of an employee and no private matters. Since criminal liability is not imposed for making such recordings, they can be used as evidence consistent with the rules of criminal procedure.

The use of witness testimony of testing operations has been blessed by the *Cour de cassation* as a legitimate means of proving discrimination in violation of *Code pénal* Articles 225–1 and 2. Initially, some lower courts were excluding testimony by witnesses to testing operations organized by groups like SOS–Racisme on the grounds that allowing such testimony violated the defendant's right to a fair defense and the presumption of innocence. Some judges dismissed the probative value of such witness testimony, particularly due to the lack of supervision by a police officer or bailiff. In a June 2002 decision, the *Cour de cassation* held that "[n]o legal provision permits criminal judges to dismiss methods of proof produced by the parties for the sole motive that they were obtained through an illicit or disloyal means." Rather, the judges were instructed to consider the probative value of the testimony after having submitted it to an adversarial discussion.

As a result, testing operations and recordings have played an important role in highly publicized cases of discrimination that resulted in convictions over the last few years. Most notably, in November 2002, Moulin Rouge, the famous Parisian nightclub, was convicted for discrimination in hiring, with a fine of €10,000. After Moulin Rouge had advertised a position for a host in the main cabaret hall, an employment agency recommended a young man of Senegalese origin, Abdoulaye Marega. A Moulin Rouge representative told the employment agency representative over the telephone "[w]e only hire people of color in the kitchen, not in the main hall." To obtain proof, SOS–Racisme organized a testing operation in which two black men presented themselves, with hidden recording devices, as candidates for the position. They were told that they would not be hired because the job required fluency in both English and Spanish, a requirement that had not been included in the job description. After these events, the employment agency representative visited Moulin Rouge, asking for an explanation of these new requirements. This conversation was recorded by hidden camera, in which the Moulin Rouge representative said that they do not hire people of color in the main hall.

If a plaintiff in a civil proceeding presented such evidence to prove disparate treatment, it would not be admissible under Article 9 of the *Code de procédure civile*. But when the evidence was submitted to the prosecutor, the prosecutor referred the case for an investigation, during which it was confirmed that all of the persons of color employed by Moulin Rouge worked in the kitchen, not in the main hall. The *Tribunal correctionnel de Paris* convicted Moulin Rouge under *Code pénal* Articles 225–1 and 225–2. In addition to the €10,000 fine imposed on Moulin Rouge, the nightclub was ordered to pay damages in the amount of €4,500 to the victim and €2,300 to SOS–Racisme for its participation as *partie civile*. The Moulin Rouge personnel director who communicated the discriminatory preferences was also convicted and fined €3,000. These judgments were affirmed on appeal. These examples highlight the ways in which criminal procedure enables persons who purport to be victims of discrimination to discover evidence confirming their assertions. In France, because anti-racist organizations have developed testing operations as their primary means of aiding persons claiming discrimination, the difficulty of using nonconsensual recordings as evidence in civil proceedings effectively excludes the only proof that a victim is likely to have. Establishing something as seemingly straightforward as the existence of disparate treatment of candidates of different races (whether motivated by racial animus or not) can be difficult without evidence from the testing operations. Because the job candidate cannot compel discovery of employer documents without first presenting some evidence of disparity, the difficulties of using testing evidence and the difficulties of obtaining employer documents are the main problems faced by employment discrimination plaintiffs in civil cases. Both of these problems are overcome by commencing criminal proceedings.

Furthermore, because victims can participate as civil parties to criminal proceedings and obtain damages through such proceedings, victims have little incentive to proceed in civil proceedings with the aid of a private attorney. Filing a criminal complaint that gives rise to a state-funded investigation is more cost-effective for victims of discrimination. As a result, racial discrimination in hiring is, for the most part, a matter of criminal law in France.

F. The Persistence of Criminal Intent

One consequence of concentrating discriminatory hiring cases in criminal proceedings is that criminal law's emphasis on the element of intent shapes the legal concept of discrimination. Combined with the defendant's presumption of innocence, it is very difficult for prosecutors to prove infractions of the criminal anti-discrimination provision, even when there is evidence of disparate treatment. As a result, even when personnel documents and testing operations unearth strong evidence of the disparate treatment, the burden is never on the employer to justify the disparity with a nondiscriminatory reason. Rather, the prosecution carries the burden of showing that the disparate treatment is motivated by the discriminatory intent of the employer. This is crucial because it is a fundamental and general principle of the *Code pénal* that there is no *crime* or *délit* without the intention to commit it.

In criminal proceedings, the defendant benefits from the presumption of innocence. As a practical matter, this presumption functions to raise the prosecutor's burden of proof. French criminal procedure does not employ different levels of standards of proof like the U.S. system. There is nothing like a "beyond a reasonable doubt" standard to be distinguished from the "preponderance of evidence" standard in civil cases. There is only one standard of proof for both civil and criminal proceedings: the *"intime conviction"* or "inner conviction" of the judge. Nonetheless, because the accused is presumed innocent, the prosecutor must prove the element of intent and cannot benefit from the burden-shifting framework that has been introduced into the civil liability regime, wherein simply establishing disparity of treatment between members of different groups could shift the burden to the employer to show that the disparity has a nondiscriminatory justification.

It appears that all of the recent cases in which an employer has been found liable of discrimination have included clear, direct evidence of intent to discriminate on the basis of race or origin, the "smoking gun" in American parlance. In all the examples discussed, it was not merely evidence of disparity, that is, the failure to hire persons of color, that sufficed to find discrimination. There was always a document or testimony that clearly stated the intent of the defendant to exclude persons of color. Prosecutors tend not to attempt to prove discrimination without direct evidence of discriminatory intent that can be clearly attributed to an identifiable defendant. Thus, even when criminal proceedings are brought, the vast majority result in dismissal for insufficiency of evidence.

The 2001 law, in adopting a burden-shifting framework for circumstantial cases, explicitly reserved this framework for civil cases only. As employers and their human resources departments become more and more aware of the legal prohibition of discrimination, they will likely be more cautious to prevent traces of discriminatory intent, even if they do consciously exclude racial minorities when they hire.

————

NOTES

1. Would this work in the U.S.? Could discrimination be a crime? Would prosecutors take discrimination cases seriously? Would plaintiffs prefer seeing perpetrators punished instead of suing them for damages? (Of course, the two are not mutually exclusive). Would juries convict companies of discrimination? How strong would the evidence need to be to gain a conviction? Would white juries (and most juries are mostly white) convict white executives of discriminating against Black employees? Consider that under U.S. law, a criminal conviction requires proof beyond a reasonable doubt, and the defendant cannot be required to testify.

2. The India Protection of Civil Rights Act of 1955, excerpted earlier in this chapter in note 4 following the D.H. case, provides that a violation of the Act is punishable by one to six months imprisonment and a fine of between Rs 100–Rs 500. The Prevention of Atrocities Act of 1989 provides for punishment of up to five years imprisonment.

There are conflicting reports of how successful criminal prosecutions have been under the Acts. According to the Ministry of Social Welfare's report on the Prevention of Atrocities Act in 2007, there were 35,352 cases registered with the police in 2007. The report indicates that 31 percent of cases end in conviction. The report reveals that under the Protection of Civil Rights Act in 2007, there were 211 cases registered with the police. The report indicates that 14.3 percent of cases end in conviction. ANNUAL REPORT ON THE SCHEDULED CASTES AND THE SCHEDULED TRIBES (PREVENTION OF ATROCITIES) ACT, 1989 FOR 2007, 11, *available at* http://socialjustice.nic.in/policiesacts1.php. ANNUAL REPORT ON THE PROTECTION OF CIVIL RIGHTS ACT, 1955 FOR 2007, 9, *available at* http://socialjustice.nic.in/policiesacts1.php. *See also*, Sanjoy Ghose, *Untouchability and the Law*, 13 INTERIGHTS BULLETIN: A REVIEW OF THE INTERNATIONAL CENTRE FOR THE LEGAL PROTECTION OF HUMAN RIGHTS 98, 99 (2001). But the Human Rights Watch report on "untouchables" indicates that ignorance of the law, non-registration of cases because of the complicity of the police with high caste Hindus, and the lack of special courts all pose serious obstacles to the prosecution of crimes. *See* Smita Narula, BROKEN PEOPLE: CASTE VIOLENCE AGAINST INDIA'S "UNTOUCHABLES" 191–94 (Patricia Gossman ed., 1999).

3.   The European Union's Council Framework Decision 2008/913/JHA of 28 November 2008 requires each Member State to make certain forms of hate speech a crime. For a discussion of hate speech as an equality issue, see Chapter IX.

4.   Brazil also makes some forms of employment discrimination a crime, as further discussed in chapter III.

EQUALITY & DISCRIMINATION IN EMPLOYMENT

INTRODUCTION

The previous chapter reviewed various conceptions of inequality and their legal proof structures. Those conceptions and proof structures will resonate in the following chapters as we begin to examine contextually how issues of inequality and equality are addressed by different legal systems. As you read the materials in this chapter, think about the role that concepts of second class citizenship, unconscious and cognitive bias, and other conceptions of inequality are addressed by employment discrimination laws. How do the legal rules account for the various types of inequality discussed in Chapter II? What vision or visions of equality do they promote? What do the laws, and the history of their development, tell us about how a particular society views its most persistent forms of inequality? Consider the following problems as you read the materials in this chapter.

PROBLEMS

- An employer forbids pregnant women from working in positions which might pose a danger to their unborn children. The employer justifies this policy by pointing to recent scientific studies that indicate that exposure to certain chemicals carries the risk of contracting a rare disease if exposed in vitro. The employer fears being held legally responsible for harm to the child of a worker born with this disease after being exposed to chemicals in its workplace. Can the employer legally exclude pregnant women from certain positions based on a well-founded risk to their unborn children?

- A theater wants to hire an actor to play a historical figure in a forthcoming production about the country's founding. Can the theater hire only white Americans if in the United States? Only white Frenchmen or women if in France? Only Han Chinese if in China?

- An employer has a history of not inviting back for follow-up job interviews candidates with a heavy foreign accent. The employer denies that it is using race or ethnicity to screen job applicants but admits that communication ability is central to the job requirement since the positions at issue requiring ongoing contact with customers. Is this an adequate justification for relying on someone's accent as a proxy for good communication skills?

- An employer rejects all job applicants who have a poor credit history. Statistical studies demonstrate, however, that this practice tends to disproportionately exclude members of an ethnic or racial minority group from qualification for the jobs at issue. Can the employer defend this practice by arguing that the criterion (poor credit history) is a neutral one and is not intended to exclude any particular group?

- A senior manager at a top finance company constantly remarks to his colleagues that women are "dumb" and "bimbos" but that he puts up with them because he "loves" and "worships" women. Most of his colleagues ignore him and think that he is just trying to draw attention to himself. In fact, many of them note, he has gone out of his way to promote women into management positions. One female employee, however, takes offense at his remarks finding them distressing and demeaning. Because he is very loud, she does not feel that she is able to escape hearing them throughout the day. Is this a form of prohibited sexual harassment?

A. THE UNITED STATES

The Fourteenth Amendment to the United States Constitution provides that "No state shall...deny to any person within its jurisdiction the equal protection of the laws." Pursuant to this equality provision, as well as the Commerce Clause, the United States Congress has passed a number of laws prohibiting discrimination in employment against its citizens on the basis of a number of personal characteristics. The first of these laws was passed in the late nineteenth century, following the freeing of slaves upon the signing of the Emancipation Declaration in 1863 and the passage of the Thirteenth Amendment abolishing slavery. During this period of "Reconstruction," Congress passed the first Civil Rights Acts which gave the newly freed slaves the right to the same freedoms as white persons enjoyed, including the freedom to "make and enforce contracts." (e.g. employment contracts). *See* Civil Rights Act of 1866, 42 United States Code Section 1981.

Following the period of legalized racial segregation in the early and mid-twentieth century, Congress again passed a number of Civil Rights Acts to address the inequalities suffered by African Americans in society. These Acts prohibited discrimination across a variety of contexts, including employment. The relevant language of the most prominent U.S. employment discrimination law, Title VII of the 1964 Civil Rights Act, provides: "It shall be an unlawful employment practice for an employer (1) to fail or refuse to hire or to discharge any individual, or otherwise to discriminate against any individual with respect to his compensation, terms, conditions, or privileges of employment, because of such individual's race, color, religion, sex, or national origin; or, (2) to limit, segregate, or classify his employees or applicants for employment in any way which would deprive or tend to deprive any individual of employment opportunities or otherwise adversely affect his status as an employee, because of such individual's race, color, religion, sex, or national origin." Section 703(a) of the Civil Rights Act of 1964, 78 Stat. 255, as amended, 42 U.S.C. § 2000e–2(a). Title VII applies to both public and private employers.

The term "discriminate" is not defined by the Act but, as we have seen in Chapter II and will see here, the U.S. Supreme Court has interpreted the term to prohibit a variety of forms of conduct and practices by employers.

They include disparate treatment (or direct discrimination), disparate impact (or indirect discrimination), pattern and practice discrimination, and sexual harassment, among others. The crux of any discrimination claim under U.S. antidiscrimination laws is that the plaintiff must prove not only that she or he was discriminated against but that such discrimination was "because of" the individual's race, color, religion, sex of national origin. Discrimination claims require courts to evaluate whether and how a particular personal or group characteristic has influenced an empoloyer's decision-making process and/or its outcomes. The following cases are examples of how the U.S. Supreme Court reasons through this evaluative process across a variety of employment discrimination claims.

------

1. DISPARATE TREATMENT

Price Waterhouse v. Hopkins

490 U.S. 228 (1989)

■ JUSTICE BRENNAN announced the judgment of the Court and delivered an opinion, in which JUSTICE MARSHALL, JUSTICE BLACKMUN, and JUSTICE STEVENS join.

I

At Price Waterhouse, a nationwide professional accounting partnership, a senior manager becomes a candidate for partnership when the partners in her local office submit her name as a candidate. * * *

Ann Hopkins had worked at Price Waterhouse's Office of Government Services in Washington, D.C., for five years when the partners in that office proposed her as a candidate for partnership. Of the 662 partners at the firm at that time, 7 were women. Of the 88 persons proposed for partnership that year, only one—Hopkins—was a woman. Forty-seven of these candidates were admitted to the partnership, 21 were rejected, and 20—including Hopkins—were "held" for reconsideration the following year. Thirteen of the 32 partners who had submitted comments on Hopkins supported her bid for partnership. Three partners recommended that her candidacy be placed on hold, eight stated that they did not have an informed opinion about her, and eight recommended that she be denied partnership. * * *

The partners in Hopkins' office praised her character as well as her accomplishments, describing her in their joint statement as "an outstanding professional" who had a "deft touch," a "strong character, independence and integrity." Clients appear to have agreed with these assessments.

* * * Virtually all of the partners' negative remarks about Hopkins— even those of partners supporting her—had to do with her "interpersonal

skills." Both "[s]upporters and opponents of her candidacy," stressed [District Court] Judge Gesell, "indicated that she was sometimes overly aggressive, unduly harsh, difficult to work with and impatient with staff."

There were clear signs, though, that some of the partners reacted negatively to Hopkins' personality because she was a woman. One partner described her as "macho"; another suggested that she "overcompensated for being a woman"; a third advised her to take "a course at charm school...." But it was the man who, as Judge Gesell found, bore responsibility for explaining to Hopkins the reasons for the Policy Board's decision to place her candidacy on hold who delivered the *coup de grace:* in order to improve her chances for partnership, Thomas Beyer advised, Hopkins should "walk more femininely, talk more femininely, dress more femininely, wear make-up, have her hair styled, and wear jewelry." * * *

II

The specification of the standard of causation under Title VII is a decision about the kind of conduct that violates that statute. According to Price Waterhouse, an employer violates Title VII only if it gives decisive consideration to an employee's gender, race, national origin, or religion in making a decision that affects that employee. On Price Waterhouse's theory, even if a plaintiff shows that her gender played a part in an employment decision, it is still her burden to show that the decision would have been different if the employer had not discriminated. In Hopkins' view, on the other hand, an employer violates the statute whenever it allows one of these attributes to play any part in an employment decision. Once a plaintiff shows that this occurred, according to Hopkins, the employer's proof that it would have made the same decision in the absence of discrimination can serve to limit equitable relief but not to avoid a finding of liability. We conclude that, as often happens, the truth lies somewhere in between.

A

In passing Title VII, Congress made the simple but momentous announcement that sex, race, religion, and national origin are not relevant to the selection, evaluation, or compensation of employees. Yet, the statute does not purport to limit the other qualities and characteristics that employers *may* take into account in making employment decisions. The converse, therefore, of "for cause" legislation, Title VII eliminates certain bases for distinguishing among employees while otherwise preserving employers' freedom of choice. This balance between employee rights and employer prerogatives turns out to be decisive in the case before us.

Congress' intent to forbid employers to take gender into account in making employment decisions appears on the face of the statute. In now-familiar language, the statute forbids an employer to "fail or refuse to hire or to discharge any individual, or otherwise to discriminate with respect to his compensation, terms, conditions, or privileges of employment," or to "limit, segregate, or classify his employees or applicants for employment in any way which would deprive or tend to deprive any individual of employment opportunities or otherwise adversely affect his status as an employee, *because of* such individual's ... sex." 42 U.S.C. §§ 2000e–2(a)(1), (2) (emphasis added). We take these words to mean that gender must be irrelevant to employment decisions. To construe the words "because of" as colloquial shorthand for "but-for causation," as does Price Waterhouse, is to misunderstand them.

But-for causation is a hypothetical construct. In determining whether a particular factor was a but-for cause of a given event, we begin by assuming that that factor was present at the time of the event, and then ask whether, even if that factor had been absent, the event nevertheless would have transpired in the same way. The present, active tense of the operative verbs of § 703(a)(1) ("to fail or refuse"), in contrast, turns our attention to the actual moment of the event in question, the adverse employment decision. The critical inquiry, the one commanded by the words of § 703(a)(1), is whether gender was a factor in the employment decision *at the moment it was made.* Moreover, since we know that the words "because of" do not mean "*solely* because of," we also know that Title VII meant to condemn even those decisions based on a mixture of legitimate and illegitimate considerations. When, therefore, an employer considers both gender and legitimate factors at the time of making a decision, that decision was "because of" sex and the other, legitimate considerations—even if we may say later, in the context of litigation, that the decision would have been the same if gender had not been taken into account. * * *

We need not leave our common sense at the doorstep when we interpret a statute. It is difficult for us to imagine that, in the simple words "because of," Congress meant to obligate a plaintiff to identify the precise causal role played by legitimate and illegitimate motivations in the employment decision she challenges. We conclude, instead, that Congress meant to obligate her to prove that the employer relied upon sex-based considerations in coming to its decision.

Our interpretation of the words "because of" also is supported by the fact that Title VII does identify one circumstance in which an employer may take gender into account in making an employment decision, namely, when gender is a "bona fide occupational qualification [(BFOQ)] reasonably necessary to the normal operation of th[e] particular business or enterprise." 42 U.S.C. § 2000e–2(e). The only plausible inference to draw from this provision is that, in all other circumstances, a person's gender may not be considered in making decisions that affect her. Indeed, Title VII even forbids employers to make gender an indirect stumbling block to employment opportunities. An employer may not, we have held, condition employment opportunities on the satisfaction of facially neutral tests or qualifications that have a disproportionate, adverse impact on members of protected groups when those tests or qualifications are not required for performance of the job.

To say that an employer may not take gender into account is not, however, the end of the matter, for that describes only one aspect of Title VII. The other important aspect of the statute is its preservation of an employer's remaining freedom of choice. We conclude that the preservation of this freedom means that an employer shall not be liable if it can prove that, even if it had not taken gender into account, it would have come to the same decision regarding a particular person. The statute's maintenance of employer prerogatives is evident from the statute itself and from its history, both in Congress and in this Court. * * *

* * *The central point is this: while an employer may not take gender into account in making an employment decision (except in those very narrow circumstances in which gender is a BFOQ), it is free to decide against a woman for other reasons. We think these principles require that, once a plaintiff in a Title VII case shows that gender played a motivating part in an employment decision, the defendant may avoid a finding of liability only by proving that it would have made the same decision even if it had not allowed gender to play such a role. This balance of burdens is the direct result of Title VII's balance of rights.

* * *In saying that gender played a motivating part in an employment decision, we mean that, if we asked the employer at the moment of the decision what its reasons were and if we received a truthful response, one of those reasons would be that the applicant or employee was a woman. In the specific context of sex stereotyping, an employer who acts on the basis of a belief that a woman cannot be aggressive, or that she must not be, has acted on the basis of gender.

. . . As for the legal relevance of sex stereotyping, we are beyond the day when an employer could evaluate employees by assuming or insisting that they matched the stereotype associated with their group, for " '[i]n forbidding employers to discriminate against individuals because of their sex, Congress intended to strike at the entire spectrum of disparate treatment of men and women resulting from sex stereotypes.' " [citations omitted]. An employer who objects to aggressiveness in women but whose positions require this trait places women in an intolerable and impermissible catch 22: out of a job if they behave aggressively and out of a job if they do not. Title VII lifts women out of this bind.

Remarks at work that are based on sex stereotypes do not inevitably prove that gender played a part in a particular employment decision. The plaintiff must show that the employer actually relied on her gender in making its decision. In making this showing, stereotyped remarks can certainly be *evidence* that gender played a part. In any event, the stereotyping in this case did not simply consist of stray remarks. On the contrary, Hopkins proved that Price Waterhouse invited partners to submit comments; that some of the comments stemmed from sex stereotypes; that an important part of the Policy Board's decision on Hopkins was an assessment of the submitted comments; and that Price Waterhouse in no way disclaimed reliance on the sex-linked evaluations. This is not, as Price Waterhouse suggests, "discrimination in the air"; rather, it is, as Hopkins puts it, "discrimination brought to ground and visited upon" an employee. . . .

As to the employer's proof, in most cases, the employer should be able to present some objective evidence as to its probable decision in the absence of an impermissible motive. Moreover, proving " 'that the same decision would have been justified . . . is not the same as proving that the same decision would have been made.' " [citations omitted]. An employer may not, in other words, prevail in a mixed-motives case by offering a legitimate and sufficient reason for its decision if that reason did not motivate it at the time of the decision. Finally, an employer may not meet its burden in such a case by merely showing that at the time of the decision it was motivated only in part by a legitimate reason. The very premise of a mixed-motives case is that a legitimate reason was present, and indeed, in this case, Price Waterhouse already has made this showing by convincing Judge Gesell that Hopkins' interpersonal problems were a legitimate concern. The employer instead must show that its legitimate reason, standing alone, would have induced it to make the same decision. * * *

■ JUSTICE WHITE, concurring in the judgment.

* * * Hopkins was not required to prove that the illegitimate factor was the only, principal, or true reason for petitioner's action. Rather, as Justice O'CONNOR states, her burden was to show that the unlawful motive was a *substantial* factor in the adverse employment action. The District Court, as its opinion was construed by the Court of Appeals, so found . . . and I agree that the finding was supported by the record. The burden of persuasion then should have shifted to Price Waterhouse to prove "by a preponderance of the evidence that it would have reached the same decision . . . in the absence of" the unlawful motive. * * *

■ JUSTICE O'CONNOR, concurring in the judgment.

I agree with the plurality that, on the facts presented in this case, the burden of persuasion should shift to the employer to demonstrate by a preponderance of the evidence that it would have reached the same decision concerning Ann Hopkins' candidacy absent consideration of her gender. . . . I thus concur in the judgment of the Court. My disagreement stems from the plurality's conclusions concerning the substantive requirement of causation under the statute and its broad statements regarding the applicability of the allocation of the burden of proof applied in this case. * * *

* * * The legislative history of Title VII bears out what its plain language suggests: a substantive violation of the statute only occurs when consideration of an illegitimate criterion is the "but-for" cause of an adverse employment action. The legislative history makes it clear that Congress was attempting to eradicate discriminatory actions in the employment setting, not mere discriminatory thoughts. Critics of the bill that became Title VII labeled it a "thought control bill," and argued that it created a "punishable crime that does not require an illegal external act as a basis for judgment." * * *

Thus, I disagree with the plurality's dictum that the words "because of" do not mean "but-for" causation; manifestly they do. [citation omitted]. The question for decision in this case is what allocation of the burden of persuasion on the issue of causation best conforms with the intent of Congress and the purposes behind Title VII. * * *

* * * There is no doubt that Congress considered reliance on gender or race in making employment decisions an evil in itself. As Senator Clark put it, "[t]he bill simply eliminates consideration of color [or other forbidden criteria] from the decision to hire or promote." [citation omitted]. Reliance on such factors is exactly what the threat of Title VII liability was meant to deter. While the main concern of the statute was with employment oppor-

tunity, Congress was certainly not blind to the stigmatic harm which comes from being evaluated by a process which treats one as an inferior by reason of one's race or sex. This Court's decisions under the Equal Protection Clause have long recognized that whatever the final outcome of a decisional process, the inclusion of race or sex as a consideration within it harms both society and the individual. [citation omitted]. At the same time, Congress clearly conditioned legal liability on a determination that the consideration of an illegitimate factor *caused* a tangible employment injury of some kind.

Where an individual disparate treatment plaintiff has shown by a preponderance of the evidence that an illegitimate criterion was a *substantial* factor in an adverse employment decision, the deterrent purpose of the statute has clearly been triggered. More importantly, as an evidentiary matter, a reasonable factfinder could conclude that absent further explanation, the employer's discriminatory motivation "caused" the employment decision. The employer has not yet been shown to be a violator, but neither is it entitled to the same presumption of good faith concerning its employment decisions which is accorded employers facing only circumstantial evidence of discrimination. Both the policies behind the statute, and the evidentiary principles developed in the analogous area of causation in the law of torts, suggest that at this point the employer may be required to convince the factfinder that, despite the smoke, there is no fire.

Civil Rights Act of 1991

(amending Title VII of the Civil Rights Act of 1964)
§ 109, 42 U.S.C. § 2000e et. seq. (1991)

SEC. 107. CLARIFYING PROHIBITION AGAINST IMPERMISSIBLE CONSIDERATION OF RACE, COLOR, RELIGION, SEX, OR NATIONAL ORIGIN IN EMPLOYMENT PRACTICES.

(a) IN GENERAL—Section 703 of the Civil Rights Act of 1964 (42 U.S.C. 2000e–2) (as amended by sections 105 and 106) is further amended by adding at the end the following new subsection:

(m) Except as otherwise provided in this title, an unlawful employment practice is established when the complaining party demonstrates that race, color, religion, sex, or national origin was a motivating factor for any employment practice, even though other factors also motivated the practice.

(b) ENFORCEMENT PROVISIONS—Section 706(g) of such Act (42 U.S.C. 2000e–5(g)) is amended—

* * *(3) by adding at the end the following new subparagraph:

(B) On a claim in which an individual proves a violation under section 703(m) and a respondent demonstrates that the respondent would have taken the same action in the absence of the impermissible motivating factor, the court—'(i) may grant declaratory relief, injunctive relief (except as provided in clause (ii)), and attorney's fees and costs demonstrated to be directly attributable only to the pursuit of a claim under section 703(m); and'(ii) shall not award damages or issue an order requiring any admission, reinstatement, hiring, promotion, or payment, described in subparagraph (A).'

International Union, United Automobile Workers v. Johnson Controls, Inc.

499 U.S. 187 (1991)

■ JUSTICE BLACKMUN delivered the opinion of the Court.

In this case we are concerned with an employer's gender-based fetal-protection policy. May an employer exclude a fertile female employee from certain jobs because of its concern for the health of the fetus the woman might conceive?

I.

Respondent Johnson Controls, Inc., manufactures batteries. In the manufacturing process, the element lead is a primary ingredient. Occupational exposure to lead entails health risks, including the risk of harm to any fetus carried by a female employee. Before the Civil Rights Act of 1964, 78 Stat. 241, became law, Johnson Controls did not employ any woman in a battery-manufacturing job. In June 1977, however, it announced its first official policy concerning its employment of women in lead-exposure work:

> "[P]rotection of the health of the unborn child is the immediate and direct responsibility of the prospective parents. While the medical profession and the company can support them in the exercise of this responsibility, it cannot assume it for them without simultaneously infringing their rights as persons. . . . . Since not all women who can become mothers wish to become mothers (or will become mothers), it would appear to be illegal discrimination to treat all who are capable of pregnancy as though they will become pregnant."

Consistent with that view, Johnson Controls "stopped short of excluding women capable of bearing children from lead exposure," but emphasized that a woman who expected to have a child should not choose a job in which she would have such exposure. The company also required a woman who wished to be considered for employment to sign a statement that she had been advised of the risk of having a child while she was exposed to lead. The statement informed the woman that although there was evidence "that women exposed to lead have a higher rate of abortion," this evidence was "not as clear . . . as the relationship between cigarette smoking and cancer," but that it was, "medically speaking, just good sense not to run that risk if you want children and do not want to expose the unborn child to risk, however small. . . ."

Five years later, in 1982, Johnson Controls shifted from a policy of warning to a policy of exclusion. Between 1979 and 1983, eight employees became pregnant while maintaining blood lead levels in excess of 30 micrograms per deciliter. This appeared to be the critical level noted by the Occupational Safety and Health Administration (OSHA) for a worker who was planning to have a family. The company responded by announcing a broad exclusion of women from jobs that exposed them to lead:

"... [I]t is [Johnson Controls'] policy that women who are pregnant or who are capable of bearing children will not be placed into jobs involving lead exposure or which could expose them to lead through the exercise of job bidding, bumping, transfer or promotion rights."

The policy defined "women ... capable of bearing children" as "[a]ll women except those whose inability to bear children is medically documented." It further stated that an unacceptable work station was one where, "over the past year," an employee had recorded a blood lead level of more than 30 micrograms per deciliter or the work site had yielded an air sample containing a lead level in excess of 30 micrograms per cubic meter.

II

In April 1984, petitioners filed in the United States District Court for the Eastern District of Wisconsin a class action challenging Johnson Controls' fetal-protection policy as sex discrimination that violated Title VII of the Civil Rights Act of 1964, as amended. Among the individual plaintiffs were petitioners Mary Craig, who had chosen to be sterilized in order to avoid losing her job, Elsie Nason, a 50–year–old divorcee, who had suffered a loss in compensation when she was transferred out of a job where she was exposed to lead, and Donald Penney, who had been denied a request for a leave of absence for the purpose of lowering his lead level because he intended to become a father. Upon stipulation of the parties, the District Court certified a class consisting of "all past, present and future production and maintenance employees" in United Auto Workers bargaining units at nine of Johnson Controls' plants "who have been and continue to be affected by [the employer's] Fetal Protection Policy implemented in 1982." * * *

III

The bias in Johnson Controls' policy is obvious. Fertile men, but not fertile women, are given a choice as to whether they wish to risk their reproductive health for a particular job. . . . Respondent's fetal-protection policy explicitly discriminates against women on the basis of their sex. The policy excludes women with childbearing capacity from lead-exposed jobs and so creates a facial classification based on gender. * * *

First, Johnson Controls' policy classifies on the basis of gender and childbearing capacity, rather than fertility alone. Respondent does not seek to protect the unconceived children of all its employees. Despite evidence in the record about the debilitating effect of lead exposure on the male reproductive system, Johnson Controls is concerned only with the harms that may befall the unborn offspring of its female employees. . . . This Court faced a conceptually similar situation in *Phillips v. Martin Marietta Corp.*, 400 U.S. 542, 91 S.Ct. 496, 27 L.Ed.2d 613 (1971), and found sex discrimination because the policy established "one hiring policy for women and another for men-each having pre-school-age children." Johnson Controls' policy is facially discriminatory because it requires only a female employee to produce proof that she is not capable of reproducing.

Our conclusion is bolstered by the Pregnancy Discrimination Act (PDA), 42 U.S.C. § 2000e(k), in which Congress explicitly provided that, for purposes of Title VII, discrimination " 'on the basis of sex' " includes discrimination "because of or on the basis of pregnancy, childbirth, or related medical conditions." "The Pregnancy Discrimination Act has now made clear that, for all Title VII purposes, discrimination based on a woman's pregnancy is, on its face, discrimination because of her sex." [citation omitted]. In its use of the words "capable of bearing children" in the 1982 policy statement as the criterion for exclusion, Johnson Controls explicitly classifies on the basis of potential for pregnancy. Under the PDA, such a classification must be regarded, for Title VII purposes, in the same light as explicit sex discrimination. Respondent has chosen to treat all its female employees as potentially pregnant; that choice evinces discrimination on the basis of sex.

We concluded above that Johnson Controls' policy is not neutral because it does not apply to the reproductive capacity of the company's male employees in the same way as it applies to that of the females. Moreover, the absence of a malevolent motive does not convert a facially discriminatory policy into a neutral policy with a discriminatory effect. Whether an employment practice involves disparate treatment through explicit facial discrimination does not depend on why the employer discriminates but rather on the explicit terms of the discrimination. * * *

In sum, Johnson Controls' policy "does not pass the simple test of whether the evidence shows 'treatment of a person in a manner which but for that person's sex would be different.' " [citation omitted]. We hold that Johnson Controls' fetal-protection policy is sex discrimination forbidden under Title VII unless respondent can establish that sex is a "bona fide occupational qualification."

IV

Under § 703(e)(1) of Title VII, an employer may discriminate on the basis of "religion, sex, or national origin in those certain instances where religion, sex, or national origin is a bona fide occupational qualification reasonably necessary to the normal operation of that particular business or enterprise." [citation omitted].We therefore turn to the question whether Johnson Controls' fetal-protection policy is one of those "certain instances" that come within the BFOQ exception.

The BFOQ defense is written narrowly, and this Court has read it narrowly. We have read the BFOQ language of § 4(f) of the Age Discrimination in Employment Act of 1967 (ADEA), which tracks the BFOQ provision in Title VII, just as narrowly. Our emphasis on the restrictive scope of the BFOQ defense is grounded on both the language and the legislative history of § 703. The wording of the BFOQ defense contains several terms of restriction that indicate that the exception reaches only special situations. The statute thus limits the situations in which discrimination is permissible to "certain instances" where sex discrimination is "reasonably necessary" to the "normal operation" of the "particular" business. Each one of these terms—certain, normal, particular—prevents the use of general subjective standards and favors an objective, verifiable requirement. But the most telling term is "occupational"; this indicates that these objective, verifiable requirements must concern job-related skills and aptitudes.

* * *

Johnson Controls argues that its fetal-protection policy falls within the so-called safety exception to the BFOQ. Our cases have stressed that discrimination on the basis of sex because of safety concerns is allowed only in narrow circumstances. In *Dothard v. Rawlinson,* this Court indicated that danger to a woman herself does not justify discrimination. We there allowed the employer to hire only male guards in contact areas of maximum-security male penitentiaries only because more was at stake than the "individual woman's decision to weigh and accept the risks of employment." We found sex to be a BFOQ inasmuch as the employment of a female guard would create real risks of safety to others if violence broke out because the guard was a woman. Sex discrimination was tolerated because sex was related to the guard's ability to do the job-maintaining prison security. We also required in *Dothard* a high correlation between sex and ability to perform job functions and refused to allow employers to use sex as a proxy for strength although it might be a fairly accurate one. Similarly, some courts have approved airlines' layoffs of pregnant flight attendants at different points during the first five months of pregnancy on the ground that the employer's policy was necessary to ensure the safety of passengers. [citations omitted]. In two of these cases, the courts pointedly indicated that fetal, as opposed to passenger, safety was best left to the mother.

We considered safety to third parties in *Western Airlines, Inc. v. Criswell, supra,* in the context of the ADEA. We focused upon "the nature of the flight engineer's tasks," and the "actual capabilities of persons over age 60" in relation to those tasks. Our safety concerns were not independent of the individual's ability to perform the assigned tasks, but rather involved the possibility that, because of age-connected debility, a flight engineer might not properly assist the pilot, and might thereby cause a safety emergency. Furthermore, although we considered the safety of third parties in *Dothard* and *Criswell,* those third parties were indispensable to the particular business at issue. In *Dothard,* the third parties were the inmates; in *Criswell,* the third parties were the passengers on the plane. We stressed that in order to qualify as a BFOQ, a job qualification must relate to the " 'essence,' " or to the "central mission of the employer's business."

* * * Justice White attempts to transform this case into one of customer safety. The unconceived fetuses of Johnson Controls' female employees, however, are neither customers nor third parties whose safety is essential to the business of battery manufacturing. No one can disregard the possibility of injury to future children; the BFOQ, however, is not so broad that it transforms this deep social concern into an essential aspect of battery making.

Our case law, therefore, makes clear that the safety exception is limited to instances in which sex or pregnancy actually interferes with the employee's ability to perform the job. This approach is consistent with the language of the BFOQ provision itself, for it suggests that permissible distinctions based on sex must relate to ability to perform the duties of the job. Johnson Controls suggests, however, that we expand the exception to allow fetal-protection policies that mandate particular standards for pregnant or fertile women. We decline to do so. Such an expansion contradicts not only the language of the BFOQ and the narrowness of its exception, but also the plain language and history of the PDA.

The PDA's amendment to Title VII contains a BFOQ standard of its own: Unless pregnant employees differ from others "in their ability or inability to work," they must be "treated the same" as other employees "for all employment-related purposes." This language clearly sets forth Congress' remedy for discrimination on the basis of pregnancy and potential pregnancy. Women who are either pregnant or potentially pregnant must be treated like others "similar in their ability . . . to work." In other words, women as capable of doing their jobs as their male counterparts may not be forced to choose between having a child and having a job. * * *

We conclude that the language of both the BFOQ provision and the PDA which amended it, as well as the legislative history and the case law, prohibit an employer from discriminating against a woman because of her capacity to become pregnant unless her reproductive potential prevents her from performing the duties of her job. We reiterate our holdings in *Criswell* and *Dothard* that an employer must direct its concerns about a woman's ability to perform her job safely and efficiently to those aspects of the woman's job-related activities that fall within the "essence" of the particular business.

V

We have no difficulty concluding that Johnson Controls cannot establish a BFOQ. Fertile women, as far as appears in the record, participate in the manufacture of batteries as efficiently as anyone else. Johnson Controls' professed moral and ethical concerns about the welfare of the next generation do not suffice to establish a BFOQ of female sterility. Decisions about the welfare of future children must be left to the parents who conceive, bear, support, and raise them rather than to the employers who hire those parents. Congress has mandated this choice through Title VII, as amended by the PDA. Johnson Controls has attempted to exclude women because of their reproductive capacity. Title VII and the PDA simply do not allow a woman's dismissal because of her failure to submit to sterilization.

Nor can concerns about the welfare of the next generation be considered a part of the "essence" of Johnson Controls' business. Judge Easterbrook in this case pertinently observed: "It is word play to say that 'the job' at Johnson [Controls] is to make batteries without risk to fetuses in the same way 'the job' at Western Air Lines is to fly planes without crashing."

Johnson Controls argues that it must exclude all fertile women because it is impossible to tell which women will become pregnant while working with lead. This argument is somewhat academic in light of our conclusion that the company may not exclude fertile women at all; it perhaps is worth noting, however, that Johnson Controls has shown no "factual basis for believing that all or substantially all women would be unable to perform safely and efficiently the duties of the job involved." [citation omitted]. Even on this sparse record, it is apparent that Johnson Controls is concerned about only a small minority of women. Of the eight pregnancies reported among the female employees, it has not been shown that any of the babies have birth defects or other abnormalities. The record does not reveal the birth rate for Johnson Controls' female workers, but national statistics show that approximately nine percent of all fertile women become pregnant each year. The birthrate drops to two percent for blue collar workers over age 30. Johnson Controls' fear of prenatal injury, no matter how sincere, does not begin to show that substantially all of its fertile women employees are incapable of doing their jobs. * * *

VII

Our holding today that Title VII, as so amended, forbids sex-specific fetal-protection policies is neither remarkable nor unprecedented. Concern for a woman's existing or potential offspring historically has been the excuse for denying women equal employment opportunities. Congress in the PDA prohibited discrimination on the basis of a woman's ability to become pregnant. We do no more than hold that the PDA means what it says.

It is no more appropriate for the courts than it is for individual employers to decide whether a woman's reproductive role is more important to herself and her family than her economic role. Congress has left this choice to the woman as hers to make.* * *

■ JUSTICE WHITE, with whom THE CHIEF JUSTICE and JUSTICE KENNEDY join, concurring in part and concurring in the judgment.

The Court properly holds that Johnson Controls' fetal-protection policy overtly discriminates against women, and thus is prohibited by Title VII of the Civil Rights Act of 1964 unless it falls within the bona fide occupational qualification (BFOQ) exception, set forth at 42 U.S.C. § 2000e–2(e). The Court erroneously holds, however, that the BFOQ defense is so narrow that it could never justify a sex-specific fetal-protection policy. * * *

Prior decisions construing the BFOQ defense confirm that the defense is broad enough to include considerations of cost and safety of the sort that could form the basis for an employer's adoption of a fetal-protection policy.* * *

In enacting the BFOQ standard, "Congress did not ignore the public interest in safety." [citation omitted]. The Court's narrow interpretation of the BFOQ defense in this case, however, means that an employer cannot exclude even *pregnant* women from an environment highly toxic to their fetuses. It is foolish to think that Congress intended such a result, and neither the language of the BFOQ exception nor our cases require it.
* * *

■ JUSTICE SCALIA, concurring in the judgment.

I generally agree with the Court's analysis, but have some reservations, several of which bear mention.

First, I think it irrelevant that there was "evidence in the record about the debilitating effect of lead exposure on the male reproductive system" [citation omitted]. Even without such evidence, treating women differently "on the basis of pregnancy" constitutes discrimination "on the basis of sex," because Congress has unequivocally said so. Pregnancy Discrimination Act, 92 Stat. 2076, 42 U.S.C. § 2000e(k).

Second, the Court points out that "Johnson Controls has shown no factual basis for believing that all or substantially all women would be unable to perform safely ... the duties of the job involved," [citation omitted]. In my view, this is not only "somewhat academic in light of our conclusion that the company may not exclude fertile women at all," it is entirely irrelevant. By reason of the Pregnancy Discrimination Act, it would not matter if all pregnant women placed their children at risk in taking these jobs, just as it does not matter if no men do so. As Judge Easterbrook put it in his dissent below: "Title VII gives parents the power to make occupational decisions affecting their families. A legislative forum is available to those who believe that such decisions should be made elsewhere." * * *

Last, the Court goes far afield, it seems to me, in suggesting that increased cost alone—short of "costs ... so prohibitive as to threaten the survival of the employer's business,"—cannot support a BFOQ defense. I agree with Justice White's concurrence, that nothing in our prior cases suggests this, and in my view it is wrong. I think, for example, that a shipping company may refuse to hire pregnant women as crew members on long voyages because the on-board facilities for foreseeable emergencies, though quite feasible, would be inordinately expensive. In the present case, however, Johnson has not asserted a cost-based BFOQ. [citations omitted]

---

2.   Disparate Impact

Wards Cove Packing Co. v. Atonio
490 U.S. 642 (1989)

■ Justice White delivered the opinion of the Court.

[From Court Syllabus: Jobs at petitioners' Alaskan salmon canneries are of two general types: unskilled "cannery jobs" on the cannery lines, which are filled predominantly by nonwhites; and "noncannery jobs," most of which are classified as skilled positions and filled predominantly with white workers, and virtually all of which pay more than cannery positions. Respondents, a class of nonwhite cannery workers at petitioners' facilities, filed suit in the District Court under Title VII of the Civil Rights Act of 1964, alleging, inter alia, that various of petitioners' hiring/promotion practices were responsible for the work force's racial stratification and had denied them employment as noncannery workers on the basis of race. The District Court rejected respondents' claims, finding, among other things, that nonwhite workers were overrepresented in cannery jobs because many of those jobs were filled under a hiring hall agreement with a predominantly nonwhite union. The Court of Appeals ultimately reversed in pertinent part, holding, inter alia, that respondents had made out a *prima facie* case of disparate impact in hiring for both skilled and unskilled noncannery jobs, relying solely on respondents' statistics showing a high percentage of nonwhite workers in cannery jobs and a low percentage of such workers in noncannery positions. The court also concluded that once a plaintiff class has shown disparate impact caused by specific, identifiable employment practices or criteria, the burden shifts to the employer to prove the challenged practice's business necessity.]

* * * *Griggs v. Duke Power Co.*, 401 U.S. 424, 431 (1971), construed Title VII to proscribe "not only overt discrimination but also practices that are fair in form but discriminatory in practice." Under this basis for liability, which is known as the "disparate-impact" theory and which is involved in this case, a facially neutral employment practice may be deemed violative of Title VII without evidence of the employer's subjective intent to discriminate that is required in a "disparate-treatment" case. * * *

II

In holding that respondents had made out a *prima facie* case of disparate impact, the Court of Appeals relied solely on respondents' statistics showing a high percentage of nonwhite workers in the cannery jobs and a low percentage of such workers in the noncannery positions. Although statistical proof can alone make out a *prima facie* case, *see Teamsters v. United States*, 431 U.S. 324, 339 (1977); *Hazelwood School Dist. v. United States*, 433 U.S. 299, 307–308 (1977), the Court of Appeals' ruling here misapprehends our precedents and the purposes of Title VII, and we therefore reverse.

* * * The "proper comparison [is] between the racial composition of [the at-issue jobs] and the racial composition of the qualified ... population in the relevant labor market." *Ibid.* It is such a comparison—between the racial composition of the qualified persons in the labor market and the persons holding at-issue jobs—that generally forms ... the proper basis for the initial inquiry in a disparate-impact case. Alternatively, in cases where such labor market statistics will be difficult if not impossible to ascertain, we have recognized that certain other statistics—such as measures indicating the racial composition of "otherwise-qualified applicants" for at-issue jobs—are equally probative for this purpose. *See, e.g., New York City Transit Authority v. Beazer*, 440 U.S. 568, 585 (1979).

It is clear to us that the Court of Appeals' acceptance of the comparison between the racial composition of the cannery work force and that of the noncannery work force, as probative of a *prima facie* case of disparate impact in the selection of the latter group of workers, was flawed for several reasons. Most obviously, with respect to the skilled noncannery jobs at issue here, the cannery work force in no way reflected "the pool of qualified job applicants" or the "qualified population in the labor force." Measuring alleged discrimination in the selection of accountants, managers, boat captains, electricians, doctors, and engineers—and the long list of other "skilled" noncannery positions found to exist by the District Court,

* * * by comparing the number of nonwhites occupying these jobs to the number of nonwhites filling cannery worker positions is nonsensical. If the absence of minorities holding such skilled positions is due to a dearth of qualified nonwhite applicants (for reasons that are not petitioners' fault), petitioners' selection methods or employment practices cannot be said to have had a "disparate impact" on nonwhites.

* * * The Court of Appeals' theory, at the very least, would mean that any employer who had a segment of his work force that was—for some reason—racially imbalanced, could be haled into court and forced to engage in the expensive and time-consuming task of defending the "business necessity" of the methods used to select the other members of his work force. The only practicable option for many employers would be to adopt racial quotas, insuring that no portion of their work forces deviated in racial composition from the other portions thereof; this is a result that Congress expressly rejected in drafting Title VII. See 42 U.S.C. § 2000e–2(j); ... The Court of Appeals' theory would "leave the employer little choice ... but to engage in a subjective quota system of employment selection. This, of course, is far from the intent of Title VII." * * *

The Court of Appeals also erred with respect to the unskilled noncannery positions. Racial imbalance in one segment of an employer's workforce does not, without more, establish a *prima facie* case of disparate impact with respect to the selection of workers for the employer's other positions, even where workers for the different positions may have somewhat fungible skills (as is arguably the case for cannery and unskilled noncannery workers). As long as there are no barriers or practices deterring qualified nonwhites from applying for noncannery positions, ... if the percentage of selected applicants who are nonwhite is not significantly less than the percentage of qualified applicants who are nonwhite, the employer's selection mechanism probably does not operate with a disparate impact on minorities. Where this is the case, the percentage of nonwhite workers found in other positions in the employer's labor force is irrelevant to the question of a *prima facie* statistical case of disparate impact. As noted above, a contrary ruling on this point would almost inexorably lead to the use of numerical quotas in the workplace, a result that Congress and this Court have rejected repeatedly in the past.

Moreover, isolating the cannery workers as the potential "labor force" for unskilled noncannery positions is at once both too broad and too narrow in its focus. It is too broad because the vast majority of these cannery workers did not seek jobs in unskilled noncannery positions; there is no showing that many of them would have done so even if none of the arguably "deterring" practices existed. Thus, the pool of cannery workers cannot be used as a surrogate for the class of qualified job applicants, because it contains many persons who have not (and would not) be noncannery job applicants. Conversely, if respondents propose to use the cannery workers for comparison purposes because they represent the "qualified labor population" generally, the group is too narrow, because there are obviously many qualified persons in the labor market for noncannery jobs who are not cannery workers.

The peculiar facts of this case further illustrate why a comparison between the percentage of nonwhite cannery workers and nonwhite non-cannery workers is an improper basis for making out a claim of disparate impact. Here, the District Court found that nonwhites were "overrepresent[ed]" among cannery workers because petitioners had contracted with a predominantly nonwhite union (local 37) to fill these positions. *See App. to Pet. for Cert.* I–42. As a result, if petitioners (for some permissible reason) ceased using local 37 as its hiring channel for cannery positions, it appears (according to the District Court's findings) that the racial stratification between the cannery and noncannery workers might diminish to statistical insignificance. Under the Court of Appeals' approach, therefore, it is possible that, *with no change whatsoever* in their hiring practices for noncannery workers—the jobs at issue in this lawsuit—petitioners could make respondents' *prima facie* case of disparate impact "disappear." But if there would be no *prima facie* case of disparate impact in the selection of noncannery workers absent petitioners' use of local 37 to hire cannery workers, surely petitioners' reliance on the union to fill the cannery jobs not at issue here (and its resulting "overrepresentation" of nonwhites in those positions) does not—standing alone—make out a *prima facie* case of disparate impact. Yet it is precisely such an ironic result that the Court of Appeals reached below.

Consequently, we reverse the Court of Appeals' ruling that a comparison between the percentage of cannery workers who are nonwhite and the percentage of noncannery workers who are nonwhite makes out a *prima facie* case of disparate impact. Of course, this leaves unresolved whether the record made in the District Court will support a conclusion that a *prima facie* case of disparate impact has been established on some basis other than the racial disparity between cannery and noncannery workers. This is an issue that the Court of Appeals or the District Court should address in the first instance.

III

* * * Because we remand for further proceedings, however, on whether a *prima facie* case of disparate impact has been made in defensible fashion in this case, we address two other challenges petitioners have made to the decision of the Court of Appeals.

A

First is the question of causation in a disparate-impact case. The law in this respect was correctly stated by Justice O'CONNOR's opinion last Term in *Watson v. Fort Worth Bank & Trust*, 487 U.S., at 994:

> "[W]e note that the plaintiff's burden in establishing a *prima facie* case goes beyond the need to show that there are statistical disparities in the employer's work force. The plaintiff must begin by identifying the specific employment practice that is challenged. . . . Especially in cases where an employer combines subjective criteria with the use of more rigid standardized rules or tests, the plaintiff is in our view responsible for isolating and identifying the specific employment practices that are allegedly responsible for any observed statistical disparities." * * *

* * * [A] Title VII plaintiff does not make out a case of disparate impact simply by showing that, "at the bottom line," there is racial imbalance in the work force. As a general matter, a plaintiff must demonstrate that it is the application of a specific or particular employment practice that has created the disparate impact under attack. Such a showing is an integral part of the plaintiff's *prima facie* case in a disparate-impact suit under Title VII.

Here, respondents have alleged that several "objective" employment practices (e. g., nepotism, separate hiring channels, rehire preferences), as well as the use of "subjective decision making" to select noncannery workers, have had a disparate impact on nonwhites. Respondents base this claim on statistics that allegedly show a disproportionately low percentage of nonwhites in the at-issue positions. However, even if on remand respondents can show that nonwhites are underrepresented in the at-issue jobs in a manner that is acceptable under the standards set forth in Part II, *supra*, this alone will not suffice to make out a *prima facie* case of disparate impact. Respondents will also have to demonstrate that the disparity they complain of is the result of one or more of the employment practices that they are attacking here, specifically showing that each challenged practice has a significantly disparate impact on employment opportunities for whites and nonwhites. To hold otherwise would result in employers being potentially liable for "the myriad of innocent causes that may lead to statistical imbalances in the composition of their work forces." * * *

* * * Consequently, on remand, the courts below are instructed to require, as part of respondents' *prima facie* case, a demonstration that specific elements of the petitioners' hiring process have a significantly disparate impact on nonwhites.

B

If, on remand, respondents meet the proof burdens outlined above, and establish a *prima facie* case of disparate impact with respect to any of petitioners' employment practices, the case will shift to any business justification petitioners offer for their use of these practices. This phase of the disparate-impact case contains two components: first, a consideration of the justifications an employer offers for his use of these practices; and second, the availability of alternative practices to achieve the same business ends, with less racial impact. *See, e.g., Albemarle Paper Co. v. Moody*, 422 U.S., at 425. We consider these two components in turn.

(1)

Though we have phrased the query differently in different cases, it is generally well established that at the justification stage of such a disparate-impact case, the dispositive issue is whether a challenged practice serves, in a significant way, the legitimate employment goals of the employer.... The touchstone of this inquiry is a reasoned review of the employer's justification for his use of the challenged practice. A mere insubstantial justification in this regard will not suffice, because such a low standard of review would permit discrimination to be practiced through the use of spurious, seemingly neutral employment practices. At the same time, though, there is no requirement that the challenged practice be "essential" or "indispensable" to the employer's business for it to pass muster: this degree of scrutiny would be almost impossible for most employers to meet, and would result in a host of evils we have identified above. * * *

In this phase, the employer carries the burden of producing evidence of a business justification for his employment practice. The burden of persuasion, however, remains with the disparate-impact plaintiff. * * *

(2)

Finally, if on remand the case reaches this point, and respondents cannot persuade the trier of fact on the question of petitioners' business necessity defense, respondents may still be able to prevail. To do so, respondents will have to persuade the factfinder that "other tests or selection devices, without a similarly undesirable racial effect, would also serve the employer's legitimate [hiring] interest[s]"; by so demonstrating, respondents would prove that "[petitioners were] using [their] tests merely as a 'pretext' for discrimination. . . ." If respondents, having established a *prima facie* case, come forward with alternatives to petitioners' hiring practices that reduce the racially disparate impact of practices currently being used, and petitioners refuse to adopt these alternatives, such a refusal would belie a claim by petitioners that their incumbent practices are being employed for nondiscriminatory reasons.

Of course, any alternative practices which respondents offer up in this respect must be equally effective as petitioners' chosen hiring procedures in achieving petitioners' legitimate employment goals. Moreover, "[f]actors such as the cost or other burdens of proposed alternative selection devices are relevant in determining whether they would be equally as effective as the challenged practice in serving the employer's legitimate business goals." *Watson, supra,* at 998 (O'CONNOR, J.). "Courts are generally less competent than employers to restructure business practices," *Furnco Construction Corp. v. Waters,* 438 U.S. 567, 578 (1978); consequently, the judiciary should proceed with care before mandating that an employer must adopt a plaintiff's alternative selection or hiring practice in response to a Title VII suit.

IV

For the reasons given above, the judgment of the Court of Appeals is reversed, and the case is remanded for further proceedings consistent with this opinion. * * *

■ JUSTICE BLACKMUN, with whom JUSTICE BRENNAN and JUSTICE MARSHALL join, dissenting.

* * *Today a bare majority of the Court takes three major strides backwards in the battle against race discrimination. * * * It bars the use of internal workforce comparisons in the making of a *prima facie* case of discrimination, even where the structure of the industry in question renders any other statistical comparison meaningless. And it requires practice-by-practice statistical proof of causation, even where, as here, such proof would be impossible.

The harshness of these results is well demonstrated by the facts of this case. The salmon industry as described by this record takes us back to a kind of overt and institutionalized discrimination we have not dealt with in years: a total residential and work environment organized on principles of racial stratification and segregation, which, as Justice STEVENS points out, resembles a plantation economy. . . . This industry long has been characterized by a taste for discrimination of the old-fashioned sort: a preference for hiring nonwhites to fill its lowest level positions, on the condition that they stay there. The majority's legal rulings essentially immunize these practices from attack under a Title VII disparate impact analysis.

Sadly, this comes as no surprise. One wonders whether the majority still believes that race discrimination—or, more accurately, race discrimination against nonwhites—is a problem in our society, or even remembers that it ever was. * * *

■ JUSTICE STEVENS, with whom JUSTICE BRENNAN, JUSTICE MARSHALL, and JUSTICE BLACKMUN join, dissenting.

Fully 18 years ago, this Court unanimously held that Title VII of the Civil Rights Act of 1964 . . . prohibits employment practices that have discriminatory effects, as well as those that are intended to discriminate. *Griggs v. Duke Power Co.,* 401 U.S. 424 (1971). Federal courts and agencies consistently have enforced that interpretation, thus promoting our national goal of eliminating barriers that define economic opportunity not by aptitude and ability, but by race, color, national origin, and other traits that are easily identified but utterly irrelevant to one's qualification for a particular job. Regrettably, the Court retreats from these efforts in its review of an interlocutory judgment respecting the "peculiar facts" of this lawsuit. Turning a blind eye to the meaning and purpose of Title VII, the majority's opinion perfunctorily rejects a longstanding rule of law and underestimates the probative value of evidence of a racially stratified workforce. I cannot join this latest sojourn into judicial activism. * * *

* * *The District Court's findings of fact depict a unique industry. Canneries often are located in remote, sparsely populated areas of Alaska. * * * Most jobs are seasonal, with the season's length and the canneries' personnel needs varying not just year to year, but day to day. To fill their employment requirements, petitioners must recruit and transport many cannery workers and noncannery workers from States in the Pacific Northwest. Most cannery workers come from a union local based outside Alaska or from Native villages near the canneries.. Employees in the noncannery positions—the positions that are "at issue"—learn of openings by word of mouth; the jobs seldom are posted or advertised, and there is no promotion to noncannery jobs from within the cannery workers' ranks.

In general, the District Court found the at-issue jobs to require "skills," ranging from English literacy, typing, and "ability to use seam micrometers, gauges, and mechanic's hand tools" to "good health" and a driver's license. . . . All cannery workers' jobs, like a handful of at-issue positions, are unskilled, and the court found that the intensity of the work during canning season precludes on-the-job training for skilled noncannery positions. It made no findings regarding the extent to which the cannery workers already are qualified for at-issue jobs: individual plaintiffs testified persuasively that they were fully qualified for such jobs, but the court neither credited nor discredited this testimony. Although there are no findings concerning wage differentials, the parties seem to agree that wages for cannery workers are lower than those for noncannery workers, skilled or unskilled. The District Court found that "nearly all" cannery workers are nonwhite, while the percentage of nonwhites employed in the entire Alaska salmon canning industry "has stabilized at about 47% to 50%...." The precise stratification of the workforce is not described in the findings, but the parties seem to agree that the noncannery jobs are predominantly held by whites.

Petitioners contend that the relevant labor market in this case is the general population of the "external' labor market for the jobs at issue." *Brief for Petitioners* 17. While they would rely on the District Court's findings in this regard, those findings are ambiguous. At one point, the District Court specifies "Alaska, the Pacific Northwest, and California" as "the geographical region from which [petitioners] draw their employees," but its next finding refers to "this relevant geographical area for cannery worker, laborer, and other nonskilled jobs," [citations omitted]. There is no express finding of the relevant labor market for noncannery Jobs.

Even assuming that the District Court properly defined the relevant geographical area, its apparent assumption that the population in that area constituted the "available labor supply," *ibid.,* is not adequately founded. An undisputed requirement for employment either as a cannery or noncannery worker is availability for seasonal employment in the far reaches of Alaska. Many noncannery workers, furthermore, must be available for preseason work. [citations omitted]. Yet the record does not identify the portion of the general population in Alaska, California, and the Pacific Northwest that would accept this type of employment.... This deficiency respecting a crucial job qualification diminishes the usefulness of petitioners' statistical evidence. In contrast, respondents' evidence, comparing racial compositions within the workforce, identifies a pool of workers willing to work during the relevant times and familiar with the workings of the industry. Surely this is more probative than the untailored general population statistics on which petitioners focus. * * *

Evidence that virtually all the employees in the major categories of at-issue jobs were white, whereas about two-thirds of the cannery workers were nonwhite, may not by itself suffice to establish a *prima facie* case of discrimination. But such evidence of racial stratification puts the specific employment practices challenged by respondents into perspective. Petitioners recruit employees for at-issue jobs from outside the workforce, rather than from lower paying, overwhelmingly nonwhite cannery worker positions. [citations omitted]. Information about availability of at-issue positions is conducted by word of mouth; therefore, the maintenance of housing and mess halls that separate the largely white noncannery workforce from the cannery workers ... coupled with the tendency toward nepotistic hiring are obvious barriers to employment opportunities for nonwhites. Putting to one side the issue of business justifications, it would be quite wrong to conclude that these practices have no discriminatory consequence. Thus, I agree with the Court of Appeals ... that, when the District Court makes the additional findings prescribed today, it should treat the evidence of racial stratification in the workforce as a significant element of respondents' *prima facie* case. * * *

———

Civil Rights Act of 1991

(amending Title VII of the Civil Rights Act of 1964)
§ 109, 42 U.S.C. § 2000e et. seq. (1991)

SEC. 105. BURDEN OF PROOF IN DISPARATE IMPACT CASES.

(a) Section 703 of the Civil Rights Act of 1964 (42 U.S.C. 2000e–2) is amended by adding at the end the following new subsection:

'(k)(1)(A) An unlawful employment practice based on disparate impact is established under this title only if—

(i) a complaining party demonstrates that a respondent uses a particular employment practice that causes a disparate impact on the basis of race, color, religion, sex, or national origin and the respondent fails to demonstrate that the challenged practice is job related for the position in question and consistent with business necessity; or

(ii) the complaining party makes the demonstration described in subparagraph (C) with respect to an alternative employment practice and the respondent refuses to adopt such alternative employment practice.

(B)(i) With respect to demonstrating that a particular employment practice causes a disparate impact as described in subparagraph (A)(i), the complaining party shall demonstrate that each particular challenged employment practice causes a disparate impact, except that if the complaining party can demonstrate to the court that the elements of a respondent's decisionmaking process are not capable of separation for analysis, the decisionmaking process may be analyzed as one employment practice.

(ii) If the respondent demonstrates that a specific employment practice does not cause the disparate impact, the respondent shall not be required to demonstrate that such practice is required by business necessity.

(C) The demonstration referred to by subparagraph (A)(ii) shall be in accordance with the law as it existed on June 4, 1989, with respect to the concept of 'alternative employment practice'.

2) A demonstration that an employment practice is required by business necessity may not be used as a defense against a claim of intentional discrimination under this title. * * *

———

3. SEXUAL HARASSMENT

Meritor Savings Bank v. Vinson

477 U.S. 57 (1986)

■ JUSTICE REHNQUIST delivered the opinion of the Court.

This case presents important questions concerning claims of workplace "sexual harassment" brought under Title VII of the Civil Rights Act of 1964, 78 Stat. 253, as amended, 42 U.S.C. § 2000e *et seq.*

I

In 1974, respondent Mechelle Vinson met Sidney Taylor, a vice president of what is now petitioner Meritor Savings Bank (bank) and manager of one of its branch offices. When respondent asked whether she might obtain employment at the bank, Taylor gave her an application, which she completed and returned the next day; later that same day Taylor called her to say that she had been hired. With Taylor as her supervisor, respondent started as a teller-trainee, and thereafter was promoted to teller, head teller, and assistant branch manager. She worked at the same branch for four years, and it is undisputed that her advancement there was based on merit alone. In September 1978, respondent notified Taylor that she was taking sick leave for an indefinite period. On November 1, 1978, the bank discharged her for excessive use of that leave.

Respondent brought this action against Taylor and the bank, claiming that during her four years at the bank she "had constantly been subjected to sexual harassment" by Taylor in violation of Title VII. She sought injunctive relief, compensatory and punitive damages against Taylor and the bank, and attorney's fees.

At the 11–day bench trial, the parties presented conflicting testimony about Taylor's behavior during respondent's employment. Respondent testified that during her probationary period as a teller-trainee, Taylor treated her in a fatherly way and made no sexual advances. Shortly thereafter, however, he invited her out to dinner and, during the course of the meal, suggested that they go to a motel to have sexual relations. At first she refused, but out of what she described as fear of losing her job she eventually agreed. According to respondent, Taylor thereafter made repeated demands upon her for sexual favors, usually at the branch, both during and after business hours; she estimated that over the next several years she had intercourse with him some 40 or 50 times. In addition, respondent testified that Taylor fondled her in front of other employees, followed her into the women's restroom when she went there alone, exposed himself to her, and even forcibly raped her on several occasions. These activities ceased after 1977, respondent stated, when she started going with a steady boyfriend.

Respondent also testified that Taylor touched and fondled other women employees of the bank, and she attempted to call witnesses to support this charge. But while some supporting testimony apparently was admitted without objection, the District Court did not allow her "to present wholesale evidence of a pattern and practice relating to sexual advances to other female employees in her case in chief, but advised her that she might well be able to present such evidence in rebuttal to the defendants' cases." [citation omitted]. Respondent did not offer such evidence in rebuttal. Finally, respondent testified that because she was afraid of Taylor she never reported his harassment to any of his supervisors and never attempted to use the bank's complaint procedure.

Taylor denied respondent's allegations of sexual activity, testifying that he never fondled her, never made suggestive remarks to her, never engaged in sexual intercourse with her, and never asked her to do so. He contended instead that respondent made her accusations in response to a business-related dispute. The bank also denied respondent's allegations and asserted that any sexual harassment by Taylor was unknown to the bank and engaged in without its consent or approval.

The District Court denied relief, but did not resolve the conflicting testimony about the existence of a sexual relationship between respondent and Taylor. It found instead that

> "[i]f [respondent] and Taylor did engage in an intimate or sexual relationship during the time of [respondent's] employment with [the bank], that relationship was a voluntary one having nothing to do with her continued employment at [the bank] or her advancement or promotions at that institution."

The court ultimately found that respondent "was not the victim of sexual harassment and was not the victim of sexual discrimination" while employed at the bank. * * *

The Court of Appeals for the District of Columbia Circuit reversed. [citation omitted]. [T]he court stated that a violation of Title VII may be predicated on either of two types of sexual harassment: harassment that involves the conditioning of concrete employment benefits on sexual favors, and harassment that, while not affecting economic benefits, creates a hostile or offensive working environment. The court drew additional support for this position from the Equal Employment Opportunity Commission's Guidelines on Discrimination Because of Sex, 29 CFR § 1604.11(a) (1985), which set out these two types of sexual harassment claims. Believing that "Vinson's grievance was clearly of the [hostile environment] type . . ." and that the District Court had not considered whether a violation of this type had occurred, the court concluded that a remand was necessary. * * *

II

* * *

The prohibition against discrimination based on sex was added to Title VII at the last minute on the floor of the House of Representatives. 110 Cong.Rec. 2577–2584 (1964). The principal argument in opposition to the amendment was that "sex discrimination" was sufficiently different from other types of discrimination that it ought to receive separate legislative treatment. See id., at 2577 (statement of Rep. Celler quoting letter from United States Department of Labor); id., at 2584 (statement of Rep. Green). This argument was defeated, the bill quickly passed as amended, and we are left with little legislative history to guide us in interpreting the Act's prohibition against discrimination based on "sex."

Respondent argues, and the Court of Appeals held, that unwelcome sexual advances that create an offensive or hostile working environment violate Title VII. Without question, when a supervisor sexually harasses a subordinate because of the subordinate's sex, that supervisor "discriminate[s]" on the basis of sex. Petitioner apparently does not challenge this proposition. It contends instead that in prohibiting discrimination with respect to "compensation, terms, conditions, or privileges" of employment, Congress was concerned with what petitioner describes as "tangible loss" of "an economic character," not "purely psychological aspects of the workplace environment ....." In support of this claim petitioner observes that in both the legislative history of Title VII and this Court's Title VII decisions, the focus has been on tangible, economic barriers erected by discrimination.

We reject petitioner's view. First, the language of Title VII is not limited to "economic" or "tangible" discrimination. The phrase "terms, conditions, or privileges of employment" evinces a congressional intent "to strike at the entire spectrum of disparate treatment of men and women" in employment. [citation omitted]. Petitioner has pointed to nothing in the Act to suggest that Congress contemplated the limitation urged here.

Second, in 1980 the EEOC issued Guidelines specifying that "sexual harassment," as there defined, is a form of sex discrimination prohibited by Title VII. As an "administrative interpretation of the Act by the enforcing agency," these Guidelines, " 'while not controlling upon the courts by reason of their authority, do constitute a body of experience and informed judgment to which courts and litigants may properly resort for guidance.' " [citations omitted]. The EEOC Guidelines fully support the view that harassment leading to noneconomic injury can violate Title VII.

In defining "sexual harassment," the Guidelines first describe the kinds of workplace conduct that may be actionable under Title VII. These include "[u]nwelcome sexual advances, requests for sexual favors, and other verbal or physical conduct of a sexual nature." [citation omitted]. Relevant to the charges at issue in this case, the Guidelines provide that such sexual misconduct constitutes prohibited "sexual harassment," whether or not it is directly linked to the grant or denial of an economic quid pro quo, where "such conduct has the purpose or effect of unreasonably interfering with an individual's work performance or creating an intimidating, hostile, or offensive working environment." * * *

Nothing in Title VII suggests that a hostile environment based on discriminatory sexual harassment should not be likewise prohibited. The Guidelines thus appropriately drew from, and were fully consistent with, the existing case law.

Since the Guidelines were issued, courts have uniformly held, and we agree, that a plaintiff may establish a violation of Title VII by proving that discrimination based on sex has created a hostile or abusive work environment. As the Court of Appeals for the Eleventh Circuit wrote in *Henson v. Dundee*, 682 F.2d 897, 902 (1982):

"Sexual harassment which creates a hostile or offensive environment for members of one sex is every bit the arbitrary barrier to sexual equality at the workplace that racial harassment is to racial equality. Surely, a requirement that a man or woman run a gauntlet of sexual abuse in return for the privilege of being allowed to work and make a living can be as demeaning and disconcerting as the harshest of racial epithets."

Of course ... not all workplace conduct that may be described as "harassment" affects a "term, condition, or privilege" of employment within the meaning of Title VII. *See Rogers v. EEOC, supra*, at 238 ("mere utterance of an ethnic or racial epithet which engenders offensive feelings in an employee" would not affect the conditions of employment to sufficiently significant degree to violate Title VII); *Henson*, 682 F.2d, at 904 (quoting same). For sexual harassment to be actionable, it must be sufficiently severe or pervasive "to alter the conditions of [the victim's] employment and create an abusive working environment." *Ibid.* Respondent's allegations in this case—which include not only pervasive harassment but also criminal conduct of the most serious nature—are plainly sufficient to state a claim for "hostile environment" sexual harassment. * * *

Petitioner contends that even if this case must be remanded to the District Court, the Court of Appeals erred in one of the terms of its remand. Specifically, the Court of Appeals stated that testimony about respondent's "dress and personal fantasies," [citation omitted] which the District Court apparently admitted into evidence, "had no place in this litigation." [citation omitted]. The apparent ground for this conclusion was that respondent's voluntariness *vel non* in submitting to Taylor's advances was immaterial to her sexual harassment claim. While "voluntariness" in the sense of consent is not a defense to such a claim, it does not follow that a complainant's sexually provocative speech or dress is irrelevant as a matter of law in determining whether he or she found particular sexual advances unwelcome. To the contrary, such evidence is obviously relevant. The EEOC Guidelines emphasize that the trier of fact must determine the existence of sexual harassment in light of "the record as a whole" and "the totality of circumstances, such as the nature of the sexual advances and the context in which the alleged incidents occurred." [citation omitted]. Respondent's claim that any marginal relevance of the evidence in question was outweighed by the potential for unfair prejudice is the sort of argument properly addressed to the District Court. In this case the District Court concluded that the evidence should be admitted, and the Court of Appeals' contrary conclusion was based upon the erroneous, categorical view that testimony about provocative dress and publicly expressed sexual fantasies "had no place in this litigation." [Citation omitted.] While the District Court must carefully weigh the applicable considerations in deciding whether to admit evidence of this kind, there is no per se rule against its admissibility.

[Court's section on employer liability omitted].

IV

In sum, we hold that a claim of "hostile environment" sex discrimination is actionable under Title VII, that the District Court's findings were insufficient to dispose of respondent's hostile environment claim, and that the District Court did not err in admitting testimony about respondent's sexually provocative speech and dress. As to employer liability, we conclude that the Court of Appeals was wrong to entirely disregard agency principles and impose absolute liability on employers for the acts of their supervisors, regardless of the circumstances of a particular case.

■ [Concurring Opinion by JUSTICE MARSHALL, JUSTICE BRENNAN, JUSTICE BLACKMUN, and JUSTICE STEVENS omitted].

———

Sexual Harassment Law in the United States, the United Kingdom and the European Union: Discriminatory Wrongs and Dignitary Harms

36 Common Law World Review 79, 80–84; 86–88 (2007)

■ LINDA CLARKE

It is generally accepted that, although the behaviour it describes has been around for a very long time, the term 'sexual harassment' was first coined during a brainstorming session involving three feminist activists at Cornell University in 1975. One of those activists, Lynn Farley, wrote a book on the subject and activists and lawyers began to take cases on behalf of women forced out of jobs because of sexual harassment at work. But the key legal development was the argument that sexual harassment was not just individualized bad behaviour, or simply 'personal', but that it was sex discrimination, and unlawful under Title VII of the Civil Rights Act 1964. Catherine MacKinnon argued forcefully that:

> [s]exual harassment perpetuates the interlocked structure by which women have been kept sexually in thrall to men and at the bottom of the labour market. Two forces of American society converge: men's control over women's sexuality and capital's control over employees' work lives.

MacKinnon rejected the idea of using traditional tort-based actions, such as intentional infliction of emotional distress, because 'by treating the incidents [of sexual harassment] as if they are outrages particular to an individual woman rather than integral to her social status as a woman worker, the personal approach on the legal level fails to analyze the relevant dimensions of the problem'. For MacKinnon, it was essential to recognize that sexual harassment was a group harm, a form of discrimination against women as women.

Her arguments were successful: by 1980 the Equal Employment Opportunity Commission (EEOC) had issued guidelines declaring that sexual harassment was a breach of section 703(a)(1) of Title VII of the Civil Rights Act 1964 and in 1986 the Supreme Court confirmed that sexual harassment was actionable sex discrimination. Public awareness of sexual harassment increased following the intensive media coverage of the allegations of sexual harassment made by Anita Hill against Clarence Thomas during the course of his nomination hearings for appointment to the Supreme Court, and in 1991, Congress extended Title VII relief to include compensatory and punitive damages. In 1998 the Supreme Court clarified employer liability, holding that employers were strictly liable where sexual harassment had tangible employment consequences, such as demotion or dismissal, though in 'hostile environment' cases, where there were no tangible employment actions, employers would have a defence where they had acted reasonably to prevent harassment, and the employee had unreasonably failed to take advantage of any preventative or corrective action.

* * * Exactly why is sexual harassment sex discrimination? This key question troubled some feminist legal scholars early on, as they tried to find an adequate theoretical basis for the assertions so readily accepted by the courts. Katherine M. Franke identified three different explanations. Firstly, sexual harassment violates the equality principle, in that a woman is treated differently from a man, and would not have been so treated 'but for' her sex. Early cases involved arguments that the issue was about sexual attraction, not sex discrimination: had the (male) harasser been attracted to a male employee, he would have subjected the man to exactly the same treatment as the woman. This was firmly quashed in *Barnes v. Costle* [citation omitted] in 1977 when Judge Spottiswood Robinson noted that the heterosexual (male) supervisor would not have demanded sexual relations from a male employee as a condition of keeping his job. Franke sees this as 'the central judicial conception' of sexual harassment.

Secondly, sexual harassment is sex discrimination simply because the conduct is sexual in nature: 'sex' equals 'sexual'. Franke has shown that after a while the courts began to ignore the 'because of sex' element whenever the conduct was explicitly sexual. It was the sexual nature of the conduct, doled out by (heterosexual) men to women, that the courts began to look for. Vicki Schultz has also argued that US case law has placed *sexual* conduct (rather than sex discriminatory conduct) at the heart of 'hostile environment' harassment in the United States. But the question then becomes, why is *sexual* conduct per se a form of sex discrimination?

Thirdly, sexual harassment is sex discrimination because it is an example of the subordination of women by men. This theory, for MacKinnon, best articulates sex discrimination as being concerned with *inequality* rather than *difference*. Under this approach, what is wrong with sexual harassment is that 'it participates in the systemic social deprivation of one sex because of sex'. Sexual harassment becomes a tool which men as a group use to subordinate women.

The weaknesses of each of these theoretical accounts were exposed by the difficulties the courts experienced in adjudicating cases of same-sex harassment. When the issue finally came before the Supreme Court in 1998 in *Oncale v. Sundowner Offshore Services* the court was forced to attempt to articulate more clearly why sexual harassment was actionable sex discrimination. Joseph Oncale was working on an offshore oil platform when he was subjected to sex-related humiliating conduct, sexual assault, and threat of rape, by male co-workers, two of whom were in a supervisory position. Was this sex discrimination, and if so, why?

The Supreme Court began by noting that lower courts had taken 'a bewildering variety of stances' to same-sex harassment claims, and identified three main approaches, which broadly follow those identified by Franke. Firstly, some courts held that same-sex sexual harassment could never be actionable as sex discrimination. This could, very loosely, be seen as endorsing MacKinnon's approach that sexual harassment is about the subordination of women by men. Secondly, some courts found that such harassment was actionable only if the harasser was homosexual, presumably motivated by sexual desire. This adopts the 'but for' approach, assuming the harasser would not have approached someone of the opposite sex. Thirdly, other courts suggested that workplace harassment that is sexual in nature is always actionable, regardless of the harasser's sex, sexual orientation, or motivations.

Justice Scalia, delivering the opinion of a unanimous court, ruled that same-sex harassment could be actionable as sex discrimination, if courts and juries were able to draw the inference that it was sex discrimination: 'whether members of one sex are exposed to disadvantageous terms or conditions of employment to which members of the other sex are not exposed'. This inference could be drawn in three situations: where the harasser was homosexual (presumably motivated by desire); where 'for example, a female victim is harassed by another woman so as to make it clear that the harasser is motivated by general hostility to the presence of women in the workplace'; and if the plaintiff can offer 'direct comparative evidence about how the alleged harasser treated members of both sexes in a mixed-sex workplace'. All of these are variations on the 'but for' explanation: the harassment would not have occurred if the victim had been of the opposite sex. Although commentators broadly welcomed the result in *Oncale*, the reasoning itself has been criticized for continuing to fail to explain why exactly, and when, sexual harassment is sex discrimination, and for ignoring broader theories about gender roles.

* * * The difficulties of fitting harassment within a discrimination framework have also arisen in UK law. In *Porcelli v. Strathclyde Regional Council*, the first British case on harassment to go to a higher court, two newly appointed male laboratory workers mounted a campaign of harassment against a female colleague, for no apparent reason. Although the harassment involved some sexual comments and behaviour, most of it did not, consisting of matters such as hiding her keys, emptying out her drawers, upsetting experiments and blocking her path. The employer's defence was that the behaviour was not motivated by any reason connected with Mrs. Porcelli's sex, but by dislike: the two men would have also harassed a male employee similarly disliked. This argument was successful before the Industrial Tribunal, but on appeal, the Court of Session held that because the *form* of the treatment involved (some) sex-specific conduct, and was 'very different in a material respect from that which would have been inflicted on a male colleague', there was sex discrimination. The men had used 'a sexual sword'.

Porcelli can be read as a very sophisticated understanding of gender relationships, with its concentration on the effect of the conduct on the victim, rather than the motive of the harassers, and the way in which sexualized conduct and language is used as a particularly effective way of putting women in their place. But it was a difficult case in other respects for the 'sex discrimination' framework: much of the harassment was not sexual or sex-specific, the Court of Session spoke of 'the equality of overall unpleasantness', and accepted that the men disliked Mrs Porcelli as a person, not as a woman. Nor was this a case of male employees harassing a new female employee in a previously male environment. In later cases, some of the reasoning in *Porcelli* was criticized, and tribunals refused to accept that the same treatment (such as the display of pornography in a workplace, or the use of foul language) was sex discrimination simply on the grounds that the treatment might have different effects or consequences for men and women. In *Pearce v. Mayfield School* the House of Lords firmly quashed the idea that harassment consisting of sex-specific language was sex discrimination: instead tribunals should treat it as part of the evidence, in determining whether the reason for the treatment was 'on the ground of her sex'.

So the problem is that, although some sexual harassment is clearly sex discrimination (such as where male workers use sexual insults and sexualized behaviour with the explicit aim of driving women out of previously male working environments), it is not always easy to explain why other forms of sexual harassment are sex discriminatory, though instinctively one may feel this is so.

* * *

Aside from these theoretical concerns, it has also been argued in the United States that, on a pragmatic and practical level, sexual harassment law has not been the great success story for women's rights at work as claimed in the past. Much of the criticism focuses on the apparent need for plaintiffs to show sexual conduct and sexualized behaviour, rather than sex discriminatory behaviour. In a comprehensive examination of hostile environment claims in the US, Vicki Schultz has demonstrated that the courts look for *sexual* conduct alone to establish hostile environment harassment. This has led to the law being both under-inclusive and over-inclusive. It is under-inclusive, in that it either ignores non-sexualized discriminatory harassment, or subjects it to the stricter requirements of a disparate impact claim. It is over-inclusive, in that it has encouraged employers, fearful of expensive sexual harassment suits, to prohibit 'a broad range of relatively harmless sexual conduct, even where that conduct does not threaten gender equality on the job'. Schultz argues that the courts have missed an important link between gender discrimination and gender segregation, and that 'hostile work environment harassment is driven not by a need for sexual domination but by a desire to preserve favoured lines of work as masculine'.

* * * There are a number of consequences to this over-inclusiveness. Firstly, if all forms of sexual expression are suspect, this can lead to overzealous disciplinary measures being taken against transgressors. This has been a particular issue in the United States, where the vast majority of employees work under so-called 'fire at will' contracts, with no legal protection against an unfair or unreasonable dismissal. The very success of sexual harassment claims in the United States has meant that employers are well advised to fire an alleged harasser, rather than risk an expensive hostile environment claim. Schultz also demonstrates that management in the United States have sometimes seized upon sexual harassment issues as a subterfuge for getting rid of employees who violate the norm of asexuality, regardless of whether such conduct is sex discriminatory: '[I]n some cases, the accused's offence is so small, its connection to any sexist

motivation or pattern so slight, and the managerial response so overblown, that it is hard to resist the conclusion that management is using sexual harassment as a justification for punishing an employee they want to punish for other reasons'. These sanctions have been used disproportionately against non-white men, gay men, and older men.

* * * There are also concerns that sexual harassment policies can actually increase sex segregation and make it more difficult for women to achieve workplace equality. Recent research from the United States has identified a 'glass partition', a barrier to cross-sex friendship at work, which has arisen partly as a result of increased awareness of sexual harassment: 75 per cent of the male participants in the survey reported that they think about sexual harassment issues when interacting with women at work. Further, this 'glass partition' disadvantages women in gaining access to information, networking and mentoring opportunities. Schultz notes that some employers resort to informal sex-segregation policies to avoid potential sexual harassment suits: 'If the presence of sex is a problem, then one way to deal with it is to segregate "the sexes"'. Quinn's research demonstrates that 'the mere fear of sexual harassment charges is used to further isolate women and to justify men's hostility towards them'.

An approach to harassment that emphasizes the sexual nature of harassing conduct also perpetuates a damaging stereotype: 'the belief that sexual expression is demeaning to women invites legal protection for the wrong reasons. It positions women as a sexually pure and vulnerable victim class whose virtue or special sensibilities require protection from men, positioned as natural sexual predators'.

This moralistic, puritanical approach to sexual conduct has also been attacked by post-modern and queer theorists. Cohen, describing post-modern feminist theory, notes that '[t]he ideology that women's sexuality is nonexistent or shameful accounts for why sexualization can become a means to discredit and silence them. It also deprives women of their own legitimate sexual expression'. Janet Halley questions the alleged 'harms' of sexual harassment, asking whether women are really more injured 'when a male supervisor asks to sleep with us than when he forgets to sign us up for a reskilling conference or power lunch'? Katherine M. Franke has noted that 'when it comes to sex, [legal feminists] have done a more than adequate job of theorizing the right to say no, but we have left to others the task of understanding what it might mean to say yes'.

It has also been suggested that much of the 'success' of sexual harassment law in the United States might be explained as much by its appeal to the business mindset of American capitalism as to American values of equality and non-discrimination. Prohibiting sexual conduct at work falls neatly within the neo-Taylorist project of advancing efficiency within the workplace by excluding irrational and emotional behaviour, argues Schultz, and this is a major reason why American employers have embraced anti-sexual harassment policies so readily, whilst ignoring issues such as maternity rights and equal pay. Saguy, comparing American and French attitudes to sexual harassment, and sexuality at work, noted that American respondents frequently used a 'business frame', saying that sexual relations were 'bad for business', without tying sexual behaviour to gender inequality.

————

NOTES

1.   The U.S. Supreme Court's jurisprudence on Title VII, including allocation of burdens of proof and employer defenses, has been used as a model for other civil rights statutes which cover characteristics such as age and disability. Although these other statutes are not covered in this chapter, it is important to note the conceptual and practical links between Title VII and those other statutes. Like Title VII, most employment discrimination statutes cover various forms of discrimination, many of which we have seen in Chapter II—including disparate treatment discrimination, disparate impact discrimination, harassment, and reasonable accommodation. Moreover, courts' interpretation of the type of discrimination covered under Title VII, and the evidentiary requirements to prove each type of discrimination, has shaped the drafting and interpretation of other employment discrimination statutes. The Age Discrimination in Employment Act ("ADEA") of 1967 prohibits discrimination in hiring, promotion, wages, termination and layoffs against anyone over the age of 40 years old. 29 U.S.C. section 621–634. It also prohibits discrimination in benefits for older workers and prohibits mandatory retirement based on age in most employment sectors (one exception is certain executives over 65 in high policy-making positions). Age discrimination is allowable, as it is under Title VII, if age is a "bona fide occupational qualification reasonably necessary to the normal operation of the particular business." *Id.*

2.   The Americans with Disabilities Act ("ADA") of 1990 prohibits discrimination against individuals with a disability in various sectors of life. 42 U.S.C. Chapter 26. An individual with a disability is defined as a person who has (or has a history of having) a physical or mental impairment that substantially limits one or more major life activities or a person who is perceived by others as having such an impairment. 42 U.S.C. section 12102. The Act does not define what kinds of impairments constitute a disability and this has been the subject of a number of important Supreme Court cases interpreting the Act. *See e.g. Toyota Motor Mfg. v. Williams*, 534 U.S. 184 (2002) (interpreting "substantial limitation" of "major life activities" to mean that claimants must demonstrate permanent or long-term impairment in ability to perform "activities that are of central importance to most people's daily lives."). Title I of the ADA prohibits discrimination in employment and explicitly prohibits both disparate treatment and disparate impact discrimination and, additionally, requires that employers make reasonable accommodations to the known physical or mental limitations of otherwise qualified individuals with disabilities, unless it results in undue hardship to the employer. 42 U.S.C. section 12112.

3.   Title VII prohibits most employers from discriminating on the basis of religion. The term "religion" includes all aspects of religious observance and practice, as well as belief, unless an employer demonstrates that he is unable to reasonably accommodate an employee's or prospective

employee's religious observance or practice without undue hardship on the conduct of the employer's business. 42 U.S.C. section 2000e(j). The Supreme Court has interpreted the reasonable accommodation requirement in a fairly de minimis way, and highly sensitive to the cost such accommodations impose on employers. *See e.g. TWA v. Hardison*, 432 U.S. 63 (1977) (to require the employer to expend more than a de minimis cost to give the plaintiff his Sabbath off would be an undue hardship); *Ansonia Board of Education v. Philbrook*, 479 U.S. 60 (1986) (neither the statute nor the legislative history require an employer to accept a particular accommodation; once an employer has reasonably accommodated an employee's needs, the statutory inquiry is at an end and the employer does not have to show that the other desired accommodations would cause undue hardship).

4. The Equal Pay Act of 1963 prohibits sex discrimination in the payment of wages and requires employers to pay men and women equally for doing the same work—equal pay for equal work. 29 U.S.C. § 206. Congress passed the Act to invalidate blatant discriminatory practices that resulted in paying women lower wages and to rectify the wage disparity between men and women. Even as those practices have been swept aside, however, the pay gap between men and women has persisted into the 21st Century. In 2009, President Obama signed the Lily Ledbetter Fair Pay Restoration Act, which allows victims of pay discrimination to file a complaint with the government against their employer within 180 days of their last paycheck. Previously, victims were only allowed 180 days from the date of the initial discriminatory decision by the employer under a Supreme Court ruling. *See Ledbetter v. Goodyear Tire & Rubber Co.*, 550 U.S. 618 (2007).

5. There is no law forbidding discrimination on the basis of sexual orientation in the United States, at least on the federal level. Members of Congress have introduced the Employment Non–Discrimination Act ("ENDA") many times over the past decade and each time it has fallen short of the votes needed for passage. The current version of the Bill would provide workplace protections on the basis of both sexual orientation and gender identity, but it would exempt a number of employers—including small businesses, religious organizations and the military. Twenty one states and the District of Columbia currently have laws which prohibit discrimination in employment based on sexual orientation. Fifteen states and the District of Columbia also prohibit discrimination based on gender identity. According to the prominent gay rights advocacy organization, the Human Rights Campaign, hundreds of companies have enacted policies protecting their lesbian, gay, bisexual and transgender employees. As of March 2011, 433 (87 percent) of the Fortune 500 companies had implemented non-discrimination policies that include sexual orientation, and 229 (46 percent) had policies that include gender identity. http://www.hrc.org/laws_and_elections/enda.asp.

6. Consider the following assessment of courts' treatment of discrimination claims based on national origin under Title VII:

"Despite its parallel status and equal longevity in Title VII, the prohibition against "national origin" discrimination remains, as it began, largely undeveloped and ineffective. For example, what is usually referred to as the legislative history of the "national origin" term consists of a few un-illuminating paragraphs of the House debate that discuss what national origin meant." The national origin term ended up in Title VII because it was part of the "boilerplate" statutory language of fair employment in executive orders and legislation preceding the Civil Rights Act of 1964. At the time, Congress gave no serious thought to the content of the national origin term nor to its proper scope. Since that time, as well, there has been a remarkable scarcity of analysis regarding the "national origin" term and whether it remains adequate for the forms of discrimination common today.

Courts have been largely unsympathetic to claims of discrimination as experienced by persons whose "ethnicity" differs from that of the majority. Thus Mexican American employees must endure insults such as "wetback" and demeaning labor which "Americans [do] not have to do." Employees may be fired or disciplined for speaking languages other than English in the workplace, even if employees are doing their jobs at the time or if their conversations do not interfere with job performance. Persons who speak with "foreign" accents may be denied employment, despite excellent qualifications and verbal skills, because of the discomfort and displeasure they cause interviewers. African American women may be denied the ability to express their ethnic identity by wearing their hair in cornrows. All of these situations occur, and recur, despite Title VII's prohibitions against national origin and race discrimination."

Juan F. Perea, *Ethnicity and Prejudice: Reevaluating "National Origin" Discrimination Under Title VII*, 35 WM. & MARY L. REV. 805 (1994).

7.   Some courts have also interpreted Title VII as not prohibiting discrimination on the basis of "voluntary" behaviors that workers may perceive to be an essential part of their racial or ethnic identity. For instance, an employer may ban certain kinds of hairstyles—such as braids or dreadlocks—from a workplace even though such a ban effectively screens out large numbers of blacks from the employment pool. Or an employer may adopt a grooming policy that forbids employees from wearing head wraps, even if those wraps are required by their religious beliefs. The judicial tolerance for these kind of employer policies is, some scholars have argued, indicative of courts' tendency to embrace biological conceptions of race and ethnicity and to exempt from protection the "performative" aspects of racial and ethnic identity, even though discrimination on the basis of these racial proxies can be based on racial bias and animus. *See e.g.* Camille Gear Rich, *Performing Racial And Ethnic Identity: Discrimination By Proxy And The Future Of Title VII*, 79 N.Y.U. LAW REVIEW 1134 (2004).

8.   What is the effect of the Civil Rights Act of 1991, excerpted above (and also known as the Civil Rights Restoration Act), passed by Congress partially in response to the Price Waterhouse and Wards Cove decisions? In what ways, if any, does the Act change the law of those cases?

9.   What is the relationship between the structure of proof set out in Section 107 of the 1991 act for proving discrimination and the burden of proof structure set out in cases like *McDonnell Douglas* and *Hicks*, covered in Chapter II, as it relates to how a plaintiff demonstrates that s/he was

discriminated against "because of" race, sex, or other prohibited characteristic? It may be that the two proof structures merge together after the Civil Rights Act of 1991. That is, the *McDonnell Douglas/Hicks* evidentiary framework can still be employed to raise an inference, circumstantially, that an illegitimate consideration (e.g. race or sex) was part of the employer's decision making process. Once this is demonstrated, either by circumstantial or direct evidence, the employer has available to it the defense made available by Price Waterhouse and the 1991 Act—that it would have made same decision even if the prohibited characteristic had played no role in the employment decision. *See Desert Palace v. Costa*, 539 U.S. 90 (2003).

10. Note that Title VII tolerates classification on basis of religion, sex or national origin in those certain instances where religion, sex or national origin is a BFOQ—a trait that is reasonably necessary to the normal operation of a particular business enterprise. What it is about race that makes it different from sex, national origin, or religion that there would never be a legitimate reason for an employer to only hire people of one race? Might there be a BFOQ defense if a theater decided to hire only women to fulfill female roles, or only men to fulfill male roles, but not blacks to fill only a black role or whites to fill only a white role? What about if it decided to hire French or Cuban person to fill, respectively, a French or Cuban role; or a Jewish person to fill a Jewish role? Are there some roles for which the theater could argue that national origin or religion are reasonably necessary or essential to the role. Note that regulations promulgated by the Equal Employment Opportunity Commission (EEOC) indicate that the BFOQ exception "shall be strictly construed." 29 Code Federal Regulations section 1606.4 (2010).

11. In the *Vinson* case the Court held that "While "voluntariness" in the sense of consent is not a defense to [a claim of sexual harassment], it does not follow that a complainant's sexually provocative speech or dress is irrelevant as a matter of law in determining whether he or she found particular sexual advances unwelcome. To the contrary, such evidence is obviously relevant." In what way is it relevant?

12. The Supreme Court in *Harris v. Forklift*, 510 U.S. 17 (1993), considered the question "whether conduct, to be actionable as 'abusive work environment' harassment (no *quid pro quo* harassment issue is present here), must 'seriously affect [an employee's] psychological well being' or lead the plaintiff to 'suffe[r] injury.' The Court unanimously held that sexual harassment need not lead to psychological harm in order for it to be actionable under Title VII. Rather, sexual harassment occurs when "the environment would reasonably be perceived, and is perceived, as hostile or abusive" even if such conduct would not seriously affect a reasonable person's psychological well being. The Court also gave further guidance on how to evaluate a sexual harassment claim:

> "[W]hether an environment is 'hostile' or 'abusive' can be determined only by looking at all the circumstances. These may include the frequency of the discriminatory conduct; its severity; whether it is physically threatening or humiliating, or a mere offensive utterance; and whether it unreasonably interferes with an employee's work performance. The effect on the employee's psychological well being is,

of course, relevant to determining whether the plaintiff actually found the environment abusive. But while psychological harm, like any other relevant factor, may be taken into account, no single factor is required."

Id. at 23.

B. EUROPE

Article 13 of the Treaty of Amsterdam, ratified by the member states of the European Union in 1999, introduced the power of the European Council ("EC") to adopt measures to combat discrimination based on sex, racial or ethnic origin, religion or belief, disability, age or sexual orientation. Pursuant to this Treaty, the Council has established a number of "Directives" prohibiting employment discrimination in each of the grounds listed above. Each member state is obligated to conform its national law to the terms of the EC Directives. These Directives set a minimum standard, or floor, below which each member state cannot go. States may adopt antidiscrimination measures that go above the standards set by the Directives. The European Court of Justice (ECJ) may determine that a member state has failed to comply with a Directive, either by failing to conform its laws to the Directives or by failing, through its national courts, to properly enforce the Directives. In this regard, recall the relationship between the EC and the ECJ (European Court of Justice), discussed briefly in chapter II.

This section is organized by the various Directives which cover employment discrimination at the European Community level. These Directives separately cover antidiscrimination prohibitions by sex (76/207/EEC) and race (2000/43/EC), and there is a general employment Directive which covers age, disability, religion or belief, and sexual orientation (2000/78/EC). Each of the Directives prohibit direct and indirect discrimination, as well as harassment on the basis of the covered characteristic. Unlike Title VII under U.S. law, the Directives are very specific about what kind of discrimination is outlawed and neither courts nor member states have had to define the term "discrimination." In other ways, however, the Directives leave open important questions about their reach—specifically, how far do they go to define and enforce racial, gender and other forms of equality?

The grounds of discrimination covered in the various Directives largely mirror those prohibited by the EU Charter on Fundamental Rights, which is also binding on members states pursuant to the Treaty of Lisbon. Article 12(1) of that charter prohibits any discrimination on the grounds of age, race, color, ethnic or social origin, genetic features, language, religion or belief, political or any other opinion, membership of a national minority, property, birth, disability, age or sexual orientation. As with the EC Directives, discrimination under the EU Charter is adjudicated by the European Court of Justice (ECJ) in Luxemburg; the European Court of Human Rights (ECtHR) in Strasburg also has jurisdiction (or "competence") over discrimination, but only when it violates the European Convention of Human Rights. A point worth noting is that fundamental rights protection in Europe has been a sphere of law which is particularly open to judicial cross-fertilization. The Strasburg Court has been referring more and more frequently to the EU Charter of Fundamental Rights, and the Luxemburg Court has always been quite receptive to the European Convention on Human Rights. Antidiscrimination law is thus a good example of this dialogue between courts since it has produced similar case law on certain discrimination issues and some cases on discrimination have even been tried by both courts.

1. SEX DISCRIMINATION

The principle of equality between men and women was an original principle contained in the Treaty of Rome (1957) which required, among other things, Member states to ensure that men and women should receive equal pay for equal work. The Treaty of Rome's principle of equality contained the twin aims of seeking equality both as a matter of market conditions and as a matter of human rights and social policy. The European Council has since adopted a number of Directives aimed at implementing the principle of equal treatment between men and women in a variety of contexts. Due to the long history of recognizing the equal treatment principle between men and women, its legal status is much more developed than other areas of non-discrimination law in Europe. Key concepts of non-discrimination law—such as the concepts of direct and indirect discrimination as well as the rules on burden of proof in discrimination cases—were developed within the context of sex equality laws.

Much of the jurisprudence developed over time has been incorporated into the Directives as they are amended by the Council. The latest Directive, excerpted below, amends earlier Directives prohibiting sex discrimination in employment and "recasts" them in one Directive. The Directive incorporates much of the jurisprudence interpreting earlier Directives and thus is quite specific about the type of discrimination covered as well as the scope of the prohibition. The Directive contains provisions to implement the equal treatment principle in relation to (a) access to employment, including promotion, and to vocational training; (b) working conditions, including pay; and (c) occupational social security schemes. Following the Directive is an example of a recent case which raises new questions regarding the reach of sex discrimination laws.

Council Directive 2006/54/EC of 5 July 2006

(on the implementation of the principle of equal opportunities and equal treatment of men and women in matters of employment and occupation (recast))

(amending, *inter alia*, Council Directive 76/207/EEC of 9 February 1976)

■ THE COUNCIL OF THE EUROPEAN UNION

Preamble

Whereas:

(2) Equality between men and women is a fundamental principle of Community law under Article 2 and Article 3(2) of the Treaty and the case-law of the Court of Justice. Those Treaty provisions proclaim equality between men and women as a 'task' and an 'aim' of the Community and impose a positive obligation to promote it in all its activities.

(3) The Court of Justice has held that the scope of the principle of equal treatment for men and women cannot be confined to the prohibition of discrimination based on the fact that a person is of one or other sex. In view of its purpose and the nature of the rights which it seeks to safeguard, it also applies to discrimination arising from the gender reassignment of a person.

(8) The principle of equal pay for equal work or work of equal value as laid down by Article 141 of the Treaty and consistently upheld in the case-law of the Court of Justice constitutes an important aspect of the principle of equal treatment between men and women and an essential and indispensable part of the *acquis communautaire*, including the case-law of the Court concerning sex discrimination. It is therefore appropriate to make further provision for its implementation.

(11) The Member States, in collaboration with the social partners, should continue to address the problem of the continuing gender-based wage differentials and marked gender segregation on the labour market by means such as flexible working time arrangements which enable both men and women to combine family and work commitments more successfully. This could also include appropriate parental leave arrangements which could be taken up by either parent as well as the provision of accessible and affordable child-care facilities and care for dependent persons.

(21) The prohibition of discrimination should be without prejudice to the maintenance or adoption of measures intended to prevent or compensate for disadvantages suffered by a group of persons of one sex. Such measures permit organisations of persons of one sex where their main object is the promotion of the special needs of those persons and the promotion of equality between men and women.

Article 2—

1. For the purposes of this Directive, the following definitions shall apply: (a) 'direct discrimination': where one person is treated less favourably on grounds of sex than another is, has been or would be treated in a comparable situation; (b) 'indirect discrimination': where an apparently neutral provision, criterion or practice would put persons of one sex at a particular disadvantage compared with persons of the other sex, unless that provision, criterion or practice is objectively justified by a legitimate aim, and the means of achieving that aim are appropriate and necessary; (c) 'harassment': where unwanted conduct related to the sex of a person occurs with the purpose or effect of violating the dignity of a person, and of creating an intimidating, hostile, degrading, humiliating or offensive environment; (d) 'sexual harassment': where any form of unwanted verbal, non-verbal or physical conduct of a sexual nature occurs, with the purpose or effect of violating the dignity of a person, in particular when creating an intimidating, hostile, degrading, humiliating or offensive environment; (e)

'pay': the ordinary basic or minimum wage or salary and any other consideration, whether in cash or in kind, which the worker receives directly or indirectly, in respect of his/her employment from his/her employer, * * *

2. For the purposes of this Directive, discrimination includes: (a) harassment and sexual harassment, as well as any less favourable treatment based on a person's rejection of or submission to such conduct; (b) instruction to discriminate against persons on grounds of sex; (c) any less favourable treatment of a woman related to pregnancy or maternity leave within the meaning of Directive 92/85/EEC.

Article 4—

For the same work or for work to which equal value is attributed, direct and indirect discrimination on grounds of sex with regard to all aspects and conditions of remuneration shall be eliminated. In particular, where a job classification system is used for determining pay, it shall be based on the same criteria for both men and women and so drawn up as to exclude any discrimination on grounds of sex.

Article 5—

Without prejudice to Article 4, there shall be no direct or indirect discrimination on grounds of sex in occupational social security schemes, in particular as regards: (a) the scope of such schemes and the conditions of access to them; (b) the obligation to contribute and the calculation of contributions; (c) the calculation of benefits, including supplementary benefits due in respect of a spouse or dependants, and the conditions governing the duration and retention of entitlement to benefits.

Article 6—

This Chapter shall apply to members of the working population, including self-employed persons, persons whose activity is interrupted by illness, maternity, accident or involuntary unemployment and persons seeking employment and to retired and disabled workers, and to those claiming under them, in accordance with national law and/or practice.

Article 14—

1. There shall be no direct or indirect discrimination on grounds of sex in the public or private sectors, including public bodies, in relation to: (a) conditions for access to employment, to self-employment or to occupation, including selection criteria and recruitment conditions, whatever the branch of activity and at all levels of the professional hierarchy, including promotion; (b) access to all types and to all levels of vocational guidance, vocational training, advanced vocational training and retraining, including practical work experience; (c) employment and working conditions, including dismissals, as well as pay ... (d) membership of, and involvement in, an organisation of workers or employers, or any organisation whose members carry on a particular profession, including the benefits provided for by such organisations.

2. Member States may provide, as regards access to employment including the training leading thereto, that a difference of treatment which is based on a characteristic related to sex shall not constitute discrimination where, by reason of the nature of the particular occupational activities concerned or of the context in which they are carried out, such a characteristic constitutes a genuine and determining occupational requirement, provided that its objective is legitimate and the requirement is proportionate.

Article 15—

A woman on maternity leave shall be entitled, after the end of her period of maternity leave, to return to her job or to an equivalent post on terms and conditions which are no less favourable to her and to benefit from any improvement in working conditions to which she would have been entitled during her absence.

Article 16—

This Directive is without prejudice to the right of Member States to recognise distinct rights to paternity and/or adoption leave. Those Member States which recognise such rights shall take the necessary measures to protect working men and women against dismissal due to exercising those rights and ensure that, at the end of such leave, they are entitled to return to their jobs or to equivalent posts on terms and conditions which are no less favourable to them, and to benefit from any improvement in working conditions to which they would have been entitled during their absence.

Commission of the European Communities v. Republic of Austria

Case C–203/03, 1 February 2005

■ EUROPEAN COURT OF JUSTICE (Grand Chamber)

1. By its application, the Commission of the European Communities requests the Court to declare that, by maintaining, contrary to the provisions of Council Directive 76/207/EEC of 9 February 1976 on the implementation of the principle of equal treatment for men and women as regards access to employment ... a general prohibition of the employment of women, with a limited number of exceptions, in the sector of the underground mining industry and in Articles 8 and 31 of the Druckluft-und TaucherarbeitenVerordnung (Regulation on work in high-pressure atmosphere and diving work) of 25 July 1973 (BGBl. 501/1973, 'the regulation of 1973'), a general prohibition of the employment of women in that kind of work, the Republic of Austria has failed to fulfil its obligations under Articles 2 and 3 of that directive and under Articles 10 EC and 249 EC, and to order the Republic of Austria to pay the costs.

Legal context

The relevant provisions of international law

3. Article 2 of Convention No 45 of the International Labour Organisation ('the I.L.O.') of 21 June 1935 concerning the employment of women on underground work in mines of all kinds, ratified by the Republic of Austria in 1937, stipulates that: 'No female, whatever her age, shall be employed on underground work in any mine.'

4. In accordance with Article 3 of that Convention: 'National law or regulations may exempt from the above prohibition: (a) females holding positions of management who do not perform manual work; (b) females employed in health and welfare services; (c) females who, in the course of their studies, spend a period of training in the underground parts of a mine; and (d) any other females who may occasionally have to enter the underground parts of a mine for the purpose of a non-manual occupation.'

5. Article 7 of that Convention stipulates: '1. A Member which has ratified this Convention may denounce it after the expiration of ten years from the date on which the Convention first comes into force, by an act communicated to the Director–General of the International Labour Office for registration.... 2. Each Member which has ratified this Convention and which does not, within the year following the expiration of the period of ten years mentioned in the preceding paragraph, exercise the right of denunciation provided for in this Article, will be bound for another period of ten years and, thereafter, may denounce this Convention at the expiration of each period of ten years under the terms provided for in this Article.'

6. Convention No 45 of the I.L.O. entered into force on 30 May 1937.

7. Convention No 176 of the I.L.O. of 22 June 1995 on safety and health in mines does not refer to men only but lays down rules on safety and health irrespective of the worker's sex.

8. The Republic of Austria ratified that convention on 26 May 1999, but it has not denounced Convention No 45 of the I.L.O.

The relevant provisions of Community law

9. The first and second paragraphs of Article 307 EC provide: 'The rights and obligations arising from agreements concluded before 1 January 1958 or, for acceding States, before the date of their accession, between one or more Member States on the one hand, and one or more third countries on the other, shall not be affected by the provisions of this Treaty. To the extent that such agreements are not compatible with this Treaty, the Member State or States concerned shall take all appropriate steps to eliminate the incompatibilities established. Member States shall, where necessary, assist each other to this end and shall, where appropriate, adopt a common attitude.'

10. Article 2(1) to (3) of Directive 76/207 provides: '1. For the purposes of the following provisions, the principle of equal treatment shall mean that there shall be no discrimination whatsoever on grounds of sex either directly or indirectly by reference in particular to marital or family status. 2. This Directive shall be without prejudice to the right of Member States to exclude from its field of application those occupational activities and, where appropriate, the training leading thereto, for which, by reason of their nature or the context in which they are carried out, the sex of the

worker constitutes a determining factor. 3. This Directive shall be without prejudice to provisions concerning the protection of women, particularly as regards pregnancy and maternity.'

11. Under Article 3 of that directive: '1. Application of the principle of equal treatment means that there shall be no discrimination whatsoever on grounds of sex in the conditions, including selection criteria, for access to all jobs or posts, whatever the sector or branch of activity, and to all levels of the occupational hierarchy. 2. To this end, Member States shall take the measures necessary to ensure that: (a) any laws, regulations and administrative provisions contrary to the principle of equal treatment shall be abolished,' * * *

The relevant provisions of national law

18. Article 16 of the Arbeitszeitordnung (rules on working time) of 30 April 1938 (Deutsches RGBl. I, p. 447; GBl.f.d.L.Ö 231/1939, 'the 1938 rules') provided: 'Prohibited employment (1) Female workers shall not be employed in mines, saltworks, processing plants, underground quarries or opencast mines, nor shall they be employed above ground in extraction, except processing (separation and washing), transport or loading. (2) Female workers shall further not be employed in coking plants or in the transport of raw materials for any type of construction. (3) The Minister for Employment may totally prohibit the employment of female workers, or make it dependent on certain conditions, for particular types of undertakings or work which entails particular risks for health and morality.'

19. In 1972 that provision was repealed, except where applicable to underground mines.

20. With effect from 1 August 2001 the employment of women in the underground mining industry has been regulated by the Regulation of 2001.

21. Article 2 of that regulation, headed 'Employment in the underground mining industry', is worded as follows: '(1) Female workers shall not be employed in the underground mining industry. (2) Paragraph 1 shall not apply to: 1. female workers with management or technical responsibilities who do not carry out strenuous physical work; 2. female workers who work in a social or health service; 3. female workers who must do vocational training as part of their studies or comparable instruction, for the duration of that training; 4. female workers who are employed only on an occasional basis in the underground mining industry in an occupation which is not physically strenuous.' * * *

23. Article 8 of the regulation of 1973 provides: '(1) Only male workers aged 21 or over who are fit for it from the point of view of health may be employed in work in a hyperbaric atmosphere. ...(2) ... Where the health requirement in paragraph 1 is satisfied, female workers aged 21 or over may also be employed as supervisory staff or in other work in a hyperbaric atmosphere which does not involve any greater physical effort....'

24. Under Article 31 of the regulation of 1973: '(1) Only those male workers aged 21 or over who are fit for it from the point of view of health

and who possess the specialised knowledge and professional experience necessary for health and safety purposes may be employed as divers. . . .'

The pre-litigation procedure

25.   Being of the view that both the prohibition laid down in the 1938 rules of the employment of women in the underground mining industry and the similar prohibition concerning work in a hyperbaric atmosphere and diving work were contrary to Community law, the Commission initiated the proceedings under Article 226 EC. Having given the Republic of Austria notice to submit its observations, the Commission issued a reasoned opinion on 7 February 2002 inviting that State to take the measures necessary to comply therewith within a period of two months from its notification. So far as employment in the underground mining industry was concerned, that opinion referred to the 1938 rules and not to the regulation of 2001 which forms the subject-matter of this action and which was cited for the first time in the Austrian Government's reply to the reasoned opinion.

26.   Considering that the information imparted by the Austrian authorities showed that the failure to fulfill obligations invoked in the reasoned opinion still subsisted, the Commission decided to bring this action.

Concerning the action

* * *

The prohibition of the employment of women in the underground mining industry

Concerning Directive 76/207

—Arguments of the parties

33.   The Commission maintains that Article 2 of the regulation of 2001, which authorises women to be employed in the underground mining industry only in respect of certain restricted activities, is contrary to Article 3(1) of Directive 76/207. In so far as the directive itself contains various restrictions of the prohibition of discrimination, the Commission submits that it cannot be prayed in aid in order to justify the prohibition of employment at issue.

34.   According to the Commission, the activity carried on in the sector of the underground mining industry does not relate to an occupation of the kind referred to in Article 2(2) of that directive.

35.   With regard to the derogation from the principle of equal treatment for men and women provided for by Article 2(3) of Directive 76/207, the Commission argues that the risks to which women are exposed in the underground mining industry are not, generally, different in kind from those to which men are equally exposed.

36.   The Austrian Government, relying on that last provision, contends that Article 2 of the regulation of 2001 is in keeping with Directive 76/207.

37.   According to that Government, working in the underground mining industry involves permanent stress on the locomotory system, in a strained position, linked to work often carried out with the arms raised, in an atmosphere heavy with, inter alia, quartz dust, nitrogen oxide and carbon monoxide with values for temperature and humidity which are most often above average. The consequence for the workers concerned is frequent diseases of the lungs, joints and spinal column (miners' knee, damage to the intervertebral discs, muscular rheumatism).

38.   On average, mass and muscular strength, vital capacity, absorption of oxygen, blood volume and the number of red blood cells are less in women than they are in men. Women bearing strong physical stresses in their place of work would be exposed to higher risks of abortion and also of osteoporosis when menopausal and would suffer more migraines.

39.   Since women have on average smaller vertebrae, they run more risks than men when carrying heavy loads. Moreover, when they have given birth several times there is an increased risk of injury to the lumbar vertebrae.

40.   According to the Austrian Government, it is clear, therefore, that on account of the morphological differences to be found on average between men and women very strenuous physical labour in the underground mining industry exposes women to more risks, in contrast to the situation with respect, for example, to night work, which exposes women and men to the same stresses.

41.   On this point, the Commission argues in particular that the Austrian Government itself declared during the pre-litigation procedure that 'the range of energy variables is wide, there are considerable areas of overlap with values for men and an individual assessment ought to be carried out'.

—Findings of the Court

42.   In accordance with Article 3(1) of Directive 76/207, application of the principle of equal treatment means that there is to be no discrimination whatsoever on grounds of sex in the conditions for access to all jobs or posts. It is not disputed that Article 2(1) of the regulation of 2001 treats men and women differently so far as employment in the mining industry is concerned. Since the Austrian Government has pleaded the derogation provided for by Article 2(3) of that directive, it has to be considered whether such a difference in treatment is covered by that provision and is therefore authorised.

43.   As the Court pointed out in Case C–394/96 *Brown* [1998] ECR I–4185, paragraph 17, by reserving to Member States the right to retain or introduce provisions which are intended to protect women in connection with 'pregnancy and maternity', Article 2(3) of Directive 76/207 recognises the legitimacy, in terms of the principle of equal treatment, first, of protecting a woman's biological condition during and after pregnancy and, second, of protecting the special relationship between a woman and her child over the period which follows pregnancy and childbirth.

44. It is precisely because certain activities may present a specific risk of exposure to hazardous agents, processes or working conditions for a pregnant worker or for one who is breast-feeding or who has recently given birth that the Community legislature, by adopting Directive 92/85, introduced the requirement to evaluate and communicate risks, and a prohibition of the exercise of certain activities.

45. Nevertheless, Article 2(3) of Directive 76/207 does not allow women to be excluded from a certain type of employment solely on the ground that they ought to be given greater protection than men against risks which affect men and women in the same way and which are distinct from women's specific needs of protection, such as those expressly mentioned (*see*, to this effect, Case 222/84 *Johnston* [1986] ECR 1651, paragraph 44, and Case C–285/98 *Kreil* [2000] ECR I–69, paragraph 30).

46. Nor may women be excluded from a certain type of employment solely because they are on average smaller and less strong than average men, while men with similar physical features are accepted for that employment.

47. In this case, while it is true that the regulation of 2001 does not prohibit the employment of women in the underground mining industry without having provided exceptions to that prohibition, the fact nevertheless remains that the ambit of the general prohibition in Article 2(1) of that regulation is very wide, inasmuch as it excludes women even from work that is not physically strenuous and that does not, therefore, present any specific risk to the preservation of a woman's biological capacity to become pregnant and to give birth, or to the safety or health of the pregnant worker or for one who is breast-feeding or who has recently given birth, or to the fetus.

48. The exception provided for by Article 2(2)(1) of that regulation in fact refers only to management posts and technical tasks undertaken by women with management responsibilities who are therefore situated at a high grade in the hierarchy. The exception contained in Article 2(2)(2) concerns only female workers employed in the social or health services, and Article 2(2)(3) and (4) deal only with specific situations limited in time.

49. Such legislation goes beyond what is necessary in order to ensure that women are protected within the meaning of Article 2(3) of Directive 76/207.

50. It follows that the general prohibition of the employment of women in the underground mining industry laid down in Article 2(1) of the regulation of 2001, even though read in conjunction with subparagraph 2 of that article, does not constitute a difference in treatment permissible under Article 2(3) of Directive 76/207.

Concerning Article 307 EC and Convention No 45 of the I.L.O.

—Arguments of the parties

51. The Austrian Government argues that, irrespective of the medical reasons relied on, restrictions on the employment of women in the underground mining industry, within the limits laid down by the new legislation,

are also justified by the fact that the Republic of Austria is bound by Convention No 45 of the I.L.O., which it ratified in 1937.

52. According to that Government, having regard to Case C–158/91 *Levy* [1993] ECR I–4287, paragraph 17 *et seq.*, and Case C–13/93 *Minne* [1994] ECR I–371, paragraph 19, it is in any case licit for the Member States to assert the rights conferred on them by such treaties. It follows that the Austrian Government, being bound to transpose into domestic law the prohibition of employment laid down in Convention No 45 of the I.L.O., is not obliged to apply in this respect Articles 2 and 3 of Directive 76/207.

53. The Commission argues that the conclusion drawn by the Austrian Government from *Levy* and *Minne* is too general.

54. According to the Commission, the interpretation of Article 307 EC given by the Court in Case C–84/98 *Commission* v. *Portugal* [2000] ECR I–5215, paragraphs 51 and 53, can be transposed direct to the present case. Article 7 of Convention No 45 of the I.L.O. contains a denunciation clause. It is unarguable that the Republic of Austria could have denounced that convention with effect from 30 May 1997, that is to say, a date after that on which the directive became binding on it by reason of the ratification of the Agreement on the European Economic Area of 2 May 1992 (OJ 1994 L 1, p. 3). The Republic of Austria was, in the Commission's view, required to denounce the convention pursuant to Article 3(2) of Directive 76/207.

55. The Austrian Government counters that it could not have known that the law applicable in that field in Austria was contrary to Community law, or that the Commission considered the provisions in question to be contrary to Community law. The Commission's first letter on the subject was dated 29 September 1998. It follows that Convention No 45 of the I.L.O. could be denounced on 30 May 2007 at the earliest.

56. *Commission* v. *Portugal* does not, according to the Austrian Government, impose any general obligation on the Member States to denounce international agreements when they are contrary to Community law. That interpretation, it argues, follows also from Case C–475/98 *Commission* v. *Austria* [2002] ECR I–9797, paragraph 49, in which the Court held, concerning 'open skies' agreements, that in the case of amendments to such an agreement concluded before accession, the Member States are prevented not only from contracting new international commitments but also from maintaining such commitments in force if they infringe Community law. If there existed a general obligation to denounce agreements contrary to Community law, it would not have been necessary to establish that the entire agreement was confirmed when certain parts of it were amended.

—Findings of the Court

57. It follows from the third paragraph of Article 307 EC that the obligations arising from agreements concluded, by acceding States before the date of their accession, between one or more Member States on the one hand, and one or more third countries on the other, are not affected by the provisions of the EC Treaty.

58. The Republic of Austria, which acceded to the European Community with effect from 1 January 1995, ratified Convention No 45 of the I.L.O. before that date. Article 2 of that convention contains a general prohibition of the employment of women in underground work in mines and Article 3 permits a few exceptions of the same kind as those provided for in the regulation of 2001. It is common ground that that regulation implements the obligations imposed by the convention without going beyond the restrictions on the employment of women laid down therein.

59. In those circumstances, while it is true that the Republic of Austria may, in principle, rely on the first paragraph of Article 307 EC to maintain in force the provisions of domestic law implementing the above-mentioned obligations, the fact remains that the second paragraph of that article states that, to the extent that earlier agreements within the meaning of the first paragraph of the article are not compatible with the Treaty, the Member State or States concerned are to take all appropriate steps to eliminate the incompatibilities established.

60. In light of the conclusion reached by the Court in paragraph 50 above, the obligations imposed on the Republic of Austria by Convention No 45 of the I.L.O. are incompatible with Articles 2 and 3 of Directive 76/207.

61. As is apparent from paragraph 50 of Case C–62/98 *Commission* v. *Portugal* [2000] ECR I–5171, the appropriate steps for the elimination of such incompatibility referred to in the second paragraph of Article 307 EC include, inter alia, denunciation of the agreements in question.

62. None the less, it must be noted that the only occasion on which the Republic of Austria could, following its accession to the European Community, have denounced Convention No 45 of the I.L.O. was, in accordance with the rules laid down in Article 7(2) of the convention, during the year following 30 May 1997. At that time, the incompatibility of the prohibition laid down by that convention with the provisions of Directive 76/207 had not been sufficiently clearly established for that Member State to be bound to denounce the convention.

63. It may appropriately be added that, as Article 7(2) of Convention No 45 of the I.L.O. makes clear, the next opportunity for the Republic of Austria to denounce the convention will occur on the expiry of another period of ten years running from 30 May 1997.

64. It follows that, by maintaining in force national provisions such as those contained in the regulation of 2001, the Republic of Austria has not failed to fulfill its obligations under Community law.

65. It follows from the foregoing considerations that the action must be dismissed in so far as it concerns the prohibition of the employment of women in the sector of the underground mining industry.

The prohibition of the employment of women in work in a high-pressure atmosphere and in diving work

—Arguments of the parties

66. The Commission considers that its observations on the prohibition of the employment of women in the underground mining industry

apply in the same way to the prohibition of the employment of women in work to be carried out in a high-pressure atmosphere and in diving work. A general prohibition of the employment of women laid down without any individual assessment cannot be justified by women's alleged special needs of protection.

67.   In the Austrian Government's opinion, the restrictions on employment contained in Articles 8 and 31 of the regulation of 1973 are also justified on medical grounds relating specifically to women's activity.

68.   That Government argues that in most cases work to be carried out in a high-pressure atmosphere and diving work involve significant physical stress, for example, in the construction of underground railways in a high-pressure atmosphere or in the carrying out of under-water repairs to bridges. Prohibiting the employment of women in physically very demanding work in a high-pressure atmosphere and their employment in diving work is justified because their respiratory capacity is less than men's and because they have a lower red blood cell count.

Findings of the Court

69.   An absolute prohibition of the employment of women in diving work does not constitute a difference in treatment permitted under Article 2(3) of Directive 76/207.

70.   The range of diving work is wide and includes, for instance, activity in the fields of biology, archaeology, tourism and police work.

71.   The absolute prohibition laid down in Article 31 of the regulation of 1973 excludes women even from work that does not involve significant physical stress and thus clearly goes beyond what is necessary to ensure that women are protected.

72.   With regard to employment in a high-pressure atmosphere, the regulation of 1973 excludes women from work that places excessive strain on their bodies.

73.   In so far as the Austrian Government claims that women have lesser respiratory capacity and a lower red blood cell count in order to justify such exclusion, it relies on an argument based on measured average values for women to compare them with those for men. However, as that Government itself acknowledged during the pre-litigation procedure, as regards those variables there are significant areas of overlap of individual values for women and individual values for men.

74.   In those circumstances legislation that precludes any individual assessment and prohibits women from entering the employment in question, when that employment is not forbidden to men whose vital capacity and red blood cell count are equal to or lower than the average values of those variables measured for women, is not authorised by virtue of Article 2(3) of Directive 76/207 and constitutes discrimination on grounds of sex.

75.   In light of the foregoing considerations, it must be declared that, by maintaining in Articles 8 and 31 of the regulation of 1973 a general prohibition of the employment of women in work in a high-pressure atmosphere and in diving work, providing a limited number of exceptions

in the former case, the Republic of Austria has failed to fulfill its obligations under Articles 2 and 3 of Directive 76/207.

————

Sexual Harassment Law in the United States, the United Kingdom and the European Union: Discriminatory Wrongs and Dignitary Harms

36 Common Law World Review 79, 80, 81, 89–94, 97–98 (2007)

■ LINDA CLARKE

The law of sexual harassment in the United Kingdom also originated in sex discrimination law, but has not provoked the same level of debate. Continental Europe has generally been less receptive to arguments about the discriminatory harms of sexual harassment, although general anti-bullying measures designed to combat behaviour, usually described as 'mobbing' or 'moral harassment' have hit a popular chord as an affront to human dignity, and led to legal prohibition.

* * * Although there was no specific legal wrong of 'sexual harassment' [in the U.K.], it was accepted early on that such behaviour fell within the general provisions of the Sex Discrimination Act 1975 if it could be shown that a woman had been treated less favourably than a comparable man, on the grounds of her sex. Tribunals were generally very ready to find 'less favourable treatment', particularly where the behaviour consisted of sexual demands or sexual comments.

[In contrast to the U.S.], continental European civil law systems did not offer the same opportunities for a litigation strategy, and the demands for new laws against sexual harassment have instead been made in the political and legislative spheres. Kathrin S. Zippel has charted how sexual harassment slowly emerged as an issue in Germany in the 1980s, with pressure coming from feminist groups, politicians, 'femocrats' (state Women's Officers), and the European Union, with the law playing a very limited role. Abigail Saguy has shown how in France, it was necessary for feminists to campaign for the introduction of new criminal statutes in order to tackle sexual harassment. Although in both Germany and France, feminists and others recognize the way in which sexual harassment operates as a tool in women's oppression, nevertheless mainstream opinion did not see sexual harassment as sex discrimination in the way that that happened in the USA and the UK. Indeed, as both Zippel and Saguy show, there was considerable antipathy towards perceptions of the law of sexual harassment in the United States, with Americans portrayed as puritanical, unsophisticated about sexual matters, over-litigious, and motivated by greed. Instead, sexual harassment was seen either through a 'violence' framework, as individualized criminal behaviour akin to rape, sexual assault and sexual exposure, or as simply one type of harassment that occurs in the workplace. It is this latter perspective that has been most influential in shaping the legal and social response to harassment.

In Sweden in 1984 the psychologist Dr Heinz Leymann first used the term 'mobbing' to describe adult behaviour in the workplace, the term having previously been used for animal behaviour. Concern over 'mobbing' spread throughout continental Europe in the 1990s, and in 1998 the French psychotherapist Marie–France Hirigoyen published her book *Le Harcelement moral: la violence perverse au quotidien* which had an enormous impact in France. Hirigoyen's 'moral harassment' focused on the psychological impact of harassment at work, defining 'moral harassment' as: any abusive conduct-whether by words, looks, gestures or in writing— that [through repetition or systematization] infringes upon the personality, the dignity, or the physical or psychical integrity of a person: also behaviour that endangers the employment of the said person or degrades the climate of the workplace.

But although Hirigoyen linked the practice to the United States' concept of 'sexual harassment', she interpreted 'moral harassment' as 'a form of interpersonal violence' and it has been argued that her title 'contained an implicit polemic against the American notion that the primary form of harassment was sexual'.

The book generated both large sales and considerable media discussion, and caught the popular imagination in a way that 'sexual harassment' had failed to do. Following publication, the French Labour Code was amended in 2001, and the French Penal Code in 2002, to prohibit 'moral harassment'. The debates over moral harassment in France also led to amendment of the sexual harassment provisions in the Labour Code, so that the restriction to conduct involving hierarchical relationships was removed, in line with the provisions on moral harassment.

In Germany also, 'mobbing' has proved to be a greater concern for employers, unions and employees than sexual harassment. The Federal Employee Protection Act 1994 prohibited sexual harassment in the workplace, but treated the issue as a breach of the contract between employer and employee, rather than a violation of a civil right. However, the law 'lacked effective implementation and enforcement mechanisms' and has been little used by victims of sexual harassment, with 80 per cent of the cases heard in the labour courts involving men claiming unfair dismissal, following accusations of sexual harassment. After the introduction of the 1994 Act, employers adopted anti-mobbing policies, rather than sexual harassment policies: as in France, this has proved to be a more powerful concept for unions, workers and employers to rally around than sexual harassment as a form of sex discrimination.

The harm caused by mobbing, or 'moral harassment', is not characterized as discrimination on grounds of sex, or race, or some other prohibited ground, but rather as a violation of dignity. The definition of moral harassment in the French Penal Code refers to conduct 'liable to harm his rights and his dignity'. Sexual harassment is defined in German law as 'any wilful sexual behaviour that violates the dignity of employees at their place of work'. 'Dignity' has a long history as a European value but has been described as recently having 'a meteoric rise to the top of the European Union's value system'. The concept of dignity as a legal value can be traced back to Roman law in the delict of *inuria* but its modern incarnation, both in national and international legal texts, is generally ascribed to Europe's (and more specifically Germany's) reaction to Nazism: '. . . the basic right to human dignity is understood as an explicit answer to the Holocaust—the "never again" in constitutional law', though this account has been challenged.

Whatever its origins, the concept of dignity is now firmly at the centre of the European Union's legal framework, though what exactly is meant (or perhaps more accurately, understood) by the concept of dignity is less clear. As Millns has noted, 'With no precise definition, dignity is simply announced'. Dignity is generally viewed as a value which underlies other human rights, rather than a right in itself, and Brownsword has argued that 'it is the duty to respect human dignity that is fundamental', rather than any 'right' to dignity. This duty is something that is owed to others. Further, consent is deemed irrelevant for those wishing to protect dignity, something which may be problematic in treating harassment as a dignitary harm, as existing definitions always refer to behaviour which is unwanted or unwelcome.

* * * But 'dignity' also has its critics. James Q. Whitman has argued that, rather than having its origins in a reaction to the horrors of Nazism, the legal protection of dignity, honour and status in continental Europe stems instead from seventeenth- and eighteenth-century etiquette codes: rather than 'dignity' expressing some grand vision of humanity and the inviolability of the human spirit, it is more concerned with insults to honour and status. Whitman links this with the European conception of privacy, concerned primarily with personal integrity and autonomy, an attachment to dignity and a concern for one's position in society. As a result, European privacy law is concerned with matters such as preventing press intrusion, controlling one's image and respecting privacy in the workplace. In the United States, however, privacy is seen as an application of liberty, and in particular, freedom from intervention by the state. * * *

European Union involvement with the issue of harassment at work was originally only concerned with harassment on grounds of sex but following the Treaty of Amsterdam in 1998, Directives were issued which required Member States to outlaw harassment on grounds of race, ethnic origin, disability, sexuality, religion or belief and age. This was then followed by an amended Equal Treatment Directive which explicitly outlawed harassment on grounds of sex.

These Directives all treat harassment as a third form of discrimination, separate from direct or indirect discrimination: harassing conduct, on the specified grounds, is deemed to be unlawful discrimination. It is no longer necessary to point to a similarly situated comparator who has not been harassed. The Directives define harassment as unwanted conduct, related to the prohibited grounds, which has the purpose or effect of violating the dignity of a person, *and* of creating an intimidating, hostile, degrading, or humiliating or offensive environment. Dignity and discrimination are thus linked: the harasser's conduct must be related to the victim's race, disability, etc., and the conduct must both violate the victim's dignity *and* create an intimidating etc. working environment. It is unclear whether the need for a 'violation of dignity' adds anything other than a rhetorical flourish: it is difficult to think of examples where conduct created an intimidating, hostile, degrading, or humiliating or offensive environment without also violating dignity (although the concept of 'violating dignity' is nowhere defined).

However, the Equal Treatment Directive, dealing with sex discrimination, does something more. In addition to outlawing harassing conduct related to the sex of the victim (retaining the discrimination framework), it also outlaws a specific type of conduct, which need not be related to the sex of the victim in any way at all. Rather, where any form of unwanted verbal, non-verbal or physical conduct of a sexual nature occurs, with the purpose or effect of violating the dignity of a person, in particular when creating an intimidating, hostile, degrading, humiliating or offensive environment, then this too is outlawed conduct.

Although Article 2.3 deems both forms of harassment to be prohibited discrimination on the grounds of sex, the second form does not contain any element of a discrimination framework: there is no need to show that a comparable man would have been treated differently, or that the behaviour was linked in some way to the sex of the complainant. Instead, sexual conduct is singled out, and is unlawful where it is unwanted, and violates a person's dignity. The use of the words 'in particular', rather than 'and', suggests that where the unwanted conduct is sexual in nature, there is no essential requirement to show also that the working environment is affected. This looks like a purely dignitary harm.

———

2.   RACIAL DISCRIMINATION

The European Union established protection against race and ethnic employment discrimination under Council Directive 2000/43/EC. The legal backdrop of the Directive includes the broader European Union's fight against race and ethnic discrimination. The Directive points to a number of other directives, guidelines, and communications of the European Union and the United Nations which predate and shape the Directive. (These include Article 6 of the Treaty on European Union; Universal Declaration of Human Rights by the United Nations, The European Council, on 15 and 16 October 1999, Article 13 of the EC Treaty, The Employment Guidelines 2000, a communication on racism, xenophobia and anti-Semitism, and Joint Action 96/443/HA). The Directive cites these documents as establishing the principles, rule of law, and fundamental freedoms "as they result from the constitutional traditions common to the Member States, as general principles of Community Law." Council Directive 2000/43 Preamble 2.

———

Council Directive 2000/43/EC of 29 June 2000

(implementing the principle of equal treatment between persons irrespective of racial or ethnic origin)

■ THE COUNCIL OF THE EUROPEAN UNION

Article 2—

   1.   For the purposes of this Directive, the principle of equal treatment shall mean that there shall be no direct or indirect discrimination based on racial or ethnic origin.

   2.   For the purposes of paragraph 1: (a) direct discrimination shall be taken to occur where one person is treated less favourably than another is, has been or would be treated in a comparable situation on grounds of racial or ethnic origin; (b) indirect discrimination shall be taken to occur where an apparently neutral provision, criterion or practice would put persons of a racial or ethnic origin at a particular disadvantage compared with other persons, unless that provision, criterion or practice is objectively justified by a legitimate aim and the means of achieving that aim are appropriate and necessary.

   3.   Harassment shall be deemed to be discrimination within the meaning of paragraph 1, when an unwanted conduct related to racial or ethnic origin takes place with the purpose or effect of violating the dignity of a person and of creating an intimidating, hostile, degrading, humiliating or offensive environment. In this context, the concept of harassment may be defined in accordance with the national laws and practice of the Member States.

   4.   An instruction to discriminate against persons on grounds of racial or ethnic origin shall be deemed to be discrimination within the meaning of paragraph 1.

Article 3—

   1.   Within the limits of the powers conferred upon the Community, this Directive shall apply to all persons, as regards both the public and private sectors, including public bodies, in relation to: (a) conditions for access to employment, to self-employment and to occupation, including selection criteria and recruitment conditions, whatever the branch of activity and at all levels of the professional hierarchy, including promotion; (b) access to all types and to all levels of vocational guidance, vocational training, advanced vocational training and retraining, including practical work experience; (c) employment and working conditions, including dismissals and pay; (d) membership of and involvement in an organisation of workers or employers, or any organisation whose members carry on a particular profession, including the benefits provided for by such organisations; (e) social protection, including social security and healthcare; (f) social advantages; (g) education; (h) access to and supply of goods and services which are available to the public, including housing.

   2.   This Directive does not cover difference of treatment based on nationality and is without prejudice to provisions and conditions relating to the entry into and residence of third country nationals and stateless persons on the territory of Member States, and to any treatment which arises from the legal status of the third-country nationals and stateless persons concerned.

Article 4—

Notwithstanding Article 2(1) and (2), Member States may provide that a difference of treatment which is based on a characteristic related to racial or ethnic origin shall not constitute discrimination where, by reason of the nature of the particular occupational activities concerned or of the context in which they are carried out, such a characteristic constitutes a genuine and determining occupational requirement, provided that the objective is legitimate and the requirement is proportionate.

———

Equal Rights Versus Special Rights? Minority Protection and the Prohibition of Discrimination

(Report Prepared for European Commission, Directorate–General Employment, Social Affairs and Equal Opportunities, June 2007, pp. 22–29; 55–59, footnotes omitted)

■ KRISTIN HENRARD

Part II—Racial Equality Directive

2.1 Reach of the Prohibition of Discrimination

* * * It should be pointed out that while the title of the Directive refers to the principle of equal treatment, this is equated in article 2(1) with the prohibition of discrimination.

As there is no case law yet of the ECJ which clarifies the actual meaning of provisions of the Racial Equality Directive, relevant interpretative questions will be identified, and likely scenarios will be outlined, based on the existing case law in terms of the prohibition of gender discrimination. It is generally accepted that the ECJ will base its reasoning vis-à-vis other grounds, like racial and ethnic origin, on its gender jurisprudence, while it is also acknowledged that the textual divergencies and the different social contexts provided by these different grounds, might make it unlikely that the case law can (and will) be transposed just like that.

As the full title of the Racial Equality Directive demonstrates, it is concerned with equal treatment on the basis of racial or ethnic origin. It is striking though that neither the Directive itself, nor the Explanatory Memorandum contains a definition of these concepts. The preamble only indicates that the Union rejects theories with attempt to determine the existence of separate human races. Since 'ethnic origin' is also explicitly addressed, the relevance of the Racial Equality Directive for ethnic groups, including ethnic minorities is however obvious and is confirmed by the reference to ethnic minorities in recital 8. Nevertheless, the failure to define these concepts in the Racial Equality Directive has been criticized, inter alia because it would play in the cards of member states that deny the existence of races (and racism) at a conceptual level.

Since minorities are often defined in terms of their own language and/or own religion, it is important to determine to what extent differentiations on the basis of language or religion are qualified as indirect racial discrimination by the ECJ. The fact that religion as prohibited ground of discrimination is taken up in Directive 2000/78 and has been left out of the Racial Equality Directive may make it 'more difficult to argue that discrimination which is primarily based on religion can be formulated as racial or ethnic origin discrimination. Nevertheless recital 10 acknowledges that religion may play a part in defining ethnicity.

In regard to the scope of application *ratione personae* it should be highlighted that recital 13 of the preamble explicitly states that it applies to third country nationals. However, article 3(2) shows that when sensitive issues arise, like immigration, states are getting anxious, potentially problematic exclusions are made. Article 3(2) reads as follows: 'this directive does not cover difference of treatment based on nationality and is without prejudice to provisions and conditions relating to entry into and residence of third-country nationals and stateless persons on the territory of the Member States, and to any treatment which arises from the legal status of third-country nationals and stateless persons'. In relation to the exclusion of differentiations on the basis of nationality it is generally known that there is an extensive overlap in most countries between ethnic origin (and race) and foreign nationality. Hence, targeted restrictions on the basis of nationality could amount to indirect discrimination on grounds of race and ethnicity. Arguably, to the extent that there would not be an objective and reasonable justification for differentiations on the basis of nationality, they should be qualified as indirect racial discrimination. * * *

2.2 Opening Towards Substantive Equality?

Prior to reviewing the provisions of the Racial Equality Directive, it seems appropriate to point out that it is widely agreed that the prohibition of discrimination does not require identical treatment, in other words, not every differentiation amounts to a prohibited discrimination. Consequently, it is important to know what are the criteria used to determine whether a differentiation amounts to a prohibited discrimination or, in other words, what is an acceptable justification for a differential treatment. By way of starting point, it can be put forward that a differentiation of treatment would amount to a prohibited discrimination when and in so far as there would not be a reasonable and objective justification for this differentiation. Such a justification is often further broken down in a requirement of a legitimate aim and a proportionality test. The proportionality test in the broad sense has at least two components. First, proportionality requires there to be a reasonable relation between the legitimate aim on the one hand and the differential treatment (and the underlying interests which it interferes with) on the other hand. In other words, the differential treatment should not go beyond what is necessary in order to achieve the goal. This first component is also called the proportionality test in the narrow sense. A more specific aspect of the proportionality test concerns the subsidiarity test. This test implies an investigation of whether there are no alternatives which can achieve the desired legitimate aim while implying less of an interference with the right to equal treatment.

* * * It should be highlighted that in terms of EU law, the above general justification possibility is only accepted in relation to indirect discrimination. Direct differentiations are only considered to be legitimate

(in that they would not amount to a prohibited discrimination) when there is an explicit ground in the treaties or secondary legislation, and in addition the demands of the proportionality principle would be met. In view of the fact that the Racial Equality Directive only allows two exceptions to the prohibition of direct discrimination, the protection against explicit differentiations on the basis of racial or ethnic origin is considerable.

2.2.1 Indirect Discrimination

Notwithstanding the absence of a generally accepted definition of indirect discrimination in terms of international law, there is a broad understanding of the core of this concept, which addresses measures that without differentiating explicitly on a certain ground, (are likely to) have a disproportionate impact on a group defined according to that ground, without objective justification.

There are arguably two related reasons why indirect discrimination is relevant for minorities and an adequate minority protection. First of all, and this is inherent in the description of the phenomenon, the prohibition of indirect discrimination reflects a concern for the underlying reality, or better for the actual effect of certain policies and rules. When the effects of an at first sight neutral rule are disproportional, in the sense that it has a disparate negative impact on a particular group without reasonable and objective justification, this would be illegitimate. In other words, prohibiting such indirect discrimination tends to contribute to the realization of full or real equality, of crucial importance for minorities. The prohibition of indirect discrimination tends to further the accommodation of diversity, by revealing that apparently neutral criteria de facto favour the dominant culture. A second reason why this prohibition of indirect discrimination is important, is because of the inherent group focus it has, ...

The extent to which a legal system provides protection against indirect discrimination, arguably depends on several issues, including whether the concept of indirect discrimination is acknowledged, and what is needed for a *prima facie* case of indirect discrimination. In the framework of EC equality law, the concept of indirect discrimination was early on accepted, and the case law of the ECJ has acknowledged several times that the concept of indirect discrimination is vital for the effective protection against discrimination. However, ample confusion and uncertainty remained as to the latter issue.

The case law of the ECJ in terms of gender discrimination was essentially codified in Article 2(2) of the Burden of Proof Directive (Council Directive 97/80/EC on the Burden of Proof in cases of Discrimination based on Sex) and required proof of actual disparity, while this 'disparity' would have to concern a 'disadvantage of a substantially higher level'. The definition of indirect discrimination in the Racial Equality Directive (article 2(2)(b)) in several respects represents an improvement in that it facilitates the burden (of proof) on the victim (claimant).

First of all, the level of disparate impact required has been lowered in that there is no longer a reference to specific proportions. It suffices that it concerns a 'particular disadvantage'. Furthermore, and this is really a remarkable progress, it is no longer necessary to proof that this disadvantage has actually occurred. It suffices that the measure is of such a nature that would put a certain group at a disadvantage. This seems to negate the need for statistical evidence in terms of EC law, which is especially important in regard of racial or ethnic origin as statistics are unlikely to be obtainable.

Unfortunately, recital 15 of the Directive indicates that national legislation or practice concerning proof may still provide 'in particular for indirect discrimination to be established by any means including on the basis of statistical evidence'. This arguably implies that the directive still allows national legislation to require statistical evidence. The ECJ's future case law will reveal to what extent this new approach to indirect discrimination actually facilitates the case for victims and leads to higher levels of protection against indirect discrimination.

2.2.2. Duty to Differentiate?

An obligation to differentiate in terms of the demands of equality can be traced back to Aristotle's formula that unequal or different things should be treated differently to the extent of the difference. The underlying vision of equality is clearly substantive equality. To the extent that more recently such an obligation to differentiate is being identified in terms of non-discrimination, this development would equally imply an opening towards substantive or real, full equality.

There is a steady line of jurisprudence of the ECJ in terms of both the general principle of equal treatment which it has developed in its case law and which is argued to be embodied in the Racial Equality Directive, and of the prohibition of discrimination, that when people find themselves in substantially different circumstances, they should be treated differently, unless 'same' treatment is objectively justified by the pursuit of a legitimate aim and is appropriate and necessary to achieve that aim.

* * * The famous *Groener* case [Case C 379/87, Groener, 1989, ECR 1967, para 19 and 23] already showed that a general application of language requirements (affecting the free movement of workers) can be denounced as indirectly discriminatory on the basis of nationality, when these requirements do not pursue a legitimate objective and/or are not proportionate to that objective. According to de Schutter, 'a similar obligation to treat differently situations which are substantively different may be derived from the definition of indirect discrimination in article 2(2)(b) of the Racial Equality Directive'. * * *

* * * It is important to realize that this type of differential measures are not necessarily temporary (in contrast to affirmative action measure). In view of the need for enduring differential treatment in order to protect and promote the separate identity of minorities, this jurisprudential line is especially relevant for minorities, for example in relation to language rights in communications with public authorities.

Part IV—Country Studies

4.1 Legislative Texts

In view of the absence of a definition of the concept 'race' in the Racial Equality Directive, it is to be welcomed that certain countries use (incorporate) the broad definition in article 1 of the International Convention on the Elimination of all forms of Racial Discrimination (ICERD), including colour, descent and national or ethnic origin. While suggestions were made to consider the extensive UK case law on the meaning of 'ethnic group', this seems questionable in view of the problematic distinctions this has entailed: Jews and Gypsies are considered to be ethnic groups, while Muslims and Rastafarians are not. The fact that in the Austrian legal system a more culturally oriented view of racial and ethnic discrimination prevails, is arguably in line with recital 6 of the Racial Equality Directive, in which the existence of separate legal races is rejected.

As was highlighted in Chapter 2, it seems commendable that the exclusion of differentiations on the basis of nationality from the scope of the Racial Equality Directive (and implementing legislation) should be narrowly constructed because of the danger that an important category of indirect discrimination on the basis of race 'escapes' scrutiny. Fortunately, this is a position which is acknowledged and taken on board in various countries. In regard to the Danish legal system it was pointed out that the Act on Ethnic Equality does not cover unequal treatment due to citizenship, but it was immediately added that 'discrimination in the labour market on account of citizenship must not indirectly reflect discrimination due to, for instance, national origin (which is covered by the definition of racial discrimination in ICERD, incorporated in the Danish legal system). This is also nicely captured in the Austrian country report, where it is pointed out that the 'issue of protection against discrimination on the basis of nationality or citizenship is crucial for the Austrian situation as most of the racist discourse is not labeled with terms like race or ethnic origin, but the scape goats and concept of the enemies is to a very large extent about 'foreigners', 'asylum seekers', 'asylum frauds'. While the Equal Treatment Act itself takes up a provision like article 3(2) Racial Equality Directive, the Explanatory Notes to the Act underline that 'this exception can not be used to legitimate discriminations on the grounds covered in this act. The prohibition of discrimination also protects third country nationals'. It should be acknowledged though that case law and interpretations by the courts, that will clarify the actual amount of protection against possible indirect racial discrimination, are awaited. * * *

It should also be highlighted that the prohibition of discrimination on the basis of nationality is especially important in countries where many residents do not have citizenship. This point was explicitly made by the Advisory Committee (FCNM) when it reviewed the periodic state report of Estonia, in relation to the draft equality legislation. In this respect, Thematic Comment no 3 of the EU Network of Independent Experts on Fundamental Rights highlights that in these circumstances it cannot be ruled out that the very conditions for granting nationality could constitute indirect discrimination on the basis of racial or ethnic origin.* * *

4.2   Case Law

In view of the importance of an effective protection against discrimination for persons belonging to minorities, it is important that also potential (in the sense of not actually materialized) discrimination would be covered by the prohibition. In this respect, an interesting case in Belgium can be highlighted, in which the court accepts that public statements of a discriminatory nature by employers might result in a finding of discrimination, even in the absence of any proven instance in which a practice or policy has been implemented vis-à-vis a particular person.

It was highlighted in chapter 2 that certain differentiations on the basis of language could potentially be qualified as indirect racial discrimination, which would be of obvious importance for linguistic minorities. A few national examples bear this out. A Swedish Labour Court decision of October 2005 might not have found indirect racial discrimination on the facts, it did acknowledge that language requirements for a position would amount to indirect racial discrimination if they were not objective justified, adequate and necessary for an adequate performance of the position at hand. Similarly, the Belgian Centre of Equality of Chances and the Fight against Racism indicated to the Flemish Government that an obligation to pass a Dutch course in order to become eligible for social housing would amount to a prohibited indirect discrimination on the basis of racial or ethnic origin.

A judgment of the House of Lords should be singled out as it demonstrates the prevalence of discrimination on the basis of racial or ethnic origin in the immigration context, which in light of article 3(2), unfortunately, runs the risk of falling outside the scope of application of the Racial Equality Directive. [*Regina v. Immigration Officer at Prague Airport and another ex parte European Roma rights Centre and others*] concerns the treatment of Roma in the pre-clearance procedure by UK authorities in Prague airport. Evidence was produced that Roma were subjected to longer, more intensive interviews and were 400 times more likely to be refused leave (to go to the UK). The House of Lords qualified this as less favourable treatment on racial grounds, and underscored that it would not be possible to justify this direct discrimination. A stronger confirmation of the need to be attentive for cases of indirect racial discrimination in this context will be difficult to find.

Finally, the tremendous amount of case law in relation to Roma and discriminatory access not only to employment, but also to public facilities, like restaurants, bars and discotheques is striking, and confirms clearly the relevance of the inclusion of article 3(1)(h) in the scope of the Racial Equality Directive.

---

3. RELIGION, DISABILITY, AGE, AND SEXUAL ORIENTATION DISCRIMINATION

As we have seen, sex equality between men and women has been the predominant focus of anti-discrimination law in Europe for the past 30 years. However, recently with the newer Directives, other forms of discrimination are now receiving increased attention. One of the most important Directives to emerge in recent years is the "general framework" Directive,

2000/78/EC, which covers many other forms of discrimination in employment and occupation.

————

Council Directive 2000/78/EC of 27 November 2000

(establishing a general framework for equal treatment in employment and occupation)

■ THE COUNCIL OF THE EUROPEAN UNION

WHEREAS * * *

(11) Discrimination based on religion or belief, disability, age or sexual orientation may undermine the achievement of the objectives of the EC Treaty, in particular the attainment of a high level of employment and social protection, raising the standard of living and the quality of life, economic and social cohesion and solidarity, and the free movement of persons.

(12) To this end, any direct or indirect discrimination based on religion or belief, disability, age or sexual orientation as regards the areas covered by this Directive should be prohibited throughout the Community. This prohibition of discrimination should also apply to nationals of third countries but does not cover differences of treatment based on nationality and is without prejudice to provisions governing the entry and residence of third-country nationals and their access to employment and occupation. * * *

(23) In very limited circumstances, a difference of treatment may be justified where a characteristic related to religion or belief, disability, age or sexual orientation constitutes a genuine and determining occupational requirement, when the objective is legitimate and the requirement is proportionate. Such circumstances should be included in the information provided by the Member States to the Commission. * * *

(31) The rules on the burden of proof must be adapted when there is a *prima facie* case of discrimination and, for the principle of equal treatment to be applied effectively, the burden of proof must shift back to the respondent when evidence of such discrimination is brought. However, it is not for the respondent to prove that the plaintiff adheres to a particular religion or belief, has a particular disability, is of a particular age or has a particular sexual orientation. * * *

Article I—Purpose

The purpose of this Directive is to lay down a general framework for combating discrimination on the grounds of religion or belief, disability, age or sexual orientation as regards employment and occupation, with a view to putting into effect in the Member States the principle of equal treatment.

————

The 2000/78 Directive specifically does not cover differences of treatment based on nationality. Article 3. This Directive prohibits both direct or indirect discrimination, as well as harassment, on the basis of religion or belief, disability, age or sexual orientation. The definitions of direct, indirect and harassment track closely those definitions in the Race and Gender Directives. The Directive applies to both the public and private sectors but has some important limitations—including its inapplicability to social security and benefit systems and its inapplicability to the armed forces where disability and age are concerned. Article 3.

A.   Religion

There is a long history of religious conflict in Europe and this history inevitably shapes equality law in the EU. Many of the major Treaties speak to freedom of religion—including the EU Charter on Fundamental Rights and the European Convention on Human Rights, among others. See Chapters VII and VIII. In the 1990s, "belief" was added to the already protected category of religion and is reflected in the 2000/78 Directive's coverage of "religion or belief" as a prohibited grounds of employment discrimination. The use of "belief" was to ensure that non-religious beliefs such as atheism were covered similarly to religious beliefs. Religion or belief is a unique protected category compared with the other grounds protected by Article 13 of the Amsterdam Treaty in that it is the only one which also appears as a positive freedom in the European Convention on Human Rights.

The 2000/78 Directive does not define the terms "religion or belief," nor do other international human rights treaties (including the ECHR). Thus, there are a number of questions left open by the Directive, including whether the definitional tests used in other legal contexts should be applicable to the Directive. There is also a question whether political beliefs fall under the protection of the Directive. Another question commentators have raised is whether the covered categories of "religion or belief" will be judged objectively by a court or subjectively according to the conscience of the individual worker.

There do not appear to be any cases interpreting the scope of "religion or belief" under the 2000/78 Directive. However, there are a number of decisions by the European Court of Human Rights that adjudicate the rights of religious minorities in Europe to express their religion and beliefs, particularly when it involves wearing religious garments (e.g. Muslim headscarf). See Chapter VIII.

Discrimination on the basis of religion and belief is sometimes permitted under the Directive. One exception is where religion or belief is a genuine and determining occupational requirement for the job. Article 4(1). The second is for organizations the "ethos" of which is based on religion or belief and the nature of the job requires that a person's religion or belief is a genuine, legitimate and justified occupational requirement. Article 4(2).

B.   Disability

The 2000/78 general framework Directive imposes a positive duty to provide reasonable accommodation to persons with disabilities. Specifically, employers are required to "take appropriate measures, where needed in a particular case, to enable a person with a disability to have access to, participate in, or advance in employment, or to undergo training, unless such measures would impose a disproportionate burden on the employer."

Article 5. Although there is no EU case law on the scope of the reasonable accommodation duty, the European Commission, in response to a question asked of it regarding 2000/78, stated: "[i]n practical terms such accommodation includes measures to adapt the workplace for people with disabilities, for example adapting premises and equipment, patterns of working time in order to facilitate their access to employment." *See* Written Question E–2112/03, by Proinsias De Rossa (PSE) to the Commission (25 June 2003). *See generally* Richard Whittle, *The Framework Directive for Equal Treatment in Employment and Occupation: An Analysis From a Disability Rights Perspective*, 27 EUROPEAN LAW REVIEW 303 (2002).

The Directive also does not define what constitutes a "disability," thus leaving considerable flexibility to member states to craft the scope of their disability anti-discrimination laws. However, two EU cases interpreting the directive provide some guidance. In *Chacon Navas v. Eurest Colectividades SA*, the Court dismissed a case in which an employee argued that dismissal on the basis of her sickness constituted disability discrimination under the 2000/78 Directive. Case C–13/05 (Grand Chamber, 11 July 2006). The Court ruled that the concept of "disability" within the meaning of the Directive must be understood as referring to a limitation which results from physical, mental or psychological impairments and which hinders the participation of the person in professional life over a long period of time; as such, the Court refused to equate the concepts of "disability" and "sickness." Paras 43–47. In *Coleman v. Law & Law*, the Court considered as disability discrimination the dismissal of an employee who is not himself disabled but whose child is disabled. Case C–303/06 (Grand Chamber, 17 July 2008). The Court interpreted the general 2000/78 Directive's prohibition on harassment on the basis of disability as not limited to those who themselves are disabled, so long as it is disability that is the basis of less favorable treatment. Paras 48–51.

C.   Age

The preamble to the 2000/78 Directive emphasizes the need to pay particular attention to supporting older workers, in order to increase their participation in the European labour force and to encourage diversity in the workforce. Paras 8 and 25. Age discrimination is justified, however, in certain circumstances. In addition to potentially constituting a genuine and determining occupational requirement, "differences of treatment on grounds of age shall not constitute discrimination, if, within the context of national law, they are objectively and reasonably justified by a legitimate aim, including legitimate employment policy, labour market and vocational training objectives, and if the means of achieving that aim are appropriate and necessary." Article 6(1). According to the Directive, age discrimination may be justified, for example, under the following circumstances:

> (a) the setting of special conditions on access to employment and vocational training, employment and occupation, including dismissal and remuneration conditions, for young people, older workers and persons with caring responsibilities in order to promote their vocational integration or ensure their protection;

(b) the fixing of minimum conditions of age, professional experience or seniority in service for access to employment or to certain advantages linked to employment;

(c) the fixing of a maximum age for recruitment which is based on the training requirements of the post in question or the need for a reasonable period of employment before retirement.

Article 6(1). In addition, the Directive provides that:

Member States may provide that the fixing for occupational social security schemes of ages for admission or entitlement to retirement or invalidity benefits, including the fixing under those schemes of different ages for employees or groups or categories of employees, and the use, in the context of such schemes, of age criteria in actuarial calculations, does not constitute discrimination on the grounds of age, provided this does not result in discrimination on the grounds of sex.

Article 6(2). The exceptions to age discrimination provided by Article 6 of the 2000/78 Directive have sometimes been interpreted narrowly and sometimes more loosely using a proportionality test. Thus the scope of age discrimination has been defined negatively, through what it is not.

Courts have given fairly wide deference to member states in setting national policy in employment and retirement matters based on age. Age discrimination law does not prohibit age distinctions within retirement or employment policies based on age as long as they are justified by objective aims and the means of achieving those aims are necessary and proportionate. The *Mangold* case was the first to apply the exception provided by article 6 of the Directive to employment policies for older workers. *Mangold v. Rudiger Helm*, Case C–144/04 (2005). There, the Court found that Article 6(1) must be interpreted as precluding a provision of domestic law that allows for the conclusion of fixed-term contracts of employment once the worker has reached the age of 52. Two other cases, the *Palacio* and *Age Concern* judgments, further clarify the standard to apply to the exception of age distinctions with regards to retirement policies. In both cases, the Court gives considerable latitude and deference to member states in determining the legitimacy of age restrictions in retirement policies. In *Palacios de la Villa*, Case C–411/05 (2007), the Court held that compulsory retirement clauses contained in collective agreements are lawful where such clauses provide as sole requirements that workers must have reached retirement age, set at 65 years by the national legislation, and must fulfil the other social security conditions for entitlement to draw a contributory retirement pension. In *Age Concern England*, Case C–388/07 (2009), the Court interpreted Article 6(1) as allowing a national measure that does not contain a precise list of the aims justifying derogation from the principle prohibiting age discrimination. More recent cases continue the trend of deference to member states, beyond retirement policies, to allow member states to set the maximum age for recruitment to certain career posts and to set maximum ages for compulsory retirement. *See Wolf v. Stadt Frakfurt am Main*, Case C–229/08 (2010) and *Vasil v. Tenicheski universitet-Sofia, filial Plovdiv*, Joined Cases C–250/09 and C–258/09 (2010).

D. Sexual Orientation

Recognition of sexual orientation in the 2000/78 framework mirrors its recognition by the ECtHR and the ECJ as a subject of human rights law. A number of cases by the ECtHR have vindicated the rights of gays and lesbians to be treated in equal terms in a variety of contexts. In recent rulings, the ECtHR has decriminalized homosexual acts between consenting adults (*Dudgeon v. the United Kingdom*, application no. 7525/76, judgment of 24 February 1983), banned sexual orientation discrimination in custody rights and family life (*Salgueiro da Silva Mouta v. Portugal*, application no. 33290/96, judgment of 21 December 1999), and prohibited discrimination in adoption on the basis of sexual orientation (E. B. v. France, application no. 43546/02, judgment 22 January 2008). More generally, it is noteworthy that in several cases the ECtHR required serious reasons to justify discrimination based on sexual orientation. In some occasions, the ECtHR even went as far as to compare discrimination based on sexual orientation to discrimination based on sex or on race.

Maruko v. Versorgungsanstalt der deutschen Buhnen

Case C–276/06, 1 April 2008

■ EUROPEAN COURT OF JUSTICE (Grand Chamber)

[Mr. Maruko filed an action against the pension fund of his deceased life partner. Mr. Maruko and his partner had a gay relationship recognised under the German Law on registered life partnerships. This law applied to gay relationships only, while marriage was open to heterosexual couples only. Mr. Maruko's deceased partner was a costume designer who had worked in the theatre sector. He was therefore a member of the German Theatre Pension Fund, which was created under the framework of the Collective Agreement for Germany's theatres. At the death of his partner, Mr. Maruko asked the pension fund for a widower's pension. The pension fund, however, refused this request on the grounds that, according to its own regulations, such a pension was only granted to a widow or a widower who had been legally married. Mr. Maruko alleged that this refusal constituted discrimination based on sexual orientation and therefore violated the 2000/78 Directive. On the specific issue of whether the refusal of the pension to Mr. Maruko violated the prohibition of discrimination based on sexual orientation, as provided by Directive 2000/78/EC, the Court ruled as follows:]

62. (...) [T]he referring court seeks to know whether the combined provisions of Articles 1 and 2 of Directive 2000/78 preclude legislation such as that at issue in the main proceedings under which, after the death of his life partner, the surviving partner does not receive a survivor's benefit equivalent to that granted to a surviving spouse, even though, like spouses, the life partners have been living in a union of mutual support and assistance which had been formally constituted for life.

Observations submitted to the Court

63. Mr Maruko and the Commission maintain that refusal to grant the survivor's benefit at issue in the main proceedings to surviving life partners constitutes indirect discrimination within the meaning of Directive 2000/78, since two persons of the same sex cannot marry in Germany and, consequently, cannot qualify for that benefit, entitlement to which is reserved to surviving spouses. In their opinion, spouses and life partners are in a comparable legal situation which justifies the granting of that benefit to surviving life partners.

64. According to the VddB [the German theatre pension fund], there is no constitutional obligation to treat marriage and life partnership identically, so far as concerns the law of social security or pensions. Life partnership is an institution *sui generis* and represents a new form of civil status. It cannot be inferred from the German legislation that there is any obligation to grant equal treatment to life partners, on the one hand, and spouses, on the other.

The Court's reply

65. In accordance with Article 1 thereof, the purpose of Directive 2000/78 is to combat, as regards employment and occupation, certain forms of discrimination including that on grounds of sexual orientation, with a view to putting into effect in the Member States the principle of equal treatment.

66. Under Article 2 of Directive 2000/78, the 'principle of equal treatment' means that there is to be no direct or indirect discrimination whatsoever on any of the grounds referred to in Article 1 of the Directive. According to Article 2(2)(a) of Directive 2000/78, direct discrimination occurs where one person is treated less favourably than another person who is in a comparable situation, on any of the grounds referred to in Article 1 of the Directive. Article 2(2)(b)(i) states that indirect discrimination occurs where an apparently neutral provision, criterion or practice would put persons having a particular religion or belief, a particular disability, a particular age, or a particular sexual orientation at a particular disadvantage compared with other persons unless that provision, criterion or practice is objectively justified by a legitimate aim and the means of achieving that aim are appropriate and necessary.

67. It is clear from the information provided in the order of reference that, from 2001—the year when the LPartG [the German law on Law on registered life partnerships], in its initial version, entered into force—the Federal Republic of Germany altered its legal system to allow persons of the same sex to live in a union of mutual support and assistance which is formally constituted for life. Having chosen not to permit those persons to enter into marriage, which remains reserved solely to persons of different sex, that Member State created for persons of the same sex a separate regime, the life partnership, the conditions of which have been gradually made equivalent to those applicable to marriage.

68. The referring court observes that the Law of 15 December 2004 contributed to the gradual harmonisation of the regime put in place for the life partnership with that applicable to marriage. By that law, the German legislature introduced amendments to Book VI of the Social Security

Code—statutory old age pension scheme, by adding *inter alia* a fourth paragraph to Paragraph 46 of that Book, from which it is clear that life partnership is to be treated as equivalent to marriage as regards the widow's or widower's pension referred to in that provision. Analogous amendments were made to other provisions of Book VI.

69.   The referring court considers that, in view of the harmonisation between marriage and life partnership, which it regards as a gradual movement towards recognising equivalence, as a consequence of the rules introduced by the LPartG and, in particular, of the amendments made by the Law of 15 December 2004, a life partnership, while not identical to marriage, places persons of the same sex in a situation comparable to that of spouses so far as concerns the survivor's benefit at issue in the main proceedings.

70.   However, the referring court finds that entitlement to that survivor's benefit is restricted, under the provisions of the VddB [the theatre pension fund] Regulations, to surviving spouses and is denied to surviving life partners.

71.   That being the case, those life partners are treated less favourably than surviving spouses as regards entitlement to that survivor's benefit.

72.   If the referring court decides that surviving spouses and surviving life partners are in a comparable situation so far as concerns that survivor's benefit, legislation such as that at issue in the main proceedings must, as a consequence, be considered to constitute direct discrimination on grounds of sexual orientation, within the meaning of Articles 1 and 2(2)(a) of Directive 2000/78.

73.   It follows from the foregoing that the answer to the third question must be that the combined provisions of Articles 1 and 2 of Directive 2000/78 preclude legislation such as that at issue in the main proceedings under which, after the death of his life partner, the surviving partner does not receive a survivor's benefit equivalent to that granted to a surviving spouse, even though, under national law, life partnership places persons of the same sex in a situation comparable to that of spouses so far as concerns that survivor's benefit. It is for the referring court to determine whether a surviving life partner is in a situation comparable to that of a spouse who is entitled to the survivor's benefit provided for under the occupational pension scheme managed by the VddB.

[. . .]

On those grounds, the Court (Grand Chamber) hereby rules:

1.   A survivor's benefit granted under an occupational pension scheme such as that [at stake in this case] falls within the scope of Council Directive 2000/78/EC of 27 November 2000 establishing a general framework for equal treatment in employment and occupation.

2.   The combined provisions of Articles 1 and 2 of Directive 2000/78 preclude legislation such as that at issue in the main proceedings under which, after the death of his life partner, the surviving partner does not receive a survivor's benefit equivalent to that granted to a surviving spouse, even though, under national law, life

partnership places persons of the same sex in a situation comparable to that of spouses so far as concerns that survivor's benefit. It
is for the referring court to determine whether a surviving life
partner is in a situation comparable to that of a spouse who is
entitled to the survivor's benefit provided for under the occupational pension scheme managed by the Versorgungsanstalt der
deutschen Bühnen.

————

NOTES

1. What are the key similarities and differences between the structure
of U.S. and E.U. employment discrimination law? How do the defenses
under the E.U. directives compare with U.S. law?

2. The Belgium case referenced by the Henrad excerpt seems to be
the one major case in which the European Court of Justice addressed the
issue of race and ethnic origin employment discrimination, and more
specifically Directive 43/2000. In that case, a company looking to hire
employees stated that it would not employ 'immigrants' "because its
customers were reluctant to give them access to their private residences for
the period of the work." Case C–54/07 *Centrum voor Gelijkheid van Kansen
en voor Racismebestrijding [Case Centre for Equal Opportunities and Fight
Against Racism] v. Firma Feryn NV*, 2008 ECR I–5187 ¶ 16. The court held
that this was direct discrimination as it would likely strongly dissuade
certain candidates from applying, which would ultimately hinder their
access to the labor market. *Id.* at ¶ 15. The court also found that it did not
matter that there was no "identifiable victim." *Id.*

3. Compare the Wards Cove reasoning and Hernard's analysis regarding the reach of disparate impact or "indirect" discrimination under
equality law in the U.S. and Europe, respectively. What assumptions are
embedded in each about the operation of race discrimination in the respective society (United States, Europe) and its prevalence in each society?

4. Would a law similar to the employer's policy in the Johnson
Controls case (U.S. Supreme Court) be upheld by the European Court of
Justice under the ruling in Commission of European Council v. Austria?
Compare the Courts' reasoning in both cases. What are the key similarities
in their reasoning? What are the differences, if any?

5. Compare Article 15 of the 2006 Directive on Sex Discrimination
with the gender-neutral U.S. Family and Medical Leave Act ("FMLA") of
1993. The FMLA entitles eligible employees of covered employers to take
unpaid, job-protected leave for specified family and medical reasons with
continuation of group health insurance coverage under the same terms and
conditions as if the employee had not taken leave. Eligible employees are
entitled to: twelve workweeks of leave in a 12–month period for the birth of
a child and to care for the newborn child within one year of birth; the
placement with the employee of a child for adoption or foster care and to
care for the newly placed child within one year of placement; to care for the
employee's spouse, child, or parent who has a serious health condition; a

serious health condition that makes the employee unable to perform the essential functions of his or her job; any qualifying exigency arising out of the fact that the employee's spouse, son, daughter, or parent is a covered military member on "covered active duty;" or twenty-six workweeks of leave during a single 12–month period to care for a covered servicemember with a serious injury or illness who is the spouse, son, daughter, parent, or next of kin to the employee (military caregiver leave). 29 U.S.C. sec. 2601 (as amended by the 2008 National Defense Authorization Act). The Department of Labor administers the FMLA. For additional information, *see* http://www.dol.gov/dol/topic/benefits-leave/fmla.htm

The FMLA specifically recognizes that "the primary responsibility for family caregiving often falls on women, and such responsibility affects the working lives of women more than it affects the working lives of men," but it does not specifically target working mothers or otherwise seek to alter workplace structures which continue to favor non-caregivers. *See* Laura Kessler, *The Attachment Gap: Employment Discrimination Law, Women's Cultural Caregiving, And The Limits Of Economic And Liberal Legal Theory*, 34 U. MICH. J.L. Ref. 371, 386–389 (2001). Does this mean that the FMLA should not be considered a part of the antidiscrimination framework, as compared to the inclusion of provisions for work leave in the sex discrimination EC Directive?

6.   In 1998, the European Commission issued a comprehensive overview of the problem of sexual harassment in the European Union. *See generally* European Commission, Sexual Harassment in the Workplace in the European Union (1998). The Commission compiled the results of many studies on sexual harassment performed in eleven northern European countries, and concluded that the scope of the problem was staggering. *Id.* at 9. The studies found that "approximately 30% to 50% of women" experience some form of sexual harassment. *Id.* at 13. Also, the studies found that "the most common forms were verbal forms such as 'sexual jokes' and 'sexual remarks about body, clothes and sex life'; physical forms as 'unsolicited physical contact', and nonverbal forms such as 'staring and whistling'." European Commission *Id.* at 5. There were more severe forms of sexual harassment found, such as 'quid quo pro,' experienced by 10% to 26% of the employees, and 'sexual assault or rape' experienced by 1% to 6% of the women. *Id.* at 5.

7.   French law has long prohibited upper age limits for recruitment. See Article 311–4 of the (previous) Labor Code. However the oil crisis brought about massive lay-offs in companies and exclusion of older workers who were systematically offered early retirement incentives. As a result, France has a very low employment rate of workers over 50. With the aging of the population, and to deal with its future financial burden on the retirement system, the government started to promote employment of older workers with the adoption of the first reform of the retirement system in 2004. The European 2000/78 Framework Directive which covers age discrimination gave France the impetus to adopt the law of November 16, 2001 which introduced age as a prohibited ground of discrimination which is included in the current article L 1132–1 and article L 1133–2 of the Labor Code. The law of November 27, 2008 modified article L 1133–2 to

include the same examples of exceptions as article 6 of the 2000/78 Directive. The widespread practice of massive early retirement of older workers from the workforce could have meant courts would resist applying age discrimination legislation, even more so than other forms of discrimination. Curiously, French case law has actually been quite quick at applying European case law and even recognizing antidiscrimination based on age as a principle, inspired by ECJ case law.

8. Consider whether EU law embraces a hierarchy of discrimination between the categories:

> Age differs from other non-discrimination grounds covered under EU law in certain important aspects. To begin with, there appears to be a great range of circumstances where age may constitute a rational and legitimate reason for distinguishing between different groups of persons than is the case for the other non-discrimination grounds. Age-based distinctions are often based upon stereotypes and prejudice. However, the use of such distinctions may also at times be rooted in rational considerations and serve valuable social and economic objectives: the same is rarely true of the other non-discrimination grounds such as sexual orientation, gender, race or religion.
>
> In particular, age may be a useful and fair method of selecting which groups of individuals may benefit from particular measures, or to identify groups for differential treatment, especially when age serves as a rational "proxy" or indicator that particular groups possess certain characteristics in general, such as experience, maturity, good physical capability, or financial stability. Age is often used in such cases to categorise groups in very general and sweeping terms: however, such generalisations are often necessary in the field of social and employment policy and experience indicates that it is harder to avoid the use of age in making these generalisations than it is for the other non-discrimination grounds. As a result, age discrimination legislation must establish a framework for distinguishing between circumstances where use of age to differentiate between individuals is justified, and when it is not. That framework is provided by Article 6 of the Directive (2000/78) . . . .

> *Palacios* and *Age Concern* are important judgments. They confirm the Court's general approach to the age discrimination provisions of the Directive that was initially set out in Mangold. In both cases, the ECJ has clarified that age discrimination is to be treated similarly as other forms of discrimination, and the objective justification test is to be applied with similar rigour across the different discrimination grounds. However the Court also made it clear in both cases that the specific nature of age discrimination would be taken into account in applying this objective justification test, and Members States enjoy wide discretion in areas where legitimate aims relating to national employment policy and other general interests were at issue. Age is thus treated as both similar and different to the other discrimination grounds: it is treated as a "suspect" category which warrants the rigorous application of the objective justification test, but nevertheless

the special nature of age and the potential for age-based distinctions to serve rational ends is also factored into the application of the test.''

Colin O'Cinneide, *Age discrimination and the European Court of Justice: EU Equality Law Comes of Age*, LAW AND EUROPEAN AFFAIRS, 2009–2010/2, p. 254, p. 269.

9.   The boldness of the Maruko ruling comes, arguably, from the Court's surprising move in ruling that the differential treatment of married couples and partnered couples constitutes direct discrimination. In this ruling, the Court goes beyond what the plaintiff and the Commission had argued. They alleged the existence of indirect discrimination only—since there was no provision that made explicit reference to sexual orientation. They argued that it could be considered an ''apparently neutral provision'', one that puts persons having a particular sexual orientation at a particular disadvantage, without objective justification. But the Court considers that the discrimination is directly based on sexual orientation, since ''life partners are treated less favourably than surviving spouses'' and marriage is only open to heterosexual couples, while life partnerships are only for gay couples.

10.   Notice the interplay of the Directive and national law in the *Maruko* case. On the one hand, the Court states that, even if family law (''civil status'') is a competence of Member States, in the exercise of that competence Members States must comply with European Union law. On the other hand, it leaves for the German court to decide whether or not spouses and gay life partners are in a comparable situation for the purposes of the concrete pension in question. If the German court decides that they are in a comparable position, then the European Court of Justice says that the different treatment is direct discrimination on the grounds of sexual orientation, prohibited under Directive 2000/78. The European Court of Justice gives a clear indication on how the German court should decide the case. But since it is for the latter to make a decision, the former cannot be accused of violating national competence. In practice, meanwhile, the highest German courts have progressively accepted the similarity of the situation of married couples and gay partners. However, what would the European Court of Justice rule if the case concerned Italy or Poland, for example, where the law does not accept gay marriage, nor even recognise gay partnerships? Would it make sense to give clear indications about the ideal outcome of the case and, subsequently, leave it for the national court to decide the main issue: whether or not gay and married couples are in a similar position?

C.   HONG KONG

Much like the E.U., Hong Kong has fairly extensive and defoiled employment discrimination laws in place, codified in four Ordinances on the subject. The Ordinances provide protection against: family status discrimination, race discrimination, disability discrimination, and sex discrimination. The Ordinances were created in two waves. The first wave occurred in 1996–1997, when the sex, disability, and family status Ordinances were enacted. It took more than ten years for Hong Kong to add a race discrimination ordinance, which they did in 2008. Each of these

Ordinances protects against broad types of discrimination, and includes a section on employment discrimination in the third part of each respective Ordinance. Enforcement of these Ordinances is the primary responsibility of the Equal Opportunities Commission (EOC). The Commission receives complaints and can give legal assistance, or can bring the proceeding in their own name.

There are a few notable items of commonality among the Ordinances. Each Ordinance provides that if an action is taken for more than one reason, prohibited discrimination occurs so long as one of those reasons is based on sex, disability, family status, or race. Family Status Discrimination Ordinance, No. 527 (1997) Part I, Section 4; Race Discrimination Ordinance, No. 602 (2008) Part II, Section 9; Disability Discrimination Ordinance, No. 487 (1996) Part I, Section 3; Sex Discrimination Ordinance, No. 480 (1996) Sex Part I, Section 4. Another commonality is that prohibited discrimination applies to the hiring and firing of an employee, and promotion opportunities, transfers, training, or any benefits, services, or facilities, while that person is an employee. Family Status Discrimination Ordinance, No. 527 (1997) Part III, Section 1–2; Race Discrimination Ordinance, No. 602 (2008) Part III, Section 1–2; Disability Discrimination Ordinance, No. 487 (1996) Part III, Section 1–2; Sex Discrimination Ordinance, No. 480 (1996) Sex Part III, Section 1–2. Finally, none of the Ordinances define discrimination, leaving it to "Codes of Practice" created to enforce each Ordinance to do so. These codes specifically prohibit direct and indirect discrimination as well as various forms of harassment.

Each Ordinance has a corresponding Code of Practice that is designed to help guide employers in aligning themselves with the dictates of each Ordinance. The Codes themselves do not create any additional legal duties, but failure to follow the recommendations in the Codes can be used as evidence in court. "Thus, while not technically enforceable, the Codes will have the practical effect of imposing duties on employers—duties which reflect the Commission's application of the laws to specific facts and which therefore are often more specific and detailed than the general duties stated in the actual laws." Carole Petersen, *Hong Kong's First Anti-Discrimination Laws and Their Potential Impact on the Employment Market*, 27 Hong Kong L.J. 324, 334 (1997).

The text below offers a general overview of the scope of the Ordinances on Sex, Race and Disability Discrimination and excerpts from their corresponding Codes.

———

1. Sex Discrimination

The sex discrimination Ordinance applies to women as well as men. Sex Discrimination Ordinance, No. 480 (1996) See Part II Section 5 and 6. It also applies to discrimination against persons because they are married, or a woman because she is pregnant. Part II Section 7 and 8. The Ordinance has one exception or defense—when "sex is a genuine occupational qualification." Part III, Section 12. It lists the "only" situations where being a man is a genuine occupational qualification for a job, and the situations are: where the job calls for a man "for reasons of physiology" or "in dramatic performances or other entertainment;" where the job "needs to be held by a man to preserve decency or privacy;" where workers live on site and there are no facilities for women; where the nature of the establishment requires it; where personal services are provided and these services "can most effectively be provided by a man;" where travel is involved to countries that would not allow a women to fully perform the job requirements. *Id.* at Part III, Section 12(2).

Excerpts from the Code of Practice on Employment Under the Sex Discrimination Ordinance

3.1. In line with the SDO, the Code stipulates equal protection for men and women. For practical purposes, listed below are the definitions of discrimination (direct and indirect), sexual harassment and victimisation that apply throughout this document.

3.1.1. *Direct discrimination* means treating a person less favourably than another person in comparable circumstances, because of a person's sex, marital status or pregnancy.

3.1.2. *Indirect discrimination* consists of applying the same treatment as between the sexes, persons with different marital status and persons who are pregnant or not, but is in practice discriminatory in its effect.

For example, applying a certain minimum height or weight requirement to applicants could exclude a large proportion of female applicants and could be to their detriment. This would constitute indirect discrimination unless there was justification for a minimum height or weight requirement in the particular job.

3.1.3. *Sexual harassment* consists of any unwelcome sexual behaviour in circumstances where a reasonable person would have anticipated that the harassed person would be offended, humiliated or intimidated. It includes unwelcome sexual advances, unwelcome requests for sexual favours, and other unwelcome conduct of a sexual nature. It also includes creating a sexually hostile work environment.

6.1. Under the SDO, sexual harassment in employment is unlawful. Without limiting the meaning of sexual harassment as defined in the SDO, the following behaviour can be regarded as sexual harassment:

6.1.1. unwelcome sexual advances—e.g. leering and lewd gestures; touching, grabbing or deliberately brushing up against another person;

6.1.2. unwelcome requests for sexual favours—e.g. suggestions that sexual co-operation or the toleration of sexual advances may further a person's career;

6.1.3. unwelcome verbal, non-verbal or physical conduct of a sexual nature—e.g. sexually derogatory or stereotypical remarks; persistent questioning about a person's sex life; and

6.1.4. conduct of a sexual nature that creates a hostile or intimidating work environment—e.g. sexual or obscene jokes around the workplace; displaying sexist or other sexually offensive pictures or posters.

6.3. A series of incidents may constitute sexual harassment. However, depending on the circumstances, it is not necessary for there to be a series of incidents. One incident may be sufficient to constitute sexual harassment.

6.4. On the other hand, an employee may be the victim of a hostile work environment where he or she is harassed in a pattern of incidents that may not be, in and of themselves, offensive, but when considered together amount to sexual harassment.

10.6. Sex discrimination by an employer in recruiting for a job, or in providing opportunities for promotion or transfer to, or training for, a job is not unlawful where a person's sex is a ***genuine occupational qualification*** (GOQ) for the job. The criteria for determining whether a person's sex is a GOQ for a particular job are set out in the SDO and are explained below:

10.6.1. the essential nature of the job calls for a man or woman for reasons of (i) physiology (excluding physical strength or stamina); or (ii) authenticity in dramatic performances or other entertainment, e.g. actors and actresses, artists'; models and fashion models;

10.6.2. the job calls for a man or a woman to preserve decency or privacy, e.g. changing room or bathroom attendants for the respective sexes;

10.6.3. the job is likely to involve the employee working or living in someone else's house and have significant physical or social contact with the person living there;

10.6.4. the nature or location of the establishment makes it impracticable for the employee to live somewhere else other than in the premises provided by the employer and no suitable premises are available, e.g. a resident janitor at a single-sex school where there are no separate accommodation or sanitary facilities for the other sex;

10.6.5. the employing establishment is a hospital, prison or other establishment for persons requiring special supervision or attention (only that part of the establishment dealing with such persons may claim sex as a GOQ);

10.6.6. the holder of the job provides individuals with personal services promoting their welfare or education, or similar personal services, and those services can most effectively be performed by one sex, e.g. a female counsellor at a shelter home for battered women; and

10.6.7. the job needs to be held by a man because it is likely to involve the performance of duties outside Hong Kong in a place where the customs or laws are such that the duties could not be performed effectively by a woman, e.g. a sales manager who is required to spend considerable time in countries where customs forbid the involvement of women in this type of work.

10.7. The GOQ is not an automatic exception for general categories of jobs; in every case it will be necessary for the employer to show, if the exception is to be claimed, that it applies to the particular job in question.

―――――

2. RACE DISCRIMINATION

Race is quite broadly construed in Hong Kong employment discrimination law. Race means "the race, colour, descent, national or ethnic origin of the person." Race Discrimination Ordinance, No. 602 (2008) Part II, Section 8. There are three major exceptions to the Race Discrimination Ordinance. *Id.* at Part III, Sections 11, 12, 13. The first is an exception for genuine occupational qualification. *Id.* at Part III, Section 11. The ordinance states that being of a particular racial group is a genuine occupational qualification only where:

a) the job involves participation in a dramatic performance or other entertainment in a capacity for which a person of that racial group is required for reasons of authenticity;

(b) the job involves participation as an artist or photographic model in the production of a work of art, visual images or sequence of visual images for which a person of that racial group is required for reasons of authenticity;

(c) the job involves working in a place where food or drink is (for payment or not) provided to and consumed by members of the public or a section of the public in a particular setting for which, in that job, a person of that racial group is required for reasons of authenticity;

(d) the holder of the job provides persons of that racial group with personal services promoting their welfare, and those services can most effectively be provided by a person of that racial group; or

(e) the job involves providing persons of that racial group with personal services of such nature or in such circumstances as to require familiarity with the language, culture and customs of and sensitivity to the needs of that racial group, and those services can most effectively be provided by a person of that racial group. *Id.* at Part III, Section 11(2).

Next is the exception for employment intended to "provide training in skills to be exercised outside Hong Kong." Part III, Section 12. This exception exempts an act that is done by an employer to benefit a non-resident of Hong Kong, or if an employee is trained in Hong Kong, but the skills will be exercised "wholly outside Hong Kong." Part III, Section 12. The last exception is the exception for employment of persons with "special skills, knowledge or experience." Part III, Section 13. The ordinance does not apply if "the employment requires special skills, knowledge or experience not readily available in Hong Kong" and the "person possesses those skills, knowledge or experience; and is recruited or transferred from a place outside Hong Kong." Part III, Section 13.

―――――

Excerpts from Code of Practice on Employment Under the Race Discrimination Ordinance

2.1   What is meant by race under the RDO

2.1.1   The RDO provides that race means a person's "race", "colour", "descent", "national" or "ethnic origin". A racial group is a group of persons defined by reference to these characteristics. In this respect, the RDO is in line with the meaning of racial discrimination in Article 1 of the International Convention on the Elimination of All Forms of Racial Discrimination (ICERD).

2.1.2   The RDO further elaborates on the meaning of "descent" by providing that discrimination on the ground of descent means discrimination against members of communities based on forms of social stratification such as a caste system or similar systems of inherited status which nullify or impair their equal enjoyment of human rights.

2.1.3   There is no elaboration in the RDO relating to the meaning of "race", "colour", "national" or "ethnic origin". In applying these terms, the following are useful references: (1) ICERD and related documents (2) Case law and other materials in other jurisdictions (for example, common law jurisdictions).

2.1.4   The above reference materials indicate that:—

(1) Racism and racial discrimination are the result of social processes that seek to classify people into different groups with the effect of marginalizing some of them in society. In this context, the words "race", "colour, "national" or "ethnic origins" in discrimination laws have broad popular meanings. They are not mutually exclusive and a person may fall into more than one racial group. For example, identifying people as Asian is an act done on the ground of race. The same is true of identifying people as having Chinese origin. A person living in Hong Kong may be in the Asian racial group as well as in the Chinese origin group.

(2) National origin includes origin in a nation that no longer exists or a nation that was never a nation state in the modern sense. National origin is not the same thing as nationality. The national origin of a person can be different from his nationality or citizenship. For example, a person living in Hong Kong of Indian origin may have Malaysian nationality.

(3) A group is an ethnic group (and its members having the ethnic origin of the group) if it is a distinct segment of the population distinguished from others by a sufficient combination of shared customs, beliefs, traditions and characteristics derived from a long common history or presumed common history. On this basis, Jews and Sikhs have been held to be ethnic groups. Other groups in the same nature will also be regarded as ethnic groups.

2.2   Religion

2.2.1   Religion in itself is not race. A group of people defined by reference to religion is not a racial group under the RDO. The RDO does not apply to discrimination on the ground of religion. But requirements or conditions having an impact on people's religious practices may indirectly discriminate against certain racial groups, and when this is so the RDO applies (see for example the blanket ban on beards in Illustration 9 below may indirectly discriminate against ethnic groups whose religious practice or custom is to wear beards).

2.3   Language

2.3.1   As language used by people is often associated with their race, treatment based on language may discriminate against certain racial groups or may amount to racial harassment. Since language issues may arise in different aspects of employment matters, they will be mentioned and dealt with in different parts of the Code below * * *

2.4   What is not regarded as an act done on the ground of race under the RDO

2.4.1   The RDO provides that acts done on the ground of the matters specified in section 8(3) are not acts done on the ground of race under the RDO. Acts done on the ground of these matters also do not constitute requirements or conditions within the definition of indirect discrimination under the RDO. These matters are:—

(1) Whether or not a person is an indigenous villager;

(2) Whether or not a person is a permanent resident, or has the right of abode or right to land, or is subject to any restriction or condition of stay, or has permission to land and remain in Hong Kong;

(3) How long is a person's length of residency in Hong Kong;

(4) Whether or not a person has a particular nationality and citizenship.

2.4.2   Although acts done on the grounds of the above matters would not constitute discrimination under the RDO because they do not come within the meaning of race under the RDO, these matters should not be used as a mask to hide what is in fact race discrimination under RDO. Where there is in fact race discrimination, the person discriminated against may bring legal proceedings in Court or complain to the EOC for investigation and conciliation.

Illustration 1:—A Hong Kong resident of Pakistani origin applies for a job as a manager with a company. She meets all the requirements of the job, but she is not a permanent resident in Hong Kong. The company declined to consider her application and told her that it only employs people who are permanent residents in Hong Kong. In fact, the company does not employ only people who are permanent residents in Hong Kong and there are managers working in the company who are of various national or ethnic origins and who are not permanent residents in Hong Kong. Although whether or not a person is a permanent resident is not a ground of race under the RDO, on the information above, the court can draw an inference that the real reason for declining to consider the job applicant's application was on the ground of her Pakistani origin, which is a ground of race under the RDO.

6.1 Types of discrimination under the RDO The RDO defines different types of discrimination. They are:—

6.1.1 Racial discrimination Racial discrimination occurs in the following situations under the RDO75:—

(1) Direct discrimination. Direct discrimination occurs when person A treats person B (belonging to one racial group) less favourably than person C (belonging to a different racial group) on the ground of person B's race, when person B and person C are in same or materially similar situation.

> ***Illustration 7:***—*A person of Pakistani origin who speaks fluent Cantonese and has adopted a Chinese name applies by telephone for the job of a sales person and is invited for an interview. But, because his appearance indicates that he is of Pakistani origin, when he turns up to the interview he is falsely told that someone else has already been hired and the interview is declined. This is less favourable treatment on the ground of race if another job seeker not of Pakistani origin would not have been declined.*

> ***Illustration 8:***—*A manager of Chinese origin is treated less favourably on the ground of race (directly discriminated against), if a manager of English origin is paid a higher amount of salary than the manager of Chinese origin on the ground of their difference in origin, when they are both in the same or materially similar employment situation (such as they both do the same job and have similar experience and their performance are both good).*

The following points should be noted:—(a) RDO section 9 provides that if an act is done for more than one reason and one of the reasons is the race of a person (whether or not it is the dominant or substantial reason), then it is taken to be done for the reason of the race of the person; (b) RDO section 4(3) provides that segregation of a person on the ground of his or her race from other persons is direct discrimination; for example, segregation occurs if employees of non-Chinese origins are required to have their meals in a separate part of the staff canteen from employees of Chinese origin; (c) A person's command of a language, including the accent, can be related to his or her race, and employers should ensure that employees and workers are not treated less favourably because of their accent or language.

(2) Indirect discrimination. Indirect discrimination occurs when a person applies an apparently non-discriminatory requirement or condition to everyone of all racial groups, but:—(a) Only a considerably smaller proportion of people from a particular racial group can meet the requirement or condition than the proportion of people not from that racial group; (b) The person applying the requirement or condition cannot show the requirement or condition to be justified on non-racial grounds; (c) The requirement or condition is to the detriment of a person of that particular racial group because he or she cannot meet it.

Illustration 9:—A blanket ban on beards for health and safety reasons in a food packaging factory is a requirement or condition that indirectly discriminates ethnic groups such as the Sikhs (who by their custom have to keep a beard), when compared to other racial groups, if information shows that the blanket ban is not justifiable as face masks could have been used satisfactorily to meet health and safety standards.

The following points should be noted:—

(i) Preferences and factors to be taken into account (as opposed to an absolute requirement or condition for achieving an objective) are not within the meaning of requirement or condition under the RDO.

(ii) A requirement or condition cannot be met if a person cannot meet it consistently with the customs and cultural conditions of his or her racial group.

(iii) RDO section 4(2) provides that a requirement or condition is justifiable if it serves a legitimate objective and bears a rational and proportionate connection to the objective.

(iv) Reference case law indicates that requirement or conditions in relation to work times and appearance can lead to claims of indirect discrimination. To determine whether a requirement or condition is justifiable, each case has to be examined on its own merits, considering any discriminatory effects against any significant degree of increased cost, decreased efficiency, or serious safety problem in accommodating individuals from particular racial groups.

Illustration 10:—A blanket ban on beards in a food packaging factory in Illustration 9 above is justifiable if information shows that face masks could not satisfactorily meet health and safety standards.

Illustration 11:—An employer who decides not to accommodate Jewish employees (who have to observe Sabbath and cannot work on Saturdays) but requires them to work on Saturdays is able to justify this requirement with information showing that accommodation would lead to a significant degree of increased safety risk, increased cost and decreased efficiency.

Illustration 12:—A requirement to wear protective headgear in a repair workshop, even if indirectly discriminatory for Sikhs (who by their custom have to wear a turban), is justifiable given information on the risk of injury, and the possibility of liability on the employers, and that the requirement would be more difficult to enforce if an exception is made for one person.

(v) Reference case law also indicates that requirement or condition in relation to academic or language standard can lead to claims of indirect discrimination. Employers must be able to justify any such requirement or condition by showing that it is relevant to and not more demanding than what is required for doing the job. Each case depends on its own facts and Illustration 13 below is for reference only.

Illustration 13:—For a job as a clerical officer or clerical assistant in a government department in the UK, successful applicants would be required to deal with inquiries from the public in person and by telephone. An ability to understand and communicate in English was a prime requirement, and a requirement that candidates must possess an English Language "O" Level or equivalent was overall fair and not arbitrary. Such a requirement is justified on grounds unconnected with race because it bears a rational and proportionate connection to the objective of communication in English which is legitimate and required for the job.

6.1.2 Discrimination on the ground of near relative's race. Discrimination on the ground of the race of a near relative happens when person A treats person B less favourably than other people on the ground of person B's near relative's race. A near relative means a person's spouse, parent or child (including born out of wedlock, adopted or step child), grandparent or grandchild, sibling and in-laws.

Illustration 14:—A manager is discriminated against on the ground of his near relative's race when he applies for promotion to the post of director but is declined because the company considered he and his wife are not suitable for company social functions on the ground that his wife is of Indonesian origin, and another manager whose wife is not of Indonesian origin is appointed.

6.3.2 Harassment on the ground of race occurs in the following situations under the RDO:—

(1) Unwelcome conduct harassment. Person A engages in unwelcome conduct (which may include an oral or a written statement) towards person B on the ground of person B's race or person B's near relative's race, in circumstances where a reasonable person would have anticipated that person B would be offended, humiliated or intimidated. There is liability for harassment even if there is no intention or motive to offend, humiliate or intimidate.

(2) Hostile environment harassment. Person A engages, on the ground of person B's race or person B's near relative's race, in conduct alone or together with other persons that create a hostile environment for person B.

———

3.   Disability Discrimination

The term "disability" is broadly defined in the Ordinance. Disability Discrimination Ordinance, No. 487 (1996) Part I, Definition of disability. It means: "totally or partial loss of the person's bodily or mental functions; total or partial loss of part of the person's body; the presence in the body of organisms causing disease or illness; the presence in the body of organism capable of causing disease or illness; malfunction, malformation or disfigurement of a part of the person's body; a disorder or malfunction that results in the person learning differently from a person without the disorder or malfunction; or a disorder, illness or disease that affects a person's thought process, perception of reality, emotions, or judgment or that results in disturbed behavior." Also included in the definition, if the above is met, is a disability that "presently exists; previously existed but no longer exists; may exist in the future; or is imputed to a person."

The Disability Discrimination Ordinance has an "[e]xception where absence of disability is a genuine occupational qualification." Part III, Section 12. This section allows an employer, when considering a person with a disability, to consider whether they "would be unable to carry out the inherent requirements of the particular employment; or would, in order to carry out those requirements, require services or facilities that are not required by persons without a disability and the provision of which would impose an unjustifiable hardship on the employer." Part III, Section 12(2)(c)(i)–(ii).

Excerpts from the Code of Practice on Employment Under the Disability Discrimination Ordinance

3.1 "Disability" is an evolving concept; it results from the interaction between persons with disabilities and attitudinal and environmental barriers that hinders full and effective participation of persons with disabilities in society on an equal basis with others. The Convention on the Rights of Persons with Disabilities (the CRPD) marks a major shift in attitudes and approaches to persons with disabilities. Adopting a rights-based approach, persons with disabilities are no longer regarded as *objects* of charity, medical treatment and social protection; but as *subjects* with rights, who are capable of being active members of society. The CRPD also affirms the right of persons with disabilities to work on an equal basis with others.

3.2 Recognising the progression in disability rights, in particular the diversity of persons with disabilities, the DDO adopts a fairly broad definition of disability to encompass most situations where a person should be regarded as having a disability and thus effectively protected by the law.

4.1 There are two forms of disability discrimination, namely direct discrimination and indirect discrimination. **Direct discrimination** arises from a differential and less favourable treatment accorded to job applicant(s) or employee(s) because of their disability. *See* paragraphs 4.12–4.22 below: An employer refused to hire persons on wheelchair because he thought persons with mobility disability were more prone to work injuries. Because of this stereotypical assumption, F, a candidate with mobility disability, was refused an opportunity to have an interview. F has therefore been discriminated against on the ground of her disability by being deprived of a chance to an interview.

4.2 **Indirect discrimination** involves imposing a seemingly neutral condition or requirement on everyone, but such condition or requirement has a disproportionate adverse effect on persons with disability(ies) and the application of such condition or requirement is not justified in the relevant circumstances. *See* paragraphs 4.23–4.28 below: All job applicants for a clerical position were required to pass a physical fitness test before further consideration for employment opportunity. Although passing the physical fitness test was a requirement applicable to all who were interested in the job, persons lacking the physical fitness because of particular disabilities would more likely to be screened out. This would give rise to indirect discrimination unless the requirement was imposed with justifiable cause.

4.3   **Disability harassment** is an unwelcome conduct towards an employee in relation to his/her disability in circumstances where a reasonable person would have anticipated that the person being harassed would feel offended, humiliated or intimidated. Name calling and mimicking gesture are common examples of disability harassment.

4.12   Section 6(a) of the DDO stipulates that: a person discriminates against another person in any circumstances relevant for the purposes of any provision of the DDO if on the ground of that other person's disability he treats that other person less favourably than he treats or would treat a person without a disability.

4.13   In short, direct disability discrimination in employment means treating an employee with a disability less favourably than another employee without a disability or without the same disability in comparable circumstances on the ground of the former's disability. There are three components of this definition which are essential: 1) cause of treatment (on the ground of), 2) comparator in relevant circumstances (comparable circumstances), and 3) detriment (less favourable treatment).

4.15   The "But-for-Test" is an objective test that helps to determine the cause of treatment. To apply this test, one needs to look into the incident as a whole from an objective point of view and ask the question: Would the aggrieved person have received the same treatment ***but for*** his/her disability? Compare the following two scenarios:

> Employee K has recovered from depression. The supervisor doubted Employee K's ability to handle the stress and workload in a more senior position and therefore did not recommend her for promotion despite her good appraisal ratings in the past years. Ask the question: Would Employee K have been recommended for promotion ***but for*** her having depression in the past? It appears that Employee K was passed over in the promotion exercise because of her past disability. The employer's decision would constitute direct discrimination on the ground of Employee K's disability.

> Employee L who suffered from migraine headache had a record of repeated tardiness and neglect of duties. He has been warned numerous times of his poor performance both verbally and in writing. The employer finally dismissed him after no improvement was shown on his part. Would Employee L have been dismissed ***but for*** his disability? It appears that L was dismissed because of his substandard performance. His disability was part of the background information irrelevant to his dismissal.

4.16   Section 3 of the DDO provides that if an act is done for two or more reasons and one of the reasons is the disability of a person then the act is taken to be done for the reason of a person's disability. The disability of that person does not have to be shown as the only reason for the unlawful discrimination.

It suffices if it is one of the reasons amongst others, whether or not it is the dominant or a substantial reason for doing the unlawful act. Genuine performance issues should be dealt with in a fair and clear manner so as to avoid misunderstanding.

4.17   It is not necessary to show that an employer has intended to commit an act of discrimination. It can be an unintended result of a decision or an action. Sometimes, it could even be a well intended *See R v. Birmingham City Council ex parte Equal Opportunities Commission* [1989] IRLR 173 HL 23 gesture on the employer's part that the treatment is done in the interest of the employee with a disability.

4.18   Direct discrimination requires a comparison between the aggrieved person and another person who does not have a disability or the same disability, in the same or not materially different circumstances. This means that there must be a sufficient degree of similarity or common features to form the basis of an appropriate comparison. The purpose is to ascertain whether the disability in question is the ground on which the aggrieved person is discriminated.

4.21   One of the crucial components of the definition of direct discrimination is that of "less favourable treatment".The term "less favourable treatment" entails a detriment suffered by the employee with a disability. In establishing detriment, it is not necessary to show financial loss. Items such as injury to feeling, training and career opportunities could also qualify as detriment in discrimination claims. Whether a treatment is detrimental to the person affected depends on an objective assessment of the relevant circumstances on a case by case basis.

4.22   One needs to bear in mind that subjective reasoning on the part of employer for the differential treatment may neither be a defence nor be relevant if it is objectively detrimental to the person affected.

4.24   Emanating from Section 6(b) of the DDO, indirect discrimination means 1) imposing the **same requirement or condition** which is applicable to everyone else, 2) where the **proportion of persons with disabilities** who can comply is considerably smaller than persons without disabilities, 3) which requirement or condition concerned **cannot be objectively justified**, and 4) as a result the person with disability suffers a **detriment**.

> Company Q required all employees not to be regularly absent from work for operational reasons. Employee R had a chronic illness and had taken sick leave for an extended period of time. The employer decided to terminate R's employment because R could not meet the company's operational needs. The company claimed that their operational needs required all employees "not to be regularly absent from work" and they would dismiss any employee who could not meet this requirement. The uniform requirement applying to all employees was the condition "not to be regularly absent from work". It is likely that

persons on valid extended period of sick leave would encounter difficulty in satisfying such attendance requirement. The onus would then be on the employer to justify the imposition of such a requirement.

4.25   The initial step in the analysis of an indirect discrimination claim is the identification of the "requirement" or "condition" which is applicable to all. It also requires a determination that the requirement or condition cannot be complied with by the person with disability in the relevant situation. These are factual matters which need to be established.

4.26   Establishing the proportion of people who can comply may require complex statistical or other technical information if a comprehensive analysis is to be undertaken. The consideration would be relatively less complicated where the comparison between the proportion of persons with disabilities who cannot comply with the requirement and the proportion of people who can is obvious. For instance, it would not be difficult to demonstrate that persons who have serious illness require taking longer sick leave and that it is proportionally more difficult for them to comply with a full attendance requirement. A common sense approach should be adopted in determining proportionality, and whether the comparison between pools of persons in a particular situation would make natural sense.

4.27   A balancing exercise of reasonableness weighing the following factors is relevant in determining the justifiability of imposing a requirement or condition:

4.27.1   Effect on the person with a disability or group of persons with the particular disability;

4.27.2   Effect on the employer's operations including the resources of the business and administrative efficiency;

4.27.3   Reasonableness of the alternative arrangements that could be provided to the person with a disability.

5.1   Some disabilities are so serious making the persons having them genuinely incapable of carrying out the inherent requirement(s) of the jobs concerned. Most disabilities, however, could be overcome with workplace adjustments and reasonable accommodation by the employer and the employer is encouraged to make the necessary adjustment and accommodation unless there is unjustifiable hardship on his part in doing so.

5.3   The DDO recognises that in some situations, a person because of his/her disability would not be able to carry out the inherent requirement(s) of the job even with reasonable accommodation. It would be unrealistic to expect an employer to recruit or continue employing a person in a job for which requirements he /she cannot fulfill.

5.18   Although there is no legal obligation on an employer to provide accommodation in order for the employee with a disability to fulfill the inherent requirement(s) of a job, the court would consider whether services or facilities have been considered or reasonably afforded to the employee with a disability before an employer could successfully avail itself of the defence of inability to perform the inherent requirement and/or unjustifiable hardship.

5.21   In determining hardship on the employer's part, the court would have to consider all aspects in the particular circumstances of individual cases. For example, while costly alteration to premises' access to accommodate an employee in wheelchair may seem unreasonable, its benefits to other users/occupants and hence the potential for cost sharing by others could well be taken into account.

————

NOTES

1.   The Ordinance on Family status is not discussed here but it covers much of the same conceptual ground as the other Ordinances in outlawing various types of discrimination on the basis of family status. Family status, according to the ordinance, "means the status of having responsibility for the care of an immediate family member." Immediate family member "means a person who is related to the person by blood, marriage, adoption or affinity." Family Status Discrimination Ordinance, No. 527 (1997) Part I, Immediate Family Member defined.

2.   Compare the definition and scope of the BFOQ defense under Hong Kong law with its counterpart in the United States? Which is more restrictive?

3.   What does the Code on Race Discrimination mean when it says, under the definition of indirect discrimination, that "preferences and factors to be taken into account (as opposed to an absolute requirement or condition for achieving an objective) are not within the meaning of requirement or condition under the RDO"? 6.11(2)(i). What is the significance of this language for someone wanting to prove that indirect discrimination has occurred?

4.   There is currently no legal prohibition of sexual orientation-based employment discrimination in Hong Kong's private sector, but such legislation has been proposed. The first major attempt to pass such legislation occurred in 1994, when legislator Anna Wu proposed a comprehensive antidiscrimination law that would have included sexual orientation. In 2001, Hong Kong's Legislative Council established a Subcommittee to study sexual orientation discrimination, but the Subcommittee never introduced a bill for consideration. The Hong Kong government has, however, launched public education campaigns to confront sexual orientation discrimination, issued non-binding declarations against sexual orientation discrimination in the workplace, and established its Gender Identity and Sexual Orientation Unit (GISOU). GISOU takes complaints of sexual orientation and gender identity discrimination and seeks to mediate claims of discrimination. However, GISOU does not offer enforceable remedies. *See generally* Holning Lau & Rebecca L. Stotzer, *Employment Discrimination Based on Sexual Orientation: A Hong Kong Study*, EMPLOY RESPONS RIGHTS J. (Springer, 2010).

5.   As was mentioned, the employment discrimination laws in Hong Kong were enacted in two waves. It was a struggle to enact these ordinances as Hong Kong had long "pursued a policy known as 'positive non-

interventionism,' " which meant "that the government provides an impartial legal system and the infrastructure necessary for industry and commerce, but avoids enacting legislation that would be viewed as unduly burdensome to business." Carole Petersen, *Hong Kong's First Anti–Discrimination Laws and Their Potential Impact on the Employment Market*, 27 HONG KONG L.J. 324, 324 (1997). Hong Kong attributed much of its economic success to this non-interventionism practice, which became an obstacle to passage of the employment discrimination ordinances. "The business community was firmly opposed to [employment discrimination laws], viewing them as interventionist, costly to enforce, and unnecessary," and the Hong Kong government backed this position. *Id.* at 325. It took very smart political maneuvering and a strong women's movement to essentially force the government into enacting the first wave of anti-discrimination laws. *Id.* at 329–333. The fight over the Sex Discrimination Ordinance made it an easier fight to pass the Disability Discrimination Ordinance, and presumably the Family Status Ordinance. *Id.* at 349.

6.   There has been a struggle with racial discrimination in Hong Kong for a long time and, as such, Hong Kong was quite slow in passing the Race Discrimination Ordinance. Consider this brief history: The government of Hong Kong asserted that their city was the "Manhattan of Asia" and at the "forefront of developed societies," which led the government to deny "the existence of significant [racial] discrimination despite strong evidence of its substantiality." Barry Sautman, *The Politics of Racial Discrimination in Hong Kong*, MARYLAND SERIES IN CONTEMPORARY ASIAN STUDIES, Number 2 at 3 (2002). In 1998, just a few years after the other ordinances were enacted, a survey was done which showed "that two-thirds of ethnic minority respondents had witnessed or been victims of discrimination." *Id.* The response from the government was that, compared to other cities of comparable size, this level of discrimination was not that bad. *Id.* at 6.

D. SOUTH AFRICA

On April 27, 1994, South Africa adopted a revolutionary Constitution, ending the era of apartheid. The final version of the Constitution became effective on February 4th 1997. Chapter 2, Section 9 of the South African Constitution created the foundation for the country to implement very strong employment discrimination laws, and, more generally, to protect against inequality. Chapter 2 is the Bill of Rights for the country, and Section 9 is the provision on "Equality." Section 9 provides that "[e]veryone is equal before the law and has the right to equal protection and benefit of the law." It also provides for the power of the state to "promote the achievement of equality" through "legislative and other measures designed to protect or advance persons, or categories of persons, disadvantaged by unfair discrimination." The latter part of this provision has been interpreted to allow for various forms of affirmative action. *See* Chapter IV on Affirmative Action. Finally, Article 9 protects against discrimination against anyone because of: "race, gender, sex, pregnancy, marital status, ethnic or social origin, colour, sexual orientation, age, disability, religion, conscience, belief, culture, language and birth." Discrimination on one or more of these grounds is "unfair unless it is established that the discrimination is fair."

A few years after the South African Constitution was put into effect, the Employment Equity Act was made law. Employment Equity Act, No. 55 of 1998. This Act specifically protects against employment discrimination, but it also requires that employers implement affirmative action measures "for people from designated groups" in the Act. The scope of the Employment Equity Act has three main components worth highlighting at the outset. First, according to Chapter 1, Section 4, the prohibition of unfair discrimination "applies to all employees and employers." Second, the categories that are protected, which are very broad and largely mirror those in the Constitution, are listed under Chapter 2, Section 6(1), as: "race, gender, sex, pregnancy, marital status, family responsibility, ethnic or social origin, colour, sexual orientation, age, disability, religion, HIV status, conscience, belief, political opinion, culture, language and birth." Third, under Chapter 2, Section 11, "whenever unfair discrimination is alleged in terms of this act, the employer against whom the allegation is made must establish that it is fair." This appears to put the burden squarely on the employer.

---

1.   THE EMPLOYMENT EQUITY ACT

Employment Equity Act, No. 55 of 1998

1998 SA Labour 55

Preamble.—Recognising—that as a result of apartheid and other discriminatory laws and practices, there are disparities in employment, occupation and income within the national labour market; and that those disparities create such pronounced disadvantages for certain categories of people that they cannot be redressed simply by repealing discriminatory laws,

Therefore, in order to—promote the constitutional right of equality and the exercise of true democracy; eliminate unfair discrimination in employment; ensure the implementation of employment equity to redress the effects of discrimination; achieve a diverse workforce broadly representative of our people; promote economic development and efficiency in the workforce; and give effect to the obligations of the Republic as a member of the International Labour Organisation,

* * *

CHAPTER II—PROHIBITION OF UNFAIR DISCRIMINATION

5.   Elimination of unfair discrimination.—Every employer must take steps to promote equal opportunity in the work—place by eliminating unfair discrimination in any employment policy or practice.

6.   Prohibition of unfair discrimination.—(1) No person may unfairly discriminate, directly or indirectly, against an employee, in any employment policy or practice, on one or more grounds, including race, gender, sex,

pregnancy, marital status, family responsibility, ethnic or social origin, colour, sexual orientation, age, disability, religion, HIV status, conscience, belief, political opinion, culture, language and birth.

(2) It is not unfair discrimination to—

(a) take affirmative action measures consistent with the purpose of this Act; or

(b) distinguish, exclude or prefer any person on the basis of an inherent requirement of a job.

(3) Harassment of an employee is a form of unfair discrimination and is prohibited on any one, or a combination of grounds of unfair discrimination listed in subsection (1).

———

2. THE CONSTITUTIONAL COURT

The Constitutional Court was established in 1994 by the new Constitution and is the highest court in South Africa. As in the United States, the Court is the final interpreter of the Constitution, the supreme law of the land, and has the power to overturn Acts of Parliament that it deems unconstitutional. On matters of constitutional law, it may review decisions of the "High Court of South Africa." The Constitutional Court has ruled only once in a case applying Section 9 of the Constitution [equality] to an allegation of employment discrimination. In *Hoffmann v. South Africa Airways* 2001 (1) SA 1 (CC) (S.Afr.), South African Airways refused to hire Jacques Hoffman because of his HIV positive status. South African Airways had an employment practice that "required the exclusion from employment as cabin attendant of all persons who were HIV positive." The rationale given by the Airline for these practices was based on medical and operational grounds. The medical rationale was that people with HIV might have a bad reaction to yellow fever vaccination, and might contract and transmit other diseases to passengers. The operational rationale was that the short life expectancy of people with HIV makes the airline unable to recoup the training costs. The High Court of South Africa (the appellate court) found merit in these arguments, but on an appeal to the Constitutional Court, the High Court was overturned.

The Constitutional Court went to some length to describe the injustice and vulnerability facing people living with HIV and AIDS before turning its attention to the constitutional standard for equality:

———

Hoffman v. South African Airways

Constitutional Court of South Africa, Case CCT 17/00, 28 September 2000

■ Ngcobo J:

* * *

[23] Transnet is a statutory body, under the control of the state, which has public powers and performs public functions in the public

interest.17 It was common cause that SAA is a business unit of Transnet. As such, it is an organ of state and is bound by the provisions of the Bill of Rights in terms of section 8(1), read with section 239, of the Constitution. It is, therefore, expressly prohibited from discriminating unfairly.

[24]   This Court has previously dealt with challenges to statutory provisions and government conduct alleged to infringe the right to equality. Its approach to such matters involves three basic enquiries: first, whether the provision under attack makes a differentiation that bears a rational connection to a legitimate government purpose. If the differentiation bears no such rational connection, there is a violation of section 9(1). If it bears such a rational connection, the second enquiry arises. That enquiry is whether the differentiation amounts to unfair discrimination. If the differentiation does not amount to unfair discrimination, the enquiry ends there and there is no violation of section 9(3). If the discrimination is found to be unfair, this will trigger the third enquiry, namely, whether it can be justified under the limitations provision. Whether the third stage, however, arises will further be dependent on whether the measure complained of is contained in a law of general application.

[25]   Mr Trengove sought to apply this analysis to SAA.'s employment practice in the present case. He contended that the practice was irrational because: first, it disqualified from employment as cabin attendants all people who are HIV positive, yet objective medical evidence shows that not all such people are unsuitable for employment as cabin attendants; second, the policy excludes prospective cabin attendants who are HIV positive but does not exclude existing cabin attendants who are likewise HIV positive, yet the existing cabin attendants who are HIV positive would pose the same health, safety and operational hazards asserted by SAA as the basis on which it was justifiable to discriminate against applicants for employment who are HIV positive. * * *

[27]   At the heart of the prohibition of unfair discrimination is the recognition that under our Constitution all human beings, regardless of their position in society, must be accorded equal dignity. That dignity is impaired when a person is unfairly discriminated against. The determining factor regarding the unfairness of the discrimination is its impact on the person discriminated against. Relevant considerations in this regard include the position of the victim of the discrimination in society, the purpose sought to be achieved by the discrimination, the extent to which the rights or interests of the victim of the discrimination have been affected, and whether the discrimination has impaired the human dignity of the victim.

[28]   The appellant is living with HIV. People who are living with HIV constitute a minority. Society has responded to their plight with intense prejudice. They have been subjected to systemic disadvantage and discrimination. They have been stigmatised and marginalised. As the present case demonstrates, they have been denied employment because of their HIV positive status without regard to their ability to perform the duties of the position from which they have been excluded. Society's response to them has forced many of them not to reveal their HIV status for fear of

prejudice. This in turn has deprived them of the help they would otherwise have received. People who are living with HIV/AIDS are one of the most vulnerable groups in our society. Notwithstanding the availability of compelling medical evidence as to how this disease is transmitted, the prejudices and stereotypes against HIV positive people still persist. In view of the prevailing prejudice against HIV positive people, any discrimination against them can, to my mind, be interpreted as a fresh instance of stigmatisation and I consider this to be an assault on their dignity. The impact of discrimination on HIV positive people is devastating. It is even more so when it occurs in the context of employment. It denies them the right to earn a living. For this reason, they enjoy special protection in our law.

[29] There can be no doubt that SAA discriminated against the appellant because of his HIV status. Neither the purpose of the discrimination nor the objective medical evidence justifies such discrimination. * * *

[30] SAA refused to employ the appellant saying that he was unfit for world-wide duty because of his HIV status. But, on its own medical evidence, not all persons living with HIV cannot be vaccinated against yellow fever, or are prone to contracting infectious diseases—it is only those persons whose infection has reached the stage of immunosuppression, and whose CD4 + count has dropped below 350 cells per microlitre of blood. Therefore, the considerations that dictated its practice as advanced in the High Court did not apply to all persons who are living with HIV. Its practice, therefore, judged and treated all persons who are living with HIV on the same basis. It judged all of them to be unfit for employment as cabin attendants on the basis of assumptions that are true only for an identifiable group of people who are living with HIV. On SAA.'s own evidence, the appellant could have been at the asymptomatic stage of infection. Yet, because the appellant happened to have been HIV positive, he was automatically excluded from employment as a cabin attendant. * * *

[32] The fact that some people who are HIV positive may, under certain circumstances, be unsuitable for employment as cabin attendants does not justify the exclusion from employment as cabin attendants of all people who are living with HIV. * * *

[34] Legitimate commercial requirements are, of course, an important consideration in determining whether to employ an individual. However, we must guard against allowing stereotyping and prejudice to creep in under the guise of commercial interests. The greater interests of society require the recognition of the inherent dignity of every human being, and the elimination of all forms of discrimination. Our Constitution protects the weak, the marginalised, the socially outcast, and the victims of prejudice and stereotyping. It is only when these groups are protected that we can be secure that our own rights are protected. * * *

[37] Prejudice can never justify unfair discrimination. This country has recently emerged from institutionalised prejudice. Our law reports are replete with cases in which prejudice was taken into consideration in denying the rights that we now take for granted. Our constitutional democracy has ushered in a new era—it is an era characterised by respect for human dignity for all human beings. In this era, prejudice and stereo-

typing have no place. Indeed, if as a nation we are to achieve the goal of equality that we have fashioned in our Constitution we must never tolerate prejudice, either directly or indirectly. * * *

[40]   Having regard to all these considerations, the denial of employment to the appellant because he was living with HIV impaired his dignity and constituted unfair discrimination.* * *

[41]   I conclude, therefore, that the refusal by SAA to employ the appellant as a cabin attendant because he was HIV positive violated his right to equality guaranteed by section 9 of the Constitution. The third enquiry, namely whether this violation was justified, does not arise. We are not dealing here with a law of general application. This conclusion makes it unnecessary to consider the other constitutional attacks based on human dignity and fair labour practices.

* * *.

NOTES

1.   Consider the 2011 annual report on the effect of the Employment Equity Act. The report reveals that: whites, who make up only 12.1% of the economically active population, continue to occupy 73.1% of 'top management' positions. African people, who make up 73.6% of the population, occupy only 12.7%. http://www.workinfo.co.za/Articles/34394_cee_annual_report_2011a.pdf.

2.   The Constitution and the Employment Equity Act are the two main devices used to prevent employment discrimination, but another act worth mentioning is the Labour Relations Act of 1995. Labour Relations Act, No. 66 of 1995 (S. Afr.). This Act was South Africa's attempt, before the Constitution and Employment Equity Act, to reform South Africa's labour laws. The Act contains one main area dealing with employment discrimination. Paragraph 187 "Automatically Unfair Dismissals" states:

'A dismissal is automatically unfair if the employer, in dismissing the employee, acts contrary to section 5, if the reason for the dismissal is—

* * *

(e) the employee's pregnancy, intended pregnancy, or any reason related to her pregnancy;

(f) that the employer unfairly discriminated against an employee, directly or indirectly, on any arbitrary ground, including, but not limited to race, gender, sex, ethnic or social origin, colour, sexual orientation, age, disability, religion, conscience, belief, political opinion, culture, language, marital status or family responsibility;'

This Act protects many of the same categories as the Employment Equity Act. The Employment Equity Act protects two more areas against discrimination as compared to the Labour Relations Act—HIV Status and Birth.

3.   The problem of sex discrimination in South Africa is evident when looking at the disparity in pay between men and women. According to a South African newspaper, "South African men are earning up to 65 percent more than their female counterparts—for doing the same job." *Equality for all? Not by a Long Shot—Statistics; Men are Earning Up to 65% More than Their Female Counterparts*, THE STAR (South Africa), Oct. 06, 2010, at E1. The disparity is even worse for women with children. *Id.* Does anything in the Employment Equity Act prohibit a disparity in pay between men and women?

4.   National origin discrimination is also evident in South Africa, in part because, after the end of Apartheid, the nation was not prepared for "the flood of people who would descend on the country in search of that same better life." Mondli Makhanya, *We Must Now Get to Grips with the New, Diverse South African Family,* SUNDAY TIMES (South Africa), May 18, 2008, at 20. These immigrants were fighting for the same jobs as the South Africans, but some felt the immigrants "were willing to work longer hours for less money and in less conducive conditions." *Id.* In May 2008, the country exploded with violence against immigrants. The riots left 62 people dead; at least 670 wounded; dozens of women raped; and at least 100,000 people displaced. Int'l Organization for Migration, Towards Tolerance, Law, and Dignity: Addressing Violence against Foreign Nationals in South Africa, 01/2009, at 2 (February 2009). The University of Cape Town's Graduate School of Business released a study, focusing "on the negative psychological effects which foreign employees experience" and it found that xenophobia is rampant throughout the South African workplace. Kurt April, *Reactions to Discrimination: Exclusive Identity of Foreign Workers in South Africa*, in EQUALITY, DIVERSITY AND INCLUSION AT WORK: A RESEARCH COMPANION 216 (ed. M.F. Özbilgin 2009). Could xenophobia in the workplace be prohibited under the Employment Equity Act or the South African constitution?

5.   Changes have been proposed in employment law through bills which would amend the Employment Equity Act, the Labour Relations Act, The Basic Conditions of Employment Act, and create an Employment Services Act. However, there is resistance. "The four bills, which were proposed last year, have met with resistance from business and civil society groups. Critics argue the bills will make South African labour legislation even more constraining than it already is, thereby deterring companies from hiring and from retaining people already in jobs." Alistair Anderson, *World Bank Warns about too Many Labour Rules*, BUSINESS DAY (South Africa), Mar. 4, 2011. The only bill that would have significant impact on employment discrimination is the Employment Equity Amendment Bill. This Bill would add an equal pay for work of equal value clause. Meaning that employers would be prohibited from paying employees who do "the same or substantially the same work" differently. The bill would also strengthen enforcement and compliance with the Employment Equity Act by empowering "the Director General to impose fines on non-complying employers as a percentage of the annual turnover of the company, at two percent for first contraventions, escalating to a maximum of ten percent for repeated contraventions." *Media Briefing on the Bills Amending the Labour Relations Act*, http://www.labour.gov.za/media-desk/media-statements/2010/media-briefing-on-the-bills-amending-the-labour-relations-act-the-basic-conditions-of-employment-act-employment-equity-act-and-the-employ ment-services-bill–2010.

6. The Employment Equity Act prohibits harassment in Chapter 2, Section 3 where it states: "[h]arassment of an employee is a form of unfair discrimination and is prohibited on any one, or a combination of grounds of unfair discrimination listed in subsection (1)." Subsection (1) includes sex and other grounds for discrimination, which make sexual harassment illegal. It appears that the labour courts are quite plaintiff friendly in their sexual harassment jurisprudence. The major case in the field is *Ntsabo v. Real Security CC* (2003) 24 ILJ 2341 (LC). In this case the plaintiff's supervisor touched, grabbed, and even simulated a sex act on her. The court believed the plaintiff's story. The court interpreted the statute favorably for the plaintiff in two ways. First, it interpreted section 60 of the Employment Equity Act, which requires "immediate" reporting if the employer is to be liable, as:

> "The requirement that the reporting procedure be reported immediately cannot be construed to mean within minutes of the incident complained of. There are circumstances of which one is reminded in such considerations. It is trite that such a requirement is regarded as being complied with when it has been done within a reasonable time in the circumstances." *Id.*

The court also found that since her employer did not take any action after the plaintiff complained about the sexual harassment, the employer was guilty of discrimination based on sexual harassment by omission. The Court held that: "For the purpose of the EEA, failure of the Respondent to attend to the problem brings the whole issue within the bounds of discrimination. The nub of the complaint laid with the Respondent involved sexual harassment. Its failure to attend to the matter is by definition as envisaged by section 6(3) read with section 6(1) of the EEA, discrimination based on sexual harassment." *Id.*

E. BRAZIL

Brazil, like many other Latin American countries, makes employment discrimination a crime. There are two main pieces of anti-discrimination legislation. Lei No. 1.390, enacted in 1951, was the first piece of legislation to confront the problem of discrimination in Brazil. The law established acts resulting from "race or color prejudice" as a criminal misdemeanor, including denial of employment, service, lodging or admittance. The focus of this law was on race and color, and these were the only protected categories for forty years in Brazil. A subsequent anti-discrimination law, Lei No. 7.716, offered additional protection against discrimination. Lei No. 7.716 adds three more prohibited categories—ethnicity, religion, and national origin,—and increases the punishment of a violation beyond a simple misdemeanor. This provision specifies that "crimes resulting from prejudice or discrimination of race, color, ethnicity, religion, or national origin," including "to deny or obstruct employment in private enterprise," are offenses punishable by two to five years imprisonment. *See* Benjamin Hensler, *Nao Vale a Pena? (Not Worth the Trouble?) Afro–Brazilian Work-*

ers and Brazilian Anti-discrimination Law 30 HASTINGS INT'L & COMP. L. REV.
267, 287–289 (2007).

There is a high evidentiary standard to use one of these statutes to
bring a criminal claim of overt discrimination. It is such a high standard
that even direct expressions of prejudice do not necessarily trigger judicial
scrutiny. Most judges in Brazil require that three prongs are met for a
"viable allegation of racial discrimination"; they are: (1) the discriminatory
act, (2) the defendant's prejudice toward the complainant, and (3) the
causal relationship between the prejudice and the act. While the defendant
can argue any or all the prongs are not met as a defense, the third prong is
particularly hard to meet because judges typically require direct evidence of
causality rather than inferring causality. As an example, a "defendant
cannot simply disparage black Brazilians, but must reveal his action to
have been motivated by the prejudicial attitude, 'that I will not hire you
because you are black.' " *See* Seth Racusen, *The Ideology of the Brazilian
Nation and the Brazilian Legal Theory of Racial Discrimination*, 10 SOCIAL
IDENTITIES 775, 783–784 (2004).

Another protection against employment discrimination is the Brazilian
Constitution. Brazil's Constitution explicitly states that "all persons are
equal before the law, without any distinction whatsoever." Chapter 1,
Article 5. It also declares that "men and women have equal rights and
duties" and generally prohibits discrimination. Paragraph 41 of Article 5
adds that "the law will punish any discrimination which would offend
rights and fundamental liberties," while paragraph 42 states that the
"practice of racism constitutes an unbailable crime, subject to the punishment of imprisonment, under the terms of the law." *Also*, Article 7,
paragraph 30, of the Constitution prohibits "difference of salary, exercise of
functions, and criteria of admission for motive of sex, age, color or civil
status." For employment cases brought under the Constitution, there is the
possibility of a type of burden shifting analysis which can, according to
scholars, reach a broader range of discriminatory practices than if brought
under the criminal anti-discrimination laws. The requirement of direct
evidence of prejudicial motive under the two Leis make it difficult to shift
the burden to the employer. Racusen, *supra* at 780.

NOTES

1. The choice between criminal enforcement of the prohibition
against employment discrimination and constitutional claims of employment discrimination will depend on the resources dedicated to enforcement,
as well as the presence of enforcement incentives in the laws. As one
commentator notes:

> The vast majority of Latin American countries have mandates against
> race discrimination in their constitutions. However, most lack either
> legislation to implement the antidiscrimination policy or a governmen-
> tal agency dedicated to enforcing them. In fact, an examination of civil
> rights structures in six Latin American countries, sponsored by the
> Inter–American Development Bank, characterizes Latin American
> countries as generally lacking government agencies dedicated to han-
> dling or investigating charges of discrimination. The few countries with

enabling statutes have tended to focus on criminal law provisions as the primary vehicle for combating acts of discrimination, in part because the criminal law venue does not require an investment of financial resources on the part of the victim.

While criminal law enforcement carries a strong normative statement about the evils of racism, it has proven a poor means for handling incidents of race discrimination. In the case of Brazil, for example, because the criminal justice system is overloaded with traditional crimes involving physical harm to individuals and property, few race discrimination allegations are investigated. In turn, the few allegations that are investigated encounter a judicial system that is reluctant to impose the sanction of prison for such a harm. The aforementioned survey of legal systems also notes that Latin American civil rights structures are hampered by the lack of provisions for attorney's fees and other financial incentives for client representation, as well as the absence of an active civil rights bar."

Tanya Katerí Hernández, *Multiracial Matrix: The Role Of Race Ideology In The Enforcement Of Antidiscrimination Laws, A United States–Latin America Comparison*, 87 CORNELL L. REV. 1093, 1129 (2002).

2. Another set of laws that can be used for employment discrimination are the Consolidacao das Leis Trabalhistas (CLT), Brazil's extensive labor code which established the country's Labor Courts and which regulate every aspect of the employment relationship. The CLT was amended in 1999. The 1999 amendments make it a violation of the CLT for employers to consider sex, age, color or marital status as: (1) a qualification for hiring; (2) a reason for termination or denying promotion; (3) a variable for determining compensation, qualifications or opportunities for advancement; or (4) a criteria for taking or passing job-related examinations. Cases brought under this law enjoy a few advantages, such as beneficial burden-shifting, the lack of a requirement to prove discriminatory intent (as required under the criminal laws), and an accessible venue for workers to bring claims not likely to be pursued by prosecutors. However, there are also restrictions to bringing claims under the CLT. Most Afro–Brazilian workers who are most likely to bring such a claim are employed informally and thus are not covered by these laws (although these workers can challenge discriminatory hiring practices that bar access to the formal sector). The CLT is also most useful as a tool for after a person is terminated but has less usefulness if a claim is brought during the course of employment. Hensler, *supra*, at 318–319.

3. That civil claims are a more friendly and viable alternative is demonstrated by recent cases in which the Labor Courts have granted relief to claimants subjected to discriminatory treatment. Consider the following two cases, as detailed in Seth Racusen, A MULATO CANNOT BE PREJUDICED: THE LEGAL CONSTRUCTION OF RACIAL DISCRIMINATION IN CONTEMPORARY BRAZIL (June 2002) 306 (unpublished Ph.D. dissertation, Massachusetts Institute of Technology, http://hdl.handle.net/1721.1/31104). Vicente Espirito do Santo was fired after three witnesses overheard his supervisor saying "[l]et's clean the department and fire that crioulo." A "crioulo" is a person of African descent. The case was brought to the Public Prosecutor, but the

prosecutor argued that because white people were dismissed at the same time as Vicente the dismissal "was economic and not racially motivated." *Id.* at 306. The claim was then brought to Brazil's Labor Courts, a distinct forum from the civil or criminal courts, composed of three judges selected by employers, labor representatives, these courts, and the judiciary. Most Brazilians view the Labor Courts as a more sympathetic forum than the criminal courts. *Id.* at 303. The Regional Labor Court (on appeal from a lower Labor Court) found that "the dismissal process did not stand up to [constitutional] scrutiny." *Id.* at 308. The Court asked how a large firm could possibly determine which 2,000 employees to dismiss on technical grounds without issuing a written record of those technical criteria— "evaluations of the technical capacities of all workers, and a method to indicate the relative assessments." *Id.* The Court did not find definitely that the dismissal was racist but nevertheless concluded that the dismissal process was "discretionary" and likely made with "racial motivation." *Id.* The judge ordered that the plaintiff be reinstated. *Id.*

In a different case, a supervisor made an extremely racist comment about an employee, when he "was overheard calling him a 'worthless Black' who should return to the tronco (slave quarters)." *Id.* at 308. The plaintiff had been reassigned to another department, which paid 10% less than he was making, and protested this reassignment as a violation of company policy. He then was subjected to harassment by a supervisor and was subsequently fired. *Id.* at 309. After an appeal from an unsuccessful claim brought in the Regional Labor Court, the Superior Labor Tribunal reinstated the plaintiff and awarded back pay. *Id.* at 310. The court found that there was documented evidence of a prejudicial motive, and this was the reason for the reassignment and dismissal of the plaintiff. *Id.* "In support of its holding about the discriminatory nature of [the supervisor's] behavior, the court cited four constitutional clauses, including the clause protecting against employment discrimination, and two international conventions (ILO111/58 & 117/62) which Brazil had signed." *Id.*

4.   Since the end of slavery in Brazil, the country has embraced the idea that it is a colourblind nation. "Brazilian colourblindness . . . projects the melding of persons into a unified nation with no salient differences, which generates claims about harmonious private relations." Racusen, *supra* at 777. This notion was formed in part by the idea of "racial democracy." During the 1930s Brazil was going through an important state-building process, and at this time a work by Gilberto Freyre, which articulated the theory of "racial democracy," became increasingly accepted in the country. "Put simply, racial democracy posits that Brazilian society is relatively free of racial discrimination because extensive interracial parentage has created a large, mixed race population incapable of prejudice against each other." Hensler, *supra,* at 282. His theory was so popular that it was found in "state policy," "official pronouncements," and the curriculum of school children. Racusen, *supra*, at 786. His work on "racial democracy" had three "basic tenets":

> "First, he inverted the racist pessimism about 'degenerate Mulatos' into the counter claim that the rise of the Moreno represented 'racial progress' that would 'resolve racial problems.' He claimed that 'racial

mixing' would inherently produce social harmony. Second, he compared this Brazilian model with the US, which generated two other claims. Freyre defined racism as a US phenomenon such as segregation, lynching, and the resultant tension between groups. That notion of racial discrimination enabled the denial of Brazilian racial discrimination. Freyre argued that the absence of North American phenomena, visible tensions and explicit state organized discrimination indicated the lack of a Brazilian problem.

Id. [citations omitted].

5.   The 1951 anti-discrimination law, Lei No. 1.390, was created under the belief of a racial democracy. "Unlike in the U.S. where civil rights laws were enacted in recognition of the need to counteract domestic systems of racial subordination, in Brazil the influence of the racial democracy thesis meant that the purpose articulated for the anti-discrimination laws was to protect Brazilian society from the importation of racism from abroad." Hensler, *supra*, at 287. The push for the law happened after "prominent African–American dancer Katherine Dunham was denied admittance to a Sao Paulo hotel." *Id.* at 288. The advocate of the bill, Senator Afonso Arionos, blamed the racial discrimination on "gringos who are ... insensitive to our old customs of racial fraternity." *Id.* Those social practices were perceived as more characteristic of North America than Brazil:

> The Lei Afonso Arinos established "acts resulting from race or color prejudice" as a criminal misdemeanor, including denial of employment, service, lodging or admittance. Thus, until the late 1980s Brazil's main anti-discrimination law was one "which prohibited social practices of the North American segregationist past," but failed to address the covert forms of discrimination far more common in Brazilian society. Within the rubric of racial democracy, however, these less explicit forms of exclusion were not covered because they did not fit a conception of discrimination based on the U.S. model of Jim Crow laws. This "narrow construction of racial discrimination," has severely limited its usefulness to the persons it purports to protect.

> The logic behind making discrimination merely a misdemeanor offense was that the law's purpose was not to uproot an already entrenched social problem, but to prevent the emergence of one that did not currently exist. As one Brazilian author notes, "the legislator of the penal code considered the practice of racism ... like the illegal carrying of arms, or vandalism, etc. These acts are punished because they can cause future prejudice or danger to the security of society." This focus on deterring the introduction of racist practices, typically of foreign origin, into society, is a persistent preoccupation in Brazilian anti-discrimination law. In a text on employment discrimination law, Francisco Gerson Marques de Lima cites, as his chief example of racial discrimination in Brazil, incidents of prejudice towards mixed race Brazilians by "groups of ''Aryans'' " among the country's large German immigrant population. "This is the result," charges de Lima, "of discrimination against Brazilians in our own land by foreigners!"

Id. at 288–289. The ideology of racial democracy thus helps explain why Brazil seems to have employment discrimination laws that are hard to use.

If racism and discrimination is not acknowledged as a real problem in Brazil, it is hard to work up a claim that it exists in a particular situation.

The racial ideology of Brazil, and other Latin American countries, might also account for "the refusal of many Latin American nations to collect census data according to racial identity, or otherwise collect systematic information on the status of its racial and ethnic populations." Tanya Katerí Hernández, *Multiracial Matrix: The Role Of Race Ideology In The Enforcement Of Antidiscrimination Laws, A United States–Latin America Comparison*, 87 CORNELL L. REV. 1093, 1130 (2002). Hernandez reports that "Only 4 out of 26 countries in Latin America have census data on populations of African descent" and concludes that the lack of census racial data "obstructs the attempt to address widespread patterns of inequality that could, inter alia, more effectively address societal inequality through litigating individual acts of discrimination." *Id.* at 1130–31.

6. There is some evidence that Brazil is shifting away from the "racial democracy" theory. In 2005, Brazilian prosecutors brought civil complaints and charged five of the country's leading banks with violating the Brazilian constitution by discriminating against Afro–Brazilian employees and job applicants in hiring, promotion and compensation:

> In almost every significant aspect, these lawsuits represented a dramatic break with the traditional treatment of racial discrimination claims in Brazilian courts. Up until the mid–1990s public prosecutors considered protection of minority rights at the bottom of their list of law enforcement priorities. Brazil's statutory anti-discrimination law was comprised of a single provision of the penal code prohibiting acts "motivated by racial prejudice." Brazilian courts held that liability for racial discrimination could only be established through direct evidence of a defendant's prejudicial motive. Instances of Afro–Brazilian workers successfully challenging racial discrimination through the court system were so rare that a 1997 documentary film chronicling a case where a plaintiff actually prevailed was entitled 'The Exception and the Rule.'

> * * * The recent employment discrimination suits brought against the banks on behalf of Afro–Brazilian workers also reflect a broader shift in the country's treatment of racial inequality. For most of the last century the Brazilian state claimed that it was a "racial democracy' whose colorblind society stood in contrast to the segregationist practices of other nations, a claim that was accepted by numerous scholars, Brazilian and foreign. By the century's end, however, both scholars and state officials increasingly recognized that despite longstanding traditions of formal legal equality and widespread interracial mixing, Brazilian racial relations were characterized by deep and persistent inequalities between the white and non-white populations. In place of the claim that Brazil was a racial democracy came a realization that in areas such as formal employment and higher education, the exclusion of persons of African descent—a group that is generally understood to include more than 40 percent of the country's population—rivaled that of countries such as South Africa and the

United States, that have only recently emerged from decades of legally-enforced apartheid.

Hensler, *supra*, at 267–269.

F. INDIA

India's Constitution is quite progressive and it is often heralded as a landmark document. There are a number of places in the document that focus on equality and discrimination; the most important for employment discrimination is Article 15, which prohibits discrimination on the grounds of religion, race, caste, sex, or place of birth. Article 15 reads:

(1) The State shall not discriminate against any citizen on grounds only of religion, race, caste, sex, place of birth or any of them.

(2) No citizen shall, on grounds only of religion, race, caste, sex, place of birth or any of them, be subject to any disability, liability, restriction or condition with regard to—

(a) access to shops, public restaurants, hotels and places of public entertainment; or

(b) the use of wells, tanks, bathing ghats, roads and places of public resort maintained wholly or partly out of State funds or dedicated to the use of the general public.

(3) Nothing in this article shall prevent the State from making any special provision for women and children.

The Constitution also mentions equality of opportunity for employment, but is limited to "public employment." Article 16 provides that:

(1) There shall be equality of opportunity for all citizens in matters relating to employment or appointment to any office under the State.

(2) No citizen shall, on grounds only of religion, race, caste, sex, descent, place of birth, residence or any of them, be ineligible for, or discriminated against in respect of, any employment or office under the State.

Although India's Constitution offers protection against discrimination, the main anti-discrimination laws in India are the Persons with Disabilities Act, 1995, the Scheduled Caste and Scheduled Tribe (Prevention of Atrocities) Act, 1989, the Equal Remuneration Act, 1976, and the Protection of Civil Rights Act, 1955. The Protection of Civil Rights Act, 1955 only covers one class of individuals, the "untouchables." The Act states that a person cannot bar an "untouchable" from "the practice of any profession or the carrying on of any occupation, trade or business [or employment in any job]." 4(iii).

The Equal Remuneration Act of 1976 focuses solely on gender discrimination. The Equal Remuneration Act, No. 25 of 1976, India Code (1976). This Act defines employer with no distinction between a government and private employer. This Act "advocates nondiscrimination on the basis of gender in matters related to fixing wages and determining transfers, training and promotion." Anuradha Saibaba Rajesh, *Women in India:*

*Abysmal Protection, Peripheral Rights and Subservient Citizenship,*16 NEW ENG. J. INT'L & COMP. L. 111, 126 (2008).

The Disabilities Act protects persons with disabilities in India, but the scope of the enforceable prohibitions of the Act is fairly limited. First, the Act defines employer to mean only organizations run by the government, or sectors of the government, and as such it does not apply to any private employers. Ch. I, 2(j). Second, there is no mention of discrimination during the hiring process under the Act; the discrimination that is prohibited refers only to situations where the person with a disability is already an employee of the government. Ch. I, 2(j). Thus, if a government employee is disabled they can be protected by the act if only when they meet the definition of "disability" and are discriminated against while on the job. The term "disability" includes: blindness; low vision; leprosy-cured; hearing impairment; locomotor disability; mental retardation; mental illness. Ch. I, 2(i). Act Ch. I–Definitions. The relevant part of the statute is:

> (1) No establishment shall dispense with, or reduce in rank, an employee who acquires a disability during his service:
>
>> Provided that, if an employee, after acquiring disability is not suitable for the post he was holding, could be shifted to some other post with the same pay scale and service benefits:
>>
>> Provided further that it is not possible to adjust the employee against and post, he may be kept on a supernumerary post until a suitable post is available or he attains the age of superannuation, whichever is earlier.
>
> (2) No promotion shall be denied to a person merely on the ground of his disability:
>
>> Provided that the appropriate Government may, having regard to the type of work carried on in any establishment, by notification and subject to such conditions, if any, as may be specified in such notification, exempt any establishment from the provisions of this section.

Ch.VIII ¶ 46.

Finally, the Act requires government authorities to provide incentives to public and private employers to "ensure that at least five percent of their work force is composed of persons with disabilities." Id.

————

NOTES

1. The Supreme Court of India has interpreted certain Constitutional equality prohibitions somewhat narrowly, particularly in the case of sex discrimination. The Supreme Court of India has held that: "what Articles 15(1) and 16(2) prohibit is that discrimination should not be made only and only on the ground of sex. These Articles of the Constitution do not prohibit the State from making discrimination on the ground of sex coupled with other considerations." *AIR India v. Meerza and Ors*, (1981) 1 S.C.C. 335 (India) ¶ 70. The Court reviewed Air India regulations forcing airhos-

tesses, who were women, to retire because of marriage or first pregnancy. The Court upheld the basic scheme of classification by sex, holding that air hostesses were a category of workers distinct from other airline employees. Moreover, the Court concluded that the marital restriction was neither unreasonable nor arbitrary because requiring air hostesses to delay marriage until they were "fully mature" would improve their health and their chances of a successful marriage, promote India's family planning program, and prevent the airlines from having to incur the cost of recruiting new airhostesses if the airhostesses who married became pregnant and quit their jobs. On the other hand, the Court struck down as unconstitutionally unreasonable and arbitrary the requirement that airhostesses terminate employment at the time of pregnancy. The Court reasoned that the difference between male and female with regard to pregnancy does not license a regulation that "amounts to compelling the poor air hostess not to have any children and thus interfere with and divert the ordinary course of human nature." *See* ¶¶ 70–84.

2. There is no specific legislation on sexual harassment in India but the Supreme Court has construed the Constitution to prohibit it under various constitutional provisions and international conventions. *Vishakha & Others v. State of Rajasthan*, A.I.R. 1997 S.C. 3011. As a result of the Supreme Court's opinion in *Vishaka*, there has been additional momentum to pass a statutory prohibition of sexual harassment in the workplace:

> The Supreme Court defines sexual harassment to include any unwelcome physical contact or advances, demands or requests for sexual favours, sexually coloured remarks, displaying of pornography and other unwelcome physical, verbal or nonverbal conduct of a sexual nature. The Supreme Court requires all workplaces, educational institutions and organised service sectors, private or public, with more than 50 employees to introduce sexual harassment prevention policy and set up a complaints committee to investigate into sexual harassment complaints. The complaints committee is required to submit an inquiry report which is treated as the last word on the incident. Prior to *Vishakha*, the only remedy for sexual harassment was to initiate a criminal proceeding. The then law did not specifically provide for awarding monetary compensation. In *Vishakha*, the Supreme Court did not deal with the question of compensation to the victim. However in subsequent cases the courts have granted tort damages to sexual harassment victims.

> The National Commission for Women (NCW) can intervene where the *Vishakha* guidelines are not followed by an employer. The NCW drafted the Sexual Harassment of Women at their Workplace (Prevention) Bill which is still pending before Parliament. The Bill does not apply to agriculture, construction and home based unorganised work sectors, among others and excludes men and same sex harassment from its purview. However it relaxes the burden of proof on a woman complaining of sexual harassment, and there is a proposal to amend the Bill to specifically cover students, research scholars and those working in unorganised sector.

There is an all-out attempt to protect women. The Sexual Harassment Bill is but one example. There are national laws on eve teasing (street sexual harassment) and a Bill to reserve 33% of seats in the national Parliament and provisional assemblies to women in the pipeline. In big cities like Delhi and Mumbai, seats are reserved for women in local trains, ladies special buses are running, and there are women-only taxis driven by women drivers. . .

D.K. Srivastava, *Progress of Sexual Harassment Law in India, China and Hong Kong: Prognosis for Further Reform*, 51 HARVARD INTERNATIONAL LAW JOURNAL ONLINE 172, 175–76 (August 11, 2010).

3.   The most rigorously enforced system of social hierarchy in India is the caste system. Although "untouchability" was officially abolished under Article 17 of the Constitution of India, the practice remains "determinative of the social and economic outcomes of those at the bottom of the caste hierarchy." Smita Narula, *Equal by Law, Unequal by Caste: The "Untouchable" Condition in Critical Race Perspective* 26, WIS. INT'L L.J. 255, 280–81 (2010). The "caste divisions . . . dominate in housing, marriage, employment, and general social interaction—divisions that are reinforced through the practice and threat of social ostracism, economic boycotts, and physical violence." *Id.* at 273. The specific labor conditions these outcasts face can be downright offensive; they are subject to "exploitative labor arrangements such as bonded labor, migratory labor, and forced prostitution." *Id.* at 274. Even if they are not forced to work these jobs the outcasts are discriminated against in hiring and in the payment of wages by private employers. *Id.* at 274. This system is a great hurdle in combating employment discrimination and in crafting effective laws in the country to combat it. The laws, specifically the Protection of Civil Rights Act, challenge a system that has been ingrained in the country over many years. When these two systems do conflict, it seems that the caste system often takes precedence. Narula writes:

> The Rule of Law in India lives in the shadow of the Rule of Caste. If law is understood as a set of rules backed by sanction, then both the legal system and the caste system can lay claim to the mantle of law with one significant difference: the caste system operates more efficiently, more swiftly, and more punitively than any rights-protecting law on the books.

Id. at 295.

4.   According to the above author, even among the untouchables, or "Dalits," it is the women who endure the brunt of discrimination in Indian society. She describes the "multiple forms of discrimination" that Dalit women suffer:

> Dalit women have unequal access to services, employment opportunities, and justice mechanisms as compared to Dalit men. In relation to employment opportunities, Dalit women are allotted some of the most menial and arduous tasks and experience greater discrimination in the payment of wages than Dalit men. In relation to services, Dalit women have less access to education and health facilities, ensuring that their literacy, nutrition, and health standards fall far below that of Dalit

men and non-Dalit men and women. The number of Dalit women in decision-making positions is also very low, and in some central services Dalit women are not represented at all. * * *

Dalit women make up the majority of manual scavengers—a caste-based occupation wherein Dalits remove excrement from public and private dry pit latrines and carry it to dumping grounds and disposal sites. Indeed, the "occupation" of manual scavenging is the only economic opportunity available to many Dalit women hailing from scavenger sub-castes, with the result that more Dalit women and girls work as manual scavengers than Dalit men. Manual scavengers are situated at the very bottom of the graded inequality structure of the caste system and as a result face discrimination from other non-scavenger caste Dalits who treat them as "untouchables," creating an unquestioned " "untouchability' within the "untouchables'." The entrenched discrimination against manual scavengers makes it difficult to find alternative employment and even more difficult to convince scavengers that they are able to take on, or are "worthy of performing," different occupations.

Narula, *Id.*, at 278–280.

5. There are laws that prevent compulsory labor on people who are "untouchable." The Civil Rights Act of 1995, discussed above and in Chapter II, provides that: "[w]hoever compels any person, on the ground of "untouchability", to do any scavenging or sweeping or to remove any carcass or to flay any animal or to remove the umbilical cord or to do any other job of a similar nature, shall be deemed to have enforced a disability arising out of "untouchability." Chapter 7A. The Scheduled Castes and the Scheduled Tribes (Prevention of Atrocities) Act, 1989 is focused on the commitment of "atrocities against the members of the Scheduled Castes and the Scheduled Tribes." It makes a punishable crime, among other things, to "compel[] or entice[] a member of a Scheduled Caste or a Scheduled Tribe to do 'begar' or other similar forms of forced or bonded labour other than any compulsory service for public purposes imposed by Government." Chapter 2(3)(vi). Although the Atrocities Act is a powerful weapon to enforce the rights of Dalits through the criminal justice system, advocates argue that it has suffered from a lack of enforcement:

> Ironically, the primary obstacles to implementation are intended to be the primary enforcers of the Act—the lowest rungs of the police and bureaucracy that form the primary mode of interaction between state and society in the rural areas. Policemen have displayed a consistent unwillingness to register offenses under the act. This reluctance stems partially from ignorance. According to a 1999 study, nearly a quarter of those government officials charged with enforcing the Act are unaware of its existence.

> In most cases, unwillingness to file a First Information Report (FIR) under the Act comes from caste-bias. Upper caste policemen are reluctant to file cases against fellow caste-members because of the severity of the penalties imposed by the Act; most offenses are non-bailable and carry minimum punishments of five years imprisonment

> . . .

A bigger obstacle faces victims who actually manage to lodge a complaint. Failure to follow through with cases is alarmingly apparent at the lowest echelons of the judicial system. The statistics speak for themselves: out of 147,000 POA cases pending in the courts in 1998, only 31,011 were brought to trial. Such delay is endemic to the Indian judicial system. Although the POA mandated the creation of Special Courts precisely to circumvent this problem, only two states have created separate Special Courts in accordance with the law. In other states, existing sessions courts have been designated Special Courts, while still being asked to process their usual caseloads. Since many different Acts require the creation of Special Courts, such sessions courts are often overloaded with a number of different kinds of "priority" cases, virtually guaranteeing that none of these cases receive the attention they are mandated to receive.

Even if cases make it to trial, the POA also suffers from abysmal rates of conviction. Out of the 31,011 cases tried under the POA in 1998, only a paltry 1,677 instances or 5.4% resulted in a conviction and 29,334 ended in acquittal. Compare this to the conviction rate in cases tried under the Indian Penal Code: in 1999, 39.4% of cases ended in a conviction and in 2000, 41.8%. Judicial delay is just one cause of this low conviction rate; the lapse between the case being registered and the trial means that witnesses who are often poor and face intimidation in the interim, turn hostile and the case becomes too weak for a conviction. The long wait also results in many plaintiffs losing interest. Judicial bias against Dalits is rampant and unchecked, and court decisions frequently bear the mark of such bias.

South Asian Human Rights Documentation Centre, *Prevention of Atrocities Act: Unused Ammunition*, http://www.hrdc.net/sahrdc/hrfeatures/HRF83.htm (August 2003); *See also Justice Undelivered*, Public Hearing on the Lack of Enforcement of The Scheduled Castes and The Scheduled Tribes (Prevention of Atrocities) Act, 1989 in Gujarat (31 March 2008), http://navsarjan.org/Documents/Public% 20Hearing% 20Report.pdf.

CHAPTER IV

EQUALITY & AFFIRMATIVE ACTION

INTRODUCTION

When a society in which inequality and discrimination are widespread, decides to reform itself, how should it proceed? Is it enough to say "from this point forward, all people will be treated equally?" Recall President Lyndon Johnson's speech from Chapter 1, in which he compared life to a footrace, and asserted that we could not take someone who had suffered systemic disadvantage and expect him or her to have an equal chance to win the race simply by now placing all runners at the same starting line.

This was the question faced by the United States in the Reconstruction period, and again during the civil rights era (and in response to the feminist movement). It was the question faced by South Africa when the apartheid system was democratically overthrown. It was the question faced by India as it responded to "Brahmanism," the caste system and colonialism. It was the question faced by Brazil as it committed to creating a "racial democracy." It continues to be a critical question in each of these countries, and is now being discussed throughout much of Europe, largely with regard to gender, and at times with regard to race/ethnicity.

In the United States one principal remedy used to address inequality, developed during the civil rights era, is affirmative action. Affirmative action is a contested term, and a highly contested policy. Some view it as a policy of inclusion and representation, or as a remedy; others see it as simply discrimination (or "reverse discrimination").

The term affirmative action is sometimes used to describe quotas (called "reservations" in India) or preferences, but it is also used to describe race-conscious (or ethnicity or gender-conscious) outreach programs, self-inspection programs, mentoring programs, or sensitivity training programs. As these race-conscious policies become increasingly benign, the line between affirmative action policies intended to remedy discrimination and policies intended to reduce discrimination is unsettled.

Affirmative action is used in several areas of American life, including admissions to colleges and graduate/professional schools, selection of employees, and selection of government or business contractors and subcontractors. In this chapter, we will focus on the use of race-conscious affirmative action (sometimes called "positive action" or "positive discrimination" in Europe and "compensatory action" In Brazil) in selecting students in higher education. We will focus on affirmative action policies in the United States, South Africa and India, with a more limited discussion of France and Brazil. In the concluding notes, we will briefly discuss comparative affirmative action in other contexts, principally employment and democratic participation, and broaden the discussion to include gender-based affirmative action.

PROBLEM

Paul is an upper middle class white college graduate who has been denied admission to a public law school (or PhD program in law). He learns that an applicant who is of Black African ancestry (for the U.S., France, Brazil, or South Africa) (or is of the caste formerly known as "untouchable" for India) was admitted to the school with lower grades and test scores than his, pursuant to the school's special admissions policies to (promote racial diversity—U.S.) (promote geographic diversity—France) (remedy societal discrimination—South Africa, Brazil, India).

If Paul sues, what outcome should we expect in the U.S., France, South Africa, Brazil, or India?

A. THE UNITED STATES

Regents of the University of California v. Bakke

438 U.S. 265 (1978)

■ JUSTICE POWELL announced the judgment of the Court. [Each of the other eight Justices concurred in part and dissented in part, as described below.] * * *

This case presents a challenge to the special admissions program of the petitioner, the Medical School of the University of California at Davis, which is designed to assure the admission of a specified number of students from certain minority groups. The Superior Court of California sustained respondent's challenge, holding that petitioner's program violated the California Constitution, Title VI of the Civil Rights Act of 1964, 42 U.S.C. § 2000d *et seq.*, and the Equal Protection Clause of the Fourteenth Amendment. The court enjoined petitioner from considering respondent's race or the race of any other applicant in making admissions decisions. * * *

For the reasons stated in the following opinion, I believe that so much of the judgment of the California court as holds petitioner's special admissions program unlawful and directs that respondent be admitted to the Medical School must be affirmed. For the reasons expressed in a separate opinion, my Brothers the Chief Justice, Mr. Justice Stewart, Mr. Justice Rehnquist and Mr. Justice Stevens concur in this judgment.

I also conclude for the reasons stated in the following opinion that the portion of the court's judgment enjoining petitioner from according any consideration to race in its admissions process must be reversed. For reasons expressed in separate opinions, my Brothers Mr. Justice Brennan, Mr. Justice White, Mr. Justice Marshall, and Mr. Justice Blackmun concur in this judgment.

The Medical School of the University of California at Davis opened in 1968 with an entering class of 50 students. In 1971, the size of the entering class was increased to 100 students, a level at which it remains. No admissions program for disadvantaged or minority students existed when the school opened, and the first class contained three Asians but no blacks, no Mexican–Americans, and no American Indians. Over the next two years, the faculty devised a special admissions program to increase the representation of "disadvantaged" students in each Medical School class. The special program consisted of a separate admissions system operating in coordination with the regular admissions process. * * *

The special admissions program operated with a separate committee, a majority of whom were members of minority groups.... The special committee continued to recommend special applicants until a number prescribed by faculty vote were admitted. While the overall class size was still 50, the prescribed number was 8; in 1973 and 1974, when the class size had doubled to 100, the prescribed number of special admissions also doubled, to 16.

From the year of the increase in class size—1971—through 1974, the special program resulted in the admission of 21 black students, 30 Mexican–Americans, and 12 Asians, for a total of 63 minority students. Over the same period, the regular admissions program produced 1 black, 6 Mexican–Americans, and 37 Asians, for a total of 44 minority students. Although disadvantaged whites applied to the special program in large numbers, none received an offer of admission through that process....

Allan Bakke is a white male who applied to the Davis Medical School in both 1973 and 1974. In both years Bakke's application was considered under the general admissions program ... In both years, applicants were admitted under the special program with grade point averages, MCAT scores, and benchmark scores significantly lower than Bakke's.

After the second rejection, Bakke filed the instant suit in the Superior Court of California.... The trial court found that the special program operated as a racial quota, because minority applicants in the special program were rated only against one another and 16 places in the class of 100 were reserved for them. * * *

* * * The Supreme Court of California transferred the case directly from the trial court, "because of the importance of the issues involved." The California court accepted the findings of the trial court with respect to the University's program. Because the special admissions program involved a racial classification, the Supreme Court held itself bound to apply strict scrutiny.... Although the court agreed that the goals of integrating the medical profession and increasing the number of physicians willing to serve members of minority groups were compelling state interests, it concluded that the special admissions program was not the least intrusive means of achieving those goals. Without passing on the state constitutional or the federal statutory grounds cited in the trial court's judgment, the California court held that the Equal Protection Clause of the Fourteenth Amendment required that "no applicant may be rejected because of his race, in favor of another who is less qualified, as measured by standards applied without regard to race." * * *

III

A

Petitioner does not deny that decisions based on race or ethnic origin by faculties and administrations of state universities are reviewable under the Fourteenth Amendment. For his part, respondent does not argue that all racial or ethnic classifications are per se invalid. The parties do disagree as to the level of judicial scrutiny to be applied to the special admissions program. * * *

* * * The special admissions program is undeniably a classification based on race and ethnic background. To the extent that there existed a pool of at least minimally qualified minority applicants to fill the 16 special admissions seats, white applicants could compete only for 84 seats in the entering class, rather than the 100 open to minority applicants. Whether this limitation is described as a quota or a goal, it is a line drawn on the basis of race and ethnic status.

The guarantees of the Fourteenth Amendment extend to all persons. Its language is explicit: "No State shall ... deny to any person within its jurisdiction the equal protection of the laws." It is settled beyond question that the "rights created by the first section of the Fourteenth Amendment are, by its terms, guaranteed to the individual. The rights established are personal rights." The guarantee of equal protection cannot mean one thing when applied to one individual and something else when applied to a person of another color. If both are not accorded the same protection, then it is not equal. * * *

B

* * * Although many of the Framers of the Fourteenth Amendment conceived of its primary function as bridging the vast distance between members of the Negro race and the white "majority," the Amendment itself was framed in universal terms, without reference to color, ethnic origin, or condition of prior servitude.

* * * Petitioner urges us to adopt for the first time a more restrictive view of the Equal Protection Clause and hold that discrimination against members of the white "majority" cannot be suspect if its purpose can be characterized as "benign." The clock of our liberties, however, cannot be turned back to 1868. It is far too late to argue that the guarantee of equal protection to all persons permits the recognition of special wards entitled to a degree of protection greater than that accorded others. * * *

IV

We have held that in "order to justify the use of a suspect classification, a State must show that its purpose or interest is both constitutionally permissible and substantial, and that its use of the classification is 'necessary ... to the accomplishment' of its purpose or the safeguarding of its interest." The special admissions program purports to serve the purposes of: (i) "reducing the historic deficit of traditionally disfavored minorities in medical schools and in the medical profession,"; (ii) countering the effects of societal discrimination; (iii) increasing the number of physicians who will practice in communities currently underserved; and (iv) obtaining the educational benefits that flow from an ethnically diverse student body. It is necessary to decide which, if any, of these purposes is substantial enough to support the use of a suspect classification.

Racial classifications in admissions conceivably could serve a fifth purpose, one which petitioner does not articulate: fair appraisal of each individual's academic promise in the light of some cultural bias in grading or testing procedures. To the extent that race and ethnic background were considered only to the extent of curing established inaccuracies in predicting academic performance, it might be argued that there is no "preference" at all. Nothing in this record, however, suggests either that any of the quantitative factors considered by the Medical School were culturally biased or that petitioner's special admissions program was formulated to correct for any such biases. Furthermore, if race or ethnic background were used solely to arrive at an unbiased prediction of academic success, the reservation of fixed numbers of seats would be inexplicable.

A

If petitioner's purpose is to assure within its student body some specified percentage of a particular group merely because of its race or ethnic origin, such a preferential purpose must be rejected not as insubstantial but as facially invalid. Preferring members of any one group for no reason other than race or ethnic origin is discrimination for its own sake. This the Constitution forbids.

B

* * *

We have never approved a classification that aids persons perceived as members of relatively victimized groups at the expense of other innocent individuals in the absence of judicial, legislative, or administrative findings of constitutional or statutory violations. After such findings have been made, the governmental interest in preferring members of the injured groups at the expense of others is substantial, since the legal rights of the victims must be vindicated. In such a case, the extent of the injury and the consequent remedy will have been judicially, legislatively, or administratively defined. Also, the remedial action usually remains subject to continuing oversight to assure that it will work the least harm possible to other innocent persons competing for the benefit. Without such findings of constitutional or statutory violations, it cannot be said that the government has any greater interest in helping one individual than in refraining from harming another. Thus, the government has no compelling justification for inflicting such harm.

Petitioner does not purport to have made, and is in no position to make, such findings. Its broad mission is education, not the formulation of any legislative policy or the adjudication of particular claims of illegality. . . .

Hence, the purpose of helping certain groups whom the faculty of the Davis Medical School perceived as victims of "societal discrimination" does not justify a classification that imposes disadvantages upon persons like respondent, who bear no responsibility for whatever harm the beneficiaries of the special admissions program are thought to have suffered. To hold otherwise would be to convert a remedy heretofore reserved for violations of legal rights into a privilege that all institutions throughout the Nation could grant at their pleasure to whatever groups are perceived as victims of societal discrimination. That is a step we have never approved.

C

Petitioner identifies, as another purpose of its program, improving the delivery of health-care services to communities currently underserved. It may be assumed that in some situations a State's interest in facilitating the health care of its citizens is sufficiently compelling to support the use of a suspect classification. But there is virtually no evidence in the record indicating that petitioner's special admissions program is either needed or geared to promote that goal. . . .

Petitioner simply has not carried its burden of demonstrating that it must prefer members of particular ethnic groups over all other individuals in order to promote better health-care delivery to deprived citizens. Indeed, petitioner has not shown that its preferential classification is likely to have any significant effect on the problem.

D

The fourth goal asserted by petitioner is the attainment of a diverse student body. This clearly is a constitutionally permissible goal for an institution of higher education. Academic freedom, though not a specifically enumerated constitutional right, long has been viewed as a special concern of the First Amendment. The freedom of a university to make its own judgments as to education includes the selection of its student body. Mr. Justice Frankfurter summarized the "four essential freedoms" that constitute academic freedom:

> It is the business of a university to provide that atmosphere which is most conducive to speculation, experiment and creation. It is an atmosphere in which there prevail "the four essential freedoms" of a university—to determine for itself on academic grounds who may teach, what may be taught, how it shall be taught, and who may be admitted to study. *Sweezy v. New Hampshire*, 354 U.S. 234, 263 (1957) (concurring in result).

* * *

The atmosphere of "speculation, experiment and creation"—so essential to the quality of higher education—is widely believed to be promoted by a diverse student body. As the Court noted in *Keyishian*, it is not too much to say that the "nation's future depends upon leaders trained through wide exposure" to the ideas and mores of students as diverse as this Nation of many peoples.

Thus, in arguing that its universities must be accorded the right to select those students who will contribute the most to the "robust exchange of ideas," petitioner invokes a countervailing constitutional interest, that of the First Amendment. In this light, petitioner must be viewed as seeking to achieve a goal that is of paramount importance in the fulfillment of its mission.

It may be argued that there is greater force to these views at the undergraduate level than in a medical school where the training is centered primarily on professional competency. But even at the graduate level, our tradition and experience lend support to the view that the contribution of diversity is substantial. In *Sweatt v. Painter*, 339 U.S., at 634 the Court made a similar point with specific reference to legal education:

> The law school, the proving ground for legal learning and practice, cannot be effective in isolation from the individuals and institutions with which the law interacts. Few students and no one who has practiced law would choose to study in an academic vacuum, removed from the interplay of ideas and the exchange of views with which the law is concerned.

Physicians serve a heterogeneous population. An otherwise qualified medical student with a particular background—whether it be ethnic, geographic, culturally advantaged or disadvantaged—may bring to a professional school of medicine experiences, outlooks, and ideas that enrich the training of its student body and better equip its graduates to render with understanding their vital service to humanity.

Ethnic diversity, however, is only one element in a range of factors a university properly may consider in attaining the goal of a heterogeneous student body. Although a university must have wide discretion in making the sensitive judgments as to who should be admitted, constitutional limitations protecting individual rights may not be disregarded. Respondent urges—and the courts below have held—that petitioner's dual admissions program is a racial classification that impermissibly infringes his rights under the Fourteenth Amendment. As the interest of diversity is compelling in the context of a university's admissions program, the question remains whether the program's racial classification is necessary to promote this interest.

V

A

It may be assumed that the reservation of a specified number of seats in each class for individuals from the preferred ethnic groups would contribute to the attainment of considerable ethnic diversity in the student body. But petitioner's argument that this is the only effective means of serving the interest of diversity is seriously flawed. In a most fundamental sense the argument misconceives the nature of the state interest that would justify consideration of race or ethnic background. It is not an interest in simple ethnic diversity, in which a specified percentage of the student body is in effect guaranteed to be members of selected ethnic groups, with the remaining percentage an undifferentiated aggregation of students. The diversity that furthers a compelling state interest encompasses a far broader array of qualifications and characteristics of which racial or ethnic origin is but a single though important element. Petitioner's special admissions program, focused solely on ethnic diversity, would hinder rather than further attainment of genuine diversity.

Nor would the state interest in genuine diversity be served by expanding petitioner's two-track system into a multitrack program with a prescribed number of seats set aside for each identifiable category of applicants. Indeed, it is inconceivable that a university would thus pursue the logic of petitioner's two-track program to the illogical end of insulating each category of applicants with certain desired qualifications from competition with all other applicants.

The experience of other university admissions programs, which take race into account in achieving the educational diversity valued by the First Amendment, demonstrates that the assignment of a fixed number of places to a minority group is not a necessary means toward that end. An illuminating example is found in the Harvard College program:

> In recent years Harvard College has expanded the concept of diversity to include students from disadvantaged economic, racial and ethnic groups. Harvard College now recruits not only Californians or Louisianans but also blacks and Chicanos and other minority students . . .

> In practice, this new definition of diversity has meant that race has been a factor in some admission decisions. When the Committee on Admissions reviews the large middle group of applicants who are 'admissible' and deemed capable of doing good work in their courses, the race of an applicant may tip the balance in his favor just as geographic origin or a life spent on a farm may tip the balance in other candidates' cases. A farm boy from Idaho can bring something to Harvard College that a Bostonian cannot offer. Similarly, a black student can usually bring something that a white person cannot offer. [See Appendix hereto.] . . .

> In Harvard College admissions the Committee has not set target-quotas for the number of blacks, or of musicians, football players, physicists or Californians to be admitted in a given year.... But that awareness [of the necessity of including more than a token number of black students] does not mean that the Committee sets a minimum number of blacks or of people from west of the Mississippi who are to be admitted. It means only that in choosing among thousands of applicants who are not only 'admissible' academically but have other strong qualities, the Committee, with a number of criteria in mind, pays some attention to distribution among many types and categories of students. *App. to Brief for Columbia University, Harvard University, Stanford University, and the University of Pennsylvania, as Amici Curiae* 2–3.

In such an admissions program, race or ethnic background may be deemed a "plus" in a particular applicant's file, yet it does not insulate the individual from comparison with all other candidates for the available seats. The file of a particular black applicant may be examined for his potential contribution to diversity without the factor of race being decisive when compared, for example, with that of an applicant identified as an Italian–American if the latter is thought to exhibit qualities more likely to promote beneficial educational pluralism. Such qualities could include exceptional personal talents, unique work or service experience, leadership potential, maturity, demonstrated compassion, a history of overcoming disadvantage, ability to communicate with the poor, or other qualifications deemed important. In short, an admissions program operated in this way is flexible enough to consider all pertinent elements of diversity in light of the particular qualifications of each applicant, and to place them on the same footing for consideration, although not necessarily according them the same weight. Indeed, the weight attributed to a particular quality may vary from year to year depending upon the "mix" both of the student body and the applicants for the incoming class.

This kind of program treats each applicant as an individual in the admissions process. The applicant who loses out on the last available seat to another candidate receiving a "plus" on the basis of ethnic background will not have been foreclosed from all consideration for that seat simply because he was not the right color or had the wrong surname. It would mean only that his combined qualifications, which may have included similar nonobjective factors, did not outweigh those of the other applicant. His qualifications would have been weighed fairly and competitively, and he would have no basis to complain of unequal treatment under the Fourteenth Amendment.

It has been suggested that an admissions program which considers race only as one factor is simply a subtle and more sophisticated—but no less effective—means of according racial preference than the Davis program. A facial intent to discriminate, however, is evident in petitioner's preference program and not denied in this case. No such facial infirmity exists in an admissions program where race or ethnic background is simply one element—to be weighed fairly against other elements—in the selection process. * * *

B

In summary, it is evident that the Davis special admissions program involves the use of an explicit racial classification never before countenanced by this Court. It tells applicants who are not Negro, Asian, or Chicano that they are totally excluded from a specific percentage of the seats in an entering class. No matter how strong their qualifications, quantitative and extracurricular, including their own potential for contribution to educational diversity, they are never afforded the chance to compete with applicants from the preferred groups for the special admissions seats. At the same time, the preferred applicants have the opportunity to compete for every seat in the class.

The fatal flaw in petitioner's preferential program is its disregard of individual rights as guaranteed by the Fourteenth Amendment. Such rights are not absolute. But when a State's distribution of benefits or imposition of burdens hinges on ancestry or the color of a person's skin, that individual is entitled to a demonstration that the challenged classification is necessary to promote a substantial state interest. Petitioner has failed to carry this burden. For this reason, that portion of the California court's judgment holding petitioner's special admissions program invalid under the Fourteenth Amendment must be affirmed. * * *

■ Opinion of MR. JUSTICE BRENNAN, MR. JUSTICE WHITE, MR. JUSTICE MARSHALL, and MR. JUSTICE BLACKMUN, concurring in the judgment in part and dissenting in part.

The Court today, in reversing in part the judgment of the Supreme Court of California, affirms the constitutional power of Federal and State Governments to act affirmatively to achieve equal opportunity for all. The difficulty of the issue presented—whether government may use race-conscious programs to redress the continuing effects of past discrimination—and the mature consideration which each of our Brethren has brought to it have resulted in many opinions, no single one speaking for the Court. But this should not and must not mask the central meaning of today's opinions: Government may take race into account when it acts not to demean or insult any racial group, but to remedy disadvantages cast on minorities by past racial prejudice, at least when appropriate findings have been made by judicial, legislative, or administrative bodies with competence to act in this area.

The Chief Justice and our Brothers Stewart, Rehnquist, and Stevens, have concluded that Title VI of the Civil Rights Act of 1964, prohibits programs such as that at the Davis Medical School. On this statutory theory alone, they would hold that respondent Allan Bakke's rights have been violated and that he must, therefore, be admitted to the Medical School. Our Brother Powell, reaching the Constitution, concludes that, although race may be taken into account in university admissions, the particular special admissions program used by petitioner, which resulted in the exclusion of respondent Bakke, was not shown to be necessary to achieve petitioner's stated goals. Accordingly, these Members of the Court form a majority of five affirming the judgment of the Supreme Court of California insofar as it holds that respondent Bakke "is entitled to an order that he be admitted to the University."

* * * Since we conclude that the affirmative admissions program at the Davis Medical School is constitutional, we would reverse the judgment below in all respects. Mr. Justice Powell agrees that some uses of race in university admissions are permissible and, therefore, he joins with us to make five votes reversing the judgment below insofar as it prohibits the University from establishing race-conscious programs in the future.

I

Our Nation was founded on the principle that "all Men are created equal." Yet candor requires acknowledgment that the Framers of our Constitution, to forge the 13 Colonies into one Nation, openly compromised this principle of equality with its antithesis: slavery. The consequences of this compromise are well known and have aptly been called our "American Dilemma." Still, it is well to recount how recent the time has been, if it has yet come, when the promise of our principles has flowered into the actuality of equal opportunity for all regardless of race or color.

The Fourteenth Amendment, the embodiment in the Constitution of our abiding belief in human equality, has been the law of our land for only slightly more than half its 200 years. And for half of that half, the Equal Protection Clause of the Amendment was largely moribund so that, as late as 1927, Mr. Justice Holmes could sum up the importance of that Clause by remarking that it was the "last resort of constitutional arguments." Worse than desuetude, the Clause was early turned against those whom it was intended to set free, condemning them to a "separate but equal" status before the law, a status always separate but seldom equal. Not until 1954— only 24 years ago—was this odious doctrine interred by our decision in *Brown v. Board of Education* and its progeny, which proclaimed that separate schools and public facilities of all sorts were inherently unequal and forbidden under our Constitution. Even then inequality was not eliminated with "all deliberate speed." In 1968 and again in 1971, for example, we were forced to remind school boards of their obligation to eliminate racial discrimination root and branch. And a glance at our docket and at dockets of lower courts will show that even today officially sanctioned discrimination is not a thing of the past.

Against this background, claims that law must be "color-blind" or that the datum of race is no longer relevant to public policy must be seen as aspiration rather than as description of reality. This is not to denigrate aspiration; for reality rebukes us that race has too often been used by those who would stigmatize and oppress minorities. Yet we cannot—and, as we shall demonstrate, need not under our Constitution or Title VI, which merely extends the constraints of the Fourteenth Amendment to private parties who receive federal funds—let color blindness become myopia which masks the reality that many "created equal" have been treated within our lifetimes as inferior both by the law and by their fellow citizens. * * *

IV

B

Properly construed, therefore, our prior cases unequivocally show that a state government may adopt race-conscious programs if the purpose of such programs is to remove the disparate racial impact its actions might otherwise have and if there is reason to believe that the disparate impact is itself the product of past discrimination, whether its own or that of society at large. There is no question that Davis' program is valid under this test.

Certainly, on the basis of the undisputed factual submissions before this Court, Davis had a sound basis for believing that the problem of underrepresentation of minorities was substantial and chronic and that the problem was attributable to handicaps imposed on minority applicants by past and present racial discrimination. Until at least 1973, the practice of medicine in this country was, in fact, if not in law, largely the prerogative of whites. In 1950, for example, while Negroes constituted 10% of the total population, Negro physicians constituted only 2.2% of the total number of physicians. The overwhelming majority of these, moreover, were educated in two predominantly Negro medical schools, Howard and Meharry. By 1970, the gap between the proportion of Negroes in medicine and their proportion in the population had widened: The number of Negroes employed in medicine remained frozen at 2.2% while the Negro population had increased to 11.1%. The number of Negro admittees to predominantly white medical schools, moreover, had declined in absolute numbers during the years 1955 to 1964.

Moreover, Davis had very good reason to believe that the national pattern of underrepresentation of minorities in medicine would be perpetuated if it retained a single admissions standard. For example, the entering classes in 1968 and 1969, the years in which such a standard was used, included only 1 Chicano and 2 Negroes out of the 50 admittees for each year. Nor is there any relief from this pattern of underrepresentation in the statistics for the regular admissions program in later years.

Davis clearly could conclude that the serious and persistent underrepresentation of minorities in medicine depicted by these statistics is the result of handicaps under which minority applicants labor as a consequence of a background of deliberate, purposeful discrimination against minorities in education and in society generally, as well as in the medical profession. From the inception of our national life, Negroes have been subjected to unique legal disabilities impairing access to equal educational opportunity. Under slavery, penal sanctions were imposed upon anyone attempting to educate Negroes. After enactment of the Fourteenth Amendment the States continued to deny Negroes equal educational opportunity, enforcing a strict policy of segregation that itself stamped Negroes as inferior, that relegated minorities to inferior educational institutions, and that denied them intercourse in the mainstream of professional life necessary to advancement. Segregation was not limited to public facilities, moreover, but was enforced by criminal penalties against private action as well. Thus, as late as 1908, this Court enforced a state criminal conviction against a private college for teaching Negroes together with whites. * * *

Moreover, we need not rest solely on our own conclusion that Davis had sound reason to believe that the effects of past discrimination were handicapping minority applicants to the Medical School, because the Department of Health, Education, and Welfare, the expert agency charged by Congress with promulgating regulations enforcing Title VI of the Civil Rights Act of 1964, has also reached the conclusion that race may be taken into account in situations where a failure to do so would limit participation by minorities in federally funded programs, and regulations promulgated by the Department expressly contemplate that appropriate race-conscious programs may be adopted by universities to remedy unequal access to university programs caused by their own or by past societal discrimination. It cannot be questioned that, in the absence of the special admissions program, access of minority students to the Medical School would be severely limited and, accordingly, race-conscious admissions would be deemed an appropriate response under these federal regulations. * * *

V

Accordingly, we would reverse the judgment of the Supreme Court of California holding the Medical School's special admissions program unconstitutional and directing respondent's admission, as well as that portion of the judgment enjoining the Medical School from according any consideration to race in the admissions process. * * *

■ JUSTICE MARSHALL.

I agree with the judgment of the Court only insofar as it permits a university to consider the race of an applicant in making admissions decisions. I do not agree that petitioner's admissions program violates the Constitution. For it must be remembered that, during most of the past 200 years, the Constitution as interpreted by this Court did not prohibit the most ingenious and pervasive forms of discrimination against the Negro. Now, when a State acts to remedy the effects of that legacy of discrimination, I cannot believe that this same Constitution stands as a barrier. * * *

II

The position of the Negro today in America is the tragic but inevitable consequence of centuries of unequal treatment. Measured by any benchmark of comfort or achievement, meaningful equality remains a distant dream for the Negro.

A Negro child today has a life expectancy which is shorter by more than five years than that of a white child. The Negro child's mother is over three times more likely to die of complications in childbirth, and the infant mortality rate for Negroes is nearly twice that for whites. The median income of the Negro family is only 60% that of the median of a white family, and the percentage of Negroes who live in families with incomes below the poverty line is nearly four times greater than that of whites.

When the Negro child reaches working age, he finds that America offers him significantly less than it offers his white counterpart. For Negro adults, the unemployment rate is twice that of whites, and the unemployment rate for Negro teenagers is nearly three times that of white teenagers. A Negro male who completes four years of college can expect a median annual income of merely $110 more than a white male who has only a high school diploma. Although Negroes represent 11.5% of the population, they are only 1.2% of the lawyers, and judges, 2% of the physicians, 2.3% of the dentists, 1.1% of the engineers and 2.6% of the college and university professors.

The relationship between those figures and the history of unequal treatment afforded to the Negro cannot be denied. At every point from birth to death the impact of the past is reflected in the still disfavored position of the Negro.

In light of the sorry history of discrimination and its devastating impact on the lives of Negroes, bringing the Negro into the mainstream of American life should be a state interest of the highest order. To fail to do so is to ensure that America will forever remain a divided society.

III

I do not believe that the Fourteenth Amendment requires us to accept that fate. Neither its history nor our past cases lend any support to the conclusion that a university may not remedy the cumulative effects of society's discrimination by giving consideration to race in an effort to increase the number and percentage of Negro doctors. * * *

IV

While I applaud the judgment of the Court that a university may consider race in its admissions process, it is more than a little ironic that, after several hundred years of class-based discrimination against Negroes, the Court is unwilling to hold that a class-based remedy for that discrimination is permissible. In declining to so hold, today's judgment ignores the fact that for several hundred years Negroes have been discriminated against, not as individuals, but rather solely because of the color of their skins. It is unnecessary in 20th-century America to have individual Negroes demonstrate that they have been victims of racial discrimination; the racism of our society has been so pervasive that none, regardless of wealth or position, has managed to escape its impact. The experience of Negroes in America has been different in kind, not just in degree, from that of other ethnic groups. It is not merely the history of slavery alone but also that a whole people were marked as inferior by the law. And that mark has endured. The dream of America as the great melting pot has not been realized for the Negro; because of his skin color he never even made it into the pot.

These differences in the experience of the Negro make it difficult for me to accept that Negroes cannot be afforded greater protection under the Fourteenth Amendment where it is necessary to remedy the effects of past discrimination. * * *

■ Justice Blackmun.

  * * *

I suspect that it would be impossible to arrange an affirmative-action program in a racially neutral way and have it successful. To ask that this be so is to demand the impossible. In order to get beyond racism, we must first take account of race. There is no other way. And in order to treat some persons equally, we must treat them differently. We cannot—we dare not—let the Equal Protection Clause perpetuate racial supremacy. * * *

————

From Regents of University of California v. Bakke
Harvard College Admissions Program

■ Appendix to Opinion of Powell, J.

For the past 30 years Harvard College has received each year applications for admission that greatly exceed the number of places in the freshman class. The number of applicants who are deemed to be not "qualified" is comparatively small. The vast majority of applicants demonstrate through test scores, high school records and teachers' recommendations that they have the academic ability to do adequate work at Harvard, and perhaps to do it with distinction. Faced with the dilemma of choosing among a large number of "qualified" candidates, the Committee on Admissions could use the single criterion of scholarly excellence and attempt to determine who among the candidates were likely to perform best academically. But for the past 30 years the Committee on Admissions has never adopted this approach. The belief has been that if scholarly excellence were the sole or even predominant criterion, Harvard College would lose a great deal of its vitality and intellectual excellence and that the quality of the educational experience offered to all students would suffer. Final Report of W. J. Bender, Chairman of the Admission and Scholarship Committee and Dean of Admissions and Financial Aid, pp. 20 *et seq.* (Cambridge, 1960). Consequently, after selecting those students whose intellectual potential will seem extraordinary to the faculty—perhaps 150 or so out of an entering class of over 1,100—the Committee seeks—variety in making its choices. This has seemed important ... in part because it adds a critical ingredient to the effectiveness of the educational experience [in Harvard College].... The effectiveness of our students' educational experience has seemed to the Committee to be affected as importantly by a wide variety of interests, talents, backgrounds and career goals as it is by a fine faculty and our libraries, laboratories and housing arrangements. (Dean of Admissions Fred L. Glimp, *Final Report to the Faculty of Arts and Sciences*, 65 Official Register of Harvard University No. 25, 93, 104–105 (1968).

The belief that diversity adds an essential ingredient to the educational process has long been a tenet of Harvard College admissions. Fifteen or twenty years ago, however, diversity meant students from California, New York, and Massachusetts; city dwellers and farm boys; violinists, painters and football players; biologists, historians and classicists; potential stockbrokers, academics and politicians. The result was that very few ethnic or racial minorities attended Harvard College. In recent years Harvard College has expanded the concept of diversity to include students from disadvantaged economic, racial and ethnic groups. Harvard College now recruits not only Californians or Louisianans but also blacks and Chicanos and other minority students. Contemporary conditions in the United States mean that if Harvard College is to continue to offer a first-rate education to its students, minority representation in the undergraduate body cannot be ignored by the Committee on Admissions.

In practice, this new definition of diversity has meant that race has been a factor in some admission decisions. When the Committee on Admissions reviews the large middle group of applicants who are "admissible" and deemed capable of doing good work in their courses, the race of an applicant may tip the balance in his favor just as geographic origin or a life spent on a farm may tip the balance in other candidates' cases. A farm boy from Idaho can bring something to Harvard College that a Bostonian cannot offer. Similarly, a black student can usually bring something that a white person cannot offer. The quality of the educational experience of all the students in Harvard College depends in part on these differences in the background and outlook that students bring with them.

In Harvard College admissions the Committee has not set target-quotas for the number of blacks, or of musicians, football players, physicists or Californians to be admitted in a given year. At the same time the Committee is aware that if Harvard College is to provide a truly heterogeneous environment that reflects the rich diversity of the United States, it cannot be provided without some attention to numbers. It would not make sense, for example, to have 10 or 20 students out of 1,100 whose homes are west of the Mississippi. Comparably, 10 or 20 black students could not begin to bring to their classmates and to each other the variety of points of view, backgrounds and experiences of blacks in the United States. Their small numbers might also create a sense of isolation among the black students themselves and thus make it more difficult for them to develop and achieve their potential. Consequently, when making its decisions, the

Committee on Admissions is aware that there is some relationship between numbers and achieving the benefits to be derived from a diverse student body, and between numbers and providing a reasonable environment for those students admitted. But that awareness does not mean that the Committee sets a minimum number of blacks or of people from west of the Mississippi who are to be admitted. It means only that in choosing among thousands of applicants who are not only "admissible" academically but have other strong qualities, the Committee, with a number of criteria in mind, pays some attention to distribution among many types and categories of students.

The further refinements sometimes required help to illustrate the kind of significance attached to race. The Admissions Committee, with only a few places left to fill, might find itself forced to choose between A, the child of a successful black physician in an academic community with promise of superior academic performance, and B, a black who grew up in an inner-city ghetto of semi-literate parents whose academic achievement was lower but who had demonstrated energy and leadership as well as an apparently abiding interest in black power. If a good number of black students much like A but few like B had already been admitted, the Committee might prefer B; and vice versa. If C, a white student with extraordinary artistic talent, were also seeking one of the remaining places, his unique quality might give him an edge over both A and B. Thus, the critical criteria are often individual qualities or experience not dependent upon race but sometimes associated with it.

NOTES

1. The description of the Harvard College admissions program, provided to the Court in an *amicus curie* brief filed by Columbia University, Harvard University, Stanford University and the University of Pennsylvania, was appended to the decision by Justice Powell, and quoted extensively in his opinion. It has been treated as a roadmap for a permissible college admissions affirmative action program.

2. Justice Powell's opinion was joined by no other justice, but his opinion was generally viewed as authoritative because he commanded a majority in support of his reasoning on his two critical conclusions (that racial quotas are prohibited by the Constitution, and that consideration of race to promote diversity is permissible). The eight other Justices split evenly, with four joining each of these conclusions, while rejecting the other.

3. Clearly Alan Bakke won, but did the University of California lose? Who spoke for the interests of the minority group applicants? Were their interests aligned with those of the University?

4. In *Parents Involved in Community Schools v. Seattle School District No. 1*, 551 U.S. 701 (2007), the Supreme Court held that the Seattle school district had violated the 14th Amendment rights of its students by assigning them to schools based on their race. The school district had

considered race as a factor in school assignment to avoid re-segregation of the schools. The five member majority held that avoiding unintentional segregation was not a compelling state interest, though one of the five, Justice Kennedy, wrote in a concurring opinion that schools could consider race to achieve diversity if their plans were sufficiently narrowly tailored.

5. Professor Michelle Adams argues that integration is now regarded by the Court as a discriminatory purpose for 14th Amendment purposes. Michelle Adams, *Is Integration a Discriminatory Purpose?*, 96:3 IOWA LAW REVIEW 837 (2011).

6. In his *Bakke* opinion Justice Blackmun wrote: "In order to get beyond racism, we must first take account of race. There is no other way." By contrast, in the Parents Involved case, Chief Justice Roberts wrote: "The way to stop discrimination on the basis of race is to stop discriminating on the basis of race." Which of them has the better argument?

7. Kathleen M. Sullivan has argued that one problem with the Supreme Court's affirmative action decisions is that they have been "backward-looking," focused on affirmative action as a remedy, instead of "forward-looking," focused on affirmative action as a policy. She writes: "affirmative action was permissible to 'remedy,' 'repair[],' or 'cure' past sins of discrimination. Underrepresentation of minorities was evil not in itself, but only insofar as it signaled that there had been specific injury in the past. Those who had caused it were now free under both the Constitution and title VII to mend it themselves, or to be made to do so, through affirmative action. Such a remedial focus need not have emerged in these cases. After all, *Bakke, Weber,* and *Fullilove* alike involved voluntary affirmative action plans undertaken by policymaking bodies, not affirmative action imposed by courts on parties found to have violated laws against race discrimination. Thus other justifications besides remedy might have defended those plans against challenges by disgruntled whites. For example, those plans might have been justified by goals for the future that depend on accelerating the racial integration of social institutions now. But such forward-looking visions appeared only fleetingly in the Court's opinions." Kathleen M. Sullivan, *Sins of Discrimination: Last Term's Affirmative Action Cases*, 100 HARV. L. REV. 78, 83–84 (1986). Is Justice Powell's opinion in *Bakke* backward or forward looking? Does it focus on a remedial justification for affirmative action, or the need for new policies to promote diversity?

8. Twenty-five years after the *Bakke* decision, the Court again considered the legitimacy of affirmative action in higher education in two cases brought against the University of Michigan. In a case challenging the University's undergraduate affirmative action program, the Court held that an admissions procedure that gave all underrepresented minorities 20 points (out of a possible 150 points) was not narrowly tailored to achieve a compelling purpose of admitting a diverse class. The program was thus struck down. *See, Gratz v. Bollinger*, 539 U.S. 244 (2003). In a companion case challenging the University's law school admission process, a more individualized process was upheld. *See, Grutter v. Bollinger*, 539 U.S. 306 (2003) [reproduced infra.]. Four members of the Court voted in favor of both plans (Justice Stevens, Justice Souter, Justice Ginsberg and Justice

Breyer), and four voted against both (Chief Justice Rehnquist, Justice Scalia, Justice Kennedy and Justice Thomas); Justice O'Connor formed the majority in each case.

9. Does the affirmation of the *Bakke* decision in *Gruter* validate Professor Sullivan's argument that forward-looking affirmative action policies are less likely to be rejected?

10. In a dissenting opinion in Parents Involved, Justice Stevens wrote "It is my firm conviction that no Member of the Court that I joined in 1975 would have agreed with today's decision."

11. By his final years on the Court, Justice Stevens was described as the Court's reigning liberal. He frequently responded that he hadn't moved from his position as a Republican centrist when appointed by President Ford in 1975, but that the Court had shifted to the right. *See, e.g.*, Richard Brust, *Practical Meaning: As the Court Shifted Right: Stevens Kept His Place*, AMERICAN BAR ASSOCIATION JOURNAL, April 9, 2010. But in the *Bakke* case, decided in his third term on the Court, he not only joined, but helped lead, the conservative block, in voting against any use of race in college admissions. Twenty-five years later, In the *Grutter* case, which appears below, he supported diversity-based affirmative action.

12. In the years following the *Bakke* decision, the Supreme Court handed down several decisions involving government contracting that raised doubts about the continuing validity of *Bakke*. The most important stood for the proposition that racial preferences in contracting could only be justified as a remedy for past discrimination. *See City of Richmond v. J.A. Croson Co.*, 488 U.S. 469 (1989).

13. Relying on *Croson*, the Fifth Circuit essentially nullified the *Bakke* decision within its region in 1996. In *Hopwood v. Texas*, 78 F.3d 932 (5th Cir.1996); *cert. denied* 518 U.S. 1033 (1996), the circuit court held that the University of Texas law school's affirmative action program was in violation of the Fourteenth Amendment, even if it complied with Justice Powell's opinion in the *Bakke* decision. The court reasoned that Justice Powell's opinion was not the authoritative decision of the Court, and in any case the diversity justification had been subsequently abandoned by the Court. Between 1996 and the decision in *Grutter*, the status of diversity-based affirmative action was thus uncertain.

Grutter v. Bollinger

539 U.S. 306 (2003)

■ JUSTICE O'CONNOR delivered the opinion of the Court.

This case requires us to decide whether the use of race as a factor in student admissions by the University of Michigan Law School (Law School) is unlawful.

I

A

The Law School ranks among the Nation's top law schools. It receives more than 3,500 applications each year for a class of around 350 students.

Seeking to "admit a group of students who individually and collectively are among the most capable," the Law School looks for individuals with "substantial promise for success in law school" and "a strong likelihood of succeeding in the practice of law and contributing in diverse ways to the well-being of others." More broadly, the Law School seeks "a mix of students with varying backgrounds and experiences who will respect and learn from each other." In 1992, the dean of the Law School charged a faculty committee with crafting a written admissions policy to implement these goals. In particular, the Law School sought to ensure that its efforts to achieve student body diversity complied with this Court's most recent ruling on the use of race in university admissions. *See Regents of Univ. of Cal. v. Bakke*, 438 U.S. 265 (1978). Upon the unanimous adoption of the committee's report by the Law School faculty, it became the Law School's official admissions policy.

The hallmark of that policy is its focus on academic ability coupled with a flexible assessment of applicants' talents, experiences, and potential "to contribute to the learning of those around them." The policy requires admissions officials to evaluate each applicant based on all the information available in the file, including a personal statement, letters of recommendation, and an essay describing the ways in which the applicant will contribute to the life and diversity of the Law School. In reviewing an applicant's file, admissions officials must consider the applicant's undergraduate grade point average (GPA) and Law School Admission Test (LSAT) score because they are important (if imperfect) predictors of academic success in law school. The policy stresses that "no applicant should be admitted unless we expect that applicant to do well enough to graduate with no serious academic problems."

The policy makes clear, however, that even the highest possible score does not guarantee admission to the Law School. Nor does a low score automatically disqualify an applicant. Rather, the policy requires admissions officials to look beyond grades and test scores to other criteria that are important to the Law School's educational objectives. So-called " 'soft' variables" such as "the enthusiasm of recommenders, the quality of the undergraduate institution, the quality of the applicant's essay, and the areas and difficulty of undergraduate course selection" are all brought to bear in assessing an "applicant's likely contributions to the intellectual and social life of the institution."

The policy aspires to "achieve that diversity which has the potential to enrich everyone's education and thus make a law school class stronger than the sum of its parts." The policy does not restrict the types of diversity contributions eligible for "substantial weight" in the admissions process, but instead recognizes "many possible bases for diversity admissions." The policy does, however, reaffirm the Law School's longstanding commitment to "one particular type of diversity," that is, "racial and ethnic diversity with special reference to the inclusion of students from groups which have been historically discriminated against, like African–Americans, Hispanics and Native Americans, who without this commitment might not be represented in our student body in meaningful numbers." By enrolling a " 'critical mass' of [underrepresented] minority students," the Law School seeks to "ensur[e] their ability to make unique contributions to the character of the Law School."

The policy does not define diversity "solely in terms of racial and ethnic status." Nor is the policy "insensitive to the competition among all students for admission to the [L]aw [S]chool." Rather, the policy seeks to guide admissions officers in "producing classes both diverse and academically outstanding, classes made up of students who promise to continue the tradition of outstanding contribution by Michigan Graduates to the legal profession."

B

Petitioner Barbara Grutter is a white Michigan resident who applied to the Law School in 1996 with a 3.8 GPA and 161 LSAT score. The Law School initially placed petitioner on a waiting list, but subsequently rejected her application. In December 1997, petitioner filed suit.... Petitioner alleged that respondents discriminated against her on the basis of race in violation of the Fourteenth Amendment. * * *

During the 15–day bench trial, the parties introduced extensive evidence concerning the Law School's use of race in the admissions process. Dennis Shields, Director of Admissions when petitioner applied to the Law School, testified that he did not direct his staff to admit a particular percentage or number of minority students, but rather to consider an applicant's race along with all other factors....

Erica Munzel, who succeeded Shields as Director of Admissions, testified that " 'critical mass' " means " 'meaningful numbers' " or " 'meaningful representation,' " which she understood to mean a number that encourages underrepresented minority students to participate in the classroom and not feel isolated. Munzel stated there is no number, percentage, or range of numbers or percentages that constitute critical mass. * * *

Dr. Stephen Raudenbush, the Law School's expert, focused on the predicted effect of eliminating race as a factor in the Law School's admission process. In Dr. Raudenbush's view, a race-blind admissions system would have a " 'very dramatic,' " negative effect on underrepresented minority admissions. He testified that in 2000, 35 percent of underrepresented minority applicants were admitted. Dr. Raudenbush predicted that if race were not considered, only 10 percent of those applicants would have been admitted. Under this scenario, underrepresented minority students would have constituted 4 percent of the entering class in 2000 instead of the actual figure of 14.5 percent.

In the end, the District Court concluded that the Law School's use of race as a factor in admissions decisions was unlawful. Applying strict scrutiny, the District Court determined that the Law School's asserted interest in assembling a diverse student body was not compelling because "the attainment of a racially diverse class ... was not recognized as such by *Bakke* and it is not a remedy for past discrimination." The District Court went on to hold that even if diversity were compelling, the Law School had not narrowly tailored its use of race to further that interest. * * *

Sitting en banc, the Court of Appeals reversed the District Court's judgment and vacated the injunction. The Court of Appeals first held that Justice Powell's opinion in *Bakke* was binding precedent establishing diversity as a compelling state interest.... The Court of Appeals also held that the Law School's use of race was narrowly tailored because race was merely a "potential 'plus' factor" and because the Law School's program was "virtually identical" to the Harvard admissions program described approvingly by Justice Powell and appended to his *Bakke* opinion. 288 F.3d 732, 746, 749 (C.A.6 2002). * * *

II

A

We last addressed the use of race in public higher education over 25 years ago. In the landmark *Bakke* case, we reviewed a racial set-aside program that reserved 16 out of 100 seats in a medical school class for members of certain minority groups. 438 U.S. 265 (1978). The decision produced six separate opinions, none of which commanded a majority of the Court. Four Justices would have upheld the program against all attack on the ground that the government can use race to "remedy disadvantages cast on minorities by past racial prejudice." (joint opinion of Brennan, White, Marshall, and Blackmun, JJ., concurring in judgment in part and dissenting in part). Four other Justices avoided the constitutional question altogether and struck down the program on statutory grounds. (opinion of Stevens, J., joined by Burger, C. J., and Stewart and Rehnquist, JJ., concurring in judgment in part and dissenting in part). Justice Powell provided a fifth vote not only for invalidating the set-aside program, but also for reversing the state court's injunction against any use of race whatsoever. The only holding for the Court in *Bakke* was that a "State has a substantial interest that legitimately may be served by a properly devised admissions program involving the competitive consideration of race and ethnic origin." Thus, we reversed that part of the lower court's judgment that enjoined the university "from any consideration of the race of any applicant." * * *

Justice Powell approved the university's use of race to further only one interest: "the attainment of a diverse student body." With the important proviso that "constitutional limitations protecting individual rights may not be disregarded," Justice Powell grounded his analysis in the academic freedom that "long has been viewed as a special concern of the First Amendment." Justice Powell emphasized that nothing less than the " 'nation's future depends upon leaders trained through wide exposure' to the ideas and mores of students as diverse as this Nation of many peoples." (quoting *Keyishian v. Board of Regents of Univ. of State of N. Y.*, 385 U.S. 589, 603 (1967)). In seeking the "right to select those students who will contribute the most to the 'robust exchange of ideas,' " a university seeks "to achieve a goal that is of paramount importance in the fulfillment of its mission." Both "tradition and experience lend support to the view that the contribution of diversity is substantial."

Justice Powell was, however, careful to emphasize that in his view race "is only one element in a range of factors a university properly may consider in attaining the goal of a heterogeneous student body." For Justice Powell, "[i]t is not an interest in simple ethnic diversity, in which a specified percentage of the student body is in effect guaranteed to be members of selected ethnic groups," that can justify the use of race. Rather, "[t]he diversity that furthers a compelling state interest encompasses a far broader array of qualifications and characteristics of which racial or ethnic origin is but a single though important element." * * *

B

* * * Context matters when reviewing race-based governmental action under the Equal Protection Clause. *See Gomillion v. Lightfoot*, 364 U.S. 339 (1960) (admonishing that, "in dealing with claims under broad provisions of the Constitution, which derive content by an interpretive process of inclusion and exclusion, it is imperative that generalizations, based on and qualified by the concrete situations that gave rise to them, must not be applied out of context in disregard of variant controlling facts"). In *Adarand Constructors, Inc. v. Peña*, we made clear that strict scrutiny must take " 'relevant differences' into account." 515 U.S., at 228. Indeed, as we explained, that is its "fundamental purpose." Not every decision influenced by race is equally objectionable, and strict scrutiny is designed to provide a framework for carefully examining the importance and the sincerity of the reasons advanced by the governmental decisionmaker for the use of race in that particular context.

III

A

With these principles in mind, we turn to the question whether the Law School's use of race is justified by a compelling state interest. Before this Court, as they have throughout this litigation, respondents assert only one justification for their use of race in the admissions process: obtaining "the educational benefits that flow from a diverse student body." In other words, the Law School asks us to recognize, in the context of higher education, a compelling state interest in student body diversity.

We first wish to dispel the notion that the Law School's argument has been foreclosed, either expressly or implicitly, by our affirmative-action cases decided since *Bakke*. It is true that some language in those opinions might be read to suggest that remedying past discrimination is the only permissible justification for race-based governmental action. *See, e.g., Richmond v. J.A. Croson Co.*, supra, at 493 (plurality opinion) (stating that unless classifications based on race are "strictly reserved for remedial settings, they may in fact promote notions of racial inferiority and lead to a politics of racial hostility"). But we have never held that the only governmental use of race that can survive strict scrutiny is remedying past discrimination. Nor, since *Bakke*, have we directly addressed the use of race in the context of public higher education. Today, we hold that the Law School has a compelling interest in attaining a diverse student body.

The Law School's educational judgment that such diversity is essential to its educational mission is one to which we defer. The Law School's assessment that diversity will, in fact, yield educational benefits is substantiated by respondents and their *amici*. Our scrutiny of the interest asserted by the Law School is no less strict for taking into account complex educational judgments in an area that lies primarily within the expertise of the university. Our holding today is in keeping with our tradition of giving a degree of deference to a university's academic decisions, within constitutionally prescribed limits. * * *

The Law School's claim of a compelling interest is further bolstered by its amici, who point to the educational benefits that flow from student body diversity. In addition to the expert studies and reports entered into evidence at trial, numerous studies show that student body diversity promotes learning outcomes, and "better prepares students for an increasingly diverse workforce and society, and better prepares them as professionals." *Brief for American Educational Research Association et al. as Amici Curiae 3*; *see, e.g.*, W. Bowen & D. Bok, THE SHAPE OF THE RIVER (1998); DIVERSITY CHALLENGED: EVIDENCE ON THE IMPACT OF AFFIRMATIVE ACTION (G. Orfield & M. Kurlaender eds.2001); COMPELLING INTEREST: EXAMINING THE EVIDENCE ON RACIAL DYNAMICS IN COLLEGES AND UNIVERSITIES (M. Chang, D. Witt, J. Jones, & K. Hakuta eds.2003).

These benefits are not theoretical but real, as major American businesses have made clear that the skills needed in today's increasingly global marketplace can only be developed through exposure to widely diverse people, cultures, ideas, and viewpoints. *Brief for 3M et al. as Amici Curiae 5; Brief for General Motors Corp. as Amicus Curiae 3–4*. What is more, high-ranking retired officers and civilian leaders of the United States military assert that, "[b]ased on [their] decades of experience," a "highly qualified, racially diverse officer corps ... is essential to the military's ability to fulfill its principle mission to provide national security." *Brief for Julius W. Becton, Jr., et al. as Amici Curiae 5*. The primary sources for the Nation's officer corps are the service academies and the Reserve Officers Training Corps (ROTC), the latter comprising students already admitted to participating colleges and universities. At present, "the military cannot achieve an officer corps that is both highly qualified and racially diverse unless the service academies and the ROTC used limited race-conscious recruiting and admissions policies." * * *

B

Even in the limited circumstance when drawing racial distinctions is permissible to further a compelling state interest, government is still "constrained in how it may pursue that end: [T]he means chosen to accomplish the [government's] asserted purpose must be specifically and narrowly framed to accomplish that purpose." *Shaw v. Hunt*, 517 U.S. 899 (1996) (internal quotation marks and citation omitted)....

Since *Bakke*, we have had no occasion to define the contours of the narrow-tailoring inquiry with respect to race-conscious university admissions programs. That inquiry must be calibrated to fit the distinct issues raised by the use of race to achieve student body diversity in public higher education. Contrary to Justice Kennedy's assertions, we do not "abando[n] strict scrutiny," Rather, as we have already explained, we adhere to Adarand's teaching that the very purpose of strict scrutiny is to take such "relevant differences into account." 515 U.S., at 228 (internal quotation marks omitted).

To be narrowly tailored, a race-conscious admissions program cannot use a quota system—it cannot "insulat[e] each category of applicants with certain desired qualifications from competition with all other applicants." *Bakke*, 438 U.S., at 315 (opinion of Powell, J.). Instead, a university may consider race or ethnicity only as a " 'plus' in a particular applicant's file," without "insulat[ing] the individual from comparison with all other candidates for the available seats." *Id.*, at 317. In other words, an admissions program must be "flexible enough to consider all pertinent elements of diversity in light of the particular qualifications of each applicant, and to place them on the same footing for consideration, although not necessarily according them the same weight."

We find that the Law School's admissions program bears the hallmarks of a narrowly tailored plan. * * *

The Law School's goal of attaining a critical mass of underrepresented minority students does not transform its program into a quota. As the Harvard plan described by Justice Powell recognized, there is of course "some relationship between numbers and achieving the benefits to be derived from a diverse student body, and between numbers and providing a reasonable environment for those students admitted." *Id.*, at 323. "[S]ome attention to numbers," without more, does not transform a flexible admissions system into a rigid quota. * * *

That a race-conscious admissions program does not operate as a quota does not, by itself, satisfy the requirement of individualized consideration. When using race as a "plus" factor in university admissions, a university's admissions program must remain flexible enough to ensure that each applicant is evaluated as an individual and not in a way that makes an applicant's race or ethnicity the defining feature of his or her application. The importance of this individualized consideration in the context of a race-conscious admissions program is paramount. * * *

We are mindful, however, that "[a] core purpose of the Fourteenth Amendment was to do away with all governmentally imposed discrimination based on race." *Palmore v. Sidoti*, 466 U.S. 429. Accordingly, race-conscious admissions policies must be limited in time. This requirement reflects that racial classifications, however compelling their goals, are potentially so dangerous that they may be employed no more broadly than the interest demands. Enshrining a permanent justification for racial preferences would offend this fundamental equal protection principle. We see no reason to exempt race-conscious admissions programs from the requirement that all governmental use of race must have a logical end point. The Law School, too, concedes that all "race-conscious programs must have reasonable durational limits." * * *

It has been 25 years since Justice Powell first approved the use of race to further an interest in student body diversity in the context of public higher education. Since that time, the number of minority applicants with high grades and test scores has indeed increased. We expect that 25 years from now, the use of racial preferences will no longer be necessary to further the interest approved today.

IV

In summary, the Equal Protection Clause does not prohibit the Law School's narrowly tailored use of race in admissions decisions to further a compelling interest in obtaining the educational benefits that flow from a diverse student body....

■ JUSTICE GINSBURG, with whom JUSTICE BREYER joins, concurring.

The Court's observation that race-conscious programs "must have a logical end point," accords with the international understanding of the office of affirmative action. The International Convention on the Elimination of All Forms of Racial Discrimination, ratified by the United States in 1994, *see* State Dept., Treaties in Force 422–423 (June 1996), endorses "special and concrete measures to ensure the adequate development and protection of certain racial groups or individuals belonging to them, for the purpose of guaranteeing them the full and equal enjoyment of human rights and fundamental freedoms." Annex to G.A. Res. 2106, 20 U.N. GAOR, 20th Sess., Res. Supp. (No. 14), p. 47, U.N. Doc. A/6014, Art. 2(2) (1965). But such measures, the Convention instructs, "shall in no case entail as a consequence the maintenance of unequal or separate rights for different racial groups after the objectives for which they were taken have been achieved."; *see also* Art. 1(4) (similarly providing for temporally limited affirmative action); Convention on the Elimination of All Forms of Discrimination against Women, Annex to G.A. Res. 34/180, 34 U.N. GAOR, 34th Sess., Res. Supp. (No. 46), p. 194, U.N. Doc. A/34/46, Art. 4(1) (1979) (authorizing "temporary special measures aimed at accelerating de facto equality" that "shall be discontinued when the objectives of equality of opportunity and treatment have been achieved"). * * *

However strong the public's desire for improved education systems may be, *see* P. Hart & R. Teeter, *A National Priority: Americans Speak on Teacher Quality* 2, 11 (2002) (public opinion research conducted for Educational Testing Service); No Child Left Behind Act of 2001, Pub.L. 107–110, 115 Stat. 1806, 20 U.S.C. § 7231 (2000 ed., Supp. I), it remains the current reality that many minority students encounter markedly inadequate and unequal educational opportunities. Despite these inequalities, some minority students are able to meet the high threshold requirements set for admission to the country's finest undergraduate and graduate educational institutions. As lower school education in minority communities improves, an increase in the number of such students may be anticipated. From today's vantage point, one may hope, but not firmly forecast, that over the next generation's span, progress toward nondiscrimination and genuinely equal opportunity will make it safe to sunset affirmative action.

■ JUSTICE THOMAS, with whom JUSTICE SCALIA joins as to Parts I–VII, concurring in part and dissenting in part.

Frederick Douglass, speaking to a group of abolitionists almost 140 years ago, delivered a message lost on today's majority:

"[I]n regard to the colored people, there is always more that is benevolent, I perceive, than just, manifested towards us. What I ask for the Negro is not benevolence, not pity, not sympathy, but simply justice. The American people have always been anxious to know what they shall do with us. . . . I have had but one answer from the beginning. Do nothing with us! Your doing with us has already played the mischief with us. Do nothing with us! If the apples will not remain on the tree of their own strength, if they are worm-eaten at the core, if they are early ripe and disposed to fall, let them fall! . . . And if the Negro cannot stand on his own legs, let him fall also. All I ask is, give him a chance to stand on his own legs! Let him alone! . . . [Y]our interference is doing him positive injury." *What the Black Man Wants: An Address Delivered in Boston, Massachusetts, on 26 January 1865*, reprinted in 4 THE FREDERICK DOUGLASS PAPERS 59, 68 (J. Blassingame & J. McKivigan eds.1991).

Like Douglass, I believe blacks can achieve in every avenue of American life without the meddling of university administrators. Because I wish to see all students succeed whatever their color, I share, in some respect, the sympathies of those who sponsor the type of discrimination advanced by the University of Michigan Law School (Law School). The Constitution does not, however, tolerate institutional devotion to the status quo in admissions policies when such devotion ripens into racial discrimination. Nor does the Constitution countenance the unprecedented deference the Court gives to the Law School, an approach inconsistent with the very concept of "strict scrutiny."

No one would argue that a university could set up a lower general admissions standard and then impose heightened requirements only on black applicants. Similarly, a university may not maintain a high admissions standard and grant exemptions to favored races. The Law School, of its own choosing, and for its own purposes, maintains an exclusionary admissions system that it knows produces racially disproportionate results. Racial discrimination is not a permissible solution to the self-inflicted wounds of this elitist admissions policy.

The majority upholds the Law School's racial discrimination not by interpreting the people's Constitution, but by responding to a faddish slogan of the cognoscenti. Nevertheless, I concur in part in the Court's opinion. First, I agree with the Court insofar as its decision, which approves of only one racial classification, confirms that further use of race in admissions remains unlawful. Second, I agree with the Court's holding that racial discrimination in higher education admissions will be illegal in 25 years. *See* ante (stating that racial discrimination will no longer be narrowly tailored, or "necessary to further" a compelling state interest, in 25 years). I respectfully dissent from the remainder of the Court's opinion and the judgment, however, because I believe that the Law School's current use of race violates the Equal Protection Clause and that the Constitution means the same thing today as it will in 300 months. * * *

V

* * * [T]here is nothing ancient, honorable, or constitutionally protected about "selective" admissions. . . .

... [S]elective admissions [began] in the beginning of the 20th century, as universities sought to exercise more control over the composition of their student bodies. Since its inception, selective admissions has been the vehicle for racial, ethnic, and religious tinkering and experimentation by university administrators. The initial driving force for the relocation of the selective function from the high school to the universities was the same desire to select racial winners and losers that the Law School exhibits today. Columbia, Harvard, and others infamously determined that they had "too many" Jews, just as today the Law School argues it would have "too many" whites if it could not discriminate in its admissions process.

Columbia employed intelligence tests precisely because Jewish applicants, who were predominantly immigrants, scored worse on such tests. Thus, Columbia could claim (falsely) that " '[w]e have not eliminated boys because they were Jews and do not propose to do so. We have honestly attempted to eliminate the lowest grade of applicant [through the use of intelligence testing] and it turns out that a good many of the low grade men are New York City Jews.' " Letter from Herbert E. Hawkes, dean of Columbia College, to E.B. Wilson, June 16, 1922 (reprinted in *Qualified Student* 160–161). In other words, the tests were adopted with full knowledge of their disparate impact. Cf. *DeFunis v. Odegaard*, 416 U.S. 312 (1974) (per curiam) (Douglas, J., dissenting).

Similarly no modern law school can claim ignorance of the poor performance of blacks, relatively speaking, on the Law School Admission Test (LSAT). Nevertheless, law schools continue to use the test and then attempt to "correct" for black underperformance by using racial discrimination in admissions so as to obtain their aesthetic student body. The Law School's continued adherence to measures it knows produce racially skewed results is not entitled to deference by this Court....

Having decided to use the LSAT, the Law School must accept the constitutional burdens that come with this decision. The Law School may freely continue to employ the LSAT and other allegedly merit-based standards in whatever fashion it likes. What the Equal Protection Clause forbids, but the Court today allows, is the use of these standards hand-in-hand with racial discrimination. An infinite variety of admissions methods are available to the Law School. Considering all of the radical thinking that has historically occurred at this country's universities, the Law School's intractable approach toward admissions is striking.

The Court will not even deign to make the Law School try other methods, however, preferring instead to grant a 25–year license to violate the Constitution. And the same Court that had the courage to order the desegregation of all public schools in the South now fears, on the basis of platitudes rather than principle, to force the Law School to abandon a decidedly imperfect admissions regime that provides the basis for racial discrimination. * * *

———

Proposition 209

(California Constitution, Article 1, Section 31)

In 1996, Ward Connerly, a member of the Regents of the University of California, took the lead role in campaigning for a California ballot initiative to amend the State's Constitution to prohibit State government affirmative action. Termed the "California Civil Rights Initiative," and avoiding any use of the term "affirmative action," the initiative campaign attracted world-wide attention. The initiative, which appears below, was adopted by the voters by a 54–46 margin. According to exit polls, it was opposed by women, and by members of racial, ethnic and religious minority groups (including African Americans, Hispanic Americans, Asian Americans, and Jews), but it was overwhelmingly supported by white male voters. *See* L.A. Times exit poll results, November 7, 1996 at http://www.acri.org/209vote demographics.html.

The proposition provides:

... [T]he state shall not discriminate against, or grant preferential treatment to, any individual or group on the basis of race, sex, color, ethnicity, or national origin in the operation of public employment, public education, or public contracting.

―――――

NOTES

1. In *Bakke*, Justice Marshall offered a statistical portrait of the inequality of African Americans in American life as of 1978. Twenty-five years later a similar statistical portrait was presented by Justice Ginsburg in her dissent in *Gratz v. Bollinger*, 539 U.S. 244, at 298–99 (2003), the undergraduate companion case to *Grutter*. Compare the portraits; they are stunningly similar. At the statistical level there had been few improvements in the lives of African Americans in the twenty five years between the two decisions. What does this suggest about Justice O'Connor's prediction that by 2028 there will be no need for affirmative action? For a further discussion of the effect of inequality on college admissions, *see*, David B. Oppenheimer, *The Legality of Promoting Inclusiveness: May the University of California use race or ethnicity as factors in applicant outreach?* 27 UCLA Chicano-Latino Law Review 11, 23–27 (2008).

2. Proposition 209 is generally understood to prohibit the kind of diversity-based affirmative action preferences subsequently approved by the Supreme Court in the *Grutter* case. Ward Connerly successfully campaigned for similar measures in Washington in 1998, in Michigan in 2006 (where it effectively nullified the *Grutter* decision's applicability to the University of Michigan), and in Nebraska in 2008. He campaigned for a similar initiative In Colorado in 2008, which was rejected by the voters.

3. Connerly also sponsored Proposition 54, a California initiative in 2003 that would have prohibited the State of California from collecting data about race or ethnicity; it was rejected by the voters. As you'll read in the

next section, such a law already exists in France. Consider how the passage of such a law in the United States would affect affirmative action programs.

4. In 1998, in response to the *Hopwood* decision, Texas Governor George W. Bush and the Texas Legislature adopted a university admissions plan that guarantees admission to any Texas university (including the highly ranked University of Texas at Austin) to any student finishing in the top 10% of his/her high school class. The effect was to increase opportunities at schools in poor communities, where few students had previously qualified for the most selective university campuses. Given the high degree of residential and school segregation (which is true in Texas, and in most of the United States), and the link between race, ethnicity and poverty, some hoped that the "Texas Plan" would prove to be an effective "race-neutral" alternative to race-based affirmative action. The jury is still out, with some praising it, and others asserting that it is insufficient. *See, e.g.*, Danielle Holley and Delia Spencer, *The Texas Ten Percent Plan*, 34 HARVARD CIVIL RIGHTS–CIVIL LIBERTIES LAW REVIEW 264 (1999); *See also* http:// www.inside highered.com/news/2007/05/29/percent; http://www.civilrights. org/publications/blend-it/.

――――

The Struggle for Access from *Sweatt* To *Grutter:* A History of African American, Latino, and American Indian Law School Admissions, 1950–2000

19 Harvard BlackLetter Law Journal 1, 2, 3, 6, 13, 15–17, 19, 22–23, 25–32, 36, 38 (2003)

■ WILLIAM C. KIDDER

* * * In this Article, using a wide array of published and unpublished data, I attempt to document and analyze law school admissions opportunities for African American, Latino, and American Indian students over the past fifty years. . . .

The historical and contemporary law school admissions and enrollment data, I argue, will support four claims. First, before law schools adopted affirmative action programs in the late 1960s, law schools and the legal profession were overwhelmingly de facto segregated. Second, even with the tool of affirmative action, White students have consistently had higher admissions rates than students of color since the mid–1970s. Third, a comprehensive review of the consequences of ending affirmative action at public law schools in California, Texas, and Washington reveal that there is little evidence that race-neutral alternatives to affirmative action are viable in legal education. When affirmative action was prohibited at law schools that are similar to the University of Michigan, the number of underrepresented minorities sank to levels not seen since the late 1960s. Finally, recent national admissions data are consistent with the conclusion that student activism can have a positive influence on admissions rates. Conversely, affirmative action bans and threats of litigation are associated with a widening of the gap in admissions rates in recent years between Whites and students of color nationwide. * * *

In the 1950s and early 1960s, aspiring minority attorneys outside the South did not confront Jim Crow segregation, yet the barriers of racial and ethnic exclusion in legal education were nonetheless quite formidable. While 1950s national law school enrollment figures broken down by race and ethnicity are unavailable due to poor data collection, it is safe to conclude that American law schools were approximately 99% White during this period. For example, there were an estimated 1450 African American attorneys in 1950 out of a total of 221,605 lawyers, meaning that African Americans were 0.65% of the legal profession. In 1960, there were 2180 African American attorneys out of a total of 285,933 lawyers, or 0.76% of the profession. Erwin Smigel, author of a major 1964 study of Wall Street lawyers, reported, "In the year and a half that was spent interviewing, I heard of only three Negroes who had been hired by large law firms. Two of these were women who did not meet the client." Likewise, a 1963 study of firm lawyers and solo practitioners in Detroit found that all 206 of the attorneys surveyed were White. . . .

Comprehensive data on African American law school enrollment are also difficult to come by for much of the 1960s. The ABA and other national organizations did not collect data on Latino, American Indian, and Asian Pacific American students until 1969. In 1965, the AALS Committee on Minority Groups, in the most comprehensive effort up to that point, surveyed ABA-accredited law schools about minority enrollment figures. The AALS Committee found that most law schools could not provide information on either Latin American or Puerto Rican students for two reasons: (1) there was confusion among deans over what these terms meant; and (2) most schools simply had no idea of the past or present enrollment levels of these groups. Even after reluctantly restricting the focus of their study to African Americans, the AALS Committee had to rely on help from faculty members, students, and personal visits to law schools, because some uncooperative deans would not provide the requisite data. The Committee eventually estimated that there were a total of 701 African American law students in the 1964–1965 academic year (combining first, second, and third year students), with 267 at six predominantly Black law schools, including 165 at Howard. Thus, African Americans were about 1.3% of national law school enrollments and less than 1.0% of enrollments excluding these six schools. Prior to 1968, there were about 200 African Americans graduating from law school annually.

U.S. Census data indicate that between 1960 and 1970, the number of African American attorneys grew by 76% (from 2180 to 3845), while the total number of American lawyers grew by 24% during that span. Not surprisingly, the shortage of Black attorneys was most severe in the South. Alabama, Arkansas, Florida, Georgia, Louisiana, Mississippi, North Carolina, South Carolina, Tennessee, and Virginia had a combined total of 393 African American lawyers in 1970, even though the total Black population of these states was over 8.8 million at that time. In 1970, the number of African American lawyers in states outside the South with Black populations over one million were as follows: 373 in California, 667 in Illinois, 650 in New York, and 141 in Pennsylvania. * * *

A decade after *Brown v. Board of Education*, the Civil Rights Movement was at its height, and the Civil Rights Act of 1964 was just approved by Congress and signed into law by President Johnson. Yet at this time, American law schools, especially elite schools, were still almost completely segregated. . . . In the fall of 1965, Boalt, Michigan, New York University (NYU), and UCLA had a combined total of four African Americans out of 4843 students, which, shockingly, is one fewer than the University of Mississippi (Ole Miss), where the law school begrudgingly enrolled five Blacks in 1965 to avoid jeopardizing a substantial grant from the Ford Foundation. Similarly, between 1948 and 1968, the University of Texas enrolled a total of 8018 White first-year law students and only 37 African Americans. Between 1956 and 1967, there were between zero and two African American enrollments at UTLS annually. * * *

The minuscule number of students of color in law schools began to improve in the late 1960s as a result of early affirmative action programs. . . . Harvard Law School's affirmative action program, started in 1964, predates those of other law schools by three or four years. In 1965, Harvard also began a "special summer program" funded by the Rockefeller Foundation that introduced about forty African American college students from the South to the possibilities of a legal career by bringing them to Cambridge for eight weeks. Between 1964 and 1966, about half of the African Americans enrolled at Harvard Law School came from the same schools that traditionally sent a large number of White students (Harvard, Yale, Columbia, Brown, etc.), and half came from historically Black colleges in the South. A couple years later, other schools like Columbia, Boalt, and UCLA started "weak" forms of affirmative action such as increased outreach, recruiting, financial aid, and summer preparation programs. However, it was the 1967 revolts in Detroit and Newark—and especially the urban uprisings that swept across America after the assassination of Martin Luther King, Jr. on April 4, 1968—which ruptured long-established practices of exclusion in legal education and other institutions, and, at a national level, quickly prompted "strong" affirmative action in the form of race-conscious admissions. By the late 1960s, UCLA and Boalt Hall had become the leading producers of Chicano law students in California. * * *

At the same time that affirmative action programs were taking root at American law schools, other demographic trends were transforming the structure of opportunity to attend law schools. Applications to ABA law schools increased sharply between 1960 and 1975, particularly between 1968 and 1973. * * *

A second factor driving the increased competition to law schools in the 1970s was the steady rise in applications from women. In the 1950s and 1960s, law schools adopted policies and practices that excluded women. In those days, it was not seen as contradictory for the legal education establishment to advocate racial desegregation, yet support discrimination against women. * * *

Likewise, in 1964, Erwin Griswold of Harvard Law School assured students and alumni, "[T]here could never be a great influx of women into the school . . . because the policy was never to give any man's place to a woman." This institutionalized policy of male privilege was also reflected in the Harvard Special Summer Program, the first significant affirmative action outreach program in legal education designed to encourage African Americans in the South to apply to law school. In 1966, Harvard's assistant dean coolly remarked that "women suffered heavily when selections were made" regarding admission into the program because admitting a substantial proportion of women made no sense in light of the "relatively low proportion of women" at Harvard and other law schools. In 1968, ten ABA-accredited law schools, including Notre Dame, still had zero female students. Other schools in the mid–1960s, like Columbia, placed ceilings on the number of women who could enroll.

In the 1960s and 1970s, feminism, the Civil Rights Movement, and other social forces put pressure on law schools to open their doors to women—that is at least White women from middle- to upper-class backgrounds. At the same time, these same forces contributed to the substantial expansion of the pool of female applicants. [Thus, there were] . . . 1064 women first-year students at ABA law schools in 1965 (4% of total enrollments), compared to 3542 in 1970 (10%), 10,472 in 1975 (27%), and 15,272 in 1980 (36%). This trend has continued, with 18,592 women in 1990 (42%) and 21,499 in 2000 (49%).

Prior to the application explosion resulting in part from the aforementioned factors, only a few law schools, including Ole Miss and Tulane, relied extensively on the LSAT in law school admissions decisions. These schools likely adopted such policies as a pretense for maintaining segregation, which is consistent with other pro-segregation maneuvers by Southern universities during that period. The more common practice at that time, however, was for schools to weigh undergraduate grade point average (UGPA) more heavily than the LSAT. This fact was reflected in a 1965 survey of eighty-eight law schools, which reported that a majority of law schools, including Boalt, Harvard, Pennsylvania, and Yale, relied on UGPA more than the LSAT. For example, prior to 1961, Boalt Hall admitted virtually all applicants with at least a B average in college; the LSAT was only used as a factor for applicants with less than a B average. Likewise, in the early 1960s, the University of Texas Law School admitted all applicants who had a 2.2 UGPA and took the LSAT, regardless of their test scores.

* * *

An overlooked irony amidst all these trends is that while critics argued that affirmative action meant admitting "unqualified" and "unprepared" students and led to the "general debasement of academic standards," admission standards were relatively more relaxed during the 1950s and early 1960s, when White men maintained virtually total control over access to legal education. For instance, at the University of Michigan Law School, the students of color in the entering class of 1971 had equivalent index scores to Michigan's White male-dominated class of 1957. Yet nationally, these White males of the 1950s and early 1960s, the majority of whom would have been denied access to an ABA education under the more extreme competition that was the norm by the early 1970s, apparently performed well enough as the judges, professors, government officials, and law firm partners of their generation. Likewise, a recent study of minority (mostly African American) alumni of the University of Michigan Law

School found that they were equally successful as Whites in terms of income and career satisfaction and that they also had significantly higher civic service contributions than their White classmates. * * *

... Black, Chicano, and American Indian first-year enrollments at ABA law schools were flat in the mid-to late–1970s.* * *

A crucial point is that while the unavailability of data makes it impossible to know whether Black and Chicano applicants had higher admissions rates than Whites at ABA law schools in the late 1960s or early 1970s, such was certainly not true by the 1975–1976 admissions cycle or thereafter. During the period shortly before and after *Bakke*, White applicants were substantially more likely to be admitted to ABA law schools than Blacks, Chicanos, or other minority applicants. Indeed, the highest acceptance rate for African Americans (55% in 1985) is still lower than the lowest acceptance rate for Whites (59% in 1976), and in each of the five years reported, the cumulative acceptance rate for African Americans is only about two-thirds of the White acceptance rate. * * *

TABLE 2: CUMULATIVE ACCEPTANCE RATES (AND APPLICANT VOLUME) TO ABA LAW SCHOOLS: 1975–79, 1985

Year	BLACK	CHICANO	WHITE
1976	39% (4299)	47% (1085)	59% (66994)
1977	41% (3914)	53% (1091)	63% (66030)
1978	42% (4230)	53% (1187)	65% (68184)
1979	46% (3721)	62% (1053)	69% (60280)
1985	55% (3776)	67% (693)	78% (48166)
5–Year Total	44.6% (19,940)	55.4% (5,109)	65.9% (309,654)

* * * Combined data from 1976 to 1979 and 1985 reveal that 26% of African Americans with 3.25+ UGPAs were denied admission from every ABA law school to which they applied, compared to 14% of Chicanos and 15% of Whites. Moreover, these results are not an artifact of group differences in the distribution of applicants with 3.25–4.0 UGPAs. More detailed data from 1976 and 1985 indicate that White applicants consistently had higher admissions rates than African Americans among those with 3.75+ UGPAs, 3.5–3.74 UGPAs, 3.25–3.49 UGPAs, and so forth. Since this pattern occurred at a time when nearly all American law schools practiced affirmative action to some extent, the depressed admissions rates for African American "high achievers" is most likely attributable to law schools giving the greatest weight to precisely the criterion that disadvantages students of color most: the LSAT.

This conclusion is consistent with the finding that in the 1970s, African American law students were disproportionately clustered in a few dozen ABA law schools and that Chicanos were disproportionately clustered in public law schools in the Southwest. While these few schools practiced energetic affirmative action in the 1970s, a much larger number of law schools had more modest affirmative action programs that were overshadowed by the disparate impact of an LSAT-driven definition of merit. Therefore, while affirmative action critics charged that law schools had become havens of widespread "reverse discrimination," the actual national admissions practices that were locked in by the mid–1970s and which were further institutionalized by *Bakke* significantly favored Whites.

TABLE 3: CUMULATIVE ACCEPTANCE RATES (AND APPLICANT VOLUME) TO ABA LAW SCHOOLS FOR APPLICANTS WITH 3.25+ UGPAS: 1976–79, 1985

Year	BLACK	CHICANO	WHITE
1976	74% (556)	77% (243)	80% (26753)
1977	71% (557)	87% (234)	82% (27876)
1978	73% (592)	84% (274)	82% (29802)
1979	73% (557)	88% (291)	85% (27189)
1985	83% (488)	88% (139)	89% (19698)
5–Year Total	74.2% (2,753)	85.9% (1,181)	85.0% (131,318)

* * * In the wake of the Fifth Circuit's decision in *Hopwood v. Texas*, California's Proposition 209, the University of California Regents' SP–1 Resolution, Washington's 1–200 Initiative, and the "One Florida" plan, a substantial number of America's leading public law schools terminated race-sensitive affirmative action in recent years.

Ending race-sensitive admissions at public law schools in California, Texas, and Washington has had significant negative consequences for African Americans, Latinos, and American Indians. The first prohibition on affirmative action occurred when the UC Regents approved SP–1 in July 1995, which ended race-conscious admissions at the graduate and professional levels beginning on January 1, 1997, and the undergraduate level one year later. This was followed up with Proposition 209, a November 1996 voter-backed amendment to the California Constitution that took effect in January of 1998. In the 1996 case of *Hopwood v. Texas*, a challenge to the affirmative action program at the University of Texas Law School, the Fifth Circuit ruled that diversity (i.e., the educational benefits that flow from having racially diverse learning environments) was not a compelling governmental interest. This ruling had the effect of prohibiting race-conscious admissions at public and private higher educational institutions in Texas, Louisiana, and Mississippi.

Washington voters passed Initiative 200, a ballot initiative with wording identical to Proposition 209, in November 1998. Finally, the "One Florida" plan, adopted in November 1999 by Governor Jeb Bush's executive order, discontinued race-conscious affirmative action in the Florida public university system beginning in 2000 at the undergraduate level and in 2001 at the graduate and professional levels. Although the "One Florida" plan grants students who graduate in the top twenty percent of their high school class a spot in at least one public university, there is no analogous admissions plan for law, medical, business, and graduate schools.

UC Berkeley (Boalt Hall), UCLA, UC Davis, the University of Texas (UT), and the University of Washington (UW) have been greatly impacted by the end of affirmative action. The law schools at the University of Florida and Florida State University are not discussed here because the One Florida Plan only took effect for the entering class of 2001 and because Florida still has race-conscious financial aid. For Boalt Hall, UCLA, UC Davis, and UT, the admissions data include the five years after Prop. 209/SP–1 and *Hopwood* (1997–2001), which are compared to the four years before the ban on affirmative action from 1993 to 1996. For UW, the three post-Initiative 200 admissions cycles (1999–2001) are compared to the admissions cycles for the last three years with affirmative action (1996–1998).

... The data reveal a precipitous drop in African American enrollments after affirmative action was banned. Across the five schools, African Americans were 6.65% of enrollments with affirmative action, but 2.25% of enrollments without affirmative action. In effect, the clock was turned back on three decades of affirmative action in California. At Boalt Hall, African Americans were 2.7% of enrollments from 1997 to 2001. By comparison, Blacks were 9.0% of enrollments in the first five years in which affirmative action took full effect (1968–1972). Likewise, African Americans were 7.5% of enrollments at UCLA in the first five years of affirmative action (1967–1971) but only 2.3% of enrollments thirty years later (1997–2001). The University of Texas came full circle as well, as a half-century of hard-fought yet halting progress was erased. In 1951, Heman Sweatt and the five other African American entrants to the first *post-de jure* segregation class at UT constituted 2.1% of enrollments. African Americans were a nearly identical proportion of enrollments (2.2%) at UT in 1997–2001. The extent to which Boalt, UCLA, and UT became resegregated is particularly disheartening in light of the recent history of those institutions. Boalt Hall and UCLA combined to award nearly 600 law degrees to African Americans between 1987 and 1997, and UT produced some 650 Black attorneys prior to *Hopwood*. It should also be noted that African Americans were 11.1% of the national applicant pool from 1993 to 1996 and a slightly higher 11.4% from 1997 to 2000.

TABLE 4: AFRICAN AMERICAN ENROLLMENTS AT SELECTIVE PUBLIC LAW SCHOOLS BEFORE AFFIRMATIVE ACTION WAS PROHIBITED

Year	BOALT	UCLA	DAVIS	U. TEXAS	U. WASH
1993	21 (269)	20 (340)	5 (160)	1 (556)	-
1994	31 (269)	46 (335)	10 (153)	37 (568)	-
1995	21 (266)	20 (272)	3 (136)	36 (509)	-
1996	20 (263)	19 (307)	4 (152)	29 (500)	6 (172)
1997	-	-	-	-	3 (166)
1998	-	-	-	-	8 (173)
Average	23.3 (266.8)	26.3 (313/5)	5.5 (150.3)	33.3 (533.3)	5.7 (170.3)

TABLE 5: AFRICAN AMERICAN ENROLLMENTS AT SELECTIVE PUBLIC LAW SCHOOLS AFTER AFFIRMATIVE ACTION WAS PROHIBITED

Year	BOALT	UCLA	DAVIS	U. TEXAS	U. WASH
1997	1 (268)	10 (381)	5 (172)	4 (464)	-
1998	8 (269)	8 (277)	3 (183)	9 (489)	-
1999	7 (269)	3 (289)	6 (161)	9 (519)	2 (158)
2000	7 (270)	5 (305)	2 (168)	17 (518)	1 (163)
2001	14 (299)	10 (304)	4 (214)	16 (527)	3 (177)
Average	7.4 (275)	7.2 (311)	4.0 (179.6)	11.0 (503.4)	2.0 (166)

* * * This fifty-year history concludes with an analysis of the current national landscape of law school admissions. As in the late 1970s and mid–1980s, White applicants to ABA law schools continue to have higher cumulative admissions rates to ABA-accredited law schools compared to African American, Latino, and American Indian candidates. * * *

Although *Hopwood* and Prop. 209 affected only a handful of schools, the data ... show that the fall of affirmative action has had a wider impact.... What is most noticeable ... is how admissions rates for underrepresented minorities (URMs) are basically flat between 1992 and 2000. In contrast, admissions rates for White applicants, in most cases already higher than those for URMS with the same UGPAs, increased significantly between the mid–1990s and the late 1990s. Thus, ... by 1996, White applicants with 3.0–3.24 UGPAs had admissions rates similar to URM applicants with 3.5–3.74 UGPAs. Likewise, ... in the late 1990s, White applicants with 3.25–3.49 UGPAs had admissions rates similar to URM applicants with 3.75+ UGPAs. * * *

The findings presented in this Article support four central claims. First, before affirmative action began in the late 1960s, legal education and the legal profession were almost entirely de facto segregated. Second, affirmative action must be placed in its proper context, because even when these programs exist, nationally, White students consistently have higher admissions rates than students of color in the years since *Bakke*. Third, race-neutral alternatives to affirmative action in law schools are ineffective at producing significant levels of diversity. When public law schools in California, Texas, and Washington banned affirmative action the number of underrepresented minorities was lower than it had been in three decades. Fourth, recent national admissions data indicate that student activism has a tangible effect on admissions rates. Affirmative action bans and threats of litigation have had a chilling effect on admissions rates for students of color nationwide.

In summary, efforts to diversify legal education have met with mixed success. On one hand, as the figures in the Appendix indicate, total first-year enrollment levels for American Indian, Chicano, Latino, and African American students have risen significantly in the last two decades, even though overall enrollment levels have been nearly flat. On the other hand, admissions rates for students of color, both cumulatively and among those with equivalent UGPAs, continue to lag behind those of White applicants. In fact, it is discouraging to note that the Black–White acceptance ratio was lower overall between 1996 and 2001 than for any other period since *Bakke*. Much remains to be done before it can be said with a straight face that law school admissions operate on an equal playing field. It is also clear from the pre-affirmative action era as well as from data on recent affirmative action bans in California, Texas, and Washington, that if the Supreme Court prohibits institutions of higher learning from using race and ethnicity as a significant plus factor in admissions, law schools will experience substantial resegregation.

———

NOTES

1. In the years since Kidder's article, enrollments of minority students at Boalt Hall and the other University of California law schools have increased only slightly. A 2011 article reveals: "At Berkeley Law School (Boalt Hall), [enrollment] . . . has since increased to 5%, less than half the pre-Proposition 209 enrollment. Meanwhile, the overall percentage of African American graduate students at all University of California (UC) campuses has dropped from approximately 4% of the student body in 1994 to approximately 2.6% in 2008." David B. Oppenheimer, *Color–Blindness, Racism–Blindness, and Racism–Awareness: Revisiting Judge Henderson's Proposition 209 Decision*, 12 Berkeley Journal of African American Law & Policy 229 (2011).

2. In 2010, the Law School Admission Council reported that 39,570 out of 52,790 white applicants were admitted to at least one law school, an acceptance rate of 75%. By contrast, just 4,290 out of 9,720 Black applicants were admitted to at least one school, an acceptance rate of only 44%. http://www.lsac.org/LSACResources/Data/volume-summary-ethnic-gender. asp.

3. Recall that in the *Bakke* case Justice Powell's opinion cited as influential an amicus curie brief filed by four elite universities: Columbia, Stanford, Harvard and the University of Pennsylvania. Twenty-five years later, Justice O'Connor's opinion in the *Grutter* case cited three amicus curie briefs as influential—briefs by 65 Fortune 500 companies (described as the *3M brief*), General Motors, and Lt. Gen. Julius W. Becton, Jr. (ret.) (on behalf of a group of former high-ranking officers and civilian leaders of the United States armed forces.) The corporate briefs argued that their ability to consider racial and ethnic diversity was necessary to their ability to compete in world markets. The military brief argued that the ability to consider racial and ethnic diversity in selecting military officers was essential to the military defense of the United States.

4. One of the procedural disputes in *Bakke, Gratz* and *Grutter* was whether groups representing the interests of minority applicants should be permitted to intervene. Charles Lawrence and Joanne Villanueva have argued that such intervention is essential to protect the rights of these students, because the university defendants have a different set of interests in defending their affirmative action programs. *See,* Charles Lawrence, *"When the Defendants are Foxes Too: The Need for Intervention by Minorities in 'Reverse Discrimination' Suits Like Bakke,"* 34 Guild Practitioner 1 (1976–77); Joanne Villanueva, *The Power of Procedure: The Critical Role of Minority Intervention in the Wake of Ricci v. DeStefano*, 99:4 California Law Review 1083 (2011).

5. Justice Thomas argues that affirmative action is an unconstitutional remedy used by elite law schools to counter their use of a discriminatory test, the LSAT. Do schools have a choice? Professors Marjorie M. Shultz and Sheldon Zedeck have developed a series of tests that measure lawyer effectiveness, and predict professional achievement among law school applicants, with few or no racial disparities. *See,* Shultz and Zedeck, *Predicting Lawyer Effectiveness: A New Assessment for Use in Law School Admission*

Decisions (2009), http://papers.ssrn.com/sol3/papers.cfm?abstract_id= 1442118.

6. One controversial objection to affirmative action is that it results in a "mismatch," in which minority students are admitted to schools for which they are only barely qualified, and thus deprived of being top performing students. *See, e.g.*, Richard H. Sander, *A Systematic Analysis of Affirmative Action in American Law Schools*, 57 STAN. L. REV. 367 (2004). For a response to Professor Sander, *see* Richard O. Lempert, William C. Kidder, Timothy T. Clydesdale, & David L. Chambers, *Affirmative Action In American Law Schools: A Critical Response to Richard Sander's "A Reply to Critics"* (February 2006) U. of Michigan Law & Economics, Olin Working Paper No. 06-001.

7. The Convention on the Elimination of All Forms of Racial Discrimination (ICERD), which was signed by the U.S. in 1966 and ratified in 1994, provides in Article 2, section 2 that "States Parties shall, when the circumstances so warrant, take, in the social, economic, cultural and other fields, special and concrete measures to ensure the adequate development and protection of certain racial groups or individuals belonging to them, for the purpose of guaranteeing them the full and equal enjoyment of human rights and fundamental freedoms." The section is understood to permit, and arguably require, affirmative action efforts.

B. SOUTH AFRICA

Constitution of the Republic of South Africa, 1996

Section 9: Equality

(1) Everyone is equal before the law and has the right to equal protection and benefit of the law.

(2) Equality includes the full and equal enjoyment of all rights and freedoms. To promote the achievement of equality, legislative and other measures designed to protect or advance persons, or categories of persons, disadvantaged by unfair discrimination may be taken.

(3) The state may not unfairly discriminate directly or indirectly against anyone on one or more grounds, including race, gender, sex, pregnancy, marital status, ethnic or social origin, colour, sexual orientation, age, disability, religion, conscience, belief, culture, language, and birth.

(4) No person may unfairly discriminate directly or indirectly against anyone on one or more grounds in terms of subsection (3). National legislation must be enacted to prevent or prohibit unfair discrimination.

(5) Discrimination on one or more of the grounds listed in subsection (3) is unfair unless it is established that the discrimination is fair.

http://www.justice.gov.za/legislation/acts/1996-108.pdf, pp.5–6.

Motala and Another v. University of Natal

Supreme Court, Durban and Coast Local Division; 1995 (3) BCLR 374 (D); 1995 SACLR Lexis 256 Judgment Date: 24//02/1995

■ Judgment By: HURT, J.

Fathima Motala, the daughter of the applicants, is a highly gifted pupil. At the end of 1993 she passed her standard nine examinations with an aggregate of 81%. In the matriculation at the end of 1994, conducted under the aegis of what is referred to in the papers as the "ex-house of delegates," she achieved five A's and a B, all in higher grade subjects. These subjects were all in the "pure science matriculation course (course S17)," which is specifically intended for pupils intending to take a degree in medicine. She achieved A's in all the science courses for which she sat. During 1994, and prior to obtaining these excellent results, she had applied for admission to the faculty of medicine at the University of Natal. This application met with a somewhat terse refusal; no reasons were given and her father, the first applicant, was asked not to contact the medical faculty about any second choice she might make as a proposed course of study. At about the end of January 1995, the applicants learnt of another prospective student, Karen Singh, who, like Fathima, had achieved excellent matriculation results in the ex-house of delegates examination and who had likewise been refused admission to the faculty of medicine. They learnt, apparently from a Mr K Pillay who, in an affidavit in these proceedings, describes himself as "a community leader in the Indian community in Durban," that the representatives of the University of Natal in the faculty of medicine had been approached for an explanation for their refusal of Karen Singh's application. Mr Pillay had been given certain explanations which he and those whom he represented had regarded as unsatisfactory. I quote Mr Pillay's evidence in this regard: "On Friday, 13 January 1995, I met with Professor Loening, the chairman of the selection committee for the admission of first year medical students (and assistant dean undergraduate) at the University of Natal. He informed me that: (a) By reason of the affirmative action policy of the University of Natal only forty Indian students would be accepted. (b) More black, coloured and white students would be accepted. (c) Only Indian students with six 'A' passes in the ex-house of delegates matriculation examination would be considered for admission. On Monday, 16 January 1994, I met with the dean of the faculty of medicine, Natal, Professor Van Dellen, who informed me: (a) Over the years many Indian doctors had qualified at the medical faculty of the University of Natal, and relatively, not many blacks and coloureds had qualified. It was therefore the policy of the faculty to admit more blacks and coloured students. Only forty Indian students would be admitted.

... The applicants founded their application on ... the following contention: that the limitation of the number of Indian students to be admitted to the faculty amounts to discrimination on a racial basis and is accordingly contrary to the provisions of the Constitution Act 200 of 1993 ...

The respondent replied to the applicants' contentions at some length. It emerges from the answering affidavits that the respondent has, for a number of years, been faced with a dilemma about the selection of students for first year medicine. The source of this dilemma is the very poor standard of education available to African students under the aegis of what was previously known as the Department of Education and Training. Professor Van Dellen, the dean of the respondents' faculty of medicine, describes how the respondent endeavoured to circumvent this difficulty by means of what he describes as "an affirmative action programme," in the following terms:

> The university's affirmative action programme is an attempt to take into account the educational disadvantages to which students have been subjected in certain of the school education departments, and is directed at determining the true potential of each aspirant student. In the faculty of medicine, this means that an attempt must be made to evaluate the potential the student has to succeed in his/her university studies, and the potential he or she has to be a good medical doctor. A similar situation obtains in other faculties.

> The faculty evaluates the performance at school of African students in a way which is different to that employed in relation to students schooled under other education departments. Since 1951 the respondent's school of medicine has trained the most African doctors in South Africa. I believe that it is therefore in a better position than any other medical faculty to make an evaluation of the potential of aspirant African medical students. It follows, from what I have said above, that the matriculation results of accepted African applicants will in almost all cases be lower than those of other applicants who are accepted, and indeed lower than those of other applicants who are not accepted.

> By these means, it is possible to identify a pool of African students who satisfy the university's requirements for admission to the medical faculty.

Professor Van Dellen goes on to explain the procedure which is then adopted, as follows:

> The principal difficulty then becomes the matter of comparing students who have been assessed on different bases. It is almost impossible to do this. A policy decision has to be made. In the ideal world, if all students had the same educational background, and each could be compared to any other on his/her academic performance at school, one would expect to find that the top 120 students, graded according to their matriculation results, would constitute a cultural mix which is more or less the same as the cultural mix of the society from which they are drawn. That being the case, if the respondent starts its selection process by looking at any one of the cultural groups involved, it is safe for the respondent to assume that there is no question of the selection process being unfair for so long as the numbers chosen from that cultural group, expressed as a percentage of the total admission, does not exceed the representation that cultural group has in society. There is no other way of overcoming the circumstance that it is almost impossible to compare potentials across the cultural groups emanating from the various educational systems. * * *

It was not seriously disputed in argument that the procedure adopted by the respondent in order to compensate for the defect in the education available to African matriculants, involves assessing African applicants on a different basis to Indian applicants.... [T]he principal submission on behalf of the applicants was that the Indian community had itself suffered substantial disadvantages as a result of discrimination prior to April 1994. Accordingly, it was contended, discrimination between members of the African community and those of the Indian community under the policy adopted by the respondent for selection of first year medical students was "unfair discrimination" which fell to be prohibited by the operation of sections 8(1) and 8(2).... On the papers before me I was satisfied that the policy described by the deponents for the respondent was a "measure designed to achieve the adequate protection and advancement of ... a group ... of persons disadvantages by unfair discrimination" within the meaning of that expression as used in section 8(3)(a) of the Constitution. The contention by counsel for the applicants appears to be based upon the premise that there were no degrees of "disadvantage." While there is no doubt whatsoever that the Indian group was decidedly disadvantaged by the apartheid system, the evidence before me establishes clearly that the degree of disadvantage to which African pupils were subjected under the "four tier" system of education was significantly greater than that suffered by their Indian counterparts. I do not consider that a selection system which compensates for this discrepancy runs counter to the provisions of sections 8(1) and 8(2)....

Achieving Substantive Equality in a Society Founded Upon Inequality: The South African Constitutional Experience (1997)

http://law.wustl.edu/Library/Guides/Equality/papers.html

■ KARTHIGASEN GOVENDER

* * * Prior to the accession to power of the National Party, South Africa was a segregated and unequal society. It is beyond the scope of this paper to list all the discriminatory laws that were passed against Black people. But some are worth mentioning because of their contribution to the inequality which presently burdens this society. *The Black (Urban Areas Consolidation Act)* 25 of 1945 prevented Africans from remaining in an urban area for more than 72 hours except if they were in possession of a permit. *The Land Acts* of 1913 and 1936 provided that, except with ministerial approval, a Black person could not acquire any land or rights to land outside a Black area. This effectively meant that 87% of South Africa's land area could not be owned by Africans except with the permission of the Minister concerned. *The Group Areas Act* 36 of 1966, allowed for areas to be proclaimed for the exclusive use of a particular race group. Once the area was proclaimed as exclusive to that particular racial group then it became a criminal offence for a person not belonging to that racial group to live in that area. These so-called disqualified persons were moved out of the

area and resettled in areas that were zoned for their racial group. *The Group Areas Act* caused considerable suffering and bitterness. * * *

The *Reservation of Separate Amenities Act* 49 of 1953 allowed a person in charge or in control of public premises to reserve part of the premises for the exclusive use of persons belonging to a particular race or class. The Act made it an offence to willfully disregard notices segregating public premises. . . .

Legislation provided for job reservations, regulations and acts restricted the occupation of industrial land and land in the central business districts to whites thus ensuring exclusive control over the means of production, legislation and regulations provided for separate education departments which offered qualitatively different education to children of different race groups. Segregated social security and health services resulted in vastly inferior facilities and services for Africans. In summary, a plethora of legislation and subordinate legislation was passed both in order to keep the races separated and to ensure vastly superior treatment for whites. * * *

The new constitutional order has, at its core, a commitment to substantive equality and seeks to map out a vision for the nation based on this commitment. This vision reflects the need to remedy the ills of the past and to establish a less divided society in which a constitutional democracy can survive and flourish. The following provisions cumulatively seek to realise this vision:

The preamble recognises that one of the functions of the Constitution is to . . . [l]ay the foundations for a democratic and open society in which government is based on the will of the people and every citizen is equally protected by the law . . . and [i]mprove the quality of life of all citizens and free the potential of each person. Section 1 identifies human dignity, the achievement of equality and the advancement of human rights and freedoms as one of the basic values upon which the Republic of South Africa is founded. Section 9, the first substantive right in the Constitution, protects the right to equality before the law, guarantees that the law will both protect people and benefit them equally and prohibits unfair discrimination. The limitation clause only allows a right in the bill of rights to be limited if the limitation is reasonable and justifiable in an open and democratic society based on human dignity, equality and freedom. Courts, tribunals and forums are directed, when interpreting the bill of rights to promote the values that underlie an open and democratic society based on human dignity, equality and freedom.

* * * The constitution seeks, unlike many other constitutions, to protect socio-economic rights. Some socio-economic rights are protected and are as directly enforceable as the right to free speech. These include the right to basic education, including adult basic education, the right not to be refused emergency medical treatment, and the right of a child to basic nutrition, shelter, basic health care services and social services. The intensity with which other socio-economic rights are protected has been reduced to reflect economic realities. Everyone has the *right to have access* to adequate housing, to health care services, sufficient food and water and social security. In order to bolster the access rights and prevent them from

simply being a wish list, a positive obligation is imposed on the state to take reasonable legislative and other measures, within its available resources, to achieve the progressive realisation of this right. In the Madisonian tradition of checks and balances, the Human Rights Commission, an institution set up by the Constitution to support democracy, is empowered to require the relevant organs of state "to supply it with information on the measures that they have taken towards the realisation of rights in the bill of rights concerning housing, health care, food, water, social security, education and the environment." The constitution thus has guards guarding the guards. The effectiveness of this overseeing function by the Commission is debatable. It would appear that exposing ineffectual government departments to public scrutiny and consequent embarrassment would be its most effective sanction. Seeking interdicts from the courts directing action is likely to be less successful except in the extreme instance of a government department that is not performing at any level. Courts are likely to adopt a deferential attitude to the executive on issues that have complex budgetary implications. * * *

Description of the right to equality

Section 9(1) guarantees the right to be treated equally by the law, to be afforded equal protection of the law and to equally enjoy the benefits of the law.

Section 9(2) provides that the right to equality includes the right to full and equal enjoyment of all rights and freedoms. In order to achieve this, legislative measures designed to advance persons previously disadvantaged by racial discrimination may be undertaken.

Section 9(3) prohibits unfair discrimination, directly or indirectly, on any one or more grounds including race, gender, sex, pregnancy, marital status, ethnic or social origin, colour, sexual orientation, age, disability, religion, conscience, belief, culture, language and birth.

Section 9(4) prohibits individuals and juristic persons from unfairly discriminating directly or indirectly on any of the grounds listed in subsection 9(3). National legislation must be enacted to give more content to this right.

Section 9(5) contains a presumption that assists the person alleging discrimination to prove unfair discrimination. Unfair discrimination is presumed if the person proves that he or she has been discriminated against directly or indirectly on any one of the grounds mentioned in section 9(3).

* * * Our equality provision in its structure and content bears a resemblance to the Canadian equality provision. However the Constitutional Court in *Brink v. Kitshoff NO* pointed out that the text protecting the right to equality is worded differently in the various national constitutions. These differences reflect the different historical backgrounds of the countries and their different jurisprudential and philosophical understanding of equality. Interpretations of the equality clause of the South African Constitution must therefore be based on the wording of the right within the constitutional context and cognisance must be taken of our history. This

interpretation directive must be borne in mind prior to having recourse to the extensive foreign jurisprudence on equality. * * *

Affirmative action

It is imperative that any assessment of affirmative action programmes be placed in the South African context. Attempts to emulate the reasoning of foreign courts must be approached with a heightened measure of circumspection. A useful starting point is the constitutional principles. The Constitutional Court identified the following as one of the basic structures and premises of the new constitutional text contemplated by the constitutional principles:

> a legal system which ensures equality of all persons before the law, which includes laws, programmes or activities that have as their objective the amelioration of the conditions of the disadvantaged, including those disadvantaged on the grounds of race, colour or creed.

Because of the commitment to substantive or real equality, the draftspersons clearly intended the affirmative action programmes to be seen as essential and integral to attaining equality and not to be viewed as a limitation or exception to the right to equality. As affirmative action is seen as part of the right to equality, it would appear that persons challenging such programmes bear the onus of proving the illegality of such programmes. Affirmative action legislation is expressly sanctioned by the constitution, thus forestalling any argument as to whether preferential treatment for disadvantaged persons is permitted or not. Affirmative action programs must:

1) promote the achievement of substantive equality; and

2) be *designed* to protect and advance persons *disadvantaged by unfair discrimination. (Emphasis added)*

* * * Hurt J in *Motala and Another v University of Natal* adopted a highly deferential standard in reviewing the admission policies of the University of Natal Medical School. A "gifted" Indian student who had obtained 5 distinctions and a "B" symbol in matric was refused admission into the medical school. The medical school decided to limit to 40 the number of Indian students admitted to its programme. The poor standards of education available to African students under the control of the Department of Education and Training meant that a merit based entrance programme would result in few African students being accepted. It was argued that as the Indian community were also disadvantaged by apartheid, discrimination between African students and Indian students amounted to unfair discrimination. The court held that the admission policy adopted by the medical school was a measure designed to achieve the adequate protection and advancement of a group disadvantaged by unfair discrimination.

———

NOTES

1. The South African Constitution prohibits "unfair discrimination." Why the qualifier? How is this different than a general prohibition of

discrimination? How might it affect U.S. law if our Equal Protection Clause were read to prohibit only unfair discrimination? Or, is that what it does, under the strict scrutiny and compelling state interest test?

2.   Is the affirmative action program upheld by the *Motala* decision an example of unfair discrimination? In the essay excerpted above, Professor Govender went on to write: "The apartheid society had a distinct hierarchy of races. Whites were at the top and Africans firmly rooted at the bottom. The coloured and Indian communities were situated in between. It is perfectly legitimate, therefore, if we are seeking to achieve genuine equality to apply the affirmative action programme in proportion to the measure of disadvantage suffered under apartheid. However, when the effect of the programme is to disadvantage people who had also been disadvantaged in the past, the court must be satisfied that the programme is reasonable. Reasonableness on the facts of *Motala* would require that, at least, some explanation be provided as to how the number of 40 was arrived at, the extent to which this operated as a guideline or as a rigid figure, the extent to which the socio-economic backgrounds of students were taken into account, the demographics of the area in which the medical school was located and the extent to which society as a whole benefitted from such a decision. Hurt's acceptance of the programme simply on the basis that Africans were more disadvantaged than Indians is, it is submitted, incorrect." Do you agree?

3.   One criticism, or fear, of affirmative action, is that quotas intended to act as a floor (providing a minimum number of spaces for a particular group) will instead act as a ceiling (imposing a maximum number for each group). Some critics worry that the position expressed by Judge Hurt in the *Motala* case, that absent discrimination there should be a balance in the professions equal to the population balance, is a proscription for quotas as ceilings, limiting the opportunity of some minority groups. There's good reason to worry; in the twentieth century, such quotas were commonly used by U.S. colleges and graduate/professional schools, to limit the number of Jewish students, and then later to limit the number of Asian–American students. And, in the United States (and, as it turns out, South Africa), Jews and Asians are "over-represented" in the medical and legal professions. Thus, a decision to limit admissions based on population balance would fall quite hard on both groups.

But affirmative action floors usually leave much room for majorities and over-represented minorities. (But see the section on India, for an exception.) Judge Hurt's observation can also be understood as calling for a presumption about identifying discrimination, as we discussed in Chapter II. In the absence of discrimination, shouldn't we expect some racial and/or ethnic balance in graduate school admissions?

If an imbalance is per se illegal, we end up with discriminatory quotas. If an imbalance requires further inquiry, we end up with a test for discrimination, requiring an explanation. Are these two expressions of the same idea?

In *Richmond v. J.A. Croson Co.*, Justice O'Connor disagreed with the underlying assumption that a lack of balance indicates discrimination. She wrote that a particular racial quota to grant public construction contracts to minority-owned contractors rested on "the 'completely unrealistic' assumption that minorities will choose a particular trade in lockstep proportion to their representation in the local population."

To what extent does the disagreement about the meaning of imbalance reflect skepticism about or support for the use of affirmative action remedies?

4. Less than 10 percent of the population of South Africa is white, while nearly 80 percent are Black. At the highly selective University of Cape Town, 45 percent of the students are white, while 25 percent are Black. An affirmative action program there is under debate, with critics complaining that affirmative action based on race is a continuation of the apartheid policies of racial discrimination, while supporters assert that it is necessary to provide opportunities to Black students. The school requires nearly all A's for admission of white applicants, while admitting Black applicants with a mixture of A's and B's. Is this a form of "unfair discrimination?" *See* Celia Dugger, *Campus that Apartheid Ruled Faces a Policy Rift*, NY TIMES, Nov. 22, 2010, http://www.nytimes.com/2010/11/23/world/africa/23safrica.html?partner=rss&emc=rss; Anders Kelto, *Inequalities Complicate S. Africa College Admissions*, NATIONAL PUBLIC RADIO, May 10, 2011, http://www.npr.org/2011/05/10/136173961/inequalities-compli cate-s-africa-college-admissions.

C. INDIA

INTRODUCTION

India has adopted a system of caste-based affirmative action, which extends to political representation, government employment, and education. Its roots can be traced to policies introduced by the British during the colonial period, which were based upon the elaborate system of caste and religious groups in India. The British initially offered preferential treatment to Muslims at the beginning of the twentieth century, and in the subsequent decades offered separate electoral representation to other groups including Sikhs, Christians, Anglo–Indians, and "untouchables."

After Independence, India adopted a constitution that prohibited the practice of untouchability and discrimination on the basis of religion, race, caste, sex, or place of birth. The Constitution limited earlier British quotas (called "reservations") based on religion, but Article 46 provided that the State would promote the educational and economic interests of the "Scheduled Castes," the "Scheduled Tribes," and "other backward classes." ("OBCs") The category of Scheduled Castes and Scheduled Tribes ("SC/STs") encompasses those who were at the bottom of the Indian social order, including castes that were formerly known as untouchable. SC/STs encompass caste groups that were historically excluded from the Hindu social order in particular ways, while OBCs include castes that are considered underprivileged based on social and educational criteria. Scheduled Castes used to perform tasks considered ritually impure like scavenging and working in leather; for this reason they were often excluded from temples, forced to live outside the boundary of villages, and denied access to wells. Recall the discussion of untouchability and caste, in Chapter II.) Scheduled Tribes, the indigenous minority of India, often were considered outside of or beneath the caste system and faced geographical isolation and poverty. The meaning of "Backward Classes" shifted throughout the twentieth century, but in relation to reservations, the government of India classifies certain castes as OBCs based on social, educational, and economic factors. For further discussion of the shifting meanings of Backward Classes, *see* Marc Galanter, COMPETING EQUALITIES: LAW AND THE BACKWARD CLASSES IN INDIA (1984).

Article 46 and Article 15(4) provided the basis for a wide array of preferential policies including seats in academic institutions. The Constitution also specifically reserved seats for SC/STs in the lower house of Parliament and in the lower houses of state legislatures. Article 335 provided that the claims of SC/STs would be taken into account in making governmental appointments. Originally, the Constitution provided that reservations would expire in ten years, but they are routinely extended every ten years.

————

The Constitution of India

Article 14. Equality before law.

The State shall not deny to any person equality before the law or the equal protection of the laws within the territory of India.

Article 15. Prohibition of discrimination on grounds of religion, race, caste, sex or place of birth.

(1) The State shall not discriminate against any citizen on grounds only of religion, race, caste, sex, place of birth or any of them.

(2) No citizen shall, on grounds only of religion, race, caste, sex, place of birth or any of them, be subject to any disability, liability, restriction or condition with regard to:

>(a) access to shops, public restaurants, hotels and places of public entertainment; or

>(b) the use of wells, tanks, bathing ghats, roads and places of public resort maintained wholly or partly out of State funds or dedicated to the use of the general public.

(3) Nothing in this article shall prevent the State from making any special provision for women and children.

(4) Nothing in this article or in clause (2) of article 29 shall prevent the State from making any special provision for the advancement of any socially and educationally backward classes of citizens or for the Scheduled Castes and the Scheduled Tribes.

(5) Nothing in this article or in sub-clause (g) of clause (1) of article 19 shall prevent the State from making any special provision, by law, for the

advancement of any socially and educationally backward classes of citizens or for the Scheduled Castes or the Scheduled Tribes in so far as such special provisions relate to their admission to educational institutions including private educational institutions, whether aided or unaided by the State, other than the minority educational institutions referred to in clause (1) of article 30.

Article 16. Equality of opportunity in matters of public employment.

(1) There shall be equality of opportunity for all citizens in matters relating to employment or appointment to any office under the State.

(2) No citizen shall, on grounds only of religion, race, caste, sex, descent, place of birth, residence or any of them, be ineligible for, or discriminated against in respect of, any employment or office under the State.

(3) Nothing in this article shall prevent Parliament from making any law prescribing, in regard to a class or classes of employment or appointment to an office under the Government of, or any local or other authority within, a State or Union territory, any requirement as to residence within that State or Union territory prior to such employment or appointment.

(4) Nothing in this article shall prevent the State from making any provision for the reservation of appointments or posts in favour of any backward class of citizens which, in the opinion of the State, is not adequately represented in the services under the State.

(4A) Nothing in this article shall prevent the State from making any provision for reservation in matters of promotion, with consequential seniority, to any class or classes of posts in the services under the State in favour of the Scheduled Castes and the Scheduled Tribes which, in the opinion of the State, are not adequately represented in the services under the State.

(4B) Nothing in this article shall prevent the State from considering any unfilled vacancies of a year which are reserved for being filled up in that year in accordance with any provision for reservation made under clause (4) or clause (4A) as a separate class of vacancies to be filled up in any succeeding year or years and such class of vacancies shall not be considered together with the vacancies of the year in which they are being filled up for determining the ceiling of fifty per cent reservation on total number of vacancies of that year.

(5) Nothing in this article shall affect the operation of any law which provides that the incumbent of an office in connection with the affairs of any religious or denominational institution or any member of the governing body thereof shall be a person professing a particular religion or belonging to a particular denomination.

Article 17. Abolition of Untouchability.

"Untouchability" is abolished and its practice in any form is forbidden. The enforcement of any disability arising out of "Untouchability" shall be an offence punishable in accordance with law.

Article 29. Protection of interests of minorities.

(1) Any section of the citizens residing in the territory of India or any part thereof having a distinct language, script or culture of its own shall have the right to conserve the same.

(2) No citizen shall be denied admission into any educational institution maintained by the State or receiving aid out of State funds on grounds only of religion, race, caste, language or any of them.

Article 46. Promotion of educational and economic interests of Scheduled Castes, Scheduled Tribes and other weaker sections.

The State shall promote with special care the educational and economic interests of the weaker sections of the people, and, in particular, of the Scheduled Castes and the Scheduled Tribes, and shall protect them from social injustice and all forms of exploitation."

[Note: Art 15 sec 4 was added after the *State of Madras v. Dorairajan* decision in 1951, which is discussed in the excerpt below.]

Affirmative Action: India's Example

Fall 1999 Civil Rights Journal (United States Civil Rights Commission), pp. 22–24, 27

■ CLARK D. CUNNINGHAM

* * * India has developed a legal system that is probably more similar to that of the United States than that of any other country, particularly in the field of constitutional law. Both countries use a federal system with power shared between states and a central government. Both have written constitutions containing similar guaranteed rights; both have supreme courts with vast powers including the power to declare statutes unconstitutional; both countries turn to their courts to resolve their most important public controversies. (Indian law is also very accessible to U.S. readers because, like American law, it rests on the foundation of the English common law and because the constitution, statutes and appellate court decisions are all written in English.) * * *

Although cognitive bias-type discrimination based on caste status is treated as a serious, continuing problem in India, affirmative action there is focused more on eradicating the enduring effects from centuries' of oppression and segregation. There appears to be a more conscious commitment than in the U.S. to change the basic social structure of the country. The Indian approach perhaps can be understood best using the economic theory pioneered by Glenn Loury that distinguishes between "human capital" and "social capital." Human capital refers to an individual's own characteristics that are valued by the labor market; social capital refers to value an individual receives from membership in a community, such as access to information networks, mentoring and reciprocal favors. Potential human capital can be augmented or stunted depending on available social capital. Economic models demonstrate how labor market discrimination, even several generations in the past, when combined with ongoing segregated social structure can perpetuate indefinitely huge differences in social capital between ethnic communities. The limitation of human potential caused when access to social capital is blocked is viewed in India not only as a personal tragedy, calling out for compassion and justice, but also as a huge loss to the society itself, that must be remedied given the vast needs and aspirations of the world's largest democracy. Although, for historical reasons, affirmative action in India is phrased largely in terms of assisting "backward" groups, "backwardness" should be understood as a comparative rather than a pejorative or patronizing term. Indians are acutely aware that the problem of unevenly distributed social capital can arise as much from the concentration of social capital in a few "forward" groups as from any deficiency in "backward" groups.

In 1951, only a year after the newly independent India adopted its constitution containing guarantees of equality taken in part from U.S. law, the Indian Supreme Court was faced with a case remarkably like the landmark 1978 *Bakke* case (in which the U.S. Supreme Court barred the use of racial quotas for admission to a state medical school but permitted consideration of race to achieve diversity). A medical school had used a detailed and rigid quota system based on caste and religious categories to assure that its entering class had a demographic make up similar to that of the general population. The Court ruled in favor of the petitioner, a high caste Hindu denied admission. The Parliament immediately modified the ruling by using its power to amend the constitution by a two-thirds vote of each house to add an explicit "affirmative action" exception to the constitutional guarantee of equality, authorizing "special provision" for the advancement of "socially and educationally backward classes of citizens."

For the next thirty years different states in India experimented with a variety of ways to interpret and implement this constitutional "special provision" with a pendulum swing from overemphasis on caste identity to purely economic criteria. A continuing problem was the extension of affirmative action to caste groups apparently based more on their political clout in a particular state than their actual need for preferential treatment relative to other groups, leading to repeated Supreme Court decisions ordering states to redesign their programs using more objective and transparent processes.

In 1980 a Presidential Commission (known as the "Mandal Commission" after the name of its Chairperson) issued a comprehensive report and set of recommendations for national standards. Although the Mandal Report did not use the term "social capital," its central premise was that the mere prohibition of discrimination and a policy of "equal opportunity" were insufficient to remedy the profound social effects of the caste system. It stated: "People who start their lives at a disadvantage rarely benefit significantly from equality of opportunity ... Equality of opportunity is also an asocial principle, because it ignores the many invisible and cumulative hindrances in the way of the disadvantaged."

Responding to the Supreme Court's concern about objective and transparent processes, the Mandal Commission conducted a national survey that started with generally recognized group categories (typically based on caste name or hereditary occupation) and tested each group using standardized criteria of "backwardness" (such as comparing the percentage of group members who married before the age of 17 or did not complete high school with other groups in the same state). Eleven numerical factors, given varying weights, were assigned to each group based on the survey results and those groups with total scores below a specified cut-off point appeared in a list of Other Backward Classes (OBCs). The Commission then recommended that a percentage of new hires for most central government jobs be reserved for OBC members under a quota system.

The Mandal Report generated lively debate but it was not until 1990 that the national government actually proposed implementation of the Report. This announcement, by then-Prime Minister V.P. Singh, prompted widespread civil disturbance, instances of self-immolation by high-caste Hindus in protest, and litigation leading to an epic three months of oral argument before the Supreme Court. In 1992 the Supreme Court reached a 6–3, decision, largely approving the Report and its recommendations, and issuing a book-long set of judicial opinions. A majority of the Supreme Court justices approved the following basic principles:

1.   Reservation of government positions for OBCs should not be interpreted as a narrow exception to the constitutional guarantee of equality but rather as a way of achieving true, substantive equality. ("Turning the caste system on its head" in the words of Justice Jeevan Reddy, author of the majority opinion.)

2.   Traditional caste categories can be used as a starting point for identifying OBCs but selection criteria must include empirical factors beyond conventional assumptions that certain castes are "backward."

3.   Identification of a group as an OBC cannot be based on economic criteria alone.

4.   Because the Mandal Commission used objective, empirical criteria to create these new group categories, distribution of government benefits based on OBC membership does not perpetuate the stigma of traditional caste categories.

5.   OBC membership only creates a rebuttable presumption that a person needs preferential treatment; therefore, the state must also use an individualized economic means test to eliminate persons from affluent or professional families (termed "the creamy layer test"). * * *

Other useful insights can be gained by looking at India, for example from the many critiques by Indian intellectuals of the Mandal Report. Those critiques suggest some cautionary lessons about the use of affirmative action: the continuing pressure to expand beneficiaries by adding categories; the risk that affirmative action will be used primarily to mobilize voting blocks; the despair and resentment by members of the younger generation who feel their opportunities are restricted by their non-OBC status; the persistence and indeed revitalization of the very social categories that the state seeks to eliminate in creating a "casteless society" due to the value they are given by affirmative action; the way debate over affirmative action can distract attention from continuing acts of intentional discrimination, particularly in the private section; and the impact on the efficiency of government when merit in hiring and promotion is de-emphasized. Perhaps the most valuable lesson, though, that Americans might learn from India and other countries is greater humility: our problems may be more fundamental than we realize and, at the same time, our methods for addressing them may be less imaginative than we assume.

———

[EDITORS' NOTE: A portion of the lead majority opinion in the Mandal Commission case, *Indira Sawhney v. Union of India*, appears below, followed by a subsequent decision on medical school admissions, *Ajay Kumar Singh v. State of Bihar*.]

Sawhney v. Union of India

AIR 1993 SC 477 (Supreme Court of India 1993)

■ Judgment delivered by B.P. JEEVAN REDDY, J.

1. Forty and three years ago was founded this republic with the fourfold objective of securing to its citizens justice, liberty, equality and fraternity. Statesmen of the highest order the like of which this country has not seen since—belonging to the fields of law, politics and public life came together to fashion the instrument of change—the Constitution of India. They did not rest content with evolving the framework of the State; they also pointed out the goal-and the methodology for reaching that goal. In the preamble, they spelt out the goal and in parts III and IV, they elaborated the methodology to be followed for reaching that goal.

2. The Constituent Assembly, though elected on the basis of a limited franchise, was yet representative of all sections of society. Above all, it was composed of men of vision, conscious of the historic but difficult task of carving an egalitarian society from out of a bewildering mass of religions, communities, castes, races, languages, beliefs and practices. They knew their country well. They understood their society perfectly. They were aware of the historic injustices and inequities afflicting the society. They realised the imperative of redressing them by constitutional means, as early as possible—for the alternative was frightening. Ignorance, illiteracy and above all, mass poverty, they took note of. They were conscious of the fact that the Hindu religion—the religion of the overwhelming majority—as it was being practiced, was not known for its egalitarian ethos. It divided its adherents into four watertight compartments. Those outside this fourtier system (chaturvarnya) were the outcastes (Panchamas), the lowliest. ... The lowliness attached to them (Shudras and Panchamas) by virtue of their birth in these castes, unconnected with their deeds. There was to be no deliverance for them from this social stigma, except perhaps death. They were condemned to be inferior. All lowly, menial and unsavoury occupations were assigned to them. In the rural life, they had no alternative but to follow these occupations, generation after generation, century after century.

It was their 'karma', they were told, the penalty for the sins they allegedly committed in their previous birth. Pity is, they believed all this. They were conditioned to believe it. This mental blindfold had to be removed first. This was a phenomenon peculiar to this country. Poverty there has been—and there is—in every country. But none had the misfortune of having this social division—or as some call it, degradation—superimposed on poverty. Poverty, low social status in Hindu caste system and the lowly occupation constituted—and do still constitute—a vicious circle. The founding fathers were aware of all this—and more.

3. 'Liberty, equality and fraternity' was the battle cry of the French Revolution. It is also the motto of our Constitution, with the concept of 'Justice–Social Economic and Political'—the sum-total of modern political thought—super-added to it. Equality has been and is the single greatest craving of all human beings at all points of time. It has inspired many a great thinker and philosopher. All religious and political schools of thought swear by it, including the Hindu religious thought, if one looks to it ignoring the later crudities and distortions. Liberty of thought, expression, belief, faith and worship has equally been an abiding faith with all human beings, and at all times in this country in particular. Fraternity assuring the dignity of the individual has a special relevance in the Indian context, as this Judgment will illustrate in due course.

4. The doctrine of equality has many facets. It is a dynamic, and an evolving concept. Its main facets, relevant to Indian Society, have been referred to in the preamble and the articles under the sub-heading "Right to equality"—(Articles 14 to 18). In short, the goal is "equality of status and of opportunity". Articles 14 to 18 must be understood not merely with reference to what they say but also in the light of the several articles in Part IV (Directive Principles of State Policy). "Justice, Social, Economic and Political", is the sum total of the aspirations incorporated in part IV.

5. Article 14 enjoins upon the state not to deny to any person "equality before the law" or "the equal protection of the laws" within the territory of India. Most constitutions speak of either "equality before the law" or "the equal protection of the laws", but very few of both. Section 1 of the XIV. Amendment to the U.S. Constitution uses only the latter expression while the Austrian Constitution (1920), the Irish Constitution (1937) and the West German Constitution (1949) use the expression "equal before the law". (Article 7 of the Universal Declaration of Human Rights, 1948, of course, declares that "all are equal before the law and are entitled without any discrimination to equal protection of the law".) The content and sweep of these two concepts is not the same though there may be much in common. The content of the expression "equality before the law" is illustrated not only by Articles 15 to 18 but also by the several articles in Part IV, in particular, Articles 38, 39, 39A, 41 and 46. Among others, the concept of equality before the law contemplates minimising the inequalities in income and eliminating the inequalities in status, facilities and opportunities not only amongst individuals but also amongst groups of people, securing adequate means of livelihood to its citizens and to promote with special care the educational and economic interests of the weaker sections of the people, including in particular the Scheduled Castes and Scheduled

Tribes and to protect them from social injustice and all forms of exploitation. Indeed, in a society where equality of status and opportunity do not obtain and where there are glaring inequalities in incomes, there is no room for equality—either equality before law or equality in any other respect.* * *

Article 46 contains a very significant directive to the State. It says:

46. Promotion of educational and economic interests of Scheduled Castes, Scheduled Tribes and other weaker sections.—The State shall promote with special care the educational and economic interests of the weaker sections of the people, and, in particular, of the Scheduled Castes and the Scheduled Tribes, and shall protect them from social injustice and all forms of exploitation.

It is evident that "the weaker sections of the people" do include the "backward class of citizens" contemplated by Article 16(4).

Part XVI of the Constitution contains "special provisions relating to certain classes". The "classes" for which special provisions are made are, Scheduled Castes, Scheduled Tribes and the Anglo–Indian Community. It also provides for appointment of a Commission to investigate the conditions of and the difficulties faced by the socially and educationally backward classes and to make appropriate recommendations. * * *

[The opinion concludes that reservations in favor of the backward classes are permissible under the Indian Constitution; that reservations should be made based on caste membership, which is equated with social class; that reservations should generally be limited to 50%; that classification should be based on degrees of social backwardness; that wealthy members of a backward class (the "creamy layer") should be excluded from reservations; that reservations should be limited to appointments, and should not be used for promotions; and that the Government should appoint a permanent body to determine lists of backward classes.]

Singh v. State of Bihar

4 Supreme Court Cases 401 (1994)

■ The Judgment of the Court was delivered by B.P. JEEVAN REDDY, J.— Permissibility of providing-reservations under clause (4) of Article 15 of the Constitution of India in postgraduate medical courses is the issue raised in these appeals. The State of Bihar issued a prospectus relating to Postgraduate Medical Admission Test, 1992 providing inter alia reservation in favour of socially and educationally backward classes, Scheduled Castes, Scheduled Tribes and women. The percentages reserved are Scheduled Castes—14%, Scheduled Tribes—10%, extremely backward classes—14%, backward classes—9% and ladies—3%. The appellants questioned the aforesaid provision for reservation by way of two writ petitions in the Patna High Court. The writ petitions were dismissed whereupon they have approached this Court by way of these appeals. The Indian Medical Council has filed an affidavit in these proceedings putting forward its point of view in the matter. It has supported the appellants' stand.* * *

4. ... Article 15(4) says that nothing in Article 15 or in clause (2) of Article 29 shall prevent the State from making "any special provision" for the advancement of classes mentioned therein. The words "any special provision" are of wide amplitude and do certainly take in a provision reserving-certain number of seats in educational institutions. Indeed, the first major case arising under Article 15 before this Court (*M.R. Balaji v. State of Mysore*) was one relating to reservation of seats in educational institutions. At no time was it questioned that such a course was not permissible, evidently in view of the width of the words "any special provision" occurring in Article 15(4). In this connection, we may refer to the holding in *Indra Sawhney v. Union of India* with respect to a similar argument vis-a-vis Article 16(1). It was argued for the petitioners that Article 16(1)—which guarantees equality of opportunity to all citizens in matters relating to employment—does not warrant providing of reservations. The contention was rejected. It was held that just as Article 14 permits classification so does Article 16(1), which is but a facet of rule of equality in Article 14. For bringing about and ensuring equality, it was held, appropriate measures including reservations can be adopted. What kind of special provision should be made in favour of a particular class, it was observed, is a matter for the State to decide having regard to the facts and circumstances of a given situation. For the above reasons, the first contention of Shri Singh is rejected.

5.   The second submission of Shri Singh is premised on the assumption that reservations are basically anti-meritarian. We are afraid, this assumption is without any basis. It is true that in *R. Chitralekha v. State of Mysore, Janki Prasad Parimoo v. State of J & K* as also in *Balaji* it seems to have been assumed that reservation necessarily implies selection of less meritorious persons but this aspect was explained in the majority judgment in *Indra Sawhney* in the following words: (SCC p. 75 1, para. 836) the relevance and significance of merit at the stage of initial recruitment cannot be ignored. It cannot also be ignored that the very idea of reservation implies selection of a less meritorious person. At the same time, we recognise that this much cost has to be paid, if the constitutional promise of social justice is to be redeemed. We also firmly believe that given an opportunity, members of these classes are bound to overcome their initial disadvantages and would compete with—and may, in some cases, excel—members of open competition. It is undeniable that nature has endowed merit upon members of backward classes as much as it has endowed upon members of other classes and that what is required is an opportunity to prove it. It may not, therefore, be said that reservations are anti-meritarian. Merit there is even among the reserved candidates and the small difference, that may be allowed at the stage of initial recruitment is bound to disappear in course of time. These members too will compete with and improve their efficiency along with others."

6.   The said observations apply equally under Article 15(4)—only read 'admission' for 'recruitment'. It is necessary to reiterate that reservation is provided only at the stage of entry and not at the stage of exit. In the matter of passing of the examination, no concession is shown to members of reserved classes. The pass marks are uniform for all. This means that even if a less meritorious student is admitted under a reserved category, he

has to improve his standard and has to acquire the same proficiency as any other candidate (including the general candidates) while passing the examination. This circumstance is a complete answer to the argument of 'less merit'. No empirical study has been brought to our notice to establish that candidates admitted under reserved quotas generally lag behind in the matter of marks or proficiency in the final examinations. They may enter under different categories but they come out as one single class. * * *

9. We are unable to appreciate the argument of detriment to the interests of society. As we have said hereinbefore, there is no distinction in the matter of passing the examination. No one will be passed unless he acquires the requisite level of proficiency. Secondly, the academic performance is no guarantee of efficiency in practice. We have seen both in law and medicine that persons with brilliant academic record do not succeed in practice while students who were supposed to be less intelligent come out successful in profession/practice. It is, therefore,, wrong to presume that a doctor with good academic record is bound to prove a better doctor in practice. It may happen or may not.

———

NOTES

1. For more on this topic, *see* Marc Galanter, Competing Equalities: Law and the Backward Classes in India (1984); Sunita Parikh, THE POLITICS OF PREFERENCE: DEMOCRATIC INSTITUTIONS AND AFFIRMATIVE ACTION IN THE UNITED STATES AND INDIA (1997); Laura Dudley Jenkins, IDENTITY AND IDENTIFICATION IN INDIA (2003); Thomas E. Weisskopf, Affirmative Action in the United States and India (2004).

2. On December 22, 2005 the Indian Parliament amended the Constitution of India to allow admissions preferences at nearly all colleges, including private colleges that receive no government aid. *See* THE CHRONICLE OF HIGHER EDUCATION, January 3, 2006. However, the amendment was not self-executing, so state and federal governments had to pass legislation to implement reservations in private institutions. Kevin D. Brown & Vinay Sitapati, *Lessons Learned From Comparing the Application of Constitutional Law and Federal Anti–Discrimination Law to African–Americans in the U.S. and Dalits in India in the Context of Higher Education*, 24 HARV. BLACKLETTER L.J. 3, 46. As of 2011, the federal government has not passed a law that establishes reservations in private institutions. Kerala and Uttar Pradesh have established reservations in private institutions, but these laws are being challenged in court. Akshaya Mukul, *Centre supports UP's law on quota in private institutes*, TIMES OF INDIA, Mar. 26, 2010.

3. Justice Reddy draws a distinction between the Indian Constitution, which provides for both "equality before the law" and "equal protection of the laws," and the U.S. Constitution, which provides only the latter. Do you find it convincing?

4. In its affirmative action decisions, the Indian Supreme Court extensively discusses equal protection decisions of the U.S. Supreme Court.

Are they authoritative as to the meaning of the Indian Constitution? Would you expect to see the U.S. Supreme Court discuss decisions of the Indian Supreme Court? The question of when (or even whether) U.S. courts should consider non-U.S. decisions has stirred considerable controversy recently. *See, e.g.,* David M. Herszenhorn, *Court Nominee Criticized as Relying on Foreign Law,* NY TIMES, June 25, 2008, http://www.nytimes.com/2009/06/26/us/ politics/26sessions.html; Ganesh Sitaraman, *The Use and Abuse of Foreign Law in Constitutional Interpretation,* 32 H.V.J.L.P.P. 653 (Spring, 2009); Jacob Foster, *The Use of Foreign Law in Constitutional Interpretation: Lessons from South Africa,* 45 U.S.F.L.R. 79 (Summer, 2010); Daniel J. Frank, *Constitutional Interpretation Revisited: the Effects of a Delicate Supreme Court Balance on the Inclusion of Foreign Law in American Jurisprudence,* 92 I.A.L.R. 1037 (March, 2007).

5.   The "creamy layer" exception applies to individuals who have attained a certain level of income or acquired a certain amount of property even though they technically come from castes designated as backward; this exception allows the Indian government to exclude them from the benefits of reservation.

6.   In *Meera Kanwaria v. Sunita and Others,* AIR 2006 SC 597, 2006 1 SCC 344, a woman from the Rajput caste (a higher caste) married a man from a scheduled caste, and thereafter ran for public office (the municipal counsel), seeking a seat reserved for members of the scheduled castes. Although by marrying a member of a scheduled caste she had taken on his social status, the Indian Supreme Court held that she was ineligible for the reserved seat, because the reservation was intended to compensate for disadvantages she had not suffered, having been born in a "forward caste." Should reservations only apply to those who lived through certain experiences illustrative of a protected group? Should the "creamy layer" exception extend not only to those who are wealthy members of a protected class, but also those who had a life experience atypical of that caste? Where is the line drawn?

7.   How does public reaction to affirmative action in the United States compare to the public reaction to the proposed expansion of reservation in India in 1990? Cunningham notes that this reaction included protests and instances of self-immolation. Although former Prime Minister V.P. Singh has called for a referendum on reservation in India, it has not yet come to pass. *Face the Nation:Reservation row,* IBN LIVE, June 19, 2007, http://ibnlive.in.com/news/face-the-nation-reservation-row/37311–3.html.   How does the unavailability of state-level referendums like Proposition 209 and the more limited economic opportunities compared to America modulate public reaction to reservation in India?

8.   In *Thakur v. Union of India,* 2007 (5) SCALE 179; (2007) 4 SCC 361, the Indian Supreme Court re-affirmed that a 50 percent reservation of jobs and higher education placements for "socially and educationally backward classes of society" is reasonable, and that the "creamy layer" should be excluded from those eligible for reservations.

9.   Would U.S. opponents of affirmative action be less critical of current U.S. policies if U.S. affirmative action policies had a "creamy layer" exception? Many of these critics complain that most U.S. minority

students benefitting from affirmative action are from the U.S. equivalent of a creamy layer, and that affirmative action thus fails to serve those for whom it is needed. For example, Stephan and Abigail Thernstrom, in AMERICA IN BLACK AND WHITE, argue that 64 percent of Black students at highly selective colleges have at least one parent who graduated from college, while only 14 percent of Black students at highly selective colleges came from poor families in which neither parent attended college. Should anyone with a parent who graduated from college be considered a member of the creamy layer? Bowen and Bok, in THE SHAPE OF THE RIVER, argue that only 2 percent of the White students at the most selective schools came from poor families where neither parent attended college. And, 15 percent of white students, but only 3 percent of Black students, came from the highest socio-economic group. Thomas Weisskopf, In AFFIRMATIVE ACTION IN THE UNITED STATES AND INDIA, concludes that even without a creamy layer exception, "admitting more Blacks and fewer White applicants to selective schools redistributes educational opportunities from better-off to less well-off students rather than the other way around." Thomas Weisskopf, AFFIRMATIVE ACTION IN THE UNITED STATES AND INDIA (Routledge 2004) at 144.

10. Could one argue that African Americans in the United States are in a similar position to the SC/STs in India? Are other minority groups that benefit from affirmative action but have not faced the same history of social exclusion comparable to India's OBCs? Some scholars, like Pratap Mehta, argue that to lump Other Backward Classes into the same narrative of social exclusion as that of the Scheduled Castes/Tribes is disingenuous, and that the same policies should not be used for both categories. *See* Pratap Bhanu Mehta, *Dear Prime Minister*, INDIAN EXPRESS (May 23, 2009), http://www.indianexpress.com/news/dear-prime-minister/4916/.

D. FRANCE

The founding document of the French Republic, comparable to (and influenced by) the U.S. Declaration of Independence, is the Declaration of the Rights of Man and Citizen, adopted by the French National Assembly on August 26, 1789. It forms the first articles of the current (1958) French Constitution. It declares:

Article 1—Men are born and remain free and equal in rights.

Article 6—Law must be the same for all, both when it protects and punishes. All citizens being equal before the law, they shall have equal access to all honors, public positions and employments, depending on their merits and without other distinctions than those resulting from their virtues and talents.

How should we expect French law to grapple with affirmative (or positive) action based on race, ethnicity or religion? Does the Constitutional provision quoted above require formal equality, or does it permit remedial efforts that treat people differently to promote substantive equality?

The "Sciences Po" Decision of Le Conseil Consitutionnel

Decision No. 2001–450 cd.—July 11, 2001
http://www.conseil-constitutionnel.fr/decision/2001/2001450/2001450dc.htm

■ THE CONSTITUTIONAL COUNCIL—(OR CONSTITUTIONAL COURT)—OF THE REPUBLIC OF FRANCE

* * * [We are asked to review a statute amending the Education Code to provide that] "the Directing Council of the Institute of Political Studies of Paris may determine ... conditions and procedures for admission to the Institute.... It may adopt admission procedures ... comprising methods intended to ensure diversified recruitment among students.... The admission procedures may be implemented by way of agreements concluded with high schools or higher, French and foreign ...";

Considering that under the thirteenth subparagraph of the Preamble to the Constitution of 1946: "the Nation guarantees equal access of children and adults to instruction ...";

Considering that, if it is permissible for the legislature to amend the Education Code in order to allow diversification of access for students to enter the Institute of Political Studies of Paris, it is with the condition that the methods used for this purpose under the amended Code, by the Directing Council of the Institute, will rest on objective criteria likely to guarantee respect for the constitutional requirement of equal access to education; that, under this reserve, the amendment is in conformity with the Constitution; * * *

————

Affirmative Action at Sciences Po

(Institut D'études Politiques De Paris)
French Politics, Culture and Society, Fall 2002 v20 i3 p52–58

■ DANIEL SABBAGH

In the United States, the expression "affirmative action" generally refers to a wide array of measures set up at the end of the 1960s by executive agencies and the federal judiciary. These measures grant some (more or less flexible) kind of preferential treatment in the allocation of scarce resources—jobs, university admissions and government contracts—to the members of groups formerly targeted for legal discrimination (African Americans, Hispanics, Native Americans, women, sometimes Asians). In France, by contrast, the main operational criterion for identifying the beneficiaries of affirmative action policies (in French, "discrimination positive") is not race or gender, but geographical location: residents of a socioeconomically disadvantaged area will indirectly benefit from the additional input of financial resources allocated by state agencies to that area as a whole. In this respect, the first affirmative action plan recently designed in the sphere of higher education by one of France's most famous *grandes écoles*, the Institut d'études politiques de Paris, while not departing significantly from this broader pattern of redistributive, territory-based public policies, has given rise to a controversy of an unprecedented scale, some features of which may actually suggest the existence of a deeper similarity between French and American affirmative action programs—and the difficulties that they face.

The Program and the Attending Controversy

Heir to the École libre des sciences politiques founded by Émile Boutmy in 1872 to provide for the Third Republic's political and administrative elites, the Institut d'études politiques de Paris (also known as Sciences Po), a publicly Financed—though largely autonomous—selective institution of higher education, has been performing that mission ever since. Partly because it imparts the training required for taking the admission exam of the even more prestigious École nationale d'administration, its alumni include two of the past three French presidents (Valéry Giscard d'Estaing and Jacques Chirac), six of the past eight prime ministers, and also half of the chief executives of France's top 200 companies. Eighty percent of Sciences Po graduates are now employed in the private sector, with the remaining twenty percent unevenly divided between public administration (fifteen percent) and the research and academic community (five percent).

Yet, just like in all other French *grandes écoles*—but even more so—Sciences Po's student body also displays a striking (and increasing) social homogeneity. Thus, according to a recent study based on 1998's admission data, 81.5 percent of the students came from the upper and upper-middle classes (up from 77 percent in 1987); 53.5 percent had parents who were upper-level management or academics, and 28 percent had parents who were professionals or entrepreneurs. Less than one percent of the students came from working-class backgrounds, as opposed to 12.5 percent of those enrolled at other, non-selective universities. On that basis, and with the full support of Jack Lang, the Socialist government's education minister, the director of Sciences Po, Richard Descoings, by way of experiment, decided to create a special admission track for the students of seven high schools located in economically disadvantaged areas ("zones d'éducation prioritaire," or ZEP), with a view to "diversifying and democratizing" the school's admission process. Instead of having to take the competitive exam imposed on all other applicants, those students were asked to write two papers—one a synthesis of several press articles collected on a chosen topic, the other an analytical essay on that same subject—and defend them before a jury made up of teachers and administrators of their high school. Then, the best candidates were invited for an interview at Sciences Po itself. Those who received an admission offer at the end of the day were also provided with financial aid, as well as with a specific kind of tutoring (available on an optional basis) to help them adjust to their new educational environment. In the fall of 2001, eighteen ZEP students were thus admitted to Sciences Po.

As one might have expected, this group of students has several distinctive features. First, its economic profile is clearly different from that of the student body as a whole, a fact all the more noticeable since there was no guarantee that the individuals eventually selected from this specific pool of candidates would turn out to be personally disadvantaged. Thus, in 2001–2002, while the children whose parents were *ouvriers* or *employés* made up only 0.5 percent and 2.5 percent respectively of the students admitted to Sciences Po after taking the "traditional" entrance exam, they comprised 16.5 percent and 34 percent of those admitted through this new affirmative action program. Second, although Sciences Po insists that the admission rates in the two populations of applicants are roughly comparable (11.5 percent for those taking the exam, 19 percent for the ZEP students), there is a substantial gap between their levels of academic performance as measured by the grades and distinctions obtained at the *baccalauréat*, a gap that underlines the existing tension between the corrective dimension of the project and the meritocratic principle strictly conceived. But that is only one dimension of the wide-ranging controversy raised by this program—to which I now turn.

Leaving aside the unsavory—or flatly abusive—comments made by a few of its opponents, Science Po's initiative has been criticized on several grounds. For one thing, many people believe that any departure from the practice of universal competitive entrance examinations to selective institutions of higher education is inherently unfair and contrary to the principle of equal treatment as understood within the French republican conception of citizenship. Some also object to the additional inequality inherent in the selection of the high schools involved, whose students will thus be given an advantage over other poor-neighborhood residents. Others fear that the existence of this separate admission track will actually prove detrimental to its intended beneficiaries and cast a cloud of suspicion over their academic achievements, leading employers to draw new distinctions among the population of Sciences Po graduates and to dismiss the degrees earned by the ZEP students as a less certain certificate of quality—despite the fact that, in theory, these students would have received exactly the same training and fulfilled the same requirements as their peers. Another, supposedly more "radical," criticism, voiced by some left-wing student unions such as the Union Nationale des Étudiants de France, advocates helping the ZEP students acquire the skills that would give them a better chance of successfully participating in a meritocratic game whose rules could thus remain identical for all participants. They denounce this affirmative action program as a cheap substitute for the much more demanding changes required—namely, a modification in the nature of the entrance exam that would take into account the unequal distribution of cultural resources among Sciences Po applicants.

The proponents of the project, on the other hand, argue that, even aside from the extra opportunity enjoyed by the individuals who will actually gain admission to Sciences Po as a result of this reform, the simple prospect of being in a position to do so may well work to stimulate the ambitions of many more ZEP students by enlarging the set of options that they will perceive to be within their reach, thus triggering a chain reaction that might eventually lead to a general improvement in their educational achievements. From another, quite different perspective, Richard Descoings and several members of Sciences Po's governing council also emphasize the specific "political, social, and moral responsibility" entailed by that institution's role in training tomorrow's government and business elites, whose future decision-making power over other citizens' lives requires that they become aware of the diversity of contemporary French society before reaching such distinguished positions. For the "recruitment by caste and class" of French *grandes écoles* in general and Sciences Po in particular necessarily stands as a dangerous anomaly in a democratic regime, which needs "to diversify the social origin of its elites" in order for them to preserve their own legitimacy. In that respect, and in the long run, the project may thus help consolidate the existing political order.

Affirmative Action *À La Francaise*: How Different Is It?

In some ways, Sciences Po's affirmative action program is clearly different from American ones. First, since it does not entail any decrease in the number of places reserved for the "traditional" candidates entering on the basis of exam scores coupled with the usual interview, an individual belonging to the vast majority of *non-beneficiaries* can hardly claim to be a *victim* of the program. While many people will still reject it on grounds of principle, it will be more difficult than in the United States for anyone to argue that he or she was personally disadvantaged by the additional creation of a few slots reserved for ZEP students. Second, and most important, because Article 1 of the 1958 French Constitution provides that "the Republic [. . .] guarantees the equality of all citizens in the eyes of the law, regardless of origin, race or religion," race is not supposed to play any part in the process leading to the identification of the program's actual beneficiaries. As a matter of fact, in France, only those who oppose the reform openly discuss what they consider to be its unspoken racial subtext (for reasons to be discussed below), while its supporters usually avoid the topic altogether by pretending not to notice that a substantial proportion of ZEP residents are also of North African extraction. Strikingly enough, both sides seem to agree on viewing the American experience of race-based affirmative action policies (*"discrimination positive"*) in a negative light, as a too risky—or straightforwardly repulsive—model, from which one ought to remain as distant as possible.

To be sure, the Sciences Po program is clearly predicated upon an acknowledgment of the "adverse impact" that the traditional exam has on candidates from underprivileged backgrounds and on the need to reduce the resulting discrepancy, thus relying implicitly on the American-born notion of *indirect discrimination*, as defined in the 1971 US Supreme Court decision, *Griggs v. Duke Power Company*. But here again, there are also major differences. First, for the reason mentioned above, only groups defined on an economic and occupational—but not ethno-racial—basis will be (indirectly) targeted for this kind of small-scale compensation. In the United States, it is just the opposite: as a practical matter, only women, racial minorities and the disabled may be protected against indirect discrimination. Second, contrary to what the *Griggs* standard would prescribe in the American context, acknowledging that the Sciences Po entrance exam has a disparate impact on students living in economically and culturally impoverished neighborhoods does not lead to the more drastic conclusion that, instead of being supplemented by a corrective scheme of some kind, it ought simply to be eliminated and replaced by other, equally functional but disparate-impact-free procedures, since those are considered not to exist. Last but not least—and partly because doing otherwise would seem to compel that unwanted conclusion—, the proponents of this affirmative action program (identified as such by most French and foreign newspapers) not only reject the suggestion that it has anything to do with "discrimination positive" as they (mis)understand it, but they also refrain from making any connection between their initiative and the emerging policy debate over the broader issue of "negative" discrimination and how to fight it. This may be due to either lack of information about this debate or, more probably, their belief that the very notion of "discrimination" runs the risk of calling to mind the—socially salient but legally nonexistent—ethno-racial features of many ZEP residents.

Indeed, since one of the main criteria used for delineating a ZEP—the rate of failure in high school—is itself correlated with the proportion of children whose parents are foreign nationals, the Sciences Po program, although officially embodying an area-based and class-based approach of affirmative action, may also be understood as indirectly and implicitly targeting groups that, in the American context, would be considered as "ethnic" or "racial" groups, in particular, second-generation North African immigrants. It may then seem at least plausible to read this formally color-blind policy as partaking of a "hidden agenda" specially directed at accelerating the integration of these immigrants through an ingenious "substitution strategy." In this light, the Sciences Po initiative—as well as the urban development policies ("la politique de la ville") that are also typical of affirmative action à la francaise—would simply work as an (admittedly imperfect) functional equivalent of the openly color-conscious US affirmative action programs, insofar as they do have an expected, positive disparate impact on individuals of North African extraction.

Besides, even if one rules out this last hypothesis and takes at face value the denials by Sciences Po officials of any infringement on the republican principle of color blindness, another striking similarity between U.S. and French affirmative action policies lies in the attempts made by their supporters to systematically minimize any negative side effects on their beneficiaries' public image potentially induced by the visibility of such programs. Supporters play down the unusualness of the measures involved and deliberately de-emphasize their antimeritocratic component. * * *

Thus, the goal is clearly to downplay the peculiarity of the program involved as perceived by both Sciences Po students and faculty and the general public. School officials apparently believe that this requires them to emphasize any feature that may seem to sharpen the distinction between their program and the American "counter-model," even though in the United States, affirmative action in admissions to selective universities actually may *not* use explicit quotas for racial minorities. In addition, more specific steps were taken to alleviate any stigmatizing effect that the program might have on its intended beneficiaries as far as their perceived ability to meet Science Po's standard academic requirements is concerned. For instance, in order to counter in advance any suggestion as to the lack of seriousness of the admission process designed for ZEP students, a decision was made that the committees in charge of the final interviews would comprise six members instead of three. Interestingly enough, it was also decided not to inform faculty members of whether one or several of their own students had been admitted as a result of that new program, in order to ensure that then would not consciously or unconsciously indulge in and kind of (negative or positive) discriminatory treatment towards them.

Yet within a French–American comparative framework, the most salient feature of Sciences Po's rhetoric in defending the reform remains its reliance on the equivocal notion of "diversity." Thus, the very title of the program is "Conventions ZEP: L'excellence dans la diversité,".... One cannot but notice how similar these arguments are to the position eventually endorsed by the US Supreme Court in the 1978 *Regents of the University of California v. Bakke* decision, where Justice Lewis Powell declared that, as a practical matter, race and ethnicity could be taken into account in university admissions only insofar as this reflected a legitimate concern for increasing the diversity of "experiences, outlooks and ideas' among members of the student body.

Moreover, a case can be made that, in both instances, this emphasis on the benefits of social and cultural pluralism actually served the same purpose: to legitimize a highly controversial kind of affirmative action by linking it to a pre-existing pattern of academic institutions possessing enough discretionary power to select students according to the requirements of diversity promotion. Thus, on the American side, the argument was that, just as diversity in the applicants' geographical origins as well as in their academic and extracurricular interests and talents was usually considered in admission decisions, racial diversity should be viewed as one more component of the kind of global diversity traditionally favored by university officials. On the French side, Sciences Po's spokespersons also attempted to defuse the issue by pretending to include the fact of coming from a ZEP into a larger set of supposedly similar, diversity-increasing characteristics, such as entering Sciences Po after having earned another B.A.-level degree instead of just after the *baccalauréat*, or being a foreign student.

But these legitimization strategies, designed in part to minimize *ex ante* some of the expected negative side effects of the project at hand, have their own costs as well. Thus, from a symbolic point of view, it may not be such a wise idea for the proponents of the program to ground one of its main justifications—the "diversity" argument—on this bizarre analogy between ZEP students and foreign students. For not only are a vast majority of ZEP students full-fledged French citizens, but the fact that a fair number of them often are not treated as such on account of their foreign (North African) extraction is precisely one of the factors that account for their being disadvantaged in the first place. Therefore, a policy that seems to incorporate an assumption that ZEP students are actually quite similar to foreign students—in their proclaimed (but less obviously explainable) inability to enter Sciences Po without a specific admission track being instituted to that end—does run the risk of indirectly reinforcing their perceived "deficiency" of some kind as compared to non-ZEP French students, a "deficiency" upon which other, more far-reaching and less benign, discriminating practices are also predicated. * * *

NOTES

1.   For more on the Science Po plan, and the controversy it stirred, *see* Craig S. Smith, *Elite French Schools Block the Poor's Path to Power*, NY TIMES, Dec. 18, 2005; Aisha Labi, *Lessons From—Quelle Horreur!—les Américains: France's venerable political-science institute adopts controversial reforms*, THE CHRONICLE OF HIGHER EDUCATION, Sept. 2, 2005. By 2006, over 250 students had entered Science Po through their affirmative action program, with the number rising from 17 in the first year to 75 in 2006. Four other elite schools have started similar admissions programs. *See* Anita Joshua, *A French Experiment in Affirmative Action*, THE HINDU, Feb. 3, 2007. By 2010, the program had spread throughout the French Republic, reaching thousands of students. *See,* Steven Erlanger, *Top French Schools, Asked to Diversify, Fear for Standards*, NY TIMES, June 30, 2010, p. 1, http://www.nytimes.com/2010/07/01/world/europe/01ecoles.html?scp=1& sq=Sciences% 20Po&st=cse.

2.   The size of the minority population of France is unknown, because it is a violation of French law for the government to collect data about race or ethnicity. But a significant number of French residents, many of whom are French citizens, would be described as "people of color" or "non-white" in the United States. Many of them are the descendants of residents of French territories and colonies in North Africa (sometimes called the "Maghreb"), and are often Muslim. Others, who are descended from residents of Sub–Saharan Africa, and the Caribbean, are Black. Whether they are French-born citizens of France, whose ancestors moved to France generations ago, or new arrivals, they are commonly described as "immigrants." What significance, if any, should we attribute to describing French citizens as "immigrants?"

3.   A survey released in January 2007 revealed that 56 percent of French adults who described themselves as Black said they suffered from discrimination, with 37 percent saying the situation had become worse in the past year. It was the first such poll ever conducted in France. "If you're not counted, you don't count," explained Patrick Lozes, head of the Representative Council of Black Associations in France, which commissioned the poll. *See* Lisa Bryant, *Survey: Blacks in France Say They Face Racial Discrimination*, VOICE OF AMERICA NEWS, Feb. 2, 2007.

4.   Azouz Begag, the Chirac government's minister for equal opportunities (and the first descendent from North African immigrants to join the French cabinet), called for amending the French census to measure diversity. *See* Katrin Bennhold, *French Minister Urges Collecting Minority Data*, INTERNATIONAL HERALD TRIBUNE, December 15, 2005. In 2007, a bill to permit the French census to collect such data for the purpose of measuring inequality was passed by the French Parliament, but ruled unconstitutional by the Constitutional Council. CC decision no. 2007–557DC, Nov. 15, 2007, J.O. Nov. 21, 2007 p. 19001.

5.   The 2005 riots in and around Paris ignited a great debate about race, ethnicity, discrimination, the legitimacy of racial identity, data collection, diversity and affirmative action throughout France. Presidential candidate Nicolas Sarkozy called for affirmative action in the form of scholar-

ships and recruitment of minorities for jobs and education. President Jacques Chirac objected to Sarkozy's plan, calling it an unjust system of quotas. In response to a suggestion that private companies consider diversity in their hiring decisions, Gereard Larcher, the Chirac government's deputy minister for employment, remarked that "companies are not the Salvation Army." *See* Thomas Fuller, *A Loud 'Non' to Quotas Based on Race*, INTERNATIONAL HERALD TRIBUNE, November 15, 2005. But in 2006, a group of French companies, now numbering over 3,000, signed a "Diversity Charter." The signatories agree, in charter section 3, to "endeavor to reflect the diversity of the French society particularly in its cultural and ethnic dimension at every level of our workforce." *See Charte de la Diversite en Enterprise*, http://www.diversity-charter.com/index.php. Many of the largest companies of France are signatories. May we conclude from this that there is a widespread commitment to what Americans would call voluntary affirmative action in employment throughout France?

6. The diversity charter movement has spread across Europe. German companies adopted a charter in 2006. Austria, Italy, Spain, and Sweden followed in 2009. In 2010, Belgium adopted three, one each for Wallonia, Flanders, and Brussels. Does the adoption of three diversity charters for one country suggest a certain lack of clarity on the concept, or is it simply the political necessity of a country divided by language?

7. For other articles discussing discrimination, affirmative action and diversity in France, *see* Craig S. Smith, *France is Trying, Discretely, To Integrate Television A Bit*, NEW YORK TIMES, Nov. 16, 2005; Elaine Sciolino, *Appointment Of Arab Prefect Fans French Angst Over Affirmative Action*, INTERNATIONAL HERALD TRIBUNE, Jan. 15, 2004; John Tagliabue, *French Lesson: Taunts on Race Can Boomerang*, NEW YORK TIMES, Sept. 21, 2005; Craig S. Smith, *France Has an Underclass, but Its Roots Are Still Shallow*, NEW YORK TIMES, Nov. 6, 2005; Craig S. Smith, *Paris Journal: Poor and Muslim? Jewish? Soup Kitchen Is Not for You*; NEW YORK TIMES, Feb. 28, 2006.

8. In the Trentino Alto–Adige region of Italy, along the Austrian border, a system called "proporzionale etnica" ("ethnic proportion") provides proportional guarantees to German-speakers whose citizenship changed from Austrian to Italian as part of the settlement of World War II. *See* Costanza Hermanin, *'Counts' in the Italian 'nomad camps': an incautious ethnic census of Roma*, ETHNIC AND RACIAL STUDIES 2011 (Routledge) 1–20, at 10. Should we regard this form of ethno-linguistic proportional representation system as a form of affirmative action?

E. BRAZIL

Brazil is a self-described "racial democracy" in which equality is a founding principal of the modern state. An estimated 70 percent of Brazil's universities have adopted affirmative action programs for Black and mixed-race students, and the courts and legislature are actively debating the legality of affirmative action.

All Things Being Equal: The Promise of Affirmative Efforts to Eradicate Color–Coded Inequality in the United States and Brazil

21 National Black Law Journal 1, 9–10, 34–35 (2009)

■ TANYA MONIQUE WASHINGTON

While Brazil and the United States share a history of the enslavement of African captives and the conquest of indigenous populations, the two nations had very different slavery and post-slavery experiences. From 1532 to 1888 Brazil imported an estimated 4 million African captives, earning it the distinction as the largest slave economy in the world. "The centrality of slavery to Brazil's economy gradually diminished with the ending of the slave trade in 1853." The enactment of the Law of the Free Womb in 1871 hastened the end of slavery by freeing the children of slave women when they turned 21 years of age. By 1888, when Brazil became the last nation to abolish slavery, its slave population outnumbered whites by almost 2–to–1. Foreshadowing Brazil's reputation as a Racial Democracy in which blacks, mulattoes and whites lived under conditions of equality, the key author of the 1891 Constitution "ordered the burning of all documentation related to the slave trade, thereby erasing what he considered to be a shameful chapter of Brazil's history. . . ."

The prospect of freedom for the slaves inspired insecurity among white Brazilians, and created the need for structures and policies that would maintain their status as the ruling elite. Responding to this exigency, the Brazilian government engaged in large scale immigration of European whites and encouraged miscegenation in order to improve the racial balance between blacks and whites. The "whitening" of the Brazilian population, through miscegenation, was believed to have a civilizing effect on the Brazilian population of observable African ancestry and reinforced normative whiteness (i.e., whiteness as the value standard). A popular slogan of the day, "Marry White to Improve the Race," captured the pervasive sentiment. * * *

The Brazilian Constitution characterizes equality as an inviolable right; authorizes government action to achieve equality; and establishes racial discrimination as a crime punishable by incarceration, for which bail may not be posted, and to which no statute of limitations applies. The Constitution also characterizes education as a social right to which all are equally entitled.

———

NOTES

1. Despite the claim of racial democracy, statistics and sociological studies reveal a long legacy of racial/color inequality. Overall, approximately 50 percent of Brazilians now describe themselves as white, and fewer than 7 percent describe themselves as Black. Most of the rest are mixed-race, with less than 1 percent descended from the indigenous people who were present before the colonial period. Fewer than 3 percent of Brazil's

university students are Black, and a minority is of mixed racial descent. Other indicia also point to ongoing discrimination, and in the early Twenty–First Century Brazil began to experiment with affirmative action in higher education. *See* Andrew Downie and Marion Lloyd, *At Brazil's Universities, Affirmative Action Faces Crucial Tests*, THE CHRONICLE OF HIGHER EDUCATION, August 1, 2010, http://chronicle.com/article/At–Brazils–Universities/123720.

2. "One of the most striking features of income inequality in Brazil is the large socioeconomic discrepancy between population groups based on skin colour. As a result of three and a half centuries of a slavery-based economy, Brazil has the second largest population of people of African descent after Nigeria. They account for almost one-half of all Brazilians: there were 11.6 million pretos (blacks) and 79.6 million pardos (persons of mixed race) in a total population of 184.4 million in 2005. Despite the absence of legally-sanctioned racism since slavery was abolished in 1888, this system has left a legacy of social discrimination against Afro–Brazilians, who are more likely to be members of socially disadvantaged groups. Indeed, the 2005 UNDP report specified the indicator for human development for Brazil in 2000 separately for each race. Whites alone (0.814) were placed among those countries with the highest human development level, ranking 44th (between Costa Rica and Kuwait), while Afro–Brazilians (0.703) fell in an intermediate group, ranking 105th (between El Salvador and Moldova). According to the main Brazilian household survey, the Pesquisa Nacional por Amostra de Domicílios, the mean per-capita income of Afro–Brazilians was only half that of whites. Furthermore, in 2005 about 33 percent of Afro–Brazilians lived in poor households whose incomes were below 50 percent of the median income of the country, in contrast to 14 percent of whites falling into this group." Carlos Gradin, WHY IS POVERTY SO HIGH AMONG AFRO-BRAZILIANS? (Universidade de Vigo, 2008); *see also*, Tanya M. Washington *supra* at 28. Should the UNDP rank human development for the United States separately for each race?

3. Tanya Katerí Hernández writes, "In December 2000 and September 2001, Rio de Janeiro was the first state in Brazil to enact a set of laws establishing that fifty percent of state university entrance admissions would be reserved for public high school graduates (most of whom are of Afro–Brazilian descent). Thereafter, the law was modified to establish an outright quota of forty percent for top scoring 'Black/negra' or 'brown/parda' students and a ten percent quota for students with disabilities. The affirmative action policy was initially challenged before the Supreme Federal Court of Brazil by a state legislator and an association of private schools (CONFENEN) as a violation of the Brazilian constitutional provision for proportionality in the exercise of legislative discretion ('razoabilidade'). This lawsuit was ruled moot when the state legislature revised the policy in September 2003, to establish the more limited quotas of twenty percent for self-declared 'Blacks/negras,' twenty percent for public school students, and five percent for other disabled students and indigenous Brazilians in total. In addition, all students admitted under the new policy had to meet financial eligibility requirements. This revised affirmative action policy was then challenged in court once again." Tanya Katerí Hernández, *To Be*

Brown in Brazil: Education and Segregation Latin American Style, 29 N.Y.U. REV. L. & SOC. CHANGE 683, 699 (2005).

4. Additional affirmative action programs from the universities of Brasilia and of Rio Grande do Sul were subsequently brought to court and as of June 2011 are pending before the Brazilian Supreme Court, which held extensive hearings on the matter in March 2010. Cases reference: ADPF 186/09 and Recurso Extraordinário 597.285/RS.

5. "An interesting aspect of the Brazilian approach to affirmative action is that, different from the United States, its justification consistently emphasizes the constitutional principle of equality (*isonomia*), which mandates compensation for the past discrimination that created current racial inequalities. This has been true from the outset; in his legislative proposals, Abdias do Nascimento [a former senator, and prominent Afro–Brazilian scholar and artist] preferred the term *compensatory action* to affirmative action. The idea is to implement the constitutional principle of equality by paying what former Supreme Federal Tribunal President Mello (2001) calls 'historical debts' owned by the Brazilian State to social minorities, in particular African Brazilians." Sérgio Da Silva Martins, Carlos Alberto Medeiros, Elisa Larkin Nascimento, *Paving Paradise: The Road From "Racial Democracy" to Affirmative Action in Brazil*, JOURNAL OF BLACK STUDIES, Vol. 34, No. 6 (Jul. 2004), p. 811.

6. The Superior Tribunal de Justiça ("STJ"), Brazil's high court which hears all cases except constitutional law matters, has decided numerous cases involving affirmative action. In a notable case brought against the Chancellor of the teaching hospital at the State University of West Paraná (UNIOESTE), the STJ upheld a state law which reserved quotas for persons of African descent ("afro-descendentes") seeking public service positions at the hospital. In its opinion, the STJ defended quotas as consistent with Brazil's National Affirmative Action Program and deemed such quotas legal in the areas of federal employment, public service, and university admissions. *See*, Christopher DiSchino, *Affirmative Action in Brazil: Reverse Discrimination and the Creation of a Constitutionally Protected Color–Line*, 17 U. MIAMI INT'L & COMP. L. REV. 155 (Spring 2010).

F. AFFIRMATIVE ACTION IN EMPLOYMENT

Most of this chapter has focused on affirmative action in higher education. This section provides a few notes on the topic of affirmative action in employment.

NOTES

1. In the United States, the Supreme Court has allowed private employers (and public employers in suits limited to Title VII) to engage in

race-based and gender-based affirmative action, subject to certain limitations. Plans are permitted if (1) limited in time, (2) established to correct a manifest imbalance in the workplace, (3) without using quotas, and (4) without requiring that white male workers be fired or deprived of settled expectations. *See United Steelworkers of America v. Weber*, 443 U.S. 193 (1979) and *Johnson v. Transportation Agency, Santa Clara County*, 480 U.S. 616 (1987).

2. U.S. public employers may adopt affirmative action employment plans only if they comply with the requirements of the Fourteenth Amendment. The leading Supreme Court decision on point produced a fractured majority, with 5 separate opinions. See *Wygant v. Jackson Board of Education*, 476 U.S. 267 (1986). The Court rejected a race-based teacher layoff plan, which preserved some jobs for Black teachers in a largely Black school district, either because the plan was not justified by "convincing evidence of prior discrimination" (Justices Powell, Burger and Rehnquist) or because the plan was not linked to the number of qualified Black teachers in the district (Justice O'Connor) or because none of the Black teachers whose jobs were protected had themselves been identified as victims of discrimination (Justice White). Wygant generally stated, and subsequent decisions involving public contracting have reiterated, that a state actor may only engage in race-based affirmative action in contracting if the plan is narrowly tailored to achieve a compelling governmental interest. *See Adarand Constructors v. Pena*, 515 U.S. 200 (1995) and *City of Richmond v. J.A. Croson Co.*, 488 U.S. 469 (1989).

3. Many U.S. employers, public and private, engage in "diversity management" to promote racial, ethnic, gender and gender identity diversity in their workforce. They use targeted outreach, mentoring, diversity training and other techniques to increase their hiring and promotion of women and minorities (and increasingly, of LGBT employees). Diversity management has become increasingly popular in Europe as well. For example, over 3,000 French companies, including many of the largest in the country, have signed a diversity pledge. *See*, http://www.diversity-charter. com/index.php.

4. The French labor code (Art. 323–1) requires employers of 20 or more employees meet a 6 percent quota, employing as a minimum of 6 percent of its workers persons with disabilities. Many European countries have similar arrangements in their legislation. This is regarded, however, as social welfare legislation, not civil rights or non-discrimination legislation. It is premised on the idea that it is costly to employ people who have disabilities, and that the cost should be spread evenly.

5. In the European Union, one of its founding documents, the 1957 Treaty of Rome, required the then-six member states (Belgium, Germany, France, Italy, Luxembourg, and the Netherlands) to provide for gender equality regarding pay (Art. 119). At the time of its adoption, the Union was primarily an economic institution (then known as the "European Economic Community" and often described in the U.S. as the "common market"); the purpose of the gender equality requirement was to reduce unfair competition between member states, and thus assure economic equality between them.

6. In the ensuing years, the institutions of the EU have taken an increasingly assertive role in promoting gender equality in the workplace. In 1976 the Council of the European Communities issued Directive 76/207/EEC permitting "measures to promote equal opportunity for men and women, in particular by removing existing inequalities which affect women's opportunities." In 1984 the Council explicitly recommended that member states engage in "positive action policies" to "promote a better balance between the sexes in employment." *See* Recommendation 84/635/EEC on the promotion of positive action for women. The 1997 Treaty of Amsterdam elevated the importance of gender equality, declaring that one of the major tasks of the then called "European Community" was the promotion of equality between men and women (new Art. 2 of the EC Treaty). The 2000 European Union Charter of Fundamental Rights provides that gender equality is a fundamental right (Art. 23) and permits positive action to promote gender equality, providing that "the principle of equality shall not prevent the maintenance or adoption of measures providing for specific advantages in favour of the under-represented sex." (Art. 23.2). The importance of gender equality was further reinforced in December 2009, with the entry into force of the Treaty of Lisbon. The latter inserted the new Art. 8 of the Treaty on the Functioning of the European Union, which provides that "in all its activities, the Union shall aim to eliminate inequalities and to promote equality, between men and women."

7. Pursuant to these provisions, beginning in 1997 the European Court of Justice has upheld gender-based affirmative action plans as a means of promoting equality between men and women. *See, Marschall v. Land Nordrhein–Westfalen*, C–409/95, ECJ 11 November 1997; *George Badeck and others*, C–158/97, ECJ 28 March 2000. The court has upheld gender preferences, while disallowing absolute quotas. The relevant measure which gives priority to women has to fulfill certain conditions. It must (1) concern a labor sector where women are under-represented; (2) the concerned women and men should be equally qualified; (3) the priority given to women can not be automatic and unconditional, and (4) the candidates must be subject to an objective assessment which takes account of the specific personal situations of all candidates. *See Katarina Abrahamsson, Lief Anderson and Elisabet Fogelqvist*, C–407/98, ECJ 6 July 2000 (paragraph 43).

8. The Court's justification for positive action, beginning with the *Hellmuth Marschall* case, was the need to remedy existing sex discrimination. The Court explained: "it appears that even where male and female candidates are equally qualified, male candidates tend to be promoted in preference to female candidates particularly because of prejudices and stereotypes concerning the role and capacities of women in working life and the fear, for example, that women will interrupt their careers more frequently, that owing to household and family duties they will be less flexible in their working hours, or that they will be absent from work more frequently because of pregnancy, childbirth and breastfeeding." (Par. 29). "For these reasons, the mere fact that a male candidate and a female candidate are equally qualified does not mean that they have the same chances." (Par. 30).

9. European Court of Justice decisions prior to the 1997 *Hellmuth Marschall* case were highly skeptical of positive action programs. In particular, in the *Kalanke* case, Case C–450/93 [1995] ECR I–3051, the Court rejected a German civil service preference for women. In response, the next revision of the treaties forming the E.U., the Amsterdam Treaty (1997), provided: "With a view to ensuring full equality in practice between men and women in working life, the principle of equal treatment shall not prevent any Member State from maintaining or adopting measures providing for specific advantages in order to make it easier for the underrepresented sex to pursue a vocational activity or to prevent or compensate for disadvantages in professional careers." Despite this language, some critics argue that the Court's subsequent decisions permit positive action as an exception to the principle of equality, rather than treating it as an instrument for creating equality.

10. In 2000, the European Union's then 15 member states unanimously adopted two equality directives. One concerned racial and ethnic equality, in all parts of life. (The Racial Equality Directive—EC Council Directive 2000/43/EC of 29 June 2000.) The other concerned employment equality, prohibiting discrimination based on religion or belief, disability, age or sexual orientation. (The Employment Equality Directive—EC Council Directive 2000/78/EC of 27 November 2000.) The 12 states that have joined the Union since 2000 have automatically come under the jurisdiction of these directives as well.

On positive action, The Racial Equality Directive provides:

Article 1—Purpose

The purpose of this Directive is to lay down a framework for combating discrimination on the grounds of racial or ethnic origin, with a view to putting into effect in the Member States the principle of equal treatment.

Article 5—Positive action

With a view to ensuring full equality in practice, the principle of equal treatment shall not prevent any Member State from maintaining or adopting specific measures to prevent or compensate for disadvantages linked to racial or ethnic origin.

The Employment Equality Directive provides:

Article 1—Purpose

The purpose of this Directive is to lay down a general framework for combating discrimination on the grounds of religion or belief, disability, age or sexual orientation as regards employment and occupation, with a view to putting into effect in the Member States the principle of equal treatment.

Article 7—Positive action

1. With a view to ensuring full equality in practice, the principle of equal treatment shall not prevent any Member State from maintaining or adopting specific measures to prevent or compensate for disadvantages linked to any of the grounds referred to in Article 1.

For the moment there is no European case-law on these latter provisions.

11.   The Canadian Charter of Rights and Freedoms provides:

Equality Rights

15(1) Every individual is equal before and under the law and has the right to the equal protection and equal benefit of the law without discrimination and, in particular, without discrimination based on race, national or ethnic origin, colour, religion, sex, age or mental or physical disability.

(2) Subsection (1) does not preclude any law, program or activity that has as its object the amelioration of conditions of disadvantaged individuals or groups including those that are disadvantaged because of race, national or ethnic origin, colour, religion, sex, age or mental or physical disability.

12.   The Canadian Employment Equity Act requires employers to correct disadvantages in the workplace experienced by women, Aboriginal peoples, persons with disabilities, and visible minorities. Should this be regarded as a form of affirmative action?

G. AFFIRMATIVE ACTION IN THE REGULATION OF DECISION-MAKING ("PARITY DEMOCRACY")

Another form of positive or affirmative action is "parity democracy" efforts. These efforts are found in electoral and representative systems, and in corporate governance systems. Some are voluntary; some are required.

_____

NOTES

1.   Could the U.S. Congress require gender quotas in the election of its members? For example, could the Senate provide that each State select two Senators, one male and one female? What Constitutional problems would this raise? Many nations around the world do have parity democracy gender quotas for electoral participation.

2.   The U.S. Democratic Party requires gender parity in the selection of delegates to its national convention. This is sometimes described as "voluntary quotas." Does this raise Constitutional problems? Is it a good idea? Could the U.S. Congress require that all political parties nominate equal numbers of men and women?

3.   At least twelve Latin American countries require minimum numbers of women be nominated to run for national office, with minimums between 20–40%. They are Argentina, Bolivia, Brazil, Colombia, Costa Rica, the Dominican Republic, Ecuador, Mexico, Panama, Paraguay, Peru and Venezuela. _See_ Tricia Gray, _Electoral Gender Quotas: Lessons from Argentina and Chile_, 22:1 BULLETIN OF LATIN AMERICAN RESEARCH 52–78 (2003).

4.   In Africa, twelve nations have national legislative seats reserved for women, while four have legislative candidate quotas and seven have voluntary quotas adopted by political parties. *See* http://www.quotaproject. org.

5.   In Asia, five states have legislative seats reserved for women, while six have legislative candidate quotas and another six have voluntary quotas adopted by political parties. *See* http://www.quotaproject.org. Also, recall that the Indian Constitution specifically reserves seats for Scheduled Castes and Scheduled Tribes in the lower house of Parliament and in the lower houses of state legislatures.

6.   In Europe, no country has national legislative seats reserved for women, but nine have legislative candidate quotas and eighteen have voluntary quotas adopted by political parties. *See* http://www.quotaproject. org. *See also*, Drude Dahlerup and Lenita Freidenvall, ELECTORAL GENDER QUOTAS AND THEIR IMPLEMENTATION IN EUROPE (2008).

7.   As of 2008, two European countries had over 40 percent of their legislative seats filled by women (Sweden 47 percent, Finland 42 percent), while eight more had over 30 percent (Norway 38 percent, Denmark, the Netherlands and Belgium 37 percent, Spain 36 percent, Austria, Germany and Iceland 32 percent.) Eight of the ten had either voluntary party quotas or legislated quotas. Belgium, France, Portugal, Slovenia and Spain have legislated quotas that are binding on all political parties. Drude Dahlerup and Lenita Freidenvall, ELECTORAL GENDER QUOTAS AND THEIR IMPLEMENTATION IN EUROPE (2008) at Table 1.

8.   France amended its constitution in 2000 to require that half of all political candidates be women. Think about the adoption of quotas by a country like France in light of its "universalist" equality mandate—i.e., its belief that all citizens are equal before the law and its opposition to identity classifications on the basis of race or ethnicity. Why doesn't a law that attempts to enforce gender parity not violate this universalism? It does, held the Constitutional Council, in an earlier attempt, to institute a 25 percent quota for women in French elections. But in support of the new law, feminists argued that "women are not a group, but rather women cut across all interest groups and would not be a unified element in the legislature. In the end, advocates succeeded with this argument—that women are half of the universal, and do not constitute a group that would conflict with French universalist traditions." Darren Rosenblum, *Parity/Disparity: Electoral Gender Inequality On The Tightrope Of Liberal Constitutional Traditions*, 39 UNIVERSITY OF CALIFORNIA DAVIS L. REV. 1119, 1163–65 (2006).

9.   In several European states, publicly traded companies are required to have a minimum number of women on the board. Norway requires that 40 percent of corporate board seats be held by women. Iceland requires 40 percent by 2013. France requires 20 percent by 2013 and 40 percent by 2016. Spain recommends (but does not require) 40 percent by 2015. The Netherlands has no target date, but requires noncompliance be disclosed. Rohini Pande and Deanna Ford, *Gender Quotas and Female Leadership: A Review* (Harvard University, Kennedy School of Government, 2011). In March 2011, the European Commission established the objective of bring-

ing women's presence on the boards of the major European publicly listed companies to 30 percent in 2015 and to 40 percent by 2020. It declared that if companies did not take action by March 2012, it would propose legislation. (http://europa.eu/rapid/pressReleasesAction.do?reference=MEMO/11/124&format=HTML&aged=0&language=EN&guiLanguage=fr).

10. Fewer than 10 percent of the board members of publicly traded U.S. corporations are women. Should Congress require parity democracy in the selection of corporate boards? Could it?

CHAPTER V

MARRIAGE EQUALITY

INTRODUCTION

Marriage has been at the crossroads of modern discussions of equality since at least the eighteenth century, when Mary Wollstonecraft published *A Vindication of the Rights of Woman* (1792). In the twentieth century, feminist critiques of marriage shared the stage with conflict over the "anti-miscegenation" laws that prohibited "intermarriage" between whites and blacks (and, more broadly, ethnic minorities regarded as non-white). Those laws were in force in many states until the decision in *Loving v. Virginia*, 388 U.S. 1 (1967). One effect of emancipation for the newly freed former slaves in the southern United States was the right to marry. Prior to the civil war, quasi-marriages were performed, but had no legal effect. *See* Leon F. Litwack, BEEN IN THE STORM SO LONG 239–241 (Vintage 1979). Today the focus has shifted to the question of same-sex marriage.

As the cases, codes, constitutions and commentary below reveal, the issue of marriage concerns more than whether same-sex couples may marry. It concerns issues in adoption, family planning and procreation, estate planning, taxes, and pensions/social security. It raises questions about how laws, cultures and families intersect. It implicates other chapters in this book on the equality issues raised by church/state relations, employment discrimination, and hate speech.

PROBLEM

As you study these materials, consider the options available to a same-sex couple, perhaps two men who love each other and wish to make the strongest commitment to each other that the law of their jurisdiction will permit; let's think of them as John and Peter (or, as we circle the globe, Johano, Jean, Hans, Jan, or Johan and Pieter, Pierre, Pedro, or Petrus). What are their options in San Francisco, Boston, Toronto, Paris, Madrid, Buenos Aires, Mexico City, Berlin, Tehran, or Johannesburg? And, what options will they have to adopt children, raise a family, make medical decisions for each other, pay their taxes, and protect each other through their pensions?

A. THE UNITED STATES

Loving v. Virginia

388 U.S. 1 (1967)

■ CHIEF JUSTICE WARREN delivered the opinion of the Court.

This case presents a constitutional question never addressed by this Court: whether a statutory scheme adopted by the State of Virginia to prevent marriages between persons solely on the basis of racial classifications violates the Equal Protection and Due Process Clauses of the Fourteenth Amendment. * * *

In June, 1958, two residents of Virginia, Mildred Jeter, a Negro woman, and Richard Loving, a white man, were married in the District of Columbia pursuant to its laws. Shortly after their marriage, the Lovings returned to Virginia and established their marital abode in Caroline County. At the October Term, 1958, of the Circuit Court of Caroline County, a grand jury issued an indictment charging the Lovings with violating Virginia's ban on interracial marriages. On January 6, 1959, the Lovings pleaded guilty to the charge, and were sentenced to one year in jail; however, the trial judge suspended the sentence for a period of 25 years on the condition that the Lovings leave the State and not return to Virginia together for 25 years. He stated in an opinion that:

> Almighty God created the races white, black, yellow, malay and red, and he placed them on separate continents. And, but for the interference with his arrangement, there would be no cause for such marriage. The fact that he separated the races shows that he did not intend for the races to mix.

After their convictions, the Lovings took up residence in the District of Columbia. On November 6, 1963, they filed a motion in the state trial court to vacate the judgment and set aside the sentence on the ground that the statutes which they had violated were repugnant to the Fourteenth Amendment. * * * The [State] Supreme Court of Appeals upheld the constitutionality of the anti-miscegenation statutes and, after modifying the sentence, affirmed the convictions. The Lovings appealed this decision * * *

The two statutes under which appellants were convicted and sentenced are part of a comprehensive statutory scheme aimed at prohibiting and punishing interracial marriages. The Lovings were convicted of violating § 258 of the Virginia Code:

> Leaving State to evade law.—If any white person and colored person shall go out of this State, for the purpose of being married, and with the intention of returning, and be married out of it, and afterwards return to and reside in it, cohabiting as man and wife, they shall be punished as provided in § 20–59, and the marriage shall be governed by the same law as if it had been solemnized in this State. The fact of their cohabitation here as man and wife shall be evidence of their marriage.

Section 259, which defines the penalty for miscegenation, provides:

> Punishment for marriage.—If any white person intermarry with a colored person, or any colored person intermarry with a white person, he shall be guilty of a felony and shall be punished by confinement in the penitentiary for not less than one nor more than five years.

Other central provisions in the Virginia statutory scheme are § 20–57, which automatically voids all marriages between "a white person and a colored person" without any judicial proceeding, and §§ 20–54 and 1–14 which, respectively, define "white persons" and "colored persons and Indians" for purposes of the statutory prohibitions. The Lovings have never disputed in the course of this litigation that Mrs. Loving is a "colored person" or that Mr. Loving is a "white person" within the meanings given those terms by the Virginia statutes. [footnotes omitted]

Virginia is now one of 16 States which prohibit and punish marriages on the basis of racial classifications. Penalties for miscegenation arose as an incident to slavery, and have been common in Virginia since the colonial period. The present statutory scheme dates from the adoption of the Racial Integrity Act of 1924, passed during the period of extreme nativism which followed the end of the First World War. The central features of this Act, and current Virginia law, are the absolute prohibition of a "white person" marrying other than another "white person," a prohibition against issuing marriage licenses until the issuing official is satisfied that the applicants' statements as to their race are correct, certificates of "racial composition" to be kept by both local and state registrars, and the carrying forward of earlier prohibitions against racial intermarriage. [footnotes omitted]

I

In upholding the constitutionality of these provisions in the decision below, the Supreme Court of Appeals of Virginia referred to its 1965 decision in *Naim v. Naim*, 197 Va. 80, 87 S.E.2d 749, as stating the reasons supporting the validity of these laws. In *Naim*, the state court concluded that the State's legitimate purposes were "to preserve the racial integrity of its citizens," and to prevent "the corruption of blood," "a mongrel breed of citizens," and "the obliteration of racial pride," obviously an endorsement of the doctrine of White Supremacy. The court also reasoned that marriage has traditionally been subject to state regulation without federal intervention, and, consequently, the regulation of marriage should be left to exclusive state control by the Tenth Amendment.

While the state court is no doubt correct in asserting that marriage is a social relation subject to the State's police power, *Maynard v. Hill*, 125 U.S. 190 (1888), the State does not contend in its argument before this Court that its powers to regulate marriage are unlimited notwithstanding the commands of the Fourteenth Amendment. * * * Instead, the State argues that the meaning of the Equal Protection Clause, as illuminated by the statements of the Framers, is only that state penal laws containing an interracial element as part of the definition of the offense must apply equally to whites and Negroes in the sense that members of each race are punished to the same degree. Thus, the State contends that, because its miscegenation statutes punish equally both the white and the Negro participants in an interracial marriage, these statutes, despite their reliance on racial classifications, do not constitute an invidious discrimination based upon race. The second argument advanced by the State assumes the validity of its equal application theory. The argument is that, if the Equal Protection Clause does not outlaw miscegenation statutes because of their reliance on racial classifications, the question of constitutionality would thus become whether there was any rational basis for a State to treat interracial marriages differently from other marriages. On this question, the State argues, the scientific evidence is substantially in doubt and, consequently, this Court should defer to the wisdom of the state legislature in adopting its policy of discouraging interracial marriages.

Because we reject the notion that the mere "equal application" of a statute containing racial classifications is enough to remove the classifications from the Fourteenth Amendment's proscription of all invidious racial discriminations, we do not accept the State's contention that these statutes should be upheld if there is any possible basis for concluding that they serve a rational purpose. The mere fact of equal application does not mean that our analysis of these statutes should follow the approach we have taken in cases involving no racial discrimination where the Equal Protection Clause has been arrayed against a statute discriminating between the kinds of advertising which may be displayed on trucks in New York City, *Railway Express Agency, Inc. v. New York*, 336 U.S. 106 (1949), or an exemption in Ohio's ad valorem tax for merchandise owned by a nonresident in a storage warehouse, *Allied Stores of Ohio, Inc. v. Bowers*, 358 U.S. 522 (1959). In these cases, involving distinctions not drawn according to race, the Court has merely asked whether there is any rational foundation for the discriminations, and has deferred to the wisdom of the state legislatures. In the case at bar, however, we deal with statutes containing racial classifications, and the fact of equal application does not immunize the statute from the very heavy burden of justification which the Fourteenth Amendment has traditionally required of state statutes drawn according to race.

The State argues that statements in the Thirty-ninth Congress about the time of the passage of the Fourteenth Amendment indicate that the Framers did not intend the Amendment to make unconstitutional state miscegenation laws. Many of the statements alluded to by the State concern the debates over the Freedmen's Bureau Bill, which President Johnson vetoed, and the Civil Rights Act of 1866, 14 Stat. 27, enacted over his veto. While these statements have some relevance to the intention of Congress in submitting the Fourteenth Amendment, it must be understood that they pertained to the passage of specific statutes, and not to the broader, organic purpose of a constitutional amendment. As for the various statements directly concerning the Fourteenth Amendment, we have said in connection with a related problem that, although these historical sources "cast some light" they are not sufficient to resolve the problem;

> [a]t best, they are inconclusive. The most avid proponents of the post-War Amendments undoubtedly intended them to remove all legal distinctions among "all persons born or naturalized in the United States." Their opponents, just as certainly, were antagonistic to both the letter and the spirit of the Amendments, and wished them to have the most limited effect.

Brown v. Board of Education, 347 U.S. 483, 489 (1954). *See also Strauder* v. West Virginia, 100 U.S. 303, 310 (1880). We have rejected the proposition that the debates in the Thirty-ninth Congress or in the state legislatures which ratified the Fourteenth Amendment supported the theory advanced by the State, that the requirement of equal protection of the laws is satisfied by penal laws defining offenses based on racial classifications so long as white and Negro participants in the offense were similarly punished. *McLaughlin v. Florida*, 379 U.S. 184 (1964).

* * * There can be no question but that Virginia's miscegenation statutes rest solely upon distinctions drawn according to race. The statutes proscribe generally accepted conduct if engaged in by members of different races. Over the years, this Court has consistently repudiated "[d]istinctions between citizens solely because of their ancestry" as being "odious to a free people whose institutions are founded upon the doctrine of equality." *Hirabayashi v. United States*, 320 U.S. 81, 100 (1943). At the very least, the Equal Protection Clause demands that racial classifications, especially suspect in criminal statutes, be subjected to the "most rigid scrutiny," *Korematsu v. United States*, 323 U.S. 214, 216 (1944), and, if they are ever to be upheld, they must be shown to be necessary to the accomplishment of some permissible state objective, independent of the racial discrimination which it was the object of the Fourteenth Amendment to eliminate. * * *

There is patently no legitimate overriding purpose independent of invidious racial discrimination which justifies this classification. The fact that Virginia prohibits only interracial marriages involving white persons demonstrates that the racial classifications must stand on their own justification, as measures designed to maintain White Supremacy. We have consistently denied the constitutionality of measures which restrict the rights of citizens on account of race. There can be no doubt that restricting the freedom to marry solely because of racial classifications violates the central meaning of the Equal Protection Clause. [footnotes omitted]

II

These statutes also deprive the Lovings of liberty without due process of law in violation of the Due Process Clause of the Fourteenth Amendment. The freedom to marry has long been recognized as one of the vital personal rights essential to the orderly pursuit of happiness by free men.

Marriage is one of the "basic civil rights of man," fundamental to our very existence and survival. *Skinner v. Oklahoma*, 316 U.S. 535, 541 (1942). *See also Maynard v. Hill*, 125 U.S. 190 (1888). To deny this fundamental freedom on so unsupportable a basis as the racial classifications embodied in these statutes, classifications so directly subversive of the principle of equality at the heart of the Fourteenth Amendment, is surely to deprive all the State's citizens of liberty without due process of law. The Fourteenth Amendment requires that the freedom of choice to marry not be restricted by invidious racial discriminations. Under our Constitution, the freedom to marry, or not marry, a person of another race resides with the individual, and cannot be infringed by the State.

These convictions must be reversed.

It is so ordered.

Beyond Analogy: *Perez v. Sharp*, Antimiscegenation Law, and the Fight for Same–Sex Marriage

96 California Law Review 839, 840–45, 854–62 (2008)

■ R.A. LENHARDT

Sixty-five years ago, two California factory workers, Sylvester Davis and Andrea Pérez, committed an act that would transform the terrain of race and ethnicity in the United States. They fell in love. Determined to share the rest of their lives together, Sylvester, an African American just returning from service abroad in World War II, and Andrea, the daughter of Mexican immigrants, went to the Los Angeles county clerk several years later to obtain a marriage license. The county clerk, however, refused to grant them one. Sylvester and Andrea had run afoul of California's antimiscegenation law.

On its face, this antimiscegenation law, which had been in effect from California's entry into the union in 1850, did not appear to apply to Sylvester and Andrea. It declared that "marriages of white persons with negroes, Mongolians, members of the Malay race, or mulattoes" would be deemed illegal and void. Individuals of Mexican descent were nowhere mentioned in the statute. But, in California, Mexican Americans had long been regarded as white for purposes of marriage. Andrea was a mestizo who, by all accounts, did not appear phenotypically white and who, given the racial politics of California at the time, likely received none of the social privileges associated with whiteness. Ironically, though, she was deemed to fall among those whose blood had to be protected from contamination by non-Whites.

Devout Catholics interested in marrying in their neighborhood church, Sylvester and Andrea refused to resort to the strategies employed by other couples ensnared in the bramble bush of California's race regulations. They were unwilling to cohabitate, misrepresent their racial identity, or even to seek a marriage license in a sister-state without an antimiscegenation law, as many others did. They sought legal marriage on the same terms available to all Californians. And so, with the help of a civil rights attorney named Dan Marshall, they resolved to challenge California's antimiscegenation law.

* * * On October 1, 1948, the California Supreme Court issued an opinion [*Perez v. Sharp*, 32 Cal. 2d 711] holding the state's antimiscegenation law unconstitutional under the Fourteenth Amendment of the U.S. Constitution. Its ground-breaking decision, which marked the first time since Reconstruction that any antimiscegenation statute had been invalidated, led to significant changes in the lives of interracial couples in California. But outside California, other state courts rarely relied on or even cited it. Indeed, for years, a footnote mention in the Supreme Court's *Loving v. Virginia* decision was *Perez*'s greatest claim to fame.

But for the efforts of advocates in recent litigation to secure civil marriage rights for same-sex couples, *Perez* would have been consigned to legal obscurity. Advocates for same-sex marriage have been "loving" *Perez*. In cases such as *In re Marriage Cases*, in which the California Supreme Court recently held that "the failure to designate the official [domestic partnership] relationship of same-sex couples as marriage violates the California Constitution," advocates have treated *Perez* as a landmark case that sheds light on the core meaning of marriage, perhaps even more so than *Loving* itself. * * *

Far from distorting the meaning of *Loving* and other cases, the use of *Perez* in recent litigation helps to focus attention on the problems inherent in identity-based marriage restrictions in a way that *Loving* failed to do. *Loving* identifies marriage as one of the "basic civil rights of man," but focuses principally on the white supremacist subtext of the antimiscegenation laws. *Perez*, in contrast, both engages issues of race and its social construction through such law, and develops a more fulsome account of the marriage rights with which interracial marriage bans interfered. It makes clear that the fundamental right to marry involves the freedom to marry not just anyone, but the "person of [one's] choice." In this sense, *Perez*, with its emphasis on choice and self-expression, goes beyond the more limited articulation of marriage rights that appears in the Supreme Court's decision in *Loving*.

* * * Were it not for advocates of marriage rights for gay men and lesbians, the footnote mention *Perez* received in *Loving* might have been the most recognition it ever received. In recent years, however, advocates in these cases have successfully cast *Perez* as a foundational decision, one without which discussions about the place of marriage in current society cannot be meaningfully conducted. Indeed, the briefs filed and/or oral arguments made in almost every case challenging gender-based marriage restrictions in the last ten years has featured *Perez* in some way. * * *

... Of course, *Loving* also plays a central role in current litigation. But, given the context in which it was decided, *Loving*'s message to lower courts is comparatively muted. The U.S. Supreme Court actively avoided addressing the constitutionality of bars on interracial marriage—widely regarded as the third rail of race relations—for years, and then only did so after they had already decided comparatively less controversial issues, such as those concerning racial segregation in public schools, parks, restaurants, hotels, housing, transportation, and voting, among other things. By the time the Court decided *Loving*, nearly half of the states that had antimiscegenation laws on their books when Andrea and Sylvester filed their lawsuit had repealed them. In many respects, some of the hardest work had already been done.

The context for the California Supreme Court's decision in *Perez* was quite different. In 1948, a full majority of states had antimiscegenation provisions in effect. Additionally, all of the judicial opinions in the area had upheld these statutes against challenge. Further, public opinion was firmly against interracial marriage. For judges hearing cases seeking marriage rights for gay and lesbian couples, the *Perez* context is more analogous to their situation than that of *Loving*, where the Court was asked to deliver the final blow to a discriminatory regime already in decline.

* * * *Perez* shows that, where precious constitutional rights are at stake, judges need not give deference to discrimination, whether supported by the legislature, tradition, public opinion, or all three. And in invoking it, advocates not only underscore that that precedent exists for the bold rulings they seek, but also remind state courts in particular that a courageous decision on civil rights grounds now may very well help to effect a significant change in doctrine later. * * *

The deployment of *Perez* in recent marriage cases also adds substantive content to advocates' claims for gay and lesbian marriage rights. Advocates use *Perez's* "person of one's choice" language to focus attention on what gay and lesbian couples seek in current marriage cases: the recognition of a shared humanity with others whose intimate relationships are eligible to be recognized by the state. *Loving*, of course, includes language very relevant to the claims for marriage rights advanced by gay and lesbian litigants. Chief Justice Warren's assertion that "[m]arriage is one of the 'basic civil rights of man,' fundamental to our very existence and survival" arguably provides strong support for the extension of marriage to same-sex couples. Other aspects of the majority opinion in *Loving* work to reinforce assertions about the effect of identity-based restrictions on civil marriage. Consider Warren's conclusion that "[t]he Fourteenth Amendment requires that the freedom of choice to marry not be restricted by invidious racial discriminations. Under our Constitution, the freedom to marry, or not marry, a person of another race resides with the individual and cannot be infringed by the State." * * *

A survey of relevant briefs makes clear that *Perez* gets employed to make a wide variety of substantive points. Chief among these is the argument that, as a constitutional matter, a meaningful analogy can be drawn between the antimiscegenation and same-sex marriage contexts. The claim here is not that the oppression experienced by African Americans is exactly the same as that confronted by members of the LGBT community. Rather, it is that the marriage rights sought by gay and lesbian couples are not fundamentally different. *Loving*, of course, suggests this in holding that the right to marry is among the " 'basic civil rights of man.' " But advocates in cases such as *Goodridge v.Department of Public Health* and *Lewis v. Harris* have still had to defend against claims that *Loving* is only a case about race and, thus, does not encompass the right to marry sought by LGBT couples, and that the marriage right afforded by the Constitution extends to heterosexual marriage alone. Here *Perez*, which purports to interpret the Fourteenth Amendment rather than just California law, has been employed to good effect.

* * * *Perez* also surfaces frequently in efforts to rebut the argument that equal application of the prohibition of same-sex marriage to both sexes renders it constitutionally legitimate. Echoing the arguments of Alabama in *Pace* and Virginia in *Loving*, the state defenders in recent marriage cases have argued that, since all men are prevented from marrying men and all women are barred from marrying women, provisions banning civil marriage for same-sex couples do not violate state and federal equal protection guarantees. Advocates, however, point to *Perez* to make the case that the Constitution guarantees a more robust conception of equality than such arguments suggest. In this connection, they cite Justice Traynor's insight that the right to marriage in modern society must mean the right of an individual to select the "person of one's choice" as a life partner. * * *

Defense of Marriage Act (1996)

Public Law 104–199–104th Congress

An Act to define and protect the institution of marriage. This Act may be cited as the "Defense of Marriage Act".

SEC. 2. POWERS RESERVED TO THE STATES.

(a) In General.—Chapter 115 of title 28, United States Code, is amended by adding after section 1738B the following:

Sec. 1738C. Certain acts, records, and proceedings and the effect thereof

No State, territory, or possession of the United States, or Indian tribe, shall be required to give effect to any public act, record, or judicial proceeding of any other State, territory, possession, or tribe respecting a relationship between persons of the same sex that is treated as a marriage under the laws of such other State, territory, possession, or tribe, or a right or claim arising from such relationship.'

SEC. 3. DEFINITION OF MARRIAGE.

(a) In General.—Chapter 1 of title 1, United States Code, is amended by adding at the end the following:

Sec. 7. Definition of 'marriage' and 'spouse'

In determining the meaning of any Act of Congress, or of any ruling, regulation, or interpretation of the various administrative bureaus and agencies of the United States, the word 'marriage' means only a legal union between one man and one woman as husband and wife, and the word 'spouse' refers only to a person of the opposite sex who is a husband or a wife.

[EDITORS' NOTE: The "Defense of Marriage Act" passed the House of Representatives by a vote of 342–67 and the Senate by a vote of 85–14. It was signed into law by President Clinton on September 21, 1996.]

————

Proposed Constitutional Amendment

110th Congress—H. J. Res. 22 (February 6, 2007)

Proposing an Amendment to the Constitution of the United States Relating to Marriage.

Resolved by the Senate and House of Representatives of the United States of America in Congress assembled, That the following article is proposed as an amendment to the Constitution of the United States, which shall be valid to all intents and purposes as part of the Constitution when ratified by the legislatures of three-fourths of the several States within seven years after the date of its submission for ratification:

Section 1. Marriage in the United States shall consist only of a legal union of one man and one woman.

Section 2. No court of the United States or of any State shall have jurisdiction to determine whether this Constitution or the constitution of any State requires that the legal incidents of marriage be conferred upon any union other than a legal union between one man and one woman.

Section 3. No State shall be required to give effect to any public act, record, or judicial proceeding of any other State concerning a union between persons of the same sex that is treated as a marriage, or as having the legal incidents of marriage, under the laws of such other State.

––––––

[EDITORS' NOTE: On June 6, 2006 an earlier version of this Amendment was abandoned when a cloture vote to end debate was rejected by the U.S. Senate by a vote of 49–48. Despite the failure to bring the amendment to a vote in the Senate, the House of Representatives voted on amendment on July 18, 2006. The vote of 236 yea to 187 nay failed to achieve the requisite two-third votes (290) to send the amendment to the states for ratification.]

––––––

Massachusetts

Goodridge v. Department of Public Health

440 Mass. 309 (2003)

■ Opinion: MARSHALL, C.J.

The question before us is whether, consistent with the Massachusetts Constitution, the Commonwealth may deny the protections, benefits, and obligations conferred by civil marriage to two individuals of the same sex who wish to marry. We conclude that it may not. The Massachusetts Constitution affirms the dignity and equality of all individuals. It forbids the creation of second-class citizens. In reaching our conclusion we have given full deference to the arguments made by the Commonwealth. But it has failed to identify any constitutionally adequate reason for denying civil marriage to same-sex couples.

We are mindful that our decision marks a change in the history of our marriage law. Many people hold deep-seated religious, moral, and ethical convictions that marriage should be limited to the union of one man and one woman, and that homosexual conduct is immoral. Many hold equally strong religious, moral, and ethical convictions that same-sex couples are entitled to be married, and that homosexual persons should be treated no differently than their heterosexual neighbors. Neither view answers the question before us. Our concern is with the Massachusetts Constitution as a charter of governance for every person properly within its reach. "Our obligation is to define the liberty of all, not to mandate our own moral code." *Lawrence v. Texas* (2003) (Lawrence), quoting *Planned Parenthood of Southeastern Pa. v. Casey* (1992).

Barred access to the protections, benefits, and obligations of civil marriage, a person who enters into an intimate, exclusive union with another of the same sex is arbitrarily deprived of membership in one of our community's most rewarding and cherished institutions. That exclusion is incompatible with the constitutional principles of respect for individual autonomy and equality under law.

I

The plaintiffs are fourteen individuals from five Massachusetts counties. As of April 11, 2001, the date they filed their complaint, the plaintiffs Gloria Bailey, sixty years old, and Linda Davies, fifty-five years old, had been in a committed relationship for thirty years; the plaintiffs Maureen Brodoff, forty-nine years old, and Ellen Wade, fifty-two years old, had been in a committed relationship for twenty years and lived with their twelve year old daughter; the plaintiffs Hillary Goodridge, forty-four years old, and Julie Goodridge, forty-three years old, had been in a committed relationship for thirteen years and lived with their five year old daughter; the plaintiffs Gary Chalmers, thirty-five years old, and Richard Linnell, thirty-seven years old, had been in a committed relationship for thirteen years and lived with their eight year old daughter and Richard's mother; the plaintiffs Heidi Norton, thirty-six years old, and Gina Smith, thirty-six years old, had been in a committed relationship for eleven years and lived with their two sons, ages five years and one year; the plaintiffs Michael Horgan, forty-one years old, and Edward Balmelli, forty-one years old, had been in a committed relationship for seven years; and the plaintiffs David Wilson, fifty-seven years old, and Robert Compton, fifty-one years old, had been in a committed relationship for four years and had cared for David's mother in their home after a serious illness until she died.

The plaintiffs include business executives, lawyers, an investment banker, educators, therapists, and a computer engineer. Many are active in church, community, and school groups. They have employed such legal means as are available to them—for example, joint adoption, powers of attorney, and joint ownership of real property—to secure aspects of their relationships. Each plaintiff attests a desire to marry his or her partner in order to affirm publicly their commitment to each other and to secure the legal protections and benefits afforded to married couples and their children.

In March and April, 2001, each of the plaintiff couples attempted to obtain a marriage license from a city or town clerk's office. As required under G. L. c. 207, they completed notices of intention to marry on forms provided by the registry, and presented these forms to a Massachusetts town or city clerk, together with the required health forms and marriage license fees. In each case, the clerk either refused to accept the notice of intention to marry or denied a marriage license to the couple on the ground that Massachusetts does not recognize same-sex marriage.

The department, represented by the Attorney General, admitted to a policy and practice of denying marriage licenses to same-sex couples. It denied that its actions violated any law or that the plaintiffs were entitled to relief. The parties filed cross motions for summary judgment. * * *

III

A

* * * The plaintiffs' claim that the marriage restriction violates the Massachusetts Constitution can be analyzed in two ways. Does it offend the Constitution's guarantees of equality before the law? Or do the liberty and due process provisions of the Massachusetts Constitution secure the plaintiffs' right to marry their chosen partner? In matters implicating marriage, family life, and the upbringing of children, the two constitutional concepts frequently overlap, as they do here. Much of what we say concerning one standard applies to the other.

We begin by considering the nature of civil marriage itself. Simply put, the government creates civil marriage. In Massachusetts, civil marriage is, and since pre-Colonial days has been, precisely what its name implies: a wholly secular institution.... No religious ceremony has ever been required to validate a Massachusetts marriage.

In a real sense, there are three partners to every civil marriage: two willing spouses and an approving State.... While only the parties can mutually assent to marriage, the terms of the marriage—who may marry and what obligations, benefits, and liabilities attach to civil marriage—are set by the Commonwealth. Conversely, while only the parties can agree to end the marriage (absent the death of one of them or a marriage void ab initio), the Commonwealth defines the exit terms. *See* G. L. c. 208.

Marriage also bestows enormous private and social advantages on those who choose to marry. Civil marriage is at once a deeply personal commitment to another human being and a highly public celebration of the ideals of mutuality, companionship, intimacy, fidelity, and family. "It is an association that promotes a way of life, not causes; a harmony in living, not political faiths; a bilateral loyalty, not commercial or social projects." *Griswold v. Connecticut* (1965). Because it fulfils yearnings for security, safe haven, and connection that express our common humanity, civil marriage is an esteemed institution, and the decision whether and whom to marry is among life's momentous acts of self-definition.

Tangible as well as intangible benefits flow from marriage. The marriage license grants valuable property rights to those who meet the entry requirements, and who agree to what might otherwise be a burdensome degree of government regulation of their activities. The Legislature has conferred on "each party [in a civil marriage] substantial rights concerning the assets of the other which unmarried cohabitants do not have." *Wilcox v. Trautz* (1998). *See Collins v. Guggenheim* (1994) (rejecting claim for equitable distribution of property where plaintiff cohabited with but did not marry defendant); *Feliciano v. Rosemar Silver Co.* (1987) (government interest in promoting marriage would be "subverted" by recognition of "a right to recover for loss of consortium by a person who has not accepted the correlative responsibilities of marriage"); *Davis v. Misiano* (1977) (unmarried partners not entitled to rights of separate support or alimony).

The benefits accessible only by way of a marriage license are enormous, touching nearly every aspect of life and death. The department states that "hundreds of statutes" are related to marriage and to marital benefits.

With no attempt to be comprehensive, we note that some of the statutory benefits conferred by the Legislature on those who enter into civil marriage include, as to property: joint Massachusetts income tax filing; tenancy by the entirety (a form of ownership that provides certain protections against creditors and allows for the automatic descent of property to the surviving spouse without probate); extension of the benefit of the homestead protection (securing up to $300,000 in equity from creditors) to one's spouse and children; automatic rights to inherit the property of a deceased spouse who does not leave a will (G. L. c. 190, § 1); the rights of elective share and of dower (which allow surviving spouses certain property rights where the decedent spouse has not made adequate provision for the survivor in a will); entitlement to wages owed to a deceased employee; eligibility to continue certain businesses of a deceased spouse; the right to share the medical policy of one's spouse; thirty-nine week continuation of health coverage for the spouse of a person who is laid off or dies; preferential options under the Commonwealth's pension system; preferential benefits in the Commonwealth's medical program, MassHealth; access to veterans' spousal benefits and preferences; financial protections for spouses of certain Commonwealth employees (fire fighters, police officers, prosecutors, among others) killed in the performance of duty; the equitable division of marital property on divorce; temporary and permanent alimony rights; the right to separate support on separation of the parties that does not result in divorce; and the right to bring claims for wrongful death and loss of consortium, and for funeral and burial expenses and punitive damages resulting from tort actions.

Exclusive marital benefits that are not directly tied to property rights include the presumptions of legitimacy and parentage of children born to a married couple; and evidentiary rights, such as the prohibition against spouses testifying against one another about their private conversations, applicable in both civil and criminal cases. Other statutory benefits of a personal nature available only to married individuals include qualification for bereavement or medical leave to care for individuals related by blood or marriage; an automatic "family member" preference to make medical decisions for an incompetent or disabled spouse who does not have a contrary health care proxy; the application of predictable rules of child custody, visitation, support, and removal out-of-State when married parents divorce; priority rights to administer the estate of a deceased spouse who dies without a will, and requirement that surviving spouse must consent to the appointment of any other person as administrator; and the right to interment in the lot or tomb owned by one's deceased spouse.

Where a married couple has children, their children are also directly or indirectly, but no less auspiciously, the recipients of the special legal and economic protections obtained by civil marriage. Notwithstanding the Commonwealth's strong public policy to abolish legal distinctions between marital and nonmarital children in providing for the support and care of minors, the fact remains that marital children reap a measure of family stability and economic security based on their parents' legally privileged status that is largely inaccessible, or not as readily accessible, to nonmarital children. Some of these benefits are social, such as the enhanced approval that still attends the status of being a marital child. Others are material, such as the greater ease of access to family-based State and Federal benefits that attend the presumptions of one's parentage.

It is undoubtedly for these concrete reasons, as well as for its intimately personal significance, that civil marriage has long been termed a "civil right." *See, e.g., Loving v. Virginia* (1967) ("Marriage is one of the 'basic civil rights of man,' fundamental to our very existence and survival") . . . The United States Supreme Court has described the right to marry as "of fundamental importance for all individuals" and as "part of the fundamental 'right of privacy' implicit in the Fourteenth Amendment's Due Process Clause." *Zablocki v. Redhail* (1978). *See Loving v. Virginia* ("The freedom to marry has long been recognized as one of the vital personal rights essential to the orderly pursuit of happiness by free men"). * * *

B

For decades, indeed centuries, in much of this country (including Massachusetts) no lawful marriage was possible between white and black Americans. That long history availed not when the Supreme Court of California held in 1948 that a legislative prohibition against interracial marriage violated the due process and equality guarantees of the Fourteenth Amendment, *Perez v. Sharp* (1948), or when, nineteen years later, the United States Supreme Court also held that a statutory bar to interracial marriage violated the Fourteenth Amendment, *Loving v. Virginia* (1967). As both *Perez* and *Loving* make clear, the right to marry means little if it does not include the right to marry the person of one's choice, subject to appropriate government restrictions in the interests of public health, safety, and welfare. *See Perez v. Sharp* ("the essence of the right to marry is freedom to join in marriage with the person of one's choice"). In this case, as in *Perez* and *Loving*, a statute deprives individuals of access to an institution of fundamental legal, personal, and social significance—the institution of marriage—because of a single trait: skin color in *Perez* and *Loving*, sexual orientation here. As it did in *Perez* and *Loving*, history must yield to a more fully developed understanding of the invidious quality of the discrimination.

The plaintiffs challenge the marriage statute on both equal protection and due process grounds. With respect to each such claim, we must first determine the appropriate standard of review. Where a statute implicates a fundamental right or uses a suspect classification, we employ "strict judicial scrutiny." For all other statutes, we employ the " 'rational basis' test." . . .

The department argues that no fundamental right or "suspect" class is at issue here, and rational basis is the appropriate standard of review. For the reasons we explain below, we conclude that the marriage ban does not meet the rational basis test for either due process or equal protection. Because the statute does not survive rational basis review, we do not consider the plaintiffs' arguments that this case merits strict judicial scrutiny.

The department posits three legislative rationales for prohibiting same-sex couples from marrying: (1) providing a "favorable setting for procreation"; (2) ensuring the optimal setting for child rearing, which the department defines as "a two-parent family with one parent of each sex"; and (3) preserving scarce State and private financial resources. We consider each in turn.

The judge in the Superior Court endorsed the first rationale, holding that "the state's interest in regulating marriage is based on the traditional concept that marriage's primary purpose is procreation." This is incorrect. Our laws of civil marriage do not privilege procreative heterosexual intercourse between married people above every other form of adult intimacy and every other means of creating a family. General Laws c. 207 contains no requirement that the applicants for a marriage license attest to their ability or intention to conceive children by coitus. Fertility is not a condition of marriage, nor is it grounds for divorce. People who have never consummated their marriage, and never plan to, may be and stay married. *See Franklin v. Franklin* (1891) ("The consummation of a marriage by coition is not necessary to its validity"). People who cannot stir from their deathbed may marry. While it is certainly true that many, perhaps most, married couples have children together (assisted or unassisted), it is the exclusive and permanent commitment of the marriage partners to one another, not the begetting of children, that is the sine qua non of civil marriage.

The department's first stated rationale, equating marriage with unassisted heterosexual procreation, shades imperceptibly into its second: that confining marriage to opposite-sex couples ensures that children are raised in the "optimal" setting. Protecting the welfare of children is a paramount State policy. Restricting marriage to opposite-sex couples, however, cannot plausibly further this policy. "The demographic changes of the past century make it difficult to speak of an average American family. The composition of families varies greatly from household to household." *Troxel v. Granville* (2000). Massachusetts has responded supportively to "the changing realities of the American family" and has moved vigorously to strengthen the modern family in its many variations.

The department has offered no evidence that forbidding marriage to people of the same sex will increase the number of couples choosing to enter into opposite-sex marriages in order to have and raise children. There is thus no rational relationship between the marriage statute and the Commonwealth's proffered goal of protecting the "optimal" child rearing unit. Moreover, the department readily concedes that people in same-sex couples may be "excellent" parents. These couples (including four of the plaintiff couples) have children for the reasons others do—to love them, to care for them, to nurture them. But the task of child rearing for same-sex couples is made infinitely harder by their status as outliers to the marriage laws.

No one disputes that the plaintiff couples are families, that many are parents, and that the children they are raising, like all children, need and should have the fullest opportunity to grow up in a secure, protected family unit. Similarly, no one disputes that, under the rubric of marriage, the State provides a cornucopia of substantial benefits to married parents and their children. The preferential treatment of civil marriage reflects the Legislature's conclusion that marriage "is the foremost setting for the education and socialization of children" precisely because it "encourages parents to remain committed to each other and to their children as they grow." Post at (CORDY, J., dissenting).

The marriage ban works a deep and scarring hardship on a very real segment of the community for no rational reason. The absence of any reasonable relationship between, on the one hand, an absolute disqualification of same-sex couples who wish to enter into civil marriage and, on the other, protection of public health, safety, or general welfare, suggests that the marriage restriction is rooted in persistent prejudices against persons who are (or who are believed to be) homosexual. "The Constitution cannot control such prejudices but neither can it tolerate them. Private biases may be outside the reach of the law, but the law cannot, directly or indirectly, give them effect." *Palmore v. Sidoti* (1984) (construing Fourteenth Amendment). Limiting the protections, benefits, and obligations of civil marriage to opposite-sex couples violates the basic premises of individual liberty and equality under law protected by the Massachusetts Constitution.

IV

We consider next the plaintiffs' request for relief. We preserve as much of the statute as may be preserved in the face of the successful constitutional challenge.

Here, no one argues that striking down the marriage laws is an appropriate form of relief. Eliminating civil marriage would be wholly inconsistent with the Legislature's deep commitment to fostering stable families and would dismantle a vital organizing principle of our society. We face a problem similar to one that recently confronted the Court of Appeal for Ontario, the highest court of that Canadian province, when it considered the constitutionality of the same-sex marriage ban under Canada's Federal Constitution, the Charter of Rights and Freedoms (Charter). *See Halpern v. Toronto* (2003). Canada, like the United States, adopted the common law of England that civil marriage is "the voluntary union for life of one man and one woman, to the exclusion of all others." In holding that the limitation of civil marriage to opposite-sex couples violated the Charter, the Court of Appeal refined the common-law meaning of marriage. We concur with this remedy, which is entirely consonant with established principles of jurisprudence empowering a court to refine a common-law principle in light of evolving constitutional standards. *See Powers v. Wilkinson* (1987) (reforming common-law rule of construction of "issue"); *Lewis v. Lewis* (1976) (abolishing common-law rule of certain inter-spousal immunity).

We construe civil marriage to mean the voluntary union of two persons as spouses, to the exclusion of all others. This reformulation redresses the plaintiffs' constitutional injury and furthers the aim of marriage to promote stable, exclusive relationships. It advances the two legitimate State interests the department has identified: providing a stable setting for child rearing and conserving State resources. It leaves intact the Legislature's broad discretion to regulate marriage.

So ordered.

GREANEY, J. (concurring). I agree with the result reached by the court, the remedy ordered, and much of the reasoning in the court's opinion. In my view, however, the case is more directly resolved using traditional equal protection analysis.

* * *

■ SPINA, J. (dissenting, with whom SOSMAN and CORDY, JJ., join).

What is at stake in this case is not the unequal treatment of individuals or whether individual rights have been impermissibly burdened, but the power of the Legislature to effectuate social change without interference from the courts, pursuant to art. 30 of the Massachusetts Declaration of Rights. The power to regulate marriage lies with the Legislature, not with the judiciary. Today, the court has transformed its role as protector of individual rights into the role of creator of rights, and I respectfully dissent.

1.   Equal protection. Although the court did not address the plaintiffs' gender discrimination claim, G. L. c. 207 does not unconstitutionally discriminate on the basis of gender. A claim of gender discrimination will lie where it is shown that differential treatment disadvantages one sex over the other. General Laws c. 207 enumerates certain qualifications for obtaining a marriage license. It creates no distinction between the sexes, but applies to men and women in precisely the same way. It does not create any disadvantage identified with gender, as both men and women are similarly limited to marrying a person of the opposite sex.

Similarly, the marriage statutes do not discriminate on the basis of sexual orientation. As the court correctly recognizes, constitutional protections are extended to individuals, not couples. Ante n.15. The marriage statutes do not disqualify individuals on the basis of sexual orientation from entering into marriage. All individuals, with certain exceptions not relevant here, are free to marry. Whether an individual chooses not to marry because of sexual orientation or any other reason should be of no concern to the court.

The court concludes, however, that G. L. c. 207 unconstitutionally discriminates against the individual plaintiffs because it denies them the "right to marry the person of one's choice" where that person is of the same sex. To reach this result the court relies on *Loving v. Virginia* and transforms "choice" into the essential element of the institution of marriage. The *Loving* case did not use the word "choice" in this manner, and it did not point to the result that the court reaches today. In *Loving*, the Supreme Court struck down as unconstitutional a statute that prohibited Caucasians from marrying non-Caucasians. It concluded that the statute was intended to preserve white supremacy and invidiously discriminated against non-Caucasians because of their race. The "choice" to which the Supreme Court referred was the "choice to marry," and it concluded that with respect to the institution of marriage, the State had no compelling interest in limiting the choice to marry along racial lines. The Supreme Court did not imply the existence of a right to marry a person of the same sex. To the same effect is *Perez v. Sharp*, on which the court also relies.

Unlike the *Loving* and *Sharp* cases, the Massachusetts Legislature has erected no barrier to marriage that intentionally discriminates against anyone. Within the institution of marriage, anyone is free to marry, with certain exceptions that are not challenged. In the absence of any discriminatory purpose, the State's marriage statutes do not violate principles of equal protection. *See Washington v. Davis* (1976). This court should not have invoked even the most deferential standard of review within equal protection analysis because no individual was denied access to the institution of marriage.

2. Due process. The marriage statutes do not impermissibly burden a right protected by our constitutional guarantee of due process implicit in art. 10 of our Declaration of Rights. There is no restriction on the right of any plaintiff to enter into marriage. Each is free to marry a willing person of the opposite sex. *Cf. Zablocki v. Redhail* (1978) (fundamental right to marry impermissibly burdened by statute requiring court approval when subject to child support order).

Substantive due process protects individual rights against unwarranted government intrusion. The court states, as we have said on many occasions, that the Massachusetts Declaration of Rights may protect a right in ways that exceed the protection afforded by the Federal Constitution. *See Arizona v. Evans*, (1995) (State courts afforded broader protection of rights than granted by United States Constitution). However, today the court does not fashion a remedy that affords greater protection of a right. Instead, using the rubric of due process, it has redefined marriage.

3. Remedy. The remedy that the court has fashioned both in the name of equal protection and due process exceeds the bounds of judicial restraint mandated by art. 30. The remedy that construes gender-specific language as gender-neutral amounts to a statutory revision that replaces the intent of the Legislature with that of the court. Article 30 permits the court to apply principles of equal protection and to modify statutory language only if legislative intent is preserved. *See, e.g., Commonwealth v. Chou* (2001) (judicial rewriting of gender language permissible only when Legislature intended to include both men and women). Here, the alteration of the gender-specific language alters precisely what the Legislature unambiguously intended to preserve, the marital rights of single men and women. Such a dramatic change in social institutions must remain at the behest of the people through the democratic process.

New Jersey

The Supreme Court of New Jersey followed a different route in its 2006 marriage equality decision, *Lewis v. Harris*, 188 N.J. 415. Similar to the Massachusetts court, the New Jersey Court held that "denying rights and benefits to committed same-sex couples that are statutorily given to their heterosexual counterparts violates the equal protection guarantee of Article I, Paragraph 1 [of the New Jersey Constitution]" and required the legislature to "either amend the marriage statutes to include same-sex couples or create a parallel statutory structure, which will provide for, on equal terms, the rights and benefits enjoyed and burdens and obligations borne by married couples."

However, the New Jersey Court viewed as a distinct issue whether "committed same-sex partners have a constitutional right to define their relationship by the name of marriage, the word that historically has characterized the union of a man and a woman." While the Court agreed unanimously that the full rights and benefits of marriage must be provided to same-sex couples, four of the seven justices held that the name applied to same-sex relationships was "a matter left to the democratic process" and they would "not presume that a separate statutory scheme, which uses a title other than marriage, contravenes equal protection principles, so long as the rights and benefits of civil marriage are made equally available to same-sex couples."

Three of the seven judges dissented from the latter element of the holding, quoting favourably from Professor Ronald Dworkin's essay Three Questions for America (2006):

> We can no more now create an alternate mode of commitment carrying a parallel intensity of meaning than we can now create a substitute for poetry or for love. The status of marriage is therefore a social resource of irreplaceable value to those to whom it is offered: it enables two people together to create value in their lives that they could not create if that institution had never existed. We know that people of the same sex often love one another with the same passion as people of different sexes do and that they want as much as heterosexuals to have the benefits and experience of the married state.

———

California

In the 2000 primary election, California voters passed Proposition 22 (with a vote of 61.4% yes to 38.6% no) through the state's statutory initiative process. Proposition 22 reiterated the decades-long statutory ban on same-sex marriage and further prohibited the recognition of valid same-sex marriages performed in other jurisdictions. The legislature of California, which had created a statutory domestic partnership scheme in 1999, continued to expand the legal rights, benefits and responsibilities accorded to same-sex couples in the years following Proposition 22. By 2005, same-sex couples in California were accorded nearly equal legal status with heterosexual married couples, but were still denied the terminology of "marriage" as a result of Proposition 22. This issue came to the California Supreme court in six consolidated cases in 2008.

The issue before the California Supreme Court in *In Re: Marriage Cases*, excerpted in Chapter 2, was the constitutionality under the California Constitution of the state's statutory scheme in which both opposite-sex and same-sex couples are granted the right to enter into an officially recognized relationship that affords all of the significant legal rights and obligations traditionally associated with marriage, but under which the union of an opposite-sex couple is designated a "marriage" whereas the union of a same-sex couple is designated a "domestic partnership." The Court invalidated this statutory scheme by applying the highest level of constitutional scrutiny—strict scrutiny—to that scheme. The Court chose to apply strict scrutiny because it found that the statutory designations discriminated on the basis of sexual orientation, a characteristic that represents—like gender, race and religion—a constitutionally "suspect" basis upon which to impose differential treatment. Moreover, it reasoned, the differential treatment impinged upon a same-sex couple's fundamental interest in having their family relationship accorded the same respect and dignity enjoyed by opposite-sex couples. The interest that the State offered to justify the differential treatment—the interest in retaining the traditional and well-established definition of marriage—was, the Court concluded, insufficiently compelling.

———

In November 2008 (six months after the *In Re: Marriages* decision), California voters voted to amend the California Constitution with passage of Proposition 8 (52.2% yes to 47.8% no). Proposition 8 added limiting language ("Only marriage between a man and a woman is valid or recognized in California") to the Constitution and thereby amended its privacy, due process and equality protections to permit discrimination in the area of civil marriage. On the day after the election, same-sex marriages were again prohibited in California.

In a subsequent case before the California Supreme Court, the validity of Proposition 8 was challenged. Opponents of Proposition 8 argued that the mere majority-based process of the constitutional initiative was insufficient under the requirements of the Constitution and that a popular initiative could not revoke inalienable rights without a compelling justification. The Court also considered the validity of the approximately 18,000 same-sex marriages that occurred between June 16 and November 5, 2008. On May 26, 2009, the Court ruled that the initiative constitutional amendment process was sufficient to amend the rights provisions of the California Constitution, thereby upholding the validity of Proposition 8. The Court nevertheless determined that the marriages performed in the months prior to the passage of Proposition 8 remained valid.

———

Connecticut

The Connecticut Supreme court ruled in a 4–3 opinion, *Kerrigan v. Commissioner of Public Health* 957 A.2d 407 (2008), that the state's ban on same-sex marriage violated the state constitution's guarantee of equal protection and that gay people had a right to "marry the otherwise qualified same-sex partner of their choice." Interestingly, the state did not attempt to justify the ban by reference to heterosexual procreation or providing an optimal setting to raise children. Instead, the state argued that the ban furthered the government's interest in maintaining uniformity with the marriage laws of most other states which prohibited same-sex marriage. The court dismissed this argument because the state "offered no reason" why this was an important goal and, moreover, the goal was not "sufficiently compelling" to justify the discrimination. The court also dismissed the state's other justification for the marriage limitation—preserving the longstanding tradition of limiting marriage to a union between a woman and a man. Neither a strong belief in this tradition, nor moral disapproval of homosexuality, provide sufficient cause for discriminating against a disfavored minority, the court reasoned.

——

Iowa

A unanimous Iowa Supreme Court in *Varnum v. Brien*, 763 N.W.2d 862 (2009), followed a very similar path as the California Supreme Court in *In re Marriage Cases*, above. The Court addressed the question whether a statute which limited marriage to a union between a man and a woman violated the equal protection clause of the state constitution. The court reasoned that "[t]he benefit denied by the marriage statute—the status of civil marriage for same-sex couples—is so 'closely correlated with being homosexual' as to make it apparent the law is targeted at gay and lesbian people as a class." Because the legislation was class based, and thus "suspect", the court applied heightened (intermediate) scrutiny to the law and concluded that "the exclusion of gay and lesbian people from the institution of civil marriage [did] not substantially further any important governmental objectives." Limiting marriage to opposite sex-couples, for instance, did not substantially contribute to the government objective of creating an optimal environment to raise children. The court found the statute under-inclusive because it did not exclude from marriage other groups of parents—such as child abusers, sexual predators, parents neglecting to provide child support, and violent felons—that are undeniably less than optimal parents. If the marriage statute was truly focused on optimal parenting, many classifications of people would be excluded, not merely gay and lesbian people. The statute was also under-inclusive because it did not prohibit same-sex couples from raising children in Iowa. The statute was over-inclusive because not all same-sex couples choose to raise children. The court also concluded that limiting marriage to opposite-sex couples did not promote the government's objective of promoting stability in opposite-sex relationships. In fact, "there was no evidence to support that excluding gay and lesbian people from civil marriage makes opposite sex-marriage more stable." The court required the state legislature to remove from its laws any language limiting marriage to a man and a woman and to interpret and apply its laws "in a manner allowing gay and lesbian people full access to the institution of marriage."

——

Virginia

Constitution of the Commonwealth of Virginia Section 15–A

Only a union between one man and one woman may be a marriage valid in or recognized by this Commonwealth and its political subdivisions.

This Commonwealth and its political subdivisions shall not create or recognize a legal status for relationships of unmarried individuals that intends to approximate the design, qualities, significance, or effects of marriage. Nor shall this Commonwealth or its political subdivisions create or recognize another union, partnership, or other legal status to which is assigned the rights, benefits, obligations, qualities, or effects of marriage.

(Effective date January 1, 2007. Approved by 57% of voters on Tuesday, November 7, 2006)

States with constitutional amendments prohibiting same-sex marriage

Alabama (2006)	Alaska (1998)	Arizona (2008)
Arkansas (2004)	California (2008)	Colorado (2006)
Florida (2008)	Georgia (2004)	Idaho (2006)
Kansas (2005)	Kentucky (2004)	Louisiana (2004)
Michigan (2004)	Mississippi (2004)	Montana (2004)
Nebraska (2000)	Nevada (2002)	North Dakota (2004)
Ohio (2004)	Oklahoma (2004)	Oregon (2004)
South Carolina (2006)	South Dakota (2006)	Tennessee (2006)
Texas (2005)	Utah (2004)	Virginia (2006)
Wisconsin (2006)		

Many gay and lesbian legal organizations initially followed a state-by-state strategy for marriage equality. However, given the significant number of state constitutional amendments and the rejection of equality arguments by some state courts, there is renewed interest in federal impact litigation. In early 2010, federal trial courts heard two significant challenges to prohibitions against same-sex marriage that have their basis in the *Goodridge* and *In Re: Marriages* cases. In *Gill v. Office of Personnel Management*, 699 F.Supp.2d 374 (2010), equality advocates challenged the federal Defense of Marriage Act provision that prohibits the federal government from providing certain tangible federal rights and benefits to legally married individuals who entered into same-sex marriages in Massachusetts. The district court held that provision of DOMA unconstitutional. That ruling has been stayed while the case is on appeal. In *Perry v. Schwarzenegger*, discussed in note 6 below, advocates are challenging the constitutionality of California's Proposition 8 in light of the successful equal protection arguments in *Romer v. Evans,* 517 U.S. 620 (1996) (holding that anti-gay animus, a "bare … desire to harm a politically unpopular group," was an insufficient legal basis to uphold an electoral initiative that broadly burdened the advancement of gay and lesbian anti-discrimination laws; and the successful federal fundamental rights arguments in *Lawrence v. Texas,* discussed in note 7, below.

NOTES

1. As of October 2011, the United States jurisdictions that perform and recognize same-sex marriages are Massachusetts (2003), Connecticut

(2009), Coquille (American Indian nation located in Oregon) (2008), Vermont (2009), the District of Columbia (2009), Iowa (2009), New Hampshire (2010), and New York (2011).

2. As of October 2011, the United States jurisdictions that do not perform, but recognize out-of-state and foreign same-sex marriages, are California (pre-November 2008 marriages only), Maryland, New Mexico, and Rhode Island.

3. As of October 2011, the United States jurisdictions that recognize ("all but marriage") civil unions are California (2003–08, 2009), New Jersey (2003), Oregon (2008), Washington (2009). Illinois (2011), Delaware (2012), and Hawaii (2012).

4. Public support for same-sex marriage in the United States has exhibited a slow but steady upward trajectory over time, at an increase of approximately 1% annually. Patrick J. Egan and Nathaniel Persily, Court Decisions and Trends in Support for Same Sex Marriage, Polling Report, (August 2009), http://www.pollingreport.com/penp0908.htm. Recent polling indicates support at an all time high, although there is considerable variation in public sentiment depending on age, political affiliation, church attendance and other demographic factors. A May 2011 Gallup poll, for example, indicated that a majority of Americans support recognition of same-sex marriages, polling 53% to 45% in favor, with older Americans, Republicans, and frequent churchgoers polling significantly less support. *For the First Time, Majority of Americans Favor Legal Gay Marriages*, Gallup, May 20, 2011, http://www.gallup.com/poll/147662/First–Time–Majority–Americans–Favor–Legal–Gay–Marriage.aspx.

5. Compare the relatively brisk upward pace of acceptance of same-sex marriage to the relatively glacial pace of acceptance of interracial marriage. Even decades after the Supreme Court invalidated bans on such marriages in *Loving v. Virginia*, such marriages were disapproved by a majority of the public. The well respected Gallup organization recently reported the following:

> According to [Gallup's 2007 poll], 77% of Americans say they approve of marriages between blacks and whites, while 17% say they disapprove. Public support for black-white marriages is now at the high end of the range of approval seen on this question since Gallup first asked it almost 50 years ago ... Gallup's long-term trend on this question documents a sea change in public attitudes about interracial marriage. In 1958, only 4% of Americans said they approved of marriages between whites and blacks.... Approval gradually increased over the next few decades, but at least half of Americans disapproved of black-white unions through 1983. Then, in the next measure eight years later, disapproval had fallen to 42%, with 48% approving. In 1997, the next time Gallup asked the question, approval had jumped well into the majority, with nearly two in three Americans saying they approved of marriages between blacks and whites. Disapproval fell to 27% in that same year. Support remained at about the two-thirds level until 2002, but increased to 73% in 2003. Since then, there have only been modest variations in attitudes about interracial marriages.

Most Americans Approve of Interracial Marriages: Blacks more Likely than Whites to approve of Black–White Unions, Gallup. August 16, 2007, http://www.gallup.com/poll/28417/ most-americans-approve-interracial-marriages.aspx. A more recent Gallup poll found an even sharper increase in approval of black-white marriage over the past decade, with 96% of blacks and 84% of whites now approving of such marriages and an overall approval high of 86%. Record High 86% *Approval of Black–White Marriages*, Gallup, September 12, 2011, http://www. gallup.com/poll/149390/Record–High–Approve–Black–White–Marriages.aspx.

6. In *Perry v. Schwarzenegger*, the opponents of California Proposition 8 claimed victory in a federal district court. The District Court for the Northern District of California found that Proposition 8 was unconstitutional under the Due Process Clause and the Equal Protection Clause. *Perry v. Schwarzenegger*, 704 F. Supp. 2d 921, 1003 (N.D. Cal. 2010). After the district court enjoined Proposition 8 from being enforced, proponents of Proposition 8 appealed the district court's holding, but the named officials did not. The Ninth Circuit, recognizing that there were no longer two sides represented in the case, presented a certified question to the Supreme Court of California on January 4, 2011. The Ninth Circuit asked:

> Whether under Article II, Section 8 of the California Constitution, or otherwise under California law, the official proponents of an initiative measure possess either a particularized interest in the initiative's validity or the authority to assert the State's interest in the initiative's validity, which would enable them to defend the constitutionality of the initiative upon its adoption or appeal a judgment invalidating the initiative, when the public officials charged with that duty refuse to do so. *Perry v. Schwarzenegger* 628 F.3d 1191, 1193 (9th Cir. 2011).

On November 17, 2011 the California Supreme Court advised the Ninth Circuit that under California law the district court's holding can be appealed by the proponents of Proposition 8. *Perry v. Brown* (S189476, order of 11/17/11). On February 7, 2012, the U.S. Court of Appeals for the Ninth Circuit affirmed that California's ban on same-sex marriage, Proposition 8, was unconstitutional. The Court ruled that the ban serves no purpose other than to "lessen the status and human dignity" of gays and lesbians and to "officially reclassify their relationships and families as inferior to those of opposite-sex couples." The Court opined that "the Constitution simply does not allow for laws of this sort." *Perry v. Brown*, http://www.ca9.uscourts.gov/datastore/general/2012/02/07/1016696com.pdf. The case will likely be appealed to the Supreme Court of the United States.

7. In *Lawrence v. Texas*, 539 U.S. 558 (2003), the U.S. Supreme Court struck down a law in the state of Texas that made it a crime for two persons of the same sex to engage in certain intimate conduct. The Court invalidated the law on the ground of due process, or personal autonomy, ruling that:

> "... adults may choose to enter upon this relationship in the confines of their homes and their own private lives and still retain their dignity as free persons. When sexuality finds overt expression in

intimate conduct with another person, the conduct can be but one element in a personal bond that is more enduring. The liberty protected by the Constitution allows homosexual persons the right to make this choice. . ." *Id.* at 567.

The Court's ruling overturned its earlier ruling in *Bowers v. Hardwick*, 478 U.S. 186 (1986), in which the Court upheld the constitutionality of a Georgia statute which criminalizes certain intimate acts when applied to homosexuals. In overturning *Bowers*, the *Lawrence* Court referred to the fact that the European Court of Human Rights and other nations have rejected the reasoning and holding in *Bowers* and consistently affirmed "the right of homosexual adults to engage in intimate, consensual conduct" as an "integral part of human freedom." *Id.* at 572–577.

8. Did *Lawrence* pave the way for the more recent invalidation of state statutes limiting marriage between a man and a woman? One of the points of tension between the majority opinion in *Lawrence*, authored by Justice Kennedy, and the dissenting opinion, authored by Justice Scalia, is this point:

> One of the benefits of leaving regulation of this matter to the people rather than to the courts is that the people, unlike judges, need not carry things to their logical conclusion. The people may feel that their disapprobation of homosexual conduct is strong enough to disallow homosexual marriage, but not strong enough to criminalize private homosexual acts—and may legislate accordingly. The Court today pretends that it possesses a similar freedom of action, so that we need not fear judicial imposition of homosexual marriage, as has recently occurred in Canada (in a decision that the Canadian Government has chosen not to appeal). * * * At the end of its opinion—after having laid waste the foundations of our rational-basis jurisprudence—the Court says that the present case "does not involve whether the government must give formal recognition to any relationship that homosexual persons seek to enter." Do not believe it.

Lawrence v. Texas, 539 U.S. at 604–605 (Scalia, dissenting)

9. President Barack Obama has decided to stop defending the Defense of Marriage Act (DOMA) in federal court in lawsuits claiming that the Act is unconstitutional. In a Statement by the Department of Justice, Attorney General Eric Holder explained the reason for this policy reversal:

> After careful consideration, including a review of my recommendation, the President has concluded that given a number of factors, including a documented history of discrimination, classifications based on sexual orientation should be subject to a more heightened standard of scrutiny. The President has also concluded that Section 3 of DOMA, as applied to legally married same-sex couples, fails to meet that standard and is therefore unconstitutional. Given that conclusion, the President has instructed the Department not to defend the statute in such cases. I fully concur with the President's determination.

> Consequently, the Department will not defend the constitutionality of Section 3 of DOMA as applied to same-sex married couples in the two cases filed in the Second Circuit. We will, however, remain parties

to the cases and continue to represent the interests of the United States throughout the litigation. I have informed Members of Congress of this decision, so Members who wish to defend the statute may pursue that option. The Department will also work closely with the courts to ensure that Congress has a full and fair opportunity to participate in pending litigation.

Statement of the Attorney General on Litigation Involving the Defense of Marriage Act, http://www.justice.gov/opa/pr/2011/February/11–ag–222.html. Republican House Speaker John Boehner has vowed that the House of Representatives will take over the legal responsibility of defending DOMA in court. Boehner said: "[t]he constitutionality of this law should be determined by the courts—not by the president unilaterally—and this action by the House will ensure the matter is addressed in a manner consistent with our Constitution." Statement by House Speaker John Boehner (R–OH) Regarding the Defense of Marriage Act, http://www.speaker.gov/ News/DocumentSingle.aspx?DocumentID=227372.

10. Adoption by individuals who are LGBT is now legal in all states. In 2010, a federal court struck down the one explicit ban against gays and lesbians from adopting. In the case *In re Gill*, a Florida district court ruled that the State of Florida's ban violated the Florida Constitution's equal protection clause. The Third Circuit Court of Appeals of Florida upheld the district court ruling reasoning that the ban had no rational relationship to the best interests of children. http://www.aclu.org/lgbt-rights_hiv-aids/re-gill-case-profile. The laws vary widely, however, for gays and lesbians who want to adopt as a couple. The state of Utah, for example, specifically prohibits unmarried, co-habitating couples from adopting. Utah Code Section 78B–6–117(3). Other states allow "second-parent" adoption by the partner of an existing legal parent. For a discussion of the rights of children of same-sex couples, *see* Catherine Smith, *Equal Protection for Children of Gay and Lesbian Parents: Challenging the Three Pillars of Exclusion—Legitimacy, Dual–Gender Parenting, and Biology,* 28 LAW AND INEQUALITY 307 (2010).

B. CANADA

Canadian Charter of Rights and Freedoms

Guarantee of Rights and Freedoms

1. The Canadian Charter of Rights and Freedoms guarantees the rights and freedoms set out in it subject only to such reasonable limits prescribed by law as can be demonstrably justified in a free and democratic society.

Equality Rights

15. (1) Every individual is equal before and under the law and has the right to equal protection and equal benefit of the law without discrimina-

tion and, in particular, without discrimination based on race, national or ethnic origin, colour, religion, sex, age or mental or physical disability.

(2) Subsection (1) does not preclude any law, program or activity that has as its object the amelioration of conditions of disadvantaged individuals or groups including those that are disadvantaged because of race, national or ethnic origin, colour, religion, sex, age or mental or physical disability.

———

Halpern v. Canada

Docket: C39172 and C39174 Court of Appeal for Ontario (2003)

INTRODUCTION

[1] The definition of marriage in Canada, for all of the nation's 136 years, has been based on the classic formulation of Lord Penzance in *Hyde v. Hyde and Woodmansee* (1866), L.R. 1 P. & D. 130 at 133: "I conceive that marriage, as understood in Christendom, may for this purpose be defined as the voluntary union for life of one man and one woman, to the exclusion of all others." The central question in this appeal is whether the exclusion of same-sex couples from this common law definition of marriage breaches ss. 2(a) or 15(1) of the Canadian Charter of Rights and Freedoms ("the Charter") in a manner that is not justified in a free and democratic society under s. 1 of the Charter.

[2] This appeal raises significant constitutional issues that require serious legal analysis. That said, this case is ultimately about the recognition and protection of human dignity and equality in the context of the social structures available to conjugal couples in Canada.

[3] In *Law v. Canada* (Minister of Employment and Immigration), [1999] 1 S.C.R. 497 at 530, Iacobucci J., writing for a unanimous court, described the importance of human dignity:

> Human dignity means that an individual or group feels self-respect and self-worth. It is concerned with physical and psychological integrity and empowerment. Human dignity is harmed by unfair treatment premised upon personal traits or circumstances which do not relate to individual needs, capacities, or merits. It is enhanced by laws which are sensitive to the needs, capacities, and merits of different individuals, taking into account the context underlying their differences. Human dignity is harmed when individuals and groups are marginalized, ignored, or devalued, and is enhanced when laws recognize the full place of all individuals and groups within Canadian society.

[4] The Ontario Human Rights Code, R.S.O. 1990, c. H.19, also recognizes the importance of protecting the dignity of all persons. The preamble affirms that "the inherent dignity and the equal and inalienable rights of all members of the human family is the foundation of freedom, justice and peace in the world". It states:

[I]t is public policy in Ontario to recognize the dignity and worth of every person and to provide for equal rights and opportunities without discrimination that is contrary to law, and having as its aim the creation of a climate of understanding and mutual respect for the dignity and worth of each person so that each person feels a part of the community and able to contribute fully to the development and well-being of the community and the Province;

[5]   Marriage is, without dispute, one of the most significant forms of personal relationships. For centuries, marriage has been a basic element of social organization in societies around the world. Through the institution of marriage, individuals can publicly express their love and commitment to each other. Through this institution, society publicly recognizes expressions of love and commitment between individuals, granting them respect and legitimacy as a couple. This public recognition and sanction of marital relationships reflect society's approbation of the personal hopes, desires and aspirations that underlie loving, committed conjugal relationships. This can only enhance an individual's sense of self-worth and dignity.

[6]   The ability to marry, and to thereby participate in this fundamental societal institution, is something that most Canadians take for granted. Same-sex couples do not; they are denied access to this institution simply on the basis of their sexual orientation.

[7]   Sexual orientation is an analogous ground that comes under the umbrella of protection in s. 15(1) of the Charter: *see Egan v. Canada*, [1995] 2 S.C.R. 513, and *M. v. H.*, [1999] 2 S.C.R. 3. As explained by Cory J. in *M. v. H.* at 52–53:

In *Egan* ... this Court unanimously affirmed that sexual orientation is an analogous ground to those enumerated in s. 15(1). Sexual orientation is "a deeply personal characteristic that is either unchangeable or changeable only at unacceptable personal costs" (para. 5). In addition, a majority of this Court explicitly recognized that gays, lesbians and bisexuals, "whether as individuals or couples, form an identifiable minority who have suffered and continue to suffer serious social, political and economic disadvantage" (para. 175, per Cory J.; *see also* para. 89, per L'Heureux–Dubé J.).

[8]   Historically, same-sex equality litigation has focused on achieving equality in some of the most basic elements of civic life, such as bereavement leave, health care benefits, pensions benefits, spousal support, name changes and adoption. The question at the heart of this appeal is whether excluding same-sex couples from another of the most basic elements of civic life—marriage—infringes human dignity and violates the Canadian Constitution.

FACTS

* * *

[9]   Seven gay and lesbian couples ("the Couples") want to celebrate their love and commitment to each other by getting married in civil ceremonies. In this respect, they share the same goal as countless other

Canadian couples. Their reasons for wanting to engage in a formal civil ceremony of marriage are the same as the reasons of heterosexual couples. * * *

ANALYSIS

* * *

[42] [T]o freeze the definition of marriage to whatever meaning it had in 1867 is contrary to this country's jurisprudence of progressive constitutional interpretation. This jurisprudence is rooted in Lord Sankey's words in *Edwards v. A.G. Canada*, [1930] A.C. 124 at 136 (P.C.): "The British North America Act planted in Canada a living tree capable of growth and expansion within its natural limits." Dickson J. reiterated the correctness of this approach to constitutional interpretation in *Hunter v. Southam Inc.*, [1984] 2 S.C.R. 145 at 155:

> The task of expounding a constitution is crucially different from that of construing a statute. A statute defines present rights and obligations. It is easily enacted and as easily repealed. A constitution, by contrast, is drafted with an eye to the future. Its function is to provide a continuing framework for the legitimate exercise of governmental power and, when joined by a Bill or a Charter of Rights, for the unremitting protection of individual rights and liberties. Once enacted, its provisions cannot easily be repealed or amended. It must, therefore, be capable of growth and development over time to meet new social, political and historical realities often unimagined by its framers. The judiciary is the guardian of the constitution and must, in interpreting its provisions, bear these considerations in mind. * * *

[60] In *Law*, Iacobucci J., writing for a unanimous court, described the purpose of s. 15(1) in the following terms, at p. 529:

> It may be said that the purpose of s. 15(1) is to prevent the violation of essential human dignity and freedom through the imposition of disadvantage, stereotyping, or political or social prejudice, and to promote a society in which all persons enjoy equal recognition at law as human beings or as members of Canadian society, equally capable and equally deserving of concern, respect and consideration.

[61] Iacobucci J. emphasized that a s. 15(1) violation will be found to exist only where the impugned law conflicts with the purpose of s. 15(1). The determination of whether such a conflict exists must be approached in a purposive and contextual manner: *Law* at 525. To that end, Iacobucci J. articulated a three-stage inquiry, at pp. 548–49:

> (A) Does the impugned law (a) draw a formal distinction between the claimant and others on the basis of one or more personal characteristics, or (b) fail to take into account the claimant's already disadvantaged position within Canadian society resulting in substantively differential treatment between the claimant and others on the basis of one or more personal characteristics?

> (B) Is the claimant subject to differential treatment based on one or more enumerated and analogous grounds? and

(C) Does the differential treatment discriminate, by imposing a burden upon or withholding a benefit from the claimant in a manner which reflects the stereotypical application of presumed group or personal characteristics, or which otherwise has the effect of perpetuating or promoting the view that the individual is less capable or worthy of recognition or value as a human being or as a member of Canadian society, equally deserving of concern, respect, and consideration?

The claimant has the burden of establishing each of these factors on a balance of probabilities. * * *

[77] The third stage of the s. 15(1) inquiry ... is concerned with substantive equality, not formal equality: *Gosselin v. Quebec* (2002). The emphasis is on human dignity. In *Law* at 530, Iacobucci J. elaborated on the meaning and importance of respecting human dignity, particularly within the framework of equality rights:

> Human dignity means that an individual or group feels self-respect and self-worth. It is concerned with physical and psychological integrity and empowerment. Human dignity is harmed by unfair treatment premised upon personal traits or circumstances which do not relate to individual needs, capacities, or merits. It is enhanced by laws which are sensitive to the needs, capacities, and merits of different individuals, taking into account the context underlying their differences. Human dignity is harmed when individuals and groups are marginalized, ignored, or devalued, and is enhanced when laws recognize the full place of all individuals and groups within Canadian society. Human dignity within the meaning of the equality guarantee does not relate to the status or position of an individual in society per se, but rather concerns the manner in which a person legitimately feels when confronted with a particular law. Does the law treat him or her unfairly, taking into account all of the circumstances regarding the individuals affected and excluded by the law?

[79] The assessment of whether a law has the effect of demeaning a claimant's dignity should be undertaken from a subjective-objective perspective. The relevant point of view is not solely that of a "reasonable person", but that of a "reasonable person, dispassionate and fully apprised of the circumstances, possessed of similar attributes to, and under similar circumstances as, the group of which the rights claimant is a member": *Egan* at 553; *Law* at 533–34. This requires a court to consider the individual's or group's traits, history, and circumstances in order to evaluate whether a reasonable person, in circumstances similar to the claimant, would find that the impugned law differentiates in a manner that demeans his or her dignity: *Law* at 533. * * *

[82] The first contextual factor to be examined is the existence of a pre-existing disadvantage, stereotyping, prejudice or vulnerability experienced by the individual or group at issue. While this contextual factor is not determinative, it is "probably the most compelling factor favouring a conclusion that differential treatment imposed by legislation is truly discriminatory". . . .

These factors are relevant because, to the extent that the claimant is already subject to unfair circumstances or treatment in society by virtue of personal characteristics or circumstances, persons like him or her have often not been given equal concern, respect, and consideration. It is logical to conclude that, in most cases, further differential treatment will contribute to the perpetuation or promotion of their unfair social characterization, and will have a more severe impact upon them, since they are already vulnerable. * * *

[89]   The Attorney General of Canada ("AGC") submits that marriage relates to the capacities, needs and circumstances of opposite-sex couples. The concept of marriage—across time, societies and legal cultures—is that of an institution to facilitate, shelter and nurture the unique union of a man and woman who, together, have the possibility to bear children from their relationship and shelter them within it.

[90]   We cannot accept the AGC's argument for several reasons.

[91]   First, it is important to remember that the purpose and effects of the impugned law must at all times be viewed from the perspective of the claimant. The question to be asked is whether the law takes into account the actual needs, capacities and circumstances of same-sex couples, not whether the law takes into account the needs, capacities and circumstances of opposite-sex couples. In *Law* at 538, Iacobucci J. cautioned that "[t]he fact that the impugned legislation may achieve a valid social purpose for one group of individuals cannot function to deny an equality claim where the effects of the legislation upon another person or group conflict with the purpose of the s. 15(1) guarantee."

[92]   Second, the AGC's argument on this point is more appropriately considered in the context of a s. 1 justification analysis. We find the comments of Bastarache J. in *Lavoie v. Canada*, [2002] 1 S.C.R. 769 at 809–10 to be apposite:

In measuring the appellants' subjective experience of discrimination against an objective standard, it is crucial not to elide the distinction between the claimant's onus to establish a prima facie s. 15(1) violation and the state's onus to justify such a violation under s. 1. Section 15(1) requires the claimant to show that her human dignity and/or freedom is adversely affected. The concepts of dignity and freedom are not amorphous and, in my view, do not invite the kind of balancing of individual against state interest that is required under s. 1 of the Charter. On the contrary, the subjective inquiry into human dignity requires the claimant to provide a rational foundation for her experience of discrimination in the sense that a reasonable person similarly situated would share that experience.

By contrast, the government's burden under s. 1 is to justify a breach of human dignity, not to explain it or deny its existence. This justification may be established by the practical, moral, economic, or social underpinnings of the legislation in question, or by the need to protect other rights and values embodied in the Charter. It may further be established based on the requirements of proportionality, that is, whether the interest pursued by the legislation outweighs its impact on human dignity and freedom.

However, the exigencies of public policy do not undermine the prima facie legitimacy of an equality claim. A law is not "non-discriminatory" simply because it pursues a pressing objective or impairs equality rights as little as possible. Much less is it "non-discriminatory" because it reflects an international consensus as to the appropriate limits on equality rights. * * *

[94]   Importantly, no one, including the AGC, is suggesting that procreation and childrearing are the only purposes of marriage, or the only reasons why couples choose to marry. Intimacy, companionship, societal recognition, economic benefits, the blending of two families, to name a few, are other reasons that couples choose to marry. As recognized in *M. v. H.* at 50, same-sex couples are capable of forming "long, lasting, loving and intimate relationships." Denying same-sex couples the right to marry perpetuates the contrary view, namely, that same-sex couples are not capable of forming loving and lasting relationships, and thus same-sex relationships are not worthy of the same respect and recognition as opposite-sex relationships.

[95]   Accordingly, in our view, the common law requirement that marriage be between persons of the opposite sex does not accord with the needs, capacities and circumstances of same-sex couples. This factor weighs in favour of a finding of discrimination. * * *

Conclusion [to the first question: Is there a violation of Section 15?]

[108]   Based on the foregoing analysis, it is our view that the dignity of persons in same-sex relationships is violated by the exclusion of same-sex couples from the institution of marriage. Accordingly, we conclude that the common-law definition of marriage as "the voluntary union for life of one man and one woman to the exclusion of all others" violates s. 15(1) of the Charter. The next step is to determine whether this violation can be justified under s. 1 of the Charter. * * *

Reasonable Limits under Section 1 of the Charter [Limitations Clause] * * *

However, the Couples submit that a s. 1 analysis is not required because this case concerns a challenge to a common law or "judge-made" rule rather than a legislative provision.

Proportionality analysis
* * *

[141]   Since we have already concluded that the objectives are not rationally connected to the opposite-sex requirement of marriage, and the means chosen to achieve the objectives do not impair the Couples' rights as minimally as possible, it is axiomatic that the deleterious effects of the exclusion of same-sex couples from marriage outweigh its objectives.

Conclusion

[142]   Accordingly, we conclude that the violation of the Couples' equality rights under s. 15(1) of the Charter is not justified under s. 1 of the Charter. The AGC has not demonstrated that the objectives of excluding same-sex couples from marriage are pressing and substantial. The AGC

has also failed to show that the means chosen to achieve its objectives are reasonable and justified in a free and democratic society.

Remedy

* * *

[148]   [I]n our view the remedy that best corrects the inconsistency is to declare invalid the existing definition of marriage to the extent that it refers to "one man and one woman", and to reformulate the definition of marriage as "the voluntary union for life of two persons to the exclusion of all others". This remedy achieves the equality required by s. 15(1) of the Charter but ensures that the legal status of marriage is not left in a state of uncertainty.

[151]   We are also of the view that the argument made by the AGC and several of the intervenors that we should defer to Parliament once we issue a declaration of invalidity is not apposite in these circumstances. Schachter provides that the role of the legislature and legislative objectives is to be considered at the second step of the remedy analysis when a court is deciding whether severance or reading in is an appropriate remedy to cure a legislative provision that breaches the Charter. These considerations do not arise where the genesis of the Charter breach is found in the common law and there is no legislation to be altered. Any lacunae created by a declaration of invalidity of a common law rule are common law lacunae that should be remedied by the courts, unless to do so would conflict with the principles of fundamental justice. * * *

DISPOSITION

[155]   In summary, we have concluded the following:

(1) the existing common law definition of marriage is "the voluntary union for life of one man and one woman to the exclusion of all others";

(2) the courts have jurisdiction to alter the common law definition of marriage; resort to constitutional amendment procedures is not required; * * *

(4) the existing common law definition of marriage violates the Couples' equality rights on the basis of sexual orientation under s. 15(1) of the Charter; and

(5) the violation of the Couples' equality rights under s. 15(1) of the Charter cannot be justified in a free and democratic society under s. 1 of the Charter.

[156]   To remedy the infringement of these constitutional rights, we:

(1) declare the existing common law definition of marriage to be invalid to the extent that it refers to "one man and one woman";

(2) reformulate the common law definition of marriage as "the voluntary union for life of two persons to the exclusion of all others";

(3) order the declaration of invalidity in (1) and the reformulated definition in (2) to have immediate effect;

(4) order the Clerk of the City of Toronto to issue marriage licenses to the Couples* * *

————

[EDITORS' NOTE: In June 2003, then Prime Minister Chrétien announced that the federal government would not appeal the Halpern decision. In July, the government referred draft marriage legislation to the Supreme Court of Canada in a constitutional reference. In December 2004, the Supreme Court of Canada held that the draft bill was consistent with the Canadian Charter of Rights and Freedoms. (*See* Clifford Krauss, *Court Says Canada's Constitution Does Not Bar Same–Sex Marriage*, NEW YORK TIMES, December 9, 2004). On February 1, 2005 the government introduced Bill C–38, The Civil Marriage Act.]

————

Bill C–38—The Civil Marriage Act

Royal Assent: July 20, 2005
Statutes of Canada S.C. 2005, c. 33

Preamble

WHEREAS the Parliament of Canada is committed to upholding the Constitution of Canada, and section 15 of the Canadian Charter of Rights and Freedoms guarantees that every individual is equal before and under the law and has the right to equal protection and equal benefit of the law without discrimination;

WHEREAS the courts in a majority of the provinces and in one territory have recognized that the right to equality without discrimination requires that couples of the same sex and couples of the opposite sex have equal access to marriage for civil purposes; * * *

WHEREAS nothing in this Act affects the guarantee of freedom of conscience and religion and, in particular, the freedom of members of religious groups to hold and declare their religious beliefs and the freedom of officials of religious groups to refuse to perform marriages that are not in accordance with their religious beliefs;

WHEREAS it is not against the public interest to hold and publicly express diverse views on marriage;

WHEREAS, in light of those considerations, the Parliament of Canada's commitment to uphold the right to equality without discrimination precludes the use of section 33 of the Canadian Charter of Rights and Freedoms to deny the right of couples of the same sex to equal access to marriage for civil purposes;

WHEREAS marriage is a fundamental institution in Canadian society and the Parliament of Canada has a responsibility to support that institution because it strengthens commitment in relationships and represents the foundation of family life for many Canadians;

AND WHEREAS, in order to reflect values of tolerance, respect and equality consistent with the Canadian Charter of Rights and Freedoms, access to marriage for civil purposes should be extended by legislation to couples of the same sex;

NOW, THEREFORE, Her Majesty, by and with the advice and consent of the Senate and House of Commons of Canada, enacts as follows:

Short title

1. This Act may be cited as the Civil Marriage Act.

Marriage—certain aspects of capacity

2. Marriage, for civil purposes, is the lawful union of two persons to the exclusion of all others.

Religious officials

3. It is recognized that officials of religious groups are free to refuse to perform marriages that are not in accordance with their religious beliefs.

Freedom of conscience and religion and expression of beliefs

3.1 For greater certainty, no person or organization shall be deprived of any benefit, or be subject to any obligation or sanction, under any law of the Parliament of Canada solely by reason of their exercise, in respect of marriage between persons of the same sex, of the freedom of conscience and religion guaranteed under the Canadian Charter of Rights and Freedoms or the expression of their beliefs in respect of marriage as the union of a man and woman to the exclusion of all others based on that guaranteed freedom.

Marriage not void or voidable

4. For greater certainty, a marriage is not void or voidable by reason only that the spouses are of the same sex.

———

NOTES

1. The *Halpern* case was the first of many judicial decisions striking down bans on same-sex marriage in various Canadian provinces and territories. Prior to the 2005 Civil Marriage Act, same-sex marriage was recognized in Ontario (2003), British Columbia (2003), Quebec (2004), Yukon Territory (2004), Manitoba (2004), Nova Scotia (2004), Saskatchewan (2004), Newfoundland and Labrador (2004), and New Brunswick (2005).

2. The definition of marriage in Canada is properly a matter of federal law. In *Reference re Same–Sex Marriage* [2004] 3 S.C.R. 698, 2004 SCC 79, the Supreme Court of Canada ruled that it was within the power of the Parliament of Canada to enact marriage legislation that stated: "[m]arriage, for civil purposes, is the lawful union of two persons to the exclusion of all others." The court then found that this legislation was

consistent with the Canadian Charter of Rights and Freedoms. Finally, the court held that the guarantee of freedom of religion in Canada protects religious officials from "being compelled by the state to perform marriages between two persons of the same sex contrary to their religious beliefs."

3. In December 2006, the House of Commons essentially reaffirmed the Civil Marriage Act, defeating a conservative government motion to examine the issue again. *MPs Defeat Bid to Reopen Same–Sex Marriage*, CBC News, December 7, 2006, http://www.cbc.ca/news/canada/story/2006/12/07/vote-samesex.html.

4. Canada's progressive stance on same-sex marriage has carried over to same-sex adoption.

> The gay community made great progress when courts at the lower levels (*i.e.*, in Ontario, Alberta, and Nova Scotia) initiated changes in provincial legislation to allow same-sex couples to jointly apply for adoption. Other jurisdictions, such as Saskatchewan, voluntarily amended its legislation in response to the Supreme Court of Canada decision in *M v. H* (discussed in more detail below).

> In regard to same-sex unions and adoption, the Ontario provincial court decision K and B (Re) is especially noteworthy because it made important factual findings about same-sex relationships and parenting, and has been referred to, considered, and applied in various jurisdictions. In that case, the Court found that the definition of spouse under the Act operated to deny lesbian couples' protected equality rights under s. 15 (1) of the Charter and could not be saved by s. 1. In particular, the applicants were denied the benefit of applying to adopt a child on the basis of sexual orientation, which was not found to be in violation of the best interests of the child. Indeed, the Court held that the same-sex relationships, including parenting, were virtually identical to those of the opposite sex in finding that each of the lesbian couples had been "living together in committed relationships for varying lengths of time," which "might be termed 'conjugal,' in that they ha[d] all the characteristics of a relationship formalized by marriage." Further, the Court held that "[h]omosexual individuals do not exhibit higher levels of psychopathology than do heterosexual individuals" in that "there is no good evidence to suggest that homosexual individuals are less healthy psychologically and therefore less able to be emotionally available to their children."

Jane Adolphe, *The Case Against Same–Sex Marriage in Canada: Law and Policy Considerations*, 18 BYU J. Pub. L. 479, 490–91 (2004).

5. While the judicial and legislative movement toward approval of same-sex marriage signals its increasing acceptance in a particular society, it is also the case that overreliance on these legal and legislative victories can obscure deeper cultural (and even legal) conflicts of the issue, and even provoke considerable social and political backlash. Using the case of Canada's recent judicial and legislative victories on behalf of gays and lesbians, one commentator cautions both against overreliance on constitutional rulings within a particular social movement, as well as for purposes of

comparative analysis, when trying to secure constitutional rights in different legal and political cultures:

> Comparative reading of the judgments of constitutional courts emphasizes the judiciary as the site of a constitution's operation, whereas the executive branch of government affects individuals much more in their daily lives. Contrary to the implication of the repeated comparisons of high court judgments, constitutional meaning is appropriately understood as found and invented in a variety of locations and practices. Taking constitutional courts as the crucial site of constitutional action, and their judgments as the primary texts for scrutiny, may misrepresent the state of constitutional rights on the ground. The comparative constitutional scholarship on gay rights seems to assume that changes in constitutional interpretation by the highest court change the constitution's operation. Put bluntly, however, constitutional judgments do not represent the state of rights in practice. Textual analysis of constitutional judgments may exclude "the actual political practices" and the "concrete political impact" of homophobic laws on "the real, live, flesh-and-blood bodies of the empirical individuals to whom those laws are addressed." It has been intriguingly argued that for feminists—and, one might fairly add, gay or queer justiceseekers—"to engage with the discursive power of Constitutions, it is strategically imperative to identify both the external local and global forces that make up the whole of the discursive frame." Those authors argue for "an embedded approach to constitutional rights, one that acknowledges all of the diverse ways in which rights are filtered, translated, upheld, or undermined." A fuller understanding of the operation of constitutionally protected freedoms may require a focus, not on the judiciary, but on the executive branch of government.

Two Canadian examples are instructive. First, in 2005, following a string of court decisions striking down the opposite-sex definition of marriage as unconstitutional, the Parliament of Canada enacted legislation so as to apply a new definition of marriage uniformly across the federation. Marriage, "for civil purposes," is henceforth "the lawful union of two persons to the exclusion of all others." More than a year after the legislative introduction of same-sex marriage by the Parliament of Canada, immigration officials continued to use a handbook predating the change, one distinguishing same-sex from opposite-sex relationships in a way inconsistent with the new statute. Second, scrutiny of administrative practices by Customs officials underscores that an ostensible victory in a constitutional law judgment may not secure the end of unlawful bureaucratic conduct.

Little Sisters Book and Art Emporium v. Canada (Minister of Justice) addresses the disproportionate seizure by customs officials of erotic materials destined for a gay bookstore. The bookstore won a partial victory, having the Customs' actions declared discriminatory. It would be a mistake, though, to trumpet a victory for gay rights in the comparative rights law reviews in optimistic reliance on the Court's judgment. The case wound up a second time in the Supreme Court of Canada because, seven years after its partial defeat in that forum,

Customs had not yet rectified its discriminatory practices. This example recalls the law and society observation that "the meaning of any specific law, and of law as a social institution, can only be understood by examining the ways in which it is actually used." The differences between the majority and minority judges arguably enact the different understandings of laws and of constitutions. Justice Binnie, writing for the majority, rejected the bookstore's request to strike down parts of the customs legislation. He held that, while Customs officials had repeatedly and systemically applied the law discriminatorily, such administrative action did not indicate a problem with the law. The law could, in theory, be applied evenhandedly. By contrast, the minority, Justices Iacobucci and Arbour, took repeated discriminatory implementation of the law to signal a constitutional defect in the law and the need for a more robust remedy. The importance of these administrative practices—their ability to eviscerate a constitutional judgment—hints that public administration, sociology, and criminology likely have insights to offer comparative constitutionalism. Those committed to enhancing justice for vulnerable minorities ignore, at their peril, evidence of the complexity of constitutional operation and change.

Robert Leckey, *Thick Instrumentalism and Comparative Constitutionalism: The Case of Gay Rights,* 40 COLUM. HUM. RTS. L. REV. 425, 452–455 (2009).

C.   EUROPE

[EDITORS' NOTE: In this section we will, for the first time, read full opinions by the European Court of Human Rights. The excerpt below offers an overview of the Court's role in the development of individual rights jurisprudence in Europe.]

European Federalism: The Nations of Europe, the European Union and the Council of Europe

■ SOPHIE ROBIN-OLIVIER

The structure of European federalism

European law is the product of two major European organizations: the European Union (EU), a small Europe of 27 nations (or "Member States"); and the Council of Europe (COE), a bigger Europe of 47 nations. An examination of European federalism requires considering the relationship between national laws and the two systems of law created by these organizations. These two systems are separate and independent, yet they serve as a source of inspiration to one another and cooperate on many issues.

EU law has its source in two treaties creating the EU: the Treaty on the EU and the Treaty on the Functioning of the EU, from which all other legal instruments derive. The Council of Europe has as its source a great number of international conventions, including several on discrimination. The most famous of these is the European Convention for the protection of Human rights and fundamental freedoms (ECHR) of 1950. Both the EU and the Council of Europe have high courts that interpret their laws. The high court of the EU is the European Court of Justice (ECJ), which sits in Luxembourg. The high court of the Council of Europe is the European Court of Human Rights (ECtHR), which sits in Strasbourg, France.

European federalism considered from Strasbourg

The ECHR draws its particular strength, in comparison to other international conventions, from the existence of a European Court of Human Rights (ECtHR), located in Strasbourg. Individuals have standing before this court whenever a member state violates the ECHR and the individual has exhausted available actions at the national level. The ECtHR functions as a Constitutional court in order to ensure the development of the protection of fundamental rights in Europe. Not only are its decisions binding on States, they must also be respected by domestic courts when the Convention is directly applicable (which depends on national Constitutions).

The case law of the ECtHR has profoundly transformed the laws of European States. These transformations have been most obvious in the fields of due process and the protection of private and family life, and in more discrete ways, have contributed to the fight against discrimination.

Article 14 of the Convention provides that:

> "The enjoyment of the rights and freedoms set forth in this Convention shall be secured without discrimination on any ground such as sex, race, colour, language, religion, political or other opinion, national or social origin, association with a national minority, property, birth or other status."

Note that Article 14 concerns only the "enjoyment of the rights and freedoms set forth in this Convention." This prohibition against discrimination is technically not a central provision of the ECHR; instead, the right not to be discriminated against depends upon other provisions of the Convention, and requires an equality violation to be tied to the central rights and freedoms protected under these provisions. (See ECtHR, 23 July 1968, Affaire linguistique belge, Appl. nos 1474/62, 1677/62, 1691/62, 1769/63, 1994/63, 2126/64.) Yet, the Court is increasingly less demanding of proof linking the claim of discrimination with another provision of the convention. (See, e.g., ECtHR, 16 Sept. 1996, Gaygusuz v. Austria, Appl. no 17371/90.) Thus, although the ECtHR has progressively developed a more robust conception of discrimination that reads Article 14 to provide for an autonomous cause of action, technically Article 14 cannot be invoked absent the violation of another article of the Convention. (See, e.g., ECtHR, 22 Jan. 2008, E.B. v. France, Appl. no 43546/02.)

To compensate for the initial weakness of the ECHR to provide protection against discrimination, Protocol n° 12 (adopted on Nov. 4, 2000, and in force since Apr. 4, 2005), includes a general and autonomous prohibition of discrimination. However, its ratification has been rather slow; only eighteen States had ratified by 2011. Of EU Member States, France and the UK have neither signed nor ratified; and Germany and Italy have signed but have not ratified. Only one case has been decided, in 2011, using the Protocol against discrimination.

Nonetheless, the ECtHR has managed to buttress the strength of Article 14. It has extended the list of prohibited criteria beyond the letter of the text, and adapted its scrutiny of national measures. Distinctions based on sexual orientation, for instance, a criterion added by the court to the list of Article 14, are subject to "strict scrutiny." (See, e.g., CEDH, 21 déc. 1999, Salgueiro da Silva Mouta c/ Portugal, Req. n° 33290/96.) This means that States' "margin of appreciation" (or room for deviation from the rule) is limited and the State has the burden of proving that no discrimination was involved. (See, e.g., CEDH, S. L. c/ Autriche, 9 janv. 2003, Req. n° 45330/99; CEDH, 24 juill. 2003, Karner c/ Autriche, Req n° 40016/98; 2 mars 2010, Kozak c. Pologne, Req. n° 13102/02 et sur l'adoption par les couples de même sexe: CEDH, 22 janv. 2008, E. B. c/ France, préc.) This same standard applies to racial discrimination. (See, CEDH, D.H. et autres c/ République Tchèque, Grande Chambre, 13 nov. 2007, Requête no 57325/00.) And, the ECtHR accepts the use of statistics to prove indirect discrimination. (Id.)

The ability of an individual to bring a claim directly to the ECtHR is one of the most distinctive features of the ECHR. In recent times, individual actions have escalated, in part due to the growing number of States within the COE. As such, under Protocol n° 14 (adopted on 13 May 2004, in force since June 1st 2010) the Court's procedure has been reformed to allow elimination of inadmissible cases and faster treatment of repetitive ones, in order to accommodate the increasing numbers of cases before the Court. Despite these procedural changes, the ECtHR remains a central actor in the protection of human rights in Europe, including the right to be free from discrimination, especially for those who seek transformation of national conceptions of these rights that maintain more traditional approaches to equality.

European Federalism in the European Union

Initially, the European Union was not generally concerned with fundamental rights, nor the more specific right to equality or non-discrimination. The European Communities (European Coal and Steel Community in 1951, Euratom and the European Economic Community in 1957) focused on economic freedoms. But the roots of an equality jurisprudence were there from the beginning, because for economic purposes the treaty on the EEC included a prohibition against discrimination based on nationality, and a requirement of equal pay for men and women.

As the economic community became a political union, this general lack of interest in providing for human rights and non-discrimination was transformed. Article 6, § 1 of the Treaty on the European Union, in the version of the text deriving from the Treaty of Amsterdam (1997), stated unequivocally that the Union is founded on the principles of liberty, democracy, respect for human rights and fundamental freedoms, and the rule of law. The reform of this initial Treaty with the Lisbon Treaty entered into force in 2009 provides that: "The Union is founded on the values of respect for human dignity, freedom, democracy, equality, the rule of law and respect for human rights, including the rights of persons belonging to minorities. These values are common to the Member States in a society in which pluralism, non-discrimination, tolerance, justice, solidarity and equality between women and men prevail." Article 6, § 1 of the Treaty now explicitly mentions that "the Union recognizes the rights, freedoms and principles set out in the Charter of Fundamental Rights of the European Union of 7 December 2000, as adopted at Strasbourg, on 12 December 2007, which shall have the same legal value as the Treaties." It goes on to further confirm in Article 6, § 3 that "[f]undamental rights, as guaranteed by the European Convention for the Protection of Human Rights and Fundamental Freedoms and as they result from the constitutional traditions common to the Member States, shall constitute general principles of the Union's law." Finally, the charter of fundamental rights of the European Union distributes rights, freedoms and principles across six chapters, including equality, dignity, freedoms, solidarity, citizens' rights, and justice. Together, these references to human rights and fundamental freedoms participate in the "constitutionalization" of the EU, developing Europe beyond simply a free trade zone or an economic union.

———

Schalk and Kopf v. Austria

Application No. 30141/04 ECtHR (3 June 2010)

■ EUROPEAN COURT OF HUMAN RIGHTS

1. The case originated in an application (no. 30141/04) against the Republic of Austria lodged with the Court under Article 34 of the Convention for the Protection of Human Rights and Fundamental Freedoms ("the Convention") by two Austrian nationals, Mr Horst Michael Schalk and Mr Johan Franz Kopf ("the applicants"), on 5 August 2004.

3. The applicants alleged in particular, that they were discriminated against as, being a same-sex couple, they were denied the possibility to marry or to have their relationship otherwise recognised by law.

THE FACTS

I. THE CIRCUMSTANCES OF THE CASE

7. The applicants were born in 1962 and 1960, respectively. They are a same-sex couple living in Vienna.

8. On 10 September 2002 the applicants requested the Office for matters of Personal Status (*Standesamt*) to proceed with the formalities to enable them to contract marriage.

9. By decision of 20 December 2002 the Vienna Municipal Office (*Magistrat*) refused the applicants' request. Referring to Article 44 of the Civil Code (*Allgemeines Bürgerliches Gesetzbuch*), it held that marriage could only be contracted between two persons of opposite sex. According to constant case-law, a marriage concluded by two persons of the same sex was null and void. Since the applicants were two men, they lacked the capacity for contracting marriage.

10. The applicants lodged an appeal with the Vienna Regional Governor (*Landeshauptmann*), but to no avail. In his decision of 11 April 2003 the Governor confirmed the Municipal Office's legal view. In addition he

referred to the Administrative Court's case-law according to which it constituted an impediment to marriage if the two persons concerned were of the same sex. Moreover, Article 12 of the European Convention for the Protection of Human Rights and Fundamental Freedoms reserved the right to contract marriage to persons of different sex.

11.   In a constitutional complaint the applicants alleged that the legal impossibility for them to get married constituted a violation of their right to respect for private and family life and of the principle of non-discrimination. They argued that the notion of marriage had evolved since the entry into force of the Civil Code in 1812. In particular, the procreation and education of children no longer formed an integral part of marriage. In present-day perception, marriage was rather a permanent union encompassing all aspects of life. There was no objective justification for excluding same-sex couples from concluding marriage, all the more so since the European Court of Human Rights had acknowledged that differences based on sexual orientation required particularly weighty reasons. Other European countries either allowed homosexual marriages or had otherwise amended their legislation in order to give equal status to same-sex partnerships.

12.   Finally, the applicants alleged a breach of their right to peaceful enjoyment of their possessions. They argued that in the event that one partner in a homosexual couple died, the other was discriminated against since he would be in a much less favourable position under tax law than the surviving partner in a married couple.

13.   On 12 December 2003 the Constitutional Court (*Verfassungsgerichtshof*) dismissed the applicants' complaint. The relevant parts of its judgment read as follows:

> "The administrative proceedings that resulted in the impugned decision were exclusively concerned with the issue of the legitimacy of the marriage. Accordingly, the complainants' sole applicable grievance is that Article 44 of the Civil Code only recognises and provides for marriage between "persons of opposite sex". The allegation of a breach of the right of property is simply a further means of seeking to show that this state of affairs is unjustified.
>
> With regard to marriage, Article 12 of the ECHR, which ranks as constitutional law, provides:
>
>> 'Men and women of marriageable age have the right to marry and to found a family, according to the national laws governing the exercise of this right.'
>
> Neither the principle of equality set forth in the Austrian Federal Constitution nor the European Convention on Human Rights (as evidenced by "men and women" in Article 12) require that the concept of marriage as being geared to the fundamental possibility of parenthood should be extended to relationships of a different kind. The essence of marriage is, moreover, not affected in any way by the fact that divorce (or separation) is possible and that it is a matter for the spouses whether in fact they are able or wish to have children. The European Court of Human Rights found in its *Cossey* judgment of 27 September 1990 (no. 10843/84, concerning the particular position of

transsexual persons) that the restriction of marriage to this "traditional" concept was objectively justified, observing

'... that attachment to the traditional concept of marriage provides sufficient reason for the continued adoption of biological criteria for determining a person's sex for the purposes of marriage.'

[The subsequent change in the case-law concerning the particular issue of transsexuals (ECtHR, *Goodwin*, no. 28957/95, 11 July 2002) does not permit the conclusion that there should be any change in the assessment of the general question at issue here.]

The fact that same-sex relationships fall within the concept of private life and as such enjoy the protection of Article 8 of the ECHR—which also prohibits discrimination on non-objective grounds (Article 14 of the ECHR)—does not give rise to an obligation to change the law of marriage.

It is unnecessary in the instant case to examine whether, and in which areas, the law unjustifiably discriminates against same-sex relationships by providing for special rules for married couples. Nor is it the task of this court to advise the legislature on constitutional issues or even matters of legal policy.

Instead, the complaint must be dismissed as ill-founded."

II. RELEVANT DOMESTIC AND COMPARATIVE LAW

A. Austrian law

1. The Civil Code

15. Article 44 of the Civil Code (*Allgemeines Bürgerliches Gesetzbuch*) provides:

"The marriage contract shall form the basis for family relationships. Under the marriage contract two persons of opposite sex declare their lawful intention to live together in indissoluble matrimony, to beget and raise children and to support each other."

The provision has been unchanged since its entry into force on 1 January 1812.

2. The Registered Partnership Act

16. The purpose of the Registered Partnership Act (*Eingetragene Partnerschaft–Gesetz*) was to provide same-sex couples with a formal mechanism for recognising and giving legal effect to their relationships. In introducing the said Act the legislator had particular regard to developments in other European states (*see* the explanatory report on the draft law—*Erläuterungen zur Regierungsvorlage*, 485 *der Beilagen* XXIV GP).

17. The Registered Partnership Act, Federal Law Gazette (*Bundesgesetzblatt*) vol. I, no. 135/2009, entered into force on 1 January 2010. Its section 2 provides as follows:

"A registered partnership may be formed only by two persons of the same sex (registered partners). They thereby commit themselves to a lasting relationship with mutual rights and obligations."

19.   Registered partnership involves co-habitation on a permanent basis and may be entered into between two persons of the same sex having legal capacity and having reached the age of majority (section 3). A registered partnership must not be established between close relatives or with a person who is already married or has established a still valid registered partnership with another person (section 5).

20.   Like married couples, registered partners are expected to live together like spouses in every respect, to share a common home, to treat each other with respect and to provide mutual assistance (section 8(2) and (3)). As in the case of spouses, the partner who is in charge of the common household and has no income has legal authority to represent the other partner in everyday legal transactions (section 10). Registered partners have the same obligations regarding maintenance as spouses (section 12).

21.   The reasons for dissolution of registered partnership are the same as for dissolution of marriage or divorce. Dissolution of a registered partnership occurs in the event of the death of one partner (section 13). It may also be pronounced by a judicial decision on various other grounds: lack of intent to establish a registered partnership (section 14), fault of one or both partners, or breakdown of the partnership due to irreconcilable differences (section 15).

22.   The Registered Partnership Act also contains a comprehensive range of amendments to existing legislation in order to provide registered partners with the same status as spouses in various other fields of law, such as inheritance law, labour, social and social insurance law, fiscal law, the law on administrative procedure, the law on data protection and public service, passport and registration issues, as well as the law on foreigners.

23.   However, some differences between marriage and registered partnership remain, apart from the fact that only two persons of the same sex can enter into a registered partnership. The following differences were the subject of some public debate before the adoption of the Registered Partnership Act: while marriage is contracted before the Office for matters of Personal Status, registered partnerships are concluded before the District Administrative Authority. The rules on the choice of name differ from those for married couples: for instance, the law speaks of "last name" where a registered couple chooses a common name, but of "family name" in reference to a married couple's common name. The most important differences, however, concern parental rights: unlike married couples, registered partners are not allowed to adopt a child; nor is step-child adoption permitted, that is to say, the adoption of one partner's child by the other partner (section 8(4)). Artificial insemination is also excluded (section 2 (1) of the Artificial Procreation Act—*Fortpflanzungsmedizingesetz*).

B.   Comparative law

1.   European Union law

24.   Article 9 of the Charter of Fundamental Rights of the European Union, which was signed on 7 December 2000 and entered into force on 1 December 2009, reads as follows:

"The right to marry and to found a family shall be guaranteed in accordance with the national laws governing the exercise of these rights."

25. The relevant part of the Commentary of the Charter states as follows:

"Modern trends and developments in the domestic laws in a number of countries toward greater openness and acceptance of same-sex couples notwithstanding, a few states still have public policies and/or regulations that explicitly forbid the notion that same-sex couples have the right to marry. At present there is very limited legal recognition of same-sex relationships in the sense that marriage is not available to same-sex couples. The domestic laws of the majority of states presuppose, in other words, that the intending spouses are of different sexes. Nevertheless, in a few countries, *e.g.*, in the Netherlands and in Belgium, marriage between people of the same sex is legally recognized. Others, like the Nordic countries, have endorsed a registered partnership legislation, which implies, among other things, that most provisions concerning marriage, *i.e.* its legal consequences such as property distribution, rights of inheritance, etc., are also applicable to these unions. At the same time it is important to point out that the name 'registered partnership' has intentionally been chosen not to confuse it with marriage and it has been established as an alternative method of recognizing personal relationships. This new institution is, consequently, as a rule only accessible to couples who cannot marry, and the same-sex partnership does not have the same status and the same benefits as marriage. (. . .)

In order to take into account the diversity of domestic regulations on marriage, Article 9 of the Charter refers to domestic legislation. As it appears from its formulation, the provision is broader in its scope than the corresponding articles in other international instruments. Since there is no explicit reference to 'men and women' as the case is in other human rights instruments, it may be argued that there is no obstacle to recognize same-sex relationships in the context of marriage. There is, however, no explicit requirement that domestic laws should facilitate such marriages. International courts and committees have so far hesitated to extend the application of the right to marry to same-sex couples. (. . .)"

26. A number of Directives are also of interest in the present case:

European Council Directive 2003/86/EC of 22 September 2003, on the right to family reunification, deals with the conditions for the exercise of the right to family reunification by third country nationals residing lawfully in the territory of the Member States.

Its Article 4, which carries the heading "family members", provides:

"(3) The Member States may, by law or regulation, authorise the entry and residence, pursuant to this Directive und subject to compliance with the conditions laid down in Chapter IV, of the unmarried partner, being a third country national, with whom the sponsor is in a duly attested stable long-term relationship, or of a third country national who is bound to the sponsor by a registered partnership in accordance with Article 5(2) . . ."

Directive 2004/38/EC of the European Parliament and Council of 29 April 2004 concerns the right of citizens of the Union and their family members to move and reside freely within the territory of the Member States.

Its Article 2 contains the following definition:

"(2) 'Family member' means:

(a) the spouse

(b) the partner with whom the Union citizen has contracted a registered parternship, on the basis of the legislation of a Member State, if the legislation of the host Member State treats registered partnerships as equivalent to marriage in accordance with the conditions laid down in the relevant legislation of the host Member State.

(c) the direct descendants who are under the age of 21 or are dependants and those of the spouse or partner as defined in point (b)

(d) the dependent direct relative in the ascending line and those of the spouse or partner as defined in point (b)."

2.   The state of relevant legislation in Council of Europe member States

27.   Currently six out of forty-seven member States grant same-sex couples equal access to marriage, namely Belgium, the Netherlands, Norway, Portugal, Spain and Sweden.

28.   In addition there are thirteen member States, which do not grant same-sex couples access to marriage, but have passed some kind of legislation permitting same-sex couples to register their relationships: Andorra, Austria, the Czech Republic, Denmark, Finland, France, Germany, Hungary, Iceland, Luxembourg, Slovenia, Switzerland and the United Kingdom. In sum, there are nineteen member States in which same sex couples either have the possibility to marry or to enter into a registered partnership (*see* also the overview in *Burden v. the United Kingdom* [GC], no. 13378/05, § 26, ECtHR 2008).

29.   In two States, namely in Ireland and Liechtenstein reforms intending to give same-sex couples access to some form of registered partnership are pending or planned. In addition Croatia has a Law on Same–Sex Civil Unions which recognises cohabiting same-sex couples for limited purposes, but does not offer them the possibility of registration.

30.   According to the information available to the Court, the vast majority of the States concerned have introduced the relevant legislation in the last decade.

31.   The legal consequences of registered partnership vary from almost equivalent to marriage to giving relatively limited rights. Among the legal consequences of registered partnerships, three main categories can be distinguished: material consequences, parental consequences and other consequences.

32.   Material consequences cover the impact of registered partnership on different kinds of tax, health insurance, social security payments and pensions. In most of the States concerned registered partners obtain a status similar to marriage. This also applies to other material consequences, such as regulations on joint property and debt, application of rules of alimony upon break-up, entitlement to compensation on wrongful death of partner and inheritance rights.

33.   When it comes to parental consequences, however, the possibilities for registered partners to undergo medically assisted insemination or to foster or adopt children vary greatly from one country to another.

34.   Other consequences include the use of the partner's surname, the impact on a foreign partner's obtaining a residence permit and citizenship, refusal to testify, next-of-kin status for medical purposes, continued status as tenant upon death of the partner, and lawful organ donations.

II.   ALLEGED VIOLATION OF ARTICLE 12 OF THE CONVENTION

39.   The applicants complained that the authorities' refusal to allow them to contract marriage violated Article 12 of the Convention, which provides as follows:

"Men and women of marriageable age have the right to marry and to found a family, according to the national laws governing the exercise of this right."

The Government contested that argument.

B.   Merits

1.   The parties' submissions

43.   In their oral pleadings before the Court, the Government maintained that both the clear wording of Article 12 and the Court's case-law as it stood indicated that the right to marry was by its very nature limited to different-sex couples. They conceded that there had been major social changes in the institution of marriage since the adoption of the Convention, but there was not yet any European consensus to grant same-sex couples the right to marry, nor could such a right be inferred from Article 9 of the Charter of Fundamental Rights of the European Union. Despite the difference in wording, the latter referred the issue of same-sex marriage to national legislation.

44.   The applicants argued that in today's society civil marriage was a union of two persons which encompassed all aspects of their lives, while the procreation and education of children was no longer a decisive element. As the institution of marriage had undergone considerable changes there was no longer any reason to refuse same-sex couples access to marriage. The wording of Article 12 did not necessarily have to be read in the sense that men and women only had the right to marry a person of the opposite sex. Furthermore, the applicants considered that the reference in Article 12 to "the relevant national laws" could not mean that States were given unlimited discretion in regulating the right to marry.

2.   The third party interveners' submissions

45.   The Government of the United Kingdom asserted that the Court's case-law as it stood considered Article 12 to refer to the "traditional marriage between persons of the opposite biological sex" (*see Sheffield and Horsham v. the United Kingdom*, 30 July 1998, § 66, *Reports of Judgments and Decisions* 1998–V). In their view there were no reasons to depart from that position.

46.   While the Court had often underlined that the Convention was a living instrument which had to be interpreted in present-day conditions, it had only used that approach to develop its jurisprudence where it had perceived a convergence of standards among member States. In *Christine Goodwin v. the United Kingdom* [GC] (no. 28957/95, ECtHR 2002–VI), for instance, the Court had reviewed its position regarding the possibility of post-operative transsexuals to marry a person of the sex opposite to their acquired gender, having regard to the fact that a majority of Contracting States permitted such marriages. In contrast there was no convergence of standards as regards same-sex marriage. At the time when the third-party Government submitted their observations only three member States permitted same-sex marriage, and in two others proposals to this effect were under consideration. The issue of same-sex marriage concerned a sensitive area of social, political and religious controversy. In the absence of consensus, the State enjoyed a particularly wide margin of appreciation.

47.   The four non-governmental organisations called on the Court to use the opportunity to extend access to civil marriage to same-sex couples. The fact that different-sex couples were able to marry, while same-sex couples were not, constituted a difference in treatment based on sexual orientation. Referring to *Karner v. Austria*, (no. 40016/98, § 37, ECtHR 2003–IX), they argued that such a difference could only be justified by "particularly serious reasons". In their contention, no such reasons existed: the exclusion of same-sex couples from entering into marriage did not serve to protect marriage or the family in the traditional sense. Nor would giving same-sex couples access to marriage devalue marriage in the traditional sense. Moreover, the institution of marriage had undergone considerable changes and, as the Court had held in *Christine Goodwin* (cited above, § 98), the inability to procreate children could not be regarded as *per se* removing the right to marry. The four non-governmental organisations conceded that the difference between the case of *Christine Goodwin* and the present case lay in the state of European consensus. However, they argued that in the absence of any objective and rational justification for the difference in treatment, considerably less weight should be attached to European consensus.

48.   Finally, the four non-governmental organisations referred to judgments from the Constitutional Court of South Africa, the Courts of Appeal of Ontario and British Columbia in Canada, and the Supreme Courts of California, Connecticut, Iowa and Massachusetts in the United States, which had found that denying same-sex couples access to civil marriage was discriminatory.

3.   The Court's assessment

a.   General principles

49.   According to the Court's established case-law Article 12 secures the fundamental right of a man and woman to marry and to found a family. The exercise of this right gives rise to personal, social and legal consequences. It is "subject to the national laws of the Contracting States", but the limitations thereby introduced must not restrict or reduce the right in such a way or to such an extent that the very essence of the right is

impaired (*see B. and L. v. the United Kingdom*, no. 36536/02, § 34, 13 September 2005, and *F. v. Switzerland*, 18 December 1987, § 32, Series A no. 128).

50. The Court observes at the outset that it has not yet had an opportunity to examine whether two persons who are of the same sex can claim to have a right to marry. However, certain principles might be derived from the Court's case-law relating to transsexuals.

51. In a number of cases the question arose whether refusal to allow a post-operative transsexual to marry a person of the opposite sex to his or her assigned gender violated Article 12. In its earlier case-law the Court found that the attachment to the traditional concept of marriage which underpins Article 12 provided sufficient reason for the continued adoption by the respondent State of biological criteria for determining a person's sex for the purposes of marriage. Consequently, this was considered a matter encompassed within the power of the Contracting States to regulate by national law the exercise of the right to marry (*see Sheffield and Horsham*, cited above, § 67; *Cossey v. the United Kingdom*, 27 September 1990, § 46, Series A no. 184; *see also Rees v. the United Kingdom*, 17 October 1986, §§ 49–50, Series A no. 106).

52. In *Christine Goodwin* (cited above, §§ 100–104) the Court departed from that case-law: It considered that the terms used by Article 12 which referred to the right of a man and woman to marry no longer had to be understood as determining gender by purely biological criteria. In that context, the Court noted that there had been major social changes in the institution of marriage since the adoption of the Convention. Furthermore, it referred to Article 9 of the Charter of Fundamental Rights of the European Union, which departed from the wording of Article 12. Finally, the Court noted that there was widespread acceptance of the marriage of transsexuals in their assigned gender. In conclusion the Court found that the impossibility for a post-operative transsexual to marry in her assigned gender violated Article 12 of the Convention.

53. Two further cases are of interest in the present context: (*Parry v. the United Kingdom* (dec.), no. 42971/05, ECtHR 2006-XV, and *R. and F. v. the United Kingdom* (dec.), no. 35748/05, 28 November 2006). In both cases the applicants were a married couple, consisting of a woman and a male-to-female post-operative transsexual. They complained *inter alia* under Article 12 of the Convention that they were required to end their marriage if the second applicant wished to obtain full legal recognition of her change of gender. The Court dismissed that complaint as being manifestly ill-founded. It noted that domestic law only permitted marriage between persons of opposite gender, whether such gender derived from attribution at birth or from a gender recognition procedure, while same-sex marriages were not permitted. Similarly, Article 12 enshrined the traditional concept of marriage as being between a man and a woman. The Court acknowledged that a number of Contracting States had extended marriage to same-sex partners, but went on to say that this reflected their own vision of the role of marriage in their societies and did not flow from an interpretation of the fundamental right as laid down by the Contracting States in the Convention in 1950. The Court concluded that it fell within the State's margin of

appreciation how to regulate the effects of the change of gender on pre-existing marriages. In addition it considered that, should they chose to divorce in order to allow the transsexual partner to obtain full gender recognition, the fact that the applicants had the possibility to enter into a civil partnership contributed to the proportionality of the gender recognition regime complained of.

b. Application in the present case

54. The Court notes that Article 12 grants the right to marry to "men and women". The French version provides ≪ *l'homme et la femme ont le droit de se marier* ≫. Furthermore, Article 12 grants the right to found a family.

55. The applicants argued that the wording did not necessarily imply that a man could only marry a woman and vice versa. The Court observes that, looked at in isolation, the wording of Article 12 might be interpreted so as not to exclude the marriage between two men or two women. However, in contrast, all other substantive Articles of the Convention grant rights and freedoms to "everyone" or state that "no one" is to be subjected to certain types of prohibited treatment. The choice of wording in Article 12 must thus be regarded as deliberate. Moreover, regard must be had to the historical context in which the Convention was adopted. In the 1950s marriage was clearly understood in the traditional sense of being a union between partners of different sex.

56. As regards the connection between the right to marry and the right to found a family, the Court has already held that the inability of any couple to conceive or parent a child cannot be regarded as *per se* removing the right to marry (*Christine Goodwin*, cited above, § 98). However, this finding does not allow any conclusion regarding the issue of same-sex marriage.

57. In any case, the applicants did not rely mainly on the textual interpretation of Article 12. In essence they relied on the Court's case-law according to which the Convention is a living instrument which is to be interpreted in present-day conditions (*see E.B. v. France* [GC], no. 43546/02, § 92, ECtHR 2008–___, and *Christine Goodwin*, cited above, §§ 74–75). In the applicants' contention Article 12 should in present-day conditions be read as granting same-sex couples access to marriage or, in other words, as obliging member States to provide for such access in their national laws.

58. The Court is not persuaded by the applicants' argument. Although, as it noted in *Christine Goodwin*, the institution of marriage has undergone major social changes since the adoption of the Convention, the Court notes that there is no European consensus regarding same-sex marriage. At present no more than six out of forty-seven Convention States allow same-sex marriage (*see* paragraph 27 above).

59. As the respondent Government as well as the third-party Government have rightly pointed out, the present case has to be distinguished from *Christine Goodwin*. In that case (cited above, § 103) the Court perceived a convergence of standards regarding marriage of transsexuals in their assigned gender. Moreover, *Christine Goodwin* is concerned with marriage of partners who are of different gender, if gender is defined not by

purely biological criteria but by taking other factors including gender reassignment of one of the partners into account.

60.   Turning to the comparison between Article 12 of the Convention and Article 9 of the Charter of Fundamental Rights of the European Union (the Charter), the Court has already noted that the latter has deliberately dropped the reference to men and women (*see Christine Goodwin*, cited above, § 100). The commentary to the Charter, which became legally binding in December 2009, confirms that Article 9 is meant to be broader in scope than the corresponding articles in other human rights instruments (*see* paragraph 25 above). At the same time the reference to domestic law reflects the diversity of national regulations, which range from allowing same-sex marriage to explicitly forbidding it. By referring to national law, Article 9 of the Charter leaves the decision whether or not to allow same-sex marriage to the States. In the words of the commentary: "... it may be argued that there is no obstacle to recognize same-sex relationships in the context of marriage. There is however, no explicit requirement that domestic laws should facilitate such marriages."

61.   Regard being had to Article 9 of the Charter, therefore, the Court would no longer consider that the right to marry enshrined in Article 12 must in all circumstances be limited to marriage between two persons of the opposite sex. Consequently, it cannot be said that Article 12 is inapplicable to the applicants' complaint. However, as matters stand, the question whether or not to allow same-sex marriage is left to regulation by the national law of the Contracting State.

62.   In that connection the Court observes that marriage has deep-rooted social and cultural connotations which may differ largely from one society to another. The Court reiterates that it must not rush to substitute its own judgment in place of that of the national authorities, who are best placed to assess and respond to the needs of society (*see B. and L. v. the United Kingdom*, cited above, § 36).

63.   In conclusion, the Court finds that Article 12 of the Convention does not impose an obligation on the respondent Government to grant a same-sex couple like the applicants access to marriage.

64.   Consequently, there has been no violation of Article 12 of the Convention.

III.   ALLEGED VIOLATION OF ARTICLE 14 TAKEN IN CONJUNCTION WITH ARTICLE 8 OF THE CONVENTION

65.   The applicants complained under Article 14 taken in conjunction with Article 8 of the Convention that they were discriminated against on account of their sexual orientation, since they were denied the right to marry and did not have any other possibility to have their relationship recognised by law before the entry into force of the Registered Partnership Act.

Article 8 reads as follows:

1.   Everyone has the right to respect for his private and family life ...

2.   There shall be no interference by a public authority with the exercise of this right except such as is in accordance with the law and is necessary in a

democratic society in the interests of national security, public safety or the economic well-being of the country, for the prevention of disorder or crime, for the protection of health or morals, or for the protection of the rights and freedoms of others.

Article 14 provides as follows:

The enjoyment of the rights and freedoms set forth in [the] Convention shall be secured without discrimination on any ground such as sex, race, colour, language, religion, political or other opinion, national or social origin, association with a national minority, property, birth or other status.

B.   Merits

1.   The parties' submissions

76.   The applicants maintained that the heart of their complaint was that they were discriminated against as a same-sex couple. Agreeing with the Government on the applicability of Article 14 taken in conjunction with Article 8, they asserted that just like differences based on sex, differences based on sexual orientation required particularly serious reasons for justification. In the applicants' contention the Government had failed to submit any such reasons for excluding them from access to marriage.

77.   It followed from the Court's *Karner* judgment (cited above, § 40) that the protection of the traditional family was a weighty and legitimate reason, but it had to be shown that a given difference was also necessary to achieve that aim. In the applicants' assertion nothing showed that the exclusion of same-sex couples from marriage was necessary to protect the traditional family.

78.   In their oral pleadings, reacting to the introduction of the Registered Partnership Act, the applicants argued that the remaining differences between marriage on the one hand and registered partnership on the other were still discriminatory. They mentioned in particular that the Registered Partnership Act did not provide a possibility to enter into an engagement; that, unlike marriages, registered partnerships were not concluded at the Office for matters of Personal Status but at the District Administrative Authority; that there was no entitlement to compensation in the event of wrongful death of the partner; and that it was unclear whether certain benefits which were granted to "families" would also be granted to registered partners and the children of one of them living in the common household. Although differences based on sexual orientation required particularly weighty reasons, no such reasons had been given by the Government.

79.   The Government accepted that Article 14 taken in conjunction with Article 8 of the Convention applied. So far the Court's case-law had considered homosexual relationships to fall within the notion of "private life" but there might be good reasons to include the relationship of a same-sex couple living together in the scope of "family life".

80.   Regarding compliance with the requirements of Article 14 taken in conjunction with Article 8, the Government maintained that it was within the legislator's margin of appreciation whether or not same-sex couples were given a possibility to have their relationship recognised by law

in any other form than marriage. The Austrian legislator had made the policy choice to give same-sex couples such a possibility. Under the Registered Partnership Act which had entered into force on 1 January 2010 same-sex partners were able to enter into a registered partnership which provided them with a status very similar to marriage. The new law covered such diverse fields as civil and criminal law, labour, social and social insurance law, fiscal law, the law on administrative procedure, the law on data protection and public service, passport and registration issues, as well as the law on foreigners.

2. The third parties' submissions

81. As to the applicability of Article 8, the third-party Government submitted that although the Court's case-law as it stood did not consider same-sex relationships to fall within the notion of "family life", this should not be excluded in the future. Nonetheless Article 8 read in conjunction with Article 14 should not be interpreted so as to require either access to marriage or the creation of alternative forms of legal recognition for same-sex partnerships.

82. Regarding the justification for that difference in treatment, the third-party Government contested the applicants' argument drawn from the Court's *Karner* judgment. In that case the Court had found that excluding same-sex couples from protection provided to different-sex couples under the Rent Act was not necessary for achieving the legitimate aim of protecting the family in the traditional sense. The issue in the present case was different: what was at stake was the question of access to marriage or alternative legal recognition. The justification for that particular difference in treatment between different-sex and same-sex couples was laid down in Article 12 of the Convention itself.

83. Finally, the third-party Government submitted that in the United Kingdom the Civil Partnership Act 2004 which had come into force in December 2005 had introduced a system of partnership registration for same-sex couples. However, the said Act was introduced as a policy choice in order to promote social justice and equality, while it was not considered that the Convention imposed a positive obligation to provide such a possibility. In the Government's view this position was supported by the Court's decision in *Courten v. the United Kingdom* (no. 4479/06, 4 November 2008).

84. The four non-governmental organisations pleaded in their joint comments that the Court should rule on the question whether a same-sex relationship of cohabiting partners fell under the notion of "family life" within the meaning of Article 8 of the Convention. They noted that the question had been left open in *Karner* (cited above, § 33). They argued that by now it was generally accepted that same-sex couples had the same capacity to establish a long-term emotional and sexual relationship as different-sex couples and, thus, had the same needs as different-sex couples to have their relationship recognised by law.

85. Were the Court not to find that Article 12 required Contracting States to grant same-sex couples access to marriage, it should address the question whether there was an obligation under Article 14 taken together

with Article 8 to provide alternative means of legal recognition of a same-sex partnership.

86.   The non-governmental organisations answered that question in the affirmative: firstly, excluding same-sex couples from particular rights and benefits attached to marriage (such as for instance the right to a survivor's pension) without giving them access to any alternative means to qualify would amount to indirect discrimination (*see Thlimmenos v. Greece* [GC], no. 34369/97, § 44, ECtHR 2000–IV). Secondly, they agreed with the applicants' argument drawn from *Karner* (cited above). Thirdly, they asserted that the state of European consensus increasingly supported the idea that member States were under an obligation to provide, if not access to marriage, alternative means of legal recognition. By now almost 40% had legislation allowing same-sex couples to register their relationships as marriages or under an alternative name (*see* paragraphs 27–28 above).

3.   The Court's assessment

a.   Applicability of Article 14 taken in conjunction with Article 8

87.   The Court has dealt with a number of cases concerning discrimination on account of sexual orientation. Some were examined under Article 8 alone, namely cases concerning the prohibition under criminal law of homosexual relations between adults (*see Dudgeon v. the United Kingdom,* 22 October 1981, Series A no. 45; *Norris v. Ireland,* 26 October 1988, Series A no. 142; and *Modinos v. Cyprus,* 22 April 1993, Series A no. 259) and the discharge of homosexuals from the armed forces (*see Smith and Grady v. the United Kingdom,* nos. 33985/96 and 33986/96, ECtHR 1999–VI). Others were examined under Article 14 taken in conjunction with Article 8. These included, *inter alia*, different age of consent under criminal law for homosexual relations (*L. and V. v. Austria*, nos. 39392/98 and 39829/98, ECtHR 2003–I), the attribution of parental rights (*Salgueiro da Silva Mouta v. Portugal*, no. 33290/96, ECtHR 1999–IX), permission to adopt a child (*Fretté v. France*, no. 36515/97, ECtHR 2002–I, and *E.B. v. France*, cited above) and the right to succeed to the deceased partner's tenancy (*Karner,* cited above).

88.   In the present case, the applicants have formulated their complaint under Article 14 taken in conjunction with Article 8. The Court finds it appropriate to follow this approach.

89.   As the Court has consistently held, Article 14 complements the other substantive provisions of the Convention and its Protocols. It has no independent existence since it has effect solely in relation to "the enjoyment of the rights and freedoms" safeguarded by those provisions. Although the application of Article 14 does not presuppose a breach of those provisions—and to this extent it is autonomous—, there can be no room for its application unless the facts at issue fall within the ambit of one or more of the latter (*see*, for instance, *E.B. v. France*, cited above, § 47; *Karner*, cited above, § 32; and *Petrovic v. Austria*, 27 March 1998, § 22, *Reports* 1998–II).

90.   It is undisputed in the present case that the relationship of a same-sex couple like the applicants' falls within the notion of "private life"

within the meaning of Article 8. However, in the light of the parties' comments the Court finds it appropriate to address the issue whether their relationship also constitutes "family life".

91.   The Courts reiterates its established case-law in respect of different-sex couples, namely that the notion of family under this provision is not confined to marriage-based relationships and may encompass other *de facto* "family" ties where the parties are living together out of wedlock. A child born out of such a relationship is *ipso jure* part of that "family" unit from the moment and by the very fact of his birth (*see Elsholz v. Germany* [GC], no. 25735/94, § 43, ECtHR 2000–VIII; *Keegan v. Ireland*, 26 May 1994, § 44, Series A no. 290; and also *Johnston and Others v. Ireland*, 18 December 1986, § 56, Series A no. 112).

92.   In contrast, the Court's case-law has only accepted that the emotional and sexual relationship of a same-sex couple constitutes "private life" but has not found that it constitutes "family life", even where a long-term relationship of cohabiting partners was at stake. In coming to that conclusion, the Court observed that despite the growing tendency in a number of European States towards the legal and judicial recognition of stable *de facto* partnerships between homosexuals, given the existence of little common ground between the Contracting States, this was an area in which they still enjoyed a wide margin of appreciation (*see Mata Estevez v. Spain* (dec.), no. 56501/00, ECtHR 2001–VI, with further references). In the case of *Karner* (cited above, § 33), concerning the succession of a same-sex couples' surviving partner to the deceased's tenancy rights, which fell under the notion of "home", the Court explicitly left open the question whether the case also concerned the applicant's "private and family life".

93.   The Court notes that since 2001, when the decision in *Mata Estevez* was given, a rapid evolution of social attitudes towards same-sex couples has taken place in many member States. Since then a considerable number of member States have afforded legal recognition to same-sex couples (*see* above, paragraphs 27–30). Certain provisions of EU law also reflect a growing tendency to include same-sex couples in the notion of "family" (see paragraph 26 above).

94.   In view of this evolution the Court considers it artificial to maintain the view that, in contrast to a different-sex couple, a same-sex couple cannot enjoy "family life" for the purposes of Article 8. Consequently the relationship of the applicants, a cohabiting same-sex couple living in a stable *de facto* partnership, falls within the notion of "family life", just as the relationship of a different-sex couple in the same situation would.

95.   The Court therefore concludes that the facts of the present case fall within the notion of "private life" as well as "family life" within the meaning of Article 8. Consequently, Article 14 taken in conjunction with Article 8 applies.

b.   Compliance with Article 14 taken together with Article 8

96.   The Court has established in its case-law that in order for an issue to arise under Article 14 there must be a difference in treatment of persons in relevantly similar situations. Such a difference of treatment is

discriminatory if it has no objective and reasonable justification; in other words, if it does not pursue a legitimate aim or if there is not a reasonable relationship of proportionality between the means employed and the aim sought to be realised. The Contracting States enjoy a margin of appreciation in assessing whether and to what extent differences in otherwise similar situations justify a difference in treatment (*see Burden,* cited above, § 60).

97.   On the one hand the Court has held repeatedly that, just like differences based on sex, differences based on sexual orientation require particularly serious reasons by way of justification (*see Karner,* cited above, § 37; *L. and V. v. Austria,* cited above, § 45; and *Smith and Grady,* cited above, § 90). On the other hand, a wide margin is usually allowed to the State under the Convention when it comes to general measures of economic or social strategy (*see,* for instance, *Stec and Others v. the United Kingdom* [GC], no. 65731/01, § 52, ECtHR 2006–VI).

98.   The scope of the margin of appreciation will vary according to the circumstances, the subject matter and its background; in this respect, one of the relevant factors may be the existence or non-existence of common ground between the laws of the Contracting States (*see Petrovic,* cited above, § 38).

99.   While the parties have not explicitly addressed the issue whether the applicants were in a relevantly similar situation to different-sex couples, the Court would start from the premise that same-sex couples are just as capable as different-sex couples of entering into stable committed relationships. Consequently, they are in a relevantly similar situation to a different-sex couple as regards their need for legal recognition and protection of their relationship.

100.   The applicants argued that they were discriminated against as a same-sex couple, firstly, in that they still did not have access to marriage and, secondly, in that no alternative means of legal recognition were available to them until the entry into force of the Registered Partnership Act.

101.   Insofar as the applicants appear to contend that, if not included in Article 12, the right to marry might be derived from Article 14 taken in conjunction with Article 8, the Court is unable to share their view. It reiterates that the Convention is to be read as a whole and its Articles should therefore be construed in harmony with one another (*see Johnston and Others,* cited above, § 57). Having regard to the conclusion reached above, namely that Article 12 does not impose an obligation on Contracting States to grant same-sex couples access to marriage, Article 14 taken in conjunction with Article 8, a provision of more general purpose and scope, cannot be interpreted as imposing such an obligation either.

102.   Turning to the second limb of the applicants' complaint, namely the lack of alternative legal recognition, the Court notes that at the time when the applicants lodged their application they did not have any possibility to have their relationship recognised under Austrian law. That situation obtained until 1 January 2010, when the Registered Partnership Act entered into force.

103. The Court reiterates in this connection that in proceedings originating in an individual application it has to confine itself, as far as possible, to an examination of the concrete case before it (*see F. v. Switzerland*, cited above, § 31). Given that at present it is open to the applicants to enter into a registered partnership, the Court is not called upon to examine whether the lack of any means of legal recognition for same-sex couples would constitute a violation of Article 14 taken in conjunction with Article 8 if it still obtained today.

104. What remains to be examined in the circumstances of the present case is whether the respondent State should have provided the applicants with an alternative means of legal recognition of their partnership any earlier than it did.

105. The Court cannot but note that there is an emerging European consensus towards legal recognition of same-sex couples. Moreover, this tendency has developed rapidly over the past decade. Nevertheless, there is not yet a majority of States providing for legal recognition of same-sex couples. The area in question must therefore still be regarded as one of evolving rights with no established consensus, where States must also enjoy a margin of appreciation in the timing of the introduction of legislative changes (*see Courten*, cited above; *see also M.W. v. the United Kingdom* (dec.), no. 11313/02, 23 June 2009, both relating to the introduction of the Civil Partnership Act in the United Kingdom).

106. The Austrian Registered Partnership Act, which entered into force on 1 January 2010, reflects the evolution described above and is thus part of the emerging European consensus. Though not in the vanguard, the Austrian legislator cannot be reproached for not having introduced the Registered Partnership Act any earlier (*see, mutatis mutandis, Petrovic*, cited above, § 41).

107. Finally, the Court will examine the applicants' argument that they are still discriminated against as a same sex-couple on account of certain differences conferred by the status of marriage on the one hand and registered partnership on the other.

108. The Court starts from its findings above, that States are still free, under Article 12 of the Convention as well as under Article 14 taken in conjunction with Article 8, to restrict access to marriage to different-sex couples. Nevertheless the applicants appear to argue that if a State chooses to provide same-sex couples with an alternative means of recognition, it is obliged to confer a status on them which—though carrying a different name—corresponds to marriage in each and every respect. The Court is not convinced by that argument. It considers on the contrary that States enjoy a certain margin of appreciation as regards the exact status conferred by alternative means of recognition.

109. The Court observes that the Registered Partnership Act gives the applicants a possibility to obtain a legal status equal or similar to marriage in many respects (*see* paragraphs 18–23 above). While there are only slight differences in respect of material consequences, some substantial differences remain in respect of parental rights. However, this corresponds on the whole to the trend in other member States (*see* paragraphs

32–33 above). Moreover, the Court is not called upon in the present case to examine each and every one of these differences in detail. For instance, as the applicants have not claimed that they are directly affected by the remaining restrictions concerning artificial insemination or adoption, it would go beyond the scope of the present application to examine whether these differences are justified. On the whole, the Court does not see any indication that the respondent State exceeded its margin of appreciation in its choice of rights and obligations conferred by registered partnership.

110.   In conclusion, the Court finds there has been no violation of Article 14 of the Convention taken in conjunction with Article 8.

■ JOINT DISSENTING OPINION OF JUDGES ROZAKIS, SPIELMANN AND JEBENS

1.   We have voted against point 6 of the operative part. We cannot agree with the majority that there has been no violation of Article 14 taken in conjunction with Article 8 of the Convention, for the following reasons.

2.   In this very important case, the Court, after a careful examination of previous case-law, has taken a major step forward in its jurisprudence by extending the notion of "family life" to same-sex couples. Relying in particular on developments in European Union law (*see* Directives 2003/86/EC of 22 September 2003 on the right to family reunification and 2004/38/EC concerning the right to citizens of the Union and their family members to move and reside freely within the territory of the Member States), the Court identified in paragraph 93 of the judgment *"a growing tendency to include same-sex couples in the notion of 'family'"*.

3.   The Court solemnly affirmed this in paragraph 94 of the judgment:

In view of this evolution the Court considers it artificial to maintain the view that, in contrast to a different-sex couple, a same-sex couple cannot enjoy 'family life' for the purposes of Article 8. Consequently the relationship of the applicants, a cohabiting same-sex couple living in a stable *de facto* partnership, falls within the notion of 'family life', just as the relationship of a different-sex couple in the same situation would.

4.   The lack of any legal framework before the entry into force of the Registered Partnership Act ("the Act") raises a serious problem. In this respect we note a contradiction in the Court's reasoning. Having decided in paragraph 94 that *"the relationship of the applicants falls within the notion of 'family life'"*, the Court should have drawn inferences from this finding. However, by deciding that there has been no violation, the Court at the same time endorses the legal vacuum at stake, without imposing on the respondent State any positive obligation to provide a satisfactory framework, offering the applicants, at least to a certain extent, the protection any family should enjoy.

5.   In paragraph 99, the Court also decided, of its own motion, that

same-sex couples are just as capable as different-sex couples of entering into stable committed relationships [and that] [c]onsequently, they are in a relevantly similar situation to a different-sex couple as regards their need for legal recognition and protection of their relationship.

6. The applicants complained not only that they were discriminated against in that they were denied the right to marry, but also—and this is important—that they did not have any other possibility of having their relationship recognised by law before the entry into force of the Act.

7. We do not want to dwell on the impact of the Act, which entered into force only in 2010, and in particular on the question whether the particular features of this Act, as identified by the Court in paragraphs 18 to 23 of the judgment, comply with Article 14 taken together with Article 8 of the Convention, since in our view the violation of the combination of these provisions occurred in any event prior to the Act.

8. Having identified a *"relevantly similar situation"* (paragraph 99), and emphasised that *"differences based on sexual orientation require particularly serious reasons by way of justification"* (paragraph 97), the Court should have found a violation of Article 14 taken in conjunction with Article 8 of the Convention because the respondent Government did not advance any argument to justify the difference of treatment, relying in this connection mainly on their margin of appreciation (paragraph 80). However, in the absence of any cogent reasons offered by the respondent Government to justify the difference of treatment, there should be no room to apply the margin of appreciation. Consequently, the *"existence or non-existence of common ground between the laws of the Contracting States"* (paragraph 98) is irrelevant as such considerations are only a *subordinate* basis for the application of the concept of the margin of appreciation. Indeed, it is only in the event that the national authorities offer grounds for justification that the Court can be satisfied, taking into account the presence or the absence of a common approach, that they are better placed than it is to deal effectively with the matter.

9. Today it is widely recognised and also accepted by society that same-sex couples enter into stable relationships. Any absence of a legal framework offering them, at least to a certain extent, the same rights or benefits attached to marriage (*see* paragraph 4 of this dissent) would need robust justification, especially taking into account the growing trend in Europe to offer some means of qualifying for such rights or benefits.

10. Consequently, in our view, there has been a violation of Article 14 in conjunction with Article 8 of the Convention.

[Concurring opinion omitted]

———

E.B. v. France

Judgment (22 January 2008)

■ EUROPEAN COURT OF HUMAN RIGHTS

1. The case originated in an application (no. 43546/02) against the French Republic lodged with the Court under Article 34 of the Convention for the Protection of Human Rights and Fundamental Freedoms ("the Convention") by a French national, Ms E.B. ("the applicant"), on 2

December 2002. The President of the Grand Chamber acceded to the applicant's request not to have her name disclosed (Rule 47 § 3 of the Rules of Court).

2.   The applicant alleged that at every stage of her application for authorisation to adopt she had suffered discriminatory treatment that had been based on her sexual orientation and had interfered with her right to respect for her private life.

THE FACTS

I.   THE CIRCUMSTANCES OF THE CASE

7.   The applicant was born in 1961 and lives in Lons-le-Saunier.

8.   She has been a nursery school teacher since 1985 and, since 1990, has been in a stable relationship with a woman, Ms R., who is a psychologist.

9.   On 26 February 1998 the applicant made an application to the Jura Social Services Department for authorisation to adopt a child. She wanted to investigate the possibility of international adoption, in particular in Asia, South America and Madagascar. She mentioned her sexual orientation and her relationship with her partner, Ms R.

10.   In a report dated 11 August 1998 the socio-educational assistant and paediatric nurse noted the following points among others:

Ms B. and Ms R. do not regard themselves as a couple, and Ms R., although concerned by her partner's application to adopt a child, does not feel committed by it. Ms B. considers that she will have to play the role of mother and father, and her partner does not lay claim to any right *vis-à-vis* the child but will be at hand if necessary.

. . .

Ms B. is seeking to adopt following her decision not to have a child herself. She would prefer to explain to a child that he or she has had a father and mother and that what she wants is the child's happiness than to tell the child that she does not want to live with a man.

. . .

Ms B. thinks of a father as a stable, reassuring and reliable figure. She proposes to provide a future adopted child with this father figure in the persons of her own father and her brother-in-law. But she also says that the child will be able to choose a surrogate father in his or her environment (a friend's relatives, a teacher, or a male friend . . .).

. . .

CONCLUSION

"On account of her personality and her occupation, Ms B. is a good listener, is broad-minded and cultured, and is emotionally receptive. We also appreciated her clear-sighted approach to analysing problems and her child-raising and emotional capacities. However, regard being had to her current lifestyle: unmarried and cohabiting with a female partner, we have not been able to assess her ability to provide a child with a family image revolving around a parental couple such as to afford safeguards for that child's stable and well-adjusted development.

Opinion reserved regarding authorisation to adopt a child"

11. On 28 August 1998, in her report on the interviews she had had with the applicant, the psychologist examining her application recommended in the following terms that authorisation be refused:

... Ms [B.] has many personal qualities. She is enthusiastic and warm-hearted and comes across as very protective of others. Her ideas about child-rearing appear very positive. Several question marks remain, however, regarding a number of factors pertaining to her background, the context in which the child will be cared for and her desire for a child.

Is she not seeking to avoid the "violence" of giving birth and genetic anxiety regarding a biological child?

Idealisation of a child and under-estimation of the difficulties inherent in providing one with a home: is she not fantasising about being able to fully mend a child's past? How certain can we be that the child will find a stable and reliable paternal referent? The possibilities of identification with a paternal role model are somewhat unclear. Let us not forget that children forge their identity with an image of both parents. Children need adults who will assume their parental function: if the parent is alone, what effects will that have on the child's development?

. . .

We do not wish to diminish Ms [B.]'s confidence in herself in any way, still less insinuate that she would be harmful to a child; what we are saying is that all the studies on parenthood show that a child needs both its parents. Moreover, when asked whether she would have wanted to be brought up by only one of her parents, Ms B. answered no.

. . .

A number of grey areas remain, relating to the illusion of having a direct perception of her desire for a child: would it not be wiser to defer this request pending a more thorough analysis of the various—complex—aspects of the situation? ..."

12. On 21 September 1998 a technical officer from the children's welfare service recommended that authorisation be refused, observing that the applicant had not given enough thought to the question of a paternal and male role model, and assumed that she could easily take on the role of father and mother herself, while mentioning a possible role for her father and/or brother-in-law, who lived a long way away, however, meaning that meetings with the child would be difficult. The officer also wondered about the presence of Ms R. in the applicant's life, noting that they refused to regard themselves as a couple and that Ms R. had not at any time been involved in the plan to adopt.

The reasoning of the opinion ended as follows:

I find myself faced with a lot of uncertainties about important matters concerning the psychological development of a child who has already experienced abandonment and a complete change of culture and language....

13. On 12 October 1998 the psychologist from the children's welfare service, who was a member of the adoption board, recommended that authorisation be refused on the ground that placing a child with the applicant would expose the child to a certain number of risks relating to the construction of his or her personality. He referred among other things to the fact that the applicant lived with a girlfriend but did not consider herself to be in a couple, which gave rise to an unclear or even an unspoken situation involving ambiguity and a risk that the child would have only a maternal role model. The psychologist went on to make the following comments:—

> . . . It is as though the reasons for wanting a child derived from a complicated personal background that has not been resolved with regard to the role as child-parent that [the applicant] appears to have had to play (*vis-à-vis* one of her sisters, protection of her parents), and were based on emotional difficulties. Has this given rise to a feeling of worthlessness or uselessness that she is trying to overcome by becoming a mother? Unusual attitude towards men in that men are rejected. In the extreme, how can rejection of the male figure not amount to rejection of the child's own image? (A child eligible for adoption has a biological father whose symbolic existence must be preserved, but will this be within [the applicant's] capabilities?) . . .

14. On 28 October 1998 the Adoption Board's representative from the Family Council for the association of children currently or formerly in State care recommended refusing authorisation to adopt in the following terms:—

> . . . From my personal experience of life with a foster family I am now, with the benefit of hindsight, in a position to assess the importance of a mixed couple (man and woman) in providing a child with a home. The role of the "adoptive mother" and the "adoptive father" in the child's day-to-day upbringing are complementary, but different. It is a balance that will be shaken by the child to a degree that may sometimes vary in intensity according to how he or she experiences the realisation and acceptance of the truth about his or her origins and history.I therefore think it necessary, in the interests of the child, for there to be a solid balance between an "adoptive mother" and an "adoptive father" where adoption is being envisaged. . . .

15. On 4 November 1998 the Board's representative from the Family Council, present on behalf of the union of family associations for the *département* (UDAF), referring to the Convention on the Rights of the Child of 20 November 1989, recommended that authorisation be refused on the ground of the lack of a paternal referent and added:

> . . . It appears impossible to build a family and bring up a child without the full support of this partner [R.] for the plan. The psychologists' and welfare reports show her clear lack of interest in Ms [B.]'s plan . . . In the further alternative, the material conditions for providing a child with a suitable home are not met. It will be necessary to move house, solve the issue of how to divide expenses between both partners, whose plans differ at least in this respect.

16.   On 24 November 1998 the head of the children's welfare service also recommended that authorisation be refused, noting expressly that

Ms [B.] lives with a female partner who does not appear to be a party to the plan. The role this partner would play in the adopted child's life is not clearly defined. There does not appear to be room for a male referent who would actually be present in the child's life. In these circumstances, there is a risk that the child would not find within this household the various family markers necessary to the development of his or her personality and well-being.

17.   In a letter of 26 November 1998 the decision of the president of the council for the *département* refusing authorisation to adopt was served on the applicant. The following reasons, among others, were given:

... in examining any application for authorisation to adopt I have to consider the child's interests alone and ensure that all the relevant safeguards are in place. Your plan to adopt reveals the lack of a paternal role model or referent capable of fostering the well-adjusted development of an adopted child. Moreover, the place that your partner would occupy in the child's life is not sufficiently clear: although she does not appear to oppose your plan, neither does she seem to be involved, which would make it difficult for the child to find its bearings. Accordingly, all the foregoing factors do not appear to ensure that an adopted child will have a sufficiently structured family framework in which to flourish....

18.   On 20 January 1999 the applicant asked the president of the council for the *département* to reconsider the decision refusing her authorisation to adopt.

19.   The children's welfare service asked a clinical psychologist to prepare a psychological assessment. In her report of 7 March 1999, drawn up after an interview with the applicant, the psychologist concluded that "Ms B. ha[d] plenty to offer in providing a home for a child (patience-values-creativity-time)", but considered that adoption was premature having regard to a number of problematic points (confusion between a non-directive and *laissez-faire* attitude, and ignorance of the effects of the introduction of a third person into the home set-up).

20.   On 17 March 1999 the president of the council for the *département* of the Jura confirmed the refusal to grant the request for authorisation.

21.   On 13 May 1999 the applicant applied to the Besançon Administrative Court seeking to have the administrative decisions of 26 November 1998 and 17 March 1999 set aside. She also contested the manner in which the screening process in respect of her request for authorisation had been conducted. She pointed out that many people involved in the process had not met her, including the psychologist from the adoption board.

22.   In a judgment of 24 February 2000 the Administrative Court set aside the decisions of 26 November 1998 and 19 March 1999, ruling as follows:

... the president of the council for the *département* of the Jura based his decision both on "the lack of a paternal role model or referent capable of fostering the well-adjusted development of an adopted child" and on "the place [her] partner would occupy in the child's life". The reasons cited are not in themselves capable of justifying a refusal to grant authorisation to adopt. The documents in the case file show that Ms B., who has undisputed personal qualities and an aptitude for bringing up children, and who is a nursery school teacher by profession and well integrated into her social environment, does offer sufficient guarantees—from a family, child-rearing and psychological perspective—that she would provide an adopted child with a suitable home. ... Ms B. is justified, in the circumstances of this case, in seeking to have the decisions refusing her authorisation set aside ...

23.   The *département* of the Jura appealed. The Nancy Administrative Court of Appeal, in a judgment of 21 December 2000, set aside the lower court's judgment. It found, first, that "B. maintain[ed] that she ha[d] not been sent a personality test, but [did] not allege that she [had] asked for the document and that her request [had been] refused" and that the 4th paragraph of Article 63 of the Family and Social Welfare Code "[did] not have the effect of precluding a report from being drawn up on the basis of a summary of the main points of other documents. Hence, the fact that a psychologist [had drawn] up a report just on the basis of information obtained by other people working on the case and without hearing submissions from the applicant [did] not invalidate the screening process carried out in respect of Ms B.'s application for authorisation to adopt ...".

24.   The court went on to find that

... the reasons for the decisions of 26 November 1998 and 17 March 1999, which were taken following an application for reconsideration of the decision of the president of the council for the *département* of the Jura rejecting the application for authorisation to adopt submitted by Ms B., are the absence of identificational markers" due to the lack of a paternal role model or referent and the ambivalence of the commitment of each member of the household to the adoptive child. It can be seen from the documents in the file, and particularly the evidence gathered during the examination of Ms B.'s application, that having regard to the latter's lifestyle and despite her undoubted personal qualities and aptitude for bringing up children, she did not provide the requisite safeguards—from a family, child-rearing and psychological perspective—for adopting a child ... contrary to Ms B.'s contentions, the president of the council for the *département* did not refuse her authorisation on the basis of a position of principle regarding her choice of lifestyle. Accordingly, and in any event, the applicant is not justified in alleging a breach ... of the requirements of Articles 8 and 14 of the Convention....

25.   The applicant appealed on points of law. On 5 June 2002 the *Conseil d'Etat* dismissed her appeal in a judgment giving the following reasons:

... Regarding the grounds for refusing Ms B. authorisation:

...

Firstly, the fact that a request for authorisation to adopt a child is submitted by a single person, as is permitted by Article 343-1 of the Civil Code, does not prevent the administrative authority from ascertaining, in terms of childrearing and psychological factors that foster the development of the child's personality, whether the prospective adoptive parent can offer—in her circle of family and friends—a paternal "role model or referent" where the application is submitted by a woman . . .; nor, where a single person seeking to adopt is in a stable relationship with another person, who will inevitably be required to contribute to providing the child with a suitable home for the purposes of the above-mentioned provisions, does this fact prevent the authority from determining—even if the relationship in question is not a legally binding one—whether the conduct or personality of the third person, considered on the basis of objective considerations, is conducive to providing a suitable home. Accordingly, the Administrative Court of Appeal did not err in law in considering that the two grounds on which the application by Ms [B.] for authorisation as a single person was refused— namely, the "absence of identificational markers due to the lack of a paternal role model or referent" and "the ambivalence of the commitment of each member of the household to the adoptive child"—were capable of justifying, under the above-mentioned provisions of the decree of 1 September 1998, the refusal to grant authorisation;

Secondly, with regard to Ms [B.]'s assertion that, in referring to her "lifestyle" to justify the refusal to grant her authorisation to adopt, the Administrative Court of Appeal had implicitly referred to her sexual orientation, it can be seen from the documents submitted to the tribunals of fact that Ms [B.] was, at the time of the examination of her application, in a stable homosexual relationship. As that relationship had to be taken into consideration in the needs and interests of an adopted child, the court neither based its decision on a position of principle in view of the applicant's sexual orientation nor breached the combined requirements of Articles 8 and 14 of the European Convention for the Protection of Human Rights and Fundamental Freedoms; nor did it breach the provisions of Article L. 225–2 of the Criminal Code prohibiting sexual discrimination;

Thirdly, in considering that Ms [B.], "having regard to her lifestyle and despite her undoubted personal qualities and aptitude for bringing up children, did not provide the requisite safeguards— from a family, child-rearing and psychological perspective—for adopting a child", the Administrative Court of Appeal, which did not disregard the elements favourable to the applicant in the file submitted to it, did not distort the contents of the file; It follows from the foregoing that Ms [B.] is not justified in seeking to have set aside the above-mentioned judgment, which contains adequate reasons. . . .

THE LAW

32. The applicant alleged that she had suffered discriminatory treatment that had been based on her sexual orientation and had interfered

with her right to respect for her private life. She relied on Article 14 of the Convention taken in conjunction with Article 8, which provide:

Article 8

"1.   Everyone has the right to respect for his private and family life, his home and his correspondence.

2.   There shall be no interference by a public authority with the exercise of this right except such as is in accordance with the law and is necessary in a democratic society in the interests of national security, public safety or the economic well-being of the country, for the prevention of disorder or crime, for the protection of health or morals, or for the protection of the rights and freedoms of others."

Article 14

"The enjoyment of the rights and freedoms set forth in [the] Convention shall be secured without discrimination on any ground such as sex, race, colour, language, religion, political or other opinion, national or social origin, association with a national minority, property, birth or other status."

II.   ALLEGED VIOLATION OF ARTICLE 14 OF THE CONVENTION TAKEN IN CONJUNCTION WITH ARTICLE 8

A.   Submissions of the parties

1.   The applicant

53.   The applicant maintained that the refusal to grant her authorisation to adopt had been based on her "lifestyle", in other words her homosexuality. In her view, this was borne out by the screening of her application and the opinion of the adoption board. She also considered that part of the judgment delivered by the *Conseil d'Etat* was worded in the same terms as the judgment it had rendered in the case of *Fretté* (cited above), which showed that the *Conseil d'Etat* adopted a discriminatory approach.

54.   With regard to the ground based on the lack of a paternal referent, she argued that while the majority of French psychoanalysts believed that a child needed a dual maternal and paternal referent, there was no empirical evidence for that belief and it had been disputed by many other psychotherapists. Moreover, in the present case the Government had not shown that there was a practice of excluding single heterosexual women who did not have a male partner.

55.   With regard to the argument based on her partner's place in and attitude to her plan to adopt, she submitted that this was an illegal ground. Articles 343 and 343–1 of the Civil Code provided that adoption was open to married couples and single persons: partners were not concerned and therefore were not a party to the adoption procedure and did not enjoy any legal status once the child was adopted. Having regard to her right to be subject to foreseeable legal rules, the applicant contested a ground for rejection of her application that had no basis in the law itself.

56.   The applicant went on to stress that she and her partner had had a meeting with the social worker and that subsequently the various officials

involved in screening her application for authorisation had never asked to meet her partner. Either steps should have been taken to interview her partner or this ground had in reality served as a pretext for rejecting her application purely on the basis of her sexual orientation.

57. The applicant submitted that the difference in treatment in her regard had no objective and reasonable justification. Particularly serious reasons were required to justify a difference in treatment based on sexual orientation. There were no such reasons in this case.

58. With regard to the division in the scientific community (*Fretté*, § 42), particularly serious reasons were required to justify a difference in treatment of homosexuals. The burden of proving the existence of any scientific reasons was on the Government and if they had failed to prove in *Fretté* and in the instant case that there was a consensus in the scientific community, this was because there was no known study on the subject.

59. The applicant disputed the existence of a "legitimate aim", since children's health was not really in issue here and the *Conseil d'Etat* had not explained how the child's health might be endangered. She submitted that three risks were generally cited: first, the alleged risk of the child becoming homosexual, which, quite apart from the fact that there was nothing reprehensible about such an eventuality and that the majority of homosexuals had heterosexual parents, was a prejudiced notion; second, the child would be exposed to the risk of developing psychological problems: that risk had never been proved and recent studies showed that being raised in a homoparental family did not incline a child to any particular disorder; besides that, the right to adopt that existed in some democratic countries showed that there was no risk for the child. Lastly, there was no long-term risk that the child would suffer on account of homophobic prejudices towards the parents and, in any event, the prejudices of a sexual majority did not constitute sufficient justification.

60. She pointed out that the practice of the administrative authorities was inconsistent in France, where some *départements* no longer refused authorisation to single homosexual applicants. She also stated that the civil courts allowed adoption by the same-sex partner of the original parent.

61. In Europe there had been a steady development in the law in favour of adoption by same-sex couples since the *Fretté* judgment (cited above, § 41), with some ten European States now allowing it. The applicant also referred to a European consensus in favour of making adoption available to single homosexuals in the member States of the Council of Europe which allowed adoption by single persons, other than France where decisions were made on a discretionary basis. The same was true outside Europe, where case-law developments were in favour of adoption by homosexuals in the interests of children needing a home.

62. Lastly, she disputed the argument that there were insufficient numbers of children eligible for adoption, to which the Court had adhered in its *Fretté* judgment (cited above, § 42), arguing that the number of children eligible for adoption in the world exceeded the number of prospective adoptive parents and that making a legal possibility available should not depend on the effective possibility of exercising the right in question.

2.   The Government

63.   The Government pointed out that authorisation to adopt was issued at local, and not national, level by the president of the council for the *département* after obtaining the opinion of an adoption board at *département* level. In 2005, 13,563 new applications had been submitted, of which barely 8% had not been satisfied (with less than 6% being refused authorisation and about 2% being withdrawn). In 2006, 4,000 visas had been granted by the relevant authorities to foreign children being adopted. The Government stated that they could not provide statistics relating to the applicants' sexual orientation, as the collecting or processing of personal data about a person's sexual life were prohibited under French law.

64.   The Government submitted, in the alternative, that the present case did not lend itself to a review of the Court's finding in the *Fretté* judgment (cited above), since present-day conditions had not sufficiently changed to justify a departure from precedent.

65.   With regard to national laws, there was no European consensus on the subject, with only nine out of forty-six member States of the Council of Europe moving towards adoption by same-sex couples and some countries not making adoption available to single persons or allowing it under more restrictive conditions than in France. Moreover, that observation should be qualified by the nature of those laws and the conditions that had to be met.

66.   The conclusion reached by the Court in *Fretté* regarding the division in the scientific community was still valid today. The Government justified the failure to produce studies identifying problems or differences in development in children raised by homosexual couples by the fact that the number of children raised by a homosexual couple was unknown and the estimated numbers highly variable. Besides the complexity of the various situations that might be encountered, the existing studies were insufficiently thorough because they were based on insufficiently large samples, failed to take a detached approach and did not indicate the profile of the single-parent families in question. Child psychiatrists or psychoanalysts defended different theories, with a majority arguing that a dual maternal and paternal referent in the home was necessary.

67.   There were also still wide differences in public opinion since *Fretté* (cited above, § 42).

68.   The Government confirmed that the reality was that applications to adopt outnumbered children eligible for adoption. Their international obligations, particularly Articles 5 and 15 of the Hague convention, compelled them to select candidates on the basis of those best able to provide the child with a suitable home.

69.   Lastly, they pointed out that none of the sixty or so countries from which French people adopted children authorised adoption by same-sex couples. International adoption might therefore remain a purely theoretical possibility for homosexuals despite the fact that their domestic law allowed it.

B.   The Court's assessment

70.   The Court observes that in *Fretté v. France* (cited above) the Chamber held that the decisions to reject the application for authorisation

had pursued a legitimate aim, namely to protect the health and rights of children who could be involved in an adoption procedure (§ 38). With regard to whether a difference in treatment was justified, and after observing that there was no common ground between the legal systems of the Contracting States, the Chamber found it quite natural that the national authorities should enjoy a wide margin of appreciation when they were asked to make rulings on such matters, subject to review by the Court (§ 41). Having regard to the competing interests of the applicant and children who were eligible for adoption, and to the paramountcy of the latter's best interests, it noted that the scientific community was divided over the possible consequences of a child being adopted by one or more homosexual parents, that there were wide differences in national and international opinion and that there were not enough children to adopt to satisfy demand (§ 42). Taking account of the broad margin of appreciation to be left to States in this area and to the need to protect children's best interests to achieve the desired balance, the Chamber considered that the refusal to authorise adoption had not infringed the principle of proportionality and that, accordingly, the justification given by the Government appeared objective and reasonable and the difference in treatment complained of was not discriminatory within the meaning of Article 14 of the Convention (§§ 42 and 43).

71.   The Court notes that the present case also concerns the question of how an application for authorisation to adopt submitted by a homosexual single person is dealt with; it nonetheless differs in a number of respects from the above-cited case of *Fretté*. The Court notes in particular that whilst the ground relating to the lack of a referent of the other sex features in both cases, the domestic administrative authorities did not—expressly at least—refer to E.B.'s "choice of lifestyle" (*see Fretté*, cited above, § 32). Furthermore, they also mentioned the applicant's qualities and her child-raising and emotional capacities, unlike in *Fretté* where the applicant was deemed to have had difficulties in envisaging the practical consequences of the upheaval occasioned by the arrival of a child (§§ 28 and 29). Moreover, in the instant case the domestic authorities had regard to the attitude of E.B.'s partner, with whom she had stated that she was in a stable and permanent relationship, which was a factor that had not featured in the application lodged by Mr Fretté.

72.   In the instant case the Court notes that the domestic administrative authorities, and then the courts that heard the applicant's appeal, based their decision to reject her application for authorisation to adopt on two main grounds.

73.   With regard to the ground relied on by the domestic authorities relating to the lack of a paternal or maternal referent in the household of a person seeking authorisation to adopt, the Court considers that this does not necessarily raise a problem in itself. However, in the circumstances of the present case it is permissible to question the merits of such a ground, the ultimate effect of which is to require the applicant to establish the presence of a referent of the other sex among her immediate circle of family and friends, thereby running the risk of rendering ineffective the right of single persons to apply for authorisation. The point is germane here

because the case does not concern an application for authorisation to adopt by a—married or unmarried—couple, but by a single person. In the Court's view, that ground might therefore have led to an arbitrary refusal and have served as a pretext for rejecting the applicant's application on grounds of her homosexuality.

74. The Court observes, moreover, that the Government, on whom the burden of proof lay (*see, mutatis mutandis, Karner v. Austria,* no. 40016/98, §§ 41–42, ECtHR 2003–IX), were unable to produce statistical information on the frequency of reliance on that ground according to the—declared or known—sexual orientation of the persons applying for adoption, which alone could provide an accurate picture of administrative practice and establish the absence of discrimination when relying on that ground.

75. In the Court's view, the second ground relied on by the domestic authorities, based on the attitude of the applicant's partner, calls for a different approach. Although she was the long-standing and declared partner of the applicant, Ms R. did not feel committed by her partner's application to adopt. The authorities, which constantly remarked on this point—expressly and giving reasons—concluded that the applicant did not provide the requisite safeguards for adopting a child.

76. It should first be noted that, contrary to the applicant's submissions, the question of the attitude of her partner, with whom she stated that she was in a stable and lasting relationship, is not without interest or relevance in assessing her application. It is legitimate for the authorities to ensure that all safeguards are in place before a child is taken into a family. Accordingly, where a male or female applicant, although unmarried, has already set up home with a partner, that partner's attitude and the role he or she will necessarily play on a daily basis in the life of the child joining the home set-up require a full examination in the child's best interests. It would moreover be surprising, to say the least, if the relevant authorities, having been informed of the existence of a *de facto* couple, pretended to be unaware of that fact when assessing the conditions in which the child would be given a home and his future life in that new home. The legal status of a person seeking to adopt is not incompatible with an examination of his or her actual situation and the subsequent finding of not one but two adults in the household.

77. The Court notes, moreover, that Article 4 of the Decree of 1 September 1998 (*see* paragraph 28 above) requires the president of the council for the relevant *département* to satisfy himself that the conditions in which the applicant is proposing to provide the child with a home meet the needs of an adopted child from a family, child-rearing and psychological perspective. The importance of these safeguards—of which the authorities must be satisfied before authorising a person to adopt a child—can also be seen in the relevant international instruments, be it the United Nations Convention on the Rights of the Child of 20 November 1989, the Hague Convention of 29 May 1993 or the draft European Convention on the Adoption of Children (*see* paragraphs 29–31 above).

78. In the Court's view, there is no evidence to establish that the ground in question was based on the applicant's sexual orientation. On the contrary, the Court considers that this ground, which has nothing to do

with any consideration relating to the applicant's sexual orientation, is based on a simple analysis of the known, *de facto* situation and its consequences for the adoption of a child.

79.   The applicant cannot therefore be deemed to have been discriminated against on the ground of her sexual orientation in that regard.

80.   Nonetheless, these two main grounds form part of an overall assessment of the applicant's situation. For this reason, the Court considers that they should not be considered alternatively, but concurrently. Consequently, the illegitimacy of one of the grounds has the effect of contaminating the entire decision.

81.   With regard to the administrative phase, the Court observes that the president of the council for the *département* did not base his decision exclusively or principally on the second ground, but on "all" the factors involved—that is, both grounds—without it being possible to consider that one of them was predominant or that one of them alone was sufficient to make him decide to refuse authorisation (*see* paragraph 17 above).

82.   With regard to the judicial phase, the Nancy Administrative Court of Appeal noted that the decision was based on two grounds: the lack of a paternal referent and the ambivalence of the commitment of each member of the household. It added that the documents in the file and the conclusions reached after examining the application showed that the applicant's lifestyle did not provide the requisite safeguards for adopting a child, but disputed that the president of the council for the *département* had refused authorisation on the basis of a position of principle regarding her choice of lifestyle, namely, her homosexuality (*see* paragraph 24 above).

83.   Subsequently, the *Conseil d'Etat* held that the two grounds on which the applicant had been refused authorisation to adopt were in keeping with the statutory provisions. It also held that the reference to the applicant's "lifestyle" could be explained by the documents in the file submitted to the tribunals of fact, which showed that the applicant was, at the time of her application, in a stable homosexual relationship, but that this could not be construed as a decision based on a position of principle regarding her sexual orientation or as any form of discrimination (*see* paragraph 25 above).

84.   The Court therefore notes that the administrative courts went to some lengths to rule that although regard had been had to the applicant's sexual orientation, it had not been the basis for the decision in question and had not been considered from a hostile position of principle.

85.   However, in the Court's opinion the fact that the applicant's homosexuality featured to such an extent in the reasoning of the domestic authorities is significant. Besides their considerations regarding the applicant's "lifestyle", they above all confirmed the decision of the president of the council for the *département*. The Court points out that the latter reached his decision in the light of the opinion given by the adoption board whose various members had expressed themselves individually in writing, mainly recommending, with reasons in support of that recommendation, that the application be refused on the basis of the two grounds in question. It observes that the manner in which certain opinions were expressed was indeed revealing in that the applicant's homosexuality was a determining

factor. In particular, the Court notes that in his opinion of 12 October 1998 the psychologist from the children's welfare service recommended that authorisation be refused, referring to, among other things, an "unusual attitude [on the part of the applicant] to men in that men are rejected" (*see* paragraph 13 above).

86.   The Court observes that at times it was her status as a single person that was relied on as a ground for refusing the applicant authorisation to adopt, whereas the law makes express provision for the right of single persons to apply for authorisation to adopt. This emerges particularly clearly from the conclusions of the psychologist who, in her report on her interviews with the applicant of 28 August 1998, stated, with express reference to the applicant's case and not as a general comment—since she prefaces her remark with the statement that she is not seeking to diminish the applicant's confidence in herself or to insinuate that she would be harmful to a child—that "all the studies on parenthood show that a child needs both its parents" (*see* paragraph 11 above). On 28 October 1998 the adoption board's representative from the Family Council for the association of children currently or formerly in State care recommended refusing authorisation on the ground that an adoptive family had to be composed "of a mixed couple (man and woman)" (*see* paragraph 14 above).

87.   Regarding the systematic reference to the lack of a "paternal referent", the Court disputes not the desirability of addressing the issue, but the importance attached to it by the domestic authorities in the context of adoption by a single person. The fact that it is legitimate for this factor to be taken into account should not lead the Court to overlook the excessive reference to it in the circumstances of the present case.

88.   Thus, notwithstanding the precautions taken by the Nancy Administrative Court of Appeal, and subsequently by the *Conseil d'Etat*, to justify taking account of the applicant's "lifestyle", the inescapable conclusion is that her sexual orientation was consistently at the centre of deliberations in her regard and omnipresent at every stage of the administrative and judicial proceedings.

89.   The Court considers that the reference to the applicant's homosexuality was, if not explicit, at least implicit. The influence of the applicant's avowed homosexuality on the assessment of her application has been established and, having regard to the foregoing, was a decisive factor leading to the decision to refuse her authorisation to adopt (*see, mutatis mutandis, Salgueiro da Silva Mouta*, cited above, § 35).

90.   The applicant therefore suffered a difference in treatment. Regard must be had to the aim behind that difference in treatment and, if the aim was legitimate, to whether the different treatment was justified.

91.   The Court reiterates that, for the purposes of Article 14, a difference in treatment is discriminatory if it has no objective and reasonable justification, which means that it does not pursue a "legitimate aim" or that there is no "reasonable proportionality between the means employed and the aim sought to be realised" (*see, inter alia, Karlheinz Schmidt*, cited above, § 24; *Petrovic*, cited above, § 30; and *Salgueiro da Silva Mouta*, cited above, § 29). Where sexual orientation is in issue, there

is a need for particularly convincing and weighty reasons to justify a difference in treatment regarding rights falling within Article 8 (*see, mutatis mutandis, Smith and Grady v. the United Kingdom*, nos. 33985/96 and 33986/96, § 89, ECtHR 1999–VI; *Lustig–Prean and Beckett v. the United Kingdom*, nos. 31417/96 and 32377/96, § 82, 27 September 1999; and *S.L. v. Austria*, no. 45330/99, § 37, ECtHR 2003–I).

92. In that connection the Court observes that the Convention is a living instrument, to be interpreted in the light of present-day conditions (*see, inter alia, Johnston and Others*, cited above, § 53).

93. In the Court's opinion, if the reasons advanced for such a difference in treatment were based solely on considerations regarding the applicant's sexual orientation this would amount to discrimination under the Convention (*see Salgueiro da Silva Mouta*, cited above, § 36).

94. The Court points out that French law allows single persons to adopt a child (*see* paragraph 49 above), thereby opening up the possibility of adoption by a single homosexual, which is not disputed. Against the background of the domestic legal provisions, it considers that the reasons put forward by the Government cannot be regarded as particularly convincing and weighty such as to justify refusing to grant the applicant authorisation.

95. The Court notes, lastly, that the relevant provisions of the Civil Code are silent as to the necessity of a referent of the other sex, which would not, in any event, be dependent on the sexual orientation of the adoptive single parent. In this case, moreover, the applicant presented, in the terms of the judgment of the *Conseil d'Etat*, "undoubted personal qualities and an aptitude for bringing up children", which were assuredly in the child's best interests, a key notion in the relevant international instruments (*see* paragraphs 29–31 above).

96. Having regard to the foregoing, the Court cannot but observe that, in rejecting the applicant's application for authorisation to adopt, the domestic authorities made a distinction based on considerations regarding her sexual orientation, a distinction which is not acceptable under the Convention (*see Salgueiro da Silva Mouta*, cited above, § 36).

97. Consequently, having regard to its finding under paragraph 80 above, the Court considers that the decision in question is incompatible with the provisions of Article 14 taken in conjunction with Article 8.

98. There has accordingly been a breach of Article 14 of the Convention taken in conjunction with Article 8.

■ DISSENTING OPINION OF JUDGE COSTA JOINED BY JUDGES TÜRMEN, UGREKHELIDZE AND JOČIENÖ (*Translation*)

2. In so far as the Court has adopted a position of principle I can, I think, accept it, but I am not at all sure that in this specific case the interference attributed to the respondent State has proved to be contrary to that position or incompatible with the Convention provisions. I shall attempt to explain what I mean.

3. With regard to the question of principle, the main thrust of the majority's reasoning—making particular reference to the Court's earlier

decision in *Salgueiro da Silva Mouta v. Portugal* (*Reports* 1999–IX)—is based on alleged discrimination against the applicant because her application for authorisation to adopt a child was allegedly refused on the ground of her homosexual orientation, and she considers such discrimination to be unjustified.

In *Fretté v. France* (*Reports* 2002–I), which the present judgment overturns (as of course the Grand Chamber can), the majority of the Chamber had considered that such a ground was not contrary to Article 14 and 8, or—to be more precise—that the reasons for which the French authorities had rejected the application for authorisation to adopt made by the applicant, who was a homosexual, were justified (in the best interests of the child likely to be adopted). I did not subscribe to that reasoning, and whilst I did vote with the majority in favour of finding that there had not been a violation that was because, in my view, the Articles of the Convention relied on were not applicable because the Convention does not guarantee a right to adopt (but the Chamber did not agree with my reasoning on that point, and I will not go into it again here—*perseverare diabolicum*).

In my concurring opinion, in which I was joined by my colleagues Judge Jungwiert and Judge Traja, I pointed out that the French Civil Code (since 1966) allowed adoption by a single person and did not in any way prohibit adoption by a homosexual (or, which comes down to the same thing, did not require that the applicant be heterosexual). I therefore thought—and see no reason to change my view now—that a refusal to grant authorisation based exclusively on the avowed or established homosexuality of the applicant in question would be contrary to both the Civil Code and the Convention.

I am equally convinced that the message sent by our Court to the States Parties is clear: a person seeking to adopt cannot be prevented from doing so merely on the ground of his or her homosexuality. This point of view might not be shared by all, for good or not so good reasons, but—rightly or wrongly—our Court, whose duty under the Convention is to interpret and ultimately apply it, considers that a person can no more be refused authorisation to adopt on grounds of their homosexuality than have their parental responsibility withdrawn on those grounds (*Salgueiro da Silva Mouta*). I agree.

4. If we leave the theoretical domain, however, and address the specific case of the applicant—which even in a judgment that sets out be a leading judgment it is the Court's primary duty to do—I do not agree. The domestic administrative and judicial case files show, unequivocally in my view, that authorisation was refused (and that that refusal was deemed legal) for two reasons, which can be summarised as follows. Firstly, there would be no male or "paternal" referent among Ms E.B.'s circle of family and friends. Secondly, the woman with whom she was in a stable relationship at the time of her application did not feel concerned by her partner's plan to adopt; although she might not have been actually opposed or hostile to it, she was certainly indifferent.

5. To my mind, the first of these grounds is illegal under French law because if the law allows a single person to adopt it is against the law to require that person, be they a man or a woman, to have a member of the

opposite sex among their circle of family and friends who could serve as a "referent" (to use bureaucratico-psychological jargon). A single person cannot be required to artificially rebuild a "home" for the purpose of being able to exercise a statutory subjective right; would a single person have to be single only in name in order to be able to adopt? I note, though, that however illegal it may be the first ground should not be confused with homophobic discrimination. Whether or not Ms E.B. had been homosexual, the council for the *département* would still have refused her—or could still have refused her—authorisation on the ground of the lack of a "referent" of the other sex. It is not therefore clear that even this bizarre reasoning was based on the applicant's sexual orientation or that it alone suffices to justify the conclusion reached by the majority, at least by their reasoning.

6. The second ground, in any case, does not appear to me to be unreasonable or disproportionate. It is a fact that Ms E.B. was living with another person. Regardless of the latter's sex or sexual orientation, it is established and moreover not seriously disputed that this person did not support the adoption plan. In these conditions, if approval had been granted and the civil courts had subsequently allowed Ms E.B. to adopt it is very unlikely that the guarantees required under French law (from a "family, child-rearing and psychological" perspective—*see* paragraph 28 of the judgment), in the child's best interests, would have been met and it is assuredly not for the Court, if it is not to set itself up as a fourth instance, to decide otherwise.

7. A delicate problem of law therefore arises. Was the first ground (which moreover I have just said is not discriminatory, at least as far as the applicant's sexual orientation is concerned) decisive? Did it suffice to "contaminate" the administrative decision in question? Is it not more realistic to consider that, regarding a specific application by a person in a specific situation, the authorities were entitled to undertake an assessment of all the factors pertaining to that situation? Just as our court is not a court of fourth instance, nor is it a court of cassation that considers a particular ground to be founded, holds that it is not necessary to examine the other grounds and contents itself with the well-foundedness of the first ground to quash the decision and remit the case. This is what the judgment actually does however.

In that connection my position is close to that of my colleague Judge Mularoni, who, in her own dissenting opinion, criticises the majority for finding that Ms E.B.'s homosexual orientation was the *decisive* ground for refusing her authorisation. I, like her, consider this assertion to be somewhat gratuitous.

8. In my opinion, the Grand Chamber could have solemnly declared that a refusal of this kind could not be based on homosexuality without violating Articles 14 and 8, and thus given an important leading judgment, while dismissing Ms E.B.'s application because in this case it was not her homosexuality that had prevented her from obtaining authorisation. In my view, this would have corresponded more closely to the reality of the case, at least as regards my own interpretation of it.

9. This is why—in the present case—I cannot follow the majority's reasoning, and I consider that France has not violated the Convention.

■ [Dissenting opinions of JUDGES ZUPANČIČ, LOUCAIDES, and MULARONI omitted]

————

NOTES

1. As of October 2011, the following European States currently permit full same-sex marriage. Netherlands (2001), Belgium (2003), Spain (2005), Norway (2009), Sweden (2009), Portugal (2010), and Iceland (2010).

2. As of October 2011, the following European States permit civil partnerships Denmark (1989), Netherlands (1998), France (1999), Germany (2001), Finland (2002), Luxembourg (2004), UK (2004), Andorra (2005), Czech Republic (2006), Slovenia (2006), Switzerland (2007), Hungary (2009), Austria (2010), Ireland (2010), Liechtenstein (2011), Scotland (2011).

3. In E.B. v. France the ECJ rejects discrimination against GBLT persons in adoption. But in Kopf v. Austria, the Court accepts, for now, that marriage can be limited to opposite-sex couples, and holds that the definition of marriage should be left to national laws. Starting from the consideration that States are still free under the Convention to restrict access to marriage only to different-sex couples, the Court derives that States enjoy a certain margin of freedom regarding the exact status conferred by alternative means of recognition of same-sex partners, such as registered partnerships. However, this solution is not set in stone. As the Court explains, its deference to national choices, derived from an examination of the comparative law of the COE member states, depends on the lack of consensus of national laws. If these national laws were to change to favor a more inclusive conception of marriage, the interpretation of the ECtHR would have to evolve in the same direction.

4. In another recent case involving gay rights in the context of family life, the European Court of Human Rights held that a rule governing child support in the UK discriminated against those in same-sex relationships. In *J.M. v. The United Kingdom* (2010) (Application No. 37060/06) The rule, part of the Child Support Act of 1991, required that the parent who does not have primary care of the child is required to pay child support to the other parent. It also provides that child support should be reduced when the non-custodial parent enters into a new relationship. The mother of the child, the non-custodial parent, was living in a domestic partnership with another woman at the time that she was assessed child support, but did not receive this discount. In the applicant's case this was a difference between the £47 she was required to pay as opposed to the £14 she would have been liable for if she had formed a new relationship with a man. The applicant claimed that, in setting the amount of child maintenance, British authorities discriminated against her on the grounds of sexual orientation. She relied on Article 14 (prohibition of discrimination), submitting that Article applied to her situation either in conjunction with Article 8 (right to respect for private and family life) and/or Article 1 of Protocol No. 1 (protection of property). The Court ruled that there was a violation of Article 14 in conjunction with Article 1 of Protocol No. 1, reasoning that

the applicant could compare her situation to that of an absent parent who had formed a new relationship with a person of the opposite sex. Her maintenance obligation towards her children had been assessed differently on account of the nature of her new relationship. The reforms introduced in the 2004 UK Civil Partnership Law remove the difference in treatment complained of in this case.

5.   The French Courts, prior to the European Court of Human Rights judgment in *E.B. v. France* were, as a general matter, quite inhospitable to same-sex couple rights. In 2007 the French Supreme Court for civil matters (the Cour de Cassation) ruled that a civil marriage of a same-sex couple which had been performed in Bordeaux in 2004 was invalid, holding that in France, marriage was between a man and a woman. (*Cour de Cassation*, No. 05–16627, Mar 13, 2007). Again, in 2007, the French Supreme Court for civil matters (the Cour de Cassation) ruled that an adoption by the same-sex partner (joined under the French civil partnership law) of a biological mother was impermissible, because it would be contrary to the best interests of the child. (Cour de Cassation, No. 06–15647, Feb. 20, 2007.). In January 2011, France's Constitutional Council ruled that laws restricting marriage to a man and a woman did not violate the French Constitution. (*Mme Corinne C. et autre*, Le Conseil Constitutionnel, Decision 2010–92). Do you find it odd, given the general french openness to sexuality, that the culture has been resistant to recognition of gay marriage and family rights?

6.   The Spanish code allowing same-sex marriage does not create a new category of marriage or civil union, but amends the existing law to expand the definition of marriage. The Civil Code, Article 44, amended on July 1, 2005 provides that: "Marriage will have the same requirements and same effects when the two people entering into the contract are of the same sex or of different sexes." (Translation by Michelle Chang.). Later, Spain's bill on assisted reproduction was amended to allow the non-biological woman of a child born to her female partner to be regarded as a legal parent. *See* Marina, et al., *Sharing motherhood: biological lesbian co-mothers, a new IVF indication*, HUMAN REPRODUCTION, Vol.25, No.4 pp. 938–941, 2010, available at: http://humrep.oxfordjournals.org/content/25/4/938.full.pdf.

7.   The simple statutory language "Marriage will have the same requirements and same effects when the two people entering into the contract are of the same sex or of different sexes" masks a remarkable transformation in perhaps the most volatilely Catholic country in Europe. Catholicism was the official religion of the Iberian Peninsula from the late Fifteenth Century, which marked both the beginning of the Spanish Inquisition (1478) and the end of the centuries-long wars between Spanish Christians and Muslims (Treaty of Grenada–1491) until the establishment of the Second Republic in 1931. The founding of the Second Republic as a secular state helped spark the Spanish Civil War, in which the Catholic Church sided with General Franco and his Fascist army in his war against the secular Republicans. At the war's end, Franco restored Catholicism as the state religion. In 1975 Franco died, having named Juan Carlos, heir to the Spanish thrown, as his successor. Juan Carlos was proclaimed King,

but in 1978, under his leadership, a new constitution was adopted, disestablishing the church, and establishing a secular democracy. In 2004 a socialist government was elected, and began a series of social reforms in the areas of marriage, divorce, and violence against women. The government's proposal in the spring of 2005 to permit same-sex marriage provoked large demonstrations organized by the church opposing the law (and thus the government). The proposed law was enacted without changes, and in the first year after its passage over 4,500 same-sex couples were married. But the fear of conflict between church and state, or between establishmentiarenists and secularists, remains close to the surface.

8.   The Netherlands was the first country to grant same-sex couples the right to marry. The legislation, strongly opposed by the Christian parties, was adopted by a sizeable majority in both houses of Parliament. Also passed was an adoption rights law giving same-sex partners the same rights at heterosexual spouses. Since the passage of that law, come commentators have tried to use the Dutch experience to warn other countries against the peril of legalizing gay marriage, particularly given the historic low rate of marriage in Europe. *See e.g.* Andy McSmith, *The Big Question: Why Does the Marriage Rate Continue to Decline, and Does the Trend Matter?* THE INDEPENDENT (UK), 13 February 2009. Consider the following response to that challenge:

> . . . [A] few Dutch scholars have issued what might at first appear to be a serious warning to Canada and the rest of the world: Learn from the Dutch mistake and stop gay marriage before it undermines traditional marriage, as it did in the Netherlands. . . .
>
> A minority warns that heterosexuals are now voting against marriage with their feet. Falling numbers of marriages and rising numbers of children born out of wedlock since 1990 supposedly confirm a serious crisis in marriage in the Netherlands that began as gay marriage was debated in Parliament. But these alarmist claims are based on the selective use of statistics. In fact, the annual number of marriages fluctuates. In their open letter, the Dutch scholars point to a decline from 95,000 marriages in 1990 to 82,000 in 2003. But one might just as well point to an increase over the past two decades from 78,000 in 1983 to 82,000 in 2003.
>
> In fact, the propensity to get married declined steeply in the 1970s and early 1980s, but stabilized thereafter. The likelihood that a Dutch person would ever marry fell from nearly 100% around 1970 to about 60% around 1980, and has remained fairly stable since then. This demographic change obviously occurred long before the public discussion on same-sex marriage.
>
> The Dutch have become more likely to have children before marrying, but that shift also started before gay couples got partnership or marriage rights. It's true that the non-marital birth rate rose from 11% in 1990 to 31% in 2003. However, a similar increase in non-marital births occurred in Ireland, Luxembourg, Hungary and Lithuania, all countries that do not give same-sex couples partnership or marriage rights. We obviously can't blame the rise in non-marital

births in those countries on gay marriage, so why should we think that's what happened in the Netherlands?

The focus on parents' marital status when a child is born is also, in itself, misleading. For most of these child-bearing couples, the wedding is simply postponed, not cancelled. Although about a third of Dutch children are now born out of wedlock, only 11% live with unmarried parents by age five. As a result, 79% of Dutch families with children (up to age 16) are headed by married parents, and 91% are headed by a couple, either married or unmarried. Marriage remains relevant for Dutch couples because it is still the easiest way to arrange the financial and legal aspects of a family's life once children are in the picture.

These data do not describe a crisis in family stability that will hurt children: The large majority of Dutch children live with two parents, so the research on the possible dangers of single parenthood is irrelevant. One in 12 young children (up to the age of four) live without a father in the household, a share that is well below the European average.

. . . Overall, as the dissenting Dutch scholars whose article appears on this page have themselves admitted, there is no definitive evidence that the debate over gay marriage contributed to recent trends in marriage and births. Our interpretation of the Dutch figures is that they reflect the continuation of long-term trends, not an effect of allowing gay couples to marry. These trends may be rooted in increasing pragmatism with respect to marriage. But they have little, if anything, to do with a decline in family values, let alone a lack of responsibility toward children. The Dutch experience confirms common sense: Equality for gay and lesbian couples does not harm either heterosexual couples or their children.

Joop Garssen and M.V. Lee Badgett, *Comment: Equality doesn't harm 'family values'*, NATIONAL POST (Toronto, Canada), Wednesday, August 11, 2004. *This article was re-published by the Williams Institute at UCLA at: http://www.law.ucla.edu/williamsinstitute/issues/dueling.html.*

9. A European wide opinion poll ("Eurobarometer") taken in 2006 asked Europeans questions about the following subjects, among others: equality versus individual freedom; the place of religion in society; and attitudes towards homosexuality. On the latter issue, it concluded that:

Openness towards homosexuality tends to be quite limited. On average, only 32% of Europeans feel that homosexual couples should be allowed to adopt children throughout Europe. In fact, in 14 of the 25 Member States less than a quarter of the public accepts adoption by homosexual couples. Public opinion tends to be somewhat more tolerant as regards homosexual marriages: 44% of EU citizens agree that such marriages should be allowed throughout Europe. It should be noted that some Member States distinguish themselves from the average result by very high acceptance levels: the Netherlands tops the list with 82% of respondents in favour of homosexual marriages and 69% supporting the idea of adoption by homosexual couples. Opposition is strongest in Greece, Latvia (both 84% and 89%, respectively) and

Poland (76% and 89%). One has to remember that [in 2006] homosexual marriages (or similar union between to persons of the same gender) are allowed in the Netherlands, Belgium, Spain, Sweden and in the UK.

A summary of the full results of this survey (including percentages per country) can be found here: http://ec.europa.eu/public_opinion/archives/eb/eb66/eb66_highlights_en.pdf.

10.   Free movement and gay couples: The right to free movement of persons is explicitly and generally provided for by the Treaty on the Functioning of the European Union (article 45 for workers, for example) and has been progressively developed to also cover people who do not have an economic activity, including students and retired people. At present, the right to free movement of persons is implemented by Directive 2004/38/EC of 29 April 2004, which concerns the right of citizens of the Union and their family members to move and reside freely within the territory of the Member States. According to its Article 2, paragraph 2, the following people are entitled to follow a worker when he or she moves to another EU Member State:

(a) the spouse

(b) the partner with whom the Union citizen has contracted a registered partnership, on the basis of the legislation of a Member State, if the legislation of the host Member State treats registered partnerships as equivalent to marriage in accordance with the conditions laid down in the relevant legislation of the host Member State.

(c) the direct descendants who are under the age of 21 or are dependants and those of the spouse or partner as defined in point (b)

(d) the dependent direct relative in the ascending line and those of the spouse or partner as defined in point (b).

Recital 5 of the Directive explains that: "For the purposes of this Directive, the definition of 'family member' should also include the registered partner if the legislation of the host Member State treats registered partnership as equivalent to marriage."

D.   SOUTH AFRICA

Constitution of the Republic of South Africa
(As adopted by the Constitutional Assembly on 8 May 1996)

Section 9: Equality

(1) Everyone is equal before the law and has the right to equal protection and benefit of the law.

(2) Equality includes the full and equal enjoyment of all rights and freedoms. To promote the achievement of equality, legislative and other measures designed to protect or advance persons, or categories of persons, disadvantaged by unfair discrimination may be taken.

(3) The state may not unfairly discriminate directly or indirectly against anyone on one or more grounds, including race, gender, sex, pregnancy, marital status, ethnic or social origin, colour, sexual orientation, age, disability, religion, conscience, belief, culture, language, and birth.

(4) No person may unfairly discriminate directly or indirectly against anyone on one or more grounds in terms of subsection (3). National legislation must be enacted to prevent or prohibit unfair discrimination.

(5) Discrimination on one or more of the grounds listed in subsection (3) is unfair unless it is established that the discrimination is fair.

————

Ending the Apartheid of the Closet: Sexual Orientation in the South African Constitutional Process

32 NYU J Int'l L & Pol 997, 997–1000, 1042–1043, 1046, 1051–1052, 1056, 1058 (2000)

■ ERIC C. CHRISTIANSEN

In 1994, the Republic of South Africa became the first country in the world to grant explicit constitutional-level protections to gays and lesbians. Those interim constitutional protections were enhanced and included in the subsequent "final" Constitution, ratified by the democratically elected Constitutional Assembly two years later. Section Nine of the Bill of Rights of the 1996 South African Constitution prohibits public and private discrimination based on sexual orientation. Textually, these protections are located amid a collection of enumerated rights and basic constitutional values, the core of what was meant to be a 'rainbow nation of God' built on "democratic values, social justice, and fundamental human rights." Socially, although they are at conflict with strong public opinion, these protections are a dramatic expression of the new democracy's commitment to expansive human rights protections.

The process of adopting a new constitution for South Africa was a complex, intentionally reflective process set against the dramatic historical backdrop of the end of apartheid and the fundamental reformulation of the political and societal structure of the entire nation.... In light of [the] avowal of a participatory process, the inclusion of sexual orientation protections in the constitution of a conservative, intensely religious, southern African nation is astounding.

The current South African posture towards its gay and lesbian citizens contrasts starkly with the legal status of gays and same-sex sexual activity in other countries. From a global perspective, torture, incarceration, forcible "medical treatment," and the death penalty are more common legal responses to homosexuality than rights protections. * * *

While such attitudes were not absent from South African society at the end of the apartheid era, they utterly failed to dominate the constitutional discourse about homosexuality. This paper seeks to discover and explain why South Africa rejected violent oppression of gays and lesbians and chose instead to provide legal protection in its first democratic Constitution.

In the early 1990s, South Africa was a country in which gays and lesbians had little genuine political power. They were poorly organized, racially divided, and mostly without sympathy from the general population. Before ratification of the post-apartheid constitution, there was no domestic legal precedent for treating gays and lesbians in any manner other than as criminals—even as the apartheid government was lifting criminal sanctions against inter-racial sexual activity in 1988, the Parliament was considering an expansion of laws against same-sex sexual activity. Indeed, a 1987 survey of Cape Town residents revealed that 71% believed homosexuality to be morally wrong.

Attempts by the gay and lesbian community to organize were further challenged by the strength of conservative churches in South Africa, the often virulent anti-gay sentiments among both Africans and Afrikaners, and the countless restrictive laws upon movement and meeting for black South Africans. Moreover, as the constitutional drafting process began there was almost no favorable foreign or international legal precedent. And yet, South Africa developed sexual orientation protections surpassing those of any other nation—despite lacking the visibility, history of organizing, and domestic networks of well-funded rights organizations that exist in numerous countries which have succeeded in instituting only limited protections based on sexual orientation. How? * * *

Examination of the process of constitutional drafting in South Africa, of policy development by the dominant political parties, of organizational development by gay institutions, and of the legal history of gay and lesbian South Africans yields a tripartite explanation of how South Africa came to be the first nation to prohibit discrimination against gays and lesbians in its Constitution. First, the stage for this unprecedented protection was set by the unique history of South Africa and its gay and lesbian citizens: the rise of gay and lesbian visibility contemporaneous with the fundamental constitutional re-creation of a state that had existed for forty-seven years with discrimination as its primary political and social reality. Second, justification for such an innovative legal protection was provided by the dominant ideology of the liberation movements, yielding the prohibition of discrimination based on sexual orientation as a presumptive corollary of the ANC policy of non-racialism. And third, an autocratic constitutional drafting process codified progressive human rights standards including explicit protections for gays and lesbians supported by uncertain claims of public support and international law precedent. * * *

[First,] the consequence of three historically congruent factors—simultaneous maturation of the ANC and the burgeoning South African gay community, newly-formed linkages between the two distinct liberation movements, and changing international legal precedent related to sexual orientation—set the stage for the legal transformation of the status of gays and lesbians in the context of a new, multi-racial South Africa. * * *

[Second,] the content of South Africa's history and its tremendously formative influence on ANC ideology are vital, additional factors: history set the stage, but it was the ideology of the liberation movements that provided the philosophical justification and indeed the affirmative argument for inclusion of anti-gay discrimination prohibitions in the Constitution. * * *

The philosophical underpinnings of the Constitution, in form and spirit, were meant to destroy and repudiate apartheid legal norms.... The ANC ideology of non-racialism was both a philosophy and a tool. As a philosophy, it espoused an end to all forms of discrimination and the inviolability of human rights by the state. It also acted as a tool for ending apartheid, creating democratic government, and healing the nation. The presumptive inclusion of gays and lesbians as a class of citizens to benefit from the end to an era of discrimination combined with the centrality of non-racialism in ANC discourse about a post-apartheid nation, strongly supported the development of anti-discrimination policies that could include protections for gays and lesbians. * * *

The third factor contributing to the inclusion of protections for gays and lesbians was the particular method of drafting the Constitution. The final draft of the Constitution was the result of a sequential process that moved from draft to draft under tight time constraints and strong political pressures on some aspects. The earliest decisions—indeed the entire Interim Constitution—and most of the weightiest decisions throughout the process were made by party-based negotiating committees behind closed doors. Additionally, small groups directed most of the textual decisions—theme committees of experts for the interim text and technical committees in the final drafting process. And the party-based Constitutional Committee approved most final decisions before the last draft was put to a vote—a vote uniformly decided along party lines. The consequence of this controlled, sequential process and the limited number of only indirectly-accountable drafters was a rather autocratic result. Gay and lesbian advocates were beneficiaries of this process because of the specific historical moment of its occurrence, the congruence of their concerns to the dominant ideology of the process, and the pro-gay attitudes of several important constitutional actors. * * *

While the constitutional drafting process was far from perfect, there are several ways in which inclusion of sexual orientation protections reflected some of the best aspects of the constitutional process. It reflected a commitment to human rights broadly defined, reflected liberal and progressive interpretation of international and foreign legal precedent, and represented a dramatic denial of the politics of division and acceptance of inclusivity and difference. Furthermore, while the efforts of gay rights advocates in the South African constitutional process offer little direct application in other countries, they set an important legal precedent. The human rights decisions of the South African Constitution are uniquely valued because of the nation's history. Hence, inclusion of gay rights discourse as a "universally accepted fundamental human right" ratifies the aspirations of gay and lesbian activists world wide and affirms South African claims that their Constitution creates a nation that "belongs to all who live in it, united in our diversity."

Since the conclusion of the drafting process, hopes have remained high for many South African gay and lesbian activists. Legally, the Constitutional Court has risen to the challenge presented by unprecedented legal protection for an unpopular segment of South African society. In the 1998 decision of *NCGLE v. Minister of Justice and Others*, the Court decriminalized consensual same-sex sexual activity between adults, and in the 1999 decision of *NCGLE v. Minister of Home Affairs and Others*, the Court examined immigration provisions and "read in" comparable benefits for "same-sex life partners" as those available for heterosexual "spouses." * * *

Nevertheless, the path ahead is somewhat unclear. For South African gays and lesbians, the Constitution means everything and nothing. It is a statement of dramatic importance and value and yet neither a sufficient nor even a necessary precondition for genuine social equality. * * *

Fourie and Another v. Minister of Home Affairs and Another

Constitutional Court of South Africa Case CCT 60/04 (Dec. 1, 2005)

■ Sachs J.

INTRODUCTION

[1]   Finding themselves strongly attracted to each other, two people went out regularly and eventually decided to set up home together. After being acknowledged by their friends as a couple for more than a decade, they decided that the time had come to get public recognition and registration of their relationship, and formally to embrace the rights and responsibilities they felt should flow from and attach to it. Like many persons in their situation, they wanted to get married. There was one impediment. They are both women.

[2]   Ms Marié Adriaana Fourie and Ms Cecelia Johanna Bonthuys are the applicants in the first of two cases that were set down for hearing on the same day in this Court. Their complaint has been that the law excludes them from publicly celebrating their love and commitment to each other in marriage. Far from enabling them to regularise their union, it shuts them out, unfairly and unconstitutionally, they claim.

[3]   They contend that the exclusion comes from the common law definition which states that marriage in South Africa is "a union of one man with one woman, to the exclusion, while it lasts, of all others." The common law is not self-enforcing, and in order for such a union to be formalised and have legal effect, the provisions of the Marriage Act have to be invoked. * * *

[5]   The matter before us accordingly raises the question: does the fact that no provision is made for the applicants, and all those in like situation, to marry each other, amount to denial of equal protection of the law and unfair discrimination by the state against them because of their sexual orientation? And if it does, what is the appropriate remedy that this Court should order? * * *

[32]   To summarise: both judgments [below] were in agreement that the SCA could and should rule that the common law definition discriminated unfairly against same-sex couples. The majority judgment by Cameron JA held, however, that although the common law definition should be developed so as to embrace same-sex couples, the Marriage Act could not be read in such a way as to include them. [Because the validity of the Marriage Act was not challenged in the initial suit,], the only way the parties could marry would be under the auspices of a religious body that recognised same-sex marriages, and whose marriage formula was approved by the Minister of Home Affairs. The right of same-sex couples to celebrate a secular marriage would have to await a challenge to the Marriage Act.
* * *

[34]   In the meantime, accepting the need to challenge the Marriage Act as well as the common law, the Lesbian and Gay Equality Project (the Equality Project) and eighteen others had launched an application in the Johannesburg High Court for the following relief:

1.   Declaring that the common law definition of marriage and the prescribed marriage formula in section 30(1) of the Marriage Act 25 of 1961 ('the Marriage Act') are unconstitutional in that they violate the rights of lesbian and gay people to:

1.1.   equality in terms of section 9 of the Constitution of the Republic of South Africa, 1996 ('the Constitution');

1.2.   dignity in terms of section 10 of the Constitution; and

1.3.   privacy in terms of section 14 of the Constitution;

2.   Declaring that the common law definition of marriage is henceforth to be read as follows:

'Marriage is the lawful and voluntary union of two persons to the exclusion of all others while it lasts';

3.   Declaring that the words 'or spouse' are to be read into the prescribed marriage formula in section 30(1) of the Marriage Act immediately after the words 'or husband'; * * *

Does the law deny equal protection to and discriminate unfairly against same-sex couples by not including them in the provisions of the Marriage Act?

[46]   Counsel for the Minister of Justice argued that the Constitution did not protect the right to marry. It merely guaranteed to same-sex couples the right to establish their own forms of family life without interference from the state. This was a negative liberty, not to be equated with a right to be assimilated into the institution of marriage, which in terms of its historic genesis and evolution, was heterosexual by nature. International law recognised and protected marriage as so understood. Same-sex couples accordingly had no constitutional right to enter into or manipulate that institution. If their form of family life suffered from particular disadvantages, then these should be dealt with by appropriate legal remedies in response to each of the identified problems, not by entry into the global set of rights and entitlements established by marriage. Marriage law appropri-

ately confined itself to marriage, it was contended, and not to all forms of family relationship. * * *

[57]   In [earlier equalty case] Du Toit, the issue flowed from a provision in child care legislation which confined the right to adopt children jointly to married couples. Holding that the exclusion of same-sex life partners conflicted both with the best interests of the child and the right to dignity of same-sex couples, Skweyiya AJ emphasised that family life as contemplated by the Constitution could be provided in different ways, and that legal conceptions of the family and what constituted family life should change as social practices and traditions changed. He pointed out further that it was a matter of our history, and that of many countries, that same-sex relationships had been the subject of unfair discrimination in the past. The Constitution required that unfairly discriminatory treatment cease. It was significant that there had been a number of recent cases, statutes and government consultation documents in South Africa which broadened the scopes of 'family', 'spouse' and 'domestic relationship' to include same-sex life partners. These legislative and jurisprudential developments indicated the growing recognition afforded to same-sex relationships. * * *

[59]   This Court has ... in five consecutive decisions highlighted at least four unambiguous features of the context in which the prohibition against unfair discrimination on grounds of sexual orientation must be analysed. The first is that South Africa has a multitude of family formations that are evolving rapidly as our society develops, so that it is inappropriate to entrench any particular form as the only socially and legally acceptable one. The second is the existence of an imperative constitutional need to acknowledge the long history in our country and abroad of marginalisation and persecution of gays and lesbians, that is, of persons who had the same general characteristics as the rest of the population, save for the fact that their sexual orientation was such that they expressed erotic desire and affinity for individuals of their own sex, and were socially defined as homosexual. The third is that although a number of breakthroughs have been made in particular areas, there is no comprehensive legal regulation of the family law rights of gays and lesbians. Finally, our Constitution represents a radical rupture with a past based on intolerance and exclusion, and the movement forward to the acceptance of the need to develop a society based on equality and respect by all for all. Small gestures in favour of equality, however meaningful, are not enough. In the memorable words of Mahomed J:

> In some countries, the Constitution only formalises, in a legal instrument, a historical consensus of values and aspirations evolved incrementally from a stable and unbroken past to accommodate the needs of the future. The South African Constitution is different: it retains from the past only what is defensible and represents a decisive break from, and a ringing rejection of, that part of the past which is disgracefully racist, authoritarian, insular, and repressive, and a vigorous identification of and commitment to a democratic, universalistic, caring and aspirationally egalitarian ethos expressly articulated in the Constitution. The contrast between the past which it repudiates and the future to which it seeks to commit the nation is stark and dramatic.

[60] A democratic, universalistic, caring and aspirationally egalitarian society embraces everyone and accepts people for who they are. To penalise people for being who and what they are is profoundly disrespectful of the human personality and violatory of equality. Equality means equal concern and respect across difference. It does not presuppose the elimination or suppression of difference. Respect for human rights requires the affirmation of self, not the denial of self. Equality therefore does not imply a levelling or homogenisation of behaviour or extolling one form as supreme, and another as inferior, but an acknowledgement and acceptance of difference. At the very least, it affirms that difference should not be the basis for exclusion, marginalisation and stigma. At best, it celebrates the vitality that difference brings to any society. The issue goes well beyond assumptions of heterosexual exclusivity, a source of contention in the present case. The acknowledgement and acceptance of difference is particularly important in our country where for centuries group membership based on supposed biological characteristics such as skin colour has been the express basis of advantage and disadvantage. South Africans come in all shapes and sizes. The development of an active rather than a purely formal sense of enjoying a common citizenship depends on recognising and accepting people with all their differences, as they are. The Constitution thus acknowledges the variability of human beings (genetic and socio-cultural), affirms the right to be different, and celebrates the diversity of the nation. Accordingly, what is at stake is not simply a question of removing an injustice experienced by a particular section of the community. At issue is a need to affirm the very character of our society as one based on tolerance and mutual respect. The test of tolerance is not how one finds space for people with whom, and practices with which, one feels comfortable, but how one accommodates the expression of what is discomfiting.

[61] . . . For present purposes it needs to be added that acknowledgement of the diversity that flows from different forms of sexual orientation will provide an extra and distinctive thread to the national tapestry. The strength of the nation envisaged by the Constitution comes from its capacity to embrace all its members with dignity and respect. In the words of the Preamble, South Africa belongs to all who live in it, united in diversity. What is at stake in this case, then, is how to respond to legal arrangements of great social significance under which same-sex couples are made to feel like outsiders who do not fully belong in the universe of equals. * * *

[71] The exclusion of same-sex couples from the benefits and responsibilities of marriage . . . is not a small and tangential inconvenience resulting from a few surviving relics of societal prejudice destined to evaporate like the morning dew. It represents a harsh if oblique statement by the law that same-sex couples are outsiders, and that their need for affirmation and protection of their intimate relations as human beings is somehow less than that of heterosexual couples. It reinforces the wounding notion that they are to be treated as biological oddities, as failed or lapsed human beings who do not fit into normal society, and, as such, do not qualify for the full moral concern and respect that our Constitution seeks to secure for everyone. It signifies that their capacity for love, commitment and accept-

ing responsibility is by definition less worthy of regard than that of heterosexual couples. * * *

[73]   Equally important as far as family law is concerned, is the right of same-sex couples to fall back upon state regulation when things go wrong in their relationship. Bipolar by its very nature, the law of marriage is invoked both at moments of blissful creation and at times of sad cessation. There is nothing to suggest that same-sex couples are any less affected than are heterosexual ones by the emotional and material consequences of a rupture of their union. The need for comprehensive judicial regulation of their separation or divorce, or of devolution of property, or rights to maintenance or continuation of tenancy after death, is no different. Again, what requires legal attention concerns both status and practical regulation.

[74]   The law should not turn its back on any persons requiring legal support in times of family breakdown. It should certainly not do so on a discriminatory basis; the antiquity of a prejudice is no reason for its survival. Slavery lasted for a century and a half in this country, colonialism for twice as long, the prohibition of interracial marriages for even longer, and overt male domination for millennia. All were based on apparently self-evident biological and social facts; all were once sanctioned by religion and imposed by law; the first two are today regarded with total disdain, and the third with varying degrees of denial, shame or embarrassment. Similarly, the fact that the law today embodies conventional majoritarian views in no way mitigates its discriminatory impact. It is precisely those groups that cannot count on popular support and strong representation in the legislature that have a claim to vindicate their fundamental rights through application of the Bill of Rights. * * *

Marriage and recognition of same-sex unions

[80]   I will now deal with the contention that respect for the traditional institution of marriage requires that any recognition of same-sex unions must be accomplished outside of the law of marriage. The applicants submitted that as a matter of simple logic flowing from the above analysis, the Marriage Act is inconsistent with the Constitution and must be declared to be invalid to the extent that it makes no provision for same-sex couples to enjoy the status, entitlements and responsibilities which it accords to heterosexual couples. The state and amici, however, argued that the fault in not furnishing same-sex couples with the possibility of regularising and giving legal effect to their unions, lay outside the Marriage Act itself. Instead, they contended, it stemmed from the failure of the law to provide an appropriate remedial mechanism that was alternative and supplementary to the Marriage Act.

[81]   There is an immediate answer to this proposition. A law that creates institutions which enable heterosexual couples to declare their public commitment to each other and achieve the status, entitlements and responsibilities that flow from marriage, but does not provide any mechanism for same-sex couples to achieve the same, discriminates unfairly against same-sex couples. It gives to the one and not to the other. The instruments created by the legal system exclude from their reach persons entitled to be protected by them. It is those instruments that stand to be identified as

being inconsistent with the Constitution, and not 'the law' as an abstraction. The law must be measured in the context of what is provided for by the legal system as a whole. In this respect, exclusion by silence and omission is as effective in law and practice as if effected by express language. Same-sex unions continue in fact to be treated with the same degree of repudiation that the state until two decades ago reserved for interracial unions; the statutory format might be different, but the effect is the same. The negative impact is not only symbolic but also practical, and each aspect has to be responded to. Thus, it would not be sufficient merely to deal with all the practical consequences of exclusion from marriage. It would also have to accord to same-sex couples a public and private status equal to that which heterosexual couples achieve from being married.

[82]   The conclusion is that when evaluated in the context of the legal regime as a whole, the common law definition and section 30(1) are under-inclusive and unconstitutional to the extent that they make no appropriate provision for gay and lesbian people to celebrate their unions in the same way that they enable heterosexual couples to do. * * *

Respect for religion arguments

[88]   The two amici submitted a number of arguments from an avowedly religious point of view in support of the view that by its origins and nature, the institution of marriage simply cannot sustain the intrusion of same-sex unions. The corollary is that such unions can never be regarded as marriages, or even marriage-like or equivalent to marriages. To disrupt and radically alter an institution of centuries-old significance to many religions, would accordingly infringe the Constitution by violating religious freedom in a most substantial way.

[89]   Their arguments raise important issues concerning the relationship foreshadowed by the Constitution between the sacred and the secular. They underline the fact that in the open and democratic society contemplated by the Constitution, although the rights of non-believers and minority faiths must be fully respected, the religious beliefs held by the great majority of South Africans must be taken seriously. As this Court pointed out in Christian Education, freedom of religion goes beyond protecting the inviolability of the individual conscience. For many believers, their relationship with God or creation is central to all their activities. It concerns their capacity to relate in an intensely meaningful fashion to their sense of themselves, their community and their universe. For millions in all walks of life, religion provides support and nurture and a framework for individual and social stability and growth. Religious belief has the capacity to awaken concepts of self-worth and human dignity which form the cornerstone of human rights. Such belief affects the believer's view of society and founds a distinction between right and wrong. It expresses itself in the affirmation and continuity of powerful traditions that frequently have an ancient character transcending historical epochs and national boundaries.For believers, then, what is at stake is not merely a question of convenience or comfort, but an intensely held sense about what constitutes the good and proper life and their place in creation.

[90]   Religious bodies play a large and important part in public life, through schools, hospitals and poverty relief programmes. They command ethical behaviour from their members and bear witness to the exercise of power by state and private agencies; they promote music, art and theatre; they provide halls for community activities, and conduct a great variety of social activities for their members and the general public. They are part of the fabric of public life, and constitute active elements of the diverse and pluralistic nation contemplated by the Constitution. Religion is not just a question of belief or doctrine. It is part of a people's temper and culture, and for many believers a significant part of their way of life. Religious organisations constitute important sectors of national life and accordingly have a right to express themselves to government and the courts on the great issues of the day. They are active participants in public affairs fully entitled to have their say with regard to the way law is made and applied.

[91]   Furthermore, in relation to the extensive national debates concerning rights for homosexuals, it needs to be acknowledged that though religious strife may have produced its own forms of intolerance, and religion may have been used in this country to justify the most egregious forms of racial discrimination, it would be wrong and unhelpful to dismiss opposition to homosexuality on religious grounds simply as an expression of bigotry to be equated to racism. As Ackermann J said in the Sodomy case:

> The issues in this case touch on deep convictions and evoke strong emotions. It must not be thought that the view which holds that sexual expression should be limited to marriage between men and women with procreation as its dominant or sole purpose, is held by crude bigots only. On the contrary, it is also sincerely held, for considered and nuanced religious and other reasons, by persons who would not wish to have the physical expression of sexual orientation differing from their own proscribed by the law.

[92]   It is also necessary, however, to highlight his qualification:

> It is nevertheless equally important to point out that such views, however honestly and sincerely held, cannot influence what the Constitution dictates in regard to discrimination on the grounds of sexual orientation.

It is one thing for the Court to acknowledge the important role that religion plays in our public life. It is quite another to use religious doctrine as a source for interpreting the Constitution. It would be out of order to employ the religious sentiments of some as a guide to the constitutional rights of others. Between and within religions there are vastly different and at times highly disputed views on how to respond to the fact that members of their congregations and clergy are themselves homosexual. Judges would be placed in an intolerable situation if they were called upon to construe religious texts and take sides on issues which have caused deep schisms within religious bodies. * * *

[97]   State accommodation of religious belief goes further. Section 31 provides:

> Certain marriage officers may refuse to solemnize certain marriages.- Nothing in this Act contained shall be construed so as to compel a

marriage officer who is a minister of religion or a person holding a responsible position in a religious denomination or organization to solemnize a marriage which would not conform to the rites, formularies, tenets, doctrines or discipline of his religious denomination or organization.

The effect of this provision is that no minister of religion could be compelled to solemnise a same-sex marriage if such a marriage would not conform to the doctrines of the religion concerned. There is nothing in the matters before us that either directly or indirectly trenches in any way on this strong protection of the right of religious communities not to be obliged to celebrate marriages not conforming to their tenets. * * *

The international law argument

[99] Considerable stress was placed by the state on the contention that international law recognises and protects heterosexual marriage only. As such, the state contended, it could not be regarded as unfair discrimination to exclude same-sex couples from the institution of marriage. The remedy to the plight of same-sex couples should therefore be found outside of rather than inside marriage. Thus, reference was made to article 16 of the 1948 Universal Declaration of Human Rights (UDHR) which states:

"16(1) Men and women of full age, without any limitation due to race, nationality or religion, have the right to marry and to found a family. They are entitled to equal rights as to marriage, during marriage and at its dissolution.

16(2) Marriage shall be entered into only with the free and full consent of the intending spouses.

16(3) The family is the natural and fundamental group unit of society and is entitled to protection by society and the State."

Similar provisions from a number of different instruments were referred to, as was a decision of the United Nations Human Rights Committee to the effect that a New Zealand law denying marriage licences to same-sex couples does not violate the International Covenant on Civil and Political Rights (ICCPR). Support for the argument was sought from the provision in our Constitution requiring that customary international law be recognised as part of the law in the Republic and that when interpreting the Bill of Rights a court must consider international law. * * *

[103] The decision of the United Nations Human Rights Committee is clearly distinguishable. The Committee held that there was no provision in the ICCPR which forbade discrimination on sexual orientation. This is a far cry from declaring that the ICCPR forbids the recognition of same-sex marriages and seals off same-sex couples from participating in marriage or establishing families. Even more directly to the point, in contradistinction to the ICCPR, our Constitution explicitly proclaims the anti-discriminatory right which was held to lack support from the text of the ICCPR. Indeed, discrimination on the grounds of sexual orientation is expressly stated by our Constitution to be presumptively unfair.

[104] It would be a strange reading of the Constitution that utilised the principles of international human rights law to take away a guaranteed

right. This would be the more so when the right concerned was openly, expressly and consciously adopted by the Constitutional Assembly as an integral part of the first of all rights mentioned in the Bill of Rights, namely, the right to equality.

[105]   I conclude that while it is true that international law expressly protects heterosexual marriage it is not true that it does so in a way that necessarily excludes equal recognition being given now or in the future to the right of same-sex couples to enjoy the status, entitlements, and responsibilities accorded by marriage to heterosexual couples. * * *

Should the order of invalidity be suspended?

[132]   Having concluded that the law of marriage as it stands is inconsistent with the Constitution and invalid to the extent outlined above, an appropriate declaration of invalidity needs to be made. The question that arises is whether this Court is obliged to provide immediate relief in the terms sought by the applicants and the Equality Project, or whether it should suspend the order of invalidity to give Parliament a chance to remedy the defect. The test is what is just and equitable, taking account of all the circumstances. * * *

[135]   .... In the present matter I have considered ordering with immediate effect reading-in of the words "or spouse" after the words "or husband" in section 30(1) of the Marriage Act. This would remedy the invalidity while at the same time leaving Parliament free, if it chose, to amend the law so as to provide an alternative statutory mechanism to enable same-sex couples to enjoy their constitutional rights as outlined in this judgment. For reasons which follow, however, I have come to the conclusion that correction by the Court itself should be delayed for an appropriate period so as to give Parliament itself the opportunity to correct the defect. * * *

[139]   This judgment serves to vindicate the rights of the applicants by declaring the manner in which the law at present fails to meet their equality claims. At the same time, it is my view that it would best serve those equality claims by respecting the separation of powers and giving Parliament an opportunity to deal appropriately with the matter. In this respect it is necessary to bear in mind that there are different ways in which the legislature could legitimately deal with the gap that exists in the law. * * *

[153]   In the present matter, ... whatever legislative remedy is chosen must be as generous and accepting towards same-sex couples as it is to heterosexual couples, both in terms of the intangibles as well as the tangibles involved. In a context of patterns of deep past discrimination and continuing homophobia, appropriate sensitivity must be shown to providing a remedy that is truly and manifestly respectful of the dignity of same-sex couples. * * *

The period of suspension of invalidity

[156]   As I have shown, Parliament has already undertaken a number of legislative initiatives which demonstrate its concern to end discrimination on the ground of sexual orientation. Aided by the extensive research and

specific proposals made by the SALRC, there is no reason to believe that Parliament will not be able to fulfill its responsibilities in the light of this judgment within a relatively short time. As was pointed out in argument, what is in issue is not a fundamental new start in legislation but the culmination of a process that has been underway for many years. In the circumstances it would be appropriate to give Parliament one year from the date of the delivery of this judgment to cure the defect. * * *

[161] In keeping with this approach it is necessary that the orders of this Court, read together, make it clear that if Parliament fails to cure the defect within twelve months, the words "or spouse" will automatically be read into section 30(1) of the Marriage Act. In this event the Marriage Act will, without more, become the legal vehicle to enable same-sex couples to achieve the status and benefits coupled with responsibilities which it presently makes available to heterosexual couples. * * *

■ *Langa CJ, Moseneke DCJ, Mokgoro J, Ngcobo J, Skweyiya J, Van der Westhuizen J and Yacoob J concur in the judgment of Sachs J.*

■ O'Regan J: * * *

[169] In my view, this Court should develop the common-law rule as suggested by the majority in the Supreme Court of Appeal, and at the same time read in words to section 30 of the Act that would with immediate effect permit gays and lesbians to be married by civil marriage officers (and such religious marriage officers as consider such marriages not to fall outside the tenets of their religion). Such an order would mean simply that there would be gay and lesbian married couples at common law which marriages would have to be regulated by any new marital regime the legislature chooses to adopt. I cannot see that there would be any greater uncertainty or instability relating to the status of gay and lesbian couples than in relation to heterosexual couples. The fact that Parliament faces choices does not, in this case, seem to me to be sufficient for this Court to refuse to develop the common law and, in an ancillary order, to remedy a statutory provision, reliant on the common law definition, which is also unconstitutional.

NOTES

1. On November 30, 2006, one day before the Lesbian and Gay Equality case would have taken effect without legislative action, the National Assembly of South Africa adopted a "Civil Union Bill." The legislation made marriage or civil unions available to heterosexual and homosexual couples, at the couple's choice. Civil Union Act, Article 17. 2006 (S. Afr.). The Bill places civil unions on an equal level with marriage, providing that any reference to "marriage" in any law includes a civil union and that any reference to "husband, wife or spouse" in any law includes a civil union partner. *Id.* at section 13.

2. While most same-sex marriage reforms have occurred in North America and Europe, South Africa is not the only Southern Hemisphere nation to support it. In July 2010, Argentina became the first nation in

Latin America to legalize same-sex marriage when the Argentina National Congress amended the marriage provisions of the Argentine Civil Code to remove reference to "man and woman" and replace it with "couple." This law grants to married same-sex couples the exact same rights as married heterosexual couples, including the right to adopt and the right of inheritance. Law No. 26.618, July 22, 2010, [CXVIII] B.O. 31.949 (Arg.). Buenos Aires was the first city in Latin America to legalize same-sex marriage, in 2002, but although marriage rights were extended to gays and lesbians, the rights to adoption and inheritance were not. The recent law passed despite fierce opposition by the Catholic Church and the vast majority of Catholics in the country: "Although a recent poll showed that 60% of Argentines favor same-sex marriages, representatives of the country's Catholic majority—as much as 90% of the populace—have been vocal in their opposition." Uki Goni, *Defying Church, Argentina Legalizes Gay Marriage*, TIME MAGAZINE, July 15, 2010.

In 2009, the Mexico City legislature legalized same-sex marriage, and same-sex common law marriage, by amending its civil code to define marriage as "the free uniting of two people" and gives gay couples access to adoption as married couples; although the law applied only to Mexico City, the Mexico Supreme has not only upheld the constitutionality of the law but also ruled that marriages performed in Mexico City are valid throughout the entire country. Alejandro Madrazo & Estefania Vela, *Constitutional Review: The Mexican Supreme Court's (Sexual) Revolution?*, 89 TEX. L. REV. 1863,1878–1879 (2011). Although Argentina is the only Latin American country to grant marriage, other Latin American countries have adopted civil union laws which grant the same, or many of the same, rights and benefits of marriage. Uruguay's civil union law (2008) allows same-sex couples to adopt in addition to granting other rights similar to marriage. Unión Concubinaria No. 18.246, Pub. D.O. 2008 No. 27402 (Uru.). The Brazilian Supreme Court, in a 2011 decision, ruled that same-sex couples should have nearly the same rights and benefits as opposite sex couples, although it did not rule that same-sex couples have the right to marry. Ruling of the Supreme Tribunal of Brazil regarding ADPF–RJ no 132 (Arguicao de Descumprimento de Preceito Fundamental del gobierno del estado de Rio de Janeiro) and ADI 4.277–DF (Acao Direita de Inconstitucionalidade, de la Procuradoria Geral da Republica) (May 6, 2011).

3. While most of the cases and codes in this chapter concerned countries with liberal views on sexual orientation, there are, of course, nations in which there is severe repression of gays, lesbians and transsexuals. In some cases, legal repression can be tied to the presence of a state religion, a topic we will explore further in Chapters VII and VIII. Consider, for example, the Islamic Republic of Iran (formerly Persia), where homosexuality is regarded as both a sin and a crime. Under Article(s) 108—113 and 127—134 of Iran's Penal Code, "Lavat" (sodomy), or homosexuality amongst men, is punishable by death (Article 110), while for homosexuality amongst women, called "mosahegheh," the penalty is 100 lashes for the first three times that the crime is committed. Upon the occurrence of the fourth incident, the women involved will also face execution.

4.   In many parts of Africa, not only is same-sex activity criminalized but so are same-sex marriages or ceremonies. In Malawi, a court sentenced a gay couple to 14 years of hard labor in prison for conducting what some news articles described as the country's first same-sex engagement ceremony. *Malawi Gay Couple Get Maximum Sentence of 14 Years*, British Broadcasting Corporation (May 20, 20010), http://www.bbc.co.uk/news/ 10130240. In an even more dramatic move, Uganda nearly implemented the Anti–Homosexuality Bill, which would have allowed the death penalty for certain gay acts. The Bill would also implement criminal sanctions for anyone that did not report gay acts that they knew about. The Bill has yet to be implemented, but could remerge at some point. *Uganda's Parliament Takes No Action on Anti–Gay Bill*, CNN (May 13, 2011), http://edition.cnn. com/2011/WORLD/africa/05/13/uganda.gay/. This type of activity is prevalent throughout the country. Even the small country of Senegal, which is considered one of the more tolerant countries in the continent, has laws making certain same-sex acts illegal. *Anti–Gay Abuse Rife in Africa*, The Washington Times (April 22, 2010), http://www.washingtontimes.com/news/ 2010/apr/22/anti-gay-abuse-rife-in-africa/.

In Asia there has been relatively little movement on the same-sex marriage front. However, some laws exist that criminalize same-sex activity, even if they are rarely enforced. Taiwan seems to be the most likely country to implement same-sex marriage and it has been suggested that once one country in Asia allows same-sex marriage others could follow. *Taiwan Could Lead Asia with Full Recognition of Gay Rights*, The China Post (September 10, 2011), http://www. chinapost.com.tw/editorial/taiwan-issues/2011/09/10/316140/Taiwan-could.htm.

E.   Notes Regarding a Feminist Perspective on Marriage and Equality

It's easy to understand why gays and lesbians want the same right to marry the person of their choice as heterosexuals. In spite of one scholar's deep skepticism about assimilating gays and lesbians into the heterosexual marriage model, she stated, "[I]t is clear to me that marriage is more than simply a set of legal rules. It has a symbolic significance that exists beyond, and sometimes in spite of, the legal and material reality. Marriage confers upon individuals the highest social status and approval." Rosemary Auchmuty, *Same Sex Marriage Revived: Feminist Critique and Legal Strategy*, Feminism & Psychology 2004 14: 101, available at: http://fap.sagepub.com/ content/14/1/101.

But one may ask: Does the institution of marriage promote equality for anyone? In particular, feminist critics have raised myriad equality concerns about the impact of marriage on women.

1.   While some studies show that marriage doesn't bring about greater happiness for either spouse past the initial boost in happiness, or "honeymoon period," other research has shown that married men are happier than married women. *Compare* Robert H. Coombs, *Marital Status and Personal Well–Being: A Literature Review*, Family Relations, Vol. 40, No. 1

(Jan., 1991), pp. 97–102, available at http://www.jstor.org/stable/pdfplus/585665.pdf ("[M]arried men are more likely than married women to receive emotional gratification from their spouse") and L. Radloff, *Sex differences in Depression: The Effects of Occupation on Marital Status*, SEX ROLES, 1, 249–265 (1975) (finding that men benefit more from marriage than women do) with *Reexaming Adaptation and the Set Point Model of Happiness: Reactions to Changes in Marital Status*, Richard E. Lucas, Michigan State University, Andrew E. Clark, Departement et Laboratoire d'Economie Theorique et Appliquee, Yannis Georgellis, Brunel University, and Ed Diener, University of Illinois at Urbana–Champaign; JOURNAL OF PERSONALITY AND SOCIAL PSYCHOLOGY, Vol. 84, No. 3 (2003) (finding that marriage does not increase either spouse's happiness long-term).

2.   The feminist critique of marriage is not simply a modern notion. For a list of important works criticizing marriage, compiled by feminist legal scholar Clare Chambers, *see* her article *Feminism, Liberalism, and Marriage*, page 8, listing: Mary Wollstonecraft, A VINDICATION OF THE RIGHTS OF WOMAN (1792) (London: Constable and Company Ltd., 1996); John Stuart Mill, ON LIBERTY AND THE SUBJECTION OF WOMEN (1879) (Ware: Wordsworth, 1996); Simone de Beauvoir THE SECOND SEX (1949) (London: Vintage, 1997); Betty Friedan, THE FEMININE MYSTIQUE (London: Penguin Books, 1963); Shulamith Firestone, THE DIALECTIC OF SEX (1970) (London: The Women's Press, 1979); Carole Pateman, THE SEXUAL CONTRACT (Cambridge: Polity Press, 1988); and Susan Moller Okin, JUSTICE, GENDER AND THE FAMILY (New York: Basic Books, 1989). As Chambers discusses, marriage has historically been "a fundamental site of women's oppression, with married women having few independent rights in law. Currently, it is associated with the gendered division of labour, with women taking on the lion's share of domestic and caring work and being paid less than men for work outside the home. Symbolically, the white wedding asserts that women's ultimate dream and purpose is to marry, and remains replete with sexist imagery: the father 'giving away' the bride; the white dress symbolising the bride's virginity (and emphasising the importance of her appearance); the vows to obey the husband; the minister telling the husband 'you may now kiss the bride' (rather than the bride herself giving permission, or indeed initiating or at least equally participating in the act of kissing); the reception at which, traditionally, all the speeches are given by men; the wife surrendering her own name and taking her husband's." Chambers, FEMINISM, LIBERALISM, AND MARRIAGE, 1 University of Cambridge, on file at http://www.brown.edu/Research/ppw/past_07_08.html

Some argue that inequalities in marriage "persist not because of legal barriers related to marriage, but rather because of the set of gender-role expectations that have historically been, and for some—for example, the conservative opponents of same-sex marriage—continue to be, attached to the legal institution of marriage. In this view, marriage denies women access to equal status and recognition as citizens by controlling women's bodies and sexuality, and by denying access to key aspects of 'social citizenship'. . . ." Jyl Josephson, *Citizenship, Same–Sex Marriage, and Feminist Critiques of Marriage*, PERSPECTIVES ON POLITICS, Vol. 3, No. 2 (Jun., 2005), p. 269–284, published by: American Political Science Association, available at http://www.jstor.org/stable/3688030.

3. More concretely, much sociological and economic research has supported the feminist critique of inequality in heterosexual marriage by pointing out that women are economically disadvantaged by marriage. Feminist legal scholar Catharine MacKinnon discusses that, while "many marriages today look nontraditional because both partners work outside the home, in reality labor and resources are divided in ways that usually subordinate one career to the other and create economic disadvantage to one"—usually the woman. *Sex Equality* (Foundation Press 2d Edition 2007), p. 668. Often the wife foregoes educational and career advancement for the family, therefore sacrificing earning potential for herself and allowing the husband to pursue more educational and career advancements for himself. *See Moge v. Moge*, Supreme Court of Canada, 3 S.C.R. 813, 1992 ("The reality... is that in many if not most marriages, the wife still remains the economically disadvantaged partner.") This disparity is often highlighted by divorce. For example, if the wife stayed home to take care of the children during the marriage, she remains dependent on the husband for financial support and will likely find it difficult to seek employment after years out of the workforce. Further, if the wife worked, she will often inherit all of childcare responsibilities after the divorce, perpetuating the ex-husband's flexibility in his career pursuits. *Id.*; *see also* Jane Lewis, The End of Marriage? Individualism and Intimate Relations (Cheltenham: Edward Elgar, 2001).

4. A number of feminists, legal scholars, and economists have compared marriage to prostitution: "The only difference between women who sell themselves in prostitution and those who sell themselves in marriage is in the price and the length of time the contract runs." Simone de Beauvoir, The Second Sex, 1972 [1949], p. 569; *see* Kate Millett, The Prostitution Papers: A Candid Dialogue; Catharine MacKinnon, Sex Equality (Foundation Press 2d Edition 2007), p. 1265 (explaining the parallel that, similar to how a "John" pays a prostitute per each sexual encounter, a husband supports his wife for continual access to her body, in MacKinnon's discussion of *United States v. Harris*, 942 F.2d 1125 (7th Cir.) (IRS sought to tax the income that a man paid to his two mistresses)); Lena Edlund and Evelyn Korn, *A Theory of Prostitution*, 110 Journal of Political Economy, (2002), (1), 181–214 (stipulating that wives are more economically valuable than prostitutes because they are more likely to offer the market "good" of reproductive sex). Others have taken a more extreme view: "Marriage as an institution developed from rape as a practice. Rape, originally defined as abduction, became marriage by capture. Marriage meant the taking was to extend in time, to be not only use of but possession of, or ownership." Andrea Dworkin, Letters From a War Zone, Dutton Publishing, 1989.

5. One may argue that marriage is so advantageous to men that where they can't find a woman who will voluntarily become their spouse, they'll buy one via mail-order. *See* MacKinnon, Sex Equality 2d, n.3; Eddy Meng, *Mail–Order Brides: Gilded Prostitution and the Legal Response*, 28 U. Mich. J.L. Reform 197 (1994–1995); Donna R. Lee, *Mail Fantasy: Global Sexual Exploitation in the Mail–Order Bride Industry and Proposed Legal Solutions*, 5 Asian L. J. 139 (1998).

6. Another issue of gender equality that arises in the law of marriage is child marriage. In rural India, for example, pre-teen girls are frequently

forced into marriage by their parents, requiring them to marry older men, not of their choosing, and leading to substantial exploitation and abuse. *See* Vaibhav Mahajan, *Lacunae in Laws against Child Marriages in India*, (May 29, 2010), available at SSRN: http://papers.ssrn.com/sol3/cf_dev/Abs ByAuth.cfm?per_id=1490587.

7. Some feminist and gay and lesbian rights activists argue "[g]ay liberation is inexorably linked to women's liberation" and that "[e]ach is essential to the other." Clare Chambers, Feminism, Liberalism, and Marriage, University of Cambridge, unpublished manuscript, p. 8, quoting Paula L. Ettelbrick, *Since When is Marriage a Path to Liberation?* in Mark Blasius and Shane Phelan (eds.), We Are Everywhere: Historical Sourcebook of Gay and Lesbian Politics (London: Routledge, 1997) p. 758. They thus argue that "although it is unjust that marriage is denied to homosexuals, the injustice of the institution as a whole means that lesbians and gay men should not fight for the right to marry—just as white women should not have fought for the (equal) right to be slave-owners." *Id.* quoting Claudia Card, *Against Marriage and Motherhood*, Hypatia vol. 11, no. 3 (Summer 1996). Indeed, some feminists have called for the abolition of marriage to end male hegemony. *See* Sheila Cronan, *Marriage*, in Koedt, Levine, and Rapone, eds., Radical Feminism, p. 219; Chambers, Feminism, Liberalism, and Marriage.

CHAPTER VI

EQUALITY & REPRODUCTIVE RIGHTS

INTRODUCTION

For many women around the world, control over their reproductive choices is a, if not the, central issue in their quest for gender equality. This chapter examines how reproductive choice is regulated by the state in the United States, Mexico, Colombia, Ireland, and China. As you read these cases, constitutions, codes, and commentary, ask yourself how the various countries negotiate the value of individual autonomy, and how they decide when a living entity becomes a legal personality entitled to certain basic rights and protections. How do their courts understand women's equality in the reproductive rights context? How do they balance equality rights between women and the living entity, as well as between women and men? Additionally, consider the cultural and social forces that shape the way the law understands women's autonomy to make choices about how they will or will not reproduce—via abortion, birth control, in vitro fertilization (IVF), and any number of other recent reproductive technologies. How and why do the courts' decisions about these various methods reflect or not reflect these societies' cultural and social norms? And how do they reflect the norms of the Catholic Church, particularly in countries such as Ireland, Mexico, and Colombia?

PROBLEMS

- Michelle is a 16 year old high school junior. While drunk at a party, she had sex with Jack, a 28 year old graduate student. She is now pregnant. She has decided she wants an abortion, but she doesn't want to tell Jack (if she could even find him) or her parents. What rights does she have in Philadelphia, Mexico City, Bogotá, or Dublin?

- Would the answer to problem 1 be different if Michelle were pregnant by her father?

- What if Michelle is 19 and married, wants an abortion, and doesn't want to tell her husband?

- What if Michelle is 43, married with three grown children, and she and her husband have decided together that she should have an abortion? Does their reason matter? What if they feel that they don't want to take on the financial burden of raising another child? Alternatively, what if they feel it would compromise Michelle's health? Does it matter whether Michelle's doctor agrees?

- Finally, consider whether your answer changes depending on what week of pregnancy Michelle is in when she decides to have an abortion.

A. THE UNITED STATES

Fourteenth Amendment to the United States Constitution

All persons born or naturalized in the United States, and subject to the jurisdiction thereof, are citizens of the United States and of the State wherein they reside. No State shall make or enforce any law which shall abridge the privileges or immunities of citizens of the United States; nor shall any State deprive any person of life, liberty, or property, without due process of law; nor deny to any person within its jurisdiction the equal protection of the laws.

———

Roe v. Wade

410 U.S. 113 (1973)

■ JUSTICE BLACKMUN delivered the opinion of the Court.

This [appeal presents] constitutional challenges to state criminal abortion legislation. The Texas statutes under attack here are typical of those that have been in effect in many States for approximately a century. * * *

Our task, of course, is to resolve the issue by constitutional measurement, free of emotion and of predilection. We seek earnestly to do this, and, because we do, we have inquired into, and in this opinion place some emphasis upon, medical and medical-legal history and what that history reveals about man's attitudes toward the abortion procedure over the centuries. * * *

The Texas statutes that concern us here are Arts. 1191–1194 and 1196 of the State's Penal Code. These make it a crime to 'procure an abortion,' as therein defined, or to attempt one, except with respect to 'an abortion procured or attempted by medical advice for the purpose of saving the life of the mother.' Similar statutes are in existence in a majority of the States. * * *

Jane Roe, a single woman who was residing in Dallas County, Texas, instituted this federal action in March 1970 against the District Attorney of the county. She sought a declaratory judgment that the Texas criminal abortion statutes were unconstitutional on their face, and an injunction restraining the defendant from enforcing the statutes. * * *

The principal thrust of appellant's attack on the Texas statutes is that they improperly invade a right, said to be possessed by the pregnant woman, to choose to terminate her pregnancy. Appellant would discover this right in the concept of personal 'liberty' embodied in the Fourteenth Amendment's Due Process Clause; or in personal marital, familial, and sexual privacy said to be protected by the Bill of Rights or its penumbras, *see Griswold v. Connecticut*, 381 U.S. 479 (1965); or among those rights reserved to the people by the Ninth Amendment, Griswold v. Connecticut, 381 U.S. at 486, (Goldberg, J., concurring). * * *

Three reasons have been advanced to explain historically the enactment of criminal abortion laws in the 19th century and to justify their continued existence.

It has been argued occasionally that these laws were the product of a Victorian social concern to discourage illicit sexual conduct. Texas, however, does not advance this justification in the present case. * * *

A second reason is concerned with abortion as a medical procedure. When most criminal abortion laws were first enacted, the procedure was a hazardous one for the woman. This was particularly true prior to the development of antisepsis. . . . Thus, it has been argued that a State's real concern in enacting a criminal abortion law was to protect the pregnant woman, that is, to restrain her from submitting to a procedure that placed her life in serious jeopardy.

Modern medical techniques have altered this situation. . . . Mortality rates for women undergoing early abortions, where the procedure is legal, appear to be as low or lower than the rates of normal childbirth. Consequently, any interest of the State in protecting the woman from an inherently hazardous procedure . . . has largely disappeared. . . . The State has a legitimate interest in seeing to it that abortion, like any other medical procedure, is performed under circumstances that insure maximum safety for the patient. . . . The prevalence of high mortality rates at illegal 'abortion mills' strengthens, rather than weakens, the State's interest in regulating the conditions under which abortions are performed. Moreover, the risk to the woman increases as her pregnancy continues. Thus, the State retains a definite interest in protecting the woman's own health and safety when an abortion is proposed at a late stage of pregnancy.

The third reason is the State's interest . . . in protecting prenatal life. Some of the argument for this justification rests on the theory that a new human life is present from the moment of conception. . . . Logically, of course, a legitimate state interest in this area need not stand or fall on acceptance of the belief that life begins at conception or at some other point prior to life birth. In assessing the State's interest, recognition may be given to the less rigid claim that as long as at least potential life is involved, the State may assert interests beyond the protection of the pregnant woman alone. * * *

The Constitution does not explicitly mention any right of privacy. . . . [But] the Court has recognized that a right of personal privacy, or a guarantee of certain areas or zones of privacy, does exist under the Constitution. In varying contexts, the Court or individual Justices have, indeed, found at least the roots of that right in the First Amendment, *Stanley v. Georgia*, 394 U.S. 557, 564 (1969); in the Fourth and Fifth Amendments, *Terry v. Ohio*, 392 U.S. 1, 8–9 (1968); in the penumbras of the Bill of Rights, *Griswold v. Connecticut*, 381 U.S., at 484–485; in the Ninth Amendment, (Goldberg, J., concurring); or in the concept of liberty guaranteed by the first section of the Fourteenth Amendment, *see Meyer v.*

Nebraska, *262 U.S. 390, 399 (1923). These decisions make it clear that only personal rights that can be deemed 'fundamental' or 'implicit in the concept of ordered liberty,' are included in this guarantee of personal privacy. They also make it clear that the right has some extension to activities relating to marriage,* Loving v. Virginia, *388 U.S. 1, 12 (1967); procreation,* Skinner v. Oklahoma, *316 U.S. 535, 541–542 (1942); contraception,* Eisenstadt v. Baird, *405 U.S.438, 453–454 (1972) (White, J., concurring in result); family relationships,* Prince v. Massachusetts, *321 U.S. 158, 166 (1944); and child rearing and education,* Pierce v. Society of Sisters, *268 U.S. 510, 535 (1925),* Meyer v. Nebraska, *supra.*

This right of privacy, whether it be founded in the Fourteenth Amendment's concept of personal liberty and restrictions upon state action, as we feel it is, or, as the District Court determined, in the Ninth Amendment's reservation of rights to the people, is broad enough to encompass a woman's decision whether or not to terminate her pregnancy. The detriment that the State would impose upon the pregnant woman by denying this choice altogether is apparent. Specific and direct harm medically diagnosable even in early pregnancy may be involved. Maternity, or additional offspring, may force upon the woman a distressful life and future. Psychological harm may be imminent. Mental and physical health may be taxed by child care. There is also the distress, for all concerned, associated with the unwanted child, and there is the problem of bringing a child into a family already unable, psychologically and otherwise, to care for it. In other cases, as in this one, the additional difficulties and continuing stigma of unwed motherhood may be involved. All these are factors the woman and her responsible physician necessarily will consider in consultation.

On the basis of elements such as these, appellant and some amici argue that the woman's right is absolute and that she is entitled to terminate her pregnancy at whatever time, in whatever way, and for whatever reason she alone chooses. With this we do not agree. . . . The Court's decisions recognizing a right of privacy also acknowledge that some state regulation in areas protected by that right is appropriate. As noted above, a State may properly assert important interests in safeguarding health, in maintaining medical standards, and in protecting potential life. At some point in pregnancy, these respective interests become sufficiently compelling to sustain regulation of the factors that govern the abortion decision. The privacy right involved, therefore, cannot be said to be absolute. * * *

We, therefore, conclude that the right of personal privacy includes the abortion decision, but that this right is not unqualified and must be considered against important state interests in regulation. * * *

Where certain 'fundamental rights' are involved, the Court has held that regulation limiting these rights may be justified only by a 'compelling state interest,' [citations omitted] and that legislative enactments must be narrowly drawn to express only the legitimate state interests at stake. * * *

* * * Appellant, as has been indicated, claims an absolute right that bars any state imposition of criminal penalties in the area. Appellee argues that the State's determination to recognize and protect prenatal life from

and after conception constitutes a compelling state interest. As noted above, we do not agree fully with either formulation.

The appellee and certain amici argue that the fetus is a 'person' within the language and meaning of the Fourteenth Amendment....

The Constitution does not define 'person' in so many words. Section 1 of the Fourteenth Amendment contains three references to 'person.' The first, in defining 'citizens,' speaks of 'persons born or naturalized in the United States.' The word also appears both in the Due Process Clause and in the Equal Protection Clause. 'Person' is used in other places in the Constitution. [citations omitted] But in nearly all these instances, the use of the word is such that it has application only postnatally. None indicates, with any assurance, that it has any possible prenatal application.

All this, together with our observation that throughout the major portion of the 19th century prevailing legal abortion practices were far freer than they are today, persuades us that the word 'person,' as used in the Fourteenth Amendment, does not include the unborn. * * *

The pregnant woman cannot be isolated in her privacy. She carries an embryo and, later, a fetus, if one accepts the medical definitions of the developing young in the human uterus. [citation omitted] The situation therefore is inherently different from marital intimacy, or bedroom possession of obscene material, or marriage, or procreation, or education, with which Eisenstadt and Griswold, Stanley, Loving, Skinner and Pierce and Meyer were respectively concerned. As we have intimated above, it is reasonable and appropriate for a State to decide that at some point in time another interest, that of health of the mother or that of potential human life, becomes significantly involved. * * *

Texas urges that, apart from the Fourteenth Amendment, life begins at conception and is present throughout pregnancy, and that, therefore, the State has a compelling interest in protecting that life from and after conception. We need not resolve the difficult question of when life begins. When those trained in the respective disciplines of medicine, philosophy, and theology are unable to arrive at any consensus, the judiciary, at this point in the development of man's knowledge, is not in a position to speculate as to the answer.

It should be sufficient to note briefly the wide divergence of thinking on this most sensitive and difficult question. There has always been strong support for the view that life does not begin until live birth. This was the belief of the Stoics. It appears to be the predominant, though not the unanimous, attitude of the Jewish faith. It may be taken to represent also the position of a large segment of the Protestant community.... [T]he common law found greater significance in quickening. Physicians and their scientific colleagues have regarded that event with less interest and have tended to focus either upon conception, upon live birth, or upon the interim point at which the fetus becomes 'viable,' that is, potentially able to live outside the mother's womb, albeit with artificial aid. Viability is usually placed at about seven months (28 weeks) but may occur earlier, even at 24 weeks.... [The Catholic] Church recognize[s] the existence of life from the moment of conception.... [T]his is a view strongly held by many non-Catholics as well, and by many physicians. Substantial problems for precise definition of this view are posed, however, by new embryological data that purport to indicate that conception is a 'process' over time, rather than an event, and by new medical techniques such as menstrual extraction, the 'morning-after' pill, implantation of embryos, artificial insemination, and even artificial wombs. * * *

In view of all this, we do not agree that, by adopting one theory of life, Texas may override the rights of the pregnant woman that are at stake. We repeat, however, that the State does have an important and legitimate interest in preserving and protecting the health of the pregnant woman, whether she be a resident of the State or a non-resident who seeks medical consultation and treatment there, and that it has still another important and legitimate interest in protecting the potentiality of human life. These interests are separate and distinct. Each grows in substantiality as the woman approaches term and, at a point during pregnancy, each becomes 'compelling.'

With respect to the State's important and legitimate interest in the health of the mother, the 'compelling' point, in the light of present medical knowledge, is at approximately the end of the first trimester. This is so because of the now-established medical fact ... that until the end of the first trimester mortality in abortion may be less than mortality in normal childbirth. It follows that, from and after this point, a State may regulate the abortion procedure to the extent that the regulation reasonably relates to the preservation and protection of maternal health. Examples of permissible state regulation in this area are requirements as to the qualifications of the person who is to perform the abortion; as to the licensure of that person; as to the facility in which the procedure is to be performed; and the like.

This means, on the other hand, that, for the period of pregnancy prior to this 'compelling' point, the attending physician, in consultation with his patient, is free to determine, without regulation by the State, that, in his medical judgment, the patient's pregnancy should be terminated. If that decision is reached, the judgment may be effectuated by an abortion free of interference by the State.

With respect to the State's important and legitimate interest in potential life, the 'compelling' point is at viability. This is so because the fetus then presumably has the capability of meaningful life outside the mother's womb. State regulation protective of fetal life after viability thus has both logical and biological justifications. If the State is interested in protecting fetal life after viability, it may go so far as to proscribe abortion during that period, except when it is necessary to preserve the life or health of the mother.

Measured against these standards, [the Texas statute,] in restricting legal abortions to those 'procured or attempted by medical advice for the purpose of saving the life of the mother,' sweeps too broadly. The statute makes no distinction between abortions performed early in pregnancy and those performed later, and it limits to a single reason, 'saving' the mother's life, the legal justification for the procedure. The statute, therefore, cannot survive the constitutional attack made upon it here. * * *

Affirmed in part and reversed in part.

———

Planned Parenthood of Southeastern Pennsylvania v. Casey

505 U.S. 833 (1992)

■ O'CONNOR, KENNEDY, and SOUTER, JJ., announced the judgment of the Court and delivered the opinion of the Court with respect to Parts I, II, III, V–A, V–C, and VI, in which BLACKMUN and STEVENS, JJ., joined, an opinion with respect to Part V–E, in which STEVENS, J., joined, and an opinion with respect to Parts IV, V–B, and V–D.

I

Liberty finds no refuge in a jurisprudence of doubt. Yet 19 years after our holding that the Constitution protects a woman's right to terminate her pregnancy in its early stages, *Roe v. Wade*, 410 U.S. 113 (1973), that definition of liberty is still questioned. Joining the respondents as *amicus curiae*, the United States, as it has done in five other cases in the last decade, again asks us to overrule *Roe*.

At issue in these cases are five provisions of the Pennsylvania Abortion Control Act of 1982, as amended in 1988 and 1989.... The Act requires that a woman seeking an abortion give her informed consent prior to the abortion procedure, and specifies that she be provided with certain information at least 24 hours before the abortion is performed. For a minor to obtain an abortion, the Act requires the informed consent of one of her parents, but provides for a judicial bypass option if the minor does not wish to or cannot obtain a parent's consent. Another provision of the Act requires that, unless certain exceptions apply, a married woman seeking an abortion must sign a statement indicating that she has notified her husband of her intended abortion. The Act exempts compliance with these three requirements in the event of a "medical emergency." In addition to the above provisions regulating the performance of abortions, the Act imposes certain reporting requirements on facilities that provide abortion services.

Before any of these provisions took effect, the petitioners, who are five abortion clinics and one physician representing himself as well as a class of physicians who provide abortion services, brought this suit seeking declaratory and injunctive relief. * * *

It must be stated at the outset and with clarity that *Roe*'s essential holding, the holding we reaffirm, has three parts. First is a recognition of the right of the woman to choose to have an abortion before viability and to obtain it without undue interference from the State. Before viability, the State's interests are not strong enough to support a prohibition of abortion or the imposition of a substantial obstacle to the woman's effective right to elect the procedure. Second is a confirmation of the State's power to restrict abortions after fetal viability, if the law contains exceptions for pregnancies which endanger the woman's life or health. And third is the principle that the State has legitimate interests from the outset of the pregnancy in protecting the health of the woman and the life of the fetus that may become a child. These principles do not contradict one another; and we adhere to each.

II

* * * Men and women of good conscience can disagree, and we suppose some always shall disagree, about the profound moral and spiritual implications of terminating a pregnancy, even in its earliest stage. Some of us as individuals find abortion offensive to our most basic principles of morality, but that cannot control our decision. Our obligation is to define the liberty of all, not to mandate our own moral code. The underlying constitutional issue is whether the State can resolve these philosophic questions in such a definitive way that a woman lacks all choice in the matter, except perhaps in those rare circumstances in which the pregnancy is itself a danger to her own life or health, or is the result of rape or incest. * * *

* * * Abortion is a unique act. It is an act fraught with consequences for others: for the woman who must live with the implications of her decision; for the persons who perform and assist in the procedure; for the spouse, family, and society which must confront the knowledge that these procedures exist, procedures some deem nothing short of an act of violence against innocent human life; and, depending on one's beliefs, for the life or potential life that is aborted. Though abortion is conduct, it does not follow that the State is entitled to proscribe it in all instances. That is because the liberty of the woman is at stake in a sense unique to the human condition and so unique to the law. The mother who carries a child to full term is subject to anxieties, to physical constraints, to pain that only she must bear. That these sacrifices have from the beginning of the human race been endured by woman with a pride that ennobles her in the eyes of others and gives to the infant a bond of love cannot alone be grounds for the State to insist she make the sacrifice. Her suffering is too intimate and personal for the State to insist, without more, upon its own vision of the woman's role, however dominant that vision has been in the course of our history and our culture. The destiny of the woman must be shaped to a large extent on her own conception of her spiritual imperatives and her place in society.

It should be recognized, moreover, that in some critical respects the abortion decision is of the same character as the decision to use contraception, to which *Griswold v. Connecticut, Eisenstadt v. Baird,* and *Carey v. Population Services International* afford constitutional protection. We have no doubt as to the correctness of those decisions. They support the reasoning in *Roe* relating to the woman's liberty because they involve personal decisions concerning not only the meaning of procreation but also human responsibility and respect for it. * * *

IV

From what we have said so far it follows that it is a constitutional liberty of the woman to have some freedom to terminate her pregnancy. We conclude that the basic decision in *Roe* was based on a constitutional analysis which we cannot now repudiate. The woman's liberty is not so unlimited, however, that from the outset the State cannot show its concern for the life of the unborn, and at a later point in fetal development the State's interest in life has sufficient force so that the right of the woman to terminate the pregnancy can be restricted. * * *

We conclude the line should be drawn at viability, so that before that time the woman has a right to choose to terminate her pregnancy. We adhere to this principle for two reasons. First, as we have said, is the doctrine of *stare decisis....* The second reason is that the concept of viability, as we noted in *Roe,* is the time at which there is a realistic possibility of maintaining and nourishing a life outside the womb, so that the independent existence of the second life can in reason and all fairness be the object of state protection that now overrides the rights of the woman. See *Roe v. Wade,* 410 U.S. at 163. * * *

The woman's right to terminate her pregnancy before viability is the most central principle of *Roe v. Wade.* It is a rule of law and a component of liberty we cannot renounce. * * *

Yet it must be remembered that *Roe v. Wade* speaks with clarity in establishing not only the woman's liberty but also the State's "important and legitimate interest in potential life." *Roe, supra,* at 163. That portion of the decision in *Roe* has been given too little acknowledgment and implementation by the Court in its subsequent cases. * * *

We reject the trimester framework, which we do not consider to be part of the essential holding of *Roe.* Measures aimed at ensuring that a woman's choice contemplates the consequences for the fetus do not necessarily interfere with the right recognized in *Roe,* although those measures have been found to be inconsistent with the rigid trimester framework announced in that case. A logical reading of the central holding in *Roe* itself, and a necessary reconciliation of the liberty of the woman and the interest of the State in promoting prenatal life, require, in our view, that we abandon the trimester framework as a rigid prohibition on all previability regulation aimed at the protection of fetal life. The trimester framework suffers from these basic flaws: in its formulation it misconceives the nature of the pregnant woman's interest; and in practice it undervalues the State's interest in potential life, as recognized in *Roe.*

As our jurisprudence relating to all liberties save perhaps abortion has recognized, not every law which makes a right more difficult to exercise is, *ipso facto,* an infringement of that right. * * *

The abortion right is similar. Numerous forms of state regulation might have the incidental effect of increasing the cost or decreasing the availability of medical care, whether for abortion or any other medical procedure. The fact that a law which serves a valid purpose, one not designed to strike at the right itself, has the incidental effect of making it more difficult or more expensive to procure an abortion cannot be enough to invalidate it. Only where state regulation imposes an undue burden on a woman's ability to make this decision does the power of the State reach into the heart of the liberty protected by the Due Process Clause. * * *

* * * Before viability, *Roe* and subsequent cases treat all governmental attempts to influence a woman's decision on behalf of the potential life

within her as unwarranted. This treatment is, in our judgment, incompatible with the recognition that there is a substantial state interest in potential life throughout pregnancy.

The very notion that the State has a substantial interest in potential life leads to the conclusion that not all regulations must be deemed unwarranted. Not all burdens on the right to decide whether to terminate a pregnancy will be undue. In our view, the undue burden standard is the appropriate means of reconciling the State's interest with the woman's constitutionally protected liberty. * * *

Some guiding principles should emerge. What is at stake is the woman's right to make the ultimate decision, not a right to be insulated from all others in doing so. Regulations which do no more than create a structural mechanism by which the State, or the parent or guardian of a minor, may express profound respect for the life of the unborn are permitted, if they are not a substantial obstacle to the woman's exercise of the right to choose. Unless it has that effect on her right of choice, a state measure designed to persuade her to choose childbirth over abortion will be upheld if reasonably related to that goal. Regulations designed to foster the health of a woman seeking an abortion are valid if they do not constitute an undue burden.

* * * We give this summary:

(a) To protect the central right recognized by *Roe v. Wade* while at the same time accommodating the State's profound interest in potential life, we will employ the undue burden analysis as explained in this opinion. An undue burden exists, and therefore a provision of law is invalid, if its purpose or effect is to place a substantial obstacle in the path of a woman seeking an abortion before the fetus attains viability.

(b) We reject the rigid trimester framework of *Roe v. Wade.* To promote the State's profound interest in potential life, throughout pregnancy the State may take measures to ensure that the woman's choice is informed, and measures designed to advance this interest will not be invalidated as long as their purpose is to persuade the woman to choose childbirth over abortion. These measures must not be an undue burden on the right.

(c) As with any medical procedure, the State may enact regulations to further the health or safety of a woman seeking an abortion. Unnecessary health regulations that have the purpose or effect of presenting a substantial obstacle to a woman seeking an abortion impose an undue burden on the right.

(d) Our adoption of the undue burden analysis does not disturb the central holding of *Roe v. Wade,* and we reaffirm that holding. Regardless of whether exceptions are made for particular circumstances, a State may not prohibit any woman from making the ultimate decision to terminate her pregnancy before viability.

(e) We also reaffirm *Roe*'s holding that "subsequent to viability, the State in promoting its interest in the potentiality of human life may, if it chooses, regulate, and even proscribe, abortion except where it is necessary, in appropriate medical judgment, for the preservation of the life or health of the mother.''

These principles control our assessment of the Pennsylvania statute, and we now turn to the issue of the validity of its challenged provisions. * * *

V

B

* * * Except in a medical emergency, the statute requires that at least 24 hours before performing an abortion a physician inform the woman of the nature of the procedure, the health risks of the abortion and of childbirth, and the "probable gestational age of the unborn child." The physician or a qualified nonphysician must inform the woman of the availability of printed materials published by the State describing the fetus and providing information about medical assistance for childbirth, information about child support from the father, and a list of agencies which provide adoption and other services as alternatives to abortion. An abortion may not be performed unless the woman certifies in writing that she has been informed of the availability of these printed materials and has been provided them if she chooses to view them. * * *

* * * In attempting to ensure that a woman apprehend the full consequences of her decision, the State furthers the legitimate purpose of reducing the risk that a woman may elect an abortion, only to discover later, with devastating psychological consequences, that her decision was not fully informed. If the information the State requires to be made available to the woman is truthful and not misleading, the requirement may be permissible.

We also see no reason why the State may not require doctors to inform a woman seeking an abortion of the availability of materials relating to the consequences to the fetus, even when those consequences have no direct relation to her health. . . . [W]e permit a State to further its legitimate goal of protecting the life of the unborn by enacting legislation aimed at ensuring a decision that is mature and informed, even when in so doing the State expresses a preference for childbirth over abortion. . . . This requirement cannot be considered a substantial obstacle to obtaining an abortion, and, it follows, there is no undue burden. * * *

Whether the mandatory 24–hour waiting period is nonetheless invalid because in practice it is a substantial obstacle to a woman's choice to terminate her pregnancy is a closer question. The findings of fact by the District Court indicate that because of the distances many women must travel to reach an abortion provider, the practical effect will often be a delay of much more than a day because the waiting period requires that a woman seeking an abortion make at least two visits to the doctor. The District Court also found that in many instances this will increase the exposure of women seeking abortions to "the harassment and hostility of anti-abortion protestors demonstrating outside a clinic." As a result, the District Court found that for those women who have the fewest financial resources, those who must travel long distances, and those who have difficulty explaining their whereabouts to husbands, employers, or others, the 24–hour waiting period will be "particularly burdensome."

These findings are troubling in some respects, but they do not demonstrate that the waiting period constitutes an undue burden. * * *

We also disagree with the District Court's conclusion that the "particularly burdensome" effects of the waiting period on some women require its invalidation.... [O]n the record before us, and in the context of this facial challenge, we are not convinced that the 24–hour waiting period constitutes an undue burden. * * *

C

Section 3209 of Pennsylvania's abortion law provides, except in cases of medical emergency, that no physician shall perform an abortion on a married woman without receiving a signed statement from the woman that she has notified her spouse that she is about to undergo an abortion. The woman has the option of providing an alternative signed statement certifying that her husband is not the man who impregnated her; that her husband could not be located; that the pregnancy is the result of spousal sexual assault which she has reported; or that the woman believes that notifying her husband will cause him or someone else to inflict bodily injury upon her. A physician who performs an abortion on a married woman without receiving the appropriate signed statement will have his or her license revoked, and is liable to the husband for damages. * * *

* * * In well functioning marriages, spouses discuss important intimate decisions such as whether to bear a child. But there are millions of women in this country who are the victims of regular physical and psychological abuse at the hands of their husbands. Should these women become pregnant, they may have very good reasons for not wishing to inform their husbands of their decision to obtain an abortion. Many may have justifiable fears of physical abuse, but may be no less fearful of the consequences of reporting prior abuse to the Commonwealth of Pennsylvania. Many may have a reasonable fear that notifying their husbands will provoke further instances of child abuse; these women are not exempt from § 3209's notification requirement.... Many may fear devastating forms of psychological abuse from their husbands, including verbal harassment, threats of future violence, the destruction of possessions, physical confinement to the home, the withdrawal of financial support, or the disclosure of the abortion to family and friends. These methods of psychological abuse may act as even more of a deterrent to notification than the possibility of physical violence, but women who are the victims of the abuse are not exempt from § 3209's notification requirement.

The spousal notification requirement is thus likely to prevent a significant number of women from obtaining an abortion. It does not merely make abortions a little more difficult or expensive to obtain; for many women, it will impose a substantial obstacle. * * *

Respondents attempt to avoid the conclusion that § 3209 is invalid by pointing out that ... the effects of § 3209 are felt by only one percent of the women who obtain abortions.... We disagree with respondents' basic method of analysis.

The analysis does not end with the one percent of women upon whom the statute operates; it begins there. Legislation is measured for consistency with the Constitution by its impact on those whose conduct it affects.... The proper focus of constitutional inquiry is the group for whom the law is a restriction, not the group for whom the law is irrelevant. * * *

* * * For the great many women who are victims of abuse inflicted by their husbands, or whose children are the victims of such abuse, a spousal notice requirement enables the husband to wield an effective veto over his wife's decision. Whether the prospect of notification itself deters such women from seeking abortions, or whether the husband, through physical force or psychological pressure or economic coercion, prevents his wife from obtaining an abortion until it is too late, the notice requirement will often be tantamount to the veto found unconstitutional in *Danforth*. The women most affected by this law—those who most reasonably fear the consequences of notifying their husbands that they are pregnant—are in the gravest danger.

The husband's interest in the life of the child his wife is carrying does not permit the State to empower him with this troubling degree of authority over his wife. The contrary view leads to consequences reminiscent of the common law. A husband has no enforceable right to require a wife to advise him before she exercises her personal choices.... A State may not give to a man the kind of dominion over his wife that parents exercise over their children. * * *

D

We next consider the parental consent provision. Except in a medical emergency, an unemancipated young woman under 18 may not obtain an abortion unless she and one of her parents (or guardian) provides informed consent as defined above. If neither a parent nor a guardian provides consent, a court may authorize the performance of an abortion upon a determination that the young woman is mature and capable of giving informed consent and has in fact given her informed consent, or that an abortion would be in her best interests. * * *

* * * For the most part, petitioners' argument is a reprise of their argument with respect to the informed consent requirement in general, and we reject it for the reasons given above. * * *

VI

* * * Each generation must learn anew that the Constitution's written terms embody ideas and aspirations that must survive more ages than one. We accept our responsibility not to retreat from interpreting the full meaning of the covenant in light of all of our precedents. We invoke it once again to define the freedom guaranteed by the Constitution's own promise, the promise of liberty.

■ JUSTICE BLACKMUN, concurring in part, concurring in the judgment in part, and dissenting in part.

* * * State restrictions on abortion violate a woman's right of privacy in two ways. First, compelled continuation of a pregnancy infringes upon a woman's right to bodily integrity by imposing substantial physical intrusions and significant risks of physical harm. During pregnancy, women experience dramatic physical changes and a wide range of health consequences. Labor and delivery pose additional health risks and physical demands. In short, restrictive abortion laws force women to endure physical invasions far more substantial than those this Court has held to violate the constitutional principle of bodily integrity in other contexts.

Further, when the State restricts a woman's right to terminate her pregnancy, it deprives a woman of the right to make her own decision about reproduction and family planning—critical life choices that this Court long has deemed central to the right to privacy. The decision to terminate or continue a pregnancy has no less an impact on a woman's life than decisions about contraception or marriage. * * *

The Court has held that limitations on the right of privacy are permissible only if they survive "strict" constitutional scrutiny—that is, only if the governmental entity imposing the restriction can demonstrate that the limitation is both necessary and narrowly tailored to serve a compelling governmental interest. * * *

Roe implemented these principles through a framework that was designed "to ensure that the woman's right to choose not become so subordinate to the State's interest in promoting fetal life that her choice exists in theory but not in fact." * * *

In my view, application of this analytical framework is no less warranted than when it was approved by seven Members of this Court in *Roe.* Strict scrutiny of state limitations on reproductive choice still offers the most secure protection of the woman's right to make her own reproductive decisions, free from state coercion. No majority of this Court has ever agreed upon an alternative approach. The factual premises of the trimester framework have not been undermined, and the *Roe* framework is far more administrable, and far less manipulable, than the "undue burden" standard adopted by the joint opinion. * * *

The final, and more genuine, criticism of the trimester framework is that it fails to find the State's interest in potential human life compelling throughout pregnancy. No Member of this Court ... has ever questioned our holding in *Roe* that an abortion is not "the termination of life entitled to Fourteenth Amendment protection." Accordingly, a State's interest in protecting fetal life is not grounded in the Constitution. Nor, consistent with our Establishment Clause, can it be a theological or sectarian interest. It is, instead, a legitimate interest grounded in humanitarian or pragmatic concerns.

But while a State has "legitimate interests from the outset of the pregnancy in protecting the health of the woman and the life of the fetus that may become a child," *ante,* at 2804, legitimate interests are not enough. To overcome the burden of strict scrutiny, the interests must be compelling. * * *

Gonzales v. Carhart

550 U.S. 124 (2007)

■ JUSTICE KENNEDY delivered the opinion of the Court.

These cases require us to consider the validity of the Partial–Birth Abortion Ban Act of 2003, a federal statute regulating abortion procedures. * * *

Abortion methods vary depending to some extent on the preferences of the physician and, of course, on the term of the pregnancy and the resulting stage of the unborn child's development. Between 85 and 90 percent of the approximately 1.3 million abortions performed each year in the United States take place in the first three months of pregnancy, which is to say in the first trimester. . . . The most common first-trimester abortion method is vacuum aspiration (otherwise known as suction curettage) in which the physician vacuums out the embryonic tissue. Early in this trimester an alternative is to use medication, such as mifepristone (commonly known as RU–486), to terminate the pregnancy. . . . The Act does not regulate these procedures.

Of the remaining abortions that take place each year, most occur in the second trimester. The surgical procedure referred to as "dilation and evacuation" or "D & E" is the usual abortion method in this trimester. . . . Although individual techniques for performing D & E differ, the general steps are the same.

A doctor must first dilate the cervix at least to the extent needed to insert surgical instruments into the uterus and to maneuver them to evacuate the fetus. * * *

After sufficient dilation the surgical operation can commence. The woman is placed under general anesthesia or conscious sedation. The doctor, often guided by ultrasound, inserts grasping forceps through the woman's cervix and into the uterus to grab the fetus. . . . A doctor may make 10 to 15 passes with the forceps to evacuate the fetus in its entirety, though sometimes removal is completed with fewer passes. * * *

The abortion procedure that was the impetus for the numerous bans on "partial-birth abortion," including the Act, is a variation of this standard D & E. *See* M. Haskell, DILATION AND EXTRACTION FOR LATE SECOND TRIMESTER ABORTION (1992), 1 Appellant's App. in No. 04–3379 (CA8), p 109 (hereinafter Dilation and Extraction). . . . The main difference between the two procedures is that in intact D & E a doctor extracts the fetus intact or largely intact with only a few passes. There are no comprehensive statistics indicating what percentage of all D & Es are performed in this manner. * * *

Casey involved a challenge to *Roe* v. *Wade*, 410 U.S. 113, 93 S. Ct. 705, 35 L. Ed. 2d 147 (1973). The opinion contains this summary:

> "It must be stated at the outset and with clarity that *Roe's* essential holding, the holding we reaffirm, has three parts. First is a recognition of the right of the woman to choose to have an abortion before viability and to obtain it without undue interference from the State. Before viability, the State's interests are not strong enough to

support a prohibition of abortion or the imposition of a substantial obstacle to the woman's effective right to elect the procedure. Second is a confirmation of the State's power to restrict abortions after fetal viability, if the law contains exceptions for pregnancies which endanger the woman's life or health. And third is the principle that the State has legitimate interests from the outset of the pregnancy in protecting the health of the woman and the life of the fetus that may become a child. These principles do not contradict one another; and we adhere to each." 505 U.S., at 846 (opinion of the Court).

Though all three holdings are implicated in the instant cases, it is the third that requires the most extended discussion; for we must determine whether the Act furthers the legitimate interest of the Government in protecting the life of the fetus that may become a child.

* * * The Act's ban on abortions that involve partial delivery of a living fetus furthers the Government's objectives. No one would dispute that, for many, D & E is a procedure itself laden with the power to devalue human life. Congress could nonetheless conclude that the type of abortion proscribed by the Act requires specific regulation because it implicates additional ethical and moral concerns that justify a special prohibition. Congress determined that the abortion methods it proscribed had a "disturbing similarity to the killing of a newborn infant," and thus it was concerned with "draw[ing] a bright line that clearly distinguishes abortion and infanticide," Congressional Findings (14)(G). * * *

In a decision so fraught with emotional consequence some doctors may prefer not to disclose precise details of the means that will be used, confining themselves to the required statement of risks the procedure entails. From one standpoint this ought not to be surprising. Any number of patients facing imminent surgical procedures would prefer not to hear all details, lest the usual anxiety preceding invasive medical procedures become the more intense. This is likely the case with the abortion procedures here in issue. *See, e.g., National Abortion Federation*, 330 F. Supp. 2d, at 466, n. 22 ("Most of [the plaintiffs'] experts acknowledged that they do not describe to their patients what [the D & E and intact D & E] procedures entail in clear and precise terms"); *see also id.,* at 479.

It is, however, precisely this lack of information concerning the way in which the fetus will be killed that is of legitimate concern to the State. *Casey, supra,* at 873, (plurality opinion) ("States are free to enact laws to provide a reasonable framework for a woman to make a decision that has such profound and lasting meaning"). The State has an interest in ensuring so grave a choice is well informed. It is self-evident that a mother who comes to regret her choice to abort must struggle with grief more anguished and sorrow more profound when she learns, only after the event, what she once did not know: that she allowed a doctor to pierce the skull and vacuum the fast-developing brain of her unborn child, a child assuming the human form.

It is a reasonable inference that a necessary effect of the regulation and the knowledge it conveys will be to encourage some women to carry the infant to full term, thus reducing the absolute number of late-term abortions. The medical profession, furthermore, may find different and less shocking methods to abort the fetus in the second trimester, thereby accommodating legislative demand. The State's interest in respect for life is advanced by the dialogue that better informs the political and legal systems, the medical profession, expectant mothers, and society as a whole of the consequences that follow from a decision to elect a late-term abortion.

* * * The Act's furtherance of legitimate government interests bears upon, but does not resolve, the next question: whether the Act has the effect of imposing an unconstitutional burden on the abortion right because it does not allow use of the barred procedure where " 'necessary, in appropriate medical judgment, for the preservation of the . . . health of the mother.' " *Ayotte,* 546 U.S., at 327–328 (quoting *Casey, supra,* at 879 (plurality opinion)). The prohibition in the Act would be unconstitutional, under precedents we here assume to be controlling, if it "subject[ed] [women] to significant health risks." *Ayotte, supra,* at 328; *see also Casey, supra,* at 880 (opinion of the Court). * * *

There is documented medical disagreement whether the Act's prohibition would ever impose significant health risks on women. . . . The three District Courts that considered the Act's constitutionality appeared to be in some disagreement on this central factual question. The District Court for the District of Nebraska concluded "the banned procedure is, sometimes, the safest abortion procedure to preserve the health of women." *Carhart, supra,* at 1017. The District Court for the Northern District of California reached a similar conclusion. *Planned Parenthood, supra,* at 1002 (finding intact D & E was "under certain circumstances . . . significantly safer than D & E by disarticulation"). The District Court for the Southern District of New York was more skeptical of the purported health benefits of intact D & E. It found the Attorney General's "expert witnesses reasonably and effectively refuted [the plaintiffs'] proffered bases for the opinion that [intact D & E] has safety advantages over other second-trimester abortion procedures." *National Abortion Federation,* 330 F. Supp. 2d, at 479. In addition it did "not believe that many of [the plaintiffs'] purported reasons for why [intact D & E] is medically necessary [were] credible; rather [it found them to be] theoretical or false." *Id.,* at 480. The court nonetheless invalidated the Act because it determined "a significant body of medical opinion . . . holds that D & E has safety advantages over induction and that [intact D & E] has some safety advantages (however hypothetical and unsubstantiated by scientific evidence) over D & E for some women in some circumstances." *Ibid.*

* * * Medical uncertainty does not foreclose the exercise of legislative power in the abortion context any more than it does in other contexts. *See Hendricks, supra,* at 360, n. 3. The medical uncertainty over whether the Act's prohibition creates significant health risks provides a sufficient basis to conclude in this facial attack that the Act does not impose an undue burden.

The conclusion that the Act does not impose an undue burden is supported by other considerations. Alternatives are available to the prohibited procedure. As we have noted, the Act does not proscribe D & E. One District Court found D & E to have extremely low rates of medical complications. *Planned Parenthood, supra,* at 1000. Another indicated D &

E was "generally the safest method of abortion during the second trimester." *Carhart*, 331 F. Supp. 2d, at 1031; *see also National Abortion Federation, supra*, at 467–468 (explaining that "[e]xperts testifying for both sides" agreed D & E was safe). In addition the Act's prohibition only applies to the delivery of "a living fetus." 18 U.S.C. § 1531(b)(1)(A) (2000 ed., Supp. IV). If the intact D & E procedure is truly necessary in some circumstances, it appears likely an injection that kills the fetus is an alternative under the Act that allows the doctor to perform the procedure.

* * * Respondents have not demonstrated that the Act, as a facial matter, is void for vagueness, or that it imposes an undue burden on a woman's right to abortion based on its overbreadth or lack of a health exception. For these reasons the judgments of the Courts of Appeals for the Eighth and Ninth Circuits are reversed.

It is so ordered.

■ JUSTICE GINSBURG, with whom JUSTICE STEVENS, JUSTICE SOUTER, and JUSTICE BREYER join, dissenting.

* * * I dissent from the Court's disposition. Retreating from prior rulings that abortion restrictions cannot be imposed absent an exception safeguarding a woman's health, the Court upholds an Act that surely would not survive under the close scrutiny that previously attended state-decreed limitations on a woman's reproductive choices.

As *Casey* comprehended, at stake in cases challenging abortion restrictions is a woman's "control over her [own] destiny." 505 U.S., at 869 (plurality opinion). *See also id.*, at 852 (majority opinion). "There was a time, not so long ago," when women were "regarded as the center of home and family life, with attendant special responsibilities that precluded full and independent legal status under the Constitution." *Id.*, at 896–897 (quoting *Hoyt* v. *Florida*, 368 U.S. 57, 62 (1961)). Those views, this Court made clear in *Casey*, "are no longer consistent with our understanding of the family, the individual, or the Constitution." 505 U.S., at 897. Women, it is now acknowledged, have the talent, capacity, and right "to participate equally in the economic and social life of the Nation." *Id.*, at 856. Their ability to realize their full potential, the Court recognized, is intimately connected to "their ability to control their reproductive lives." *Ibid.* Thus, legal challenges to undue restrictions on abortion procedures do not seek to vindicate some generalized notion of privacy; rather, they center on a woman's autonomy to determine her life's course, and thus to enjoy equal citizenship stature.

* * * Ultimately, the Court admits that "moral concerns" are at work, concerns that could yield prohibitions on any abortion. *See ante*, at 158 ("Congress could ... conclude that the type of abortion proscribed by the Act requires specific regulation because it implicates additional ethical and moral concerns that justify a special prohibition."). Notably, the concerns expressed are untethered to any ground genuinely serving the Government's interest in preserving life. By allowing such concerns to carry the day and case, overriding fundamental rights, the Court dishonors our precedent. *See, e.g., Casey*, 505 U.S., at 850 ("Some of us as individuals find abortion offensive to our most basic principles of morality, but that cannot

control our decision. Our obligation is to define the liberty of all, not to mandate our own moral code."); *Lawrence* v. *Texas*, 539 U.S. 558, (2003) (Though "[f]or many persons [objections to homosexual conduct] are not trivial concerns but profound and deep convictions accepted as ethical and moral principles," the power of the State may not be used "to enforce these views on the whole society through operation of the criminal law." (citing *Casey*, 505 U.S., at 850).

* * * Today, the Court blurs that line, maintaining that "[t]he Act [legitimately] appl[ies] both previability and postviability because ... a fetus is a living organism while within the womb, whether or not it is viable outside the womb." *Ante*, at 147. Instead of drawing the line at viability, the Court refers to Congress' purpose to differentiate "abortion and infanticide" based not on whether a fetus can survive outside the womb, but on where a fetus is anatomically located when a particular medical procedure is performed. *See ante*, at 158.

One wonders how long a line that saves no fetus from destruction will hold in face of the Court's "moral concerns." *See supra*, at 182; cf. *ante*, at 147 (noting that "[i]n this litigation" the Attorney General "does not dispute that the Act would impose an undue burden if it covered standard D & E"). The Court's hostility to the right *Roe* and *Casey* secured is not concealed. Throughout, the opinion refers to obstetrician-gynecologists and surgeons who perform abortions not by the titles of their medical specialties, but by the pejorative label "abortion doctor." *Ante*, at 144, 145, 155, 161, 163. A fetus is described as an "unborn child," and as a "baby," *ante*, at 134, 138; second-trimester, previability abortions are referred to as "late-term," *ante*, at 156; and the reasoned medical judgments of highly trained doctors are dismissed as "preferences" motivated by "mere convenience," *ante*, at 134, 166. Instead of the heightened scrutiny we have previously applied, the Court determines that a "rational" ground is enough to uphold the Act, *ante*, at 158, 166. And, most troubling, *Casey*'s principles, confirming the continuing vitality of "the essential holding of *Roe*," are merely "assume[d]" for the moment, *ante*, at 146, 161, rather than "retained" or "reaffirmed," *Casey*, 505 U.S., at 846.

————

NOTES

1.   How does U.S. jurisprudence on abortion shift from a strict scrutiny analysis of the fundamental right to "personal privacy" (*Roe*) to an undue burden analysis (*Casey* and *Carhart*)?

2.   In a 2007 law review article, "Sex Equality Arguments for Reproductive Rights," Reva Siegel argues that because of the rise of the "woman-protective antiabortion argument" of the type we saw in *Carhart*, we must re-articulate the right to abortion in terms of constitutional values of sex equality. 56 Emory L.J. 815. What kinds of arguments would you make in that vein? What other constitutional provisions, in addition to the Equal Protection Clause of the Fourteenth Amendment, might be available?

3. Justice Ginsburg's dissent in *Carhart* includes a footnote documenting the unequal effects the ban on intact D & E's would have among women:

> Dilation and evacuation (D & E) is the most frequently used abortion procedure during the second trimester of pregnancy; intact D & E is a variant of the D & E procedure. [. . .] Adolescents and indigent women, research suggests, are more likely than other women to have difficulty obtaining an abortion during the first trimester of pregnancy. Minors may be unaware they are pregnant until relatively late in pregnancy, while poor women's financial constraints are an obstacle to timely receipt of services. *See* Finer, Frohwirth, Dauphinee, Singh, & Moore, *Timing of Steps and Reasons for Delays in Obtaining Abortions in the United States*, 74 CONTRACEPTION 334, 341–343 (2006). . . .

Not only do restrictions on abortions have unequal effects between women, but the right to choose whether or not to have an abortion has not had universal meaning for all women. The reproductive capacities of poor women and women of color in the U.S., as well as women in developing countries, have been subject to forms of disciplinary and even compulsory sterilization. From federal welfare reforms drastically cutting resources and subsidies for women and children to medical experimentation of Quinacrine and Norplant on women of the global South, the socio-economic context, more than the abortion right, determines and limits the complex family planning choices these women face. *See* Andrea Smith, *Beyond Pro–Choice Versus Pro–Life*, NATIONAL WOMEN'S STUDIES ASSOCIATION JOURNAL, Vol. 17, No. 1 (Spring 2005), pp. 129–133. How can equality arguments supporting women's reproductive autonomy attend to these differences between women?

4. Abortion law state-by-state: After *Casey* and *Carhart*, wide disparities developed from state-to-state in regulating abortion. Because of strict regulation, combined with the ostracism and physical threats faced by physicians who perform abortions, in large parts of the United States there are very few doctors willing to provide abortions to their patients. We encourage U.S. students using this casebook to research the availability of abortions in their states. A good place to start is the website of the Guttmacher Institute. See: http://www.guttmacher.org/statecenter/abortion.html.

5. The dissent in *Carhart* invokes powerful language from several personal liberty and privacy cases, including *Lawrence v. Texas,* discussed in Chapter V. In doing so, the dissenters contend that the Court should not use the country's moral code to control the outcome of such cases, but rather should focus on defining the parameters of individual liberty. Where is the line drawn between protecting individual liberty, and protecting widely held moral values, such as opposition to killing another human being? Does the majority or dissent provide guidance as to how to separate the two in cases such as abortion, where both individual liberty and moral values are at stake?

B. Mexico

Constitution of Mexico (as amended)

http://www.juridicas.unam.mx/infjur/leg/constmex/pdf/consting.pdf
Translation by Carlos Perez Vasquez

TITLE ONE

Chapter I, Individual Guarantees

Article 1. In the Mexican United States all individuals shall be entitled to the privileges and immunities granted by this Constitution. Such privileges and immunities shall not be restricted or suspended, but in the cases and under the conditions established by this Constitution itself. * * *

Discrimination based on ethical or national origin as well as discrimination based on gender, age, disabilities of any kind, social status, health condition, religious opinions, preferences of any kind, civil status or on any other reason which attempts against human dignity and which is directed to either cancel or restrain the individuals' privileges and immunities, shall be prohibited.

Article 4. Men and women are equal under the law. The law shall protect family organization and development.

Every person has a right to decide in a free, mature and informed way, the number and spacing of their children.

————

[EDITORS' NOTE: In April 2007 the legislature for the state encompassing Mexico City passed a law permitting abortion during the first trimester without restrictions. The law was affirmed by the Mexican Supreme Court, by a vote of 8–3, in the opinion reproduced below. In most states within the Mexican Republic, abortion is prohibited except under very limited circumstances.]

In re Mexico City's Law of Legal Interruption of Pregnancy

Case #146/2007–00–147/2000–00 (August 28, 2008)

■ In the Supreme Court of Mexico

[In Part I of the decision, the Court finds that the Mexico City law neither violates the Mexican Constitution's implied right to life, nor the right to life provided in various international treaties to which Mexico is a signatory, and begins a discussion of equality.]

* * *

The general justification to de-penalize abortion was to give an end to a public health problem arising from clandestine abortions. The de-penalization of abortion will allow women to voluntarily interrupt their pregnancy in safe and hygienic conditions; additionally, it will guarantee an equal treatment to women, specifically low income women, as well as it will recognize their freedom and determination in the way in which they choose to have sexual intercourse and reproduce; it will recognize that forced maternity must not exist, and a woman should be allowed to pursue her life project in the terms in which she finds it convenient. It was also justified, that the procedure for an abortion must take place within 12 weeks. The interruption of a pregnancy will only be de-penalized during the embryonic and not fetal period, before the product of conception develops its sensory and cognitive faculties. Additionally, the legislature, when enacting the decree that modified the previously analyzed article, given its temporary nature, took into consideration the development of the embryo and how safely and easily a pregnancy could be interrupted without grave consequences for the health of the woman. If said interruption takes place clandestinely and outside of the parameters given by the Legislature, it is not possible to guarantee the health of the mother. On the other hand, the penalization of the interruption during this first state of pregnancy is not ideal to safeguard the continuation of the process of gestation, given that the legislature took into consideration that it is a social reality that women who do not want to be mothers, will recur to the clandestine practice of interrupting their pregnancies with the consequent detriment to their health, and even with the possibility of losing their lives. * * *

Imposing penal consequences then, does not serve the purpose to ensure the correct development of the process of gestation, given that our social reality is different, and therefore, would discriminate against women. Therefore, a penal threat is neither the best nor the only solution to eradicate clandestine abortion practices, since in spite of what we may argue to justify the imposition of a state penalty, sanctioning abortion cannot ignore the rationality and necessity, since, conversely, we would be allowing the entrance of revenge to our penal system as the foundation for this sanction. * * *

For all those reasons, because life, as a constitutional and internationally protected right, cannot be put in front of other rights, and also is a right that could not be considered in any moment as absolute; and that specific provisions at the national and international level refer only to the arbitrary deprivation of life, and prohibit the establishment of the death penalty; this is a problem that deals with the de-criminalization of a specific conduct and there is no specific mandate for its penalization; and, finally, the evaluation of the social conditions and the analysis done by the Legislative Assembly of the Distrito Federal [the district in which Mexico City is located] is constitutional and it is within the democratic powers of the Assembly, this Court considers that the presently analyzed arguments related to the nature and existence of the right to life are unfounded.

I. Do These Dispositions Violate the Equality Principles?

    (A) In respect to the problem presented on the first place, related to the equality between men and women, it is necessary to make a series of distinctions. * * *

[T]he argument that males have the right to be fathers seems to ignore the difference between what people can do, and what they have the right to impose on other people, or on the State, as well as the fact that the norms analyzed that are there to establish the criteria that must take place in cases of disagreement. As it is natural, cases in which it is necessary or relevant to look into the content of the jurisdictional norms now under analysis are those where there is a disagreement between the person that is involved in the continuation of an unwanted pregnancy and other people, cases where what is to be determined by the law is who can veto whose decision. The decision of the local legislature that the one who can make the final decision is the female carrying the embryo, is not discriminatory, and therefore, responds to the clear difference of the position of the woman before any other person (i.e. the male who believes he has participated in the creation of the embryo, or any other person.) The continuation of an unwanted pregnancy has consequences that are distinctively permanent and profound for women, independently of the fact that she may count on the support of other people for the continuation and later the care and education of the child, and it is this asymmetric consequence to a woman's life plan, which establishes the basis for the distinct treatment that the legislature granted when it decided to grant women the final decision over whether the pregnancy must be interrupted or not. This is what makes it not unreasonable to deny the male participant the capacity to make that decision.

[Translation by Felipa Quiroz.]

The Abortion Debate in Mexico

26 Bulletin of Latin American Research 50, 57–59 (2007)

■ Andrzej Kulczycki

Before the Church regained full legal status and the state restored diplomatic relations with the Vatican in 1992, Church-state relations were governed by a *modus vivendi* whereby the authoritarian state did not enforce anticlerical laws while the Church kept clear of the political forum and was expected to help keep social order (Loaeza–Lajous, 1990; Puente, 1992). At the same time the clergy maintained influence by developing a network of lay organisations, such as the National Parents' Union; by implicitly supporting PAN [National Action Party], the voice of national conservatism which has favoured Church activism; and by educating Mexican elites through private Church schools and colleges. Consequently, the Church can still count on many devout followers, in spite of growing secularisation and the spread of evangelical Protestantism. . . .

Mexican bishops assumed a greater public role in the 1980s due to the political bankruptcy and economic mismanagement of the ruling Institutional Revolutionary Party (PRI), as well as the electoral gains made by PAN. They were also emboldened by Pope John Paul II, a strong advocate of human rights, who visited Mexico five times during his papacy. The Church hierarchy and Church-backed groups have since become more assertive in rallying against abortion. However, there are continued sensitivities surrounding Church-state relations and clerical opinion over issues neither strictly moral nor religious.

The Episcopal Commission for the Family promotes Church teaching on the family. Its board includes representatives of various Catholic groups and religious orders who vigorously oppose abortion under any circumstances. The commission's President—since appointed as Archbishop of Mexico City, the largest diocese in the world, and the leader of the Catholic Church in Mexico—explained [...] that it seeks to stop publications and media messages 'dealing with AIDS, sex education, non-natural methods of family planning, as promoted by non-governmental agencies and sometimes by the government, and which are part of the worldwide plan to undermine such [Catholic] values'. * * *

It is by no means certain that Mexican Catholics are listening closely to these injunctions, as most do not practice their faith rigidly (Blancarte, 1991, 2003). Beyond the public level, the Church has become more tolerant of family planning activities and has muted its criticism of condom use as an HIV/AIDS preventive measure. * * *

Several Catholic groups have recently attempted to open up debate about their Church's teaching on women, sexuality and reproductive health, including abortion. The most prominent, *Católicas por el Derecho a Decidir* [Catholics for a Free Choice], is a small but active group that publishes a quarterly opinion journal on these matters, along the lines of its U.S. parent organisation.

* * * On World AIDS Day, 2001, the Church hierarchy even granted it permission to hold a religious celebration in Mexico City's cathedral as part of the group's campaign to promote condom use to prevent the spread of AIDS. This shows that a plurality of opinions exists within the Church, despite initial appearances to the contrary.

NOTES

1. Since Mexico City's decision to permit legal abortion in 2007 and the Supreme Court's judgment upholding the legislation in 2008, there has been a broad movement to enforce long-standing anti-abortion laws in other parts of Mexico. In addition, seventeen states have passed constitutional amendments declaring that life begins at conception. Legal scholar at the National Autonomous University of Mexico, Pedro Salazar, has described these actions as a well-coordinated political response against the pro-choice movement in Mexico. Elizabeth Malkin, *Many States in Mexico Crack Down on Abortion*, N.Y. TIMES, Sept. 22, 2010, www.nytimes.com/2010/09/23/world/americas/23mexico.html.

2. The opposition to abortion in Mexico is often ascribed to Roman Catholic conservatives. *See id.* If this is correct, does the prohibition on abortion cast doubt on Mexico's status as a secular state? For a further discussion of secularism in Mexico, see Chapter VII.

C. Colombia

The Political Constitution Of Colombia, 1991 (as Amended 2005)

[English Translation found online at: http://confinder.richmond.edu/admin/docs/colombia_const2.pdf]

CONCERNING FUNDAMENTAL PRINCIPLES

Article 1. Colombia is a legal social state organized in the form of a unitary republic, decentralized, with the autonomy of its territorial units, democratic, participatory, and pluralistic, based on the respect of human dignity, on the work and solidarity of the individuals who belong to it, and the prevalence of the general interest.

CONCERNING FUNDAMENTAL RIGHTS

Article 11. The right to life is inviolate. There will be no death penalty.

Article 12. No one will be subjected to forced imprisonment, nor submitted to torture or cruel, inhuman, or degrading treatment or punishment.

Article 13. All individuals are born free and equal before the law and entitled to equal protection and treatment by the authorities, and tol enjoy the same rights, freedoms, and opportunities without discrimination on the basis of gender, race, national or family origin, language, religion, political opinion, or philosophy.

The State will promote the conditions necessary in order that equality may be real and effective and will adopt measures in favor of groups that are discriminated against or marginalized.

Article 16. All persons are entitled to their free personal development without limitations other than those imposed by the rights of others and those which are prescribed by the legal system.

Article 21. The right to dignity is guaranteed. The law will provide the manner in which it will be upheld.

CONCERNING SOCIAL, ECONOMIC, AND CULTURAL RIGHTS

Article 42. The family is the basic nucleus of society. It is formed on the basis of natural or legal ties, through the free decision of a man and woman to contract matrimony or by their responsible resolve to comply with it.

The State and society guarantee the integral protection of the family. The law may determine the inalienable and unseizable family patrimony. The family's honor, dignity, and intimacy are inviolable.

Family relations are based on the equality of rights and duties of the couple and on the mutual respect of all its members. Any form of violence in the family is considered destructive of its harmony and unity, and will be sanctioned according to law.

The couple has the right to decide freely and responsibly the number of their children and will have to support them and educate them while they are minors or non-self-supporting.

Article 43. Women and men have equal rights and opportunities. Women cannot be subjected to any type of discrimination. During their periods of pregnancy and following delivery, women will benefit from the special assistance and protection of the State and will receive from the latter food subsidies if they should thereafter find themselves unemployed or abandoned.

The State will support the female head of household in a special way.

Article 49. Public health and environmental protection are public services for which the State is responsible. All individuals are guaranteed access to services that promote, protect, and rehabilitate public health.

It is the responsibility of the State to organize, direct, and regulate the delivery of health services and environmental protection to the population in accordance with the principles of efficiency, universality, and cooperation, and to establish policies for the provision of health services by private entities and to exercise supervision and control over them. In the area of public health, the state will establish the jurisdiction of the nation, territorial entities, and individuals, and determine the shares of their responsibilities within the limits and under the conditions determined by law. Public health services will be organized in a decentralized manner, accordance with levels of responsibility and with the participation of the community.

The law will determine the limits within which basic care for all the people will be free of charge and mandatory.

Every person has the obligation to attend to the integral care of his/her health and that of his/her community.

In Re Abortion Law

Constitutional Court of Colombia (2006) C–355/2006
Women's Link Worldwide

■ Writing for the majority of the Court: JUSTICE ARAÚJO RENTERÍA and JUSTICE VARGAS HERNÁNDEZ

* * * The Plaintiffs assert that the [Colombian penal code sections criminalizing abortion] ... violate the following constitutional rights: the right to dignity (Constitutional Preamble and article 1 of the Constitution); the right to life (article 11 of the Constitution); the right to bodily integrity (article 12 of the Constitution); the right to equality and the general right to liberty (article 13 of the Constitution); the right to the free development of the individual (article 16 of the Constitution); the right to reproductive autonomy (article 42 of the Constitution); the right to health (article 49 of the Constitution) and obligations under international human rights law (article 93 of the Constitution). * * *

In general, the arguments of the Plaintiffs revolve around the fact that the articles of the Penal Code that criminalize abortion (article 122) and abortion without consent (article 123), together with the mitigating circumstances therein (article 124), are unconstitutional because they disproportionately and unreasonably limit the rights and liberties of the pregnant woman, including when she is a minor of less than 14 years of age.

The Plaintiffs also assert that the articles in question violate various international human rights law treaties, which are part of the Constitutional Bundle in accordance with article 93 of the Constitution, as well as with the opinions issued by the various bodies charged with interpreting and applying such international treaties. In particular, the challenge to paragraph 7 of article 32 of the Penal Code revolves around the fact that the state of necessity prescribed therein breaches a woman's fundamental right to life and physical integrity because she is forced to resort to a clandestine abortion "which is humiliating and potentially dangerous to her integrity." * * *

* * * The Preamble of the Constitution establishes "life" as one of the values that the constitutional legal system aims to protect. Article 2 notes that the authorities of the Republic exist in order to protect the life of the people residing in Colombia. Article 11 affirms, along with other references in the Constitution, that "the right to life is inviolable." In the Constitution of 1991, these various references give "life" a multiplicity of functions, as both a value and a fundamental right. * * *

Within the legal system, life receives different normative treatments. For instance, there is a distinction between the right to life in article 11 of the Constitution and life as a value protected by the Constitution. The right to life requires that an individual be entitled to it and claim the right. As with all other rights, the right to life is restricted to human persons, while the protection of life can be afforded to those who have not yet reached the human condition. * * *

Following this reasoning, "life" and "the right to life" are different phenomena. Human life passes through various stages and manifests in various forms, which are entitled to different forms of legal protection. Even though the legal system protects the fetus, it does not grant it the same level or degree of protection it grants a human person. * * *

These considerations must be taken into account by the legislature if it finds it appropriate to enact public policies regarding abortion, including imposing criminal penalties where the Constitution permits, while respecting the rights of women. * * *

7. Fundamental rights of women under the Colombian National Constitution and international law

The 1991 Constitution expressly sets out the goal of recognizing and enhancing the rights of women, as well as of reinforcing these rights by protecting them in an effective and decisive manner. Thus, women are now entitled to special constitutional protection and their rights must be recognized and protected by government authorities, including those within the legal system, without exception. * * *

In effect, various international treaties form the basis for the recognition and protection of women's reproductive rights, which derive from the protection of other fundamental rights such as the right to life, health, equality, the right to be free from discrimination, the right to liberty, bodily integrity and the right to be free from violence—all of which constitute the essential core of reproductive rights. Other fundamental rights, such as the right to work and the right to education—which are also affected when women's reproductive rights are violated—serve as parameters to protect and guarantee sexual and reproductive rights.

It must be noted that in addition to the protections for women's rights in the Universal Declaration of Human Rights; the International Covenant on Civil and Political Rights; the International Covenant on Economic, Social and Cultural Rights; and the American Convention on Human Rights, special protection for the rights of Latin American women are found in the Convention on the Elimination of All Forms of Discrimination against Women (CEDAW), which entered into force in Colombia on February 19, 1982, with the passage of Law 51, 1981, and the Inter–American Convention on the Prevention, Punishment and Eradication of Violence Against Women (Convention of Belém do Pará), which entered into force in Colombia on December 15, 1996, by means of Law 248, 1995. These documents, together with those signed by the governments of the signatory countries in the World Conferences, are fundamental to the protection and guarantee of the rights of women as they form the point of reference for establishing concepts which contribute to their interpretation both in the national and international spheres. * * *

Other sexual and reproductive rights are based on the right of freedom to marry and start a family. The right to privacy is also connected to reproductive rights and is infringed upon when the state or private citizens interfere with a woman's right to make decisions about her body and her reproductive capacity. The right to privacy includes the right of a patient to have her confidentiality respected by her doctor. Therefore, the right to intimacy is infringed upon when the doctor is legally obliged to report a woman who has undergone an abortion.

With regard to the right to equality and to be free from discrimination, the Women's Convention (CEDAW) establishes women's right to enjoy human rights in conditions of equality with men. It also prescribes the elimination of barriers impeding women's effective enjoyment of their internationally recognized rights, as well as of those found in national legislation. It also establishes measures to prevent and sanction acts of discrimination. * * *

Sexual and reproductive rights also emerge from the recognition that equality in general, gender equality in particular, and the emancipation of women and girls are essential to society. Protecting sexual and reproductive rights is a direct path to promoting the dignity of all human beings and a step forward in humanity's advancement towards social justice.

Nonetheless, neither a mandate to decriminalize abortion nor a prohibition on the legislature's adoption of criminal abortion laws derives from international treaties or constitutional articles on the topic. Congress has a wide range of discretion to adopt public policies on abortion. However, this discretion is not unlimited. As this Court has held, even in criminal matters, the legislature must respect two constitutional limits. First, the legislature cannot disproportionately encroach upon constitutional rights. Second, the legislature must not leave certain constitutional values unprotected. At the same time, the legislature must recognize the principle that criminal law, due to its potential to restrict liberties, must always be a measure of last resort.

Below, the Court will set out the limits to the legislature's discretion to utilize criminal law to penalize abortion, first examining the more general limits and then turning to the particulars of the case before it.

8. Limits on legislative discretion over criminal matters

* * * Congress may introduce variations in the criminalization and punishment of different conducts that threaten life, a value found in the Constitution. Colombia's legal system includes various laws that aim to protect life, such as laws against genocide, homicide, abortion, abandoning a minor or a person with disabilities, or genetic manipulation. Another example is failing to aid a person at risk. The criminalization of these acts all aim to protect life. Although all these laws have the same objective, that of protecting life, the penalties assigned are different, in accordance with the specific situation and the stage of life in question. In this manner, birth is a relevant event in determining the protection accorded by the law, as is reflected in the penalty associated with the crime.

8.1. The fundamental right to dignity as a limit on the legislature's discretion over criminal matters

As with "life," the concept of "dignity" has various functions in Colombian constitutional law, as has been recognized by constitutional jurisprudence. This Court has stated that "human dignity" has three different roles: (i) it is a foundational principle of the legal system and as such, it has an axiological dimension as a constitutional value; (ii) it is a constitutional principle; and (iii) it is a fundamental right. * * *

[T]he rules which flow from the concept of human dignity—both the constitutional principle and the fundamental right to dignity—coincide in protecting the same type of conduct. This Court has held that in those cases where dignity is used as a criterion in a judicial decision, it must be understood that dignity protects the following: (i) autonomy, or the possibility of designing one's life plan and living in accordance with it (to live life as one wishes); (ii) certain material conditions of existence (to live well); and (iii) intangible goods such as physical integrity and moral integrity (to live free of humiliation). * * *

Therefore, when the legislature enacts criminal laws, it cannot ignore that a woman is a human being entitled to dignity and that she must be treated as such, as opposed to being treated as a reproductive instrument for the human race. The legislature must not impose the role of procreator on a woman against her will.

8.2. The right to the free development of the individual as a limit on the legislature's discretion over criminal matters

The right to the free development of the individual stems from axiological considerations: the principle of human dignity and the strong libertarian characteristics of the 1991 Constitution. This right is understood as the necessary result of a new conception of the state's role. In this new role, the state is "an instrument at the service of the citizens, as opposed to the citizen as a servant of the state." In this new light, individual autonomy—understood as the vital sphere of matters solely within the decisional ambit of the individual—becomes a constitutional principle, binding on public authorities, who are therefore prevented from infringing on this private sphere and making decisions on behalf of citizens because such infringement would amount to "a brutal usurpation of a citizen's ethical condition, reducing him/her to the condition of an object, converting him/her into a means to ends imposed from outside...."

The substance of the right is found within the realm of an individual's private decisions, which result in a person's life plan or in an individual's ideal of personal achievement. Throughout time, constitutional jurisprudence has identified a spectrum of conduct that is protected under the right to the free development of the individual, among which the following must be mentioned due to their importance in the present analysis.

The freedom of every individual to choose his or her marital status without coercion of any type; this includes, among others options, the freedom to choose whether to marry, to live in a common law relationship or remain single.

The right to be a mother, or in other words, the right to opt for motherhood as a "life choice," is a decision of the utmost private nature for each woman. Therefore, the Constitution does not permit the state, the family, the employer or educational institutions to introduce any regulation or policy that infringes upon the right of a woman to choose to be a mother or that interferes with the rightful exercise of motherhood. Any discriminatory or unfavorable treatment of a woman on the basis of special circumstances she might be facing at the time of making the decision of whether to be a mother (for example, at an early age, within marriage or not, with a partner or without one, while working, etc.) is a flagrant violation of the constitutional right to the free development of the individual. * * *

8.3. Health, life and bodily integrity as limits on the discretion of the legislature over criminal matters

* * * The Constitutional Court has said on various occasions that the right to health, even though it is not expressly found in the Constitution as a fundamental right, has a fundamental character when it is in close relation to the right to life. That is, when its protection becomes necessary in order to guarantee the continuity of life in dignified conditions.

The Court has also said that human life as protected in the Constitution refers not only to a biological existence, but also to life with a minimum degree of dignity. Human beings are multifaceted and their existence involves more than purely material aspects; it incorporates physical, biological, spiritual, mental and psychological factors, all of which must be taken into consideration when defining human dignity. * * *

Also, as mentioned above, the right to health has a dimension related to decision-making about one's own health, which is closely linked to the right to autonomy and the right to the free development of the individual. Thus, the Constitutional Court has understood that every person has the autonomy to make decisions related to his or her health, and that therefore the informed consent of the patient prevails over the views of the treating physician, and the interest of society and the state in preserving the health of the people. From this perspective, medical treatment or intervention should always take place with the consent of the patient, except in very exceptional circumstances. * * *

10.   The case before the Court

10.1.   The unconstitutionality of a total prohibition of abortion

* * * In the case at hand, as has been held numerous times, the life of the fetus is entitled to protection under constitutional law and therefore the decisions of the pregnant woman regarding the termination of her pregnancy go beyond the sphere of her private autonomy and implicate the interests of both the state and the legislature. * * *

Even though the protection of the fetus through criminal law is not in itself disproportionate and penalizing abortion may be constitutional, the criminalization of abortion in all circumstances entails the complete pre-eminence of the life of the fetus and the absolute sacrifice of the pregnant woman's fundamental rights. This result is, without a doubt, unconstitutional.

In effect, one of the characteristics of constitutional regimes with a high degree of axiological content, such as the Colombian Constitution of 1991, is the coexistence of different values, rights and principles, none of which is absolute and none of which prevails over the rest. This is one of the fundamental pillars of proportionality that must be utilized as an instrument to resolve the tension amongst laws in a structured and principled manner.

Thus, a criminal law that prohibits abortion in all circumstances extinguishes the woman's fundamental rights, and thereby violates her dignity by reducing her to a mere receptacle for the fetus, without rights or interests of constitutional relevance worthy of protection. * * *

This Court is of the view that under the enumerated circumstances, abortion does not constitute a crime. This is not only because that result was originally contemplated by the legislature, but also because the absolute prevalence of the fetus' rights in these circumstances implies a complete disregard for human dignity and the right to the free development of the pregnant woman whose pregnancy is not the result of a free and conscious decision, but the result of arbitrary, criminal acts against her in violation of her autonomy; acts that are penalized in the Penal Code. * * *

When the pregnancy is the result of rape, sexual abuse, non-consensual artificial insemination or implantation of a fertilized ovule, or incest, it is necessary that such criminal acts be reported accordingly to the competent authorities.

To this end, the legislature may enact regulations as long as the regulations do not preclude access to abortion and do not impose a disproportionate burden on the rights of women. For instance, the regulations cannot require forensic evidence of actual penetration after a report of rape or require evidence to establish lack of consent to the sexual relationship. Nor can they require that a judge or a police officer find that the rape actually occurred; or require that the woman obtain permission from, or be required to notify, her husband or her parents. * * *

For the present analysis, it is relevant to consider various international human rights bodies' interpretation of international treaties that guarantee women's right to life and health. For instance, article 6 of the International Covenant on Civil and Political Rights, article 12.1 of the Convention on the Elimination of All Forms of Discrimination against Women and article 12 of the International Covenant on Economic, Social and Cultural Rights, are all part of the Constitutional Bundle and thus impose an obligation on the state to adopt measures to protect life and health. The prohibition of abortion where the life and health of the mother are at risk may therefore violate Colombia's obligations under international law.

These obligations do not pertain only where the woman's physical health is at risk, but also where her mental health is at risk. It must be noted that the right to health, under article 12 of the International Covenant on Economic, Social and Cultural Rights, includes the right to the highest achievable level of both physical and mental well-being. Pregnancy may at times cause severe anguish or even mental disorders, which may justify its termination if so certified by a doctor. * * *

A final circumstance that must be addressed involves medically-certified malformations of the fetus. Although there are different types of malformations, those extreme malformations incompatible with life outside the womb pose a constitutional issue that must be resolved. Those circumstances are different from having identified an illness of the fetus that may be cured during pregnancy or after birth. Rather, those circumstances involve a fetus that is unlikely to survive due to a severe malformation, as certified by a doctor. In these cases, the duty of the state to protect the fetus loses weight, since this life is in fact not viable. Thus, the rights of the woman prevail and the legislature cannot require her, under the threat of a criminal penalty, to carry a pregnancy to term.

An additional reason for the decriminalization of abortion in these extreme circumstances is that imposing a criminal penalty in order to protect the fetus results in the imposition of an unreasonable burden on the pregnant woman, who is forced to go through a pregnancy only to lose the growing life due to the malformation.

Furthermore, in a situation where the fetus is not viable, forcing the mother, under the threat of criminal charges, to carry the pregnancy to term amounts to cruel, inhumane and degrading treatment, which affects her moral well-being and her right to dignity.

In both cases described above, where the continuation of the pregnancy puts the life or health of the pregnant woman at risk or when there are serious malformations of the fetus incompatible with life outside the womb, there should be a medical certificate to validate the circumstances under which the abortion cannot be penalized. * * *

To conclude, under the principle that calls for the preservation of laws, it is necessary to declare the conditional constitutionality of the challenged article. In accordance with this decision, abortion will not be considered a crime in the circumstances described herein. In this manner, protection for the life of the fetus will not disproportionately override the rights of the pregnant woman.

The Court declares that article 122 of the Penal Code is constitutional with the understanding that abortion is not criminal in the following circumstances: a) when the continuation of the pregnancy presents risks to the life or the health of the woman, as certified by a medical doctor; b) when there are serious malformations of the fetus that make the fetus not viable, as certified by a medical doctor; and c) when the pregnancy is the result of any of the following criminal acts, duly reported to the authorities: incest, rape, sexual abuse, or artificial insemination or implantation of a fertilized ovule without the consent of the woman. * * *

11. Final considerations

Having weighed the duty to protect the life of the fetus against the fundamental rights of the pregnant woman, this Court concludes that the total prohibition of abortion is unconstitutional and that article 122 of the Penal Code is constitutional on the condition that the three circumstances described in this decision are excluded from its ambit and on the under-standing that all three circumstances are autonomous and independent of one another.

However, the legislature in its discretion may decide that abortion is not penalized in additional circumstances. In the present decision, the Court has limited itself to the three extreme circumstances that violate the Constitution when the pregnant woman has consented to the abortion and the pertinent requirements have been met. However, aside from these circumstances, the legislature may foresee others in which public policy calls for the decriminalization of abortion, taking into consideration the circumstances under which abortions are performed, as well as socio-economic situations and other public health policy objectives. * * *

[Translated by Monica Roa]

NOTES

1. How does Colombia's proportionality inquiry compare with the U.S.'s strict scrutiny or undue burden analyses?

2. The Constitutional Court of Colombia describes its constitution as one containing a "high degree of axiological content." "Dignity" and "life" are philosophical values, in addition to being rights or principles, and the Constitutional Court spends much time elaborating on these values. But so does *Roe*, even as the decision ultimately ends up separating its philosoph-

ical discussion from its legal analysis. What do you think are the benefits and/or limitations of bridging philosophical and legal questions?

3. In October 2009, the Court re-visited its 2006 decision and reaffirmed a woman's right to seek an abortion "when a pregnancy threatens a woman's life or health, in cases of rape, incest and in cases where the fetus has malformations incompatible with life outside the womb." The Court ruled that in those circumstances, women "enjoy a right to decide, free from any pressure, coercion, urging, manipulation and, in general, any sort of inadmissible intervention, to terminate a pregnancy. . . . [I]t is forbidden to raise any obstacles, requirements or additional barriers." *Momentous Decision in Abortion Case in Colombia*, CHOICE IRELAND BLOG (Oct. 28, 2009, 11:15), http://www.choiceireland.org/content/momentous-decision-abortion-case-colombia.

4. Colombia's constitution and cases refer heavily to a right to bodily integrity. What does the right to bodily integrity entail, especially in the context of pregnant women? Are there comparable rights in the United States, Mexico, and Ireland, for example? For a comparative look at how different countries' constitutions and declarations of human rights articulate a right to bodily integrity, *see* Rights of Individuals—Civil and Political (chart), Human and Constitutional Rights, Columbia Law School Library, http://www.hrcr.org/chart/civil+political/personal_security.html.   (current as of 2008.)

5. Colombia's ruling on abortion mentions that as a signatory of international human rights treaties such as the International Covenant on Economic, Social and Cultural Rights, Colombia is obligated to uphold women's rights in accordance with international law. The United States is a signatory to several of the international human rights treaties listed in the opinion. Why does the Colombian court bestow greater importance on Colombia's status as a signatory to these treaties than the United States does in its major Supreme Court opinions on abortion? Does it seem the treaties are equally binding on both countries when it comes to women's, and human, rights?

D. IRELAND

In 1922, Ireland declared its independence from English rule and adopted its own constitution, which combined British common law with indigenous Irish norms and aspects of American law. Ireland as a nation is majority Catholic, and many aspects of the Irish law have been shaped by its strong Catholic identity. With regard to abortion, Ireland's current criminal code deems individuals who perform an abortion as committing a felony subject to a lifetime sentence, while those who assist in an abortion are considered to have committed a misdemeanor. The 1937 Constitution also includes an amendment that provides an explicit right to life for the unborn. But in 1992 the constitution was amended by popular referendum to provide a right to information about abortion, and a right to travel (to secure an abortion abroad). A narrow and diminishing majority of the Irish public continues to support anti-abortion laws.

————

The Constitution of Ireland, 1937 (as Amended 2004)

[Excerpted from The Constitution of Ireland, 1937, found online at http://www.taoiseach.gov.ie/attached_files/ Pdffiles/Constitution% 20of% 20Ireland.pdf]

FUNDAMENTAL RIGHTS

Personal Rights.

Article 40.

1. All citizens shall, as human persons, be held equal before the law.

This shall not be held to mean that the State shall not in its enactments have due regard to differences of capacity, physical and moral, and of social function.

3. 1° The State guarantees in its laws to respect, and, as far as practicable, by its laws to defend and vindicate the personal rights of the citizen.

2° The State shall, in particular, by its laws protect as best it may from unjust attack and, in the case of injustice done, vindicate the life, person, good name, and property rights of every citizen.

3° The State acknowledges the right to life of the unborn and, with due regard to the equal right to life of the mother, guarantees in its laws to respect, and, as far as practicable, by its laws to defend and vindicate that right.

This subsection shall not limit freedom to travel between the State and another state.

This subsection shall not limit freedom to obtain or make available, in the State, subject to such conditions as may be laid down by law, information relating to services lawfully available in another state.

————

Attorney General v. X and Others

Supreme Court of Ireland (1992)

■ FINLAY CJ, (delivered his judgment on 5 March 1992)

This is an appeal brought by the defendants against an order made by Costello J in the High Court on 17 February 1992 [. . .].

The first-named defendant is a fourteen and a half year old girl and the second and third-named defendants are her parents.

Upon the facts proved in the High Court, the first-named defendant was, in the month of December 1991 raped, and as a result of such rape became pregnant of which fact she and her parents became aware at the very end of January 1992. The rape was then reported to the Garda Siochana and a statement given by the first-named defendant to them of the facts surrounding the alleged rape.

All the defendants were distraught as a result of the revelation of the fact of rape and as a result of the fact that the first-named defendant was pregnant and after careful consideration all of them reached a decision that she should travel to the United Kingdom and undergo an operation for abortion. The family informed the Garda Siochana of that fact and inquired from them whether any particular process was available for testing the foetus so aborted in order to provide proof in any subsequent charge of the paternity of the accused. The Garda Siochana apparently submitted that inquiry to the Director of Public Prosecutions and he in turn communicated the information thus arising to the Attorney General.

The Attorney General on 7 February 1992 having applied ex parte to Costello J in the High Court, obtained an order of interim injunction restraining the first-named defendant and the other defendants from leaving the country or from arranging or carrying out a termination of the pregnancy of the first named defendant. At the time that order was ready to be served on the defendants they apparently had left this country and were in England arranging for the carrying out of the termination of the pregnancy. Upon being informed whilst there of the order which had been made by the court, they returned to this country.

* * * With regard to the finding by the learned trial judge concerning the disparity between the risk to life of the unborn and the risk to life of the mother, the following submission was made [by the defendants]. It was contended that the true test, having regard to the proper interpretation of Article 40.3.3 of the Constitution, was that if it was established as a matter of probability that the continuation of the life of the unborn child constituted a real and substantial risk to the life of the mother then the conflict thus arising should be resolved by preferring the life of the mother. This submission was based upon an assertion, having regard to the meaning which should be placed upon the two phrases 'as far as practicable' and 'with due regard to' contained in Article 40.3.3, that the protection of the life of the mother must, by reason of it being a life in being as distinct from an unborn life, in the circumstances where a real and substantial risk to it was established, be preferred. It was further submitted that the learned trial judge's judgment did not appear to apply this test, but rather the test that with regard to the unborn life a certainty of termination arose if an abortion operation was not prevented, whereas there was no certainty that the mother's life would be terminated if the pregnancy continued. It was further contended that, applying this submitted test to the facts which without conflict or question had been deposed to before the learned trial judge, it had been established that a real and substantial risk to the life of the mother would occur if the pregnancy were not terminated.

* * * With regard to the question of the true interpretation of the provisions of Article 40.3.3, it was submitted on behalf of the Attorney General, firstly, that the terms of that subsection must not be interpreted in isolation from the other provisions of the Constitution; that the use of the phrase 'due regard' and of the phrase 'as far as practicable' necessarily

involved, for the interpretation of the provisions of the subsection of the article, a consideration of the entire provisions of the Constitution, of the principles in accordance with which the courts should approach its interpretation, and with the need for harmonisation between this particular provision of the Constitution and other rights and obligations identified, granted or guaranteed by it. In this context reliance was placed by counsel on the judgments of this Court in *McGee v Attorney General* [1974] IR 284; on the judgment of O'Higgins CJ [1981] IR 412. Having regard to the principles thus laid down by this Court, it was submitted on behalf of the Attorney General that the phrases 'due regard' and 'as far as practicable' contained in the subarticle of the Constitution made it necessary that in interpreting this sub-article one looked elsewhere at the position of a woman who is a mother and a member of a family group and a member of society in the terms of the rights and obligations which, as such, she may have, together with, in relevant cases, the rights and obligations of her parents as well.

Having regard to these principles, it was submitted that the true test to be applied was that under the terms of the sub-article if it was established in any case that the continuation of the life of the unborn constituted a risk of immediate or inevitable death to the mother, the termination of the pregnancy would be justified and lawful.

* * * Interpretation of Article 40.3.3

In the course of his judgment in *McGee v Attorney General* [1974] IR 284 Walsh J at p. 318, stated as follows:

> In this country, it falls finally upon the judges to interpret the Constitution and in doing so to determine, where necessary, the rights which are superior or antecedent to positive law or which are imprescriptible or inalienable. In the performance of this difficult duty there are certain guidelines laid down in the Constitution for the judge. The very structure and content of the articles dealing with fundamental rights clearly indicate that justice is not subordinate to the law. In particular, the terms of s. 3 of Article 40 expressly subordinate the law to justice. Both Aristotle and the Christian philosophers have regarded justice as the highest human virtue. The virtue of prudence was also esteemed by Aristotle, as by the philosophers of the Christian world. But the great additional virtue introduced by Christianity was that of charity—not the charity which consists of giving to the deserving, for that is justice, but the charity which is also called mercy. According to the preamble, the people gave themselves the Constitution to promote the common good, with due observance of prudence, justice and charity so that the dignity and freedom of the individual might be assured. The judges must, therefore, as best they can from their training and their experience interpret these rights in accordance with their ideas of prudence, justice and charity. It is but natural that from time to time the prevailing ideas of these virtues may be conditioned by the passage of time; no interpretation of the Constitution is intended to be final for all time. It is given in the light of prevailing ideas and concepts.

* * * I accept the submission made on behalf of the Attorney General, that the doctrine of the harmonious interpretation of the Constitution

involves in this case a consideration of the constitutional rights and obligations of the mother of the unborn child and the interrelation of those rights and obligations with the rights and obligations of other people and, of course, with the right to life of the unborn child as well.

Such a harmonious interpretation of the Constitution carried out in accordance with concepts of prudence, justice and charity, as they have been explained in the judgment of Walsh J in *McGee v Attorney General* leads me to the conclusion that in vindicating and defending as far as practicable the right of the unborn to life but at the same time giving due regard to the right of the mother to life, the court must, amongst the matters to be so regarded, concern itself with the position of the mother within a family group, with persons on whom she is dependent, with, in other instances, persons who are dependent upon her and her interaction with other citizens and members of society in the areas in which her activities occur. Having regard to that conclusion, I am satisfied that the test proposed on behalf of the Attorney General that the life of the unborn could only be terminated if it were established that an inevitable or immediate risk to the life of the mother existed, for the avoidance of which a termination of the pregnancy was necessary, insufficiently vindicates the mother's right to life.

* * * I am satisfied that the only risk put forward in this case to the life of the mother is the risk of self-destruction. I agree with the conclusion reached by the learned trial judge in the High Court that that was a risk which, as would be appropriate in any other form of risk to the life of the mother, must be taken into account in reconciling the right of the unborn to life and the rights of the mother to life. Such a risk to the life of a young mother, in particular, has it seems to me, a particular characteristic which is relevant to the question of whether the evidence in this case justifies a conclusion that it constitutes a real and substantial risk to life.

If a physical condition emanating from a pregnancy occurs in a mother, it may be that a decision to terminate the pregnancy in order to save her life can be postponed for a significant period in order to monitor the progress of the physical condition, and that there are diagnostic warning signs which can readily be relied upon during such postponement.

In my view, it is common sense that a threat of self-destruction such as is outlined in the evidence in this case, which the psychologist clearly believes to be a very real threat, cannot be monitored in that sense and that it is almost impossible to prevent self-destruction in a young girl in the situation in which this defendant is if she were to decide to carry out her threat of suicide.

I am, therefore, satisfied that on the evidence before the learned trial judge, which was in no way contested, and on the findings which he has made, that the defendants/appellants have satisfied the test which I have laid down as being appropriate and have established, as a matter of probability, that there is a real and substantial risk to the life of the mother by self-destruction which can only be avoided by termination of her pregnancy.

It is for this reason that, in my view, the defendants were entitled to succeed in this appeal, and the orders made in the High Court have been set aside. * * *

————

Case of A, B, and C v. Ireland

Application no. 25579/05 (16 December 2010)

■ EUROPEAN COURT OF HUMAN RIGHTS

I. THE CIRCUMSTANCES OF THE CASE

[Facts for Applicants A and B omitted]

* * *

C. The third applicant (C)

22.   On 3 March 2005 the third applicant had an abortion in England believing that she could not establish her right to an abortion in Ireland. She was in her first trimester of pregnancy at the time.

23.   Prior to that, she had been treated for 3 years with chemotherapy for a rare form of cancer. She had asked her doctor before the treatment about the implications of her illness as regards her desire to have children and was advised that it was not possible to predict the effect of pregnancy on her cancer and that, if she did become pregnant, it would be dangerous for the foetus if she were to have chemotherapy during the first trimester.

24.   The cancer went into remission and the applicant unintentionally became pregnant. She was unaware of this fact when she underwent a series of tests for cancer, contraindicated during pregnancy. When she discovered she was pregnant, the first applicant consulted her General Practitioner ("GP") as well as several medical consultants. She alleged that, as a result of the chilling effect of the Irish legal framework, she received insufficient information as to the impact of the pregnancy on her health and life and of her prior tests for cancer on the foetus.

25.   She therefore researched the risks on the internet. Given the uncertainty about the risks involved, the third applicant travelled to England for an abortion. She maintained that she wanted a medical abortion (drugs to induce a miscarriage) as her pregnancy was at an early stage but that she could not find a clinic which would provide this treatment as she was a non-resident and because of the need for follow-up. She therefore alleged she had to wait a further 8 weeks until a surgical abortion was possible.

26.   On returning to Ireland after the abortion, the third applicant suffered complications of an incomplete abortion, including prolonged bleeding and infection. She alleges that doctors provided inadequate medical care. She consulted her own GP several months after the abortion and her GP made no reference to the fact that she was visibly no longer pregnant.

* * *

H. Relevant European and international material

1. *The Maastricht and Lisbon Treaties*

100. Efforts to preserve, *inter alia*, the existing Irish prohibition on abortion gave rise to Protocol No. 17 to the Maastricht Treaty on European Union which was signed in February 1992. It reads as follows:

> "Nothing in the Treaty on European Union, or in the treaties establishing the European Communities, or in the Treaties or Acts modifying or supplementing those treaties, shall affect the application in Ireland of Article 40.3.3 of the Constitution of Ireland" * * *

2. *The International Conference on Population and Development ("the Cairo ICPD, 1994")*

(a) The Programme of Action of the Cairo ICPD, 1994

104. At this conference 179 countries adopted a twenty-year Programme of Action which focused on individuals' needs and rights rather than on achieving demographic targets. Article 8.25 of the programme provided, in so far as relevant, as follows:

> "... All Governments ... are urged to strengthen their commitment to women's health, to deal with the health impact of unsafe abortion as a major public health concern and to reduce the recourse to abortion through expanded and improved family-planning services. ...Any measures or changes related to abortion within the health system can only be determined at the national or local level according to the national legislative process."

(b) The Fourth World Conference on Women, Beijing 1995

105. The Platform for Action adopted at this conference recalled the above-noted paragraph 8.25 of the Programme of Action of the Cairo ICPD 1994 and the Governments resolved to consider reviewing laws containing punitive measures against women who have undergone illegal abortions.

(c) Parliamentary Assembly of the Council of Europe ("PACE") Recommendation 1903(2010) entitled: Fifteen years since the International Conference on Population and Development Programme of Action

106. The PACE noted some progress has been made since the Cairo ICPD 1994. However, "achievements on education enrolment, gender equity and equality, infant child and maternal mortality and morbidity and the provision of universal access to sexual and reproductive health services, including family planning and safe abortion services, remain mixed." The PACE called on European governments to "review, update and compare Council of Europe members states' national and international population and sexual and reproductive health and rights policies and strategies," as well as to review and compare funding to ensure the full implementation of the Programme of Action of the Cairo ICPD 1994 by 2015.

* * *

7. The Assembly invites the member states of the Council of Europe to:

7.1. decriminalise abortion within reasonable gestational limits, if they have not already done so;

7.2. guarantee women's effective exercise of their right of access to a safe and legal abortion;

7.3. allow women freedom of choice and offer the conditions for a free and enlightened choice without specifically promoting abortion;

7.4. lift restrictions which hinder, *de jure* or *de facto*, access to safe abortion, and, in particular, take the necessary steps to create the appropriate conditions for health, medical and psychological care and offer suitable financial cover ..."

4. *Report of the Commissioner for Human Rights on his visit to Ireland, 26–30 November 2007, adopted on 30 April 2008, CommDH(2008)9*

109. The Commissioner noted that there was still no legislation in place implementing the *X* judgment and, consequently, no legal certainty when a doctor might legally perform a life-saving abortion. He opined that, in practice, abortion was largely unavailable in Ireland in almost all circumstances. * * *

5. *Office of the High Commissioner for Human Rights, Committee on the Elimination of Discrimination Against Women ("CEDAW")* * * *

In the Committee's concluding comments, it responded as follows:

"396. While acknowledging positive developments ... the Committee reiterates its concern about the consequences of the very restrictive abortion laws, under which abortion is prohibited except where it is established as a matter of probability that there is a real and substantial risk to the life of the mother that can be averted only by the termination of her pregnancy." * * *

6. *The Human Rights Committee*

111. In the Committee's Concluding Comments on the third periodic Report of Ireland on observance of the UN Covenant on Civil and Political Rights (CCPR/C/IRL/CO/3 dated 30 July 2008), it noted:

"13. The Committee reiterates its concern regarding the highly restrictive circumstances under which women can lawfully have an abortion in the State party. While noting the establishment of the [CPA], the Committee regrets that the progress in this regard is slow...." * * *

7. *Laws on abortion in Contracting States*

112. Abortion is available on request (according to certain criteria including gestational limits) in some 30 Contracting States. An abortion justified on health grounds is available in some 40 Contracting States and justified on well-being grounds in some 35 such States. Three Contracting States prohibit abortion in all circumstances (Andorra, Malta and San Marino). In recent years, certain States have extended the grounds on which abortion can be obtained (Monaco, Montenegro, Portugal and Spain).

* * *

II. ALLEGED VIOLATION OF ARTICLE 8 OF THE CONVENTION

A. The observations of the applicants

168. The applicants maintained that Article 8 clearly applied to their complaints since the relevant restrictions on abortion interfered with the most intimate part of their family and private lives including their physical integrity. * * *

170. While they accepted that the abortion restrictions pursued the aim of protecting foetal life, they took issue with a number of related matters.

They considered that it had not been shown that the restrictions were effective in achieving that aim: the abortion rate for women in Ireland was similar to States where abortion was legal since, *inter alia*, Irish women chose to travel abroad for abortions in any event.

Even if they were effective, the applicants questioned how the State could maintain the legitimacy of that aim given the opposite moral viewpoint espoused by human rights bodies worldwide.

The applicants also suggested that the current prohibition on abortion in Ireland (protecting foetal life unless the life of the woman was at risk) no longer reflected the position of the Irish people, arguing that there was evidence of greater support for broader access to legal abortion. * * *

171. The applicants also maintained that the means chosen to achieve that aim was disproportionate.

172. While the State was entitled to a margin of appreciation to protect pre-natal life, it was not an absolute one. The Court could not give unqualified deference to the State's interest in protecting pre-natal life as that would allow a State to employ any means necessary to restrict abortion without any regard to the mother's life (*Open Door*, cited above, at §§ 68–69 and 73).... Preserving pre-natal life was an acceptable goal only when the health and well-being of the mother were given proportionate value (*Vo v. France* [GC], no. 53924/00, § 80, ECHR 2004–VIII and *Tysiąc v. Poland* judgment, § 113).

173. The restrictive nature of the legal regime in Ireland disproportionately harmed women. There was a medical risk due to a late, and therefore often surgical, abortion and an inevitable reduction in pre- and post-abortion medical support. The financial burden impacted more on poor women and, indirectly, on their families. Women experienced the stigma and psychological burden of doing something abroad which was a serious criminal offence in their own country.

The core Convention values necessitated that the State adopt alternative methods of protecting pre-natal life without criminalising necessary health care. Such methods existed and this was the approach favoured by human rights bodies (the Office of the Commissioner for Human Rights and the CEDAW). Instead of punitive criminal measures, State resources should be directed towards reproductive health and support. * * *

174. Moreover, the extent of the prohibition on abortion in Ireland stood in stark contrast to more flexible regimes for which there was a clear European and international consensus. This Court's case law had previously found reliance on consensus instructive in considering the scope of Convention rights, including the consensus amongst Contracting States and the provisions in specialised international instruments and evolving norms and principles of international law (*Opuz v. Turkey*, no. 33401/02, §§ 164 and 184, ECHR 2009– . . .; and *Christine Goodwin v. the United Kingdom* [GC], no. 28957/95, § 85, ECHR 2002–VI).

* * * In addition, the laws of the vast majority of the Contracting States also constituted strong evidence: 31 out of 47 States allowed abortion on request during the first trimester, 42 out of 47 States allowed abortion when the woman's health was at risk; and 32 out of 47 States expressly allowed the termination of pregnancy where there was a foetal abnormality. Ireland was in a small minority of 4 States that still enforced highly restrictive criminal abortion laws (with Malta, San Marino and Andorra). They further argued that the recent trend was towards further easing of restrictions on access to abortions including decriminalisation. * * *

177. The third applicant impugned the lack of a legal framework through which the relevant risk to her life and her entitlement to an abortion in Ireland could have been established which, she maintained, left her with no choice but to travel to England.

178. She underlined that Article 40.3.3, as interpreted by the *X* case, was a general provision. That provision did not define ''unborn'' and the *X* case did not define a real and substantial risk to life. A legal distinction, without more, between a woman's life and her health was also an unworkable distinction in practice. There were no legally binding and/or relevant professional guidelines and none of the professional bodies provided any clear guidance as to the precise steps to be taken or the criteria to be considered. Accordingly, none of her doctors could inform the third applicant of any official procedures to assist her. The doctors, who had treated her for cancer, were unable to offer her basic assistance as to the impact her pregnancy could have on her health. She stated that her own GP failed to advise her about abortion options and did not refer to the fact that she had been pregnant when she visited him several months later. This hesitancy on the part of doctors was explained by the chilling effect of a lack of clear legal procedures combined with the risk of serious criminal and professional sanctions. It was not a problem that could be reduced, as the Government suggested, to the dereliction by doctors of their duties. Accordingly, the normal medical consultation process relied on by the Government to establish an entitlement to a lawful abortion was simply insufficient given the lack of clarity as to what constitutes a ''real and substantial risk'' to life combined with the chilling effect of severe criminal sanctions for doctors whose assessment could be considered *ex post facto* to fall outside that qualifying risk. * * *

B. The observations of the Irish Government

180. The Government argued that the Convention organs had never held that Article 8 was engaged where States failed to provide for certain

types of abortion and any conclusion in that direction would raise serious issues for all Contracting States and, particularly for Ireland, where the prohibition was constitutionally enshrined. The Convention (*see* the *travaux préparatoires*) did not intend to make this Court the arbiter of the substantive law of abortion. The issue attracted strong opinions in Contracting States and was resolved by domestic decision-making often following extensive political debate. The protection accorded under Irish law to the right to life of the unborn was based on profound moral values deeply embedded in the fabric of society in Ireland and the legal position was defined through equally intense debate. * * *

181.   Even if Article 8 applied, the impugned restrictions satisfied the requirements of its second paragraph. In particular, Article 40.3.3, as interpreted in the *X* case, was a fundamental law of the State, was clear and foreseeable and pursued the legitimate aims of the protection of morals and the rights and freedoms of others including the protection of pre-natal life. * * *

183.   In any event, the Government disputed the applicants' suggestion that the current will of the Irish people was not reflected in the restrictions on abortion in Ireland: the opinion of the Irish people had been measured in referenda in 1983, 1992 and 2002. * * *

The Government also underlined that the impugned restrictions had led to a significant reduction in Irish women travelling to the United Kingdom for an abortion (6673 women in 2001 travelled and 4686 women did so in 2007) and to one of the lowest levels of maternal deaths in the European Union and they disputed the assertion of Doctors for Choice/ BPAS that the reduction in recent years in Irish women going to the United Kingdom for an abortion was explained by travel to other countries for an abortion, * * *

184.   Moreover, the impugned restrictions were proportionate.

185.   The protection accorded under Irish domestic law to the right to life of the unborn and the restrictions on lawful abortion in Ireland were based on profound moral and ethical values to which the Convention afforded a significant margin of appreciation. A broad margin was specifically accorded to determining what persons were protected by Article 2 of the Convention: the Court had conclusively answered in its judgments in *Vo v. France* and in *Evans v. the United Kingdom* ([GC], no. 6339/05, ECHR 2007–IV) that there was no European scientific or legal definition of the beginning of life so that the question of the legal protection of the right to life fell within the States' margin of appreciation. * * *

186.   As to the role of any consensus, the Government noted that it was not only the State's concern to protect pre-natal life that must to be factored into the balance but also the legitimate choice made, in the absence of any European consensus on when life begins, that the unborn was deserving of protection. The Government did not accept the contention that there was a European and/or international consensus in favour of greater access to abortion, including for social reasons: while in some countries, access to abortion was indeed broader, the conditions of access greatly varied * * *

In the first place, they maintained in response to a question from the Court [regarding the third applicant's claim], that the procedure for obtaining a lawful abortion in Ireland was clear. The decision was made, like any other major medical matter, by a patient in consultation with her doctor. On the rare occasion there was a possibility of a risk to the life of a woman, there was "a very clear and bright line rule provided by Irish law which is neither difficult to understand or to apply because it is the same law that has been applied under Section 58 of the 1861 Act, under Article 40.3.3 of the Irish Constitution and under the legislative provisions of every country which permits a pregnancy to be terminated on that ground." As to the precise procedures to be followed by a pregnant woman and her doctor where an issue arose as to such a possible risk, it was the responsibility of the doctor and a termination could occur when the risk was real and substantial. If the patient did not agree with that advice, she was free to seek another medical opinion and, in the last resort, she could make an emergency application to the High Court (as outlined above). The grounds for lawful abortion in Ireland were well known and applied. [. . .] While the Irish Institute of Obstetricians and Gynaecologists had no published guidelines concerning a pregnant woman presenting with life threatening conditions, that Institute would be in agreement with the Guidelines of the United Kingdom Royal College of Obstetricians and Gynaecologists concerning the management of ectopic pregnancies and it was probable that Irish gynaecologists would "by and large" follow the latter Guidelines with or without minor amendments or additions. * * *

* * *

E. The Court's assessment

1. Whether Article 8 applied to the applicants' complaints

212. The Court recalls that the notion of "private life" within the meaning of Article 8 of the Convention is a broad concept which encompasses, *inter alia*, the right to personal autonomy and personal development (*see Pretty v. the United Kingdom*, cited above, § 61). It concerns subjects such as gender identification, sexual orientation and sexual life (for example, *Dudgeon v. the United Kingdom*, judgment of 22 October 1981, Series A no. 45, pp. 18–19, § 41; and *Laskey, Jaggard and Brown v. the United Kingdom,* judgment of 19 February 1997, *Reports of Judgments and Decisions* 1997–I, p. 131, § 36), a person's physical and psychological integrity (*Tysiąc v. Poland* judgment, cited above, § 107) as well as decisions both to have and not to have a child or to become genetic parents (*Evans v. the United Kingdom* [GC], cited above, § 71).

213. The Court has also previously found, citing with approval the case-law of the former Commission, that legislation regulating the interruption of pregnancy touches upon the sphere of the private life of the woman, the Court emphasising that Article 8 cannot be interpreted as meaning that pregnancy and its termination pertain uniquely to the woman's private life as, whenever a woman is pregnant, her private life becomes closely connected with the developing foetus. The woman's right to respect for her private life must be weighed against other competing rights and freedoms invoked

including those of the unborn child (*Tysiąc v. Poland* judgment, cited above, § 106; and *Vo v. France* [GC], cited above, §§ 76, 80 and 82).

214.   While Article 8 cannot, accordingly, be interpreted as conferring a right to abortion, the Court finds that the prohibition in Ireland of abortion where sought for reasons of health and/or well-being about which the first and second applicants complained, and the third applicant's alleged inability to establish her qualification for a lawful abortion in Ireland, come within the scope of their right to respect for their private lives and accordingly Article 8. * * *

218.   To determine whether this interference entailed a violation of Article 8, the Court must examine whether or not it was justified under the second paragraph of that Article namely, whether the interference was "in accordance with the law" and "necessary in a democratic society" for one of the "legitimate aims" specified in Article 8 of the Convention. * * *

(c) Did the interference pursue a legitimate aim?

222.   The Court recalls that, in the *Open Door* case, it found that the protection afforded under Irish law to the right to life of the unborn was based on profound moral values concerning the nature of life which were reflected in the stance of the majority of the Irish people against abortion during the 1983 referendum. The impugned restriction in that case was found to pursue the legitimate aim of the protection of morals of which the protection in Ireland of the right to life of the unborn was one aspect. * * *

(e) Was the interference "necessary in a democratic society"?

229.   In this respect, the Court must examine whether there existed a pressing social need for the measure in question and, in particular, whether the interference was proportionate to the legitimate aim pursued, regard being had to the fair balance which has to be struck between the relevant competing interests in respect of which the State enjoys a margin of appreciation (*Open Door*, § 70; *Odièvre v. France* [GC], no. 42326/98, § 40, ECHR 2003–III; and *Evans v. the United Kingdom* [GC], § 75). * * *

232.   The Court recalls that a number of factors must be taken into account when determining the breadth of the margin of appreciation to be enjoyed by the State when determining any case under Article 8 of the Convention. Where a particularly important facet of an individual's existence or identity is at stake, the margin allowed to the State will normally be restricted (*see Evans v. the United Kingdom* [GC], cited above, § 77). Where, however, there is no consensus within the Member States of the Council of Europe, either as to the relative importance of the interest at stake or as to the best means of protecting it, particularly where the case raises sensitive moral or ethical issues, the margin will be wider (*Evans v. the United Kingdom* [GC], cited above, § 77; *X., Y. and Z. v. the United Kingdom*, judgment of 22 April 1997, *Reports of Judgments and Decisions 1997–II*, § 44; *Frette v. France*, no. 36515/97, § 41, ECHR 2002–I; *Christine Goodwin*, cited above, § 85). As noted above, by reason of their direct and continuous contact with the vital forces of their countries, the State authorities are, in principle, in a better position than the international judge to give an opinion, not only on the "exact content of the require-

ments of morals" in their country, but also on the necessity of a restriction intended to meet them (*Handyside v. the United Kingdom* judgment and the other references cited at paragraph 223 above).

233.   There can be no doubt as to the acute sensitivity of the moral and ethical issues raised by the question of abortion or as to the importance of the public interest at stake. A broad margin of appreciation is, therefore, in principle to be accorded to the Irish State in determining the question whether a fair balance was struck between the protection of that public interest. * * *

234.   However, the question remains whether this wide margin of appreciation is narrowed by the existence of a relevant consensus. * * *

235.   In the present case, and contrary to the Government's submission, the Court considers that there is indeed a consensus amongst a substantial majority of the Contracting States of the Council of Europe towards allowing abortion on broader grounds than accorded under Irish law. * * *

236.   However, the Court does not consider that this consensus decisively narrows the broad margin of appreciation of the State.

237.   * * * Since the rights claimed on behalf of the foetus and those of the mother are inextricably interconnected (*see* the review of the Convention case law at paragraphs 75–80 in the above-cited *Vo v. France* [GC] judgment), the margin of appreciation accorded to a State's protection of the unborn necessarily translates into a margin of appreciation for that State as to how it balances the conflicting rights of the mother. It follows that, even if it appears from the national laws referred to that most Contracting Parties may in their legislation have resolved those conflicting rights and interests in favour of greater legal access to abortion, this consensus cannot be a decisive factor in the Court's examination of whether the impugned prohibition on abortion in Ireland for health and well-being reasons struck a fair balance between the conflicting rights and interests, notwithstanding an evolutive interpretation of the Convention (*Tyrer v. the United Kingdom*, § 31; and *Vo v. France* [GC], § 82, both cited above). * * *

241.   Accordingly, having regard to the right to lawfully travel abroad for an abortion with access to appropriate information and medical care in Ireland, the Court does not consider that the prohibition in Ireland of abortion for health and well-being reasons, based as it is on the profound moral views of the Irish people as to the nature of life (paragraphs 222–227 above) and as to the consequent protection to be accorded to the right to life of the unborn, exceeds the margin of appreciation accorded in that respect to the Irish State. * * *

   3.   *The third applicant*

              * * *

   (a) Does her complaint fall to be examined under the positive or negative obligations of Article 8 of the Convention?

244. While the essential object of Article 8 is, as noted above, to protect individuals against arbitrary interference by public authorities, it may also impose on a State certain positive obligations to ensure effective respect for the rights protected by Article 8 (*see*, among other authorities, *X and Y v. the Netherlands*, judgment of 26 March 1985, Series A no. 91, § 23). * * *

246. Accordingly, the Court considers that the third applicant's complaint falls to be analysed under the positive aspect of Article 8. In particular, the question to the determined by the Court is whether there is a positive obligation on the State to provide an effective and accessible procedure allowing the third applicant to establish her entitlement to a lawful abortion in Ireland and thereby affording due respect to her interests safeguarded by Article 8 of the Convention.

(b) General principles applicable to assessing a State's positive obligations

247. The principles applicable to assessing a State's positive and negative obligations under the Convention are similar. Regard must be had to the fair balance that has to be struck between the competing interests of the individual and of the community as a whole, the aims in the second paragraph of Article 8 being of a certain relevance (*Gaskin v. the United Kingdom*, 7 July 1989, § 42, Series A no. 160; and *Roche v. the United Kingdom* [GC], cited above, § 157).

248. * * * [C]ertain factors have been considered relevant for the assessment of the content of those positive obligations on States. Some factors concern the applicant: the importance of the interest at stake and whether "fundamental values" or "essential aspects" of private life are in issue (*X and Y v. the Netherlands*, 26 March 1985, § 27, Series A no. 91; and *Gaskin v. the United Kingdom*, 7 July 1989, § 49, Series A no. 160); and the impact on an applicant of a discordance between the social reality and the law, the coherence of the administrative and legal practices within the domestic system being regarded as an important factor in the assessment carried out under Article 8 (*B. v. France*, 25 March 1992, § 63, Series A no. 232–C; and *Christine Goodwin v. the United Kingdom* [GC], cited above, §§ 77–78). Some factors concern the position of the State: whether the alleged obligation is narrow and defined or broad and indeterminate (*Botta v. Italy*, 24 February 1998, § 35, *Reports of Judgments and Decisions* 1998–I); and the extent of any burden the obligation would impose on the State (*Rees v. the United Kingdom*, 17 October 1986, §§ 43–44, Series A no. 106; *Christine Goodwin v. the United Kingdom* [GC], cited above, §§ 86–88).

* * *

(c) Application of the general principles to the third applicant's case

250. The third applicant had a rare form of cancer. When she discovered she was pregnant she feared for her life as she believed that her pregnancy increased the risk of her cancer returning and that she would not obtain treatment for that cancer in Ireland while pregnant (*see* paragraph 125 above). The Court considers that the establishment of any such

relevant risk to her life caused by her pregnancy clearly concerned funda-mental values and essential aspects of her right to respect for her private life (*X and Y v. the Netherlands*, 26 March 1985, cited above, § 27 and paragraph 248 above). Contrary to the Government's submissions, it is not necessary for the applicant to further substantiate the alleged medical risk, her complaint concerning as it did the absence of any effective domestic procedure for establishing that risk. * * *

253.   However, the Court has a number of concerns as to the effective-ness of this consultation procedure as a means of establishing the third applicant's qualification for a lawful abortion in Ireland.

It is first noted that the ground upon which a woman can seek a lawful abortion in Ireland is expressed in broad terms: Article 40.3.3, as interpret-ed by the Supreme Court in the *X* case, provides that an abortion is available in Ireland if it is established as a matter of probability that there is a real and substantial risk to the life, as distinct from the health, of the mother, including a risk of self harm, which can only be avoided by a termination of the pregnancy (the *X* case, cited at paragraphs 39–44 above). While a constitutional provision of this scope is not unusual, no criteria or procedures have been subsequently laid down in Irish law, whether in legislation, case law or otherwise, by which that risk is to be measured or determined, leading to uncertainty as to its precise application. Indeed, while this constitutional provision (as interpreted by the Supreme Court in the X case) qualified sections 58 and 59 of the earlier 1861 Act (*see* paragraph 145 above), those sections have never been amended so that, on their face, they remain in force with their absolute prohibition on abortion and associated serious criminal offences thereby contributing to the lack of certainty for a woman seeking a lawful abortion in Ireland.

Moreover, whether or not the broad right to a lawful abortion in Ireland for which Article 40.3.3 provides could be clarified by Irish profes-sional medical guidelines as suggested by the Government (and *see* the High Court judgment in *MR v. TR and Others*, at paragraph 97 above), the guidelines do not in any event provide any relevant precision as to the criteria by which a doctor is to assess that risk. [. . .]

Furthermore, there is no framework whereby any difference of opinion between the woman and her doctor or between different doctors consulted, or whereby an understandable hesitancy on the part of a woman or doctor, could be examined and resolved through a decision which would establish as a matter of law whether a particular case presented a qualifying risk to a woman's life such that a lawful abortion might be performed.

254.   Against this background of substantial uncertainty, the Court considers it evident that the criminal provisions of the 1861 Act would constitute a significant chilling factor for both women and doctors in the medical consultation process, regardless of whether or not prosecutions have in fact been pursued under that Act. Both the third applicant and any doctor ran a risk of a serious criminal conviction and imprisonment in the event that a decision taken in medical consultation, that the woman was entitled to an abortion in Ireland given the risk to her life, was later found not to accord with Article 40.3.3 of the Constitution. * * *

256. Secondly, the Government argued that her interests would be protected by the availability of judicial proceedings, submitting also that the third applicant had failed to exhaust domestic remedies, an argument which was joined to the merits of the present complaint (paragraph 155 above). * * *

258. The Court does not consider that the constitutional courts are the appropriate *fora* for the primary determination as to whether a woman qualifies for an abortion which is lawfully available in a State. In particular, this process would amount to requiring the constitutional courts to set down on a case by case basis the legal criteria by which the relevant risk to a woman's life would be measured and, further, to resolve through evidence, largely of a medical nature, whether a woman had established that qualifying risk.... The High Court in the "C" case (paragraphs 95–96 above) referred to the same issue more succinctly, finding that it would be wrong to turn the High Court into a "licensing authority" for abortions.

259. In addition, it would be equally inappropriate to require women to take on such complex constitutional proceedings when their underlying constitutional right to an abortion in the case of a qualifying risk to life was not disputable (the Green Paper 1999, paragraph 68 above). * * *

263. Consequently, the Court considers that neither the medical consultation nor litigation options relied on by the Government constituted effective and accessible procedures which allowed the third applicant to establish her right to a lawful abortion in Ireland. The Court is not, therefore, required to address the parties' additional submissions concerning the timing, speed, costs and confidentiality of such domestic proceedings. * * *

266. As to the burden which implementation of Article 40.3.3 would impose on the State, the Court accepts that this would be a sensitive and complex task. However, while it is not for this Court to indicate the most appropriate means for the State to comply with its positive obligations (*Marckx v. Belgium* judgment, § 58; *Airey v. Ireland* judgment, § 26; and *B. v. France*, § 63, all cited above), the Court notes that legislation in many Contracting States has specified the conditions governing access to a lawful abortion and put in place various implementing procedural and institutional procedures (*Tysiąc v. Poland* judgment, § 123). Equally, implementation could not be considered to involve significant detriment to the Irish public since it would amount to rendering effective a right already accorded, after referendum, by Article 40.3.3 of the Constitution.

(d) The Court's conclusion as regards the third applicant

* * *

268. Accordingly, the Court finds that there has been a violation of Article 8 of the Convention. * * *

JOINT PARTLY DISSENTING OPINION OF JUDGES ROZAKIS, TULKENS, FURA, HIRVELÄ, MALINVERNI AND POALELUNGI

2. * * * The issue before the Court was whether, regardless of when life begins—before birth or not—the right to life of the foetus can be balanced against the right to life of the mother, or her right to personal autonomy and development, and possibly found to weigh less than the

latter rights or interests. And the answer seems to be clear: there is an undeniably strong consensus among European States—and we will come back to this below—to the effect that, regardless of the answer to be given to the scientific, religious or philosophical question of the beginning of life, the right to life of the mother, and, in most countries' legislation, her well-being and health, are considered more valuable than the right to life of the foetus.

This seems to us a reasonable stance for European legislation and practice to take, given that the values protected—the rights of the foetus and the rights of a living person—are, by their nature, unequal: on the one hand there are the rights of a person already participating, in an active manner, in social interaction, and on the other hand there are the rights of a foetus within the mother's body, whose life has not been definitively determined as long as the process leading to the birth is not yet complete, and whose participation in social interaction has not even started. In Convention terms, it can also be argued that the rights enshrined in that text are mainly designed to protect individuals against State acts or omissions while the former participate actively in the normal everyday life of a democratic society.

Consequently, we believe that the majority erred when it inappropriately conflated in paragraph 237 of the judgment the question of the beginning of life (and as a consequence the right to life), and the States' margin of appreciation in this regard, with the margin of appreciation that States have in weighing the right to life of the foetus against the right to life of the mother or her right to health and well-being.

3. When we come to the proportionality test which the Court should properly apply in the circumstances of the case, there are two elements which should be taken into consideration and which weigh heavily in determining whether the interference with the private life of the two applicants was justified: the first is the existence of a European consensus in favour of allowing abortion; the second is the sanctions provided for by Irish law in cases of abortions performed for health or well-being reasons in breach of the prohibition on abortion in the territory of Ireland.

4. It emerges clearly from the material in our possession that there exists a consensus amongst a substantial majority of the Contracting States of the Council of Europe towards allowing abortion "on broader grounds than accorded under Irish law" (paragraph 235).... Only 3 States have more restrictive access to abortion services than in Ireland namely, a prohibition on abortion regardless of the risk to the woman's life". (ibid.).

5. According to the Convention case-law, in situations where the Court finds that a consensus exists among European States on a matter touching upon a human right, it usually concludes that that consensus decisively narrows the margin of appreciation which might otherwise exist if no such consensus were demonstrated. This approach is commensurate with the "harmonising" role of the Convention's case-law: indeed, one of the paramount functions of the case-law is to gradually create a harmonious application of human rights protection, cutting across the national boundaries of the Contracting States and allowing the individuals within their jurisdiction to enjoy, without discrimination, equal protection regardless of their place of residence. * * *

6. Yet in the case before us a European consensus (and, indeed, a strong one) exists. We believe that this will be one of the rare times in the Court's case-law that Strasbourg considers that such consensus does not narrow the broad margin of appreciation of the State concerned; the argument used is that the fact that the applicants had the right "to lawfully travel abroad for an abortion with access to appropriate information and medical care in Ireland" suffices to justify the prohibition of abortion in the country for health and well-being reasons, "based as it is on the profound moral views of the Irish people as to the nature of life" (paragraph 241 *in limine*).

7. We strongly disagree with this finding. Quite apart from the fact, as we have emphasised above, that such an approach shifts the focus of this case away from the core issue, which is the balancing of the right to life of the foetus against the right to health and well-being of the mother, and not the question of when life begins or the margin of appreciation afforded to States on the latter issue, the majority bases its reasoning on two disputable premises: first, that the fact that Irish law allows abortion for those who can travel abroad suffices to satisfy the requirements of the Convention concerning applicants' right to respect for their private life; and, second, that the fact that the Irish people have profound moral views as to the nature of life impacts on the European consensus and overrides it, allowing the State to enjoy a wide margin of appreciation.

8. On the first premise, the Court's argument seems to be circular. The applicants' complaints concern their inability to have an abortion in their country of residence and they consider, rightly, that travelling abroad to have an abortion is a process which is not only financially costly but also entails a number of practical difficulties well illustrated in their observations. Hence, the position taken by the Court on the matter does not truly address the real issue of unjustified interference in the applicants' private life as a result of the prohibition of abortion in Ireland.

9. As to the second premise, it is the first time that the Court has disregarded the existence of a European consensus on the basis of "profound moral views." Even assuming that these profound moral views are still well embedded in the conscience of the majority of Irish people, to consider that this can override the European consensus, which tends in a completely different direction, is a real and dangerous new departure in the Court's case-law. * * *

NOTES

1. *A, B and C v. Ireland* marks the extension of Ireland's exception to its total ban on abortion to a different set of circumstances. On the one hand, interpreting the health risks of cancer and suicide as circumstances that indicate a "substantial" threat to a pregnant woman's life reflects a narrow understanding of the "life" of the woman. On the other, in this narrow interpretation, both the ECtHR and Ireland's domestic courts had to explicitly engage the question of to what extent a community's morals should be reflected in the law, as well as how to gauge this community

sensibility. Where else in this chapter have we seen similar questions engaged? How does the ECtHR's engagement compare with these other instances?

2.   Has Irish law defined when "life" begins? Contrary to its disavowals, has EU law perhaps, also, settled on a definition of when life begins? U.S. jurisprudence on abortion contains similar disavowals, and yet, might we infer an implicit assumption that the law makes about when life begins? Do you agree or disagree with the idea that the law should not try to attempt a definition of life's beginning point? Why?

3.   For a thorough discussion of the ECtHR's decision and the emergence of a right to abortion in EU law, *see* Paolo Ronchi, *A, B and C v. Ireland: Europe's Roe v Wade still has to wait?*, LAW QUARTERLY REVIEW (forthcoming), 365–369.

4.   Following the Supreme Court's decision in the X case, but before an abortion could be arranged, X had a miscarriage. The rapist was subsequently convicted and sentenced to prison.

5.   The *C* case affirmed the X test, which permits an abortion if there is a substantial risk to the woman's life, and provided that the state could fund an abortion if necessary. Jason MacLeod argues that the Court in the C case "declared a rule without any democratic process. If proposed legislation mirrored the High Court's opinion, both the legislators and the electorate would contest it. Here, the Court declared policy, thus an action of judicial lawmaking." The Court in the *C* case expressly stated that it would not rely on changing public opinions regarding abortion to influence its decision. Should the general public and legislature's views on the issue have had a greater impact on the outcome of the case? *See* Jason MacLeod, *Abortion and Ireland's Supreme Court*, 14 November 2008, http://www.jasonmacleod.com/?page_id=60.

6.   The C case, which was decided in the European Court of Human Rights, applies not only Irish law to the facts of the case, but also international human rights conventions, specifically Article 8 of The Programme of Action of the Cairo ICPD. Examine the conflicts between Ireland's abortion laws and the mandates of the international laws discussed by the ECtHR. In what ways does Article 8 conflict with Ireland's laws on abortion, and how does the Court resolve these conflicts? Which set of laws should determine abortion policy in Ireland? Compare the ECtHR's discussion of international human rights treaties binding on Ireland with Colombia's ruling on abortion, *supra*.

E.   CHINA

The Constitution of the People's Republic of China
Adopted December 4, 1982
http://www.usconstitution.net/china.html

Article 4. **Minority rights**

All nationalities in the People's Republic of China are equal. The state protects the lawful rights and interests of the minority nationalities and upholds and develops a relationship of equality, unity and mutual assistance among all of China's nationalities. Discrimination against and oppression of any nationality are prohibited; any act which undermines the unity of the nationalities or instigates division is prohibited.

Article 25. **Family planning**

The state promotes family planning so that population growth may fit the plans for economic and social development.

Article 48. **Equal rights for women**

Women in the People's Republic of China enjoy equal rights with men in all spheres of life, political, economic, cultural, social, and family life.

The state protects the rights and interests of women, applies the principle of equal pay for equal work for men and women alike and trains and selects cadres from among women.

Article 49. **Protection of marriage and family**

Marriage, the family and mother and child are protected by the state.

Both husband and wife have the duty to practice family planning.

Parents have the duty to rear and educate their children who are minors, and children who have come of age have the duty to support and assist their parents.

Violation of the freedom of marriage is prohibited. Maltreatment of old people, women and children is prohibited.

1. LEGISLATION

In 1979, the Chinese government introduced what is known as the One Child Policy, a set of rules and regulations requiring a substantial segment of the population to have only one child per couple. Implementation of the policy has varied considerably from place to place, and China's central legislative body, the National People's Congress, struggled for two decades to draft and pass a national family planning law. The following, China's first Population and Family Planning Law, was finally enacted in September 2002.

————

Population and Family Planning Law of the People's Republic of China

http://www.gov.cn/english/laws/2005–10/11/content_75954.htm

Article 1 This Law is enacted, in accordance with the Constitution, for the purpose of bringing about a coordinated development between population on the one side and the economy, society, resources and environment on the other, promoting family planning, protecting the legitimate rights and interests of citizens, enhancing happiness of families, and contributing to prosperity of the nation and progress of the society.

* * *

Article 3 The population and family planning programs shall be combined with the efforts to offer more opportunities for women to receive education and get employed, improve their health and elevate their status.

* * *

Article 17 Citizens have the right to reproduction as well as the obligation to practise family planning according to law. Both husband and wife bear equal responsibility for family planning.

Article 18 The State maintains its current policy for reproduction, encouraging late marriage and childbearing and advocating one child per couple. Where the requirements specified by laws and regulations are met, plans for a second child, if requested, may be made. Specific measures in this regard shall be formulated by the people's congress or its standing committee of a province, autonomous region, or municipality directly under the Central Government.

Family planning shall also be introduced to the ethnic peoples. Specific measures in this regard shall be formulated by the people's congress or its standing committee of a province, autonomous region, or municipality directly under the Central Government.

Article 19 Family planning shall be practised chiefly by means of contraception.

The State creates conditions to ensure that individual citizens knowingly choose safe, effective, and appropriate contraceptive methods. Where birth control operations are performed, the recipients' safety shall be ensured.

Article 20 Couples of reproductive age shall conscientiously adopt contraceptive methods and accept technical services and guidance for family planning.

Incidence of unwanted pregnancies shall be prevented and reduced.

* * *

Article 22 Discrimination against and maltreatment of women who give birth to baby girls or who suffer from infertility are prohibited. Discrimination against, maltreatment, and abandonment of baby girls are prohibited.

* * *

Article 25 Citizens who marry late and delay childbearing may be entitled to longer nuptial and maternity leaves or other welfare benefits.

Article 26 In accordance with relevant State regulations, women shall enjoy special occupational protection and be entitled to assistance and subsidies during the period of pregnancy, delivery, and breast-feeding.

Citizens who undergo surgical operation for family planning shall enjoy leaves as specified by the State. Local people's governments may give them rewards.

* * *

Article 35 Use of ultrasonography or other techniques to identify fetal sex for non-medical purposes is strictly prohibited. Sex-selective pregnancy termination for non-medical purposes is strictly prohibited.

* * *

Article 41 Citizens who give birth to babies not in compliance with the provisions of Article 18 of this Law shall pay a social maintenance fee prescribed by law.

———

2.   EXAMPLE OF LOCAL REGULATIONS

Population and Family Planning Regulations for Ningxia Ethnic Autonomous Region

http://www.chinapop.gov.cn/zcfg/dffg/201003/t20100326_199567.html

Article 17 If both spouses are urban residents, or if one spouse is an urban resident and the other a rural resident, the couple can have only one child. But couples who fulfill one of the following conditions may apply to have a second child:

1) One or both spouses belong to an ethnic minority;

2) Both spouses are "only children" themselves;

3) Couples who were unable to conceive and lawfully adopted a child, but who subsequently conceive;

4) If the first child is certified as disabled and unable to grow up to be a normal member of the labor force, and when the couple is medically suitable for further reproduction; * * *

Article 25 In the following circumstances, approval will not be granted for further reproduction; where approval has been granted already, it will be rescinded by the issuing population and family planning agency; where another child has been born, the parents will be treated as unlawfully giving birth:

1) Forging medical certification of disabled children;

2) Termination of pregnancy that is not medically necessary and for the purpose of gender selection;

3) Abandonment of children;

4) Giving up of children for adoption;

5) Claiming the death of babies without proof thereof;

6) Intentionally causing the death or disabling of babies;

7) Other circumstances where further reproduction will not be permitted.

———

3.   HISTORY AND BACKGROUND OF THE POLICY

The Effect of China's One Child Policy After 25 Years

353 New Eng. J. Med. 1171, 1171–1172 (2005)

■ THERESE HESKETH, LI LU, and ZHU WEI XING

* * * In 1979, the Chinese government embarked on an ambitious program of market reform following the economic stagnation of the Cultur-

al Revolution. At the time, China was home to a quarter of the world's people, who were occupying just 7 percent of world's arable land. Two thirds of the population were under the age of 30 years, and the baby boomers of the 1950s and 1960s were entering their reproductive years. The government saw strict population containment as essential to economic reform and to an improvement in living standards. So the one-child family policy was introduced.

The policy consists of a set of regulations governing the approved size of Chinese families. These regulations include restrictions on family size, late marriage and childbearing, and the spacing of children (in cases in which second children are permitted). The State Family Planning Bureau sets the overall targets and policy direction. Family-planning committees at provincial and county levels devise local strategies for implementation. Despite its name, the one-child rule applies to a minority of the population; for urban residents and government employees, the policy is strictly enforced, with few exceptions. The exceptions include families in which the first child has a disability or both parents work in high-risk occupations (such as mining) or are themselves from one-child families (in some areas).

In rural areas, where approximately 70 percent of the people live, a second child is generally allowed after five years, but this provision sometimes applies only if the first child is a girl—a clear acknowledgment of the traditional preference for boys. A third child is allowed among some ethnic minorities and in remote, underpopulated areas. The policy is underpinned by a system of rewards and penalties, which are largely meted out at the discretion of local officials and hence vary widely. They include economic incentives for compliance and substantial fines, confiscation of belongings, and dismissal from work for noncompliance.

The policy depends on virtually universal access to contraception and abortion. A total of 87 percent of all married women use contraception; this statistic compares with about one third in most developing countries. There is heavy reliance on long-term contraception, with intrauterine devices and sterilizations together accounting for more than 90 percent of contraceptive methods used since the mid–1980s. The number of sterilizations has declined since the peak in the early 1990s. For the majority of women, no choice in contraception is offered; 80 percent of women in a recent large study said they had no choice and just accepted the method recommended by the family-planning worker. The use of these long-term methods keeps abortion rates relatively low, with 25 percent of women of reproductive age having had at least one abortion, as compared with 43 percent in the United States. The main reasons given for abortion are contraceptive failure and a lack of government approval for the pregnancy under the one-child policy. Women who proceed with an unapproved pregnancy are known to be reluctant to use antenatal and obstetric services because they fear they will face pressure to have an abortion or fines for violating the one-child policy. Many deliveries of babies that have not been officially sanctioned occur at home without trained personnel, a practice that is associated with the risk of maternal or neonatal mortality. A study carried out in rural Sichuan province in 1990 reported a doubling of maternal deaths for unapproved pregnancies as compared with those receiving government sanction. * * *

————

China's Local and National Fertility Policies at the End of the Twentieth Century

33 Population & Development Review 129, 130, 132–133 (2007)

■ GU BAOCHANG, WANG FENG, GUO ZHIGANG, and ZHANG ERLI

Since the early days of the one-child policy, its implementation has varied from one locale to another, often down to the level of rural villages.... When China's first [national] Population and Family Planning Law was finally enacted in September 2002, it "advocated," rather than "required," that each couple have only one child. Modifications to the state policy of population control have been left to each province, under the general principle of slowing down population growth and encouraging only one child per couple. * * *

Fertility policy: A look at provincial birth control regulations

The localized nature of China's fertility policy can be seen in the birth control regulations designed by each of China's provinces. Throughout the 1990s, under the general guidelines of and with the permission of the national birth control agency, China's State Family Planning Commission (now renamed the National Population and Family Planning Commission), provinces revised their own regulations on the number of children a couple could have and the conditions under which exceptions could be made to the one-child-per couple rule. These regulations were drafted by provincial Family Planning Commissions and discussed in and adopted by the provincial People's Congresses. After adoption by the provincial People's Congresses, these birth control regulations were published in local newspapers and, more recently, on websites. Altogether, these regulations contain more than 100 articles concerning the allowable number of children and criteria for exemptions. From this large list of articles, we identify 22 unique exemptions for allowing a second child. [...] The large number of exemptions contained in the provincial-level birth control regulations reflects considerations of rationales for and feasibility of implementation. These exemptions can be grouped into four broad categories, from the most general to the most specific.

1) *Gender-based/demographic.* Exemptions under this category include rural couples with only one daughter, as well as exemptions conferred on individuals who are only children themselves. Allowing a second birth when the first child is a girl has created the broadest category of exemptions to the one-child rule in most parts of rural China. But it has to some extent contributed to increasing the sex ratio at birth in recent decades, caused mostly by sex-selective induced abortion.

2) *Economic*. These exemptions recognize the need for family labor or encourage participation in certain risky occupations. Exemptions in the latter category include miners who work underground, fishermen, farmers in mountainous or poor areas, and those deemed to have economic difficulties. Concern with rural/urban differences is the most important factor prompting such exemptions.

3) *Political/ethnic/social*. Exemptions are granted to persons who belong to an ethnic minority population group, those in a uxorilocal marriage (a man marrying into a woman's family, but only one son per family is allowed), returning overseas Chinese, and persons with the status of being the single child of a revolutionary martyr.

4) *Entitlement/replacement*. Couples are allowed to have a second child if their first child has died or is physically handicapped. Pregnancy and childbirth is also allowed after adopting a child following an initial diagnosis of infertility (such a condition requires a five-year observation following marriage and a medical certificate from a city or a higher-level hospital), as is childbearing in a remarriage (for those divorced or widowed). Being the only second son in a family of multiple children (in a rural setting) also falls into this category.

According to the fertility policies in effect at the provincial level, the 31 mainland Chinese provincial-level administrative regions can be classified as follows. First, there is an urban-rural differentiation. For Chinese with an urban (nonagricultural) household registration status, one child per couple is the rule. Second, for the majority of the Chinese population with rural or agricultural household registration status, provincial-level fertility policy can be grouped into three categories: 1) One-child policy; in six provinces, [. . .] almost all residents are expected to follow the one-child-per-couple policy. 2) "1.5–children" policy; in 19 provinces, rural residents are allowed to have a second child after a specified birth interval if the first birth is a girl. 3) Two-children policy; in five provinces, [. . .] all rural couples are allowed to have two children. In provinces that require a one-child or a 1.5–children policy, married couples who are only children themselves can have more than one child. . . . * * *

---

4. SEX DISCRIMINATION

Sex discrimination in China, particularly in the form of the deep-rooted traditional preference for sons, has been exacerbated by the one child policy. This is evident in the severe sex ratio imbalance in the country's population. As one study has found:

"The highest sex ratios are seen in countries with a combination of preference for sons, easy access to sex selective technology, and a low fertility rate, as births of girls must be prevented to allow for the desired number of sons within the family size. In the era of the one child policy the fact that the problem of excess males in China seems to outstrip that of all other countries is perhaps no surprise." *See* Wei Xing Zhu et al., *China's*

Excess Males, Sex Selective Abortion, and One Child Policy: Analysis of Data from 2005 National Intercensus Survey, 338 Brit. Med. J. 1211 (2009).

The Chinese Academy of Social Sciences predicted in 2010 that by 2020, there would be 24 million excess males of reproductive age. The study also warned that the worsening sex ratio could exacerbate social problems, especially sex trafficking, abduction of women, and prostitution. (Chinese Academy of Social Sciences, *Blue Book of China's Society: Analysis and Forecast* (2010), relevant section summarized at http://www.worldjournal.com/view/full_china/8619816/article-% E7% 94% B7% E5% A5% B3% E5% A4% B1% E8% A1% A1–10% E5% B9% B4% E   5% BE% 8C-% E5% 85% 89% E6% A3% 8D2400% E8% 90% AC% E4% BA% BA?instance=china2).   The urgency of the situation has been increasingly recognized, and a number of measures taken to correct the sex ratio imbalance.

————

5. ANTI-DISCRIMINATION MEASURES

Prohibition of Medically Unnecessary Procedures to Identify Fetal Sex, and of Gender–Selective Artificial Termination of Pregnancy

Translated regulation issued by the Eighth Department of the National Population and Family Planning Committee, http://www.gov.cn/banshi/2005–10/24/content_82759.htm (last accessed June 2010)

Article 1 This regulation is issued in order to implement the National Population and Family Planning Law, and to maintain the sex ratio at birth within the normal range. . . . * * *

Article 3 Medically unnecessary procedures to identify fetal sex, and gender-selective artificial termination of pregnancy are prohibited. Except as otherwise provided by law, no institution or individual may conduct procedures to identify the sex of fetuses or to artificially terminate pregnancy. * * *

Article 7 If a woman more than 14 weeks into her pregnancy wishes to have a medically unnecessary abortion, she must first obtain permission and relevant certification from the appropriate local government and family planning agency.

Those who willfully terminate their pregnancy for non-medical reasons without permission will be subject to disciplinary action by the local family planning agency. No permission to have another child will be granted until the facts are ascertained. * * *

Article 14 When a newborn infant dies in a medical facility, the facility must provide a certificate of death, and report the death to the local family planning agency. . . . When a newborn infant dies outside a medical facility, its parents must report to the appropriate governmental and family planning agency within 48 hours; the appropriate agency must verify the circumstances of the death. * * *

Article 20 This regulation will go into effect as of January 1, 2003.

The "Caring for Girls" Project

In 2003, China's National Population and Family Planning Committee ("Committee") launched the "Caring for Girls" project in order to safeguard the right to life of female fetuses and right to survival of female infants, and to address the severe sex ratio imbalance in the population. The project is an annual propaganda campaign to enforce the notion of gender equality, and to promote awareness of the illegality of actions such as gender-selective abortion. The following are excerpts of the Committee's agenda.

The Main Contents of the "Caring for Girls" Campaign

Translated from the Committee's website: http://www.chinapop.gov.cn/rdzt/ganhxd/gddt/200403/t20040302_138437.html (last accessed June 2010)

1) The Liberation of Women and Gender Equality

After the foundation of the People's Republic, the Party and the Government established a series of laws, regulations and policies aimed at the liberation of women and the attainment of gender equality.... Family planning is an essential step in achieving this goal.

First, family planning liberates women from the inferior position of a household servant whose whole life is taken up by frequent pregnancies, bringing up numerous children, housework and taking care of the elderly. This gives women the time and opportunity to acquire education and skills, and allows them to participate in the labor force and in mainstream social and cultural life.

Second, late marriage and birth, with fewer births, allow couples who participate in family planning to conserve their economic resources and achieve better quality of life.

Third, the women's liberation movement has weakened the tradition in rural areas whereby a woman moves into her husband's family after marriage ... and strengthened the woman's equal right to inherit from her husband's family. * * *

2) Protecting the Legal Rights of Women and Children

Our government has always viewed as highly important the safeguard of the legal rights of women and children. This is demonstrated in the Constitution, in national legislation, and in local regulations.

Article 48 of the Constitution provides: "Women in the People's Republic of China enjoy equal rights with men in all spheres of life, including in political, economic, cultural, social, and family life. The state protects the rights and interests of women."

Article 49 of the Constitution provides: "The institutions of marriage and family, and the mother and her children are protected by the state...."

Many laws, executive legislation, provincial regulations, family planning agency regulations and local government policies include special provisions to safeguard the rights of women and children. These include the Civil Code, the Labor Code, the Education Code, the Marriage Code, the Population and Family Planning Law ... the Resolution of the National People's Congress Concerning the Severe Punishment of Criminals who Abduct and Traffic Women and Children. ...

The Population and Family Planning Law ... Article 22, provides: Discrimination against and maltreatment of women who give birth to baby girls or who suffer from infertility are prohibited. Discrimination against, maltreatment, and abandonment of baby girls are prohibited. It is essential to achieve greater public awareness and knowledge of laws concerning the rights of women and children ... and to increase the strength of enforcement of these laws, and to severely punish illegal and criminal activities that violate these rights.

3) Promoting the Modern Reproductive Attitude that Daughters are as good as Sons

It is a relic of thousands of years of feudal society that men are superior to women and that wives must move into and become a member of their husbands' families. In rural areas, the notion of the inferiority of women and the traditional preference for sons are still widespread. This has a negative effect on the education of children, the choice of residence after marriage, the choice of gender in giving birth.... To firmly establish the attitude that daughters are just as desirable as sons requires persistent, difficult and long-term efforts, as well as outside factors such as the development of society and culture.

Our country has many structural and legislative tools to promote gender equality:

First, the Constitution expressly provides that men and women have equal rights.... Third, our country has a system of nine years of compulsory education for all children, guaranteeing the equal right of girls to education.... Fourth, our laws guarantee that daughters and sons have equal rights to inheritance ... * * *

6) Severe Punishment of Female Infanticide, Abandonment of Female Infants, and Sex–Selective Abortions

Our laws strictly prohibit the discrimination and maltreatment of infertile women and women who give birth to girls. Discrimination against, maltreatment and abandonment of female infants is strictly prohibited. In serious abandonment cases, offending persons are subject to a maximum of five years in prison. Those guilty of infanticide are treated as guilty of intentional murder, subject to the death penalty, life in prison, or imprisonment of a minimum of ten years....

Sex identification of fetuses and sex-selective abortion are strictly prohibited. The Population and Family Planning Law provides that family planning should be conducted chiefly through contraception.... Identification of the sex of the fetus through ultrasound and other medically unnecessary procedures is strictly prohibited.

———

The "Caring for Girls" Project: Social Background and Implications for Public Administration

Translated Research Paper of the China Population and Development Research Center http://www.cpdrc.org.cn/yjwx/yjwx_detail.asp?id=4245 (last accessed June 2010)

■ JIANG XIANGQUN et al.

The "caring for girls" project is aimed at eradicating the traditional preference for boys, eliminating gender discrimination, and especially at eliminating the discrimination against female infants in some areas, in order to achieve the goal of equality between the sexes in society. As an essential task of public administration, the project also shows our government's dedication to solving the problems of population development and management.

1. The Social Background of the "Caring for Girls" Project

With the development of society and civilization, great progress has been made towards equality between the sexes, as can be seen in the legal recognition of gender equality in many countries, and in our country's fundamental policy that gender equality is essential for social progress. However, there is still a great distance between equality in law and equality in fact. In reality, there are still inequalities between men and women in our country, such as in the areas of marriage, reproduction, education, employment, social security, allocation of benefits, and women's position in the family and in society.

What is the cause for the long-term existence of the problem of discrimination against women? The author believes that it is partly because we have too long focused only on adult women, and neglected the problem of discrimination against girls and female infants. The study of women has not included girls in its scope, while research on children has often not distinguished between boys and girls. Yet since girls are both children and females, they have to bear double the negative effects of powerlessness and discrimination.

The upbringing and quality of girls have an impact on the progress of society, and we must pay special attention to the problem of discrimination against girls. . . . The current gender inequality manifests itself mainly in three aspects: political power, skills, and opportunity. Of these, the disparity in skills is the most easy to solve, since there is no difference between the aptitude of girls and boys as infants. The disparity in skills between males and females arise later, from environmental factors and conditioning. The key to good conditioning is during infancy, childhood and adolescence, and the availability of good healthcare and education is essential. * * *

3. Legal and structural guarantees are the fundamental solution to the problem of discrimination against girls

* * * In order to solve the problem of discrimination against girls, we must address the overall problem of discrimination against the female gender in society. This is a long-term social development goal. Our direct goal is to elevate the social status and quality of life of girls and female infants; our deeper aim is inextricably related to population control and family planning.

From a public administration perspective, it is urgent that this problem be addressed through legislative and structural channels, including addressing gender inequality and gender-based poverty through public policy and social security.

First, we must enforce the notion of equality of genders throughout society, and improve the social status and treatment of women.

Second, we must target elementary education in rural areas and enforce the notion of gender equality by teaching it to children. We must strengthen the indoctrination of gender equality especially in rural areas where the traditional preference for boys is deep-seated. In addition, there must be legal protection for the right of girls to receive education, especially in extremely poor rural areas.

Third, we must use the public media in order to convey the message of the "caring for girls" project.

The "caring for girls" project is an extension of the women's liberation movement, and is crucial for the security and balance of our country's population, as well as the protection of women's legal rights.... It requires the collaboration of different governmental departments as well as NGOs.

————

NOTES

1. Although the right to procreation is not mentioned in China's Constitution, Article 17 of the Population and Family Planning Law does state that "citizens have the right to reproduction." The duty to practice family planning, however, is mentioned in the Constitution (Articles 25 and 49). The implication, then, is that the individual right to reproduce is trumped by the state's interest in shaping population growth to "fit the plans for economic and social development." How does this state interest in restricting population growth compare with the state interest articulated by Ireland in protecting unborn life? Are these two interests two sides of the same coin—alternate articulations of a state's general duty to regulate the size of its national population given its economic resources, cultural commitments and political aspirations?

2. Although Article 4 of the Constitution provides that all nationalities in China are equal and that discrimination against any nationality is prohibited, the population planning policies favor ethnic minorities—*i.e.* ethnicities other than the Han majority. It is a well-established exemption that couples belonging to ethnic minorities may have more than one child. How would you expect this policy to fare in the U.S., under the Equal Protection Clause of the Fourteenth Amendment? Would it be subject to an

"affirmative action" exception? (Could U.S. law permit anything like a "one child" policy?)

3.   In assessing the one child policy, Penny Kane and Ching Y. Choi argue that the "main criticism of the policy, though, is undoubtedly its stimulus to sex discrimination. Faced with hard choices about overall numbers, the Chinese girl child has once again become expendable. Too many girls, if not aborted, face orphanages or second class lives concealed from the world and with reduced chances of schooling and health care. China has one of the world's highest rates of suicide of women in the reproductive years. Increased pressure to produce the desired child, and a perceived reduction in the value of females, can only have exacerbated the problems of rural women. At the same time, the successes of the policy should not be underrated. In the context of rising costs and rising aspirations throughout China, there is increasing recognition among the four fifths of the population that is rural of the burden to the family of having a third child, and some are even willing to avoid a second. Moreover, since its inception reductions in Chinese fertility have reduced the country's (and the world's) population growth by some 250 million. These reductions in fertility have eased at least some of the pressures on communities, state, and the environment in a country which still carries one fifth of the world's people." Penny Kane and Ching Y. Choi, *China's One Child Family Policy*, 319 Brit. Med. J. 922 (1999).

4.   Although the overarching aim of the policy is population control, one of the main justifications for the policy advanced by the Chinese government mirrors the sex equality arguments for abortion rights (*supra* United States, note 2, Siegel). Article 3 of the Population and Family Planning Law provides that the policy should be combined with efforts to offer more opportunities for women to receive education, better employment, improved health and elevated status. Much of the government's rationale also ties the family planning law to the women's liberation movement, and the effort to achieve gender equality in society. Might we read China's policies as a type of standardization and codification of the choice argument used in other countries to provide women with more control over their lives to achieve social-economic equality with men? Does it matter that women in China exercise their reproductive rights to fulfill a preference for male children—a preference likely borne of a history of patriarchy? In comparing "choice" in these two contexts, is choice in fact freely available in one, and absolutely impossible in another? Or do the laws and policies across these contexts suggest a more complicated relationship between equality and reproductive rights?

F.   Abortion Law Globally

According to the United Nations Population Division, the overwhelming majority of countries—97 percent—permit abortion to save the woman's life. In five countries, Chile, El Salvador, Nicaragua, Malta and Vatican City, abortion is not permitted for any reason. In countries where some form of abortion is legal, a total of seven grounds on which abortion is permitted are identified: (1) to save the woman's life; (2) to preserve physical health; (3) to preserve mental health; (4) in case of rape or incest; (5) for fetal impairment; (6) for economic or social reasons and (7) on request.

The following chart summarizes the percentage of countries that allow abortion for the various different reasons. *See*, United Nations Department of Economic and Social Affairs, Population Division, *World Abortion Policies 2007*, available at: http://www.un.org/esa/population/publications/2007_Abortion_Policies_Chart/2007_WallChart.pdf.

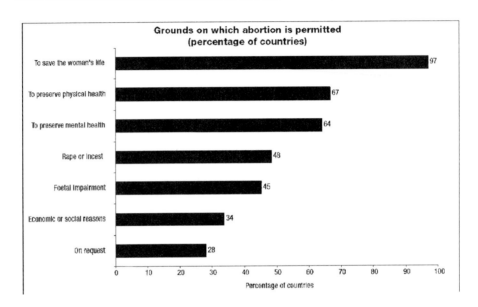

Abortion laws and policies are significantly more restrictive in the developing world. In developed countries, abortion is permitted for economic or social reasons in 78 percent of countries and on request in 67 percent of countries. In contrast, 19 percent of developing countries permit abortion for economic or social reasons, while in 15 percent of developing countries abortion is available on request. Many countries have additional procedural requirements that must be met before an abortion may be legally performed. Additional requirements may relate to the gestational limits within which abortion may be performed, mandatory waiting period, parental or spousal consent, third-party authorization, the categories of health providers permitted to perform abortions, the types of medical facilities where abortions may be performed and mandatory counseling. In addition, even when abortion is legally permitted, access to abortion services may be limited.

International law has ruled on abortion in certain instances. In their 2005 decision, *Karen Noelia Llantoy Huaman v. Peru*, the United Nations Human Rights Committee found that Peru had violated Article 17 of the "Optional Protocol to the International Covenant on Civil and Political Rights," which prohibits arbitrary or unlawful interference with privacy by denying a woman an abortion to which she was legally entitled under Peruvian law. *See*, R.J. Cook, J.N. Erdman & B.M. Dickens, *Achieving*

Transparency in Implementing Abortion Laws, in INTERNATIONAL JOURNAL OF GYNECOLOGY AND OBSTETRICS (2007) 99, 157–161.

————

NOTES

1. The Chilean abortion law is one of the most restrictive in the world—all forms of abortion are deemed criminal, without exception. The current laws against abortion are codified in the Penal Code, Articles 342–345, under the title "Crimes and Offences against Family Order, Public Morality and Sexual Integrity." The law punishes those seeking abortions with 3–5 years in jail, as well as those providing abortions with 541 days–3 years in jail. (http://www.leychile.cl/Navegar?idNorma=1984).

Furthermore, the life of the fetus is constitutionally protected, where the Chilean Constitution, Article 19–1, provides that "the law protects the life of those about to be born." (http://www.leychile.cl/Navegar?idNorma= 242302) Various United Nations agencies, including the committee monitoring compliance with the International Covenant on Economic, Social and Cultural Rights (CESCR), and the Human Rights Council, have expressed concern over the restrictiveness of Chile's abortion laws. Many abortion-related bills have been submitted to its Congress for discussion, and some are currently under review.

2. In Indonesia, under Fatwa MUI No. 4/2005, abortion is *haram*, forbidden by God, except for the following reasons:

1. Pregnant woman has a severe physical illness, like advanced stage of cancer or tuberculosis, which should be decided by a team of doctors.

2. In cases where pregnancy is dangerous for the life of the pregnant woman.

3. Where the embryo or fetus has a genetic disadvantage or illness that is difficult to cure.

4. Where the pregnancy is the result of rape. Whether rape occurred is decided by a team with special authority, including the victim's family, doctors, and Muslim ulama.

The Fatwa, however, is not legally binding but a religious guideline. Under the Indonesian Penal Code and Law No.23/1992 on Health, abortion is punished as a crime except "with the purpose of saving the life of a pregnant woman." There are no legal exceptions for rape, fetal impairment, or physical illness.

Indonesia is a heavily Muslim country, and its views on abortion are thus influenced by the teachings of Islam. Most Islamic scholars agree that abortions are allowed before the soul enters the fetus, although different Muslim leaders disagree as to when precisely this takes place. A survey showed that perceptions of Muslim thought on abortion are similar to those of other religions like Catholicism or other forms of Christianity in Indonesia. Most religious leaders believe that a woman's life is more important that the fetus's life, because she is needed to take care of her children and family. *See* Erlangga Agustino Landiyanto, *Abortion Policy in Indonesia: Rights, Law and Religious Perspectives* (April 2, 2010), available at http://ssrn.com/abstract=1583403.

3. In the Tamil Nadu province of India, the practice of female infanticide was so prevalent—one estimate put it at 3,000 female infant deaths per year—that the government launched the Cradle Baby Scheme in 1992, following continued efforts of NGOs and the media. Instead of resorting to female infanticide, parents who were unwilling to bring up their female babies could place them anonymously in cradles located at health centres, selected orphanages and NGOs, where they would be cared for and placed for adoption. The scheme at first had little success, but saw a sharp increase from the turn of the century: between May 2001 and November 2007, 2,410 baby girls had been received. As of March 2009, the figure stood at 3,418 babies (486 male and 2,932 female).

Although the scheme has had some success in reducing female infanticide, it has been criticized by NGOs and activists because it encourages son preference, and absolves parents of their responsibility towards their daughters. Women can continue to 'dump baby girls in the cradles' until they have the desired number of sons. The Campaign against Sex Selective Abortion rejects the scheme, arguing that it violates articles 7 and 9 of the UN Convention on the Rights of the Child, which deal with the child's right to be cared for by her biological parents. Supporters of the scheme counter these criticisms by arguing that handing over babies is a more humane option than murder. Yet among local people, the scheme is unpopular precisely because of the belief that 'we may give (children) to *Yama* (the Hindu God of death) but none to others (in adoption).' *See* Sharada Srinivasan and Arjun Bedi, *Daughter Elimination and the Cradle Baby Scheme in Tamil Nadu* (March 1, 2010), available at http://ssrn.com/abstract=1610144.

4. According to a 2007 study by the Population Reference Bureau, Israel has one of the highest fertility rates in the world. "[T]he fertility rate was 2.9 in Israel, whereas in Northern America it was 2.0 and only 1.5 in Europe. To illustrate, the fertility rate in Israel was also higher than the average fertility rates in Latin America (2.3), Central America (2.5), South America (2.2), and Asia (2.3)." This high fertility rate is an effect of both religious tradition and national policy. The Jewish faith contains a biblical commandment to "be fruitful and multiply" accompanied by matriarchal figures with strong desires for children. Additionally, the historical memory of the Holocaust and resettlement, with national concerns about sustaining a demographic presence in the Middle East has created a culture that views reproduction as a form of patriotism.

Israeli law and public policy thus protects the right to pursue in vitro fertilization (IVF). The Supreme Court of Israel in its 1996 landmark decision, *Nachmani v. Nachmani*, recognized parenthood as a right. And District Courts have found such a right under the Human Dignity and Liberty Basic Act. As well, the Women's Labor Act protects the right of men and women to miss work for fertility treatment. And finally, Israeli case law has ruled that fertility clinics have an obligation to protect frozen eggs from damage during their storage. *See* Daniel Sperling, *Commanding the "Be Fruitful and Multiply" Directive: Reproductive Ethics, Law and Policy in Israel*, 1 CAMBRIDGE QUARTERLY OF HEALTHCARE ETHICS, Vol. 19, pp. 363–371 (2010).

———

CHAPTER VII

EQUALITY & RELIGION: SECULARISM AND ESTABLISHMENT

INTRODUCTION

One of the vexing problems of equality around the globe is the status of members of minority religious groups. For Christians in China, Hindus in Pakistan, Muslims and Jews in Europe, Sikhs in North America, Catholics in Northern Ireland, Baha'i in Iran, and non-believers nearly anywhere, their position as members of a religious minority group often endangers their ability to live their lives with the same rights and privileges as their neighbors. Most of the horrific instances of mass murder in the past century can be traced, at least in part, to a religious majority's intolerance of a religious minority.

In much of the world the response to religious oppression, strife and inequality has been the establishment of the principle of secularism—the separation of church and state. In the United States, secularism has two elements, each guaranteed under the First Amendment. The first is the non-establishment of a state religion; the second is the freedom to exercise one's religion without interference from the state. Other nations have different approaches. For example, in England there is a state religion—the Church of England (or Anglicanism), but members of religious minorities are entitled to practice their religion without state interference. The same is true in Denmark, where the state religion is Lutheranism. By contrast, China is secular, in that there is no state religion, but the practice of religion is largely prohibited or circumscribed. In Germany, some spheres of life are secular, while others are regarded as requiring respect for religion; German law distinguishes between "positive" and "negative" religious freedom. Under the German Basic Law, positive religious freedom is the right to freely exercise one's religion, while negative religious freedom is the right to be free of any religion. Positive freedom, then, is comparable to the U.S. concept of free exercise, while negative freedom is comparable to at least part of the U.S. concept of non-establishment (if with a different balance).

This chapter and the chapter that follows adopt the U.S. paradigm to compare the equality rights of religious minorities within these two contexts of secularism: establishment and free exercise. Some people think equality is furthered by separation of church and state, while others think that separation leads to inequality for religious people. In this chapter, which addresses establishment, we consider the question of whether the state may provide support to a religion without violating principles of equality. As with affirmative action (Chapter IV), these problems often arise in the context of education. For example, may a state help support private religious schools? (And, to take up the potential conflict between these two principles of secularism, is it discrimination against persons of faith if the state declines to support private religious schools?) Or, may a state require prayer in the public schools, or the display of a religious symbol in public school classrooms?

Another area of life where establishment problems arise is the state's regulation of marriage, which we addressed in part in Chapter V. For example, should there be a separation between civil marriage and religious marriage? Should a state enforce religious law in regulating marriage? A third is the right of women to control reproduction, as discussed in Chapter VI. As we have seen, when a state is closely tied to a religion that calls for regulation over women's reproductive choices, the religious directive is often adopted as the law of the state. Are secular states thus more likely to guarantee equal rights to reproductive choice?

PROBLEMS

After an opening essay on the different forms of church-state relations by Winfried Brugger, we examine how these problems are addressed in the United States, France, Germany, and Mexico. Before you read these materials, ask yourself the following questions:

- Who owns the great cathedrals of France?

- Who determines the salary of a rabbi in Germany?

- Is the mandatory display of a cross in a public school classroom consistent with a guarantee of freedom of religion?

- Who appoints the Roman Catholic Archbishop of Alsace?

- If a town provides free school bus service for students attending its public schools, may it also provide the service without charge to students attending religious schools? If so, may it buy buses for the schools instead?

- In Britain, must state-supported schools provide an act of Christian collective worship each day?

You may be surprised by some of the answers.

Then, in the following chapter, we compare how the equality right of free exercise of religion is enforced. We again examine the United States and France, and also consider Great Britain, Canada, India, and Turkey, a secular state ruled by a religious political party. There, again, we focus on the problem of enforcing equality rights for religious minorities in the setting of public schools.

————

On the Relationship between Structural Norms and Constitutional Rights in Church–State–Relations

In *Religion in the Public Sphere: A Comparative Analysis of German, Israeli, American and International Law* (eds. Winfried Brugger & Michael Karayanni, 2007), pp. 31–48, (citations omitted)

■ WINFRIED BRUGGER

* * *

III.   Six Models on the Relationship between Church and State

Six Models of State–Church Relationships

1. Aggressive Animosity between State and Church	2. Strict Separation in Theory and Practice	3. Strict Separation in Theory, Accommodation in Practice	4. Division and Cooperation	5. Formal Unity of Church & State, with Substantive Division	6. - Formal and Substantive Unity of Church and State

1.   Animosity between Church and State

The political regime of a country may have an anti-religious attitude in its official ideology, constitution or political practice. It may force religions and churches to go underground or perhaps attempt to eliminate them altogether. For example, the communists in Albania were fiercely against religion. Article 37 of the 1976 Constitution stated: "The state recognizes no religion of any kind and supports and develops the atheistic view so as to ingrain in the people the scientific and materialistic world-view." A hostile attitude toward religion was dominant in most communist governments before the collapse of the Soviet Union at the end of the 1980s. This is hardly surprising when one considers that Karl Marx in his 1844 criticism of Hegel's legal philosophy referred to religion as the opium of the people. Animosity toward religion is not, however, limited to Marxist–Leninist ideology and practice.

Time and time again anti-clerical political and intellectual efforts have been mounted advocating against the influence of religious representatives in state affairs in general as well as against church attempts to claim dominance in particular. France is often cited as an example. This variant of hostility, though, is different from aggressive Marxism–Leninism. Whereas the latter sees in religion a genuine hoax and manipulation (or, unspoken, a powerful critic of all totalitarian powers), the former in its religion-friendly version challenges domination of state power by religious power. Thus, in anti-clericalism or laicism there exists no categorical hostility between church and state, but a sense of danger if a religion—usually the dominant one in a country—wants to usurp the messages and instruments of governmental power for its aggrandizement. A secular outlook on life can be combined with this mistrust and then lead to general anticlericalism, but this variant is still different from militant atheism á la Marxism–Leninism. One is well advised to distinguish these three different kinds of animosity or hostility. (1) Adversarial tones towards religion in general point to militant secularism, often combined with the goal of not only eliminating but also replacing religious themes and promises with secular ones. (2) Hostility towards religion in its "softer" version renounces totalitarian annihilation of religion and religious believers, but fights "civilly" for a secular outlook on life. (3) Adversarial tones towards one particular religion, such as Catholicism in France, can also be expressive of the wish to keep the two organizations separate, for their respective best interest. If the latter is the case, one moves to the following model 2.

2. *Strict Separation in Theory and Practice*

This model is a variation of the wall-of-separation doctrine to the extent that it refers to spatial and organizational entanglements as well as common policies of church and state, and it is strictly applied in practice. An example is the above-mentioned case of *Everson v. Board of Education*. In 1941, New Jersey enacted a law that provided funds for school bussing to both public and private schools, including Catholic schools. The dissenting opinions of the Supreme Court saw this as a benefit to the Catholic religion and therefore as an infraction of the Non-establishment Clause. The justices did express their sympathy for Christian parents who were forced to pay taxes for the support of state schools but could not enjoy the privileges of school bussing. This was obviously a financial burden and perhaps even a penalty against religiously oriented students and parents. Yet, this was found to be tolerable, for once the state begins financially giving benefits to churches, more far-reaching regulation could no longer be prevented. Justice Jackson noted, "[i]f the state may aid these religious schools, it may therefore regulate them. Many groups have sought aid from tax funds only to find that it carried political control with it." The financial disadvantage was weighed against the concrete advantage—a strict separation provided for maximum freedom for minority religions in relation to hostile mainstream religions or other majority preferences. "[It] is the same constitution that alone assures Catholics the right to maintain these [parochial] schools ... when predominant local sentiment would forbid them." Thus, as Justice Rutledge concluded, the complete separation of church and state, covering spatial and organizational as well as substantive and financial aspects was "best for the state and best for religion." Furthermore, it "is only by observing the prohibition rigidly that the state can maintain its neutrality and avoid partisanship in dissensions inevitable when sect opposes sect over demands for public funds to further religious education, teaching or training in any form or degree, directly or indirectly."

Model Elements of Strict Separation

Strict separation applies to	1. Substantive policies of the state (worldly/common good instead of salvation) 2. Locality (state as opposed to religious facilities) 3. Organization (no cooperation)
Unconstitutional	Accommodation and support, whether direct or indirect, whether substantive or marginal
Consequences for the private sphere	Strong positive and negative religious freedom
Consequences for the public sphere	Strong positive and negative religious freedom
Consequences for the state sphere	Maximization of negative religious freedoms against state paternalism; beneficial for "radical" and/or suppressed religions

3.   Strict Separation in Theory, Accommodation in Practice

The majority of the Justices in *Everson* arrived at a different conclusion, although they accepted the wall-of-separation doctrine. The Non-establishment Clause admittedly forbids the government from levying church taxes for religious purposes. A different assessment, however, is legitimate when taxes are raised neutrally and the state provides a service not only for public but also private schools. This is a traditional state duty similar to providing police protection, trash collection, firefighting or ensuring the safety of public streets. As such, the Non-establishment Clause does not exclude religious schools and students from receiving state support. A different conclusion would limit the positive freedom of religion and may be understood as a hostile attitude towards religion. "[The First Amendment] requires the state to be neutral in its relations with groups of religious believers and non-believers; it does not require the state to be their adversary. State power is no more to be used to handicap religions than it is to favor them."

This moderate, accommodating view of the separation-wall doctrine suggests that the wall need not be quite as high and thick as the other, stricter version. Doctrinally speaking, one religious clause (i.e., the Free Exercise Clause) is used to limit the strict-structural Non-establishment Clause. In the terminology of the German Constitutional Court (*Bundesverfassungsgericht*, hereafter BVerfG), a "practical concordance" between two norms must be found. Exactly where the line of separation is to be drawn was not answered in *Everson*. In the 1971 case *Lemon v. Kurtzman*, the U.S. Supreme Court developed the *Lemon* Test, which distinguished three components of the Non-establishment Clause: "First, the statute must have a secular legislative purpose; second, its principle or primary effect must be one that neither advances nor inhibits religion; finally, the statute must not foster 'an excessive government entanglement with religion.'" If even one element is lacking, the statute is unconstitutional.

The divergence from the strict separation approach is clear—marginal and indirect support as well as weak, organizational entanglement are not alone sufficient to be deemed unconstitutional. This also applies to the intent and purpose of the subsidy. However, it should be noted that all three parts of this test as well as the burden of proof can still be "strictly" or "loosely" applied (this also pertains to the following "endorsement test" and the corresponding basic-rights criteria of "force" and "discrimination"). A lenient interpretation of the *Lemon* Test was suggested in the dissenting opinion in *Allegheny v. ACLU*: "The requirement of neutrality inherent in the *Lemon* formulation does not require a relentless extirpation of all contact between government and religion. Government policies of accommodation, acknowledgement and support for religion are an accepted part of our political and cultural heritage, and the Establishment Clause permits government some latitude in recognizing the central role of religion in society. Any approach less sensitive to our heritage would border on latent hostility to religion, as it would require government in all its multifaceted roles to acknowledge only the secular, to the exclusion and to the detriment of the religious."

Elements of the *Lemon* Test

I. Unconstitutional Statutes	II. Constitutional Statutes
1. Exclusive or primary intent is the support of (one) religion, or	1. Goal of religious support is secondary or marginal
2. Exclusive or primary effect is the support of (one) religion, or	2. Supportive effect is secondary, weak or marginal
3. Excessive or strong organizational entanglement of the state and a church/religion	3. Only weak or marginal organizational entanglement

4. Division and Cooperation

No wall of separation between church and state exists where the two actually cooperate, i.e., beyond mere accommodation, in certain areas in the larger context of fundamental division. In this model, the third element of the *Lemon* Test is clearly implicated, but also relativized—organizational entanglements beyond the categories of "weak" and "marginal" are legal. Depending on the type and scope of cooperation, the first and second elements will also be interpreted more openly, as in the case of Germany. For example, the basic division between church and state is a result of the individual and collective religious/philosophical freedoms in Article 4(1) and (2) Basic Law. This provision establishes a clear distinction. Religion and churches are the subjects of basic rights, and the state has the duty to respect those rights. Article 140 Basic Law, in connection with Article 137 (1) Weimar Constitution, is also significant in that it stipulates that state churches are not allowed. Followers and the faithful are to build religious communities from bottom to top. Despite this, the division does not lead to a strict separation but rather to partial cooperation and mutual coordination. This is demonstrated in Articles 7(3) (religious instruction in schools) and 140 Basic Law in connection with Articles 137, 138 and 141 Weimar Constitution allowing for various methods of cooperation and support by means of the constitutions of the German *Laender*, by statutes, as well as public contracts (*Konkordate*) with churches. Such contracts include the terms of cooperation between churches and the state with regard to the administration of cemeteries, spiritual care for prison inmates and members of the military, the organization of religious classes in public schools and the funding of those education, medical and social activities of churches that the state determines to be in the public interest.

Granting churches the status of a public law corporation as stipulated in Article 140 Basic Law in connection with Article 137(5) and (6) Weimar Constitution could be understood as an abdication of the separation-wall doctrine. However, this would be a misunderstanding. It is only a formal incorporation of a church as a public body—the church remains a religious institution not subject to direct governmental regulation, but with some "governmental" powers of its own, e.g., the right to hire personnel in civil service status and disciplinary and judicial powers. The state supports these corporations by withholding church taxes from member salaries (Article 137[6]), as well as allowing certain other privileges in tax and zoning law. In exchange, the respective churches must make certain concessions to adhere to the German Basic Law in general and to its state-church system in particular (*Rechtstreue*). Thus, the incorporated church is not completely unencumbered, as in the model of strict separation, to advocate radical messages in its doctrine contradicting the most elementary elements of the German Constitution. The advantages are thus juxtaposed against the disadvantages. With the exception, however, state influence is greatly limited. No religious group can be forced to obtain the status of a public law corporation, and the church retains the right to regulate its own affairs without state interference (excessive entanglement in terms of the *Lemon Test*), Article 137(3) Weimar Constitution. Religious organizations of a private law as well as a public law character may also claim their "corporate" rights under the "collective" aspect of the guarantee of freedom of religion in Article 4 Basic Law.

5. *Formal Unity of Church and State with Substantive Division*

The organizational convergence of church and state may go well beyond granting the status of a public law corporation as in Germany. For instance, the political community may form a state church or identify itself with a particular national church. Two models must be distinguished: on the one hand a formal union, and on the other hand a material union or identification of the two authorities. Formal identification occurs when despite an official commitment of the state to a state or national church, (1) both entities primarily retain separate organizational structures, (2) pursue differing objectives (worldly/common good vs. eternal salvation), (3) have independent decision-making processes, (4) the church does not exercise state authority and external force, and (5) the religions/confessional freedom of all followers as well as non-followers is largely respected. This is the case, for example, in Great Britain, Greece and Israel.

The situation in Great Britain is quite complex. Sociologically speaking, the country is largely influenced by the Christian faith. However, the internal legal order reflects clear regional differences in state competencies. The dominant Christian denominations must be differentiated by their formal connection with state authority: "[the] law does identify regions within [the United Kingdom] with Christianity in the sense that regions are identified with distinct denominational Christian churches. The law identifies the State in part of the United Kingdom which is England with the Church of England; the law identifies the Principality of Wales with the Church of Wales; the law identifies the nation with the Church of Scotland in Scotland." As for the formal and in some aspects material union between church and state, "the Monarch is the head of the Church of England; royal succession is denied to those married to Roman Catholics; the Monarch must promise at accession to uphold and maintain the established church; the Monarch has a statutory power to appoint candidates as bishops of the church; some bishops are members of the House of Lords...." Moreover, the following elements are to be noted: "Christianity is one of the principal beneficiaries ... religious education must be broadly Christian as must school worship; only Christianity is protected by the law of blasphemy (Islam is not); the law of the Church of England is treated as part of the law of the land, the law of the Roman Catholic Church is not...."

Despite this, according to the English viewpoint, a material union between church and state does not exist. "[The] state has accepted the

Church [of England] as a religious body in its opinion truly teaching the Christian faith, and [has] given to it a certain legal position, and its decrees, if rendered under certain legal conditions, certain legal sanctions." However, the church "is not thereby made a department of the State." The bottom line is that differential treatment of the Church of England in comparison with other churches has remained within a manageable scope.

In its 1975 constitution, Greece established the Orthodox Church as a national church in Article 3 (1): "The dominant religion in Greece is that of the Christian Eastern Orthodox Church. The Greek Orthodox Church, which recognises as its head Our Lord Jesus Christ, is indissolubly united, doctrinally, with the Great Church of Constantinople and with any other Christian Church in communion with it (oxodoxi), immutably observing, like other churches, the holy apostolic and synodical canons and the holy traditions...." Partly, this is understood as a mere factual acknowledgement of the current situation, due to the fact that 96% of the population are members of the faith. This view, however, contradicts numerous legal provisions, which provide distinct advantages for the Orthodox Church. These advantages include: State ceremonies are conducted along the lines of Orthodox Church rituals; the Greek state remunerates the clergy of the Orthodox Church; obligatory religious instruction based on Orthodox teaching is conducted in public elementary and secondary schools (however, a teaching waiver is available for non-believers or followers or other religions); and, in the process of issuing building permits for religious buildings, the competent Orthodox bishop has a legal say in the matter. Article 3 of the Greek Constitution is completed and qualified by Article 13, which guarantees religious freedom: "1. Freedom of conscience in religious matters is inviolable. The enjoyment of personal and political rights shall not depend on an individual's religious beliefs. 2. There shall be freedom to practice any known religion; individuals shall be free to perform their rites of worship without hinderance and under the protection of the law...." As such, it is clear that even though a state church formally does exist, in many areas it is not complemented by a substantive union between church and state. * * *

6. *Formal and Substantive Unity of Church and State*

In this model, the state church or national religion is not merely symbolically and formally, or even "softly," associated with state authority. Rather, the practical policies and organizational structures of the two are extensively intertwined. In this sense, one approaches theocracy. The models of division and separation no longer apply: legal obligations often are identical to religious duties, and illegal acts tend to be seen as "sins." Internal and external coercion can combine, intensifying the coercive force. In terms of fundamental rights, a theocratic system devalues the negative freedom of religion and limits the exercise of worldly authority, which may not, even in a state of emergency, contradict religious commandments. The level of paternalism and suppression also increases, precisely because binding precepts with the threat of penalty are made regarding ultimate, personal beliefs about the meaning of the world and moral accountability. The duties to belong to the one, true religion or church and to profess the right faith fit seamlessly into the union of church and state, as exemplified in some Muslim countries by the prohibition on leaving the one, true religion. An example of an extreme form of this model was the reign of the Taliban in Afghanistan prior to the US/NATO intervention in 2002. A second example of a Muslim theocracy can be noted in the summary of the Supreme Court of Pakistan, which described the elements of the predominant Islamic Law in the decision of *Zaheeruddin v. State:*

> "(i) Islamic law of Shari'ah is the supreme law of the land, and all legislation, including the Constitution, must yield to it; (ii) Islamic law is a self-evident and fixed normative code, one that can be deployed without any revision of development to seek answers to all problems confronting a state in modern times, including issues of constitutional governance and fundamental individual rights ... (iii) in a Muslim/majority state, no protection needs to be provided to religious beliefs and practices which are out of step with, and offend, the majority; and (iv) the dictates of international human rights law must yield to the pronouncements of Islamic law and are thus irrelevant with respect to questions regarding the freedom of religion in a Muslim state."

More moderate forms exist in other Muslim countries. A material moderation occurs when tolerance towards other faiths is fostered to a greater or lesser extent, but there is no true guarantee of basic rights, and an institutional division does not occur. Organizational moderation can be observed when political and religious leaders are separate persons; however, in this case, the real question is how much influence one person or group exercises over the other. If there is significant tolerance of distance between church and state, one is approaching the fifth model outlined above.

NOTE

1. How do these six models each balance the values of secularism, religious liberty, and equality? Which is most beneficial for equality? What additional values seem to be driving them?

A.   THE UNITED STATES

First Amendment
United States Constitution

Congress shall make no law respecting an establishment of religion, Or prohibiting the free exercise thereof. . . .

Everson v. Board of Education of the Township of Ewing

330 U.S. 1 (1947)

■ JUSTICE BLACK delivered the opinion of the Court.

A New Jersey statute authorizes its local school districts to make rules and contracts for the transportation of children to and from schools. The appellee, a township board of education, acting pursuant to this statute authorized reimbursement to parents of money expended by them for the bus transportation of their children on regular busses operated by the public transportation system. Part of this money was for the payment of transportation of some children in the community to Catholic parochial schools. These church schools give their students, in addition to secular education, regular religious instruction conforming to the religious tenets and modes of worship of the Catholic Faith. The superintendent of these schools is a Catholic priest.

The appellant, in his capacity as a district taxpayer, filed suit in a State court challenging the right of the Board to reimburse parents of parochial school students. He contended that the statute and the resolution passed pursuant to it violated both the State and the Federal Constitutions. That court held that the legislature was without power to authorize such payment under the State constitution. 132 N.J.L. 98, 39 A.2d 75. The New Jersey Court of Errors and Appeals reversed, holding that neither the statute nor the resolution passed pursuant to it was in conflict with the State constitution or the provisions of the Federal Constitution in issue. 133 N.J.L. 350, 44 A.2d 333. The case is here on appeal under 28 U.S.C. § 344(a), 28 U.S.C.A. § 344(a). * * *

The New Jersey statute is challenged as a "law respecting an establishment of religion." The First Amendment, as made applicable to the states by the Fourteenth, *Murdock v. Commonwealth of Pennsylvania*, 319 U.S. 105 (1943) commands that a state "shall make no law respecting an establishment of religion, or prohibiting the free exercise thereof." * * *

The "establishment of religion" clause of the First Amendment means at least this: neither a state nor the Federal Government can set up a church. Neither can pass laws which aid one religion, aid all religions, or prefer one religion over another. Neither can force nor influence a person to go to or to remain away from church against his will or force him to profess a belief or disbelief in any religion. No person can be punished for entertaining or professing religious beliefs or disbeliefs, for church attendance or non-attendance. No tax in any amount, large or small, can be levied to support any religious activities or institutions, whatever they may be called, or whatever form they may adopt to teach or practice religion. Neither a state nor the Federal Government can, openly or secretly, participate in the affairs of any religious organizations or groups and vice versa. In the words of Jefferson, the clause against establishment of religion by law was intended to erect "a wall of separation between Church and State." *Reynolds v. United States*, supra, 98 U.S. at page 164.

We must consider the New Jersey statute in accordance with the foregoing limitations imposed by the First Amendment. But we must not strike that state statute down if it is within the state's constitutional power even though it approaches the verge of that power. *See Interstate Consolidated Street Ry. Co. v. Commonwealth of Massachusetts*, Holmes, J., *supra* 207 U.S. at 85, 88. New Jersey cannot consistently with the "establishment of religion" clause of the First Amendment contribute tax-raised funds to the support of an institution which teaches the tenets and faith of any church. On the other hand, other language of the amendment commands that New Jersey cannot hamper its citizens in the free exercise of their own religion. Consequently, it cannot exclude individual Catholics, Lutherans, Mohammedans, Baptists, Jews, Methodists, Nonbelievers, Presbyterians, or the members of any other faith, because of their faith, or lack of it, from receiving the benefits of public welfare legislation. While we do not mean to intimate that a state could not provide transportation only to children attending public schools, we must be careful, in protecting the citizens of New Jersey against state-established churches, to be sure that we do not inadvertently prohibit New Jersey from extending its general State law benefits to all its citizens without regard to their religious belief.

Measured by these standards, we cannot say that the First Amendment prohibits New Jersey from spending tax raised funds to pay the bus fares of parochial school pupils as a part of a general program under which it pays the fares of pupils attending public and other schools. It is undoubtedly true that children are helped to get to church schools.... Of course, cutting off church schools from these services, so separate and so indisputably marked off from the religious function, would make it far more difficult for the schools to operate. But such is obviously not the purpose of the First Amendment. That Amendment requires the state to be neutral in its relations with groups of religious believers and nonbelievers; it does not require the state to be their adversary. State power is no more to be used so as to handicap religions, than it is to favor them. * * *

This Court has said that parents may, in the discharge of their duty under state compulsory education laws, send their children to a religious rather than a public school if the school meets the secular educational requirements which the state has power to impose. *See Pierce v. Society of Sisters*, 268 U.S. 510. It appears that these parochial schools meet New Jersey's requirements. The State contributes no money to the schools. It does not support them. Its legislation, as applied, does no more than provide a general program to help parents get their children, regardless of their religion, safely and expeditiously to and from accredited schools.

The First Amendment has erected a wall between church and state. That wall must be kept high and impregnable. We could not approve the slightest breach. New Jersey has not breached it here.

■ JUSTICE RUTLEDGE, with whom JUSTICE FRANKFURTER, JUSTICE JACKSON and JUSTICE BURTON agree, dissenting.

* * * Does New Jersey's action furnish support for religion by use of the taxing power? Certainly it does, if the test remains undiluted as Jefferson and Madison made it, that money taken by taxation from one is not to be used or given to support another's religious training or belief, or indeed one's own. Today, as then, the furnishing of "contributions of money for the propagation of opinions which he disbelieves" is the forbid-

den exaction, and the prohibition is absolute for whatever measure brings that consequence and whatever amount may be sought or given to that end.

The funds used here were raised by taxation. The Court does not dispute, nor could it, that their use does, in fact, give aid and encouragement to religious instruction. It only concludes that this aid is not "support" in law. But Madison and Jefferson were concerned with aid and support in fact, not as a legal conclusion "entangled in precedents." Here, parents pay money to send their children to parochial schools, and funds raised by taxation are used to reimburse them. This not only helps the children to get to school and the parents to send them. It aids them in a substantial way to get the very thing which they are sent to the particular school to secure, namely, religious training and teaching. * * *

New Jersey's action therefore exactly fits the type of exaction and the kind of evil at which Madison and Jefferson struck. Under the test they framed, it cannot be said that the cost of transportation is no part of the cost of education or of the religious instruction given. That it is a substantial and a necessary element is shown most plainly by the continuing and increasing demand for the state to assume it. Nor is there pretense that it relates only to the secular instruction given in religious schools, or that any attempt is or could be made toward allocating proportional shares as between the secular and the religious instruction. It is precisely because the instruction is religious and relates to a particular faith, whether one or another, that parents send their children to religious schools under the *Pierce* doctrine. * * *

Two great drives are constantly in motion to abridge, in the name of education, the complete division of religion and civil authority which our forefathers made. One is to introduce religious education and observances into the public schools. The other, to obtain public funds for the aid and support of various private religious schools. *See* Johnson, The Legal Status of Church–State Relationships in the United States (1934); Thayer, Religion in Public Education (1947); Note (1941) 50 YALE L.J. 917. In my opinion, both avenues were closed by the Constitution. Neither should be opened by this Court. The matter is not one of quantity, to be measured by the amount of money expended. Now, as in Madison's day, it is one of principle, to keep separate the separate spheres as the First Amendment drew them, to prevent the first experiment upon our liberties, and to keep the question from becoming entangled in corrosive precedents. We should not be less strict to keep strong and untarnished the one side of the shield of religious freedom than we have been of the other.

———

Lemon v. Kurtzman

403 U.S. 602 (1971)

■ CHIEF JUSTICE BURGER delivered the opinion of the Court.

* * * Pennsylvania has adopted a statutory program that provides financial support to nonpublic elementary and secondary schools by way of

reimbursement for the cost of teachers' salaries, textbooks, and instructional materials in specified secular subjects. Rhode Island has adopted a statute under which the State pays directly to teachers in nonpublic elementary schools a supplement of 15% of their annual salary. Under each statute state aid has been given to church-related educational institutions. We hold that both statutes are unconstitutional.

I

The Rhode Island Statute

The Rhode Island Salary Supplement Act was enacted in 1969. It rests on the legislative finding that the quality of education available in nonpublic elementary schools has been jeopardized by the rapidly rising salaries needed to attract competent and dedicated teachers. The Act authorizes state officials to supplement the salaries of teachers of secular subjects in nonpublic elementary schools by paying directly to a teacher an amount not in excess of 15% of his current annual salary. * * *

A three-judge federal court was convened pursuant to 28 U.S.C. §§ 2281, 2284. It found that Rhode Island's nonpublic elementary schools accommodated approximately 25% of the State's pupils. About 95% of these pupils attended schools affiliated with the Roman Catholic church. To date some 250 teachers have applied for benefits under the Act. All of them are employed by Roman Catholic schools.

The court held a hearing at which extensive evidence was introduced concerning the nature of the secular instruction offered in the Roman Catholic schools whose teachers would be eligible for salary assistance under the Act. Although the court found that concern for religious values does not necessarily affect the content of secular subjects, it also found that the parochial school system was 'an integral part of the religious mission of the Catholic Church.'

The District Court concluded that the Act violated the Establishment Clause, holding that it fostered 'excessive entanglement' between government and religion. In addition two judges thought that the Act had the impermissible effect of giving 'significant aid to a religious enterprise.' 316 F.Supp. 112. We affirm. * * *

II

The language of the Religion Clauses of the First Amendment is at best opaque, particularly when compared with other portions of the Amendment. Its authors did not simply prohibit the establishment of a state church or a state religion, an area history shows they regarded as very important and fraught with great dangers. Instead they commanded that there should be "no law respecting an establishment of religion." A law may be one "respecting" the forbidden objective while falling short of its total realization. A law 'respecting' the proscribed result, that is, the establishment of religion, is not always easily identifiable as one violative of the Clause. A given law might not establish a state religion but nevertheless be one "respecting" that end in the sense of being a step that could lead to such establishment and hence offend the First Amendment. * * *

Every analysis in this area must begin with consideration of the cumulative criteria developed by the Court over many years. Three such tests may be gleaned from our cases. First, the statute must have a secular legislative purpose; second, its principal or primary effect must be one that neither advances nor inhibits religion, *Board of Education v. Allen*, 392 U.S. 236, 243 (1968); finally, the statute must not foster "an excessive government entanglement with religion." *Walz v. Tax Commission*, 397 U.S. 664 (1970), at 674. * * *

III

In *Walz v. Tax Commission, supra*, the Court upheld state tax exemptions for real property owned by religious organizations and used for religious worship. That holding, however, tended to confine rather than enlarge the area of permissible state involvement with religious institutions by calling for close scrutiny of the degree of entanglement involved in the relationship. The objective is to prevent, as far as possible, the intrusion of either into the precincts of the other.

Our prior holdings do not call for total separation between church and state; total separation is not possible in an absolute sense. Some relationship between government and religious organizations is inevitable. *Zorach v. Clauson*, 343 U.S. 306, 312 (1952); *Sherbert v. Verner*, 374 U.S. 398 (1963) (Harlan, J., dissenting). Fire inspections, building and zoning regulations and state requirements under compulsory school-attendance laws are examples of necessary and permissible contacts. Indeed, under the statutory exemption before us in *Walz*, the State had a continuing burden to ascertain that the exempt property was in fact being used for religious worship. Judicial caveats against entanglement must recognize that the line of separation, far from being a "wall," is a blurred, indistinct, and variable barrier depending on all the circumstances of a particular relationship.

* * * In order to determine whether the government entanglement with religion is excessive, we must examine the character and purposes of the institutions that are benefited, the nature of the aid that the State provides, and the resulting relationship between the government and the religious authority. Mr. Justice Harlan, in a separate opinion in *Walz*, supra, echoed the classic warning as to "programs, whose very nature is apt to entangle the state in details of administration...." Here we find that both statutes foster an impermissible degree of entanglement.

(a) Rhode Island program

* * * We need not and do not assume that teachers in parochial schools will be guilty of bad faith or any conscious design to evade the limitations imposed by the statute and the First Amendment. We simply recognize that a dedicated religious person, teaching in a school affiliated with his or her faith and operated to inculcate its tenets, will inevitably experience great difficulty in remaining religiously neutral. Doctrines and faith are not inculcated or advanced by neutrals. With the best of intentions such a teacher would find it hard to make a total separation between secular teaching and religious doctrine. What would appear to some to be essential to good citizenship might well for others border on or constitute

instruction in religion. Further difficulties are inherent in the combination of religious discipline and the possibility of disagreement between teacher and religious authorities over the meaning of the statutory restrictions.

We do not assume, however, that parochial school teachers will be unsuccessful in their attempts to segregate their religious beliefs from their secular educational responsibilities. But the potential for impermissible fostering of religion is present. The Rhode Island Legislature has not, and could not, provide state aid on the basis of a mere assumption that secular teachers under religious discipline can avoid conflicts. The State must be certain, given the Religion Clauses, that subsidized teachers do not inculcate religion-indeed the State here has undertaken to do so. To ensure that no trespass occurs, the State has therefore carefully conditioned its aid with pervasive restrictions. An eligible recipient must teach only those courses that are offered in the public schools and use only those texts and materials that are found in the public schools. In addition the teacher must not engage in teaching any course in religion.

A comprehensive, discriminating, and continuing state surveillance will inevitably be required to ensure that these restrictions are obeyed and the First Amendment otherwise respected. Unlike a book, a teacher cannot be inspected once so as to determine the extent and intent of his or her personal beliefs and subjective acceptance of the limitations imposed by the First Amendment. These prophylactic contacts will involve excessive and enduring entanglement between state and church. * * *

IV

A broader base of entanglement of yet a different character is presented by the divisive political potential of these state programs. In a community where such a large number of pupils are served by church-related schools, it can be assumed that state assistance will entail considerable political activity. Partisans of parochial schools, understandably concerned with rising costs and sincerely dedicated to both the religious and secular educational missions of their schools, will inevitably champion this cause and promote political action to achieve their goals. Those who oppose state aid, whether for constitutional, religious, or fiscal reasons, will inevitably respond and employ all of the usual political campaign techniques to prevail. Candidates will be forced to declare and voters to choose. It would be unrealistic to ignore the fact that many people confronted with issues of this kind will find their votes aligned with their faith.

Ordinarily political debate and division, however vigorous or even partisan, are normal and healthy manifestations of our democratic system of government, but political division along religious lines was one of the principal evils against which the First Amendment was intended to protect. * * *

V

In *Walz* it was argued that a tax exemption for places of religious worship would prove to be the first step in an inevitable progression leading to the establishment of state churches and state religion. That claim could not stand up against more than 200 years of virtually universal practice imbedded in our colonial experience and continuing into the present.

The progression argument, however, is more persuasive here. We have no long history of state aid to church-related educational institutions comparable to 200 years of tax exemption for churches. Indeed, the state programs before us today represent something of an innovation. * * *

Under our system the choice has been made that government is to be entirely excluded from the area of religious instruction and churches excluded from the affairs of government. The Constitution decrees that religion must be a private matter for the individual, the family, and the institutions of private choice, and that while some involvement and entanglement are inevitable, lines must be drawn. * * *

Zelman v. Simmons–Harris

536 U.S. 639 (2002)

■ CHIEF JUSTICE REHNQUIST delivered the opinion of the Court.

* * * There are more than 75,000 children enrolled in the Cleveland City School District. The majority of these children are from low-income and minority families. Few of these families enjoy the means to send their children to any school other than an inner-city public school. For more than a generation, however, Cleveland's public schools have been among the worst performing public schools in the Nation. In 1995, a Federal District Court declared a "crisis of magnitude" and placed the entire Cleveland school district under state control. *See Reed v. Rhodes,* No. 1:73 CV 1300 (N.D. Ohio, Mar. 3, 1995). Shortly thereafter, the state auditor found that Cleveland's public schools were in the midst of a "crisis that is perhaps unprecedented in the history of American education." Cleveland City School District Performance Audit 2–1 (Mar. 1996). The district had failed to meet any of the 18 state standards for minimal acceptable performance. Only 1 in 10 ninth graders could pass a basic proficiency examination, and students at all levels performed at a dismal rate compared with students in other Ohio public schools. More than two-thirds of high school students either dropped or failed out before graduation. Of those students who managed to reach their senior year, one of every four still failed to graduate. Of those students who did graduate, few could read, write, or compute at levels comparable to their counterparts in other cities.

It is against this backdrop that Ohio enacted, among other initiatives, its Pilot Project Scholarship Program ("program"). The program provides two basic kinds of assistance to parents of children in a covered district. First, the program provides tuition aid for students in kindergarten through third grade, expanding each year through eighth grade, to attend a participating public or private school of their parent's choosing. Second, the program provides tutorial aid for students who choose to remain enrolled in public school.

The tuition aid portion of the program is designed to provide educational choices to parents who reside in a covered district. Any private school, whether religious or nonreligious, may participate in the program and accept program students so long as the school is located within the boundaries of a covered district and meets statewide educational standards. Participating private schools must agree not to discriminate on the basis of race, religion, or ethnic background, or to "advocate or foster unlawful behavior or teach hatred of any person or group on the basis of race, ethnicity, national origin, or religion." Any public school located in a school district adjacent to the covered district may also participate in the program. Adjacent public schools are eligible to receive a $2,250 tuition grant for each program student accepted in addition to the full amount of per-pupil state funding attributable to each additional student. All participating schools, whether public or private, are required to accept students in accordance with rules and procedures established by the state superintendent.

The program has been in operation within the Cleveland City School District since the 1996–1997 school year. In the 1999–2000 school year, 56 private schools participated in the program, 46 (or 82%) of which had a religious affiliation. None of the public schools in districts adjacent to Cleveland have elected to participate. More than 3,700 students participated in the scholarship program, most of whom (96%) enrolled in religiously affiliated schools. Sixty percent of these students were from families at or below the poverty line. In the 1998–1999 school year, approximately 1,400 Cleveland public school students received tutorial aid. This number was expected to double during the 1999–2000 school year.

In July 1999, respondents filed this action in United States District Court, seeking to enjoin the reenacted program on the ground that it violated the Establishment Clause of the United States Constitution. In December 1999, the District Court granted summary judgment for respondents. 72 F.Supp.2d 834. In December 2000, a divided panel of the Court of Appeals affirmed the judgment of the District Court, finding that the program had the "primary effect" of advancing religion in violation of the Establishment Clause. 234 F.3d 945 (C.A.6). The Court of Appeals stayed its mandate pending disposition in this Court. App. to Pet. for Cert. in No. 00–1779, p. 151. We granted certiorari, 533 U.S. 976 (2001), and now reverse the Court of Appeals.

The Establishment Clause of the First Amendment, applied to the States through the Fourteenth Amendment, prevents a State from enacting laws that have the "purpose" or "effect" of advancing or inhibiting religion. *Agostini v. Felton,* 521 U.S. 203, 222–223 (1997) ("[W]e continue to ask whether the government acted with the purpose of advancing or inhibiting religion [and] whether the aid has the 'effect' of advancing or inhibiting religion" (citations omitted)). There is no dispute that the program challenged here was enacted for the valid secular purpose of providing educational assistance to poor children in a demonstrably failing public school system. Thus, the question presented is whether the Ohio program nonetheless has the forbidden "effect" of advancing or inhibiting religion.

To answer that question, our decisions have drawn a consistent distinction between government programs that provide aid directly to religious schools, *Mitchell v. Helms,* 530 U.S. 793, 810–814 (2000) (plurality opinion); *id.,* at 841–844 (O'Connor, J., concurring in judgment); *Agostini, supra,* at 225–227; *Rosenberger v. Rector and Visitors of Univ. of Va.,* 515 U.S. 819, 842 (1995) (collecting cases), and programs of true private choice, in which government aid reaches religious schools only as a result of the genuine and independent choices of private individuals, *Mueller v. Allen,* 463 U.S. 388 (1983); *Witters v. Washington Dept. of Servs. for Blind,* 474 U.S. 481 (1986); *Zobrest v. Catalina Foothills School Dist.,* 509 U.S. 1 (1993). While our jurisprudence with respect to the constitutionality of direct aid programs has "changed significantly" over the past two decades, *Agostini, supra,* at 236, our jurisprudence with respect to true private choice programs has remained consistent and unbroken. Three times we have confronted Establishment Clause challenges to neutral government programs that provide aid directly to a broad class of individuals, who, in turn, direct the aid to religious schools or institutions of their own choosing. Three times we have rejected such challenges. * * *

Mueller, Witters, and *Zobrest* thus make clear that where a government aid program is neutral with respect to religion, and provides assistance directly to a broad class of citizens who, in turn, direct government aid to religious schools wholly as a result of their own genuine and independent private choice, the program is not readily subject to challenge under the Establishment Clause. A program that shares these features permits government aid to reach religious institutions only by way of the deliberate choices of numerous individual recipients. The incidental advancement of a religious mission, or the perceived endorsement of a religious message, is reasonably attributable to the individual recipient, not to the government, whose role ends with the disbursement of benefits. As a plurality of this Court recently observed:

"[I]f numerous private choices, rather than the single choice of a government, determine the distribution of aid, pursuant to neutral eligibility criteria, then a government cannot, or at least cannot easily, grant special favors that might lead to a religious establishment." *Mitchell,* 530 U.S., at 810. * * *

We believe that the program challenged here is a program of true private choice, consistent with *Mueller, Witters,* and *Zobrest,* and thus constitutional. As was true in those cases, the Ohio program is neutral in all respects toward religion. It is part of a general and multifaceted undertaking by the State of Ohio to provide educational opportunities to the children of a failed school district. It confers educational assistance directly to a broad class of individuals defined without reference to religion, *i.e.,* any parent of a school-age child who resides in the Cleveland City School District. The program permits the participation of *all* schools within the district, religious or nonreligious. Adjacent public schools also may participate and have a financial incentive to do so. Program benefits are available to participating families on neutral terms, with no reference to religion. The only preference stated anywhere in the program is a preference for low-income families, who receive greater assistance and are given priority for admission at participating schools. * * *

Any objective observer familiar with the full history and context of the Ohio program would reasonably view it as one aspect of a broader undertaking to assist poor children in failed schools, not as an endorsement of religious schooling in general.

There also is no evidence that the program fails to provide genuine opportunities for Cleveland parents to select secular educational options for their school-age children. Cleveland schoolchildren enjoy a range of educational choices: They may remain in public school as before, remain in public school with publicly funded tutoring aid, obtain a scholarship and choose a religious school, obtain a scholarship and choose a nonreligious private school, enroll in a community school, or enroll in a magnet school. That 46 of the 56 private schools now participating in the program are religious schools does not condemn it as a violation of the Establishment Clause. The Establishment Clause question is whether Ohio is coercing parents into sending their children to religious schools, and that question must be answered by evaluating *all* options Ohio provides Cleveland schoolchildren, only one of which is to obtain a program scholarship and then choose a religious school. * * *

In sum, the Ohio program is entirely neutral with respect to religion. It provides benefits directly to a wide spectrum of individuals, defined only by financial need and residence in a particular school district. It permits such individuals to exercise genuine choice among options public and private, secular and religious. The program is therefore a program of true private choice. In keeping with an unbroken line of decisions rejecting challenges to similar programs, we hold that the program does not offend the Establishment Clause.

The judgment of the Court of Appeals is reversed.

■ Justice Souter, with whom Justice Stevens, Justice Ginsburg, and Justice Breyer join, dissenting.

* * * The record indicates that the schools are failing to serve their objective, and the vouchers in issue here are said to be needed to provide adequate alternatives to them. If there were an excuse for giving short shrift to the Establishment Clause, it would probably apply here. But there is no excuse. Constitutional limitations are placed on government to preserve constitutional values in hard cases, like these. * * *

In the city of Cleveland the overwhelming proportion of large appropriations for voucher money must be spent on religious schools if it is to be spent at all, and will be spent in amounts that cover almost all of tuition. The money will thus pay for eligible students' instruction not only in secular subjects but in religion as well, in schools that can fairly be characterized as founded to teach religious doctrine and to imbue teaching in all subjects with a religious dimension. Public tax money will pay at a systemic level for teaching the covenant with Israel and Mosaic law in Jewish schools, the primacy of the Apostle Peter and the Papacy in Catholic schools, the truth of reformed Christianity in Protestant schools, and the revelation to the Prophet in Muslim schools, to speak only of major religious groupings in the Republic. * * *

I

The majority's statements of Establishment Clause doctrine cannot be appreciated without some historical perspective on the Court's announced limitations on government aid to religious education, and its repeated repudiation of limits previously set. My object here is not to give any nuanced exposition of the cases, which I tried to classify in some detail in an earlier opinion, *see Mitchell v. Helms*, 530 U.S. 793, 873–899 (2000) (dissenting opinion), but to set out the broad doctrinal stages covered in the modern era, and to show that doctrinal bankruptcy has been reached today.

Viewed with the necessary generality, the cases can be categorized in three groups. In the period from 1947 to 1968, the basic principle of no aid to religion through school benefits was unquestioned. Thereafter for some 15 years, the Court termed its efforts as attempts to draw a line against aid that would be divertible to support the religious, as distinct from the secular, activity of an institutional beneficiary. Then, starting in 1983, concern with divertibility was gradually lost in favor of approving aid in amounts unlikely to afford substantial benefits to religious schools, when offered evenhandedly without regard to a recipient's religious character, and when channeled to a religious institution only by the genuinely free choice of some private individual. Now, the three stages are succeeded by a fourth, in which the substantial character of government aid is held to have no constitutional significance, and the espoused criteria of neutrality in offering aid, and private choice in directing it, are shown to be nothing but examples of verbal formalism.

A

Everson v. Board of Ed. of Ewing inaugurated the modern development of Establishment Clause doctrine at the behest of a taxpayer challenging state provision of "tax-raised funds to pay the bus fares of parochial school pupils" on regular city buses as part of a general scheme to reimburse the public-transportation costs of children attending both public and private nonprofit schools. 330 U.S., at 17. Although the Court split, no Justice disagreed with the basic doctrinal principle already quoted, that "[n]o tax in any amount ... can be levied to support any religious activities or institutions ... whatever form they may adopt to teach ... religion." *Id.*, at 16. Nor did any Member of the Court deny the tension between the New Jersey program and the aims of the Establishment Clause. The majority upheld the state law on the strength of rights of religious-school students under the Free Exercise Clause, *id.*, at 17–18, which was thought to entitle them to free public transportation when offered as a "general government servic[e]" to all schoolchildren, *id.*, at 17. Despite the indirect benefit to religious education, the transportation was simply treated like "ordinary police and fire protection, connections for sewage disposal, public highways and sidewalks," *id.*, at 17–18, and, most significantly, "state-paid policemen, detailed to protect children going to and from church schools from the very real hazards of traffic," *id.*, at 17. The dissenters, however, found the benefit to religion too pronounced to survive the general principle of no establishment, no aid, and they described it as running counter to every objective served by the establishment ban: New Jersey's use of tax-raised funds forced a taxpayer to "contribut[e] to the propagation of opinions which he disbelieves in so far as ... religions differ,"*id.,* at 45 (internal quotation marks omitted); it exposed religious liberty to the threat of dependence on state money, *id.,* at 53; and it had already sparked political conflicts with opponents of public funding, *id.,* at 54.

The difficulty of drawing a line that preserved the basic principle of no aid was no less obvious some 20 years later in *Board of Ed. of Central School Dist. No. 1 v. Allen,* 392 U.S. 236 (1968), which upheld a New York law authorizing local school boards to lend textbooks in secular subjects to children attending religious schools, a result not self-evident from *Everson's* "general government services" rationale.* * *

B

Allen recognized the reality that "religious schools pursue two goals, religious instruction and secular education," 392 U.S., at 245; if state aid could be restricted to serve the second, it might be permissible under the Establishment Clause. But in the retrenchment that followed, the Court saw that the two educational functions were so intertwined in religious primary and secondary schools that aid to secular education could not readily be segregated, and the intrusive monitoring required to enforce the line itself raised Establishment Clause concerns about the entanglement of church and state. *See Lemon v. Kurtzman,* 403 U.S. 602, 620 (1971) (striking down program supplementing salaries for teachers of secular subjects in private schools). To avoid the entanglement, the Court's focus in the post-*Allen* cases was on the principle of divertibility, on discerning when ostensibly secular government aid to religious schools was susceptible to religious uses. The greater the risk of diversion to religion (and the monitoring necessary to avoid it), the less legitimate the aid scheme was under the no-aid principle. On the one hand, the Court tried to be practical, and when the aid recipients were not so "pervasively sectarian" that their secular and religious functions were inextricably intertwined, the Court generally upheld aid earmarked for secular use.

The fact that the Court's suspicion of divertibility reflected a concern with the substance of the no-aid principle is apparent in its rejection of stratagems invented to dodge it. In *Committee for Public Ed. & Religious Liberty v. Nyquist,* 413 U.S. 756 (1973), for example, the Court struck down a New York program of tuition grants for poor parents and tax deductions for more affluent ones who sent their children to private schools. The *Nyquist* Court dismissed warranties of a "statistical guarantee," that the scheme provided at most 15% of the total cost of an education at a religious school, *id.,* at 787–788, which could presumably be matched to a secular 15% of a child's education at the school. And it rejected the idea that the path of state aid to religious schools might be dispositive: "far from providing a *per se* immunity from examination of the substance of the State's program, the fact that aid is disbursed to parents rather than to the schools is only one among many factors to be considered." *Id.,* at 781. The point was that "the effect of the aid is unmistakably to provide desired financial support for nonpublic, sectarian institutions." *Id.,* at 783. *Nyquist* thus held that aid to parents through tax deductions was no different from forbidden direct aid to religious schools for religious uses. The focus remained on what the public money bought when it reached the end point of its disbursement. * * *

II

Although it has taken half a century since *Everson* to reach the majority's twin standards of neutrality and free choice, the facts show that, in the majority's hands, even these criteria cannot convincingly legitimize the Ohio scheme.

A

Consider first the criterion of neutrality. As recently as two Terms ago, a majority of the Court recognized that neutrality conceived of as evenhandedness toward aid recipients had never been treated as alone sufficient to satisfy the Establishment Clause, *Mitchell*, 530 U.S., at 838–839 (O'CONNOR, J., concurring in judgment); *id.*, at 884 (SOUTER, J., dissenting). But at least in its limited significance, formal neutrality seemed to serve some purpose. Today, however, the majority employs the neutrality criterion in a way that renders it impossible to understand. * * *

In order to apply the neutrality test, then, it makes sense to focus on a category of aid that may be directed to religious as well as secular schools, and ask whether the scheme favors a religious direction. Here, one would ask whether the voucher provisions, allowing for as much as $2,250 toward private school tuition (or a grant to a public school in an adjacent district), were written in a way that skewed the scheme toward benefiting religious schools.

This, however, is not what the majority asks. The majority looks not to the provisions for tuition vouchers, Ohio Rev.Code Ann. § 3313.976 (West Supp.2002), but to every provision for educational opportunity: "The program permits the participation of *all* schools within the district, [as well as public schools in adjacent districts], religious or nonreligious." The majority then finds confirmation that "participation of *all* schools" satisfies neutrality by noting that the better part of total state educational expenditure goes to public schools, thus showing there is no favor of religion.

The illogic is patent. If regular, public schools (which can get no voucher payments) "participate" in a voucher scheme with schools that can, and public expenditure is still predominantly on public schools, then the majority's reasoning would find neutrality in a scheme of vouchers available for private tuition in districts with no secular private schools at all. "Neutrality" as the majority employs the term is, literally, verbal and nothing more. * * *

B

The majority addresses the issue of choice the same way it addresses neutrality, by asking whether recipients or potential recipients of voucher aid have a choice of public schools among secular alternatives to religious schools. Again, however, the majority asks the wrong question and misapplies the criterion. The majority has confused choice in spending scholarships with choice from the entire menu of possible educational placements, most of them open to anyone willing to attend a public school. I say "confused" because the majority's new use of the choice criterion, which it frames negatively as "whether Ohio is coercing parents into sending their children to religious schools," *ante,* at 2469, ignores the reason for having a private choice enquiry in the first place. Cases since *Mueller* have found private choice relevant under a rule that aid to religious schools can be permissible so long as it first passes through the hands of students or parents. The majority's view that all educational choices are comparable for purposes of choice thus ignores the whole point of the choice test: it is a criterion for deciding whether indirect aid to a religious school is legitimate because it passes through private hands that can spend or use the aid in a secular school. The question is whether the private hand is genuinely free to send the money in either a secular direction or a religious one. The majority now has transformed this question about private choice in channeling aid into a question about selecting from examples of state spending (on education) including direct spending on magnet and community public schools that goes through no private hands and could never reach a religious school under any circumstance. When the choice test is transformed from where to spend the money to where to go to school, it is cut loose from its very purpose.

Defining choice as choice in spending the money or channeling the aid is, moreover, necessary if the choice criterion is to function as a limiting principle at all. If "choice" is present whenever there is any educational alternative to the religious school to which vouchers can be endorsed, then there will always be a choice and the voucher can always be constitutional, even in a system in which there is not a single private secular school as an alternative to the religious school. *See supra,* at 2491 (noting the same result under the majority's formulation of the neutrality criterion). And because it is unlikely that any participating private religious school will enroll more pupils than the generally available public system, it will be easy to generate numbers suggesting that aid to religion is not the significant intent or effect of the voucher scheme. * * *

It is not, of course, that I think even a genuine choice criterion is up to the task of the Establishment Clause when substantial state funds go to religious teaching; the discussion in Part III, *infra,* shows that it is not. The point is simply that if the majority wishes to claim that choice is a criterion, it must define choice in a way that can function as a criterion with a practical capacity to screen something out.

If, contrary to the majority, we ask the right question about genuine choice to use the vouchers, the answer shows that something is influencing choices in a way that aims the money in a religious direction: of 56 private schools in the district participating in the voucher program (only 53 of which accepted voucher students in 1999–2000), 46 of them are religious; 96.6% of all voucher recipients go to religious schools, only 3.4% to nonreligious ones. Unfortunately for the majority position, there is no explanation for this that suggests the religious direction results simply from free choices by parents. One answer to these statistics, for example, which would be consistent with the genuine choice claimed to be operating, might be that 96.6% of families choosing to avail themselves of vouchers choose to educate their children in schools of their own religion. This would not, in my view, render the scheme constitutional, but it would speak to the majority's choice criterion. * * *

If the divisiveness permitted by today's majority is to be avoided in the short term, it will be avoided only by action of the political branches at the state and national levels. Legislatures not driven to desperation by the problems of public education may be able to see the threat in vouchers negotiable in sectarian schools. Perhaps even cities with problems like Cleveland's will perceive the danger, now that they know a federal court will not save them from it.

My own course as a judge on the Court cannot, however, simply be to hope that the political branches will save us from the consequences of the majority's decision. *Everson's* statement is still the touchstone of sound law, even though the reality is that in the matter of educational aid the Establishment Clause has largely been read away. True, the majority has not approved vouchers for religious schools alone, or aid earmarked for religious instruction. But no scheme so clumsy will ever get before us, and in the cases that we may see, like these, the Establishment Clause is largely silenced. I do not have the option to leave it silent, and I hope that a future Court will reconsider today's dramatic departure from basic Establishment Clause principle.

————

NOTES

1. Is the United States a "Christian Nation?" Sixty-two percent of Americans answered "yes" in a 2009 Newsweek poll. *See* http://www.news week.com/2009/ 04/06/one-nation-under-god.html. Is the statement "The United States is a Christian nation" merely descriptive (a majority of Americans describe themselves as Christians) or is it prescriptive (U.S. law should be governed by Christian principles)? Does this affect how we should read the meaning of the Establishment Clause?

2. In a U.S. public (secular) school, should organized prayer be permitted? In *Engel v. Vitale*, 370 U.S. 421 (1962) the Supreme Court held that organized daily classroom prayers, even if nonsectarian and voluntary, violated the Establishment Clause. *See also, School Dist. of Abington Township School District v. Schempp*, 374 U.S. 203 (1963) (same for mandatory Bible reading); *Wallace v. Jaffree*, 472 U.S. 38 (1985) (same for moment of silence); *Lee v. Weisman*, 505 U.S. 577 (1992) (same for clergy-led prayers at graduation). Following *Lee v. Weisman*, some commentators thought that student-led prayers would be permitted. The Fifth Circuit so ruled in *Jones v. Clear Creek Independent School District*, 977 F.2d 963 (5th Cir. 1992), permitting a student-delivered nonsectarian prayer. But in *Santa Fe Independent School Dist. v. Doe*, 530 U.S. 290 (2000), the Supreme Court disagreed, at least at high school football games. The Santa Fe Unified School District allowed Christian students to lead a prayer at home football games over the public address system. A group of students filed suit claiming a violation of the Establishment Clause. The district court allowed the prayer so long as it was nonsectarian and nonproselytiz-

ing. The Fifth Circuit held that "nonsectarian, nonproselytizing" prayers were permissible at graduation, but not at football games. The Supreme Court held that the student-led prayer was impermissible under the Establishment Clause because "an objective Santa Fe High School student will unquestionably perceive the inevitable pre-game prayer as stamped with her school's seal of approval." Part of what makes the issue of school prayer difficult is that truly voluntary prayer, in which the school authorities have no role, is not simply permitted, but protected, by the Free Exercise Clause. We will take this up in Chapter VIII.

3. In the United Kingdom, the 1998 School Standards and Framework Act provides that publicly funded schools must provide religious education (Sec. 69), and that students in government schools must participate in a daily act of "collective worship" (Sec. 70). Collective worship is defined as worship "of a broadly Christian character if it reflects the broad traditions of Christian belief without being distinctive of any particular Christian denomination." (Schedule 20, Part 3.) It is subject to exceptions for religious schools (which may be state-supported), to schools where the government has determined that Christian worship is inappropriate, and to an individual opt-out procedure by parents. *See* http://www.legislation.gov.uk/ukpga/1998/31/contents.

4. A 2006 reform of the UK 1998 School Standards and Framework Act provides that 16-year-olds may opt out of school prayer without parental permission. The Archbishop of Wales objected to the new law, explaining that "group prayer offered pupils a rare opportunity for 'recognition, affirmation and celebration of shared values' and should be encouraged." He "warned that strict secularists should take caution from the examples of the U.S. and France and 'their struggle to build a sense of cultural understanding and mutual respect.'" Jon Swaine, Allowing Pupils to opt out of school prayer is wrong, says Archbishop of Wales, Aug 7, 2009 The Telegraph, http://www.telegraph.co.uk/news/religion/5988771/Allowing-pupils-to-opt-out-of-school-prayer-is-wrong-says-Archbishop-of-Wales.html. School prayer in France is discussed in the next section of this chapter.

5. The Indian Constitution, Article 28, Section 1, provides, "No religious instruction shall be provided in any educational institution wholly maintained out of State funds." However, Section 2 of the same article stipulates that "Nothing in clause (1) shall apply to an educational institution which is administered by the State but has been established under any endowment or trust which requires that religious instruction shall be imparted in such institution."

6. Does a requirement that students recite the "pledge of allegiance" violate the Establishment Clause? In *Elk Grove Unified School District v. Newdow*, 542 U.S. 1 (2004), Newdow, an atheist, sued the school district on behalf of his daughter, a public school student, claiming that the phrase "Under God" in the pledge of allegiance offended his ability to impart his own religious beliefs to his daughter. Newdow appealed the district court's dismissal of the suit and the Ninth Circuit reversed, holding that the phrase did indeed violate the Establishment Clause and was unconstitutional. The U.S. Supreme Court reversed on procedural grounds.

7. Does a public display of the "Ten Commandments" violate the Establishment Clause? Two cases raising this question, *McCreary County v. ACLU*, 545 U.S. 844 (2005) and *Van Orden v. Perry*, 545 U.S. 677 (2005) were released by the Court on the same day with seemingly contradictory results. Justice Breyer was the swing vote in the two cases, siding with the majority in *McCreary* to hold that a Kentucky display was prohibited and concurring in Perry to say that a Texas display was permitted. In *McCreary*, the Kentucky case, the objection was to a government sponsored display of the Ten Commandments in two Kentucky courthouses. The District Court found that the displays were unconstitutional since they were "purely religious" and had "no secular purpose." The Sixth Circuit affirmed, as did the Supreme Court. In *Perry*, the Texas case, the objection was to a government sponsored display of the Ten Commandments at the State Capitol in Austin, TX. The Fifth Circuit held that the display was constitutional because it contained both a secular and religious purpose. The Supreme Court, in a plurality decision, agreed, finding a secular purpose.

8. Recall our discussion in Chapter V of the issue of same-sex marriage, and more broadly, of equality rights for gays and lesbians. Religious opposition to gay rights can implicate state neutrality under the Establishment Clause. For example, in *Christian Legal Society, Hastings College of the Law v. Martinez*, 561 U. S. ___ (2010) the Court reviewed a decision by Hastings to withhold student funds from the Christian Legal Society, an otherwise eligible student group, because they refused to agree to the Hastings non-discrimination pledge, which prohibited student groups from discriminating based on sexual orientation. The Court upheld the school's decision by a 5–4 vote.

9. Is the Latin cross a Christian religious symbol? Does its use by the state constitute a violation of the Establishment Clause, or may it be used in a permissibly secular manner? In *Salazar v. Buono*, 130 S.Ct. 1803 (2010), the Supreme Court, in a fractured series of opinions, declined to affirm an injunction which had enjoined an Act of Congress that transferred one acre of public park lands to the Veterans of Foreign Wars (VFW) in order to avoid an Establishment Clause violation. On the land was a cross that the VFW had erected as a war memorial. Justice Kennedy wrote that "certainly a Christian symbol, the cross was not emplaced on Sunrise Rock to promote a Christian message," and that a reasonable observer would not see its display as a government endorsement of Christianity.

10. In oral argument in *Salazar v. Buono*, attorney Peter Eliasberg of the ACLU argued that Jewish war veterans would not want to be honored by "the predominant symbol of Christianity." Justice Scalia replied that "The cross is the most common symbol of the resting place of the dead." When Eliasberg replied that there were no crosses in Jewish cemeteries, Justice Scalia, according to the New York Times, "grew visibly angry." *See* Adam Liptak, *Religion Largely Absent in Argument About Cross*, NY TIMES, Oct. 7, 2009, http://www.nytimes.com/2009/10/08/us/08scotus.html?_r=2.n Assume Justice Scalia is correct (he may well be within the U.S., but he is almost certainly incorrect as to the whole world); does his observation rebut the objection?

11.   According to the 2011 CIA World Factbook, the population of the United States (approximately 313 million) is 51.3% Protestant and 23.9% Roman Catholic. The remainder of the population counted in the data are, by percentage, unaffiliated, none, other, Mormon, other Christian, Jewish, Buddhist, and Muslim. https://www.cia.gov/library/publications/the-world-factbook/geos/us.html.

12.   Opponents of Establishment Clause claims consistently argue that secularism threatens their religious liberty interests, or is "hostile" to religion. Stephen Carter, in his book *The Culture of Disbelief*, examines how the Supreme Court's interpretation of the Establishment Clause in hallmark First Amendment cases such as *Lemon v. Kurtzman* has made the public square a seemingly hostile place for the religiously devout in the U.S. Carter writes:

> "One must be careful not to misunderstand what the [Establishment Clause] doctrine and the First Amendment that is said to embody it were designed to do. Simply put, the metaphorical separation of church and state originated in an effort to protect religion from the state, not the state from religion. The religion clauses of the First Amendment were crafted to permit maximum freedom to the religious. In modern, religiously pluralistic America, where, as we have seen, the religions play vital roles as independent sources of meaning for adherents, this means that the government should neither force people into sectarian religious observances . . . nor punish people for their religiosity without a very strong reason other than prejudice. It does not mean, however, that people whose motivations are religious are banned from trying to influence government, nor that the government is banned from listening to them. Understanding this distinction is key to preserving the necessary separation of church and state without resorting to a philosophical rhetoric that treats religion as an inferior way for citizens to come to public judgment." Stephen Carter, The Culture of Disbelief, Basic Books (1994), pp. 105–106.

13.   Later in this chapter we will examine two cases, one from Germany one from Italy, determining whether the cross can be displayed in public school classrooms.

B. France

Secularism (laïcité) in France

■ Marie-Christine Pauwels

Before 1789, France had a state religion, Roman Catholicism. The Revolution brought about a massive shifting of powers from the Roman Catholic Church to the state, and a period of turmoil and conflict set in, with a brief separation of Church and State in 1795. In 1801, with the signing of the Concordat, an agreement concluded with the Pope (Pius VII), Napoleon reestablished the Church in France. Roman Catholicism was officially recognized as the majority religion of the French people and rules for a relationship between the Catholic Church and the French State were established. Napoleon also officially recognized Judaism and the Lutheran and Reformed churches. These groups received official state recognition and support until the 1905 law which put an end to the Concordat regime.

1. The Constitutional & Statutory Law of laïcité

When we speak of secularism—or secularity—the French use the word laïcité. What does it mean exactly? Here is the definition Catherine Kintzler, a professor of philosophy at the University of Lille and author of "Qu'est-ce que la laïcité?" (Vrin, 2007), offers:

Laïcité is a philosophical concept which, unlike 'tolerance' does not ask how antagonistic freedoms can coexist in a society where diverse communities live side by side. Laïcité is about constructing a space *a priori* that will allow every individual to enjoy freedom of opinion.

This space is defined by the public authority. It produces and enforces the law. And the individual does not need to be a member of a specific group to enjoy freedom of opinion within civil society, because the public authority is entirely impervious in its approach to religious and non-religious forms of belief.

A. Constitutional Texts

Secularism in France is framed by three constitutional documents:

1. Declaration of the Rights of Man and Citizen, August 26, 1789

An important document in the evolution toward religious liberty, this document stated that "no one may be disturbed on account of his opinions, even religious ones, as long as the manifestation of such opinions does not interfere with the established Law and Order."

2. Preamble to the Constitution of the 4th Republic, October 27, 1946:

This preamble guarantees, among other things, equal access to education, professional training and culture for both children and adults. The State has the duty to organize free public and secular education at all levels. The term "secular" (laïc) first appears as a constitutional term.

3. Constitution of the 5th Republic, October 4, 1958

The current Constitution of France, which established the 5th Republic in 1958, makes explicit reference to the former two texts in its preamble: "The French people solemnly proclaim their attachment to the Rights of Man and the principles of national sovereignty as defined by the Declaration of 1789, confirmed and complemented by the preamble to the Constitution of 1946."

Secularism is established as a core principle of French society: "France is a Republic that is indivisible, secular, democratic, and social. France assures the equality before the law of all its citizens without any distinction based on origin, race, or religion. It respects all beliefs." (Art. 1).

B.   Legislative Texts

In 1881 and 1882, passage of the "Jules Ferry Laws" mark the beginning of the secularization of education in France; Jules Ferry is regarded as the founder of the modern Republican and secular school system. The first law establishes the principle of free education; the second makes education compulsory for all boys and girls aged 6 to 13, and reaffirms its secular nature. Primary schools are instructed to free one day a week to enable children to worship outside the school.

In 1886, passage of the "Goblet Law" ordered a large-scale secularization of the teaching staff and of the entire public education system (also called the Education Nationale). Priests were banned from teaching in public schools, religious education was forbidden from taking place on school premises, and the holy cross disappears from the classroom.

In 1905, France adopted a formal separation between Church and State. This was the most important law reform regarding the status of secularism in France. It separates Church and State and prohibits the State from recognizing, funding, or endorsing any religion. Because of a long history of violent conflict between religious groups, the state decided to break its ties to the Catholic Church and adopt a strong commitment to maintaining a totally secular public sector. The 1905 law is based on two main principles: freedom of conscience and separation between Church and State. This means that France does not recognize any religion in particular, but protects them all, and that religious beliefs have no room in the public sphere. It guarantees freedom of worship: "the Republic ensures freedom of conscience. It guarantees the free exercise of worship." It puts an end to the funding of religious groups: "The Republic neither recognizes, nor salaries, nor subsidizes any religion." Affixing religious signs on public buildings is prohibited. All religious buildings are declared property of the state and local governments. Under the 1905 law, secularism means neutrality in religious matters: the state does not recognize nor fund any religion, yet it recognizes religious organizations (association cultuelles). Religions are recognized as private-law bodies. A follow-up law in 1907 organized the public exercise of religion. In a spirit of conciliation, religious buildings were put at the disposal of religious organizations at no expense, provided they continued to use the buildings for worship purposes.

In 1959, with the passage of the Debré law, which establishes the basic operating and financing rules of private schools, the old quarrel over state aid to religious schools was put to rest. The French government agreed to subsidize private elementary and secondary schools, and to pay their teachers, as long as they applied the same curriculum as the public schools, with the same academic standards, and did not discriminate on grounds of religious affiliation nor make religious education compulsory.

In 1984, the Savary Law reaffirmed the secular nature of higher education and its independence from political, religious, or ideological influence.

Secularism was challenged in the mid-eighties under the pressure of a growing Muslim community. In 2004, after five years of tensions over whether to allow the wearing of religious symbols inside public schools, a law was finally adopted, reaffirming the principle of secularism and banning conspicuous religious attire, behaviors, and symbols in schools. In practice, this ban applied to Muslim headscarves, Sikh turbans, Jewish skullcaps, and large Christian crosses, but was primarily directed at the Muslim headscarf (hijab).

C. High Court Decisions

[EDITORS' NOTE: France can be described as having three supreme courts. Civil or Criminal cases are heard in the last resort by the Cour de Cassation, while claims against the administration or cancellation of administrative decisions, are decided by the Conseil d'Etat. The Conseil d'Etat has the final power to assure the unity of jurisprudence and the power to appeal all administrative rulings. It is also an advisory body which can be solicited by the State and has the capacity to advise State authorities on various legal issues, including how conflicting interpretations of the law should be applied in particular cases. Finally, constitutional challenges regarding statute law are examined by the Conseil Constitutionnel.]

November 23, 1977: The Conseil Constitutionnel acknowledges freedom of education as a fundamental principle of the Republic.

May 3, 2000: The Conseil d'Etat prohibits all agents in the public education system from displaying their religious beliefs during working hours. This advice was confirmed by a court decision from the Paris administrative court on October 17, 2002 which extended this prohibition to all public services.

April 21, 2005: Should religious facts and history be taught at school? Faced with the pressing need to address misinterpretations about different religions and calm down misplaced fears about their influence in today's world, the Conseil Constitutionnel released a decision (n°2005–512–DC) aimed at brushing up curricula and redefining the missions of education. Children should be taught about religious facts and the role religions have played in the shaping of civilizations, all the while respecting freedom of conscience and the principles of secularism and neutrality which are at the heart of the French model.

2. Applications of the French Law of laïcité

A. State financing and religion: an "open" secularism

1. Places of worship

Statute

December 9, 1905: law affirming separation of Church and State.

Article 2: "The Republic does not grant recognition nor pay nor subsidize any church."

The French government is prohibited by law from granting official recognition to religions, and is also prohibited from subsidizing them or paying their clergy. Churches, temples, and synagogues existing before 1905 are the property of the state, and local governments (les communes) are in charge of their maintenance. Cathedrals are under the supervision of the Ministry of Culture and their upkeep falls under the responsibility of the state. Churches and places of worship built after 1905 cannot be subsidized by the state. The Cathédrale de la Résurrection, for example, which is the only new cathedral built in France after 1905, in the Paris suburb of Evry in 1996, is a private building.

In practice, as the government grants legal recognition and a tax-exempt status to entities supporting religious activities (associations cult-uelles), municipalities lease land to these associations of worship via "emphyteutic leases" which are very long-term (generally 99 years) and extremely cheap leases enabling them to build places of worship. And while local governments may not directly subsidize the construction of a religious building, they can finance the cultural space linked to it; the sacred art museum located under the Evry cathedral was thus subsidized by public funding.

Over the years, similar flexible arrangements were adopted by the state to help places of worship survive and to ensure their upkeep. The Law of December 21, 1942 allows public subsidies for repairing religious build-ings. The Law of 1961 allows the state to secure loans subscribed to build religious buildings. The Law of July 23, 1987 on sponsoring, authorizes tax deductions for donations to religious associations.

Adjustments have constantly been made to the principle of strict separation between Church and State: A good example is the August 21, 1920 law which enabled the building of the Great Mosque of Paris (inaugu-rated in 1926) thanks to the vote of a public subsidy of 500,000 francs (around $120,000), while the municipal council of Paris gave out for free the necessary tract of land, as a gesture of gratefulness for all the Muslim soldiers who had given their lives for France during World War I. Subse-quent renovation in 2004 was also partly financed on public funds, by the city of Paris, the government, the Ile-de-France region, as well as the foreign governments of Algeria and Qatar.

As for the clergy, priests are paid by funds collected during mass or annual contributions to parish upkeep (denier de l'Eglise) for which donors can benefit from tax relief. A Catholic priest earns around € 950 a month. The law of 1978 integrates religious personnel into the national system of social security.

B.   Religious schools

Another exception to the strict principle of non-intervention from the state is the way it subsidizes religious schools, yet another example of the "open secularism" practiced by the French.

December 31, 1959: Vote of the Debré law (n°59–1557) which organizes the financing by the State of private schools, 90% of which are Catholic. Two types of schools are identified:

1.   Private/parochial schools receiving government subsidies (enseigne-ment privé sous contrat), the vast majority of private schools;

2.   Private/parochial schools not receiving government subsidies (ens-eignement privé hors contrat)

The French government subsidizes private elementary and secondary schools, and pays their teachers, as long as they apply the same curriculum as the public schools, with the same academic standards, and do not discriminate on grounds of religious affiliation nor make religious education compulsory. The state covers around 85% of the costs at qualifying parochial schools in order to keep the church out of the public classroom. The same educational opportunities are given to children studying in public and private schools, thus preserving the right of families to choose the kind of education they desire for their children. In practice today, it is not uncommon to see Muslim or Jewish children educated in Catholic schools.

In the same vein, the state subsidizes chaplaincies that provide religious education in public high schools and in other public institutions (boarding schools, prisons, asylums, etc.), so as to enable citizens to worship freely.

In August 2004, the law went even further: Article 89 of this law on the freedoms and responsibilities of local governments makes it compulsory for local governments to contribute to the tuition of resident children who decide to attend a private school located outside their jurisdiction. Until then, only the children attending private schools inside their jurisdiction could benefit from public aid.

3. The case of Alsace & Moselle/overseas territories

The most striking exception to this rigorous separation of Church and State is the case of three departments in the east of France, Haut–Rhin and Bas–Rhin (which together make up the Alsace region), and Moselle (part of the Lorraine region), which were under German rule when the 1905 law was voted. When World War I ended in 1918, they were returned to France, which agreed as a pacifying gesture to keep in place the Concordat dating back to Napoleon. Under this regime, there is no separation of Church and State, even though freedom of religion is guaranteed. This Concordat, signed in 1801 between Napoleon and the Vatican, recognizes and subsidizes four religions, Roman Catholic, Lutheran, Calvinist and Jewish, as well as public school education in those religions.

Clergy for these religions, Catholic priests, Protestant ministers and Jewish rabbis are thus civil servants, and are paid by the state. Catholic bishops are named by the French President on the proposal of the Pope. Controversy periodically erupts over this public funding of certain religions, while others argue that since Islam has now become the second largest religion in France, it should enjoy comparable status with the four official religions. The overseas territories of French Guiana and Mayotte, dating back to colonial times, also have public financing of Catholic priests and Muslim imams.

C. Religious Representative Bodies

The full title of the Minister of the Interior, France's Secretary of State, is ''Ministre de l'Intérieur et des Cultes.'' Part of his duty is to ensure the respect of the principles of secularism hand in hand with the official representative bodies of the main religions. All major religions are organized at the national level, and all have legal existence in a national representative body.

Roman Catholicism: While there is no French Catholic Church, nor a single religious authority in France, there is a "Conférence des évêques de France" (CEF) which is the national conference of Roman Catholic bishops of France.

Protestantism: The Protestant Federation of France (FPF) was created in 1905. An estimated 1.1 million (2% of the population) French are of Protestant faith.

Judaism: The CRIF (Conseil Représentatif des Institutions Juives de France), established in 1944 federates the largest French Jewish associations. The Jewish population of France is estimated to be approximately 500,000 (1% of the population).

Islam: Islam is now the second largest religion in France, with an estimated 5 to 7 million Muslims. Islam, in which religion and society are tightly interwoven, poses a great challenge to the principle of secularism as the French understand it. The CFCM (French Council of the Muslim Faith/Conseil National du Culte Musulman), was created by Nicolas Sarkozy when he was Minister of the Interior in 2002, as the controversy over headscarves had begun to build and French Islamic rage toward Israel was increasing. The government pulled together three very different Muslim organizations, ranging from modern assimilationist to Islamic fundamentalist, into a single "French Council of the Muslim Faith," making sure that the leadership was of the first tendency. It held its first meeting in May 2003. In this case, state intervention and pragmatism have been overriding secularism. Attempting to make up for lost time, during which the lack of French-oriented imams (religious leaders) had led to an influx of frequently fundamentalist imams from abroad, the new Muslim council is now trying to figure how to train religious leaders in France. A series of non-religious courses for imams thus opened in January 2008 in Paris, to give trainees a good background in the secular principles of France and French law. Ironically, the institution hosting this new program is none other than ... the Institut Catholique, a private Catholic university!

D. Hospitals

A government recommendation of February 2, 2005 gives guidelines as to the application of secularism within public hospitals. Personnel must respect the principle of secularism as well as strict neutrality. Hospital agents are thus forbidden to display religious symbols. The headscarf issue for nurses was solved by replacing it by a disposable head cover (like those used in operating theaters). Concerning patients, rules respect religious practice. There is no discrimination between patients of different creeds who may worship freely. This includes respecting burial rites. But propaganda and proselytism are prohibited. Women patients may choose the gender of their practitioner, except in emergency cases. This was to prevent objections from more traditional Muslims who opposed examination of their wives by male doctors. On January 24, 2007, a 23–year–old Frenchman named Fouad ben Moussa was charged in Paris with a 6–month prison sentence for violent behavior against a male doctor who had just examined his wife after giving birth.

E. Miscellaneous

Civil Status/Record: Religious ceremonies (weddings, baptism, burials) have no legal status and apart from baptism can take place only after their civil equivalent is recorded. Census forms do not mention religion. The State organizes religious funerals for French Presidents.

Religious holidays: France has not entirely cut itself off from its Catholic religious roots. The six "obligatory feast days" of the Catholic Church—Easter Monday, Pentecost, Christmas, Ascension, Assumption of Mary and All Saints Day—are all public holidays. The holy days of other religions—such as Judaism, Islam or Buddhism—are recognized only in the granting of individual leave of absence for civil servants and schoolchildren.

Public broadcasting: Public television is required to provide religious broadcasting for certain religions, currently Catholicism, Protestantism, the Eastern Orthodox Church, Judaism, Islam and Buddhism. This takes place on Sunday morning.

Dietary laws in public places (school dining halls, etc.): While it is not an obligation, many schools and public places now accommodate dietary restrictions (dishes containing pork meat can always be replaced for example). And most schools still serve fish on Fridays, a remnant of the old Catholic tradition.

F. The current controversy over the 1905 law

The 1905 law has recently come under increased scrutiny in connection with the integration of Muslim and other religious minority groups in French society. As with the headscarf controversy, the financing of mosques is a contentious topic. Since the State is forbidden to chip in, and few French Muslims are wealthy, most Muslim mosques are built via foreign donors like Saudi Arabia, arousing the fear of foreign influence and the rise of fundamentalism. While most Catholic churches were built before 1905, and thus are maintained largely at the expense of the government, followers of Islam and other religions more recently implanted in France have to pay the full price of founding and maintaining religious places of worship.

President Sarkozy is one of the most active advocates of change. In a book published in 2004, (La République, les religions, l'espérance, Cerf Publishers), he had already stated his belief that secularism should be reinterpreted according to the realities of the time, including the proposal that France should help Muslims build and maintain a sufficient number of mosques, in order to encourage Islamic integration into French society. Although committed to secular democracy, he sees the 1905 law as promoting a "negative laïcité" to which he opposes a "positive laïcité" that would allow, among other things, state subsidies for faith-based groups.

In 2005, a commission chaired by Professor Jean–Pierre Machelon was set up with a view to revising the 1905 law, and suggested that local authorities should contribute financial aid to the construction of religious places of worship.

In yet another example of his sometimes confusing wish to revise tradition, the French President, who is also honorary canon of the Basilica of St. John Lateran in Rome, a tradition dating back to 1604, broke a taboo when he delivered his honorary speech on December 20, 2007 and reminded the audience of the Catholic heritage of France, "the eldest daughter of the Church," with "roots [that] are essentially Christian." He also made a controversial comparison between priests and secular teachers, implying that the former had a moral superiority in educating young souls, since "someone who believes is someone who hopes." Presenting the development of religious beliefs as "an asset" for the country is clearly a breach of secularism as the French know it and his overall approach to the question of the place of religion in society is drawing much fire from the advocates of neutrality.

G.   The different perspectives on religion in the U.S. and France

In their attitudes toward the relationship between religion and the state, France and the United States are in fact "two nations divided by a common similarity." Religion is probably one of the major differences (if not the main one) between the U.S. and France. Whereas "religious freedom" in the United States means freedom to practice religion and freedom from state-imposed religion, in France laïcité often means the state protecting citizens from the excesses of religion. For example, whereas in the American tradition, the Islamic faith and its manifestations are fully compatible with religious freedom, in the French tradition, some aspects of Judaism, Islam, and the Sikh religion, such as wearing head coverings in public places (including schools), which are considered neutral ground, are seen as contradictory with the governing principle of laïcité. Laïcité is not only restricted to tolerance, it goes further than that. Everyone can choose to practice a religion or not to practice one, and the freedom of each is actively guaranteed.

This does not mean that the French are anti-religious. Laïcité does not mean opposition to religion. It promotes the free expression of opinion and only rejects the claim of religion as a basis for law or political membership. Conversely, religion is very present in the American public sphere, where a form of civic religion prevails. In the U.S., it is normal and natural to express one's religious beliefs, while in France it is considered a private matter. A marked difference is also the fact that Americans have erected a higher wall of separation between Church and State than the French, who have always tried to accommodate religious practice with the requirements of secularism. For example, religious buildings built before 1905 are the property of the state; the government pays the salaries of teachers in religious schools and these schools are subsidized by public authorities.

———

NOTES

1.   For further reading on French secularism *see*:

Jean Baubérot, The Secular Principle, 2005, http://www.ambafrance-us.org/atoz/secular.asp (Professor at the Ecole des Hautes Etudes en Sciences Sociales (EHESS–Paris) and head of the sociology of religion and secularity department at the National Center for Scientific Research (CNRS).)

Re-examining French-style Secularism, an interview with Catherine Kintzler, professor of philosophy and aesthetics at the University of Lille–III and author of, *Qu'est-ce que la laïcité?* (What is Laicism?), Middle East Times, February 26, 2008, http://www.metimes.com/Opinion/ 2008/02/26/op-ed_catherine_kintzler_on_laicite/3852/.

On President Sarkozy's re-interpretation of "laïcité": Agnès Poirier, *Vive la laïcité! President Nicolas Sarkozy's plan for 'positive secularism' will be fought by the French—and rightly so*, The Guardian, February 13 2008, http://commentisfree.guardian.co.uk/ agnes_poirier/2008/02/vive_la_laicite.html.

Timothy Lehmann, *Man and God in France*, review of La République, les religions, l'espérance by Nicolas Sarkozy, Policy Review, Vol. 130 (April–May 2005). http://www.hoover.org/publications/policyreview/3399376.html.

On the differences between the U.S. and France: Decherf Dominique, *French Views of Religious Freedom: U.S.–France Analysis*, Harvard Center for International Affairs, July 2001, http://www.brookings.edu/articles/2001/07france_decherf.aspx.

2. Professor Pauwels' essay reveals the following practices under French laïcité. Which of them would also be consistent with your understanding of the First Amendment to the United States Constitution?

- Priests cannot teach in public schools, but state-employed chaplains are placed in public high schools to provide religious instruction.
- All religious buildings built before 1905, including churches, mosques and synagogues, are the property of the state, but may be used without charge by their respective religious groups. Clearly, this rule mostly benefits Catholics.
- Teachers in religious schools are paid by the state.
- Teachers in public schools may not express their religious beliefs.
- Contributions to religious associations are tax-deductible.
- In the eastern region of France, and some of the overseas territories, priests, ministers, imams and rabbis are civil servants.
- Religious weddings have no legal status.
- The six "obligatory feast days" of the Roman Catholic Church are public holidays.

C. Germany and Italy

Basic Law for the Federal Republic of Germany
(Grundgesetz, GG)

Article 3 [Equality before the law]

(1) All persons shall be equal before the law.

(2) Men and women shall have equal rights. The state shall promote the actual implementation of equal rights for women and men and take steps to eliminate disadvantages that now exist.

(3) No person shall be favored or disfavored because of sex, parentage, race, language, homeland and origin, faith, or religious or political opinions. No person shall be disfavored because of disability.

Article 4 [Freedom of faith, conscience, and creed]

(1) Freedom of faith and of conscience, and freedom to profess a religious or philosophical creed, shall be inviolable.

(2) The undisturbed practice of religion shall be guaranteed.

"The Crucifix Case"

BVerfGE 93, 1 1 BvR 1087/91 Kruzifix-decision

■ Decided by the German Federal Constitutional Court on May 16, 1995

* * *

1.   By § 13(1), third sentence, of the School Regulations for Elementary Schools in Bavaria (Volksschulordnung—VSO) of 21 June 1983 (GVBl. p. 597), a cross is to be affixed in every classroom in the public elementary schools. The Volksschulordnung is a legal regulation issued by the Bavarian State Ministry for Education and Cultural Affairs, based on a power delegated in the Bavarian Act on Education and Public Instruction (Bay-EUG).... § 13(1) VSO reads:

The school shall support those having parental power in the religious upbringing of children. School prayer, school services, and school worship are possibilities for such support. In every classroom a cross shall be affixed. Teachers and pupils are obliged to respect the religious feelings of all.

2.   Complainants 3–5 are the school-age minor children of complainants 1 and 2. The latter are followers of the anthroposophical philosophy of life as taught by Rudolf Steiner, and bring up their children accordingly. Since their eldest daughter, complainant 3), went to school they have been objecting to the fact that in the schoolrooms attended by their children first of all crucifixes and later in part crosses without a body have been affixed. They assert that through this symbol, in particular through the portrayal of a "dying male body," their children are being influenced in a Christian direction; which runs counter to their educational notions, in particular their philosophy of life.

When complainant 3) entered school in late summer 1986, in her classroom there was a crucifix with a total height of 80 cm and a 60 cm high representation of the body affixed, directly in the field of view of the blackboard. Complainants 1) and 2) asked for removal of this crucifix and declined to send complainant 3) to school as long as she was exposed to that sight. The conflict was initially settled by exchanging the crucifix for a smaller cross without body, affixed over the door. The disputes between complainants 1) and 2) and the school administration however flared up again when their other children went to school and when complainant 3) changed class and finally school, because crucifixes were again affixed in the schoolrooms. By not sending their children to school, sometimes for fairly long periods, complainants 1) and 2) repeatedly secured the compromise solution again (small cross with no body, at the side above the door) for the classrooms, but not for the other schoolrooms. The school administration, moreover, gave complainants 1) and 2) no assurance that the compromise would be kept to at every change of class.

For a time the three children attended a Waldorf school; however, for lack of the necessary funds, this remained only a transitory attempt at resolving the conflict.

3. In February 1991 complainants 1) and 2) brought an action against the Free State of Bavaria before the administrative court, in their own behalf and that of their children, with the aim of having the crosses removed from all rooms frequented or yet to be frequented in public schools by their children in connection with attending school. At the same time they applied for the issuing of a temporary order pending conclusion of the action for removal of crucifixes.

a) The administrative court refused the urgent request. The affixation of crosses in schoolrooms infringed neither the parents' rights regarding upbringing nor the children's fundamental rights. § 13(1), third sentence, VSO did not provide that the cross be used as a means of education and made into an object of the overall school teaching. It served merely for constitutionally unobjectionable support to parents in the religious upbringing of their children. The constitutionally admissible bounds of religious or philosophical references in schooling were not overstepped. The principle of non-identification could not claim the same respect in schooling—by contrast with the purely secular sphere—because in the educational sphere religious and philosophical conceptions had always been of importance. The tension between positive and negative religious freedom had to be resolved having regard to the precept of tolerance in accordance with the principle of concordancy. That meant the complainants could not demand absolute primacy for their negative confessional freedom over the positive confessional freedom of those pupils who were brought up in a religious confession and wished to manifest that. Instead, tolerance and respect were to be expected of the complainants for the religious convictions of others when encountering their exercise of religion at school (for details *see* VG Regensburg, BayVBl 1991, p. 345). * * *

III.

1. The Bavarian Minister–President, expressing the view of the Bavarian State Government, regards the constitutional complaint as unjustified. § 13(1), third sentence, VSO was an emanation of the precept contained in Art. 135, second sentence, of the Bavarian Constitution (BV), found constitutional by the Federal Constitutional Court (BVerfGE 41, 65), that pupils in Bavarian elementary schools were to be taught and brought up in accordance with the principles of the Christian confessions. That meant the values and standards which, decisively marked by Christianity,

had also largely become the common property of the Western cultural area. By affixing school crosses the Bavarian elementary school was giving an upbringing in accordance with those very principles, without thereby becoming involved in theological questions in a way that conflicted with the State's religious and philosophical neutrality. The fact that other pupils might feel themselves addressed in their positive religious freedom did not affect the rights of the complainants. Missionary propaganda through the cross did not occur in general teaching. Nor were rights of the complainants affected when, in the context of religious instruction or school prayer, the cross in the schoolroom abandoned its general symbolic character and was turned into a specific symbol of faith. The complainants need not take part in religious instruction, and could acceptably avoid school prayer. The right to apply their own philosophy of life met its limit in the positive religious freedom of third parties and the concomitant precept of tolerance.... The preamble to the Basic Law spoke of responsibility before God. According to the prevailing overall picture, it was a Christian, Western concept of God the constitutional legislators had had in mind. The school cross did not go beyond that statement, but on the other hand gave concrete form to just this responsibility that the constitutional legislators had at the time themselves felt.

2. On the position of the Catholic Church, the Secretariat of the German Bishops' Conference presented an opinion of the Institute for Law on Church–State Relations of the Dioceses of Germany. It stated that religious references like those objected to here were admissible in public nondenominational schools. The affixation of a wall cross in a schoolroom in no way identified the State with the Christian religion. The cross was not a means of instruction, nor did § 13(1), third sentence, VSO call for associating the content of all teaching with the cross. The provision was instead connected with the constitutionally unobjectionable intent that the school should support parents in the religious upbringing of children, and promote this; all that followed from the State's duty of neutrality was that the school ought not to be a missionary school nor claim any binding validity for the content of Christian beliefs. The complainant's view was by contrast advocacy of a secular or religion-free school from which all religious references were to be excluded. This was a failure to recognize that Art. 4 Basic Law protected both negative and positive forms of expression of religious freedom equally against encroachments by the State. For attendance at compulsory school, religious and philosophical views had always been relevant.... The complainants' negative religious freedom was limited here by the positive religious freedom of those parents who desired a Christian upbringing for their children, and by State law on school organization. The secular State of the Basic Law, while subjecting itself to the precept of non-identification, on the other hand strove for positive, open neutrality. This was closely connected with the precept of tolerance as a further objective definition of the content of Art. 4 Basic Law. The conflicting fundamental rights were to be reconciled in a spirit of practical concordancy. This meant that while the complainants could call for other religions and philosophies of life not to be excluded from the life of the school even at a school run in accordance with Art. 135, 2nd sentence, BV, and for tolerance to be shown to their philosophy of life, in the sense of

respect and acknowledgment, they could not however claim that their negative religious freedom should be allotted absolute primacy, to the detriment of pupils brought up in a religious confession and wishing to profess it, since no room would then be left over for the exercise of positive religious freedom. While the presentation of the cross as a symbol of Christian faith spanning the confessions did confront the complainants with a religious view of the world in which the decisive force of Christian conceptions of faith was affirmed, they were not thereby brought into a constitutionally unacceptable religious or philosophical conflict. They were not forced daily to disclose their position of rejection; instead, they were left the possibility of purely passive non-observance.

3.   The Evangelical Lutheran Church in Bavaria's State–Church Council referred to an expert opinion by the Ecclesiastical Law Institute of the Evangelical Church in Germany. In summary, it stated that the State, pursuant to Art. 7(1) Basic Law, had a separate, equal educational mandate alongside the parents. The Christian nondenominational school in accordance with Art. 135 BV was constitutionally unobjectionable as long as it was not a missionary school and did not claim any binding validity for the content of Christian beliefs. The cross in the classroom was a symbol for the common principles of the Christian confessions in accordance with which pupils in elementary schools were taught and brought up. The cross emblem was not the expression of a particular denominational confession, and certainly not the expression of a Christian State. Negative freedom of religion had no primacy over the positive side of this fundamental right. The State's neutrality in the context of its educational mandate in schools was expressed in the fact that, in a spirit of tolerance and consideration for others, the positive and negative religious freedom of pupils and parents was allowed sway. Since given a reasonably acceptable setting a jointly spoken school prayer did not encroach on the negative religious freedom of dissenters, this was certainly true a fortiori for equipping a schoolroom with a cross. By contrast with school prayers, the cross emblem did not challenge the individual pupil to a decision to take part or not. * * *

IV

* * *

1.   Art. 4(1) Basic Law protects freedom of religion. The decision for or against a faith is according to it a matter for the individual, not the State. The State may neither prescribe nor forbid a faith or religion. Freedom of religion does not however mean just the freedom to have a faith, but also the freedom to live and act in accordance with one's own religious convictions (cf. BVerfGE 32, 98 [106]). In particular, freedom of religion guarantees participation in acts of worship a faith prescribes or is expressed in. This implies, conversely, the freedom to stay away from acts of worship of a faith not shared. This freedom relates similarly to the symbols in which a faith or religion presents itself. Art. 4(1) Basic Law leaves it to the individual to decide what religious symbols to acknowledge and venerate and what to reject. Certainly, in a society that allows room for differing religious convictions, the individual has no right to be spared from others' manifestations of faith, acts of worship or religious symbols. This is

however to be distinguished from a situation created by the State where the individual is exposed without possibility of escape to the influence of a particular faith, to the acts through which it is manifested and to the symbols in which it is presented. Accordingly, Art. 4(1) Basic Law develops its effect of guaranteeing freedom in the very areas of life that are not left to society's spontaneous organization but taken in hand by the State (cf. BVerfGE 41, 29 [49]). Art. 140 Basic Law taken together with Art. 136(4) of the Weimar Constitution (WRV) takes account of this by explicitly prohibiting compelling anyone to take part in religious practices.

Art. 4(1) Basic Law does not however confine itself to barring the State from intervening in the religious convictions, actions, and presentations of individuals or of religious communities. Instead, it further imposes the duty on it to guarantee room for them to operate in which the personality can develop in the philosophical and religious area (cf. BVerfGE 41, 29 [49]), and to protect them against attacks or obstruction by adherents of other religious tendencies or competing religious groups. Art. 4(1) Basic Law, however, does not confer on the individual or on religious communities any entitlement in principle to give expression to their religious conviction with State support. On the contrary, the freedom of religion of Art. 4(1) Basic Law implies the principle of State neutrality towards the various religions and confessions. The State, in which adherents of different or even opposing religious and philosophical convictions live together, can guarantee peaceful coexistence only if it itself maintains neutrality in questions of belief. It may thus not itself endanger religious peace in a society. * * *

Taken together with Art. 6(2) first sentence Basic Law, which guarantees parents the care and upbringing of their children as a natural right, Art. 4(1) Basic Law also covers the right to bring up children in religious and philosophical respects. It is a matter for the parents to convey to their children those convictions in matters of belief and philosophy of life that they find right (cf. BVerfGE 41, 29 [44, 47 f.]). This implies the right to keep the children away from religious convictions that seem to the parents wrong or harmful.

2. This fundamental right is infringed by § 13(1) third sentence VSO, and by the decisions challenged, which are based on this provision.

a) * * * Taken together with universal compulsory schooling, crosses in schoolrooms mean that pupils are, during teaching, under State auspices and with no possibility of escape, confronted with this symbol and compelled to learn "under the cross." This distinguishes the affixing of crosses in classrooms from the frequent confrontation with religious symbols of the most varied religious tendencies arising in everyday life. Firstly, the latter does not proceed from the State but is a consequence of the spread of various religious convictions or religious communities in society. Secondly, it does not have the same degree of inescapability. Certainly, the individual cannot control encounters in the street, in public transport or when entering buildings with religious symbols or manifestations. As a rule, however, these are fleeting encounters, but even in the case of longer confrontation this is not based on a compulsion enforceable where necessary through sanctions. * * *

b) The cross is a symbol of a particular religious conviction and not merely an expression of the Western culture marked partly by Christianity. * * *

The cross continues to be one of the specific faith symbols of Christianity. It is, indeed, its symbol of faith as such. It symbolizes the salvation of man from original sin brought about through Christ's sacrificial death, but at the same time also Christ's victory over Satan and death and his lordship over the world: suffering and triumph simultaneously.... For the believing Christian it is accordingly in many ways an object of reverence and of piety. The equipping of a building or a room with a cross is still today understood as an enhanced profession of the Christian faith by the owner. For the non-Christian or the atheist, just because of the importance that Christianity attaches to it and that it has had in history, the cross becomes a symbolic expression of particular religious convictions and a symbol of their missionary dissemination. It would be a profanation of the cross running counter to the self-perception of Christianity and the Christian churches to regard it, as the decisions challenged do, as a mere expression of Western tradition or cult token without a specific reference to faith. That the cross has a religious reference is also clear from the context of § 13(1) VSO. * * *

3. The basic right to religious freedom is guaranteed without reservation. This does not however mean that it might not be subject to some sort of restrictions. These would, however, have to follow from the constitution itself. The setting up of limits not already laid out in the constitution is not something the legislature can do. Constitutional grounds that might have justified intervention are not however present here. * * *

a) * * * Resolving the unavoidable tension between negative and positive religious freedom while taking account of the precept of tolerance is a matter for the Land legislature, which must through the public decision-making process seek a compromise acceptable to all. In its arrangements it may take as a guide the fact that on the one hand Art. 7 Basic Law allows religious and philosophical influences in the area of schooling, and on the other Art. 4 Basic Law commands the exclusion as far as at all possible of religious and philosophical compulsions when opting for a particular form of school. Both provisions have to be seen together and reconciled with each other through interpretation, since it is only concordance of the objects of legal protection under both articles that can do justice to the decision contained in the Basic Law (cf. BVerfGE 41, 29 [50 f.]). * * *

The affixing of crosses in classrooms goes beyond the boundary thereby drawn to the religious and philosophical orientation of schools. As already established, the cross cannot be divested of its specific reference to the beliefs of Christianity and reduced to a general token of the Western cultural tradition. It symbolizes the essential core of the conviction of the Christian faith, which has undoubtedly shaped the Western world in particular in many ways, but is certainly not shared by all members of society, and is indeed rejected by many in the exercise of their fundamental right under Art. 4(1) Basic Law. Its affixation in State elementary schools is accordingly incompatible with Art. 4(1) Basic Law insofar as these are not Christian nondenominational schools.

b) The affixation of the cross cannot be justified from the positive religious freedom of parents and pupils of the Christian faith either. Positive religious freedom is due to all parents and pupils equally, not just the Christian ones. * * *

Accordingly, the provision of § 13(1), third sentence, VSO that underlies the dispute is incompatible with the fundamental rights mentioned and is to be pronounced null and void. The decisions in the proceedings for provisional protection of rights challenged are to be set aside.... Judges: Henschel, Seidl, Grimm, Söllner, Kühling, Seibert, Jaeger, Haas.

Dissenting opinion

■ JUDGES SEIDL, SÖLLNER and HAAS from the order of the First Panel of 16 May 1995–1BvR 1087/91–* * *

Affixing crosses in classrooms does not infringe the State's duty of philosophical and religious neutrality. Within the validity of the Basic Law, the precept of philosophical and religious neutrality ought not to be understood as an obligation on the State to indifference or secularism. * * *

* * * The mere presence of a cross in the classroom does not compel the pupils to particular modes of conduct nor make the school into a missionary organization. Nor does the cross change the nature of the Christian nondenominational school; instead it is, as a symbol common to the Christian confessions, particularly suitable for acting as a symbol for the constitutionally admissible educational content of that form of school. The affixation of a cross in a classroom does not exclude consideration for other philosophical and religious contents and values in education. The form of teaching is, additionally, subject to the precept of Art. 136(1) BV, according to which, at all schools, the religious feelings of others are to be respected. * * *

Admittedly, this is not a problem of the relation between majority and minority, but one of how in the area of State compulsory schools the positive and negative religious freedom of pupils and their parents can in general be brought into harmony. Resolving this tension, unavoidable in the area of schooling, between negative and positive religious freedom is a matter for the democratic State legislature, which must in the public decision-making process seek a compromise acceptable to all, taking account of the various views (cf. BVerfGE 41, 29 [50]; 52, 223 [247]). Here negative religious freedom is not some superior fundamental right that displaces the positive expressions of religious freedom where they come together. The right of religious freedom is not a right to prevent religion. The necessary adjustment between the two manifestations of religious freedom must be brought about through tolerance (cf. Schlaich, in Kirche und Staat in der neueren Entwicklung, 1980, p. 427 [439]; *Starck, in: v. Mangoldt/Klein, Das Bonner Grundgesetz*, Art. 4(1), 2 Rdnr. 17, with further references). * * *

The psychic impairment and mental burden that non-Christian pupils have to endure from the enforced perception of the cross in class is of only relatively slight weight. The minimum of elements of compulsion which in this respect is to be accepted by pupils and their parents (cf. BVerfGE 41, 29 [51]) is not exceeded. The pupils are not obliged to particular modes of conduct or religious exercises before the cross. They are accordingly—by contrast with school prayer (cf. BVerfGE 52, 223 [245 ff.])—not forced to display their differing philosophical or religious conviction by non-partic-ipation. The danger of their being discriminated against accordingly does not exist from the outset.

Nor are the pupils constitutionally inadmissibly influenced in mission-ary fashion by the cross in the classroom (cf. BVerfGE 41, 29 [51]). Direct influence on the content of teaching or educational objectives in the sense of propaganda for Christian beliefs does not proceed from the cross in the classroom. Moreover, the particular conditions in Bavaria must be taken as a starting point. Pupils are there confronted, even outside the narrower church sphere, with the sight of crosses in many other areas of life. As examples mention will be made only of the roadside crosses frequently to be met with in Bavaria, the many crosses in secular buildings (such as hospitals and old-age homes, but also hotels and restaurants), and finally also the crosses present in private dwellings. In such circumstances the cross in the classroom too remains within the framework of the ordinary; no missionary character attaches to it. * * *

NOTES

1.   The dissenters write that "negative religious freedom is not some superior fundamental right that displaces the positive expressions of reli-gious freedom where they come together. The right of religious freedom is not a right to prevent religion." In American terms, "positive religious freedom" is the right to freely exercise one's religion, while "negative religious freedom" is the right to be free of a state-established religion. Striking the right balance between them is the great challenge of U.S. law, as well as German law.

2.   As in Bavaria (and many European states, as set forth below), Italian law requires the display of the crucifix in every public school classroom. In *Lautsi v. Italy*, the atheist mother of two school-age children challenged this policy. Her claim was rejected by the Italian courts, includ-ing the Constitutional Court. She then brought the case to the European Court of Human Rights, arguing that Italy was violating Article 9 of the European Convention of Human Rights, which requires its signatory states to guarantee freedom of religion. A panel of the Court ruled in her favor. Italy then appealed to the Court's Grand Chamber, which reversed the panel decision by a vote of 15–2, and held that the crucifixes could remain in Italian classrooms. The Court accepted as legitimate the Italian govern-ment's argument that "beyond its religious meaning, the crucifix symbol-ized the principles and values which formed the foundation of democracy and western civilization, and that its presence in classrooms was justifiable on that account." (Par. 67).

3.   The Italian Constitutional Court in *Lautsi* (2011) found that "in Italy the crucifix is capable of expressing, symbolically of course, but appropriately, the religious origin of those values—tolerance, mutual re-spect, valorisation of the person, affirmation of one's rights, consideration

for one's freedom, the autonomy of one's moral conscience vis-à-vis authority, human solidarity and the refusal of any form of discrimination—which characterize Italian civilization. Those values, which have pervaded traditions, a way of life, the culture of the Italian people, form the basis for and spring from the . . . form of secularism appropriate to the Italian State." (*Lautsi*, Par. 16). That is, the crucifix is a symbol of secularism. Italy had a state religion, Roman Catholicism, until 1948. It is now described by its Constitutional Court as a secular (laicita) parliamentary republic. Its Constitution provides that the "State and the Catholic Church are, each within their own sphere, independent and sovereign." (Article 7). Does this language, and the language from the Constitutional Court's decision in *Lautsi*, suggest a different form of secularism than the French secularism described by Professor Pauwels?

4. As set forth by the Court in *Lautsi*, the display of the crucifix in public school classrooms is "expressly prescribed—in addition to Italy—in a few member States, namely: Austria, certain administrative regions of Germany (Länder) and Switzerland (communes), and Poland. Nevertheless, such symbols are found in the State schools of some member States where the question is not specifically regulated, such as Spain, Greece, Ireland, Malta, San Marino, and Romania." (Par. 27).

5. In his dissent, Judge Malinverni argued that "negative freedom of religion is not restricted to the absence of religious services or religious education. It also extends to symbols expressing a belief or a religion. That negative right deserves special protection if it is the State which displays a religious symbol and dissenters are placed in a situation from which they cannot extract themselves." *Lautsi* dissenting opinion at Par. 5.

6. For more on the *Lautsi* case, and on the distinction between positive and negative religious freedom as an emerging European norm, *see* Tommaso Pavone, *Redefining Religious Neutrality: Lautsi vs. Italy and the European Court of Human Rights* (April 3, 2011), http://ssrn.com/abstract=1763412.

7. Just as the presence of religious symbols in public school classrooms raises establishment concerns and affects the religious equality of students who are members of minority religions, state regulation of religious symbols worn by students raises free exercise concerns for all students, whether members of minority or majority religious groups. We will turn to this question in the next chapter, on equality and free exercise.

8. According to the U.S. Department of State's International Religious Freedom Report 2010, the German population (82 million people) is comprised of the following belief systems: 25 million Catholics; 25 million Evangelical Protestants; 4 million Muslims; 1.4 million Christian Orthodox; 245,000 Buddhists; 200,00 Jews; 100,000 Hindus; and 28 million classified as having no religion.

D.   Mexico

The clash between adopting a state religion and embracing secularism has been a central force in Mexican history.

Under Spanish colonial rule, the Roman Catholic Church was the established religion. The Church was responsible for oversight of education, hospitals, and public registry services, and received a 10 percent surcharge on all taxes collected known as the *diezmo*.

The Church played a key role in Mexico's struggle for independence in 1821, and was established as the state religion in Article 1 of the first Constitution of Mexico (1824). ("The Religion of the Mexican Nation, is, and will be perpetually, the Roman Catholic Apostolic. The Nation will protect it by wise and just laws, and prohibit the exercise of any other whatever.")

In 1857, liberal forces introduced a more secular constitution, which led to civil war (the Reform War, 1857–1860). In combination with the Reform laws of 1859, the 1857 Constitution ended legal recognition of the Church. It secularized education, and banned the acquisition of property by religious institutions. Nonetheless, the Church had strong support, and continued to wield substantial influence until the Mexican Revolution (1910–1917).

The Mexican Revolution had a strong secular, anti-clerical component. The adoption of the 1917 Constitution (which remains the current Constitution, as amended) originally placed severe restrictions on Church ownership of property, excluded religious groups from political activity, disallowed religious participation in public education, forbade religious services outside churches, banned clerical dress in public, and granted the government broad powers to expropriate private property in the public interest and to redistribute land. After a period of repression of the Church, however, many of the secular reforms were eased in practice, and the Church regained significant influence. Major amendments in 1992 gave the Church legal capacity as a "religious institution" and authorized the Church to own assets, if "indispensable" for their purposes. Religious instruction is not permitted in public schools; private religious schools are permitted, but cannot receive public funds.

The Constitution continues to provide that there be no established religion (Art. 130), and that religious groups be closely supervised. For example, Article 130 regulates the building of places of worship, and Article 24 provides that "[e]very religious act of public worship must be performed strictly inside places of public worship, which shall at all times be under governmental supervision."

For more on secularism in Mexico, *see* Ricardo Hernandez–Forcada, *The Effect of International Treaties on Religious Freedom in Mexico*, 2002 B.Y.U.L. REV. 301; Jorge A. Vargas, *Freedom of Religion and Public Worship in Mexico: A Legal Commentary on the 1992 Federal Act on Religious Matters*, 1998 B.Y.U.L. REV. 421; Roderic Ai Camp, CROSSING SWORDS: POLITICS AND RELIGION IN MEXICO 3 (1997); Peter Lester Reich, MEXICO'S HIDDEN REVOLUTION, 9 (1995).

NOTES

1. According to the U.S. Department of State's International Religious Freedom Report 2010, of the population of Mexico (approximately 111 million people), 88 percent consider themselves Roman Catholic.

2. According to the Berkley Center for Religion, Peace & World Affairs at Georgetown University, "The growth of Protestantism has resulted in local tensions and hostilities between traditional Catholic populations and Protestant converts, particularly in rural towns of southern Mexico. Between the 1960s and 1990s, the federal government largely turned a blind eye to religious persecution in this region. By 2000, such discrimination had led to hundreds of deaths and the displacement of approximately 30,000 Protestants." Eric Patterson, Mexico: Persecution of Religious Minorities (August 11, 2011), http://berkleycenter.georgetown. edu/publications/mexico-persecution-of-religious-minorities.

CHAPTER VIII

EQUALITY & RELIGION: FREE EXERCISE OF RELIGION FOR RELIGIOUS MINORITIES

INTRODUCTION

As we saw in Chapter VII, in the United States secularism, or the separation of church and state, embraces two concepts. First, the state will not adopt a particular religion; it will remain neutral between religions (non-establishment). This was the subject of Chapter VII, and is comparable to what German law describes as "negative freedom of religion." Second, people are free to practice the religion of their choice without state interference (free exercise of religion). This is the subject of this chapter, and is comparable to what German law describes as "positive freedom of religion." These two concepts do not necessarily go hand in hand, and may at times be in conflict. For example, when the state deprives religious groups of access to public facilities to maintain its neutrality, is it interfering with the free exercise of religion?

As the following cases and materials reveal, free exercise and non-establishment are not mutually dependent. For example, Great Britain has a state-established religion (the Church of England, or Anglicanism) but guarantees freedom of religion to all its citizens. So does Iran, though it is often criticized by human rights groups for failing to adhere to its constitutional guarantees. The United States, France, Turkey, Italy, Canada and India describe themselves as "secular" but, as we have seen and will further explore herein, their secularity has very different meanings.

Issues of equality law arise when members of religious minorities are not afforded the same rights as others. The problems can arise in the context of free exercise rights, as in this chapter, or in state establishment problems, as in chapter VII. Many of the conflicts between the principle of equal treatment for all religious groups and a state's preference for a particular religion occur in public school settings. In this chapter, we focus on secularism, free exercise, and the rights of students. In the past decade, many of the most heated controversies in this area have concerned the right of Muslim girls and women to wear the headscarf, or hijab. We will focus on the regulation of the hijab in France, Turkey and Britain. Note that some of the cases and problems below are approached by courts as problems of speech and political expression rights, but they are applicable to religion as well.

PROBLEM

- Isabelle, a 17 year old high school student, arrived at her public high school wearing a head scarf, as required by her religion. The principal instructed her to remove it. When Isabelle refused, she was indefinitely suspended, and told she could not return to school until she did so with her head uncovered.

What action may Isabelle take in New York, Paris, London, Toronto, or Istanbul?

A.   THE UNITED STATES

Tinker v. Des Moines

393 U.S. 503 (1969)

■ JUSTICE FORTAS delivered the opinion of the Court.

Petitioner John F. Tinker, 15 years old, and petitioner Christopher Eckhardt, 16 years old, attended high schools in Des Moines, Iowa. Petitioner Mary Beth Tinker, John's sister, was a 13–year–old student in junior high school.

In December 1965, a group of adults and students in Des Moines held a meeting at the Eckhardt home. The group determined to publicize their objections to the hostilities in Vietnam and their support for a truce by wearing black armbands during the holiday season and by fasting on December 16 and New Year's Eve. Petitioners and their parents had previously engaged in similar activities, and they decided to participate in the program.

The principals of the Des Moines schools became aware of the plan to wear armbands. On December 14, 1965, they met and adopted a policy that any student wearing an armband to school would be asked to remove it, and if he refused he would be suspended until he returned without the armband. Petitioners were aware of the regulation that the school authorities adopted.

On December 16, Mary Beth and Christopher wore black armbands to their schools. John Tinker wore his armband the next day. They were all sent home and suspended from school until they would come back without their armbands. They did not return to school until after the planned period for wearing armbands had expired—that is, until after New Year's Day.

I.

The District Court recognized that the wearing of an armband for the purpose of expressing certain views is the type of symbolic act that is within the Free Speech Clause of the First Amendment. *See West Virginia State Board of Education v. Barnette*, 319 U.S. 624 (1943); *Stromberg v. California*, 283 U.S. 359 (1931). *Cf. Thornhill v. Alabama*, 310 U.S. 88 (1940); *Edwards v. South Carolina*, 372 U.S. 229 (1963); *Brown v. Louisiana*, 383 U.S. 131 (1966). As we shall discuss, the wearing of armbands in the circumstances of this case was entirely divorced from actually or potentially disruptive conduct by those participating in it. It was closely akin to 'pure speech' which, we have repeatedly held, is entitled to comprehensive protection under the First Amendment. *Cf. Cox v. Louisiana*, 379 U.S. 536, 555 (1965); *Adderley v. Florida*, 385 U.S. 39 (1966).

First Amendment rights, applied in light of the special characteristics of the school environment, are available to teachers and students. It can hardly be argued that either students or teachers shed their constitutional rights to freedom of speech or expression at the schoolhouse gate. This has been the unmistakable holding of this Court for almost 50 years. In *Meyer v. Nebraska*, 262 U.S. 390 (1923), and *Bartels v. Iowa*, 262 U.S. 404 (1923), this Court, in opinions by Mr. Justice McReynolds, held that the Due Process Clause of the Fourteenth Amendment prevents States from forbidding the teaching of a foreign language to young students. Statutes to this effect, the Court held, unconstitutionally interfere with the liberty of teacher, student, and parent.

In *West Virginia State Board of Education v. Barnette*, supra, this Court held that under the First Amendment, the student in public school may not be compelled to salute the flag. Speaking through Mr. Justice Jackson, the Court said:

'The Fourteenth Amendment, as now applied to the States, protects the citizen against the State itself and all of its creatures—Boards of Education not excepted. These have, of course, important, delicate, and highly discretionary functions, but none that they may not perform within the limits of the Bill of Rights. That they are educating the young for citizenship is reason for scrupulous protection of Constitutional freedoms of the individual, if we are not to strangle the free mind at its source and teach youth to discount important principles of our government as mere platitudes.' 319 U.S., at 637.

On the other hand, the Court has repeatedly emphasized the need for affirming the comprehensive authority of the States and of school officials, consistent with fundamental constitutional safeguards, to prescribe and control conduct in the schools. *See Epperson v. Arkansas, supra*, 393 U.S. at 104; *Meyer v. Nebraska, supra*, 262 U.S. at 402. Our problem lies in the area where students in the exercise of First Amendment rights collide with the rules of the school authorities.

II.

The problem posed by the present case does not relate to regulation of the length of skirts or the type of clothing, to hair style, or deportment. *Cf. Ferrell v. Dallas Independent School District*, 392 F.2d 697 (C.A.5th Cir. 1968); *Pugsley v. Sellmeyer*, 158 Ark. 247 (1923). It does not concern aggressive, disruptive action or even group demonstrations. Our problem involves direct, primary First Amendment rights akin to 'pure speech.'

The school officials banned and sought to punish petitioners for a silent, passive expression of opinion, unaccompanied by any disorder or disturbance on the part of petitioners. There is here no evidence whatever of petitioners' interference, actual or nascent, with the schools' work or of collision with the rights of other students to be secure and to be let alone.

Accordingly, this case does not concern speech or action that intrudes upon the work of the schools or the rights of other students.

Only a few of the 18,000 students in the school system wore the black armbands. Only five students were suspended for wearing them. There is no indication that the work of the schools or any class was disrupted. Outside the classrooms, a few students made hostile remarks to the children wearing armbands, but there were no threats or acts of violence on school premises.

The District Court concluded that the action of the school authorities was reasonable because it was based upon their fear of a disturbance from the wearing of the armbands. But, in our system, undifferentiated fear or apprehension of disturbance is not enough to overcome the right to freedom of expression. Any departure from absolute regimentation may cause trouble. Any variation from the majority's opinion may inspire fear. Any word spoken, in class, in the lunchroom, or on the campus, that deviates from the views of another person may start an argument or cause a disturbance. But our Constitution says we must take this risk, *Terminiello v. Chicago*, 337 U.S. 1 (1949); and our history says that it is this sort of hazardous freedom—this kind of openness—that is the basis of our national strength and of the independence and vigor of Americans who grow up and live in this relatively permissive, often disputatious, society.

In order for the State in the person of school officials to justify prohibition of a particular expression of opinion, it must be able to show that its action was caused by something more than a mere desire to avoid the discomfort and unpleasantness that always accompany an unpopular viewpoint. Certainly where there is no finding and no showing that engaging in the forbidden conduct would 'materially and substantially interfere with the requirements of appropriate discipline in the operation of the school,' the prohibition cannot be sustained. *Burnside v. Byars, supra*, 363 F.2d at 749.

In the present case, the District Court made no such finding, and our independent examination of the record fails to yield evidence that the school authorities had reason to anticipate that the wearing of the armbands would substantially interfere with the work of the school or impinge upon the rights of other students. Even an official memorandum prepared after the suspension that listed the reasons for the ban on wearing the armbands made no reference to the anticipation of such disruption.

Moreover, the testimony of school authorities at trial indicates that it was not fear of disruption that motivated the regulation prohibiting the armbands; and regulation was directed against 'the principle of the demonstration' itself. School authorities simply felt that 'the schools are no place for demonstrations,' and if the students 'didn't like the way our elected officials were handling things, it should be handled with the ballot box and not in the halls of our public schools.'

On the contrary, the action of the school authorities appears to have been based upon an urgent wish to avoid the controversy which might result from the expression, even by the silent symbol of armbands, of opposition to this Nation's part in the conflagration in Vietnam. It is revealing, in this respect, that the meeting at which the school principals decided to issue the contested regulation was called in response to a student's statement to the journalism teacher in one of the schools that he wanted to write an article on Vietnam and have it published in the school paper. (The student was dissuaded.)

It is also relevant that the school authorities did not purport to prohibit the wearing of all symbols of political or controversial significance. The record shows that students in some of the schools wore buttons relating to national political campaigns, and some even wore the Iron Cross, traditionally a symbol of Nazism. The order prohibiting the wearing of armbands did not extend to these. Instead, a particular symbol—black armbands worn to exhibit opposition to this Nation's involvement in Vietnam—was singled out for prohibition. Clearly, the prohibition of expression of one particular opinion, at least without evidence that it is necessary to avoid material and substantial interference with schoolwork or discipline, is not constitutionally permissible.

* * *

We reverse and remand for further proceedings consistent with this opinion.

■ [Dissenting opinion by Justice Black omitted.]

—————

NOTES

1. Why begin a discussion of the free exercise of religion with a case about freedom of speech? The two are closely related. The conflicts that arise under the Free Exercise Clause often concern public expressions of religious views, and the right of free exercise is often exercised as a right of free speech on the topic of religion. Consider the relationship as you read the following note.

2. In 2003 the Secretary of Education issued a Guidance on Constitutionally Protected Prayer in Public Elementary and Secondary Schools. It provides, in part, "Students may pray when not engaged in school activities or instruction, subject to the same rules designed to prevent material disruption of the educational program that are applied to other privately initiated expressive activities. Among other things, students may read their Bibles or other scriptures, say grace before meals, and pray or study religious materials with fellow students during recess, the lunch hour, or other noninstructional time to the same extent that they may engage in nonreligious activities. While school authorities may impose rules of order and pedagogical restrictions on student activities, they may not discriminate against student prayer or religious speech in applying such rules and restrictions.... Students may organize prayer groups, religious clubs, and "see you at the pole" gatherings before school to the same extent that students are permitted to organize other non-curricular student activities groups. Such groups must be given the same access to school facilities for assembling as is given to other non-curricular groups, without discrimination because of the religious content of their expression.... Students may

express their beliefs about religion in homework, artwork, and other written and oral assignments free from discrimination based on the religious content of their submissions. Such home and classroom work should be judged by ordinary academic standards of substance and relevance and against other legitimate pedagogical concerns identified by the school." Guidance on Constitutionally Protected Prayer in Public Elementary and Secondary Schools, http://www2.ed.gov/policy/gen/guid/religionandschools/ prayer_guidance.html.

———

Cooper v. Eugene

301 Oregon Supreme Court 358 (1986)

■ LINDE, JUSTICE.

When Janet Cooper, a special education teacher in the Eugene public schools, became a Sikh, she donned white clothes and a white turban and wore them while teaching her sixth and eighth grade classes. In a letter to the staff of the school where she taught, she wrote that she would wear the turban and often wear white clothing as part of her religious practice, and that she had explained this and other changes in her life to her students. She continued to wear her white garb after being warned that she faced suspension if she violated a law against wearing religious dress at her work.

The law provides, in ORS 342.650:

"No teacher in any public school shall wear any religious dress while engaged in the performance of duties as a teacher." * * *

[T]he school superintendent, acting for the school board, suspended Cooper from teaching and reported this action to the Superintendent of Public Instruction, who, after a hearing, revoked Cooper's teaching certificate.

* * *

II.   OREGON'S GUARANTEES OF RELIGIOUS FREEDOM

Cooper's case is not one of declining to comply with an otherwise valid law on grounds of personal religious belief. The law here at issue is not a general regulation, neutral toward religion on its face and in its policy, like the unemployment benefits standards that we sustained against attack under the Oregon Constitution (though not under the First Amendment) by claimants who had been discharged for religiously motivated conduct in *Smith v. Employment Division*, 301 Or. 209 (1986) and *Black v. Employment Division*, 301 Or. 221 (1986). The cases would be comparable if a school regulation prescribed how teachers should dress while on duty without taking account of religious considerations. Then we would have only an issue of statutory authority to make such a regulation, *see Hysong v. Gallitzin School Dist.*, 164 Pa. 629 (1894); *Neuhaus v. Federico*, 12 Or.App. 314 (1973), and an individual claim to exemption on religious grounds. *See, e.g., Goldman v. Weinberger*, 475 U.S. 503 (1986) (military regulation prohibiting headgear indoors applied to Jewish servicemen's yarmulkes); *Menora v. Illinois High School Ass'n*, 683 F.2d 1030 (7th Cir.1982) (rule forbidding headwear while playing basketball applied to yarmulkes). But ORS 342.650 is not neutral toward religion. On the contrary, the religious significance of the teacher's dress is the specific target of this law. The law singles out a teacher's religious dress because it is religious and to the extent that its religious significance is apparent when the wearer is engaged in teaching. The issue therefore is whether the law infringes the right guaranteed to "all men" by Article I, section 2, of the Oregon Constitution "to worship Almighty God according to the dictates of their own consciences," or "control[s] the free exercise, and enjoyment of religious opinions, or interfere[s] with the rights of conscience" contrary to Article I, section 3. . . . The religion clauses of Oregon's Bill of Rights, Article I, sections 2, 3, 4, 5, 6 and 7, are more than a code. They are specifications of a larger vision of freedom for a diversity of religious beliefs and modes of worship and freedom from state-supported official faiths or modes of worship. * * *

The courts' tolerance of overt religious symbolism in public schools has differed over time and perhaps with the religious composition of different communities. Looking beyond the specific facts of the cases, however, the decisions generally have been that more than a teacher's religious dress is needed to show a forbidden sectarian influence in the classroom, but that a rule against such religious dress is permissible to avoid the appearance of sectarian influence, favoritism, or official approval in the public school. The policy choice must be made in the first instance by those with lawmaking or delegated authority to make rules for the schools. The courts' role is to see whether the rule stays within that authority and within the constitution and, if necessary, to give the rule a constitutional interpretation. * * *

IV. THE PERMISSIBLE REACH OF ORS 342.650

* * *

To forbid a teacher to disclose personal views that are identified as such and not attributed to the school, including religious views, involves issues of free speech as well as religion. A program hermetically sealed to exclude all controversy and potentially offensive ideas can hardly be defended as education for the world beyond the classroom. Teachers as well as students have been held free to express their objection to national policy symbolically by their dress. A distinction between privileged personal expression and forbidden "indoctrination" or "proselytizing" is easier to assert than to apply; one teacher's personal views and acts can carry more unintended persuasion than another's most determined teaching efforts. Yet if Janet Cooper on December 6, 1983, only had told her class that she had changed her name because she became a Sikh and what this meant, the school district could hardly have discharged her in order to protect her pupils against religious proselytizing. To disqualify her from teaching under ORS 342.650 for dressing as a Sikh one must find greater significance in the forbidden religious dress than in the verbal religious self-identification.

* * * "[R]eligious dress" must be judged from the perspective both of the wearer and of the observer, that it is dress which is worn by reason of

its religious importance to the teacher and also conveys to children of the age, background, and sophistication typical of students in the teacher's class a degree of religious commitment beyond the choice to wear common decorations that a person might draw from a religious heritage, such as a necklace with a small cross or Star of David. A teacher does not violate the statute by wearing a garment or a color that unintentionally happens to imply membership in some religious group, nor, for instance, by dressing in clerical garb to assume a role in a classroom historical exercise or a performance of, say, George Bernard Shaw's Saint Joan. * * *

The additional element . . . is the continual or frequent repetition of a teacher's appearance in specifically religious (not merely ethnic) dress. The religious influence on children while in the public school that laws like ORS 342.650, in their concern with the employment of nuns wearing their special garb as public school teachers, legitimately seek to prevent is not the mere knowledge that a teacher is an adherent of a particular religion. Their concern is that the teacher's appearance in religious garb may leave a conscious or unconscious impression among young people and their parents that the school endorses the particular religious commitment of the person whom it has assigned the public role of teacher. This is what makes the otherwise privileged display of a teacher's religious commitment by her dress incompatible with the atmosphere of religious neutrality that ORS 342.650 aims to preserve, or so the school authorities may decide. The statute therefore would not be violated whenever a teacher makes an occasional appearance in religious dress, for instance on her way to or from a seasonal ceremony. It is the same distinction as that between an occasional religious meeting, parade or brief display in a public park or building and the permanent erection of a religious symbol, as in *Lowe v. City of Eugene, supra*. Only wearing religious dress as a regular or frequently repeated practice while teaching is grounds for disqualification.

V. CONCLUSION

We conclude that, when correctly interpreted and applied, ORS 342.650 survives challenge under Oregon's guarantees of religious freedom. As interpreted in this opinion, we believe it also does not violate the federal First Amendment.

NOTES

1. In the Cooper case, on appeal to the US Supreme Court, the Court noted probable jurisdiction, but then dismissed for want of a substantial federal question. 480 U.S. 942 (1987).

2. In BVerwG Second Senate 2 BvR 1436/02 ("HEADSCARF CASE") (September 24, 2003), (http://www.utexas.edu/law/academics/centers/trans national/work_new/german/table.php?id=130) the German Federal Constitutional Court held that absent a statute, a school teacher could not be fired for wearing the hijab. "There is an unavoidable tension between the teachers positive freedom of religion on the one hand and, on the other, the states duty to observe neutrality in matters of religion and ideology and the

parents' right to educate their children and the schoolchildren's freedom not to believe. It is for the democratic legislator in the Länder to resolve this tension in the tolerant spirit of the requisite evenhandedness." The court thus left it open to the legislature, on balance, to ban the hijab, if it concluded that a ban was warranted. Following the decision, eight German states passed laws banning the Hijab. *See German Court Upholds Muslim Headscarf Ban in Schools*, http://www.spiegel.de/international/germany/0, 1518,542211,00.html.

3. In *Dahlab v. Switzerland* (no. 42393/98, ECtHR 2001–V), the European Court of Human Rights ruled that Switzerland may not prohibit an elementary public school teacher from wearing the Hijab in class. The case was decided in 2001. Would you expect the same decision today?

4. There have been a number of cases in which students were suspended from schools for wearing the hijab. They will be discussed in the text and notes found in Sections B (Turkey) and C (France) of this chapter.

5. Considering that many forms of Protestantism do not stipulate specific religious dress, does Oregon's law apply evenly to all religions?

Wisconsin v. Yoder

406 U.S. 205 (1972)

■ CHIEF JUSTICE BURGER delivered the opinion of the Court.

On petition of the State of Wisconsin, we granted the writ of certiorari in this case to review a decision of the Wisconsin Supreme Court holding that respondents' convictions of violating the State's compulsory school-attendance law were invalid under the Free Exercise Clause of the First Amendment to the United States Constitution made applicable to the States by the Fourteenth Amendment. For the reasons hereafter stated we affirm the judgment of the Supreme Court of Wisconsin.

Respondents Jonas Yoder and Wallace Miller are members of the Old Order Amish religion, and respondent Adin Yutzy is a member of the Conservative Amish Mennonite Church. They and their families are residents of Green County, Wisconsin. Wisconsin's compulsory school-attendance law required them to cause their children to attend public or private school until reaching age 16 but the respondents declined to send their children, ages 14 and 15, to public school after they completed the eighth grade. The children were not enrolled in any private school, or within any recognized exception to the compulsory-attendance law, and they are conceded to be subject to the Wisconsin statute.

On complaint of the school district administrator for the public schools, respondents were charged, tried, and convicted of violating the compulsory-attendance law in Green County Court and were fined the sum of $5 each. Respondents defended on the ground that the application of the compulsory-attendance law violated their rights under the First and Fourteenth Amendments. The trial testimony showed that respondents believed, in accordance with the tenets of Old Order Amish communities generally, that their children's attendance at high school, public or private, was contrary to the Amish religion and way of life. They believed that by sending their children to high school, they would not only expose themselves to the danger of the censure of the church community, but, as found by the county court, also endanger their own salvation and that of their children. The State stipulated that respondents' religious beliefs were sincere.

Amish objection to formal education beyond the eighth grade is firmly grounded in these central religious concepts. They object to the high school and higher education generally, because the values they teach are in marked variance with Amish values and the Amish way of life; they view secondary school education as an impermissible exposure of their children to a "worldly" influence in conflict with their beliefs. The high school tends to emphasize intellectual and scientific accomplishments, self-distinction, competitiveness, worldly success, and social life with other students. Amish society emphasizes informal learning-through-doing; a life of "goodness," rather than a life of intellect; wisdom, rather than technical knowledge; community welfare, rather than competition; and separation from, rather than integration with, contemporary worldly society.

... The Wisconsin Circuit Court affirmed the convictions. The Wisconsin Supreme Court, however, sustained respondents' claim under the Free Exercise Clause of the First Amendment and reversed the convictions. A majority of the court was of the opinion that the State had failed to make an adequate showing that its interest in "establishing and maintaining an educational system overrides the defendants' right to the free exercise of their religion." 49 Wis. 2d 430, 447 (1971).

I

There is no doubt as to the power of a State, having a high responsibility for education of its citizens, to impose reasonable regulations for the control and duration of basic education. *See, e.g., Pierce v. Society of Sisters*, 268 U.S. 510, 534 (1925). Providing public schools ranks at the very apex of the function of a State. Yet even this paramount responsibility was, in Pierce, made to yield to the right of parents to provide an equivalent education in a privately operated system. There the Court held that Oregon's statute compelling attendance in a public school from age eight to age 16 unreasonably interfered with the interest of parents in directing the rearing of their offspring, including their education in church-operated schools. As that case suggests, the values of parental direction of the religious upbringing and education of their children in their early and formative years have a high place in our society. *See also Ginsberg v. New York*, 390 U.S. 629, 639 (1968); *Meyer v. Nebraska*, 262 U.S. 390 (1923); *cf. Rowan v. Post Office Dept.*, 397 U.S. 728 (1970). Thus, a State's interest in universal education, however highly we rank it, is not totally free from a balancing process when it impinges on fundamental rights and interests, such as those specifically protected by the Free Exercise Clause of the First Amendment, and the traditional interest of parents with respect to the religious upbringing of their children so long as they, in the words of Pierce, "prepare [them] for additional obligations." 268 U.S. at 535.

It follows that in order for Wisconsin to compel school attendance beyond the eighth grade against a claim that such attendance interferes with the practice of a legitimate religious belief, it must appear either that the State does not deny the free exercise of religious belief by its requirement, or that there is a state interest of sufficient magnitude to override the interest claiming protection under the Free Exercise Clause.

II

We come then to the quality of the claims of the respondents concerning the alleged encroachment of Wisconsin's compulsory school-attendance statute on their rights and the rights of their children to the free exercise of the religious beliefs they and their forebears have adhered to for almost three centuries. In evaluating those claims we must be careful to determine whether the Amish religious faith and their mode of life are, as they claim, inseparable and interdependent. A way of life, however virtuous and admirable, may not be interposed as a barrier to reasonable state regulation of education if it is based on purely secular considerations; to have the protection of the Religion Clauses, the claims must be rooted in religious belief.

Giving no weight to such secular considerations, however, we see that the record in this case abundantly supports the claim that the traditional way of life of the Amish is not merely a matter of personal preference, but one of deep religious conviction, shared by an organized group, and intimately related to daily living.

The impact of the compulsory-attendance law on respondents' practice of the Amish religion is not only severe, but inescapable, for the Wisconsin law affirmatively compels them, under threat of criminal sanction, to perform acts undeniably at odds with fundamental tenets of their religious beliefs. *See Braunfeld v. Brown*, 366 U.S. 599, 605 (1961).

In sum, the unchallenged testimony of acknowledged experts in education and religious history, almost 300 years of consistent practice, and strong evidence of a sustained faith pervading and regulating respondents' entire mode of life support the claim that enforcement of the State's requirement of compulsory formal education after the eighth grade would gravely endanger if not destroy the free exercise of respondents' religious beliefs.

III

* * *

We turn, then, to the State's broader contention that its interest in its system of compulsory education is so compelling that even the established religious practices of the Amish must give way. Where fundamental claims of religious freedom are at stake, however, we cannot accept such a sweeping claim; despite its admitted validity in the generality of cases, we must searchingly examine the interests that the State seeks to promote by its requirement for compulsory education to age 16, and the impediment to those objectives that would flow from recognizing the claimed Amish exemption. *See, e. g., Sherbert v. Verner, supra; Martin v. City of Struthers*, 319 U.S. 141 (1943); *Schneider v. State*, 308 U.S. 147 (1939).

The State advances two primary arguments in support of its system of compulsory education. It notes, as Thomas Jefferson pointed out early in our history, that some degree of education is necessary to prepare citizens to participate effectively and intelligently in our open political system if we are to preserve freedom and independence. Further, education prepares individuals to be self-reliant and self-sufficient participants in society. We accept these propositions.

However, the evidence adduced by the Amish in this case is persuasively to the effect that an additional one or two years of formal high school for Amish children in place of their long-established program of informal vocational education would do little to serve those interests. Respondents' experts testified at trial, without challenge, that the value of all education must be assessed in terms of its capacity to prepare the child for life. It is one thing to say that compulsory education for a year or two beyond the eighth grade may be necessary when its goal is the preparation of the child for life in modern society as the majority live, but it is quite another if the goal of education be viewed as the preparation of the child for life in the separated agrarian community that is the keystone of the Amish faith. *See Meyer v. Nebraska*, 262 U.S., at 400.

We must not forget that in the Middle Ages important values of the civilization of the Western World were preserved by members of religious orders who isolated themselves from all worldly influences against great obstacles. There can be no assumption that today's majority is "right" and the Amish and others like them are "wrong." A way of life that is odd or even erratic but interferes with no rights or interests of others is not to be condemned because it is different.

Wisconsin's interest in compelling the school attendance of Amish children to age 16 emerges as somewhat less substantial than requiring such attendance for children generally. For, while agricultural employment is not totally outside the legitimate concerns of the child labor laws, employment of children under parental guidance and on the family farm from age 14 to age 16 is an ancient tradition that lies at the periphery of the objectives of such laws. There is no intimation that the Amish employment of their children on family farms is in any way deleterious to their health or that Amish parents exploit children at tender years. Any such inference would be contrary to the record before us. Moreover, employment of Amish children on the family farm does not present the undesirable economic aspects of eliminating jobs that might otherwise be held by adults.

IV

* * *

Contrary to the suggestion of the dissenting opinion of Mr. Justice DOUGLAS, our holding today in no degree depends on the assertion of the religious interest of the child as contrasted with that of the parents. It is the parents who are subject to prosecution here for failing to cause their children to attend school, and it is their right of free exercise, not that of their children, that must determine Wisconsin's power to impose criminal penalties on the parent. The dissent argues that a child who expresses a desire to attend public high school in conflict with the wishes of his parents should not be prevented from doing so. There is no reason for the Court to consider that point since it is not an issue in the case. The children are not parties to this litigation. The State has at no point tried this case on the theory that respondents were preventing their children from attending school against their expressed desires, and indeed the record is to the contrary. The State's position from the outset has been that it is empowered to apply its compulsory-attendance law to Amish parents in the same manner as to other parents—that is, without regard to the wishes of the child. That is the claim we reject today.

Our holding in no way determines the proper resolution of possible competing interests of parents, children, and the State in an appropriate state court proceeding in which the power of the State is asserted on the theory that Amish parents are preventing their minor children from attending high school despite their expressed desires to the contrary. Recognition of the claim of the State in such a proceeding would, of course, call into question traditional concepts of parental control over the religious upbringing and education of their minor children recognized in this Court's past decisions. It is clear that such an intrusion by a State into family decisions in the area of religious training would give rise to grave questions of religious freedom comparable to those raised here and those presented in *Pierce v. Society of Sisters*, 268 U.S. 510 (1925). On this record we neither reach nor decide those issues.

Indeed it seems clear that if the State is empowered, as parens patriae, to "save" a child from himself or his Amish parents by requiring an additional two years of compulsory formal high school education, the State will in large measure influence, if not determine, the religious future of the child. Even more markedly than in *Prince*, therefore, this case involves the fundamental interest of parents, as contrasted with that of the State, to guide the religious future and education of their children. The history and culture of Western civilization reflect a strong tradition of parental concern for the nurture and upbringing of their children. This primary role of the parents in the upbringing of their children is now established beyond debate as an enduring American tradition.

In the face of our consistent emphasis on the central values underlying the Religion Clauses in our constitutional scheme of government, we cannot accept a parens patriae claim of such all-encompassing scope and with such sweeping potential for broad and unforeseeable application as that urged by the State.

V

For the reasons stated we hold, with the Supreme Court of Wisconsin, that the First and Fourteenth Amendments prevent the State from compelling respondents to cause their children to attend formal high school to age 16. Our disposition of this case, however, in no way alters our recognition of the obvious fact that courts are not school boards or legislatures, and are ill-equipped to determine the "necessity" of discrete aspects of a State's program of compulsory education. This should suggest that courts must move with great circumspection in performing the sensitive and delicate task of weighing a State's legitimate social concern when faced with religious claims for exemption from generally applicable educational requirements. It cannot be overemphasized that we are not dealing with a way of life and mode of education by a group claiming to have recently discovered some "progressive" or more enlightened process for rearing children for modern life.

Aided by a history of three centuries as an identifiable religious sect and a long history as a successful and self-sufficient segment of American society, the Amish in this case have convincingly demonstrated the sincerity of their religious beliefs, the interrelationship of belief with their mode of life, the vital role that belief and daily conduct play in the continued survival of Old Order Amish communities and their religious organization, and the hazards presented by the State's enforcement of a statute generally valid as to others. Beyond this, they have carried the even more difficult burden of demonstrating the adequacy of their alternative mode of continuing informal vocational education in terms of precisely those overall interests that the State advances in support of its program of compulsory high school education. In light of this convincing showing, one that probably few other religious groups or sects could make, and weighing the minimal difference between what the State would require and what the Amish already accept, it was incumbent on the State to show with more particularity how its admittedly strong interest in compulsory education would be adversely affected by granting an exemption to the Amish.

Affirmed.

■ JUSTICE DOUGLAS, dissenting in part.

I

I agree with the Court that the religious scruples of the Amish are opposed to the education of their children beyond the grade schools, yet I disagree with the Court's conclusion that the matter is within the dispensation of parents alone. The Court's analysis assumes that the only interests at stake in the case are those of the Amish parents on the one hand, and those of the State on the other. The difficulty with this approach is that, despite the Court's claim, the parents are seeking to vindicate not only their own free exercise claims, but also those of their high-school-age children.

II

* * *

On this important and vital matter of education, I think the children should be entitled to be heard. While the parents, absent dissent, normally speak for the entire family, the education of the child is a matter on which the child will often have decided views. He may want to be a pianist or an astronaut or an oceanographer. To do so he will have to break from the Amish tradition.

It is the future of the student, not the future of the parents, that is imperiled by today's decision. If a parent keeps his child out of school beyond the grade school, then the child will be forever barred from entry into the new and amazing world of diversity that we have today. The child may decide that that is the preferred course, or he may rebel. It is the student's judgment, not his parents', that is essential if we are to give full meaning to what we have said about the Bill of Rights and of the right of students to be masters of their own destiny. If he is harnessed to the Amish way of life by those in authority over him and if his education is truncated, his entire life may be stunted and deformed. The child, therefore, should be given an opportunity to be heard before the State gives the exemption which we honor today.

NOTES

1. The majority here had to draw a distinction between ways of life based upon religious considerations versus secular considerations. In this vein, they write that "the traditional way of life of the Amish is not merely a matter of personal preference, but one of deep religious conviction, shared by an organized group, and intimately related to daily living." If we take deep conviction, group organization, and relation to daily living as criteria, would certain choices—like living on a commune—be considered religious ways of life? Has the Court convincingly treated the distinction between religious and secular ways of life?

2. According to the majority, the long history of the Amish demonstrated "the sincerity of their religious beliefs." How would newer religions like Scientology fare under this Court's analysis?

Cheema v. Thompson

67 F.3d 883 (9th Cir. 1995)

■ HALL, CIRCUIT JUDGE:

Appellants Livingston Union School District (the "school district") appeal the district court's preliminary injunction ordering them to accommodate three schoolchildren's religious practices until this dispute under the Religious Freedoms Restoration Act of 1993 ("RFRA"), 42 U.S.C. §§ 2000bb et seq., can be litigated on the merits. * * *

I.

Three young Khalsa Sikh children stand at the center of this controversy: Rajinder, Sukhjinder, and Jaspreet Cheema (together, the "children" or "Cheemas"). A central tenet of their religion requires them to wear at all times five symbols of their faith: "kes" (long hair), "kangha" (comb), "kachch" (sacred underwear), "kara" (steel bracelet), and a "kirpan" (ceremonial knife). This case began when the school district in which the Cheemas reside refused to allow the children to wear kirpans to school.

The school district relied on its total ban of all weapons, including knives, from school grounds. It also pointed to two state statutes, both of which it thought compelled its policy. *See* Cal. Pen. Code § 626.10(a) (making it a crime to carry a knife with a blade longer than 2 1/2 inches on school property); Cal. Educ. Code § 48915(a) (authorizing expulsion for the possession of "any knife . . . of no reasonable use to the pupil" on school grounds). As far as the school district was concerned, there was nothing left to discuss; a kirpan was unquestionably a knife, and as such it fell squarely within the absolute ban.

This left the Cheema children with two choices if they wished to attend school: either leave their kirpans at home (and violate a fundamental tenet of their religion) or bring them to school (and face expulsion and/or criminal prosecution).

II.

The Cheemas claimed in their lawsuit that the district's policy, as applied to them, violated their statutory right to the free exercise of religion as guaranteed by 42 U.S.C. §§ 2000bb et seq. The children immediately asked for a preliminary injunction enjoining enforcement of the ban. The district court denied the motion, and the children appealed.

To prevail under RFRA, the children had to prove that their insistence on wearing kirpans was animated by a sincere religious belief and that the school district's refusal to accommodate that belief put a substantial burden on their exercise of religion. *See* 42 U.S.C. § 2000bb–1(a). The children unquestionably carried their burden.

We concluded, as did the district court, that the school district had a compelling interest in campus safety. *See, e.g., Wisconsin v. Yoder*, 406 U.S. 205, 213 (1972). We even agreed that the kirpan ban served that interest, despite the almost total lack of evidentiary support in the record. But we simply could not conclude that nothing short of a wholesale ban would adequately protect student safety. The problem was a total failure of proof; the school district refused to produce any evidence whatever to demonstrate the lack of a less restrictive alternative. Its stance, both before the district court and the panel, was that it had no obligation to do so. It was quite mistaken. *See* 42 U.S.C. § 2000bb–2(3) (putting burdens of production and persuasion on the government).

The district court overlooked this problem. When it denied the children's motion for a preliminary injunction, it simply declared that the absolute ban was necessary to protect the school district's compelling interest in, among other things, student safety. Order of May 27, 1995. The district court's failure to consider RFRA's "no less restrictive alternative" requirement left us no choice but to reverse.

III.

On remand the district court invited the parties to negotiate the terms of the preliminary injunction. The parties, however, failed to agree on a compromise solution, so the district court, as we specifically instructed, imposed its own plan. It ordered the school district to lift its wholesale kirpan ban and allow the children (and their kirpans) back to school under the following conditions:

1) the kirpan will be of the type demonstrated to the Board and to the District Court, that is: a dull blade, approximately 3–3 1/2 inches in length with a total length of approximately 6 1/2–7 inches including its sheath;

2) the kirpan will be sewn tightly to its sheath;

3) the kirpan will be worn on a cloth strap under the children's clothing so that it is not readily visible;

4) a designated official of the District may make reasonable inspections to confirm that the conditions specified about are being adhered to;

5) if any of the conditions specified above are violated, the student's privilege of wearing his or her kirpan may be suspended; and

6) the District will take all reasonable steps to prevent any harassment, intimidation or provocation of the Cheema children by any employee or student in the District and will take appropriate disciplinary action to prevent and redress such action, should it occur. . . .

The school district now appeals. Again, our review is for abuse of discretion. This time we find none.

■ WIGGINS, CIRCUIT JUDGE, dissenting.

The majority affirms the district court's pre-trial "plan of accommodation," under which a school district is enjoined from enforcing both its own no-knives policy and a state statutory limitation on the size of knives on campuses against Sikh children who carry their knives ("kirpans") for religious reasons. Further, the plan of accommodation bars the school district from requiring that the kirpans in question be riveted to their sheaths. As a result of the majority's ruling, the school district must allow 7, 8 and 10 year-old children to carry 7-inch knives to school, as long as the knives are worn under the children's clothing and are sewn to their sheaths, even though: the district court originally concluded that the knives in question are dangerous; the children's own expert testified that sewing the knives to the sheaths does not render them unremovable; no evidence was presented showing that the 7, 8 and 10 year-olds in question are any more mature than other children of the same age; evidence was presented that the children in question, despite their religious dictates, have exposed their knives during play; evidence was presented that one of the children has stated his willingness to use his knife when wronged; the children's expert testified that the children's faith allows, or even mandates, that they use their knives in propagation of "God's justice"; and the same expert testified, and the district court found, that the children's faith allows them to use their knives for defensive purposes. I dissent.

————

NOTES

1. The *Cheema* case was brought under the Religious Freedom Restoration act, which was subsequently declared unconstitutional in *City of*

Boerne v. Flores, 521 U.S. 507 (1997). Had it been brought as a Section 1983 case, the result would have probably been unchanged.

2. Other cases in which Sikh children have been permitted to wear kirpans to school include *New York v. Partap Singh*, 516 N.Y.S.2d 412 (1987) (U.S. First Amendment) and *Multani v. Commission scolaire Marguerite–Bourgeoys*, (2006) 1 S.C.R. 256 (Supreme Court of Canada, Canadian Charter of Rights and Freedoms section 2(a)) (further discussed in section E of this chapter).

3. Article 25, Explanation 1 of the Constitution of India permits the carrying of the kirpan by Sikhs as part of its guarantee of the "right freely to profess, practice and propagate religion."

4. Under UK law, carrying a knife in public is prohibited, but an exception is made when it is carried for religious reasons. *See* Criminal Justice Act of 1988, Section 139.

5. In Denmark, research scientist Ripudamen Singh was convicted of carrying a knife (his kirpan) and sentenced to six days imprisonment, or a DKK 3,000 (approximately $550) fine. The court rejected his religious defense. *See*, http://www.unp.me/f46/danish-court-sentences-sikh-youth-for-carrying-kirpan–11303/.

6. There have been a number of cases in which Muslim students were suspended from schools in various parts of the world for wearing a headscarf (or hijab). They will be discussed in the text and notes found in the Sections B (Turkey) and C (France) of this chapter.

———

Goldman v. Weinberger

475 U.S. 503 (1986)

■ JUSTICE REHNQUIST delivered the opinion of the Court.

Petitioner Goldman is an Orthodox Jew and ordained rabbi. In 1973, he was accepted into the Armed Forces Health Professions Scholarship Program and placed on inactive reserve status in the Air Force while he studied clinical psychology at Loyola University of Chicago. During his three years in the scholarship program, he received a monthly stipend and an allowance for tuition, books, and fees. After completing his Ph.D. in psychology, petitioner entered active service in the United States Air Force as a commissioned officer, in accordance with a requirement that participants in the scholarship program serve one year of active duty for each year of subsidized education. Petitioner was stationed at March Air Force Base in Riverside, California, and served as a clinical psychologist at the mental health clinic on the base.

Until 1981, petitioner was not prevented from wearing his yarmulke on the base. He avoided controversy by remaining close to his duty station in the health clinic and by wearing his service cap over the yarmulke when out of doors. But in April 1981, after he testified as a defense witness at a court-martial wearing his yarmulke but not his service cap, opposing counsel lodged a complaint with Colonel Joseph Gregory, the Hospital

Commander, arguing that petitioner's practice of wearing his yarmulke was a violation of Air Force Regulation (AFR) 35–10. This regulation states in pertinent part that "[h]eadgear will not be worn ... [w]hile indoors except by armed security police in the performance of their duties." AFR 35–10, ¶ 1–6.h(2)(f) (1980).

Colonel Gregory informed petitioner that wearing a yarmulke while on duty does indeed violate AFR 35–10, and ordered him not to violate this regulation outside the hospital. Although virtually all of petitioner's time on the base was spent in the hospital, he refused. Later, after petitioner's attorney protested to the Air Force General Counsel, Colonel Gregory revised his order to prohibit petitioner from wearing the yarmulke even in the hospital. Petitioner's request to report for duty in civilian clothing pending legal resolution of the issue was denied. The next day he received a formal letter of reprimand, and was warned that failure to obey AFR 35–10 could subject him to a court-martial. Colonel Gregory also withdrew a recommendation that petitioner's application to extend the term of his active service be approved, and substituted a negative recommendation.

Petitioner then sued respondent Secretary of Defense and others, claiming that the application of AFR 35–10 to prevent him from wearing his yarmulke infringed upon his First Amendment freedom to exercise his religious beliefs.

* * *

The considered professional judgment of the Air Force is that the traditional outfitting of personnel in standardized uniforms encourages the subordination of personal preferences and identities in favor of the overall group mission. Uniforms encourage a sense of hierarchical unity by tending to eliminate outward individual distinctions except for those of rank. The Air Force considers them as vital during peacetime as during war because its personnel must be ready to provide an effective defense on a moment's notice; the necessary habits of discipline and unity must be developed in advance of trouble. We have acknowledged that "[t]he inescapable demands of military discipline and obedience to orders cannot be taught on battle-fields; the habit of immediate compliance with military procedures and orders must be virtually reflex with no time for debate or reflection...." A narrow exception to this rule exists for headgear worn during indoor religious ceremonies. *See* AFR 35–10, ¶ 1–6.h(2)(d) (1980). In addition, military commanders may in their discretion permit visible religious headgear and other such apparel in designated living quarters and nonvisible items generally. *See* Department of Defense Directive 1300.17 (June 18, 1985).

Petitioner Goldman contends that the Free Exercise Clause of the First Amendment requires the Air Force to make an exception to its uniform dress requirements for religious apparel unless the accouterments create a "clear danger" of undermining discipline and esprit de corps. He asserts that in general, visible but "unobtrusive" apparel will not create such a danger and must therefore be accommodated. He argues that the Air Force failed to prove that a specific exception for his practice of wearing an unobtrusive yarmulke would threaten discipline. He contends that the Air Force's assertion to the contrary is mere *ipse dixit*, with no support from actual experience or a scientific study in the record, and is contradicted by expert testimony that religious exceptions to AFR 35–10 are in fact desirable and will increase morale by making the Air Force a more humane place.

But whether or not expert witnesses may feel that religious exceptions to AFR 35–10 are desirable is quite beside the point. The desirability of dress regulations in the military is decided by the appropriate military officials, and they are under no constitutional mandate to abandon their considered professional judgment. Quite obviously, to the extent the regulations do not permit the wearing of religious apparel such as a yarmulke, a practice described by petitioner as silent devotion akin to prayer, military life may be more objectionable for petitioner and probably others. But the First Amendment does not require the military to accommodate such practices in the face of its view that they would detract from the uniformity sought by the dress regulations. The Air Force has drawn the line essentially between religious apparel that is visible and that which is not, and we hold that those portions of the regulations challenged here reasonably and evenhandedly regulate dress in the interest of the military's perceived need for uniformity. The First Amendment therefore does not prohibit them from being applied to petitioner even though their effect is to restrict the wearing of the headgear required by his religious beliefs.

■ JUSTICE STEVENS, with whom JUSTICE WHITE and JUSTICE POWELL join, concurring.

Captain Goldman presents an especially attractive case for an exception from the uniform regulations that are applicable to all other Air Force personnel. His devotion to his faith is readily apparent. The yarmulke is a familiar and accepted sight. In addition to its religious significance for the wearer, the yarmulke may evoke the deepest respect and admiration—the symbol of a distinguished tradition and an eloquent rebuke to the ugliness of anti-Semitism. Captain Goldman's military duties are performed in a setting in which a modest departure from the uniform regulation creates almost no danger of impairment of the Air Force's military mission. Moreover, on the record before us, there is reason to believe that the policy of strict enforcement against Captain Goldman had a retaliatory motive—he had worn his yarmulke while testifying on behalf of a defendant in a court-martial proceeding. Nevertheless, as the case has been argued, I believe we must test the validity of the Air Force's rule not merely as it applies to Captain Goldman but also as it applies to all service personnel who have sincere religious beliefs that may conflict with one or more military commands.

* * *

■ JUSTICE BRENNAN, with whom JUSTICE MARSHALL joins, dissenting.

Simcha Goldman invokes this Court's protection of his First Amendment right to fulfill one of the traditional religious obligations of a male Orthodox Jew—to cover his head before an omnipresent God. The Court's response to Goldman's request is to abdicate its role as principal expositor of the Constitution and protector of individual liberties in favor of credu-

lous deference to unsupported assertions of military necessity. I dissent.
* * *

B.   TURKEY

Sahin v. Turkey

Case #44774/98, European Court of Human Rights (10 November 2005)

■ GRAND CHAMBER

PROCEDURE

1.   The case originated in an application against the Republic of
Turkey lodged with the European Commission of Human Rights ("the
Commission") under former Article 25 of the Convention for the Protection
of Human Rights and Fundamental Freedoms ("the Convention") by a
Turkish national, Ms Leyla Şahin ("the applicant"), on 21 July 1998.

3.   The applicant alleged that her rights and freedoms under Articles
8, 9, 10 and 14 of the Convention and Article 2 of Protocol No. 1 had been
violated by regulations on wearing the Islamic headscarf in institutions of
higher education.

8.   In its judgment of 29 June 2004 ("the Chamber judgment"), the
Chamber held unanimously that there had been no violation of Article 9 of
the Convention on account of the ban on wearing the headscarf and that no
separate question arose under Articles 8 and 10, Article 14 taken in
conjunction with Article 9 of the Convention, and Article 2 of Protocol No.
1.

THE FACTS

I.   THE CIRCUMSTANCES OF THE CASE

14.   The applicant was born in 1973 and has lived in Vienna since
1999, when she left Istanbul to pursue her medical studies at the Faculty of
Medicine at Vienna University. She comes from a traditional family of
practising Muslims and considers it her religious duty to wear the Islamic
headscarf.

A.   The circular of 23 February 1998

15.   On 26 August 1997 the applicant, then in her fifth year at the
Faculty of Medicine at Bursa University, enrolled at the Cerrahpaşa Faculty of Medicine at Istanbul University. She says she wore the Islamic
headscarf during the four years she spent studying medicine at the University of Bursa and continued to do so until February 1998.

16.   On 23 February 1998 the Vice–Chancellor of Istanbul University
issued a circular, the relevant part of which provides:

"By virtue of the Constitution, the law and regulations, and in accordance with the case-law of the Supreme Administrative Court and the
European Commission of Human Rights and the resolutions adopted by the

university administrative boards, students whose 'heads are covered' (who wear the Islamic headscarf) and students (including overseas students) with beards must not be admitted to lectures, courses or tutorials. . . .

17. On 12 March 1998, in accordance with the aforementioned circular, the applicant was denied access by invigilators to a written examination on oncology because she was wearing the Islamic headscarf. On 20 March 1998 the secretariat of the chair of orthopaedic traumatology refused to allow her to enrol because she was wearing a headscarf. On 16 April 1998 she was refused admission to a neurology lecture and on 10 June 1998 to a written examination on public health, again for the same reason.

B. The application for an order setting aside the circular of 23 February 1998

18. On 29 July 1998 the applicant lodged an application for an order setting aside the circular of 23 February 1998. In her written pleadings, she submitted that the circular and its implementation had infringed her rights guaranteed by Articles 8, 9 and 14 of the Convention and Article 2 of Protocol No. 1, in that there was no statutory basis for the circular and the Vice–Chancellor's Office had no regulatory power in that sphere.

19. In a judgment of 19 March 1999, the Istanbul Administrative Court dismissed the application. . . .

C. The disciplinary measures taken against the applicant

21. In May 1998 disciplinary proceedings were brought against the applicant under paragraph 6 (a) of the Students Disciplinary Procedure Rules (*see* paragraph 50 below) as a result of her failure to comply with the rules on dress.

22. On 26 May 1998, in view of the fact that the applicant had shown by her actions that she intended to continue wearing the headscarf to lectures and/or tutorials, the dean of the faculty declared that her attitude and failure to comply with the rules on dress were not befitting of a student. He therefore decided to issue her with a warning.

23. On 15 February 1999 an unauthorised assembly gathered outside the deanery of the Cerrahpaşa Faculty of Medicine to protest against the rules on dress.

24. On 26 February 1999 the dean of the faculty began disciplinary proceedings against various students, including the applicant, for joining the assembly. On 13 April 1999, after hearing her representations, he suspended her from the university for a semester pursuant to Article 9 (j) of the Students Disciplinary Procedure Rules (*see* paragraph 50 below).

25. On 10 June 1999 the applicant lodged an application with the Istanbul Administrative Court for an order quashing the decision to suspend her. The application was dismissed on 30 November 1999 by the Istanbul Administrative Court on the ground that, in the light of the material in the case file and the settled case-law on the subject, the impugned measure could not be regarded as illegal.

28.   In the meantime, on 16 September 1999, the applicant abandoned her studies in Turkey and enrolled at Vienna University, where she pursued her university education.

II.   RELEVANT LAW AND PRACTICE

A.   The Constitution

29.   The relevant provisions of the Constitution provide:

Article 2

"The Republic of Turkey is a democratic, secular [laik] and social State based on the rule of law that is respectful of human rights in a spirit of social peace, national solidarity and justice, adheres to the nationalism of Atatürk and is underpinned by the fundamental principles set out in the Preamble."

* * *

Article 10

"All individuals shall be equal before the law without any distinction based on language, race, colour, sex, political opinion, philosophical belief, religion, membership of a religious sect or other similar grounds.

Men and women shall have equal rights. The State shall take action to achieve such equality in practice.

No privileges shall be granted to any individual, family, group or class.

State bodies and administrative authorities shall act in compliance with the principle of equality before the law in all circumstances."

* * *

Article 24

"Everyone shall have the right to freedom of conscience, belief and religious conviction.

* * *

Article 42

"No one may be deprived of the right to instruction and education.

* * *

B.   History and background

1.   *Religious dress and the principle of secularism*

30.   The Turkish Republic was founded on the principle that the State should be secular (*laik*). Before and after the proclamation of the Republic on 29 October 1923, the public and religious spheres were separated through a series of revolutionary reforms: the abolition of the caliphate on 3 March 1923; the repeal of the constitutional provision declaring Islam the religion of the State on 10 April 1928; and, lastly, on 5 February 1937, a constitutional amendment according constitutional status to the principle

of secularism (*see* Article 2 of the Constitution of 1924 and Article 2 of the Constitutions of 1961 and 1982, as set out in paragraph 29 above).

31.   The principle of secularism was inspired by developments in Ottoman society in the period between the nineteenth century and the proclamation of the Republic. The idea of creating a modern public society in which equality was guaranteed to all citizens without distinction on grounds of religion, denomination or sex had already been mooted in the Ottoman debates of the nineteenth century. Significant advances in women's rights were made during this period (equality of treatment in education, the introduction of a ban on polygamy in 1914, the transfer of jurisdiction in matrimonial cases to the secular courts that had been established in the nineteenth century).

32.   The defining feature of the Republican ideal was the presence of women in public life and their active participation in society. Consequently, the ideas that women should be freed from religious constraints and that society should be modernised had a common origin. Thus, on 17 February 1926 the Civil Code was adopted, which provided for equality of the sexes in the enjoyment of civic rights, in particular with regard to divorce and succession. Subsequently, through a constitutional amendment of 5 December 1934 (Article 10 of the 1924 Constitution), women obtained equal political rights to men.

33.   The first legislation to regulate dress was the Headgear Act of 28 November 1925 (Law no. 671), which treated dress as a modernity issue. Similarly, a ban was imposed on wearing religious attire other than in places of worship or at religious ceremonies, irrespective of the religion or belief concerned, by the Dress (Regulations) Act of 3 December 1934 (Law no. 2596).

34.   Under the Education Services (Merger) Act of 3 March 1924 (Law no. 430), religious schools were closed and all schools came under the control of the Ministry of Education. The Act is one of the laws with constitutional status that are protected by Article 174 of the Turkish Constitution.

35.   In Turkey, wearing the Islamic headscarf to school and university is a recent phenomenon which only really began to emerge in the 1980s. There has been extensive discussion on the issue and it continues to be the subject of lively debate in Turkish society. Those in favour of the headscarf see wearing it as a duty and/or a form of expression linked to religious identity. However, the supporters of secularism, who draw a distinction between the *başörtüsü* (traditional Anatolian headscarf, worn loosely) and the *türban* (tight, knotted headscarf hiding the hair and the throat), see the Islamic headscarf as a symbol of a political Islam. As a result of the accession to power on 28 June 1996 of a coalition government comprising the Islamist Refah Partisi, and the centre-right Doğru Yol Partisi, the debate has taken on strong political overtones. The ambivalence displayed by the leaders of the Refah Partisi, including the then Prime Minister, over their attachment to democratic values, and their advocacy of a plurality of legal systems functioning according to different religious rules for each religious community was perceived in Turkish society as a genuine threat to republican values and civil peace (*see Refah Partisi (the Welfare Party)*

and Others v. Turkey [GC], nos. 41340/98, 41342/98, 41343/98 and
41344/98, ECtHR 2003–II).

2. *The rules on dress in institutions of higher education and the case-law
of the Constitutional Court*

37. On 20 December 1982 the Higher Education Authority issued a
circular on the wearing of headscarves in institutions of higher education.
The Islamic headscarf was banned in lecture theatres. In a judgment of 13
December 1984, the Supreme Administrative Court held that the regulations were lawful, noting:

"Beyond being a mere innocent practice, wearing the headscarf is in
the process of becoming the symbol of a vision that is contrary to the
freedoms of women and the fundamental principles of the Republic."

D. Comparative law

55. For more than twenty years the place of the Islamic headscarf in
State education has been the subject of debate across Europe. In most
European countries, the debate has focused mainly on primary and secondary schools. However, in Turkey, Azerbaijan and Albania it has concerned
not just the question of individual liberty, but also the political meaning of
the Islamic headscarf. These are the only member States to have introduced regulations on wearing the Islamic headscarf in universities.

56. In France, where secularism is regarded as one of the corner-
stones of republican values, legislation was passed on 15 March 2004
regulating, in accordance with the principle of secularism, the wearing of
signs or dress manifesting a religious affiliation in State primary and
secondary schools. The legislation inserted a new Article L. 141–5–1 in the
Education Code which provides: "In State primary and secondary schools,
the wearing of signs or dress by which pupils overtly manifest a religious
affiliation is prohibited. The school rules shall state that the institution of
disciplinary proceedings shall be preceded by dialogue with the pupil."

The Act applies to all State schools and educational institutions,
including post-baccalaureate courses (preparatory classes for entrance to
the *grandes écoles* and vocational training courses). It does not apply to
State universities. In addition, as a circular of 18 May 2004 makes clear, it
only concerns "... signs, such as the Islamic headscarf, however named,
the kippa or a cross that is manifestly oversized, which make the wearer's
religious affiliation immediately identifiable".

57. In Belgium there is no general ban on wearing religious signs at
school. In the French Community a decree of 13 March 1994 stipulates that
education shall be neutral within the Community. Pupils are in principle
allowed to wear religious signs. However, they may do so only if human
rights, the reputation of others, national security, public order, and public
health and morals are protected and internal rules complied with. Further,
teachers must not permit religious or philosophical proselytism under their
authority or the organisation of political militancy by or on behalf of pupils.
The decree stipulates that restrictions may be imposed by school rules. On
19 May 2004 the French Community issued a decree intended to institute
equality of treatment. In the Flemish Community, there is no uniform

policy among schools on whether to allow religious or philosophical signs to be worn. Some do, others do not. When pupils are permitted to wear such signs, restrictions may be imposed on grounds of hygiene or safety.

58. In other countries (Austria, Germany, the Netherlands, Spain, Sweden, Switzerland and the United Kingdom), in some cases following a protracted legal debate, the State education authorities permit Muslim pupils and students to wear the Islamic headscarf.

59. In Germany, where the debate focused on whether teachers should be allowed to wear the Islamic headscarf, the Constitutional Court stated on 24 September 2003 in a case between a teacher and the *Land* of Baden–Württemberg that the lack of any express statutory prohibition meant that teachers were entitled to wear the headscarf. Consequently, it imposed a duty on the *Länder* to lay down rules on dress if they wished to prohibit the wearing of the Islamic headscarf in State schools.

60. In Austria there is no special legislation governing the wearing of the headscarf, turban or kippa. In general, it is considered that a ban on wearing the headscarf will only be justified if it poses a health or safety hazard for pupils.

61. In the United Kingdom a tolerant attitude is shown to pupils who wear religious signs. Difficulties with respect to the Islamic headscarf are rare. The issue has also been debated in the context of the elimination of racial discrimination in schools in order to preserve their multicultural character (*see*, in particular, *Mandla v. Dowell*, The Law Reports 1983, pp. 548–70). The Commission for Racial Equality, whose opinions have recommendation status only, also considered the issue of the Islamic headscarf in 1988 in the *Altrincham Grammar School* case, which ended in a compromise between a private school and members of the family of two sisters who wished to be allowed to wear the Islamic headscarf at the school. The school agreed to allow them to wear the headscarf provided it was navy blue (the colour of the school uniform), kept fastened at the neck and not decorated.

In *R. (On the application of Begum) v. Headteacher and Governors of Denbigh High School* ([2004] EWHC 1389 (Admin)), the High Court had to decide a dispute between the school and a Muslim pupil wishing to wear the *jilbab* (a full-length gown). The school required pupils to wear a uniform, one of the possible options being the headscarf and the *shalwar kameeze* (long traditional garments from the Indian subcontinent). In June 2004 the High Court dismissed the pupil's application, holding that there had been no violation of her freedom of religion. However, that judgment was reversed in March 2005 by the Court of Appeal, which accepted that there had been interference with the pupil's freedom of religion, as a minority of Muslims in the United Kingdom considered that a religious duty to wear the *jilbab* from the age of puberty existed and the pupil was genuinely of that opinion. No justification for the interference had been provided by the school authorities, as the decision-making process was not compatible with freedom of religion.

62. In Spain there is no express statutory prohibition on pupils' wearing religious head coverings in State schools. By virtue of two royal

decrees of 26 January 1996, which are applicable in primary and secondary schools unless the competent authority—the autonomous community—has introduced specific measures, the school governors have power to issue school rules which may include provisions on dress. Generally speaking, State schools allow the headscarf to be worn.

63. In Finland and Sweden the veil can be worn at school. However, a distinction is made between the *burka* (the term used to describe the full veil covering the whole of the body and the face) and the *niqab* (a veil covering all the upper body with the exception of the eyes). In Sweden mandatory directives were issued in 2003 by the National Education Agency. These allow schools to prohibit the *burka* and *niqab*, provided they do so in a spirit of dialogue on the common values of equality of the sexes and respect for the democratic principle on which the education system is based.

64. In the Netherlands, where the question of the Islamic headscarf is considered from the standpoint of discrimination rather than of freedom of religion, it is generally tolerated. In 2003 a non-binding directive was issued. Schools may require pupils to wear a uniform provided that the rules are not discriminatory and are included in the school prospectus and that the punishment for transgressions is not disproportionate. A ban on the *burka* is regarded as justified by the need to be able to identify and communicate with pupils. In addition, the Equal Treatment Commission ruled in 1997 that a ban on wearing the veil during physical education classes for safety reasons was not discriminatory.

65. In a number of other countries (Russia, Romania, Hungary, Greece, the Czech Republic, Slovakia and Poland), the issue of the Islamic headscarf does not yet appear to have given rise to any detailed legal debate.

E. The relevant Council of Europe texts on higher education

66. Among the various texts adopted by the Council of Europe on higher education, should be cited, first of all, Parliamentary Assembly Recommendation 1353 (1998) on the access of minorities to higher education, which was adopted on 27 January 1998, and Committee of Ministers Recommendation No. R (98) 3 on access to higher education, which was adopted on 17 March 1998.

Another relevant instrument in this sphere is the joint Council of Europe/UNESCO Convention on the Recognition of Qualifications concerning Higher Education in the European Region, which was signed in Lisbon on 11 April 1997 and came into force on 1 February 1999.

67. The preamble to the Convention on the Recognition of Qualifications concerning Higher Education in the European Region states:

"Conscious of the fact that the right to education is a human right, and that higher education, which is instrumental in the pursuit and advancement of knowledge, constitutes an exceptionally rich cultural and scientific asset for both individuals and society ..."

68. On 17 March 1998 the Committee of Ministers of the Council of Europe adopted Recommendation No. R (98) 3 on access to higher education. In the preamble to the recommendation it is stated:

"... higher education has a key role to play in the promotion of human rights and fundamental freedoms and the strengthening of pluralistic democracy and tolerance [and] ... widening opportunities for members of all groups in society to participate in higher education can contribute to securing democracy and building confidence in situations of social tension ..."

69. Likewise, Article 2 of Recommendation 1353 (1998) on the access of minorities to higher education, which was adopted by the Parliamentary Assembly of the Council of Europe on 27 January 1998, provides:

"Education is a fundamental human right and therefore access to all levels, including higher education, should be equally available to all permanent residents of the States signatories to the European Cultural Convention."

THE LAW

I. ALLEGED VIOLATION OF ARTICLE 9 OF THE CONVENTION

70. The applicant submitted that the ban on wearing the Islamic headscarf in institutions of higher education constituted an unjustified interference with her right to freedom of religion, in particular, her right to manifest her religion.

She relied on Article 9 of the Convention, which provides:

"1. Everyone has the right to freedom of thought, conscience and religion; this right includes freedom to change his religion or belief and freedom, either alone or in community with others and in public or private, to manifest his religion or belief, in worship, teaching, practice and observance.

2. Freedom to manifest one's religion or beliefs shall be subject only to such limitations as are prescribed by law and are necessary in a democratic society in the interests of public safety, for the protection of public order, health or morals, or for the protection of the rights and freedoms of others."

A. The Chamber judgment

71. The Chamber found that the Istanbul University regulations restricting the right to wear the Islamic headscarf and the measures taken thereunder had interfered with the applicant's right to manifest her religion. It went on to find that the interference was prescribed by law and pursued one of the legitimate aims set out in the second paragraph of Article 9 of the Convention. It was justified in principle and proportionate to the aims pursued and could therefore be regarded as having been "necessary in a democratic society" (see paragraphs 66–116 of the Chamber judgment).

B. The parties' submissions to the Grand Chamber

72. In her request for a referral to the Grand Chamber dated 27 September 2004 and in her oral submissions at the hearing, the applicant contested the grounds on which the Chamber had concluded that there had been no violation of Article 9 of the Convention.

73. However, in the observations she submitted to the Grand Chamber on 27 January 2005 she said that she was not seeking legal recognition of a right for all women to wear the Islamic headscarf in all places, and stated in particular: "Implicit in the section judgment is the notion that the right to wear the headscarf will not always be protected by freedom of religion. [I] do not contest that approach."

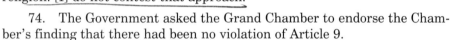

Interesting c.p.p.n...g

74. The Government asked the Grand Chamber to endorse the Chamber's finding that there had been no violation of Article 9.

C. The Court's assessment

75. The Court must consider whether the applicant's right under Article 9 was interfered with and, if so, whether the interference was "prescribed by law", pursued a legitimate aim and was "necessary in a democratic society" within the meaning of Article 9 § 2 of the Convention.

Standard.

1. Whether there was interference

76. The applicant said that her choice of dress had to be treated as obedience to a religious rule which she regarded as "recognised practice". She maintained that the restriction in issue, namely the rules on wearing the Islamic headscarf on university premises, was a clear interference with her right to freedom to manifest her religion.

77. The Government did not make any submissions to the Grand Chamber on this question.

78. As to whether there was interference, the Grand Chamber endorses the following findings of the Chamber (*see* paragraph 71 of the Chamber judgment):

"The applicant said that, by wearing the headscarf, she was obeying a religious precept and thereby manifesting her desire to comply strictly with the duties imposed by the Islamic faith. Accordingly, her decision to wear the headscarf may be regarded as motivated or inspired by a religion or belief and, without deciding whether such decisions are in every case taken to fulfil a religious duty, the Court proceeds on the assumption that the regulations in issue, which placed restrictions of place and manner on the right to wear the Islamic headscarf in universities, constituted an interference with the applicant's right to manifest her religion."

2. "Prescribed by law"

    (b) The Court's assessment

84. The Court reiterates its settled case-law that the expression "prescribed by law" requires firstly that the impugned measure should have a basis in domestic law. It also refers to the quality of the law in question, requiring that it be accessible to the persons concerned and

formulated with sufficient precision to enable them—if need be, with appropriate advice—to foresee, to a degree that is reasonable in the circumstances, the consequences which a given action may entail and to regulate their conduct (*see Gorzelik and Others v. Poland* [GC], no. 44158/98, § 64, ECtHR 2004–I).

98. ... the Court finds that there was a legal basis for the interference in Turkish law. ... It would have been clear to the applicant, from the moment she entered Istanbul University, that there were restrictions on wearing the Islamic headscarf on the university premises and, from 23 February 1998, that she was liable to be refused access to lectures and examinations if she continued to do so.

3. Legitimate aim

99. Having regard to the circumstances of the case and the terms of the domestic courts' decisions, the Court is able to accept that the impugned interference primarily pursued the legitimate aims of protecting the rights and freedoms of others and of protecting public order, a point which is not in issue between the parties.

4. "Necessary in a democratic society"

    (a) The parties' submissions to the Grand Chamber

       (i) The applicant

101. The applicant further explained in her aforementioned observations that students were discerning adults who enjoyed full legal capacity and were capable of deciding for themselves what was appropriate conduct. Consequently, the allegation that, by wearing the Islamic headscarf, she had shown a lack of respect for the convictions of others or sought to influence fellow students and to undermine their rights and freedoms was wholly unfounded. Nor had she created an external restriction on any freedom with the support or authority of the State. Her choice had been based on religious conviction, which was the most important fundamental right that pluralistic, liberal democracy had granted her. It was, to her mind, indisputable that people were free to subject themselves to restrictions if they considered it appropriate. It was also unjust to say that merely wearing the Islamic headscarf was contrary to the principle of equality between men and women, as all religions imposed such restrictions on dress which people were free to choose whether or not to comply with.

    (b) The Court's assessment

       (i) General principles

106. In democratic societies, in which several religions coexist within one and the same population, it may be necessary to place restrictions on freedom to manifest one's religion or belief in order to reconcile the interests of the various groups and ensure that everyone's beliefs are respected (*see Kokkinakis*, cited above, p. 18, § 33). This follows both from paragraph 2 of Article 9 and the State's positive obligation under Article 1 of the Convention to secure to everyone within its jurisdiction the rights and freedoms defined therein.

108. Pluralism, tolerance and broadmindedness are hallmarks of a "democratic society". Although individual interests must on occasion be subordinated to those of a group, democracy does not simply mean that the views of a majority must always prevail: a balance must be achieved which ensures the fair and proper treatment of people from minorities and avoids any abuse of a dominant position (*see, mutatis mutandis, Young, James and Webster v. the United Kingdom*, judgment of 13 August 1981, Series A no. 44, p. 25, § 63, and *Chassagnou and Others v. France* [GC], nos. 25088/94, 28331/95 and 28443/95, § 112, ECtHR 1999–III). Pluralism and democracy must also be based on dialogue and a spirit of compromise necessarily entailing various concessions on the part of individuals or groups of individuals which are justified in order to maintain and promote the ideals and values of a democratic society (*see, mutatis mutandis, the United Communist Party of Turkey and Others*, cited above, pp. 21–22, § 45, and *Refah Partisi (the Welfare Party) and Others*, cited above § 99). Where these "rights and freedoms" are themselves among those guaranteed by the Convention or its Protocols, it must be accepted that the need to protect them may lead States to restrict other rights or freedoms likewise set forth in the Convention. It is precisely this constant search for a balance between the fundamental rights of each individual which constitutes the foundation of a "democratic society" (*see Chassagnou and Others*, cited above, § 113).

109. Where questions concerning the relationship between State and religions are at stake, on which opinion in a democratic society may reasonably differ widely, the role of the national decision-making body must be given special importance (*see, mutatis mutandis, Cha'are Shalom Ve Tsedek*, cited above, § 84, and *Wingrove v. the United Kingdom*, judgment of 25 November 1996, *Reports* 1996–V, pp. 1957–58, § 58). This will notably be the case when it comes to regulating the wearing of religious symbols in educational institutions, especially (as the comparative-law materials illustrate—*see* paragraphs 55–65 above) in view of the diversity of the approaches taken by national authorities on the issue. It is not possible to discern throughout Europe a uniform conception of the significance of religion in society (*see Otto–Preminger–Institut v. Austria*, judgment of 20 September 1994, Series A no. 295–A, p. 19, § 50), and the meaning or impact of the public expression of a religious belief will differ according to time and context (*see*, among other authorities, *Dahlab v. Switzerland* (dec.), no. 42393/98, ECtHR 2001–V). Rules in this sphere will consequently vary from one country to another according to national traditions and the requirements imposed by the need to protect the rights and freedoms of others and to maintain public order (*see, mutatis mutandis, Wingrove*, cited above, p. 1957, § 57). Accordingly, the choice of the extent and form such regulations should take must inevitably be left up to a point to the State concerned, as it will depend on the specific domestic context (*see, mutatis mutandis, Gorzelik and Others*, cited above, § 67, and *Murphy v. Ireland*, no. 44179/98, § 73, ECtHR 2003–IX).

110. This margin of appreciation goes hand in hand with a European supervision embracing both the law and the decisions applying it. The Court's task is to determine whether the measures taken at national level were justified in principle and proportionate (*see Manoussakis and Others*,

cited above, p. 1364, § 44). In delimiting the extent of the margin of appreciation in the present case, the Court must have regard to what is at stake, namely the need to protect the rights and freedoms of others, to preserve public order and to secure civil peace and true religious pluralism, which is vital to the survival of a democratic society (*see, mutatis mutandis, Kokkinakis*, cited above, p. 17, § 31; *Manoussakis and Others*, cited above, p. 1364, § 44; and *Casado Coca*, cited above, p. 21, § 55).

111. The Court also notes that in the decisions in *Karaduman v. Turkey* (no. 16278/90, Commission decision of 3 May 1993, DR 74, p. 93) and *Dahlab* (cited above) the Convention institutions found that in a democratic society the State was entitled to place restrictions on the wearing of the Islamic headscarf if it was incompatible with the pursued aim of protecting the rights and freedoms of others, public order and public safety. In *Karaduman*, measures taken in universities to prevent certain fundamentalist religious movements from exerting pressure on students who did not practise their religion or who belonged to another religion were not considered to constitute interference for the purposes of Article 9 of the Convention. Consequently, it is established that institutions of higher education may regulate the manifestation of the rites and symbols of a religion by imposing restrictions as to the place and manner of such manifestation with the aim of ensuring peaceful coexistence between students of various faiths and thus protecting public order and the beliefs of others (*see*, among other authorities, *Refah Partisi (the Welfare Party) and Others*, cited above, § 95). In *Dahlab*, which concerned the teacher of a class of small children, the Court stressed among other matters the "powerful external symbol" which her wearing a headscarf represented and questioned whether it might have some kind of proselytising effect, seeing that it appeared to be imposed on women by a religious precept that was hard to reconcile with the principle of gender equality. It also noted that wearing the Islamic headscarf could not easily be reconciled with the message of tolerance, respect for others and, above all, equality and non-discrimination that all teachers in a democratic society should convey to their pupils.

(ii) Application of the foregoing principles to the present case

113. In its judgment of 7 March 1989, the Constitutional Court stated that secularism, as the guarantor of democratic values, was the meeting point of liberty and equality. The principle prevented the State from manifesting a preference for a particular religion or belief; it thereby guided the State in its role of impartial arbiter, and necessarily entailed freedom of religion and conscience. It also served to protect the individual not only against arbitrary interference by the State but from external pressure from extremist movements. The Constitutional Court added that freedom to manifest one's religion could be restricted in order to defend those values and principles (*see* paragraph 39 above).

114. As the Chamber rightly stated (*see* paragraph 106 of its judgment), the Court considers this notion of secularism to be consistent with the values underpinning the Convention. It finds that upholding that principle, which is undoubtedly one of the fundamental principles of the Turkish State which are in harmony with the rule of law and respect for

human rights, may be considered necessary to protect the democratic system in Turkey. An attitude which fails to respect that principle will not necessarily be accepted as being covered by the freedom to manifest one's religion and will not enjoy the protection of Article 9 of the Convention (*see Refah Partisi (the Welfare Party) and Others*, cited above, § 93).

115. After examining the parties' submissions, the Grand Chamber sees no good reason to depart from the approach taken by the Chamber (*see* paragraphs 107–09 of the Chamber judgment) as follows:

"... The Court ... notes the emphasis placed in the Turkish constitutional system on the protection of the rights of women ... Gender equality—recognised by the European Court as one of the key principles underlying the Convention and a goal to be achieved by member States of the Council of Europe (*see*, among other authorities, *Abdulaziz, Cabales and Balkandali v. the United Kingdom*, judgment of 28 May 1985, Series A no. 94, pp. 37–38, § 78; *Schuler-Zgraggen v. Switzerland*, judgment of 24 June 1993, Series A no. 263, pp. 21–22, § 67; *Burgharz v. Switzerland*, judgment of 22 February 1994, Series A no. 280–B, p. 29, § 27; *Van Raalte v. the Netherlands*, judgment of 21 February 1997, *Reports* 1997–I, p. 186, § 39 *in fine*; and *Petrovic v. Austria*, judgment of 27 March 1998, *Reports* 1998–II, p. 587, § 37)—was also found by the Turkish Constitutional Court to be a principle implicit in the values underlying the Constitution ...

... In addition, like the Constitutional Court ..., the Court considers that, when examining the question of the Islamic headscarf in the Turkish context, it must be borne in mind the impact which wearing such a symbol, which is presented or perceived as a compulsory religious duty, may have on those who choose not to wear it. As has already been noted (see *Karaduman*, decision cited above, and *Refah Partisi (the Welfare Party) and Others*, cited above, § 95), the issues at stake include the protection of the 'rights and freedoms of others' and the 'maintenance of public order' in a country in which the majority of the population, while professing a strong attachment to the rights of women and a secular way of life, adhere to the Islamic faith. Imposing limitations on freedom in this sphere may, therefore, be regarded as meeting a pressing social need by seeking to achieve those two legitimate aims, especially since, as the Turkish courts stated ..., this religious symbol has taken on political significance in Turkey in recent years.

... The Court does not lose sight of the fact that there are extremist political movements in Turkey which seek to impose on society as a whole their religious symbols and conception of a society founded on religious precepts ... It has previously said that each Contracting State may, in accordance with the Convention provisions, take a stance against such political movements, based on its historical experience (*see Refah Partisi (the Welfare Party) and Others*, cited above, § 124). The regulations concerned have to be viewed in that context and constitute a measure intended to achieve the legitimate aims referred to above and thereby to preserve pluralism in the university."

122. In the light of the foregoing and having regard to the Contracting States' margin of appreciation in this sphere, the Court finds that the

interference in issue was justified in principle and proportionate to the aim pursued.

123. Consequently, there has been no breach of Article 9 of the Convention.

■ Dissenting Opinion of JUDGE TULKENS

(Translation)

2. Once the majority had accepted that the ban on wearing the Islamic headscarf on university premises constituted interference with the applicant's right under Article 9 of the Convention to manifest her religion, and that the ban was prescribed by law and pursued a legitimate aim—in this case the protection of the rights and freedom of others and of public order—the main issue became whether such interference was "necessary in a democratic society". Owing to its nature, the Court's review must be conducted *in concreto*, in principle by reference to three criteria: firstly, whether the interference, which must be capable of protecting the legitimate interest that has been put at risk, was appropriate; secondly, whether the measure that has been chosen is the measure that is the least restrictive of the right or freedom concerned; and, lastly, whether the measure was proportionate, a question which entails a balancing of the competing interests.

Underlying the majority's approach is the margin of appreciation which the national authorities are recognised as possessing and which reflects, *inter alia*, the notion that they are "better placed" to decide how best to discharge their Convention obligations in what is a sensitive area (*see* paragraph 109 of the judgment). The Court's jurisdiction is, of course, subsidiary and its role is not to impose uniform solutions, especially "with regard to establishment of the delicate relations between the Churches and the State" (*see Cha'are Shalom Ve Tsedek v. France* [GC], no. 27417/95, § 84, ECtHR 2000–VII), even if, in certain other judgments concerning conflicts between religious communities, the Court has not always shown the same judicial restraint (*see Serif v. Greece*, no. 38178/97, ECtHR 1999–IX, and *Metropolitan Church of Bessarabia and Others v. Moldova*, no. 45701/99, ECtHR 2001–XII). I therefore entirely agree with the view that the Court must seek to reconcile universality and diversity and that it is not its role to express an opinion on any religious model whatsoever.

3. I would perhaps have been able to follow the margin-of-appreciation approach had two factors not drastically reduced its relevance in the instant case. The first concerns the argument the majority use to justify the width of the margin, namely the diversity of practice between the States on the issue of regulating the wearing of religious symbols in educational institutions and, thus, the lack of a European consensus in this sphere. The comparative-law materials do not allow of such a conclusion, as in none of the member States has the ban on wearing religious symbols extended to university education, which is intended for young adults, who are less amenable to pressure. * * *

4. On what grounds was the interference with the applicant's right to freedom of religion through the ban on wearing the headscarf based? In the

present case, relying exclusively on the reasons cited by the national authorities and courts, the majority put forward, in general and abstract terms, two main arguments: secularism and equality. While I fully and totally subscribe to each of these principles, I disagree with the manner in which they were applied here and to the way they were interpreted in relation to the practice of wearing the headscarf. In a democratic society, I believe that it is necessary to seek to harmonise the principles of secularism, equality and liberty, not to weigh one against the other.

5.   As regards, firstly, *secularism*, I would reiterate that I consider it an essential principle and one which, as the Constitutional Court stated in its judgment of 7 March 1989, is undoubtedly necessary for the protection of the democratic system in Turkey. Religious freedom is, however, also a founding principle of democratic societies. Accordingly, the fact that the Grand Chamber recognised the force of the principle of secularism did not release it from its obligation to establish that the ban on wearing the Islamic headscarf to which the applicant was subject was necessary to secure compliance with that principle and, therefore, met a "pressing social need". Only indisputable facts and reasons whose legitimacy is beyond doubt—not mere worries or fears—are capable of satisfying that requirement and justifying interference with a right guaranteed by the Convention. Moreover, where there has been interference with a fundamental right, the Court's case-law clearly establishes that mere affirmations do not suffice: they must be supported by concrete examples (*see Smith and Grady v. the United Kingdom*, nos. 33985/96 and 33986/96, § 89, ECtHR 1999–VI). Such examples do not appear to have been forthcoming in the present case.

6.   Under Article 9 of the Convention, the freedom with which this case is concerned is not freedom to have a religion (the internal conviction) but to manifest one's religion (the expression of that conviction). If the Court has been very protective (perhaps overprotective) of religious sentiment (*see Otto–Preminger–Institut v. Austria*, judgment of 20 September 1994, Series A no. 295–A, and *Wingrove v. the United Kingdom*, judgment of 25 November 1996, *Reports of Judgments and Decisions* 1996–V), it has shown itself less willing to intervene in cases concerning religious practices (*see Cha'are Shalom Ve Tsedek*, cited above, and *Dahlab v. Switzerland* (dec.), no. 42393/98, ECtHR 2001–V), which only appear to receive a subsidiary form of protection (*see* paragraph 105 of the judgment). This is, in fact, an aspect of freedom of religion with which the Court has rarely been confronted up to now and on which it has not yet had an opportunity to form an opinion with regard to external symbols of religious practice, such as particular items of clothing, whose symbolic importance may vary greatly according to the faith concerned.

7.   Referring to *Refah Partisi (the Welfare Party) and Others v. Turkey* ([GC], nos. 41340/98, 41342/98, 41343/98 and 41344/98, ECtHR 2003–II), the judgment states: "An attitude which fails to respect that principle [of secularism] will not necessarily be accepted as being covered by the freedom to manifest one's religion" (*see* paragraph 114). The majority thus consider that wearing the headscarf contravenes the principle of secularism. In so doing, they take up a position on an issue that has been the

subject of much debate, namely the signification of wearing the headscarf and its relationship with the principle of secularism.

In the present case, a generalised assessment of that type gives rise to at least three difficulties. Firstly, the judgment does not address the applicant's argument—which the Government did not dispute—that she had no intention of calling the principle of secularism, a principle with which she agreed, into question. Secondly, there is no evidence to show that the applicant, through her attitude, conduct or acts, contravened that principle. This is a test the Court has always applied in its case-law (*see* *Kokkinakis v. Greece*, judgment of 25 May 1993, Series A no. 260–A, and *United Communist Party of Turkey and Others v. Turkey*, judgment of 30 January 1998, *Reports* 1998–I). Lastly, the judgment makes no distinction between teachers and students, whereas in *Dahlab* (decision cited above), which concerned a teacher, the Court expressly noted the role-model aspect which the teacher's wearing the headscarf had. While the principle of secularism requires education to be provided without any manifestation of religion and while it has to be compulsory for teachers and all public servants, as they have voluntarily taken up posts in a neutral environment, the position of pupils and students seems to me to be different.

8. Freedom to manifest a religion entails everyone being allowed to exercise that right, whether individually or collectively, in public or in private, subject to the dual condition that they do not infringe the rights and freedoms of others and do not prejudice public order (Article 9 § 2).
* * *

9. The majority maintain, however, that, "when examining the question of the Islamic headscarf in the Turkish context, it must be borne in mind the impact which wearing such a symbol, which is presented or perceived as a compulsory religious duty, may have on those who choose not to wear it" (*see* paragraph 115 of the judgment).

Unless the level of protection of the right to freedom of religion is reduced to take account of the context, the possible effect which wearing the headscarf, which is presented as a symbol, may have on those who do not wear it does not appear to me, in the light of the Court's case-law, to satisfy the requirement of a pressing social need. *Mutatis mutandis*, in the sphere of freedom of expression (Article 10), the Court has never accepted that interference with the exercise of the right to freedom of expression can be justified by the fact that the ideas or views concerned are not shared by everyone and may even offend some people. Recently, in *Gündüz v. Turkey* (no. 35071/97, ECtHR 2003–XI), the Court held that there had been a violation of freedom of expression where a Muslim religious leader had been convicted for violently criticising the secular regime in Turkey, calling for the introduction of the sharia and referring to children born of marriages celebrated solely before the secular authorities as "bastards". Thus, manifesting one's religion by peacefully wearing a headscarf may be prohibited whereas, in the same context, remarks which could be construed as incitement to religious hatred are covered by freedom of expression.

10. In fact, it is the threat posed by "extremist political movements" seeking to "impose on society as a whole their religious symbols and conception of a society founded on religious precepts" which, in the Court's

view, serves to justify the regulations in issue, which constitute "a measure intended to ... preserve pluralism in the university" (*see* paragraph 115 *in fine* of the judgment). The Court had already made this clear in *Refah Partisi (the Welfare Party) and Others* (cited above, § 95), when it stated: "In a country like Turkey, where the great majority of the population belong to a particular religion, measures taken in universities to prevent certain fundamentalist religious movements from exerting pressure on students who do not practise that religion or on those who belong to another religion may be justified under Article 9 § 2 of the Convention."

While everyone agrees on the need to prevent radical Islamism, a serious objection may nevertheless be made to such reasoning. Merely wearing the headscarf cannot be associated with fundamentalism and it is vital to distinguish between those who wear the headscarf and "extremists" who seek to impose the headscarf as they do other religious symbols. Not all women who wear the headscarf are fundamentalists and there is nothing to suggest that the applicant held fundamentalist views. She is a young adult woman and a university student, and might reasonably be expected to have a heightened capacity to resist pressure, it being noted in this connection that the judgment fails to provide any concrete example of the type of pressure concerned. The applicant's personal interest in exercising the right to freedom of religion and to manifest her religion by an external symbol cannot be wholly absorbed by the public interest in fighting extremism.

11. Turning to *equality*, the majority focus on the protection of women's rights and the principle of sexual equality (*see* paragraphs 115 and 116 of the judgment). Wearing the headscarf is considered on the contrary to be synonymous with the alienation of women. The ban on wearing the headscarf is therefore seen as promoting equality between men and women. However, what, in fact, is the connection between the ban and sexual equality? The judgment does not say. Indeed, what is the signification of wearing the headscarf? As the German Constitutional Court noted in its judgment of 24 September 2003, wearing the headscarf has no single meaning; it is a practice that is engaged in for a variety of reasons. It does not necessarily symbolise the submission of women to men and there are those who maintain that, in certain cases, it can even be a means of emancipating women. What is lacking in this debate is the opinion of women, both those who wear the headscarf and those who choose not to.

12. On this issue, the Grand Chamber refers in its judgment to *Dahlab* (cited above), taking up what to my mind is the most questionable part of the reasoning in that decision, namely that wearing the headscarf represents a "powerful external symbol", which "appeared to be imposed on women by a religious precept that was hard to reconcile with the principle of gender equality" and that the practice could not easily be "reconciled with the message of tolerance, respect for others and, above all, equality and non-discrimination that all teachers in a democratic society should convey to their pupils" (*see* paragraph 111 *in fine* of the judgment).

It is not the Court's role to make an appraisal of this type—in this instance a unilateral and negative one—of a religion or religious practice, just as it is not its role to determine in a general and abstract way the signification of wearing the headscarf or to impose its viewpoint on the applicant. The applicant, a young adult university student, said—and there is nothing to suggest that she was not telling the truth—that she wore the headscarf of her own free will. In this connection, I fail to see how the principle of sexual equality can justify prohibiting a woman from following a practice which, in the absence of proof to the contrary, she must be taken to have freely adopted. Equality and non-discrimination are subjective rights which must remain under the control of those who are entitled to benefit from them. "Paternalism" of this sort runs counter to the case-law of the Court, which has developed a real right to personal autonomy on the basis of Article 8 (*see Keenan v. the United Kingdom*, no. 27229/95, § 92, ECtHR 2001–III; *Pretty v. the United Kingdom*, no. 2346/02, §§ 65–67, ECtHR 2002–III; and *Christine Goodwin v. the United Kingdom* [GC], no. 28957/95, § 90, ECtHR 2002–VI). Finally, if wearing the headscarf really was contrary to the principle of equality between men and women in any event, the State would have a positive obligation to prohibit it in all places, whether public or private.

13.   Since, to my mind, the ban on wearing the Islamic headscarf on the university premises was not based on reasons that were relevant and sufficient, it cannot be considered to be interference that was "necessary in a democratic society" within the meaning of Article 9 § 2 of the Convention. In these circumstances, there has been a violation of the applicant's right to freedom of religion, as guaranteed by the Convention. * * *

NOTES

1.   The controversy over the headscarf has rocked Turkey to its Constitutional foundations. In May 1999, Merve Kavakci was prohibited from taking her seat in the Turkish Parliament because she was wearing a headscarf. She was later stripped of her Turkish citizenship as well. In February 2008, the Turkish Parliament voted to permit university students to wear the headscarf; in June 2008, that decision was overruled by the Turkish Constitutional Court.

2.   Despite the June 2008 decision of the Constitutional Court, in 2010 the Higher Education Board announced that university students may wear the headscarf. The Board's decision has not been challenged. *See*, http:// www.bbc.co.uk/news/world-europe–11880622.

3.   For an insightful article on the head-scarf and the growing political controversy in Turkey, *see Sabrina Tavernise, Under A Scarf, A Turkish Lawyer Fighting to Wear it*, NY TIMES, Feb. 9, 2008. As Tavernise reports therein, in 2002 the Justice & Development Party (AKP), an Islamic party, won the Parliamentary elections and selected its founder Recep Tayyip Erdogan as Prime Minister. The party has declared itself committed to the Turkish principle of secularism, but growing conflicts between the ruling party's Islamic identity and the Turkish elite's commitment to protecting secularism (with the support of the Turkish army), has led to a series of crises. By 2008 the the Army was threatening to carry out its fifth coup since 1960. *See, e.g., Sabrina Tavernise, Elected Chief of Turkey Warns*

Army, NY TIMES, April 29, 2007; *In Turkey, Fear About Religious Lifestyle*, NY TIMES, April 30, 2007. But in 2010 and 2011 Mr. Erdogan turned the tables on the army, as a series of arrests of military leaders accused of conspiring to overthrow the government culminated in an en masse resignation by the country's top military commanders. See, *Sabrina Tavernise, Top Generals Quit in Group, Stunning Turks*, NY TIMES, July 30, 2011.

C. FRANCE

Education Code Article L141–5–1

www.legifrance.gouv.fr.

In public elementary and secondary schools, students are prohibited from wearing signs or symbols by which they express conspicuously a religious membership.

Timeline of the Headscarf (Hijab) Issue in France

■ MARIE-CHRISTINE PAUWELS

October 1989: Controversy erupts when three young girls of Moroccan ancestry who refuse to take their hijab off during class are expelled from the school.

November 27 1989: Asked to provide some guidelines, the Conseil d'Etat (Council of State, the French Supreme Court for Administrative Law, and advisor to the government on matters of administration) rules in an advisory opinion that in principle, the wearing of the Islamic headscarf, as a symbol of religious expression in public schools, is not incompatible with the French school system and the system of laïcité (secularism), yet warns against any propaganda, proselytism, or threats to the public order.

December 1989: First ministerial recommendation (circulaire) released by Education Minister Lionel Jospin, stating that schools should be responsible in deciding whether or not to accept the headscarf inside the classroom. School principals are left to address the problem case by case.

1990: A second recommendation from the Education Minister reminds the educational community of the need to respect the principle of secularism (laïcité) within the public school system.

November 2 1992: The Conseil d'Etat confirms its tolerant position (C.E. November 2 1992, Kherouaa case, n°130394, Rec.p.389), and condemns any sweeping condemnation, preferring a case by case approach. This tolerant principle is reiterated several times, including by lower courts.

September 1994: Third recommendation by new Education Minister François Bayrou distinguishes between "discrete" symbols of faith which may be worn to school and "conspicuous" symbols to be banned.

Between 1994 and 2003, around 100 young women were expelled from public schools. Half the expulsions were subsequently cancelled in court.

December 2003: President Jacques Chirac decides a law is necessary to clarify the debate. He appoints an investigative committee (la commission Stasi) whose December 2003 report led to the vote of a law the following year.

March 15 2004: Vote of law n° 2004–228 against the wearing of "conspicuous" symbols of faith. Reaffirming the principle of secularism and of the separation of Church and State, the law prohibits the wearing in public primary and secondary schools of conspicuous symbols or clothing which are religious in nature or appearance. This includes the Islamic headscarf, the Jewish yarmulke and large Christian crosses. Although the law does not mention any particular symbol, it is considered by many to specifically target the wearing of headscarves and was referred to as the "French headscarf ban".

May 18 2004: A recommendation published by then Education Minister François Fillon specifies that the law also applies to all teaching personnel working in public schools, who must respect the neutrality principle.

Secularism and Human Rights: A Contextual Analysis of Headscarves, Religious Expression, and Women's Equality Under International Law

45 Columbia Journal of Transnational Law 367 (2007)

■ KARIMA BENNOUNE

For some living in countries where Muslims are in the minority, headscarves may reflect minority identification and pride, or criticism of government policies toward the Muslim world. Some appear to adopt such clothing as the best way to rebel against more liberal parents or parents whose religiosity is deemed insufficiently pure. And yet other women may wear headscarves and veils as an affiliation to an Islamist political project aimed at theocracy, which is an antithesis to women's human rights as conceived in international human rights law.

Note that many of these personal beliefs about the imperative to cover may have implications for other women, especially other Muslim women, in the same environment who choose, or believe there is no need, to veil. Either they are seen by some as not identifying with their ethnic or religious group and therefore may be coded as "assimilated." Or they are seen as not expressing their religious beliefs as required by certain interpretations of Islamic dogma and thus are labled "bad" Muslims by some. Or they may be considered "loose" or "shameful." In particular environments, this may yield a range of consequences, including pressure to cover, stigma, or even threats, violence, and death. The ECtHR appeared to have precisely this problem in mind when it warned of "the impact which wearing such a symbol, which is presented or perceived as a compulsory religious duty, may have on those who choose not to wear it."

Of course, all of this is contextual. In Turkey, commentators have suggested that "[t]he importance of fights over Islamic symbols cannot be underestimated." Yet, in some other environments, either because there are few other Muslim women or little pressure to dress in such a manner, the impact on others may be relatively minor. For example, at Rutgers Law School–Newark where this author teaches, there are only a negligible number of Muslim students, a tiny number who wear the headscarf, and little interest in the law school from area Muslim fundamentalist groups. Here headscarving may have no impact on the rights of other students. A contextual approach leads to a different conclusion on the balancing in human rights law than in *Sahin* or *Begum*. However, were one of the local fundamentalist groups (which reportedly are very active in New Jersey) to begin campaigning for "modest" dress in area educational institutions, or were more women to begin to cover, this contextual determination could shift. Indeed, one of the benefits of the contextual approach is its ability to respond to changes on the ground.

Any thoughtful analysis must also contend with the range of positive and negative significations of veils. However, the meaning of the choice of garment in the head and heart of the wearer is not the only meaning to consider in the human rights framework. Some of these garments are now particularly associated, both in the minds of some Muslims and some non-Muslims, with Taliban, Iranian, and Saudi practices, according to which wearing headscarves or veils is, or was, required by law and violators subject to punishments, including corporal punishments banned under international law. Similar associations are made with fundamentalist or conservative social movements seeking to impose or "strongly encourage" veils. Given these echoes, such coverings come to represent for many a threat to secularism and to basic notions of gender equality which secularism makes possible, especially when deployed in the public school system.

For some secular feminist women, wearing the headscarf or veils in this political moment means choosing to wear "a sign of male domination over women's bodies and lives." As French Muslim women's rights activist Fadela Amara has written, "[i]t is a mistake to see the veil as only a religious issue. We must remember that it is first of all a tool of oppression, alienation, discrimination, and an instrument of men's power over women. It is not an accident that men do not wear the veil." The veil is not just or even primarily a religious symbol, but a highly contested social and political sign. Some Muslim and Arab women's organizations and many Muslim and Arab intellectuals have long campaigned against it in their home countries. This leads Ghais Jasser angrily to assert that:

> If, then, you claim that the veil is simply a manifestation of cultural particularity, you lack solidarity with women opposing purdah—of which the head-covering is but one expression among others— at the cost of their very lives. You also abandon to their destiny the young girls courageously confronting daily their own families and neighborhoods.

Fundamentalist movements seeking to challenge governments deemed insufficiently religious in the Muslim world have often sought to encourage or impose this range of garments as a way of indicating support for their project. Conservative movements that lash back against women's rights invoke these symbols, an effect magnified in education. Moroccan scholar Fatna Aït Sabbah has described this phenomenon as follows: "So the number of women with secondary and university degrees has been increasing non-stop? They require her to don the veil to remind her that in high places of knowledge ... she is merely accepted on sufferance." These garments thus can become affiliated with these social projects which seek to limit women's rights and increase the role of religion in the rule of law. In certain contexts, then, it is not mere paranoia which leads to restrictions on such coverings.

Most paradoxically, the veil may be all, or many, or some of these contradictory things at the same time. It is against the complex weave of this tapestry of meanings that human rights norms must be applied. Headscarves and other "modest" garments for women in specific contexts cannot be seen as mere innocent symbols of personal religious beliefs nor simply as flags of gender discrimination in the abstract. One criticism of the French law has been that it risks imbuing the headscarf with only one meaning, and one that is derogatory to women, leading to abusive treatment of veiled women in broader French society. On the other hand, rejections of restrictions sometimes focus only on the positive meanings, dismissing or overlooking the negative connotations and their consequences. Hence, this Article's plea for careful, contextual consideration of any proposed limitations on such symbols, in light of their many meanings. Where that consideration leads to the conclusion that the restrictions are necessary in public education to prevent women's subordination, and are in accordance with international human rights norms, they are permissible.

Banning the veil or headscarf feels repressive because it concerns a choice about the public presentation of one's body. Given that efforts to control the female body have been crucial in maintaining women's subordination historically, this may feel viscerally wrong. Yet women's freedom to make physical choices is not defended across the board on human rights grounds. Ironically, some mainstream human rights organizations have been reluctant to battle the imposition of religious garments on women, even by governments, nor do prominent human rights groups have clear positions defending nudity. Clearly some limits are deemed acceptable when religion is taken out of the picture. Given the presence of religion in this debate, for those who are committed to tolerance, openness suggests itself. Yet being tolerant of intolerance can have paradoxical results. In some contexts, the decision which one woman makes about covering her body in particular ways directly affects the choices other women may have to make about the public presentation of their persons. Mediating all these realities is an extremely sensitive task.

Here we begin to grapple with tensions between simultaneous commitments to transnational cosmopolitanism and civic republicanism, to borrow a paradigm articulated by Seyla Benhabib. What do we do when secularism is a prerequisite to democracy and women's human rights in certain contexts, yet its defense may require limitations which might be uncomfortable in a traditional international human rights approach? The first step toward an answer is that we proceed with great caution, bearing in mind the specifics of the particular context and the actual result our approach is likely to produce for women seeking to dress in certain ways and for their peers. Conversely, if we proceed oblivious to context, we may see human rights used as a strategy to curb women's equality and promote their further subordination, a result specifically forbidden by the limitations clauses in human rights law discussed below. Still, one must concede that the potential misuse of such restrictions on headscarves in a context of increasing anti-Muslim sentiment poses yet other risks.

Case of Dogru v. France

Application no. 27058/05, 4 December 2008

■ EUROPEAN COURT OF HUMAN RIGHTS

I. THE CIRCUMSTANCES OF THE CASE

5. The applicant was born in 1987 and lives in Flers.

6. The applicant, a Muslim aged eleven at the material time, was enrolled in the first year of a state secondary school in Flers for the academic year 1998–1999. From January 1999 onwards she wore a headscarf to school.

7. On seven occasions in January 1999 the applicant went to physical education and sports classes wearing her headscarf and refused to take it off despite repeated requests to do so by her teacher, who explained that wearing a headscarf was incompatible with physical education classes. The teacher sent two reports to the headmaster dated 22 January and 8 February 1999.

8. At a meeting on 11 February 1999 the school's pupil discipline committee decided to expel the applicant from the school for breaching the duty of assiduity by failing to participate actively in physical education and sports classes. * * *

14. ... On 31 July 2003 the Nantes Administrative Court of Appeal dismissed their appeal ... finding that the applicant, by behaving as she had done, had overstepped the limits of the right to express and manifest her religious beliefs on the school premises.

15. The applicant's parents lodged an appeal on points of law with the *Conseil d'Etat*, relying, *inter alia*, on their daughter's right to freedom of conscience and expression.

16. On 29 December 2004 the *Conseil d'Etat* declared the appeal inadmissible.

[SECTION II omitted]

THE LAW

I. ALLEGED VIOLATION OF ARTICLE 9 OF THE CONVENTION

33.   The applicant complained of an infringement of her right to manifest her religion within the meaning of Article 9 of the Convention, which reads as follows:

"1. Everyone has the right to freedom of thought, conscience and religion; this right includes freedom to change his religion or belief and freedom, either alone or in community with others and in public or private, to manifest his religion or belief, in worship, teaching, practice and observance.

2.   Freedom to manifest one's religion or beliefs shall be subject only to such limitations as are prescribed by law and are necessary in a democratic society in the interests of public safety, for the protection of public order, health or morals, or for the protection of the rights and freedoms of others."

A.   The parties' submissions

1.   The Government

34.   The Government acknowledged that the restrictions imposed on the applicant regarding wearing the Islamic headscarf at school amounted to an interference with the exercise of her right to manifest her religion. They submitted, however, that as in the case of *Leyla Sahin v. Turkey* ([GC], no. 44774/98, ECtHR 2005–XI) the requirements of legality, legitimacy and proportionality stipulated in paragraph 2 of Article 9 of the Convention were satisfied.

35.   The Government pointed out, first of all, that the measure in question had a legal basis in French law. They observed that the events had occurred in January 1999, that is, ten years after the *Conseil d'Etat* had given its opinion of 27 November 1989, which had provided a very specific legal framework regarding the wearing of the headscarf in State schools and had been the subject of much analysis by legal commentators, and of still wider coverage by the media, and the publication of circulars by the Minister for Education. The Government added that the established case-law of the administrative courts had confirmed and specified the rules thus defined. The Government also pointed out that the internal rules of the school that the applicant had attended were very specific on these points.

36.   In the Government's submission, the measure in question had pursued a legitimate aim, namely, the protection of order and the rights and freedoms of others, in the present case compliance by pupils with the duty to wear clothes adapted to and compatible with the proper conduct of classes, both for safety reasons and on public-health grounds.

37.   Lastly, the interference had been necessary in a democratic society. The Government referred in that connection to the case of *Leyla Sahin* (cited above), and recommended that the same solution be adopted in the present case, having regard to the fact that the measure in question had mainly been based on the constitutional principles of secularism and gender equality. In that connection they submitted that the French conception of

secularism respected the principles and values protected by the Convention. It permitted the peaceful coexistence of people belonging to different faiths, while maintaining the neutrality of the public arena. Accordingly, religions benefited from a protection in principle, it being impossible to restrict religious practice other than by limitations enacted in laws applicable to all, and by the principle of respect for secularism and the neutrality of the State. The Government added that respect for religious freedom did not, however, mean that manifestations of religious beliefs could not be subject to restrictions.

39. The Government also submitted that the applicant's proposal to wear a hat or balaclava instead of her headscarf did not in itself constitute proof of her willingness to find a compromise solution or enter into dialogue. The school, however, had initiated a dialogue with the pupil before and during the disciplinary proceedings (ban limited to physical education classes alone, repeated explanations by the teachers, time for reflection granted and extended, etc.). By way of example, the director for education had observed during the meeting of the appeal panel on 17 March 1999 that "the teachers having agreed, in the end, that she could wear the headscarf during classes demonstrated a conciliatory approach. They expected a gesture on the part of the pupil in the form of an agreement to abide by the rules commonly accepted in P.E. classes ... the words 'we're going to win' were illustrative of the family's refusal to compromise and their intention to confine themselves to the legal position." Apart from the disruption of physical education and sports classes, the authorities had legitimate grounds to fear that the pupil's behaviour would interfere with order in the school or the normal functioning of the State education service. The Caen Administrative Court had accordingly observed that her attitude had created a general atmosphere of tension in the school.

41. Lastly, the Government noted that, as in *Leyla Sahin* (cited above, § 120), the rules that the applicant had refused to obey had been the fruit of a broad debate within French society and the teaching profession. Their implementation had, moreover, been guided by the competent authorities (by means of circulars and internal rules) and accompanied by a series of court decisions on the subject.

42. The Government concluded that the applicant's conduct had overstepped the limits of the right to manifest her religious beliefs within the school premises and that, accordingly, the measures taken had been proportionate to the aim pursued and necessary in a democratic society.

2. The applicant

* * *

44. The applicant alleged, lastly, that the restrictions in question had not pursued a legitimate aim that was necessary in a democratic society. Contrary to the Government's submissions, she had not failed to comply with her duty of assiduity but had been confronted with the teacher's refusal to allow her to take part in the class. Despite her proposal to wear a hat or balaclava instead of her headscarf, she had continually been refused permission to participate in sports classes. The teacher had refused to allow

her to take part in the class on grounds of her safety. However, when the teacher had been asked, at the session of the pupil discipline committee, how wearing the headscarf or a hat during his classes would endanger the child's safety, he had refused to answer the question. The Government had not provided any further explanations on this point.

45.   The applicant concluded that expelling her for wearing the headscarf had amounted to an interference with her religious freedom that did not satisfy the criteria set forth in paragraph 2 of Article 9 of the Convention.

B.   The Court's assessment

[SECTION 1 omitted]

2.   The merits

* * *

48.   The Court considers that in the present case the ban on wearing the headscarf during physical education and sports classes and the expulsion of the applicant from the school on grounds of her refusal to remove it constitute a "restriction" on the exercise by the applicant of her right to freedom of religion, as is, moreover, undisputed by the parties. Such interference will infringe the Convention if it does not meet the requirements of paragraph 2 of Article 9. The Court must therefore determine whether it was "prescribed by law", was directed towards one or more of the legitimate aims set out in that paragraph and was "necessary in a democratic society" to achieve the aims concerned. * * *

73.   In the present case the Court considers that the conclusion reached by the national authorities that the wearing of a veil, such as the Islamic headscarf, was incompatible with sports classes for reasons of health or safety is not unreasonable. It accepts that the penalty imposed is merely the consequence of the applicant's refusal to comply with the rules applicable on the school premises—of which she had been properly informed—and not of her religious convictions, as she alleged.

74.   The Court also notes that the disciplinary proceedings against the applicant fully satisfied the duty to undertake a balancing exercise of the various interests at stake. In the first place, before proceedings were instituted, the applicant refused on seven occasions to remove her headscarf during physical education classes, despite her teacher's requests and explanations for those requests. Subsequently, according to the information provided by the Government, the authorities concerned made many unsuccessful attempts over a long period of time to enter into dialogue with the applicant and a period of reflection was granted her and subsequently extended. Furthermore, the ban was limited to the physical education class, so cannot be regarded as a ban in the strict sense of the term (*see Köse and Others*, cited above). Moreover, it can be seen from the circumstances of the case that these events had led to a general atmosphere of tension within the school. Lastly, the disciplinary process also appears to have been accompanied by safeguards—the rule requiring conformity with statute and judicial review—that were apt to protect the pupils' interests (*see, mutatis mutandis, Leyla Sahin*, cited above, § 159).

75. As regards the choice of the most severe penalty, it should be pointed out that, where the ways and means of ensuring respect for internal rules are concerned, it is not within the province of the Court to substitute its own vision for that of the disciplinary authorities which, being in direct and continuous contact with the educational community, are best placed to evaluate local needs and conditions or the requirements of a particular training (*see, mutatis mutandis, Valsamis v. Greece*, 18 December 1996, § 32, *Reports of Judgments and Decisions* 1996–VI). With regard to the applicant's proposal to replace the headscarf by a hat, apart from the fact that it is difficult for the Court to judge whether wearing a hat instead would be compatible with sports classes, the question whether the pupil expressed a willingness to compromise, as she maintains, or whether—on the contrary—she overstepped the limits of the right to express and manifest her religious beliefs on the school premises, as the Government maintain and appears to conflict with the principle of secularism, falls squarely within the margin of appreciation of the State.

76. The Court considers, having regard to the foregoing, that the penalty of expulsion does not appear disproportionate, and notes that the applicant was able to continue her schooling by correspondence classes. It can be seen that the applicant's religious convictions were fully taken into account in relation to the requirements of protecting the rights and freedoms of others and public order. It is also clear that the decision complained of was based on those requirements and not on any objections to the applicant's religious beliefs (*see Dahlab*, cited above).

77. Accordingly, having regard to the circumstances of the case, and taking account of the margin of appreciation that should be left to the States in this domain, the Court concludes that the interference in question was justified as a matter of principle and proportionate to the aim pursued.

78. Accordingly, there has been no violation of Article 9 of the Convention.

———

NOTES

1. Paragraph 39 of *Dogru* begins: "The Government also submitted that the applicant's proposal to wear a hat or balaclava instead of her headscarf did not in itself constitute proof of her willingness to find a compromise solution or enter into dialogue." Why not? In Paragraph 73 the Court states: "In the present case the Court considers that the conclusion reached by the national authorities that the wearing of a veil, such as the Islamic headscarf, was incompatible with sports classes for reasons of health or safety is not unreasonable." But wasn't it a refusal to cover her head by wearing a headscarf, hat or balaclava? Is it unsafe to wear any kind of hat while playing sports? What should we conclude from the teacher's refusal to respond when asked in the disciplinary hearing why it was dangerous to wear a hat? Or of the fact that the school had permitted Dogru to wear her hijab to all classes other than physical education?

2.   Does the French law prohibit students from wearing headscarves for non-religious reasons? Scarves are a common fashion accessory in France. If Christian French school girls begin wearing head scarves to class as a fashion statement, will it violate the law? If not, may the schools expel the Muslim girls wearing scarves, while taking no action against the Christian girls? How should the schools determine which girls are wearing scarves for inappropriate religious reasons?

3.   As described by Professor Pauwels, the French law prohibiting the display of conspicuous religious symbols in schools was adopted in 2004, following a recommendation by a commission convened by French President Jacques Chirac. The commission made dozens of recommendations, including adding Muslim and Jewish holidays as French national holidays, but the only proposal to be adopted by the Parliament was the headscarf ban.

4.   On July 13, 2010, the French National assembly, by a vote of 355–1, at the request of President Sarkosy, passed a bill prohibiting women from wearing clothing that covers the face in any public place in France. The law was approved by the French Constitution Council, holding that "women who conceal their face, voluntarily or otherwise, are placed in a situation of exclusion and inferiority patently incompatible with constitutional principles of liberty and equality." Décision n° 2010–613 DC du 07 octobre 2010. The law took effect on April 11, 2011. In the first month, nearly 50 women had been detained. *See*, http://www.voanews.com/english/news/europe/France–Detains–Several–People–Enforcing–Veil–Ban–121794489.html. Should the decision in the Dogru case govern a challenge to the new French law?

5.   Several German states prohibit Muslim teachers, but not students, from wearing headscarves in the classroom. *See German Court Upholds Muslim Headscarf Ban in Schools,* http://www.spiegel.de/international/germany/0,1518,542211,00.html.

6.   In Flanders, the Flemish speaking part of Belgium, schools had been free to allow students to wear headscarves or to ban them, and one third had allowed them while another one third had banned them (and the rest had no rule). But in 2009 a decision was made to ban the headscarf in all state-run schools. *See Flanders to ban Muslim headscarf in schools,* http:// www.earthtimes.org/articles/news/285264,flanders-to-ban-muslim-headscarf-in-schools.html.

7.   In March 2009 Kyrgyzstan banned head scarves from its schools. "We are a secular state," Education Ministry official Damira Kudaibergenova said on March 3. "Children are coming under a massive attack and we will protect them. . . . When the choice is between education and a headscarf we choose education." *See Kyrgystan Bans Head Scarves from Schools,*   http://www.rferl.org/content/Kyrgyzstan_Bans_Head_Scarves_From_Schools/1503459. html.

8.   In December 2010 the secular government of Azerbaijan banned Muslim girls from wearing the headscarf in school. *See, Azeri Activists Protest Against School Ban on Islamic Headscarf,* http://www.bloomberg.

com/news/2011–05–06/azeri-activists-protest-against-school-ban-on-islamic-headscarf.html.

9. Kosovo, which is 90% Muslim and mostly secular, banned the headscarf from schools in 2010. *See, Ban on headscarves in school upsets devout Muslims in Kosovo*, http:// blogs.reuters.com/faithworld/2010/06/24/ban-on-headscarves-in-schools-upsets-devout-muslims-in-kosovo/.

10. In 2011, a Dutch court held that a publicly-funded Catholic school could ban a Muslim student from wearing the Hijab. *See* http://zoeken.recht spraak.nl/detailpage.aspx?ljn= BQ0063. In France, Catholic schools generally allow students to wear religious symbols, including headscarves.

11. For a nuanced and detailed discussion of how the headscarf restrictions were experienced by French Muslim students and their teachers, principals and parents, *see*, Jane Kramer, *Taking The Veil: How France's Public Schools Became A Battleground In A Culture War*, THE NEW YORKER, November 22, 2004 (Letter From Europe; Pg. 58).

12. There have been several cases in which students were suspended from public schools in the United States for wearing religious head coverings, but no published court decisions. In March 2004 the U.S. Department of Justice intervened in a case in Muskogee Oklahoma where an 11 year old Muslim girl had been suspended for wearing a head scarf (hijab), leading to a settlement in which the school agreed to amend its rule. The government argued that the school's dress code violated the girl's rights under the equal protection clause of the Fourteenth Amendment. *See* http://www.cnn.com/2004/LAW/03/30/us.school.headscarves/.

D. BRITAIN

Begum v. Headteacher & Governors of Denbigh High School

House of Lords [2006] UKHL 15

■ LORD BINGHAM of Cornhill

My Lords,

1. The respondent, Shabina Begum, is now aged 17. She contends that the appellants, who are the head teacher and governors of Denbigh High School in Luton ("the school"), excluded her from that school, unjustifiably limited her right under article 9 of the European Convention on Human Rights to manifest her religion or beliefs and violated her right not to be denied education under article 2 of the First Protocol to the Convention. . . .

2. It is important to stress at the outset that this case concerns a particular pupil and a particular school in a particular place at a particular time. It must be resolved on facts which are now, for purposes of the appeal, agreed. The House is not, and could not be, invited to rule whether Islamic dress, or any feature of Islamic dress, should or should not be permitted in the schools of this country. That would be a most inappropri-

ate question for the House in its judicial capacity, and it is not one which I shall seek to address.

The agreed facts

3.   The school is a maintained secondary community school taking pupils of both sexes aged 11–16. It has a very diverse intake, with 21 different ethnic groups and 10 religious groupings represented. About 79% of its pupils are now Muslim, the percentage having fallen from 90% in 1993. It is not a faith school, and is therefore open to children of all faiths and none. Its high percentage of Muslim pupils is reflected in its exemption from the ordinary duty of maintained schools to secure an act of collective worship each day wholly or mainly of a broadly Christian character.

4.   The governing body of the school always contained a balanced representation of different sections of the school community. At the time of these proceedings, four out of six parent governors were Muslim, the chairman of the Luton Council of Mosques was a community governor and three of the LEA governors were also Muslim. The school makes a significant contribution to social cohesion in a catchment area that is racially, culturally and religiously diverse.

5.   The head teacher, Mrs Yasmin Bevan, was born into a Bengali Muslim family and grew up in India, Pakistan and Bangladesh before coming to this country. She has had much involvement with Bengali Muslim communities here and abroad, and is familiar with the codes and practices governing the dress of Muslim women. Since her appointment as head teacher in 1991, when it was not performing well, the school has come to enjoy an outstanding measure of success.

6.   The head teacher believes that school uniform plays an integral part in securing high and improving standards, serving the needs of a diverse community, promoting a positive sense of communal identity and avoiding manifest disparities of wealth and style. The school offered three uniform options. One of these was the shalwar kameeze: a combination of the kameeze, a sleeveless smock-like dress with a square neckline, revealing the wearer's collar and tie, with the shalwar, loose trousers, tapering at the ankles. A long-sleeved white shirt is worn beneath the kameeze and, save in hot weather, a uniform long-sleeved school jersey is worn on top. It has been worn by some Muslim, Hindu and Sikh female pupils. * * *

9.   The respondent is Muslim. Her father died before she entered the school, and at the material times she lived with her mother (who did not speak English and has since died), a sister two years older, and a brother (Rahman), five years older, who is now her litigation friend. The family lived outside the school's catchment area, but chose it for the respondent and her elder sister, and were told in clear terms of the school's uniform policy. For two years before September 2002 the respondent wore the shalwar kameeze happily and without complaint. It was also worn by the respondent's sister, who continued to wear it without objection throughout her time at the school.

10.   On 3 September 2002, the first day of the autumn term, the respondent (then aged nearly 14) went to the school with her brother and another young man. They asked to speak to the head teacher, who was not

available, and they spoke to the assistant head teacher, Mr Moore. They insisted that the respondent be allowed to attend the school wearing the long garment she had on that day, which was a long coatlike garment known as a jilbab. They talked of human rights and legal proceedings. Mr Moore felt that their approach was unreasonable and he felt threatened. He decided that the respondent should wear the correct school uniform and told her to go home, change and return wearing school uniform. His previous experience in such situations, with one exception, was that pupils always complied. He did not believe he was excluding the respondent, which he had no authority to do, but did not allow her to enter the school dressed as she was, this being (it was said) the only garment which met her religious requirements because it concealed, to a greater extent than the shalwar kameeze, the contours of the female body, and was said to be appropriate for maturing girls. The respondent then left with her brother and the other young man. The young men said they were not prepared to compromise over this issue.

11. On the same day the head teacher, who had been informed of the incident, wrote to the respondent's mother and brother. After setting out an account of the incident, she stated that the uniform had been agreed with the governing body, and that it was her view, and that of the LEA, that the school's uniform rules were more than reasonable in taking into account cultural and religious concerns. She noted that the respondent had not attended school because she had been removed by those representing her and stated that the respondent was required to attend school dressed in the correct uniform. She further stated that the matter would be referred to the Education Welfare Service (the "EWS") should the respondent fail to attend. * * *

18. The respondent issued her claim for judicial review on 13 February 2004. Since then, according to the appellants, a number of Muslim girls at the school have said that they do not wish to wear the jilbab and fear they will be pressured into wearing it. A demonstration outside the school gates by an extreme Muslim group (unconnected with the respondent) in February 2004, protesting against the education of Muslim children in secular schools, caused a number of pupils to complain to staff of interference and harassment. Some pupils were resistant to wearing the jilbab as unnecessarily restrictive and associated with an extremist group. The head teacher and her assistant, and also some parents, were concerned that acceptance of the jilbab as a permissible variant of the school uniform would lead to undesirable differentiation between Muslim groups according to the strictness of their views. The head teacher in particular felt that adherence to the school uniform policy was necessary to promote inclusion and social cohesion, fearing that new variants would encourage the formation of groups or cliques identified by their clothing. The school had in the past suffered the ill-effects of groups of pupils defining themselves along racial lines, with consequent conflict between them. The school uniform had been designed to avoid the development of sub-groups identified by dress. * * *

20. So far as relevant to this case article 9 provides:

"Freedom of thought, conscience and religion

1. Everyone has the right to freedom of thought, conscience and religion; this right includes freedom to change his religion or belief and freedom, either alone or in community with others and in public or private, to manifest his religion or belief, in worship, teaching, practice and observance.

2. Freedom to manifest one's religion or beliefs shall be subject only to such limitations as are prescribed by law and are necessary in a democratic society . . . for the protection of the rights and freedoms of others.'' * * *

23. The Strasbourg institutions have not been at all ready to find an interference with the right to manifest religious belief in practice or observance where a person has voluntarily accepted an employment or role which does not accommodate that practice or observance and there are other means open to the person to practice or observe his or her religion without undue hardship or inconvenience. Thus in *X v Denmark* (1976) 5 DR 157 a clergyman was held to have accepted the discipline of his church when he took employment, and his right to leave the church guaranteed his freedom of religion. His claim under article 9 failed. In Kjeldsen, Busk Madsen and *Pedersen v Denmark* (1976) 1 EHRR 711, paras 54 and 57, parents' philosophical and religious objections to sex education in state schools was rejected on the ground that they could send their children to state schools or educate them at home. The applicant's article 9 claim in Ahmad, above, paras 13, 14 and 15, failed because he had accepted a contract which did not provide for him to absent himself from his teaching duties to attend prayers, he had not brought his religious requirements to the employer's notice when seeking employment and he was at all times free to seek other employment which would accommodate his religious observance. *Karaduman v Turkey* (1993) 74 DR 93 is a strong case. The applicant was denied a certificate of graduation because a photograph of her without a headscarf was required and she was unwilling for religious reasons to be photographed without a headscarf. The Commission found (p 109) no interference with her article 9 right because (p 108) ''by choosing to pursue her higher education in a secular university a student submits to those university rules, which may make the freedom of students to manifest their religion subject to restrictions as to place and manner intended to ensure harmonious coexistence between students of different beliefs''. In rejecting the applicant's claim in *Konttinen v Finland* (1996) 87–A DR 68 the Commission pointed out, in para 1, page 75, that he had not been pressured to change his religious views or prevented from manifesting his religion or belief; having found that his working hours conflicted with his religious convictions, he was free to relinquish his post. An application by a child punished for refusing to attend a National Day parade in contravention of her beliefs as a Jehovah's Witness, to which her parents were also party, was similarly unsuccessful in *Valsamis v Greece* (1996) 24 EHRR 294. It was held (para 38) that article 9 did not confer a right to exemption from disciplinary rules which applied generally and in a neutral manner and that there had been no interference with the child's right to freedom to manifest her religion or belief. In *Stedman v United Kingdom* (1997) 23 EHRR CD 168 it was fatal to the applicant's article 9 claim that she was free to resign rather than work on Sundays. The applicant in Kalaç, above,

paras 28–29, failed because he had, in choosing a military career, accepted of his own accord a system of military discipline that by its nature implied the possibility of special limitations on certain rights and freedoms, and he had been able to fulfil the ordinary obligations of Muslim belief. In *Jewish Liturgical Association Cha'are Shalom Ve Tsedek v France* (2000) 9 BHRC 27, para 81, the applicants' challenge to the regulation of ritual slaughter in France, which did not satisfy their exacting religious standards, was rejected because they could easily obtain supplies of meat, slaughtered in accordance with those standards, from Belgium. * * *

25. In the present case the respondent's family chose for her a school outside their own catchment area. It was a school which went to unusual lengths to inform parents of its uniform policy. The shalwar kameeze, and not the jilbab, was worn by the respondent's elder sister throughout her time at the school, and by the respondent for her first two years, without objection. It was of course open to the respondent, as she grew older, to modify her beliefs, but she did so against a background of free and informed consent by her and her family. It is also clear that there were three schools in the area at which the wearing of the jilbab was permitted. The respondent's application for admission to one of these was unsuccessful because the school was full, and it was asserted in argument that the other two were more distant. There is, however, no evidence to show that there was any real difficulty in her attending one or other of these schools, as she has in fact done and could no doubt have done sooner had she chosen. On the facts here, and endeavouring to apply the Strasbourg jurisprudence in a reasonable way, I am of opinion that in this case (unlike Williamson, above, para 41, where a different conclusion was reached) there was no interference with the respondent's right to manifest her belief in practice or observance. I appreciate, however, that my noble and learned friends Lord Nicholls and Lady Hale of Richmond incline to a different opinion. It follows that this is a debatable question, which gives the issue of justification under article 9(2) particular significance.

Justification

26. To be justified under article 9(2) a limitation or interference must be (a) prescribed by law and (b) necessary in a democratic society for a permissible purpose, that is, it must be directed to a legitimate purpose and must be proportionate in scope and effect. It was faintly argued for the respondent that the school's uniform policy was not prescribed by law, but both the judge (para 78) and the Court of Appeal (paras 61, 83 and 90) held otherwise, and rightly so. The school authorities had statutory authority to lay down rules on uniform, and those rules were very clearly communicated to those affected by them. It was not suggested that the rules were not made for the legitimate purpose of protecting the rights and freedoms of others. So the issue is whether the rules and the school's insistence on them were in all the circumstances proportionate. This raises an important procedural question on the court's approach to proportionality and, depending on the answer to that, a question of substance. * * *

32. It is therefore necessary to consider the proportionality of the school's interference with the respondent's right to manifest her religious belief by wearing the jilbab to the school. In doing so we have the valuable

guidance of the Grand Chamber of the Strasbourg court in Sahin, above, paras 104–111. The court there recognises the high importance of the rights protected by article 9; the need in some situations to restrict freedom to manifest religious belief; the value of religious harmony and tolerance between opposing or competing groups and of pluralism and broadmindedness; the need for compromise and balance; the role of the state in deciding what is necessary to protect the rights and freedoms of others; the variation of practice and tradition among member states; and the permissibility in some contexts of restricting the wearing of religious dress. * * *

34. On the agreed facts, the school was in my opinion fully justified in acting as it did. It had taken immense pains to devise a uniform policy which respected Muslim beliefs but did so in an inclusive, unthreatening and uncompetitive way. The rules laid down were as far from being mindless as uniform rules could ever be. The school had enjoyed a period of harmony and success to which the uniform policy was thought to contribute. On further enquiry it still appeared that the rules were acceptable to mainstream Muslim opinion. It was feared that acceding to the respondent's request would or might have significant adverse repercussions. It would in my opinion be irresponsible of any court, lacking the experience, background and detailed knowledge of the head teacher, staff and governors, to overrule their judgment on a matter as sensitive as this. The power of decision has been given to them for the compelling reason that they are best placed to exercise it, and I see no reason to disturb their decision. * * *

40. For these reasons, and those given by Lord Hoffmann, with which I agree, I would allow the appeal, set aside the order of the Court of Appeal, and restore the order of the judge. * * *

■ LORD HOFFMANN

My Lords,

* * *

50. I accept that wearing a jilbab to a mixed school was, for her, a manifestation of her religion. The fact that most other Muslims might not have thought it necessary is irrelevant. But her right was not in my opinion infringed because there was nothing to stop her from going to a school where her religion did not require a jilbab or where she was allowed to wear one. Article 9 does not require that one should be allowed to manifest one's religion at any time and place of one's own choosing. Common civility also has a place in the religious life. Shabina's discovery that her religion did not allow her to wear the uniform she had been wearing for the past two years created a problem for her. Her family had chosen that school for her with knowledge of its uniform requirements. She could have sought the help of the school and the local education authority in solving the problem. They would no doubt have advised her that if she was firm in her belief, she should change schools. That might not have been entirely convenient for her, particularly when her sister was remaining at Denbigh High, but people sometimes have to suffer some inconvenience for their beliefs. Instead, she and her brother decided that it was the school's problem. They

sought a confrontation and claimed that she had a right to attend the school of her own choosing in the clothes she chose to wear. * * *

■ Baroness Hale of Richmond

My Lords,

92. I too agree that this appeal should be allowed. Most of your lordships take the view that Shabina Begum's right to manifest her religion was not infringed because she had chosen to attend this school knowing full well what the school uniform was. It was she who had changed her mind about what her religion required of her, rather than the school which had changed its policy. I am uneasy about this. The reality is that the choice of secondary school is usually made by parents or guardians rather than by the child herself. The child is on the brink of, but has not yet reached, adolescence. She may have views but they are unlikely to be decisive. More importantly, she has not yet reached the critical stage in her development where this particular choice may matter to her.

93. Important physical, cognitive and psychological developments take place during adolescence. Adolescence begins with the onset of puberty; from puberty to adulthood, the 'capacity to acquire and utilise knowledge reaches its peak efficiency'; and the capacity for formal operational thought is the forerunner to developing the capacity to make autonomous moral judgments. Obviously, these developments happen at different times and at different rates for different people. But it is not at all surprising to find adolescents making different moral judgments from those of their parents. It is part of growing up. The fact that they are not yet fully adult may help to justify interference with the choices they have made. It cannot be assumed, as it can with adults, that these choices are the product of a fully developed individual autonomy. But it may still count as an interference. I am therefore inclined to agree with my noble and learned friend, Lord Nicholls of Birkenhead, that there was an interference with Shabina Begum's right to manifest her religion.

94. However, I am in no doubt that that interference was justified. It had the legitimate aim of protecting the rights and freedoms of others. The question is whether it was proportionate to that aim. This is a more difficult and delicate question in this case than it would be in the case of many similar manifestations of religious belief. If a Sikh man wears a turban or a Jewish man a yamoulka, we can readily assume that it was his free choice to adopt the dress dictated by the teachings of his religion. I would make the same assumption about an adult Muslim woman who chooses to wear the Islamic headscarf. There are many reasons why she might wish to do this. As Yasmin Alibhai–Brown (WHO do WE THINK we ARE?, (2000), p 246) explains: "What critics of Islam fail to understand is that when they see a young woman in a hijab she may have chosen the garment as a mark of her defiant political identity and also as a way of regaining control over her body." Bhikhu Parekh makes the same point (in *A Varied Moral World, A Response to Susan Okin's 'Is Multiculturalism Bad for Women'*, Boston Review, October/November 1997): "In France and the Netherlands several Muslim girls freely wore the hijab (headscarf), partly to reassure their conservative parents that they would not be corrupted by the public culture of the school, and partly to reshape the

latter by indicating to white boys how they wished to be treated. The hijab in their case was a highly complex autonomous act intended to use the resources of the tradition both to change and to preserve it." Hence I have found the dissenting opinion of Judge Tulkens in the case of the Turkish University student, *Leyla Sahin v Turkey*, Application No 44774/98, Judgment of 10 November 2005, very persuasive.

95.   But it must be the woman's choice, not something imposed upon her by others. It is quite clear from the evidence in this case that there are different views in different communities about what is required of a Muslim woman who leaves the privacy of her home and family and goes out into the public world. There is also a view that the more extreme requirements are imposed as much for political and social as for religious reasons. If this is so, it is not a uniquely Muslim phenomenon. *The Parekh Report on The Future of Multi-Ethnic Britain* (Runnymede Trust, 2000, at pp 236–237, para 17.3), for example, points out that: "In all traditions, religious claims and rituals may be used to legitimise power structures rather than to promote ethical principles, and may foster bigotry, sectarianism and fundamentalism. Notoriously, religion often accepts and gives its blessing to gender inequalities." Gita Saghal and Nira Yuval–Davis, discussing *Fundamentalism, Multiculturalism and Women in Britain* (in REFUSING HOLY ORDERS, WOMEN AND FUNDAMENTALISM IN BRITAIN, (2000), p 14) argue that the effect of and on women is "... central to the project of fundamentalism, which attempts to impose its own unitary religious definition on the grouping and its symbolic order. The 'proper' behaviour of women is used to signify the difference between those who belong and those who do not; women are also seen as the 'cultural carriers' of the grouping, who transmit group culture to the future generation; and proper control in terms of marriage and divorce ensures that children who are born to those women are within the boundaries of the collectivity, not only biologically but also symbolically."

According to this view, strict dress codes may be imposed upon women, not for their own sake but to serve the ends of others. Hence they may be denied equal freedom to choose for themselves. They may also be denied equal treatment. A dress code which requires women to conceal all but their face and hands, while leaving men much freer to decide what they will wear, does not treat them equally. Although a different issue from seclusion, the assumption may be that women will play their part in the private domestic sphere while men will play theirs in the public world. Of course, from a woman's point of view, this may be a safer and more comfortable place to be. Gita Saghal and Nira Yuval Davis go on to point out that, at p 15: "One of the paradoxes ... is the fact that women collude, seek comfort, and even at times gain a sense of empowerment within the spaces allocated to them by fundamentalist movements."

96.   If a woman freely chooses to adopt a way of life for herself, it is not for others, including other women who have chosen differently, to criticise or prevent her. Judge Tulkens, in *Sahin v Turkey*, at p 46, draws the analogy with freedom of speech. The European Court of Human Rights has never accepted that interference with the right of freedom of expression is justified by the fact that the ideas expressed may offend someone.

Likewise, the sight of a woman in full purdah may offend some people, and especially those western feminists who believe that it is a symbol of her oppression, but that could not be a good reason for prohibiting her from wearing it.

97.   But schools are different. Their task is to educate the young from all the many and diverse families and communities in this country in accordance with the national curriculum. Their task is to help all of their pupils achieve their full potential. This includes growing up to play whatever part they choose in the society in which they are living. The school's task is also to promote the ability of people of diverse races, religions and cultures to live together in harmony. Fostering a sense of community and cohesion within the school is an important part of that. A uniform dress code can play its role in smoothing over ethnic, religious and social divisions. But it does more than that. Like it or not, this is a society committed, in principle and in law, to equal freedom for men and women to choose how they will lead their lives within the law. Young girls from ethnic, cultural or religious minorities growing up here face particularly difficult choices: how far to adopt or to distance themselves from the dominant culture. A good school will enable and support them. This particular school is a good school: that, it appears, is one reason why Shabina Begum wanted to stay there. It is also a mixed school. That was what led to the difficulty. It would not have arisen in a girls' school with an all-female staff.

98.   In deciding how far to go in accommodating religious requirements within its dress code, such a school has to accommodate some complex considerations. These are helpfully explained by Professor Frances Radnay in *Culture, Religion and Gender* [2003] 1 International Journal of Constitutional Law 663: "... genuine individual consent to a discriminatory practice or dissent from it may not be feasible where these girls are not yet adult. The question is whether patriarchal family control should be allowed to result in girls being socialised according to the implications of veiling while still attending public educational institutions.... A mandatory policy that rejects veiling in state educational institutions may provide a crucial opportunity for girls to choose the feminist freedom of state education over the patriarchal dominance of their families. Also, for the families, such a policy may send a clear message that the benefits of state education are tied to the obligation to respect women's and girls' rights to equality and freedom ... On the other hand, a prohibition of veiling risks violating the liberal principle of respect for individual autonomy and cultural diversity for parents as well as students. It may also result in traditionalist families not sending their children to the state educational institutions. In this educational context, implementation of the right to equality is a complex matter, and the determination of the way it should be achieved depends upon the balance between these two conflicting policy priorities in a specific social environment." It seems to me that that was exactly what this school was trying to do when it devised the school uniform policy to suit the social conditions in that school, in that town, and at that time. Its requirements are clearly set out by my noble and learned friend, Lord Scott of Foscote, in para 76 of his opinion. Social cohesion is promoted by the uniform elements of shirt, tie and jumper, and the

requirement that all outer garments be in the school colour. But cultural and religious diversity is respected by allowing girls to wear either a skirt, trousers, or the shalwar kameez, and by allowing those who wished to do so to wear the hijab. This was indeed a thoughtful and proportionate response to reconciling the complexities of the situation. This is demonstrated by the fact that girls have subsequently expressed their concern that if the jilbab were to be allowed they would face pressure to adopt it even though they do not wish to do so. Here is the evidence to support the justification which Judge Tulkens found lacking in the Sahin case.

(Not Yet) Taking Rights Seriously: The House of Lords In Begum v. Headteacher and Governors of Denbigh High School

Human Rights & Human Welfare: A Forum for Works in Progress. Working paper no. 37, pp. 20–27

http://ssrn.com/abstract=945319

■ GARETH DAVIES

... That schools may be allowed a degree of discretion and variation in judging where lines should be drawn, according to local circumstances, may be seen as a decentralisation of the margin of appreciation, and perhaps fair enough. At any rate, it is indeed the way UK law works. However, there is also the question of the degree to which courts should require schools to explain their decisions, in order to ensure adequate review and protection of rights. This is not about decentralisation, it is about intensity of review. Conflating the two creates the risk that decisions which are in fact contemptuous of rights will not be exposed because review is superficial, but this will be treated as a margin of discretion matter. Schools may be allowed some variation in value choices and balancing, but to ensure the protection of rights courts must engage in review sufficiently intense to establish what choices and balances the school has in fact made.

Evidence

Their lordships mentioned the reasons above as justifications for the school's interference. However, a mere statement of possible justifications does not suffice to decide a case. A court must also indicate why it believes the facts on which the justifications are based to be true. Were the negative scenarios associated with wearing the jilbab merely hypothetical and unrealistic scaremongering, or a reasonable and accurate assessment of the situation?

Lord Hoffman addressed this issue by reference. He stated that the trial judge had had ample material for deciding that the scenarios were plausible. That may be true. However, in an appeal judgment in the common law tradition it is hardly adequate. Some indication of what that evidence was and why it was convincing would have been appropriate. There was no such indication.

In fact a reading of Lord Hoffman's judgment indicates to the reader that, as with the other judges, his primary reason for accepting that permitting the jilbab brought serious consequence for the rights and freedoms of others was because the head teacher, and to a lesser extent the school governors, said so. The views of the head teacher were repeated, accorded respect, and acceded to, without any consideration of arguments or evidence against them. It is hard to believe that such arguments were not made, and indeed even if they were not, it is the duty of a judge to consider the evidence of parties sceptically and critically. In a contested case, the fact that one party says a thing is true cannot as such decide the matter. It is necessary to consider arguments against the view, and the view of the opposing party, before coming to a conclusion.

Their lordships did not do this. They adopted wholesale the opinions of one party to the case without any discussion or consideration of reasons why these might in fact not be accurate. This is surely rather scandalous. After all, it is perfectly apparent that even a well-meaning and experienced person in authority may well succumb to the temptation to prize a peaceful life and the status quo over the desires and rights of particular individuals, and may tend to over-estimate the risks of change. Perhaps that did not occur in this case. But is it asking too much to expect the House of Lords to at least consider the extent to which the school may possibly have got it wrong?

Lord Bingham explained that to do so was out of the question (having earlier said that the court could not avoid the difficult question of the ban's proportionality, and must face up to it, and decide it objectively). The school had the relevant expertise and was best placed to decide, and for a court to overrule them on "a matter as sensitive as this" would be "irresponsible" What then is the function of judicial review, one is tempted to ask?

Rather than consider directly the factual plausibility of the threats to freedom that the jilbab allegedly comprised, their Lordships supported their decision to support the school in an indirect way. They accepted the school's version because it was a good school, and in particular because the head teacher seemed to be a good head teacher. The judgments abound with references to how the school had improved since the head teacher came to it, how it achieved above average results and had been harmonious and successful in recent years. Moreover, the head teacher could not be accused of being anti-Muslim. She was herself born in Bengal, and permitted headscarves and the shalwar kameeze. Therefore she both understood and respected Islam.

An additional factor which seemed to greatly impress some of their Lordships, as it indeed had had a peculiar fascination for the judges in the Court of Appeal, was that the uniform policy had been drawn up after wide consultation with Muslim authorities and was held by many to be compatible with mainstream Muslim dress requirements.

One consequence of this point was that Ms Begum's desire to wear the jilbab was taken less seriously. Lord Scott even thought it "extraordinary" that a Muslim girl might not regard the shalwar kameeze as sufficiently modest. It is, it is submitted, far more extraordinary that a senior judge should make such a statement. It is manifestly the case that religions have different streams, and the authority of one, even the dominant one, is therefore of very little use in a case concerning another. Would his Lordship find it extraordinary if a Methodist or Lutheran in the United Kingdom disagreed on doctrine with the Archbishop of Canterbury? Or if a practicing Anglican felt that his freedom of religion encompassed the capacity to disagree with the Catholic Church, still the dominant Christian Church worldwide? Only Lord Hoffman explicitly stated that whether or not the majority of Muslims wore one outfit did not make the belief of a minority that another was necessary any less genuine or worthy of respect.

The opinions of the Muslim authorities, however genuine, sincere and founded in knowledge and scholarship, clearly apply to many branches of Islam but not all, and as such are not relevant to the case except insofar as the wide consultation indicates that the school and head teacher were doing their best to construct a fair and tolerant policy. This was the second, and understandable, message that their Lordships took from the point. They mentioned the school's concessions to mainstream Islam as evidence of the fairness and tolerance of the decision-makers. Thus the basis of the substantive finding that an interference with religious liberty was justified is remarkably *ad personem*. The evidence relied upon does not go to the threat itself but to the character of the decision maker. Since this character seemed worthy, the decision was accepted too.

The personal emphasis is further highlighted by repeated, and rather oblique, suggestions that Ms Begum was in some way a less deserving party. Several of their Lordships mention that the teachers found her behaviour in demanding to wear the jilbab "unreasonable" and that her brother seemed even "threatening". Lord Bingham and Lord Scott mention that when they came to school to discuss the matter they talked of "human rights and legal proceedings". The clear implication is that this was unreasonable, confrontational, and not appropriate. Schoolchildren should defer. Perhaps they should beg?

These comments are unfortunate. In many cases there is an equitable element; the merit of the parties and the quality of their behaviour is relevant to the decision. However, this is not one of them. The questions upon which the entire case turns are whether a prohibition of the jilbab is a restriction of religious freedom, and, if so, whether it is necessary to protect the rights and freedoms of others, and proportionate to that goal. The character, nor even behaviour, of the individual who wishes to wear the jilbab does not play a role in either of these. The right of socially unskilled and insecure, or as Lord Hoffman would put it, uncivil, people to manifest their religion is no less than that of the charming and urbane—or if it is, this had better be argued and explained. Hence the comments about Ms Begum and her brother's attitude, combined with the frequent praise of the teacher, combine to nurture the unpleasant thought that this case may have been decided, however subconsciously, on inappropriate grounds. The absence of any other good reasoning magnifies the concern, of course.

Indeed, the evident distaste with which Lords Bingham and Scott refer to Ms Begum and her brother's mention of "human rights" is rather startling. It is as if they consider this something outrageous and wrongful. Indeed, it is probably not the most attractive or skilful commencement of a negotiation, particularly of a school pupil with her teacher. However, precisely in that situation the pupil starts with a disadvantage, and may need to play their strongest card in order to be taken seriously. We may reasonably surmise, given the position of the school, now endorsed by their Lordships, that the initial reaction of the school to her request was a simple refusal, on the basis of the dress code. How then, is a pupil to protect their rights, if they may not refer to them? Even if Ms Begum was wrong, if she believed that she had a fundamental right to religious freedom that was being restricted, and the school refused to adapt its behaviour, was it therefore wrong of her to raise the point? One can imagine that it is difficult for teachers in an age of legalism, when pupils know their rights and sometimes expect them to be respected, but this is the price of treating pupils as human beings, indeed of rights themselves. They are precisely a tool of individual assertion, and if we think, as even their Lordships do, that pupils are human beings with rights too, then they can hardly be blamed for using them. The sneering and accusatory tone directed at Ms Begum because she dared to mention her rights may well be authentic to the non-rights tradition of the common law, but since the Human Rights Act has in fact been passed it amounts almost to contempt for parliament. The capacity of the weak to challenge authority is the price paid for rights, and if their Lordships dislike this they should properly voice their criticisms in the political arena rather than in court.

————

NOTES

1. The *Begum* case was decided by the "Law Lords" of the House of Lords, which until 2009 was the United Kingdom's high court. In 2005, Parliament passed the Constitutional Reform Act of 2005, creating a separate institution that took over the work of the Law Lords, named the Supreme Court of the United Kingdom. It assumed its judicial functions in 2009.

2. In March 2007, British authorities proposed new rules to allow schools to forbid Muslim students to wear full-face veils in class. *See Alan Cowell, Britain Proposes Allowing Schools to Forbid Full–Face Muslim Veils*, NEW YORK TIMES, March 21, 2007.

3. In the *Begum* case, as well as the *Yoder* case, the respective courts addressed the question of whether the plaintiffs' explanation of their religious beliefs correctly stated the governing dogma of their religion. Does addressing this question in a "free exercise" context interfere with the requirement of neutrality under the non-establishment principle? Is it within the jurisdiction of the House of Lords (or now the Supreme Court of the United Kingdom) to decide whether the tenets of Islam required Ms. Begum to wear a jilbab?

4. In *R v. Governing Body of JFS, [2009] UKSC15*, the Supreme Court of the United Kingdom held that the Jewish Free School discriminated on the basis of ethnic origin when it refused admission to the son of a woman who had converted to Judaism, on the grounds that the child was not Jewish. The school used a traditional religious test—was M the child of a Jewish woman—in determining that he was not Jewish. M's mother had

converted in a Progressive synagogue; the school authorities only recognized conversions conducted in Orthodox synagogues, thus concluding that the mother was not Jewish. The Court rejected the test as a form of ethnic or racial discrimination, not based on religious beliefs. *See* Sarah Lyall, *British High Court Says Jewish School's Ethnic–Based Admissions Policy is Illegal*, December 16, 2009. http://www.nytimes.com/2009/12/17/world/europe/17britain.html. Is the determination of whether M's mother is Jewish better left to the Court, or the school?

E. CANADA

Multani v. Commission Scolaire Marguerite–Bourgeoys

Supreme Court of Canada [2006] 1 S.C.R. 256, 2006 SCC 6

OFFICIAL ENGLISH TRANSLATION

G and his father B are orthodox Sikhs. G believes that his religion requires him to wear a kirpan at all times; a kirpan is a religious object that resembles a dagger and must be made of metal. In 2001, G accidentally dropped the kirpan he was wearing under his clothes in the yard of the school he was attending. The school board sent G's parents a letter in which, as a reasonable accommodation, it authorized their son to wear his kirpan to school provided that he complied with certain conditions to ensure that it was sealed inside his clothing. G and his parents agreed to this arrangement. The governing board of the school refused to ratify the agreement on the basis that wearing a kirpan at the school violated art. 5 of the school's *Code de vie* (code of conduct), which prohibited the carrying of weapons. The school board's council of commissioners upheld that decision and notified G and his parents that a symbolic kirpan in the form of a pendant or one in another form made of a material rendering it harmless would be acceptable in the place of a real kirpan. B then filed in the Superior Court a motion for a declaratory judgment to the effect that the council of commissioners' decision was of no force or effect. The Superior Court granted the motion, declared the decision to be null, and authorized G to wear his kirpan under certain conditions. The Court of Appeal set aside the Superior Court's judgment. After deciding that the applicable standard of review was reasonableness *simpliciter*, the Court of Appeal restored the council of commissioners' decision. It concluded that the decision in question infringed G's freedom of religion under s. 2(*a*) of the *Canadian Charter of Rights and Freedoms* ("*Canadian Charter*") and s. 3 of Quebec's *Charter of human rights and freedoms* ("*Quebec Charter*"), but that the infringement was justified for the purposes of s. 1 of the *Canadian Charter* and s. 9.1 of the *Quebec Charter*.

Held: The appeal should be allowed. The decision of the Court of Appeal should be set aside and the decision of the council of commissioners should be declared to be null.

Per McLachlin C.J. and Bastarache, Binnie, Fish and Charron JJ.: In the case at bar, it is the compliance of the commissioners' decision with the requirements of the *Canadian Charter* that is central to the dispute, not the decision's validity from the point of view of administrative law. There is no suggestion that the council of commissioners did not have jurisdiction, from an administrative law standpoint, to approve the *Code de vie*. Nor is the administrative and constitutional validity of the rule against carrying weapons in issue. Since the complaint is based entirely on freedom of religion, the Court of Appeal erred in applying the reasonableness standard to its constitutional analysis. The administrative law standard of review was not relevant.

The *Canadian Charter* applies to the decision of the council of commissioners, despite the decision's individual nature. Any infringement of a guaranteed right that results from the actions of a decision maker acting pursuant to its enabling statute is also a limit "prescribed by law" within the meaning of s. 1. Where the legislation pursuant to which an administrative body has made a contested decision confers a discretion and does not confer, either expressly or by implication, the power to limit the rights and freedoms guaranteed by the *Canadian Charter*, the decision should, if there is an infringement, be subjected to the test set out in s. 1 to ascertain whether it constitutes a reasonable limit.

In the instant case, the Court does not at the outset have to reconcile two constitutional rights, as only freedom of religion is in issue here. However, that freedom is not absolute and can conflict with other constitutional rights. Since the test governing limits on rights was developed in *Oakes*, the Court has never called into question the principle that rights are reconciled through the constitutional justification required by s. 1 of the *Canadian Charter*. Since the decision genuinely affects both parties and was made by an administrative body exercising statutory powers, a contextual analysis under s. 1 will make it possible to balance the relevant competing values in a more comprehensive manner.

The council of commissioners' decision prohibiting G from wearing his kirpan to school infringes his freedom of religion. G genuinely believes that he would not be complying with the requirements of his religion were he to wear a plastic or wooden kirpan, and none of the parties have contested the sincerity of his belief. The interference with G's freedom of religion is neither trivial nor insignificant, as it has deprived him of his right to attend a public school. The infringement of G's freedom of religion cannot be justified under s. 1 of the *Canadian Charter*. Although the council's decision to prohibit the wearing of a kirpan was motivated by a pressing and substantial objective, namely to ensure a reasonable level of safety at the school, and although the decision had a rational connection with the objective, it has not been shown that such a prohibition minimally impairs G's rights.

The analogy with the duty of reasonable accommodation is helpful to explain the burden resulting from the minimal impairment test with respect to an individual. In the circumstances of the instant case, the decision to establish an absolute prohibition against wearing a kirpan does not fall within a range of reasonable alternatives. The arguments in support of such a prohibition must fail. The risk of G using his kirpan for violent purposes or of another student taking it away from him is very low, especially if the kirpan is worn under conditions such as were imposed by the Superior Court. It should be added that G has never claimed a right to wear his kirpan to school without restrictions. Furthermore, there are many objects in schools that could be used to commit violent acts and that are much more easily obtained by students, such as scissors, pencils and baseball bats. The evidence also reveals that not a single violent incident related to the presence of kirpans in schools has been reported. Although it is not necessary to wait for harm to be done before acting, the existence of concerns relating to safety must be unequivocally established for the infringement of a constitutional right to be justified. Nor does the evidence support the argument that allowing G to wear his kirpan to school could have a ripple effect. Lastly, the argument that the wearing of kirpans should be prohibited because the kirpan is a symbol of violence and because it sends the message that using force is necessary to assert rights and resolve conflict is not only contradicted by the evidence regarding the symbolic nature of the kirpan, but is also disrespectful to believers in the Sikh religion and does not take into account Canadian values based on multiculturalism. Religious tolerance is a very important value of Canadian society. If some students consider it unfair that G may wear his kirpan to school while they are not allowed to have knives in their possession, it is incumbent on the schools to discharge their obligation to instill in their students this value that is at the very foundation of our democracy. A total prohibition against wearing a kirpan to school undermines the value of this religious symbol and sends students the message that some religious practices do not merit the same protection as others. Accommodating G and allowing him to wear his kirpan under certain conditions demonstrates the importance that our society attaches to protecting freedom of religion and to showing respect for its minorities. The deleterious effects of a total prohibition thus outweigh its salutary effects.

Given that G no longer attends his school, the appropriate and just remedy is to declare the decision prohibiting him from wearing his kirpan to be null.

F. INDIA

The Constitution of India

Article 25. Freedom of conscience and free profession, practice and propagation of religion.

(1) Subject to public order, morality and health and to the other provisions of this Part, all persons are equally entitled to freedom of conscience and the right freely to profess, practice and propagate religion.

(2) Nothing in this article shall affect the operation of any existing law or prevent the State from making any law—

(a) regulating or restricting any economic, financial, political or other secular activity which may be associated with religious practice;

(b) providing for social welfare and reform or the throwing open of Hindu religious institutions of a public character to all classes and sections of Hindus.

Explanation I: The wearing and carrying of kirpans shall be deemed to be included in the profession of the Sikh religion.

Explanation II: In sub-Clause (b) of clause (2), the reference to Hindus shall be construed as including a reference to persons professing the Sikh, Jains or Buddhist religion, and the reference to Hindu religious institutions shall be construed accordingly.

Article 26. Freedom to manage religious affairs.

Subject to public order, morality and health, every religious denomination or any section thereof shall have the right—

(a) to establish and maintain institutions for religious and charitable purposes;

(b) to manage its own affairs in matters of religion;

(c) to own and acquire movable and immovable property; and

(d) to administer such property in accordance with law.

Article 28. Freedom as to attendance at religious instruction or religious worship in certain educational institutions.

(1) No religious instruction shall be provided in any educational institution wholly maintained out of State funds.

(2) Nothing in clause (1) shall apply to an educational institution which is administered by the State but has been established under any endowment or trust which requires that religious instruction shall be imparted in such institution.

(3) No person attending any educational institution recognised by the State or receiving aid out of State funds shall be required to take part in any religious instruction that may be imparted in such institution or to attend any religious worship that may be conducted in such institution or in any premises attached thereto unless such person or, if such person is minor, his guardian has given his consent thereto.

Article 29 Protection of interests of minorities.

(2) No citizen shall be denied admission into any educational institution maintained by the State or receiving aid out of State funds on grounds only of religion, race, caste, language or any of them.

Article 30. Right of minorities to establish and administer educational institutions.

(1) All minorities, whether based on religion or language, shall have the right to establish and administer educational institutions of their choice.

(1A) In making any law providing for the compulsory acquisition of any property of an educational institution established and administered by a minority, referred to in clause (1), the State shall ensure that the amount fixed by or determined under such law for the acquisition of such property is such as would not restrict or abrogate the right guaranteed under that clause.

(2) The State shall not, in granting aid to educational institutions, discriminate against any educational institution on the ground that it is under the management of a minority, whether based on religion or language.

The Ahmedabad St. Xavier's College Society v. State of Gujarat

Writ Petition Nos. 232 and 233 of 1973—Decided on: 26.04.1974, Supreme Court of India 1974

■ JUDGMENT, A.N. RAY, C.J.

1. The question for consideration is whether the minorities based on religion or language have the right to establish and administer educational institutions for imparting general secular education within the meaning of Article 30 of the Constitution.

2. The minority institutions which are in truth and reality educational institutions where education in its various aspects is imparted claim protection of Article 30.

3. This raises the question at the threshold whether Articles 30(1) and 29(1) of the Constitution are mutually exclusive.

4. Articles 29 and 30 of the Constitution are grouped under the heading "Cultural and educational rights". Article 29(1) deals with right of any section of the citizens residing in India to preserve their language, script or culture. Article 30(1) provides that all religious and linguistic minorities have the right to establish and administer educational institutions of their choice. * * *

12. The real reason embodied in Article 30(1) of the Constitution is the conscience of the nation that the minorities, religious as well as linguistic, are not prohibited from establishing and administering educational institutions of their choice for the purpose of giving their children the best general education to make them complete men and women of the country. The minorities are given this protection under Article 30 in order to preserve, and strengthen the integrity and unity of the country. The sphere of general secular education is intended to develop the commonness of boys and girls of our country. This is in the true spirit of liberty, equality and fraternity through the medium of education. If religious or linguistic minorities are not given protection under Article 30 to establish and administer educational institutions of their choice, they will feel isolated and separate. General secular education will open doors of perception and

act as the natural light of mind for our countrymen to live in the whole.
* * *

19. The entire controversy centers round the extent of the right of the religious and linguistic minorities to administer their educational institutions. * * *

21. On behalf of the petitioners, it is said that the right to administer means autonomy in administration. Emphasis is placed on the minority's claim to mould the institution as it thinks fit. It is said that the regulatory measures should not restrict the right of administration but facilitate the same through the instrumentality of the management of the minority institution. It is said that the management of the minority institution should not be displaced because that will amount to violation of the right to administer. * * *

39. The provisions contained in Section 33A(1)(a) of the Act state that every college shall be under the management of a governing body which shall include amongst its members, a representative of the university nominated by the Vice–Chancellor and representatives of teachers, non-teaching staff and students of the college. These provisions are challenged on the ground that this amounts to invasion of the fundamental right of administration. It is said that the governing body of the college is a part of its administration and therefore that administration should not be touched. The right to administer is the right to conduct and manage the affairs of the institution. This right is exercised through a body of persons in whom the founders, of the institution have faith and confidence and who have full autonomy in that sphere. The right to administer is subject to permissible regulatory measures. Permissible regulatory measures are those which do not restrict the right of administration but facilitate it and ensure better and more effective exercise of the right for the benefit of the institution and through the instrumentality of the management of the educational institutions and without displacing the management. If the administration has to be improved it should be done through the agency or instrumentality of the existing management and not by displacing it. Restrictions on the right of administration imposed in the interest of the general public alone and not in the interests of and for the benefit of minority educational institutions concerned will affect the autonomy in administration.

40. Autonomy in administration means right to administer effectively and to manage and conduct the affairs of the institutions. . . . The provisions contained in Section 33A(i)(a) of the Act have the effect of displacing the management and entrusting it to a different agency. The autonomy in administration is lost. New elements in the shape of representatives of different type are brought in. The calm waters of an institution will not only be disturbed but also mixed.

These provisions in Section 33A(1)(a) cannot therefore apply to minority institutions. . . . These provisions violate the fundamental rights of the minority institutions.

The Constitution of India

Article 44. Uniform civil code for the citizens.

The State shall endeavour to secure for the citizens a uniform civil code throughout the territory of India.

NOTES

1.   What does Article 44 mean? Is there no uniform civil code in India? Swapna Balepur explains: "The only state in India where the Uniform Civil Code is in force is Goa, where there is the Portuguese Civil Code, which is still in force despite the independence of Goa from Portuguese rule because the government chose to continue to enforce the Code for all people irrespective of their religion. In the rest of India the personal and customary law of each religion is in force. Hence Muslims continue to apply the Muslim Shariat Act which governs marriage, divorce, succession, etc. Likewise there is a Hindu marriage Act, Hindu succession Act, Hindu guardianship act, and Hindu adoption and maintenance act." Swapna Balepur, *Secularism in India: An Overview* (on file with authors). The term "Hindu" in these Acts, however, is used expansively, to include several non-Muslim religions, including Buddhists, Jains and Sikhs.

2.   In the absence of a uniform marriage law, can the State have any control over how religious marriage and divorce is regulated, without entangling itself in establishment and interfering with free exercise? This is the problem addressed by the *Khan* case, which follows.

Khan v. Shah Bano

Supreme Court of India, 1985 AIR 945, 1985 SCC(2) 556

■ JUDGMENT, SUPREME COURT OF INDIA

1.   This appeal does not involve any question of constitutional importance but, that is not to say that it does not involve any question of importance. Some questions which arise under the ordinary civil and criminal law are of a far-reaching significance to large segments of society which have been traditionally subjected to unjust treatment. Women are one such segment. * * *

2.   This appeal, arising out of an application filed by a divorced Muslim woman for maintenance under Section 125 of the CrPC [Criminal Procedure Code], raises a straightforward issue which is of common interest not only to Muslim women, not only to women generally but, to all those who, aspiring to create an equal society of men and women, lure themselves into the belief that mankind has achieved a remarkable decree of progress in that direction. The appellant, who is an advocate by profes-

sion, was married to the respondent in 1932. Three sons and two daughters were born of that marriage. In 1975 the appellant drove the respondent out of the matrimonial home, In April 1978, the respondent filed a petition against the appellant under Section 125 of the Code in the court of the learned Judicial Magistrate (First Class), Indore asking for maintenance at the rate of Rs. 500 per month. On November 6, 1978 the appellant divorced the respondent by an irrevocable talaq [a type of divorce in Islamic Law]. His defence to the respondent's petition for maintenance was that she had ceased to be his wife by reason of the divorce granted by him, to provide that he was therefore under no obligation maintenance for her, that he had already paid maintenance to her at the rate of Rs. 200 per month for about two years and that, he had deposited a sum of Rs. 3000 in the court by way of dower during the period the of iddat [the period of time a divorced woman must wait before remarrying]. * * *

3. Does the Muslim Personal Law impose no obligation upon the husband to provide for the maintenance of his divorced wife? Undoubtedly, the Muslim husband enjoys the privilege of being able to discard his wife whenever he chooses to do so, for reasons good, bad or indifferent. Indeed, for no reason at all. * * *

4. The question as to whether Section 125 of the Code applies to Muslims also is concluded by two decisions of this Court which are reported in *Bai Tahira Ali Hussain Fidaalli Chothia and Fuzlunbi v. K. Khader Vali*. Those decisions took the view that the divorced Muslim wife is entitled to apply for maintenance under Section 125. But, a Bench consisting of our learned Brethren, Murtaza Fazal Ali and A. Varadarajan, JJ. were inclined to the view that those cases are not correctly decided. Therefore, they referred this appeal to a larger Bench by an order dated February 3, 1981, which reads thus:

As this case involves substantial questions of law of far-reaching consequences, we feel that the decisions of this Court in *Bai Tahira v. Ali Hussain Fidaalli Chothia and Anr.* and *Fuzlunbi v. K. Khader Vali and Anr.* require reconsideration because, in our opinion, they are not only in direct contravention of the plain and an unambiguous language of Section 127(3)(b) of the CrPC, 1973 which far from overriding the Muslim Law on the subject protects and applies the same in cases where a wife has been divorced by the husband and the dower specified has been paid and the period of iddat has been observed. The decision also appears to us to be against the fundamental concept of divorce by the husband and its consequences under the Muslim law which has been expressly protected by Section 2 of the Muslim Personal Law. * * *

7. Under Section 125(1)(a), a person who, having sufficient means, neglects or refuses to maintain his wife who is unable to maintain herself, can be asked by the court to pay a monthly maintenance to her at a rate not exceeding Five Hundred rupees. By Clause (b) of the Explanation to Section 125(1), 'wife' includes a divorced woman who has not remarried. These provisions are too clear and precise to admit of any doubt or refinement. The religion professed by a spouse or by the spouses has no place in the scheme of these provisions. Whether the spouses are Hindus or Muslims, Christians or Parsis, pagans or heathens is wholly irrelevant in

the application of these provisions.... The liability imposed by Section 125 to maintain close relatives who are indigent is founded upon the individual's obligation to the society to prevent vagrancy and destitution. That is the moral edict of the law and morality cannot be clubbed with religion. Clause (b) of the Explanation to Section 125(1), which defines 'wife' as including a divorced wife, contains no words of limitation to justify the exclusion of Muslim women from its scope. Section 125 is truly secular in character. * * *

9.   Under Section 488 of the Code of 1898, the wife's right to maintenance depended upon the continuance of her married status. Therefore, that right could be defeated by the husband by divorcing her unilaterally as under the Muslim Personal Law, or by obtaining a decree of divorce against her under the other systems of law. It was in order to remove this hardship that the Joint Committee recommended that the benefit of the provisions regarding maintenance should be extended to a divorced woman, so long as she has not remarried after the divorce. That is the genesis of Clause (b) of the Explanation to Section 125(1), which provides that 'wife' includes a woman who has been divorced by, or has obtained a divorce from her husband and has not remarried. * * *

[The Court then examined whether there was an obligation under Muslim religious law for a divorced husband to provide support to his divorced wife, concluding that there was.]

25.   These Aiyats leave no doubt that the Quran imposes an obligation on the Muslim husband to make provision for or to provide maintenance to the divorced wife. The contrary argument does less than justice to the teaching of the Quran. * * *

30.   It is contended on behalf of the appellant that the proceedings of the Rajya Sabha dated December 18, 1973 (volume 86, column 186), when the bill which led to the Code of 1973 was on the anvil, would show that the intention of the Parliament was to leave the provisions of the Muslim Personal Law untouched. In this behalf, reliance is placed on the following statement made by Shri Ram Niwas Mirdha, the then Minister of State, Home Affairs:

> "Dr. Vyas very learnedly made certain observations that a divorced wife under the Muslim law deserves to be treated justly and she should get what is her equitable or legal due. Well, I will not go into this, but say that we would not like to interfere with the customary law of the Muslims through the Criminal Procedure Code. If there is a demand for change in the Muslim Personal Law, it should actually come from the Muslim Community itself and we should wait for the Muslim public opinion on these matters to crystalise before we try to change this customary right or make changes in their personal law. Above all, this is hardly, the place where we could do so. But as I tried to explain, the provision in the Bill is an advance over the previous situation. Divorced women have been included and brought within the admit of Clause 125, but a limitation is being imposed by this amendment to Clause 127, namely, that the maintenance orders would ceases to operate after the amounts due to her under the personal law are paid to her. This is a healthy compromise between what has been termed a

conservative interpretation of law or a concession to conservative public opinion and liberal approach to the problem. We have made an advance and not tried to transgress what are the personal rights of Muslim women. So this, I think, should satisfy Hon. Members that whatever advance we have made is in the right direction and it should be welcomed."

31. It does appear from this speech that the Government did not desire to interfere with the personal law of the Muslim through the Criminal Procedure Code. It wanted the Muslim community to take the lead and the Muslim public opinion to crystalise on the reforms in their personal law. However, we are not concerned with the question whether the Government did or did not desire to bring about changes in the Muslim Personal Law by enacting Sections 125 and 127 of the Code. As we have said earlier and, as admitted by the Minister, the Government did introduce such a change by defining the expression 'wife' to include a divorced wife. * * *

35. It is also a matter of regret that Article 44 of our Constitution has remained a dead letter. It provides that "The State shall endeavour to secure for the citizens a uniform civil code throughout the territory of India". There is no evidence of any official activity for framing a common civil code for the country. A belief seems to have gained ground that it is for the Muslim community to take a lead in the matter of reforms of their personal law. A common Civil Code will help the cause of national integration by removing disparate loyalties to laws which have conflicting ideologies. No community is likely to bell the cat by making gratuitous concessions on this issue. It is the State which is charged with the duty of securing a uniform civil code for the citizens of the country and, unquestionably, it has the legislative competence to do so. A counsel in the case whispered, somewhat audibly, that legislative competence is one thing, the political courage to use that competence is quite another. We understand the difficulties involved in bringing persons of different faiths and persuasions on a common platform. But, a beginning has to be made if the Constitution is to have any meaning. Inevitably, the role of the reformer has to be assumed by the courts, because it is beyond the endurance of sensitive minds to allow injustice to be suffered when it is so palpable. But piecemeal attempts of courts to bridge the gap between personal laws cannot take the place of a common Civil Code. Justice to all is a far more satisfactory way of dispensing justice than justice from case to case.

36. Dr. Tahir Mahmood in his book MUSLIM PERSONAL LAW (1977 Edition, pages 200–202), has made a powerful plea for framing a uniform Civil Code for all citizens of India. He says: "In pursuance of the goal of secularism, the State must stop administering religion-based personal laws". He wants the lead to come from the majority community but, we should have thought that, lead or no lead, the State must act. It would be useful to quote the appeal made by the author to the Muslim community:

"Instead of wasting their energies in exerting theological and political pressure in order to secure an "immunity" for their traditional personal law from the stated legislative jurisdiction, the Muslim will do well to begin exploring and demonstrating how the true Islamic laws, purged of their time-worn and anachronistic interpretations, can enrich the common civil code of India." * * *

NOTES

1. In editing *Shah Bano*, we have removed most of the Court's analysis of Muslim religious law. This part of the decision was highly critical of the Muslim law of divorce. Why would the Supreme Court of India publish an opinion which in effect disparaged a religion which over one hundred million Indians follow?

2. In the same portion removed by our editing, the Court engages in an extensive analysis of Muslim religious law, including its understanding of the Quran (or Koran) and many major interpretative texts, concluding that there is no conflict between the Indian law requiring spousal support and Muslim religious law. If a litigant in a U.S. court claimed that he did not have to pay alimony because his religion absolved him of responsibility, would you expect the United States Supreme Court to examine the religious law relied upon in such a fashion? What accounts for the difference?

3. The Court begins its opinion by stating: "This appeal does not involve any question of constitutional importance." Do you agree?

4. In response to the decision, the All India Muslim Personal Law Board organized Muslim opposition to the judgment. Nawaz B. Mody, *The Shah Bano Judgment and Its Aftermath,* ASIAN SURVEY, Vol. 27, No. 8 (Aug. 1987), 935, 946. This included a march of 200,000 in Mumbai. *Id.* The Prime Minister of India, Rajiv Gandhi, and the ruling Congress party passed the Muslim Women (Protection of Rights on Divorce) Act in the spring of 1986. *Id.* at 950. They passed the bill because of reports that many of the country's minorities felt that their religions were in danger. *Id.* This Act undid the judgment and required men to provide maintenance to their former wives after divorce only for the period of iddat. *Id.* at 949.

5. Why does the Indian Constitution require the state to "endeavor" to create a uniform civil code? What prevents the Indian Parliament from simply adopting a uniform civil code of marriage and divorce?

6. The Court's decision appears to be driven in part by concerns about gender equality for Muslim women. How should courts in secular nations like India balance their commitment (here required by its Constitution) to gender equality with a commitment to non-establishment and free exercise?

7. For a discussion of how the concept of secularism in India differs from the concept in Europe or the United States, *see* Partha Chatterjee, *Secularism and Toleration*, ECONOMIC AND POLITICAL WEEKLY Vol. 29 No. 28 1768, 1773 (July 9, 1994).

Secularism in India: Why is it Imperiled?

Future of Secularism (Oxford University Press, 2009)

■ Jagdish Bhagwati

Introduction

Secularism in India is widely considered to be under threat. The razing of the Babri Masjid in Ayodhya led to riots and killings by Muslims and by Hindus. The recent massacres of innocent Hindus in Godhra, presumably ignited by smouldering Muslim resentments against the Hindutva proponents over Ayodhya, touched off a larger massacre of equally innocent Muslims in tit-for-tat killings that undermined yet further the amity under which these religious communities had lived earlier in Gujerat State in an atmosphere of secularism.

And we have had unspeakable atrocities against the Sikhs in Delhi after the assassination of Prime Minister Indira Gandhi; and an occasional slaying of proselytizing Christian missionaries: a matter that has personal salience and poignancy for me as I was educated at the Catholic St. Xavier's School in Mumbai with religious tolerance and indulgence—I was allowed to spend all my Book Prize moneys each year on the writings of Swami Vivekananda and none of us who were not Christians had to attend Bible classes but were instructed in Good Manners and Morals instead—which stand in contrast to the fanatical stereotypes of forced conversions that agitate the extreme fringe among the Hindus.

Does this resurfacing of communal strife, which is disturbing even though it pales in comparison to the horrendous post-partition violence in both India and Pakistan and, I suspect, owes a great deal to the festering memories of those events, suggest that we are at the edge of a precipice? Or can we draw comfort from the fact that, just as India's democracy has survived for over half a century while nearly all other nations liberated from colonialism succumbed to civil strife and often to military takeovers and military dictatorships—four times, with General Ayub Khan, General Yahya Khan, then General Zia and now General Musharraf, in Pakistan—India will be able to survive the threat to its equally important other pillar of civic virtue, secularism? Must India land on its feet here too, even as communal turbulence threatens to throw her off balance? Perhaps; but none of us can afford to be complacent.

What I propose to do here therefore is to analyze the factors contributing to these disturbing trends, and then to offer policy and institutional correctives. I shall divide the analysis into factors that operate at home, and the external factors: though, they do interact at times, for sure.

At Home

Why are Hindus agitated? It is a cliché by now that Hindu revivalism is characterized by the paradox that a sizeable number in the majority community, constituted by Hindus who are nearly 82% of the population, act as if Hindus were a minority. The reactionary, activist fringe among the Hindus feels that the rights of the Hindus are set back by the secular state while the rights of the religious minorities, especially the Muslims, are advanced.

I have little doubt that this sense has come to prevail in India, increasingly in the post-Independence years, because of an explosive combination of three elements:

(1) The Nehruvian secularists (among whom I counted myself, having been educated at Cambridge and Oxford) founded their secularism on an equal contempt for all religions. Religion was, in the famous formulation at the time, the opium of the masses (creating the *bon mot* where, asked as to what the opium of the Chinese masses was, the wit replies: opium). Secularism, as an element of modernity, required therefore a non-discriminatory rejection of all religions and all religiosity from public, as distinct from private, affirmation.

(2) Aside from the fact that such an attitude is unrealistic when religion plays an immense role in society, just as it does in the United States (where Presidents of both Parties visibly affirm their Christian faith, whether real or simulated and politically stimulated, by going to church on Sundays, for instance), it posed a compelling problem for the majority religion. For, while this denial of religiosity could be carried through for the Hindus, it was not possible to do so for the Muslims because another principle intervened: the Muslims were a minority and their religious practices had to be respected and were not to be interfered with except in the manner, and at the pace, at which the community's leadership itself defined.

This principle had been partly inherited from the colonial times. The British had not imposed a uniform common law on all communities. Each community was to be subject to its own religious customs and laws as practiced traditionally. When Independence came, this situation continued. Each community was left with reforming its ways. When it came to Hinduism, the Hindu reformers managed to get changes in objectionable pre-modern practices implemented in legislation such as the Hindu Code Bill. But, by contrast, the Muslim reformers were less effective for several reasons, so that the reforms in Muslim religious practices as they bear on civil life fell behind the progress achieved by the Hindu reformers. But this then appeared to the regressive Hindu elements to be a bias by the secular forces in favour of the Muslims and against the Hindus.

In some cases, the provocative thoughtlessness of the secularists in this regard was quite gratuitous.... I recall that, when my father, who had retired from the Supreme Court, was the Vice Chancellor of the Benares Hindu University, which was one of the few central universities, he was suddenly confronted by the consequences of a governmental attempt to drop the word "Hindu" from the name of the University while, for the obvious reason that Muslims were to be protected against such a "reform" since few Muslims would have tolerated this, the word "Muslim" was not to be removed from the Aligarh Muslim University which too was a central university. This asymmetry fueled more outraged and protracted outbursts and violence on the Benares campus than would have been the case if this asymmetry of treatment was not present. Instead of cutting and running, as many today do, my father (who had done a great deal for the Independence movement by encouraging his many sons to take active part in the Independence struggle, with my eldest brother, later the Chief Justice of

India and a great human rights activist, having to go underground in view of a British warrant for his arrest and being caught up in a lathi charge which destroyed some of his front teeth) stuck it out but it destroyed his health. And what <u>was</u> the point of the measure in any event, except to indulge anti-religiosity, and that too in a silly act of symbolism since the university would have continued offering courses in Hindu texts, traditions etc. much the way Brandeis and Yeshiva universities do for Jewish culture and traditions in the United States, for instance?

(3) But the resulting feeling among the Hindu traditionalists that Hindus were subject to discriminatory treatment, to a kind of "reverse discrimination" if you like, because of the asymmetric treatment of the two religions, was further reinforced by the appropriate affirmative action in favour of the Muslim minority in many other ways.

The Congress Party, during Independence struggle, had done the same unsuccessfully with a view to wooing Muslims away from the demands by Jinnah for Pakistan, offering to a rejectionist Jinnah a hugely dispropor-tionately higher representation for Muslims in the provisional govern-ments, for instance, as the great secularist Muslim leader Maulana Azad has written with great passion in his celebrated AUTOBIOGRAPHY. In similar vein, the Haj travel to Mecca was widely believed to be subsidized whereas the travel for the Kumbha Mela was presumably not. Again, Muslims were noticeably and quite properly represented deliberately in the cabinet, in the courts and in the bureaucracy. All this might have been accepted in other contexts as appropriate. But, set in the context of asymmetric treatment of the two religions in the manner outlined earlier and the active reforms being legislated against unacceptable Hindu practices, it was perceived as inappropriate and as more of the unjustified bias against Hindus, the overwhelming majority in the country, and of the contrasting "pampering" of the Muslim minority.

This constellation of factors, acting in concert to produce the backlash among the anti-modern traditionalist Hindus many of whom have now rallied behind Hindutva, induces me to suggest, if only tentatively, that the correction of one or more of these factors might have produced greater harmony and might have moderated, if not avoided, the current incendiary situation. It is possible that a Gandhian approach to secularism, based instead on equal respect for all religions in the public sphere (an approach that I discuss in the next Section titled "Abroad"), and a more deliberate and decisive attempt early on in the life of our nation (in concert with progressive Muslims like the actress Shabna Azami and her celebrated poet husband, and several remarkable intellectuals in public life like former Ambassador Abid Husain and the late Professor Khusro) to bring non-fundamentalist Hindu and Muslim leadership together to converge on *common* civil laws, would have helped.

Abroad

But let me also add two external reasons one familiar and the other novel, which have also fueled the threat to secularism today.

One is, of course, the fact that Pakistan, ruled for half its life by military dictators who have exiled civilian political leaders and even hanged a former Prime Minister, has had the usual vested interest in externalizing its domestic problems of governance. Three successive defeats at the hands of India, and especially the ignominious surrender to the Indian army in East Pakistan, have fueled the desire for revenge by going after India's soft spots. These certainly include Kashmir, where the Muslim card is played cynically, and another is India's Muslims who are treated as pawns in the game of playing up their sentiments as "imagined" victims of the "Hindu state". This is obviously not the entire story of Indo–Pakistan differences, but if it is not the Prince in Hamlet, it certainly has an important part in the play. It clearly exacerbates Muslim discontent and encourages Hindu–Muslim divisiveness. While the recent dialogue between General Musharraf and Prime Minister Manmohan Singh carries the BJP initiatives of Prime Minister Vajpayee a step further in the right direction, surely the restoration of democracy in Pakistan is critical to reaching an enduring solution to the problems between the two countries and, in its wake, strengthening the amity, and weakening the strife, between Hindus and Muslims in India. There are signs today that the military dictatorship's Kashmir-baiting, and use of Indian Muslims as pawns in conflict with India, has fewer sympathizers in Pakistan's population; and democracy would only strengthen the forces for accommodation in the same way that NGOs willing to negotiate a solution to Kashmir, for instance, flourish under democratic conditions in India.

But one more external factor, operating instead on the Hindus, needs to be appreciated. It turns out that a substantial fraction of the Indian diaspora, especially in the United States, also shares the Hindu revivalist sentiments. Why do they get so hot under the collar, to the point of supporting financially and otherwise these revivalist notions? I believe there are two principal reasons, one political-philosophical and capable of heroic correction and the other cultural-sociological.

(i) The former lies in the fact that there is an interesting, partial parallel at the international level with the feeling within India among Hindu anti-modernists. While these Hindus feel that Hinduism is being discriminated against in India and other religions favoured in a discriminatory fashion, a large number of Indian abroad feel the same way about the situation in which Hinduism finds itself internationally. They look around the world and what do they find? Every major religion has nation states embracing them and playing for them, whether they profess to be secular or a theocracy. Look at Israel; it plays for the Jews, of course. The United States is clearly a Christian country, and now a Judeo–Christian country (with Clintons going to church and George W. Bush professing to be twice-born) The Vatican, the church of the Catholics, even has status at the UN and receives Ambassadors from countries worldwide in a manner that no other religious order does. The Muslim states not merely profess theocracy and embrace Islamic constitutions; they even band together in foreign policy through institutions such as the Arab League and others. It is natural therefore for Hindus abroad to ask: who plays for Hinduism? Hinduism has over a billion adherents; but it is predominantly in one country, India. And they see India embracing secularism since Independence; and they get upset. It is what I call, in the spirit of E.H.Carr on the problem of "socialism in one state", the problem of "secularism in one state".

So these Hindus, among whom there are many professionals, object to the secularist demands to treat what they see as benign Hindu cultural forms as malign anti-secularism. Therefore, they ask noisily for Hindu prayers at Indian functions; they send their children to Sunday schools like the Jewish Saturday schools to learn Sanskrit, Bharatanatyam and the Gita; and, most provocatively, they send moneys to RSS [Rashtriya Swayamsevak Sangh, or National Patriotic Organization] schools where they feel that Hindu religion and culture will be taught.

(ii) Compounding the problem of "secularism in one state" is a different issue that afflicts some of the diaspora Indians. Coming from a different culture where the women do not enjoy equality—and this is particularly true of immigrant East African Indians whose isolation from modernity has frozen them at gender attitudes that are a century behind the curve—, they react to the greater freedom and independence of their women folk by voting for Rama Rajya. What they are really looking for is Rajya over Sita. This also drives them into the arms of the RSS-type fundamentalists among the Hindus. When I offered this hypothesis to my colleague, Jack Hawley who has done much distinguished work on Religions and particularly on Hinduism, he agreed and led me to the insightful volume that he has recently edited on FUNDAMENTALISM AND GENDER (Oxford, 1994), where he writes in a related and complementary vein of the link between fundamentalism and a conservative ideology of gender that cuts across most religions:

"Why, in 1979, did the leaders of the Islamic revolution in Iran insist that women be covered in public, and why did militant Muslims demanding an independent Kashmir do the same thing ten years later? Why, in 1981, did the Akali Dal, the most influential Sikh party, demand a personal law that would bar Sikh women from using cosmetics, jewelry, or clothing that exposed their bodies? Think also of Vishwa Hindu Parishad—the group primarily responsible for the bloody agitations aimed at building a temple to Rama to mark its supposed birthplace, on a site where a mosque stood until Hindu militants destroyed it in 1992. Why did the VHP's general secretary, in 1989, list three points of Hindu honor that he held to be non-negotiable: the building of the temple, to be sure; but also the veneration of woman and the defense of "mother cow"? Why has women's wearing of the sari, not Western dresses or pants, recently become an aspect of Vishwa Hindu Parishad teaching? Is there a connection between demands like these and the behavior of Hasidic Jews who in the same year stoned a group of women who were defying tradition by carrying the Torah as they went to pray at the Wailing Wall in Jerusalem?"

In focusing on why the diaspora of educated Indians abroad seeks this link, I provide the explanation that it is the threat to their views on gender roles and the threat to them posed by migration to America that provides the fuel for their support of the RSS, VHP *et.al.* from abroad.

But if this link can be explained but not remedied, this is not true of the problem posed by "secularism in one state". To see how this might be remedied, one needs to focus on the fact that the problem arises, not from the refusal to allow Hindus freedom to practice their religion but from the fact that the public displays and affirmation of it assign to it a discriminatory and inferior status. We need to consider frontally therefore the important question of what we mean by religious freedom, a cornerstone of our fundamental political beliefs. The conventional Western view of religious freedom considers it to be what I might call, borrowing philosophical terminology in the debates on liberty, *negative* religious freedom: that we permit the free exercise of religion. But, we also need to consider what should be called *positive* religious freedom: that no religion be favored in public space, effectively dominating and marginalizing other religions.

While theocracies typically elevate the dominant religion to a status that compromises positive religious freedom, there is no excuse for self-described non-theocratic societies to do so. Consider the United States: because of historical reasons dating back to virtually mono-religious composition of the voting population, affirmation through public displays of the dominant religion, Christianity, is what hits the eye. Even in the quasi-public space, such as university convocations, one typically sees Christian ministers delivering benedictions, with an occasional rabbi thrown in: where are the Hindu and Buddhist priests and invocations? President Bush now makes an occasional nod to Islam: but that is a transparently political response to the need to demonstrate that we are not anti-Muslim as Islamic fundamentalists scream otherwise in the turbulent Middle East.

Perhaps the best example that the US can learn from is the practice of Mahatma Gandhi, one of the greatest figures of the last century, in this regard. He began his public meetings, given his own and the nation's religiosity, with prayers drawing on the sacred texts of India's principal religions, among them the Bhagawad Gita, the Koran, the Old and the New Testament, and the Granth Sahib of the Sikhs. He is known to have borrowed civil disobedience from Thoreau. It is time for Thoreau's country now to borrow from him.

Perhaps that will moderate the sense in the Indian diaspora that Hinduism is suffering from the discrimination resulting from "secularism in one state".

NOTES

1. Professor Bhagwati challenges us to imagine an India in which the Hindu majority respects accommodations for the religious practices of the Muslim minority, while confining their own religious practices to the private sphere. Can we point to any secular state we have studied as a model for his proposal?

2. Professor Bhagwati challenges us to make the United States less Judeo–Christian and more secular, hoping that India and the rest of the world will follow by example. Do you see any evidence from this chapter and the preceding one that the world looks to the United States for guidance on this question?

3. Professor Bhagwati alludes to controversy over Christian missionaries in India at the beginning of his article. As a post-colonial country, the

Indian public often reacts strongly to the actions of Christian missionaries. In 2003, states increasingly began adopting "anti-conversion bills," which purport to prevent illegal conversions. States often require thirty days notice of an intended conversion. These bills primarily target Christian conversion. Gujarat, Madhya Pradesh, Chattisgarh, Himachal Pradesh, and Rajasthan have passed such bills.

4. Some scholars believe that the Indian government restricts the free exercise of religion through the administration of reservations. For many years, Scheduled Castes and Scheduled Tribes had to identify as Hindus or Sikhs in order to receive the benefits of reservation. For this reason, Scheduled Castes and Scheduled Tribes might have been prevented from converting to Christianity or Islam. If they did convert, they would have had to profess their pre-conversion identities to receive the benefits of reservation.

5. Professor Bhagwati's description of India's relationship with Pakistan is provocative. Yet, an outside observer might note that both sides have engaged in aggressive military actions, appealed to religious prejudice, and taken narrow nationalist positions to exacerbate the dispute over Kashmir. Human Rights Watch has reported that Indian security forces have been responsible for a number of human rights violations, including extrajudicial killings, forced disappearances, and illegal detentions. See Human Rights Watch, "Everyone Lives in Fear": Patterns of Impunity in Jammu and Kashmir, vol. 18, no. 11, September 2006 (available at http://www.hrw.org/sites/default/files/reports/india0906web.pdf).

6. For further reading on constitutional secularism in India, *see* Anuradha Dingwaney Needham and Rajeswari Sunder Rajan (eds), THE CRISES OF SECULARISM IN INDIA (Duke University Press, 2007).

CHAPTER IX

EQUALITY & HATE SPEECH

INTRODUCTION

Is hate speech a concern of equality law? Although it is usually regarded as a topic of free speech law in the United States, for members of minority groups who are the objects of hate speech, it is often regarded as both a deprivation of equality rights, and as a warning of impending violence based on their status as minority group members. In this chapter, we will return to two familiar forums, the problem of equality in education, and the interaction of equality and secularism. This chapter will challenge you to apply your insights from these earlier topics, as you confront the conflict between equality for minorities, and liberty through freedom of speech.

PROBLEMS

As you consider these cases, codes, constitutions and treaties, apply them to the following problems.

- Jean is a law student at a public university. S/he is convinced that the Holocaust never occurred. S/he reserved a classroom at his/her school to make a presentation, open to other students, faculty, staff, and the public, in which s/he will argue that the Holocaust was a hoax. The dean learned of the plans and cancelled the room reservation, explaining that the topic was "impermissible." Jean wants to make a claim for a violation of the right to freedom of speech and the right to academic freedom. How will this claim be resolved in San Francisco, Paris, Berlin or Istanbul? Would it make a difference if Jean were a professor, not a student? Would it matter whether the school was public or private?

- Alex is a newspaper reporter. S/he has published a news story based on an interview with Daniel, the president of an organization named "Men Against Women (MAW)." The purpose of MAW is to return women to their role as homemakers, outlawing their participation in any occupation or profession other than housemaid or nurse. In the story, Alex quoted Daniel as saying, "We all know that women lack the intellectual capacity for higher thought. Men know. Women know. But no one wants to admit it." Alex has been charged with publishing hateful speech. Again, how will the charges be resolved in Detroit, Paris, Copenhagen, Berlin or Istanbul?

- Terri is a sociology professor at a state university. S/he published an essay describing his/her feelings about 9/11 in which s/he wrote: "All death by violence is regrettable, but the workers in the World Trade Center were participants in a system of global death and destruction that makes their own deaths look peaceful, as well as justified, if it helps eliminate the cause of untold greater suffering by people who are really innocent. I won't waste my tears on these collaborators." When the essay was distributed, there was a political outcry in the state. The university is now investigating Terri for "conduct unbecoming a faculty member," an offense usually used in cases of plagiarism or sexual harassment. Again, how will the charges be resolved in San Francisco, Detroit, Paris, Berlin or Istanbul?

A. THE UNITED STATES

First Amendment to the United States Constitution

Congress shall make no law respecting an establishment of religion, or prohibiting the free exercise thereof; or abridging the freedom of speech, or of the press; or the right of the people peaceably to assemble, and to petition the Government for a redress of grievances.

———

Brandenburg v. Ohio

395 U.S. 444 (1969)

■ PER CURIAM.

The appellant, a leader of a Ku Klux Klan group, was convicted under the Ohio Criminal Syndicalism statute for "advocat[ing] ... the duty, necessity, or propriety of crime, sabotage, violence, or unlawful methods of terrorism as a means of accomplishing industrial or political reform" and for voluntarily assembl[ing] with any society, group, or assemblage of persons formed to teach or advocate the doctrines of criminal syndicalism. Ohio Rev. Code Ann. § 2923.13. He was fined $1,000 and sentenced to one to 10 years' imprisonment. The appellant challenged the constitutionality of the criminal syndicalism statute under the First and Fourteenth Amendments to the United States Constitution, but the intermediate appellate court of Ohio affirmed his conviction without opinion. The Supreme Court of Ohio dismissed his appeal sua sponte "for the reason that no substantial constitutional question exists herein." It did not file an opinion or explain its conclusions. Appeal was taken to this Court, and we noted probable jurisdiction. 393 U.S. 948 (1968). We reverse.

The record shows that a man, identified at trial as the appellant, telephoned an announcer-reporter on the staff of a Cincinnati television station and invited him to come to a Ku Klux Klan "rally" to be held at a farm in Hamilton County. With the cooperation of the organizers, the reporter and a cameraman attended the meeting and filmed the events. Portions of the films were later broadcast on the local station and on a national network.

The prosecution's case rested on the films and on testimony identifying the appellant as the person who communicated with the reporter and who spoke at the rally. The State also introduced into evidence several articles appearing in the film, including a pistol, a rifle, a shotgun, ammunition, a Bible, and a red hood worn by the speaker in the films.

One film showed 12 hooded figures, some of whom carried firearms. They were gathered around a large wooden cross, which they burned. No one was present other than the participants and the newsmen who made the film. Most of the words uttered during the scene were incomprehensible when the film was projected, but scattered phrases could be understood that were derogatory of Negroes and, in one instance, of Jews. Another scene on the same film showed the appellant, in Klan regalia, making a speech. The speech, in full, was as follows:

> "This is an organizers' meeting. We have had quite a few members here today which are—we have hundreds, hundreds of members throughout the State of Ohio. I can quote from a newspaper clipping from the Columbus Ohio Dispatch, five weeks ago Sunday morning. The Klan has more members in the State of Ohio than does any other organization. We're not a revengent organization, but if our President, our Congress, our Supreme Court, continues to suppress the white, Caucasian race, it's possible that there might have to be some revengeance taken.

> We are marching on Congress July the Fourth, four hundred thousand strong. From there, we are dividing into two groups, one group to march on St. Augustine, Florida, the other group to march into Mississippi. Thank you."

The second film showed six hooded figures one of whom, later identified as the appellant, repeated a speech very similar to that recorded on the first film. The reference to the possibility of "revengeance" was omitted, and one sentence was added: "Personally, I believe the nigger should be returned to Africa, the Jew returned to Israel." Though some of the figures in the films carried weapons, the speaker did not.

The Ohio Criminal Syndicalism Statute was enacted in 1919. From 1917 to 1920, identical or quite similar laws were adopted by 20 States and two territories. E. Dowell, A History of Criminal Syndicalism Legislation in the United States 21 (1939). In 1927, this Court sustained the constitutionality of California's Criminal Syndicalism Act, Cal. Penal Code §§ 11400–11402, the text of which is quite similar to that of the laws of Ohio. *Whitney v. California*, 274 U.S. 357 (1927). The Court upheld the statute on the ground that, without more, "advocating" violent means to effect political and economic change involves such danger to the security of the State that the State may outlaw it. Cf. *Fiske v. Kansas*, 274 U.S. 380 (1927). But *Whitney* has been thoroughly discredited by later decisions. *See Dennis v. United States*, 341 U.S. 494, 507 (1951). These later decisions have fashioned the principle that the constitutional guarantees of free speech and free press do not permit a State to forbid or proscribe advocacy of the use of force or of law violation except where such advocacy is directed to inciting or producing imminent lawless action and is likely to incite or produce such action. As we said in *Noto v. United States*, 367 U.S. 290,

297–298 (1961), "the mere abstract teaching ... of the moral propriety or even moral necessity for a resort to force and violence is not the same as preparing a group for violent action and steeling it to such action." *See also Herndon v. Lowry*, 301 U.S. 242, 259–261 (1937); *Bond v. Floyd*, 385 U.S. 116, 134 (1966). A statute which fails to draw this distinction impermissibly intrudes upon the freedoms guaranteed by the First and Fourteenth Amendments. It sweeps within its condemnation speech which our Constitution has immunized from governmental control. *Cf. Yates v. United States*, 354 U.S. 298 (1957); *De Jonge v. Oregon*, 299 U.S. 353 (1937); *Stromberg v. California*, 283 U.S. 359 (1931). *See also United States v. Robel*, 389 U.S. 258 (1967); *Keyishian v. Board of Regents*, 385 U.S. 589 (1967); *Elfbrandt v. Russell*, 384 U.S. 11 (1966); *Aptheker v. Secretary of State*, 378 U.S. 500 (1964); *Baggett v. Bullitt*, 377 U.S. 360 (1964).

Measured by this test, Ohio's Criminal Syndicalism Act cannot be sustained. The Act punishes persons who "advocate or teach the duty, necessity, or propriety" of violence "as a means of accomplishing industrial or political reform"; or who publish or circulate or display any book or paper containing such advocacy; or who "justify" the commission of violent acts "with intent to exemplify, spread or advocate the propriety of the doctrines of criminal syndicalism"; or who "voluntarily assemble" with a group formed "to teach or advocate the doctrines of criminal syndicalism." Neither the indictment nor the trial judge's instructions to the jury in any way refined the statute's bald definition of the crime in terms of mere advocacy not distinguished from incitement to imminent lawless action.

Accordingly, we are here confronted with a statute which, by its own words and as applied, purports to punish mere advocacy and to forbid, on pain of criminal punishment, assembly with others merely to advocate the described type of action. Such a statute falls within the condemnation of the First and Fourteenth Amendments. The contrary teaching of *Whitney v. California, supra*, cannot be supported, and that decision is therefore overruled.

Reversed.

[Concurrences by JUSTICES BLACK and DOUGLAS omitted.]

Smith v. Collin

439 U.S. 916 (1978)

■ JUSTICE BLACKMUN, with whom JUSTICE WHITE joins, dissenting.

It is a matter of regret for me that the Court denies certiorari in this case, for this is litigation that rests upon critical, disturbing, and emotional facts, and the issues cut down to the very heart of the First Amendment.

The village of Skokie, Ill., a suburb of Chicago, in 1974 had a population of approximately 70,000 persons. A majority were Jewish; of the Jewish population a substantial number were survivors of World War II persecution. In March 1977, respondents Collin and the National Socialist Party of America, which Collin described as a "Nazi organization," publicly announced plans to hold an assembly in front of the Skokie Village Hall. On May 2, the village enacted three ordinances. The first established a permit system for parades and public assemblies and required applicants to post public liability and property damage insurance. The second prohibited the dissemination of material that incited racial or religious hatred with intent so to incite. The third prohibited public demonstrations by members of political parties while wearing military-style uniforms.

On June 22, respondent Collin applied for a permit under the first ordinance. His application stated that a public assembly would take place on July 4, would consist of persons demonstrating in front of the Village Hall, would last about a half hour, and would not disrupt traffic. It also stated that the participants would wear uniforms with swastikas and would carry placards proclaiming free speech for white persons, but would not distribute handbills or literature. The permit was denied.

Skokie's Village Hall stood on a street that was zoned commercial. There were residential areas, however, adjoining to the North, South, and West. The front of the Village Hall was visible from dwellings in those areas.

Upon the rejection of the permit application, respondents filed a complaint in the United States District Court for the Northern District of Illinois against the president of the village of Skokie, its manager, its corporation counsel, and the village itself. Respondents asked that the ordinances be declared void and their enforcement enjoined. The District Court, after receiving evidence, ruled that the ordinances were unconstitutional on their face, and granted the requested declaratory and injunctive relief. It filed a comprehensive opinion. 447 F. Supp. 676 (1978). The United States Court of Appeals for the Seventh Circuit, with one judge dissenting in part, affirmed. 578 F.2d 1197 (1978).

A permit then was issued to respondents for a demonstration on the afternoon of June 25, 1978, in front of the Village Hall. Respondents, however, shifted their assembly from Skokie to Chicago where activities took place on June 24 and July 9.

Other aspects of the controversy already have reached this Court. In April 1977, the Circuit Court of Cook County, Ill., entered an injunction against respondents prohibiting them, within the village, from parading in the National Socialist uniform, displaying the swastika, or displaying materials that incite or promote hatred against persons of the Jewish or any other faith. The Illinois Appellate Court denied an application for stay pending appeal. The Supreme Court of Illinois, in turn, denied a stay and also denied leave for an expedited appeal. Relief was sought here. This Court, *per curiam* but by a divided vote, reversed the denial of a stay and remanded the case for further proceedings. *National Socialist Party v. Skokie*, 432 U.S. 43 (1977).

On remand, the Illinois Appellate Court reviewed and modified the injunction the Circuit Court had entered and this time upheld only that portion thereof that prevented the display of swastikas "in the course of a demonstration, march, or parade." *Village of Skokie v. National Socialist Party*, 51 Ill.App.3d 279 (1977). The Supreme Court of Illinois denied an application for stay pending expedited review. Mr. Justice Stevens, as Circuit Justice, denied a stay of the injunction as so modified. 434 U.S. 1327 (1977). The Illinois Supreme Court ultimately reversed the remaining injunctive feature, "albeit reluctantly," and with one justice dissenting. 69 Ill.2d 605 (1978).

Thereafter, the village and its codefendants in the present federal litigation filed an application to stay the Seventh Circuit's mandate, or, in the alternative, to stay enforcement of the injunction entered by the District Court. This Court, with two Justices dissenting, denied the application. 436 U.S. 953 (1978).

These facts and this chronology demonstrate, I believe, the pervading sensitivity of the litigation. On the one hand, we have precious First Amendment rights vigorously asserted and an obvious concern that, if those asserted rights are not recognized, the precedent of a "hard" case might offer a justification for repression in the future. On the other hand, we are presented with evidence of a potentially explosive and dangerous situation, enflamed by unforgettable recollections of traumatic experiences in the second world conflict. Finally, Judge Sprecher of the Seventh Circuit observed that "each court dealing with these precise problems (the Illinois Supreme Court, the District Court and this Court) feels the need to apologize for its result." 578 F.2d at 1211.

Furthermore, in *Beauharnais v. Illinois*, 343 U.S. 250 (1952), this Court faced up to an Illinois statute that made it a crime to exhibit in any public place a publication that portrayed "depravity, criminality, unchastity, or lack of virtue of a class of citizens, of any race, color, creed or religion," thereby exposing such citizens "to contempt, derision, or obloquy." The Court, by a divided vote, held that, as construed and applied, the statute did not violate the liberty of speech guaranteed as against the States by the Due Process Clause of the Fourteenth Amendment.

I stated in dissent when the application for stay in the present litigation was denied, 436 U.S., at 953, that I feel the Seventh Circuit's decision is in some tension with *Beauharnais*. That case has not been overruled or formally limited in any way.

I therefore would grant certiorari in order to resolve any possible conflict that may exist between the ruling of the Seventh Circuit here and *Beauharnais*. I also feel that the present case affords the Court an opportunity to consider whether, in the context of the facts that this record appears to present, there is no limit whatsoever to the exercise of free speech. There indeed may be no such limit, but when citizens assert, not casually but with deep conviction, that the proposed demonstration is scheduled at a place and in a manner that is taunting and overwhelmingly offensive to the citizens of that place, that assertion, uncomfortable though it may be for judges, deserves to be examined. It just might fall into the same category as one's "right" to cry "fire" in a crowded theater, for "the character of every act depends upon the circumstances in which it is done." *Schenck v. United States*, 249 U.S. 47, 52 (1919).

[EDITORS' NOTE: *Smith v. Collin* marked the third time the Supreme Court confronted the desire of the American Nazi Party to march in the Jewish community of Skokie, Illinois. *See Crist v. Bretz*, 437 U.S. 28 (1978); *Smith v. Collin*, 436 U.S. 953 (1978); *Smith v. Collin*, 439 U.S. 916 (1978). The cases were at the center of the most contentious First Amendment dispute of the 1970's, and provoked a crisis for the American Civil Liberties Union (ACLU), which lost the support of many of its donors when it decided to represent the Nazis. For more on Skokie, *see* Lee Bollinger, THE TOLERANT SOCIETY (1986).]

R.A.V. v. City of St. Paul

505 U.S. 377 (1992)

■ SCALIA, J., delivered the opinion of the Court, in which REHNQUIST, C.J., and KENNEDY, SOUTER, and THOMAS, JJ., joined. WHITE, J., filed an opinion concurring in the judgment, in which BLACKMUN and O'CONNOR, JJ., joined, and in which STEVENS, J., joined except as to Part I–A. BLACKMUN, J., filed an opinion concurring in the judgment. STEVENS, J., filed an opinion concurring in the judgment, in Part I of which WHITE and BLACKMUN, JJ., joined.

■ JUSTICE SCALIA delivered the opinion of the Court.

In the predawn hours of June 21, 1990, petitioner and several other teenagers allegedly assembled a crudely made cross by taping together broken chair legs. They then allegedly burned the cross inside the fenced yard of a black family that lived across the street from the house where petitioner was staying. Although this conduct could have been punished under any of a number of laws, one of the two provisions under which respondent city of St. Paul chose to charge petitioner (then a juvenile) was the St. Paul Bias–Motivated Crime Ordinance, St. Paul, Minn., Legis. Code § 292.02 (1990), which provides:

> "Whoever places on public or private property a symbol, object, appellation, characterization or graffiti, including, but not limited to, a burning cross or Nazi swastika, which one knows or has reasonable grounds to know arouses anger, alarm or resentment in others on the basis of race, color, creed, religion or gender commits disorderly conduct and shall be guilty of a misdemeanor."

Petitioner moved to dismiss this count on the ground that the St. Paul ordinance was substantially overbroad and impermissibly content based and therefore facially invalid under the First Amendment. The trial court granted this motion, but the Minnesota Supreme Court reversed. That court rejected petitioner's overbreadth claim because, as construed in prior Minnesota cases, *see, e.g., In re Welfare of S.L.J.*, 263 N.W.2d 412 (Minn. 1978), the modifying phrase "arouses anger, alarm or resentment in others" limited the reach of the ordinance to conduct that amounts to "fighting words," i.e., "conduct that itself inflicts injury or tends to incite immediate violence ...," *In re Welfare of R.A.V.*, 464 N.W.2d 507, 510 (Minn. 1991) (citing *Chaplinsky v. New Hampshire*, 315 U.S. 568, 572

(1942)), and therefore the ordinance reached only expression "that the First Amendment does not protect," 464 N.W.2d, at 511. The court also concluded that the ordinance was not impermissibly content based because, in its view, "the ordinance is a narrowly tailored means toward accomplishing the compelling governmental interest in protecting the community against bias-motivated threats to public safety and order."

We granted certiorari, 501 U.S. 1204 (1991).

I

* * * Assuming, *arguendo*, that all of the expression reached by the ordinance is proscribable under the "fighting words" doctrine, we nonetheless conclude that the ordinance is facially unconstitutional in that it prohibits otherwise permitted speech solely on the basis of the subjects the speech addresses.

The First Amendment generally prevents government from proscribing speech, *see, e.g.*, *Cantwell v. Connecticut*, 310 U.S. 296, 309–311 (1940), or even expressive conduct, *see, e.g.*, *Texas v. Johnson*, 491 U.S. 397, 406 (1989), because of disapproval of the ideas expressed. Content-based regulations are presumptively invalid. *Simon & Schuster, Inc. v. Members of N.Y. State Crime Victims Bd.*, 502 U.S. 105, 115 (1991) *id.*, at 124 (KENNEDY, J., concurring in judgment); *Consolidated Edison Co. of N.Y. v. Public Serv. Comm'n of N.Y.*, 447 U.S. 530, 536 (1980); *Police Dept. of Chicago v. Mosley*, 408 U.S. 92, 95 (1972). From 1791 to the present, however, our society, like other free but civilized societies, has permitted restrictions upon the content of speech in a few limited areas, which are "of such slight social value as a step to truth that any benefit that may be derived from them is clearly outweighed by the social interest in order and morality." *Chaplinsky, supra*, 315 U.S., at 572. We have recognized that "the freedom of speech" referred to by the First Amendment does not include a freedom to disregard these traditional limitations. *See, e.g.*, *Roth v. United States*, 354 U.S. 476 (1957) (obscenity); *Beauharnais v. Illinois*, 343 U.S. 250 (1952) (defamation); *Chaplinsky v. New Hampshire, supra* (" 'fighting' words"); *see generally Simon & Schuster, supra*, 502 U.S., at 124 (KENNEDY, J., concurring in judgment). * * *

... [T]he exclusion of "fighting words" from the scope of the First Amendment simply means that, for purposes of that Amendment, the unprotected features of the words are, despite their verbal character, essentially a "nonspeech" element of communication. Fighting words are thus analogous to a noisy sound truck: Each is, as Justice Frankfurter recognized, a "mode of speech," *Niemotko v. Maryland*, 340 U.S. 268, 282 (1951) (opinion concurring in result); both can be used to convey an idea; but neither has, in and of itself, a claim upon the First Amendment. As with the sound truck, however, so also with fighting words: The government may not regulate use based on hostility—or favoritism—towards the underlying message expressed. * * *

II

Applying these principles to the St. Paul ordinance, we conclude that, even as narrowly construed by the Minnesota Supreme Court, the ordinance is facially unconstitutional. Although the phrase in the ordinance, "arouses anger, alarm or resentment in others," has been limited by the Minnesota Supreme Court's construction to reach only those symbols or displays that amount to "fighting words," the remaining, unmodified terms make clear that the ordinance applies only to "fighting words" that insult, or provoke violence, "on the basis of race, color, creed, religion or gender." Displays containing abusive invective, no matter how vicious or severe, are permissible unless they are addressed to one of the specified disfavored topics. Those who wish to use "fighting words" in connection with other ideas—to express hostility, for example, on the basis of political affiliation, union membership, or homosexuality—are not covered. The First Amendment does not permit St. Paul to impose special prohibitions on those speakers who express views on disfavored subjects. *See Simon & Schuster*, 502 U.S. at 116; *Arkansas Writers' Project, Inc. v. Ragland*, 481 U.S. 221, 229–230 (1987).

In its practical operation, moreover, the ordinance goes even beyond mere content discrimination, to actual viewpoint discrimination. Displays containing some words—odious racial epithets, for example—would be prohibited to proponents of all views. But "fighting words" that do not themselves invoke race, color, creed, religion, or gender—aspersions upon a person's mother, for example—would seemingly be usable *ad libitum* in the placards of those arguing in favor of racial, color, etc., tolerance and equality, but could not be used by those speakers' opponents. One could hold up a sign saying, for example, that all "anti-Catholic bigots" are misbegotten; but not that all "papists" are, for that would insult and provoke violence "on the basis of religion." St. Paul has no such authority to license one side of a debate to fight freestyle, while requiring the other to follow Marquis of Queensberry rules.

What we have here, it must be emphasized, is not a prohibition of fighting words that are directed at certain persons or groups (which would be facially valid if it met the requirements of the Equal Protection Clause); but rather, a prohibition of fighting words that contain (as the Minnesota Supreme Court repeatedly emphasized) messages of "bias-motivated" hatred and in particular, as applied to this case, messages "based on virulent notions of racial supremacy." 464 N.W.2d, at 508, 511. One must wholeheartedly agree with the Minnesota Supreme Court that "[i]t is the responsibility, even the obligation, of diverse communities to confront such notions in whatever form they appear," *id.*, at 508, but the manner of that confrontation cannot consist of selective limitations upon speech. St. Paul's brief asserts that a general "fighting words" law would not meet the city's needs because only a content-specific measure can communicate to minority groups that the "group hatred" aspect of such speech "is not condoned by the majority." Brief for Respondent 25. The point of the First Amendment is that majority preferences must be expressed in some fashion other than silencing speech on the basis of its content. * * *

Finally, St. Paul and its *amici* defend the conclusion of the Minnesota Supreme Court that, even if the ordinance regulates expression based on hostility towards its protected ideological content, this discrimination is nonetheless justified because it is narrowly tailored to serve compelling state interests. Specifically, they assert that the ordinance helps to ensure the basic human rights of members of groups that have historically been subjected to discrimination, including the right of such group members to live in peace where they wish. We do not doubt that these interests are compelling, and that the ordinance can be said to promote them. But the "danger of censorship" presented by a facially content-based statute, *Leathers v. Medlock*, 499 U.S., at 448 requires that that weapon be employed only where it is "necessary to serve the asserted [compelling] interest," *Burson v. Freeman*, 504 U.S. 191, 199 (1992) (plurality opinion); *Perry Ed. Assn. v. Perry Local Educators' Assn.*, 460 U.S. 37, 45 (1983). The existence of adequate content-neutral alternatives thus "undercut[s] significantly" any defense of such a statute, *Boos v. Barry, supra*, 485 U.S., at 329, casting considerable doubt on the government's protestations that "the asserted justification is in fact an accurate description of the purpose and effect of the law," *Burson, supra*, 504 U.S., at 213 (KENNEDY, J., concurring). *See Boos, supra*, 485 U.S., at 324–329; *cf. Minneapolis Star & Tribune Co. v. Minnesota Comm'r of Revenue*, 460 U.S. 575, 586–587 (1983). The dispositive question in this case, therefore, is whether content discrimination is reasonably necessary to achieve St. Paul's compelling interests; it plainly is not. An ordinance not limited to the favored topics, for example, would have precisely the same beneficial effect. In fact the only interest distinctively served by the content limitation is that of displaying the city council's special hostility towards the particular biases thus singled out. That is precisely what the First Amendment forbids. The politicians of St. Paul are entitled to express that hostility—but not through the means of imposing unique limitations upon speakers who (however benightedly) disagree. * * *

Let there be no mistake about our belief that burning a cross in someone's front yard is reprehensible. But St. Paul has sufficient means at its disposal to prevent such behavior without adding the First Amendment to the fire.

The judgment of the Minnesota Supreme Court is reversed, and the case is remanded for proceedings not inconsistent with this opinion.

It is so ordered.

■ JUSTICE WHITE, with whom JUSTICE BLACKMUN and JUSTICE O'CONNOR join, and with whom JUSTICE STEVENS joins except as to Part I–A, concurring in the judgment.

I agree with the majority that the judgment of the Minnesota Supreme Court should be reversed. However, our agreement ends there.

This case could easily be decided within the contours of established First Amendment law by holding, as petitioner argues, that the St. Paul ordinance is fatally overbroad because it criminalizes not only unprotected expression but expression protected by the First Amendment. Instead, "find[ing] it unnecessary" to consider the questions upon which we granted review, the Court holds the ordinance facially unconstitutional on a ground that was never presented to the Minnesota Supreme Court, a ground that has not been briefed by the parties before this Court, a ground that requires serious departures from the teaching of prior cases and is inconsistent with the plurality opinion in *Burson v. Freeman*, 504 U.S. 191 (1992), which was joined by two of the five Justices in the majority in the present case. * * *

I

A

This Court's decisions have plainly stated that expression falling within certain limited categories so lacks the values the First Amendment was designed to protect that the Constitution affords no protection to that expression. *Chaplinsky v. New Hampshire*, 315 U.S. 568 (1942), made the point in the clearest possible terms:

"There are certain well-defined and narrowly limited classes of speech, the prevention and punishment of which have never been thought to raise any Constitutional problem. . . . It has been well observed that such utterances are no essential part of any exposition of ideas, and are of such slight social value as a step to truth that any benefit that may be derived from them is clearly outweighed by the social interest in order and morality." *Id.*, at 571–572. *See also Bose Corp. v. Consumers Union of United States, Inc.*, 466 U.S. 485, 504 (1984) (citing *Chaplinsky*).

Thus, as the majority concedes, *see ante*, at 2543, this Court has long held certain discrete categories of expression to be proscribable on the basis of their content. For instance, the Court has held that the individual who falsely shouts "fire" in a crowded theater may not claim the protection of the First Amendment. *Schenck v. United States*, 249 U.S. 47, 52 (1919). The Court has concluded that neither child pornography nor obscenity is protected by the First Amendment. *New York v. Ferber*, 458 U.S. 747, 764 (1982); *Miller v. California*, 413 U.S. 15, 20 (1973); *Roth v. United States*, 354 U.S. 476, 484–485 (1957). And the Court has observed that, "[l]eaving aside the special considerations when public officials [and public figures] are the target, a libelous publication is not protected by the Constitution." *Ferber, supra*, 458 U.S., at 763 (citations omitted).

All of these categories are content based. But the Court has held that the First Amendment does not apply to them because their expressive content is worthless or of de minimis value to society. *Chaplinsky, supra*, 315 U.S., at 571–572. We have not departed from this principle, emphasizing repeatedly that, "within the confines of [these] given classification[s], the evil to be restricted so overwhelmingly outweighs the expressive interests, if any, at stake, that no process of case-by-case adjudication is required." *Ferber, supra*, 458 U.S., at 763–764; *Bigelow v. Virginia*, 421 U.S. 809, 819 (1975). This categorical approach has provided a principled and narrowly focused means for distinguishing between expression that the government may regulate freely and that which it may regulate on the basis of content only upon a showing of compelling need.

Today, however, the Court announces that earlier Courts did not mean their repeated statements that certain categories of expression are "not within the area of constitutionally protected speech." . . . The present Court submits that such clear statements "must be taken in context" and are not "literally true."

To the contrary, those statements meant precisely what they said: The categorical approach is a firmly entrenched part of our First Amendment jurisprudence. Indeed, the Court in *Roth* reviewed the guarantees of freedom of expression in effect at the time of the ratification of the Constitution and concluded, "In light of this history, it is apparent that the unconditional phrasing of the First Amendment was not intended to protect every utterance." 354 U.S., at 482–483.

In its decision today, the Court points to "[n]othing . . . in this Court's precedents warrant[ing] disregard of this longstanding tradition." *Burson*, 504 U.S., at 216 (SCALIA, J., concurring in judgment); *Allied–Signal, Inc.*, *supra*, 504 U.S., at 783. Nevertheless, the majority holds that the First Amendment protects those narrow categories of expression long held to be undeserving of First Amendment protection-at least to the extent that lawmakers may not regulate some fighting words more strictly than others because of their content. The Court announces that such content-based distinctions violate the First Amendment because "[t]he government may not regulate use based on hostility—or favoritism—towards the underlying message expressed." *Ante*, at 2545. Should the government want to criminalize certain fighting words, the Court now requires it to criminalize all fighting words. * * *

The majority's observation that fighting words are "quite expressive indeed," is no answer. Fighting words are not a means of exchanging views, rallying supporters, or registering a protest; they are directed against individuals to provoke violence or to inflict injury. *Chaplinsky*, 315 U.S., at 572. Therefore, a ban on all fighting words or on a subset of the fighting words category would restrict only the social evil of hate speech, without creating the danger of driving viewpoints from the marketplace. * * *

B

In a second break with precedent, the Court refuses to sustain the ordinance even though it would survive under the strict scrutiny applicable to other protected expression. Assuming, *arguendo*, that the St. Paul ordinance is a content-based regulation of protected expression, it nevertheless would pass First Amendment review under settled law upon a showing that the regulation " 'is necessary to serve a compelling state interest and is narrowly drawn to achieve that end.' " *Simon & Schuster, Inc. v. Members of N.Y. State Crime Victims Bd.*, 502 U.S. 105 (1991) (quoting *Arkansas Writers' Project, Inc. v. Ragland*, 481 U.S. 221, 231 (1987)). St. Paul has urged that its ordinance, in the words of the majority, "helps to ensure the basic human rights of members of groups that have historically been subjected to discrimination. . . ." The Court expressly concedes that this interest is compelling and is promoted by the ordinance. *Ibid.* Nevertheless, the Court treats strict scrutiny analysis as irrelevant to the constitutionality of the legislation:

"The dispositive question . . . is whether content discrimination is reasonably necessary to achieve St. Paul's compelling interests; it plainly is not. An ordinance not limited to the favored topics, for example, would have precisely the same beneficial effect."

Under the majority's view, a narrowly drawn, content-based ordinance could never pass constitutional muster if the object of that legislation could be accomplished by banning a wider category of speech. This appears to be a general renunciation of strict scrutiny review, a fundamental tool of First Amendment analysis. * * *

Turning to the St. Paul ordinance and assuming, *arguendo*, as the majority does, that the ordinance is not constitutionally overbroad (*but see* Part II, *infra*), there is no question that it would pass equal protection review. The ordinance proscribes a subset of "fighting words," those that injure "on the basis of race, color, creed, religion or gender." This selective regulation reflects the city's judgment that harms based on race, color, creed, religion, or gender are more pressing public concerns than the harms caused by other fighting words. In light of our Nation's long and painful experience with discrimination, this determination is plainly reasonable. Indeed, as the majority concedes, the interest is compelling. * * *

II

Although I disagree with the Court's analysis, I do agree with its conclusion: The St. Paul ordinance is unconstitutional. However, I would decide the case on overbreadth grounds.

We have emphasized time and again that overbreadth doctrine is an exception to the established principle that "a person to whom a statute may constitutionally be applied will not be heard to challenge that statute on the ground that it may conceivably be applied unconstitutionally to others, in other situations not before the Court." *Broadrick v. Oklahoma*, 413 U.S., at 610; *Brockett v. Spokane Arcades, Inc.*, 472 U.S., at 503–504. A defendant being prosecuted for speech or expressive conduct may challenge the law on its face if it reaches protected expression, even when that person's activities are not protected by the First Amendment. This is because "the possible harm to society in permitting some unprotected speech to go unpunished is outweighed by the possibility that protected speech of others may be muted." *Broadrick, supra*, 413 U.S., at 612; *Osborne v. Ohio*, 495 U.S., at 112, n. 8; *New York v. Ferber*, 458 U.S., at 768–769; *Schaumburg v. Citizens for a Better Environment*, 444 U.S. 620, 634; *Gooding v. Wilson*, 405 U.S. 518, 521 (1972).

However, we have consistently held that, because overbreadth analysis is "strong medicine," it may be invoked to strike an entire statute only when the overbreadth of the statute is not only "real, but substantial as well, judged in relation to the statute's plainly legitimate sweep," *Broadrick*, 413 U.S., at 615, and when the statute is not susceptible to limitation or partial invalidation, *id.*, at 613; *Board of Airport Comm'rs of Los Angeles v. Jews for Jesus, Inc.*, 482 U.S. 569 (1987). "When a federal court is dealing with a federal statute challenged as overbroad, it should ... construe the statute to avoid constitutional problems, if the statute is subject to a limiting construction." *Ferber*, 458 U.S., at 769, n. 24. Of course, "[a] state court is also free to deal with a state statute in the same way." *Ibid. See, e.g., Osborne*, 495 U.S., at 113–114. * * *

I agree with petitioner that the ordinance is invalid on its face. Although the ordinance as construed reaches categories of speech that are constitutionally unprotected, it also criminalizes a substantial amount of expression that—however repugnant—is shielded by the First Amendment. * * *

In the First Amendment context, "[c]riminal statutes must be scrutinized with particular care; those that make unlawful a substantial amount of constitutionally protected conduct may be held facially invalid even if they also have legitimate application." *Houston v. Hill*, 482 U.S. 451, 459 (1987) (citation omitted). The St. Paul antibias ordinance is such a law. Although the ordinance reaches conduct that is unprotected, it also makes criminal expressive conduct that causes only hurt feelings, offense, or resentment, and is protected by the First Amendment. *Cf. Lewis, supra*, 415 U.S., at 132. The ordinance is therefore fatally overbroad and invalid on its face.

■ JUSTICE BLACKMUN, concurring in the judgment.

I regret what the Court has done in this case. The majority opinion signals one of two possibilities: It will serve as precedent for future cases, or it will not. Either result is disheartening.

In the first instance, by deciding that a State cannot regulate speech that causes great harm unless it also regulates speech that does not (setting law and logic on their heads), the Court seems to abandon the categorical approach, and inevitably to relax the level of scrutiny applicable to content-based laws. As Justice WHITE points out, this weakens the traditional protections of speech. If all expressive activity must be accorded the same protection, that protection will be scant. The simple reality is that the Court will never provide child pornography or cigarette advertising the level of protection customarily granted political speech. If we are forbidden to categorize, as the Court has done here, we shall reduce protection across the board. It is sad that in its effort to reach a satisfying result in this case, the Court is willing to weaken First Amendment protections.

In the second instance is the possibility that this case will not significantly alter First Amendment jurisprudence but, instead, will be regarded as an aberration—a case where the Court manipulated doctrine to strike down an ordinance whose premise it opposed, namely, that racial threats and verbal assaults are of greater harm than other fighting words. I fear that the Court has been distracted from its proper mission by the temptation to decide the issue over "politically correct speech" and "cultural diversity," neither of which is presented here. If this is the meaning of today's opinion, it is perhaps even more regrettable.

I see no First Amendment values that are compromised by a law that prohibits hoodlums from driving minorities out of their homes by burning crosses on their lawns, but I see great harm in preventing the people of Saint Paul from specifically punishing the race-based fighting words that so prejudice their community.

I concur in the judgment, however, because I agree with Justice WHITE that this particular ordinance reaches beyond fighting words to speech protected by the First Amendment.

———

Virginia v. Black

538 U.S. 343 (2003)

■ JUSTICE O'CONNOR announced the judgment of the Court and delivered the opinion of the Court with respect to Parts I, II, and III, and an opinion with respect to Parts IV and V, in which the CHIEF JUSTICE, JUSTICE STEVENS, and JUSTICE BREYER join.

In this case we consider whether the Commonwealth of Virginia's statute banning cross burning with "an intent to intimidate a person or group of persons" violates the First Amendment. Va. Code Ann. § 18.2–423 (1996). We conclude that while a State, consistent with the First Amendment, may ban cross burning carried out with the intent to intimidate, the provision in the Virginia statute treating any cross burning as *prima facie* evidence of intent to intimidate renders the statute unconstitutional in its current form.

I

Respondents Barry Black, Richard Elliott, and Jonathan O'Mara were convicted separately of violating Virginia's cross-burning statute, § 18.2–423. That statute provides:

> "It shall be unlawful for any person or persons, with the intent of intimidating any person or group of persons, to burn, or cause to be burned, a cross on the property of another, a highway or other public place. Any person who shall violate any provision of this section shall be guilty of a Class 6 felony.

> "Any such burning of a cross shall be *prima facie* evidence of an intent to intimidate a person or group of persons."

On August 22, 1998, Barry Black led a Ku Klux Klan rally in Carroll County, Virginia. Twenty-five to thirty people attended this gathering, which occurred on private property with the permission of the owner, who was in attendance. The property was located on an open field just off Brushy Fork Road (State Highway 690) in Cana, Virginia.

When the sheriff of Carroll County learned that a Klan rally was occurring in his county, he went to observe it from the side of the road. During the approximately one hour that the sheriff was present, about 40 to 50 cars passed the site, a "few" of which stopped to ask the sheriff what was happening on the property. Eight to ten houses were located in the vicinity of the rally. Rebecca Sechrist, who was related to the owner of the property where the rally took place, "sat and watched to see wha[t] [was] going on" from the lawn of her in-laws' house. She looked on as the Klan prepared for the gathering and subsequently conducted the rally itself.

During the rally, Sechrist heard Klan members speak about "what they were" and "what they believed in." The speakers "talked real bad about the blacks and the Mexicans." One speaker told the assembled gathering that "he would love to take a .30/.30 and just random[ly] shoot the blacks." The speakers also talked about "President Clinton and Hillary

Clinton," and about how their tax money "goes to ... the black people." Sechrist testified that this language made her "very ... scared."

At the conclusion of the rally, the crowd circled around a 25– to 30–foot cross. The cross was between 300 and 350 yards away from the road. According to the sheriff, the cross "then all of a sudden ... went up in a flame." As the cross burned, the Klan played Amazing Grace over the loudspeakers. Sechrist stated that the cross burning made her feel "awful" and "terrible." * * *

Black was charged with burning a cross with the intent of intimidating a person or group of persons, in violation of § 18.2–423. At his trial, the jury was instructed that "intent to intimidate means the motivation to intentionally put a person or a group of persons in fear of bodily harm. Such fear must arise from the willful conduct of the accused rather than from some mere temperamental timidity of the victim." *Id.*, at 146. The trial court also instructed the jury that "the burning of a cross by itself is sufficient evidence from which you may infer the required intent." *Ibid.* When Black objected to this last instruction on First Amendment grounds, the prosecutor responded that the instruction was "taken straight out of the [Virginia] Model Instructions." The jury found Black guilty, and fined him $2,500. The Court of Appeals of Virginia affirmed Black's conviction. Rec. No. 1581–99–3 (Va. App., Dec. 19, 2000).

On May 2, 1998, respondents Richard Elliott and Jonathan O'Mara, as well as a third individual, attempted to burn a cross on the yard of James Jubilee. Jubilee, an African–American, was Elliott's next-door neighbor in Virginia Beach, Virginia. Four months prior to the incident, Jubilee and his family had moved from California to Virginia Beach. Before the cross burning, Jubilee spoke to Elliott's mother to inquire about shots being fired from behind the Elliott home. Elliott's mother explained to Jubilee that her son shot firearms as a hobby, and that he used the backyard as a firing range.

On the night of May 2, respondents drove a truck onto Jubilee's property, planted a cross, and set it on fire. Their apparent motive was to "get back" at Jubilee for complaining about the shooting in the backyard. Respondents were not affiliated with the Klan. The next morning, as Jubilee was pulling his car out of the driveway, he noticed the partially burned cross approximately 20 feet from his house. After seeing the cross, Jubilee was "very nervous" because he "didn't know what would be the next phase," and because "a cross burned in your yard ... tells you that it's just the first round."

Elliott and O'Mara were charged with attempted cross burning and conspiracy to commit cross burning. O'Mara pleaded guilty to both counts, reserving the right to challenge the constitutionality of the cross-burning statute. The judge sentenced O'Mara to 90 days in jail and fined him $2,500. The judge also suspended 45 days of the sentence and $1,000 of the fine.

At Elliott's trial, the judge originally ruled that the jury would be instructed "that the burning of a cross by itself is sufficient evidence from which you may infer the required intent." At trial, however, the court instructed the jury that the Commonwealth must prove that "the defendant intended to commit cross burning," that "the defendant did a direct act toward the commission of the cross burning," and that "the defendant had the intent of intimidating any person or group of persons." The court did not instruct the jury on the meaning of the word "intimidate," nor on the *prima facie* evidence provision of § 18.2–423. The jury found Elliott guilty of attempted cross burning and acquitted him of conspiracy to commit cross burning. It sentenced Elliott to 90 days in jail and a $2,500 fine. The Court of Appeals of Virginia affirmed the convictions of both Elliott and O'Mara. *O'Mara v. Commonwealth*, 33 Va. App. 525, 535 S.E.2d 175 (2000).

Each respondent appealed to the Supreme Court of Virginia, arguing that § 18.2–423 is facially unconstitutional. The Supreme Court of Virginia consolidated all three cases, and held that the statute is unconstitutional on its face. 262 Va. 764 (2001). It held that the Virginia cross-burning statute "is analytically indistinguishable from the ordinance found unconstitutional in *R.A.V.* [*v. St. Paul*, 505 U.S. 377 (1992)]." The Virginia statute, the court held, discriminates on the basis of content since it "selectively chooses only cross burning because of its distinctive message." The court also held that the *prima facie* evidence provision renders the statute overbroad because "[t]he enhanced probability of prosecution under the statute chills the expression of protected speech."

Three justices dissented, concluding that the Virginia cross-burning statute passes constitutional muster because it proscribes only conduct that constitutes a true threat. The justices noted that unlike the ordinance found unconstitutional in *R.A.V. v. St. Paul*, 505 U.S. 377 (1992), the Virginia statute does not just target cross burning "on the basis of race, color, creed, religion or gender." 262 Va., at 791. Rather, "the Virginia statute applies to any individual who burns a cross for any reason provided the cross is burned with the intent to intimidate." * * *

II

* * * From the inception of the second Klan, cross burnings have been used to communicate both threats of violence and messages of shared ideology. The first initiation ceremony occurred on Stone Mountain near Atlanta, Georgia. While a 40–foot cross burned on the mountain, the Klan members took their oaths of loyalty. This cross burning was the second recorded instance in the United States. The first known cross burning in the country had occurred a little over one month before the Klan initiation, when a Georgia mob celebrated the lynching of Leo Frank by burning a "gigantic cross" on Stone Mountain that was "visible throughout" Atlanta. * * *

Often, the Klan used cross burnings as a tool of intimidation and a threat of impending violence. For example, in 1939 and 1940, the Klan burned crosses in front of synagogues and churches. After one cross burning at a synagogue, a Klan member noted that if the cross burning did not "shut the Jews up, we'll cut a few throats and see what happens." In Miami in 1941, the Klan burned four crosses in front of a proposed housing

are here to keep niggers out of your town.... When
on us." * * *

of this Court in *Brown v. Board of Education*, 347 U.S.
with the Civil Rights Movement of the 1950's and 1960's,
outbreak of Klan violence. These acts of violence included
atings, shootings, stabbings, and mutilations. Members of the
crosses on the lawns of those associated with the Civil Rights
, assaulted the Freedom Riders, bombed churches, and murdered
well as whites whom the Klan viewed as sympathetic toward the
ights Movement.

Throughout the history of the Klan, cross burnings have also remained
ent symbols of shared group identity and ideology. The burning cross
ecame a symbol of the Klan itself and a central feature of Klan gatherings.
* * *

To this day, regardless of whether the message is a political one or
whether the message is also meant to intimidate, the burning of a cross is a
"symbol of hate." *Capitol Square Review and Advisory Bd. v. Pinette*, 515
U.S., at 771 (THOMAS, J., concurring). And while cross burning sometimes
carries no intimidating message, at other times the intimidating message is
the only message conveyed. * * *

In sum, while a burning cross does not inevitably convey a message of
intimidation, often the cross burner intends that the recipients of the
message fear for their lives. And when a cross burning is used to intimidate, few if any messages are more powerful.

III

A

The First Amendment, applicable to the States through the Fourteenth
Amendment, provides that "Congress shall make no law ... abridging the
freedom of speech." The hallmark of the protection of free speech is to
allow "free trade in ideas"—even ideas that the overwhelming majority of
people might find distasteful or discomforting. *Abrams v. United States*, 250
U.S. 616, 630 (1919) * * *

The protections afforded by the First Amendment, however, are not
absolute, and we have long recognized that the government may regulate
certain categories of expression consistent with the Constitution. * * *

"True threats" encompass those statements where the speaker means
to communicate a serious expression of an intent to commit an act of
unlawful violence to a particular individual or group of individuals. *See
Watts v. United States*, 394 U.S. 705, at 708 ("political hyperbole" is not a
true threat); *R.A.V. v. City of St. Paul*, 505 U.S., at 388. The speaker need
not actually intend to carry out the threat. Rather, a prohibition on true
threats "protect[s] individuals from the fear of violence" and "from the
disruption that fear engenders," in addition to protecting people "from the
possibility that the threatened violence will occur." Intimidation in th
constitutionally proscribable sense of the word is a type of true threa
where a speaker directs a threat to a person or group of persons with
intent of placing the victim in fear of bodily harm or death. Respondent

not contest that some cross burnin

ing speech, and rightly so. As note

burning in this country shows that

intended to create a pervasive fear in

violence.

B

* * * The Supreme Court of Virginia relied up

Paul, supra, to conclude that once a statute discrimin

this type of content, the law is unconstitutional. We

Virginia's statute does not run afoul of the First Amendm

it bans cross burning with intent to intimidate. Unlike the state

in *R.A.V.*, the Virginia statute does not single out for opprobrium

speech directed toward "one of the specified disfavored topics." It do

matter whether an individual burns a cross with intent to intimia

because of the victim's race, gender, or religion, or because of the victim's

"political affiliation, union membership, or homosexuality." Moreover, as a

factual matter it is not true that cross burners direct their intimidating

conduct solely to racial or religious minorities. * * *

The First Amendment permits Virginia to outlaw cross burnings done
with the intent to intimidate because burning a cross is a particularly
virulent form of intimidation. Instead of prohibiting all intimidating messages, Virginia may choose to regulate this subset of intimidating messages
in light of cross burning's long and pernicious history as a signal of
impending violence. Thus, just as a State may regulate only that obscenity
which is the most obscene due to its prurient content, so too may a State
choose to prohibit only those forms of intimidation that are most likely to
inspire fear of bodily harm. A ban on cross burning carried out with the
intent to intimidate is fully consistent with our holding in *R.A.V.* and is
proscribable under the First Amendment.

IV

* * * The *prima facie* evidence provision, as interpreted by the jury
instruction, renders the statute unconstitutional. . . .

. . . The act of burning a cross may mean that a person is engaging in
constitutionally proscribable intimidation. But that same act may mean
only that the person is engaged in core political speech. The *prima facie*
evidence provision in this statute blurs the line between these two meanings of a burning cross. As interpreted by the jury instruction, the provision
chills constitutionally protected political speech because of the possibility
that the Commonwealth will prosecute—and potentially convict—somebody
engaging only in lawful political speech at the core of what the First
Amendment is designed to protect.

As the history of cross burning indicates, a burning cross is not always
intended to intimidate. Rather, sometimes the cross burning is a statement
of ideology, a symbol of group solidarity. It is a ritual used at Klan
gatherings, and it is used to represent the Klan itself. Thus, "[b]urning a
cross at a political rally would almost certainly be protected expression."
R.A.V. v. St. Paul, 505 U.S., at 402, n. 4 (WHITE, J., concurring in judgment)

(citing *Brandenburg v. Ohio*, 395 U.S., at 445). *Cf. National Socialist Party of America v. Skokie*, 432 U.S. 43 (1977) (per curiam). . . .

The *prima facie* provision makes no effort to distinguish among these different types of cross burnings. It does not distinguish between a cross burning done with the purpose of creating anger or resentment and a cross burning done with the purpose of threatening or intimidating a victim. It does not distinguish between a cross burning at a public rally or a cross burning on a neighbor's lawn. It does not treat the cross burning directed at an individual differently from the cross burning directed at a group of like-minded believers. It allows a jury to treat a cross burning on the property of another with the owner's acquiescence in the same manner as a cross burning on the property of another without the owner's permission. * * *

For these reasons, the *prima facie* evidence provision, as interpreted through the jury instruction and as applied in Barry Black's case, is unconstitutional on its face. * * *

V

With respect to Barry Black, we agree with the Supreme Court of Virginia that his conviction cannot stand, and we affirm the judgment of the Supreme Court of Virginia. With respect to Elliott and O'Mara, we vacate the judgment of the Supreme Court of Virginia, and remand the case for further proceedings.

It is so ordered.

■ JUSTICE THOMAS, dissenting.

In every culture, certain things acquire meaning well beyond what outsiders can comprehend. That goes for both the sacred, *see Texas v. Johnson*, 491 U.S. 397, 422–429 (1989) (REHNQUIST, C. J., dissenting) (describing the unique position of the American flag in our Nation's 200 years of history), and the profane. I believe that cross burning is the paradigmatic example of the latter.

I

Although I agree with the majority's conclusion that it is constitutionally permissible to "ban . . . cross burning carried out with the intent to intimidate," I believe that the majority errs in imputing an expressive component to the activity in question (relying on one of the exceptions to the First Amendment's prohibition on content-based discrimination outlined in *R.A.V. v. St. Paul*, 505 U.S. 377 (1992)). In my view, whatever expressive value cross burning has, the legislature simply wrote it out by banning only intimidating conduct undertaken by a particular means. A conclusion that the statute prohibiting cross burning with intent to intimidate sweeps beyond a prohibition on certain conduct into the zone of expression overlooks not only the words of the statute but also reality.

A

"In holding [the ban on cross burning with intent to intimidate] unconstitutional, the Court ignores Justice Holmes' familiar aphorism that 'a page of history is worth a volume of logic.' " *Texas v. Johnson, supra*, at 421(REHNQUIST, C.J., dissenting) (quoting *New York Trust Co. v. Eisner*, 256 U.S. 345, 349 (1921)).

> "The world's oldest, most persistent terrorist organization is not European or even Middle Eastern in origin. Fifty years before the Irish Republican Army was organized, a century before Al Fatah declared its holy war on Israel, the Ku Klux Klan was actively harassing, torturing, and murdering in the United States. Today ... its members remain fanatically committed to a course of violent opposition to social progress and racial equality in the United States." M. Newton & J. Newton, The Ku Klux Klan: An Encyclopedia vii (1991) (hereinafter Newton & Newton).

To me, the majority's brief history of the Ku Klux Klan only reinforces this common understanding of the Klan as a terrorist organization, which, in its endeavor to intimidate, or even eliminate those it dislikes, uses the most brutal of methods. * * *

Because I would uphold the validity of this statute, I respectfully dissent.

NOTE

1.   Could a state pass a statute that treated the burning of the Koran as *prima facie* evidence of intent to intimidate Muslims? The Westboro Baptist Church from Topeka, Kansas set fire to a Koran on a street corner in 2008. The media largely ignored the event in 2008, but the pastor Terry Jones's decision to burn copies of the Koran on the ninth anniversary of the September 11 attacks attracted worldwide media attention. Brian Stelter, *A Fringe Pastor a Fiery Stunt and the Media Spotlight's Glare*, N.Y. TIMES, Sept. 10, 2010, http://query. nytimes.com/gst/fullpage.html?res=9F02EFDF1339F933A2575AC0A9669D8B63 & ref=terryjonespastor. President Obama condemned the plan and General David Petraeus warned that the burning could endanger American troops. *Id.* This plan coincided with public uproar over a proposed Islamic center near ground zero of the September 11 attacks in New York. *Id.* Terry Jones canceled his plan to burn the Koran after he believed that he had won a promise that the proposed Islamic center would be moved away from ground zero. Damien Cave & Anne Barnard, *Minister Wavers on Plans to Burn Koran*, N.Y. TIMES, Sept. 9, 2010, http://www.nytimes.com/2010/09/10/us/10obama.html?ref=terryjonespastor. However, the leaders behind the proposed Islamic center announced that they had not made such an agreement. *Id.* Pastor Jones presided over a "trial" and burning of the Koran in March of 2011; this sparked protests in Afghanistan in which over 24 were killed and the UN offices in Mazar-i-Sharif were overrun. Taimoor Shah & Rod Nordland, *Afghans Protest Koran Burning for Third Day*, N.Y. TIMES, April 3, 2011, http://www.nytimes.com/2011/04/04/world/asia/04afghanistan.html?ref= terryjonespastor.

Doe v. University of Michigan

721 F.Supp. 852 (E.D. Mich. 1989)

■ COHN, DISTRICT JUDGE

I. INTRODUCTION

It is an unfortunate fact of our constitutional system that the ideals of freedom and equality are often in conflict. The difficult and sometimes painful task of our political and legal institutions is to mediate the appropriate balance between these two competing values. Recently, the University of Michigan at Ann Arbor (the University), a state-chartered university, *see* Mich. Const. art. VIII, adopted a Policy on Discrimination and Discriminatory Harassment of Students in the University Environment (the Policy) in an attempt to curb what the University's governing Board of Regents (Regents) viewed as a rising tide of racial intolerance and harassment on campus. The Policy prohibited individuals, under the penalty of sanctions, from "stigmatizing or victimizing" individuals or groups on the basis of race, ethnicity, religion, sex, sexual orientation, creed, national origin, ancestry, age, marital status, handicap or Vietnam-era veteran status. However laudable or appropriate an effort this may have been, the Court found that the Policy swept within its scope a significant amount of "verbal conduct" or "verbal behavior" which is unquestionably protected speech under the First Amendment. Accordingly, the Court granted plaintiff John Doe's (Doe) prayer for a permanent injunction as to those parts of the Policy restricting speech activity, but denied the injunction as to the Policy's regulation of physical conduct. The reasons follow.

II. FACTS GENERALLY

According to the University, in the last three years incidents of racism and racial harassment appeared to become increasingly frequent at the University. For example, on January 27, 1987, unknown persons distributed a flier declaring "open season" on blacks, which it referred to as "saucer lips, porch monkeys, and jigaboos." On February 4, 1987, a student disc jockey at an on-campus radio station allowed racist jokes to be broadcast. At a demonstration protesting these incidents, a Ku Klux Klan uniform was displayed from a dormitory window. These events and others prompted the University's President on February 19, 1987 to issue a statement expressing outrage and reaffirming the University's commitment to maintaining a racially, ethnically, and culturally diverse campus. The University was unable to identify any of the perpetrators. It is unknown whether the culprits were students. Likewise, there was no evidence to suggest that these were anything other than isolated and purposeless acts. * * *

III. THE UNIVERSITY OF MICHIGAN POLICY ON DISCRIMINATION AND DISCRIMINATORY HARASSMENT

A. The Terms of the Policy

The Policy established a three-tiered system whereby the degree of regulation was dependent on the location of the conduct at issue. The broadest range of speech and dialogue was "tolerated" in variously described public parts of the campus. Only an act of physical violence or destruction of property was considered sanctionable in these settings.

Publications sponsored by the University such as the Michigan Daily and the Michigan Review were not subject to regulation. The conduct of students living in University housing is primarily governed by the standard provisions of individual leases, however the Policy appeared to apply in this setting as well. The Policy by its terms applied specifically to "[e]ducational and academic centers, such as classroom buildings, libraries, research laboratories, recreation and study centers[.]" In these areas, persons were subject to discipline for:

1.   Any behavior, verbal or physical, that stigmatizes or victimizes an individual on the basis of race, ethnicity, religion, sex, sexual orientation, creed, national origin, ancestry, age, marital status, handicap or Vietnam-era veteran status, and that

a.   Involves an express or implied threat to an individual's academic efforts, employment, participation in University sponsored extra-curricular activities or personal safety; or

b.   Has the purpose or reasonably foreseeable effect of interfering with an individual's academic efforts, employment, participation in University sponsored extra-curricular activities or personal safety; or

c.   Creates an intimidating, hostile, or demeaning environment for educational pursuits, employment or participation in University sponsored extra-curricular activities.

2.   Sexual advances, requests for sexual favors, and verbal or physical conduct that stigmatizes or victimizes an individual on the basis of sex or sexual orientation where such behavior:

a.   Involves an express or implied threat to an individual's academic efforts, employment, participation in University sponsored extra-curricular activities or personal safety; or

b.   Has the purpose or reasonably foreseeable effect of interfering with an individual's academic efforts, employment, participation in University sponsored extra-curricular activities or personal safety; or

c.   Creates an intimidating, hostile, or demeaning environment for educational pursuits, employment or participation in University sponsored extra-curricular activities.

On August 22, 1989, the University publicly announced, without prior notice to the Court or Doe, that it was withdrawing section 1(c) on the grounds that "a need exists for further explanation and clarification of [that section] of the policy."

The Policy by its terms recognizes that certain speech which might be considered in violation may not be sanctionable, stating: "The Office of the General Counsel will rule on any claim that conduct which is the subject of a formal hearing is constitutionally protected by the first amendment."

B.   Hearing Procedures

Any member of the University community could initiate the process leading to sanctions by either filing a formal complaint with an appropriate

University office or by seeking informal counseling with described University officials and support centers. The Policy states that it is the preference of the University to employ informal mechanisms for mediation and resolution of complaints whenever possible and in fact most complainants have chosen to proceed informally. * * *

Where a negotiated settlement proves impossible, a formal complaint would be filed with the Administrator of Complaints of Discriminatory Behavior in the Office of Vice–President of Student Services (Policy Administrator). * * *

C. Sanctions

The Policy provided for progressive discipline based on the severity of the violation. * * * Depending on the intent of the accused student, the effect of the conduct, and whether the accused student is a repeat offender, one or more of the following sanctions may be imposed: (1) formal reprimand; (2) community service; (3) class attendance; (4) restitution; (5) removal from University housing; (6) suspension from specific courses and activities; (7) suspension; (8) expulsion. The sanctions of suspension and expulsion could only be imposed for violent or dangerous acts, repeated offenses, or a willful failure to comply with a lesser sanction. The University President could set aside or lessen any sanction.

D. Interpretive Guide

Shortly after the promulgation of the policy in the fall of 1988, the University Office of Affirmative Action issued an interpretive guide (Guide) entitled What Students Should Know about Discrimination and Discriminatory Harassment by Students in the University Environment. The Guide purported to be an authoritative interpretation of the Policy and provided examples of sanctionable conduct. These included:

- A flyer containing racist threats distributed in a residence hall.

- Racist graffiti written on the door of an Asian student's study carrel.

- A male student makes remarks in class like "Women just aren't as good in this field as men," thus creating a hostile learning atmosphere for female classmates.

- Students in a residence hall have a floor party and invite everyone on their floor except one person because they think she might be a lesbian.

- A black student is confronted and racially insulted by two white students in a cafeteria.

- Male students leave pornographic pictures and jokes on the desk of a female graduate student.

- Two men demand that their roommate in the residence hall move out and be tested for AIDS.

In addition, the Guide contained a separate section entitled "You are a harasser when . . ." which contains the following examples of discriminatory conduct:

- You exclude someone from a study group because that person is of a different race, sex, or ethnic origin than you are.
- You tell jokes about gay men and lesbians.
- Your student organization sponsors entertainment that includes a comedian who slurs Hispanics.
- You display a confederate flag on the door of your room in the residence hall.
- You laugh at a joke about someone in your class who stutters.
- You make obscene telephone calls or send racist notes or computer messages.
- You comment in a derogatory way about a particular person or group's physical appearance or sexual orientation, or their cultural origins, or religious beliefs.

It was not clear whether each of these actions would subject a student to sanctions, although the title of the section suggests that they would. It was also unclear why these additional examples were listed separately from those in the section entitled "What is Discriminatory Harassment."

According to the University, the Guide was withdrawn at an unknown date in the winter of 1989, because "the information in it was not accurate." The withdrawal had not been announced publicly as of the date this case was filed.

IV. STANDING

Doe is a psychology graduate student. His specialty is the field of biopsychology, which he describes as the interdisciplinary study of the biological bases of individual differences in personality traits and mental abilities. Doe said that certain controversial theories positing biologically-based differences between sexes and races might be perceived as "sexist" and "racist" by some students, and he feared that discussion of such theories might be sanctionable under the Policy. He asserted that his right to freely and openly discuss these theories was impermissibly chilled, and he requested that the Policy be declared unconstitutional and enjoined on the grounds of vagueness and overbreadth.

The University in response questioned Doe's standing to challenge the Policy, saying that it has never been applied to sanction classroom discussion of legitimate ideas and that Doe did not demonstrate a credible threat of enforcement as to himself. The University also asserts that Doe could not base his claim on the free speech interests of unspecified third parties. These arguments served only to diminish the credibility of the University's argument on the merits because it appeared that it sought to avoid coming to grips with the constitutionality of the Policy. * * *

It is well settled that an individual has standing to challenge the constitutionality of a penal statute if he or she can demonstrate a realistic and credible threat of enforcement. * * *

Were the Court to look only at the plain language of the Policy, it might have to agree with the University that Doe could not have realistically alleged a genuine and credible threat of enforcement. The Policy prohibited conduct which "stigmatizes or victimizes" students on the basis of "race, ethnicity, religion, sex, sexual orientation" and other invidious factors. However, the terms "stigmatize" and "victimize" are not self defining. These words can only be understood with reference to some exogenous value system. What one individual might find victimizing or stigmatizing, another individual might not. Accordingly, the likelihood of a complaint being filed in response to Doe's anticipated classroom comments would be speculative at best. * * *

The slate was not so clean, however. The Court had before it not only the terms of the Policy, but also its legislative history, the Guide, and experiences gleaned from a year of enforcement. The record clearly shows that there existed a realistic and credible threat that Doe could be sanctioned were he to discuss certain biopsychological theories. * * *

The record before the Court thus indicated that the drafters of the policy intended that speech need only be offensive to be sanctionable.

The Guide also suggested that the kinds of ideas Doe wished to discuss would be sanctionable. The Guide was the University's authoritative interpretation of the Policy. It explicitly stated that an example of sanctionable conduct would include:

A male student makes remarks in class like "Women just aren't as good in this field as men," thus creating a hostile learning atmosphere for female classmates.

Doe said in an affidavit that he would like to discuss questions relating to sex and race differences in his capacity as a teaching assistant in Psychology 430, Comparative Animal Behavior. He went on to say:

An appropriate topic for discussion in the discussion groups is sexual differences between male and female mammals, including humans. [One] ... hypothesis regarding sex differences in mental abilities is that men as a group do better than women in some spatially related mental tasks partly because of a biological difference. This may partly explain, for example, why many more men than women chose to enter the engineering profession.

* * *

Finally, the record of the University's enforcement of the Policy over the past year suggested that students in the classroom and research setting who offended others by discussing ideas deemed controversial could be and were subject to discipline. A review of the University's discriminatory harassment complaint files suggested that on at least three separate occasions, students were disciplined or threatened with discipline for comments made in a classroom setting. * * * At least one student was subject to a formal hearing because he stated in the context of a social work research class that he believed that homosexuality was a disease that could be psychologically treated. As will be discussed below, the Policy was enforced so broadly and indiscriminately, that plaintiff's fears of prosecution were entirely reasonable. Accordingly, the Court found that Doe had standing to challenge the policy.

V. VAGUENESS AND OVERBREADTH.

Doe initially moved for a preliminary injunction against the Policy on the grounds that it was unconstitutionally vague and overbroad and that it chilled speech and conduct protected by the First Amendment. The University in response said that the Policy has never been applied to reach protected speech and a preliminary injunction should therefore be denied. * * *

What the University could not do, however, was establish an anti-discrimination policy which had the effect of prohibiting certain speech because it disagreed with ideas or messages sought to be conveyed. * * * As the Supreme Court stated in *West Virginia State Board of Education v. Barnette*, 319 U.S. 624, 642, 87 L.Ed. 1628, 63 S.Ct. 1178 (1943):

> If there is any star fixed in our constitutional constellation, it is that no official, high or petty, can prescribe what shall be orthodox in politics, nationalism, religion, or other matters of opinion or force citizens to confess by word or act their faith therein.

Nor could the University proscribe speech simply because it was found to be offensive, even gravely so, by large numbers of people. * * *

These principles acquire a special significance in the university setting, where the free and unfettered interplay of competing views is essential to the institution's educational mission. *Keyishian v. Board of Regents*, 385 U.S. 589, 603 (1967); *Sweezy v. New Hampshire*, 354 U.S. 234, 250 (1957). With these general rules in mind, the Court can now consider whether the Policy sweeps within its scope speech which is otherwise protected by the First Amendment.

B. Overbreadth

Doe claimed that the Policy was invalid because it was facially overbroad. It is fundamental that statutes regulating First Amendment activities must be narrowly drawn to address only the specific evil at hand. *Broadrick v. Oklahoma*, 413 U.S. 601, 611 (1973). "Because First Amendment freedoms need breathing space to survive, government may regulate in the area only with narrow specificity." *NAACP v. Button*, *supra* 371 U.S. at 433. A law regulating speech will be deemed overbroad if it sweeps within its ambit a substantial amount of protected speech along with that which it may legitimately regulate. *Id.* 413 U.S. at 612; *Houston v. Hill*, 482 U.S. 451, 458–60 (1987); *Kolender v. Lawson*, 461 U.S. 352, 359 n. 8 (1983); *Gooding v. Wilson*, 405 U.S. 518, 521–22 (1972).

The Supreme Court has consistently held that statutes punishing speech or conduct solely on the grounds that they are unseemly or offensive are unconstitutionally overbroad. * * *

C. Vagueness

Doe also urges that the policy be struck down on the grounds that it is impermissibly vague. A statute is unconstitutionally vague when "men of common intelligence must necessarily guess at its meaning." *Broadrick*, *supra* 413 U.S. at 607. A statute must give adequate warning of the conduct which is to be prohibited and must set out explicit standards for those who apply it. *Id.* "No one may be required at the peril of life, liberty or property to speculate as to the meaning of penal statutes. All are entitled to be informed as to what the State commands or forbids." *Lanzetta v. New Jersey*, 306 U.S. 451, 453 (1939). These considerations apply with particular force where the challenged statute acts to inhibit freedoms affirmatively protected by the constitution. *Smith v. Goguen*, 415 U.S. 566, 573 (1974). However, the chilling effect caused by an overly vague statute must be both real and substantial, *Young v. American Mini–Theatres*, 427 U.S. 50 (1976), and a narrowing construction must be unavailable before a court will set it aside, *Screws v. United States*, 325 U.S. 91, 98 (1945).

Looking at the plain language of the Policy, it was simply impossible to discern any limitation on its scope or any conceptual distinction between protected and unprotected conduct. The structure of the Policy was in two parts; one relates to cause and the other to effect. Both cause and effect must be present to state a *prima facie* violation of the Policy. The operative words in the cause section required that language must "stigmatize" or "victimize" an individual. However, both of these terms are general and elude precise definition. Moreover, it is clear that the fact that a statement may victimize or stigmatize an individual does not, in and of itself, strip it of protection under the accepted First Amendment tests.

The first of the "effects clauses" stated that in order to be sanctionable, the stigmatizing and victimizing statements had to "involve an express or implied threat to an individual's academic efforts, employment, participation in University sponsored extra-curricular activities or personal safety." It is not clear what kind of conduct would constitute a "threat" to an individual's academic efforts. It might refer to an unspecified threat of future retaliation by the speaker. Or it might equally plausibly refer to the threat to a victim's academic success because the stigmatizing and victimizing speech is so inherently distracting. Certainly the former would be unprotected speech. However, it is not clear whether the latter would.

Moving to the second "effect clause," a stigmatizing or victimizing comment is sanctionable if it has the purpose or reasonably foreseeable effect of interfering with an individual's academic efforts, etc. Again, the question is what conduct will be held to "interfere" with an individual's academic efforts. The language of the policy alone gives no inherent guidance. The one interpretive resource the University provided was withdrawn as "inaccurate," an implicit admission that even the University itself was unsure of the precise scope and meaning of the Policy.

During the oral argument, the Court asked the University's counsel how he would distinguish between speech which was merely offensive, which he conceded was protected, and speech which "stigmatizes or victimizes" on the basis of an invidious factor. Counsel replied "very carefully." The response, while refreshingly candid, illustrated the plain fact that the University never articulated any principled way to distinguish sanctionable from protected speech. Students of common understanding were necessarily forced to guess at whether a comment about a controversial issue would later be found to be sanctionable under the Policy. The terms of the Policy were so vague that its enforcement would violate the due process clause. *See Cramp v. Board of Public Instruction*, 368 U.S. 278, 285–88 (1961).

VI. CONCLUSION.

* * * While the Court is sympathetic to the University's obligation to ensure equal educational opportunities for all of its students, such efforts must not be at the expense of free speech. Unfortunately, this was precisely what the University did. From the Acting President's December 14 memorandum forward to the adoption of the Policy and continuing through the August 25 hearing, there is no evidence in the record that any officials at the University ever seriously attempted to reconcile their efforts to combat discrimination with the requirements of the First Amendment. * * *

NOTES

1. In the U. S., what steps may a public university take to reduce hate speech directed at students who are members of racial, ethnic, religious or sexual minority groups? Are these steps adequate? If minority students are unable to study with the same sense of physical security as white male Christian heterosexual students, is there a counter-balancing Fourteenth Amendment equality issue?

2. Experts on hate groups point to the internet as a primary factor leading to the growth of hate groups today. The internet allows individuals, who were once isolated in their communities, to connect with others who share supremacist beliefs and gain a sense of "national momentum." The nature of the internet also allows individuals to post supremacist and racist comments in online forums with complete anonymity. Mark P. Orbe & Tina M. Harris, INTERRACIAL COMMUNICATION: THEORY INTO PRACTICE 233 (Sage Publications) (2d ed. 2008).

3. Could Congress pass a law criminalizing the denial of slavery or asserting that slavery was not a cause of the civil war? Although most historians agree that slavery was a principle cause of the civil war, and that slavery was a horrendous violation of human rights, some Americans claim otherwise. A number of American politicians have made statements in recent years suggesting that slaves were better off than African Americans today. For instance, Congressman Trent Franks, of Arizona, stated in 2010 that although slavery is a "crushing mark on America's soul... [f]ar more of the African American community is being devastated by the policies of today than were being devastated by the policies of slavery." Ryan Grim, GOP Rep: *Blacks Worse Off Now Than Under Slavery*, HUFFINGTON POST (Apr. 28, 2010, 5:12 AM), http://www.huffingtonpost.com/2010/02/26/gop-rep-blacks-worse-off_n_478744.html. In 2011, Republican candidates running for president signed a pledge which included similar language, although the controversial language regarding slavery was eventually withdrawn. Alexandra Petri, *Michele Bachmann's slavery and pornography problem*, WASHINGTON POST (Jul. 8, 2011 4:50 PM) http://www.washington post.com/blogs/compost/post/michele-bachmanns-slavery-and-pornography problem/2011/07/08/gIQAjz053H_blog.html. Should Congress be allowed to criminalize statements such as these, which minimize the impact of slavery?

4. Justice Blackmun makes note twice, once in his dissent in *Smith* and once in his concurrence in *R.A.V.*, that the Supreme Court was

"distracted" or "uncomfortable" with the specific fact patterns these cases dealt with, and as a result, applied First Amendment analyses to these cases in a way that broke with precedent. Review the majority opinions in both cases. Are these examples of Justices "manipulating" First Amendment doctrine to arrive at an outcome they think are the just and socially acceptable outcome?

5.   Justice Thomas quotes Justice Holmes's aphorism, "A page of history is worth a volume of logic." Can certain symbols, which have unique historical significance as communicating violence or hatred, ever be realistically divorced from their historical interpretations, as the Court attempts to argue in *Virginia v. Black* regarding burning crosses? Although the burning cross serves as a symbol of group membership for the Ku Klux Klan, isn't hatred towards or intimidation of other races key to that group's identity? Can the symbol and the meaning be separated? What about a Confederate flag, as mentioned in *Doe?*

6.   Content-based regulation of speech, including unconstitutional viewpoint discrimination and censorship of ideological speech, are discussed heavily by the Court in *R.A.V.* Why do you think the Court chose not to apply this same analysis to the speech code at the University of Michigan in *Doe?* What are the key distinctions between the two cases that merited very different doctrinal analyses?

7.   As you read the Holocaust denial cases in the next two sections, ask whether (and why) Germany and France balance the conflict between equality and liberty differently than the U.S.

B.   GERMANY

ART. 1, 2, 3 (1) AND 5 (1) AND (2) OF THE GERMAN BASIC LAW

Article 1 [Human Dignity]

Human dignity shall be inviolable. To respect and protect it shall be the duty of all state authority.

The German people therefore acknowledge inviolable and inalienable human rights as the basis of every community, of peace and of justice in the world.

The following basic rights shall bind the legislature, the executive, and the judiciary as directly applicable law.

Article 2 [Personal Freedom]

Every person shall have the right to the free development of his personality insofar as he does not violate the right of others or offend against the constitutional order or the moral law.

Every person shall have the right to life and physical integrity. Freedom of the person shall be inviolable. These rights may be interfered with only pursuant to a law.

Article 3 [Equality before the law]

All persons shall be equal before the law.

Article 5 [Freedom of expression]

Every person shall have the right freely to express and disseminate his opinions in speech, writing, and pictures and to inform himself without hindrance from generally accessible sources. Freedom of the press and freedom of reporting by means of broadcasts and films shall be guaranteed. There shall be no censorship.

These rights shall find their limits in the provisions of general laws, in provisions for the protection of young persons, and in the right to personal honor.

SECTION 185 OF THE GERMAN CRIMINAL CODE

Insult will be punished by imprisonment not exceeding one year or by a fine. [Definition of insult/defamation: "an illegal attack on the honor of another person by intentionally showing disrespect or no respect at all."]

SECTION 130 OF THE GERMAN CRIMINAL CODE

(1) Whosoever, in a manner liable to disturb public peace, (1) incites hatred against segments of the population or calls for violent or arbitrary measures against them, or (2) assaults the human dignity of others by insulting, maliciously maligning or defaming segments of the population shall be punished with imprisonment from three months to five years ...

(3) Whoever publicly or in a meeting approves of, denies or [minimizes the Holocaust] in a manner capable of disturbing the public peace shall be punished with imprisonment for not more than five years or a fine.

German Holocaust Denial Case

90 BVerfGE 241 (1994)

■ German Federal Constitutional Court (Translation by Sir Basil Markesinis)

Case reference [e.g., BGHZ 56, 163] (Engl. translation) in the web site of The University of Texas School of Law, http://www.utexas.edu/law/academics/centers/transnational/work_new/, [copyright holder]. Copyright of translation held by: B. S. Markesinis, Professor of European Private Law, University College London, and Professor of Anglo–American Law, University of Leiden.

Facts:

The complainant was a district association of the National Democratic Party of Germany (NPD). It invited the historian David Irving, widely seen as a revisionist of the extreme right wing, to a lecturing event. Pursuant to § 5 no. 4 of the Meetings Act, the competent authority imposed on the complainant the condition that it ensured, by appropriate measures, that nothing was said at the meeting about the persecution of the Jews in the Third Reich that would deny or call into question that persecution. The criminality of such spoken contributions was to be pointed out at the beginning of the event, and possible relevant spoken contributions were to be immediately prevented. If necessary, the meeting was to be interrupted or brought to an end, by using the [appropriate] rights of the person in possession of the premises. The authority regarded itself as obliged to take such measures because grounds existed for the assumption that there would be criminal acts in the sense of §§ 130, 185, 189 and 194 StGB [Criminal Code] at the planned event. Proceedings in the administrative courts against this edict were unsuccessful. The Federal Constitutional Court rejected the constitutional complaint as obviously unfounded for the following

Reasons:

II

The decisions under challenge do not violate Art5 (1) sentence 1 GG [Constitution of 1949].

1. Art 5 (1) sentence 1 GG guarantees to everyone the right to express and disseminate his opinions freely.

The decisions are to be measured primarily against this basic right. It is true that the condition that the complainant challenges refers to a meeting. Its object however is certain statements which were not to be either made or tolerated by the complainant as organiser of the meeting. The assessment of the condition on the basis of constitutional law is above all dependent on whether these kinds of statements are allowed or not. A statement that cannot be prevented on constitutional grounds, can also not be a cause for a measure restricting meetings in accordance with § 5 no. 4 of the Meetings Act. But the standards for the answering of this question do not arise from the basic right of the freedom of assembly (Art 8 GG) but from that of freedom of opinion.

The object of the basic right protection of Art 5 (1) sentence 1 GG is opinions. It is to them that the freedom to make statements and disseminate them refers. Opinions are characterised by the subjective relationship of the individual to the content of his statement [reference omitted]. For them the element of taking a position and making a judgement is typical [references omitted]. In this respect they cannot be proved true or untrue. They enjoy the protection of the basic right without any question of whether the statement is well founded or unfounded, emotional or rational, valuable or worthless, dangerous or harmless [reference omitted]. The protection of the basic right also extends to the form of the statement. A statement of opinion does not lose the basic right protection by being formulated sharply or hurtfully [references omitted]. In this respect the question can only be whether and to what extent limits to the freedom of opinion arise according to the standard of Art 5(2) GG.

Assertions of fact are on the other hand in the strict sense not statements of opinion. In contrast to such statements, the objective relationship between the statement and reality predominates. In this respect they are also open to an examination of their truth content. But assertions of fact do not, for this reason, automatically fall outside the area of protection of Art 5 (1) sentence 1 GG. Since opinions are, as a rule, based on factual assumptions, or take a position in relation to factual circumstances, they are in any case protected by the basic right insofar as they are the prerequisite for the formation of opinions which Art 5 (1) GG in its totality guarantees [reference omitted].

Consequently, the protection of assertions of fact ends at the point where they cease to contribute anything to the formation of opinion that is presupposed in constitutional law. From this point of view, incorrect information is not an interest worthy of protection. The Federal Constitutional Court has thus consistently held that an assertion of fact known or proved to be untrue is not covered by the protection of freedom of opinion [references omitted]. The requirements for a duty to be truthful may nevertheless not be laid down in such a way as to harm the functioning of freedom of opinion so that even permissible statements are not made because of the fear of sanctions [references omitted].

The distinguishing of statements of opinion from assertions of facts can certainly be difficult because both are frequently connected with each other and can only together determine the sense of a statement. In this case a division of the factual and evaluating components is only permissible if the sense of the statement is not thereby falsified. Where that is not possible, the statement must in the interest of an effective protection of the basic right be, as a whole, regarded as an expression of opinion and be included within the protected area of freedom of opinion. Otherwise, there would be a threat of a substantial reduction in the protection of the basic right [references omitted].

(c) Freedom of opinion is nevertheless not guaranteed unconditionally. According to Art 5 (2) GG it is subject to limitations which arise from general laws as well as provisions of law for the protection of the young and personal honour. But in the interpretation and application of statutes which have a limiting effect on the freedom of opinion, account must be taken of the importance of freedom of opinion (*see* BVerfGE 7, 198 [208 f.]). That, as a rule, requires a balancing exercise related to the case in question, to be undertaken within the framework of the features of definition in the relevant norm, between the basic right which has been restricted and the legal interest which the statute restricting the basic right serves.

The Federal Constitutional Court has developed some rules for this balancing exercise. According to these, freedom of opinion is by no means always entitled to priority over protection of the personality, as the complainant thinks. Instead the protection of the personality will, as a rule, prevail over freedom of opinion in relation to statements of opinion which are to be regarded as "insult" in the formal sense [of the Criminal law] or abuse [references omitted]. In relation to statements of opinion which are connected with statements of fact, whether they are worthy of protection can depend on the truth content of the factual assumptions on which they are based. If these are proved to be untrue, freedom of opinion as a rule takes second place to protection of the personality [references omitted]. In other respects, what matters is which legal interest deserves the preference in the individual case. But at the same time it has to be taken into account that in questions, which substantially affect the public, there is a presumption in favour of free speech (*see* BVerfGE 7, 198 [212]). This must always be borne in mind as well in the balancing between the legal positions of the persons involved.

2. Measured against this, a violation of Art 5 (1) sentence 1 GG is obviously not present. The condition imposed on the complainant as the organiser of the meeting that it must ensure that the persecution of the Jews in the Third Reich is not denied or doubted in the meeting is reconcilable with this basic right.

a) The complainant has not challenged the prediction made by the Meetings Authority and confirmed by the administrative courts that there was a danger that in the course of the meeting statements of the kind would be made. Instead it argues that it should be able to make such assertions.

b) The prohibited statement that there was no persecution of Jews in the Third Reich is an assertion of fact which is proved to be untrue according to innumerable eye witness reports and documents, the verdicts of courts in numerous criminal proceedings, and the findings of history. Taken by itself, an assertion of this content does not, therefore, enjoy the protection of freedom of opinion. In that respect there is significant difference between the denial of persecution of the Jews in the Third Reich and the denial of German guilt at the outbreak of the Second World War, which was the issue in the decision of the Federal Constitutional Court of the 11th January 1994—1 BvR 434/87 (BVerfGE 90, 1). In relation to statements about guilt and responsibility for historical events it is always a question of complex judgements which cannot be reduced to an assertion of facts, whilst the denial of an event itself will, as a rule, have the character of an assertion of facts.

c) But even if the statement to which the condition refers is not taken by itself but is considered in connection with the subject of the meeting, and is regarded in this respect as a prerequisite for formation of opinion as to the "blackmailability" of German politics, the decisions challenged stand up to examination in constitutional law. The prohibited statement then admittedly enjoys the protection of Art 5 (1) sentence 1 GG. But the limitation of it is not open to objection on constitutional law grounds.

aa) The limitation has a statutory basis which accords with the Constitution.

The authorities and administrative courts have based the condition limiting expression of opinion on § 5 no. 4 of the Meetings Act. According to this provision a meeting in closed rooms can be forbidden if facts are established from which it follows that the organiser or his followers will defend views or tolerate statements which amount to a crime (Verbrechen), or an offence (Vergehen) of the kind which is to be pursued by the state. This provision is reconcilable with the Basic Law.

In particular such a prohibition does not violate Art 8 (1) GG. It is true that the right to hold meetings in closed rooms is guaranteed unconditionally. But that does not mean that expressions of opinion in meetings are protected beyond Art 5 (1) and (2) GG. Expressions of opinion which are threatened with punishment by a norm which is permissible according to Art 5 (2) GG remain prohibited even at such meetings. In the light of Art 8 (1) GG there is also no objection in principle to the fact that the legislator seeks to prevent criminal acts, which are with high probability to be expected at a meeting, before they are committed. The limitation of the grounds of prohibition to crimes and offences of the kind which are to be pursued by the state, as well as the principle of proportionality, which must be observed in relation to all measures by which the freedom of assembly is limited, provide protection from an excessive restriction of the freedom of assembly.

Likewise, no violation of Art 5 (1) sentence 1 GG exists. § 5 no. 4 of the Meetings Act does not contain an independent restriction of the freedom of opinion but is linked to the restrictions that are contained in the Criminal Code. Measures restricting meetings in accordance with § 5 no. 4 of the Meetings Act may therefore only be taken if in a meeting statements are threatened which are made punishable anyway and are to be pursued by the state. Nevertheless, the provision does not operate in the realm of ex post facto sanctions by the courts but in the realm of preventative prohibitions by the authorities. The dangers for freedom of opinion connected with this can however be met by placing strict requirements on the extent to which the danger must be predictable and the criminality of the statements must not, according to case law, be in any doubt.

No doubts exist as to the proportionality of the criminal provisions on which the condition here has been based. The definitions of "insult" protect personal honour, which is expressly named in Art 5 (2) GG as a legal interest that justifies the restriction of the freedom of opinion. With § 130 StGB it is a question of a general statute in the sense of Art 5 (2) GG which serves the protection of humanity [reference omitted] and in the end finds its support in constitutional law in Art 1 (1) GG.

bb) The interpretation and application of § 5 no. 4 of the Meetings Act in combination with § 185 StGB by the decisions which are being challenged are likewise reconcilable with Art 5 (1) sentence 1 GG.

(1) The administrative authorities and courts have based their decisions on the interpretation of the criminal norm, which the ordinary courts have given to them. According to this, Jews living in Germany, on the basis of the fate to which the Jewish population was exposed under National Socialist rule, form a group capable of being insulted; the denial of persecution of the Jews is judged as an insult inflicted on this group. The Bundesgerichtshof has stated on this subject that:

"The historical fact that human beings were separated in accordance with the descent criteria of the so-called Nuremberg laws and were robbed of their individuality with the objective of their extermination gives to the Jews living in the Federal Republic a special personal relationship to their fellow citizens; in this relationship the past is still present today. It is part of their personal self-image that they are seen as attached to a group of persons marked out by their fate, against which group there exists a special moral responsibility on the part of everyone else and which is a part of their dignity. Respect for this personal self-image is for each of them really one of the guarantees against a repetition of such discrimination and a basic condition for their life in the Federal Republic. Whoever seeks to deny those events denies to each of them individually this personal worth to which they have a claim. For those affected, this means the continuation of discrimination against the group of human beings to which he belongs, and with it against his own person" (BGHZ 75, 160 [162 f.]).

The legislator has made a link with this case law and inserted an exception from the requirement for a complaint (Antrag) for such insults in § 194 (1) sentence 2 StGB [reference omitted].

The opinion of the Bundesgerichtshof has, it is true, encountered criticism in the criminal law literature. It is partly seen as over-stretching the definition of insult [references omitted]. However, the Federal Constitutional Court does not test whether an interpretation of the Criminal Code is correct in ordinary law or whether other opinions would be tenable as well. The only thing that is decisive for the constitutional law assessment is whether the interpretation rests on a failure to appreciate the basic rights. That is not the case here.

There is no objection to the fact that the decisions that are challenged have seen, in the wake of this case law, a serious violation of the right of personality in the denial of the persecution of the Jews. The basic interrelation established by the Bundesgerichtshof between the denial of the racially motivated extermination of the Jewish population in the Third Reich and the attack on the claim to respect the human dignity of Jews living today is not open to objection in constitutional law. The denial of the persecution of the Jews also differs in this respect from the denial of German war guilt (*see* BVerfGE, decision of the 11th January 1994—1 BvR 434/87 (BVerfGE 90, 1)). The last named opinion, apart from being historically dubious, does not in any case interfere with legal interests of third parties.

Neither does the objection of the complainant that the conditions were supported by an understanding of § 185 StGB which was based on the draft of § 140 StGB in the 21st Criminal Law Amendment Act [reference omitted], which was not passed by the German Bundestag, make this interpretation unconstitutional. The fact that the legislature refrained from introducing a special definition with a more severe punishment for the denial of the persecution of the Jews does not allow the conclusion that the action is not punishable under the more general norm of § 185 StGB, especially as the legislature—as explained—has made a link with the case law which sees an insult in the denial of the persecution.

(2) The balancing between the injury to honour on the one hand and the limitation of the freedom of opinion on the other does not reveal any substantial error in constitutional law. The severity of the relevant interference plays a decisive role in this balancing. In the case of expressions of opinion injurious to honour, which contain an assertion of facts, weight must be given to the question of whether the assertion of facts is true or not. Assertions of facts proved to be incorrect are not an interest worthy of protection. It is true that if they are inextricably connected with opinions, the protection of Art 5 (1) sentence 1 GG will benefit them, but an invasion

will be weighted from the outset less heavily than in the case of statements of facts not shown to be untrue.

That is the state of affairs here. Even if the statement which was prohibited for the complainant at its meeting is, in connection with the subject of the meeting, regarded as an expression of opinion, that changes nothing as to the proven incorrectness of its factual content. The interference relating to this is not on that account to be weighted particularly heavily. In the face of the weight to be given to the injury to honour, there is no objection to the fact that the decisions under challenge have given the protection of the personality priority over freedom of opinion.

Nor is anything changed by consideration of the fact that the attitude of Germany to its national socialist past and its political consequences, which was the concern of this meeting, is a question substantially affecting the public. It is true that in this case there is a presumption in favour of free speech. But this does not apply for statements which are insults in the formal sense or abuse, nor when a hurtful statement is based on factual assertions which are proved to be untrue.

There need be no fear of an excessive requirement for a duty of truth, which would be irreconcilable with Art 5 (1) sentence 1 GG, in relation to the factual kernel of the statement from this outcome of the balancing exercise. The Federal Constitutional Court proceeds in the interest of free communication as well as of the functions of criticism and control by the media on the basis of a limitation of a duty of care. But this refers to factual assertions the correctness of which is still uncertain at the point in time of the statement and which cannot be cleared up within a very short period of time. It does not however take effect where the incorrectness of a statement has already been established, as is the case here.

————

NOTES

1.   Adolph Hitler came to power as the leader of the Nazi (National Socialist) party in Germany in 1933. He believed the Aryan race was the "master race" and that, even though German Jews made up less than 1% of the German population, they were responsible for Germany's economic hardships and its loss of World War I. UNITED STATES HOLOCAUST MEMORIAL MUSEUM, http://www.ushmm.org/outreach/en/article.php?ModuleId=10007687 (last visited Sept. 22, 2011). Although German Jews had long lived in Germany, and had actively contributed to German culture and fought in Germany's prior wars, the Nazis began to segregate German Jews in the 1930s. In 1935, Germany passed the Nuremburg Laws, denying German Jews citizenship, forbidding marriage between a Jew and a non-Jew, and prohibiting Jews from attending schools and participating in the military. Greg Bradsher, *The Nuremburg Laws*, National Archives, PROLOGUE MAGAZINE, Winter 2010, Vol. 42, No. 4 (available at http://www.archives.gov/publications/prologue/2010/winter/nuremberg.html).

2.   The Holocaust was the systematic attempt by the Nazi regime to "cleanse" Europe of Jews. UNITED STATES HOLOCAUST MEMORIAL MUSEUM, http://www.ushmm.org/wlc/en/article.php?ModuleId=10005143. Through enforcing a system of ghettos and death camps, the Nazi regime

was able to first concentrate and manage, and then systematically murder the Jewish population. Prior to World War II there were approximately 9 million Jews in Europe—during the course of the war nearly two out of every three European Jews, approximately 6 million people, were murdered. Also targeted as racially inferior were Roma, of whom an estimated 200,000 were murdered, and Slavs. Other victims included homosexuals, communists, socialists, disabled persons, trade unionists, and religious dissidents (such as Jehovah's Witnesses). UNITED STATES HOLOCAUST MEMORIAL MUSEUM, http://www.ushmm.org/ wlc/en/article.php?ModuleId=10005143.

3.   The Nazi attempt to exterminate those defined as Jewish extended from Germany into the territories they invaded. In Poland, where approximately 10% of the population was Jewish prior to the war, over 90% of the Jewish population was killed. *History of the Holocaust—An Introduction*, Jewish Virtual Library, http://www.jewishvirtuallibrary.org/jsource/ Holocaust/history.html (last visited Sept. 17, 2011); *Estimated Number of Jews Killed in The Final Solution*, Jewish Virtual Library, http://www. jewishvirtuallibrary.org/jsource/Holocaust/killedtable.html.

4.   The Holocaust, and the subsequent Nuremburg trials which tried the leaders of Nazi Germany, are often used today as the lens by which to view other genocides and mass human rights violations.

5.   Among reputable historians, the crimes of the Holocaust are regarded as established fact. The Holocaust Denial Movement, known in France as Négationnisme de la Shoah, consists of persons who deny the historical fact of the Holocaust, describing it as a "myth." Holocaust deniers, who misleadingly refer to themselves as "revisionists" to align themselves with other historians, argue that the Nazi regime did not have an official policy to murder Jews and that Hitler intended to deport the Jewish population rather than exterminate them. Andrew E. Mathis, HOLOCAUST DENIAL, A DEFINITION, in CONSPIRACY THEORIES IN AMERICAN HISTORY: AN ENCYCLOPEDIA, 321–324 (Peter Knight, ed. ABC–CLIO 2003) (available at http://www.holocaust-history.org/denial/abc-clio/). Holocaust deniers also argue that no gas chambers existed at the Auschwitz–Birkenau concentration camps, or that gas chambers existed but only for delousing and not for killing, and that the number of Jews who died during the Holocaust is grossly exaggerated. *Review: Contesting the Holocaust Deniers* (Aug. 24, 2000, 12:35 PM), http://edition.cnn.com/2000/books/reviews/08/24/review. denying.history/. Most Holocaust deniers argue that between 300,000 and 1.5 million Jews died during the Holocaust, contrary to the 6 million Jews most historians believe perished. Andrew E. Mathis, HOLOCAUST DENIAL, A DEFINITION IN CONSPIRACY THEORIES IN AMERICAN HISTORY: AN ENCYCLOPEDIA, 321–324 (Peter Knight, ed. ABC–CLIO 2003) (available at http://www. holocaust-history.org/denial/abc-clio/).

C. FRANCE

ART. 10 OF THE EUROPEAN CONVENTION ON HUMAN RIGHTS

Everyone has the right to freedom of expression. This right shall include freedom to hold opinions and to receive and impart information and ideas without interference by public authority and regardless of frontiers. This article shall not prevent States from requiring the licensing of broadcasting, television or cinema enterprises.

The exercise of these freedoms, since it carries with it duties and responsibilities, may be subject to such formalities, conditions, restrictions or penalties as are prescribed by law and are necessary in a democratic society, in the interests of national security, territorial integrity or public safety, for the prevention of disorder or crime, for the protection of health or morals, for the protection of the reputation or rights of others, for preventing the disclosure of information received in confidence, or for maintaining the authority and impartiality of the judiciary.

ART. 2(1), 7, 19 OF THE UNIVERSAL DECLARATION OF HUMAN RIGHTS

Article 2

Everyone is entitled to all the rights and freedoms set forth in this Declaration, without distinction of any kind, such as race, colour, sex, language, religion, political or other opinion, national or social origin, property, birth or other status.

Article 7

All are equal before the law and are entitled without any discrimination to equal protection of the law. All are entitled to equal protection against any discrimination in violation of this Declaration and against any incitement to such discrimination.

Article 19

Everyone has the right to freedom of opinion and expression; this right includes freedom to hold opinions without interference and to seek, receive and impart information and ideas through any media and regardless of frontiers.

ART. 19, 20 OF THE INTERNATIONAL COVENANT ON CIVIL AND POLITICAL RIGHTS

Article 19

1. Everyone shall have the right to hold opinions without interference.

2. Everyone shall have the right to freedom of expression; this right shall include freedom to seek, receive and impart information and ideas of all kinds, regardless of frontiers, either orally, in writing or in print, in the form of art, or through any other media of his choice.

3. The exercise of the rights provided for in paragraph 2 of this article carries with it special duties and responsibilities. It may therefore be

subject to certain restrictions, but these shall only be such as are provided by law and are necessary:

(a) For respect of the rights or reputations of others;

(b) For the protection of national security or of public order (ordre public), or of public health or morals.

Article 20

1. Any propaganda for war shall be prohibited by law.

2. Any advocacy of national, racial or religious hatred that constitutes incitement to discrimination, hostility or violence shall be prohibited by law.

———

Faurisson v. France

Comm. No. 550/1993, U.N. Doc. CCPR/C/58/D/550/1993 (1996)

■ UNITED NATIONS HUMAN RIGHTS COMMITTEE

The Human Rights Committee, established under article 28 of the International Covenant on Civil and Political Rights, Meeting on 8 November 1996,

Having concluded its consideration of communication No. 550/1993 submitted to the Human Rights Committee by Mr. Robert Faurisson under the Optional Protocol to the International Covenant on Civil and Political Rights,

Having taken into account all written information made available to it by the author of the communication and the State party,

Adopts the following:

Views under article 5, paragraph 4, of the Optional Protocol

1. The author of the communication, dated 2 January 1993, is Robert Faurisson, born in the United Kingdom in 1929 and with dual French/British citizenship, currently residing in Vichy, France. He claims to be a victim of violations of his human rights by France. The author does not invoke specific provisions of the Covenant.

The facts as submitted by the author

2.1 The author was a professor of literature at the Sorbonne University in Paris until 1973 and at the University of Lyon until 1991, when he was removed from his chair. Aware of the historical significance of the Holocaust, he has sought proof of the methods of killings, in particular by gas asphyxiation. While he does not contest the use of gas for purposes of disinfection, he doubts the existence of gas chambers for extermination purposes ("chambres à gaz homicides") at Auschwitz and in other Nazi concentration camps.

2.2 The author submits that his opinions have been rejected in numerous academic journals and ridiculed in the daily press, notably in France; nonetheless, he continues to question the existence of extermination gas chambers. As a result of public discussion of his opinions and the polemics accompanying these debates, he states that, since 1978, he has become the target of death threats and that on eight occasions he has been physically assaulted. On one occasion in 1989, he claims to have suffered serious injuries, including a broken jaw, for which he was hospitalized. He contends that although these attacks were brought to the attention of the competent judicial authorities, they were not seriously investigated and none of those responsible for the assaults has been arrested or prosecuted....

2.3   On 13 July 1990, the French legislature passed the so-called "Gayssot Act", which amends the law on the Freedom of the Press of 1881 by adding an article 24 bis; the latter makes it an offence to contest the existence of the category of crimes against humanity as defined in the London Charter of 8 August 1945, on the basis of which Nazi leaders were tried and convicted by the International Military Tribunal at Nuremberg in 1945–1946. The author submits that, in essence, the "Gayssot Act" promotes the Nuremberg trial and judgment to the status of dogma, by imposing criminal sanctions on those who dare to challenge its findings and premises. Mr. Faurisson contends that he has ample reason to believe that the records of the Nuremberg trial can indeed be challenged and that the evidence used against Nazi leaders is open to question, as is, according to him, the evidence about the number of victims exterminated at Auschwitz.

2.5   Shortly after the enactment of the "Gayssot Act", Mr. Faurisson was interviewed by the French monthly magazine Le Choc du Mois, which published the interview in its Number 32 issue of September 1990. Besides expressing his concern that the new law constituted a threat to freedom of research and freedom of expression, the author reiterated his personal conviction that there were no homicidal gas chambers for the extermination of Jews in Nazi concentration camps. Following the publication of this interview, eleven associations of French resistance fighters and of deportees to German concentration camps filed a private criminal action against Mr. Faurisson and Patrice Boizeau, the editor of the magazine Le Choc du Mois. By judgment of 18 April 1991, the 17th Chambre Correctionnelle du Tribunal de Grande Instance de Paris convicted Messrs. Faurisson and Boizeau of having committed the crime of "contestation de crimes contre l'humanité" and imposed on them fines and costs amounting to FF 326,832 [approximately $50,000].

2.6   The conviction was based, inter alia, on the following Faurisson statements:

"... No one will have me admit that two plus two make five, that the earth is flat, or that the Nuremberg Tribunal was infallible. I have excellent reasons not to believe in this policy of extermination of Jews or in the magic gas chamber ..."

"I would wish to see that 100 per cent of all French citizens realize that the myth of the gas chambers is a dishonest fabrication ('est une gredinerie'), endorsed by the victorious powers of Nuremberg in 1945–46 and officialized on 14 July 1990 by the current French Government, with the approval of the 'court historians' "".

2.7   The author and Mr. Boizeau appealed their conviction to the Court of Appeal of Paris (Eleventh Chamber). On 9 December 1992, the Eleventh Chamber, under the Presidency of Mrs. Françoise Simon, upheld the conviction and fined Messrs. Faurisson and Boizeau a total of FF 374,045.50. * * *

The complaint

3.1   The author contends that the "Gayssot Act" curtails his right to freedom of expression and academic freedom in general, and considers that the law targets him personally ("lex Faurissonia"). He complains that the incriminated provision constitutes unacceptable censorship, obstructing and penalizing historical research. * * *

Examination of the merits

9.1   The Human Rights Committee has considered the present communication in the light of all the information made available to it by the parties, as it is required to do under article 5, paragraph 1, of the Optional Protocol. * * *

9.3   Although it does not contest that the application of the terms of the Gayssot Act, which, in their effect, make it a criminal offence to challenge the conclusions and the verdict of the International Military Tribunal at Nuremberg, may lead, under different conditions than the facts of the instant case, to decisions or measures incompatible with the Covenant, the Committee is not called upon to criticize in the abstract laws enacted by States parties. The task of the Committee under the Optional Protocol is to ascertain whether the conditions of the restrictions imposed on the right to freedom of expression are met in the communications which are brought before it.

9.4   Any restriction on the right to freedom of expression must cumulatively meet the following conditions: it must be provided by law, it must address one of the aims set out in paragraph 3 (a) and (b) of article 19, and must be necessary to achieve a legitimate purpose.

9.5   The restriction on the author's freedom of expression was indeed provided by law i.e. the Act of 13 July 1990. It is the constant jurisprudence of the Committee that the restrictive law itself must be in compliance with the provisions of the Covenant. In this regard the Committee concludes, on the basis of the reading of the judgment of the 17th Chambre correctionnelle du Tribunal de grande instance de Paris that the finding of the author's guilt was based on his following two statements: "... I have excellent reasons not to believe in the policy of extermination of Jews or in the magic gas chambers ... I wish to see that 100 per cent of the French citizens realize that the myth of the gas chambers is a dishonest fabrication". His conviction therefore did not encroach upon his right to hold and express an opinion in general, rather the court convicted Mr. Faurisson for having violated the rights and reputation of others. For these reasons the Committee is satisfied that the Gayssot Act, as read, interpreted and applied to the author's case by the French courts, is in compliance with the provisions of the Covenant.

9.6   To assess whether the restrictions placed on the author's freedom of expression by his criminal conviction were applied for the purposes provided for by the Covenant, the Committee begins by noting, as it did in its General Comment 10 that the rights for the protection of which restrictions on the freedom of expression are permitted by article 19, paragraph 3, may relate to the interests of other persons or to those of the community as a whole. Since the statements made by the author, read in their full context, were of a nature as to raise or strengthen anti-semitic feelings, the restriction served the respect of the Jewish community to live free from fear of an atmosphere of anti-semitism. The Committee therefore concludes that the restriction of the author's freedom of expression was permissible under article 19, paragraph 3 (a), of the Covenant.

9.7   Lastly the Committee needs to consider whether the restriction of the author's freedom of expression was necessary. The Committee noted the State party's argument contending that the introduction of the Gayssot Act was intended to serve the struggle against racism and anti-semitism. It also noted the statement of a member of the French Government, the then Minister of Justice, which characterized the denial of the existence of the Holocaust as the principal vehicle for anti-semitism. In the absence in the material before it of any argument undermining the validity of the State party's position as to the necessity of the restriction, the Committee is satisfied that the restriction of Mr. Faurisson's freedom of expression was necessary within the meaning of article 19, paragraph 3, of the Covenant.

10.   The Human Rights Committee, acting under article 5, paragraph 4, of the Optional Protocol to the International Covenant on Civil and Political Rights, is of the view that the facts as found by the Committee do not reveal a violation by France of article 19, paragraph 3, of the Covenant.

C. Individual opinion by Elizabeth Evatt and David Kretzmer, co-signed by Eckart Klein (concurring)

1.   While we concur in the view of the Committee that in the particular circumstances of this case the right to freedom of expression of the author was not violated, given the importance of the issues involved we have decided to append our separate, concurring, opinion.

2.   ... The main issue is whether the restriction has been shown by the State party to be necessary, in terms of article 19, paragraph 3 (a), for respect of the rights or reputations of others.

3.   The State party has argued that the author's conviction was justified "by the necessity of securing respect for the judgment of the International Military Tribunal at Nuremburg, and through it the memory of the survivors and the descendants of the victims of Nazism." While we entertain no doubt whatsoever that the author's statements are highly offensive both to Holocaust survivors and to descendants of Holocaust victims (as well as to many others), the question under the Covenant is whether a restriction on freedom of expression in order to achieve this purpose may be regarded as a restriction necessary for the respect of the rights of others.

4.   Every individual has the right to be free not only from discrimination on grounds of race, religion and national origins, but also from incitement to such discrimination. This is stated expressly in article 7 of the Universal Declaration of Human Rights. It is implicit in the obligation

placed on States parties under article 20, paragraph 2, of the Covenant to prohibit by law any advocacy of national, racial or religious hatred that constitutes incitement to discrimination, hostility or violence. The crime for which the author was convicted under the Gayssot Act does not expressly include the element of incitement, nor do the statements which served as the basis for the conviction fall clearly within the boundaries of incitement, which the State party was bound to prohibit, in accordance with article 20, paragraph 2. However, there may be circumstances in which the right of a person to be free from incitement to discrimination on grounds of race, religion or national origins cannot be fully protected by a narrow, explicit law on incitement that falls precisely within the boundaries of article 20, paragraph 2. This is the case where, in a particular social and historical context, statements that do not meet the strict legal criteria of incitement can be shown to constitute part of a pattern of incitement against a given racial, religious or national group, or where those interested in spreading hostility and hatred adopt sophisticated forms of speech that are not punishable under the law against racial incitement, even though their effect may be as pernicious as explicit incitement, if not more so. * * *

6.   The notion that in the conditions of present-day France, Holocaust denial may constitute a form of incitement to anti-semitism cannot be dismissed. This is a consequence not of the mere challenge to well-documented historical facts, established both by historians of different persuasions and backgrounds as well as by international and domestic tribunals, but of the context, in which it is implied, under the guise of impartial academic research, that the victims of Nazism were guilty of dishonest fabrication, that the story of their victimization is a myth and that the gas chambers in which so many people were murdered are "magic".

7.   The Committee correctly points out, as it did in its General Comment 10, that the right for the protection of which restrictions on freedom of expression are permitted by article 19, paragraph 3, may relate to the interests of a community as a whole. This is especially the case in which the right protected is the right to be free from racial, national or religious incitement. The French courts examined the statements made by the author and came to the conclusion that his statements were of a nature as to raise or strengthen anti-semitic tendencies. It appears therefore that the restriction on the author's freedom of expression served to protect the right of the Jewish community in France to live free from fear of incitement to anti-semitism. This leads us to the conclusion that the State party has shown that the aim of the restrictions on the author's freedom of expression was to respect the right of others, mentioned in article 19, paragraph 3. The more difficult question is whether imposing liability for such statements was necessary in order to protect that right.

8.   The power given to States parties under article 19, paragraph 3, to place restrictions on freedom of expression, must not be interpreted as license to prohibit unpopular speech, or speech which some sections of the population find offensive. Much offensive speech may be regarded as speech that impinges on one of the values mentioned in article 19, paragraph 3 (a) or (b) (the rights or reputations of others, national security, ordre public,

public health or morals). The Covenant therefore stipulates that the purpose of protecting one of those values is not, of itself, sufficient reason to restrict expression. The restriction must be necessary to protect the given value. This requirement of necessity implies an element of proportionality. The scope of the restriction imposed on freedom of expression must be proportional to the value which the restriction serves to protect. It must not exceed that needed to protect that value. As the Committee stated in its General Comment 10, the restriction must not put the very right itself in jeopardy.

9. * * * Does this restriction meet the proportionality test?

10. The French courts examined the author's statements in great detail. Their decisions, and the interview itself, refute the author's argument that he is only driven by his interest in historical research. In the interview the author demanded that historians "particularly Jewish historians" ("les historiens, en particulier juifs") who agree that some of the findings of the Nuremburg Tribunal were mistaken be prosecuted. The author referred to the "magic gas chamber" ("la magique chambre à gaz") and to "the myth of the gas chambers" ("le mythe des chambres à gaz"), that was a "dirty trick" ("une gredinerie") endorsed by the victors in Nuremburg. The author has, in these statements, singled out Jewish historians over others, and has clearly implied that the Jews, the victims of the Nazis, concocted the story of gas chambers for their own purposes. While there is every reason to maintain protection of bona fide historical research against restriction, even when it challenges accepted historical truths and by so doing offends people, anti-semitic allegations of the sort made by the author, which violate the rights of others in the way described, do not have the same claim to protection against restriction. The restrictions placed on the author did not curb the core of his right to freedom of expression, nor did they in any way affect his freedom of research; they were intimately linked to the value they were meant to protect—the right to be free from incitement to racism or anti-semitism; protecting that value could not have been achieved in the circumstances by less drastic means. It is for these reasons that we joined the Committee in concluding that, in the specific circumstances of the case, the restrictions on the author's freedom of expression met the proportionality test and were necessary in order to protect the rights of others. * * *

NOTE

1. On May 10, 1940, German forces invaded France. France signed an armistice with Germany on June 22 of the same year, allowing the German military to occupy northern France and the Atlantic coastline. The treaty also created an unoccupied zone in Southern France and along the Mediterranean coast, governed by a French collaborationist government headquartered in the town of Vichy. The "Vichy regime" was led by the elderly World War I hero, Marshal Henri Philippe Pétain.

In 1943 André Lavagne, the chief of Marshal Pétain's civil cabinet, proudly declared, "It is France that, along with Germany, has persecuted the most Jews." Though the Vichy regime was nominally autonomous, it worked closely with the German government. Beginning in the fall of 1940, the Vichy government passed a series of anti-Jewish legislation barring Jews from participation in civil society, business, and the military, and coordinating the confiscation of Jewish property for the French state. In early summer of 1942, the Vichy administration agreed to surrender Jewish adults for deportation, and engaged the French police to arrest and detain Jews before sending them East by train. Shortly after, France changed its policy to support the deportation of whole families. In total, approximately 77,000 Jews, around 20% of the Jewish population living on French territory, died in concentration camps between 1942 and 1944. Because of the French government's initial resistance to deporting French citizens, many of these were Jews who had "escaped" to France, only to be sent to their death. The vast majority were arrested by the French police, deported through a transit center outside of Paris and sent directly on French trains to the Auschwitz death camp.

When the war ended in 1945, collaborationist organizations were dissolved. The provisional government led by Charles de Gaulle, formerly the leader of the militant anti-German resistance movement, rapidly executed many collaborators and began formal prosecutions of the Vichy leadership. On August 15, 1945, Marshal Pétain was condemned to death on treason charges, but de Gaulle commuted Pétain's sentence to life imprisonment; he died in 1951. Bolstered in part by de Gaulle's popularity, post-war France reified the Résistance and developed a mythology of widespread disobedience to the Germans. French patriotic identity came to rest on the notion that France had been a noncompliant occupied state during the war.

With the rise of a new generation in the late 1960s, this mass historical amnesia began to fracture. In the early 1970s director Marcel Ophuls released his epic two-part film, *"Le Chagrin et la Pitié"* ("The Sorrow and the Pity"), which investigated France's involvement in and memory of the Holocaust. The film was banned from public television until 1981, but it continued to screen in independent theaters in France and the United States, fostering awareness of France's historical revisionism both in France and internationally. Following the film's release, French courts reinvigorated their efforts to prosecute former collaborators for crimes against humanity. Their first successful effort was the 1987 conviction of Klaus Barbie, who was responsible for the deportation of a large number of Jewish children. It was in this atmosphere that France passed the Gayssot Act in 1990, making Holocaust denial a criminal offense. The Act continues to figure largely in French politics; in 2008 Jean–Marie Le Pen, the widely known founder of the National Front party, was fined $14,500 for making statements that diminished the gravity of the Holocaust.

For more information, *see* the United States Holocaust Memorial Museum website at www.ushmm.org.

———

Lehideux and Isorni v. France

(Application no. 24662/94) 23 September 1998
EUROPEAN COURT OF HUMAN RIGHTS

I. THE CIRCUMSTANCES OF THE CASE

9. Mr Lehideux, the first applicant, who was born in 1904 and died on 21 June 1998, was formerly an administrator and later a director of several companies—including Renault France—and lived in Paris. From September 1940 to April 1942 he was Minister for Industrial Production in the Government of Marshal Pétain and, from 1959 to 1964, a member of the Economic and Social Committee. He was the President of the Association for the Defence of the Memory of Marshal Pétain.

The second applicant, Mr Isorni, who was born in 1911 and died on 8 May 1995, was formerly a lawyer practising in Paris. As First Secretary of the Conference of Pupil Advocates of the Paris Bar, he was officially appointed to assist the President of the Bar Association in defending Marshal Pétain at his trial before the High Court of Justice. On 15 August 1945 the High Court of Justice sentenced Philippe Pétain to death and forfeiture of his civic rights for collusion with Germany with a view to furthering the designs of the enemy.

A. The publication in issue

10. On 13 July 1984 the daily newspaper Le Monde published a one-page advertisement bearing the title "People of France, you have short memories" in large print, beneath which appeared in small italics, "Philippe Pétain, 17 June 1941". The text ended with an invitation to readers to write to the Association for the Defence of the Memory of Marshal Pétain and the National Pétain–Verdun Association.

11. The text, which was divided into several sections each beginning with the words "People of France, you have short memories if you have forgotten . . ." in large capitals, recapitulated, in a series of assertions, the main stages of Philippe Pétain's life as a public figure from 1916 to 1945, presenting his actions, first as a soldier and later as French Head of State, in a positive light. * * *

B. The criminal proceedings against the applicants

12. On 10 October 1984 the National Association of Former Members of the Resistance filed a criminal complaint, together with an application to join the proceedings as a civil party, against a Mr L., the publication manager of Le Monde, for publicly defending the crimes of collaboration with the enemy, and against Mr Lehideux as President of the Association for the Defence of the Memory of Marshal Pétain, Mr Isorni as the author of the text complained of and a Mr M., as President of the National Pétain–Verdun Association, for aiding and abetting a public defence of the crimes of collaboration with the enemy.

The civil party argued that the text was an apologia which contravened the criminal law since it tended to justify the policy of Marshal Pétain, who had been found guilty by the High Court of Justice on 15 August 1945.

13. The applicants denied that their advertisement constituted a public defence of the crimes of collaboration with the enemy, but acknowledged that the spirit of the text was consistent with their aim of having the judgment of the High Court of Justice overturned and rehabilitating Marshal Pétain. * * *

21. On 26 January 1990 the Paris Court of Appeal declared the two civil party applications admissible ... and awarded the civil parties damages of one franc. It also ordered the publication of excerpts from the judgment in Le Monde.

In its judgment it held that the three constituent elements of the offence of making a public defence of the crimes of collaboration had been made out....

It went on to say that the text contained an "apologia" for the crimes of collaboration, and that the mental element had been made out. * * *

23. On 16 November 1993 the Criminal Division of the Court of Cassation dismissed the appeals on the following grounds:

* * * "In presenting as praiseworthy a person convicted of collusion with the enemy, the text glorified his crime and, in so doing, publicly defended it. The mental element of the offence can be inferred from the deliberate nature of the acts on account of which the defendants were charged.

In delivering that judgment, the Court of Appeal did not ... infringe the right to freedom of expression protected by Article 10, paragraph 1, of the European Convention for the Protection of Human Rights and Fundamental Freedoms, since the exercise of that right may, under paragraph 2 of that Article, be subject to certain restrictions prescribed by law, where these are necessary, as in the instant case, in the interests of national security, territorial integrity or public safety."

II. RELEVANT DOMESTIC LAW

A. The Freedom of the Press Act of 29 July 1881

24. In 1984 section 23 of the Freedom of the Press Act of 29 July 1881 read as follows:

"Where a crime or major offence is committed, anyone who, by uttering speeches, cries or threats in a public place or assembly, or by means of a written or printed text, drawing, engraving, painting, emblem, image, or any other written, spoken or pictorial item sold or distributed, offered for sale or exhibited in a public place or assembly, or by means of a placard or notice exhibited in a place where it can be seen by the public, has directly and successfully incited another or others to commit the said crime or major offence shall be punished as an accomplice thereto."

25. At the same time, section 24 provided that "anyone who, by one of the means set out in section 23, has made a public defence of ... the crimes of collaboration with the enemy" was to be liable to one to five years' imprisonment and a fine of from three hundred to three hundred thousand francs.

26. The French courts have gradually clarified the conditions for the application of the provisions making public defence of a crime a criminal offence. * * *

Publication of a text which is likely to incite any reader to judge favourably the German National Socialist Party leaders convicted of war crimes by the Nuremberg International Tribunal and constitutes an attempt to justify their crimes in part is a public defence of war crimes (Crim. 14 January 1971, Bull. crim. no. 14). * * *

27. Law no. 90–615 of 13 July 1990 ("the loi Gayssot") added to the Freedom of the Press Act a section 24 bis making liable to one year's imprisonment and a fine of 300,000 French francs, or one of those penalties only, those who "deny the existence of one or more crimes against humanity as defined in Article 6 of the Statute of the International Military Tribunal annexed to the London agreement of 8 August 1945 which have been committed either by the members of an organisation declared criminal pursuant to Article 9 of the Statute or by a person found guilty of such crimes by a French or international court".

Section 48–2 of the Freedom of the Press Act, also inserted by the loi Gayssot, provides: "Any association which has been lawfully registered for at least five years at the relevant time, and whose objects, according to its articles of association, include the defence of the moral interests and honour of the French Resistance or deportees, may exercise the rights conferred on civil parties in connection with public defence of war crimes, crimes against humanity or the crimes of collaboration with the enemy and in connection with the offence defined in section 24 bis."

PROCEEDINGS BEFORE THE COMMISSION

29. Mr Lehideux and Mr Isorni applied to the Commission on 13 May 1994, complaining of a breach of Articles 6, 10 and, in substance, 7 of the Convention. * * *

AS TO THE LAW

I. ALLEGED VIOLATION OF ARTICLE 10 OF THE CONVENTION

33. The applicants alleged that their conviction for "public defence of war crimes or the crimes of collaboration" had breached Article 10 of the Convention, which provides:

> "1. Everyone has the right to freedom of expression. This right shall include freedom to hold opinions and to receive and impart information and ideas without interference by public authority and regardless of frontiers. This Article shall not prevent States from requiring the licensing of broadcasting, television or cinema enterprises.
>
> 2. The exercise of these freedoms, since it carries with it duties and responsibilities, may be subject to such formalities, conditions, restrictions or penalties as are prescribed by law and are necessary in a democratic society, in the interests of national security, territorial integrity or public safety, for the prevention of disorder or crime, for the protection of health or morals, for the protection of the reputation or rights of others, for preventing the disclosure of information re-

ceived in confidence, or for maintaining the authority and impartiality of the judiciary."

34. The Government asked the Court to dismiss the application, pursuant to Article 17 of the Convention, on the ground of incompatibility with the provisions of the Convention. At the very least, in their submission, paragraph 2 of Article 10 should be applied in the light of the obligations arising from Article 17.

A. Application of Article 17

35. The Government considered that the publication in issue infringed the very spirit of the Convention and the essential values of democracy. The application of Mr Lehideux and Mr Isorni was accordingly barred by Article 17, which provides:

"Nothing in [the] Convention may be interpreted as implying for any State, group or person any right to engage in any activity or perform any act aimed at the destruction of any of the rights and freedoms set forth herein or at their limitation to a greater extent than is provided for in the Convention."

The justification given by the applicants for publishing the text in issue—that they sought to overturn Philippe Pétain's conviction—was unacceptable, as were their assertions about their text being a contribution to the historical debate. The text presented certain historical events in a manifestly erroneous manner, sometimes by lending them a significance they did not have, as in the way they had presented the Montoire meeting, and sometimes by ignoring events which were essential for an understanding of the relevant period of history, namely collaboration between the Vichy regime and Nazi Germany. * * *

B. Compliance with Article 10

39. The conviction in issue incontestably amounted to "interference" with the applicants' exercise of their right to freedom of expression. Those appearing before the Court agreed that it was "prescribed by law" and pursued several of the legitimate aims set forth in Article 10 § 2, namely protection of the reputation or rights of others and the prevention of disorder or crime.

The Court agrees. It must now, therefore, determine whether the interference was "necessary in a democratic society" for the achievement of those aims. * * *

45. According to the Commission, the correctness or incorrectness of the facts presented by the applicants—which it was not in any way its task to verify—had not been the basis on which they were convicted. The Court of Appeal had criticised the applicants more for their non-exhaustive presentation of facts relating to a specific period of history than for distorting or denying established historical events.

The applicants had expressed themselves on behalf of two associations which had been legally constituted in France and whose object was, precisely, to have Marshal Pétain's case reopened; they could not therefore be denied the right to pursue this object through the press or any other medium of communication. Moreover, the applicants had not failed to mention in the text and distance themselves from "Nazi atrocities and persecutions".

Lastly, the Commission emphasised the importance, in a democratic society, of historical debate about a public figure in respect of whom, as was the case with Philippe Pétain, different opinions had been and might be expressed. For these reasons, the Commission expressed the opinion that there had been a violation of Article 10. * * *

53.   There is no doubt that, like any other remark directed against the Convention's underlying values (*see, mutatis mutandis*, the *Jersild v. Denmark* judgment of 23 September 1994, Series A no. 298, p. 25, § 35), the justification of a pro-Nazi policy could not be allowed to enjoy the protection afforded by Article 10. In the present case, however, the applicants explicitly stated their disapproval of "Nazi atrocities and persecutions" and of "German omnipotence and barbarism". Thus they were not so much praising a policy as a man, and doing so for a purpose—namely securing revision of Philippe Pétain's conviction—whose pertinence and legitimacy at least, if not the means employed to achieve it, were recognised by the Court of Appeal.

54.   As to the omissions for which the authors of the text were criticised, the Court does not intend to rule on them in the abstract. These were not omissions about facts of no consequence but about events directly linked with the Holocaust. Admittedly, the authors of the text did refer to "Nazi barbarism", but without indicating that Philippe Pétain had knowingly contributed to it, particularly through his responsibility for the persecution and deportation to the death camps of tens of thousands of Jews in France. The gravity of these facts, which constitute crimes against humanity, increases the gravity of any attempt to draw a veil over them. Although it is morally reprehensible, however, the fact that the text made no mention of them must be assessed in the light of a number of other circumstances of the case.

55.   These include the fact that, as the Government observed, "this page of the history of France remains very painful in the collective memory, given the difficulties the country experienced in determining who was responsible, whether isolated individuals or entire institutions, for the policy of collaboration with Nazi Germany".

In that connection it should be pointed out, however, that it was for the prosecution, whose role it is to represent all the sensibilities which make up the general interest and to assess the rights of others, to put that case during the domestic proceedings. . . .

The Court further notes that the events referred to in the publication in issue had occurred more than forty years before. Even though remarks like those the applicants made are always likely to reopen the controversy and bring back memories of past sufferings, the lapse of time makes it inappropriate to deal with such remarks, forty years on, with the same severity as ten or twenty years previously. That forms part of the efforts that every country must make to debate its own history openly and dispassionately. The Court reiterates in that connection that, subject to paragraph 2 of Article 10, freedom of expression is applicable not only to "information" or "ideas" that are favourably received or regarded as inoffensive or as a matter of indifference, but also to those that offend, shock or disturb; such are the demands of that pluralism, tolerance and broadmindedness without which there is no "democratic society" (*see*, among many other authorities, the *Open Door* and *Dublin Well Woman v. Ireland* judgment of 29 October 1992, Series A no. 246–A, p. 30, § 71, and the *Vogt v. Germany* judgment of 26 September 1995, Series A no. 323, p. 25, § 52).

56. Furthermore, the publication in issue corresponds directly to the object of the associations which produced it, the Association for the Defence of the Memory of Marshal Pétain and the National Pétain–Verdun Association. These associations are legally constituted and no proceedings have been brought against them, either before or after 1984, for pursuing their objects.

57. Lastly, the Court notes the seriousness of a criminal conviction for publicly defending the crimes of collaboration, having regard to the existence of other means of intervention and rebuttal, particularly through civil remedies.

58. In short, the Court considers the applicants' criminal conviction disproportionate and, as such, unnecessary in a democratic society. There has therefore been a breach of Article 10.

Having reached that conclusion, the Court considers that it is not appropriate to apply Article 17.

FOR THESE REASONS, THE COURT

1. Holds by fifteen votes to six that there has been a breach of Article 10 of the Convention;

2. Holds unanimously that the finding of a breach in itself constitutes sufficient just satisfaction for the non-pecuniary damage sustained by the applicants;

■ JOINT DISSENTING OPINION OF Judges Foighel, Loizou AND Sir John Freeland

1. We agree that the conviction and sentencing of the applicants in this case amounted to an interference with their right to freedom of expression as guaranteed by Article 10 of the Convention and that the restriction which this interference represented is to be regarded as having been "prescribed by law" in the sense of paragraph 2 of that Article and as having pursued a legitimate aim under that paragraph. Where we differ from the majority is in the assessment of whether the interference is to be treated as "necessary in a democratic society".

2. As to that question, it should first be noted that the text in question was published as a full-page advertisement, paid for by the applicants' associations, in the edition of Le Monde for 13 July 1984. The text contained a series of slogans, in capital letters and bold type (People of France, you have short memories if you have forgotten . . .), interspersed with short passages in laudatory terms purporting to summarise episodes

in the career of Philippe Pétain. It was clearly intended to drum up support for the applicants' associations and, no doubt to that end, concluded with an invitation to readers to write to those associations. Nowhere, however, did it say anything about the reopening of the case of Philippe Pétain, which has been claimed by the applicants to have been the purpose of the advertisement. Nor can it be regarded as in any valid sense a contribution to genuine historical debate, given its wholly one-sided and promotional character.

3.   Secondly, it perhaps needs to be said that it is not for the Court to decide whether the conviction of the applicants of apology for serious offences of collaboration was or was not justified as a matter of French law. That conviction proceeded from the judgment of the Paris Court of Appeal of 26 January 1990, in which the text of the advertisement was carefully analysed, and was upheld by the Court of Cassation in its judgment of 16 November 1993. The relevant question for our Court is whether the Convention test of necessity in a democratic society is satisfied in the case of this outcome in the domestic courts.

4.   As is clear from the Court's case-law, the adjective "necessary", as part of the test of necessity in a democratic society, is to be understood as implying a "pressing social need" and it is in the first place for the national authorities to determine whether the interference in issue corresponds to such a need, for which they enjoy a greater or lesser margin of appreciation. In cases involving the right to freedom of expression the Court has generally been particularly restrictive in its approach to the margin of appreciation, although it has been prepared to accept a wider margin in relation to issues likely to offend personal convictions in the religious or moral domain. That latter category, based as it is on the principle that the margin of appreciation is wider where the aim pursued cannot be objectively defined on the European scale, is in our view not to be regarded as confined to those particular issues. It may include an issue such as that in question in the present case, where the aim pursued arose out of historical circumstances peculiar to France and where the French authorities were uniquely well placed, by virtue of their direct and continuous contact with the vital forces of their country, to assess the consequences for the protection of the rights of other groups, such as the associations of former Resistance fighters and of deportees who were civil parties to the domestic proceedings, and more generally for the process of healing the wounds and divisions in French society resulting from the events of the 1940s. We would particularly underline that Article 10 § 2 of the Convention refers not only to the protection of the rights of others but also to the duties and responsibilities which accompany the exercise of the freedom of expression; and we consider it entirely justifiable—indeed, only natural—that in circumstances such as those of the present case full and sympathetic account should be taken of the extent of offensiveness of the publication to the sensitivities of groups of victims affected by it.

5.   Are the French authorities, then, to be regarded as having exceeded their margin of appreciation by virtue of the facts that the legislature has (as part of a law which was primarily concerned to establish an amnesty for serious offences of collaboration) criminalised acts of apology for such offences and that the courts have determined the publication of an

advertisement in the terms in question to constitute such an act and imposed the penalties which they did? It has (unsurprisingly) not been argued before the Court that the criminalisation of acts of apology for serious offences of collaboration in itself went beyond the margin of appreciation. As regards the content of the advertisement, the applicants have, in order to distance Philippe Pétain from personal responsibility for the darker side of what was done in France during the Vichy era and as part of the vindication of his actions during the period, pointed to the references in the text to "Nazi atrocities and persecutions" and its claim that he afforded protection to the French people from "German omnipotence and barbarism". Yet, as the Paris Court of Appeal observed in its judgment of 26 January 1990, the text said nothing at all about the notorious racist, and in particular anti-Jewish, activities undertaken by the Pétain regime itself, beginning with the Act relating to aliens of Jewish race which was signed by him on 3 October 1940.

6. The distortion inherent in this contrasting silence about one of the most unsavoury features of the Pétain regime is capable of being understood as amounting to implicit support for what was done. Even if such a distortion is, however, insufficient, because too indirect or remote, to constitute an "activity or ... act aimed at the destruction of any of the rights and freedoms set forth" in the Convention, within the meaning of its Article 17, so as to disable the applicants from relying on Article 10, the principle which underlies Article 17 is a factor which can properly be taken into account in the assessment of the exercise of the margin of appreciation and the existence of necessity. That principle is one of firm discouragement of the promotion of values hostile to those embodied in the Convention. Having regard to the conclusions reached in the judgment of the Paris Court of Appeal of 26 January 1990 as to the effect to be given to the wording of the advertisement, and having regard to the concern which the French authorities, with their particular familiarity with the historical background and current context, could legitimately have to demonstrate that racism and, in particular, anti-Semitism, are not to be condoned, we consider that the margin of appreciation should not be treated as having been exceeded and that the test of necessity in a democratic society has been satisfied in this case.

7. On the question of proportionality, we would note only that the penalty imposed by the Paris Court of Appeal was limited to the requirement of a symbolic payment of one franc to the civil parties and the ordering of publication of excerpts from that Court's judgment in Le Monde.

8. We would add that our conclusion on the question of necessity in a democratic society is confined to the circumstances of the present case and should of course not be understood as suggesting in any way that it is permissible to restrict genuine debate about controversial historical figures. Such debate about the role of Philippe Pétain has been, and no doubt will continue to be, engaged in vigorously in France.

9. For the reasons indicated above, we voted against the finding of a violation of Article 10 of the Convention in this case.

————

NOTES

1.   The French prohibition of hate speech extends beyond Holocaust denial and permits the prosecution and criminal conviction of a person for any utterance of racially charged hateful speech. For example, French fashion designer John Galliano was convicted in September 2011 for comments made on two occasions in a bar in Paris, which were in both cases anti-Semitic and in one case anti-Asian. He was fired from his job as the head of the House of Dior, and was tried and convicted by a French criminal court for hate speech, and fined 6,000 euros. The fine was eventually suspended, but he was also made to pay 24,000 euros to human rights organizations that joined with state prosecutor in the case. *See* the Doreen Carvajal, *Court Convicts Galliano in Anti–Semitism Case*, NY TIMES, September 8, 2011. In how many ways does this differ from what would have happened if similar comments were made by a person of similar stature or celebrity in the United States? For example, what if Mel Gibson made similar derogatory comments during a DUI arrest in the United States?

2.   The National Front, a far-right political party in France, was founded by Jean–Marie Le Pen in 1972. The party supports French protectionism, an end to France's adoption of the euro and withdrawal from NATO. The party is frequently criticized for its anti-immigrant views, which are directed at non-European immigrants, and are widely regarded as racist. In recent years, the party has consistently won approximately 15% of the vote, with far higher totals in certain regions. In the 2002 Presidential race Le Pen surprised much of the political world when he came in second in the first round, before losing the second round to incumbent Jacques Chirac. His daughter Marine Le Pen was elected as leader of the party in 2011 and has contributed to the party's growing popularity. In late 2010, Marine Le Pen compared crowds of Muslims praying in the streets outside overcrowded mosques to the Nazi occupation of France. /July–December, *2010 International Religious Freedom Report— France/*, United States Department of State, (13 Sept. 2011), available at: http://www.unhcr.org/refworld/docid/4e734c9cc.html.; France's National Front picks Marine Le Pen as new head, BBC News (16 January 2011 06:59 AM), http://www.bbc.co.uk/news/world-europe–12201475.

3.   In September 2011 the French Parliament banned Muslims from praying in the streets outside crowded Mosques, reasoning that such public displays of religion violated the public neutrality required by French Constitutional secularism.

D. DENMARK

International Convention on the Elimination of All Forms of Racial Discrimination (1966)

Article 4:

States Parties condemn all propaganda and all organizations which are based on ideas or theories of superiority of one race or group of persons of one colour or ethnic origin, or which attempt to justify or promote racial hatred and discrimination in any form, and undertake to adopt immediate and positive measures designed to eradicate all incitement to, or acts of, such discrimination and, to this end, with due regard to the principles embodied in the Universal Declaration of Human Rights and the rights expressly set forth in article 5 of this Convention, inter alia:

(a) Shall declare an offence punishable by law all dissemination of ideas based on racial superiority or hatred, incitement to racial discrimination, as well as all acts of violence or incitement to such acts against any race or group of persons of another colour or ethnic origin, and also the provision of any assistance to racist activities, including the financing thereof;

(b) Shall declare illegal and prohibit organizations, and also organized and all other propaganda activities, which promote and incite racial discrimination, and shall recognize participation in such organizations or activities as an offence punishable by law;

(c) Shall not permit public authorities or public institutions, national or local, to promote or incite racial discrimination.

———

Jersild v. Denmark

36/1993/431/510, 22 August 1994

■ EUROPEAN COURT OF HUMAN RIGHTS

I. The particular circumstances of the case

9. Mr. Jens Olaf Jersild, a Danish national, is a journalist and lives in Copenhagen. He was at the time of the events giving rise to the present case, and still is, employed by Danmarks Radio (Danish Broadcasting Corporation, which broadcasts not only radio but also television programmes), assigned to its Sunday News Magazine (Søndagsavisen). The latter is known as a serious television programme intended for a well-informed audience, dealing with a wide range of social and political issues, including xenophobia, immigration and refugees.

A. The Greenjackets item

10. On 31 May 1985 the newspaper *Information* published an article describing the racist attitudes of members of a group of young people, calling themselves "the Greenjackets" ("grønjakkerne"), at Østerbro in Copenhagen. In the light of this article, the editors of the Sunday News Magazine decided to produce a documentary on the Greenjackets. Subsequently the applicant contacted representatives of the group, inviting three of them together with Mr Per Axholt, a social worker employed at the local youth centre, to take part in a television interview. During the interview, which was conducted by the applicant, the three Greenjackets made abusive and derogatory remarks about immigrants and ethnic groups in

Denmark. It lasted between five and six hours, of which between two and two and a half hours were video-recorded. Danmarks Radio paid the interviewees fees in accordance with its usual practice.

11. The applicant subsequently edited and cut the film of the interview down to a few minutes. On 21 July 1985 this was broadcast by Danmarks Radio as a part of the Sunday News Magazine. * * *

B. Proceedings in the City Court of Copenhagen

12. Following the programme no complaints were made to the Radio Council, which had competence in such matters, or to Danmarks Radio but the Bishop of A°lborg complained to the Minister of Justice. After undertaking investigations the Public Prosecutor instituted criminal proceedings in the City Court of Copenhagen (Københavns Byret) against the three youths interviewed by the applicant, charging them with a violation of Article 266 (b) of the Penal Code (straffeloven) (*see* paragraph 19 below) for having made the statements cited below:

"... the Northern States wanted that the niggers should be free human beings, man, they are not human beings, they are animals."

"Just take a picture of a gorilla, man, and then look at a nigger, it's the same body structure and everything, man, flat forehead and all kinds of things."

"A nigger is not a human being, it's an animal, that goes for all the other foreign workers as well, Turks, Yugoslavs and whatever they are called."

"It is the fact that they are 'Perkere', that's what we don't like, right, and we don't like their mentality ... what we don't like is when they walk around in those Zimbabwe-clothes and then speak this hula-hula language in the street ..."

"It's drugs they are selling, man, half of the prison population in 'Vestre' are in there because of drugs ... they are the people who are serving time for dealing drugs ..."

"They are in there, all the 'Perkere', because of drugs ..."

The applicant was charged, under Article 266 (b) in conjunction with Article 23 (*see* paragraph 19 below), with aiding and abetting the three youths; the same charge was brought against the head of the news section of Danmarks Radio, Mr Lasse Jensen.

* * *

II. Relevant domestic law

A. The Penal Code

19. At the relevant time Article 266 (b) of the Penal Code provided:

"Any person who, publicly or with the intention of disseminating it to a wide circle ("videre kreds") of people, makes a statement, or other communication, threatening, insulting or degrading a group of persons on account of their race, colour, national or ethnic origin or belief shall be liable to a fine or to simple detention or to imprisonment for a term not exceeding two years."

Article 23, paragraph 1, reads:

"A provision establishing a criminal offence shall apply to any person who has assisted the commission of the offence by instigation, advice or action. The punishment may be reduced if the person in question only intended to give assistance of minor importance or to strengthen an intent already resolved or if the offence has not been completed or an intended assistance failed."

* * *

III. Instruments of the United Nations

21. Provisions relating to the prohibition of racial discrimination and the prevention of propaganda of racist views and ideas are to be found in a number of international instruments, for example the 1945 United Nations Charter (paragraph 2 of the Preamble, Articles 1 para. 3, 13 para. 1 (b), 55 (c) and 76 (c)), the 1948 Universal Declaration of Human Rights (Articles 1, 2 and 7) and the 1966 International Covenant on Civil and Political Rights (Articles 2 para. 1, 20 para. 2 and 26). The most directly relevant treaty is the 1965 International Convention on the Elimination of All Forms of Racial Discrimination ("the UN Convention"), which has been ratified by a large majority of the Contracting States to the European Convention, including Denmark (9 December 1971). Articles 4 and 5 of that Convention provide:

Article 4 [*see* above]

The effects of the "due regard" clause in Article 4 has given rise to differing interpretations and the UN Committee on the Elimination of Racial Discrimination ("the UN Committee"—set up to supervise the implementation of the UN Convention) was divided in its comments on the applicant's conviction. The present case had been presented by the Danish Government in a report to the UN Committee. Whilst some members welcomed it as "the clearest statement yet, in any country, that the right to protection against racial discrimination took precedence over the right to freedom of expression", other members considered that "in such cases the facts needed to be considered in relation to both rights" (Report of the Committee to the General Assembly, Official Records, Forty–Fifth Session, Supplement No. 18 (A/45/18), p. 21, para. 56).

* * *

FINAL SUBMISSIONS MADE BY THE GOVERNMENT TO THE COURT

24. At the hearing on 20 April 1994 the Government invited the Court to hold that, as submitted in their memorial, there had been no violation of Article 10 (art. 10) of the Convention.

AS TO THE LAW

I. ALLEGED VIOLATION OF ARTICLE 10 (art. 10)

25. The applicant maintained that his conviction and sentence for having aided and abetted the dissemination of racist remarks violated his

right to freedom of expression within the meaning of Article 10 (art. 10) of the Convention. * * *

27.   It is common ground that the measures giving rise to the applicant's case constituted an interference with his right to freedom of expression.

It is moreover undisputed that this interference was "prescribed by law", the applicant's conviction being based on Articles 266 (b) and 23 (1) of the Penal Code. In this context, the Government pointed out that the former provision had been enacted in order to comply with the UN Convention. The Government's argument, as the Court understands it, is that, whilst Article 10 (art. 10) of the Convention is applicable, the Court, in applying paragraph 2 (art. 10–2), should consider that the relevant provisions of the Penal Code are to be interpreted and applied in an extensive manner, in accordance with the rationale of the UN Convention (*see* paragraph 21 above). In other words, Article 10 (art. 10) should not be interpreted in such a way as to limit, derogate from or destroy the right to protection against racial discrimination under the UN Convention.

Finally it is uncontested that the interference pursued a legitimate aim, namely the "protection of the reputation or rights of others". The only point in dispute is whether the measures were "necessary in a democratic society".

28.   The applicant and the Commission were of the view that, notwithstanding Denmark's obligations as a Party to the UN Convention (*see* paragraph 21 above), a fair balance had to be struck between the "protection of the reputation or rights of others" and the applicant's right to impart information. According to the applicant, such a balance was envisaged in a clause contained in Article 4 of the UN Convention to the effect that "due regard" should be had to "the principles in the Universal Declaration of Human Rights and the rights . . . in Article 5 of [the UN] Convention". The clause had been introduced at the drafting stage because of concern among a number of States that the requirement in Article 4 (a) that "[States Parties] shall declare an offence punishable by law all dissemination of ideas based on racial superiority or hatred" was too sweeping and could give rise to difficulties with regard to other human rights, in particular the right to freedom of opinion and expression. . . .

The applicant and the Commission emphasised that, taken in the context of the broadcast as a whole, the offending remarks had the effect of ridiculing their authors rather than promoting their racist views. The overall impression of the programme was that it sought to draw public attention to a matter of great public concern, namely racism and xenophobia. The applicant had deliberately included the offensive statements in the programme, not with the intention of disseminating racist opinions, but in order to counter them through exposure. The applicant pointed out that he tried to show, analyse and explain to his viewers a new phenomenon in Denmark at the time, that of violent racism practised by inarticulate and socially disadvantaged youths. Joined by the Commission, he considered that the broadcast could not have had any significant detrimental effects on the "reputation or rights of others". The interests in protecting the latter were therefore outweighed by those of protecting the applicant's freedom of expression. . . .

29. The Government contended that the applicant had edited the Greenjackets item in a sensationalist rather than informative manner and that its news or information value was minimal. Television was a powerful medium and a majority of Danes normally viewed the news programme in which the item was broadcast. Yet the applicant, knowing that they would incur criminal liability, had encouraged the Greenjackets to make racist statements and had failed to counter these statements in the programme. It was too subtle to assume that viewers would not take the remarks at their face value. No weight could be attached to the fact that the programme had given rise to only a few complaints, since, due to lack of information and insufficient knowledge of the Danish language and even fear of reprisals by violent racists, victims of the insulting comments were likely to be dissuaded from complaining. The applicant had thus failed to fulfil the "duties and responsibilities" incumbent on him as a television journalist. The fine imposed upon him was at the lower end of the scale of sanctions applicable to Article 266 (b) offences and was therefore not likely to deter any journalist from contributing to public discussion on racism and xenophobia; it only had the effect of a public reminder that racist expressions are to be taken seriously and cannot be tolerated. . . .

The Government stressed that at all three levels the Danish courts, which were in principle better placed than the European Court to evaluate the effects of the programme, had carried out a careful balancing exercise of all the interests involved. The review effected by those courts had been similar to that carried out under Article 10 (art. 10); their decisions fell within the margin of appreciation to be left to the national authorities and corresponded to a pressing social need. * * *

31. A significant feature of the present case is that the applicant did not make the objectionable statements himself but assisted in their dissemination in his capacity of television journalist responsible for a news programme of Danmarks Radio (*see* paragraphs 9 to 11 above). In assessing whether his conviction and sentence were "necessary", the Court will therefore have regard to the principles established in its case-law relating to the role of the press (as summarised in for instance the *Observer and Guardian v. the United Kingdom* judgment of 26 November 1991, Series A no. 216, pp. 29–30, para. 59).

The Court reiterates that freedom of expression constitutes one of the essential foundations of a democratic society and that the safeguards to be afforded to the press are of particular importance (*ibid.*). Whilst the press must not overstep the bounds set, inter alia, in the interest of "the protection of the reputation or rights of others", it is nevertheless incumbent on it to impart information and ideas of public interest. Not only does the press have the task of imparting such information and ideas: the public also has a right to receive them. Were it otherwise, the press would be unable to play its vital role of "public watchdog" (*ibid.*). Although formulated primarily with regard to the print media, these principles doubtless apply also to the audiovisual media. * * *

* * * [T]he methods of objective and balanced reporting may vary considerably, depending among other things on the media in question. It is not for this Court, nor for the national courts for that matter, to substitute their own views for those of the press as to what technique of reporting should be adopted by journalists. In this context the Court recalls that Article 10 (art. 10) protects not only the substance of the ideas and information expressed, but also the form in which they are conveyed (*see* the *Oberschlick v. Austria* judgment of 23 May 1991, Series A no. 204, p. 25, para. 57). * * *

The Court's assessment will have regard to the manner in which the Greenjackets feature was prepared, its contents, the context in which it was broadcast and the purpose of the programme. Bearing in mind the obligations on States under the UN Convention and other international instruments to take effective measures to eliminate all forms of racial discrimination and to prevent and combat racist doctrines and practices (*see* paragraph 21 above), an important factor in the Court's evaluation will be whether the item in question, when considered as a whole, appeared from an objective point of view to have had as its purpose the propagation of racist views and ideas.

32.   The national courts laid considerable emphasis on the fact that the applicant had himself taken the initiative of preparing the Greenjackets feature and that he not only knew in advance that racist statements were likely to be made during the interview but also had encouraged such statements. He had edited the programme in such a way as to include the offensive assertions. Without his involvement, the remarks would not have been disseminated to a wide circle of people and would thus not have been punishable (*see* paragraphs 14 and 18 above).

The Court is satisfied that these were relevant reasons for the purposes of paragraph 2 of Article 10 (art. 10–2).

33.   On the other hand, as to the contents of the Greenjackets item, it should be noted that the TV presenter's introduction started by a reference to recent public discussion and press comments on racism in Denmark, thus inviting the viewer to see the programme in that context. He went on to announce that the object of the programme was to address aspects of the problem, by identifying certain racist individuals and by portraying their mentality and social background. There is no reason to doubt that the ensuing interviews fulfilled that aim. Taken as a whole, the feature could not objectively have appeared to have as its purpose the propagation of racist views and ideas. On the contrary, it clearly sought—by means of an interview—to expose, analyse and explain this particular group of youths, limited and frustrated by their social situation, with criminal records and violent attitudes, thus dealing with specific aspects of a matter that already then was of great public concern.

The Supreme Court held that the news or information value of the feature was not such as to justify the dissemination of the offensive remarks (*see* paragraph 18 above). However, in view of the principles stated in paragraph 31 above, the Court sees no cause to question the Sunday News Magazine staff members' own appreciation of the news or information value of the impugned item, which formed the basis for their decisions to produce and broadcast it.

34. Furthermore, it must be borne in mind that the item was broadcast as part of a serious Danish news programme and was intended for a well-informed audience (*see* paragraph 9 above).

The Court is not convinced by the argument, also stressed by the national courts (*see* paragraphs 14 and 18 above), that the Greenjackets item was presented without any attempt to counterbalance the extremist views expressed. Both the TV presenter's introduction and the applicant's conduct during the interviews clearly dissociated him from the persons interviewed, for example by describing them as members of "a group of extremist youths" who supported the Ku Klux Klan and by referring to the criminal records of some of them. The applicant also rebutted some of the racist statements for instance by recalling that there were black people who had important jobs. It should finally not be forgotten that, taken as a whole, the filmed portrait surely conveyed the meaning that the racist statements were part of a generally anti-social attitude of the Greenjackets.

Admittedly, the item did not explicitly recall the immorality, dangers and unlawfulness of the promotion of racial hatred and of ideas of superiority of one race. However, in view of the above-mentioned counterbalancing elements and the natural limitations on spelling out such elements in a short item within a longer programme as well as the journalist's discretion as to the form of expression used, the Court does not consider the absence of such precautionary reminders to be relevant.

35. News reporting based on interviews, whether edited or not, constitutes one of the most important means whereby the press is able to play its vital role of "public watchdog" (*see*, for instance, the above-mentioned Observer and Guardian judgment, pp. 29–30, para. 59).

The punishment of a journalist for assisting in the dissemination of statements made by another person in an interview would seriously hamper the contribution of the press to discussion of matters of public interest and should not be envisaged unless there are particularly strong reasons for doing so. In this regard the Court does not accept the Government's argument that the limited nature of the fine is relevant; what matters is that the journalist was convicted.

There can be no doubt that the remarks in respect of which the Greenjackets were convicted (*see* paragraph 14 above) were more than insulting to members of the targeted groups and did not enjoy the protection of Article 10 (art. 10) (*see*, for instance, the Commission's admissibility decisions in *Glimmerveen and Hagenbeek v. the Netherlands*, applications nos. 8348/78 and 8406/78, DR 18, p. 187; and *Kuñen v. Germany,* application no. 12194/86, DR 56, p. 205). However, even having regard to the manner in which the applicant prepared the Greenjackets item (*see* paragraph 32 above), it has not been shown that, considered as a whole, the feature was such as to justify also his conviction of, and punishment for, a criminal offence under the Penal Code.

36. It is moreover undisputed that the purpose of the applicant in compiling the broadcast in question was not racist. Although he relied on

this in the domestic proceedings, it does not appear from the reasoning in the relevant judgments that they took such a factor into account (*see* paragraphs 14, 17 and 18 above).

37.   Having regard to the foregoing, the reasons adduced in support of the applicant's conviction and sentence were not sufficient to establish convincingly that the interference thereby occasioned with the enjoyment of his right to freedom of expression was "necessary in a democratic society"; in particular the means employed were disproportionate to the aim of protecting "the reputation or rights of others". Accordingly the measures gave rise to a breach of Article 10 (art. 10) of the Convention.
* * *

FOR THESE REASONS, THE COURT

1.   Holds by twelve votes to seven that there has been a violation of Article 10 (art. 10) of the Convention;

* * *

■ JOINT DISSENTING OPINION OF Judges Ryssdal, Bernhardt, Spielmann AND Loizou

1.   This is the first time that the Court has been concerned with a case of dissemination of racist remarks which deny to a large group of persons the quality of "human beings". In earlier decisions the Court has—in our view, rightly—underlined the great importance of the freedom of the press and the media in general for a democratic society, but it has never had to consider a situation in which "the reputation or rights of others" (Article 10 para. 2) (art. 10-2) were endangered to such an extent as here.

2.   We agree with the majority (paragraph 35 of the judgment) that the Greenjackets themselves "did not enjoy the protection of Article 10 (art. 10)". The same must be true of journalists who disseminate such remarks with supporting comments or with their approval. This can clearly not be said of the applicant. Therefore it is admittedly difficult to strike the right balance between the freedom of the press and the protection of others. But the majority attributes much more weight to the freedom of the journalist than to the protection of those who have to suffer from racist hatred.

3.   Neither the written text of the interview (paragraph 11 of the judgment) nor the video film we have seen makes it clear that the remarks of the Greenjackets are intolerable in a society based on respect for human rights. The applicant has cut the entire interview down to a few minutes, probably with the consequence or even the intention of retaining the most crude remarks. That being so, it was absolutely necessary to add at least a clear statement of disapproval. The majority of the Court sees such disapproval in the context of the interview, but this is an interpretation of cryptic remarks. Nobody can exclude that certain parts of the public found in the television spot support for their racist prejudices.

And what must be the feelings of those whose human dignity has been attacked, or even denied, by the Greenjackets? Can they get the impression that seen in context the television broadcast contributes to their protection? A journalist's good intentions are not enough in such a situation, especially in a case in which he has himself provoked the racist statements.

4. The International Convention on the Elimination of All Forms of Racial Discrimination probably does not require the punishment of journalists responsible for a television spot of this kind. On the other hand, it supports the opinion that the media too can be obliged to take a clear stand in the area of racial discrimination and hatred.

5. The threat of racial discrimination and persecution is certainly serious in our society, and the Court has rightly emphasised the vital importance of combating racial discrimination in all its forms and manifestations (paragraph 30 of the judgment). The Danish courts fully recognised that protection of persons whose human dignity is attacked has to be balanced against the right to freedom of expression. They carefully considered the responsibility of the applicant, and the reasons for their conclusions were relevant. The protection of racial minorities cannot have less weight than the right to impart information, and in the concrete circumstances of the present case it is in our opinion not for this Court to substitute its own balancing of the conflicting interests for that of the Danish Supreme Court. We are convinced that the Danish courts acted inside the margin of appreciation which must be left to the Contracting States in this sensitive area. Accordingly, the findings of the Danish courts cannot be considered as giving rise to a violation of Article 10 (art. 10) of the Convention.

■ JOINT DISSENTING OPINION OF JUDGES GÖLCÜKLÜ, RUSSO AND VALTICOS

(Translation)

We cannot share the opinion of the majority of the Court in the *Jersild* case. * * *

* * * [T]he statements made and willingly reproduced in the relevant broadcast on Danish television, without any significant reaction on the part of the commentator, did indeed amount to incitement to contempt not only of foreigners in general but more particularly of black people, described as belonging to an inferior, subhuman race ("the niggers . . . are not human beings . . . Just take a picture of a gorilla . . . and then look at a nigger, it's the same body structure . . . A nigger is not a human being, it's an animal, that goes for all the other foreign workers as well, Turks, Yugoslavs and whatever they are called.").

While appreciating that some judges attach particular importance to freedom of expression, the more so as their countries have largely been deprived of it in quite recent times, we cannot accept that this freedom should extend to encouraging racial hatred, contempt for races other than the one to which we belong, and defending violence against those who belong to the races in question. It has been sought to defend the broadcast on the ground that it would provoke a healthy reaction of rejection among the viewers. That is to display an optimism, which to say the least, is belied by experience. Large numbers of young people today, and even of the population at large, finding themselves overwhelmed by the difficulties of life, unemployment and poverty, are only too willing to seek scapegoats who are held up to them without any real word of caution; for—and this is an important point—the journalist responsible for the broadcast in question made no real attempt to challenge the points of view he was presenting, which was necessary if their impact was to be counterbalanced, at least for the viewers.

That being so, we consider that by taking criminal measures—which were, moreover, moderate ones—the Danish judicial institutions in no way infringed Article 10 (art. 10) of the Convention.

————

NOTES

1. For a further discussion of the application of Article 10 to journalists, *see* Regis Bismuth, *Standards of Conduct for Journalists under Europe's First Amendment*, 8:2 FIRST AMENDMENT LAW REVIEW 283 (2010).

2. In 2005, the Danish newspaper Jylland–Posten published twelve cartoons of the Prophet Muhammad. Patricia Cohen, *Danish Cartoon Controversy*, NY TIMES, Aug. 12, 2009, http://www.nytimes.com/2006/01/08/international/europe/08denmark.ready.html?ref=danishcartoon controversy. Although many Muslims interpret the Koran as forbidding depiction of Muhammad, many images of him have appeared in both Islamic and Western art without incident. The Danish newspaper, however, caricatured Muhammad. In one cartoon, he is depicted "wearing a turban shaped as a bomb with a burning fuse." *Id.* Several Muslim groups filed a complaint with the police alleging violation of Section 266b and Section 140 of the Danish Penal code. Section 266b is reproduced in the case above, and Section 140 prohibits disturbing public order by insulting the dogmas of worship of any religious community in Denmark. The regional prosecutor determined that the cartoons did not constitute a criminal offense and discontinued the investigation. The Director of Public Prosecutions in Denmark agreed. Henning Fode, Director of Public Prosecutions, Decision on possible criminal proceedings in the case of Jyllands–Posten's article *The Face of Muhammed*, March 15, 2006, http://www.rigsadvokaten.dk/media/bilag/afgorelse_engelsk.pdf. Muslims in the Middle East and Africa protested over this depiction of Muhammad. In Damascus and Beirut, protesters set fire to the Danish missions, and Afghan security forces killed protesters who tried to storm the American base at Bagram. Michael Kimmelman, *A Startling New Lesson in the Power of Imagery*, N.Y. TIMES, Feb. 8, 2006, http://www.nytimes.com/2006/02/08/arts/design/08imag.html?ref=danishcartooncontroversy. The cartoons also reignited tensions between Christians and Muslims in Nigeria, and over 100 people died in protests there. Lydia Polgreen, *Nigeria Counts 100 Deaths Over Danish Caricatures*, N.Y. TIMES, Feb. 24, 2006, http://www.nytimes.com/2006/02/24/international/africa/24nigeria.html?ref=danishcartooncontroversy. For more on this topic, *see* JYTTE KLAUSEN, THE CARTOONS THAT SHOOK THE WORLD (2009).

3. In May 2011, activists managed to qualify a measure for the ballot that would have criminalized the practice of circumcision in the City and County of San Francisco (a similar measure qualified for the ballot in Santa

Monica, but was later withdrawn). The initiative's proponents posted online a comic book series featuring the battles of a superhero named Foreskin Man with evil Monster Mohel (a Jewish religious officiant who performs circumcisions), and containing images of Jews that the City Attorney's office said in court papers were "strikingly similar to images of Jews used in Nazi propaganda during the 1930s and 1940s." The Jewish Community Relations Council, the Anti–Defamation League, and a number of other Jewish and Muslim organizations and individuals filed a pre-election challenge to the ballot measure in San Francisco Superior Court, seeking to have it removed from the ballot before the November election. California courts are traditionally reluctant to strike ballot measures before an election has been held, which is extraordinary relief that demands a "compelling showing" of "clear invalidity." The American Civil Liberties Union of Northern California filed an *amicus curiae* brief in support of the petitioners' position, which also drew support from the City Attorney and the San Francisco Medical Association. The brief argued that the measure was preempted by state law, which prohibits cities and counties from regulating recognized medical procedures such as circumcision, and threatened serious violations of protected constitutional rights including the free exercise of religion. On July 28, 2011, the San Francisco Superior Court granted the petition and ordered the measure removed from the ballot. In early September 2011, following these developments, the California Legislature unanimously enacted urgency legislation that would preclude localities from prohibiting or restricting the practice of male circumcision or the exercise of a parent's authority to have a child circumcised.

E. TURKEY

Turkish Criminal Code Sec. 312

Whosoever expressly arouses hatred and hostility in society on the basis of a distinction between social classes, races or religions, or one based on allegiance to a particular denomination or region, shall be sentenced to between one and three years' imprisonment and a fine of between nine thousand and thirty-six thousand liras. If this incitement is done in a manner likely to endanger public safety, the sentence shall be increased [by one third to one half].

———

Case of Gündüz v. Turkey

(Application no. 35071/97) 4 December 2003

■ EUROPEAN COURT OF HUMAN RIGHTS

THE FACTS

I. THE CIRCUMSTANCES OF THE CASE

    9. The applicant was born in 1941. He is a retired labourer.

A.   The television programme in issue

10.   On 12 June 1995 the applicant took part in his capacity as the leader of Tarikat Aczmendi (a community describing itself as an Islamic sect) in a television programme, *Ceviz Kabuğu* ("Nutshell"), broadcast live on HBB, an independent channel.

11.   It appears from the evidence before the Court that the programme started late in the evening of 12 June and lasted about four hours. Relevant excerpts from the programme are set out below.

> *Hulki Cevizoğlu (presenter—"H.C.")*: "Good evening ... There is a group that is grabbing public attention because of the black robes [*cüppe*] worn by its members, the sticks they carry and their habit of chanting [*zikir*]. How can this group be described—it is called a sect [*tarikat*], but is it really a community or group? We will be discussing the various characteristics of this group—the Aczmendis—with their leader, Mr Müslüm Gündüz, who will be talking to us live. We will also be phoning a number of guests to hear their views. On the subject of the black robes, we'll be talking on the phone to Ms N. Yargıcı, a stylist and expert on black clothing. We'll also be hearing the views of Mr T. Ateş and Mr B. Baykam on Kemalism. As regards Nurculuk, we'll be calling one of its most important leaders. The Aczmendi group—or sect—has views on religious matters as well. We'll be discussing those with Mr Y. İşcan, of the Religious Affairs Department. And while we are on the subject, viewers may phone in with questions for the Aczmendis' leader, Mr Gündüz ..."

Ms Yargıcı, a stylist taking part in the programme via a telephone link, asked Mr Gündüz a number of questions about women's clothing. They discussed religious apparel and whether the clothing worn by the sect's members was in keeping with fashion or with Islam.

The presenter then discussed movements claiming to represent Islam and asked the applicant a number of questions on the subject. They also talked about methods of chanting. In this context Mr Gündüz stated:

> *Mr Gündüz ("M.G.")*: "Kemalism was born recently. It is a religion—that is, it is the name of a religion that has destroyed Islam and taken its place. Kemalism is a religion and secularism has no religion. Being a democrat also means having no religion ..."

> *H.C.*: "You have already expressed those views on a programme on the Star channel ... We are now going to have Bedri Baykam on the line to see what he thinks about your comments. We are going to ask him, as a proponent of Kemalism, if it can be regarded as a religion."

> *H.C.*: "Do you agree with Mr Gündüz's views on Kemalism? You are one of Turkey's foremost Kemalists."

> *Bedri Baykam ("B.B.")*: "I don't know where to begin after so many incorrect statements. For one thing, Kemalism is not a religion

and secularism has nothing to do with having no religion. It is completely wrong to maintain that democracy has no religion."

Mr Baykam challenged Mr Gündüz's arguments and explained the concepts of democracy and secularism. He stated:

B.B.: "A sect such as the one you belong to may observe a religion. But concepts such as democracy, philosophy and free thought do not observe a religion, because they are not creatures who can establish a moral relationship with God. In a democracy all people are free to choose their religion and may choose either to adhere to a religion or to call themselves atheists. Those who wish to manifest their religion in accordance with their belief may do so. Moreover, [democracy] encompasses pluralism, liberty, democratic thought and diversity. This means that the people's desire will be fulfilled, because the people may elect party A today and party B tomorrow and then ask for a coalition to be formed the day after tomorrow. All that is dictated by the people. That is why, in a democracy, everything is free, and secularism and democracy are two related concepts. Secularism in no way means having no religion."

M.G.: "Tell me the name of the religion of secularism."

B.B.: "Secularism is freedom of the people and the principle that religious affairs may not interfere with affairs of State."

. . .

M.G.: "My brother, I say that secularism means having no religion. A democrat is a man with no religion. A Kemalist adheres to the Kemalist religion . . ."

B.B.: "[Our ancestors were not without a religion.] True, our ancestors did not allow the establishment of a system based on sharia . . . inspired by the Middle Ages, an undemocratic, totalitarian and despotic system that will not hesitate to cause bloodshed where necessary. And you call that 'having no religion'—that's your problem. But in a law-based, democratic, Kemalist and secular State all people are free to manifest their religion. Behind closed doors, they may practise their religion through chanting, worship or prayer; they may read what they like, the Koran, the Bible or philosophy—that is their choice. So I'm sorry, but your views are demagoguery. Kemalism has no connection with religion. It respects religion; all people are entitled to believe in a religion of their choice."

M.G.: "Yes. But what I am saying is that a person who has no connection with religion has no religion. Isn't that so? . . . I'm not insulting anyone. I am just saying that anyone calling himself a democrat, secularist or Kemalist has no religion . . . Democracy in Turkey is despotic, merciless and impious [*dinsiz*] . . ."

. . .

M.G.: "This secular democratic system is hypocritical [*ikiyüzlü ve münafık*] . . .; it treats some people in one way and others in another way. In other words, we do not share democratic values. I swear that we are not appropriating democracy for ourselves. I am not taking refuge in its shadow. Don't be a hypocrite."

H.C.: "But it is thanks to democracy that you can say all that."

M.G.: "No, not at all. It is not thanks to democracy. We will secure our rights no matter what. What is democracy? It has nothing to do with that."

H.C.: "I repeat that if democracy did not exist, you would not have been able to say all that."

M.G.: "Why would I not have said it? I am saying these words while fully aware that they constitute a crime under the laws of tyranny. Why would I stop speaking? Is there any other way than death?"

The participants then entered into a debate on Islam and democracy.

M.G.: "According to Islam, no distinction can be made between the administration of a State and an individual's beliefs. For example, the running of a province by a governor in accordance with the rules of the Koran is equivalent to a prayer. In other words, manifesting your religion does not only mean joining in prayer or observing Ramadan ... Any assistance from one Muslim to another also amounts to a prayer. OK, we can separate the State and religion, but if [a] person has his wedding night after being married by a council official authorised by the Republic of Turkey, the child born of the union will be a *piç* [bastard]."

H.C.: "Do you mind ..."

M.G.: "That is how Islam sees it. I am not talking about the rules of democracy ..."

B.B.: "... In Turkey people are killed for not observing Ramadan. People are beaten at university. [Mr Gündüz] claims he is innocent, but people like that oppress society because they interfere with the way of life of others. In Turkey people who say they support sharia misuse it for demagogic purposes. As Mr Gündüz said, they want to destroy democracy and set up a regime based on sharia."

M.G.: "Of course, that will happen, that will happen ..."

12. The programme continued, the participants including Mr T. Ateş, a professor, Mr Y. İşcan, a representative of the Religious Affairs Department, and Mr Mehmet Kırkıncı, a prominent figure from Erzurum.

B. The criminal proceedings against the applicant

13. In an indictment preferred on 5 October 1995, the public prosecutor at the Istanbul National Security Court instituted criminal proceedings against the applicant on the ground that he had breached Article 312 §§ 2 and 3 of the Criminal Code by making statements during the television programme that incited the people to hatred and hostility on the basis of a distinction founded on religion.

14. On 1 April 1996 the National Security Court, after ordering an expert opinion, found the applicant guilty as charged and sentenced him to

two years' imprisonment and a fine of 600,000 Turkish liras, pursuant to Article 312 §§ 2 and 3 of the Criminal Code. * * *

16. On 15 May 1996 the applicant appealed on points of law to the Court of Cassation. In his notice of appeal, referring to Article 9 of the Convention and Articles 24 (freedom of religion) and 25 (freedom of expression) of the Constitution, he relied on the protection of his right to freedom of religion and freedom of expression.

17. On 25 September 1996 the Court of Cassation upheld the judgment at first instance. * * *

THE LAW

I. ALLEGED VIOLATION OF ARTICLE 10 OF THE CONVENTION

25. The applicant submitted that his conviction under Article 312 of the Criminal Code had infringed Article 10 of the Convention. * * *

26. It was common ground between the parties that the measures giving rise to the instant case had amounted to interference with the applicant's right to freedom of expression. Such interference would constitute a breach of Article 10 unless it was "prescribed by law," pursued one or more of the legitimate aims referred to in paragraph 2 and was "necessary in a democratic society" in order to achieve the aim or aims in question.

A. "Prescribed by law"

27. It was, moreover, undisputed that the interference had been "prescribed by law," the applicant's conviction being based on Article 312 of the Criminal Code.

B. Legitimate aim

28. Nor was it disputed that the interference had pursued legitimate aims, namely the prevention of disorder or crime, the protection of morals and, in particular, the protection of the rights of others.

C. "Necessary in a democratic society"

1. The parties' submissions

29. The Government argued, firstly, that freedom of expression did not entail freedom to proffer insults. The applicant could not lay claim to the protection of freedom of expression when using insulting words such as "*piç*" (bastard). Moreover, his conduct had been punishable by law. They asserted in that connection that Articles 311 and 312 of the Criminal Code punished anyone who openly incited the people to hatred or hostility on the basis of a distinction founded on membership of a religion or denomination. * * *

31. In the Government's submission, the interference in question should be deemed to have been necessary in a democratic society and to have met a pressing need. The applicant's comments had not merely been offensive or shocking but had also been likely to cause serious harm to morals and to public order. Through his comments, which ran counter to the moral principles of a very large majority of the population, the appli-

cant had severely jeopardised social stability. Furthermore, his comment that any child born of a marriage celebrated before a mayor was a *"piç"* had touched on a subject of great sensitivity to Turkish public opinion. It had called into question the morality, indeed the legitimacy, of families, accusing them of being immoral and of failing to observe the Islamic faith. The Government also emphasised the impact of such comments, made during a television programme shown across the country.

32.   The Government further submitted that the applicant had been convicted not on account of his religion but for spreading hatred based on religious intolerance. On that account, he had also failed to comply with his duties under the second paragraph of Article 10 of the Convention.

33.   The applicant contested the Government's arguments. He submitted that he had been taking part in a television debate that had been broadcast late at night and had lasted about four hours. A number of people had taken part in order to ascertain his views and had engaged in debate with him by asking questions or submitting counter-arguments.

34.   The applicant maintained that his views, taken as a whole, were protected by freedom of expression. He had given examples and explanations on the basis of his personal beliefs. He had used the word *"piç"*, which should be interpreted as "illegitimate child", in response to a question from the programme's presenter. In doing so he had intended to stress that civil marriage was contrary to the Islamic conception of marriage requiring all marriages to be solemnised by a cleric. The word had therefore not been an insult but rather a term commonly used to describe a particular situation from the standpoint of Islam.

35.   As to the applicant's statements such as "democracy has no religion," he argued that they should be viewed in their context.

36.   The applicant further submitted that there had been no pressing social need for his conviction. Nobody to whom his comments had allegedly referred had instituted court proceedings against him for defamation or insult.

2.   The Court's assessment

(a) Relevant principles

37.   Freedom of expression constitutes one of the essential foundations of any democratic society and one of the basic conditions for its progress and for each individual's self-fulfilment. Subject to paragraph 2 of Article 10, it is applicable not only to "information" or "ideas" that are favourably received or regarded as inoffensive or as a matter of indifference, but also to those that offend, shock or disturb (*see Handyside v. the United Kingdom*, judgment of 7 December 1976, Series A no. 24, p. 23, § 49).

38.   The test of whether the interference complained of was "necessary in a democratic society" requires the Court to determine whether it corresponded to a "pressing social need," whether it was proportionate to the legitimate aim pursued and whether the reasons given by the national authorities to justify it are relevant and sufficient (*see The Sunday Times v. the United Kingdom (no. 1)*, judgment of 26 April 1979, Series A no. 30, p.

38, § 62). In assessing whether such a "need" exists and what measures should be adopted to deal with it, the national authorities are left a certain margin of appreciation. * * *

40. The present case is characterised, in particular, by the fact that the applicant was punished for statements classified by the domestic courts as "hate speech." Having regard to the relevant international instruments (*see* paragraphs 22–24 above) and to its own case-law, the Court would emphasise, in particular, that tolerance and respect for the equal dignity of all human beings constitute the foundations of a democratic, pluralistic society. That being so, as a matter of principle it may be considered necessary in certain democratic societies to sanction or even prevent all forms of expression which spread, incite, promote or justify hatred based on intolerance (including religious intolerance), provided that any "formalities," "conditions," "restrictions" or "penalties" imposed are proportionate to the legitimate aim pursued (with regard to hate speech and the glorification of violence, *see*, *mutatis mutandis*, *Sürek v. Turkey (no. 1)* [GC], no. 26682/95, § 62, ECtHR 1999–IV).

41. Furthermore, as the Court noted in *Jersild v. Denmark* (judgment of 23 September 1994, Series A no. 298, p. 25, § 35), there can be no doubt that concrete expressions constituting hate speech, which may be insulting to particular individuals or groups, are not protected by Article 10 of the Convention.

(b) Application of the above principles in the instant case

42. The Court must consider the impugned "interference" in the light of the case as a whole, including the content of the comments in issue and the context in which they were broadcast, in order to determine whether it was "proportionate to the legitimate aims pursued" and whether the reasons adduced by the national authorities to justify it are "relevant and sufficient" (*see*, among other authorities, *Fressoz and Roire v. France* [GC], no. 29183/95, ECtHR 1999–I). Furthermore, the nature and severity of the penalties imposed are also factors to be taken into account when assessing the proportionality of the interference (*see Skaka v. Poland*, no. 43425/98, § 42, 27 May 2003).

43. The Court observes, firstly, that the programme in question was about a sect whose followers had attracted public attention. The applicant, who was regarded as the leader of the sect and whose views were already known to the public, was invited to take part in the programme for a particular purpose, namely to present the sect and its nonconformist views, including the notion that democratic values were incompatible with its conception of Islam. This topic was widely debated in the Turkish media and concerned a matter of general interest, a sphere in which restrictions on freedom of expression are to be strictly construed.

44. The Court further notes that the format of the programme was designed to encourage an exchange of views or even an argument, in such a way that the opinions expressed would counterbalance each other and the debate would hold the viewers' attention. It notes, as the domestic courts did, that in so far as the debate concerned the presentation of a sect and was limited to an exchange of views on the role of religion in a democratic

society, it gave the impression of seeking to inform the public about a matter of great interest to Turkish society. It further points out that the applicant's conviction resulted not from his participation in a public discussion, but from comments which the domestic courts regarded as "hate speech" beyond the limits of acceptable criticism (*see* paragraph 15 above).

45. The main issue is therefore whether the national authorities correctly exercised their discretion in convicting the applicant for having made the statements in question (*see, mutatis mutandis, Murphy*, cited above, § 72).

46. In order to assess whether the "necessity" of the restriction on the applicant's freedom of expression has been established convincingly, the Court must examine the issue essentially from the standpoint of the reasoning adopted by the national courts. In this connection, the Court notes that the Turkish courts' conclusions related solely to the fact that the applicant had described contemporary secular institutions as "impious," had vehemently criticised concepts such as secularism and democracy and had openly campaigned for sharia (*see* paragraph 15 above).

47. The Turkish courts examined certain statements made by the applicant before reaching the conclusion that he was not entitled to the protection of freedom of expression. For the purposes of the instant case, the Court will divide the statements into three passages.

48. The first passage is the following:

"... anyone calling himself a democrat [or] secularist ... has no religion ... Democracy in Turkey is despotic, merciless and impious [*dinsiz*] ...

This secular ... system is hypocritical [*ikiyüzlü ve münafık*] ... it treats some people in one way and others in another way ...

I am making these comments while fully aware that they represent a crime against the laws of tyranny. Why would I stop speaking? Is there any other way than death?"

In the Court's view, such comments demonstrate an intransigent attitude towards and profound dissatisfaction with contemporary institutions in Turkey, such as the principle of secularism and democracy. Seen in their context, however, they cannot be construed as a call to violence or as hate speech based on religious intolerance.

49. The second passage is the following:

"... if [a] person has his wedding night after being married by a council official authorised by the Republic of Turkey, the child born of the union will be a *piç* ..."

In Turkish, "*piç*" is a pejorative term referring to children born outside marriage and/or born of adultery and is used in everyday language as an insult designed to cause offence.

Admittedly, the Court cannot overlook the fact that the Turkish people, being deeply attached to a secular way of life of which civil marriage is a part, may legitimately feel that they have been attacked in an unwarranted and offensive manner. It points out, however, that the applicant's statements were made orally during a live television broadcast, so that he had no possibility of reformulating, refining or retracting them before they were made public (*see Fuentes Bobo v. Spain*, no. 39293/98, § 46, 29 February 2000). Similarly, the Court observes that the Turkish courts, which are in a better position than an international court to assess the impact of such comments, did not attach particular importance to that factor. Accordingly, the Court considers that, in balancing the interests of free speech and those of protecting the rights of others under the necessity test in Article 10 § 2 of the Convention, it is appropriate to attach greater weight than the national courts did, in their application of domestic law, to the fact that the applicant was actively participating in a lively public discussion (*see, mutatis mutandis, Nilsen and Johnsen*, cited above, § 52).

50. Lastly, the national courts sought to establish whether the applicant was campaigning for sharia. In that connection they held, in particular (see paragraph 15 above):

> "Mr Bedri Baykam told Mr Gündüz that the aim of the latter's supporters was to 'destroy democracy and set up a regime based on sharia', and the defendant replied: 'Of course, that will happen, that will happen.' [Furthermore,] the defendant acknowledged before this Court that he had made those comments, and stated that the regime based on sharia would be established not by duress, force or weapons but by convincing and persuading the people."

The Turkish courts considered that the means by which the applicant intended to set up a regime based on religious rules were not decisive. * * *

52. In conclusion, having regard to the circumstances of the case as a whole and notwithstanding the national authorities' margin of appreciation, the Court considers that the interference with the applicant's freedom of expression was not based on sufficient reasons for the purposes of Article 10. This finding makes it unnecessary for the Court to pursue its examination in order to determine whether the two-year prison sentence imposed on the applicant, an extremely harsh penalty even taking account of the possibility of parole afforded by Turkish law, was proportionate to the aim pursued.

53. The applicant's conviction accordingly infringed Article 10 of the Convention. * * *

———

CHAPTER X

EQUALITY & FEDERALISM

INTRODUCTION

This final chapter shifts our attention from how equality is pursued in various substantive areas and examines how federalism as a system of political power sharing shapes equality. In federal systems, sovereign power is typically shared between a national or central governing body and subnational or more local entities, like states in the U.S., provinces in Canada, or "Member States" in the European Union. A decentralized national government leaves most political power to subnational governments, while a centralized government controls the exercise of subnational powers. And because people are citizens or members both of the national and subnational governments, methods of providing for equality in a decentralized federal government will tend to vary across local, regional and national scales, while equality in a centralized federal government will strive towards uniformity. Relatedly, while federalism refers to divisions of power between national and subnational entities, concerns around separation of powers between branches of government often arise as well. In other words, we can distinguish federalism as the vertical division of power from separation of powers as the horizontal division of powers in a polity. The designation of powers to legislative, executive and/or judicial bodies, are for the most part set up by respective constitutions, or in the case of the European Union, by treaty. And within this institutional design, how much power is given to the judicial body ultimately impacts how federalism issues are resolved.

The U.S. is recognized as the oldest federal government in modern history. The U.S. Constitution contains two enumerations of Congress's affirmative power to legislate to the States. Article I, Section 8, provides to Congress the power to "borrow money...[t]o regulate Commerce with foreign Nations, and among the several States" and "[t]o establish an uniform Rule of Naturalization...". And Section 5 of the 14th Amendment provides that "The Congress shall have power to enforce, by appropriate legislation, the provisions of this article." Yet, these enumerated powers are limited by the default reservation of powers to the states by the 10th Amendment, which provides that "[t]he powers not delegated to the United States by the Constitution, nor prohibited by it to the States, are reserved to the States respectively, or to the people." As well, the 11th Amendment, which provides that "The Judicial power of the United States shall not be construed to extend to any suit in law or equity, commenced or prosecuted against one of the United States by Citizens of another State, or by Citizens or Subjects of any Foreign State", has been interpreted to guarantee that nonconsenting states generally may not be sued by citizens in federal courts. One of the most significant ways Congress has exercised its federal powers over State sovereignty has been to attach conditions to receipt of federal monies, as well as to ensure the enforcement of substantive 14th Amendment rights through Section 5 legislation.

Whether and to what extent the U.S. federal structure should be or has been a template for other political systems across the world is a contested issue. Indeed, whether Europe through its various multinational treaties and supranational governing bodies has become a federal system is widely debated. Of issue here is whether European law and supranational governing bodies have been accompanied by equivalent supranational developments in more or less unified culture, identity and political ideals. However, it is still possible to discern a line of cases that grapples with issues associated with federalism without having to resolve this debate over whether Europe is today a federation. These cases, excerpted below, deal specifically with how much power the European Court of Justice (ECJ) and the European Court of Human Rights (ECtHR) have to enforce European treaties on member states.

This chapter also presents materials on the development of federalism in India, South Africa and Iraq. In these relatively new and developing countries, federalism issues emerge less as conflicts of power-sharing between definitive entities, as the U.S. with states, or in the EU with nations. Federalism issues are entangled with autonomous entities such as communities, religious institutions and ethnic groups that have not enjoyed the status of a formal political government or sovereign power. The key historical difference between federalism in these cases from the Global South and U.S. and EU federalism is that the question of how to recognize diversity and difference in new or transitional countries has been explicitly, from the outset, debated and incorporated into constitutional language and jurisprudence.

As you read through the following materials, consider how changing arrangements of national and subnational powers are more or less protective of minority group rights. Do strong federal laws provide more protection for minority groups? Or does subnational autonomy provide more protection? Are there particular historical and social conditions that call for more federal power, or more subnational power, to provide for effective equality? Overall, what options of flexible combination, or strict partitioning appear more successful? And how does this structural organization of political power then shape how people organize and imagine legal reforms?

————

A. THE UNITED STATES

California Federal Savings and Loan Assoc. v. Guerra

479 U.S. 272 (1987)

■ JUSTICE MARSHALL delivered the opinion of the Court.

The question presented is whether Title VII of the Civil Rights Act of 1964, as amended by the Pregnancy Discrimination Act of 1978, pre-empts a state statute that requires employers to provide leave and reinstatement to employees disabled by pregnancy.

I

California's Fair Employment and Housing Act (FEHA) is a comprehensive statute that prohibits discrimination in employment and housing. [* * *] Subdivision (b)(2)—the provision at issue here—is the only portion of the statute that applies to employers subject to Title VII. *See* § 12945(e). It requires these employers to provide female employees an unpaid pregnancy disability leave of up to four months. Respondent Fair Employment and Housing Commission, the state agency authorized to interpret the FEHA, has construed § 12945(b)(2) to require California employers to reinstate an employee returning from such pregnancy leave to the job she previously held, unless it is no longer available due to business necessity. In the latter case, the employer must make a reasonable, good-faith effort to place the employee in a substantially similar job. The statute does not compel employers to provide *paid* leave to pregnant employees. Accordingly, the only benefit pregnant workers actually derive from § 12945(b)(2) is a qualified right to reinstatement.

Title VII of the Civil Rights Act of 1964, 42 U.S.C. § 2000e *et seq.,* also prohibits various forms of employment discrimination, including discrimination on the basis of sex. However, in *General Electric Co. v. Gilbert,* 429 U.S. 125, 97 S.Ct. 401, 50 L.Ed.2d 343 (1976), this Court ruled that discrimination on the basis of pregnancy was not sex discrimination under Title VII. In response to the *Gilbert* decision, Congress passed the Pregnancy Discrimination Act of 1978 (PDA), 42 U.S.C. § 2000e(k). The PDA specifies that sex discrimination includes discrimination on the basis of pregnancy.

II

Petitioner California Federal Savings & Loan Association (Cal Fed) is a federally chartered savings and loan association based in Los Angeles; it is an employer covered by both Title VII and § 12945(b)(2). Cal Fed has a facially neutral leave policy that permits employees who have completed three months of service to take unpaid leaves of absence for a variety of reasons, including disability and pregnancy. Although it is Cal Fed's policy to try to provide an employee taking unpaid leave with a similar position upon returning, Cal Fed expressly reserves the right to terminate an employee who has taken a leave of absence if a similar position is not available.

Lillian Garland was employed by Cal Fed as a receptionist for several years. In January 1982, she took a pregnancy disability leave. When she was able to return to work in April of that year, Garland notified Cal Fed, but was informed that her job had been filled and that there were no receptionist or similar positions available. Garland filed a complaint with respondent Department of Fair Employment and Housing, which issued an administrative accusation against Cal Fed on her behalf. Respondent charged Cal Fed with violating § 12945(b)(2) of the FEHA. [Procedural history omitted]

III

A

In determining whether a state statute is pre-empted by federal law and therefore invalid under the Supremacy Clause of the Constitution, our sole task is to ascertain the intent of Congress. Federal law may supersede state law in several different ways. First, when acting within constitutional limits, Congress is empowered to pre-empt state law by so stating in express terms. Second, congressional intent to pre-empt state law in a particular area may be inferred where the scheme of federal regulation is sufficiently comprehensive to make reasonable the inference that Congress "left no room" for supplementary state regulation. Neither of these bases for pre-emption exists in this case. Congress has explicitly disclaimed any intent categorically to pre-empt state law or to "occupy the field" of employment discrimination law.

As a third alternative, in those areas where Congress has not completely displaced state regulation, federal law may nonetheless pre-empt state law to the extent it actually conflicts with federal law. Such a conflict occurs either because "compliance with both federal and state regulations is a physical impossibility," [citation omitted] or because the state law stands "as an obstacle to the accomplishment and execution of the full purposes and objectives of Congress." [citation omitted] Nevertheless, pre-emption is not to be lightly presumed.

This third basis for pre-emption is at issue in this case. In two sections of the 1964 Civil Rights Act, §§ 708 and 1104, Congress has indicated that state laws will be pre-empted only if they actually conflict with federal law. Section 708 of Title VII provides:

"Nothing in this title shall be deemed to exempt or relieve any person from any liability, duty, penalty, or punishment provided by any present or future law of any State or political subdivision of a State, other than any such law which purports to require or permit the doing of any act which would be an unlawful employment practice under this title." 78 Stat. 262, 42 U.S.C. § 2000e-7.

Section 1104 of Title XI, applicable to all titles of the Civil Rights Act, establishes the following standard for pre-emption:

"Nothing contained in any title of this Act shall be construed as indicating an intent on the part of Congress to occupy the field in which any such title operates to the exclusion of State laws on the same subject matter, nor shall any provision of this Act be construed as invalidating any provision of State law unless such provision is inconsistent with any of the purposes of this Act, or any provision thereof." 78 Stat. 268, 42 U.S.C. § 2000h-4.

Accordingly, there is no need to infer congressional intent to pre-empt state laws from the substantive provisions of Title VII; these two sections provide a "reliable indicium of congressional intent with respect to state authority" to regulate employment practice. [* * *]

In order to decide whether the California statute requires or permits employers to violate Title VII, as amended by the PDA, or is inconsistent with the purposes of the statute, we must determine whether the PDA prohibits the States from requiring employers to provide reinstatement to pregnant workers, regardless of their policy for disabled workers generally.

B

Petitioners argue that the language of the federal statute itself unambiguously rejects California's "special treatment" approach to pregnancy discrimination, thus rendering any resort to the legislative history unnecessary. They contend that the second clause of the PDA forbids an employer to treat pregnant employees any differently than other disabled employees. Because " '[t]he purpose of Congress is the ultimate touchstone' " of the pre-emption inquiry, [citations omitted] however, we must examine the PDA's language against the background of its legislative history and historical context. As to the language of the PDA, "[i]t is a 'familiar rule, that a thing may be within the letter of the statute and yet not within the statute, because not within its spirit, nor within the intention of its makers.' " [citations omitted]

It is well established that the PDA was passed in reaction to this Court's decision in [*Gilbert*]. "When Congress amended Title VII in 1978, it unambiguously expressed its disapproval of both the holding and the reasoning of the Court in the *Gilbert* decision." [* * *] Rather than imposing a limitation on the remedial purpose of the PDA, we believe that the second clause was intended to overrule the holding in *Gilbert* and to illustrate how discrimination against pregnancy is to be remedied. [citations omitted] Accordingly, subject to certain limitations, we agree [. . .] that Congress intended the PDA to be "a floor beneath which pregnancy disability benefits may not drop—not a ceiling above which they may not rise." [citation omitted]

The context in which Congress considered the issue of pregnancy discrimination supports this view of the PDA. Congress had before it extensive evidence of discrimination *against* pregnancy, particularly in disability and health insurance programs like those challenged in *Gilbert* [. . .]. The Reports, debates, and hearings make abundantly clear that Congress intended the PDA to provide relief for working women and to end discrimination against pregnant workers. In contrast to the thorough account of discrimination against pregnant workers, the legislative history is devoid of any discussion of preferential treatment of pregnancy, beyond acknowledgments of the existence of state statutes providing for such preferential treatment. *See infra* this page. Opposition to the PDA came from those concerned with the cost of including pregnancy in health and disability-benefit plans and the application of the bill to abortion, not from those who favored special accommodation of pregnancy.

In support of their argument that the PDA prohibits employment practices that favor pregnant women, petitioners and several *amici* cite statements in the legislative history to the effect that the PDA does not *require* employers to extend any benefits to pregnant women that they do not already provide to other disabled employees. For example, the House Report explained that the proposed legislation "does not require employers to treat pregnant employees in any particular manner. . . . H.R. 6075 in no way requires the institution of any new programs where none currently exist." We do not interpret these references to support petitioners' construction of the statute. On the contrary, if Congress had intended to *prohibit* preferential treatment, it would have been the height of understatement to say only that the legislation would not *require* such conduct. It is hardly conceivable that Congress would have extensively discussed only its intent not to require preferential treatment if in fact it had intended to prohibit such treatment.

* * * Title VII, as amended by the PDA, and California's pregnancy disability leave statute share a common goal. The purpose of Title VII is "to achieve equality of employment opportunities and remove barriers that have operated in the past to favor an identifiable group of ... employees over other employees." [citations omitted] Rather than limiting existing Title VII principles and objectives, the PDA extends them to cover pregnancy. As Senator Williams, a sponsor of the Act, stated: "The entire thrust ... behind this legislation is to guarantee women the basic right to participate fully and equally in the workforce, without denying them the fundamental right to full participation in family life."

Section 12945(b)(2) also promotes equal employment opportunity. By requiring employers to reinstate women after a reasonable pregnancy disability leave, § 12945(b)(2) ensures that they will not lose their jobs on account of pregnancy disability. California's approach is consistent with the dissenting opinion of Justice Brennan in [*Gilbert*] which Congress adopted in enacting the PDA. [* * *] By "taking pregnancy into account," California's pregnancy disability-leave statute allows women, as well as men, to have families without losing their jobs.* * *

IV

Thus, petitioners' facial challenge to § 12945(b)(2) fails. The statute is not pre-empted by Title VII, as amended by the PDA, because it is not inconsistent with the purposes of the federal statute, nor does it require the doing of an act which is unlawful under Title VII.

The judgment of the Court of Appeals is

Affirmed.

Equal Protection by Law: Federal Antidiscrimination Legislation After Morrison and Kimel

110 Yale L.J. 441 (2000), pp. 442–455

■ Robert C. Post & Reva B. Siegel

Last Term, the Supreme Court sent ominous signals about the future of federal antidiscrimination law. The Court twice ruled that Congress lacked power under Section 5 of the Fourteenth Amendment to enact laws prohibiting discrimination. In *Kimel v. Florida Board of Regents*, the Court concluded that Section 5 did not give Congress the power to abrogate state Eleventh Amendment immunity for suits under the Age Discrimination in

Employment Act of 1967, and in *United States v. Morrison*, the Court held that Congress was without power under either the Commerce Clause or Section 5 to enact a provision of the Violence Against Women Act of 1994 (VAWA) creating a federal civil remedy for victims of gender-motivated violence.

Both *Kimel* and *Morrison* are written in forceful and broad strokes that threaten large stretches of congressional authority under Section 5. Yet the Court's Section 5 holdings were rendered without dissent. Although in *Kimel* there were four Justices prepared to disagree strenuously with the decision's liberal interpretation of Eleventh Amendment immunity, and although in *Morrison* there were four Justices prepared to disagree strenuously with the decision's restrictive interpretation of federal Commerce Clause power, not a single Justice in either case was ready to vote to sustain congressional power under Section 5, even as Justice Breyer identified key deficiencies in *Morrison*'s justification for its Section 5 holding.

This silence is remarkable, yet explicable. Since the New Deal, the Commerce Clause has shaped core understandings of the contours of national power. In the early 1960s, the Supreme Court took the consequential step of upholding the public accommodations provisions of the Civil Rights Act of 1964 on Commerce Clause grounds alone, despite the fact that Congress had asserted authority to enact the legislation under both the Commerce Clause and Section 5 of the Fourteenth Amendment. We have ever since grown habituated to the use of Commerce Clause power to sustain federal antidiscrimination law, never definitively resolving the shape and reach of Section 5 authority.

What might be called the "jurisdictional" compromise of the 1960s was forged at a time when the Commerce Clause seemed to offer boundless support for Congress's authority to enact antidiscrimination laws. But this no longer appears to be the case. Given the Court's current determination to impose limits on Congress's authority to enact antidiscrimination legislation under the Commerce Clause, the time has come to examine thoroughly, at long last, a question that the Court has now rendered inescapable: the extent of Congress's power to enact antidiscrimination legislation under Section 5 of the Fourteenth Amendment.

A growing number of the Court's decisions now claim authoritatively to resolve this question within a framework that seeks to protect what the Court regards as "vital principles necessary to maintain separation of powers and the federal balance." These decisions are enormously consequential. This past Term represents the first time since Reconstruction that the Court has declared that Congress lacked power to enact legislation prohibiting discrimination. Yet the impact of last Term's decisions is still not clear. The decisions are rife with ambiguity. After *Kimel*, for example, it is uncertain whether and to what extent Congress can exercise its power under Section 5 to redress forms of discrimination that differ from those that courts prohibit in cases arising under Section 1 of the Fourteenth Amendment. It is equally unclear after *Morrison* whether and to what extent antidiscrimination legislation enacted under Section 5 can regulate the conduct of private actors. Depending upon how *Kimel* and *Morrison* are interpreted in subsequent decisions, the Court's Section 5 jurisprudence could develop in quite different directions.* * *

I. The Contemporary Significance of Section 5

The history of federal antidiscrimination law in the twentieth century features two momentous events. The first is *Brown v. Board of Education*, when the Supreme Court breathed new life into Section 1 of the Fourteenth Amendment. The second is the passage of the Civil Rights Act of 1964, the first major federal antidiscrimination legislation enacted since 1875. In debating and drafting the 1964 Act, Congress invoked its power under both the Commerce Clause and Section 5 of the Fourteenth Amendment. But when the Supreme Court came to determine the Act's constitutionality in *Heart of Atlanta Motel v. United States*, it shied away from a confrontation with its own Section 5 precedents, which dated from the first Reconstruction, and chose instead to build on the case law of the New Deal settlement, which ceded very broad powers to Congress to legislate under the Commerce Clause. It translated the question of congressional authority into the relatively simple issue of whether "Congress had a rational basis for finding that racial discrimination . . . affected commerce."

The decision fixed a fateful pattern. While Congress, in what might be called a second Reconstruction, continued to invoke its powers to enact antidiscrimination legislation under Section 5 of the Fourteenth Amendment, *Heart of Atlanta* set a precedent that invited judicial ratification of this legislation on alternative grounds, most notably on the basis of the Commerce Clause. This pattern persisted during the ensuing years, progressively obscuring the relationship of federal antidiscrimination legislation to Section 5, even as Congress and the Court continued to reason about antidiscrimination legislation as enforcing the equality values of the Fourteenth Amendment. Over time, disparities emerged between the requirements of federal antidiscrimination legislation and the constitutional requirements that courts were willing to enforce under Section 1 of the Fourteenth Amendment. But these differences were not generally understood by the Court or others as constitutionally problematic; they could always be accommodated by the broad authority of the Commerce Clause.

Recently, however, three lines of decision have combined to disturb this arrangement. First, the Court has signaled its intention to abrogate the New Deal settlement and reassert judicial control over the scope of Commerce Clause power. In *United States v. Lopez*, the Court struck down the Gun–Free School Zones Act of 1990 as exceeding Congress's authority to regulate interstate commerce. In *Morrison*, the Court expanded the logic of *Lopez* into the domain of federal civil rights law, holding that 42 U.S.C. § 13981, the provision of VAWA creating a federal civil remedy for victims of gender-motivated violence, could not be sustained as an exercise of Commerce Clause power. The Court stressed that the reach of § 13981 was not limited by any "jurisdictional element" connecting federally regulated behavior to interstate commerce and that § 13981 sought to assert federal control over "noneconomic activity" that was peculiarly within an area "of traditional state regulation." Despite extensive congressional findings documenting the adverse effects of gender-motivated violence on interstate commerce—findings far more extensive than those that the Court had found adequate to sustain the Civil Rights Act of 1964 in *Heart of Atlanta*— the Court ruled that upholding this exercise of the commerce power over an activity that is not itself "commercial" or "economic" in character would obliterate the "distinction between what is truly national and what is truly local." If § 13981 were to be upheld as a constitutional exercise of congressional power, therefore, it would have to be under Section 5 of the Fourteenth Amendment.

Lopez and *Morrison* impose uncertain restrictions on the use of the commerce power. Although the present Court does not seem inclined to attack *Heart of Atlanta* by holding that federal regulation of discrimination in public accommodations or employment involves matters that are "noneconomic" or "truly local," the Court has now begun to use criteria to restrict Congress's power under the Commerce Clause that are indifferent to the varying forms and settings in which discrimination occurs. The Court's new Commerce Clause cases tend toward equating national power with power to regulate "economic" events, activities, and transactions, a category whose definition is not especially clear, but whose purpose seems to be to restrict Congress from enacting legislation that intrudes upon "traditional" areas of state regulation, like education, the family, or the criminal regulation of intrastate violence.

Morrison dramatically illustrates how the Court's revived limitations on the commerce power now materially constrict the effective scope of federal antidiscrimination legislation. Because exercise of VAWA's civil rights remedy would impose federal constraints on violence in the family, the Court treats the law as interfering with "noneconomic" matters that, from the standpoint of the Court's new Commerce Clause jurisprudence, are "local," beyond the scope of legitimate national concern. From the standpoint of Fourteenth Amendment values, however, there is no reason to assume that sex discrimination in the administration of the criminal law is outside federal regulatory concern, because the state's failure to enforce prohibitions on assault in an evenhanded way leaves women unprotected from attack by family members as well as by others. Discrimination in state regulation of family life has no special immunity from the reach of the Fourteenth Amendment. The Court's recent limitations on Congress's powers under the Commerce Clause thus focus renewed attention on Section 5 as an alternative source of constitutional authority, one adequate to the task of combating discrimination in whatever social forms or settings it happens to manifest itself.

This reinvigorated focus on Section 5 has been intensified by a second line of recent decisions. In its 1996 opinion in *Seminole Tribe v. Florida*, the Court held that congressional legislation enacted pursuant to Article I powers, such as the Commerce Clause, cannot abrogate the Eleventh Amendment immunity of states, which "prevents congressional authorization of suits by private parties against unconsenting States" in federal courts. Two years later, in *Alden v. Maine*, the Court held that this immunity also prohibited the federal government from subjecting "nonconsenting States to private suits for damages in state courts."

The contours of Eleventh Amendment immunity are extremely complex, but suffice it to say that the Amendment bars suits by private parties that seek money or damages "resulting from a past breach of a legal duty." Since large stretches of federal law are ordinarily enforced by exactly such suits, it is fair to conclude that the "net result" of *Seminole Tribe* and *Alden* will be "that Congress may regulate the states, but in the end will lack the practical tools necessary to do so with maximum effectiveness." This would certainly be true of most federal antidiscrimination law, which is normally enforced by private suits against the states. In fact, federal antidiscrimination law that cannot be sustained as an exercise of Section 5 power will probably be enforced against the states primarily through the cumbersome and unwieldy interventions of federal agencies.

Eleventh Amendment immunity, however, can be abrogated by legislation enacted "pursuant to Congress's § 5 power." The upshot is that the scope of Section 5 power has now become the measure of what federal antidiscrimination legislation may effectively be applied to the states. The Court's evasion in *Heart of Atlanta* has thus come home to roost. In the past thirty years, Congress has exercised its commerce authority to develop a rich and complex jurisprudence of federal antidiscrimination legislation, which is in many of its particulars in tension with judicial enforcement of Section 1 of the Fourteenth Amendment. The question of whether this law may properly be applied to the states will depend upon how the Court chooses to conceptualize the relationship between Section 5 and Section 1.

Much is at stake in this issue. So, for example, the Court has interpreted Section 1 to require a showing of "discriminatory purpose" as a prerequisite for a judicial finding of constitutional invalidity, yet a violation of Title VII can be established merely upon a showing of "disparate impact." In order to uphold the application of the disparate impact standard of Title VII to a state, the Eleventh Circuit recently felt itself obliged to reconcile these two standards by concluding that "although the form of the disparate impact inquiry differs from that used in a case challenging state action directly under the Fourteenth Amendment, the core injury targeted by both methods of analysis remains the same: intentional discrimination."

If the conclusion of the Eleventh Circuit were taken seriously, it would suggest a fundamental reworking of an important area of Title VII jurisprudence. We might then imagine Title VII divided between those standards suitable for application to states, because duplicative of judicial practice under Section 1, and those standards suitable for application to private parties, because developed under the aegis of the Commerce Clause. Or we might imagine an incremental judicial reworking of the body of Title VII law so as to bring it into line with the constricted set of standards constitutionally applicable to states. Neither alternative is attractive. They can be avoided, however, only if we are able to distinguish congressional power under Section 5 from judicially enforceable standards under Section 1.

But it is just this possibility that appears to be threatened by the Court's newly developing case law on the scope of Congress's powers under the enforcement clause of the Fourteenth Amendment. We are referring, of course, to a third line of decisions, initiated by the Court's 1997 decision in

City of Boerne v. Flores, holding that the Religious Freedom Restoration Act of 1993 (RFRA) was not a constitutional exercise of Section 5 power. *Boerne* was the first significant decision explicitly to address the scope of Section 5 in almost twenty years.

Congress enacted RFRA "in direct response" to the Court's decision in *Employment Division v. Smith*, which had sharply constricted the approach of *Sherbert v. Verner* by holding that constitutional rights of free exercise of religion would not, for the most part, be violated by neutral, generally applicable regulations of conduct. Congress disagreed and passed RFRA "to restore the compelling interest test as set forth in *Sherbert v. Verner* . . . and to guarantee its application in all cases where free exercise of religion is substantially burdened." RFRA was justified as an exercise of Congress's Section 5 power "to enforce" First Amendment free exercise rights as incorporated in the Due Process Clause of Section 1 of the Fourteenth Amendment.

In *Boerne*, the Court declared that Congress lacked power under Section 5 to enact RFRA. It began its analysis by observing "that § 5 is 'a positive grant of legislative power' to Congress" and that its "scope" was therefore to be interpreted in "broad terms." Reaffirming *Katzenbach v. Morgan*, the Court stated that "[i]t is for Congress in the first instance to 'determin[e] whether and what legislation is needed to secure the guarantees of the Fourteenth Amendment,' and its conclusions are entitled to much deference." But the Court then distinguished between the power "to enforce" the provisions of the Fourteenth Amendment and "the power to determine what constitutes a constitutional violation." It held that Section 5 authorized the former, but not the latter:

> Congress's power under § 5 . . . extends only to "enforc[ing]" the provisions of the Fourteenth Amendment. The Court has described this power as "remedial[.]" The design of the Amendment and the text of § 5 are inconsistent with the suggestion that Congress has the power to decree the substance of the Fourteenth Amendment's restrictions on the States. Legislation which alters the meaning of the Free Exercise Clause cannot be said to be enforcing the Clause. Congress does not enforce a constitutional right by changing what the right is.

The Court initially argued that maintaining the distinction between the power to remedy constitutional violations and the power to determine the nature of constitutional rights was necessary in order to preserve the supremacy of the Constitution. "If Congress could define its own powers by altering the Fourteenth Amendment's meaning, no longer would the Constitution be 'superior paramount law, unchangeable by ordinary means.' It would be 'on a level with ordinary legislative acts, and, like other acts, . . . alterable when the legislature shall please to alter it.' "

But because the Constitution remains "superior, paramount law" whether interpreted by the Court or by Congress, so long as either institution chooses to regard it as such, what really seems to be at stake for the Court in the distinction between remedial and substantive legislation is the preservation of judicial control over the ultimate meaning of the Constitution, at least in the context of cases properly litigated before the Court. In *Boerne*, the Court was plainly provoked by Congress's openly expressed purpose to nullify the Court's own interpretation of the First Amendment in *Smith*. RFRA posed a direct challenge to the Court's interpretation of the Free Exercise Clause, a challenge that the Court was determined to resist:

> When the Court has interpreted the Constitution, it has acted within the province of the Judicial Branch, which embraces the duty to say what the law is.... When the political branches of the Government act against the background of a judicial interpretation of the Constitution already issued, it must be understood that in later cases and controversies the Court will treat its precedents with the respect due them under settled principles, including stare decisis, and contrary expectations must be disappointed.... [I]t is this Court's precedent, not RFRA, which must control.

Boerne thus reasserts the basic precept of *Marbury*: In the last instance, it is for "the Judicial Branch ... to say what the law is."

Boerne frankly concedes that "the line between measures that remedy or prevent unconstitutional actions and measures that make a substantive change in the governing law is not easy to discern, and [that] Congress must have wide latitude in determining where it lies." But in a context in which "common sense" suggested that RFRA was "a congressional effort to overrule the Supreme Court on a point of constitutional interpretation," the Court insisted that the line "exists and must be observed."

To ensure that Congress would not exceed its legitimate powers under the Fourteenth Amendment, Boerne proposed that the line be discerned by a test of "congruence and proportionality between the injury to be prevented or remedied and the means adopted to that end. Lacking such a connection, legislation may become substantive in operation and effect."

The Court concluded that:

> RFRA cannot be considered remedial, preventive legislation, if those terms are to have any meaning. RFRA is so out of proportion to a supposed remedial or preventive object that it cannot be understood as responsive to, or designed to prevent, unconstitutional behavior. It appears, instead, to attempt a substantive change in constitutional protections.

The Court's new interest in constraining Section 5 power, when considered in light of the developments in Commerce Clause and Eleventh Amendment jurisprudence we have just discussed, raises disconcerting questions for the future of federal antidiscrimination law. Limitations on Commerce Clause power, imposed in the name of federalism by *Lopez* and *Seminole Tribe*, have reemphasized the importance of congressional Section 5 power, while *Boerne* has simultaneously imposed a new and uncertain restriction on the nature of that power. When the 1999 Term began, the Court had not yet applied either its resurgent federalism or its intensified solicitude for separation of powers to federal antidiscrimination legislation. But this restraint ended in January 2000, when *Kimel* held that Congress was without power under Section 5 to enact the Age Discrimination in Employment Act of 1967 (ADEA). Five months later, *Morrison* held that Congress was without power under either the Commerce Clause or Section

5 to create in VAWA a civil cause of action for victims of gender-motivated violence. * * *

Board of Trustees of University of Alabama v. Garrett

531 U.S. 356 (2001)

■ CHIEF JUSTICE REHNQUIST delivered the opinion of the Court.

We decide here whether employees of the State of Alabama may recover money damages by reason of the State's failure to comply with the provisions of Title I of the Americans with Disabilities Act of 1990 (ADA or Act), 104 Stat. 330, 42 U.S.C. §§ 12111–12117. We hold that such suits are barred by the Eleventh Amendment.

The ADA prohibits certain employers, including the States, from "discriminating against a qualified individual with a disability because of the disability of such individual in regard to job application procedures, the hiring, advancement, or discharge of employees, employee compensation, job training, and other terms, conditions, and privileges of employment." §§ 12112(a), 12111(2), (5), (7). To this end, the Act requires employers to "make reasonable accommodations to the known physical or mental limitations of an otherwise qualified individual with a disability who is an applicant or employee, unless [the employer] can demonstrate that the accommodation would impose an undue hardship on the operation of the [employer's] business." § 12112(b)(5)(A).

" 'Reasonable accommodation' may include—"(A) making existing facilities used by employees readily accessible to and usable by individuals with disabilities; and (B) job restructuring, part-time or modified work schedules, reassignment to a vacant position, acquisition or modification of equipment or devices, appropriate adjustment or modifications of examinations, training materials or policies, the provision of qualified readers or interpreters, and other similar accommodations for individuals with disabilities." § 12111(9).

The Act also prohibits employers from "utilizing standards, criteria, or methods of administration . . . that have the effect of discrimination on the basis of disability." § 12112(b)(3)(A).

The Act defines "disability" to include "(A) a physical or mental impairment that substantially limits one or more of the major life activities of such individual; (B) a record of such an impairment; or (C) being regarded as having such an impairment." § 12102(2). A disabled individual is otherwise "qualified" if he or she, "with or without reasonable accommodation, can perform the essential functions of the employment position that such individual holds or desires." § 12111(8).

Respondent Patricia Garrett, a registered nurse, was employed as the Director of Nursing, OB/Gyn/Neonatal Services, for the University of Alabama in Birmingham Hospital. In 1994, Garrett was diagnosed with breast cancer and subsequently underwent a lumpectomy, radiation treatment, and chemotherapy. Garrett's treatments required her to take substantial leave from work. Upon returning to work in July 1995, Garrett's supervisor informed Garrett that she would have to give up her Director position. Garrett then applied for and received a transfer to another, lower paying position as a nurse manager.

Respondent Milton Ash worked as a security officer for the Alabama Department of Youth Services (Department). Upon commencing this employment, Ash informed the Department that he suffered from chronic asthma and that his doctor recommended he avoid carbon monoxide and cigarette smoke, and Ash requested that the Department modify his duties to minimize his exposure to these substances. Ash was later diagnosed with sleep apnea and requested, again pursuant to his doctor's recommendation, that he be reassigned to daytime shifts to accommodate his condition. Ultimately, the Department granted none of the requested relief. Shortly after Ash filed a discrimination claim with the Equal Employment Opportunity Commission, he noticed that his performance evaluations were lower than those he had received on previous occasions. * * *

I

* * *Congress may not, of course, base its abrogation of the States' Eleventh Amendment immunity upon the powers enumerated in Article I. [* * *] In *Fitzpatrick* v. *Bitzer,* [citation omitted] however, we held that "the Eleventh Amendment, and the principle of state sovereignty which it embodies, are necessarily limited by the enforcement provisions of § 5 of the Fourteenth Amendment." As a result, we concluded, Congress may subject nonconsenting States to suit in federal court when it does so pursuant to a valid exercise of its § 5 power. Our cases have adhered to this proposition. [citation omitted] Accordingly, the ADA can apply to the States only to the extent that the statute is appropriate § 5 legislation.

* * * Section 5 of the Fourteenth Amendment grants Congress the power to enforce the substantive guarantees contained in § 1 by enacting "appropriate legislation." [citation omitted] Congress is not limited to mere legislative repetition of this Court's constitutional jurisprudence. "Rather, Congress' power 'to enforce' the Amendment includes the authority both to remedy and to deter violation of rights guaranteed thereunder by prohibiting a somewhat broader swath of conduct, including that which is not itself forbidden by the Amendment's text." [citation omitted]

City of Boerne also confirmed, however, the long-settled principle that it is the responsibility of this Court, not Congress, to define the substance of constitutional guarantees. Accordingly, § 5 legislation reaching beyond the scope of § 1's actual guarantees must exhibit "congruence and proportionality between the injury to be prevented or remedied and the means adopted to that end." [citation omitted]

II

The first step in applying these now familiar principles is to identify with some precision the scope of the constitutional right at issue. Here, that inquiry requires us to examine the limitations § 1 of the Fourteenth Amendment places upon States' treatment of the disabled. As we did last

Term in *Kimel*, [citation omitted] we look to our prior decisions under the Equal Protection Clause dealing with this issue.

In *Cleburne* v. *Cleburne Living Center, Inc.*, (1985), we considered an equal protection challenge to a city ordinance requiring a special use permit for the operation of a group home for the mentally retarded. The specific question before us was whether the Court of Appeals had erred by holding that mental retardation qualified as a "quasi-suspect" classification under our equal protection jurisprudence. We answered that question in the affirmative, concluding instead that such legislation incurs only the minimum "rational-basis" review applicable to general social and economic legislation. In a statement that today seems quite prescient, we explained that

> "if the large and amorphous class of the mentally retarded were deemed quasi-suspect for the reasons given by the Court of Appeals, it would be difficult to find a principled way to distinguish a variety of other groups who have perhaps immutable disabilities setting them off from others, who cannot themselves mandate the desired legislative responses, and who can claim some degree of prejudice from at least part of the public at large. One need mention in this respect only the aging, the disabled, the mentally ill, and the infirm. We are reluctant to set out on that course, and we decline to do so."

* * * Thus, the result of *Cleburne* is that States are not required by the Fourteenth Amendment to make special accommodations for the disabled, so long as their actions towards such individuals are rational. They could quite hard headedly—and perhaps hardheartedly—hold to job-qualification requirements which do not make allowance for the disabled. If special accommodations for the disabled are to be required, they have to come from positive law and not through the Equal Protection Clause.

III

Once we have determined the metes and bounds of the constitutional right in question, we examine whether Congress identified a history and pattern of unconstitutional employment discrimination by the States against the disabled. Just as § 1 of the Fourteenth Amendment applies only to actions committed "under color of state law," Congress' § 5 authority is appropriately exercised only in response to state transgressions. [citations omitted] The legislative record of the ADA, however, simply fails to show that Congress did in fact identify a pattern of irrational state discrimination in employment against the disabled.

Respondents contend that the inquiry as to unconstitutional discrimination should extend not only to States themselves, but to units of local governments, such as cities and counties. All of these, they say, are "state actors" for purposes of the Fourteenth Amendment. This is quite true, but the Eleventh Amendment does not extend its immunity to units of local government. [citation omitted] These entities are subject to private claims for damages under the ADA without Congress' ever having to rely on § 5 of the Fourteenth Amendment to render them so. It would make no sense to consider constitutional violations on their part, as well as by the States themselves, when only the States are the beneficiaries of the Eleventh Amendment.

Congress made a general finding in the ADA that "historically, society has tended to isolate and segregate individuals with disabilities, and, despite some improvements, such forms of discrimination against individuals with disabilities continue to be a serious and pervasive social problem." 42 U.S.C. § 12101(a)(2). The record assembled by Congress includes many instances to support such a finding. But the great majority of these incidents do not deal with the activities of States.

* * * Several of these incidents undoubtedly evidence an unwillingness on the part of state officials to make the sort of accommodations for the disabled required by the ADA. Whether they were irrational under our decision in *Cleburne* is more debatable, particularly when the incident is described out of context. But even if it were to be determined that each incident upon fuller examination showed unconstitutional action on the part of the State, these incidents taken together fall far short of even suggesting the pattern of unconstitutional discrimination on which § 5 legislation must be based. [citations omitted] Congress, in enacting the ADA, found that "some 43,000,000 Americans have one or more physical or mental disabilities." 42 U.S.C. § 12101(a)(1). In 1990, the States alone employed more than 4.5 million people. [citation omitted] It is telling, we think, that given these large numbers, Congress assembled only such minimal evidence of unconstitutional state discrimination in employment against the disabled.

* * * Even were it possible to squeeze out of these examples a pattern of unconstitutional discrimination by the States, the rights and remedies created by the ADA against the States would raise the same sort of concerns as to congruence and proportionality as were found in *City of Boerne, supra.* For example, whereas it would be entirely rational (and therefore constitutional) for a state employer to conserve scarce financial resources by hiring employees who are able to use existing facilities, the ADA requires employers to "make existing facilities used by employees readily accessible to and usable by individuals with disabilities." 42 U.S.C. § 12111(9). The ADA does except employers from the "reasonable accommodation" requirement where the employer "can demonstrate that the accommodation would impose an undue hardship on the operation of the business of such covered entity." § 121119. However, even with this exception, the accommodation duty far exceeds what is constitutionally required in that it makes unlawful a range of alternate responses that would be reasonable but would fall short of imposing an "undue burden" upon the employer. The Act also makes it the employer's duty to prove that it would suffer such a burden, instead of requiring (as the Constitution does) that the complaining party negate reasonable bases for the employer's decision.

The ADA also forbids "utilizing standards, criteria, or methods of administration" that disparately impact the disabled, without regard to whether such conduct has a rational basis. § 12112(b)(3)(A). Although disparate impact may be relevant evidence of racial discrimination, *see Washington* v. *Davis,* [citation omitted] (1976) such evidence alone is insufficient even where the Fourteenth Amendment subjects state action to strict scrutiny.* * *

The ADA's constitutional shortcomings are apparent when the Act is compared to Congress' efforts in the Voting Rights Act of 1965 to respond to a serious pattern of constitutional violations. In *South Carolina* v. *Katzenbach,* [citation omitted] (1966), we considered whether the Voting Rights Act was "appropriate" legislation to enforce the Fifteenth Amendment's protection against racial discrimination in voting. Concluding that it was a valid exercise of Congress' enforcement power under § 2 of the Fifteenth Amendment, we noted that "before enacting the measure, Congress explored with great care the problem of racial discrimination in voting."

In that Act, Congress documented a marked pattern of unconstitutional action by the States. State officials, Congress found, routinely applied voting tests in order to exclude African–American citizens from registering to vote. Congress also determined that litigation had proved ineffective and that there persisted an otherwise inexplicable 50–percentage–point gap in the registration of white and African–American voters in some States. Congress' response was to promulgate in the Voting Rights Act a detailed but limited remedial scheme designed to guarantee meaningful enforcement of the Fifteenth Amendment in those areas of the Nation where abundant evidence of States' systematic denial of those rights was identified.

The contrast between this kind of evidence, and the evidence that Congress considered in the present case, is stark. Congressional enactment of the ADA represents its judgment that there should be a "comprehensive national mandate for the elimination of discrimination against individuals with disabilities." 42 U.S.C. § 12101(b)(1). Congress is the final authority as to desirable public policy, but in order to authorize private individuals to recover money damages against the States, there must be a pattern of discrimination by the States which violates the Fourteenth Amendment, and the remedy imposed by Congress must be congruent and proportional to the targeted violation. Those requirements are not met here, and to uphold the Act's application to the States would allow Congress to rewrite the Fourteenth Amendment law laid down by this Court in *Cleburne*. Section 5 does not so broadly enlarge congressional authority. The judgment of the Court of Appeals is therefore

Reversed.

■ JUSTICE BREYER, with whom JUSTICE STEVENS, JUSTICE SOUTER and JUSTICE GINSBURG join, dissenting.

* * * The Court says that its primary problem with this statutory provision is one of legislative evidence. It says that "Congress assembled only ... minimal evidence of unconstitutional state discrimination in employment." In fact, Congress compiled a vast legislative record documenting "'massive, society-wide discrimination'" against persons with disabilities. [citation omitted] In addition to the information presented at 13 congressional hearings and its own prior experience gathered over 40 years during which it contemplated and enacted considerable similar legislation

Congress created a special task force to assess the need for comprehensive legislation. That task force held hearings in every State, attended by more than 30,000 people, including thousands who had experienced discrimination first hand. [citation omitted] At the task force hearings, Congress' own hearings, and an analysis of "census data, national polls, and other studies" led Congress to conclude that "people with disabilities, as a group, occupy an inferior status in our society, and are severely disadvantaged socially, vocationally, economically, and educationally." 42 U.S.C. § 12101(a)(6). As to employment, Congress found that "two-thirds of all disabled Americans between the age of 16 and 64 [were] not working at all," even though a large majority wanted to, and were able to, work productively. And Congress found that this discrimination flowed in significant part from "stereotypic assumptions" as well as "purposeful unequal treatment." 42 U.S.C. § 12101(a)(7).

The powerful evidence of discriminatory treatment throughout society in general, including discrimination by private persons and local governments, implicates state governments as well, for state agencies form part of that same larger society. There is no particular reason to believe that they are immune from the "stereotypic assumptions" and pattern of "purposeful unequal treatment" that Congress found prevalent. The Court claims that it "makes no sense" to take into consideration constitutional violations committed by local governments. But the substantive obligation that the Equal Protection Clause creates applies to state and local governmental entities alike. [citation omitted] Local governments often work closely with, and under the supervision of, state officials, and in general, state and local government employers are similarly situated. Nor is determining whether an apparently "local" entity is entitled to Eleventh Amendment immunity as simple as the majority suggests—it often requires a "'detailed examination of the relevant provisions of [state] law.'" [citations omitted]

In any event, there is no need to rest solely upon evidence of discrimination by local governments or general societal discrimination. There are roughly 300 examples of discrimination by state governments themselves in the legislative record. I fail to see how this evidence "falls far short of even suggesting the pattern of unconstitutional discrimination on which § 5 legislation must be based." *Ante*, at 12.* * *

As the Court notes, those who presented instances of discrimination rarely provided additional, independent evidence sufficient to prove in court that, in each instance, the discrimination they suffered lacked justification from a judicial standpoint. [citation omitted] Perhaps this explains the Court's view that there is "minimal evidence of unconstitutional state discrimination." But a legislature is not a court of law. And Congress, unlike courts, must, and does, routinely draw general conclusions—for example, of likely motive or of likely relationship to legitimate need—from anecdotal and opinion-based evidence of this kind, particularly when the evidence lacks strong refutation. * * *

* * * I recognize nonetheless that this statute imposes a burden upon States in that it removes their Eleventh Amendment protection from suit, thereby subjecting them to potential monetary liability. Rules for interpreting § 5 that would provide States with special protection, however, run

counter to the very object of the Fourteenth Amendment. By its terms, that Amendment prohibits *States* from denying their citizens equal protection of the laws. U.S. Const., Amdt. 14, § 1. Hence "principles of federalism that might otherwise be an obstacle to congressional authority are necessarily overridden by the power to enforce the Civil War Amendments 'by appropriate legislation.' Those Amendments were specifically designed as an expansion of federal power and an intrusion on state sovereignty." [citations omitted] And, ironically, the greater the obstacle the Eleventh Amendment poses to the creation by Congress of the kind of remedy at issue here—the decentralized remedy of private damage actions—the more Congress, seeking to cure important national problems, such as the problem of disability discrimination before us, will have to rely on more uniform remedies, such as federal standards and court injunctions, 42 U.S.C. § 12188 (a)(2), which are sometimes draconian and typically more intrusive. [citations omitted] For these reasons, I doubt that today's decision serves any constitutionally based federalism interest.

The Court, through its evidentiary demands, its non-deferential review, and its failure to distinguish between judicial and legislative constitutional competencies, improperly invades a power that the Constitution assigns to Congress. [citations omitted] Its decision saps § 5 of independent force, effectively "confining the legislative power ... to the insignificant role of abrogating only those state laws that the judicial branch [is] prepared to adjudge unconstitutional." Whether the Commerce Clause does or does not enable Congress to enact this provision, [citation omitted] in my view, § 5 gives Congress the necessary authority. For the reasons stated, I respectfully dissent.

[Appendices omitted]

Nevada v. Hibbs

538 U.S. 721 (2003)

■ CHIEF JUSTICE REHNQUIST delivered the opinion of the Court, in which JUSTICE O'CONNOR, JUSTICE SOUTER, JUSTICE GINSBURG and JUSTICE BREYER joined.

The Family and Medical Leave Act of 1993 (FMLA or Act) entitles eligible employees to take up to 12 work weeks of unpaid leave annually for any of several reasons, including the onset of a "serious health condition" in an employee's spouse, child, or parent. 107 Stat. 9, 29 U.S.C. § 2612(a)(1)(C). The Act creates a private right of action to seek both equitable relief and money damages "against any employer (including a public agency) in any Federal or State court of competent jurisdiction," § 2617(a)(2), should that employer "interfere with, restrain, or deny the exercise of" FMLA rights, § 2615(a)(1). We hold that employees of the State of Nevada may recover money damages in the event of the State's failure to comply with the family-care provision of the Act.

Petitioners include the Nevada Department of Human Resources (Department) and two of its officers. Respondent William Hibbs (hereinafter respondent) worked for the Department's Welfare Division. In April and May 1997, he sought leave under the FMLA to care for his ailing wife, who was recovering from a car accident and neck surgery. The Department granted his request for the full 12 weeks of FMLA leave and authorized him to use the leave intermittently as needed between May and December 1997. Respondent did so until August 5, 1997, after which he did not return to work. In October 1997, the Department informed respondent that he had exhausted his FMLA leave, that no further leave would be granted, and that he must report to work by November 12, 1997. Respondent failed to do so and was terminated.

Respondent sued petitioners in the United States District Court seeking damages and injunctive and declaratory relief for, *inter alia,* violations of 29 U.S.C. § 2612(a)(1)(C). [procedural history omitted]

For over a century now, we have made clear that the Constitution does not provide for federal jurisdiction over suits against nonconsenting States. [citations omitted]

Congress may, however, abrogate such immunity in federal court if it makes its intention to abrogate unmistakably clear in the language of the statute and acts pursuant to a valid exercise of its power under § 5 of the Fourteenth Amendment. [citation omitted] The clarity of Congress' intent here is not fairly debatable. The Act enables employees to seek damages "against any employer (including a public agency) in any Federal or State court of competent jurisdiction," and Congress has defined "public agency" to include both "the government of a State or political subdivision thereof" and "any agency of ... a State, or a political subdivision of a State," §§ 203(x), 2611(4)(A)(iii). [* * *] This case turns, then, on whether Congress acted within its constitutional authority when it sought to abrogate the States' immunity for purposes of the FMLA's family-leave provision.

In enacting the FMLA, Congress relied on two of the powers vested in it by the Constitution: its Article I commerce power and its power under § 5 of the Fourteenth Amendment to enforce that Amendment's guarantees. Congress may not abrogate the States' sovereign immunity pursuant to its Article I power over commerce. Congress may, however, abrogate States' sovereign immunity through a valid exercise of its § 5 power, for "the Eleventh Amendment, and the principle of state sovereignty which it embodies, are necessarily limited by the enforcement provisions of § 5 of the Fourteenth Amendment." [citations omitted]

Two provisions of the Fourteenth Amendment are relevant here: Section 5 grants Congress the power "to enforce" the substantive guarantees of § 1—among them, equal protection of the laws—by enacting "appropriate legislation." Congress may, in the exercise of its § 5 power, do more than simply proscribe conduct that we have held unconstitutional. [* * *] Congress may enact so-called prophylactic legislation that proscribes facially constitutional conduct, in order to prevent and deter unconstitutional conduct.

City of Boerne also confirmed, however, that it falls to this Court, not Congress, to define the substance of constitutional guarantees. [* * *] We distinguish appropriate prophylactic legislation from "substantive redefinition of the Fourteenth Amendment right at issue," [citation omitted] by applying the test set forth in *City of Boerne:* Valid § 5 legislation must exhibit "congruence and proportionality between the injury to be prevented or remedied and the means adopted to that end," [citation omitted].

The FMLA aims to protect the right to be free from gender-based discrimination in the workplace. We have held that statutory classifications that distinguish between males and females are subject to heightened scrutiny. [citation omitted] For a gender-based classification to withstand such scrutiny, it must "serv[e] important governmental objectives," and "the discriminatory means employed [must be] substantially related to the achievement of those objectives." The State's justification for such a classification "must not rely on overbroad generalizations about the different talents, capacities, or preferences of males and females." [citation omitted] We now inquire whether Congress had evidence of a pattern of constitutional violations on the part of the States in this area.

The history of the many state laws limiting women's employment opportunities is chronicled in—and, until relatively recently, was sanctioned by—this Court's own opinions. [* * *] Such laws were based on the related beliefs that (1) a woman is, and should remain, "the center of home and family life," [citation omitted], and (2) "a proper discharge of [a woman's] maternal functions—having in view not merely her own health, but the well-being of the race—justif[ies] legislation to protect her from the greed as well as the passion of man," [citation omitted]. * * *

Congress responded to this history of discrimination by abrogating States' sovereign immunity in Title VII of the Civil Rights Act of 1964, [citation omitted] and we sustained this abrogation in *Fitzpatrick.* But state gender discrimination did not cease. [* * *] The long and extensive history of sex discrimination prompted us to hold that measures that differentiate on the basis of gender warrant heightened scrutiny; here, as in *Fitzpatrick,* the persistence of such unconstitutional discrimination by the States justifies Congress' passage of prophylactic § 5 legislation.

As the FMLA's legislative record reflects, a 1990 Bureau of Labor Statistics (BLS) survey stated that 37 percent of surveyed private-sector employees were covered by maternity leave policies, while only 18 percent were covered by paternity leave policies.* * *

Congress also heard testimony that "[p]arental leave for fathers . . . is rare. Even . . . [w]here child-care leave policies do exist, men, *both in the public and private sectors,* receive notoriously discriminatory treatment in their requests for such leave." [citation omitted] Many States offered women extended "maternity" leave that far exceeded the typical 4- to 8-week period of physical disability due to pregnancy and childbirth, but very few States granted men a parallel benefit: Fifteen States provided women up to one year of extended maternity leave, while only four provided men with the same. [citation omitted] This and other differential leave policies were not attributable to any differential physical needs of men and women, but rather to the pervasive sex-role stereotype that caring for family members is women's work.

Finally, Congress had evidence that, even where state laws and policies were not facially discriminatory, they were applied in discriminatory ways. It was aware of the "serious problems with the discretionary nature of family leave," because when "the authority to grant leave and to arrange the length of that leave rests with individual supervisors," it leaves "employees open to discretionary and possibly unequal treatment." * * *

In sum, the States' record of unconstitutional participation in, and fostering of, gender-based discrimination in the administration of leave benefits is weighty enough to justify the enactment of prophylactic § 5 legislation.

We reached the opposite conclusion in *Garrett* and *Kimel*. In those cases, the § 5 legislation under review responded to a purported tendency of state officials to make age- or disability-based distinctions. Under our equal protection case law, discrimination on the basis of such characteristics is not judged under a heightened review standard, and passes muster if there is "a rational basis for doing so at a class-based level, even if it 'is probably not true' that those reasons are valid in the majority of cases." * * *

Here, however, Congress directed its attention to state gender discrimination, which triggers a heightened level of scrutiny. [citation omitted] Because the standard for demonstrating the constitutionality of a gender-based classification is more difficult to meet than our rational-basis test—it must "serv[e] important governmental objectives" and be "substantially related to the achievement of those objectives," [citation omitted]—it was easier for Congress to show a pattern of state constitutional violations. Congress was similarly successful in *South Caroline v. Katzenbach* [citation omitted], where we upheld the Voting Rights Act of 1965: Because racial classifications are presumptively invalid, most of the States' acts of race discrimination violated the Fourteenth Amendment.

* * * We believe that Congress' chosen remedy, the family-care leave provision of the FMLA, is "congruent and proportional to the targeted violation," [citation omitted]. Congress had already tried unsuccessfully to address this problem through Title VII and the amendment of Title VII by the Pregnancy Discrimination Act, 42 U.S.C. § 2000e(k). * * *

By creating an across-the-board, routine employment benefit for all eligible employees, Congress sought to ensure that family-care leave would no longer be stigmatized as an inordinate drain on the workplace caused by female employees, and that employers could not evade leave obligations simply by hiring men. By setting a minimum standard of family leave for *all* eligible employees, irrespective of gender, the FMLA attacks the formerly state-sanctioned stereotype that only women are responsible for family caregiving, thereby reducing employers' incentives to engage in discrimination by basing hiring and promotion decisions on stereotypes.

Indeed, in light of the evidence before Congress, a statute mirroring Title VII, that simply mandated gender equality in the administration of leave benefits, would not have achieved Congress' remedial object. Such a law would allow States to provide for no family leave at all. Where "[t]wo-thirds of the nonprofessional caregivers for older, chronically ill, or disabled persons are working women," [citation omitted] and state practices continue to reinforce the stereotype of women as caregivers, such a policy would exclude far more women than men from the workplace.

Unlike the statutes at issue in *City of Boerne, Kimel,* and *Garrett,* which applied broadly to every aspect of state employers' operations, the FMLA is narrowly targeted at the faultline between work and family—precisely where sex-based overgeneralization has been and remains strongest—and affects only one aspect of the employment relationship. * * *

We also find significant the many other limitations that Congress placed on the scope of this measure. [citations omitted] The FMLA requires only unpaid leave, 29 U.S.C. § 2612(a)(1), and applies only to employees who have worked for the employer for at least one year and provided 1,250 hours of service within the last 12 months, § 2611(2)(A). Employees in high-ranking or sensitive positions are simply ineligible for FMLA leave; of particular importance to the States, the FMLA expressly excludes from coverage state elected officials, their staffs, and appointed policymakers. [citations omitted] Employees must give advance notice of foreseeable leave, § 2612(e), and employers may require certification by a health care provider of the need for leave, § 2613. In choosing 12 weeks as the appropriate leave floor, Congress chose "a middle ground, a period long enough to serve 'the needs of families' but not so long that it would upset 'the legitimate interests of employers.'" [citation omitted] Moreover, the cause of action under the FMLA is a restricted one: The damages recoverable are strictly defined and measured by actual monetary losses, §§ 2617(a)(1)(A)(i)–(iii), and the accrual period for backpay is limited by the Act's 2–year statute of limitations (extended to three years only for willful violations), §§ 2617(c)(1) and (2).

For the above reasons, we conclude that § 2612(a)(1)(C) is congruent and proportional to its remedial object, and can "be understood as responsive to, or designed to prevent, unconstitutional behavior." [citation omitted]

The judgment of the Court of Appeals is therefore

Affirmed.

————

NOTES

1.   Generally, unless power to regulate a specific realm of social life is enumerated to Congress, all other realms are assumed the province of state power. Yet, this Constitutional division is less clear because the federal power over interstate commerce has been able to encompass a variety of social issues that touch upon market structures. As Post and Siegel discuss, *Morrison* exemplifies the failure to establish enough of a link between a social issue and the national economy because domestic violence is seen as too local and thus "noneconomic". Perhaps, as Post and Siegel suggest, it never really made all that much sense for the Court to develop federal civil rights jurisprudence via the Commerce Clause, and the recent turn towards Section 5 is a more historically resonant legal development. Yet, Section 5

analysis, seen in *Garrett* similarly reveals the difficulties establishing links between local, state and national scales of discrimination. Is this difficulty one of evidence? Or could it be also linked to the nature of the discrimination itself?

2. States as semi-autonomous governments have been seen as important sites for developing new legal frameworks. In 1932, Justice Brandeis opined that "It is one of the happy incidents of the federal system that a single courageous state may, if its citizens choose, serve as a laboratory; and try novel social and economic experiments without risk to the rest of the country." *New State Ice Co. v. Liebmann*, 285 U.S. 262, 311 (1932). We might think of this as a trickle up effect, designating how localized innovations in equality law should culminate towards more generalizable norms and approaches at state or national levels. This might be true in the case of some states that have extended the institution of marriage to same-sex couples without risking a moral panic at the local or regional level. Yet, other states have made the exclusion more explicit, creating uneven policies that further expose same-sex couples and families to discrimination.

3. In contrast to the idea that innovations at the local level can trickle up to establish a grounded national trend if not actual reform to federal policy, we have seen, also in the context of same-sex marriage debates, an opposite, trickle down, effect. Nancy Knauer, in her article, *Same–Sex Marriage and Federalism*, 17 Temple Political & Civil Rights Law Review 421–432 (2008), illuminates how the federal articulation of inequality between same-sex and opposite-sex marriage in the 1996 Defense of Marriage Act (DOMA), defining marriage as only between one man and one woman, provided a template for states to enact what are often referred to as "mini-DOMAs". Recently, states have been going beyond the definitional purposes of DOMA-type laws, and adding on provisions which restrict recognition of civil unions and domestic partnerships, prohibit legislatures from granting parallel status, rights and privileges to same-sex couples, and in certain states, criminalize granting a marriage license to same-sex partners. "[T]his new generation of laws could be interpreted to inhibit the ability of courts to apply concepts of 'functional' family or equity to secure certain rights and standing for same-sex partners. Seventeen states have adopted these so-called 'DOMAs with teeth.'" In DOMA, we see the clash between Congress's Article IV power to legislate the kinds of things states might be exempt from giving full faith a credit to and Tenth Amendment state sovereignty over the regulation of marriage and family. What kind of federalism claim might be made in this context? In favor of states that do recognize same-sex marriage? Against these "DOMAs with teeth"? Against DOMA itself?

4. In *Guerra*, the Court looks at the intent of Congress in determining whether the Supremacy Clause preempts similar state legislation. However, if Congress is silent, how do we know whether Congress intended its legislation to create a floor or ceiling on equality? Is it always the case that to assume federal legislation is a floor would widen the possibility for effective equality? And to what extent might an interpretation of this floor/ceiling ambiguity rely on the substantive equality issue?

5.   If Section 1 of the Fourteenth Amendment articulates the substantive goal of equality, then Section 5 provides for the means by which that end could be accomplished. This means-ends structure of the Fourteenth Amendment is what lays the ground for judicial analyses of the congruence and proportionality of a federal statute to the state-perpetrated injury. When congruence or proportionality is not shown, the judicial suspicion is that Congress has used the Fourteenth Amendment as pretext for exceeding its Section 5 powers. Randy Beck, *The Heart of Federalism: Pretext Review of Means–End Relationships, 36 U.C.D.L.Rev. 407*, 440 (2003). Can this suspicion towards pretextual federal civil rights legislation be assuaged by empirical evidence? Is this suspicion a healthy mechanism for balancing powers, or does it skew judicial review in favor of states' rights?

6.   The Supreme Court of Mexico's 2008 decision declaring the constitutionality of Mexico City's legalization of abortion led to a pro-life backlash in seventeen different states which declared that life begins at conception. See Note 1 in the section on Mexico in Chapter VI. Is there a potential federalism issue here, to the extent that women's right to abortion recognized in the decision hinges on when life is regarded in the law to begin? Would a similar legal phenomenon in the U.S. raise issues of federalism? Consider, for example, Mississippi's recent attempt to ratify a constitutional amendment granting zygotes—a fertilized human egg—the status of legal personhood. Erik Eckholm, *Push for Personhood Amendment Represents New Tack in Abortion Fight*, NEW YORK TIMES, Oct. 11, 2011.

————

B.   EUROPE

Recall from Ch. V that European law is the product of two major European organizations: the European Union (EU), a small Europe of 27 nations (or "Member States"); and the Council of Europe (COE), a bigger Europe of 47 nations. An examination of European federalism requires considering the relationship between national laws and the two systems of law created by these organizations. These two systems are separate and independent, yet they serve as a source of inspiration to one another and cooperate on many issues.

EU law has its source in two treaties creating the EU: the Treaty on the EU and the Treaty on the Functioning of the EU, from which all other legal instruments derive. The Council of Europe has as its source a great number of international conventions, including several on discrimination. The most famous of these is the European Convention for the protection of Human rights and fundamental freedoms (ECHR) of 1950. Both the EU and the Council of Europe have high courts that interpret their laws. The high court of the EU is the European Court of Justice (ECJ), which sits in Luxembourg. The high court of the Council of Europe is the European Court of Human Rights (ECtHR), which sits in Strasbourg, France. For more background information on the ECtHR, see Chapter V, on marriage and equality in the EU.

Initially, the European Union was not generally concerned with fundamental rights, nor the more specific right to equality or non-discrimination. The European Communities (European Coal and Steel Community in 1951, Euratom and the European Economic Community in 1957) focused on economic freedoms. But the roots of an equality jurisprudence were there from the beginning, because for economic purposes the treaty on the EEC included a prohibition against discrimination based on nationality, and a requirement of equal pay for men and women.

As the economic community became a political union, this general lack of interest in providing for human rights and non-discrimination was transformed. Article 6, § 1 of the Treaty on the European Union, in the version of the text deriving from the Treaty of Amsterdam (1997), stated unequivocally that the Union is founded on the principles of liberty, democracy, respect for human rights and fundamental freedoms, and the rule of law. The reform of this initial Treaty with the Lisbon Treaty entered into force in 2009 provides that: "The Union is founded on the values of respect for human dignity, freedom, democracy, equality, the rule of law and respect for human rights, including the rights of persons belonging to minorities. These values are common to the Member States in a society in which pluralism, non-discrimination, tolerance, justice, solidarity and equality between women and men prevail." Article 6, § 1 of the Treaty now explicitly mentions that "the Union recognizes the rights, freedoms and principles set out in the Charter of Fundamental Rights of the European Union of 7 December 2000, as adopted at Strasbourg, on 12 December 2007, which shall have the same legal value as the Treaties." It goes on to further confirm in Article 6, § 3 that "[f]undamental rights, as guaranteed by the European Convention for the Protection of Human Rights and Fundamental Freedoms and as they result from the constitutional traditions common to the Member States, shall constitute general principles of the Union's law." Finally, the charter of fundamental rights of the European Union distributes rights, freedoms and principles across six chapters, including equality, dignity, freedoms, solidarity, citizens' rights, and justice. Together, these references to human rights and fundamental freedoms participate in the "constitutionalization" of the EU, developing Europe beyond simply a free trade zone or an economic union.

The relationship between national laws and European law is based on two basic principles: supremacy and direct effect. Supremacy has been a source of serious concern because it requires European law to prevail over national constitutions, which are no longer considered the supreme law of the land. National constitutions can be objects of judicial review by the ECJ or the ECtHR applying European rules and principles. Thus, national conceptions of equality, which historically developed through national constitutions by domestic constitutional courts, are being challenged by pan-European conceptions of equality and non-discrimination.

The notion of direct effect, allowing European law to be invoked before national courts, has also facilitated the expansion of European Law. Indeed, national courts, in their fulfillment of their obligation to respect European Law, have played a major role in the expansion of European fundamental rights. For example, the French *Cour de cassation* (the French supreme court for civil and criminal law matters) accepted the horizontal direct effect of European Law's prohibition against discrimination, thereby allowing the enforcement of European Law in a contract dispute between private parties. (*See* Cass. civ. 3ᵉ, 6 mars 1996, Office public d'habitations de la Ville de Paris c/ Mme Mel Yedei, pourvoi n° 93–11113; rental contract prohibiting the non-married partner of the party to live in the rented apartment.) As such, States have adjusted domestic legislation, directly enforced European fundamental rights, and at times, set aside conflicting legislation. Failure to fulfill this obligation would result in action against the State itself before European courts.

Direct effect is all the more important in the EU because individuals do not have standing before the EU's High Court, the European Court of Justice ("ECJ"). Individuals have no right to bring a claim against a Member State for violation of EU law, and only in rare cases are they allowed to initiate judicial review of acts adopted by the EU institutions. Insufficient as it might be to compensate for this lack of individual standing, national courts can or sometimes must, upon claimants' requests, request a preliminary ruling on an interpretation or the validity of EU law from the ECJ. In a number of cases, contested national law had to be discarded due to the ECJ's interpretation of EU anti-discrimination law (see below).

————

Kalanke v. Freie Hansestadt Bremen

Case C–450/93 (17 October 1995)

■ EUROPEAN COURT OF JUSTICE

The purpose of the Directive (76/207/EEC) is, as stated in Article 1(1), to put into effect in the Member States the principle of equal treatment for men and women as regards, inter alia, access to employment, including promotion. Article 2(1) states that the principle of equal treatment means that "there shall be no discrimination whatsoever on grounds of sex either directly or indirectly."

A national rule that, where men and women who are candidates for the same promotion are equally qualified, women are automatically to be given priority in sectors where they are under-represented, involves discrimination on grounds of sex.

It must, however, be considered whether such a national rule is permissible under Article 2(4), which provides that the Directive "shall be without prejudice to measures to promote equal opportunity for men and women, in particular by removing existing inequalities which affect women's opportunities."

That provision is specifically and exclusively designed to allow measures which, although discriminatory in appearance, are in fact intended to eliminate or reduce actual instances of inequality which may exist in the reality of social life * * *.

It thus permits national measures relating to access to employment, including promotion, which give a specific advantage to women with a view to improving their ability to compete on the labour market and to pursue a career on an equal footing with men.

As the Council considered in the third recital in the preamble to Recommendation 84/635/EEC of 13 December 1984 on the promotion of positive action for women (OJ 1984 L 331, p. 34), "existing legal provisions on equal treatment, which are designed to afford rights to individuals, are inadequate for the elimination of all existing inequalities unless parallel action is taken by governments, both sides of industry and other bodies concerned, to counteract the prejudicial effects on women in employment which arise from social attitudes, behaviour and structures."

Nevertheless, as a derogation from an individual right laid down in the Directive, Article 2(4) must be interpreted strictly * * *.

National rules which guarantee women absolute and unconditional priority for appointment or promotion go beyond promoting equal opportunities and overstep the limits of the exception in Article 2(4) of the Directive.

Furthermore, in so far as it seeks to achieve equal representation of men and women in all grades and levels within a department, such a system substitutes for equality of opportunity as envisaged in Article 2(4) the result which is only to be arrived at by providing such equality of opportunity.

The answer to the national court's questions must therefore be that Article 2(1) and (4) of the Directive precludes national rules such as those in the present case which, where candidates of different sexes shortlisted for promotion are equally qualified, automatically give priority to women in sectors where they are under-represented, under-representation being deemed to exist when women do not make up at least half of the staff in the individual pay brackets in the relevant personnel group or in the function levels provided for in the organization chart.

———

Mangold v. Helm

Case C–144/04 (22 May 2005)

■ European Court of Justice

* * * [I]t is to be noted that * * * the purpose of Directive 2000/78 is to lay down a general framework for combating discrimination on any of the grounds referred to in that article, which include age, as regards employment and occupation.

Paragraph 14(3) of the TzBfG (German statute), however, by permitting employers to conclude without restriction fixed-term contracts of employment with workers over the age of 52, introduces a difference of treatment on the grounds directly of age.

Specifically with regard to differences of treatment on grounds of age, Article 6(1) of Directive 2000/78 provides that the Member States may provide that such differences of treatment 'shall not constitute discrimination, if, within the context of national law, they are objectively and reasonably justified by a legitimate aim, including legitimate employment policy, labour market and vocational training objectives, and if the means of achieving that aim are appropriate and necessary'. According to subparagraph (a) of the second paragraph of Article 6(1), those differences may include inter alia 'the setting of special conditions on access to employment and vocational training, employment and occupation ... for young people, older workers and persons with caring responsibilities in order to promote their vocational integration or ensure their protection' and, under subparagraphs (b) and (c), the fixing of conditions of age in certain special circumstances.

As is clear from the documents sent to the Court by the national court, the purpose of that legislation is plainly to promote the vocational integration of unemployed older workers, in so far as they encounter considerable difficulties in finding work.

The legitimacy of such a public-interest objective cannot reasonably be thrown in doubt, as indeed the Commission itself has admitted.

An objective of that kind must as a rule, therefore, be regarded as justifying, 'objectively and reasonably', as provided for by the first subparagraph of Article 6(1) of Directive 2000/78, a difference of treatment on grounds of age laid down by Member States.

It still remains to be established whether, according to the actual wording of that provision, the means used to achieve that legitimate objective are 'appropriate and necessary'.

In this respect the Member States unarguably enjoy broad discretion in their choice of the measures capable of attaining their objectives in the field of social and employment policy. However, as the national court has pointed out, application of national legislation such as that at issue in the main proceedings leads to a situation in which all workers who have reached the age of 52, without distinction, whether or not they were unemployed before the contract was concluded and whatever the duration of any period of unemployment, may lawfully, until the age at which they may claim their entitlement to a retirement pension, be offered fixed-term contracts of employment which may be renewed an indefinite number of times. This significant body of workers, determined solely on the basis of age, is thus in danger, during a substantial part of its members' working life, of being excluded from the benefit of stable employment which, however, as the Framework Agreement makes clear, constitutes a major element in the protection of workers.

In so far as such legislation takes the age of the worker concerned as the only criterion for the application of a fixed-term contract of employment, when it has not been shown that fixing an age threshold, as such, regardless of any other consideration linked to the structure of the labour market in question or the personal situation of the person concerned, is objectively necessary to the attainment of the objective which is the vocational integration of unemployed older workers, it must be considered to go beyond what is appropriate and necessary in order to attain the objective pursued. Observance of the principle of proportionality requires every derogation from an individual right to reconcile, so far as is possible, the requirements of the principle of equal treatment with those of the aim pursued * * *. Such national legislation cannot, therefore, be justified under Article 6(1) of Directive 2000/78.

The fact that, when the contract was concluded, the period prescribed for the transposition into domestic law of Directive 2000/78 had not yet expired cannot call that finding into question.

First, the Court has already held that, during the period prescribed for transposition of a directive, the Member States must refrain from taking any measures liable seriously to compromise the attainment of the result prescribed by that directive * * *.

* * * [A]bove all, Directive 2000/78 does not itself lay down the principle of equal treatment in the field of employment and occupation. Indeed, in accordance with Article 1 thereof, the sole purpose of the directive is 'to lay down a general framework for combating discrimination on the grounds of religion or belief, disability, age or sexual orientation', the source of the actual principle underlying the prohibition of those forms of discrimination being found, as is clear from the third and fourth recitals in the preamble to the directive, in various international instruments and in the constitutional traditions common to the Member States.

The principle of non-discrimination on grounds of age must thus be regarded as a general principle of Community law.

* * * Consequently, observance of the general principle of equal treatment, in particular in respect of age, cannot as such be conditional upon the expiry of the period allowed the Member States for the transposition of a directive intended to lay down a general framework for combating discrimination on the grounds of age, in particular so far as the organisation of appropriate legal remedies, the burden of proof, protection against victimisation, social dialogue, affirmative action and other specific measures to implement such a directive are concerned.

In those circumstances it is the responsibility of the national court, hearing a dispute involving the principle of non-discrimination in respect of age, to provide, in a case within its jurisdiction, the legal protection which individuals derive from the rules of Community law and to ensure that those rules are fully effective, setting aside any provision of national law which may conflict with that law.

———

Sejdic and Finci v. Bosnia and Herzegovina

Application no. 27996/06 (22 December 2009)

■ European Court of Human Rights

* * * Ethnicity and race are related concepts. Whereas the notion of race is rooted in the idea of biological classification of human beings into subspecies on the basis of morphological features such as skin colour or facial characteristics, ethnicity has its origin in the idea of societal groups marked in particular by common nationality, religious faith, shared language, or cultural and traditional origins and backgrounds. Discrimination on account of a person's ethnic origin is a form of racial discrimination (see

the definition adopted by the International Convention on the Elimination of All Forms of Racial Discrimination in paragraph 19 above and that adopted by the European Commission against Racism and Intolerance in paragraph 23 above). Racial discrimination is a particularly egregious kind of discrimination and, in view of its perilous consequences, requires from the authorities special vigilance and a vigorous reaction. It is for this reason that the authorities must use all available means to combat racism, thereby reinforcing democracy's vision of a society in which diversity is not perceived as a threat but as a source of enrichment [citations omitted].

In this context, where a difference in treatment is based on race or ethnicity, the notion of objective and reasonable justification must be interpreted as strictly as possible (*see D.H. and Others*). The Court has also held that no difference in treatment which is based exclusively or to a decisive extent on a person's ethnic origin is capable of being objectively justified in a contemporary democratic society built on the principles of pluralism and respect for different cultures (ibid). That being said, Article 14 does not prohibit Contracting Parties from treating groups differently in order to correct "factual inequalities" between them. Indeed, in certain circumstances a failure to attempt to correct inequality through different treatment may, without an objective and reasonable justification, give rise to a breach of that Article [citations omitted].

Turning to the present case, the Court observes that in order to be eligible to stand for election to the House of Peoples of Bosnia and Herzegovina, one has to declare affiliation with a "constituent people." The applicants, who describe themselves to be of Roma and Jewish origin respectively and who do not wish to declare affiliation with a "constituent people," are, as a result, excluded * * *. The Court notes that this exclusion rule pursued at least one aim which is broadly compatible with the general objectives of the Convention, as reflected in the Preamble to the Convention, namely the restoration of peace. When the impugned constitutional provisions were put in place a very fragile cease-fire was in effect on the ground. The provisions were designed to end a brutal conflict marked by genocide and "ethnic cleansing." The nature of the conflict was such that the approval of the "constituent peoples" (namely, the Bosniacs, Croats and Serbs) was necessary to ensure peace. This could explain, without necessarily justifying, the absence of representatives of the other communities (such as local Roma and Jewish communities) at the peace negotiations and the participants' preoccupation with effective equality between the "constituent peoples" in the post-conflict society.

It is nevertheless the case that the Court is only competent ratione temporis to examine the period after the ratification of the Convention and Protocol No. 1 thereto by Bosnia and Herzegovina. The Court does not need to decide whether the upholding of the contested constitutional provisions after ratification of the Convention could be said to serve a "legitimate aim" since, for the reasons set out below, the maintenance of the system in any event does not satisfy the requirement of proportionality.

To begin with, the Court observes significant positive developments in Bosnia and Herzegovina since the Dayton Peace Agreement. It is true that progress might not always have been consistent and challenges remain

* * *. It is nevertheless the case that in 2005 the former parties to the conflict surrendered their control over the armed forces and transformed them into a small, professional force; in 2006 Bosnia and Herzegovina joined NATO's Partnership for Peace; in 2008 it signed and ratified a Stabilisation and Association Agreement with the European Union; in March 2009 it successfully amended the State Constitution for the first time; and it has recently been elected a member of the United Nations Security Council for a two-year term beginning on 1 January 2010. Furthermore, whereas the maintenance of an international administration as an enforcement measure under Chapter VII of the United Nations Charter implies that the situation in the region still constitutes a "threat to international peace and security", it appears that preparations for the closure of that administration are under way * * *.

In addition, while the Court agrees with the Government that there is no requirement under the Convention to abandon totally the power-sharing mechanisms peculiar to Bosnia and Herzegovina and that the time may still not be ripe for a political system which would be a simple reflection of majority rule, the Opinions of the Venice Commission * * * clearly demonstrate that there exist mechanisms of power-sharing which do not automatically lead to the total exclusion of representatives of the other communities. In this connection, it is recalled that the possibility of alternative means achieving the same end is an important factor in this sphere * * *.

Lastly, by becoming a member of the Council of Europe in 2002 and by ratifying the Convention and the Protocols thereto without reservations, the respondent State has voluntarily agreed to meet the relevant standards. * * *

Thus, the Court concludes that the applicants' continued ineligibility to stand for election to the House of Peoples of Bosnia and Herzegovina lacks an objective and reasonable justification and has therefore breached Article 14 taken in conjunction with Article 3 of Protocol No. 1.

———

Kozak v. Poland

Application no. 13102/02 (2 March 2010)

■ EUROPEAN COURT OF HUMAN RIGHTS

* * * In the enjoyment of the rights and freedoms guaranteed by the Convention, Article 14 affords protection against different treatment, without an objective and reasonable justification, of persons in similar situations * * *.

Not every difference in treatment will amount to a violation of this provision; thus, Contracting States enjoy a margin of appreciation in assessing whether and to what extent differences in otherwise similar situations justify a different treatment in law. For the purposes of Article 14, it must be established that there is no objective and reasonable justification for the impugned distinction, which means that it does not pursue a "legitimate aim" or that there is no "reasonable proportionality between the means employed and the aim sought to be realised" * * *.

Sexual orientation is a concept covered by Article 14. Furthermore, when the distinction in question operates in this intimate and vulnerable sphere of an individual's private life, particularly weighty reasons need to be advanced before the Court to justify the measure complained of. Where a difference of treatment is based on sex or sexual orientation the margin of appreciation afforded to the State is narrow and, in such situations, the principle of proportionality does not merely require that the measure chosen is in general suited for realising the aim sought, but it must also be shown that it was necessary under the circumstances. Indeed, if the reasons advanced for a difference in treatment were based solely on the applicant's sexual orientation, this would amount to discrimination under the Convention * * *.

* * * [According to the contested provision], a person seeking succession to a tenancy had, among other things, to fulfill the condition of living with the tenant in the same household in a close relationship—such as, for instance, de facto marital cohabitation * * *.

In the Government's submission, the case disclosed no element of discrimination since the applicant's claim was rejected not for reasons related to his sexual orientation but for his non-compliance with the above two statutory conditions * * *.

However, having regard to the findings of fact and law made by the District Court and the Regional Court ... the Court does not accept the Government's contention. * * *

In the Court's opinion, * * * the Regional Court considered that the principal issue material for the ruling related to the applicant's sexual orientation. In contrast to what the Government argued, the relevant element was not the question of the applicant's residence in the flat or the emotional, economic or other quality of his relationship with T.B., but the homosexual nature of that relationship, which per se excluded him from succession.

It remains for the Court to determine whether the Polish authorities can be said to have given "objective and reasonable justification" for the impugned distinction in law in respect to same-and different-sex partners, that is to say whether this measure pursued a "legitimate aim" and maintained "reasonable proportionality between the means employed and the aim sought to be realised" * * *.

It emerges from the grounds given by the Regional Court that the essential objective of the difference in treatment was to ensure the protection of the family founded on a "union of a man and a woman", as stipulated in Article 18 of the Polish Constitution * * *. The Court accepts that protection of the family in the traditional sense is, in principle, a weighty and legitimate reason which might justify a difference in treatment * * *.

However, in pursuance of that aim a broad variety of measures might be implemented by the State. Also, given that the Convention is a living instrument, to be interpreted in the light of present-day conditions * * *, the State, in its choice of means designed to protect the family and secure, as required by Article 8, respect for family life, must necessarily take into account developments in society and changes in the perception of social, civil-status and relational issues, including the fact that there is not just one way or one choice in the sphere of leading and living one's family or private life.

Striking a balance between the protection of the traditional family and the Convention rights of sexual minorities is, by the nature of things, a difficult and delicate exercise, which may require the State to reconcile conflicting views and interests perceived by the parties concerned as being in fundamental opposition. Nevertheless, having regard to the State's narrow margin of appreciation in adopting measures that result in a difference based on sexual orientation * * *, a blanket exclusion of persons living in a homosexual relationship from succession to a tenancy cannot be accepted by the Court as necessary for the protection of the family viewed in its traditional sense * * *. Nor have any convincing or compelling reasons been advanced by the Polish Government to justify the distinction in treatment of heterosexual and homosexual partners.

In view of the foregoing, the Court finds that the Polish authorities, in rejecting the applicant's claim on grounds related to the homosexual nature of his relationship with T.B., failed to maintain a reasonable relationship of proportionality between the aim sought and the means employed. The impugned distinction was not, therefore, compatible with the standards under the Convention.

The Court accordingly rejects the Government's objection regarding the applicant's victim status and holds that there has been a violation of Article 14 taken in conjunction with Article 8 of the Convention.

————

Association Belge des Consommateurs Test–Achats ASBL v. Conseil des Ministres

Case C–236/09 (1 March 2011)

■ European Court of Justice

The applicants in the main proceedings brought an action before the Cour constitutionnelle (Constitutional Court) (Belgium) for annulment of the Law of 21 December 2007 transposing Directive 2004/113 into Belgian law.

They claimed that the Law of 21 December 2007, which implements the derogation provided for in Article 5(2) of Directive 2004/113, is contrary to the principle of equality between men and women.

* * * [T]he national court asks, in substance, whether Article 5(2) of Directive 2004/113 is valid in the light of the principle of equal treatment for men and women.

* * * As is stated in recital 18 to Directive 2004/113, the use of actuarial factors related to sex was widespread in the provision of insurance services at the time when the directive was adopted.

Consequently, it was permissible for the EU legislature to implement the principle of equality for men and women—more specifically, the application of the rule of unisex premiums and benefits—gradually, with appropriate transitional periods.

Thus it was that the EU legislature provided in Article 5(1) of Directive 2004/113 that the differences in premiums and benefits arising from the use of sex as a factor in the calculation thereof must be abolished by 21 December 2007 at the latest.

By way of derogation from the general rule requiring unisex premiums and benefits established by Article 5(1) of Directive 2004/113, Article 5(2) of that directive grants certain Member States—those in which national law did not yet apply that rule at the time when Directive 2004/113 was adopted—the option of deciding before 21 December 2007 to permit proportionate differences in individuals' premiums and benefits where the use of sex is a determining factor in the assessment of risks based on relevant and accurate actuarial and statistical data.

Under Article 5(2) of Directive 2004/113, any decision to make use of that option is to be reviewed five years after 21 December 2007, account being taken of a Commission report. However, given that Directive 2004/113 is silent as to the length of time during which those differences may continue to be applied, Member States which have made use of the option are permitted to allow insurers to apply the unequal treatment without any temporal limitation.

The Council expresses its doubts as to whether, in the context of certain branches of private insurance, the respective situations of men and women policyholders may be regarded as comparable, given that, from the point of view of the modus operandi of insurers, in accordance with which risks are placed in categories on the basis of statistics, the levels of insured risk may be different for men and for women. The Council argues that the option provided for in Article 5(2) of Directive 2004/113 is intended merely to make it possible not to treat different situations in the same way.

The Court has consistently held that the principle of equal treatment requires that comparable situations must not be treated differently, and different situations must not be treated in the same way, unless such treatment is objectively justified (*see* Case C–127/07 *Arcelor Atlantique et Lorraine and Others* [2008] ECR I–9895, paragraph 23).

In that regard, it should be pointed out that the comparability of situations must be assessed in the light of the subject-matter and purpose of the EU measure which makes the distinction in question (*see*, to that effect, *Arcelor Atlantique et Lorraine and Others*, paragraph 26). In the present case, that distinction is made by Article 5(2) of Directive 2004/113.

It is not disputed that the purpose of Directive 2004/113 in the insurance services sector is, as is reflected in Article 5(1) of that directive, the application of unisex rules on premiums and benefits. Recital 18 to Directive 2004/113 expressly states that, in order to guarantee equal treatment between men and women, the use of sex as an actuarial factor must not result in differences in premiums and benefits for insured individuals. Recital 19 to that directive describes the option granted to Member States not to apply the rule of unisex premiums and benefits as an option to permit 'exemptions'. Accordingly, Directive 2004/113 is based on the premise that, for the purposes of applying the principle of equal treatment for men and women, enshrined in Articles 21 and 23 of the Charter, the respective situations of men and women with regard to insurance premiums and benefits contracted by them are comparable.

Accordingly, there is a risk that EU law may permit the derogation from the equal treatment of men and women, provided for in Article 5(2) of Directive 2004/113, to persist indefinitely. Such a provision, which enables the Member States in question to maintain without temporal limitation an exemption from the rule of unisex premiums and benefits, works against the achievement of the objective of equal treatment between men and women, which is the purpose of Directive 2004/113, and is incompatible with Articles 21 and 23 of the Charter. That provision must therefore be considered to be invalid upon the expiry of an appropriate transitional period.

———

NOTES

1. *Kozak* holds that the ECtHR will grant Member States a "margin of appreciation" in determining different social policies for different groups of people on a continuum depending on the kind of discrimination at issue. If it is sex discrimination, the margin will be narrow and conformity with EU law more strictly enforced. But if it is disability discrimination, for example, the margin might be wider and conformity with EU law less strictly enforced. Does the ECJ have a similar scale for determining how much EU law should delimit or defer to national law?

2. The *Association Belge des Consommateurs Test–Achats ASBL* case has led to a dramatic rethinking of how gender categories have traditionally been used in insurance calculation schemes in Europe. Beyond the insurance industry, the case illustrates the federal extension of anti-discrimination law to the field of goods and services, which has yet to be fully explored in EU law. Because this field consists primarily of private activities and private actors, the changes implied by this case will most likely face fierce resistance in some sectors of the industry (particularly, banking and insurance), which continue to rely on gender and age differentiations.

3. Since Directive 2000/78 was put into force in 2003 (some states obtained a delay to 2006), the number of age discrimination cases has increased, and age discrimination has been the most litigated issue among the categories of discrimination prohibited by the Directive. However, Member States have not traditionally regarded their use of age as a criterion in social policy as possible grounds for a discrimination claim. On the contrary, both private and public sectors relied upon age both to distribute advantages to seniors and to provide security for the retired class more generally. As such, the European prohibition against age discrimination has threatened public and private policies concerning retirement age as well as employment practices like those addressed in the *Mangold* case.

4. In *Age Discrimination and the European Court of Justice: EU Equality Law Comes of Age* in LAW & EUROPEAN AFFAIRS, Vol. 2 (2009–2010), p. 253, C. O'Cinneide writes:

> ... [T]he Mangold decision, as clarified by the recent ECJ decisions in the age discrimination cases of Bartsch and Kücükdeveci, appears to have established that national courts must give effect to this general principle of equal treatment by disregarding national laws linked to the transposition of Directives and other elements of EU law which conflict with this principle. As Advocate General Bot noted in his opinion in Kücükdeveci, the requirement for national courts to disapply national laws that conflict with EU legal norms is not wholly new, as it dates back to the Simmenthal decision. However, these cases appear to have developed this doctrine and taken its implications one stage further, by clarifying that national courts must disapply national laws in the case of conflict with this general principle of equal treatment, even where this has the result that in practice the Directive will become applicable in 'horizontal' disputes between private parties. This jurisprudence marks a departure by the Court from its traditional reluctance to avoid giving horizontal direct effect to Directives within national law: now, it appears that Directives may be directly applicable as between private parties when they embody and give effect to fundamental principles of EU law.

5. In the *Leyla Sahin v. Turkey* case, reprinted in Chapter VIII, the Court also looked to the comparative law of the COE member states to determine whether a national law violated the Convention. Is this a form of reverse federalism, where national law re-shapes the meaning of the (federal) Convention?

6. Similarly, *Case of Lautsi and Others v. Italy*, decided by the ECtHR on February 16, 2011, discussed in Chapter VII, concerned the issue of whether Italy's national laws expressly prescribing the display of a crucifix in a public school violated the Convention's Article 2, Protocol No. 1, providing the right of education and the right of parents to ensure an education in line with their own religious and philosophical beliefs, and Article 9, providing the right to freedom of thought, conscience and religion. It ruled that Italy was not in violation because it remained within the "margin of appreciation" the Convention grants Member States to determine whether and how to perpetuate its national and historical traditions in relation to their Art. 2, Protocol No. 1 and Article 9 obligations. It added, "the fact that there is no European consensus on the question of the presence of religious symbols in State school speaks in favour of that approach" (p. 29). Indeed, as with the *E.B.* case and the *Sahin* case, the decision includes a survey of the various national laws of the Member States on the issue (p. 13). Religious symbols are forbidden in public schools in the former Yugoslavia, France and Georgia, while religious symbols are prescribed in Italy, Austria, certain regions of Germany and Switzerland, and Poland. And religious symbols are found in public schools in Spain, Greece, Ireland, Malta, San Marino and Romania although there are no formal regulations on the matter. Could this lack of

consensus perhaps indicate the opposite of what the ECtHR argues? That the lack of consensus in fact should indicate the need for less deference towards States' "margin of appreciation" and more "European supervision" (p. 29)?

7. Imagine that the ECtHR in *Lautsi* decided that Italy was in violation of the Convention, ruling that a state may not prescribe the placement of religious symbols in public institutions. Reading this decision as the European suppression of Catholic culture and religion, could Member States with investments in their Catholic traditions terminate their membership in the COE?

8. One feature of EU federalism is that it oftentimes gives Member States some amount of latitude in how and when compliance with EU law will be achieved. However, Sophie Robin–Olivier has noted how this sometimes produces inconsistencies and ineffectiveness. "In 2008, French law adopted EC directives' definition of discrimination and, at the same time, a new definition of sexual harassment. But it has done so without getting rid of its own old conception. As a result, the two sets of provisions explicitly devoted to harassment (moral and sexual) are now competing with a definition of discrimination, which includes what EC law calls harassment. This blurred picture gives the impression that French law has only paid lip service to the European conceptions, particularly in the field of sexual harassment. Rather than directly confronting the issue of sexual harassment, French law always seems more at ease when the problem can be brought to a more general level." *French Prohibition of Harassment at Work: A Case of Complex Articulation of Moral and Sex, under European Influence*, EUROPEAN LABOR LAW JOURNAL, no. 1, 2009.

9. National laws of COE Member States rarely tolerate overt racial discrimination. However, as the *Sejdic* case reveals, when such formal discrimination exists, two factors may lead to inconsistent interpretations of national laws and the Convention. The first is the ambiguity of the EU notion of "race and ethnic origin" and what it exactly refers to in a given nation, which in turn causes difficulties in determining whether a national law conforms to EU anti-discrimination law. The second is the complexity of enforcing EU anti-discrimination law in central and eastern European countries that became member states in the aftermath of the fall of the Berlin wall. In those post-conflict countries, formal and effective equality between the major hostile groups must be legally provided for, while at the same time attending to demographic, generational and cultural shifts that might exceed the primary lines of division those anti-discrimination laws were intended to address. This is not unlike the function of the Voting Rights Act of 1965 in the U.S., which prohibited the state-sanctioned disenfranchisement of African American voters, particularly in the South after the abolition of Jim Crow. The Convention and federal legislation serve to monitor behavior, not of every nation or state, respectively, but of particular ones for particular kinds of racially discriminatory behavior. See also, note 1 in the section below on Iraq for further discussion of the role of federalism in stabilizing ethnic conflict.

10.   Consider the articulation of gender equality in Article 157 of the Treaty on the Functioning of the European Union.

Article 157

1.   Each Member State shall ensure that the principle of equal pay for male and female workers for equal work or work of equal value is applied.

2.   For the purpose of this Article, 'pay' means the ordinary basic or minimum wage or salary and any other consideration, whether in cash or in kind, which the worker receives directly or indirectly, in respect of his employment, from his employer.

Equal pay without discrimination based on sex means:

(a) that pay for the same work at piece rates shall be calculated on the basis of the same unit of measurement;

(b) that pay for work at time rates shall be the same for the same job.

3.   The European Parliament and the Council, acting in accordance with the ordinary legislative procedure, and after consulting the Economic and Social Committee, shall adopt measures to ensure the application of the principle of equal opportunities and equal treatment of men and women in matters of employment and occupation, including the principle of equal pay for equal work or work of equal value.

4.   With a view to ensuring full equality in practice between men and women in working life, the principle of equal treatment shall not prevent any Member State from maintaining or adopting measures providing for specific advantages in order to make it easier for the underrepresented sex to pursue a vocational activity or to prevent or compensate for disadvantages in professional careers.

According to Professor Alvaro Oliveira, currently on the legal staff of the European Commission, Article 157 mirrors the historical attempt of the U.S. 14th Amendment to create a federal prohibition against state-sanctioned racial discrimination. However, the last paragraph of Article 157, unlike 14th Amendment Equal Protection jurisprudence, explicitly gives Treaty force to the possibility of national affirmative action policies. This is in stark contrast to the 14th Amendment, which has served historically as justification for and prohibition against affirmative action policies adopted by states. What might account for the substantive difference between the U.S. 14th Amendment and the EU Article 157? Perhaps one reason is that the 14th Amendment was a universal declaration turning slaves into citizens imposed on states already part of postbellum America; whereas Article 157, as a treaty provision to be adopted after the fact, needed to give potential members a certain amount of flexibility.

11.   Positive action policies developed at the national level present a particularly difficult issue for European federalism. Cases arising from disputes about positive action policies oftentime require balancing individual and group rights, and as such, are politically sensitive and controversial. According to Daniela Caruso, "The case-by-case definition of the wavering line separating the hard core of individual rights from the soft periphery of collective entitlements endorsed by political consensus is still best left in

states' hands." *Limits of the Classic Method: Positive Action in the European Union after the New Equality Directives*, 44 HARVARD INTERNATIONAL LAW JOURNAL 331, 381 (2003). This might seem like an appropriate retort to the ECJ's finding in *Eckhard*, but when might supranational intervention become necessary? What about European federalism and EC law bodes against the direction U.S. caselaw on equality and federalism has taken?

12.   Note 9 of Chapter III, "Equality and Discrimination in Employment", points to an advisory relationship between the ECJ and national law. In the German *Maruko* case, developing a consistent EU-wide policy recognizing the status of same-sex partnerships seems caught between the obligation of the ECJ to respect national competence and the obligation of Member States to comply with supranational law. How does this advisory relationship compare with the U.S. Supreme Court's jurisprudence on federal preemption?

————

C. INDIA

Federalism and Diversity in India

Vasuki Nesiah, in Yash Ghai, ed. 2000. *Autonomy and Ethnicity: Negotiating Competing Claims in Multi–Ethnic States*. Cambridge University Press, pp. 54–59.

■ VASUKI NESIAH

* * * Ethnic Diversity and the constitution

India has sometimes been described as a nation where everyone is a minority. Cross-cutting lines of identity and difference can be tracked along multiple axes: language, religion, caste, tribe, region, and so on. These are layered over factors such as class and gender that add further complexity to the country's demographic profile. As Bajpai (1997:38) has noted, while these differences may divide India, 'the absence of a nationwide cleavage along ethnic lines' also provides a 'source of stability', since 'religious, caste, tribal, linguistic and regional differences do not converge on a single fault line'. * * *

If there are cross-cutting lines of diversity in the Indian polity, the constitution carries cross-cutting mechanisms to address that diversity. We can identify four approaches to diversity in the Indian constitution. First, the constitution attempts to tailor mechanisms that enable an inclusive and dialogical relationship between minority communities and the state; in this vein, federal institutions attempt to channel linguistic and regional diversity. Accompanying the federal schema is the language policy. While Hindi is the official language, English is to be used as an additional language for official matters and, most importantly, states can conduct affairs in their regional language. Similarly, the 'three language formula' recommended by the National Integration Council in 1961 required that 'all schools' have 'compulsory teaching in three languages: the regional language and English, with Hindi for the non-Hindi states and another Indian language for the Hindi-speaking states' (Hardgrave and Kochanek 1986:131).

Second, in other contexts, the constitution encourages the proactive intervention of the state in overcoming differences and their social and political consequences; affirmative action programs for scheduled castes and tribals are illustrative here. India continues to be fraught with deep caste hierarchy and discrimination. However, as Galanter (1989:185) says, 'If one reflects on the propensity of nations to neglect the claim of those at the bottom, I think it's fair to say that this policy of compensatory discrimination has been pursued with remarkable persistence and generosity (if not always with vigor and effectiveness) over the past thirty years'.

The constitution crafts a third approach to diversity by limiting state power and safeguarding a sphere of autonomy so that differences can be protected and enhanced without threat of assimilation and subjugation. This approach may be exemplified by the way in which the principle of secularism has been interpreted to offer religious minorities a protected sphere through the regime of personal laws. Secularism is sometimes understood in the classical liberal sense that religion is zoned out of the public sphere, or sometimes understood as being multi-religious, with parity in respect of all religious traditions (Sen 1997:22). Concern with religious unity has been so overwhelming that there is a determined refusal to allow federal boundaries to recognize religious divisions. Even when the federal map of India was reorganized, it was on linguistic grounds, and 'an important principle was reaffirmed: religious appeals were to be kept out of the official politics and language of the state' (Corbridge 1995:106).

Finally, a fourth approach to diversity lies in establishing a norm of equality for both individuals and groups, to guide the application of the specific guarantees and protections that run through other pieces of the constitutional framework; here we may cite those provisions entrenching the fundamental rights of all citizens against discrimination. [. . .] Ultimately, these provisions protect not only minorities but also minorities within minorities.

If the different approaches to diversity have worked in complementary ways, historical change has also added to the complexity. As illustrated by the now famous *Shah Bano* case, tensions between different approaches to diversity have gained increased urgency. New sources of diversity have been foregrounded; old approaches to diversity have begged for new strategies.* * *

Diversity and federalism

The British introduced a skeletal model of the current federal system through the Government of India Act in 1935 (Setalvad 1960:168–179). Using the boundaries drawn in this Act as a starting-point, the Constituent Assembly sought to breathe federal life into the administrative units in the constitution of independent India. The Constituent Assembly went about its project with considerable skepticism, suspicion and resentment of the 'divide and rule' motivations of the colonial legacy with which it had to work. We may infer that the stance towards federalism was itself informed by these initial sentiments. The 1956 States Reorganisation Act redrew the original borders along linguistic lines. Since then, some additional border changes have taken place, and some calls for border changes have been defeated. There have been calls for secession, citing 'cultural distinctiveness and economic and social disparities' (Hardgrave and Kochanek 1986:145). Hitherto, all calls for secession have been quelled by accommodation of some grievances and/or by force.

Indian federalism entails a basic division of powers, with a 'concurrent list' enumerating shared powers such as civil and criminal law, and planning; a 'state list' enumerating state powers such as education, agriculture and welfare; and a 'union list' enumerating the centre's powers, from defence and foreign affairs to income taxation, banking, and so on, and with all residual powers reverting to the centre as well. In addition to the wide range of powers allotted to the union list, 'the paramount position of the Centre is underscored by the power of Parliament to create new states, to alter boundaries of existing states, and even to abolish a state by ordinary legislative procedure without recourse to constitutional amendment' (Hardgrave and Kochanek 1986:116). Under emergency powers, the constitution allows the federal government to 'convert itself into a unitary one'. Moreover, even when not operating under emergency conditions, 'parliament can make laws with respect to any matter falling in the state list for a temporary period'. The constitutional structure is sometimes described as quasi-federal because of this centralising bias. 'The underlying emphasis is on the indestructibility of the Indian Union and not of the States' that make up that union (Mathur 1990:6).

Indian federalism is a contested terrain, characterised by shifts in the lines of diversity it engages with and the nature of that engagement. For instance, since the 1935 Act had drawn the borders of federalism for administrative convenience, these boundaries did not necessarily resonate with the relationships of identity and community that constituted people's lives. As Thakus (1995:71) notes, 'there was little opportunity for regional identities to coalesce around the existing political units'. The organisation of states along linguistic lines was a longstanding demand directed at the constitutional framers; however, the dynamics of Hindu–Muslim tensions, and then partition [between India and Pakistan], overtook questions of linguistic diversity in that inaugural moment of Indian federalism. However, linguistic regionalism re-emerged as a force after independence, and particularly after the reorganisation of states along linguistic and cultural lines (Thakur 1995: 71) and the establishment of Hindi as the official language in 1965. As Yash Ghai (1995:24) notes, with the States Reorganisation Act in 1956 the basis of Indian federalism was transformed from administration to ethnicity. Linguistic identity, as expressed by federal boundaries, has flowed into ethnic and regional identity, sometimes giving rise to 'sons of the soil' movements contesting internal migration from other states within India. Some assertions of regional identity can be understood as responding to the evolution of federalism in centrifugal directions, just as the centrifugal tendencies of the Indian nation-state can be located in its anxieties about an emerging regionalism.

Shifts in the relationship between federalism and diversity are also attested to by the waxing and waning of federalism as a take-off point for mobilising religious identity. While Indian federalism is said to have its basis in language and region, given that lines of diversity, and even the different components of the constitution's approach to diversity, intersect and overlap, federalism cannot but address questions that go beyond linguistic and regional identity. The shift in Punjab from linguistic nationalism to religious nationalism is but one marker of this complexity. In fact, when the constitutional framers began their project, federalism had significant purchase as part of the package of religious diversity, particularly as the Muslim League in their negotiations with the Congress Party had demanded federalism. Once partition was announced, this rationale for federalism declined considerably, although it was kept prominently alive with the crisis in Kashmir, Punjab, and so on.[. . .]

Religion is not the only cross-cutting cleavage impacted by federalism. The struggle of the left-wing government in West Bengal to resist centre directives regarding land reform, agricultural taxes, and so on conveys this dynamic along the axes of class differentiation within West Bengal. Thus, although Indian federalism is concerned principally with ethnicity, the dialectic between federalism and society, between institutional form and social relations, cuts diversity along a number of axes. These intersecting and overlapping cleavages both complicate and pluralise our conceptions of diversity, while also bringing into the federal equation various other sources of difference and hierarchy, such as class, that are not explicitly addressed by the constitutional form of federalism.

[. . .] Another layer of complexity is added by the provision for asymmetrical federalism in certain special cases. One of the most obvious instances of this is the constitutional provision (art. 370) for Kashmir's different status. Similarly, Indian federalism also entails constitutional demarcation of autonomous regions within states for tribal communities. Such internal differentiation is the norm, not the exception, of centre-state relations, as in Kashmir where explicit rules provide for institutional asymmetry, but also, as in the West Bengal example, in the more informal and everyday negotiation of federalism on substantive issues.

In sum, much of this discussion of change and continuity, intersection and overlap suggests that the defining alliances and tensions of diversity are not offered a priori for federalism to then address; rather, there is an ongoing dialectical process that is mutually constitutive.

NOTES

1. Indian law on religious freedom is less concerned about separation between church and state, and more with maintaining religious diversity. Meaningfully supporting religious diversity has, then, required that religious groups and institutions be afforded a certain level of autonomy to govern its members and/or local community. Thus, private religious institutions, like a mosque, or religious communities with their personal laws emerge as a type of subnational political unit sharing power with federal and state governments.

2.   The legal pluralism we saw in the *Shah Bano* case in Chapter XIII, which recognized the Muslim personal laws on divorce but ultimately applied the secular law (Section 125 of the Code on Criminal Procedure making it a crime to fail to provide maintenance) to grant Shah Bano maintenance, might be seen as an encroachment by the federal government on the autonomy of the Muslim religion. Yet, in response to the Supreme Court's ruling, the Indian Parliament upon lobbying by Muslim religious leaders enacted the The Muslim Woman (Protection of Rights on Divorce) Act (1986) which prohibited the application of Section 125 entitling divorced Muslim women to "reasonable and fair provision and maintenance" during the iddat period, and beyond that, promulgating a number of other sources of maintenance purportedly available to her in accordance with Muslim personal law. In the 2001 case, *Danial Latifi v. Union of India*, the Supreme Court in another Muslim divorce maintenance case, upheld the MWA but interpreted "reasonable and fair" iddat maintenance to include providing for the future of the woman. These series of decisions and legislations, indicate both a horizontal tension between the two branches of federal government on how to balance group and individual rights, but as well, a negotiation of power between the federal government and Muslim organizations about whose law has authority in this line of cases. What do you make of the fact that the Supreme Court is the final venue of interpreting the boundary of national jurisdiction, in *Latifi* ultimately interpreting state-adopted religious law against its intentions? Can there be equality between the laws of subnational religious groups and the secular government if the Supreme Court always gets the last word on interpreting religious law towards liberal or communal conceptions of equality?

D.   SOUTH AFRICA

Authorizing Subnational Constitutions in Transitional Federal States: South Africa, Democracy, and the Kwazulu–Natal Constitution

41 Vand. J. Transnat'l L. 585 (2008), pp. 591–599

■ JONATHAN L. MARSHFIELD

* * * II.   The Legal Status of Provincial Constitutions in South Africa

South Africa's current structural framework originated with the 1993 Interim Constitution (IC). The IC demarcated nine subnational units, termed provinces, and established executive and legislative branches in each province. It also authorized the provinces to adopt their own constitutions by a two-thirds majority of the provincial legislature. However, the provinces were designed to function effectively without constitutions and the IC provided "full particulars" on all necessary provincial government institutions. In 1996, the National Constitution (NC) replaced the IC and, with minor exceptions, reaffirmed the IC's constitutional structure.

A. The Provinces' Limited "Constitutional Space"

South Africa is a devolutionary federal system. A unitary state theoretically preceded any subnational units, and that state subsequently instituted the provinces. The provinces are creatures of the national government and have only those powers specifically conferred on them by the NC. Thus, the constitutional competency of the provinces is limited to the NC's express delegation of authority. Stated differently, provincial "constitutional space" is circumscribed rather than plenary.

To ensure that provincial constitutions do not contain ultra vires content, they must be certified by the national Constitutional Court (Court) before they can become law. Certification involves a two-step legal analysis. First, the Court evaluates every provision to ensure that the entire document is within one of the enumerated provincial competencies. Second, the Court must certify that no provision is inconsistent with any provision of the NC.

There are three provincial constitutional competencies. First, a provincial constitution may include any provision that would fall within the province's legislative authority. Second, a provincial constitution may establish "executive and legislative structures and procedures" that differ from the default provisions of the NC. Finally, provincial constitutions may provide for "the institution, role, authority and status of a traditional monarch."

Provincial government's legislative authority is defined in Schedules 4 and 5 of the NC. Schedule 4 lists areas of concurrent national and provincial legislative competence, with the most notable being traditional leadership, trade, tourism, housing, and education. Schedule 5 lists twelve rather insignificant areas of exclusive provincial competency. Thus, because the provinces can legislate in respect of traditional leadership under Schedule 4, government structure and procedure is the only constitutional competence that is not also within a province's legislative authority.

That overlap between constitutional and legislative competency is significant because of the NC's conflict of law rules. The NC provides specific rules with respect to how conflicts between national and provincial laws should be resolved, with national law superseding provincial law in almost all situations. Section 147 equates provincial constitutions with provincial legislation for purposes of resolving conflicts between national and provincial law. Section 147, however, does not implicate provisions relating to government structure and procedure. With that one exception, therefore, provincial constitutions are no more insulated from national preemption than provincial legislation, and the bounds of a province's constitutional space are dependant largely on the existence of preemptory national legislation.

An additional, and perhaps more significant, limitation on the competency of the provinces is their ability to tax. Under Chapter 3 of the NC, provinces are precluded from assessing any sales, property, income, or value-added tax. The provinces, however, are entitled to an equitable share of the national tax revenue. Distribution of the equitable share is determined by national legislation. The NC provides that the equitable share must be sufficient for the provinces to provide "basic services" and perform the functions allocated to them under national law. Thus, the provinces are not entitled to additional funding for expenses created by provincial law, and their ability to raise independent revenue is severely limited.

* * * C.   Individual Rights and Provincial Constitutions

Some commentators suggest that provincial constitutions may develop into an additional source of legally enforceable individual rights. Indeed, the 1996 KZN [Kwazulu–Natal] draft constitution contained an extravagant bill of rights. Although the Court refused to certify the 1996 KZN bill of rights, the Court nevertheless stated in its judgment:

> A provincial bill of rights could (in respect of matters falling within the province's powers) place greater limitations on the province's powers or confer greater rights on individuals than does the [National] Constitution, and it could even confer rights on individuals which do not exist in the [National] Constitution. However, the Court reiterated that a provincial bill of rights must not be "inconsistent" with the NC and "cannot operate in respect of matters which fall outside of its legislative or executive competence." The Court also noted that certification of a provincial bill of rights requires the additional consideration of whether the provincial right "has the effect of eliminating or limiting a right protected in the [National] Constitution."

Thus, a provincial bill of rights can operate only within areas that are not already addressed by the NC's bill of rights or preempted by national legislation. In view of the NC's exhaustive list of individual protections and the ever-growing body of national legislation, there appears to be little remaining "space" for meaningful provincial rights. Furthermore, although theoretical possibilities do exist, provincial constitutions do not currently provide any additional protections. The Western Cape and KZN are the only provinces to have enacted constitutions. As already noted, however, the Court refused to certify the KZN constitution, and KZN still operates under the NC's default provisions. The Western Cape Constitution was certified in 1997 but does not contain a bill of rights. That constitution, however, did vary from the NC's default provisions by increasing the number of provincial parliamentary seats from thirty-nine to forty-two, and the Court has subsequently upheld that variation notwithstanding conflicting national legislation. That minor aberration appears to be the only substantive contribution of the Western Cape Constitution because the remainder of the document essentially mirrors the NC. No other provinces besides the Western Cape and KZN have attempted to draft a constitution.

In sum, South Africa's structural framework is tilted heavily in favor of the national government and allocates very little constitutional space to the provinces. Additionally, as a descriptive matter, provincial constitutions have not become a significant source of substantive law. Rather, the provinces are analogous to regional administrative agencies of the national government—delivering services that are financed primarily by national funds and developing almost no independent constitutional law. * * *

[EDITORS' NOTE: Not only does South African federalism negotiate power-sharing between the federal government and provinces. It also, through its equality jurisprudence, articulates an approach to power-sharing between federal, provincial and traditional communities with their own precolonial, colonial, and postcolonial customary laws and systems of governance. In this way, South African equality jurisprudence reflects how issues of federalism overlap, inform and are shaped by a national constitutional commitment to legal pluralism. For recognizing the sovereignty of customary law and community governance was required in order to effect the ideals of equality in the South African Constitution. Yet, tensions and conflicts between national ideals and community law become particularly visible in gender-based claims, where modern legal concepts, like equality, human dignity and freedom are universally applicable to all South African citizens, at the same time that tradition and customary cultures must enjoy a certain degree if not nearly complete autonomy.]

Shilubana v. Nwamitwa

Constitutional Court of South Africa Case CCT 03/07 (2008)

◼ JUSTICE VAN DER WESTHUIZEN

Introduction

[1] This is an application for leave to appeal against a decision of the Supreme Court of Appeal, substantially confirming a decision of the Pretoria High Court. It raises issues about a traditional community's authority to develop their customs and traditions so as to promote gender equality in the succession of traditional leadership, in accordance with the Constitution. A woman was appointed to a chieftainship position for which she was previously disqualified by virtue of her gender. This Court is called on to decide whether the community has the authority to restore the position of traditional leadership to the house from which it was removed by reason of gender discrimination, even if this discrimination occurred prior to the coming into operation of the Constitution.

[2] The matter also raises issues regarding the relationship between traditional community structures and courts of law envisaged by our constitutional democracy. This Court has to consider how courts of law are to apply customary law as required by the Constitution, while acknowledging and preserving the institution and role of traditional leadership and the functioning of a traditional authority that observes customary law.

* * * *Submissions of the Parties*

[27] The applicants argue that customary law is dynamic and adaptable; the only constraints are those imposed by the Constitution and applicable legislation in terms of section 211(2) of the Constitution. The Valoyi were acting well within their power, under customary law, to amend their customs and traditions to reflect changed circumstances.

[29] The process used in appointing Ms Shilubana as Hosi [Chief] was consistent with the rules and procedures of the community, according to

the applicants. The Royal Family, including the Hosi, initiated the change and submitted the decision to the Royal Council, which approved it. The Tribal Council also considered the decision. The applicants contend that there was no evidence that this procedure was not in accordance with custom or that it was deficient in any way. All structures of the community participated in the decision.

[30] On behalf of Mr Nwamitwa it is argued that the question before the Court is not only one of gender, but also of lineage. In addition to the fact that it is not the custom that a woman may be a Hosi, it was not permissible to "elect" Ms Shilubana to the chieftainship, ignoring the traditional family line.

[31] Moreover, any discrimination that may exist in male primogeniture relating to succession is "very fair", since allowing Ms Shilubana to succeed as Hosi would result in the next Hosi not being fathered by a Hosi, which would lead to confusion and chaos in the community. Ms Shilubana was not disqualified from being Hosi simply because she was a woman. Therefore the lower courts' judgments cannot be attacked on the basis of gender discrimination. In the alternative, Mr Nwamitwa argues that any discrimination against Ms Shilubana would not be unconstitutional, being based on a reason that is acceptable, fair, reasonable and justifiable.

* * * *Determining customary law*

[42] The status of customary law in South Africa is constitutionally entrenched. Section 211 of the Constitution provides that the institution, status and role of traditional leadership are recognised subject to the Constitution. It further states that a traditional authority that observes a system of customary law may function subject to applicable legislation and customs, including amendments to or repeal of that legislation and those customs, and that courts must apply customary law where it is applicable, subject to the Constitution and relevant legislation.

[43] The import of this section, in the words of Langa DCJ in *Bhe*, is that customary law "is protected by and subject to the Constitution in its own right." Customary law, like any other law, must accord with the Constitution. Like any other law, customary law has a status that requires respect. As this Court held in *Alexkor v Richtersveld Community*, customary law must be recognised as "an integral part of our law" and "an independent source of norms within the legal system." It is a body of law by which millions of South Africans regulate their lives and must be treated accordingly.

[44] As a result, the process of determining the content of a particular customary law norm must be one informed by several factors.[* * *]

[49] [. . . W]here there is a dispute over the legal position under customary law, a court must consider both the traditions and the present practice of the community. If development happens within the community, the court must strive to recognise and give effect to that development, to the extent consistent with adequately upholding the protection of rights. In addition, the imperative of section 39(2) must be acted on when necessary, and deference should be paid to the development by a customary communi-

ty of its own laws and customs where this is possible, consistent with the continuing effective operation of the law. With that, I turn to the enquiry into the legal position in the present case.

[Sections discussing whether Mr Nwamitwa has a vested right to the Chieftainship under traditional and living customary law of male successorship omitted]

Did the traditional authorities develop their law in terms of the Constitution?

[67]   As stated earlier, when the Royal Family confirmed the appointment of Ms Shilubana as Hosi, its members noted that, in view of the new democratic dispensation under the Constitution, it is permissible for a female child to become a Hosi "since she is also equal to a male child." It must be emphasised that Hosi Richard agreed with and approved of this decision.

[68]   The Valoyi authorities intended to bring an important aspect of their customs and traditions into line with the values and rights of the Constitution. Several provisions of the Constitution require the application of the common law and customary law, as well as the practice of culture or religion, to comply with the Constitution. Sections 1(c) and 2 establish the supremacy of the Constitution over all law. Section 30 recognises the right to participate in the cultural life of one's choice, but only in a manner consistent with the Bill of Rights. Similarly, section 31 recognises the right of cultural and religious communities to enjoy their culture and practice their religion in a manner consistent with the Bill of Rights. Section 39(2) has been mentioned above. And last, but certainly not least in this context, the above-mentioned section 211(3) demands that courts apply customary law where it is applicable, subject to the Constitution.

[69]   The importance of equality in our society has been repeatedly emphasised by this Court. The remarks of Ngcobo J in his concurring judgment in *Bato Star* sum up the position:

"South Africa is a country in transition. It is a transition from a society based on inequality to one based on equality. This transition was introduced by the Interim Constitution, which was designed to 'create a new order ... in which there is equality between men and women and people of all races so that all citizens should be able to enjoy and exercise their fundamental rights and freedoms'. This commitment to the transformation of our society was affirmed and reinforced in 1997, when the Constitution came into force. The Preamble to the Constitution 'recognises the injustices of our past' and makes a commitment to establishing 'a society based on democratic values, social justice and fundamental human rights'. This society is to be built on the foundation of the values entrenched in the very first provision of the Constitution. These values include human dignity, the achievement of equality and the advancement of human rights and freedoms. The achievement of equality is one of the fundamental goals that we have fashioned for ourselves in the Constitution. Our constitutional order is committed to the transformation of our society from a grossly unequal society to one 'in which there is equality between men and women and people of all races'." (Footnotes omitted.)

[70] In deciding as they did, the Valoyi authorities restored the chieftainship to a woman who would have been appointed Hosi in 1968, were it not for the fact that she is a woman. As far as lineage is relevant, the chieftainship was also restored to the line of Hosi Fofoza from which it was taken away on the basis that he only had a female and not a male heir.

[71] If that was what the authorities purported to do, it must next be asked whether they had the authority to act as they did. It was held above that the evidence did not permit this Court to rule on the question of whether traditional authorities have a broad discretion in appointing the Chief and are not bound simply to appoint the heir by birth. Accordingly, this Court has no basis on which to overturn the High Court's finding that, in terms of the existing customary law, the role of the Royal Family is more than formal only where there is no candidate for the chieftainship or where the candidate is not suitable, which is not alleged to be the case in the present matter. However, even if the High Court was correct on this point, it must be true that the traditional authorities had the power to act as they did, for the reasons that follow.

[72] It must be noted that the traditional authorities' power is the high water mark of any power within the traditional community on matters of succession. If the authorities have only the narrow discretion the High Court found them to have had, it follows that no other body in the community has more power in this regard, since no other body has more power here than those authorities. This would mean that no body in the customary community would have the power to make constitutionally-driven changes in traditional leadership. This result can be seen if we consider what would have happened, on the narrow view, if the traditional authorities in the present case had sought simply to install a woman as Hosi. Even if she were the eldest child of the previous Chief, it would follow on the narrow view that the traditional authorities would have no power to appoint her, unless there was no other heir or the male heir was unfit to rule. It would be necessary, on this view, to approach the courts before a woman could be installed as Chief.

[73] This is not only undesirable; it is contrary to the Constitution. Section 211(2) specifically provides for the right of traditional communities to function subject to their own system of customary law, including amendment or repeal of laws. A community must be empowered to itself act so as to bring its customs into line with the norms and values of the Constitution. Any other result would be contrary to section 211(2) and would be disrespectful of the close bonds between a customary community, its leaders and its laws.

[74] It follows that if the traditional authority has only those powers accorded it by the narrow view, it would be contrary to the Constitution and frustrate the achievement of the values in the Bill of Rights. Section 39(2) of the Constitution obliges this Court to develop the customary law in accordance with the spirit, purport and aims of the Bill of Rights. This power should be exercised judiciously and sensitively, in an incremental fashion. As the Supreme Court of Canada has held in relation to the common law, "[t]he judiciary should confine itself to those incremental

changes which are necessary to keep the common law in step with the dynamic and evolving fabric of our society." The same remarks apply to customary law. It is appropriate for the Court to exercise its section 39(2) powers in a manner that will empower the community itself to continue the development.

[75]   Accordingly, if it is true that the authorities presently have no power to bring the law and practice of customary leadership into line with the Constitution, their power must be expanded. It must be held that they have the authority to act on constitutional considerations in fulfilling their role in matters of traditional leadership. Their actions, reflected in the appointment of Ms Shilubana, accordingly represent a development of customary law. The only remaining question is that posed by the third factor of the test set out above: are there considerations which outweigh the recognition of this development as determinative of the legal position?

Should this contemporary development be recognised as law?

* * * [81]   It is true that Ms Shilubana's installation leaves unanswered some questions relating to how the Valoyi succession will operate in the future. However, customary law is living law and will in the future inevitably be interpreted, applied and, when necessary, amended or developed by the community itself or by the courts. This will be done in view of existing customs and traditions, previous circumstances and practical needs, and of course the demands of the Constitution as the supreme law. It therefore suffices to say two things.

[82]   First, whereas the Valoyi people moved away from any previously existing rule that a woman could never be appointed as a Hosi, other aspects of the customs and traditions governing chieftainship are not necessarily affected. For example, to the extent that the principle that a Hosi is born and not elected indeed exists, it is not necessarily changed by this ruling. Ms Shilubana was born as the child of a Hosi. She was not elected from a number of candidates who campaigned for the position. Her birth was crucial to the decision of the Royal Family.

[83]   Second, such additional developments of the law as Ms Shilubana's installation may necessitate are in the first instance a matter for the relevant traditional authorities, acting in accordance with custom, practical needs and the Constitution. These future decisions are not before this Court, and nothing further need be said about them.

[84]   The value of recognising the development by a traditional community of its own law is not here outweighed by factors relating to legal certainty or the protection of rights. The Royal Family intended to act to affirm constitutional values in traditional leadership in its community. It had the authority to do so. A balancing of the effects of its action reveals no consideration that should prevent this Court from recognising its actions as such.

[85]   The conclusions of the High Court and Supreme Court of Appeal that the traditional authorities lacked the power to act as they did were incorrect. They erred in that their focus was too narrow, tied to the statement that a Hosi is never appointed, but born, and unable to countenance that the lineage would change from that of Hosi Richard to that of Hosi Fofoza. They gave insufficient consideration to the historical and

constitutional context of the decision, more particularly the right of traditional authorities to develop their customary law.

[86]   Accordingly, Mr Nwamitwa has no vested right to the chieftainship of the Valoyi. He has, at most, an expectation that as the eldest son of Hosi Richard, he would have been heir. However, the past practice of the Valoyi community is not determinative and does not itself guarantee that Mr Nwamitwa's possible expectation must be fulfilled. The contemporary practice of the Valoyi reflects a valid legal change, resulting in the succession of Ms Shilubana to the chieftainship. Mr Nwamitwa does not have a right to the chieftainship under this altered position. He cannot be declared the Chief in terms of the current customary law of the Valoyi traditional community.* * *

[Additional concluding matters omitted]

NOTES

1.   In *Shilubana*, we see the Constitutional Court of South Africa affirm the sovereign power of the Valoyi authorities to reform their laws of successorship, which traditionally have excluded women. The subtle language in paragraph 81, by recognizing the limit of national courts to interpret customary law where a community's governing body has acted in accordance with constitutional principles, articulates a compelling feature of South African federalism which mandates power-sharing between modern political units and traditional communities. Yet, this recognition of community autonomy is not absolute, since the courts will impose their interpretations of customary law if community authorities depart from the basic principles of the constitution. This decision, in paragraph 75, even goes so far as to say that "if it is true that the authorities presently have no power to bring the law and practice of customary leadership into line with the Constitution, their power must be expanded." Does this federal empowerment of the Valoyi authorities support or undermine community autonomy?

2.   South African constitutional rights may be enforceable against private discrimination. *See* S. Afr. Const. 1996 § 8(2), stating that "A provision of the Bill of Rights binds a natural or a juristic person if, and to the extent that, it is applicable, taking into account the nature of the right and the nature of any duty imposed by the right."; and § 9(4), stating that "No person may unfairly discriminate directly or indirectly against anyone." Jonathan Marshfield notes how the New Constitution's enforcement of individual rights against both state and private actors might give rise to an interesting federalism issue that is avoided in the U.S. "[T]here exists the possibility that a provincial right, when exercised by an individual, could infringe a national constitutional right of another individual. The absence of a state action requirement in those situations creates a legal conflict between the two individuals who both claim valid legal rights. The Court therefore articulated a test to resolve such conflicts. According to the Court, two rights provisions 'are inconsistent when they cannot stand at the same time, or cannot stand together, or cannot both be obeyed at the same time.' KZN Certification (11)BCLR 1419 at 32. In those cases, the

provincial right must yield to the national right." *Authorizing Subnational Constitutiosn in Transitional Federal States: South Africa, Democracy, and the Kwazulu–Natal Constitution*, 41 VAND. J. TRANSNAT'L L. 585 (2008), footnote 67.

3.   Similarly, the extraordinary remedy of amparo is available in many Latin American countries, as well as Haiti and the Philippines, to protect individual constitutional rights against both federal and subnational powers. In certain countries, amparo may function like a writ of habeas corpus, but in others, it goes further to protect individual rights beyond physical liberty. In Mexico, where it originated and has enjoyed the most robust elaboration, an amparo claim may be brought in federal court against infringements on constitutional rights by "responsible authority" defined by the Mexican Supreme Court as "every person who, de jure or de facto, exercises public power and is materially enabled thereby to operate as an individual who commits public acts...." Amparo suits have even been brought by governmental agencies against other governmental agencies. In Argentina, amparo may be brought against both public and private parties that interfere with constitutional rights. Brazil has a remedy called the writ of security (mandado de segurana), which functions like the amparo, and can be filed against public authorities or private individuals with governmentally delegated powers. Amparo in these contexts serve to equalize the obligation to guarantee individual rights and liberties between federal and subnational agencies, unlike the United States, where federal courts and legislation serve as the ultimate protector. Keith Rosenn, *Federalism in the Americas in Comparative Perspective*, 26 U. MIAMI INTER-AM. L. REV. 1, 41–43 (1994). In addition to Mexico, Argentina and Brazil, other Latin American countries with some form of the amparo remedy include, Bolivia, Colombia, Costa Rica, Ecuador, El Salvador, Guatemala, Honduras, Nicaragua, Panama, Paraguay, Peru, and the Dominican Republic, Uruguay and Venezuela. Allen R. Brewer–Carias, *The Constitutional Protection of Human Rights in Latin America: A Comparative Study of Amparo Proceedings*, Cambridge University Press, 2008, 425–426.

4.   Compare the Latin American remedy of amparo and South Africa's constitutionally actionable private discrimination with the U.S.'s bright-line declaration in *Shelley v. Kraemer*, 334 U.S. 1, 13 (1948), that the U.S. Bill of Rights prohibits "only such [racially discriminatory] action as may fairly be said to be that of the States".

———

E.   IRAQ

Iraq's Constitutional Mandate to Justly Distribute Water: The Implications of Federalism, Islam, International Law and Human Rights

42 Geo. Wash. Int'l L. Rev. 749 (2011), pp. 759–769

■ SHARMILA L. MURTHY

III. Iraq's Federal Structure

* * * Federalism was one of the most controversial issues when Iraq drafted its constitution. The Iraqi federalism negotiations fundamentally revolved around balancing the power between the federal authorities in Baghdad and the Kurdish regional government, which had been the de facto government in Kurdistan since the end of the Gulf War in 1991. The Kurdish government sought greater autonomy, if not independence, from Baghdad. During the constitutional negotiations, "[t]he strongest disagreements concerned the status and evolution of Iraqi federalism, and, in particular, the creation of new federal regions outside of Iraqi Kurdistan."

In its final form, Iraq's constitution recognized eighteen governorates and one region, Kurdistan, which encompassed three of these governorates entirely, as well as limited areas of other governorates. In this respect, Iraq embraced an asymmetrical form of consociational federalism. 'Consociationalism' refers to a power-sharing arrangement based on a group affinity, such as ethnicity and religion. 'Asymmetric' refers to the distinct amounts of power wielded by governments at the federal, regional, and governorate levels. If certain conditions are met, Iraq's governorates may join together to form regions. This "phased and asymmetric approach to the assumption of powers by sub-federal governments" has been lauded as providing governorates with the "crucial time to build capacity and infrastructure." In addition, it has avoided the hard partitioning of the country into Shia, Sunni, and Kurdish regions, and has allowed for a more liberal, locally-driven form of consociational federalism.

In Iraq, federalism was perceived as a way "to reduce centrifugal forces by providing an avenue for diverse ethnic, religious, and geographic groups to participate in the regional and national government, and thereby hopefully reduce the grievances that [gave] rise to their desire to separate from the state." However, disputes over control of Iraq's natural resources have tugged at these centrifugal forces, thereby fueling tensions that the federal structure was designed to accommodate. The constitutional negotiations over Iraq's vast oil and gas reserves were particularly contentious because the reserves are not evenly distributed across the country.

The constitutional negotiations over Iraq's water have received less attention than those over oil and gas. But as the Kurdistan Regional Government's President, Massoud Barzani, recently stated in an interview: "Water is now more important than oil." With the growing scarcity of fresh water in Iraq, the relationship between water governance and federalism, and the potential for these divisions of power to create jurisdictional conflict, deserve scrutiny.

Iraq's constitution gives the federal government exclusive authority over sources of water outside of Iraq, but grants the federal and regional governments concurrent authority over sources of water inside Iraq. In contrast to the regions, governorates do not have guaranteed constitutional authority over any aspect of internal water resources policy unless the federal government devolves power to a region in accordance with Article 123. Kurdistan is currently the only region in Iraq, and thus, the only sub-federal entity, that has power to determine internal water policy under Article 114.

Kurdistan is rich in water resources, as compared to the rest of Iraq. Cities in Kurdistan rely on surface water from rivers, reservoirs, and groundwater. Rural areas of this region use a traditional system of wells and aqueducts known as karez, which provide access to groundwater. Major tributaries to the Tigris River run through Kurdistan, which give the region great control over the water supply in many downstream areas, including Baghdad, that rely on surface water for drinking and sanitation. Moreover, two of Iraq's largest hydroelectric power plants, the Dokan and Darbandikhan, are located in Kurdish governorates in the north. The country's largest dam, the 320–megawatt Mosul Dam, is located just outside of the Kurdish region, in Mosul, the capital of the contested Ninawa governorate. The Mosul Dam is currently under the joint control of the Kurdish Democratic Party and the Patriotic Union of Kurdistan. According to one commentator, the dam "represents a valuable prize in the Kurds' ongoing struggle with Baghdad for increased autonomy." Another has observed that "[t]he Kurds in northern Iraq have long recognized the importance of controlling their own water resources. It is no accident that an influential Kurd, Latif Rashid, was appointed to lead the newly formed Ministry of Water Resources in Baghdad soon after the U.S. led invasion in 2003." If Kurdistan expands regional irrigation or builds new dams, the already-delicate water situation in the south of Iraq could be exacerbated.

During constitutional negotiations, the Kurds ensured that the Constitution would enshrine their autonomy over their water resources. According to Ashley Deeks and Matthew Burton, who were the Legal Adviser and Deputy Legal Adviser, respectively, at the U.S. Embassy in Baghdad, Iraq, from June until December 2005:

> The Kurds wanted as much regional control as possible over the rivers passing through Iraqi Kurdistan. Thus, they pushed the Shia to accept an "exclusive authorities" formulation that did not include central government authority to guarantee the "just distribution" of water resources within Iraq. The Shia objected to the Kurdish position, fearing that the Kurds would divert significant amounts of water from rivers flowing through the northern part of Iraq, such as the Tigris and its tributaries, away from the central and southern parts.... With the inclusion of "just distribution inside Iraq" in the exclusive authority provision, the compromise reflected something of a Shia victory. Nevertheless, the final language created significantly overlapping authority between the federal government and the regions to the extent that external water sources flowing into Iraq join with water sources originating in and remaining inside Iraq, and because both provisions appear to cover the just distribution of water inside Iraq. Ultimately, as with other areas of overlapping authority, the Federal Supreme Court could be well positioned to resolve any conflicts that arose between the federal and regional governments.

As Deeks and Burton suggest, disputes could arise if Iraq's Kurdistan region and its federal government develop conflicting internal water policies. Several provisions in Iraq's constitution suggest that in the event of such jurisdictional disputes, regional policy would take precedence. Article 115 states:

All powers not stipulated in the exclusive powers of the federal government belong to the authorities of the regions and governorates that are not organized in a region. With regard to other powers shared between the federal government and the regional government, priority shall be given to the law of the regions and governorates not organized in a region in case of dispute.

Article 114 could be interpreted as requiring the federal and regional governments to develop a single, joint policy on internal water resources. Such an interpretation, however, seems at odds with the constitutional drafting history. The language of Article 115, which gives regional law priority over federal law, anticipates jurisdictional conflict. Moreover, Article 121 of Iraq's constitution states that "[i]n case of a contradiction between regional and national legislation in respect to a matter outside the exclusive authorities of the federal government, the regional power shall have the right to amend the application of the national legislation within that region." A more likely interpretation is that under Article 114, the federal and regional governments exercise concurrent, but independent, powers.

In contrast to the regions, Iraq's governorates do not have any guaranteed constitutional power over water policy under Article 114, which begins by stating that "[t]he following competencies shall be shared between the federal authorities and regional authorities." Article 114 then lists seven enumerated concurrent powers. Of these seven powers, four—customs management, environmental regulation, health policy, and educational policy—must be exercised in consultation, in coordination, or in cooperation with the governorates. The remaining three powers—internal water policy, electricity regulation, as well as development and general planning policies—do not mention the governorates.

The constitutional provisions governing the governorates' power were influenced by several conflicting factors. The Shia Alliance initially sought a strong central government, but later in the constitutional negotiations, pushed to expand the governorates' power. Concerned that creating a region as powerful as Kurdistan may prove difficult in the future, "the Shia Alliance made a concerted effort to give governorates the same or similar governmental authority that the constitution gave regions." Despite this effort, Iraq's governorates do not share all of the concurrent powers of Article 114—and water is not one of those shared powers.* * *

Given the unequal distribution of water in Iraq, the following hypothetical example illustrates the challenges of Iraq's federated water governance approach. Imagine that the Kurds began diverting the tributaries of the Tigris River for hydropower or irrigation, which may enable the just distribution water within Kurdistan. Such a diversion would be consistent with Kurdistan's draft regional constitution, which views surface and underground water as national resources for the Region. However, the diversion could leave less water for downstream users throughout of Iraq. Does a governorate further south that relies on the Tigris River have a right to contest Kurdistan's policies under the theory that the water has not been justly distributed? What if the diversion activities in Kurdistan conflicted with efforts by the federal government to justly distribute water from outside Iraq under Article 110? Would Kurdistan's water governance policies take priority over those of the federal government under Article 115? Or, given the fungible nature of water, does the federal government's exclusive right under Article 110 to ensure the just distribution of waters from outside Iraq mean that it can preempt Kurdistan's water policies?

Brendan O'Leary, who served as an advisor to the Kurdistan Regional Government during the constitutional negotiations, offers an interpretation of the "apparent clash" between the "just distribution" provisions of Articles 110 and 114:

> [A]ny regional government is entitled to nullify (or modify) within its region any application of the law [under Article 110] as regards "just distribution," since the determination of "just distribution" is specified as a shared competence [under Article 114]. The relevant articles express the technical acknowledgement of Iraq's interdependence as regards water and grant the federal government the minimum necessary planning authority, but they also express the historic distrust of Baghdad governments by Kurdistan—and ensure that the Kurdish Regional Government can veto any law that in its judgment does not match international law and conventions on "just distribution."

> ... The relevant clauses recognize interdependence but also the hidden power and importance of Kurdistan.... Given the present and future importance of water resources for Iraq's urban populations, and for agriculture, the necessary interdependence between water policy and hydroelectric power, and Saddam's past abuse of central authority to build huge dams without any degree of local consultation or planning, these articles and subsections express a principled bargain—one which ensures that regions can block misbehavior by the federal government.

O'Leary's interpretation may make sense from Kurdistan's perspective, but it could lead to the creation of conflicting policies within Iraq. The division of power over water governance illustrates how the very concept of federalism "bears an ambivalent, even paradoxical, relationship to nation building." The Kurds were the driving force behind the definition of regional power in Iraq's constitution. Having suffered brutally at the hands of Saddam Hussein and having enjoyed a degree of autonomy since 1991, the Kurds were reluctant to surrender any authority. Although Iraq adopted a federated system largely to accommodate Kurdish demands for increased autonomy, disputes over control of vital natural resources—like oil or water—could increase tensions. It is perhaps not surprising, then, that federalism has been described as "a strategy for conflict management and not for conflict resolution." * * *

_____

NOTES

1. The history of federalism in Iraq reveals how federalism is not simply a chosen model of power-sharing by an already constituted nation, but is a complex process by which a nation is established through governmental and infrastructural development. To the extent that federalism was

envisioned in Iraq to regulate ethnic, religious and sectarian differences during the nascent stage of nation-building, especially given the scarcity of resources, perhaps in Iraq we see how federalism is a precondition for a nation, rather than an effect of it. For this reason, then, the model of consociational federalism we see in Iraq, which specifically refers to subnational units as structures of "group affinity", suggests a more dialogical process of power-sharing, as opposed to a devolutionary process of power distribution, as in the South African context. It raises interesting questions about the nature of subnational governmental structures in federal systems. How does Iraqi consociational federalism compare to the history of Indian federalism? How might race, religion, language, history and culture have shaped the formation of U.S. states or EU nations?

2.   The Iraqi Constitution lays out a relation of "interdependence" between the federal, regional and governatorial levels. Indian federalism, as argued by Nesiah, ultimately grants more power to the national government, as does South Africa. What kind of relation does U.S. equality jurisprudence suggest about U.S. federalism? EU equality jurisprudence about EU federalism? And how would an Iraqi constitutional priority of power-sharing between ethnic, religious and culturally-specific subnational units sound in a case like *Guerra*, or any of the others included in the section above?

3.   For materials on the development of equality in other federal systems, including Canada, Belgium, and Ethiopia, see Chapter VIII, *Federalism: Power Sharing and Minority Protection* in COMPARATIVE CONSTITUTIONAL LAW (eds. V. Jackson & M. Tushnet, 1999).

INDEX

References are to Pages

†